THE
HUMAN
EXPERIENCE OF
PSYCHOLOGICAL
DISORDERS

ABNORMAL PSYCHOLOGY

THE HUMAN EXPERIENCE OF PSYCHOLOGICAL DISORDERS

Richard P. Halgin
Susan Krauss Whitbourne

University of Massachusetts at Amherst

Harcourt Brace Jovanovich College Publishers

Fort Worth   Philadelphia   San Diego   New York   Orlando   Austin   San Antonio
Toronto   Montreal   London   Sydney   Tokyo

Editor-in-Chief: Ted Buchholz
Acquisitions Editor: Eve Howard
Senior Developmental Editor: Meera Dash
Project Editor: Nancy Lombardi
Senior Production Manager: Annette Dudley Wiggins
Senior Book Designer: Don Fujimoto
Photo Editor: Greg Meadors
Permissions Editor: Van E. Strength

Cover and Chapter Opening Photos: Heidi Wrage

*To
our
families,
with love
and appreciation*

In his junior year of college, a young man named Jason apprehensively approaches the instructor of his abnormal psychology course after class. Learning about the strong genetic influence involved in the development of schizophrenia, he feels frightened that his mother's lifelong struggle with this disorder means he too will experience a life of extreme emotional upheaval. Jason is concerned about his susceptibility and wants to understand the problems his mother faces. How sensitive will the instructor be to his concerns?

Kelly's interest in abnormal psychology arises from her aspiration to become a clinical psychologist. She wants to help people with psychological problems as a psychotherapist and investigate new and emerging areas of research in severe psychological disturbance. She hopes that her instructor and her textbook will translate the most current, sophisticated findings from scientific journals into terms that she can understand. At the same time, the instructor will want to challenge and guide her to the next level of inquiry.

A third student, Connie, is a management major. Her friends have told her how fascinating this course is because she will learn about many unusual kinds of disorders, such as pathological gambling, agoraphobia, and pedophilia. She wants to understand better some of the problems, such as eating disorders and substance abuse, she sees in other students on campus.

Many abnormal psychology classrooms today have students like Jason, Kelly, and Connie. Instructors face a variety of challenges. In writing this textbook, we speak to all three kinds of students in a way that is informative, scholarly, and engaging. We have achieved this balance by writing with a combined focus on human interest and scientific accuracy.

The Human Experience of Psychological Disorders

The subtitle of our textbook reflects a central approach, which makes this book unique. In discussing psychological disturbances, we prefer to view these experiences as points on a continuum of human behavior, rather than extreme phenomena that affect only other people in some faraway place. For example, we begin the discussion of anxiety disorders by urging the student to think about personal experiences involving anxiety, then to imagine what it might be like to endure fear and apprehension that is many times more intense. This conversational approach is characterized by simple and direct language and lively expression.

We use this imaginative paradigm as an illustrative method in discussion of several other disorders throughout the textbook. In each case, we qualify the example to ensure that the student extends the experience, to avoid self-diagnosis. While it illustrates the material in everyday terms, this extension also helps students distinguish between common emotional experiences and pathological disturbances, helping them answer the question, "What is abnormal?" Psychological disorders do not happen just to "the other person." They are problems that we face either directly in our own lives or indirectly through people we know. That is the crux of the "human experience" element. We hope that this approach becomes clear and useful as you read.

Logical Organization and an Integrative Approach

The table of contents reflects a building block approach. In the first five chapters, we provide the fundamentals of history and research methods (Chapter 1); diagnosis, classification, treatment planning, and legal issues (Chapter 2); assessment (Chapter 3); and theories (Chapters 4 and 5). These chapters provide a foundation for exploring many different perspectives in understanding and treating psychological disorders. We then move to a consideration of the disorders, beginning with those which we believe are more familiar to the students, such as personality disorders (Chapter 6) and anxiety disorders (Chapter 7). We progress through the major categories of psychological disorders, ending with disorders of impulse control, which are characterized by irresistible urges, (Chapter 16), and life stress disorders (Chapter 17), which are more likely to be encountered in the lives of typical undergraduates.

We have taken an integrative position, combining what researchers have demonstrated to be the most applicable and effective approaches for the disorder under consideration. We have chosen to cover relevant treatments within the context of discussing each disorder rather than in separate chapters. Many instructors prefer to have therapy discussed in the context of the disorder because it makes discussion of therapy more lively and realistic and in many cases provides further insight into the nature of the disorder.

The organization of this textbook also has required special coverage of the *Diagnostic and Statistical Manual of Mental Disorders (DSM)*. Aware of the transition from *DSM-III-R* to *DSM-IV*, we have carefully considered the major diagnostic changes proposed in the manual. Our discussions of psychological disorders focus on conceptual issues more than specific criteria used by mental health professionals in diagnosing disorders. We believe that this approach will be more helpful to students, and that the textbook will be accurate and useful both before and after the introduction of *DSM-IV*.

Interactive Case Material

The textbook includes built-in case material. We have created this approach through two special features.

First, each chapter begins with a case report that sets the stage for the didactic material in the chapter. Starting in Chapter 3, we return to the case at the end of the chapter. At this point, the student is ready to apply knowledge from the chapter, developing an understanding of the case and the kind of treatment that would be used in handling this particular case. Each case is presented from the perspective of "Dr. Sarah Tobin," a psychologist who is consulted by a different client in each chapter. The cases are based on actual clinical material. By speaking through the character of Dr. Tobin, we can illustrate the disorders more vividly, giving students an appreciation of the complexities of psychological disorders and the real-life dilemmas involved in clinical work.

Second, within the chapter, a boxed clinical vignette accompanies the discussion of each disorder or set of disorders. Thus, several clinical vignettes appear in each of the chapters on disorders, bringing the symptoms and disorders to life in interesting case examples. Two critical thinking questions follow each vignette to help the student focus on important facets of the case and the disorder.

Consistent Learning Aids

Each chapter includes a set of pedagogical features that make the material engaging and pedagogically appealing.

- **Case report**   A lively account in the words of the featured clinician, Dr. Sarah Tobin, introduces a client who has one of the disorders covered in the chapter.
- **Objectives**   In the first section of the chapter, behavioral objectives help the student anticipate the most important knowledge to be acquired in the chapter.
- **Chapter organization**   In Chapters 6 through 17, which cover specific disorders, each chapter has a similar structure. Each section on "characteristics" of the disorder is followed by a section on "theories and treatments." This format provides a reliable structure to ensure that the material on treatment is thoroughly integrated, and to help the student learn the material.
- **Key terms**   Each important term is defined the first time it appears; the term is printed in bold type. It also appears in a page-referenced "Key Terms" glossary at the end of the chapter, and in an alphabetical glossary at the end of the book.
- **Critical issues boxes**   Interspersed throughout the text are thought-provoking discussions of controversial issues such as involuntary treatment or the use of the aversive therapy in treating autism.
- **Research focus boxes**   In-depth descriptions of interesting and important research studies give students an appreciation of the complexity of investigating important issues in abnormal psychology. For example, Chapter 1 presents findings from a fascinating research project conducted by Nancy Andreasen on the relationship between creativity and psychological disorder.
- **The perspectives revisited**   A section at the end of each chapter discusses the perspectives that have had the greatest impact on the disorders. It highlights current issues regarding the disorders and their treatment.

A summary table compares and contrasts the different approaches to understanding and treating the disorders.
- **Return to the case**   At the end of the chapter, students return to the case introduced at the start of the chapter. By this point they are equipped with the knowledge to understand the diagnosis, formulation, and treatment of the case.
- **Chapter summary**   Each chapter ends with a numbered summary of the major points in the chapter.
- **Visual aids**   The ample illustrative material in each chapter includes questionnaires, graphs, and drawings that show research findings or epidemiological data, tables that integrate the topics discussed, helpful photographs, and a design that supports these visual aids.

ANCILLARIES

A comprehensive multimedial ancillary package accompanies *Abnormal Psychology: The Human Experience of Psychological Disorders*. The package consists of the following items:

- A Study Guide prepared by Richard Halgin and Susan Krauss Whitbourne that is closely integrated with the text. Each chapter includes learning objectives, a brief overview, matching items, an "identifying terms" section, short-answer questions, 20 multiple-choice items, and a unique puzzle or game. Also contained in the Study Guide are answers to the thought questions that accompany each of the case vignettes in the textbook. The Study Guide, which has been class-tested before its publication, is an innovative teaching tool that students will find helpful in mastering concepts and terminology related to abnormal psychology.
- An Instructor's Manual prepared by the textbook authors and Timothy P. Tomczak, Genesee Community College. Each chapter has teaching objectives, a lecture outline including key terms and supplementary cross-cultural lecture topics, discussions and demonstrations, additional resources, and writing assignments. The instructor's manual includes a video instructor's guide.
- A Test Bank prepared by Timothy P. Tomczak, Genesee Community College. The test bank features approximately 110 multiple-choice items per chapter. Each item is classified by level of difficulty, cognitive type, and learning objective. In addition, several questions in each chapter occur in the study guide and are so labelled.
- The Computerized Test Bank is available in IBM and Macintosh formats. The testing software, ExaMaster™, allows you to create tests using fewer keystrokes, with all steps defined in easy-to-follow screen prompts. ExaMaster™ offers instructors three easy-to-use options for test creation:

1. EasyTest lets you create a test from a screen in just a few easy steps. You can select questions from the data base or let EasyTest randomly select the questions for you, given your parameters.

2. FullTest lets you use the whole range of options available:
   - select questions as you preview them on the screen
   - edit existing questions or add your own questions
   - add or edit graphics in the MS-DOS version
   - link related questions, instructions, and graphics
   - have FullTest randomly select questions from a wider range of criteria
   - create your own criteria on two open keys
   - block specific questions from random selection
   - print up to 99 different versions of the same test and answer sheet

3. RequesTest is there for you when you do not have access to a computer. When that happens, just call 1-800-447-9457. Software specialists will compile the questions according to your criteria and either mail or fax the test master to you within 48 hours!

Included with ExaMaster is ExamRecord, a gradebook program that allows you to record, curve, graph, and print out grades. ExamRecord takes raw scores and converts them into grades by criteria you've set. You can set the curve you want and see the distribution of the grades in a bar graph or a plotted graph.

If questions arise, the Software Support Hotline is available Monday through Friday, 9 AM–4 PM Central Time at 1-800-447-9457.

- **Supershrink II: Jennifer** is an interactive microcomputer simulation program for use on an IBM system. Users take the role of a counselor at a helpline clinic and conduct an interview with the client, Jennifer. This program is especially helpful to students learning concepts in psychopathology, personality, and assessment.
- **Brainstack,** an interactive software program for Macintosh users, provides students with a self-guided tour of the cerebral cortex, giving valuable information about brain-behavior relationships. Major topics include the motor and sensory cortex, visual and auditory cortex, memory, thinking, pattern recognition, facial identity, and the language system.
- **The video library** includes video sources which are available as supplemental teaching aids. Users of *Abnormal Psychology: The Human Experience of Psychological Disorders* are able to select from a wide variety of programs by consulting with their HBJ book representatives.

ACKNOWLEDGMENTS

We are indebted to the following instructors who reviewed outlines, chapters, and entire drafts of our manuscript: Judith Armstrong, Towson State University; Bruce E. Bailey, Clinical Psychologist; Barbara Brackney, Eastern Michigan University; Dennis E. Chestnut, East Carolina University; Gerard Connors, Research Institute on Alcoholism; Eric Cooley, Western Oregon State College; Peter Ebersole, California State University, Fullerton; William Goggin, University of Southern Mississippi; Jeffrey Hecker, University of Maine; Douglas Hindman, Eastern Kentucky University; Herb Krauss, Hunter College; Joseph Lowman, University of North Carolina; Tom Marsh, Pitt Community College; Janet Matthews, Loyola University; William Miley, Richard Stockton State College; Paul Olczak, State University of New York at Geneseo; Joseph Palladino, University of Southern Indiana; Beth Rienzi, California State University, Bakersfield; Jerome Small, Youngstown State University; and Thomas Widiger, University of Kentucky.

When we started working on this textbook, little did we know that a corporate reorganization would lead us from San Diego to Fort Worth for editorial direction. Changes in the middle of a project are often disruptive, but in our case this change put us in the hands of a superb team. In particular, Eve Howard's excitement about this project, combined with her miraculous efficiency, propelled us through the final critical drafts of the manuscript. We valued her advice, respected her judgment, and appreciated her honesty. As fortunate as we were to have Eve Howard as our acquisitions editor, we were doubly blessed to have our title assigned to Meera Dash, our gifted developmental editor who helped us reshape and tighten the manuscript, and ultimately to realize our vision for the text. We came to rely upon and treasure Meera's impressive candor, expert judgment, and sophisticated perspective. The rest of the editorial team at HBJ have also proven to be enormously helpful and efficient. Greg Meadors, our photo researcher, patiently scoured a wide range of sources to find the most appropriate illustrative material to highlight the text. In addition, we are enormously grateful for benefitting from the talents of our project editor, Nancy Lombardi, our designer, Don Fujimoto, and our copyeditor, Cindy Simpson.

Every textbook requires countless hours of library research, photocopying, and bibliographic duties. We were fortunate to have found a group of wonderfully bright and conscientious graduate and undergraduate students to assist us in these tasks. Our research assistants performed all these duties with marvelous skill but gave us much more in the process. Each one of them mastered a complex reference system, a sophisticated word processing program, and a massive library system. We knew that we could ask for an article, no matter how obscure the source, and be handed a clean copy in short order. They also read drafts of the manuscript with a critical eye, and shared with us ways to enliven the material and stick to our mission of "talking to the student." The central players in this process were

Kevin Fletcher, Christine Haigney, Kelly Michaelian, and Sharon Stapel, each of whom devoted tremendous amounts of time, energy, and enthusiasm to this project. We also wish to thank the other students who assisted us, including Mark Caron, Peter Leahy, Jeris Miller, Rachel Forsythe, and Dana Weaver, and especially Michael Grunes, Heather Golm, and Jung Oh, who participated in the final, frenetic days of manuscript preparation.

Our most heartfelt appreciation goes to our families whose encouragement and patience gave both of us the energy to follow through on a task that consumed thousands more hours than either of us had ever imagined. The loving support of our spouses, Lucille Halgin and Richard O'Brien, made it possible for us to maintain a reasonable degree of emotional stability. The youthful perspectives of our children, Daniel and Kerry Halgin, and Stacey Whitbourne and Jennifer O'Brien, helped keep before us the goal of writing in a way that would answer the questions of an inquiring mind.

On a final note, we want to thank each other for a working relationship characterized by good humor, nondefensiveness, and mutual respect. We can honestly say that no part of this book is owned exclusively by either of us. In a most collaborative writing process, we created the wording of each phrase through discussion, debate, and occasional good-natured sarcasm. We recurrently argued about the order of authorship, each of us insisting that the other deserved to be first author, and ultimately yielded to the tradition of alphabetical listing.

Richard P. Halgin
Susan Krauss Whitbourne
University of Massachusetts at Amherst

Richard P. Halgin and Susan Krauss Whitbourne are professors of psychology at the University of Massachusetts at Amherst. Both teach large undergraduate classes in addition to teaching and supervising doctoral students in clinical psychology. Their clinical experience has covered both

in-patient and out-patient settings. Professors Halgin and Whitbourne have also been elected Fellows of the American Psychological Association, and have served on the editorial boards of major professional journals.

Professor Halgin received his Ph.D. from Fordham University. He is a diplomate in Clinical Psychology and has had two decades of clinical experience. He has served as Director of the University's Psychological Services Center, a primary provider of mental health services in Western Massachusetts and as a visiting professor at Amherst College. His teaching has been recognized at both the university and national levels. He received the University Distinguished Teaching Award and was recognized by Division 2 of the American Psychological Association (Teaching of Psychology). He is the author of more than three dozen journal articles and book chapters in the fields of integrative psychotherapy and professional issues in psychology.

Professor Whitbourne received her Ph.D. from Columbia University and has training and credentials both in life-span developmental psychology and clinical psychology. Prior to joining the faculty of the University of Massachusetts, she taught at the State University of New York at Geneseo and the University of Rochester. Professor Whitbourne is known on the university campus for her excellence and creativity as a teacher, and her courses are typically oversubscribed. She maintains a private practice in addition to teaching, research, and writing. The author of six books and over 50 journal articles and book chapters, she is regarded as an expert in the field of adult development and aging, with a focus on personality and mental health issues of aged people.

BRIEF CONTENTS

DETAILED CONTENTS

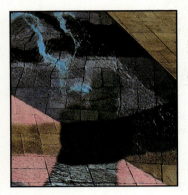
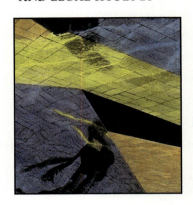

CHAPTER 3
ASSESSMENT 54

CHAPTER 8
SOMATOFORM AND DISSOCIATIVE DISORDERS 196

CHAPTER 9
SEXUAL DISORDERS 218

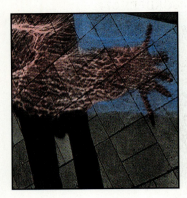

CHAPTER 12
THEORIES AND TREATMENT OF SCHIZOPHRENIC
DISORDERS 294

CHAPTER 13
DEVELOPMENT-RELATED DISORDERS 320

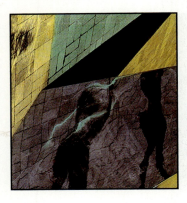

CHAPTER 14
ORGANIC DISORDERS INVOLVING COGNITIVE
    IMPAIRMENT 348

CHAPTER 15
SUBSTANCE-RELATED DISORDERS 370

CHAPTER 16
DISORDERS OF SELF-CONTROL 404

CHAPTER 17
REACTIONS TO LIFE STRESS 428

ABNORMAL PSYCHOLOGY

THE
HUMAN
EXPERIENCE OF
PSYCHOLOGICAL
DISORDERS

Case Report: Rebecca James

Rebecca is a 29-year-old woman whose brother died suddenly and without any clear cause. Shortly after his death, Rebecca began to act in many strange ways. She would wander the streets of the city in the early morning hours, mumbling to herself and sometimes wearing only her nightclothes. During these times she would be overheard "conversing" with her brother and telling him about a malicious plot on the part of her neighbors. On other occasions, she could be heard by her neighbors laughing or crying, at other times screaming that she had lost her sight.

1

UNDERSTANDING ABNORMALITY: A LOOK AT HISTORY AND RESEARCH METHODS

The field of abnormal psychology is filled with countless fascinating "cases" of people that many would regard as quite remote. In this chapter, we will try to give you some sense of the reality that psychological disturbance is certain to touch everyone, to some extent, at some point in life. Ideally, as you progress through this course, you will develop a sense of the pain and stigma often associated with psychological problems. In the pages that follow, we will consider some of the tremendous emotional, social, and financial costs associated with mental health problems.

After reading this chapter, you should be able to:

■ Recognize the problems involved in arriving at criteria for "abnormal" behavior.

■ Define an integrative approach to understanding "abnormal" behavior.

■ Be knowledgeable regarding the history of views regarding psychological problems, focusing on broad themes from the prehistoric era to the present day.

■ Understand research methods used by scientists to answer some of the difficult questions about the nature and causes of psychological problems.

WHAT IS ABNORMAL BEHAVIOR?

Think about how you would feel if you saw someone like Rebecca walking around your neighborhood. You might be shocked, upset, or afraid, or you might even laugh. Why would you respond in this manner? Perhaps Rebecca would seem abnormal to you. But think further about this. On what basis would you judge Rebecca to be abnormal? Is it her dress, the fact that she's mumbling to herself, that she sounds paranoid, or that she's emotionally unstable? And what would account for your emotional responses to seeing this woman? Why should it bother you to see Rebecca behaving in this way? Do you imagine that she will hurt you? Are you upset because she seems so helpless and out of control? Do you laugh because she seems so ridiculous, or is there something about her that makes you nervous? Perhaps you speculate on the causes of Rebecca's bizarre behavior. Is she physically ill, intoxicated, or psychologically disturbed? And if she is psychologically disturbed, how could her disturbance be explained? You might also feel concerned about Rebecca's welfare, and wonder how she might be helped. Should the police be called to take her to a hospital? Or should she just be left alone because she presents no real danger to anyone? You may not have experienced a situation involving someone exactly like Rebecca, but you have certainly encountered some people in your life whom you regard as "abnormal," and your reactions to these people probably have included the range of feelings you would experience if you saw Rebecca.

Conditions like Rebecca's are likely to touch you in a very personal way. Perhaps you have already been affected by the distressing effects of psychological disorders. Perhaps you have, in your estimation, been unusually depressed, fearful, or anxious. Or, maybe the emotional distress has been a step removed from you—your father struggles with alcoholism, or your mother has been hospitalized for severe depression; a sister has an eating disorder, or your brother has a sleep disturbance. If you have not encountered a psychological disorder within your immediate family, you have very likely encountered one in your extended family and circle of friends. You may not have known the formal psychiatric diagnosis for the problem, and you may not have understood its nature or cause. But you knew that something was wrong, and that professional help was needed.

Until they are forced to face such problems, most people believe that "bad things" happen only to other people. Other people have car accidents; other people get cancer; and other people become severely depressed. We hope that this textbook will help you to go beyond this "other people" syndrome. Psychological disorders are part of the human experience touching the life, either directly or indirectly, of every person. As you read, you will find that most of these problems are treatable and many are preventable.

What is "abnormal" behavior? You may have read this word in the title of the book without giving it much thought. Perhaps you told a friend that you were taking a course in "abnormal" psychology. Think about what you had in mind when you read or used the word "abnormal" as applied to human behavior. How would you define "abnormal" behavior? Read the following examples. Which of these behaviors would you regard as abnormal?

- Taking a "lucky" pencil to an exam.
- Being unable to sleep, eat, study, or talk to anyone else for days after one's lover says, "It's over between us."

This woman is hesitant to use the phone out of fear that her conversation might be recorded. How would you go about determining whether her concern is realistic or evidence of some kind of disturbed thinking?

- Breaking into a cold sweat at the thought of being trapped in an elevator.
- Swearing, throwing pillows, and pounding one's fist on the wall in the middle of an argument with a roommate.
- Refusing to eat solid food for days at a time in order to stay thin.
- Having to engage in a thorough hand-washing after coming home from a ride on public transportation.
- Believing that the government has agents who are listening in to one's telephone conversations.
- Drinking a six-pack of beer a day in order to be "sociable" with one's friends after work.

What is your basis for deciding between "normal" and "abnormal"? As you can see from this exercise, this distinction is often difficult to make. It may even seem arbitrary. Yet, it is essential that you arrive at a clear definition of this term to guide you in your study of the many varieties of human behavior discussed in this book.

Defining "Abnormal" Behavior

Now that you have seen how hard it is to distinguish between normal and abnormal behavior, you can see how important it is to arrive at a clear working definition of the concept of abnormality. As you begin this process, you first must decide on a point of reference. In other words, abnormal compared with what? Let's take a look at two different ways of approaching this question: deviation from the average, and deviation from the optimal.

■ Deviation from the average

The **statistical average** provides one way of thinking about normality. The average is the arithmetical mean on a given measure, calculated by dividing the sum of all scores by the number of people who are measured. You deal with averages all your life, whether it is in regard to your height, your weight, or your examination scores. When your score is significantly above or below the average, it would be considered "deviant." You will see later in the book that some psychological tests have been devised so that deviation from the average score is used as a basis for determining psychological abnormality. Consider a hypothetical test that measures anxiety. It would include items such as "When you have to speak in public, how nervous do you get?" and "Do you ever feel jittery for no reason at all?". A test of anxiety might define a score of 5 as an average level of anxiety, and 7 through 10 as progressively more deviant. This type of approach is intended to be more objective and scientific than the more subjective, informal standards involved in other approaches. However, as you might guess, the use of statistical averages is not completely objective. Someone must decide what cutoff point to use to define the extent of deviation that will indicate psychological abnormality.

■ Deviation from the optimal

Another way that you might define abnormal is by comparing a person's behavior with your notions of what represents the "optimal"—the ideal of human functioning. Think of what optimal functioning would be in a stressful situation. A person who functions optimally is able to respond to stress by keeping "cool" and solving problems rather than being overwhelmed by them. This is probably the ideal to which you would strive, for example, during final exams week. Contrast this ideal with the average of how all people contend with stress. In this case, the optimal would be quite different from the average. One problem with using the optimal as a basis for judging abnormality is that this concept is so subjectively determined. Who decides what is optimal psychological functioning, and who decides how far from optimal one has to be in order to be considered abnormal? Is it optimal to be completely stress-free? Some might contend that a certain moderate level of stress facilitates creativity and efficiency. And there are individual differences in responses to the same stress-provoking events. For example, perhaps you know someone who becomes overwhelmed with anxiety the night before an exam, when you are feeling only a minor level of concern. If your friend gets a higher grade, you might question who was showing the optimal stress reaction.

Depending on whether your basis for comparison is the average or the optimal, you would arrive at very different judgments about what is abnormal behavior. When we discuss psychological disorders, we will rely more on the no-

tion of deviation from the average, though it is important to realize that it is easy to lose sight of what would be regarded as optimal functioning.

How Do We Classify Deviation?

When psychologists attempt to define abnormal functioning, they are likely to focus on three domains of human experience: the body, the mind, and the social context of the individual. In each of these domains, there are various criteria for defining what is abnormal. The criteria for the body fall within the biological domain, for the mind within the psychological domain, and for the social context in the sociocultural domain. Throughout the book, we will return frequently to these three domains and how they pertain to abnormal human behavior, because each has relevance to understanding and treating psychological disorders.

■ Biological criteria

Most likely, you know when something is wrong with your body. You may have an elevated temperature, headache, disturbed sleep, or upset stomach. Biological criteria of abnormality include a wide range of dimensions of bodily functioning. Some biological disturbances are of particular relevance to psychological disorders. As you will see when we discuss depression, disturbances of appetite and sleep patterns are often telling clues associated with mood disorders.

Even though biological functioning may, at first, seem remote from the realm of abnormal psychology, you will see many instances throughout the book showing that biology plays a prominent role in the causes, expression, and treatment of abnormal behavior. For example, there is a theory that an excess of dopamine, a chemical substance in the brain, is responsible for the psychological disorder called schizophrenia. This excess is believed to cause a variety of symptoms associated with this disorder, such as hallucinations and disorganized thinking. The clinician's goal in treating an individual with this disorder would be to bring the amount of dopamine down to a level within the normal range.

Increasingly, as medical technology becomes more and more sophisticated, measures of brain structure and function are being used to assist mental health professionals in diagnosis. Fascinating new procedures are constantly being developed to get an inside picture of the brain in the living human being, and these procedures can provide invaluable diagnostic information about abnormalities in the brain's structures. Some of these methods can also show the activities of these brain structures, and can be used to detect any unusual functioning.

■ Psychological criteria

Psychological indices used in evaluating normality include a person's emotional state and ability to solve new

The anxiety experienced by this business executive during a sales presentation may interfere with the quality of her performance.

problems, remember what is learned, use language, adapt to stressful situations, and meet personal needs. One important criterion for psychological abnormality is personal distress. Feelings of unhappiness, lack of fulfillment, and maladjustment are often used as indications of dysfunction. If you think about Rebecca, you might regard her as abnormal because her behavior reveals that she is extremely distressed about the death of her brother.

Sometimes people do not feel particularly distressed, but their behavior is nevertheless maladaptive in that it interferes with their everyday functioning. Take the case of a college student who refuses to enter any classroom that has an odd number. Such behavior would certainly create problems for this individual, even though the person may not experience any distress about this ritualistic behavior. Think about the limitations that this person would encounter in college, and perhaps later in life if this behavior continues. Individuals may also engage in more indirect forms of maladaptive behavior, such as a person who constantly gets romantically involved with people who are exploitative. There are many other kinds of maladaptive behaviors, and very commonly these behaviors are associated with acute personal distress.

■ *Sociocultural criteria*

Returning to the case of Rebecca, in addition to your evaluation of her emotional state, your reaction to her behavior may have been based largely on the fact that her actions violated social conventions. It is not considered appropriate to wander in your nightclothes on the streets talking to yourself. The sociocultural criteria for abnormality focus on the extent to which the individual has adopted the

prevailing views of society. A behavior is abnormal if it involves stepping outside of society's expectations for appropriate behavior. These expectations are called "social norms." A **social norm** is a standard for acceptable behavior that is established in a given society or culture. When you think about Rebecca's behavior, for example, you would see it as "abnormal" because it deviates from what most people would regard as acceptable. After the loss of a family member, most people would be upset. However, would they walk the streets at night, dressed in their nightclothes and talking to themselves? Probably not. This kind of behavior would deviate, then, from what is appropriate and acceptable for people in this kind of situation.

One problem with this criterion of abnormality is, as you might imagine, that not everyone in a given society agrees on what is "acceptable" behavior. Often, there are significant differences in what is considered acceptable from one country to another and from one subculture to another. Funeral rituals, for example, vary tremendously according to the cultural and ethnic tradition of the individual. Rebecca's behavior, as odd as it might seem to most people in the United States, might actually be considered appropriate elsewhere.

Sometimes violation of social norms causes harm to the individual or other people. Failure to adapt to conventional expectations of the world may interfere with a person's ability to sustain a job, to live independently in the community, or to maintain family ties. Violating social norms may directly harm others by interfering with their freedom or by upsetting them.

Although in this book we focus primarily on psychological criteria for abnormal behavior, it is important to

Do you think that dressing as a Viking to run in the Boston marathon is normal or abnormal behavior?

remember that what is "normal" differs from situation to situation, from culture to culture, and from person to person. A behavior may be normal in one setting but not in another. It is normal to shout and yell when you are a spectator at a basketball game but usually not normal when you are walking alone in the corridor of your dormitory. A behavior that is normal in one person may not be normal in another. It is normal for the president of the United States to regard his ideas as so important that they affect the lives of millions of people. It is of doubtful normality for an ordinary citizen to place such great value on his or her own ideas.

Some social critics, such as the noted British psychiatrist R. D. Laing (1964), have taken what might be regarded as an extreme position that modern society dehumanizes the individual, and that people who refuse to abide by the norms of this society are healthier psychologically than those who blindly accept and live by such restrictive social norms. Along similar lines, the American psychiatrist Thomas Szasz (1961) argues that the concept of mental illness is a "myth" created by modern society and put into practice by the mental health profession. Szasz proposed that a better way to describe people who cannot fit into society's norms would be that they have "problems in living."

Such terminology would avoid labeling people as "sick," and instead indicate that their difficulties stem from a mismatch between their personal needs and the ability of society to meet those needs. Although most mental health professionals regard the ideas of Laing and Szasz as overly simplistic, there was great value in raising these issues. The mental health community as a whole seems more sensitive today than in decades past to the need to avoid labeling people with psychological disorders as socially deviant. Such views also help to promote acceptance of people with such problems by the larger society.

Criticisms of the mental health establishment such as those raised by Laing and Szasz became more credible when researcher David Rosenhan conducted a radical experiment that caused many people in the scientific community to take a second look at institutionalization. The Critical Issue in this chapter (page 6) describes the questions raised by Rosenhan's study.

■ *Toward a definition of abnormal behavior*

The different kinds of criteria for defining abnormal behavior are summarized in Table 1-1. Disturbances in any of these areas of human functioning can be thought of as deviating from an optimal or from an average state of functioning.

In this book, when we refer to concepts such as "abnormal" or "abnormality," we are relying on current views within the mental health profession that incorporate biological, psychological, and sociocultural dimensions. We will place different emphasis on each of these dimensions, and on deviation from the ideal or average, depending on the exact nature of the disorder or the way it is currently understood. We will use as criteria the dysfunctions of the body, the phenomena of perceived psychological distress, and violations of social norms. For example, people with

Table 1-1   Criteria for Abnormal Behavior

BIOLOGICAL	Abnormal levels of biochemical substances in the nervous system Bodily symptoms involving sleep, appetite, and energy levels Disturbances in the structure and function of parts of the brain
PSYCHOLOGICAL	Unusual sensory and perceptual experiences Peculiar or deficient cognitive functioning Disturbed emotional state Personal distress Maladaptive behavior
SOCIOCULTURAL	Violation of social norms Harm to other people

On Being Sane in Insane Places

On January 19, 1973, an article appeared in *Science* magazine that was to have an enormous impact on the entire mental health profession. This article, by David L. Rosenhan, reported the findings of a study in which eight people successfully fooled the staffs of twelve psychiatric hospitals located across the United States. These people were all "sane," and were employed in a variety of mostly professional occupations. They each presented themselves at a hospital's admissions office, complaining that they had been hearing voices that said "empty," "hollow," and "thud." The kind of "existential psychosis" that these symptoms were supposed to represent has never been reported in the psychiatric literature, which is why those symptoms were chosen. No other details about the lives of the "pseudopatients" (except their names and employment) were changed when they described themselves; consequently, their histories and current behaviors outside of their symptoms could not be considered abnormal in any way. All hospitals accepted the pseudopatients for treatment. Once admitted to the hospitals, the pseudopatients stopped fabricating any symptoms at all. None of the staff in any of the hospitals detected the sanity of the pseudopatients and instead interpreted the ordinary activities of the pseudopatients on the hospital wards

as further evidence of their abnormality. One of the most troubling experiences for the pseudopatients was a feeling of dehumanization, as they felt that no one on the staff cared about their personal issues and needs. And despite their efforts to convince the staff that they were normal, no one believed them, with the interesting exception of some of the patients who guessed that they might be either reporters or researchers trying to get an inside look at mental hospitals.

It took from 7 to 52 days for the pseudopatients to be released from the hospitals. By the time they left, each had a diagnosis of schizophrenia "in remission"; in other words, their symptoms were no longer evident, at least for the time being. Rosenhan concluded that the misattribution of abnormality was due to a general bias among hospital staff to call a healthy person sick: "Better to err on the side of caution, to suspect illness even among the healthy" (p. 179).

Rosenhan's study was criticized on both ethical and methodological grounds. Ethical concerns were raised about the fact that the study involved the deception of the mental health professionals whose job it was to diagnose and treat the pseudopatients. Methodological questions were raised by the fact that no at-

tempt was made to exercise the usual experimental controls on a study of this nature such as having a comparison group (Spitzer, 1975). Other criticisms pertained to diagnostic issues. The pseudopatients were reporting serious symptoms (hallucinations) that would understandably cause alarm in others. At the point of discharge, the fact that the pseudopatients were labelled as being in remission implied that they were symptom-free. Technically, the staff probably felt reluctant to label these individuals as "normal," in light of the fact that the pseudopatients had previously complained of schizophrenia-like symptoms (Farber, 1975).

Despite these criticisms, Rosenhan's results and the debates that followed in the study's aftermath were part of the momentum in the late 1960s and early 1970s to change attitudes toward institutionalization of psychologically disturbed individuals. At the same time, mental health professionals were in the process of changing the system for diagnosing many disorders, including schizophrenia. The point of the study, however, is still pertinent today. When a patient in a psychiatric hospital claims to be "the sane one in an insane place," would anyone believe the patient?

---

alcoholism deviate from both the average and the optimal in a variety of ways: bodily, emotionally, and interpersonally.

However, we realize that current views of abnormality in the mental health profession have limitations, and it is likely that you will, at times, question whether a certain behavior should be considered abnormal or not. For example, we will talk about people with a personality disorder characterized by a preference for social isolation. As you read about these people, you may question whether their condition should be considered a psychological disorder and therefore regarded as abnormal. As you read about each of the disorders in this text, you may want to ask yourself what you think about labeling people with this set of behaviors as "abnormal."

The Stigma of Being "Abnormal"

One of your reactions to seeing people like Rebecca might be to see them as very different from you. You may even feel a certain degree of contempt or disgust for them. This reaction is common, and it is the basis for much of the discrimination experienced by people with psychological disorders. A *stigma* is a label that causes certain people to be regarded as different, and therefore defective. It sets certain individuals apart from others who do not want to be associated with them.

There is no question that emotional disorder, and the treatments associated with it, are less socially accepted than physical illness and its accompanying treatment. Common myths about recovered psychiatric patients, shown in Table 1-2, illustrate the various forms that stigma toward these people can take.

Most people would outwardly espouse an understanding and tolerance for people with psychological disorders. Reflected more subtly in their language, humor, and stereotypes, however, are usually some fairly negative attributions. Watch television for an hour, or listen to the everyday conversation of those around you, and you will probably encounter some comment about emotional illness. Colloquialisms relating to emotional illness abound in our language. Statements about being "nuts," "crazy," "mental," "maniac," "flaky," "off-the-wall," "psycho," "schizo," or "retarded" are quite common. Popular humor is filled with jokes about "crazy people."

Why would mental illness serve as the topic of so much humor? One reason might be that people often joke about issues that make them anxious. This might be why someone would laugh at a person such as Rebecca. There is something very frightening about psychological disorder that makes people want to distance themselves from it as much as possible. Perhaps some people are frightened about the prospect of losing control over their senses and sensibilities. This experience could happen to anyone. Most people have had some experience close to a loss of control, if only for a brief spell. For example, anyone who has gone without sleep or nourishment for an extended period, or who has undergone an intense amount of stress, has had disturbing perceptual experiences and thoughts. Coming so close to losing control can prove terrifying. As a way of distancing themselves from such a possibility, people joke about it.

What about your own attitudes? Imagine the following scenario: An urgent message is waiting for you when you come back to your room. It is from the mother of Jeremy, your best friend in high school. You call Jeremy's mother, who says she wants you to meet her at the psychiatric hospital in your hometown as soon as possible. Jeremy has just been admitted there and says that he has to see you, because only you can understand what he is going through. You are puzzled and distressed by this news. You had no idea that he had any psychological problems. What will you say to him? Can you ask him what's wrong? Can you ask him how he feels? Do you dare inquire about what his doctors have told him about his chances of getting better? What will it be like to see him in a hospital that cares for "crazy" people? Does that mean he is "crazy" too? Do you think you could be friends with someone who has spent time in a mental hospital?

Now imagine the same scenario, but instead you receive news that Jeremy has just been hospitalized for treatment of a kidney dysfunction. As you imagine yourself going to visit him, you will probably not think twice about how you will respond to him. Of course you will ask him how he feels, what exactly is wrong with him, and when he will be well again. Even though you might not like hospitals very much, at least you have a pretty good idea about what hospital patients are like. It does not seem peculiar to imagine Jeremy as a patient in this kind of hospital. Your friend's physical illness would be much easier to understand and accept than his psychological disorder. You would probably not even consider whether you could be friends with him again after he is discharged.

ABNORMAL PSYCHOLOGY THROUGHOUT HISTORY

Now that you know about the complexities of defining abnormal behavior, you can appreciate how very difficult it is to understand its causes. This question has challenged the greatest thinkers of the world, from Plato to the present day. In this section, we will look at how the mental health field has gotten to present-day understandings of the causes and

Table 1-2   Fourteen Myths about Mental Illness

	True	False
1. A person who has been mentally ill can never be normal.		X
2. Even if some mentally ill persons return to normal, chronically mentally ill people remain different—in fact, crazy.		X
3. If people with other handicaps can cope on their own, recovered mental patients should be able to do so, too.		X
4. Persons with mental illness are unpredictable.		X
5. Yes, but those with schizophrenia or other severe mental disorders must remain unpredictable.		X
6. Mentally ill persons are dangerous.		X
7. But recovered mental patients are surely potentially dangerous. They could go berserk at any time.		X
8. Anyone who has had shock treatment must really be in a bad way.		X
9. When you learn a person has been mentally ill, you have learned the most important thing about his or her personality.		X
10. You can't talk to someone who has been mentally ill.		X
11. If a former mental patient has a really bad history there isn't much hope.		X
12. A former mental patient is bound to make a second-rate employee.		X
13. Perhaps recovered mental patients can work successfully at low-level jobs. But they aren't suited for really important or responsible positions.		X
14. Recovered mental patients have a tough row to hoe. But there's not much that can be done about it.		X

Source: USDHHS, (1988).

treatments of psychological disorders. You will see how ideas about psychological disorders have taken a variety of twists and turns throughout recorded history. There is every reason to expect that these concepts will continue to evolve.

Three prominent themes in explaining psychological disorders recur throughout history: the mystical, the scientific, and the humanitarian. Mystical explanations of psychological disorders regard abnormal behavior as the product of possession by evil or demonic spirits. The scientific approach looks for natural causes such as biological imbalances, faulty learning processes, or emotional stressors. Humanitarian explanations view psychological disorders as the result of cruelty, nonacceptance, or poor living conditions. Tension among these three approaches has existed throughout recorded history; at times, one or another has dominated, but all three have coexisted for centuries. Even in today's scientific world, the humanitarian and mystical approaches each have their advocates. As you read about the historical trends in understanding and treating psychological disorders, see if you can identify which theme is most prevalent at each stage.

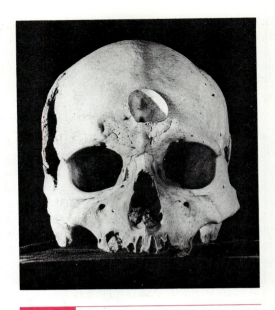

A trephined skull shows that prehistoric people tried to treat psychological disorders by releasing evil spirits from the head.

Prehistoric Times: Abnormal Behavior as Demonic Possession

There is no written record of ideas regarding psychological disorders in prehistoric times, but there is mysterious archeological evidence—skulls with holes drilled in them. Furthermore, there was evidence that the bone healed near these holes, evidence taken to indicate that the procedure was a surgical one and that people survived it. Why would prehistoric people perform such bizarre surgery?

Some psychologists have wondered whether this kind of surgery, called **trephining**, was performed as a way of treating psychological disorders. Perhaps prehistoric people thought that abnormal behavior was caused by evil spirits that were trapped inside the head, and that by releasing the evil spirits, the person would return to normal behavior. Another interpretation is that trephining was used to treat medical problems. For all we know, the procedure might have been an effective treatment for some psychological disturbances caused by physiological imbalances or abnormalities. In any case, the skulls are the only evidence we have from that period of history and we can only speculate about their meaning (Maher & Maher, 1985a).

Many thousands of years later, the idea that possession by evil spirits caused psychological disorders had firmly taken hold (Zilboorg & Henry, 1941). In the days of the ancient Hebrews, people who showed signs of "possession" were subjected to exorcism, a ritual used to expel evil spirits. At times, the procedures involved in exorcism bordered on outright torture. The possessed person might be starved, whipped, beaten, and treated in other extreme ways with the intention of driving the evil spirits away. Some were

forced to eat or drink foul-tasting and disgusting concoctions which included blood, wine, and sheep dung. Some were executed because they were considered a burden and a threat to their communities. Others were allowed to wander around the countryside, perhaps mocked by their neighbors, but never helped by them.

Considering the case of Rebecca, it is easy to imagine how her symptoms might have been interpreted as signs of demonic possession. The voices that she heard could have been devils speaking to her. Her bizarre behavior would have been perceived as evidence that she was under the control of a supernatural force. Frightened and disturbed by behaviors they could not understand, her neighbors might have sent her to a shaman or witch doctor, who would carry out the rites of exorcism. As you will see, such ideas played

A Brazilian priestess tries to control a spirit in a woman believed to be "possessed" by a saint, in a carryover of an ancient ritual.

a prominent role in the understanding and treatment of psychological disorders for centuries to follow.

Ancient Greece and Rome: The Emergence of the Scientific Model

Even though their theories were far off the mark, the early Greek philosophers such as Heraclitus and Hippocrates established the foundation for a systematic approach to psychological disorders. Heraclitus (535–475 B.C.), for example, tried to look for the causes of behavior as residing within the individual, not as the result of external forces. He believed that fire was the energy of all life, and that rationality depended on the nature of the fire within the soul. Hippocrates (c. 460–377 B.C.), whom many people consider the founder of modern medicine, was concerned not only with physical diseases but with psychological problems as well. He believed that there were four important bodily fluids that influenced physical and mental health: black bile, yellow bile, phlegm, and blood. An excess of any of these fluids could account for an individual's personality and behavior. For example, an excess of black bile would make a person depressed ("melancholic"), or an excess of yellow bile would cause a person to be anxious and irritable ("choleric"). Too much phlegm would result in a calm and placid disposition bordering perhaps on indifference ("phlegmatic"). An overabundance of blood would cause a person to experience unstable mood shifts ("sanguine"). Treatment of a psychological disorder, then, would involve ridding the body of the excess fluid through methods such as bleeding, purgation (forced excretion), and emetics (nausea-producing substances), or by establishing a healthier balance through proper nutrition.

As unlikely as it sounds, Hippocrates' classification of four types of fluid imbalances resurfaced in modern explanations of personality types. The classification proposed by Eysenck (1957) shown in Figure 1-1 is based on a psychological test that provides scores on various personality dispositions. The two dimensions of neurotic-normal and introvert-extrovert interact to produce the four personality types shown in the figure. The resurfacing of ancient ideas in the form of a modern psychological theory suggest that despite the very different philosophies that underlie these systems, there might be something to the notion that there are some enduring dimensions of personality.

For the next 500 years, the views of Hippocrates were to dominate medical thinking on the topic of psychological disorders. However, these views were countered by the more popular belief in spiritual possession and the cruel treatment of psychologically disturbed people. The next significant advances in the medical approach were made by two Greek physicians living in Rome, separated by 200 years, who introduced new and more humane ideas about psychological disorders.

In the first century B.C. Aesclepiades rebelled against the Hippocratic belief that a psychological disorder was

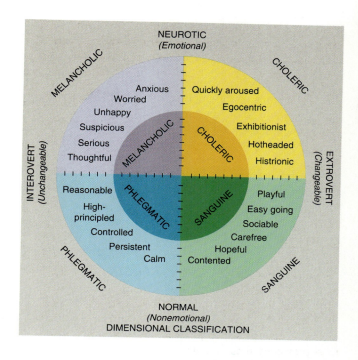

Figure 1–1 Four temperaments
An illustration of Eysenck's explanation of personality types. The two dimensions of neurotic–normal and introvert–extrovert interact to produce the four types described by Hippocrates. The resurfacing of ancient ideas in the form of a modern psychological theory suggests that there might be something to the notion of enduring dimensions of personality.

caused by the imbalance of bodily substances. Instead, he recognized that psychological problems could result from emotional disturbances. This notion is comparable to many contemporary explanations of abnormal behavior. Aesclepiades also made diagnostic distinctions, such as the difference between acute and chronic psychological disorders, and the difference between hallucinations and delusions. Today, these distinctions are taken for granted. As a therapist, Aesclepiades also developed some surprisingly modern ideas, such as music therapy. In addition, he argued strenuously against the use of bleeding, imprisonment, and other cruel treatments.

Two hundred years later, Galen (A.D. 130–200) developed a system of medical knowledge that revolutionized previous thinking about psychological as well as physical disorders. Rather than rely on philosophical speculation, Galen studied anatomy to discover answers to questions about the workings of the human body and mind. He was the first "medical researcher" who conducted experiments on animals in order to study the workings of the internal organs. Galen was also the first to suggest that abnormal behavior could have psychological origins rather than result only from abnormalities in bodily organs or fluids. The approach he advocated formed the basis for the scientific model of abnormal behavior, but it was buried under the cloud of the Middle Ages and the return to superstition and spiritual explanations of abnormality.

The Middle Ages and Renaissance: The Re-emergence of Spiritual Explanations

The Middle Ages are sometimes referred to as the "Dark Ages." In terms of the approaches to psychological disorders, this was a "dark" period. No scientific or medical advances occurred beyond those of Hippocrates and Galen. In the rare cases in which people with psychological disorders sought medical treatment, there was little the physician could offer beyond the barbaric methods of purging and bleeding, ineffectual attempts to manipulate diet, or prescribing useless drugs.

The Middle Ages are also associated with the resurgence of primitive beliefs regarding spiritual possession. During this time, people turned to superstition, astrology, and alchemy to explain many natural phenomena including psychological and physical illnesses. So-called treatments corresponding to these beliefs were widely practiced, including magical rituals, exorcism, and folk medicines. Beliefs in demonic possession were also used to account for abnormal behavior, and in some cases, people who sought help from the clergy were treated as sinners, witches, or embodiments of the devil. The punishment and execution of people thought to be witches became more widespread toward the end of the Middle Ages and especially during the Renaissance.

During the Middle Ages, the dominance of religious thinking had both positive and negative effects on the care

The inhumane treatment at the Hospital of St. Mary of Bethlehem in London is shown in William Hogarth's *The Madhouse.*

of psychologically disturbed individuals. Beliefs in spiritual possession and the treatment of people as sinners had harmful effects. By contrast, ideas about Christian charity and the need to help poor and sick people formed the basis for more humanitarian approaches to treatment. Monasteries began to open their doors to give these people a place to stay and receive whatever primitive treatments the monks could offer. Poorhouses, or homes for people who could not pay their living expenses, were built all over Europe. Many of them sheltered people who were emotionally disturbed.

Later, the poorhouses became known as **asylums.** One of the most famous of these asylums was The Hospital of St. Mary of Bethlehem in London. Originally founded as a hospital for poor people in 1247, by the year 1403 it began to house people described as "lunatics." In the centuries to follow, the term "bedlam," a derivative of the hospital's name, became synonymous with the chaotic and inhumane housing of psychologically disturbed people who languished unattended for years (MacDonald, 1981). As the hospital became more crowded and its occupants increasingly unruly, the hospital workers resorted to chains and other punishments to keep the inhabitants under control. Similar conditions prevailed in other asylums as they became more and more crowded. Unfortunately, the original intention of enlisting clergy to treat psychologically disturbed individuals with humanitarian methods ended up having disastrous consequences. It was not until several centuries later that the humanitarian ideals were reinstated.

In contrast to what you might learn in a history class about the Renaissance as a period of enlightenment, you will see that this period was far from enlightened with regard to an understanding of psychological disorders. There were virtually no scientific or humanitarian advances during this entire period, and demonic possession remained the prevalent explanation for abnormal behavior of any kind. Some historical accounts have proposed that witch hunts, conducted on a wide scale throughout Europe and later in North America, were directed at people with psychological

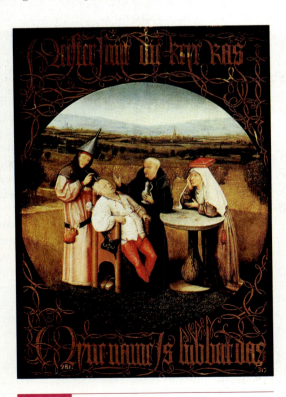

Hieronymous Bosch's *Removal of the Stone of Folly* depicted the prevailing belief that spiritual possession was the cause of psychological disorder.

disturbances. However, more careful study of this period has produced evidence that the targets of witch hunts were people, mostly women, who were accused of religious heresy and victims of fraudulent political charges (Ussher, 1991).

Were Rebecca to be treated during this era, it is possible that she might have been regarded as a witch, especially if she was heard to refer to the devil or some other supernatural force. However, it is just as likely that she would have been taken to a medical practitioner. The view that people who showed signs of demonic possession might be psychologically disturbed had been introduced in the 1500s. In 1563, a physician named Johann Weyer (1515-1588) wrote a major treatise called "The Deception of Demons" in which he tried to debunk the myth that psychologically disturbed people were possessed by the devil. Although Weyer did not abandon the notion of demonic possession, his book represented the first major advance since the time of Galen in the description and classification of forms of abnormal behavior. Weyer's approach also formed the basis for what would later become a renewal of the humanitarian approach to psychologically disturbed people. However, at the time of his writing, Weyer was severely criticized and ridiculed for challenging the views held by the powerful and influential religious and political leaders of the time. Yet, in another part of Europe, Weyer's "radical" ideas were being echoed by an Englishman, Reginald Scot (1538-1599), who deviated even further from the prevalent ideologies by denying the very existence of demons.

Europe and the United States in the 1700s: The Reform Movement

The eighteenth century was a time of massive political and social reformation throughout Europe. Public institutions housing individuals with psychological disorders had, by this point, become like dungeons where people were not even given the care that would be accorded an animal. The living conditions for poor people were miserable, but to be psychologically disturbed and poor was a horrible fate. People with psychological disorders lived in dark, cold cells with dirt floors, often chained to straw beds and surrounded by their own excrement. It was widely believed that psychologically disturbed people were insensitive to extremes of heat and cold or to the cleanliness of their surroundings. The "treatment" given to these people involved bleeding, forced vomiting, and purging. It took a few courageous people, who recognized the inhumanity of the existing practices, to bring about sweeping reforms.

The leader of the reform movement was Vincenzo Chiarugi (1759–1820), the superintendent of a mental hospital in Florence called the Ospidale di Bonifazio. Within a year of taking charge of the hospital in 1788, he instituted major changes such as eliminating most physical restraints on the patients and providing them with activities to occupy their time. Through his writings, Chiarugi also spread the word among his professional colleagues about the need to make mental hospitals safe and comfortable (Maher & Maher, 1985b).

More widely publicized were the reforms of Phillipe Pinel (1745–1826) in La Bicêtre, a hospital in Paris with conditions like those faced by Chiarugi. Upon his appointment as a hospital physician in 1792, Pinel was influenced by a hospital staff worker, Jean-Baptiste Pussin, who had begun the process of reform. Together, they made changes to improve the living conditions of the patients. When Pinel left La Bicêtre two years later, Pussin stayed behind. It was then that Pussin made the bold gesture of freeing patients from their chains, an act for which Pinel is mistakenly given credit. After leaving La Bicêtre, Pinel became director of La Salpêtrière Hospital, where he and Pussin continued to spread these reforms.

This painting shows Phillipe Pinel having the irons removed from the inmates at La Salpêtrière Hospital. It was actually Pinel's employer, Jean-Baptiste Pussin, who performed this liberating gesture.

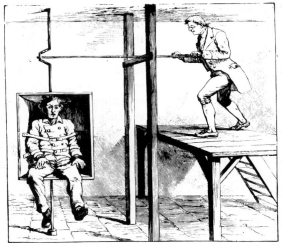

Benjamin Rush's methods of treatment, based on what he thought were scientific principles, would be considered barbaric by today's standards.

England was the third country to see major reforms in its treatment of psychologically disturbed individuals. In 1792, an English Quaker named William Tuke established the York Retreat, an institution based on the religious humanitarian principles of the Quakers. Tuke's work was carried on by succeeding generations of his family. Their methods became known as **moral treatment.** Underlying this approach was the philosophy that people can, with the proper care develop self-control over their own disturbed behaviors. Restraints would be used only if absolutely necessary, and, even in these cases the patient's comfort should come first.

At the time of Europe's revolutionary reforms, similar changes in the care of psychologically disturbed people were being initiated in the United States. Benjamin Rush (1745–1813) became known as the founder of American psychiatry for his rekindling of interest in the scientific approach to psychological disorders. Rush, who was one of the signers of the Declaration of Independence, achieved fame as a politician, statesman, surgeon general, and writer in many diverse fields ranging from philosophy to meteorology. Because of his prestigious role in American society, he was able to influence the instituting of reforms in the mental health field. In 1783, he joined the medical staff of Pennsylvania Hospital. Rush was appalled by the poor conditions in the hospital and by the fact that psychologically disturbed patients were placed on wards with the physically ill. He spoke out for changes that were considered radical at the time. He placed the psychologically disturbed patients in separate wards, giving them occupational therapy and prohibiting visits from curiosity seekers who frequented the hospital for entertainment.

In evaluating Rush's contributions, we must also mention that he advocated some rather barbaric interventions that he naively thought were based on scientific principles. Rush supported the use of bleeding to remove excess blood, which he believed to be the source of psychological problems. He also recommended invoking terror as a way to treat psychologically disturbed patients. Some of his meth-

ods were very unusual and almost sadistic. Rush's "tranquilizer" consisted of a chair to which a patient was tied. He also recommended that patients be submerged in cold shower baths and frightened with threats that they would be killed. Similar techniques were used by other physicians at the time, such as surprise immersions into tubs of cold water, and the "well-cure," where a patient was placed at the bottom of a well as water was slowly being poured into it. Rush and his contemporaries thought that the fright induced by these methods would counteract the over-excitement responsible for their violent and bizarre behavior (Deutsch, 1949). It is ironic that in the spirit of reform, methods just as primitive as those of the Middle Ages continued to be developed.

Thirty years after Rush's death, asylums were built across the United States with the intention of providing moral therapy. However, conditions in these institutions worsened as they became overcrowded. The psychologically disturbed patients were often forced to live in poorhouses and jails, where conditions were even less conducive to treatment than in the asylums. By 1841, when a retired Boston schoolteacher named Dorothea Dix (1802–1887) made her first venture into these institutions, conditions were ripe for another round of major reforms. She was shocked and repulsed by scenes that were reminiscent of the horrifying conditions faced by European reformers in the previous century. Her first encounter was with the prison system, where many psychologically disturbed people were incarcerated. Inmates were chained to the walls, no heat was provided for them, and they were forced to live in filth. Viewing these conditions was enough to set Dix off onto an investigative path. She traveled throughout Massachusetts visiting jails and poorhouses, chronicling the horrors that she witnessed. Two years later, Dix presented her findings to the Massachusetts Legislature, with the demand that more state-funded public hospitals be built to care specifically for the psychologically disturbed. From Massachusetts, Dix spread her message throughout North America, and even to Europe. She spent the next forty years campaigning for the

Dorothea Dix worked throughout the late 1800s to move psychologically disturbed people from jails and poorhouses to state-funded hospitals where they could receive more humane treatment.

Even though moral therapy was a failure, the humanitarian goals that Dix advocated had a lasting influence on the mental health system. Her work was carried forward into the 1900s by advocates of the "mental hygiene" movement, most notably Clifford Beers. In 1908, Beers wrote a very disturbing book, *A Mind That Found Itself*, which recounted in alarming detail his own harsh treatment in psychiatric institutions. Beers had become so enraged by the inhumane treatments that he established the National Committee for Mental Hygiene, a group of people who worked to improve treatment of those in psychiatric institutions.

The 1800s to the 1900s: Development of Alternative Models for Abnormal Behavior

While Dix was engaged in her reform campaign, the superintendents of existing state mental hospitals were also trying to develop better ways to manage patients. In 1844, a group of 13 mental hospital administrators formed the Association of Medical Superintendents of American Institutions for the Insane. The name of this organization was eventually changed to the American Psychiatric Association. The founding of this organization gave rise to the **medical model**, the view that abnormal behaviors result from physical problems and should be treated medically.

The goals of the American Psychiatric Association were furthered by the publication in 1845 of a book on the pathology and treatment of psychological disorders by William Greisinger, a German psychiatrist. Greisinger focused on the role of the brain rather than spiritual possession as the cause of abnormal behavior. Another German psychiatrist, Emil Kraepelin, was also influential in the development of the American psychiatric movement. Kraepelin carried further Greisinger's ideas that psychological disorder was caused by brain malfunction. He is perhaps better known, however, for his efforts to improve the way that psychological disorders were classified. Kraepelin's ideas continue to be influential even today, and some of the distinctions he introduced are reflected in contemporary systems of psychiatric diagnosis. For example, Kraepelin's concept of manic-depression was a precursor to what is now

proper treatment of psychologically disturbed people. She was a most effective champion of this cause, and her efforts resulted in the growth of the state hospital movement.

In the century to follow, scores of state hospitals were built throughout the United States. Once again, as in the Middle Ages, the best intentions of the mental health reformers became lost and ultimately backfired. These new state hospitals became so overcrowded and understaffed that treatment conditions deteriorated. The wards in these hospitals were overflowing with people whose symptoms included violent and destructive behaviors. Under these circumstances, there was no way to fulfill Dix's goals of providing moral therapy. Instead, the staff resorted to the use of physical restraints and other measures that moral therapy was intended to replace. There were some reforms, such as allowing patients to work on the hospital grounds and to participate in various forms of recreation. However, at the same time, these institutions became custodial facilities where people would spend their entire lives, an outcome that Dix had not anticipated. It simply was not possible to "cure" people of these serious disorders by providing them with the well-intentioned but ineffective interventions proposed by moral therapy. Furthermore, over the course of several decades, the emphasis of this form of treatment had shifted almost solely to disciplinary enforcement of the institution's rules and away from the more humane spirit of the original idea.

The work of Emil Kraepelin, a German psychiatrist, led to improved ways of classifying psychological disorders.

called bipolar disorder; his concept of *dementia praecox* (premature degeneration) is now known as schizophrenia.

It was not until the 1950s that scientists introduced medications that controlled some of the debilitating symptoms of severe psychological disturbance. These medicines were quickly incorporated into the treatment regimens of mental hospitals. They were seen as an easy solution to the centuries-old problem of how to control the harmful and bizarre behaviors of psychologically disturbed people and possibly even to cure them. The initial hopes for these "miracle drugs" were naive and simplistic. No one realized that these medications could have harmful physical side effects, some of which could cause irreversible neurological damage. Swept away by early enthusiasm, mental health professionals often became caught up in indiscriminate and unselective use of large doses of powerful drugs. An extreme over-emphasis on the medical model also had the unanticipated effect of inattention to the other mental health needs of these patients.

At the same time that the medical model was evolving, a very different approach to understanding psychological problems was also taking root. The **psychoanalytic model**, which seeks explanations of abnormal behavior in the workings of unconscious psychological processes, had its origins in the controversial techniques developed by Anton Mesmer (1734–1815), a Viennese physician. Mesmer gained fame and notoriety for his dramatic interventions involving hypnotic techniques. Expelled from Vienna for what were regarded as false claims of cure, Mesmer traveled to Paris, where the same misfortune befell him. Wherever he went, the medical establishment regarded him as a fraud because of his unbelievable assertions and questionable practices. In 1766, Mesmer published a book called *The In-fluence of the Planets*, which promoted the rather doubtful idea that magnetic fluid fills the universe, and thus is in the bodies of all living creatures. He maintained that physical and psychological disturbances were the result of an imbalance in this magnetic fluid, which could be corrected by a device he invented called a "magnetizer." Mesmer "cured" people in groups by having them hold hands around a tub containing chemicals and iron rods, while he walked around them holding a magnetic wand and stroking them. As bizarre as the whole concept of magnetism seems today, it was practiced widely in Europe and the United States throughout the 1800s. Many people believed it to be an effective treatment for a variety of nervous and psychological disorders.

Intrigued by claims of the supposed beneficial effects of magnetism, the English physician James Braid (1795–1860) became convinced that whatever positive effects occurred were unrelated to magnetic fluid. Instead, Braid proposed that changes took place in people's minds outside their conscious awareness that could explain the "cures" attributed to mesmerism. In 1842, Braid introduced the term **hypnotism** to describe the process of being put into a trance, which he saw as responsible for Mesmer's ability to effect changes in the minds of his subjects. He reasoned that some people treated by Mesmer's method improved because they were in a hypnotic state and were open to suggestions that could result in removal of their symptoms. The term **mesmerized,** in fact, refers to this state of heightened suggestibility brought about by the words and actions of a charismatic individual. Braid's explanation of hypnosis played an important role in leading practitioners to realize how powerful the mind can be in causing and removing symptoms.

Anton Mesmer claimed that by redistributing the magnetic fluids in the patient's body, he could cure psychological disorders. Mesmer, standing in the far right-hand corner of the room, is holding a wand while his patients hold metal rods.

Jean-Martin Charcot, a neurologist, is shown demonstrating a hypnotic technique during a medical lecture.

Two decades later Ambrose-Auguste Liébault (1823–1904), a French doctor, began to experiment with mesmerism. Many of Liébault's patients were poor farmers, whom Liébault treated in his clinic in Nancy, France. Liébault discovered that he could use hypnotic sleep induction as a substitute for drugs. Liébault's clinic eventually became well-known for innovative treatments. In 1882, Liébault was visited by another physician, Hippolyte-Marie Bernheim (1837–1919), who became one of the major proponents of hypnotism in Europe. Bernheim was seeking Liébault's help in treating a patient with severe back pains for whom other forms of therapy were unsuccessful. Liébault's cure of this patient convinced Bernheim that hypnosis was the wave of the future.

From their work at the Nancy clinic, Bernheim and Liébault gained international attention for advances in the use of hypnosis as a treatment for nervous and psychological disorders. At the same time, an esteemed neurologist in Paris, Jean-Martin Charcot (1825–1893), was testing similar techniques in La Salpêtrière hospital. However, Charcot's Salpêtrière "school" of hypnosis differed sharply in its explanation of how hypnosis works. Charcot believed that hypnotizability was actually a symptom of a neurological disorder and that only people who suffered from this disorder could be treated by hypnosis. You can see how Charcot's notion that hypnosis involved physical changes in the nervous system was a radical departure from the Nancy school's position. The weight of evidence, however, was in favor of the Nancy school, and eventually Charcot adopted its position. Hypnosis was clearly understood as a psychological process that could be very instrumental in resolving certain kinds of disorders. In particular, hypnosis became the treatment of choice for **hysteria,** a disorder in which psychological problems become expressed in physical form. The girl that Mesmer "cured" of her blindness was probably suffering from hysteria; in other words, some psychological conflict was converted into an apparent sensory deficit. Other forms of hysteria became widely known in the medical establishment, including various forms of paralysis, pain disorders, and a wide range of sensory deficits such as blindness and hearing loss.

The development of hypnosis went on to play a central role in the evolution of psychological methods for treating psychological disorders. In fact, Sigmund Freud (1856–1939) was heavily influenced by both Charcot and Bernheim in his early work with hysterical patients. Freud originally studied medicine in Vienna, where he trained as a neurologist. After graduating from the University of Vienna, Freud traveled to France to learn about hypnosis, a method of treatment that fascinated him. In *Studies in Hysteria* (1895, 1982), written with his colleague Josef Breuer (1842–1925), Freud analyzed the famous case of "Anna O." and other women suffering from hysteria. Freud and Breuer described how Anna O. was cured of her many and varied hysterical symptoms by the use of hypnosis. In addition, however, Anna O. urged Breuer, who was actually the one treating her, to allow her to engage in "chimney sweeping," which she also called the "talking cure." When she was allowed simply to talk about her problems, she felt better, and her symptoms disappeared. Freud and Breuer called this the "cathartic method," a cleansing of the mind's emotional conflicts through talking about them. The cathartic method was the forerunner of **psychotherapy**, the treatment of abnormal behavior through psychological techniques. This discovery eventually led Freud to develop **psychoanalysis**, a theory and system of practice that relied heavily on the concepts of the unconscious mind, inhibited sexual impulses, early development, and the use of the "free association" technique and dream analysis.

In the early 1900s, Freud attracted a variety of brilliant minds and courageous practitioners from across the Atlantic Ocean and all over Europe who came to work with him at his home in Vienna. Although many of these people eventually broke ranks and went on to develop their own theories and training schools, Freud's legacy continues to maintain an important position throughout the world.

The Late Twentieth Century: The Challenge of Providing Humane and Effective Treatment

When first encountering the various historical approaches to understanding and treating psychological disorders, some people may wonder how it was possible for people to have had such notions as demonic possession, moral therapy, and the utility of mechanical devices as cures. However, only in the past 50 years have we begun to move away from the almost superstitious views regarding psychological disorders. Although the scientific approach has its origins in ancient Greece, this method was not applied systematically until the mid-1900s.

As recently as the 1970s, many patients in psychiatric hospitals were restrained physically, such as in cribs with bars.

Until the 1970s, despite the growing body of knowledge about the causes of abnormal behavior, the actual practices used in the day-to-day care of psychologically disturbed people were as barbaric as those used in the Middle Ages. Even people suffering from the least severe psychological disorders were housed in what were known as the "back wards" of large and impersonal state institutions, without adequate or appropriate care. Although patients were not chained to the walls of their cells, they were severely restrained by the use of powerful tranquilizing drugs and straightjackets, coats with sleeves long enough to wrap around the patient's torso. Even more radical was the indiscriminate use of behavior-altering brain surgery, known as **psychosurgery**, and **electroconvulsive therapy (ECT)**, the application of electrical shock to the head. Both techniques were intended to correct abnormal functioning of the nervous system. Although therapeutic in intent, these methods were all too easily misused as forms of punishment or restraint. How could these practices have come about in our "modern" society? It's difficult to say, but it is probably due to a combination of population growth, limited financial resources, misguided intentions, and lack of cures.

Whatever the causes of this situation, society finally came to terms with the realization that dramatic changes were needed. Spurred on by graphic exposures to conditions in the mental hospitals, through such movies as *One Flew over the Cuckoo's Nest*, legislators began to promote a new policy designed to move people out of institutions and into less restrictive programs in the community. By the mid-1970s, the state mental hospitals which had once been overflowing with patients were practically deserted. Community programs were designed to take the place of the hospital, including social clubs, vocational rehabilitation facilities, day hospitals, and psychiatric clinics. People were placed in halfway houses after their discharge from the hospital, which provided a supportive environment where they could learn the social skills needed to reenter the community.

Like all other supposed breakthroughs in the treatment of psychologically disturbed people, the **deinstitutionalization movement** that promoted the release of psychiatric clients into community treatment sites has failed to fulfill the dreams of its originators. Rather than freeing the psychologically disturbed from the shackles of inhumane treatment, deinstitutionalization created another set of woes. Many of the promises and programs hailed as alternatives to institutionalization failed to come through because of inadequate planning and insufficient funds. The very sad phenomenon of the "revolving door" became all too frequent (Talbott, 1974; Talbott & Glick, 1986). Patients were shuttled back and forth between hospitals, halfway houses, and shabby boarding homes, never having a sense of stability or respect. Many psychologically disturbed people have become part of the homeless population (Fischer & Breakey, 1991) because of a lack of community programs and housing (Dear & Welch, 1987). Some authorities are now beginning to question whether the almost indiscriminate release of psychologically disturbed people was too radical a step. Critics of deinstitutionalization contend that the proponents of this movement have deprived psychiatric patients of the protection they need (Wasow, 1986).

As the year 2000 approaches, we still face the nightmare of seriously disturbed people wandering uncared for in the streets of every city in the country, and moving in and out of jails and shelters. Ironically, this situation is not unlike that which confronted Dorothea Dix 150 years ago.

In the decades to come, experts and lay people will continue to struggle to find the proper balance of providing asylum for those in need versus incarcerating people in institutions beyond the point where they are helped. At the same time, scientific researchers will search for the causes of

Marie Balter was misdiagnosed as having schizophrenia and placed in a state hospital for 17 years. Following discharge and a return to normal life, she went on to become the administrator of the same hospital.

abnormal behavior and the most effective forms of treatment. In the next section, we will examine research methods used by psychologists to deal with these crucial issues.

RESEARCH METHODS IN ABNORMAL PSYCHOLOGY

Psychological disorders are such a fascinating and mysterious aspect of human behavior that people feel compelled to offer explanations, even without adequate support. Popular books claiming that psychological problems are due to everything from diet to radioactivity are regularly published. You can pick up almost any newspaper and read simplistic speculations about the profile of a murderer or a person who has committed suicide. Such easy explanations can be misleading because they lack a grounding in psychological theory and scientific data.

The Scientific Method

Claims about the cause and treatment of abnormal behavior must be made on the basis of solid, scientific research rather than speculation. We will explain briefly the essentials of scientific methods as applied to abnormal psychology. In this process, we will discuss topics that you may have learned in introductory psychology or in a psychological methods course. Our review of this topic will explain those aspects of research methods that apply specifically to the study of abnormal psychology. This review should equip you to read reports in newspapers and magazines with an eye for scientific standards. An overview of research methods in abnormal psychology is contained in Table 1-3.

The essence of the scientific method is objectivity, the process of testing ideas about the nature of psychological phenomena without bias before accepting these ideas as adequate explanations. Taking a farfetched example, let's say

Table 1-3 Research Methods in Abnormal Psychology

TYPE OF METHOD	APPLICATION TO STUDYING DEPRESSION
Experimental	The effectiveness of an antidepressant drug is evaluated by comparing the scores on a test of depression of people who receive the drug with people who do not.
Purpose:	To establish whether the drug works better than no drug.
Advantages:	If the group receiving the drug improves and the other group does not, the experimenter can conclude quite confidently that the drug had a therapeutic effect.
Disadvantages:	It can be difficult to withhold treatment from people who are depressed.
Correlational	People who become depressed are tested on self-esteem to see if they have negative views about themselves.
Purpose:	To study the relationship of depression with other psychological states.
Advantages:	The experimenter can determine what other psychological qualities characterize depressed people.
Disadvantages:	The experimenter cannot determine whether depression causes people to have low self-esteem or whether low self-esteem is a cause of depression.
Case Study	A person with a history of depression is described in depth with particular emphasis on this person's development of the disorder.
Advantages:	Many circumstances in the person's life and psychological status can be explored in an attempt to gain a thorough understanding of that individual.
Disadvantages:	What characterizes one individual may not characterize others with depression.
Single-Subject Design	A depressed person is given a trial run of treatment and tested after this treatment to measure its effectiveness. Then the treatment is discontinued, and depression is measured again. This cycle is repeated one or more times.
Advantages:	By comparing the person receiving the treatment with himself or herself rather than other individuals, differences between people in their life histories or current circumstances can be ruled out.
Disadvantages:	It can be emotionally draining for the individual to be run through a cycle of on-again, off-again treatments. Later treatments may be influenced by the outcome of earlier ones.

How would this student test whether he should switch to caffeinated beverages to stay awake while studying?

you suspect that people who live on the East Coast are more stable psychologically than people who live on the West Coast (or vice versa, if you live on the West Coast). You should test this suspicion systematically before accepting it as "fact." As you set about this process, you would certainly want to hold open the possibility that your initial hunch was in error. The potential to discard an erroneous idea is an essential ingredient of the scientific method.

The underlying logic of the scientific method involves three concepts: observation, hypothesis formation, and ruling out competing explanations through proper controls. You have probably already used the scientific method yourself without referring to it in these terms. You may have found, for example, that every time you have a caffeinated drink like coffee after 6 P.M., you have trouble falling asleep. What would you need to do to test this possibility? You might go through the **observation process**, in which you mentally keep track of the differences between the nights you drink coffee and the nights you do not. The **hypothesis formation process** would be the step of predicting that drinking coffee causes you to stay awake at night. To test this hypothesis, you could try experimenting with drinking coffee on some nights but not on others. Next you must rule out competing explanations. You must be careful not to drink coffee on a night that you have just watched a scary movie, for example. Otherwise, you would have no way of knowing whether your sleep problems were due to the coffee or to the anxiety created by the movie.

Although the coffee drinking example may seem rather simple, it highlights the basic issues involved in most of the research we will encounter in this book. Researchers in abnormal psychology begin by observing a phenomenon of interest, forming hypotheses to explain it, and then designing ways to eliminate as many competing explanations as possible. This last step often is the most difficult, because abnormal behavior is such a multifaceted phenomenon.

To help make these important decisions, researchers rely on statistical procedures in which probability is a central concept. **Probability** refers to the odds or likelihood that an event will happen. The probability of a coin toss turning up heads is .5; that is, if a coin is tossed 100 times, it should show heads one-half of the time because there are only two possibilities. All conclusions about the correctness or incorrectness of hypotheses are framed in terms of probability, because it is almost impossible to study every individual whose responses might be relevant to the question under study. For example, if you are studying people with serious depression, you cannot obtain data from every person in the world who is depressed. You can study only some people from this very large group. In other words, you would select a **sample**, or selection, from the **population**, or entire group, of depressed people. After you have studied the sample, you would proceed to draw conclusions about the larger population. For example, you might find that in your sample of 50 depressed people, most of them had a disturbance in their appetite. You could then infer that appetite disturbance is a common feature of serious depression. However, you would have to be careful to state this inference in terms of probabilities. After all, you did not sample every depressed person in the population. Assuming your results were statistically "significant," there would be at most a 5 percent probability that your results were due to chance factors.

All statistics rely on some very important assumptions about the samples on which the results were based, namely, that the sample is representative of the whole population and that it was randomly selected. **Representativeness** refers to the idea that your sample adequately reflects the characteristics of the population from which it is drawn. For example, if you interviewed only 50 men, you could not draw conclusions about men and women. Random selection increases the likelihood that your sample will not be contaminated by some selective factor. Ideally, every person who is representative of the population of depressed people should have an equal likelihood of being selected for the sample. Let's say you have identified 1000 potential subjects for your study who are representative of the population of depressed people. Of these 1000, you have resources to interview only 50. To ensure that your final sample was randomly selected, you would need to use some method such as drawing names out of a hat. You can see how it would be a mistake to select your final sample by choosing the first 50 people who responded to your initial request for subjects. These people might be unusually compulsive or desperately in pursuit of relief from their depression. Either of these attributes might bias your sample so that it no longer represents the full spectrum of people with depression.

The Experimental Method

The purpose of psychological research is to develop an understanding of how and why people differ in their behavior. The dimensions along which people, things, or events differ are called **variables.** For example, depression is a variable.

HOW "CRAZY" ARE CREATIVE PEOPLE

Most of us have encountered certain people who possess a remarkable sense of creativity, wit, or insight that enables them to see the world in strikingly unique ways. Perhaps they have a keen sense of humor or an unusual perspective on life that engenders a response of awe in other people with whom they interact. Maybe it is another student in one of your classes who comes up with some "far out" ideas that captivate the imagination of others. Perhaps it is a person you know socially who is able to come up with great ideas for parties, and whose spark of creativity ignites fantasies and creative fires within others. Among the select group of very creative people you have encountered, it is quite possible that one or more of these individuals has been described by others as being just a little bit "crazy." When thinking about such people, you might have even wondered, just as some prominent researchers have wondered, whether there might actually be a relationship between some forms of creativity and some psychological disorders. Many people wonder about this possibility when they look at the art work of certain world-renowned artists like Salvador Dali or Jackson Pollock. Or they may ask this question when they watch a Woody Allen movie or read one of his books. Could such a creative person really be "normal"? In the literary world, the question of a possible connection between creativity and psychological disorder has been raised often. The suicides of famous writers such as Ernest Hemingway, Sylvia Plath, John Berryman, and Anne Sexton caused many people to wonder about the possible connection between mood disorders, particularly depression, and creativity expressed in the form of writing. Such a connection has, in fact, been uncovered by a prominent researcher.

In an effort to assess the relationship between creativity and psychological disorders, Nancy Andreasen, a leading researcher in the area of schizophrenia, examined the rate of mental illness among 30 creative writers and 30 matched control subjects. Andreasen was quite aware of the commonly held belief about a relationship between creativity and a serious form of psychological disturbance called schizophrenia. However, she was also aware that no research evidence existed to support this belief. Consequently, she set out to investigate the nature and extent of such a connection. Andreasen did not find a relationship between schizophrenia and creativity, but her research uncovered some intriguing facts about creative people. Although creative writers are not more likely than others to suffer from schizophrenia, they, and their close relatives, are more likely to suffer from a mood disorder. (As you will see later in the text, a mood disorder refers to a condition in which a person suffers from disturbances in mood in the forms of depression and/or elation.) Let's take a closer look at the way in which Andreasen came to her conclusion.

Andreasen began her investigation by systematically evaluating a sample of creative writers at the University of Iowa Writers' Workshop, an established and highly respected creative writing program which boasts of an enviable list of previous participants including internationally respected writers such as Kurt Vonnegut, John Irving, Flannery O'Connor, Philip Roth, and John Cheever. During a 15-year period, Andreasen's research team used a structured interview to evaluate 30 workshop faculty members (27 men and 3 women, with an average age of 37 years) to determine their patterns of creativity, personal history of psychological disorder, and the extent of mental health problems among their close relatives. Of course, it was necessary for Andreasen to guarantee confidentiality regarding the identity of all subjects who agreed to participate in her study. The researchers recruited a control group of 30 people matched for age, sex, and educational status, but who differed in occupation. The control subjects were professional people, including hospital administrators, lawyers, and social workers. They were comparable in intelligence (except, understandably, in their vocabulary skills) to the writers.

For each group of subjects, the researchers used specific criteria to determine the presence of a psychological disorder in the subject and among the subject's close relatives; in addition, the researchers evaluated cognitive function and style in a subset of 15 writers and control subjects.

Andreasen wanted to know whether the subjects had experienced a period of psychological disorder at any point in their lives, and the results were startling—80 percent of the writers had suffered from a mood disorder. Was mood disorder absent from the lives of the 30 controls? Interestingly, no. In fact, 30 percent of the control subjects had suffered from mood disorder at some point in life, but statistical analysis demonstrated that the higher proportion of mood disorders among the writers was much greater than chance. Andreasen realized that there was something curious about the rate of 30 percent among the control group; this figure was higher

continued

than one would expect to find in a group of individuals selected randomly from the population. However, keep in mind one important fact—these people were not randomly selected; rather they were *matched* with the controls along several dimensions. Of specific relevance is the fact that studies have shown a relationship between mood disorder and occupational achievement. This fact, and other issues pertaining to the diagnostic criteria used by Andreasen, led her to conclude that the differences in rates of psychological disorder between the two groups could be attributed to the very important variable of whether the subject was a writer, not the person's high level of occupational achievement.

When Andreasen inquired about the prevalence of psychological disorder among the subjects' relatives, once again she found that the rate of psychological disturbance, particularly mood disorder in the form of depression, was higher among the group of writers than among the control group. It was not surprising, either, to find that the creative subjects were much more likely than the controls to have relatives who were creative in diverse areas including art, music, dance, and mathematics.

Every study has its limitations, and Andreasen recognized some in her own study. One worrisome limitation she pointed out pertains to the fact that the investigator knew which of her subjects were in the creative group and which were in the control group. Ideally, the investigator would be "blind" to the status of the subject so as not to be biased in such a way that she might inadvertently look for evidence to support her hypothesis. However, keep in mind that Andreasen had set out to study a very different connection—she was looking for the connection between creativity and schizophrenia, not mood disorder. So in some ways, her findings are more credible and more valuable because she has provided us with two different sets of findings: (1) there is a relationship between creativity (as expressed in writing) and mood disorder, and (2) there is no relationship between creativity and schizophrenia.

How would you explain this puzzling relationship between creativity and mood disorder? On one level we might consider what makes creative writing so appealing to read. Certainly, one facet of creativity that others find appealing is the creative writer's ability to see the world in different, moving, and provocative ways. Perhaps successful writers are able to do this because of the inner turmoil with which they struggle. Sometimes inner pain gives people a view and understanding of the world that is not otherwise accessible.

Some people are more depressed than others; if given a test of depression, some people would receive high scores and others would receive low scores. The purpose of research on depression is to find out what accounts for these differences among people.

The experimental method is one approach to discovering the source of differences among people on psychological variables. The **experimental method** involves altering or changing the conditions to which subjects are exposed and observing the effects of this manipulation on the behavior of the subjects. In research involving this method, the experimenter attempts to ascertain whether there is a cause-effect relationship between two kinds of variables. The experimenter adjusts the level of one variable, called the **independent variable**, and observes the effect of this manipulation on the second variable, called the **dependent variable**. In our example about the effects of coffee on sleep patterns, the independent variable would be the caffeine in the coffee. The dependent variable would be ease of falling asleep. In depression research, the independent variable would be a factor that the researcher has hypothesized causes depression. For example, a current hypothesis is that some people in northern climates become more depressed in the winter, when the daylight hours are shorter and the light is less intense. To test this hypothesis, you would need to create an artificial situation in which you could manipulate light exposure for at least several days and observe the effect on depression scores in your subjects.

The experimental method usually involves making comparisons between groups exposed to varying levels of the independent variables. The simplest experimental design has two groups: an experimental and a control group. In this design, the **experimental group** receives the "treatment" thought to influence the behavior under study and the **control group** does not. Returning to the coffee example, you would test the hypothesis that caffeine causes sleeplessness by designing an experiment in which the experimental group is given caffeine and the control group is not given caffeine. By comparing sleep patterns in the two groups, you would be able to determine whether caffeine causes sleeplessness.

Many studies involve a special kind of control group—a "placebo" condition. In the **placebo condition**, people are given an inert substance or treatment that is similar in all other ways to the experimental treatment. So, to test the caffeine hypothesis, you might give one group of subjects a sugar pill that has no caffeine in it but looks identical to the caffeine pill you have given the experimental subjects. What is the purpose of the placebo condition? Think about your own experience taking pills or exposing yourself to other treatments that supposedly affect your behavior or health. Sometimes you feel better (or, perhaps, worse) just

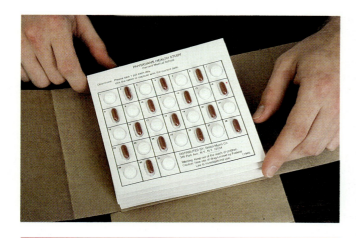

In a medication effectiveness study, placebo drugs are administered in order to control for the experience of taking pills.

knowing that you have taken a substance that you think might affect you. Again, in the case of the caffeine example, if you wanted to test the effects of "coffee" (as opposed to caffeine), you might give the experimental group a cup of caffeinated coffee and the placebo group a cup of decaffeinated coffee. That way, people in both groups would be drinking a hot, brown beverage. You might compare their sleeping patterns, then, to the "no treatment" control group who drink nothing before going to sleep.

In abnormal psychology, studies on the effectiveness of various therapeutic treatments should, ideally, include a placebo condition. For example, take the case of researchers who are investigating whether a new medication will be effective in treating a certain psychological disorder. It would be important to make sure that there is a group receiving a placebo to ensure that any therapeutic benefit in the treatment group can be attributed to the active ingredients in the medication. If the medication was found to be an effective treatment, or if the researcher was interested in establishing further control, the researcher might then make medication available to the people in the placebo and other control conditions and test the effect of the intervention at that point. Comparable procedures would be carried out in investigating the effects of certain kinds of psychotherapy. In these cases, however, the task of providing a placebo treatment is much more complicated than in the case of medication studies. What would a placebo treatment be for psychotherapy? Ideally, the researchers would want the placebo subjects to receive treatments of the same frequency and duration as the experimental group subjects who are receiving psychotherapy. As you might imagine, this would provide a real challenge for the researchers, who would be faced with trying to devise a method in which the people in the placebo condition would be meeting with a "therapist" but not participating in a therapeutic interaction. Perhaps they would talk about the weather or politics, but you might ask whether even such apparently neutral conversations might not have some therapeutic effect.

Researchers in the field of abnormal psychology must also make allowances for the **demand characteristics** of the experimental situation. People in an experiment have certain expectations about what is going to happen to them or the proper way they should respond, particularly when these people suspect that the research may reveal something very personal about themselves. For example, if you know that you will be given caffeine, you might anticipate difficulty falling asleep that night. Similarly, if the experimenter knows that you have been given caffeine, he or she might make comments that could further influence how easily you fall asleep. The "demand" in this situation is the pull towards responding in ways based not on caffeine's actual effects, but on how you or the experimenters think the caffeine will affect you. Imagine how seriously the demand characteristics could bias an experiment on the effects of an antianxiety medication. An experimenter tells subjects that they will feel relaxed in a little while. The chances are that they will feel more relaxed, but there would be no way of knowing whether this was the result of the experimenter's leading comments or a true response to the medication. Or perhaps you might notice labeling on the bottle indicating that the pill you are taking is an antianxiety drug. Just knowing this fact might influence how you feel in some way.

To control for demand characteristics on both sides, most researchers use a **double-blind technique** in which neither the person giving the treatment nor the person receiving the treatment has knowledge of whether the subject is in the experimental or control group. Even if this technique cannot be applied, as in the case of research on the effects of psychotherapy on depression, a minimal requirement for methodologically sound research is that neither the experimenter nor the subject knows the study's hypotheses. Otherwise, they will behave in ways that fulfill the expectations of the research.

In all of these cases, it is essential that the experimenter assign subjects to conditions in a totally random manner. You would not want to put all the people with sleep problems in the coffee-drinking group, or vice versa. Instead, the researcher would place people in groups according to some predetermined method of random assignment.

The experimental method can be a powerful way to determine cause-effect relationships. However, in many situations the researcher cannot clearly say whether one variable "causes" another. For example, researchers have found that depressed people have fewer friends. Are they depressed because they have fewer friends or do they have fewer friends because they are depressed? If you are planning to do an experimental study on the relationship between depression and number of friends, how would you choose which should be the independent variable? Furthermore, as this example illustrates, it is not always possible to manipulate a variable in an experiment. If you decided that number of friends should be the independent variable, there is no practical way you could control the number of friends people have. These limitations of the experimental method have contributed to the development of other methods, notably correlational procedures.

Correlational Methods

The relationship between depression and number of friends is a perfect example of a correlation. A **correlation** is an association, or co-relation, between two variables. The advantage of using a correlational procedure is that the researcher can study areas that are not easily tested by the experimental method. For example, it is theorized that people who have depressive disorders think very negatively about themselves and have very low levels of self-esteem. The most direct way to test this theory would be to measure the levels of depression and self-esteem in people and see if the scores are related to each other.

The correlation statistic is expressed in terms of a number between plus and minus one. Positive numbers represent positive correlations, meaning that as scores on one variable increase, scores on the second variable increase. Returning to our earlier example, you would expect that scores on a measure of depression are positively correlated with sleep disturbances. Conversely, negative correlations indicate that as scores on one variable increase, scores on the second variable decrease. An example of a negative correlation is the relationship between depression and self-esteem. The more depressed people are, the lower their scores will be on a measure of self-esteem. In many cases, there is no correlation between two variables. In other words, two variables show no systematic relationship with each other. For example, depression is unrelated to height. Illustrations of different types of correlations are shown in Figure 1-2.

Just knowing that there is a correlation between two variables does not tell you whether one variable causes the other. The correlation simply tells you that the two variables are associated with each other in a particular way. Sleep disturbance might cause a person to score higher on a measure of depression, just as a high degree of depression can result in disturbed sleep patterns. Furthermore, a third variable that you have not measured could account for the correlation between the two variables that you have studied. Both depression and sleep disturbance could be due to an unmeasured physical problem, such as a biochemical imbalance. People who use correlational methods in their research are always on guard for the potential existence of unmeasured variables influencing the observed results.

The Case-Study Method

Sometimes a researcher is interested in studying a condition that is very rare but has compelling features that make it worth investigating. For example, transsexualism is a disor-

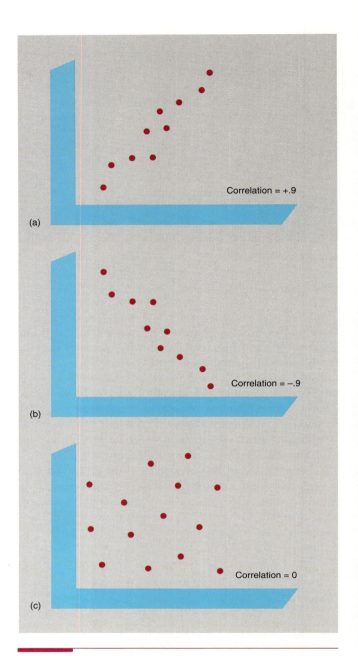

Figure 1–2 Scatter diagrams
Hypothetical scatterplots to illustrate different types of correlations: (a) a high positive correlation between sleep disturbance and depression, (b) a high negative correlation between self-esteem and depression, (c) a zero-order correlation between height and depression. It is rare in psychology to find correlations as high as those in (a) and (b).

der in which people feel that they are trapped in the body of the wrong gender. A biological male would feel that he is really a female and vice versa. This disorder affects a fraction of one percent of the population, so researchers would not have access to sufficient numbers to conduct a statistically rigorous study. Instead, they would perform a **case study**. The case study method allows the researcher to describe a single case in detail. For example, a therapist treating a transsexual client would describe the client's developmental history, psychological functioning, and response to interventions. Other clinicians and researchers reading about this case would have the opportunity to learn about a rare phenomenon to which they might otherwise not have access. Furthermore, case studies can be particularly useful in helping others to develop hypotheses either about psychological disorders or treatment.

A **single subject design** adds an experimental component to the study of the individual. In this type of research, one person at a time is studied in both the experimental and control conditions. Often, this method is used in research in which the focus is really on treatment. For example, a school psychologist wants to assess the effectiveness of a particular approach to treating a kindergartner named Bruce for temper tantrums. She could use a four-phase variant of the single subject design called the "A-B-A-B" method. The "A" phase is the **baseline**, the period in which Bruce is observed but given no treatment for a fixed period of time. During phase "B," the treatment is administered. In Bruce's case, this might consist of sending Bruce to the "time out" corner. To show this method in its simplest form, the schedule for the experiment might be conducted as follows:

■ Week 1: Condition A is followed. The frequency of Bruce's temper tantrums is observed, but no attempt is made to regulate them.

■ Week 2: Bruce is put on a time-out program. This is Condition B. Bruce's temper tantrums continue to be monitored, but every time he has one, he spends 10 minutes in the time-out corner of the classroom.

■ Week 3: The time-out program is discontinued (Condition A).

■ Week 4: The time-out program is re-instituted (Condition B).

Throughout this period, the frequency of Bruce's temper tantrums is monitored. If the treatment is effective, Bruce's temper tantrums should be less frequent in the "B" periods than in the "A." The "A-B" sequence is repeated to allow the psychologist to conclude with confidence that the treatment, rather than chance factors, caused Bruce's troublesome behavior to decrease. You can see from the graph in Figure 1-3 how an A-B-A-B design would look.

Sometimes the withdrawal of treatment in the A-B-A-B design would be considered unethical. In Bruce's case, this would be true if Bruce were physically harming himself or other children. The psychologist would not want to suspend treatment that was regarded as effective. As an alternative, the psychologist could use a **multiple baseline approach.** This method involves observing different dependent variables in the same person over the course of treatment, or observing the behavior as it occurs under different conditions. For example, the effectiveness of time outs on Bruce's temper tantrums could be determined first in the classroom, then in the playground, and finally in the cafeteria. If the time-out procedure is working, then it should result in reduced frequency of temper tantrums across these situations.

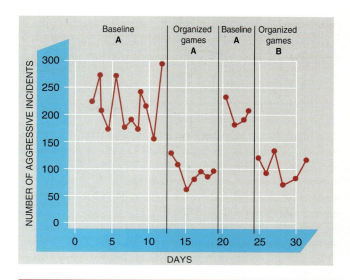

Figure 1–3 An example of an A-B-A-B design
This graph shows the frequency of aggressive incidents recorded during 20-minute morning observation periods of a child during playground activity time.

Single-subject designs are most appropriate for studying specific behaviors that are easily observed and measured; a mood state such as depression would be difficult to study using this procedure. Specific behaviors such as number of pessimistic statements, which are thought to reflect depressed mood, could be studied in this manner. One advantage of this method is that it allows the investigator to make precise manipulations whose effect can be carefully measured. The disadvantage is that the study is carried out on only one individual, thus limiting its generalizability. To avoid this problem, some researchers report the results of several single-subject designs in one study.

THE HUMAN EXPERIENCE OF PSYCHOLOGICAL DISORDERS

As researchers continue to make progress in understanding the causes of psychological disorders, interest and attention has become increasingly focused on the impact of these disorders on every level—the family, community, and society. The widespread dissemination of information, such as research findings, along with increased openness on the part of society to confront the concerns of people with psychological disorders, has led to a dramatic increase in public awareness of how psychological disorders affect many aspects of life.

Psychological problems touch upon many facets of human experience. They are not limited to the experience of a handful of people, but rather they are part of the life of every person. Not only is the individual with the problem deeply troubled; the family is disturbed, the community is moved, and society is affected.

Impact on the Family

Typically, even before a person with a psychological disorder has been seen by a professional, the family has been affected by the person's behavior and distress. The degree of the impact depends in part on the nature of the problem and in part on the dynamics of the family.

Most commonly, family members are touched by the pain of a relative who is wounded emotionally. For example, a mother loses sleep for many months as she struggles to understand what role she might have played in the development of her teenage daughter's suicidal depression. A father worries that his son might once again drink insecticide as he responds to visions of giant insects crawling down his throat. A wife feels anxious every time the phone rings, wondering whether it might be the police or an acquaintance calling to tell her that her husband has passed out in a drunken stupor at the neighborhood bar.

The stigma of a psychological disorder also taints the family. Many families speak of the shame and embarrassment they feel when neighbors, schoolmates, and co-workers discover that someone in the family is schizophrenic, depressed, addicted to drugs, or a child abuser.

For much of the twentieth century, the mental health profession in general was unsympathetic regarding the impact of psychological disorder on the family. Not only were families kept uninformed about treatment, but they were often blamed for the problem. Theories of many disorders like schizophrenia, depression, and sexual problems, typically blamed families—usually mothers. Families found themselves distressed by the turbulence caused by the problems of one of their relatives, and hurt and confused by what they heard as accusations from mental health professionals. Since the 1970s, prominent mental health profes-

Although the deinstitutionalization movement of the 1970s and 1980s resulted in the discharge of many people who could function satisfactorily outside of the hospital, some people did not fare so well. Homelessness and inadequate medical and psychiatric care have proven to be the plight of some deinstitutionalized people.

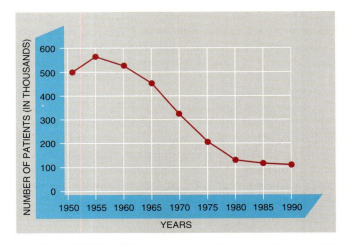

Figure 1–4 Numbers of patients in psychiatric hospitals
The number of patients in psychiatric hospitals in the United States from 1950 to 1990, showing a steady drop since 1960.

sionals have recognized the distress of these families and written books specifically directed to them (Bernheim et al., 1982; Hatfield, no date; Kanter, 1984; Park & Shapiro, 1976; Torrey, 1988). Their writings have let families know that they are not alone; that their worries, concerns, and problems are similar to those experienced by millions of other Americans.

Families also have banded together for support and mutual education. Organizations such as the National Alliance for the Mentally Ill (NAMI) have been formed across the country by families of clients with serious psychological disorders. These groups have helped many families better understand the nature of the problems they face, and the organizations have also served an important political function. Many such family advocacy groups have played a crucial role in ensuring that psychiatrically hospitalized people are properly treated, that their legal rights are respected, and that adequate post-hospitalization care is planned.

Impact on the Community and Society

Anyone who has ever lived in a community where a state psychiatric hospital is located knows that there are many challenges involved in accommodating the mental health-care needs of psychologically disturbed people following their discharge from the hospital. As we discussed earlier, beginning in the 1970s, there has been a national movement toward relocating clients from hospitals into less restrictive environments. It was commonplace in the mid-1970s for a state hospital to contain several thousand people. By the early 1990s, those numbers had dwindled. (See Figure 1-4.) Many institutions had closed; others were left open, but operated at a far smaller scale. Some of the discharged individuals moved back to the homes of their families, but the majority moved into community-based homes with several other "deinstitutionalized" people. In some programs and communities, these people are adequately cared for; however, in many areas, particularly large cities, there are dozens, even hundreds of formerly institutionalized people who go without homes, food, or health attention.

The impact of psychological disorder on society is not easily measured, but there is agreement among mental health professionals and public health experts that psychological problems exact a tremendous toll on society. Families are often torn apart and communities are divided. Our understanding of human nature is repeatedly challenged as we look for better ways to reduce the suffering of so many people.

SUMMARY

1. Everyone experiences psychological problems at some point in life, although there is a considerable range of severity in the disturbance that people experience.

2. There is no clear dividing line between what is normal and what is abnormal. It is probably best to consider abnormal behavior as existing in gradations, from slightly abnormal to extremely deviant.

3. Deviation is defined along several lines. Deviation from the average refers to a statistical measure that uses arithmetical means. The farther away from the mean, the more deviant the person or the score under consideration. Deviation from the optimal refers to variation from behavior that is considered ideal or best, a criterion that is often difficult to define.

4. Psychologists most often classify deviation within three domains of human experience: the body, the mind, and the social context of the individual. The biological domain serves as the context for understanding the body, the psychological domain for understanding the workings of the mind, and the sociocultural domain for understanding the social context.

5. Proponents of an integrative view of abnormal behavior consider the three domains—biological, psychological, and sociocultural—as they attempt to understand causes and develop interventions for psychological disorders.

6. Tremendous stigma is associated with psychological disturbance. People with psychological problems, especially serious problems, are often regarded as different and defective. They are frequently the subject of ridicule, and targets of a great deal of negatively-toned common language and humor.

7. The history of understanding and treating people with psychological problems is filled with three prominent recurring themes—the mystical, the scientific, and the humanitarian. Mystical explanations of psychological disorders regard abnormal behavior as the product of possession by evil or demonic spirits. The scientific approach looks for natural and measurable causes such as biological imbalances or faulty learning. The humanitarian approach has rested on premises of cruelty and kindness.

8. In prehistoric and early ancient times, demonic possession was regarded as the basis of psychological disorders, and people devised extreme interventions, such as trephining or exorcism. Presumed connections between demonic possession and psychological disturbance resurfaced repeatedly throughout history.

9. In the days of ancient Greece and Rome more medically based approaches surfaced, leading practitioners like Hippocrates to propose that bodily fluids influenced physical and mental health, with four main types of bodily fluids producing characteristic personality patterns and disorders. Although this idea was simplistic, the notion of personality types survives today. Other ideas dating back to Hippocrates have formed the basis for current diagnostic systems of psychological disorders. The Greeks also advocated a number of humane treatment methods that were surprisingly modern.

10. The ancient Roman physician Galen was the first to apply a scientific approach to the study of psychological disorders. He studied anatomy and conducted experiments to learn about the body's functioning, and proposed that psychological difficulties could have nonphysical origins.

11. Little changed from the time of ancient Rome until the 1700s, as the Dark Ages brought with them a return to the idea that abnormal behavior was the result of spiritual possession. Even in the Renaissance, which was a time of cultural enlightenment, ideas of possession still predominated, although pioneers such as Johann Weyer and Reginald Scot tried to return to the idea that psychological disorders needed to be approached humanely and scientifically. Starting in the year 1247, with the Bethlehem Hospital in England, asylums were built all over Europe. Rather than being cared for in asylums, people with psychological disorders were forced to live under primitive and even cruel conditions.

12. The reform movement in the 1700s, that was spearheaded by Phillipe Pinel, Vincenzo Chiarugi, and William Tuke, brought about widespread changes throughout Europe that greatly alleviated the suffering of asylum inmates. The approach advocated by the reformers was called "moral treatment," and it was based on the assumption that people with psychological disorders could recover on their own if they were given proper and humane care. At the same time that European reformers were working on behalf of asylum

inmates, Benjamin Rush in the United States began to renew interest in approaching psychological disorders scientifically. The founder of American psychiatry, Rush worked avidly on behalf of people with psychological disorders, but he also invented methods of treatment that were no less cruel than the archaic approaches used prior to the reform movement.

13. True reform in American psychiatric hospitals came about with the remarkable work of Dorothea Dix, who worked tirelessly to release people in these hospitals from their chains and overcrowded conditions. Her efforts, throughout the United States and Europe, resulted in the creation of the state "mental hospital," an institution intended to restore the basic principles of moral therapy. However, the state hospitals soon became overcrowded, and for most of the latter part of the 1800s and early 1900s, these institutions reverted to their prior, overcrowded and inhumane conditions.

14. The application of hypnotism to the treatment of certain psychological disorders, promoted largely by Mesmer and Charcot, led eventually to the psychoanalytic movement. Freud, who founded this movement, began through hypnosis to find that psychological difficulties often had their roots in the unconscious mind. Freud found that he could access the unconscious mind of his patients by allowing them to talk freely, and to recall their dreams. His methods of treatment were adopted by many psychiatrists and psychologists during the early part of the twentieth century, and paved the way for the modern emphasis on psychotherapy in treating psychological disorders.

15. In the 1950s, the discovery of tranquilizing medications enabled psychiatrists to provide the first real relief of psychotic symptoms. Over the next two decades, widespread use of these medications made it possible for people with severe psychological disorders to be treated outside the hospital. The deinstitutionalization movement gained momentum during the late 1960s; at present the number of people being treated in state mental hospitals on a long-term basis is relatively small. Deinstitutionalization has brought its own set of problems, however, adding to the growth of the homeless population, which includes psychologically disturbed people unable to cope with the stresses of living on their own in the community.

16. The scientific approach to the study of psychological disorders involves applying an objective set of methods for observing behavior, making a hypothesis about the causes of behavior, setting up proper conditions for studying this hypothesis, and drawing conclusions about its validity.

17. Four basic methods are used in psychological research: experimental, correlational, case study, and single subject design. In the experimental method, the researcher alters the amount of the independent variable and observes its effects on the dependent variable. This process is usually accomplished by comparing the performance of an experimental group who receive a treatment, a control group who receive no treatment, and a placebo group who receive an inert or inactive form of the treatment. In the correlational method, the researcher observes the naturally occurring relationship between two variables. The case study method involves a detailed and careful analysis of one individual who is studied intensively. In the single-subject design, one person at a time is studied in both the experimental and control conditions, in that treatment is applied and removed in alternating phases.

18. The human cost of psychological disorders is profound, with wide-ranging effects on family members, society, and the community.

KEY TERMS

Statistical average: the arithmetical mean on a given measure, calculated by dividing the sum of all scores by the number of scores. p. 3

Social norm: a standard for acceptable behavior that is established in a given society of culture. p. 4

Trephining: a treatment in prehistoric times, presumably for the purpose of curing psychological disorder, by drilling a hole in the skull. p. 8

Asylum: a place of refuge or safety, the term originally used to describe a psychiatric facility that later came to have negative connotations. p. 10

Moral treatment: the philosophy that people can, with the proper care, develop self-control over their own disturbed behaviors. p. 12

Medical model: the view that abnormal behaviors result from physical problems and should be treated medically. p. 13

Psychoanalytic model: an approach that seeks explanations of abnormal behavior in the workings of unconscious psychological processes. p. 14

Hypnotism: a method of using suggestion to induce a trance state. p. 14

Mesmerized: derived from the name Mesmer, used to refer to a state of heightened suggestibility brought about by the words and actions of a charismatic individual. p. 14

Hysteria: a disorder in which psychological problems become expressed in physical form. p. 15

Psychotherapy: the treatment of abnormal behavior through psychological techniques. p. 15

Psychoanalysis: a theory and system of practice that relies heavily on the concepts of the unconscious mind, inhibited sexual impulses, early development, and the use of the "free association" technique and dream analysis. p. 15

Psychosurgery: a form of brain surgery, the purpose of which is to reduce psychological disturbance. p. 16

Electroconvulsive therapy (ECT): the application of electrical shock to the head, for the purpose of inducing therapeutically effective seizures. p. 16

Deinstitutionalization movement: the release of psychiatric patients into community treatment sites as a result of dramatic changes in public policy. p. 16

Observation process: the stage of research in which the researcher watches and records the behavior of interest. p. 18

Hypothesis formation process: the stage of research in which the researcher generates ideas about cause-effect relationship between the behaviors under study. p. 18

Probability: the odds or likelihood that an event will happen. p. 18

Sample: a selection of individuals from a larger group. p. 18

Population: the entire group of individuals sharing a particular characteristic. p. 18

Representativness: the extent to which a sample adequately reflects the characteristics of the population from which it is drawn. p. 18

Variable: A dimension along which people, things, or events differ. p. 18

Experimental method: the process used in scientific research of altering or changing the conditions to which subjects are exposed and observing the effects of this manipulation on the behavior of the subjects. p. 20

Independent variable: The variable whose level is adjusted or controlled by the experimenter. p. 20

Dependent variable: The variable whose value is the outcome of the experimenter's manipulation of the independent variable. p. 20

Experimental group: the group of subjects who receive the "treatment" thought to influence the behavior under study. p. 20

Control group: the group of subjects who do not receive the "treatment" thought to influence the behavior under study. p. 20

Placebo condition: the condition used in experimental research in which people are given an inert substance or treatment that is similar in all other ways to the experimental treatment. p. 20

Demand characteristics: the expectations of people in an experiment about what is going to happen to them or the proper way to respond. p. 21

Double-blind technique: an experimental procedure in which neither the person giving the treatment nor the person receiving the treatment has knowledge of whether the subject is in the experimental or control group. p. 21

Correlation: an association, or co-relation, between two variables. p. 22

Case study: an intensive study of a single person described in detail. p. 22

Single-subject design: an experimental procedure in which one person at a time is studied in both the experimental and control conditions. p. 23

Baseline: the period in which a subject is observed prior to being given treatment for the purpose of documenting the frequency of the target behavior. p. 23

Multiple baseline approach: observing different dependent variables in the same person over the course of treatment, or observing the behavior as it occurs under different conditions. p. 23

Case Report: Peter Dickinson

Peter, a man in his early 20s, is seeking help for what he describes as bouts of "anxiety" that started over a month ago. When these episodes hit, he feels very sad, loses his appetite, cannot sleep, and contemplates suicide. As a result of these episodes, Peter lost his job as a bank teller. Four months ago, Peter went through a very different kind of experience of feeling "elated," "full of nervous energy," "sure of myself," and "ready to conquer the world." In the midst of this period, Peter went to an expensive imported car dealer, bought a brand new European luxury sportscar putting himself into enormous debt, and took off the next day for a trip to Mexico. On the way, he picked up a hitchhiker, whom he married a few days later in Tijuana. After Peter's excited state subsided, he sold the car, obtained a divorce, and moved back into his parent's house. "I sure had a lot of laughs at the time, but I really paid for it later. I'll never do anything that stupid again," said Peter regretfully.

2

CLASSIFICATION, TREATMENT PLANS, ETHICS, AND LEGAL ISSUES

In this chapter, we will discuss the system that clinicians use to classify and diagnose psychological disorders. This system has evolved over the past 50 years to provide clinicians with a consistent means of identifying and treating psychological dysfunction. This endeavor has proven to be a challenging and difficult one, as you will realize when you read about the many possible variations of psychological disorder.

After reading this chapter, you should be able to:

- Understand the nature and concerns of clients and clinicians, as well as the factors that influence their interactions.
- Give an overview of the diagnostic classification system currently in use by clinicians in the United States.
- Define the concepts of reliability and validity in terms of diagnoses.
- Summarize the definition of "mental disorder" as used in a current diagnostic systems.
- Describe a treatment plan.
- Discuss the ethical and legal issues involved in treatment of psychological disorders.

PSYCHOLOGICAL DISORDER: EXPERIENCES OF CLIENT AND CLINICIAN

The field of abnormal psychology goes beyond the academic concern of studying behavior: it encompasses the large range of human issues involved when a client and a clinician work together to help the client resolve psychological difficulties. Throughout this text, we will continually return to these human issues and focus on the individual experiences of the client and the clinician as well as the drama that unfolds when they interact with each other. Here, we orient you to these issues with a discussion of who these people are.

The Client

What do you think of when you hear that someone you know is in psychotherapy? Do you think of the person being treated as a "patient"? This is a common view, with roots in the medical model, and it is reinforced by popular characterizations of therapy on television and in films. There are, however, unfortunate associations with the term "patient." A "patient" is someone who is ill, and someone who passively ("patiently") waits to be treated. Consequently, many prefer the term **client** to refer to the person seeking psychological treatment. As you read this chapter, you will find that psychotherapy is very much a collaborative endeavor and that the term "client" aptly captures this quality. When we do use the term "patient," it is because that is the convention in some legal and ethical contexts.

Although this book focuses on people with severe psychological problems, it is important to keep in mind that everyone, at some point, faces crises, dilemmas, or a desire for greater self-understanding. It is a common human experience, when faced with these problems, to seek help from others. In some cases, this help comes from relatives, friends, clergy, or other informal sources of support. In other cases, help is sought from a mental health professional. Whether a person consults a friend or a professional, seeking help from others is a normal and natural part of life.

The Clinician

Many people respond in an understandably defensive manner to the idea of consulting a mental health professional. They fear being scrutinized and labeled by a total stranger, a stranger who is in a position to judge them as being "crazy." This negative view of the clinician accounts in part for the resistance often expressed about "seeing a shrink."

Optimally, however, a clinician is an astute observer of human nature, an expert in human relations, a facilitator of growth, and a resource who aids others in making crucial life choices. A good clinician assesses others, not out of arrogance and insensitivity, but out of concern for understanding and responding to the problems of people seeking help.

There are many types of clinicians, based on the training and orientation of these professionals. During the early 1900s, most people in need of psychological help were treated by **psychiatrists**—medical doctors (MDs) with advanced training in treating people with psychological disorders. During World War II, the mental health needs of the nation increased, necessitating an expansion of the mental health provider network. University-based doctoral (PhD) psychology programs were created to increase the number of mental health professionals with training in the behavioral sciences who provided direct service to clients. Individuals trained in such programs are known as **clinical psychologists.** Psychiatrists and clinical psychologists currently predominate in the mental health field. An important distinction between them is that psychiatrists are licensed to administer medical treatment and psychologists are not. In addition to providing psychotherapy, then, psychiatrists are responsible for prescribing medication for the treatment of psychological disorders when necessary. Psy-

In therapy, the client and clinician work jointly to help the client resolve psychological problems.

chologists and other mental health professionals often work closely with psychiatrists and consult with them when a client appears to need medication. Another difference is that clinical psychologists are trained in conducting **psychological testing**, a broad range of measurement techniques, all of which involve having people provide scorable information about their psychological functioning.

In addition to doctorally trained professionals, there are several other groups of professionals who provide mental health services including psychiatric social workers, nurse clinicians, and marriage and family counselors. The mental health field also includes a large group of individuals who do not have graduate-level training but serve a critically important role in the functioning and administration of the mental health system. Included in this group are the thousands of nurses, occupational therapists, recreational therapists, and counselors who devote their careers to working with emotionally troubled people in institutions, agencies, schools, and homes.

A clinician consults a manual to help arrive at an accurate diagnosis of his client.

■ *The Diagnostic and Statistical Manual of Mental Disorders*

In making a diagnosis, mental health professionals use the standard terms and definitions contained in the ***Diagnostic and Statistical Manual of Mental Disorders***, a publication that is periodically revised to reflect the most up-to-date knowledge concerning psychological disorders. The title of this book, and the diagnostic system it contains, is abbreviated as *DSM*; this is followed by an indication, in Roman numerals, of the edition currently in use. This diagnostic system was originally developed in 1952, when the first *DSM* was published by the American Psychiatric Association. In the years since then, *DSM-II, DSM-III, DSM-III-Revised,* and *DSM-IV* have reflected advances and refinements in the system of diagnosis that is most commonly used in the United States. We will discuss the history of the development of this system later, but first it is important for you to have a grasp of what we mean by a diagnostic system, or "nomenclature," as it is sometimes called.

The *DSM* contains descriptions of all psychological disorders, alternatively referred to as mental disorders. In developing recent editions of the *DSM*, various task forces have been appointed, each consisting of a group of expert clinicians and researchers knowledgeable about a particular subset of disorders. Several hundred disorders are listed and described, ranging from relatively minor adjustment problems to long-term chronic and incapacitating disorders. The *DSM* provides both clinicians and researchers with a common language for delineating disorders so that they can feel relatively confident that diagnostic labels have accepted meanings.

The authors of recent versions of *DSM* have taken an atheoretical approach. In other words, they have attempted to describe psychological disorders in terms that refer to observable phenomena (Millon, 1991) rather than presenting the disorders in terms of their possible causes. In describing an anxiety disorder, for example, various psychological and physical symptoms associated with the experience of anxiety are listed without consideration of whether the cause is physical or emotional.

The *DSM* classification system is based on extensive research on diagnosis and treatment of psychological disorders. By characterizing a client's symptoms in terms of a *DSM* diagnosis, the clinician can use that system of knowledge as the basis for a treatment plan. For example, a clinician would plan a very different kind of treatment for an anxiety disorder than for schizophrenia. Furthermore, the clinician often is asked to provide a diagnosis, with the accompanying *DSM* numerical code, to help a client obtain insurance payments to cover the cost of treatment.

In developing the *DSM*, its authors have faced a major challenge in arriving at a system that will be scientifically and clinically accurate (Garfield, 1984). One important standard sought in the diagnostic system is that the diagnoses meet the criterion of **reliability**, meaning that a given diagnosis will be consistently applied to anyone showing a particular set of symptoms. Returning to the case of Peter, if he were to describe his symptoms to a clinical psychologist in Spokane, Washington, that psychologist should be able to use the *DSM* to arrive at the same diagnosis as if Peter were being seen by a psychiatrist in Baton Rouge, Louisiana. Further, any knowledgeable mental health professional should be able to use the criteria specified in the *DSM* to make a diagnosis regardless of that professional's theoretical orientation or particular experience with clients. Working toward reliability of diagnoses, authors of successive versions of the *DSM* have continued to expand and refine the criteria for disorders. At the same time, teams of researchers throughout the United States have continued to investigate the **validity** of the classification system, seeking to ensure that the various diagnoses represent real and distinct clinical phenomena. It is important for anyone developing a diagnostic system to keep in mind the **base rate** of a disorder, which is its frequency of occurrence in the general population (Grove et al., 1981). Psychological disorders generally are uncommon, with base rates of 1 percent to perhaps 20 or 30 percent at most.

How the *DSM* Developed

The first edition of the American Psychiatric Association's *DSM*, which appeared in 1952, was the first official psychiatric manual to describe psychological disorders and as such was a major step forward in the search for a standard set of diagnostic criteria (Blashfield, 1984). Although a step in the right direction, these criteria were very vague and had poor reliability. A second limitation of the *DSM-I* was that it was based on the theoretical assumption that the disorders it described were caused by emotional problems or "reactions." The second edition, known as *DSM-II*, was published in 1968. This was the first classification of mental disorders based on the system contained in the *International Classification of Diseases (ICD)*. The *DSM-II* represented a movement away from the conceptualization of most psychological disorders as being emotional reactions. The authors of this edition tried to use diagnostic terms that would not imply a particular theoretical framework but, in retrospect, it is clear that they based their criteria on psychoanalytic concepts. Furthermore, these criteria were sufficiently loose that a clinician with a particular theoretical preference could fit a client's diagnosis in with his or her theory rather than with the client's actual condition. These problems in validity and reliability were reflected in studies showing that given the same symptoms in a client, clinicians in the United States gave radically different diagnoses than those made by British clinicians (Cooper et al., 1972).

To overcome these problems with low reliability, the American Psychiatric Association appointed a task force in 1974 of eminent scholars and practitioners to prepare a new and more extensive classification system that would reflect the most current information on mental disorders. The task force was directed to develop a manual that would have an empirical basis and be clinically useful, reliable, and acceptable to clinicians and researchers of different orientations (Spitzer, et al., 1980).

When *DSM-III* was published in 1980, it was widely heralded as a major improvement over its predecessors. It provided precise rating criteria and definitions for each disorder. These criteria enabled clinicians to be more quantitative and objective in assigning diagnoses. However, the *DSM-III* did not go far enough in specifying these criteria, leading the American Psychiatric Association to try once again to improve and refine the diagnostic system (American Psychiatric Association, 1987). Nevertheless, the *DSM-III*'s greater clarity and comprehensiveness compared to its predecessors led to wide acceptance among mental health professionals. *DSM-III* enabled clinicians and researchers to accumulate a body of reliable data on many of the disorders it described. Based on those new data, the American Psychiatric Association introduced the revision of the third edition, the *DSM-III-R*, in 1987. The *DSM-III-R* was similar to the *DSM-III* in its conceptualization, but further refined the diagnostic definitions and criteria.

Another important step has been taken with the development of *DSM-IV* which has focused as much on validity as on reliability. In other words, the authors of *DSM-IV* have made every effort to ensure that the diagnoses included in the manual correspond to the latest research findings (Widiger et al., 1991).

Assumptions of the *DSM*

An important assumption underlying the *DSM* is that psychological disorders cannot be considered discrete entities with sharp boundaries. As you read about each disorder in this textbook, you may be tempted for the sake of simplicity to believe that each disorder is always clearly recognizable and distinguishable from all others. This would be a mistake. Though the *DSM* has facilitated accuracy in diagnosis, many disorders are hard to identify.

■ *Definition of "mental disorder"*

In Chapter 1, we discussed the alternate conceptions of what is "abnormal," and how difficult it is to define what constitutes abnormal behavior or, for that matter, how it should be labeled. *DSM* uses the term "mental disorder"; our preference in this book is to use the term "psychological disorder," which carries a less pejorative connotation. As a starting point to our consideration, however, it is important to be clear about the current accepted meanings of terminology. The authors of recent editions of the *DSM* have had to confront the task of defining "mental disorder." An accepted definition of mental disorder is "a clinically significant behavioral or psychological syndrome or pattern that occurs in a person and that is associated with present distress (a painful symptom) or disability (impairment in one or more important areas of functioning) or with a significantly increased risk of suffering death, pain, disability, or an important loss of freedom" (American Psychiatric Association, 1987, p. xxii). The concept of mental disorders is central to the whole enterprise of diagnosis and treatment. Let's take a closer look at the definition given in *DSM* and its implications.

The disorder is "clinically significant." For each disorder, the *DSM* specifies both the length of time during which the symptoms must be present, and the extent to which the symptoms deviate from the individual's prior level of functioning. Thus, a fleeting thought or mood, an occasional strange behavior, or a temporary feeling of instability or confusion does not constitute a mental disorder. You probably can think of a time when you felt like you were losing control of your emotions. Such experiences are quite common and would not be regarded as mental disorders unless they happen repeatedly or are so severe that they result in serious consequences.

For some people psychological distress becomes so great that they feel suicide is their only option.

The disorder is reflected in a behavioral or psychological "syndrome." A **syndrome** is a collection of symptoms that together form a definable pattern. A behavioral or psychological syndrome is a collection of observable actions and the client's reported thoughts and feelings. So we are not referring to an isolated behavior or a single thought or feeling, but rather an organized unit that manifests itself in a wide range of thoughts, feelings, and behaviors. If you feel sad for a few days, and this feeling is your only symptom, a diagnosis of depression would be inappropriate.

The disorder is associated with present distress, impairment in life, or serious risk. In other words, there must be some kind of personal or social cost. For example, a woman's fear of leaving the house causes her to be very distressed. She wishes she could overcome her extreme fearfulness, but feels incapable of changing her behavior. Her syndrome, then, in addition to being severe, is also causing her a great deal of personal distress. In addition, her functioning is impaired because she is unable to hold a job or take care of household errands.

Not everyone with a psychological disorder is distressed. Consider the man who has developed an unusually cold, constricted, and impersonal style of relating to other people because of a disturbed view of interpersonal relation-

ships. Although this man might not be bothered by this style, it will make it difficult, if not impossible, to develop intimate relationships. Moreover, unless he has a job that involves absolutely no social interaction (and there are not many such jobs), this style of relating to others will invariably hurt his chances of having a productive career.

Some disorders can lead a person to commit suicide or inflict severe physical pain through self-mutilation. Other disorders place the individual at risk because they lead to acts involving physical peril. A man in a hyper-excited state of euphoria may go out and rent a hang-glider because he feels like flying, unconcerned that he lacks the proper training. Still other disorders threaten the individual with physical harm because they lead to the adoption of an unhealthy life style. A person who is driven to work excessively hard without taking time for relaxation is likely, over a period of years, to suffer from heart problems due to stress. Finally, a psychological disorder can lead a person to give up personal freedom if it leads to criminal acts resulting in punishment or incarceration.

■ *Neurosis versus psychosis*

Everyone has heard the terms "neurotic" and "psychotic." Most people understand that psychosis is relatively rare and involves some kind of serious break with reality. Neurosis is considered to be more common, and usually refers to some kind of peculiarity or undue level of concern over a minor issue. For example, you might describe your friend as "neurotic" because she seems to worry all the time over nothing. Given the common use of these words, it might be surprising to learn that these terms do not appear as official diagnoses in the *DSM*. The reason is that both terms are rather broad descriptions of certain kinds of behaviors, and they are not precise enough to be reliably used.

The term **psychosis** is used to refer to various forms of behavior involving loss of contact with reality. In other words, a person showing psychotic behavior might have bizarre thoughts and perceptions of what is happening. This might involve delusions (false beliefs) or hallucinations (false perceptions). The term psychotic may also be used to refer to behavior that is so grossly disturbed that the person seems to be out of control.

Neurosis is not part of the official nomenclature, but you will still find it in many books and articles on abnormal psychology. When you come across the term, it will usually be in reference to behavior that involves some symptoms that are distressing to an individual and are recognized by that person as unacceptable. These symptoms usually are enduring and lack any kind of physical basis. So, in the case of your friend's excessive worrying, you can see that her symptom causes her distress. Assuming that she recognizes how inappropriate her worrying is, your labeling of her behavior as neurotic might be justified. However, if she were to visit a mental health practitioner, she would be diagnosed with some form of "anxiety disorder," a more precise description of her constant worrying behavior.

Medical Model

Another feature of the *DSM*, a feature that has survived to its most recent edition, is a medical model orientation in which disorders, whether physical or psychological, are viewed as diseases. Some mental health professionals find this bias to be objectionable, and prefer to avoid using diagnostic categories in their work with clients. Often, though, the need for diagnosis and clear-cut terminology overrides philosophical objections, and for insurance purposes or other reasons, the clinician must rely on the concepts and terms in the *DSM*.

Multiaxial System

As you might imagine, when a clinician is developing a diagnostic hypothesis about a client, there may be several features of the individual's functioning that are important to capture. For example, consider the case of a young man we will call Greg, who is suffering from periods of intense depression that have troubled him for the past few months. Greg says that he has had personality problems since high school as well as a problem with ulcers. Six months ago, Greg's girlfriend was killed in an automobile accident. Before then, he was managing reasonably well, although his personality problems and ulcer sometimes made it difficult for him to function well on his job.

Each fact presented by the client is important for the clinician to take into account when making a diagnosis, not just the client's immediate symptoms. In Greg's case, the symptom of depression is merely one part of a complex diagnostic picture. Most clients, like Greg, have multiple concerns that are relevant to diagnosis and treatment. Each relevant dimension or area of functioning is categorized within what is called an "axis" in *DSM*. There are five axes along which each client is evaluated. This **multiaxial system** allows for clients to be characterized in a multidimensional way, accommodating all relevant information about their functioning in an organized and systematic fashion.

The Five Axes of the DSM

Each mental disorder in *DSM* is listed on either Axis I or Axis II. The remaining axes are used to characterize a client's physical health (Axis III), extent of stressful life circumstances (Axis IV), and overall degree of functioning (Axis V).

■ *Axis I: Clinical Syndromes*

Axis I contains mental disorders called syndromes, that is, groups of related symptoms that each form a recognizable pattern. The disorders in Axis I represent a large and diverse group, ranging from cognitive impairment disorders caused by some dysfunction of the brain, to schizo-phrenia, mood disorders, and anxiety disorders. These disorders are classified on the basis of symptoms rather than cause; remember that the *DSM* makes no assumptions about what causes people to develop these disorders. This is quite different from medical classification systems, which group diseases according to the bodily system affected rather than on the basis of the symptoms or patterns of behavior experienced by the individual.

■ *Axis II: Personality and Developmental Disorders*

Axis II includes disorders that represent enduring personality traits that are inflexible and maladaptive and cause either subjective distress or considerable impairment in the person's ability to carry out the tasks of daily living. Included in this axis are mental retardation and speech disorders in addition to personality disorders. One way to keep the distinction between the two axes clear is to regard the Axis II disorders as built into the very fabric of the individual's personality or behavioral repertoire, like the weave of a piece of cloth.

To help you understand the differences between Axis I and Axis II, consider these two clinical examples. One case involves a 29-year-old woman who, following delivery of her first child, becomes very suspicious of other people's intentions, to the point of not trusting even close relatives. After a month of treatment, she returns to normal functioning and her symptoms disappear. This woman would receive a diagnosis of an Axis I disorder because she has a condition that could be considered an overlay on an otherwise healthy personality. In contrast, the hypersensitivity to criticism and fear of closeness shown by another 29-year-old woman is a feature of her way of viewing the world that has characterized her from adolescence. She has chosen not to become involved in intimate relationships and steers clear of people who seem overly interested in her. Were she to seek treatment, these longstanding dispositions would warrant an Axis II diagnosis.

Sometimes an individual can have diagnoses on both axes. For example, a man who is struggling with substance abuse and also is characteristically very dependent on others would probably be diagnosed on both Axis I and Axis II. On Axis I he would be assigned a diagnosis pertaining to his substance abuse, and on Axis II he would receive a diagnosis of dependent personality disorder. In other words, his substance abuse is considered to be a condition and his personality disorder is considered to be part of the fabric of his character.

■ *Axis III: Physical Disorders or Conditions*

Axis III is the place where physical conditions are documented. At times physical problems can be the basis of psychological problems. For example, a person sometimes becomes depressed following the diagnosis of a serious physical illness. Conversely, conditions such as chronic anxiety can intensify some physical problems such as stomach disorders. In some cases there is no obvious connection between the physical and the psychological problems of the individual. Nevertheless, the existence of a physical disorder is considered critically important to the clinician, because it means that a major facet of the client's life is being affected by something outside the psychological realm. The clinician must keep this information in mind in developing a treatment plan. Take the example of a young man with diabetes who seeks treatment for his incapacitating irrational fear of cars. Though his physical and psychological problems are not apparently connected, it would be important for the clinician to be aware of the diabetes, because the condition would certainly have a major impact on the client's life. Furthermore, if the clinician considers recommending a prescription of antianxiety medication, the young man's physical condition and other medications must be taken into account.

■ *Axis IV: Severity of Psychosocial Stressors*

Axis IV gives the clinician an opportunity to evaluate and record the seriousness of stressful events over the past year of the client's life. It is presumed that stressful events often contribute to the development of new emotional disorders, the recurrence of prior disorders, or the worsening of existing disorders.

When most people think of an event that qualifies as a "stressor," they tend to list negative events such as losing a job, having an automobile accident, or breaking up with a lover. However, many events that seem to be positive also have stressful elements. Getting married, having a baby, and getting a job promotion are ordinarily quite happy events; even so, they introduce many new stresses into a person's life. A stressor is any event, then, positive or negative, that requires the individual to adapt emotionally and to make a major readjustment in lifestyle and daily activities.

Because stressful events differ in the extent to which they require adaptation, *DSM* provides a scale for rating the severity of a stressor (see Table 2-1 on page 36). The highest rating is 6, representing catastrophic stress. The lowest rating is 1, indicating that the client has experienced no documented stressor during the preceding year.

■ *Axis V: Global Assessment of Functioning*

Axis V helps the clinician to arrive at an overall judgment of a client's psychological, social, and occupational functioning. Two ratings are made on Axis V. One refers to the client's level of functioning at the time he or she is seen by the clinician. The other rating refers to the client's highest level of functioning for at least a few months of the previous year. Typically the ratings of a client's current functioning correspond with the client's need for treatment. The rating of the client's functioning during the preceding year provides the clinician with important information about the client's **prognosis**, or likelihood of recovering from the disorder. If a client has functioned effectively in the recent past, the clinician has more reason to hope for

improvement. The prognosis may not be so bright if a client has a lengthy history of poor adjustment. The **Global Assessment of Functioning (GAF)** scale rates the individual's overall level of psychological health, ranging from a high rating of 90, indicating good functioning in all areas, to a low rating of 1, indicating a markedly serious level of functioning, possibly including suicidal acts (see Table 2-2 on page 37).

THE DIAGNOSTIC PROCESS

The process of arriving at a diagnosis may be compared to detective work. A detective tries to piece together a coherent picture from many bits and pieces of information, some of which would not seem important to the untrained observer. Similarly, a clinician looks for clues in order to arrive at a total understanding of the client's disorder. That understanding is most conveniently expressed in terms of a diagnosis.

Introducing Dr. Sarah Tobin

We realize that an abstract discussion does not enable you to appreciate fully who the clinician is and what the clinician does. Consequently, throughout this book, we will use examples involving one clinician and some of the cases she has treated. This clinician, whom we call Dr. Sarah Tobin, is a composite of many of the qualities found in a good clinical psychologist. Her cases are similar to those in psychological clinics and psychiatric institutions. As you read about Dr. Tobin's work, think of yourself as her apprentice or intern. Imagine yourself discussing the cases with her, and consulting with her about the diagnosis and treatment of each client. At the beginning of each chapter, you will read a case report that relates to the content of that chapter. As you read the chapter, we want you to use an inquisitive and problem-solving approach to develop your own understanding of the case. Try to form your own hypotheses about the most appropriate diagnosis, the cause of the client's problems, and ways that the client might best be treated. We return now to the example of Peter to illustrate how a clinician like Dr. Tobin would formulate a diagnosis.

Client's Reported Symptoms

Remember that Peter first described his symptoms as involving "bouts of anxiety." When Dr. Tobin hears the word "anxiety," she immediately begins thinking about the *DSM* criteria for what is called an "anxiety disorder." This is the first step in the diagnostic process. Dr. Tobin listens for a key word or phrase in the client's self-report of symptoms. That gives her a clue about what to look for next. In the process of following up on this clue, Dr. Tobin will gain more information about the symptoms that Peter reports.

Table 2-1 Axis IV of the *DSM*

SEVERITY OF PSYCHOSOCIAL STRESSORS SCALE: ADULTS

Code	Term	Examples of Stressors	
		Acute Events	Enduring Circumstances
1	None	No acute events that may be relevant to the disorder.	No enduring circumstances that may be relevant to the disorder.
2	Mild	Broke up with boyfriend or girlfriend; started or graduated from school; child left home.	Family arguments; job dissatisfaction; residence in high-crime neighborhood.
3	Moderate	Marriage; marital separation; loss of job; retirement; miscarriage.	Marital discord; serious financial problems; trouble with boss; being a single parent.
4	Severe	Divorce; birth of first child.	Unemployment; poverty.
5	Extreme	Death of spouse; serious physical illness diagnosed; victim of rape.	Serious chronic illness in self or child; ongoing physical or sexual abuse.
6	Catastrophic	Death of child; suicide of spouse; devastating natural disaster.	Captivity as hostage; concentration camp experience.
0	Inadequate information, or no change in condition		

SEVERITY OF PSYCHOSOCIAL STRESSORS SCALE: CHILDREN AND ADOLESCENTS

Code	Term	Examples of Stressors	
		Acute Events	Enduring Circumstances
1	None	No acute events that may be relevant to the disorder.	No enduring circumstances that may be relevant to the disorder.
2	Mild	Broke up with boyfriend or girlfriend; change of school.	Overcrowded living quarters; family arguments.
3	Moderate	Expelled from school; birth of sibling.	Chronic disabling illness in parent; chronic parental discord.
4	Severe	Divorce of parents; unwanted pregnancy; arrest.	Harsh or rejecting parents; chronic life-threatening illness in parent; multiple foster home placements.
5	Extreme	Sexual or physical abuse; death of a parent.	Recurrent sexual or physical abuse.
6	Catastrophic	Death of both parents.	Chronic life-threatening illness.
0	Inadequate information, or no change in condition		

Source: American Psychiatric Association: *Diagnostic and Statistical Manual of Mental Disorders, Third Edition, Revised,* Washington, DC, American Psychiatric Association 1987. Reprinted by permission.

Table 2-2 Axis V: Global Assessment of Functioning Scale

Rating	Level of Symptoms	Examples
81-90	No symptoms or minimal symptoms; generally good functioning in all areas; no more than everyday problems or concerns	Occasional worries such as feeling understandably anxious before taking examinations or feeling disappointment following an athletic loss
71-80	Transient, slight symptoms that are reasonable responses to stressful situations; no more than slight impairment in social, occupational, or school functioning	Concentration difficulty following an exciting day; trouble sleeping after an argument with partner
61-70	Mild symptoms, or some difficulty in social, occupational, or school functioning	Mild insomnia; mild depression
51-60	Moderate symptoms or moderate difficulties in social, occupational, or school functioning	Occasional panic attacks; conflicts with roommates
41-50	Serious symptoms or any serious impairment in social, occupational, or school functioning	Suicidal thoughts; inability to keep job
31-40	Serious difficulties in thought or communication or major impairment in several areas of functioning	Illogical speech; inability to work; neglect of responsibilities
21-30	Behavior influenced by psychotic symptoms or serious impairment in communication or judgment or inability to function in almost all areas	Delusional and hallucinating; incoherent; preoccupied with suicide; stays in bed all day every day
11-20	Dangerous symptoms or gross impairment in communication	Suicide attempts without clear expectation of death; muteness
1-10	Persistent danger to self or others or persistent inability to maintain hygiene	Recurrent violence; serious suicidal act with clear expectation of death

Source: American Psychiatric Association: *Diagnostic and Statistical Manual of Mental Disorders, Third Edition, Revised,* Washington, DC, American Psychiatric Association, 1987. Reprinted by permission.

Diagnostic Criteria

The second step is to obtain as clear an idea as possible of the client's symptoms. What does Peter mean when he says that he has "bouts of anxiety"? After Dr. Tobin asks him this question, she listens to determine whether any of his symptoms match the *DSM* criteria for "anxiety." Do his hands tremble? Does he get "butterflies" in his stomach? Does he feel jittery and irritable, have trouble sleeping? Dr. Tobin keeps a mental tally of Peter's symptoms to see if there are enough of the appropriate ones present before she decides that his state is, in fact, "anxiety" and that he might therefore have an "anxiety disorder."

As she listens to Peter's symptoms, Dr. Tobin discovers that his anxiety bouts involve depression. This discovery leads her to decide that Peter does not have an anxiety disorder at all. Instead, what he is describing are the classic symptoms of a "mood" disturbance. Based on this decision, Dr. Tobin then refers to the guidelines called "decision trees" in the *DSM*. A **decision tree** is used for the purpose of

diagnosis, and consists of a series of simple yes/no questions that guide the questions the clinician poses to the client. Dr. Tobin can then go through an orderly process of sorting out possible alternative diagnoses by asking Peter questions that are based on the decision tree (See Figure 2-1 on page 38).

Although there are many more steps in this tree than represented here, the basic logic of the process can be seen in this simplified version. By proceeding through the decision tree, the clinician has a systematic basis for arriving at a diagnosis that helps in ruling out other possible diagnoses.

Dr. Tobin begins with the mood disturbance decision tree because she has already decided that Peter's symptoms might fit the diagnostic criteria for a mood disorder. Going through the steps of the decision tree, Dr. Tobin is able to rule out diagnoses such as a physically-based disorder, and the more chronic form of depression called dysthymic disorder. However, Dr. Tobin ascertains an important new piece of information as she reviews the decision tree. In addition to feeling sad, Peter also reported a period of feeling "elated." It sounds as though he might have had what is called a manic episode, a period of elated mood and

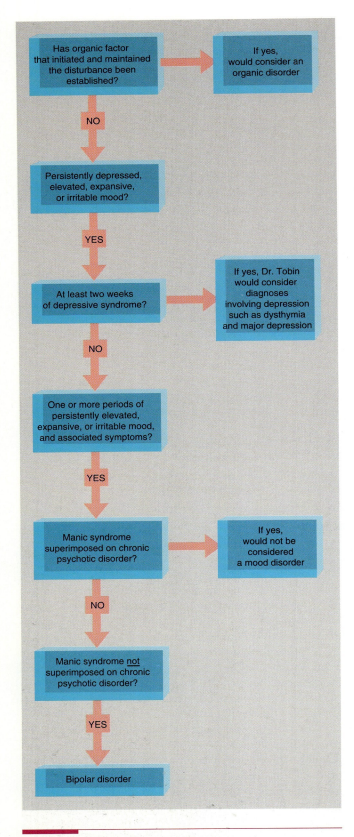

Figure 2–1 Dr. Tobin's decision tree for Peter
The decision trees in *DSM* provide choices for the clinician based on the client's history and symptoms. Follow the choices made by Dr. Tobin throughout the tree for mood disturbances, the area that seems most appropriate for Peter.

unusually high excitability. If he did, it would mean that Peter should be diagnosed as having bipolar disorder, a mood disorder which is characterized by alternating cycles of extreme depression and elation (formerly referred to as manic depression). Otherwise he would be diagnosed as suffering from major depressive disorder, a mood disorder characterized by serious impairment associated with sad mood. Had Dr. Tobin not gone through the decision tree with Peter she would have missed out on this essential clue to his diagnosis.

In moving through the decision tree, Dr. Tobin asks Peter a series of specific questions about his past and present symptoms to distinguish between the diagnoses of major depression and bipolar disorder. She gains further proof that the period in question, when Peter felt so "elated," meets the diagnostic criteria of a manic episode. A particularly telling feature was Peter's description of his extravagance in buying an expensive sportscar and impulsiveness in marrying a virtual stranger.

Differential Diagnosis

If Dr. Tobin is satisfied that Peter fits the diagnostic criteria for bipolar disorder, the final step in the diagnostic process is for her to be sure that she has ruled out all alternatives. This process is called **differential diagnosis.**

This step will probably have been completed already, because Dr. Tobin has been through the decision tree process. However, Dr. Tobin must be confident that she has not left out any other possible diagnoses. Either by questioning Peter or by reviewing the information she has already collected, Dr. Tobin attempts to establish a diagnosis that excludes any possible alternatives.

The diagnostic process often requires more than one session with the client, which is why some clinicians prefer to regard the first few psychotherapy sessions as a period of "evaluation" or "assessment." While some therapeutic work may be accomplished during this time, the major goal is for the client and clinician together to arrive at as thorough an understanding as possible of the nature of the client's disorder. This paves the way for the clinician to work with the client on an agreed-upon treatment plan.

Peter's diagnosis was fairly straightforward; however, there are many people whose problems do not fit neatly into a diagnostic category. The problems of some individuals meet the criteria for two or more disorders. The most common instance would be the case of the individual who has a long-standing personality disorder and also has another more circumscribed problem such as depression or a sexual disorder. In other cases, an individual without a personality disorder may have two concurrent problems that both warrant professional attention, as in the case of the person who suffers from both alcoholism and depression. When clinicians use multiple diagnoses, they typically consider one of the diagnoses to be the **principal diagnosis**, namely the disorder that is considered to be the primary cause for the individual seeking professional help.

Final Diagnosis

The final diagnosis that Dr. Tobin assigns to Peter incorporates all the information gained during the diagnostic phase of his treatment. The diagnosis appears as follows:

Axis I: Bipolar disorder

Axis II: Diagnosis deferred (no information yet available on Peter's long-standing personality traits)

Axis III: No physical conditions reported

Axis IV: Psychosocial stressors: 3 (marriage and subsequent divorce)

Axis V: Current Global Assessment of Functioning: 43. Highest Global Assessment of Functioning during past year: 80

Case Formulation

Once the formal diagnosis is made, the clinician is still left with a formidable challenge—to piece together a picture of how the disorder evolved. A diagnosis is a categorical judgment, and although it is very informative, it does not say much about the client as an individual. To gain a full appreciation of the client's disorder the clinician must have what is called a **case formulation.** A case formulation is an analysis of the client's development and the factors that might have influenced the client's current psychological status. The analysis provided by the case formulation transforms the diagnosis from a set of code numbers to a rich piece of descriptive information about the client's personal history, and helps the clinician in designing a treatment plan that is attentive to the client's symptoms, unique past experiences, and future potential for growth. As you might imagine, the case formulation is very much influenced by the clinician's theoretical perspective, a point that will become very obvious throughout this book.

Let's return to Peter's case. Having diagnosed Peter as having bipolar disorder, Dr. Tobin uses the next two therapy sessions with him to obtain a comprehensive review of his presenting problem as well as his life history. Based on this review, Dr. Tobin makes the following case formulation:

Peter is a 23-year-old single white male with a diagnosis of bipolar disorder. He is currently in the middle of his first major depressive episode, which follows his first manic episode by about 4 months. Relevant to Peter's condition is an important fact about his family—his mother has been treated for a period of 20 years for what also appears to be a bipolar disorder. Peter's diagnosis appears to be a function of both an inherited predisposition to a mood disorder and a set of experiences within his family. The middle child of three boys, Peter was somehow singled out by his mother to be her confidant. She would tell Peter in detail about her symptoms and the therapy she was receiving. Whenever Peter him-

self was in a slightly depressed mood, his mother told him that it was probably the first signs of a disorder he was bound to inherit from her. Her involvement in his emotional problems creates another difficulty for Peter in that it has made him very ambivalent about seeking therapy. On the one hand, he wants to get help for his problems. Counteracting this desire is Peter's reluctance to let his mother find out that he is in therapy for fear that this information will confirm her dire predictions for him.

This case formulation gives a much more complete picture of Peter's diagnosis than the simple diagnosis of "bipolar disorder." Having read this case formulation, you now know some important potential contributions to Peter's current disorder.

In effect, what a clinician does in developing a case formulation is to propose a hypothesis about the causes of the client's disorder. This hypothesis gives the clinician a logical starting point for designing a treatment and serves as a guide through the many decisions yet to be made.

A clinician works on developing a case formulation for her new client.

PLANNING A TREATMENT

We have discussed the steps through which a clinician develops an understanding of a client's problem. This understanding provides the basis for the clinician's next phase, which is to plan the most appropriate treatment for the client. With the client's cooperation, the clinician makes a series of choices. What are the goals of the treatment? What would be the best treatment setting? Who should treat the client? What kind of treatment should be used? What kind of treatment is financially feasible and available? Finally, what theoretical orientation would be best suited to the client's particular needs? All of these considerations would form Dr. Tobin's treatment plan as she moves from the diagnostic phase toward the treatment phase.

The Goals of Treatment

To help you understand what treatment planning involves, it might be useful to think of an analogous situation involving a personal relationship. Of course, you are not "treating" the person in a professional sense, but the steps you take might be very much like the approach a clinician takes with a client in developing a treatment plan. Let's take the example of a friend who knocks on your door late one night, in tears because she has had another of her many arguments on the phone with her father. Because of her problems with her father, she has had academic difficulties all semester. Tomorrow she has an important exam, and she is panic-stricken. What would you do? Your first reaction would be to help her calm down. You might talk to her and try to get her in a better frame of mind so that she will be

able to take the exam. However, you would also realize that she has other problems that she will need to attend to after she gets through the next day. In the short term, she needs to catch up on the rest of her course work. Over the long term, she will need to deal with the difficulties that recur between her and her father. A clinician treating a client would also think in terms of the three stages just discussed—immediate management, short-term goals, and long-term goals.

These three stages imply a sequential order, and in many cases this is the way that a treatment plan is conceived. First the clinician deals with the crisis, then handles problems in the near future, and finally addresses issues that require extensive work well into the future. However, in other cases, there may be a cyclical unfolding of stages. New sets of immediate crises or short-term goals may arise in the course of treatment. Or there may be a redefinition of long-term goals as the course of treatment progresses. It is perhaps more helpful to think of the three stages not as "stages" per se, but as implying different levels of treatment focus. In dealing with immediate management, the clinician is addressing the most pressing needs at the moment. Short-term goals involve some change in the client's behavior, thinking, or emotions, but do not involve a major personality restructuring. Long-term goals include more fundamental and deeply-rooted alterations in the client's personality and relationships.

Immediate management, then, is called for in situations involving intense distress or risk to the client or others. A person experiencing an acute anxiety attack would most likely be treated on the spot with antianxiety medication. A client who is severely depressed and suicidal would probably need to be hospitalized. In the case of Peter, Dr. Tobin decides that his symptoms of suicidal ideation, appetite, and

At this suicide hotline, telephone counseling is available 24 hours a day.

Clients in a psychiatric hospital engage in a group exercise called "The Spider's Web" as a means of promoting trust, support, and communication.

sleep disturbance warrant hospitalization. Not all clinical situations require that action be taken in the immediate management stage, but it is important for the clinician to think about various options to help the client deal with pressing concerns of the moment.

When a client's most troubling symptoms are under control, it is possible for the clinician to work with the client in developing more effective ways of resolving current difficulties. The plan at this point might include establishing a working relationship between the clinician and client, and setting up specific objectives for therapeutic change. If Dr. Tobin is to treat Peter's mood disorder, she must establish rapport with him, and he, in turn, must feel committed to working with her. Another short-term goal might be to stabilize Peter on medication so that his symptoms will be alleviated.

Long-term goals refer to the ultimate aims of therapeutic change. Ideally, the long-term goal for any client is to overcome the problem and develop a strategy to prevent recurrence. In reality, this goal is difficult to achieve. The restructuring of a personality can be a life-long endeavor. Dr. Tobin will work with Peter in helping him plan his life taking into account his disorder. For example he may be advised to take medication aimed at preventing a recurrence of his symptoms. He may also need help in preparing himself for some of the ways this disorder may affect his life. In addition, she will have to work with Peter on dealing with the emotional scars that he has suffered as a result of his own disorder and the troubled childhood caused by his mother's disorder.

A treatment plan, then, includes a set of goals for short- and long-range interventions. Having established these goals, the clinician's next task is to specify how to implement the plan. This requires decisions regarding the optimal treatment site, treatment modality and theoretical perspective.

Treatment Site

What enters into the clinician's decision about what kind of treatment site to recommend for a client? The severity of the client's problem is one of the first issues that a clinician considers in making this decision. Severity is assessed on several dimensions. Is the client suicidal, at risk of harming others, delusional, or otherwise incapable of maintaining control? Does the client have physical problems, such as those that might result from a brain dysfunction, an eating disorder, or illness? What is the client's support system at home—that is, are there people who can help the client deal with the problems that the disorder causes? Depending on the answers to these questions, the clinician will recommend a psychiatric hospital, outpatient treatment, or a halfway house or group home that provides a combination of services.

■ Psychiatric hospitals

Hospitalization is usually recommended by a clinician when the client is at risk of harming self or others, or seems incapable of self-care. The decision to hospitalize a client depends largely on the risk the client presents. Only those clients who appear to be at great risk of harm to themselves or others are likely to be admitted and retained in the hospital. Often, these clients are involuntarily hospitalized by a court order until their symptoms can be brought under control.

Hospitalization is particularly helpful for disorders that require medical interventions and some forms of psychotherapeutic interventions. Some medical interventions, such as a trial on a new drug regimen, are best done in a setting where risks of potential side effects and treatment efficacy can easily be monitored. Some psychotherapeutic interventions, such as the design of a system that rewards nondisturbed behavior and aversively responds to pathological behavior, are best done in a setting where most of the contingencies of the client's behavior can be monitored and reinforced.

In some cases, the clinician might recommend a specialized inpatient treatment center, as would be the case when treating adults with substance abuse problems, or children and adolescents who need professional treatment in a residential setting.

■ Outpatient treatment

Because hospitalization is such a radical and expensive intervention, most clients are treated in outpatient settings. In fact, the process of seeking help usually begins by a client's seeking help through an outpatient treatment consultation. The client may look up a private practitioner in the Yellow Pages, or obtain a recommendation from a friend. In some cases, clients seek help from a crisis intervention hotline or a telephone referral service. Once a client makes the initial contact, it is most likely that outpatient care will be recommended unless exceptional circumstances warrant hospitalization.

The particular kind of outpatient site recommended for treatment is often determined by the financial resources of the client. Clients who are able to afford it will usually seek help from a professional in private practice, or one who is part of some prepaid health insurance plan such as a health maintenance organization (HMO). In this regard, mental health professionals provide services in a manner that resembles the services offered by physicians. Like a physician, the mental health professional may have an independent private practice, be a participant in a group practice, or work as part of a prepaid health plan. In addition to the private practice and insurance-based clinics, there are many other agencies supported partially or completely by public funds. The most common of these agencies are **community mental health centers (CMHC)**, outpatient clinics that provide psychological services on a sliding fee scale for individuals who live within a certain geographic area.

■ *Halfway houses and day treatment programs*

There are many clients for whom hospitalization is not needed but for whom outpatient treatment is not sufficient. For such individuals, there are halfway houses and day treatment programs. These facilities may be connected with a hospital, a public agency, or a private corporation. The **halfway house** is designed for those deinstitutionalized clients coming out of a hospital who are not yet ready for independent living. The halfway house provides a living context with other deinstitutionalized people, and is staffed by a group of professionals who work with clients in developing the skills needed to become employed and set up their own living situations. **Day treatment programs** are designed for those clients who do not need hospitalization but do need some structured program during the day similar to that provided in the milieu of the hospital. Some of these clients reside in a halfway house and some live independently, with relatives or in apartments supervised by a paraprofessional mental health worker.

The clinician's recommendation of a treatment site is based not only on the severity of the client's problem, but on the match between the client's needs and the services provided in a particular treatment setting. On an inpatient unit, the client receives round-the-clock attention as well as a range of therapeutic activities. Outpatient services are, by necessity more limited. Most clients involved in outpatient treatment participate in weekly psychotherapy. However, in some cases this may be augmented by additional services. Perhaps a client needs vocational counseling, help with domestic management, group therapy, or the support of a self-help organization such as Alcoholics Anonymous. Formerly hospitalized psychiatric clients often participate in "day treatment" programs. Many of these are based on a social club model, in which people spend their days involved in a therapeutic milieu. The clinician's recommendation of a treatment site, then, is contingent on whether the activities provided at that site will be suitable for the client's particular problems.

Psychological treatment is provided in settings other than hospitals and clinics. This high school counselor is talking with a student about drug abuse.

Psychological treatment is also provided in settings not traditionally associated with mental health such as the schools and the workplace. Guidance counselors and school psychologists are often called upon to intervene in cases where a student is emotionally disturbed or is upset by a pathological living situation. These professionals handle much of the intervention in the school, but they often find it necessary to refer the student or family for professional help outside the school setting. In the workplace, many employers have recognized the importance of intervening in the lives of employees whose emotional problems are interfering with job performance and could possibly result in termination from employment. The most common programs are the Employee Assistance Programs (EAP) that are provided by most large companies. The EAP provides the employee with a confidential setting in which to seek help for emotional problems, substance abuse difficulties, or relationship problems. Often the EAP professional can work with the employee toward a resolution of the problem; at times, the EAP professional can help the employee to locate appropriate treatment resources for the problem at hand.

Returning to the case of Peter, a hospital would be the treatment site of choice because he is suicidal, he needs medication monitoring, and the hospital could offer him various forms of therapy. As he improves Dr. Tobin will develop a discharge plan that will undoubtedly include outpatient care.

Modality of Treatment

The **modality,** or form in which psychotherapy is offered, is another crucial component of the treatment plan. In **individual psychotherapy**, the therapist works with the client on a one-to-one basis. Typically, the therapist and client meet on a regular schedule, most commonly once a week for

In family therapy, all available members of a family are involved in treatment.

about an hour. In **family therapy**, several or all the family members participate in the treatment. One person may be identified by family members as being the "patient." The therapist, however, views the whole family system as the target of the treatment. **Group therapy** provides a modality in which troubled people can openly share their problems with others, receive feedback, develop trust, and improve interpersonal skills.

A modality found to be helpful for hospitalized clients is **milieu therapy.** Milieu therapy refers to the premise that the entire milieu, or environment, participates in treatment. Milieu therapy is based on the presumption that a new setting in which a team of treating professionals is working together for the improvement of a client's mental health is better than the home and work environment with their stresses and pressures. Ideally, the milieu is constructed in such a way that all interactions and contexts will be perceived by clients as therapeutic and constructive. In addition to traditional psychotherapy, other therapeutic endeavors are made through group therapy, occupational therapy, recreational therapy, and family therapy.

The clinician's decision to recommend a particular modality of treatment is based, again, on a match between the client's specific needs and the potential of the treatment to meet these needs. For example, a teenage girl with an eating disorder may be seen in both individual therapy and family therapy if the clinician believes that the eating disorder is rooted in disturbed parent–child interactions. As this example illustrates, the clinician has the option of recommending multiple modalities rather than being restricted to one form of therapy.

In Peter's case, three treatment modalities would be recommended, at least in the initial phase of his treatment. Along with his individual therapy needs, Peter would benefit from both family therapy and group therapy. Family therapy would be useful in helping Peter resolve his problems with his mother, and group therapy would provide Peter

with the opportunity to interact with and derive support from other clients who have similar disorders.

Theoretical Perspective on Which Treatment Is Based

Whatever modality of treatment a clinician recommends, it must be based on the choice of the most appropriate theoretical perspective or the most appropriate aspects of several different perspectives. Many clinicians are trained according to a particular set of assumptions about the origins of psychological disorders and the best methods of treating these disorders. Often, this theoretical orientation forms the basis for the clinician's treatment decisions. However, just as frequently, clinicians adapt their theoretical orientation to fit the client's particular needs. Further, the growing movement toward integrating diverse theoretical models in treatment planning is addressing the concerns of clinicians who feel that a single theoretical model is too narrow. Increasingly, clinicians are combining the best elements of various theoretical orientations in tailoring the treatment plan that will have the greatest likelihood of success for a given client (Norcross, 1992).

IMPLEMENTING TREATMENT

With the diagnostic process complete, the clinician begins to implement the treatment plan. Despite all the thinking and preparation that has gone into this plan, though, the exact way in which treatment unfolds varies according to the characteristics of the clinician, the client, and the interaction between the two. There are many individual variations among both clients and clinicians. Consequently, the potential for variation is virtually unlimited in the interactions between any one client and any one clinician. Some common issues, though, characterize all therapeutic interactions.

Above and beyond whatever techniques a clinician uses to treat a client's problems, the quality of the relationship between the client and clinician is a crucial determinant of whether therapy will succeed or not. A good clinician does more than coldly and objectively "administer" a treatment to a client. A good clinician infuses a deep personal interest, concern, and respect for the client into the therapeutic relationship. In this regard, psychotherapy is as much an art as a skill.

The Course of Treatment

■ *The clinician's role in treatment*

One of the skills the clinician develops is an ability to scan the client–clinician interaction for meaningful cues that will provide insight into the nature of the client's

Determining the Need for Treatment

Who determines whether someone is normal or abnormal? The individual or an outside agency or "expert"? The way this question is answered in a given situation can have crucial practical implications. A person may feel normally adjusted, but may be called abnormal by a mental health system that applies different standards of assessment. In some cases, the individual's own perspective is distorted by a psychological disorder so that he is incapable of recognizing that he does in fact need help. Were treatment not provided, that individual might hurt himself or other people because of his misguided judgmental abilities and erratic emotional state. In other cases, a person might think there is something wrong with her when, according to external criteria, she is undergoing a normal adjustment reaction. In that case, it would be a waste of effort and possibly even harmful to expose her to unnecessary treatment.

In both of these cases, evaluation by a professional of the individual's abnormality can be seen to have an advantage over the individual's own perspective. The professional, after all, has the experience, knowledge of psychological functioning, and objectivity to be able to make a clear determination. However, there is always the chance that the professional's judgment is erroneous. You might think this to be a remote possibility, but consider what happens in a totalitarian government as an extreme example. Political dissidents are labelled "schizophrenic" and sent away to prisons and work camps that are called hospitals. Psychologically healthy people who happen not to agree with their government are thereby condemned to years of imprisonment, forced labor, and poor living conditions, resulting possibly in premature death. The professionals in this case are the ones who are in error. They are applying a social criterion to judge psychological behavior. Often, this is the kind of categorical error committed when internal and external judgments of abnormality are discordant.

Consider the opposite possibility of the example just discussed: that a person who feels in need of psychological help is told by a mental health worker that he must be "faking it"; there is nothing the matter with him at all. Yet, the individual is miserable and despondent, on the verge of committing suicide. In this case, it appears that something important has been missed in the professional's evaluation that cannot be appreciated from an outsider's perspective. Both of these examples show that the question of which evaluative perspective is used can be one upon which someone's life may depend.

Where do you stand on this issue? With the exception of those who are politically biased, should professionals be the ones to define abnormality? Or is the individual the only one who can make that determination? Perhaps both perspectives are needed, as we believe they are. In which cases should the professional be listened to, and in which cases would you accept the individual's self-evaluation? As you try to answer these questions, keep in mind the different types of criteria of abnormality and the different ways of defining a norm.

---

problems. One important piece of information the clinician gathers is the way the client seems to respond to the clinician. Let's use Dr. Tobin as an example to illustrate this point. Dr. Tobin is a woman in her early 40s. Each of her clients forms a unique impression of the kind of person she is. One client thinks of Dr. Tobin as an authority figure because Dr. Tobin's mannerisms and appearance remind him of his seventh-grade teacher. Another client perceives Dr. Tobin as a peer because she is about the same age and professional status. A third client is in his 60s, and Dr. Tobin reminds him of his daughter. Thus, the same clinician is perceived in three different ways by three different clients. With each client, Dr. Tobin will have a markedly different basis for a therapeutic relationship.

Not only do clients have unique responses to Dr. Tobin, but she also has individualized responses to each client. As a professional, Dr. Tobin is trained to examine her reactions to each client and to try not to let her reactions interfere with her ability to help. Moreover, she has learned how to use her perception of each client, and the way she thinks she is perceived, as aids in diagnosing the client's disorder and in embarking on a therapeutic procedure.

■ *The client's role in treatment*

Psychotherapy is a joint enterprise in which the client plays an active role. It is largely up to the client to describe and identify the nature of his or her disorder, to describe his or her reactions as treatment progresses, and to initiate and follow through on whatever changes are going to be made.

The client's attitudes toward therapy and the therapist are an important part of the contribution the client makes to the therapeutic relationship. There is a special quality to the help that the client is requesting; it involves potentially painful, embarrassing, and personally revealing material which the client is not accustomed to disclosing to someone else. Most people are much more comfortable discussing their medical, legal, financial, and other problems outside the realm of the emotions. Social attitudes toward psychological disorders also play a role. People may feel that they should be able to handle their emotional problems without seeking help. They may believe that if they can't solve their own emotional problems, it means they are immature or incompetent. Moreover, having to see a clinician may make a person believe that he or she is "crazy." You would not hesitate to tell your friends that you have an appointment with a physician because of your sore knee. Most people would, though, feel less inclined to mention to acquaintances that they are in psychotherapy for personal problems. The pressure to keep therapy secret usually adds to a client's anxiety about seeking professional help. To someone who is already troubled by severe problems in living, this added anxiety can be further inhibiting. With so many potential forces driving the troubled individual away from seeking therapy, the initial step is sometimes the hardest to take.

Thus, the therapeutic relationship requires the client to be willing to work with the clinician in a partnership, and to be prepared to endure the pain and embarrassment involved in making personal revelations. Moreover, it also requires a willingness to break old patterns and try new ways of viewing the self and relating to others.

The Outcome of Treatment

In the best of all possible worlds, the treatment will work. The client will stay through the treatment, show improvement, and maintain this improved level of functioning. Many times, though, the road is not so smooth, and either the goals of the treatment plan are never attained or unanticipated problems arise. Some of the obstacles that clinicians face in their efforts to help clients include some curious and frustrating realities. The most frustrating involve the client who is unwilling to change. It may sound paradoxical, but even though a client may seem terribly distressed by a problem, that same client may fail to follow through on a very promising treatment. Mental health professionals know that change is very difficult, and in many cases a client has become so accustomed to living with a problem that the effort needed to change the problem seems overwhelming. At times clinicians also face frustration over financial constraints. They may recommend a treatment that they are quite confident can succeed, but that is financially infeasible. In other cases there may be an involved party, such as a lover or parent, who refuses to participate in the treatment even though he or she plays a central role. Other pragmatic issues can disrupt therapy: clients may move, lose jobs, or lack consistent transportation to the clinic. Over time those in the mental health field learn that they are limited in how effective they can be in changing the lives of people who come to them for help.

ETHICAL AND LEGAL ISSUES

So far, we have described psychotherapy in terms of a voluntary process in which clients are able to communicate their need for help, and in which their problems are of a personal nature. Our discussion has not dealt with issues involving other people's rights, legal implications, or the clinician's ethical responsibilities. During the last few decades, clinicians have found it necessary to become very attentive to these issues, as the whole climate of psychotherapy has changed. These changes have taken place in the context of broader changes such as deinstitutionalization, concerns about the rights of research subjects, increased attention to potential abuses in psychotherapy, and heightened publicity regarding medical malpractice.

Client's Rights

Because the therapeutic relationship involves deeply personal concerns and because of the potential for the client to become dependent on the clinician, extraordinary care must be taken by the clinician to maintain a professional and ethical relationship with the client.

■ *Informed consent*

Clients must understand what therapy is about if they are to make informed decisions about their treatment. Consequently, **informed consent**, similar to that used in research, has become standard practice in psychotherapy. Informed consent refers to the client's statement of understanding about the potential risks and benefits of therapy, confidentiality and its limits, and the expected length of therapy. You can understand how a person beginning therapy would have questions such as how much it will cost, what the risks are, how long it will take, and what gains can be expected. In cases where a risk is involved in treatment, such as when medication or electroconvulsive therapy is recommended, the client should understand possible short-term or long-term side effects. The clinician has a responsibility to ensure that the client is made aware of these issues, given answers to these questions, and given the opportunity to refuse treatment.

You can imagine that this process has some complications. Psychotherapy is an imprecise procedure, and it is not always possible to predict its course, risks, or benefits. The clinician's job, however, is to give a best estimate at the

Before being admitted to a psychiatric hospital, this client is asked to give informed consent indicating that he understands the nature of the treatment he will receive.

onset of therapy and to provide further information as therapy proceeds. Most people are able to discuss these matters with the clinician and come to an informed choice. However, what happens when prospective clients are unable to understand the issues in order to make informed consent? This would be the case with people who are out of touch with reality, people who are mentally retarded, or children. In these cases, the clinician must work with the individual's family or other legally appointed guardians. The main point is that the clinician must make every effort to ensure that the client's rights are protected.

■ *Confidentiality*

Part of the informed consent process involves informing the client that what takes place in therapy is confidential. Confidentiality has long been regarded as a sacred part of clinician-client relationship. Why is confidentiality so important? In order for clients to feel comfortable disclosing intimate details, they need to have the assurance that the clinician will protect this information. For example, if a man tells his therapist that he is having an extramarital affair, he would do so with the understanding that the therapist would not divulge this information to others. In fact, safeguards against the disclosure of confidential information exist within the laws of most states. Communications between a client and a therapist are considered "privileged." In other words, the therapist may not disclose any information without the client's expressed permission.

There are some important exceptions in which a clinician is required to breach confidentiality such as cases involving the abuse of children, elders, or handicapped people, or cases involving potential physical danger to the client or others. When a clinician hears that a client is planning to hurt another person, the clinician has a **duty to warn.** This means that the clinician is required to take action to prevent the client from harming the intended victim by informing the victim.

Duty to warn laws have their origins in a famous case that took place in 1969 in California. The "Tarasoff" case (*Tarasoff v. Regents of the University of California*, 1976) involved a young woman named Tatiana Tarasoff, who was a student at the University of California at Berkeley. She was shot and fatally stabbed by a man named Prosenjit Poddar, whom she had dated the previous year and with whom she had broken off relations. Her parents successfully sued the university following her murder on the grounds that she was not properly warned about the fact that Poddar, who was a client at the counseling center, intended to kill her. The psychologist who treated the murderer had become alarmed when Poddar told him that he was going to go after Tarasoff and kill her. The psychologist informed the police, who then interviewed Poddar. After assurances from Poddar, the police let him go. The court ruled that the psychologist had not gone far enough in preventing Tarasoff's murder. He should have told her that Poddar was intent on killing her. It took several years for this case to proceed through the legal system, and the ramifications of this case continue to

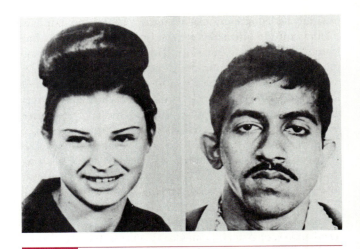

Tatiana Tarasoff, a junior at the University of California, was stabbed to death on the doorstep of her home by Prosenjit Poddar, who had told his therapist that he intended to kill her.

be felt by psychotherapists who struggle to differentiate between serious threats and random fantasies of their clients. In trying to make these distinctions, clinicians recurrently weigh the client's right of confidentiality against concern for the rights of other people.

■ *Refusal of treatment*

One client right that has engendered considerable controversy is the right to refuse unwanted treatment. You might have heard of people who, for religious reasons, refuse for themselves or their children various medical treatments that physicians deem necessary. These cases have typically generated considerable national attention, especially when they involve children at risk of dying because of a lack of medical intervention. Arguments similar to those presented in medical cases have been put forth by individuals who refuse to undergo various psychiatric interventions aimed at bettering their mental health. Generally, the more risky or intrusive the intervention, the more important it is for mental health professionals to ensure that they have received the client's informed consent. For example, patients have the right to refuse electroconvulsive therapy (ECT) or psychosurgery.

When clients are unable to make an informed decision, it is imperative that someone acting in their behalf evaluate the procedure and be given the right to refuse the intervention. The case involving the prescription of psychoactive medications is a bit more complex, however, because medications are not generally regarded as being as risky as ECT or psychosurgery. Nevertheless, many states have enacted laws that give the client the right to refuse unwanted medications. But what happens when a client's disorder is putting the individual or others at great risk?

Clients have the right to live in what is called the **least restrictive alternative** to treatment in an institution. This evolved from several legal cases brought to trial on behalf of mental patients in different states. One U.S. Supreme Court ruling in particular received national attention. This case, *O'Connor v. Donaldson* (1975), involved several issues relevant to the commitment and treatment of mental patients, including the right to refuse treatment and the right to a humane environment. Donaldson was committed at the age of 49 to a mental hospital in Chattahoochee, Florida, on the basis his father's contention that Donaldson was dangerous. However, Donaldson never exhibited signs of threatening behavior. His disorder, which was diagnosed as paranoid schizophrenia, went into remission soon after his commitment. Nevertheless, Donaldson was kept in the hospital for nearly two decades, during which time he was denied many fundamental privileges, such as the right to send and receive mail. Donaldson's successful lawsuit, along with several less well-known cases, paved the way for major changes in the mental health system. Society was forced to recognize that the presence of mental illness in a person is not sufficient reason for confinement to a mental hospital.

Forensic Issues in Psychological Treatment

Many of the issues involved in clients' rights lead to a larger consideration of forensic issues in psychological treatment. These issues involve the relationship between criminal behavior and psychological disturbance. The rapidly growing field of forensic psychology addresses concerns such as determining whether a mentally disturbed person should be held legally responsible for a criminal act, and if so, how that person should be dealt with.

Two widely publicized cases, a decade apart, focused national attention on forensic issues. The first case involved John Hinckley, who attempted to assassinate President Reagan soon after his inauguration in 1981. At the time, Hinckley was obsessed with the actress Jodie Foster.

From the photo in his 1977 highschool yearbook, would you suspect that Jeffrey L. Dahmer would become an infamous serial murderer? This July 1991 picture shows Dahmer in Milwaukee County Circuit Court where he was found guilty of killing and sexually mutilating at least 15 young men.

Hinckley believed that if he killed the president, Jodie Foster would be so impressed that she would fall in love with him and marry him. He even thought that they would live in the White House someday. When the case went to trial, the jury confronted a very difficult decision—was John Hinckley's behavior that of an "insane" person or that of a cold-blooded assassin? They ruled that he was insane, and he was sent to a mental hospital rather than a prison. This case brought to the nation's attention the rarely used but controversial insanity plea.

Ten years later the controversy surrounding the insanity plea resurfaced, and once again the U.S. judicial system struggled with some of the thorny legal issues raised in the case of John Hinckley. Partly because of the storm of criticism following the Hinckley case, however, a very different route was taken in 1992. This time the case involved a 31-year-old man, Jeffrey Dahmer, who confessed to murdering and dismembering 17 boys and young men, asserting that he was driven to kill out of a compulsion to have sex with dead bodies. The trial took place in Milwaukee for the 15 murders that Dahmer claimed to have committed in Wisconsin. Dahmer's defense attorney argued that Dahmer's bizarre acts could only be those of someone who was insane. However, the jury was not persuaded, and decided that Dahmer was sane at the time of the murders. He was found guilty and was sentenced to 15 consecutive life terms in prison. Let's take a look at some of the complex issues involved in designating a person like Hinckley or Dahmer as insane.

■ *Insanity defense*

Contrary to popular belief, insanity is not a psychological term, but rather a legal term that refers to the individual's lack of moral responsibility for committing criminal acts. The **insanity defense** refers to the argument presented by a lawyer acting on behalf of the client that because of the existence of a mental disorder, the client should not be held legally responsible for criminal actions. The insanity defense has a long history dating back to the 1800s. To understand the basis of the insanity defense, it is important to know the assumptions upon which criminal law is based—that people have free choice in their actions and that if they break the law they must be held responsible. People who are "insane," however, are considered to lack freedom of choice over controlling their behavior as well as the mental competence to distinguish right from wrong. The insanity defense originated as an attempt to protect people with mental disorders from being punished for harmful behavior resulting from their disturbed psychological state.

The insanity defense emerged from various legal precedents and attempts at clarification by the legal profession (Caplan, 1984). In 1843, the M'Naghten Rule was handed down in a disturbing case involving a Scottish woodcutter named Daniel M'Naghten. Under the delusional belief that he was being commanded by God, M'Naghten killed an official of the English government. When he went to trial, the argument was presented that he should not be held

The case of John Hinckley, who in 1981 tried to assassinate President Ronald Reagan, raised public concern over possible misuse of the insanity defense. Hinckley, who was declared insane by the courts, was not imprisoned; instead he was committed to treatment at St. Elizabeth's Hospital in Washington, D.C.

responsible for the murder because his mental disorder prevented him from knowing the difference between right and wrong. He believed that he was following the commands of a higher power, and therefore saw nothing wrong in his behavior. This is why the M'Naghten rule is often referred to as the "right-wrong test."

The M'Naghten Rule was criticized because it did not address the question of the individual's capacity to control harmful behavior. About 30 years later, the **irresistible impulse** test went a step further to add the notion that some disturbed behaviors may result from people's inability to inhibit actions that they feel compelled to carry out. They may "know" that an act is wrong, but be unable to stop themselves from acting on their impulses.

You can probably understand how the courts would be sympathetic to a person with a history of psychological disorder on trial for committing an alleged criminal act. However, it may not be possible to establish that the defendant's criminal behavior resulted from inability either to distinguish right from wrong or to control impulses. The Durham Rule, which emerged from a court decision in 1954, increased the scope of the insanity defense by asserting that a person is not criminally responsible if the "unlawful act was the product of mental disease or defect." This rule is significant because it allows for the insanity defense to be used in cases involving many forms of mental disorders. Its intent was to protect individuals with disturbed psychological functioning due to any of a variety of conditions, including personality disorders. As you can imagine, this rule, although well-intentioned, created tremendous legal difficulties because it put the burden on mental health experts to prove whether or not a defendant is mentally disturbed even when there is not overt psychosis.

In an attempt to develop uniform standards for the insanity defense, the American Law Institute (ALI) published

guidelines in 1962 (Sec. 4.01) that take a middle position between the pre-Durham Rule codes and the liberal standing taken by the Durham Rule. According to the ALI, people are not responsible for criminal behavior if their mental disorder prevents them from "appreciating" the wrongfulness of their behavior (a variation of the M'Naghten right-wrong rule) or from exerting the necessary willpower to control their acts (the irresistible impulse rule). The important term here is "appreciate." In other words, knowing what is right and wrong is not equivalent to "understanding" that one's behavior is wrong (Gutheil & Appelbaum, 1982). An important feature of the ALI code is the exclusion from the insanity defense of people whose only maladaptive behavior is repeated criminal or otherwise antisocial conduct. The ALI guideline is considered a more viable standard of insanity than the Durham Rule, because it takes the question of guilt or innocence away from mental health experts and places it into the hands of the jury, who can then make a determination based on the evidence related to the crime itself. Despite this improvement, the ALI guidelines remained problematic.

In the years following publication of the ALI standards, the insanity defense became much more widely used up to the point of the Hinckley case, which brought to national attention some of the flaws in the ALI guidelines. The public was particularly outraged about the possibility that an assassin could get away with murder on the grounds of having a mental disorder. To tighten the standards of the insanity defense, Congress passed the Insanity Defense Reform Act of 1984 (Shapiro, 1986). This Act was an attempt to clear up the ambiguity inherent in the ALI standards regarding the severity and nature of an accused person's mental disorder. In order for people to be designated as insane according to the Reform Act, they must meet criteria of severe disturbance. In other words, people with personality

John Hinckley's attempted assassination of President Reagan and Mark David Chapman's murder of John Lennon brought a troubling question to the public's attention—How possible is it to predict dangerousness among psychologically disordered individuals? Virtually every day the news includes stories about brutal murders, commonly committed by people with ostensible psychological disorders. When such terrible events occur, many people wonder why the murder couldn't have been predicted based on the personality and history of the perpetrator. Didn't people know that the murderer was dangerous? Couldn't somebody have seen the murder coming and done something to stop it? If the individual had a history of psychiatric treatment, couldn't the person's therapist have predicted the violence and done something to avert it?

Such questioning has been raised not only by the public, but by experts in both criminal justice and mental health fields. Even a decade before Hinckley and Chapman received such notoriety, researchers were struggling with the thorny issue of prediction of dangerousness. During the 1970s psychiatrists and psychologists were severely criticized as being nearly inept in this task, a conclusion that was based on a handful of studies contending that psychiatrists and psychologists were wrong at least twice as often as they were accurate when attempting such predictions. If indeed the professionals were so imprecise on this very crucial task, some very troubling questions might follow. One prominent researcher in this field, John Monahan (1981, 1984) asked professionals in both the mental health system and the criminal justice system to consider the question of how imprisoned offenders could be designated as "safe" enough to be released, if indeed these professionals were so incapable of making an accurate prediction about the future likelihood of these individuals acting in violent ways.

THE PREDICTION OF VIOLENT BEHAVIOR

During the early 1980s, notions about violence prediction evolved considerably because of more precise research methods using actuarial statistics. Violent behavior prior to admission to a psychiatric unit was found to be the best predictor of violence after admission (Janofsky, Spears, & Neubauer, 1988). However, even this one predictor, significant though it was, could not tell the whole story because of the high proportion of "false negatives." In other words, not all individuals with histories of pre-admission violence were subsequently violent. Again, the lack of precise predictors of dangerousness among psychologically disturbed individuals left researchers and experts in the fields of mental health and criminal justice looking for improved methods of prediction.

One group of Norwegian researchers (Blomhoff, Seim, & Friis, 1990) undertook a study in which they attempted to refine predictors of dangerousness among psychiatrically hospitalized patients by comparing 25 patients who committed acts of violence while psychiatrically hospitalized with 34 patients on the same ward who were not violent during their hospital stay. These researchers confirmed the notion that the best single predictor of violence was a history of previous violence. Further, they found that violent behavior was much more likely among those individuals with a history of violence in their families of origin, as well as personal histories of drug abuse.

In addition to the variables of violent history, violent family background, and history of drug abuse, certain other predictors have emerged as significant: being male, moving frequently, being unemployed, having low intelligence, growing up in a violent subculture, having weapons available, and having victims available (Beck, 1987). However, even with all of these factors present, would a professional evaluating such an individual have enough information to predict with certainty that this person will, in fact, go out and harm someone? Unfortunately not. Again, there is the problem of false negatives. A number of men with such histories do not go on to act in violent ways, thus leaving professionals reluctant to point the finger of accusatory prediction. You can probably understand that, because of the seriousness of the problem of inaccuracy in predicting dangerousness, much more research must be carried out before society can feel confident about the judgments of professionals regarding this issue.

disorders would probably not be considered insane according to the new law. This law also changed the nature of the legal arguments used to establish the insanity defense. Instead of the prosecuting attorney having the responsibility of proving that the defendant was sane, the defense must instead show that the defendant was insane. This means that the defense must provide a stronger case to convince the jury that the defendant should not go to jail. Prior to this law, the defense only needed to provide "reasonable doubt" regarding the prosecution's argument that the defendant was sane.

The upshot of the change in insanity guidelines is that it is harder now for a defendant to be judged insane. This law is a federal law that applies in federal cases, and individual states vary in the nature of the insanity defense used in criminal proceedings at the state level. Some states have moved toward separating the question of guilt from that of mental disorder by allowing the plea of "guilty, but mentally ill" (Simon & Aaronson, 1988). The defendant is not then exonerated from the crime, but is given special consideration by virtue of having a mental disorder. Another important feature of the Reform Act was developed in response to criticisms that "insane" people were often released from mental hospitals after a much shorter period of time than they would have spent in a jail. With the Reform Act, people who are designated as insane are treated in a psychiatric institution. Should their psychological condition improve, they would then be moved to a prison for the duration of the "sentence."

The effects of the Reform Act could be seen in the outcome of the Dahmer case. Unlike Hinckley, who was sent to a psychiatric hospital for treatment, Dahmer was sent to prison. His plea of "guilty but insane" was rejected by the jury, who believed him to be responsible for his crimes and able to appreciate the wrongfulness of his conduct. At numerous points during the trial questions were raised about the exact nature of his disorder. The chief psychologist for the Milwaukee County Mental Health Complex asked, "What do you think about a person who kills people and has sex with their dead bodies and eats some of them—do you think he's nuts?" (Newsweek, February 3, 1992, p. 45). In the end it was decided that he was not psychotic but rather had a sexual disorder; however, this was not considered sufficient grounds for absolving him of responsibility.

■ Competency to stand trial

There is a very important distinction between the individual's state of mind at the time a crime was committed and at the time a trial takes place. So far, we have discussed the insanity defense, which refers to a defendant's mental state at the time of the alleged crime. But as you can imagine, it is critically important for an accused person to be able to understand what is going on in a trial and to participate in the defense.

The determination of **competency to stand trial** involves a prediction regarding the defendant's future behavior at the point of the trial. The job of the mental health expert is to provide an evaluation of the defendant's cognitive capacity, emotional stamina, and ongoing symptoms. For example, if a man is hallucinating and evidently delusional, he will probably have a very difficult time participating in the court proceedings. In other cases, however, defendants whose crime was committed while they were in a disturbed mental state may appear "normal" when interviewed about the crime. The forensic expert must determine, though, whether the stress of the criminal trial would precipitate a psychotic episode.

■ Commitment

What would you do if your friend told you that she is feeling so despondent that she is planning to kill herself? Obviously, you would be very alarmed and would want to stop her any way you could. However, you would realize that your ability to do so is limited, because you cannot be with her every minute and she resists your suggestion that she be hospitalized. In order to deal with situations such as this, all states have developed **commitment** procedures designed to protect disturbed individuals from harming themselves or other people. A commitment procedure is the involuntary placement of an individual into a psychiatric facility if a professional determines that the individual is at risk to self or a danger to others due to a psychological disorder. In the hypothetical case involving your friend, you would be faced, then, with the issue of whether you should

Courts often rely on the testimony of psychologists for guidance in determining issues of insanity or competency.

take action that will result in her being committed to a psychiatric hospital.

As you think about the question of involuntary commitment, it is probably clear to you that it is a very complex issue. Does one person have the right to interfere with another's decisions or freedom of action? If your friend wants to kill herself, what right have you or anyone else to stop her? Consider the question of dangerousness. Your friend's threats are very serious, but what if her risk was less obvious? Perhaps she has stopped eating for the past few days, or perhaps she has been drinking and driving. Would these behaviors be considered dangerous enough to warrant her involuntary hospitalization?

Questions such as those raised in the case of potential suicide are tackled by professionals who do commitment evaluations. Forensic psychologists are often called upon to assess dangerousness, usually in the context of predicting whether a person will be dangerous in the future. As you might imagine, this is often a difficult determination to make. Most psychologists agree that the best prediction of future dangerousness is the level of dangerousness shown by the person in the past. An individual who has murdered several times is more likely to harm someone in the future than an individual with no previous homicidal history. But even when the probability of dangerousness is high, there is still room for error in the prediction of future behavior. The consequences of erroneous predictions are, of course, very significant. The supposedly dangerous individual might be institutionalized unnecessarily, or the person deemed nondangerous might go on to commit serious harm.

■ *Patient's rights*

In the cases that we have presented so far, most people would agree that involuntary commitment is an appropriate action. However, when people are involuntarily committed, they may feel frightened and outraged at being "incarcerated" against their will. Such reactions are natural and understandable, and to ensure that clients' rights to their own freedom are not violated, the process of commitment has important safeguards to protect patients from inappropriate hospitalizations. Such measures include informing people about the reason for their hospitalization, their right to legal assistance, the nature of their treatment, and their options for treatment.

Patients in mental hospitals are entitled by law to several basic rights. One is the right to treatment. This right emerged as the outcome of a landmark legal case, *Wyatt v. Stickney* (1971, 1972). In this case, a patient named Ricky Wyatt instituted a class action suit against the commissioner of mental health for the state of Alabama, Dr. Stickney, in response to the horrifying conditions in psychiatric and mental retardation facilities. These institutions failed to provide even a minimum of treatment, and indeed were so inhumane that they were actually detrimental to the mental health of the patients. The court invoked the constitutional right to due process in making the ruling against Alabama. In other words, people cannot be committed to an institution that is supposed to help them unless they can be guaranteed that they will be helped. Otherwise, their commitment constitutes the equivalent of imprisonment without a trial. Along these lines, patients have the right to a "humane" environment, including privacy, appropriate clothing, opportunities for social interaction, mail, telephone and visitation privileges, comfortable furnishings, physical exercise, and adequate diet.

As you can see from our discussion of forensic issues, there is a whole body of knowledge and practice regarding mental disorders that has very little to do with psychology per se. "Insanity" is a legal, not a psychological term. The definition of this term rests not on theoretical concepts such as the unconscious, self-actualization, or reinforcement. This is important to understand so that you do not confuse the concept of "mental disorder" with that of "insanity."

Yet, by the same token, you should be aware that the ethical and legal concerns we have discussed are very important to a psychological understanding of mental disorders. Mental health professionals are playing an increasingly important role in the legal system and, at the same time, are finding that they must familiarize themselves with a whole array of forensic issues. Clearly, the areas of intersection between psychology and the law will continue to grow as society looks for interventions that are humane, ethical, and effective.

SUMMARY

1. Clients are individuals who seek professional help for various psychological problems ranging from adjustment difficulties to severe disorders.

2. There are many types of clinicians, but the desire to help others and training in interpersonal skills are general characteristics of mental health professionals. Clinical psychologists are mental health professionals with training that combines knowledge of behavioral sciences with expertise in direct care to clients. Unlike psychiatrists, who are physicians with special training in mental health, clinical psychologists cannot prescribe medications; typically, clinical psychologists focus more on psychotherapy and psychological testing. The mental health profession is growing rapidly and now includes mental health professionals with degrees in areas such as education, social work, and nursing. Professionals from various disciplines often work together in a team approach when providing treatment to people with psychological disorders.

3. In making diagnoses, most clinicians rely on the classification and diagnostic system developed in the *Diagnostic and Statistical Manual (DSM)* published by the American Psychiatric Association. This manual is intended to be a comprehensive and systematic approach to the accurate diagnosis of people with

psychological disorders. The team of researchers and clinicians who developed the *DSM* have tried to develop diagnoses that will meet acceptable standards of reliability and validity.

4. The first *DSM* was developed in 1952. Over the past 40 years, the *DSM* has been revised four times, each time becoming more comprehensive and specific in its cataloging of psychological disorders. *DSM-IV* reflects the work of thousands of researchers all over the world whose findings have contributed to present-day labeling of psychological disorders and specification of symptoms.

5. According to the *DSM*, a "mental disorder" is "a clinically significant behavioral or psychological syndrome or pattern that occurs in a person and that is associated with present distress (a painful symptom) or disability (impairment in one or more important areas of functioning) or with a significantly increased risk of suffering death, pain, disability, or an important loss of freedom" (p. xxii). This means that for a person's psychological difficulty to be considered a "disorder," it must persist for some length of time, cause noticeable impairment in a person's everyday functioning, or lead to a heightened risk of harm. Often mental disorders involve psychological distress, but this is not always the case.

6. The *DSM* provides a system of describing an individual's functioning along dimensions, called "axes." There are five axes in the *DSM* (labeled with Roman numerals). Axes I and II describe psychological disorders; Axis III is used to record medical conditions; Axis IV is used for rating psychosocial stressors; and Axis V rates the individual's overall level of psychological functioning. A formal diagnosis involves rating the individual on all five axes. Often, the clinician also provides a case formulation which augments the diagnosis with additional descriptive information about the client.

7. The diagnostic process involves comparing the client's reported symptoms with the diagnostic criteria in the *DSM*. In this process, the clinician can consult a decision tree, which offers a sequence of choices for possible diagnoses based on a series of "yes/no" questions that the clinician answers. The decision tree facilitates differential diagnosis, which allows the clinician to rule out other possible diagnoses that might describe the client's disorder.

8. Creating a treatment plan is the next step after the clinician has arrived at a diagnosis. A treatment plan gives a statement of treatment goals, describes the site at which treatment will take place (such as a hospital or outpatient clinic), identifies the type of professional who will be responsible for the treatment, and describes the preferred treatment modality. Most clinicians base their treatment plan on a theoretical perspective. Both the client and clinician play roles in implementing the treatment plan, and the outcome of treatment is a function of the unique combination of factors involved in their relationship.

9. Many ethical and legal factors are involved in the provision of psychological treatment. These include the rights of the client to give informed consent regarding the nature of treatment and to have an understanding about confidentiality. Although confidentiality is regarded as an essential part of the therapist-client relationship, there are certain exceptions such as cases involving potential harm to self or others or cases involving specific forms of abuse. Clients, or someone acting on their behalf, have the right to refuse treatment. They also have the right to live in settings that provide the least restrictive alternative to treatment in an institution.

10. The field of forensic psychology is concerned with matters involving the relationship between criminal behavior and psychological disturbance. The insanity defense has a long history of use as a plea by psychologically disturbed individuals not to be held responsible for criminal acts. Controversy over the insanity defense has led to a series of revisions and refinements in the legal code. Competency to stand trial is a determination made on the basis of an individual's predicted ability to participate in legal defense. Involuntary commitment is a process initiated by others to have an individual confined to a psychiatric treatment facility. This is a drastic step taken only when there is a high likelihood that the individual presents a danger to self or others. Another forensic issue is the right to treatment, which gives each individual the right to receive adequate and humane care for psychological disorders.

KEY TERMS

Client: a person seeking psychological treatment. p. 30

Psychiatrist: a medical doctor (M.D.) with advanced training in treating people with mental disorders. p. 30

Clinical psychologist: a mental health professional with training in the behavioral sciences who provides direct service to clients. p. 30

Psychological Testing: a broad range of measurement techniques, all of which involve having people provide scorable information about their psychological functioning. p. 31

Diagnostic and Statistical Manual of Mental Disorders (DSM): a book published by the American Psychiatric Association that contains standard terms and definitions of the various psychological disorders. p. 31

Reliability: the consistency of measurements or diagnoses. p. 31

Validity: the extent to which a diagnosis or rating accurately and distinctly characterizes a person's psychological status. p. 31

Base rate: the frequency of a disorder's occurrence in the general population. p. 31

Syndrome: a collection of symptoms that together form a definable pattern. p. 33

Psychosis: a nontechnical term used to describe various forms of behavior involving loss of contact with reality. p. 33

Neurosis: a nontechnical term used to refer to behavior that involves symptoms that are distressing to an individual and are recognized by that person as unacceptable. Sometimes used to characterize certain psychological disorders considered to be less severe than psychosis. p. 33

Mulitaxial system: a multidimensional classification and diagnostic system that summarizes a variety of relevant information about an individual's physical and psychological functioning. p. 34

Prognosis: a client's likelihood of recovering from a disorder. p. 35

Global Assessment of Functioning (GAF): Axis V of the *DSM*, a scale that rates the individual's overall level of psychological health. p. 35

Decision tree: a strategy used for the purpose of diagnosis, consisting of a series of yes/no questions that guide the clinicians in ruling in or out various psychological disorders. p. 37

Differential diagnosis: the process of systematically ruling out alternative diagnoses. p. 38

Principal diagnosis: the disorder that is considered to be the primary cause for the individual's seeking professional help. p. 38

Case formulation: a clinician's analysis of the factors that might have influenced the client's current psychological status. p. 39

Community mental health centers (CMHC): outpatient clinics that provide psychological services on a sliding fee scale to serve individuals who live within a certain geographic area. p. 42

Halfway house: a community treatment facility designed for deinstitutionalized clients coming out of a hospital who are not yet ready for independent living. p. 42

Day treatment program: a structured program in a community treatment facility that provides activities similar to those provided in a psychiatric hospital. p. 42

Modality: the form in which psychotherapy is offered. p. 42

Individual psychotherapy: psychological treatment in which the therapist works on a one-to-one basis with the client. p. 42

Family therapy: psychological treatment in which the therapist works with the family. p. 43

Group therapy: psychological treatment in which the therapist facilitates discussion among a group of several clients who talk together about their problems. p. 43

Milieu therapy: the provision of a therapeutic environment on a 24-hour basis in an inpatient psychiatric facility. p. 43

Informed consent: the client's statement of understanding about the potential risks and benefits of therapy, confidentiality and its limits, and the expected length of therapy. p. 45

Duty to warn: the clinician's responsibility to notify a potential victim of a client's harmful intent toward that individual. p. 46

Least restrictive alternative: a treatment setting that provides the fewest constraints on the client's freedom. p. 46

Insanity defense: the argument presented by a lawyer acting on behalf of the client that because of the existence of a mental disorder, the client should not be held legally responsible for criminal actions. p. 47

Irresistible impulse: a legal defense claiming that because of the presence of a psychological disorder, the individual is unable to inhibit actions that he or she feels compelled to carry out. p. 48

Competency to stand trial: a determination of whether an individual is psychologically capable of testifying on his or her own behalf in a court of law. p. 50

Commitment: legal procedures designed to protect individuals from doing harm to themselves or others through institutionalization or other forms of mental health treatment. p. 50

Case Report: Ben Appleton

On the day that Ben Appleton, a 21-year-old college student, first stopped by the clinic during walk-in hours, I was terribly busy and found it difficult to accommodate our receptionist, Marie, who phoned me to ask if I could just meet with Ben for a few moments. Marie said she felt bad for Ben, because this was the third time he had stopped by the clinic during walk-in hours. Each time he had been turned away because the clinician on duty was busy with clinical crises and unable to meet with him to "answer a few questions about psychological testing."

Despite my hectic schedule, I felt it important to be responsive to Ben, thinking in the back of my mind that his simple request might be a cover for some serious problem. As I walked into the lobby to escort Ben to my office, my thoughts of concern intensified as I looked into his eyes. Although he showed no obvious distress, there was something about him that made me wonder about the stability of his emotions. For some undefinable reasons, he seemed needy and frightened.

Ben accompanied me to my office and upon taking a seat got right to the focus of his request. He stated that he thought it would be interesting to find out what it was like to be tested and to learn more about himself. Although such requests are uncommon, the notion of a college student being interested in the experience of psychological testing did not seem unreasonable. However, I was struck by the comments of Ben that followed. He asked me whether the police would ever have access to the testing results. When I queried him about why he would have such a concern, he claimed that police officers had been following him for several months. Of course, I reassured him that the test results would be kept confidential, but I felt a certain level of alarm that he would be troubled by such outlandish worries. The fact that this young man would have such unusual concerns led me to wonder about the possibility that he might be suffering from some psychological disorder and was using the pretext of psychological testing as a route by which to gain access to professional help.

Sarah Tobin, PhD

3

ASSESSMENT

As you read the opening case report about Ben's request for psychological testing, certain questions probably came to mind. Perhaps you wondered whether the police might actually be following Ben. Maybe you thought that Ben seemed paranoid. Perhaps it crossed your mind that Ben was actually looking for professional help. If you were Dr. Tobin, how would you go about finding the answers to these questions? First, you would want to talk with Ben and find out more about his concerns. You would possibly find, however, that talking with him did not really answer your questions. He could sound very convincing and present you with "facts" to document his concerns about the police. At the end of your interview, you still would not know whether his concerns were legitimate. You would want to gather more data that would include a careful study of how Ben thinks, behaves, and organizes his world. You would also want to know about his personality and emotional stability. The most efficient way to gather this information is to conduct what is called a psychological assessment.

After reading this chapter, you should be able to:

- Understand the purposes of psychological assessment.
- Compare the types of interviews used in assessment and their applications, strengths, and weaknesses.
- Describe the characteristics that clinicians look for in assessing mental status, such as disturbances of movement, perception, content of thought, and affective expression.
- Define the qualities of good psychological tests.
- Describe the major intelligence tests and the meaning of intelligence test scores.

- Describe personality tests used for the purpose of diagnosing psychological disorder and for drawing inferences about personality processes.
- Understand the rationale for and describe the types of behavioral assessment devices.
- Describe physical assessment techniques and their role in assessing psychological disorder.
- Understand testing methods used to draw inferences about brain functioning.

WHAT IS A PSYCHOLOGICAL ASSESSMENT?

When you meet people for the first time, you usually "size them up." You may try to figure out how smart they are, how nice they are, or how mature they are. In certain circumstances, you may be trying to solve other puzzles, such as whether a car salesperson really has your best interests in mind or is trying to take advantage of your naiveté. Perhaps you are trying to decide whether to accept a classmate's invitation to go on a date. You will probably base your decision on your appraisal of that person's motives and personality. Or consider what you would do if a professor suggests that members of the class pair up to study. You are faced with the task of judging the intelligence of the other students to find the best study partner. All of these scenarios involve some form of **assessment.** In psychological contexts, assessment involves the evaluation of a person's psychological status.

Psychologists approach the tasks of assessment with particular goals in mind. These goals often include establishing a diagnosis for someone with a mental disorder, determining a person's intellectual capacity, predicting a person's appropriateness for a particular job, or evaluating whether someone is mentally competent to stand trial for a crime. Depending on the questions to be answered by the assessment, the psychologist selects the most appropriate tools. For example, a psychologist asked by a teacher to evaluate a third-grader's mathematical ability would use a very different kind of assessment technique than if asked to evaluate the child's emotional adjustment.

The kinds of techniques used in assessment vary in their focus and degree of structure. Some assessment tools focus on personality; others are oriented toward intellectual functioning. Some follow very carefully defined instructions and procedures; others allow for flexibility on the part of the examiner.

INTERVIEW

The clinical interview is the most commonly used format for developing an understanding of a client and the nature of the client's current problems, past history, and future aspirations. Generally an assessment interview consists of a series of questions administered in face-to-face interaction. The questions may be constructed during the interview as the client reveals particular situations, or they may be designed prior to the interview. The interview may be tape-recorded, written down

A clinical interview is the most common format used by a clinician to develop an understanding of a client.

during the interview, or reconstructed from the clinician's memory following the interview. In clinical settings, two different kinds of interviews are most commonly used: the *flexible interview* and the *standardized interview*.

Flexible Interview

The **flexible interview** is a set of open-ended questions aimed at determining the client's reasons for being in treatment, symptoms, health status, family background, and life history. The interview is called "flexible" because the interviewer adjusts the exact content and order of the questions according to what the interviewer hypothesizes about the client's diagnosis or problems. The interviewer formulates questions during the interview on the basis of the client's verbal responses as well as such nonverbal behaviors as eye contact, body position, tone of voice, hesitations, and other emotional cues. In most instances, the clinician works toward the goal of forming a diagnosis. However, some people seek professional psychological help for problems that are not diagnosable mental disorders. For example, when working with a woman who is unhappy because of job dissatisfaction and her deteriorating marriage, a clinician may feel that it is inappropriate to focus entirely on diagnosis. Instead, the clinician works toward developing an understanding of what is causing this woman's distress.

An important part of the flexible interview is *history taking,* a process in which the clinician attempts to obtain, in the client's own words, a chronology of past events, both in the client's life and in the lives of relatives. The main objective of history taking is to gain a clear understanding of the client's life and family. By the time the history taking is complete, the clinician should have enough information to write a summary of the major turning points in the client's life and how the client's current symptoms or concerns fit into this sequence of events.

In some cases, clear links may be drawn between a particular event, such as a trauma, and the current problem. Most of the time, however, the determinants of current problems are not this precise, and the clinician proceeds to make inferences about the possible causes of current problems. For example, a man told a college counselor that he was looking for help in overcoming his intense anxiety in situations involving public speaking. The counselor first looked for connections between the student's problem and one or more specific upsetting events related to this problem. Finding no clear connection, the counselor inquired about possible relationships between the student's current problem and early family relationships and school experiences.

In most cases, history taking covers the client's *personal history* and *family history*. The **personal history** includes important events and relationships in the client's life, and is usually constructed in chronological sequence. The client is asked about experiences in realms such as school perfor-

mance, peer relationships, employment, and health. The **family history** covers the sequence of major events in the lives of the client's relatives, including those who are closest to the client as well as more distantly related family members. The clinician can gain useful information by inquiring about psychological disorders among an individual's relatives. As you will see later, there are some psychological disorders for which genetic inheritance appears to play an important role. For example, the fact that a client has several ancestors who suffered from serious depression would be an important clue to a clinician who is evaluating the nature of the client's disturbance.

Let's return to the case of Ben, so that you can get an idea of what might take place in a flexible interview. Read the excerpt from Dr. Tobin's interview focusing on Ben's history (Table 3-1 on page 58). Take note of how her questions follow naturally from Ben's answers, and how there appears to be a natural flow in the dialogue. Imagine yourself interviewing someone like Ben and try to think of some of the questions that you might want to ask in your effort to understand his needs and concerns.

What features of this interview stand out? You probably noticed that Ben seemed quite fearful and evasive as he talked about some matters, particularly his current experiences. He was particularly concerned about the issue of privacy, more so than might be warranted given the confidential nature of the professional contact. At the same time, he was also unduly worried about the possibility that he may sound so disturbed that hospitalization might be considered. Yet, he has very unusual beliefs and perceptions that might lead you to wonder whether he is, in fact, out of touch with reality. As he described some of his relationships, even the one with his father, you may have noticed some seemingly paranoid thinking. All of these issues would be of considerable concern to Dr. Tobin in her effort to understand the nature of Ben's problems.

Standardized Interview

Flexible interviews can differ from person to person depending on the interviewer and the client. It is possible that two clinicians interviewing the same client would solicit very different kinds of information, and in some cases, insufficient information to derive a diagnosis. In order to deal with this problem, experts have developed standardized interviews which are particularly useful in research on establishing the validity and reliability of psychiatric diagnoses. The **standardized interview** consists of a highly structured series of questions, with a predetermined wording and order. Several standardized interviews have been used, particularly for research purposes, such as the *Schedule for Affective Disorders and Schizophrenia* (SADS; Endicott & Spitzer, 1978), the *Structured Clinical Interview for the DSM-III-R* (Spitzer et al., 1989), and the *Diagnostic Interview Schedule* (Robins et al., 1981).

Table 3-1   Excerpts from Ben's History Taking

Dr. Tobin:	Can you tell me what brings you here today?
Ben:	I'd like to take some of the psychological tests I've heard about.
Dr. Tobin:	Explain to me what you mean.
Ben:	Well, my psychology teacher said that these tests can help you tell whether you're crazy or not.
Dr. Tobin:	Is that a concern for you?
Ben:	I've had some pretty strange experiences lately, and when I tell other people about them, they tell me I'm nuts.
Dr. Tobin:	Tell me about these experiences.
Ben:	Well, sometimes, . . . (pause) . . . I don't know if I should tell you this, but . . . (pause) . . . I know that as soon as you hear this you'll want to lock me up . . . but anyway, here goes. For the past few months, the police have been following me. It all started one day when I was walking by a student demonstration on campus where people were being arrested. I stayed away from the action because I didn't want to get involved, you know, but I know that the police were watching me. A few days after the demonstration, I saw Nazi soldiers out in my backyard taking pictures of my house and looking in through the windows. You know, this sounds so crazy, I'm not sure I believe it myself. All I know is it scares the hell out of me. So, can I please have the testing to see if I'm losing my mind or not?
Dr. Tobin:	We can talk about that a little bit later, but right now I'd like to hear more about the experiences you're having.
Ben:	I'd really rather not talk about them anymore. They're too scary.
Dr. Tobin:	I can understand that you feel scared, but it would be helpful for me to get a better sense of what you're going through.
Ben:	. . . (pause) . . . Well, okay, but you're sure no one else will hear about this? . . .

(Later in the interview, Dr. Tobin proceeded to inquire about Ben's history)

Dr. Tobin:	I'd like to hear something about your early life experiences, such as your family relationships and your school experiences. First, tell me something about your family when you were growing up.
Ben:	Well . . . there's me and my sister, Doreen. She's two years older than me. And we haven't ever really gotten along. My mother . . . well . . .

	Doreen claims that my mother treated me better than Doreen. Maybe that's true, but not because I wanted it that way.
Dr. Tobin:	Tell me more about your relationship with your mother.
Ben:	I hated the way she . . . my mother . . . hovered over me. She wouldn't let me make a move without her knowing about it. She always worried that I would get sick or that I would hurt myself. If I was outside playing in the backyard, she would keep coming outside and telling me to be careful. I would get so mad. Even my father would get angry about the way she babied me all the time.
Dr. Tobin:	What about your relationship with your father?
Ben:	I can't say that I had much of one. No one in the family did. He always came home late, after we had gone to bed. Maybe he was trying to avoid the rest of us or something. I don't know, maybe he was working against the family in some way.
Dr. Tobin:	What do you mean, "working against the family"?
Ben:	I don't want to get into it.

(Later in the interview)

Dr. Tobin:	I'd like to hear about the things that interested you as a child.
Ben:	You mean like hobbies, friends, things like that?
Dr. Tobin:	Yes.
Ben:	I was a loner. That's what Doreen always called me. She would call me a "loser and a loner." I hated those names, but she was right. I spent most of the time in my room, with earphones on, listening to rock music. It was sort of neat. I would imagine that I was a rock star, and I would get lost in these wild thoughts about being important and famous and all. Staying home was OK. But going to school stunk.
Dr. Tobin:	Let's talk about your experiences in school.
Ben:	Teachers hated me. They liked to embarrass me . . . always complaining that I wouldn't look them in the eye. Why should I? If I made the smallest mistake they made a federal case out of it. One time . . . we were studying state capitals and the teacher, Mrs. Edison, asked me to name the capital of Tennessee. I didn't know what a capital was. I said, "I don't know anything about capitalism." She got pissed off and called me a "wise guy."

As you read the sample questions from the SADS (Table 3-2), contrast their format and coding with the one used in the flexible diagnostic interview with Ben. In addition to the questions shown, other questions in the SADS cover behavior, psychiatric symptoms, affect, mood, medical problems, substance abuse, and previous treatment. To ensure that interviewers strictly adhere to the set protocol, they are usually given extensive training and supervision. The answers to the questions are designed to fit into pre-coded categories which, for research purposes, can be subjected to statistical data analysis procedures.

The goal of the standardized interview, like that of the flexible interview, is to arrive at a diagnosis. There are, though, important differences between the two. The flexible interview depends on the clinical judgment of the interviewer and requires a great deal of skill and experience before it can be properly administered and evaluated. The standardized interview does not require extensive knowledge about

Table 3-2　Sample Items from the SADS

1. Have you had any ideas that other people might not understand? If the person answers "yes," the next set of questions would then be asked, and would be coded as follows:

    0　　No information
    1　　Absent
    2　　Suspected or likely
    3　　Definite

2. Do people seem to drop hints about you or say things with a double meaning or do things in a special way so as to convey a meaning?
3. Have things seemed especially arranged?
4. Have you had the feeling that you were being controlled by some force or power outside of yourself?
5. Can people know what you are thinking?
6. Did you ever feel that your thoughts were broadcast so that other people knew what you were thinking?
7. Did you feel that thoughts were put into your head that were not your own?

Questions pertaining to hallucinations

1. Has there been anything unusual about the way things looked, or sounded, or smelled?
2. Have you heard voices or other things that weren't there or that other people couldn't hear, or seen things that were not there? [If this is answered "yes," the following questions would be asked, and coded as above]:
3. Have you noticed strange or unusual smells that other people didn't notice?
4. Why do you think the voices are saying . . . to you?

psychological disorders, either for administration or scoring. The standardized interview uses questions developed through research that can be rated according to objective criteria.

MENTAL STATUS EXAMINATION

Clinicians use the term mental status (or present status) in the context of assessment to refer to *what* the client thinks about and *how* the client thinks, talks, and acts. Later, when we discuss particular psychological disorders, we will frequently refer to symptoms reflecting disturbances in mental status. The **mental status examination** is a procedure for assessing a client's current functioning in a variety of spheres. The areas of functioning assessed in the mental status examination include behavior, orientation, content of thought, thinking style and language, affect and mood, perceptual experiences, sense of self, motivation, intelligence, and insight (Mueller et al., 1988). Clinicians conducting mental status examinations observe the behavior of the client and ask a number of questions to assess the client's functioning in these areas. A typical mental status examination is comprised of several components. Though clinicians vary the order in which the informa-

tion is recorded or collected, there are several major areas that clinicians routinely cover.

Behavior

In assessing behavior, the clinician takes note of the client's **motor behavior**, or how the client moves. Bodily movements can be very telling signs of what is going on emotionally with the individual. Consequently, clinicians pay careful attention to the motor behavior of clients and observe whether they move in unusual ways. For example, one man may be so restless that he cannot stop pacing, while another man is so slowed down that he moves in a lethargic and listless manner.

Sometimes abnormalities of bodily movements take rather extreme forms, such as rigid posturing or immobilization. **Catatonia** is the term that refers to motor disturbances in a psychotic disorder not attributable to physiological causes. Take the case of Alice, who sits motionless all day long in a catatonic state. If someone were to stand in front of her and shout or try to startle her, she would not respond. Later in the book, you will read about certain disorders that are characterized by various forms of catatonia.

Another disturbance of behavior is a **compulsion**, a repetitive and seemingly purposeful behavior performed in response to uncontrollable urges or according to a ritualistic or stereotyped set of rules. Compulsions can take over the individual's life, causing considerable distress. For example, a woman who insists upon cleaning the door knob with her handkerchief five times prior to turning the knob to open the door may feel tormented by these seemingly uncontrollable urges. There are many types of compulsive behavior, and you will learn more about them when we discuss certain anxiety and personality disorders.

A clinician conducting a mental status examination.

Orientation

People with some kinds of disorders are disoriented and out of touch with basic facts about themselves and their surroundings. **Orientation** refers to a person's awareness of time, place, and identity. For example, a woman with brain damage may have amnesia, or a man with a schizophrenic disorder may believe that he is some famous person living in the 1600s. A clinician assessing the orientation of these individuals would evaluate their awareness of who they are and where they are, and their understanding of the time and date.

Content of Thought

The clinician detects that a client is plagued by disturbing thoughts by asking questions on the mental status examination such as, "Do you have thoughts that you can't get out of your head?" Other evidence for unusual thoughts may arise elsewhere in the course of the interview as, for example, when the client reports having had previous occupations that cannot possibly have a basis in reality. A man who has spent his adult life in a state hospital and holds the false belief that he is a famous movie actor may provide answers about his occupation consistent with his belief, and in the process reveal his particular disturbance of thought content. Clinicians listen for these kinds of clues to gain a better understanding of the nature of the client's disorder.

Of particular interest to the clinician are disturbances of thought content known as obsessions and delusions. **Obsessions** are unwanted repetitive thoughts or images that invade a person's consciousness. These thoughts often concern something evil the client believes to have done or is thinking about doing. Obsessions and compulsions often go hand in hand, as in the case of a man, who was obsessively worried that a car accident might take place outside his apartment; consequently, he walked to the window every ten minutes to make sure that the streetlight had not burned out.

Obsessions are certainly irrational, but even further removed from reality are **delusions**, deeply entrenched false beliefs that are not consistent with the client's intelligence or cultural background. Despite the best efforts of others to convince an individual that his or her beliefs are irrational, delusions are highly resistant to being changed by other people presenting a contrary, more realistic, view. In determining the presence of delusional thinking the clinician needs to be aware of the person's intelligence and cultural background. For example, a very religious person may be-

---

Table 3-3   Examples of Delusions

All of these delusions involve one or another form of *false belief;* that is, they have no validity to anyone except the person who believes in them and are inconsistent with external reality.

Grandeur: a grossly exaggerated conception of the individual's own importance. Such delusions range from beliefs that the person has an important role in society to the belief that the person is actually Christ, Napoleon, or Hitler. Milton Rokeach's 1964 book entitled *The Three Christs of Ypsilanti* described the interesting situation involving three state hospital patients who each thought he was Jesus Christ; when they met, each one believed that the others were frauds.

Control: the feeling that one is being controlled by others, or even by machines or appliances. For example, a man may believe that his actions are being controlled by the radio, which is "forcing" him to enact certain actions against his will.

Nihilism: the feeling that one's self, others, or the world is nonexistent. Commonly this delusion is associated with feelings of unreality, and the individual becomes absorbed with the thought that he or she is only "part of a dream."

Reference: the belief that the behavior of others or certain objects or events are personally referring to oneself. For example, a woman believes that a soap opera is really telling the story of her life. Or a man believes that the sale items at a local food market are targeted at his own particular dietary deficiencies.

Persecution: the belief that another person or persons are trying to inflict harm on the individual or on that individual's family or social group. For example, a woman feels that an organized group of politically liberal individuals is attempting to destroy the right-wing, political organization to which she belongs.

Self-blame: feelings of remorse without justification. A man holds himself responsible for a famine in Africa because of certain unkind or sinful actions that he believes he has committed.

Somatic: inappropriate concerns about one's own body, typically relating to some disease. For example, without any justification, a woman believes that she has brain cancer. Or adding an even more bizarre note, she believes that ants have invaded her head and are eating away at her brain.

Poverty: the belief that the individual has no material possessions worth any value. Even when confronted with facts about her sound financial condition, a woman may assert that the possessions or the money do not belong to her.

Infidelity: a false belief usually associated with pathological jealousy involving the notion that one's lover is being unfaithful. A man lashes out in violent rage at his wife, insisting that she is having an affair with the mailman because of her eagerness for the mail to arrive each day.

Thought broadcasting: the idea that one's thoughts are being broadcast to others. A man believes that everyone else in the room can hear what he is thinking, or possibly that his thoughts are actually being carried over the airways on television or radio.

Thought insertion: the belief that thoughts are being inserted into one's mind by outside forces. For example, a woman concludes that her thoughts are not her own, but that they are being placed there for the sake of controlling her or upsetting her.

Thought withdrawal: the belief that thoughts are being removed from one's mind. A man believes that his forgetting of an appointment was caused by someone intentionally removing the thought from his mind.

---

lieve in miracles, which people from a different religious background might regard as delusional. Table 3-3 gives some examples of delusions.

Thinking Style and Language

In addition to listening to *what* a person thinks, the clinician also listens for evidence about *how* a person thinks. The clinician gathers information on the client's vocabulary and use of sentence structure. For example, when conversing with a man who is psychotic, you may have a difficult time grasping his words or meaning. His language may be illogical and unconnected. In listening to him during a mental status examination, a clinician would suspect that he has a **thought disorder**, a disturbance in the way the person thinks or uses language. Examples of thought disorders may be found in Table 3-4.

Affect and Mood

Affect refers to an individual's outward expression of an emotion. A feeling state becomes an affect when it can be observed by others. In the mental status examination, a clinician may refer to the client's affect with different descriptors, such as being *inappropriate* or *flat*. In **inappropriate affect**, the person's expression of emotion does not coincide with the context or the content of what is being said. For example, a woman giggled when asked how she felt about a recent death in her family. **Flat affect** refers to the virtual lack of emotional expression, as in speech that is monotonous or a face that is immobile.

Mood refers to a person's experience of emotion, the way the person feels "inside." Such emotions include depression, elation, anger, and anxiety. A clinician is particularly interested in assessing a client's mood because the way the client characteristically feels has great diagnostic and

---

Table 3-4   Examples of Thought Disorders

Incoherence: speech that is incomprehensible. Incoherent speech is impossible for others to understand because of a lack of meaningful connections between words or sentences. For example, a client who is asked how he is feeling responds, "The gutter tree ain't here go far."

Loosening of associations: a flow of thoughts that is vague, unfocused, and illogical. In response to the question how he is feeling, a man responded, "I'm feeling pretty good today, though I don't think that there is enough good in the world. I think that I should subscribe to *National Geographic.*"

Illogical thinking: thinking that is characterized by contradictions and erroneous conclusions and that characterizes the individual's entire cognitive system. People who think illogically are typically unable to see how others might perceive them as being illogical. For example, a client who likes milk thinks that she must be part cat because she knows that cats like milk.

Neologisms: a word invented by a person, or a distortion of an existing word to which a person has given a new personalized meaning. For example, a woman expressed concerns about her homicidal fantasies saying, "I can't stand these *gunly* thoughts of *murdeviousness.*"

Poverty of content of speech: speech that conveys very little information because the speaker is vague, overly abstract, overly concrete, or repetitive. A client, when asked how he is feeling, responded, "I could say that I'm OK, and I could say that I'm not OK, but I think that it's best to say that I'm like the squirrel on a rusty piece of metal."

Blocking: the experience in which a person seemingly "loses" a thought in the midst of speaking, leading to a period of silence ranging from seconds to minutes. This differs from the common experience of losing one's train of thought occasionally; by contrast, blocking involves a frequent intrusion into the thought and communication processes of some seriously disturbed people.

Circumstantiality: speech that is indirect and delayed in reaching the point because of irrelevant and tedious details. In response to a simple question about the kind of work that he does, a man responded with a long-winded description of his 20-year work history with overly detailed comments about the nature of his relationship with each of the seven supervisors he has worked under during that

period. Though his talk remains remotely connected to the topic, it is filled with unnecessary and inconsequential details.

Tangentiality: going completely off the track and never returning to the point in a conversation. For example, when asked how long she had been depressed, a woman began speaking about her unhappy mood and ended up talking about the inadequacy of care in the United States for people who are depressed.

Clanging: speech in which the sound, rather than the meaning of the words, determines the content of the individual's speech. When asked why he woke up so early, a man responded, "The bell on my clock, the smell from the sock, and the well was out of stock."

Confabulation: fabricating facts or events to fill in voids in one's memory. These are not conscious lies, but are attempts by the individual to respond to questions with answers that seem to approximate what the truth should be. For example, although a client was not fully sure of whether or not he had eaten breakfast this morning, when queried about what he had for breakfast, he replied, "Oatmeal with honey." He gave a description of a typical breakfast in his household rather than a confident reporting of precisely what he had eaten that morning.

Echolalia: persistent repetition or echoing words of phrases, as if the person is intending to be mocking or sarcastic. When a woman was asked by her roommate, "What's the time?" she responded, "the time, the time, the time."

Flight of ideas: fast-paced speech that, while usually intelligible, is marked by acceleration, abrupt changes of topic, and plays on words. A man rapidly spoke: "I have to go to work. I have to get there right away. I have to earn some money. I'll go broke. My kids need food. Food is expensive. The prices are way too high. I need the money. I need it now!"

Pressure of speech: speech that is so rapid and driven that it seems as though the individual is being inwardly compelled to utter a stream of nonstop monologue. Flight of ideas usually involves pressure of speech.

Perseveration: repeating the same idea, word, or sound over and over. A woman said, "I have to get dressed. I have to get dressed. My clothes, my clothes, I have to get dressed." Another example would be giving the same response regardless of the question.

This woman's affect seems to be an inappropriate response to her friend telling her a humorous story.

treatment significance. In Chapter 10, we will discuss some disorders whose primary symptom involves a disturbance in mood. A **normal mood** or **euthymic mood** is one that is neither unduly happy nor sad, but shows day-to-day variations within a relatively limited range considered to be appropriate. **Dysphoric mood** refers to unpleasant feelings such as sadness or irritability. An **elevated mood** is more cheerful than average, though not necessarily to the point of causing the person to be out of touch with everyday life. Your mood might be elevated after doing well on an exam. On the other hand, **euphoric mood** refers to a state in which an individual feels an exaggerated sense of happiness, elation, and excitement.

Perceptual Experiences

Individuals with psychological disorders often have disturbances in perception. A clinician would find out whether a client has these disturbances by asking whether the client hears voices or sees things of which other people are not aware. **Hallucinations** are false perceptions not corresponding to the objective stimuli present in the environment. Unlike **illusions**, which involve the misperception of a real object, such as misperceiving a tree at night to be a man, hallucinations involve the perception of an object or stimulus for which there is no real counterpart. Hallucinations are defined by the sense with which they are associated. **Auditory hallucinations** involve the hearing of sounds, often voices. **Visual hallucinations** involve the false visual perception of objects or persons. **Olfactory hallucinations** pertain to the sense of smell. **Gustatory hallucinations** involve the sense of taste, and **tactile hallucinations** involve the false perception of sensation or movement. Hallucinations often relate to the content of a person's delusions. For example, a man who had a delusion of persecution, also had olfactory hallucinations in which he believed that he constantly smelled toxic fumes.

Sense of Self

A number of psychological disorders have the effect of altering the individual's personal identity or sense of "Who I am." Clinicians assess this altered sense of self by asking clients to describe any strange bodily sensations or feelings of disconnectedness from their body. **Depersonalization** refers to an altered experience of the self such as a man feeling that his body is not connected to his mind; sometimes he feels that he is not "real." Other disturbances in sense of self become apparent when the clinician discovers that a client is experiencing **identity confusion**, a lack of clear sense of who one is, ranging from confusion about one's role in the world to actual delusional thinking in which one believes oneself to be under the control of some external person or force.

Motivation

The clinician assesses motivation across a wide range of areas by asking the client to discuss how strongly he or she desires a lasting personality change or relief of emotional distress. With some psychological disorders, the client's motivation is so severely impaired that even ordinary life tasks seem insurmountable, much less the process of embarking on the time-consuming and effortful course of therapy. As surprising as it may seem, some individuals seem to prefer to remain in their present familiar state of unhappiness rather than risk the uncertainty of facing a new and unknown set of challenges.

Intelligence and Insight

In a mental status examination, a clinician attempts to gauge a client's level of intelligence, general insight, and ability to understand the nature of his or her disorder. Grasping the client's intellectual capacity is critical in ascertaining the relationship between some symptoms and the client's apparent level of intelligence. For example, a woman with an IQ significantly above average might use unusual or abstract words that give the impression that she has a thought disorder. Appreciating the client's capacity for insight also alerts the clinician to the client's receptivity to treatment. A client who has no understanding of the debilitating nature of her paranoid delusions is certainly not going to be very receptive to intervention by a mental health professional. She may even resist any such attempts because she regards them as proof that others are trying to control or hurt her.

PSYCHOLOGICAL TESTING

Psychological testing covers a broad range of measurement techniques, all of which involve a process of having people provide scorable information about their psychological func-

Many magazines contain "personality" tests. This man is completing a quiz to measure his level of daily stress.

An air traffic controller must be able to make quick decisions under pressure. Psychological tests help in the selection of suitable candidates for this type of work.

tioning. The information that test-takers provide may concern their intellectual abilities, personalities, emotional states, attitudes, and behaviors that reflect lifestyle or interests. It is very likely that you have had some form of psychological testing in your life, and that your scores on these tests had a bearing on decisions made by you or about you, since psychological tests have become increasingly important in contemporary society. Because of this importance, psychologists have devoted intensive efforts to developing tests that accurately measure what they are designed to measure.

What Makes a Good Psychological Test?

Many popular magazines and newspapers occasionally publish so-called "psychological tests." Items on these tests claim to measure such features of your personality as your potential for loving, how lonely you are, how devoted your romantic partner is, whether you have "too much anger," or whether you worry too much. These tests contain a number of scorable items, accompanied by a scale to tell you what your responses indicate about your personality. Although

interesting and provocative, the large majority of tests published in the popular press fail to meet accepted standards for a good psychological test.

To show you the many issues involved in developing a good psychological test, we will take an in-depth look at each of the criteria that play a role in the process (see Table 3-5 on page 64). These criteria are covered by the general term **psychometrics,** whose literal meaning, "measurement of the mind," reflects the goal of finding the most suitable tests for the psychological variables of interest to the researcher and clinician.

A good psychological test is one that, first of all, follows standardized, or uniform, procedures for both test administration and scoring. When people take a national college entrance examination, they are supposed to be given the test under the strictest of standardized conditions. The room should be quiet and well-lit, the seats should be comfortable for test-taking, proctors should monitor the students so that no one has any unfair advantages, and the same instructions are given to everyone. A standardized psychological test is intended to follow the same guidelines. Particularly important is the requirement that each person

Table 3-5 Criteria for a Good Psychological Test

RELIABILITY	The consistency of test scores.	
Type of Reliability	**Definition**	**Example**
• Test–retest	The degree to which test scores obtained from people on one day (the "test") agree with test scores obtained from those people on another day (the "retest").	A test of intelligence should yield similar scores for the same person on Tuesday and on Thursday, because intelligence is aquality that is assumed not to change over short time periods.
• Interjudge	The extent to which two or more people agree on how to score a particular test response.	On a 5-point scale of thought disorder, two raters should give similar scores to a psychiatric patient's response.
• Internal consistency	How well items on a test correlate with each other.	On a test of anxiety, people answer similarly to the items designed to assess how nervous a person feels.

VALIDITY	How well the test measures what it is designed to measure.	
Type of Validity	**Definition**	**Example**
• Content	How well the test reflects the body of information it is designed to tap.	The professor's abnormal psychology exam concerns knowledge of abnormal psychology rather than familiarity with music from the 1960s.
• Criterion	The extent to which the test scores relate in expected ways to another benchmark.	(See more specific examples below.)
Concurrent	How well scores on a test relate to other measures taken at the same time.	A test of depression should produce high scores in people with known diagnoses of depression.
Predictive	The extent to which test scores relate to future performance.	People who receive high scores on college entrance examinations are expected to achieve high grade point averages in college.
• Construct	The extent to which a test measures a theoretically-derived psychological quality or attribute.	A test of depression should correlate with recognized characteristics of depression such as low self-esteem, guilt, and feelings of sadness.

taking the test receive the same instructions. At times, because people with certain psychological disorders may have problems focusing on test items or following instructions, it may be necessary for the examiner to provide extra assistance or encouragement to complete the test. However, the examiner must, under no conditions, suggest how the test-taker should answer the questions or bias the test-taker's performance in any way. It is also important that the examiner not stretch the time limits beyond those allowed for the test.

Standardization also applies to the way that tests are scored. The most straightforward scoring method involves adding up responses on a multiple-choice test or a test with items that are rated on numerical scales. Less straightfor-

Standardized tests are sometimes administered in group settings for personnel selection. These people have applied for jobs at a large manufacturing company.

ward are tests that involve judgements on the part of raters who must decide how to score the test-taker's responses. For the scoring to be standardized, the examiner must follow a prescribed set of rules that equate a given response with a particular score. The examiner must be sure not to let any biases interfere with the scoring procedure. This is particularly important when only one person does the scoring, as is the case with many established tests whose reliability has already been documented. When scoring an intelligence test, for example, it may be tempting for the examiner to try to give the test-taker the "benefit of the doubt" if the test-taker is someone who seems to have been trying hard and wants to do well. Conversely, examiners must be sensitive to their negative biases regarding certain types of clients and not inadvertently penalize them by scoring them lower than they deserve. Ideally, the scoring of a test is done without knowledge of the person who took the test, but this ideal may not always be achievable. As guarantees against the misuse of tests, people who administer and score standardized psychological tests receive extensive training and supervision in all of these procedures.

The term "standardization" is also used to refer to the basis for evaluating scores on a particular test. The college entrance examination, for example, has been given to vast numbers of high school seniors over the years, and there is a known distribution of scores on the parts of this test. When evaluating a student's potential for college, the student's scores are compared to the national scores for the student's gender, and a percentile score is given. This **percentile score**, which indicates what percent of students scored below a certain number, is considered to be an objective indication of the student's college potential and is preferable to basing such an evaluation on the personal judgment of one individual. As you will see in our discussion of intelli-

gence tests, however, there are many questions about the appropriateness of percentile scores when the person taking the test differs in important ways from the people on whom the test was standardized.

These psychometric criteria for evaluating a test's quality are applied to all methods of assessment, even those that do not involve having the person being evaluated specifically answer test questions. It is just as important for a questionnaire test of personality to have reliability and validity as it is for a rating of a person's behavior to be reliable and valid. Once the psychometric qualities of a measurement instrument have been established, the measure becomes one of many types and forms of tests that the clinician can incorporate into an assessment. Psychologists make this choice of a measure on the basis of the assessment goals and theoretical preferences. As we look at the various types of assessment devices, we will examine each from the standpoint of its most appropriate use in assessment, its theoretical assumptions, and its psychometric qualities.

Intelligence Testing

Intelligence tests serve various purposes. One important purpose is to help educators determine whether certain students might benefit from remedial or accelerated learning opportunities. Intelligence tests can also be useful for employers who wish to know whether a prospective employee has the intellectual capacity to carry out the duties of a given job. For the mental health professional, intelligence tests provide crucial information for understanding a client's cognitive capacities, and the relationship between these capacities and the expression of emotional problems. For example, an exceptionally bright young woman might

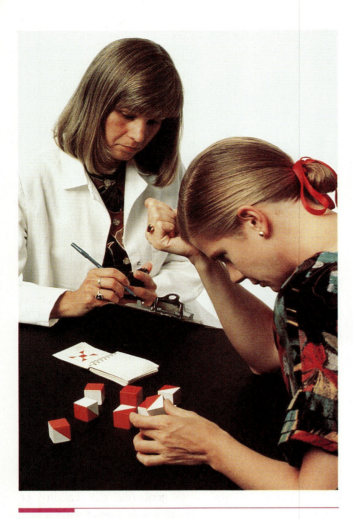

The Block Design is one of the subtests of the Wechsler Adult Intelligence Scale–Revised (WAIS–R).

make very esoteric but bizarre associations on a test of personality. Knowing that this young woman's intellect is at a higher level than the norm can provide the clinician with an understanding that such associations are probably not due to a psychological disorder. Alternatively, a man whose intelligence is significantly below average might say or do things that give the appearance of a psychotic disorder.

Intelligence tests can yield fairly specific information about a person's cognitive deficits or strengths, which can be helpful to a therapist working on a treatment plan. Clients who have little capacity for abstract thinking are likely to have difficulty in insight-oriented psychotherapy. Instead, a clinician treating a client with such cognitive deficits would focus on practical, day-to-day problems.

Some intelligence tests are designed to be administered to relatively large groups of people at a time. These tests are more commonly used in nonclinical settings such as psychological research, schools, personnel screening, and the military. Most of these tests use a multiple-choice question format, and scores are reported in terms of separate subscales assessing different facets of intellectual functioning. Group tests are used because they allow mass administration and

are easily scored, with no special training required of the examiner. However, clinicians fault these tests for their impersonality and their insensitivity to nuances in the test-taker's answers. A test-taker may give a creative but wrong answer to a question that the computer simply scores as incorrect, without taking into account the originality of the response.

Individual testing methods have the advantage of providing rich qualitative information about the client. Open-ended answers to questions regarding vocabulary, which cannot conveniently be obtained in group testing, may reveal that the client's thoughts follow a rather bizarre chain of associations. This sort of information would be lost in a group intelligence test, which does not provide any opportunities to scrutinize the client's thought processes and judgment.

■ History of intelligence testing

Psychologists have long been interested in studying intelligence, because of its wide-ranging influence on many aspects of an individual's functioning. The first intelligence test was developed by Alfred Binet in 1905 through his work for the French government in screening mentally retarded children and adults. The original test has been revised many times and scales were added in an effort to expand the test's usefulness. The current version, published in 1986, is the fourth revision.

Although the *Stanford-Binet* test can be used to measure adult intelligence, it is oriented primarily toward children. In 1939, the *Wechsler-Bellevue Intelligence Scale* was developed by the psychologist David Wechsler to measure intelligence in adults. The format of the *Wechsler-Bellevue* has persisted until the present day, serving as the basis for revisions of the original adult test and the addition of tests for younger age groups. Currently, there are three Wechsler tests: the *Wechsler Adult Intelligence Scale-Revised (WAIS-R)*, the *Wechsler Intelligence Scale for Children-III (WISC-III)* and the *Wechsler Preschool and Primary Scale of Intelligence-Revised (WPPSI-R)*. All Wechsler tests share a common organization in that they are divided into two scales: *Verbal* and *Performance*. The *Verbal* scale includes measures of vocabulary, factual knowledge, short-term memory, and verbal reasoning. The *Performance* subtests measure psychomotor abilities, nonverbal reasoning, and the ability to learn new relationships.

Scores on intelligence tests are expressed in terms of **IQ**, an abbreviation of the term **intelligence quotient**. When the term was originally proposed by psychologist Lewis Terman at Stanford University in 1916, it literally referred to a ratio measure or quotient, namely the individual's "mental age" (calculated on the basis of test performance) compared to the individual's chronogical age. An IQ of 80, in this system, meant that the child had a mental age of 8 and a chronological age of 10 or, in other words, was moderately retarded. An IQ of 100 indicated average intelligence; in other words, a child's mental age was exactly equal to his or her chronological age. This scoring system worked reasonably well for children, but it created

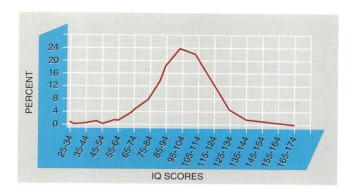

Figure 3-1

An approximate distribution of IQ scores in the population. The distribution follows a bell-shaped curve, with the highest percentage of people in the "normal" range of between 85–115.

problems with adults because the highest mental age possible to achieve on the Stanford-Binet is 16. A 32-year-old with an average level of intelligence could, using the quotient as a basis for scoring, have an IQ of 50. Obviously, this method was flawed.

Because Wechsler's tests were initially designed for adults, he developed a method of scoring, called the **deviation IQ**, which moves away from the ratio concept entirely and eventually became adopted in the 1960 revision of the Stanford-Binet. The deviation IQ score is calculated by converting a person's actual test score to a score that reflects how high or low the score is compared to others of similar age and gender. An average IQ, in Wechsler's system, is 100. (See Figure 3-1). An IQ of 80, using this calculation method, reflects the fact that relative to others in the same age group, the individual's score is significantly below the mean.

The Wechsler tests yield an overall IQ, called the Full Scale IQ. They also yield a Verbal IQ and a Performance IQ. There are a number of published guidelines for interpreting WAIS-R scores, and many of these are derived from extensive data collected over several decades. Clinicians can go beyond the numbers to gain a more in depth analysis of the client's cognitive strengths and weaknesses. By looking at how the test taker has responded to particular items and to the test situation in general, it is possible to make some inferences about the client's personality and interpersonal style. For example, a woman responded quickly on many of the tasks but was often incorrect. Her test-taking impulsivity reflected a general personality style that was probably evident in many situations in her life.

Let's return to the case of Ben and consider his WAIS–R (see Figure 3-2 on page 68). From this, you can get an idea of how a clinician would interpret intelligence test scores and fit this interpretation into the larger puzzle of arriving at a psychological assessment.

Ben has average intelligence, with no striking strengths or deficits. Considering the extent of his distress,

he was able to function adequately on the various subtests of the *WAIS-R*. This would tell you that when tasks are clear and structure is provided, Ben is able to respond appropriately. However, you might be surprised that Ben does not have a higher IQ, considering the fact that he is a college junior. It is possible that his performance on the test was lower because of emotional problems. For example, anxiety or depression can interfere with a person's ability to answer the questions and perform the manual tasks on the WAIS-R.

Assessment of an individual's intelligence must take into account the person's cultural, ethnic, and racial background. Most intelligence tests were developed with an American middle-class white orientation. Many critics have contended that these tests cannot accurately evaluate people from diverse backgrounds. Items on the WAIS-R, for example, ask the test-taker to make judgments about socially or culturally acceptable behaviors. Such judgments reflect the individual's exposure to the prevailing standards and values of the culture. People of diverse cultural backgrounds are likely to make judgments reflecting their experiences, and in the process give the "wrong" answer. Discrepancies between the test and the test-taker's background can also artificially lower the individual's scores on measures of vocabulary and general information, to name two examples.

Although test developers have attempted to rectify the potential cultural bias in intelligence tests, users still need to be very aware of this issue when assessing the intelligence of someone whose background does not match that of the test (Anastasi, 1988). More generally, the validity of WAIS-R scores has not been well-established, with few empirical attempts to relate performance on its various subtests with behaviors in everyday life presumed to have some relationship to these scores. However, the WAIS-R continues to be used in the clinical assessment of adults, and if its limitations are kept in mind, it can provide useful data on the individual's way of approaching intellectual problems (Groth-Marnat, 1990).

Personality and Diagnostic Testing

Personality and diagnostic tests are particularly useful when a clinician wishes to supplement interview data in developing a better understanding of a client or in formulating a treatment plan. For example, a psychologist completed an interview with her new client, Vanessa, and hypothesized two possible diagnoses which both seemed plausible. Vanessa told her that she was "penniless and had no hope of ever earning a cent." The psychologist, realizing that Vanessa was delusional, wondered whether this delusion of poverty was reflective of a severe depression or was a symptom of serious personality disorganization. Vanessa's performance on certain personality tests helped the psychologist conclude that Vanessa was suffering from pervasive personality disorganization.

WAIS-R RECORD FORM

WECHSLER ADULT INTELLIGENCE SCALE—REVISED

NAME Ben Appleton

ADDRESS 113 South St.

SEX M AGE 21 RACE White MARITAL STATUS S

OCCUPATION Student EDUCATION 3 years of college

PLACE OF TESTING Clinic TESTED BY Sarah Tobin PhD

TABLE OF SCALED SCORE EQUIVALENTS*

Scaled Score	RAW SCORE											Scaled Score
	VERBAL TESTS						PERFORMANCE TESTS					
	Information	Digit Span	Vocabulary	Arithmetic	Comprehension	Similarities	Picture Completion	Picture Arrangement	Block Design	Object Assembly	Digit Symbol	
19	—	28	70	—	32	—	—	—	51	—	93	**19**
18	29	27	69	—	31	28	—	—	—	41	91-92	**18**
17	—	26	68	19	—	—	20	20	50	—	89-90	**17**
16	28	25	66-67	—	30	27	—	—	49	40	84-88	**16**
15	27	24	65	18	29	26	—	19	47-48	39	79-83	**15**
14	26	22-23	63-64	17	27-28	25	19	—	44-46	38	75-78	**14**
13	25	20-21	60-62	16	26	24	—	18	42-43	37	70-74	**13**
12	23-24	18-19	55-59	15	25	23	18	17	38-41	35-36	66-69	**12**
11	22	17	52-54	13-14	23-24	22	17	15-16	35-37	34	62-65	**11**
10	19-21	15-16	47-51	12	21-22	20-21	16	14	31-34	32-33	57-61	**10**
9	17-18	14	43-46	11	19-20	18-19	15	13	27-30	30-31	53-56	**9**
8	15-16	12-13	37-42	10	17-18	16-17	14	11-12	23-26	28-29	48-52	**8**
7	13-14	11	29-36	8-9	14-16	14-15	13	8-10	20-22	24-27	44-47	**7**
6	9-12	9-10	20-28	6-7	11-13	11-13	11-12	5-7	14-19	21-23	37-43	**6**
5	6-8	8	14-19	5	8-10	7-10	8-10	3-4	8-13	16-20	30-36	**5**
4	5	7	11-13	4	6-7	5-6	5-7	2	3-7	13-15	23-29	**4**
3	4	6	9-10	3	4-5	2-4	3-4	—	2	9-12	16-22	**3**
2	3	3-5	6-8	1-2	2-3	1	2	1	1	6-8	8-15	**2**
1	0-2	0-2	0-5	0	0-1	0	0-1	0	0	0-5	0-7	**1**

*Clinicians who wish to draw a profile may do so by locating the subject's raw scores on the table above and drawing a line to connect them. See Chapter 4 in the Manual for a discussion of the significance of differences between scores on the tests.

	Year	Month	Day
Date Tested	91	9	12
Date of Birth	70	8	5
Age	21		

SUMMARY

	Raw Score	Scaled Score	
VERBAL TESTS			
Information	23	12	
Digit Span	14	9	
Vocabulary	53	11	
Arithmetic	12	10	
Comprehension	21	10	
Similarities	18	9	
Verbal Score		61	
PERFORMANCE TESTS			
Picture Completion	15	9	
Picture Arrangement	13	9	
Block Design	42	13	
Object Assembly	30	9	
Digit Symbol	67	12	
Performance Score		52	

	Sum of Scaled Scores	IQ
VERBAL	61	102
PERFORMANCE	52	100
FULL SCALE	113	101

THE PSYCHOLOGICAL CORPORATION
HARCOURT BRACE JOVANOVICH, INC.

9-991829

Figure 3-2
The WAIS-R report used by Dr. Tobin in her assessment of Ben Appleton.
Source: Wechsler Adult Intelligence Scale—Revised. Copyright © 1981, 1955 by The Psychological Corporation. Reproduced by permission. All rights reserved.

There are two main forms of personality tests: *self-report* and *projective*. These tests differ in the nature of their items and in the way they are scored.

■ Self-report clinical inventories

A **self-report clinical inventory** has standardized questions with fixed response categories that the test-taker completes independently, "self"-reporting the extent to which the responses are accurate characterizations. The scores on the test items are added together and usually combined into a number of scales. The scores on these scales are then used to construct a psychological profile of the client. This type of test is considered "objective" in the sense that scoring is completely standardized and usually does not involve any judgment on the part of the clinician. The majority of self-report inventories are now scored by computer, eliminating any form of human bias in assigning scores. However, this type of test is not entirely free of subjectivity. The questions on these tests were developed by people who hold to certain theories and beliefs about the causes of psychological disorders. Moreover, the interpretation of the test scores is anything but a mechanical affair. It typically requires that the clinician draw inferences on the basis of numerical scores, and these inferences may all too often reflect the clinician's theoretical interest and biases (Matarazzo, 1986). Even as computerized interpretations become increasingly available (Butcher, 1987), they are programmed by humans and interpreted by humans, whose theoretical biases must by necessity enter into the process (Karson & O'Dell, 1987). Nevertheless, because of the ease of administering and scoring these questionnaires, they can be given to large numbers of people. Consequently, the more well-known self-report inventories have extensive data available on their validity and reliability.

The most popular self-report inventory for clinical use is the *Minnesota Multiphasic Personality Inventory (MMPI)*. The MMPI was published in 1943, and a revised form, the *MMPI-2*, was published in 1989. The MMPI-2 has not completely replaced the MMPI, because there is some debate about whether scores on the two measures are entirely comparable. Furthermore, the original MMPI is the most widely used clinical personality inventory in the United States (Lubin et al., 1985), as well as more than 40 other countries (Butcher, 1990). Also, there is a vast amount of published research on this instrument consisting of over 10,000 studies (Graham, 1990); consequently, there is an understandable reluctance for clinicians and researchers to abandon the original test altogether.

The MMPI consists of 566 items containing self-descriptions to which the test-taker responds "true" or "false." These self-descriptions refer to particular behaviors (for example, alcohol use) as well as thoughts and feelings (such as feelings of sadness or self-doubt). The MMPI yields a profile of the test-taker's personality and psychological difficulties, and three scales that provide the clinician with information about the validity of each individual's profile.

The original MMPI was developed at the University of Minnesota in the 1930s by Starke Hathaway, a psychologist, and J. Charnley McKinley, a psychiatrist, with the goal of providing an efficiently administered and scored tool that could be used for diagnosing psychological disorders. It was hoped that the MMPI would meet the need for a diagnostic "cookbook" (Meehl, 1956) that could eliminate subjectivity, bias, and uncertainty from the diagnostic process. The scale names on the MMPI reflect this intention; for example, the "depression" scale was intended to diagnose depression.

In order to determine which items should comprise the clinical scales of the MMPI, the authors developed a method called **empirical criterion keying** (Graham, 1990). In this method, an item is included on a scale if it empirically differentiates groups of people. For example, people who are clinically depressed should have higher depression scale scores than those who are not clinically depressed. Hathaway and McKinley began work on the MMPI with a set of about 1000 self-descriptive statements taken from a variety of sources such as other tests, textbooks, and clinical reports. From this set, they arrived at a pool of 504 test items that appeared to be clearly written and relatively independent of each other. These items were then given to patients in University of Minnesota hospitals with a wide variety of psychiatric diagnoses. The same items were administered to "Minnesota normals," which included other groups of people without psychiatric diagnoses, including relatives and visitors of the patients, recent high school graduates applying to college, medical patients, and blue-collar workers. Items were included on the scales if they corresponded to the diagnosis of the psychiatric patients and differentiated them from the Minnesota normals. Further refinement and continued testing led eventually to the final set of clinical scale items. At the same time, the authors included "validity" scales that would detect whether the test-taker was confused or was attempting to deny psychiatric symptoms or, conversely, was attempting to project a false image of psychological disturbance.

The final MMPI, then, provides scores on ten "clinical" scales and three "validity" scales. The clinical scales are used to provide the clinician with a profile of the individual's personality and possible psychological disorder. The validity scales provide the clinician with important information about how defensive the test-taker was, and also whether the individual might have been careless, confused, or intentionally lying during the test. Scales 1–10 (or 1–0) are the clinical scales, and the remaining three are the validity scales (see Table 3-6 on page 70). An additional scale, the "?" or "Can't say" scale, is the number of unanswered questions, with a high score indicating carelessness, confusion, or unwillingness to self-disclose.

With the accumulation of data and clinical experience on the MMPI from the 1940s to the 1980s, it became apparent that the initial hope of using scores on the MMPI scales for diagnosis was unrealistic (Butcher, 1987). Elevated scores on individual scales can form the basis for only

Table 3-6   Scales of the MMPI

Scale	Scale Name	Content
1	Hypochondriasis	Bodily preoccupations, fear of illness and disease, and concerns about physical competence.
	Sample item:	I have a hard time with nausea and vomiting.
2	Depression	Denial of happiness and personal worth, psychomotor retardation and withdrawal, lack of interest in surroundings, somatic complaints, worry or tension, denial of hostility, difficulty controlling thought processes.
	Sample item:	I wish I were as happy as others appear to be.
3	Hysteria	Hysterical reactions to stress situations. Various somatic complaints and denial of psychological problems as well as discomfort in social situations.
	Sample item:	Frequently my head seems to hurt everywhere.
4	Psychopathic deviate	Asocial or amoral tendencies, lack of life satisfaction, family problems, delinquency, sexual problems, difficulties with authorities.
	Sample item:	I was occasionally sent to the principal's office for bad behavior.
5	Masculinity-Femininity	Extent to which individual ascribes to stereotypic sex-role behaviors and attitudes.
	Sample item:	I like reading romantic tales (male item).

Scale	Scale Name	Content
6	Paranoia	Paranoid symptoms such as ideas of reference, feelings of persecution, grandiosity, suspiciousness, excessive sensitivity, rigid opinions and attitudes.
	Sample item:	I would have been a lot more successful had others not been vindictive toward me.
7	Psychasthenia	Obsessive-compulsiveness, with doubts, compulsions, obsessions, and unreasonable fears.
	Sample item:	Sometimes, I think thoughts too awful to discuss.
8	Schizophrenia	Disturbances of thinking, mood, and behavior.
	Sample item:	I have had some rather bizarre experiences.
9	Hypomania	Elevated mood, accelerated speech and motor activity, irritability, flight of ideas, brief periods of depression.
	Sample item:	I become very excited at least once a week.
0	Social introversion	Tendency to withdraw from social contacts and responsibilities.
	Sample item:	I usually do not speak first. I wait for others to speak to me.
L	"Lie" scale	Unrealistically positive self-presentation.
K	"Faking good"	Compared to the L scale, a more sophisticated indication of a person's tendency to deny psychological problems and present oneself positively.
F	"Faking bad"	Presenting oneself in an unrealistically negative light by responding to a variety of deviant or atypical items.

limited clinical interpretations, leading most clinicians to look at patterns of high scale scores, such as elevated scores on two or three of the ten. Current interpretive guides to the MMPI and MMPI-2 provide detailed psychological descriptions that correspond to these two-point or three-point codes, as they are called. The validity scales supplement these descriptions, and in some cases can provide telling information about the individual's test-taking attitude.

An additional enhancement of the original interpretative procedure has come about through the development of a variety of scales based on item content including anxiety, alcoholism, and college maladjustment. "Critical item" scales include items that, when endorsed by the test-taker, are regarded as particularly indicative of psychological problems such as depression and worry, deviant thinking and experiences, problematic anger, and family conflict (Butcher, 1990; Graham, 1990). The vast amount of research on the MMPI has led, then, to a rich store of descriptive information to be used for clinical interpretation, going well beyond the original aim of providing a simple and straightforward psychiatric diagnosis.

Even as the MMPI gained worldwide renown as a major assessment tool, it also became the focus of debate. Critics maintained that the comparison group of "Minnesota normals" used in developing the original MMPI did not accurately reflect the population diversity of the United States. Further, the items on the MMPI, which were written in the 1930s and early 1940s, had become outdated or were considered offensive by contemporary standards. Data on the psychometric qualities of the MMPI indicate only moderate test-retest reliability and unacceptably high levels of overlap among the clinical scales. There are also serious questions about the applicability of the MMPI to diverse cultural and age groups (Groth-Marnat, 1990).

The MMPI-2 (Hathaway et al., 1989) was developed in response to these criticisms by a team of researchers commissioned in 1982 by the University of Minnesota Press to embark on a restandardization project (Graham, 1990). Over the next several years, data were collected from a sample of 2600 persons all across the United States, chosen to be representative of the general U.S. population in terms of regional, racial, occupational, and educational dimensions. Additional data from various clinical groups were also obtained, including people in psychiatric hospitals and others receiving treatment in a variety of settings.

Changes were also made in the items themselves to bring them up-to-date (Ben-Porath & Butcher, 1989). Of the original items, 82 were reworded to eliminate sexist language, expressions no longer in use, and objectionable or exclusionary statements. Subcultural biases were eliminated by changing items that left out certain groups, such as changing the word "church" in "I go to church every week" to "religious services." Other changes included the development of new and more subtle validity scales and additional scales to assess dimensions of personality.

Research evidence is beginning to accumulate on the correspondence of the MMPI-2 with the MMPI (Butcher et al., 1990; Munley & Zarantonello, 1990; Vincent 1990) but it is too soon to determine whether the MMPI-2 will come to replace its predecessor. Future research is needed to evaluate the comparability of the two instruments across a wide variety of samples and to determine the gains, if any, in validity that the MMPI-2 makes possible.

Let's return once again to the case of Ben. As you study his MMPI-2 profile (see Figure 3-3 on page 72), you will undoubtedly notice that there are several extremely high scores. First, look at the validity scale scores, which give some important clues to understanding the clinical scales. Ben's high F tells us that he reports having many unusual experiences, thoughts, and feelings. This could be due to a deliberate attempt on Ben's part to make himself appear "sick" for some ulterior motive. On the other hand, an exaggeration of symptoms sometimes reflects a person's desperation, a "call for help." Looking next at Ben's K scale, you can see that he is not particularly defensive. You might recall that Ben appeared to be quite guarded in the opening phase of his interview with Dr. Tobin. How would you reconcile these seemingly conflicting impressions? Perhaps the more anonymous nature of the MMPI-2 allowed Ben to be self-disclosing. The validity scales yield important information, then, about Ben's personality, as well as the fact that Ben's clinical profile is a valid one. The clinical scales show a picture of severe disturbance. The highest elevations are on scales 7 and 8, which measure obsessional anxiety, social withdrawal, and delusional thinking. He also suffers from physical concerns and depression, and very possibly sexual conflicts.

In summary, Ben's MMPI-2 profile is that of a young man on the verge of panic. He is extremely alarmed by very unusual thoughts, feelings, and conflicts. He is calling out for help, while at the same time, he feels conflicted about asking for it. Keep these observations about Ben in mind when you read about his responses on the other tests.

There are literally hundreds of self-report clinical inventories, many of which have been developed for specific research or clinical purposes. Researchers and clinicians interested in a quantitative measure of an individual's symptoms might use the *SCL-90-R* (Derogatis, 1975), a self-report measure in which the respondent indicates the extent to which he or she experiences 90 physical and psychological symptoms. For example, the SCL-90-R might be used to evaluate whether a certain kind of therapy is effective in reducing symptoms by giving the SCL-90-R before and after therapy. For every clinical issue and syndrome, there are inventories that can be used for the purposes of assessment. (See Table 3-7 on page 73.) Sometimes, researchers and clinicians want to assess some clinical phenomenon or theory for which there is no published scale, and they may be faced with the challenge of developing one that fits their needs. Examples of scales developed in this way measure such varied phenomena as eating disorders, fears, impulsivity, attitudes about sexuality, depressive thinking, personality style, and loneliness (Corcoran & Fisher, 1987).

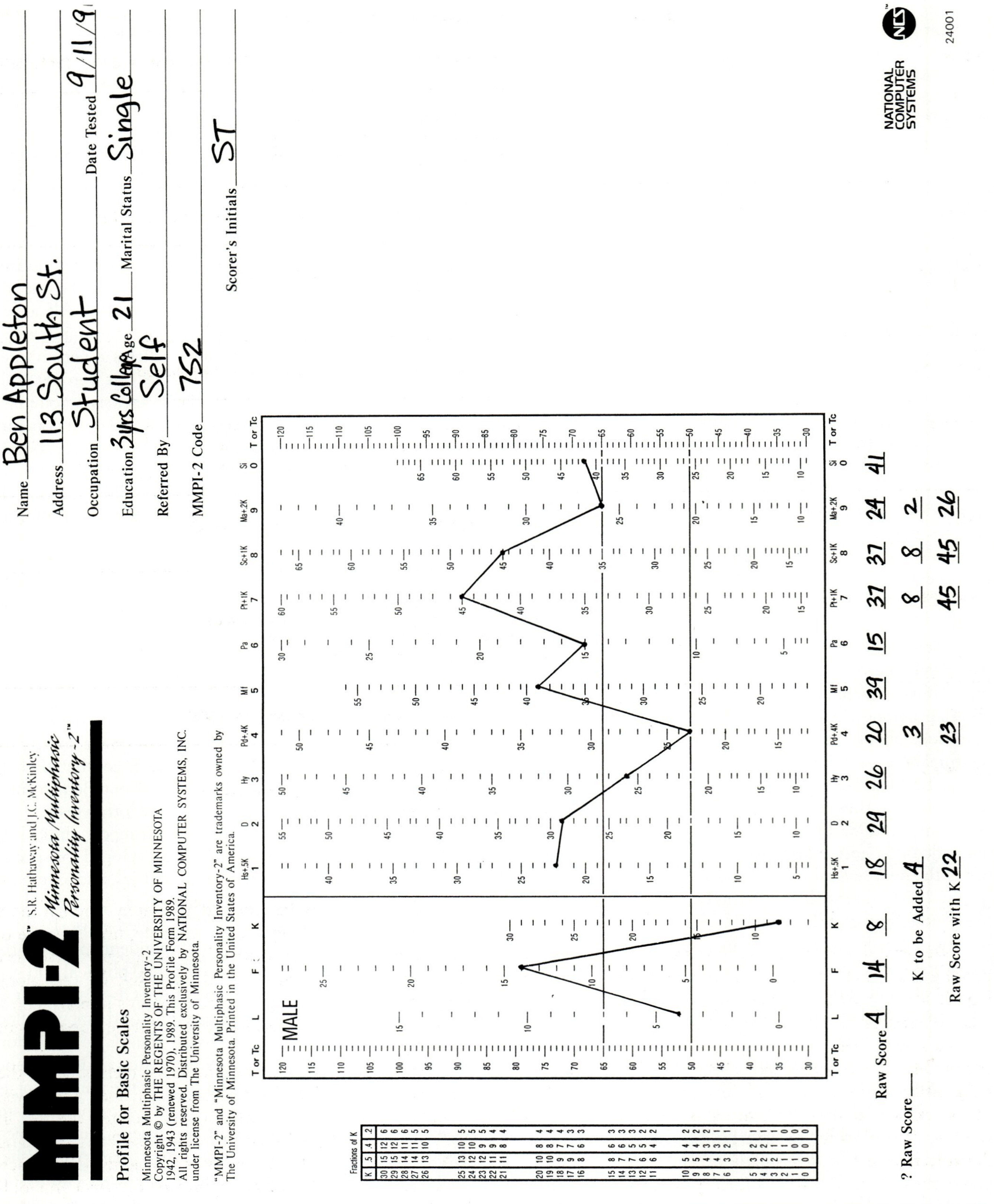

Figure 3-3
Ben Appleton's MMPI-2 profile
Source: Minnesota Multiphasic Personality Inventory–2. Copyright © by the Regents of the University of Minnesota 1942, 1943 (renewed 1970), 1989. This profile form 1989. All rights reserved. "MMPI–2" and "Minnesota Multiphasic Personality Inventory–2" are trademarks owned by the University of Minnesota.

Table 3-7 Examples of Self-Report Clinical Inventories

Name:	Sixteen Personality Factor Questionnaire (16 PF) (Cattell and IPAT Staff, 1986)
Assesses:	Personality facets reflective of normal functioning, such as emotional maturity, shrewdness, imagination, and self-sufficiency.
Name:	Symptom Check List-90 Revised (SCL-90 R) (DeRogatis, 1975)
Assesses:	Problems or complaints designed to measure symptomatic psychological distress, which respondents rate according to severity.
Name:	Millon Clinical Multiaxial Inventory-II (MCMI-II) (Millon, 1987)
Assesses:	Clinical information that corresponds to 22 DSM-III-R categories including the Axis II personality disorders and several Axis I clinical syndromes.
Name:	California Psychological Inventory-Revised (Gough, 1987)
Assesses:	Normal personality functioning, including characteristics important in everyday life such as interpersonal style, cognitive functioning, conventionality, and social maturity.
Name:	NEO Personality Inventory (Costa & McCrae, 1985)
Assesses:	Five major domains of normal adult personality, including agreeableness, openness to new experiences, and neuroticism.

■ *Projective testing*

We have discussed several tests that are based on the premise that an effective method of understanding psychological functioning involves a highly structured task that asks the test-taker to provide self-report information. In many instances, such information is sufficient to understand the individual. However, many clinicians take the theoretical position that unconscious issues exist below the surface of conscious awareness. *Projective tests* were developed with the intention of gaining access to these unconscious issues. A **projective test** is a technique in which the test-taker is presented with an ambiguous item or task and asked to respond by providing his or her own meaning. Presumably, the test-taker bases this meaning on unconscious issues or conflicts; in other words, he or she "projects" unconscious meanings onto the item. It is assumed that the respondent will disclose features of his or her personality or concerns that could not easily be reported accurately through more overt or obvious techniques. For example, take the case of Barry who, in response to items on a self-report inventory about interpersonal relationships, says that he gets along very well with other people. In contrast, his responses on a projective technique reveal hidden hostility and resentment toward others.

The most famous of the projective techniques is the *Rorschach Inkblot Test.* This technique is named after Swiss psychiatrist Hermann Rorschach, who created the test in 1911 and in 1921 published his results of 10 years of using this technique in the book *Psychodiagnostik*. Rorschach constructed the inkblots by dropping ink on paper and folding the paper, resulting in a symmetrical design. Before arriving at the final set of 10, Rorschach experimented with many hundreds, presumably until he found ones that produced the most useful responses. Although Rorschach did not invent the inkblot technique (it had been proposed by

Binet in 1896), he was the first to use standardized inkblots as the basis for assessing psychological disorder. Unfortunately, Rorschach did not live long after his book's publication; he died a year later, in his late 30s.

The initial response to the idea of the Rorschach test was unenthusiastic, and Rorschach's book was not even reviewed by the psychiatric journals in his own country. When the test made its way to the United States it created little impact, but eventually its use caught on in the mental health community. As of the early 1980s, the Rorschach test was the fourth most widely used assessment method in all clinical settings, and the most frequently used in psychiatric hospitals (Lubin et al., 1985).

The Rorschach test consists of a series of 10 cards showing ink blots. Half of these inkblots are colored and half are black-and-white. The test-taker is instructed to look at each inkblot and respond by saying what the inkblot looks like. After explaining the procedure to the test-taker, the examiner shows the inkblots one at a time, without giving the test-taker any guidance as to what is expected, except that the test-taker should indicate what the inkblot looks like. The examiner is trained to provide no clues as to how the inkblot will be scored. The test-taker is then asked to describe what about the inkblot made it look that way. While the test-taker is talking, the examiner makes a verbatim record of what the test-taker says, how the test-taker responds, and how long it takes the test-taker to respond.

Throughout the history of the Rorschach, clinicians and researchers have debated the best way to evaluate Rorschach responses. Soon after the test's introduction in the United States, clinicians and researchers began to explore ways of scoring it, developing a number of different systems until by the 1950s, there were five different approaches for administering, scoring, and interpreting the Rorschach. Some of these methods were based on the subjective judgment of the clinician, and others attempted to rely more on empirical methods (Groth-Marnat, 1990). The lack of accepted procedures for the Rorschach resulted in a failure to establish the measure's validity, and experts in the scientific community had no hesitation in attacking the measure on these grounds (Eysenck, 1959).

In response to such criticisms, the Rorschach Foundation began a concerted effort in the late 1960s to improve the psychometric qualities of the Rorschach. This effort was organized and led by psychologist John Exner, who undertook the massive job of bringing together the best features of all the available scoring systems. Exner's efforts have resulted in a method that is becoming the standard in the field, and as data based on this system accumulate, the value of the Rorschach as a diagnostic tool should become clearer. Researchers have begun to accumulate evidence supporting the Rorschach's reliability, suggesting that it is higher than critics of the test have maintained (Parker, 1983; Wagner et al., 1986). It appears now that the Rorschach meets adequate psychometric standards if it is administered and scored by professionals who have been properly trained (Karon, 1978; Parker, et al., 1988).

Ben's perception of this Rorschach inkblot was: "An evil mask that's jumping out to get you. Also a seed, some kind of seed which is dividing itself into two equal halves. It could be a sign of conception and yet it's dying. It's losing part of itself, falling apart, raging."
© Rorschach: Psychodiagnostic

You may be wondering how a set of Rorschach responses can be used to help understand an individual's personality. The Rorschach test is one of several types of projective techniques that can be integrated with the more objective information gained from a self-report clinical inventory. Let's go back to our example of Barry, who responded in different ways on self-report and projective techniques regarding his attitudes toward other people. The clinician working with Barry's test data would look for ways to integrate these divergent views, and might conclude that Barry deludes himself into believing that he feels more positively about other people than might be the case. This hypothesis about Barry's personality could be tested with other projective methods, a clinical interview, or more specific self-report inventories focusing on interpersonal styles.

It is important to remember that the choice of what test to incorporate in a battery is usually reflective of the theoretical stand of the clinician. Projective techniques are most commonly associated with approaches that focus on unconscious determinants of behavior. In contrast, a clinician who is more interested in conscious and overt behaviors might select a very different battery of tests to assess a client with serious disturbance. We have chosen to emphasize projective tests in describing Ben's case in order to show the richness of the information that can be derived from these techniques.

Ben's response to Rorschach Card I shows that the ambiguity of the projective test stimulated a variety of unusual and idiosyncratic perceptions. He sees in this card an "evil mask." Many people look at this card and see a mask. However, Ben sees this mask as "evil," a more ominous image than simply a mask. Furthermore, Ben sees the mask as "jumping out to get you." Not only does the mask have ominous elements, then, but it is seen as an attacker. In his next response to the same card, Ben sees the inkblot as a seed that is falling apart, dying, and experiencing intense anger. Is Ben talking about himself in this description?

Ben's response to another card, which contains color, reflects an even more extreme trip into fantasy. By the time Ben saw this card, which came near the end of the test, he had become preoccupied with fantasies of people and objects coming together and splitting apart. His responses had become increasingly bizarre and unconnected with the stimuli. When unusual responses such as these are paired with Ben's *MMPI-2* profile, the clinician would hypothesize that Ben is losing control and feels panicked by the experience of losing control.

The *Thematic Apperception Test (TAT)*, another widely used projective test, works on the same premise as the Rorschach, namely, that when presented with ambiguous stimuli, test-takers reveal hidden aspects of their personalities. Instead of inkblots, the stimuli are a series of black-and-white ink drawings and photographs that portray people in a variety of ambiguous contexts. Parts of these pictures are vague and sketchy. The TAT is far more structured than the Rorschach in that it presents the test-taker with more clearly defined pictures, many of which contain people. These pictures are ambiguous in that their meaning is not totally obvious, but they nevertheless provide the test-taker with a context within which to respond. The instructions for the TAT request the respondent to tell a story about what is happening in each picture, including what the main characters are thinking and feeling, what events preceded the depicted situation, and what will happen to the people in the picture. Some test-takers become very involved in the telling of these stories, as the pictures lend themselves to some fascinating interpersonal dramas.

TAT stories are interpreted on the basis of either quantitative ratings such as the number and type of different words or ideas, or qualitative interpretations based on the themes and issues present in the characters and stories. The premise of the TAT is that themes or issues can be accessed that are not conscious or that are too painful to discuss. For example, one man's stories were filled with caricatures of people acting in harsh and abusive ways, which led the clinician to hypothesize that he might have been the victim of abuse at some point in his life, or alternatively might be fearful of being exploited in the future.

The TAT was originally conceived by Christina Morgan and Henry Murray (Morgan & Murray, 1935), working at the Harvard Psychological Clinic, and was published as a method of assessing personality several years later (Murray 1938, 1943). The test was intended to uncover personality "needs" or forms of motivation proposed by Murray's theory of personality in ways that could not be assessed through self-report methods. However, within 10 years, the test became used more as a general projective assessment device both in clinical work and research, to assess a wide variety of forms of motivation and personality themes assumed to operate below the level of conscious awareness. In the process of changing the focus of the TAT from Murray's theory to a wider range of issues, researchers and clinicians began to experiment with different ways of administering the TAT and different ways of interpreting the responses. Over subsequent decades, variations on the TAT were developed for use with populations other than the white college-age individuals for whom it was designed, including children, adolescents, older adults, and minority groups. By the 1980s, the TAT ranked as the seventh most frequently used clinical assessment tool in the United States (Lubin et al., 1985), and it had become a widely used research instrument for measuring forms of motivation such as achievement, power, and affiliation (e.g., McClelland, 1980).

As much as the TAT has become a fixture among psychological assessment devices, there is still considerable debate over its psychometric qualities. In large part, this debate is a function of the way the TAT has evolved over the years, in that there is no standard way of administering or scoring it. Many who use the TAT adapt it to their own theoretical interests, and their interpretations are often based on subjective impressions and familiarity gained through experience in deriving possible meaning from test-takers' responses. However, there is moderately good evidence for the reliability of TAT ratings, and its validity, in clinical and research settings, is considered respectable (Groth-Marnat, 1990). As with other projective techniques, though, the TAT is best used as part of a set of assessment measures rather than as a single index of personality functioning (Anastasi, 1988).

Ben told the following story about this TAT card: "This is a story of a woman who has lived too long with her mother. She wants to break away but knows that she can't. Her whole life is wrapped up in her mother and the house. She's a successful businesswoman and yet she feels like a failure because she can't break out because of what she sees going on outside the house. She is looking out at the sky and sees a plane about to make a crash landing on the street. Across the street she sees a man about to jump off the top of a six-story building, but he stops when someone comes to rescue him. Because of all the crazy things going on outside, the woman thinks that maybe it is better to stay with her mother."

The themes that emerge from Ben's TAT response are consistent with the issues identified in the other personality tests in that they reflect such concerns as family problems, depression, and fears about what is going on around him. Ben described a character who is frightened by the chaos in her environment. In Ben's story the character observes someone being rescued from a suicide attempt. One might wonder whether Ben's description of the relationship between the character and her mother is a parallel of his own relationship with his mother. Interestingly, the character describes leaving home as "breaking out," as if home were a prison from which to escape. He pessimistically concludes that the character will not be able to fulfill the wish to separate. In the report at the end of this chapter, the data from this test will be integrated with the other test results as Dr. Tobin puts the pieces of Ben's puzzle together.

BEHAVIORAL ASSESSMENT

So far, we have discussed forms of assessment that involve psychological testing. These forms of assessment are the ones that most people think about when they imagine how a psychologist approaches the task of diagnosing psychological disorder. Another form of psychological assessment has emerged since the late 1960s, which relies on a very different set of assumptions than those of projective testing. **Behavioral assessment** includes a number of measurement techniques based on objective recording of the individual's behavior. Clinicians use these techniques to identify problem behaviors, to understand what maintains these behaviors, and to develop and refine appropriate interventions to change these behaviors (Barrios, 1988; Barrios & Hartmann, 1986).

As originally conceived, behavioral assessment relied almost exclusively on the recording of observable behaviors, namely actions carried out by the individual that other people could watch. This was in large part a reaction against traditional models which rely on inferences about hidden causes such as unconscious determinants or unobservable personality traits. Since the late 1970s, though, behavioral assessments have increasingly come to include the recording of thoughts and feelings as reported by the individual, in addition to outward actions. How does a clinician go about assessing behavior? There are three commonly used approaches—the behavioral self-report of the client, the clinician's observation of the client, and physiological measures.

Behavioral Self-Report

Behavioral self-report is an assessment method in which the client provides information about the frequency of particular behaviors. The rationale underlying behavioral self-report techniques is the notion that information about troublesome behavior should be derived from the client, who has the closest access to information critical for understanding and treating the problematic behavior. This information can be acquired in a number of ways, including interviews conducted by the clinician, self-monitoring of the behavior by the client, and completion of any one of a number of checklists or inventories specifically designed for this purpose.

It is commonly accepted within clinical contexts that the best way to find out what troubles clients is to ask them; the interview is the context within which to undertake such inquiry. **Behavioral interviewing** is a specialized form of interviewing in which the clinician focuses on the behavior under consideration as well as what preceded and followed the behavior. Events that precede the behavior are referred to as **antecedents**, and events following the behavior are called **consequences**.

Behavioral interviewing has long been regarded as an integral part of behavioral assessment and therapy, for it is within this context that the clinician works to understand the problem under consideration (Morganstern, 1988). When interviewing the client about the problem behavior, the clinician gathers detailed information about what happens before, during, and after the enactment of the behavior. For example, take the case of a young man who develops incapacitating levels of anxiety whenever it begins to rain while he is driving his car. In interviewing this man, the clinician tries to develop as precise an understanding as possible of the nature of these attacks of anxiety, and asks very specific questions pertaining to the time, place, frequency, and nature of these attacks. Although the clinician wants to obtain some background information, in most cases this is limited to information that seems relevant to the problem behavior. In this example, it would be more likely for the clinician to focus on particular experiences in the client's history that relate to fears of driving under risky conditions than to ask about early life relationships.

Within the behavioral interview, the clinician not only tries to understand the precise nature of the problem, but also seeks to collaborate with the client in setting goals for intervention. What is it that the client wants to change? In the example of the anxiety attacks, presumably the client wants to be able to continue driving after the rain starts, without being impaired by the anxiety that had previously afflicted him. The clinician tries to ascertain whether the client's goal is realistic or not. If the young man asserts that he wants to work toward a goal of *never* feeling any anxiety while in a car, the clinician would consider such a goal unrealistic and would help the client set a more attainable objective.

Self-monitoring is another behavioral self-report technique in which the client keeps a record of the frequency of specified behaviors, such as the number of cigarettes smoked or calories consumed, or the number of times in a day that a given unwanted thought comes to the client's mind. Perhaps a woman is instructed to keep a diary of each time she bites her fingernails, documenting the time, place, and context of the target behavior. With such careful attention to the troubling behavior, she may come to realize that it is primarily in certain situations that she is prone to bite her nails. For example, she may notice that her nail-biting is twice as likely to occur when she is speaking on the telephone.

There can be some problems involved with self-monitoring procedures. Habits such as nail-biting are so deeply ingrained that people are almost unaware of engaging in the behavior. Another problem with self-monitoring procedures is the fact that the individual must have the discipline to keep records of the behavior. As you might imagine, it could be quite disruptive for the nail-biter to take out a note pad each time she raises her fingernails to her mouth. In response to such concerns, some clinicians acknowledge that the measurement of the behavior in and of itself may be therapeutic.

Behavioral checklists and inventories have been developed to aid in the assessment or recording of troubling behaviors. In completing a behavioral checklist or inventory, the client checks off or rates whether certain events or experiences have transpired. For example, in the *Beck Depression Inventory (BDI)* (Beck, 1987), the client indicates the occurrence of depression-related thoughts. Another commonly used behavioral inventory is the *Fear Survey Schedule* (Wolpe, 1973; Wolpe & Lang, 1964), in which an individual is asked to indicate the extent to which various experiences evoke feelings of fear. Checklists and inventories such as these often appeal to both clinicians and clients because they are relatively economical and easy to use.

However, in many instances it is important to observe and measure the behavior that is the focus of concern. A client can tell a clinician about the nature and frequency of a troubling behavior, but a person may have trouble reporting a behavior that is embarrassing or otherwise upsetting.

Behavioral Observation

Behavioral observation emerged as an important component of behavioral assessment as clinicians and researchers became increasingly concerned that clients might "fake" their responses to self-report inventories in order to respond in more socially acceptable ways (Foster, Bell-Dolan, & Burge, 1988).

In behavioral observation, the clinician observes the individual and records the frequency of specific behaviors along with any relevant situational factors. For example, the nursing staff on a psychiatric unit might be instructed to observe and record the target behavior of an individual who bangs his head against a wall every time something out of the ordinary occurs. Or a classroom observer of a hyperactive boy might count the number of times each minute the boy gets out of his seat. The consequences of each behavior would also be recorded, such as the number of times the teacher tells the child to sit down.

The first step in behavioral observation involves the selection of **target behaviors**, the behaviors of interest or

Psychologists use behavior records to monitor the frequency of target behaviors, as in the case of a child whose disruptive behavior is being recorded in 16-second blocks.

concern. In the example of the hyperactive child, the target behavior would be the boy's getting up from his desk at inappropriate times. The second step is to define the target behavior clearly. Vague terms are not acceptable in a behavioral observation context. For example, a target behavior of "restlessness" in the hyperactive boy is too vague to measure. However, a measurement can be made of the number of times he jumps out of his seat.

Ideally, behavioral observation takes place in the natural context where the target behavior occurs. This is called **in vivo observation.** For the hyperactive boy the classroom setting is particularly problematic, so it is best that his behavior be observed and measured there, rather than in a laboratory. But many challenges are involved in conducting such assessment, including possible effects of the observer's presence. It is possible that the boy's behavior will be affected by the fact that he knows he is being observed, a phenomenon behaviorists refer to as **reactivity**.

To deal with some of the limitations of in vivo observation, the clinician or researcher may conduct an **analog observation**, which takes place in a setting or context specifically designed for observing the target behavior. For example, the hyperactive boy may be brought to the clinician's office, where his behavior can be observed through a one-way mirror. Perhaps other children will be included so that the boy's interactions can be observed and certain target behaviors measured. Analog observation has its limits, however, primarily because the situation is somewhat artificial (Foster et al., 1988).

PHYSIOLOGICAL ASSESSMENT

A great deal can be determined about an individual by assessing bodily responses in given situations. For example, a girl who is terrified of dogs experiences several bodily responses each time she confronts a dog. By observing this girl as she encounters a dog, you might not see any outward behavioral signs that would lead you to conclude that she is frightened. However, many changes would take place in her body reflecting her state of fear. There are several kinds of physiological assessment. Of particular utility to clinicians conducting behavioral assessment are measures of physiological processes that have a clear relationship with psychological functioning. Because of this relationship between psychological and physiological processes, they are sometimes referred to as **psychophysiological processes**.

There are other forms of physiological assessment that are of general interest and concern to all clinicians, because they provide evidence of disturbed bodily functioning that may cause a person to experience a psychological disorder. It has been well-established that there are abnormalities in the bodies of people with certain forms of severe psychological disorder. Sometimes the disturbance is localized in the brain, perhaps in the form of a structural abnormality. Or perhaps a person has a physical disorder, such as diabetes or overactive thyroid, that causes the individual to experience abnormal psychological functioning. Any comprehensive assessment should include a carefully conducted physical assessment.

Psychophysiological Assessment

Since the early days of behavior therapy, many clinicians have been interested in assessing changes in the body that are associated with psychological or emotional experiences. There are several psychophysiological systems that have been of interest to behavioral psychologists. The most commonly measured psychophysiological changes are those that take place in a person's cardiovascular system, muscles, skin, and brain. Psychophysiological assessment can provide a wealth of information about the experiences of an individual or the responses of an individual to a given situation (Sturgis & Gramling, 1988).

The cardiovascular system is concerned with functions of the heart and its distribution of blood through the body. As you know from thinking about any situation in which you have felt frightened, your heart rate can change quite drastically in a short period of time. Even thinking about something that frightens you can cause cardiovascular changes. Various measurement devices might be used to measure the activity of the heart, the most common of which is an **electrocardiogram (ECG)**, a measure of electrical impulses that pass through the heart. **Blood pressure**, the resistance offered by the arteries to the flow of blood as it is pumped from the heart, is another psychophysiological measure used to derive information about an individual's psychological functioning.

Changes in a person's muscles are assessed by means of **electromyography (EMG)**, a measure of electrical activity of the muscles. This technique is valuable in assessing the level of a person's tension, and might be used in the assessment and treatment of tension-related disorders such as headaches, which involve muscle contractions.

An individual's skin also provides important information about what the person is experiencing emotionally. As you know, most people tend to sweat when they feel nervous. Even very minor electrical changes in the skin caused by sweating, called the **electrodermal response**, can be measured. This response, also called the **galvanic skin response**, is a sensitive indicator of emotional responses such as fear and anxiety.

The most commonly used assessment of brain activity is the **electroencephalogram (EEG)**, a measure of changes in the electrical activity of the brain. In addition to the many uses of the EEG for diagnosing brain abnormalities, it can also be valuable for clinicians conducting behavioral assessment. For example, a state of relaxation is accompanied by a certain EEG pattern. By studying the EEG patterns of a client being taught relaxation methods, the clinician has a reliable measure of the electrical activity in the individual's brain and can infer the depth of the person's state of relaxation.

Physical Assessment

A clinician who is working to understand the nature of an individual's psychological problems should investigate the possibility that the problem might be caused by or aggravated by some physical disturbance. Think of a time when you have gone without food for an inordinately long time; you probably experienced some emotional changes, such as irritability, that were clearly related to your food deprivation. Or you may have become depressed as a result of a bad case of influenza that left you feeling listless and unmotivated. From experiences such as these, you can understand that an array of psychological symptoms can result from or be associated with physical problems. Using their knowledge of physiology, clinicians can sometimes rule out the

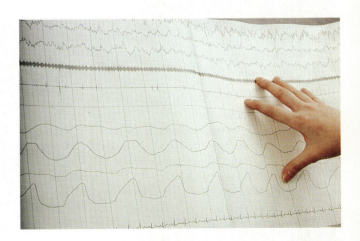

An EEG record provides information on levels of activity in the brain. High frequency waves, such as those in the top row, characterize the brain in an awake state, and the low frequency waves, near the bottom, record the brain during sleep.

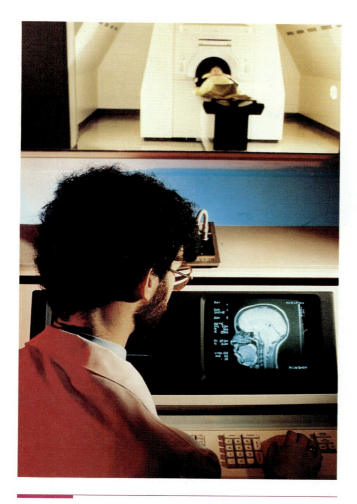

The MRI is a scanning procedure that uses magnetic fields and radio frequency pulses to construct an image of the brain.

likelihood that a client's psychological problems are physically caused. At times, however, they may refer the client to a physician for an examination focused on possible bodily causes for the problem.

In some instances, the clinician may be concerned about the possibility that a brain abnormality is associated with the client's disorder. In addition to the EEG, which is usually included in diagnostic procedures involving the brain, several other sophisticated procedures have been developed in the past two decades that provide invaluable information to clinicians about the structure and functioning of the body. If a man has an undiagnosed brain tumor that is causing him to behave in bizarre and disturbing ways, brain imaging techniques can provide the clinician with critical information, without which erroneous conclusions might be drawn.

The **computerized axial tomography (CAT or CT)** scan provides an image of the brain by means of an ingenious computerized combination of many thousands of separate x-rays taken from different vantage points or axes through a person's head. The computer provides a cross-sectional picture of the brain from any angle or level chosen.

In some settings, **magnetic resonance imaging (MRI)**, sometimes called **nuclear magnetic resonance (NMR)** has replaced the CAT scan because of its increased power and precision. This scanning procedure uses magnetic fields and radio-frequency pulses to construct an image. This technique also relies on a computer which takes the hundreds of thousands of measurements and yields a two-dimensional image of the body part being studied.

In addition to knowing about the structure of the individual's brain, the clinician may also wish to have some detailed information about the brain's neural activity. For this purpose the **positron emission tomography (PET) scan**

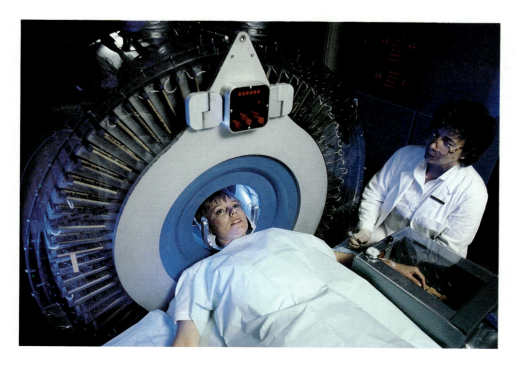

In PET scanning, radioactive sugar is injected into the individual's bloodstream to monitor the level of brain activity.

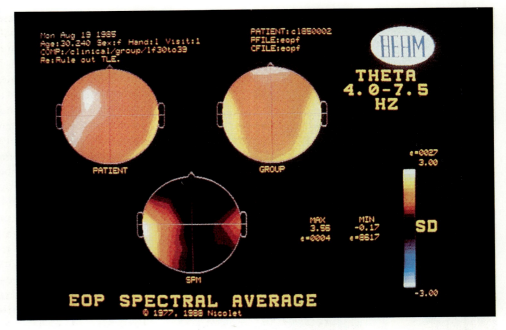

Brain map obtained from the BEAM™ topographic mapping system showing spectral analysis of eyes-open EEG data indicating excess theta over left-posterior temporal area. These topographic maps show data for the patient (upper left), data from an age-matched control group (upper right), and a statistical comparison of patient data with the control group (lower center).
Courtesy Nicolet Instruments

may be used. In this procedure, a small amount of radioactive sugar is injected into an individual's bloodstream, following which a computer measures the varying levels of radiation in different parts of the brain and yields a multicolored cross-sectional image.

A much more recently developed technology has evolved from a field of science called **neurometrics**, the measurement and analysis of brain activity. **Brain electrical activity mapping (BEAM)™** involves a procedure in which electrodes are attached to a person's head to measure brain activity.* A computer analyzes the information about the brain wave patterns, and then constructs a multicolored pattern of brain activity. Researchers have found that deviations from average patterns of brain electrical activity can provide valuable information to assist in drawing inferences about specific psychological and medical problems (John et al., 1988).

Neuropsychological Assessment

As valuable as physical assessment techniques are in pinpointing certain kinds of abnormalities in the brain or other parts of the body, they have limitations. Often the clinician needs information about the kind of cognitive impairment that has resulted from a brain abnormality such as a tumor. Or perhaps information is needed about the extent of the deterioration that the individual has suffered to that point. **Neuropsychological assessment** is the process of gathering information about a client's brain functioning on the basis of performance on psychological tests.

*BEAM is a registered trademark of the Nicolet Instrument Corporation, Madison, Wisconsin.

The most well-known neuropsychological assessment tool is the *Halstead-Reitan Neuropsychological Test Battery*, a series of tests designed to measure sensorimotor, perceptual, and speech functions. This battery was developed by psychologist Ralph Reitan, based on the earlier work of an experimental psychologist, Ward Halstead (1947). Each test involves a specific task that measures a particular hypothesized brain-behavior relationship. Clinicians can choose from an array of tests such as the *Halstead Category Test*, *Tactual Performance Test*, *Rhythm Test*, *Speech-Sounds Perception Test*, and the *Finger Oscillation Task*. These tests were developed by comparing the performance of people with different forms of brain damage as determined through independent measures such as skull x-rays, autopsies, and physical examinations. The complete Halstead-Reitan battery includes these specialized tests in addition to the WAIS-R and MMPI.

Although the Halstead-Reitan is regarded as an extremely valuable approach to neuropsychological assessment, some clinicians prefer the more recently developed *Luria-Nebraska Neuropsychological Battery*. A. R. Luria was a well-known Russian neuropsychologist who developed a variety of individualized tests intended to detect specific forms of brain damage. These tests were put into standardized form by a group of psychologists at the University of Nebraska (Golden et al., 1985). This battery comprises 269 separate tasks, organized into 11 subtests including motor function, tactile function, and receptive speech. It takes less time to administer than the Halstead-Reitan; furthermore, its content, administration, and scoring procedures are more standardized.

Though the Halstead-Reitan and the Luria-Nebraska are regarded as impressively precise, their administration involves very sophisticated skills and training. Rather than

In neuropsychological tests such as the one being taken by this woman, the ability to copy simple objects is used to assess brain functioning.

begin with these tests, most psychologists administer simpler global screening indicators such as the *Bender Visual Motor Gestalt Test* (Bender, 1938) and the *Benton Revised Visual Retention Test* (Benton, 1974). These tests are dignostic tools used to assess general visual perception, motor coordination, memory, concepts of time and space, and ability to organize. If the clinician detects some abnormality in performance, the next step would be to refer the client for more comprehensive neuropsychological testing.

PUTTING IT ALL TOGETHER

At the end of the assessment period, the clinician should have a broad-based understanding of the client as a total individual. In addition, any specific areas of concern should be identified as focuses for diagnosis and treatment. The clinician's next task is to put together a "case" that describes the client's current situation and background in a comprehensive, detailed fashion. Like a detective, the clinician be-

gins with a person's presenting problem or disorder and then collects clues that will provide an explanation of what is currently going on with the person and what led up to the client's present situation. Very few psychological problems have precise singular causes. Thus, the clinician is faced with the formidable task of discerning the roles played by environment, intelligence, personality, learning, physical functioning, and heredity in the development and maintenance of a psychological disorder. A comprehensive and well-informed understanding of these crucial factors allows the clinician to develop an individualized treatment plan that responds to the particular needs and experiences of the client.

Let's return to the case of Ben to give you an idea of what a psychological testing report would look like. Keep in mind that psychological testing is just one source of information about an individual. Within psychological testing, clinicians use one or more of the hundreds of instruments available, choosing tests that are compatible with their theoretical orientation and that seem to be most informative in the given clinical situation. In the case of Ben, Dr. Tobin responded to Ben's requests to take projective tests; with his permission, she also administered other tests that she believed would help her to understand the nature of Ben's personality.

SUMMARY

1. Psychologists use assessment for a variety of purposes, including diagnosis, measurement of intelligence, personnel selection, and evaluation of competency to stand trial. The methods used in a particular assessment depend on the context and the goals of the clinician.

2. There are two main types of clinical interviews. The flexible interview consists of open-ended questions on various topics such as reasons for being in treatment, symptoms, health status, family background, and life history. The standardized interview, used for research purposes, contains fixed questions with fixed scoring categories.

3. A mental status examination is used to evaluate the content of the client's thoughts and how the client thinks, talks, and acts. The mental status examination assesses motor behavior, orientation, content of thought (obsessions and delusions), thinking style and language, affect and mood, perceptual experiences (hallucinations and illusions), sense of self, motivation, and intelligence and insight.

4. A good psychological test is one that meets criteria of reliability and validity. A reliable test is one that produces consistent results. Reliability is assessed by test–retest reliability, internal consistency, and interjudge agreement. Validity is assessed in various forms, including content validity, criterion validity, and

Return to the Case

Testing Report on Ben Appleton

Reason for Testing

Ben Appleton's stated reason for psychological testing was curiosity. At the time of his original request, he expressed concern that the police were following him. The unusual nature of this concern warranted an assessment aimed at determining whether Ben was suffering from a serious psychological disorder.

Identifying Information

This is a 21-year-old white male college student who lives with his family and works part-time in a supermarket. He is currently a junior in college who plans to enter a career in politics.

Behavioral Observations

Ben was casually dressed, well-mannered, and cooperative in both test sessions. He seemed comfortable with the examiner, although he admitted that he felt anxious. He made frequent comments to himself such as "This really makes you take a good look at yourself." At times, he seemed defensive about his responses. For example, when questioned about the meaning of two unclear sentences on the Incomplete Sentences Blank, he curtly responded "That's what I meant." In several instances, he responded tangentially to test and conversational questions, relating personal incidents that had little to do with the task or topic.

Relevant History

A native of Minneapolis, Ben Appleton is from a middle-class family. Ben described his early childhood years as being troubled, both at home and at school. He had a very antagonistic relationship with his sister Doreen, who was 2 years older. Ben spoke of how he fought almost constantly with Doreen and how Mrs. Appleton invariably sided with Ben in any dispute. This reflected what Ben believed to be his mother's strongly overprotective style. Mr. Appleton was minimally involved with the rest of the family, according to Ben. Most of Ben's time was spent in solitary hobbies such as listening to rock music. He had no close friends and preferred to stay at home rather than to socialize.

Ben recalls how, from the earliest grades, his teachers repeatedly commented about his failure to look people in the eyes. He remembered their apparent bewilderment or annoyance when he responded to classroom questions with answers that they found difficult to understand. Ben clearly remembers one incident in which he was asked to name the capital of Tennessee, and he replied "I don't know anything about capitalism." His teacher became angry with him for sounding like a "wise guy," although Ben did not intend to make a joke. Despite his idiosyncrasies, Ben managed to get through high school and be accepted into college.

During his sophomore year of college, Ben was walking by a student demonstration protesting military funding. Upon seeing a police officer, Ben became alarmed and feared that he might be arrested. In the weeks that fol-

---

construct validity. Standardization helps ensure that tests meet these criteria of reliability and validity by controlling the conditions under which tests are given and scored.

5. Intelligence tests were first developed as a way of screening children who were likely to have difficulties in school. Current tests used in the assessment of adult intelligence attempt to provide a broad-based estimate of the individual's cognitive functioning. Individually administered tests such as the WAIS-R provide an overall intelligence estimate along with estimates of more specific functions, both verbal and nonverbal.

6. Self-report personality inventories are used for providing information used in making clinical diagnoses. Tests such as the MMPI and MMPI-2 provide the test-taker with a large number of easily scored items that provide a profile of the individual's personality. Less structured tasks are used for projective personality tests that attempt to assess unconscious psychological dynamics. The rationale behind projective tests is that test-takers will "project" their hidden feelings and impulses onto ambiguous stimuli in a way that would not be possible with more structured test items. Projective tests have been criticized for being unstandardized and as having low reliability and validity, but efforts to improve the psychometric qualities of projectives such as the Rorschach appear to be meeting with some success.

7. Behavioral assessments are conducted by psychologists who prefer quantifiable recordings of behavior to information gained from psychological testing.

Ben Appleton continued

lowed, his fears intensified. He began to worry that his phone might be tapped, his mail read, and his food treated with truth serum. Since that time, Ben reports feeling continually followed by the police and says that they are trying to put together trumped-up charges against him. According to Ben, he has seen Nazi agents whom the police have sent to trail him.

Evaluation Procedures: Diagnostic interview, WAIS-R, MMPI-2, Rorschach, and TAT.

Impressions and Interpretations

This is a very troubled young man who is desperately seeking help. He is beginning to show signs of thought disorder, emotional instability, and loss of contact with reality.

Ben is of average intelligence with no exceptional strengths or deficits. However, the quality of many of his responses reflected unusual thought processes. For example, when asked to define the word "winter" he responded, "It means death." It is possible that conflicts and unusual thought processes, as reflected by this response, interfere with his intellectual test performance, which is lower than the norm for college students.

Ben is clearly suffering from intense anxiety, frightened by his gradual loss of touch with reality. In this state of near panic, he is desperately calling out for help. Ben sees the world as an ominous place, filled with people who are either evil or on the verge of some horrible calamity. To cope with his fright, Ben escapes

into fantasy in which he imagines that he will be cared for, that people will live in happiness, and that conflict will disappear.

Ben keeps his distance from other people. His feelings about women are characterized by ambivalence. On the one hand he wishes for women to be nurturant caretakers, yet on the other hand he sees them as controlling and seductive. This ambivalence about women is further aggravated by his confusion about his own sexuality. He speaks of a secret problem that he is finally admitting to himself. Although he is not explicit about this problem, there are many allusions in his responses to anxiety about his sexual orientation.

In summary, this young man is on the verge of a break with reality and is in immediate need of professional help. Ben needs regular psychotherapy at this time, and should be immediately evaluated with the possibility of prescribing medication that can address his deteriorating mental health and his heightened level of anxiety.

Recommendation

Ben will be referred for a psychiatric consultation. It is recommended that he be evaluated for antipsychotic medication to treat his emerging signs of severe psychological disturbance: delusional thinking, hallucinations, and extreme anxiety. Ben is also being referred for long-term psychotherapy that focuses on helping him develop more appropriate adaptive behaviors such as social skills and coping strategies.

Behavioral self-report techniques involve having clients provide information about the frequency of their problematic thoughts or undesirable behaviors. This information can be gained through the behavioral interview, in which the clinician asks the client to provide the information, or through self-monitoring, in which the client reports the frequency of specified behaviors. Behavioral checklists and inventories ask clients to report on the frequency of certain thoughts and feelings. In behavioral observation, a clinician or other trained observer watches the individual and records the frequency of behaviors. These observations can be made in their naturally occurring contexts (in vivo) or in a con-trolled setting (analog).

8. Psychophysiological recordings are used to measure bodily processes that have relevance to psychological

functioning. These measures include the electrocardiogram, blood pressure, electromyography, the electrodermal response, and the electroencephalogram. Physical assessments, which detect abnormalities in the brain's structures, include computerized axial tomography (CAT scan), magnetic resonance imaging (MRI), and nuclear magnetic resonance (NMR). Positron emission tomography (PET scan) and brain electrical activity mapping (BEAM)™ are used to assess brain activity at specific sites.

9. When brain injury or damage is a suspected cause of psychological disorder, a neuropsychological assessment may be called for. The procedures involved in this type of assessment include various types of tests thought to tap some particular brain function. The Halstead-Reitan Test Battery, the Luria-Nebraska

Neuropsychological Battery, the Bender Visual Gestalt Test, and the Benton Revised Visual Retention Test are widely used neuropsychological tests.

10. Clinicians use multiple sources of information in completing a psychological assessment. Which types of information are used depend on the characteristics of the client and the client's disorder, the clinician's preferences for particular types of tests, and the goals of the assessment.

KEY TERMS

Assessment: the evaluation of a client's psychological status. p. 56

Flexible interview: a set of open-ended questions aimed at determining the client's reasons for being in treatment, symptoms, health status, family background, and life history. p. 57

Personal history: information gathered in a psychological assessment regarding important events and relationships in areas of the client's life such as school performance, peer relationships, employment, and health. p. 57

Family history: information gathered in a psychological assessment regarding the sequence of major events in the lives of the client's relatives, including those who are closest to the client as well as more distantly related family members. p. 57

Standardized interview: a highly structured series of assessment questions, with a predetermined wording and order. p. 57

Mental status examination: a focused way to provide a snapshot of the client's current functioning in the areas of behavior, orientation, content of thought, thinking style and language, affect and mood, perceptual experiences, sense of self, motivation, intelligence, and insight. p. 59

Motor behavior: how a person moves; may refer to fine movements such as handling small objects or large movements involved in walking. p. 59

Catatonia: motor disturbances in a psychotic disorder not attributable to physiological causes. p. 59

Compulsion: a repetitive and seemingly purposeful behavior performed in response to uncontrollable urges or according to a ritualistic or stereotyped set of rules. p. 59

Orientation: a person's awareness of time, place, and identity. p. 60

Obsessions: unwanted repetitive thoughts or images that invade a person's consciousness. p. 60

Delusions: deeply entrenched false beliefs that are not consistent with the client's intelligence or cultural background. p. 60

Thought disorder: a disturbance in the way the person thinks or uses language. p. 61

Affect: an individual's outward expression of an emotion. p. 61

Inappropriate affect: an inconsistency between the person's expression of emotion and the context or the content of what is being said. p. 61

Flat affect: the virtual lack of emotional expression, as in speech that is monotonous or a face that is immobile. p. 61

Mood: a person's experience of emotion, the way the person feels inside. p. 61

Normal mood or **(euthymic mood):** mood that is neither unduly happy nor sad, but shows day-to-day variations within a relatively limited range. p. 62

Dysphoric mood: unpleasant feelings such as sadness or irritability. p. 62

Elevated mood: mood that is more cheerful than average. p. 62

Euphoric mood: a state in which the individual feels an exaggerated sense of happiness, elation, and excitement. p. 62

Hallucination: a false perception, not corresponding to the objective nature of stimuli present in the environment. p. 62

Illusion: misperception of a real object. p. 62

Auditory hallucination: the false perception of a sound. p. 62

Visual hallucination: the false visual perception of objects or persons. p. 62

Olfactory hallucination: the false perception of a smell. p. 62

Gustatory hallucination: the false perception of a taste. p. 62

Tactile hallucination: the false perception of sensation or movement. p. 62

Depersonalization: an altered experience of the self ranging from feeling that one's body is not connected to one's mind to the feeling that one is not real. p. 62

Identity confusion: a lack of clear sense of who one is, ranging from confusion about one's role in the world to actual delusional thinking. p. 62

Psychometrics: literally means "measurement of the mind," reflecting the goal of finding the most suitable tests for psychological variables under study. p. 63

Reliability: the consistency of test scores. p. 64

Validity: how well the test measures what it is designed to measure. p. 64

Percentile score: the percent of those who score below a certain number on a test. p. 65

IQ: an abreviation of the term *intelligence quotient*. p. 66

Intelligence quotient: a method of quantifying performance on an intelligence test, originally calculated according to the ratio of a person's tested age to that person's chronological age, and changed in the 1960 revision of the Stanford-Binet to the deviation IQ. p. 66

Deviation IQ: an index of intelligence derived from comparing the individual's score on an intelligence test with the mean score for that individual's reference group. p. 67

Self-report clinical inventory: a psychological test with standardized questions having fixed response categories that the test-taker completes independently, "self"-reporting the extent to which the responses are accurate characterizations. p. 69

Empirical criterion keying: a method of constructing a test in which an item is included on a scale if it empirically differentiates between groups of people. p. 69

Projective test: a technique in which the test-taker is presented with an ambiguous item or task and asked to respond by providing his or her own meaning or perception. p. 73

Behavioral assessment: a number of measurement techniques based on objective recording of the individual's behavior. p. 76

Behavioral self-report: a method of behavioral assessment in which the individual provides information about the frequency of particular behaviors. p. 76

Behavioral interviewing: a specialized form of interviewing in which the clinician asks for information on the behavior under consideration as well as what preceded and followed that behavior. p. 76

Antecedents: events preceding a specified behavior. p. 76

Consequences: events following a specified behavior. p. 76

Self-monitoring: a self-report technique in which the client keeps a record of the frequency of specified behaviors. p. 76

Behavioral checklists and inventories: behavioral assessment devices in which the client checks off or rates whether or not certain events or experiences have transpired. p. 77

Target behavior: a behavior of interest or concern. p. 77

In vivo observation: a form of behavioral assessment in which the individual is observed in the natural context where the target behavior occurs. p. 77

Reactivity: change in a person's behavior in response to knowledge that he or she is being observed. p. 77

Analog observation: a form of behavioral assessment that takes place in a setting or context specifically designed for observating the target behavior. p. 77

Psychophysiological processes: physiological processes that have a clear relationship with psychological functioning. p. 78

Electrocardiogram (ECG): a measure of electrical impulses that pass through the heart. p. 78

Blood pressure: the resistance offered by the arteries to the flow of blood as it is pumped from the heart, a measure used to derive information about an individual's psychological functioning. p. 78

Electromyography (EMG): a measurement of electrical activity of the muscles. p. 78

Electrodermal response (also called **Galvanic Skin Response** or **GSR):** minor electrical changes in the skin that result from sweating. p. 78

Electroencephalogram (EEG): a measure of changes in the electrical activity of the brain. p. 78

Computerized axial tomography (CAT or CT): a measure that provides an image of the brain by means of a computerized combination of many thousands of separate x-rays taken from different vantage points or axes through a person's head. p. 79

Magnetic resonance imaging (MRI) (sometimes called **nuclear magnetic resonance** or **NMR):** a scanning procedure that uses magnetic fields and radio-frequency pulses to construct an image. p. 79

Positron emission tomography (PET) scan: a measure of brain activity in which a small amount of radioactive sugar is injected into an individual's bloodstream, following which a computer measures the varying levels of radiation in different parts of the brain and yields a multicolored cross-sectional image. p. 79

Neurometrics: the measurement and analysis of brain activity. p. 80

Brain electrical activity mapping (BEAM)™: a procedure in which electrodes are attached to a person's head to measure brain activity; a computer analyzes the information about the brainwave patterns and then constructs a multicolored pattern of brainwave activity. p. 80

Neuropsychological assessment: a process of gathering information about a client's brain functioning on the basis of performance on psychological testing. p. 80

Case Report: Kristin Pierpont

Kristin Pierpont is a 23-year-old woman who came to see me for help regarding her feelings of isolation and loneliness. Ever since graduating from college, she has been unable to meet new people. Her job as a store buyer is not particularly gratifying, and she sees herself as a "failure" because she is earning a lower salary than she feels she should be at her age. In college, Kristin had a small close-knit circle of friends, but dated very infrequently. She fears that she will "go nuts" unless she can find more ways to socialize. She also fears that she will never get married, since by the age of 23 she feels that she should have a steady relationship. In addition to her loneliness, Kristin has a number of ill-defined bodily symptoms, such as stomachaches, difficulty sleeping, and a stiff neck.

Kristin lives about 200 miles from her hometown. The youngest of a family of four girls, Kristin has little contact with her sisters, all of whom are married and have families. As a child she was very close to her father; her mother seemed more interested in the other girls in the family. After her father's death 4 years ago, Kristin was severely distraught for well over a year. When I asked Kristin for details about his death, she became tearful but assured me that she had worked through her grief, and that to be upset about his death anymore would be unnatural. My hunch is that her father's death is still very much on Kristin's mind and may be related to her current psychological distress.

Sarah Tobin, PhD

4

PSYCHODYNAMIC AND HUMANISTIC PERSPECTIVES

What do you think is the source of Kristin's loneliness? Do you think it is a matter of her childhood experiences, biological problems, or lack of a fulfilling occupation and social life? As you read Kristin's case, you probably formed your own hunches about the causes of her behavior. Most people have a general set of assumptions about why people do what they do, assumptions that form a kind of "theory." Even though you may not use the term "theory" to describe your own assumptions about human nature, you will probably find that the formal psychological theories we discuss in this chapter and the next contain ideas similar to yours. As you read about these theories, try to see which come closest to your own. You may be surprised to find your own ideas about human behavior echoed in the words of well-known psychological theorists.

After presenting a synopsis of the major ideas each perspective offers on the understanding and treatment of psychological disorder, we will illustrate how each theory would be applied to Kristin's psychotherapy. Most clinicians approach clinical cases with a somewhat broader orientation than that provided by one theory. However, in this chapter and the next, we will describe a pure version of therapy as approached by each perspective.

After reading this chapter, you should be able to:

- Describe the purpose of theories in abnormal psychology.
- Understand the historical origins of psychoanalytic theory and its main ideas as developed by Freud.
- Compare approaches within the psychodynamic perspective originated by theorists who challenged Freud's views.

- Describe principles of treatment within the psychodynamic perspective.
- Understand the humanistic perspective as represented by the theories of Rogers and Maslow.
- Describe the client-centered approach to psychotherapy advocated by Rogers.
- Evaluate research based on the humanistic perspective and the contribution of this perspective to an understanding of abnormal behavior.

THE PURPOSE OF THEORIES IN ABNORMAL PSYCHOLOGY

Theories are crucial to the understanding of abnormal behavior. They offer contrasting perspectives from which to approach the possible causes of abnormal psychological functioning. Also, a theoretical perspective provides a framework for collecting and analyzing research data. The evidence gathered on abnormal behavior takes on a very distinct flavor depending on the perspective of the researcher. Some forms of data on psychological disorder are more acceptable and relevant to one perspective than to another. Psychologists of different orientations are likely to examine different aspects of the person when gathering data on abnormal psychological functioning. When it comes to actual practice, experienced clinicians do not strictly adhere to one theoretical orientation. Although most clinicians tend to identify with one perspective or another, they freely borrow from other perspectives if the treatment of a particular client warrants it (Norcross, 1992; Norcross & Prochaska, 1988). If they do not believe they are competent to administer the needed treatment, they refer the client to another therapist who is trained to provide a particular kind of therapy.

We will examine abnormal behavior from five major theoretical perspectives that have shaped the field as it is today. In this chapter, we will examine the psychodynamic and humanistic-existential perspectives, and in the next chapter, we will examine the behavioral, family systems, and biological perspectives. Our purpose in these two chapters is to look at what answers each perspective provides to questions regarding abnormal behavior. What is the underlying model of human nature it describes, and in turn, how does it explain abnormal behavior? What are the implications of the perspective for research? What treatment approaches would follow from the perspective, and how well do these treatments work? The field of abnormal psychology is filled with lively controversies regarding the nature of psychological disorder, its causes, and its treatment. We hope not only to convey a solid basis for your academic understanding of these theories, but also to share with you the excitement that scientists, clinicians, and theorists experience as they search for answers to some of the most puzzling questions that confront humankind.

PSYCHODYNAMIC PERSPECTIVE

You will recall from Chapter 1 that Sigmund Freud's (1856–1939) view of psychological disorder focused on unconscious motives and conflicts. The **psychodynamic perspective** is the theoretical orientation that emphasizes unconscious determinants of behavior. Treatment of psychological disorder, from this perspective, involves an attempt to restructure the individual's personality. Freud's ideas about the cause and treatment of psychological disorder form the foundation for the psychodynamic perspective. As you will see, this theory has come a long way from Freud's original formulations.

Freudian Psychoanalytic Theory

Sigmund Freud's psychoanalytic theory paved the way for contemporary approaches to understanding mental disorders. As we noted in Chapter 1, prior to Freud's work, many people believed that mental illness was produced by mystical, evil spirits. Freud discovered that bizarre and exotic behaviors and symptoms could be produced by disorders of the mind and that they could be scientifically studied and explained.

- *Freud's background*

Freud claimed that the "child is father to the man," meaning that early life experiences play a formative role in personality. This observation stemmed from the analysis he conducted on his own childhood (Gay, 1988; Jones, 1953). In his thirties and forties, Freud came to the dramatic realization that the events of his early childhood had taken root in the deepest level of awareness, the region of the mind he called the "unconscious." He came to this conclusion through extensive analysis of his dreams and of the thoughts and memories they triggered (Freud, 1900). In the process of this self-analysis, he found that he was able to obtain relief from a variety of disturbing symptoms and phobias such as a train phobia he acquired during a traumatic ride from his hometown to Vienna at the age of four.

Freud's medical training led him to the conviction that disorders of the mind could be understood by scientific methods, and that all psychological phenomena could be traced to physiological processes. After he finished his medical training, Freud traveled to France where his study of hypnosis led him to search for psychological methods of communicating with the unconscious mind. From these experiences, Freud went on to develop the principles and methods that he later called psychoanalysis.

- *Freud's structural model of personality*

In order to understand Freud's views of psychopathology, it is necessary to understand how he conceived of

Psychoanalyst Sigmund Freud with his daughter, psychoanalyst Anna Freud, in 1928.

personality structure. According to Freud (1923), the mind has three structures: the id, the ego, and the superego.

THE ID   The **id** is the structure of personality that contains sexual and aggressive instincts. Freud defined the id as a "seething cauldron" of animal instincts. The id is inaccessible to conscious awareness; it lies entirely in the "unconscious" layer of the mind. The id follows the **pleasure principle**, a motivating force oriented toward the immediate and total gratification of sensual needs and desires. According to Freud, pleasure can be obtained only when the tension of an unmet drive is reduced. The way the id attempts to achieve pleasure is not necessarily through the actual gratification of a need with tangible rewards. Instead, the id uses "wish-fulfillment" to achieve its goals. Through wish-fulfillment, the id conjures up an image of whatever it is that will satisfy the needs of the moment. The id cannot distinguish between fantasy and reality: an image of a chocolate milkshake is as good to the id as an actual milkshake.

Freud (1911) used the phrase **primary process thinking**, to describe the id's loosely associated, idiosyncratic, and distorted cognitive representation of the world. In primary process thinking, the thoughts, feelings, and desires related to sexual and aggressive instincts are represented symbolically with very concrete visual images that do not necessarily fit together in a rational, logical way. Time, space, and causality do not correspond to what happens in real life. Primary process thinking is best illustrated in dreams. For example, a boy dreams that he is walking down a hallway, falls into a hole that suddenly opens up in the floor, and lands in Brazil. He thinks, "I haven't seen a hula hoop in years!" All of a sudden, a hula hoop appears out of the clear blue sky, waiting for him to give it a spin. Such images—

probabilities do not seem strange or extraordinary in primary process thinking.

THE EGO   The center of conscious awareness in personality is the **ego.** Unlike the chaotic id, the ego is a coherent organization. The ego's function is to give the individual the mental powers of judgment, memory, perception, and decision-making, which will enable the individual to adapt to the realities of the external world. Recall that the id is incapable of distinguishing between fantasy and reality. The ego is needed to transform a wish into real gratification. Freud (1911) described the ego as being governed by the **reality principle**, a motivational force that leads the individual to confront the constraints of the external world.

In contrast to the illogical and loose associational thinking characteristic of the id, the ego functions are characterized by **secondary process thinking**, which is involved in logical and rational problem-solving. How does primary process thinking differ from secondary process thinking? Consider the situation where a hungry student, working late in the library, goes to a coin-operated vending machine, inserts her last quarter and finds that the machine fails to respond. The primary process thinking of her id might lead her to bang angrily and desperately on the machine, achieving nothing in the process except injuring her hand. The secondary process thinking of her ego might cause her to search for a friend to borrow some change, to look for someone in charge of the vending machine to get a refund, or to leave the library and return to her room for a snack.

In Freud's version of psychodynamic theory, the ego has no motivating force of its own. All of the ego's energy is derived from the energy of the id, a pressure for gratification that Freud called the **libido.** The id, then, is the ego's task master. The ego performs the functions that will allow the id's desires to be gratified in reality, not just in fantasy.

Although the ego is the center of consciousness, not all of the ego's contents are accessible to conscious awareness. The unconscious part of the ego contains memories of experiences that reflect unfavorably upon the individual's conscious self. These experiences include events in which the individual acted selfishly, behaved in sexually inappropriate ways, or was unnecessarily cruel and violent.

THE SUPEREGO   In nontechnical terms, the **superego** would be called the "conscience." The superego exerts a controlling function over the ego's pursuit of the id's desires. Freud believed that without a superego, people would pursue for pleasure the satisfaction of the "taboo" or socially unacceptable desires of the id, such as rape, murder, and incest. The superego also serves an inspirational function. It includes the **ego-ideal**, which is the individual's personal model of all that is exemplary in life. The individual acquires both functions in the first few years of life from parents or primary caregivers.

■ *Psychodynamics*

The three structures of the mind, or **psyche** (the Greek word for mind), are continuously interacting with one another in a "dynamic" fashion. Freud coined the term **psychodynamics** (literally, dynamics of the mind) to describe the processes of interaction among personality structures that lie beneath the surface of observable behavior.

In the personality of a healthy individual, according to Freud (1923), the id is able to achieve at least some of its instinctual desires through the ego's ability to navigate in the external world and through the cautions imposed upon it by the superego. Even in the normal personality, though, the demands of the id and the superego can never be completely met by the ego. Freud had a very pessimistic view of human nature in this regard. He believed that human beings have a choice of being lustful and murderous happy savages (if they allow gratification of their id instincts) or unhappy but civilized neurotics (by following the dictates of the superego). Even normal individuals are destined to lack a perfect resolution of their instinctual desires and the prescriptions of their society (Freud, 1930).

In Freud's view, psychological disorder results from serious imbalance between the id's needs and the superego's restrictions. Either the id reigns unimpeded by the superego, or the id is totally restrained by an overly punitive and demanding superego. In the first case, the individual would have a psychotic disorder dominated by fantasies of wish-fulfillment and illogical primary process thinking. If the superego is dominant, the individual is overly inhibited and unable to experience sensual pleasure without feeling guilty. Such a condition also may take the form of a psychosis, because the superego's demands can be just as irrational as the id's. For example, a woman may have psychotic delusions that she deserves to be punished for crimes that she did not commit.

■ *Defense mechanisms*

Psychological disturbance can result from defects in the ego. In normally functioning individuals, the ego attempts to protect itself from recognition of the unreasonable demands of the id for satisfying sexual and aggressive instincts, and feelings such as lust and rage that can accompany these instincts. Awareness of these instincts is unacceptable to the person's conscious standards of decency and propriety. The person would experience an unpleasant degree of anxiety if the repugnant desires held by the unconscious mind were to rise to the surface of consciousness.

To protect against anxiety, a person must use a variety of tactics that keep unacceptable instincts and feelings out of conscious awareness. Freud called these tactics **defense mechanisms** because they protect the ego against anxiety. According to Freud, everyone uses defense mechanisms on an ongoing basis to screen out potentially disturbing experiences. The desires that defense mechanisms neutralize and inhibit still seek some kind of expression, however, through the indirect mechanisms of dreams and neurotic symptoms, as well as jokes, slips of the tongue, and accidents (Freud, 1901). It is when defense mechanisms are used in a rigid or extreme fashion that they become the source of psychological disorder.

The concept of defense mechanisms originated with Freud's theory (1926) and was developed more fully by his daughter, Anna Freud (1895–1982), who became a well-known psychoanalyst in her own right. She described the following defense mechanisms (A. Freud, 1936):

REPRESSION   Simply stated, **repression** is unconsciously motivated forgetting. An instinct, feeling, or thought is pushed out of the ego's realm of conscious awareness, so that the individual "forgets" something that would cause anxiety. Repression is like sweeping dirt under a rug; and once it is swept under the rug, you are not aware of its existence. Forgetting your appointment with the dentist or forgetting the name of a person you dislike are examples of repression. Sometimes it is good to forget something, such as the pain you experienced during a tooth extraction last year. However, repression becomes pathological when used too frequently. If you consistently forget important appointments or significant people in your life, then repression has begun to play a negative role for you. Taking it a step further, we enter the realm of more serious psychopathology. Some theorists believe that certain forms of amnesia are actually extreme versions of repression.

DENIAL   An individual may get rid of unpleasant feelings, thoughts, or desires by pretending that they never existed. In **denial**, the reality of an event that affected the person's ego unfavorably is simply rejected. For example, consider a young man's reaction to the death of his best friend from cancer. Rather than contend with the painful emotions that confronting his friend's death would evoke, he takes a matter-of-fact attitude toward the death and acts as though he is unaffected. Denial becomes more

After assisting in a murder, Shakespeare's Lady Macbeth developed the symptom of compulsive hand-washing in an attempt at "undoing" her feelings of guilt.

pathological when the person refuses to acknowledge that the event ever occurred. If the young man denies the fact that his friend died, then there could be concern about his loss of touch with reality. For some individuals this loss of contact with reality reaches psychotic proportions. For example, a paranoid man refused to admit that he was married to his wife; in fact, he insisted that he had never seen her before.

ISOLATION   When using **isolation**, an individual separates feelings from actions. Behaviors that would normally be associated with certain feeling states are performed without the accompanying emotion. A young man who is driving his sister to school has an accident in which his sister is seriously injured. As she lies on the side of the road bleeding, he must respond to the crisis in a level-headed manner, so he isolates his intense emotional reaction from taking care of the tasks at hand.

UNDOING   The defense mechanism of **undoing** is used to protect the ego from feeling guilt or remorse over an illicit desire or harmful action. **Undoing** refers to the ego's attempt to restore the individual to the state that existed before the need was expressed or the behavior occurred. This attempted restoration may take the form of counter-

actions intended to reverse the sequence of events that led to trouble. Such behavior was described by Shakespeare in *Macbeth*. Crying "Out, out damned spot!" Macbeth's wife scrubbed her hands repeatedly, trying to remove the stains of blood from the murder that she had provoked her husband into committing.

DISPLACEMENT   In **displacement**, unacceptable feelings or impulses are shifted from the target of those feelings to someone or something that is more acceptable. For example, a man realizes that it's not wise to respond with an angry outburst when his boss hassles him. Instead, he unconsciously displaces his anger onto a subordinate. His subordinate, in turn, may displace the anger felt toward him by kicking the wastebasket. From the standpoint of the ego, such measures are adaptive in that they allow the person to express anger without threatening the individual's sense of propriety or safety. Displacement is not adaptive, though, if it is the predominant basis for the release of feelings and impulses. Persistent failure to respond to the appropriate target of anger will at the very least result in disturbed interpersonal relationships. In its more severe forms, displacement can divert an individual's rage at a specific person onto innocent and uninvolved others.

REACTION FORMATION   A feeling or desire that the ego considers unacceptable may be transformed into its opposite in order to make it more acceptable. This defense mechanism is called **reaction formation**, a defense mechanism that protects the ego from the anxiety it would experience if it knew the "real" content of the emotion or impulse. Consider the example of the man who secretly is addicted to pornography but at school committee meetings rants and raves about teachers who assign literature with sexual themes. His behavior exemplifies reaction formation because it transforms his hidden unsavory desires into socially acceptable forms of expression.

PROJECTION   In **projection**, a person attributes undesirable personal traits or feelings to someone else. The ego is protected from the acknowledgment that such distasteful attributes actually exist within oneself. Individuals who have trouble getting along with others often "project" the difficulty onto others, perhaps perceiving acquaintances as being obnoxious when the flaw is their own. In its severe forms, projection results in very disturbed relationships. For example, a paranoid woman who is completely untrusting of others may contend that no one confides in her or initiates friendships with her.

RATIONALIZATION   In **rationalization**, the ego finds a more acceptable reason to mask the potentially threatening "real" reason for a behavior. For example, a young woman was turned down by a classmate with whom she was hoping to go out. Instead of expressing her disappointment and sense of rejection, she said to herself, "What a relief! I almost got suckered into going out with that jerk! I'm sure glad I didn't fall into that trap!" Her response is an unconscious defense against feeling the pain that would be caused

This college student's thumb-sucking might be considered regression to infantile behavior associated with an earlier psychosexual stage.

by acknowledging how badly she wanted that date. Rationalization becomes problematic for people who consistently fail to take responsibility for the consequences of their behavior or who cannot acknowledge their own shortcomings.

REGRESSION   A person using **regression** reverts to behaviors that were more acceptable or more rewarding in childhood. For example, a middle-aged man enters a restaurant eagerly awaiting a good meal. After 20 minutes of not being waited on, he pounds his fist on the table, yelling for someone to come and take his order. His behavior has regressed to what you might expect to see in a 2-year-old child whose parent is late with lunch. The stress of his hunger pangs has stimulated him to revert to an earlier way of responding.

SUBLIMATION   An individual using **sublimation** translates unacceptable impulses into more acceptable actions. Freud regarded sublimation as the basis for civilized behavior in modern society. Civilized people express their sexual instincts not by engaging in unlimited indulgence, but in intimate relationships. Aggressive instincts are satisfied not by beating and killing people, but by competing for power, status, and money in the workplace.

■ *Psychosexual development*

According to Freud, the id, ego, and superego evolve during the first 5 years of life. The id is present at birth. The ego develops out of the id as the growing infant learns to master the external world's demands. The superego emerges out of the ego in the process of socialization as the individual acquires the ways and mores of society. Subsequent development involves the further refinement of personality dynamics, particularly the building of defense mechanisms.

Freud (1905) proposed that there is a normal sequence of development through a series of what he called *psychosex-ual stages*. Each stage focuses on a different sexually excitable zone of the body (*erogenous zone*). The way the child learns to fulfill the sexual desires associated with each stage becomes an important component of the child's personality. Failure to pass through these stages in the normal manner is the cause of various psychosexual disturbances and character disorders.

Freud based his description of the psychosexual stages almost entirely on his observations of adults he treated in psychotherapy, whose recollections convinced him that their current difficulties stemmed from repressed sexual instincts left over from their early years (Freud, 1925). According to Freudian theory the notions of regression and fixation are central to the development of psychological disturbance. An individual may regress to behavior appropriate to an earlier stage, or may become stuck, or fixated, at that stage. In **fixation**, then, the individual remains at a stage of psychosexual development characteristic of childhood.

The following discussion describes the essential features of each stage. The ages listed along with these stages should be understood as approximate. As you read the descriptions, try to imagine how children in each age range behave.

ORAL STAGE   (0–18 months) The main source of pleasure for the small infant is derived from stimulation of the mouth and lips. This stage is divided into two phases. The first is the **oral-passive** or **receptive phase**, in which pleasurable feelings come from nursing or eating. In the second phase, called **oral-aggressive**, pleasure is derived from gumming and biting anything the infant can get into the mouth. Regression to or fixation at the oral-passive stage results in excessive reliance on oral sources of gratification (thumb-sucking, cigarette smoking, overeating). People who regress to or fixate at the oral-aggressive stage are overly hostile and have a critical (biting) attitude toward others.

During the oral stage of development, infants put anything they can find in their mouths.

ANAL STAGE (18 months–3 years) The toddler's sexual energy focuses on stimulation in the anal area from holding onto and expelling feces. Fixation at this stage may result in a person having an over-controlled, hoarding type of character structure whose main way of relating to the world is by holding back. Conversely, fixation at the anal stage may result in a sloppy, impulsive, and uncontrolled character. In regression to the anal stage, the individual may become excessively sloppy or, conversely, overly neat. For example, a woman who cleans out her dresser drawers in a frenzied manner every time she has an argument with her husband is regressing to anal-like behaviors.

PHALLIC STAGE (3–5 years) In this stage, the genital area of the body is the focus of the child's sexual feelings. Freud believed that the fate of the child's future psychological health is sealed during this phase, when the child must deal with the most important issue of early life. During the phallic stage, the child becomes sexually attracted to the opposite-sex parent. Freud (1913) called this scenario in boys the *Oedipus complex,* after Oedipus, the tragic character in ancient Greek literature, who unknowingly killed his father and married his mother. Freud described a parallel process in girls, the *Electra complex,* based on Electra, the ancient Greek character who conspired to kill her mother. Freud believed there were important sex differences in how the crisis is resolved, but for both sexes, it is resolved favorably when the child identifies with the same-sex parent. At the same time, the child acquires a superego, which enforces society's taboo against incest, and sets the stage for all later struggles in dealing with unacceptable sexual and aggressive desires. Freud believed that failure to resolve the Oedipus complex, as it is now referred to for both genders, becomes the major source of neurosis.

LATENCY (5–12 years) After the turmoil of the Oedipus complex quiets, the child's sexual energies recede entirely, according to Freud. The child interacts with peers and imitates the behavior of parents and other adults of the same biological gender as the child. With sex presumably out of the picture, not much of psychological interest happens during this stage.

GENITAL STAGE (12 years through adulthood) Sexual energy resurfaces just prior to puberty, causing the Oedipus complex to reappear. The adolescent must learn to transfer feelings of sexual attraction from the parent figure to opposite-sex peers. Adult **genitality**, the ability to express sexual feelings in a mature way and in appropriate contexts, is reached when an individual is able to "work and love" (in Freud's words) with another person. Prior fixations and regressions will, however, restrict the individual's ability to complete this stage satisfactorily.

■ *Freud's place in history*

You can probably imagine that Freud's theories created a great deal of controversy, especially since he was writing at a time when sex was not openly discussed. Many people today react to Freud's ideas with amusement and disbelief. Freud himself often compared his role to that of a conqueror and explorer, paving the way for revolutionary approaches to understanding the mind. During his lifetime, Freud experienced rejection from his medical colleagues, and was often the target of derision. By the time he died, however, he had achieved international renown, and his work was beginning to have a major impact on many fields besides psychology.

Even though Freud's ideas have been influential, there are areas of his theory that many people think are flawed. As you read further, you might find that some of your reactions to Freud's theory are echoed in the work of theorists who followed him. However, we must not lose sight of the major role that Freud played in redefining ways of understanding human behavior.

Post-Freudian Psychodynamic Views

Soon after the turn of the century, Freud attracted a group of followers who wanted to learn about and promote the practice of psychoanalysis. Several of these followers spent years attending weekly seminars in Freud's home, where they carried on theoretical and clinical discussions that were to prove central to Freud's development of his theory. From this group, as well as from other psychoanalytic circles throughout Europe, emerged several prominent theorists. Although these theorists had their differences, they shared certain ideas. Collectively they represented a departure from Freudian theory in that they believed Freud overemphasized sexual instincts. Instead, they focused on interpersonal and social needs and the way that society molds personalities. Because of ideological differences between Freud and these theorists, he felt bitterness and disappointment in the latter part of his life (Roazen, 1974). However, these theorists made important advances in areas that are still very alive in contemporary psychology.

■ *Jung*

Carl Jung (1875–1961) developed a theory that differed radically from Freud's in its emphasis on sexuality (Jung, 1961) and in the conceptualization of the unconscious. According to Jung (1936), the deepest layer of the

Carl Gustav Jung sought new insights into the treatment of severely disturbed psychotic patients. However, he could never accept Freud's ideas about sexuality and eventually broke from Freud's inner circle.

unconscious includes images common to all human experience. Jung called these images **archetypes.** Some of these archetypes include images of "good" versus "evil," the "hero," rebirth, and the self. Through genetic inheritance, people are programmed to respond to events in their daily lives on the basis of these archetypes. For example, Jung would assert that movies such as *Superman* are popular because they activate the hero archetype. Jung (1916) believed that the goal of healthy personality development was integration of the unconscious life with conscious thoughts, and that psychological disorders result from an imbalance between these two parts of the personality.

■ *Adler and Horney*

Alfred Adler (1870–1937) and Karen Horney (1885–1952) never actually collaborated, but we present their ideas together because they are so similar in their basic approach to understanding neurosis. They share a focus on the ego, the more conscious elements of the mind. Instead of seeing the individual as being driven by unconscious sexual and aggressive impulses, Adler and Horney regarded the individual's self-concept as a major organizer of personality. People are motivated to maintain a consistent and favorable view of the self, and psychological defenses are developed to protect this positive self-view. Another similarity between Adler and Horney is their emphasis on social concerns and interpersonal relations in the development of personality. Close relationships with friends and family and an interest in the life of the community are seen as gratifying in their own right, not because a sexual or aggressive desire is indirectly satisfied in the process.

In the theories of Adler and Horney, the neurotic adult is someone who feels very inferior or unworthy, a feeling that originated in childhood. In order to feel more self-confident, the individual begins a pattern of putting on a false front of superiority. It makes the child feel more adequate to say either "I am better than everyone else" or "I am a terrific person because I have such high standards for myself." This is the point at which the individual becomes the victim of the desire to overcome weakness. An "idealized self" is created to cover up the "real" self that feels inadequate and unlovable. The person becomes trapped by this

Both Adler and Horney differed from Freud in that they emphasized social concerns. Horney saw discrimination against women as a more important psychological influence than penis envy.

scheme when confronted with the fact that the idealized self's unrealistic goals, by definition, can never fully be met.

The neurotic does, however, discover how to feel better about the hopeless mess created in this fashion. Making "neurotic excuses" is one way of avoiding challenging situations likely to lead to failure. One excuse is to use symptoms to avoid going to places and doing things that would put personal abilities to the test ("I can't go to the sales meeting because I get so nervous when I have to speak before a large crowd," or "If only I didn't have this headache, I could finish my homework assignment"). The neurotic may also use unreasonably high standards as an "excuse" for not having attained goals ("I could have graduated from college, but I think a college education is a waste of time and money these days because colleges aren't as rigorous as they used to be").

Adler and Horney used different terms to describe the basis for psychological disorder, and each had a somewhat different focus. Adler (1931, 1958) placed more emphasis on the individual's relationship to society, and saw the basis for psychological disorder as loss of social interest, or a turning away from fellow humans.

Horney (1950) focused more on the inner world of the individual as the basis for psychological disorder. She proposed that people with psychological disorder have become distanced from their true needs and desires. Their distress results from this sense of alienation as well as the tyrannical demands of the idealized self, what she called the "shoulds." These demands form an unrealistic set of goals that eventually dominate the individual's life. For example, a man whose idealized self is a highly competent athlete might become obsessed with exercise and weight-lifting. The more he tries to meet these demands of the idealized self, the more he is doomed to unhappiness, because the idealized self is virtually insatiable in demanding perfection.

Karen Horney believed that Freud overemphasized the role of sexual instincts. She focused more on the self-concept.

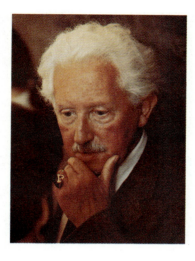

Erik Erikson was heavily influenced by the work of the Freuds after meeting Anna Freud. Before World War II, he moved to the United States, and his travels throughout the country gave his psychoanalytic approach a distinctly cross-cultural flavor.

■ *Erikson*

Erik Erikson (1902–), like Adler and Horney, gave considerable emphasis to society's influence on the devel-

opment of the psyche. However, Erikson's theory is strongly grounded in Freudian psychoanalysis, particularly in its focus on unconscious roots of personality and psychological disorder (Roazen, 1976). Further, Erikson specifically discussed personality development throughout life.

Based on observations of families in various cultures, Erikson (1963) proposed that development proceeds throughout the life span in a series of eight "crises" (see Figure 4–1). Each "crisis" is really a critical period during which the individual is maximally vulnerable to two opposing forces: one that pulls the individual to healthy age-specific ego-functioning, and another that pulls the individual to unhealthy functioning. Depending on how the crisis is resolved, the individual's ego will acquire a new "strength" unique to that stage. When the forces of a particular crisis pull the individual toward unhealthy resolution of that issue, the stage is set for the development of subsequent problems. Crisis resolutions have a cumulative effect—if one stage is unfavorably resolved, it becomes more likely that succeeding stages will also be unfavorably resolved. Failure to resolve the early psychosocial issues has particularly serious consequences for later development.

■ *Sullivan*

Like the other psychodynamic theorists, Harry Stack Sullivan (1892–1949) (1953a) focused on infancy as the primary formative period of personality. Sullivan believed that the actual mother–infant relationship is crucial. By observing the interaction between a mother and her baby, you can appreciate Sullivan's notion that a mother's child-rearing attitude is communicated nonverbally to the child. A mother who is calm and relaxed is able to convey her nurturance through the way she holds and feeds her baby. By contrast, a mother who is uncomfortable and anxious with her child is likely to communicate a very different sense. Sullivan believed that the baby picks up these cues from the mother, and that if the mother is generally anxious, the baby will develop a feeling of anxiety also. If this pattern is

Stage	1	2	3	4	5	6	7	8
Oral	Basic trust vs. mistrust							
Anal		Autonomy vs. shame doubt						
Genital			Initiative vs. guilt					
Latency				Industry vs. inferiority				
Puberty & adolescence					Identify achievement vs. diffusion			
Young adulthood						Intimacy vs. isolation		
Middle adulthood							Generativity vs. stagnation	
Later adulthood								Ego integrity vs. despair

Figure 4–1 The eight stages of development in Erikson's theory

According to this theory, in each stage of the life-span there is a theme or issue which the individual must resolve. However, earlier stages can reappear in later life, and later stages may appear before their "scheduled" time. When a young child must confront the death of a close relative, this experience may trigger the issue of ego integrity versus despair.

According to Sullivan, a mother's emotional state is sensed by her infant.

continually repeated, the child faces the difficulty of learning how to cope with the uncomfortable feelings of anxiety. You can see why Sullivan's theory is termed "interpersonal."

Sullivan substituted the term "problems in living" for what he felt were the more pejorative diagnostic labels used to describe psychological disorders (Sullivan, 1953b). Reflecting his emphasis on interpersonal relationships, Sullivan believed that problems in living are the result of the individual's feeling of anxiety in relating to parent figures. These feelings of anxiety interfere with the child's ability to develop appropriate forms of communicating with other people and leads to disturbances in thought and language.

Sullivan's position that people with schizophrenia can respond to psychotherapy was considered a breakthrough in the treatment of this disorder. The concept of the psychiatric ward of a hospital as a "therapeutic community," which was discussed in Chapter 1, was Sullivan's idea (Chapman, 1976).

■ Object relations theories

Rejecting Freud's belief that instinctual desires for sexual and aggressive release of tension are the sole basis for the formation of personality, a group of "object relations" theorists proposed instead that interpersonal relationships lie at the core of personality (Greenberg & Mitchell, 1983). These theorists believed that the unconscious mind is peopled with images of the parents and of the child's relationships to the parents. These internalized images remain at the foundation of personality throughout life. This perspective is called **object relations** because Freud used the term "object" to refer to anyone or anything that is the object of an individual's instinctual desires.

Compared with Freud, the object relations theorists placed far greater emphasis on the early mother–child relationship. The Oedipal complex was considered to have less of an impact on the child's development than the interactions with the parents in the first months and years of life. Some object relations theorists went so far as to make the attachment relationship of the child to the mother the central focus of their theories, a position similar to that proposed by Sullivan. In their focus on early attachments, these theorists moved substantially away from Freud's emphasis on instinctual desires as the driving force behind personality dynamics (Eagle, 1984).

Object relations theorists propose that various forms of psychological disorder arise from defects in the individual's sense of self. Some disorders are caused by a failure to form an integrated self early in life. A neglected child whose mother does not provide enough emotional support and physical care will lack a sense of security that comes from feeling loved. Conversely, a child who is smothered with affection by a mother who is overly involved in the child's life will fail to develop a sense of self that is separate from the mother's. An overinvolved parent impedes the child's necessary tests of personal independence and autonomy. Other

Melanie Klein was a key object relations theorist. Her work quickly became the source of bitter controversy between her advocates and the more traditional Freudians.

disorders may occur when a parent's lack of **empathy**, or sharing of the child's perspective, and failure to mirror back or take pride in the child's achievements cause the individual to develop unhealthy needs for attention.

One prominent object relations theorists, Melanie Klein, (1882–1960) developed ideas and therapy techniques that are still regarded as radical departures from standard psychoanalytic theory and practice. Proponents of her version of object relations theory believe that her unique perspective offers insights not attainable through more conventional modes of understanding personality and psychopathology.

Klein's major contribution was the idea that the infant has an active fantasy life built around the parents (Klein, 1964). The infant conjures up images of the mother as good when she is nurturing the infant, and as bad when she fails to satisfy the infant's immediate needs. Eventually, the infant must form an integrated view of the mother that incorporates both her nurturing and depriving aspects. The infant's self-image develops in relation to these feelings toward the mother.

D. W. Winnicott (1896–1971), a British pediatrician and psychiatrist, was given psychoanalytic training by Melanie Klein. Winnicott (1971) continued the tradition begun by Anna Freud and Melanie Klein of basing his ideas about personality on observations and work with young children. One of Winnicott's most astute observations was that possessions such as teddy bears and security blankets play a crucial role in development. Winnicott called these possessions "transitional objects" and suggested that they help the child form a sense of self separate from the mother.

Like Klein and Winnicott, Heinz Kohut (1913–1981) believed it was important for a child to be given enough independence to develop a separate sense of self in childhood. In addition, Kohut believed that it is important for parents to communicate to the child their pride in the child's accomplishments. Even a minor success that brings pleasure and approval from a parent can help a child to develop what Kohut considered to be a healthy degree of "narcissism," or self-love. Kohut felt that this quality forms the basis for an individual's later sense of self-esteem and self-worth. In Kohut's view, a disturbed sense of self accounts for most forms of psychological disorder (Kohut, 1971).

Integrating the work of these theorists with systematic observations of infants and young children, Margaret Mahler (1897–1985) and her co-workers sketched out a timetable for the emergence of phases in the development of object relations (Mahler et al., 1975). Mahler, a psychoanalyst who began her career as a pediatrician, became interested in the development of object relations in her observations of mothers with their children.

According to Mahler, beginning in the fourth month of life the infant must begin to grow away from the mother and become a separate individual with a unique identity. This "separation-individuation" phase begins with an early and tentative exploration by infants of their surroundings, followed by further movement away from the mother's direct presence, with the father becoming an important figure in the child's life (Mahler & McDevitt, 1982). If you have ever watched a toddler in a store wander away from his or her parents, you are familiar with this kind of exploratory behavior. However, this exploratory phase is replaced within the last few months of the second year by the "rapprochement" phase (a French term for a coming together). The toddler, having practiced autonomy, now begins to experience conflict over wanting to be with the mother but at the same time fearing that the mother will take over his or her life. In order for this conflict to be successfully negotiated, the child must achieve a rapprochement between the two counteracting tendencies. The mother must be available to the child for support but not overly intrusive or inhibiting of the child's needs to establish a sense of independence.

During the final subphase of separation-individuation, beginning at about the third year of life, the child begins to develop a symbolic representation of the mother and other important figures. These representations serve as internalized substitutes for the actual people. The child need not have the mother physically present in order to feel a sense of security because the mental image of the mother is there to serve as a source of comfort and approval. This experience continues throughout life as the individual continues to develop a sense of identity. Later theorists working in Mahler's tradition have hypothesized that the period of adolescence, in which the individual attempts to move from the relative dependence of childhood to the independent status of adulthood, involves a renegotiation of the balance established during the separation-individuation phase (Blos, 1967; Hoffman, 1984).

Psychological disturbance, according to Mahler's theory, can result from problems arising at any of these phases of development. Particularly important are deviations from the ideal pattern during the rapprochement phase, when the mother's ability to find the right balance between dependence and independence becomes crucial. Every mother can err by going too far in one direction or the other at various times, but when these deviations become extreme, the child may develop a psychotic disorder or a severe disturbance in the sense of self (Mahler, 1971; Mahler & Gosliner, 1955).

Treatment

The main goal of traditional psychoanalytic treatment as developed by Freud (1913–1915, 1963) is to bring repressed unconscious material into conscious awareness. This is done through the use of free association and dream analysis to access repressed material in the unconscious. In **free association**, the client is instructed by the clinician to speak freely in therapy, saying whatever comes to mind.

This is the couch used by Freud in his consulting room in the Vienna apartment where he invented psychoanalysis.

Dream analysis involves asking the client to tell the clinician the events of a dream and to free associate to these events. The clinician attempts to interpret the dream's meaning from the content of the dream itself and from the associations the client makes to the dream. These methods of accessing the unconscious mind were best accomplished, according to Freud, by having the client recline on a couch, in as relaxed a state as possible.

The psychoanalytic process is stimulated by what Freud called **transference.** For therapy to be effective, the client should be stimulated to relive conflictual relationships with parents by transferring feelings about them onto the clinician. The transference was best promoted by the clinician's maintaining an attitude of **neutrality,** meaning that the clinician did not provide any information that would reveal the clinician's preferences, personal background, or reactions to the client's revelations in therapy.

Once conflictual feelings about parents are aroused through the evoking of transference feelings, the clinician can begin the difficult process of **working through,** in which the client is helped to achieve a healthier resolution of these issues than had occurred in the client's actual early childhood environment. For example, the client might transfer onto the clinician feelings of having been neglected as a child. With these feelings brought out into the open within the therapeutic relationship, the clinician can explore with the client the reasons for feeling neglected. Over time, the client may learn that it is possible to trust a

parent figure (the clinician in this case), and this realization will help the client feel more secure in relationships outside therapy.

The progress of therapy, however, is often impeded by the client's **resistance,** or holding back within the therapy. It is a painful and difficult process for the client to confront unconscious fears and desires, and clients may forget important material, refuse to free associate, or stop therapy altogether as a protection from the anxiety associated with this process. An important part of the clinician's job is to help the client overcome resistance through the process of interpretation. For example, a client may consistently arrive late for therapy appointments. The clinician would try to help the client realize that this behavior reflects an unconscious desire to avoid anxiety.

Although psychoanalysts who broke with the Freudian tradition developed their own theories of personality, their methods of therapy nevertheless relied heavily on Freud's principles of encouraging the client to explore unconscious personality dynamics. Jung's theory, which emphasizes imbalance between conscious and unconscious elements of personality as the cause of psychological disorder, led him to propose methods of therapy that involved strengthening the weaker, repressed tendencies in the unconscious mind.

The psychodynamic approach offered by Adler focuses in the opposite direction from that of Jung, namely, to work more on the individual's conscious experience of the self and help the individual develop a more productive "style of

A Jungian clinician interprets dream symbols as archetypal themes seeking expression in consciousness. For example, a person who consciously feels a sense of fragmentation or "falling apart" may dream of a round object with spokes such as this amusement park ride, symbolizing the client's search for a unified self.

life." The clinician develops a collaboration with the client, a partnership that is intended to help foster the client's interest in other people. Together with the client, the clinician examines the client's feelings of inferiority and tries to reframe the client's interpretations of experiences in a way that enhances the client's sense of inner confidence. At the same time, the clinician looks at the client's excuses and other attempts to maintain an unrealistic sense of superiority, and helps the client to be more accepting of the actual self, with all its flaws.

Horney's approach to therapy involves more explicit attempts to help the individual regain lost connections to the true, inner self. Therapy would involve having the client begin to explore the unrealistic demands involved in meeting the idealized self's expectations. At the same time, as in the Adlerian approach, the client would be encouraged to gain more confidence in the true, though flawed, self. Slowly, the client would drop the "shoulds" and live according to a more realistic set of goals based on personal interest and capacities.

Erikson's approach to treatment is closer to Freud's than are the methods used by the other ego psychologists. Nevertheless, Erikson's analytic treatment is distinguished from Freud's in its emphasis on social factors in childhood and the potential for development throughout life. Erikson analyzes the individual's situation from the perspective of the psychosocial issue that is most important at the time and attempts to discover the factors impeding the individual's successful resolution of that issue.

In psychotherapy, Sullivan tried to help people overcome interpersonal problems through developing better communication. The clinician, referred to by Sullivan as a "participant observer," actively tries to correct the client's ineffective patterns of interactions with others. Sullivan believed that all clients, no matter how disturbed, had the capacity to solve their "problems in living" with the help of a concerned clinician. Furthermore, the clinician could build up the client's sense of security so that the client feels less threatened by rejection from others who are emotionally significant in the client's life.

According to object relations theorists, the purpose of therapy is to reverse the destructive processes that occurred in the client's early life through providing a new kind of relationship. The clinician attempts to restore, through good "parenting," the client's sense of self and control over the boundaries that define the self. Empathy is another crucial ingredient of the therapeutic relationship, according to Kohut, because it helps the client to feel that the clinician

According to Adler and Horney, people who push themselves too hard are attempting to overcome feelings of weakness and inadequacy.

appreciates and accepts the client as an individual (Kohut, 1984).

Returning to the case of Kristin, a clinician working from a psychodynamic perspective would assume that her difficulties stem from conflicts in early life. Pulling apart the elements of Kristin's case, you can see which themes would be of importance to each of the theorists we have covered. Freud would focus on Kristin's unconscious guilt over feelings of anger toward her father for abandoning her by his death (Freud, 1917). Interpretation of Kristin's resistance to confronting her feelings of grief would also be important. Jung would attempt to overcome Kristin's conscious unwillingness to speak about her father's death by exploring the symbolic meaning of archetypal images in Kristin's dreams. Adler would suggest that perhaps it is time for Kristin to move on to use her talents and her education in a more productive way and to try to establish new friendships. Kristin's physical ailments and even her grief over her father might be seen as excuses that keep Kristin from taking the risk of getting involved in a more challenging career or in a romantic relationship.

Horney would help Kristin realize that part of her unhappiness is due to her following various "shoulds": she "should" have a higher salary, she "should" be involved in a steady relationship, she "should" have recovered from her father's death. By accepting the reality of her situation, Kristin can become more comfortable with who she really is. Erikson would approach Kristin's depression as due to unresolved identity and intimacy issues.

Any one of the object relations theorists would focus on Kristin's early relationships to her parents, both as these relationships were perceived then and as they are perceived now. It would appear that Kristin's mother paid little attention to her, and although Kristin's father was a strong, positive figure in her life, Kristin was deprived of an early

attachment to her mother. This lack of attachment could be at the foundation of Kristin's weak sense of identity and direction in life, leading to her unhappiness. In therapy, having a stronger sense of attachment to an important figure in her life could, over time, help Kristin build a more secure image of herself.

Contributions of Psychodynamic Theories

The psychodynamic perspective, almost 100 years old, is still evolving today. Clinicians, researchers, and theorists continue to debate basic issues such as the role of instincts in shaping the unconscious mind and personality dynamics, the influence of early childhood on later adult functioning, and the role of the clinician in promoting psychological change. The debate centers around several fundamental issues, and although these issues are not likely to be resolved in the near future, the writings and research stimulated by this debate have helped to refine and clarify some of Freud's most important teachings.

Freud is often given credit for having developed the first comprehensive psychological theory and the first systematic approach to psychotherapy. Although trained in neurology, Freud discovered early in his career that physical symptoms could have psychological causes, and these discoveries formed the cornerstone of a revolutionary approach to understanding the nature and treatment of psychological disorders. Freud can also be credited for introducing into popular culture important psychological concepts that have given people insights into their behavior and have changed the way that Western society views itself.

Just as Freud's theory led to radical alterations in the way psychological disorder was conceptualized, it also led to intense debates in academic circles regarding its scientific

Freud's theory pointed out the many neurotic aspects of contemporary society that cause us to experience inner conflict.

validity. Perhaps the most serious charge levied against psychoanalysis is that its major premises are so difficult to test through empirical research. Although researchers have made efforts to translate some of Freud's ideas about the unconscious mind into experimental studies (Erdelyi, 1985; Fisher & Greenberg, 1977; Masling, 1983, 1985; see also Research Focus), these attempts have been relatively few in number and the majority of concepts have little hard data to back them up. Furthermore, on logical grounds, Freud's theory contains many assumptions that are difficult to disprove. If you challenge the Freudian position that anxiety over sexual impulses lies at the root of defense mechanisms, you might be told by a Freudian that it is your own anxiety over sexuality that keeps you from acknowledging the role of sexuality in personality.

Other criticisms of psychodynamic theory have concerned the way that women were characterized by Freud, who explained the psychology of women in terms of **penis envy.** Following the dictum that "anatomy is destiny," Freud maintained that their lack of a penis leads women to spend their lives feeling as though their bodies are incomplete. The only way to compensate for this lack is, according to Freud, to have a baby. Feminists have argued strongly against Freud's teachings about women, a position articulated by Horney during Freud's lifetime, and carried further by contemporary feminist critics (Cantor & Bernay, 1988; Chodorow, 1978; Dinnerstein, 1976; Mitchell, 1974; Sayers, 1991).

Another related and very controversial line of criticism concerns Freud's position regarding the extent to which the women he treated for hysteria actually experienced childhood trauma. Originally, Freud proposed that hysterical symptoms in women (paralysis, deafness, blindness, and miscellaneous abnormalities having no physical basis) were consequences of their having been traumatized as children by men who seduced or raped them. According to the "seduction hypothesis," a woman's hysterical symptoms developed when, as an adult, she found her sexual feelings to be unacceptable and frightening. However, Freud soon abandoned the seduction hypothesis, claiming instead that the traumatic childhood experiences reported by his women clients were products of their imagination, nothing but mere childhood fantasy. Critics charge that Freud's change of position was motivated by political, not scientific reasons and that he discounted the very real pain experienced by women who have been victims of sexual abuse (Masson, 1985). Indeed, current research on the causes of psychological disorders similar to those originally described by Freud as caused by childhood sexual trauma, is beginning to suggest that the original seduction hypothesis held some validity (Wilbur & Kluft, 1989).

In broadening the scope of psychodynamic theory to include the relationship between the individual and society, the post-Freudians set the stage for many later theorists and researchers to explore the role of cognitive processes, interpersonal relationships, and social context in the development of personality and psychological disorder. Many post-Freudian ideas have become prominent features of contemporary psychology, such as sibling rivalry (Adler), inferiority complex (Adler), identity crisis (Erikson), alienation (Horney), archetypes (Jung), personality types (Jung), and mother–child attachment (object relations theorists). Further, their approach to therapy expanded the role of clinicians beyond that of the neutral screen advocated by Freud. These theorists have been instrumental in altering the structure of therapy as well, allowing for the development of therapy models that require less time than traditional psychoanalysis because they focus on specific issues or difficulties that are more accessible to conscious awareness. Later theorists were also influenced by the more optimistic post-Freudian belief that humans by nature are social, cooperative, productive, and rational rather than destructive and oriented toward fulfillment of sexual drives.

As with traditional Freudian psychoanalysis, though, critics have charged that post-Freudian theories are difficult to test empirically and are based largely on biased clinical evidence derived from clients seeking psychoanalysis. Although the theories as a whole did not have an empirical base, later researchers have picked up many important themes and have tested various propositions related to personality and psychological disorder.

A large number of research studies have tested the hypotheses of Erikson, Adler, and the object relations theorists. Erikson's theory regarding the existence of psychosocial stages and their relationship to each other through development has been tested extensively on various age groups, including college students (Waterman, 1982), young adults (Whitbourne & Tesch, 1985), middle-aged adults (Vaillant & Milofsky, 1980; Whitbourne et al., 1992), and the elderly (Walaskay et al., 1983–1984). Adler's propositions about the influence of self-perceptions have been incorporated into the larger body of literature on self-concept and cognitive psychology (Shulman, 1985).

A great deal of research on object relations theories has accumulated since the 1970s, much of it on the social behavior of infants and young children. Advances in this line of research were made by psychologist Mary Ainsworth and her associates (Ainsworth et al., 1978), who developed the innovative "Strange Situation Test" to study attachment behavior in young children. In this test, infants are exposed to a series of eight situations intended to increase the amount of stress they experience when approached by an adult stranger and when their mother leaves them. On the basis of the infant's reaction to these situations, he or she is classified in terms of an **attachment style,** or way of relating to a caregiver figure. For example, in one situation, the infant's mother leaves the room and then returns a few minutes later. The infant's reaction to the mother's return would be rated for attachment style. A securely attached infant shows some distress when the mother leaves the room but greets her happily when she returns. In contrast, an insecurely attached child shows an ambivalent or resistant reaction to the mother or avoids her when she returns. Follow-up studies of infants studied in the Strange

In this child development study, a researcher tests her theories by observing a child at play.

Situation Test into their early childhood years (Arend et al., 1979; Sroufe et al., 1983; Waters et al., 1979) and even into adulthood (Skolnick, 1986) have yielded support for the idea that infant attachment style plays a major role in influencing competence in school and in social relationships.

On the critical side, extensive research and review of the child development literature led psychiatrist Daniel Stern to challenge Mahler's claim that there are distinct stages in the separation-individuation process (Stern, 1985). Stern maintains that attachment, trust, and dependency remain critical issues throughout life. Consistent with the views of object relations theorists, Stern agrees that psychological disorder follows from difficulties in early development, and that treatment involves a reconstruction of past childhood experiences.

From the start, psychoanalysis aroused bitter criticism for being unscientifically-based, expensive, and unduly long. Much of the data collected to test its effectiveness was obtained through the case study method without rigorous experimental controls. In many instances, the researcher was also the psychoanalyst, who naturally, would be biased toward proving that the treatment cured the client. Further, when supportive data are obtained in such a study, their validity is suspect because the client is influenced by the therapist's expectations for the success of the treatment. Jungian clients have archetypal dreams; Freudian clients have Oedipal dreams; Eriksonian clients talk of identity crises; and Adlerian clients speak of their inferiority complexes. The clinician's suggestions all too easily influence the client toward producing supportive evidence.

These criticisms of traditional psychoanalysis culminated in a major attack on the profession by H. J. Eysenck

(1952), further eroding the view of psychoanalysis as a scientifically respectable method of treatment. New interest in psychoanalysis has occurred, however, since the late 1970s. Several trends have contributed to this rebirth. One is the growing interest by historians and literary scholars in the political and social conditions that gave rise to psychoanalysis. A number of recent biographies on Freud and the other psychoanalysts have appeared, as well as historical analyses of Viennese life in the early part of the twentieth century. These accounts have shed light on the factors that influenced early psychoanalysts in the development of their theories and approaches to therapy. Psychoanalysis is now increasingly seen as a product of a certain time and place in Western society's development. As an approach to psychological disorder, it must be updated and translated into contemporary terms. Part of this process involves reexamining the myths surrounding Freud's life and uncovering the very human limitations that interfered with his attempts to unlock the secrets of the unconscious mind.

The updating of psychoanalysis is taking place along two fronts. The first involves efforts to develop brief forms of treatment that, while relying on interpretation of transference relationships, focus the therapy more intensely on circumscribed issues of current concern to the client (Luborsky, 1984; Malan, 1979; Sifneos, 1979, 1981). Instead of trying to reconstruct the client's personality, the clinician helps the client overcome disappointment in a romantic relationship or at work, or the stress of adjusting to a major life change such as parenthood. A client may receive treatment for a prearranged period of three to four months of weekly therapy. At the end of this period, the client uses the strengths gained in treatment to attempt to cope independently with the life stress or issue. Therapy may again be sought later when new circumstances arise or the gains from therapy have eroded. Brief psychotherapy is gaining acceptance not only for practical reasons of less time and expense, but also because of its demonstrated effectiveness (Crits-Cristoph, 1992; Koss & Butcher, 1986).

Along with the greater focus on specific problems permitted by brief therapy, it is also easier to test its effectiveness with controlled studies. The criteria for successful therapy can be predetermined, and progress in therapy can be weighed against these criteria. For example, researchers at the Mt. Zion Hospital in San Francisco have developed an elaborate scheme for testing the effectiveness of therapeutic interventions by having objective raters evaluate psychotherapy transcripts using pre-set categories to measure gains or losses (Weiss & Samson, 1986).

The second new focus of current psychodynamic approaches is the testing of specific hypotheses generated by object relations theory. Kohut, Klein, Winnicott, Mahler, and other theorists working in the object relations tradition generated ideas that many contemporary psychoanalysts have translated into specific hypotheses regarding personality disorders (e.g., Nigg et al., 1992). As we examine these disorders in Chapter 6, you will see that the object relations theories strongly influenced the development of the diagnostic categories themselves and the exploration of ways to understand and treat these disorders. A large part of this effort has involved systematic research and attempts to develop psychometrically sound measures of personality disorders.

Those who maintain the psychodynamic tradition are encouraged by the increasing willingness of researchers and clinicians to make their data available for scrutiny by the scientific community. Although the central concepts of psychodynamic theory will perhaps forever remain elusive and abstract, there are signs that a new generation of researchers is willing to take on the challenge.

HUMANISTIC PERSPECTIVE

The core of the humanistic perspective is the belief that human motivation is based on an inherent tendency to strive for self-fulfillment and meaning in life. According to **humanistic** theories of personality, people are motivated by the need to understand themselves and the world and to derive greater enrichment from their experiences by fulfilling their unique individual potential.

The work of humanistic theorists was heavily influenced by **existential** psychology, a theoretical position that emphasizes the importance of fully appreciating each moment as it occurs (May, 1983). According to existential psychology, people who are tuned into the world around them and experience life as fully as possible in each moment are psychologically healthy. Psychological disorder arises when people are unable to experience this kind of living "in the moment." According to this view, it is not a fundamental flaw in human nature that causes psychological disorder; people become disturbed because they must live within the restrictions on human freedom imposed by modern society (Frankl, 1963; Laing, 1959). Take the case of a woman with artistic talent who feels "stuck" in a menial job, and because of economic limitations is unable to take the time to fulfill her real interest. Her days are spent in drudgery rather than the excitement and exhilaration she would feel if she were able to be artistically creative. The type of enjoyment the existentialists speak of also includes smaller, but nevertheless rewarding, opportunities to enjoy simple pleasures such as a walk through the countryside or an intimate talk with a good friend.

By the mid-twentieth century, psychologists who were disenchanted with the major theoretical approaches to understanding human behavior and psychological disorder believed that psychology had lost its contact with the "human" side of human behavior. These humanists joined together to form the "third force" in psychology with the intention of challenging psychoanalysis and behaviorism. Two of the most prominent theorists within this tradition are Carl Rogers and Abraham Maslow.

Person-Centered Approach

Carl Rogers (1902–1987) developed the *person-centered approach* because he felt that psychoanalysis and behaviorism were overly deterministic in their emphasis on forces outside the individual's control that influence behavior and personality. Rogers' approach to therapy and personality focuses on the uniqueness of each individual, the importance of allowing each individual to achieve maximum fulfillment of potential, and the need for the individual to confront honestly the reality of his or her experiences in the world. Rogers (1951) used the term **client-centered** to describe this approach to therapy, reflecting his belief that people are innately good and that the potential for self-improvement lies within the client.

A central feature of Rogers' theory (1961, 1964) is the idea that in order to be well-adjusted, a person's self-image

Carl R. Rogers changed his career goals from ministry to psychology, maintaining a commitment to seeing the "good" in people. In reflecting on his career, Rogers observed that his interest in scientific rigor balanced his more subjective experiences as a clinician.

According to Rogers, when a parent constantly communicates the message that the child must be "good" to be loved, the child becomes insecure and anxious.

should match, or have **congruence** with, the person's experiences. When this happens, a person is said to be **fully-functioning**, with an accurate view of the self and experiences. The term "fully" implies that the individual is putting psychological resources to their maximal use. Conversely, psychological disorder is the result of a blocking of one's potential for living to full capacity, resulting in a state of **incongruence**—a mismatch between a person's self-perception and reality.

As an example of incongruence, consider people you have known whose self-image did not fit with the way others perceived them. Take the example of a high school boy who considers himself unpopular but fails to recognize that he is liked by most of his classmates. According to Rogers, this boy's views of himself are "incongruent" with the reality of his situation. By telling himself that he is unpopular, he keeps from his awareness the fact that other people try to approach him in an effort to be friendly. You can see how a situation such as this would lead to problems over time because of his distorted perceptions of reality. These distortions cause him to interact with others in ways that lead to frustration rather than happiness.

Rogers regarded the fully-functioning person as being in a process of continual evolution and movement rather than in a static or fixed place. The way in which people develop these qualities has been an important focus of Rogers' theory (1959) and is the basis for the application of this theory in schools, parent education, and counseling. According to Rogers, psychological disorder develops in an individual who, as a child, was subjected to parents who were too critical and demanding. Their criticism made the child feel overly anxious about doing things of which they did not approve. In this case, they were setting up what Rogers

referred to as **conditions of worth**, or conditions in which the child received love only when certain demands were fulfilled. The parents in effect tell the child, "If you want us to love you, you have to meet our conditions. That is the only way we will treat you as a worthy person." Under conditions of worth, children become so fearful of being punished that they cannot admit to having done something "wrong," and the stage is set for a lifetime of low self-esteem.

Self-Actualization Theory

Related to Rogers' views of the fully-functioning person is the theory developed by Abraham Maslow (1962) which centers on the notion of **self-actualization**, the maximum realization of the individual's potential for psychological growth. It is perhaps because of this focus on healthy human functioning that Maslow's theory has gained popularity as a guide to optimal living in such contexts as personnel management and human resources. Maslow's theory also focuses on motivation, in that he wanted to draw attention to the experiences that propel people toward realizing their fullest potential.

According to Maslow, self-actualized people are accurate in their self-perceptions, and are able to find rich sources of enjoyment and stimulation in their everyday activities. They are capable of **peak experiences** in which they feel a tremendous surge of inner happiness, as if they are totally in harmony with themselves and their world. But these individuals are not simply searching for sensual or spiritual pleasure. They also have a philosophy of life that is based on humanitarian and egalitarian values.

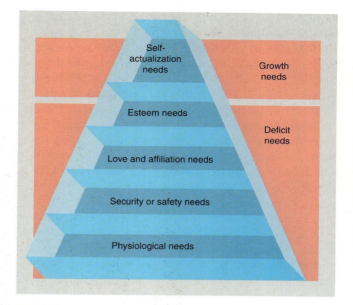

Figure 4–2 The hierarchy of needs according to Maslow's theory
In Maslow's hierarchy of needs, it is assumed that lower-order (deficit) needs must be met before the need for self-actualization can be achieved.

Maslow based his concept not on psychotherapy patients, but on the lives of extraordinary people who were extremely productive and who seemed to have reached their maximum potential. Abraham Lincoln, Harriet Tubman, Martin Luther King Jr., and Mother Theresa are examples of such self-actualized people.

Maslow's theory is best known, perhaps, for its pyramid-like structure that he called the **hierarchy of needs**, which describes the order in which human needs must be fulfilled (see Figure 4-2). The basic premise of the hierarchy is that for people to achieve a state of self-actualization, they must first have satisfied a variety of physical and psychological needs that are less uplifting than self-actualization. Needs lower on the hierarchy are called **deficit needs** because they describe a state in which the individual seeks to obtain something that is lacking. The deficit needs are, from lowest to highest on the pyramid, physiological, security or safety from harm, love and affiliation, and esteem or respect from others. An individual who is still struggling to meet those needs will not be able to progress to the top of the pyramid. For example, if you are a performer, you cannot focus your energies on putting on your best show when your stomach is rumbling with hunger. A person cannot progress to the next level of needs if a lower hierarchical need is unmet. Maslow would contend that a philosopher who is hungry is unable to philosophize.

A deficit need, once satisfied, diminishes in importance, at least until the need to satisfy it arises again. Self-actualization, by contrast, has no limit on its capacity for fulfillment. According to Maslow, the need for self-actualization feeds on itself and can continue to grow in a limitless fashion, so that even the most psychologically healthy individuals never reach a state of smug complacency about themselves. Self-actualized individuals are always looking for new areas of growth and challenge, and for ways to improve their understanding of self and the world.

Like Rogers, Maslow (1971) defined psychological disorder in terms of the degree of deviation from the ideal state of being. Self-actualization is an ideal that many people do not achieve; those who do attain self-actualization find that it usually takes many years. Maslow's views about the conditions that hamper self-actualization were similar to those of Rogers. To progress beyond the "deficit" needs, children must feel a stable sense of being physically cared for, safe from harm, loved, and esteemed. Another source of psychological problems is the suppression of the higher-level needs required to achieve actualization. For example, a person who is raised in an environment of dishonesty is deprived in satisfaction of the need for truth and as a result becomes cynical and mistrusting.

Treatment

According to Rogers' client-centered approach, therapy should focus on the needs of the client rather than be determined by the clinician. A clinician's job is to help clients discover their inherent goodness, and in the process help each client to achieve greater self-understanding.

Most adults with psychological problems, according to Rogers, were exposed to conditions of worth in childhood. To counteract the problems caused by this sort of parenting, Rogers recommended that therapists treat clients with "unconditional positive regard." This method involves total acceptance of what the client says, does, and feels. As the client's sense of being a good person grows stronger, the client becomes better able to tolerate the anxiety associated with acknowledging weaknesses. The clinician tries to be as empathic as possible and attempts to see the client's situation as it appears to the client.

Therapists working within the client-centered model often use techniques such as reflection and clarification of what the client says in therapy. In reflection, the therapist mirrors back what the client has just said, perhaps rephrasing it slightly. For example, the client might say, "I'm really down today because last week my girlfriend told me to get lost." A reflection of this statement by the therapist might take the following form: "So when your girlfriend threatens to leave you, it makes you feel sad." In clarification, the therapist provides clarity to a vague or poorly formulated statement about how the client feels. If the client says, "I'm really mad at my girlfriend for the lousy way she treated me," the therapist might say, "And perhaps you're very sad about that too."

Rogers also maintained that the clinician should provide a model of genuineness and willingness to disclose personal weaknesses and limitations. Presumably clients can learn a great deal from observing the therapist's behavior. Ideally, the client will see that it is acceptable and healthy to be honest in confronting one's experiences, even if those experiences have less than favorable implications. For example, the Rogerian clinician might admit to a client who reports feeling anxious when speaking before a group that the clinician also has such experiences. Through such self-disclosure on the part of the clinician, the client learns that having such experiences does not mean one is a bad and inadequate person.

There is no special model of psychotherapy that follows from Maslow's theory because he developed his ideas in an academic context rather than through clinical observation and treatment. His theory presents more of a map for optimal human development than a concrete basis for treatment of psychological disorders.

As an approach to treating a client like Kristin, humanistic therapists would focus on providing her with a secure sense of positive self-regard. Consistent with the Rogerian emphasis on becoming more aware of one's feelings, Kristin would be encouraged to experience more fully her feelings regarding her father's death, and to link her sadness over his passing with her sense of insecurity regarding her mother's feelings toward her. In this process, the clinician would help Kristin identify her feelings and to accept them without undue self-criticism. In keeping with the concept of therapist self-disclosure, the clinician might share with Kristin personal reactions to losses, or feelings of sadness in hearing Kristin talk about the hurt she has experienced.

Contributions of Humanistic Theories

The humanistic approach has generated a considerable body of research based on the ideas of both Rogers and Maslow. Much of this research was conducted by the originators of these theories, both of whom were interested in translating their ideas into measurable concepts.

Maslow developed his theory on the basis of case studies, gathered from 60 individuals, that involved combining biographical information about each individual's life with extensive interview data when possible. Although Maslow did not consider his own research to meet the criteria of scientific objectivity, he believed that the uniqueness of his work justified deviation from the requirements for reliability and validity of measures. His sample was purposefully limited to individuals showing signs of optimal psychological functioning, because Maslow maintained that psychology had ignored the study of healthy individuals in favor of those who suffered from various forms of psychopathology (Maslow, 1970).

Others following Maslow have attempted to translate his ideas about self-actualization into researchable terms. One of the more significant efforts was that of E. L. Shostrom (1974), who developed the *Personal Orientation Inventory (POI)* as a measure of the individual's self-actualization tendencies. The scales on the POI assess qualities that Maslow identified in self-actualizing people, such as holding certain values, being spontaneous, having positive self-regard and self-acceptance, believing that human nature is basically good, and having a capacity for close relationships with others. Examples of items from a shorter scale of self-actualization shown in Table 4-1 illustrate more clearly the qualities of self-actualized people. Low scores on this inventory would suggest that the individual is at risk for psychological distress.

In addition to stimulating systematic investigations of self-actualization, Maslow's ideas have been widely applied in industry and business as the basis for improving worker productivity and job satisfaction (e.g., Herzberg et al., 1959). The human relations movement in industry has developed around the concept that employee productivity is enhanced by satisfying self-actualization needs. It is assumed that if workers feel personally involved in what they do, they will be happier and more productive. As appealing as these ideas may sound, they have not been consistently borne out in research (Miner, 1983; Rauschenberger et al., 1980). Perhaps the problem is that Maslow's theory is too simplistic to apply to as complex a phenomenon as work motivation.

Rogers was interested in researching two central facets of the client-centered approach—people's self-concept and the therapy process. In his research on self-concept, Rogers

Table 4-1 Items from the Self-Actualization Scale

1. I do not feel ashamed of any of my emotions.
2. I feel I must do what others expect of me.
3. I believe that people are essentially good and can be trusted.
4. I feel free to be angry at those I love.
5. It is always necessary that others approve of what I do.
6. I don't accept my own weaknesses.
7. I can like people without having to approve of them.
8. I fear failure.
9. I avoid attempts to analyze and simplify complex domains.
10. It is better to be yourself than be popular.
11. I have no mission in life to which I can feel especially dedicated.
12. I can express my feelings even when they may result in undesirable consequences.
13. I do not feel responsible to help anybody.
14. I am bothered by fears of being inadequate.
15. I am loved because I give love.

High self-actualization scores result from agreeing with items 1,3,4,7,10,12, and 15, and disagreeing with the rest.

Source: Jones & Crandall, (1986)

focused on the extent to which the individual experiences an incongruence between "actual self" and "ideal self." Your actual self refers to your self-concept as you experience it; your ideal self refers to the individual you would like to be. According to Rogers, the greater the incongruence between the two, the more psychologically distressed you are. Rogers used the **Q-sort procedure** (Stephenson, 1953) in this research, a technique in which the individual sorts statements related to self-concept, such as "I am hard-working" or "I am a quiet person." In one part of this exercise the individual focuses on actual self, and in the other part on ideal self. During each part, the individual places these statements into piles according to the degree to which the statement characterizes the individual. By comparing the Q-sorts for the actual and ideal selves, the degree of incongruence can be empirically determined. The degree of incongruence can be correlated with other psychological variables such as happiness, satisfaction with life, and symptoms.

By using the Q-sort procedure, Rogers was able to turn his theoretical constructs about the experience of incongruence into measurable data. He also used the Q-sort to evaluate the effectiveness of psychotherapy as practiced through the client-centered approach. If incongruence is an unhealthy state, he reasoned, then effective psychotherapy should be able to reduce the individual's level of incongruence. This hypothesis formed the basis for a series of studies initiated by Rogers and his collaborators (Rogers & Dymond, 1954). Clients in client-centered psychotherapy were asked to perform Q-sorts at the beginning and end of therapy; these researchers did in fact find that incongruence showed a measurable decrease.

The second, much broader and more ambitious line of research concerns the therapeutic relationship, and the factors within it that contribute to successful psychotherapy. The clinician's level of empathy toward the client emerged from this research as one of the most crucial elements for successful therapy. The clinician's empathy communicates unconditional positive regard by sending the message to the client that "You are a good person." The client can feel safe, accepted, and free to explore potentially anxiety-provoking thoughts and experiences. You can probably relate to this idea from your own interactions with people. It is much easier to confide in a person who appears to like and understand you than a person who seems ready to criticize and ridicule you for your thoughts and feelings.

A number of researchers in the 1960s and 1970s, working within the client-centered tradition, were able to demonstrate the beneficial effects of therapist empathy in terms of clients' ability to engage in self-exploration and to make progress in understanding their difficulties (Bergin & Strupp, 1972; Kurtz & Grummon, 1972). Further, experienced and psychologically healthier therapists were found to be better able to offer empathy to their clients (Barrett-Lennard, 1962; Bergin & Solomon, 1970). Following from these and similar findings, programs were developed to help clinicians and paraprofessionals increase their effectiveness by becoming more empathic (Truax & Carkhuff, 1967).

The importance of empathy is widely acknowledged today by clinicians working within a variety of theoretical models (e.g., Kahn, 1991). The training of empathic communication styles has become integrated into current models of self-help, counseling, and advising programs. However, the research on the effectiveness of client-centered therapy has not gone without criticism. Lacking from this research are some of the fundamental requirements for a scientific approach. The research is flawed by failure to use appropriate control groups, to adopt acceptable levels of statistical significance in evaluating outcome, and to reduce the demand upon subjects to conform to the expectations of the researcher, who is often the therapist (Prochaska, 1982). Although advocates of the client-centered model are open to the importance of research, they have not been particularly successful at ensuring that their work is scientifically rigorous.

Limitations also exist in the way that Rogers and Maslow applied their theories to psychological disorder. In both research and treatment, the humanistic perspective relies heavily on the individual's self-report of psychological functioning. But what about psychological disorders that do not involve subjective distress? A related issue is the deemphasis by humanistic theorists on unconscious processes. Even those who do not fully accept the psychodynamic model generally agree that people are often unaware of some of the factors influencing their behavior.

With regard to therapy, the humanistic approach seems best suited for a relatively narrow range of clients, who are motivated to focus on their subjective experience and who are able to discuss their emotional concerns in

SUBLIMINAL ACTIVATION

A program of research carried out over the past 25 years by psychologist Lloyd Silverman began with the ambitious goal of translating Freud's ideas about the unconscious into experimental laboratory data (Silverman & Silverman, 1964). Silverman's investigations have focused on one of the main tenets of psychoanalytic theory: that psychological disorder follows from unconscious conflict over unacceptable sexual and agressive impulses. To test the hypothesis that such conflict underlies psychological symptoms, Silverman used a technique called *subliminal psychodynamic activation.* This procedure was intended to stimulate unacceptable wishes of the id, below the level of conscious awareness. Once these wishes are stimulated, the individual's behavior can be observed and inferences made about the connection between these unconscious wishes and forms of pathological reactions.

Silverman's method involves placing stimuli in front of a *tachistoscope,* a machine that presents visual images at a rapid rate on the order of several milliseconds per view. Two kinds of images are presented to subjects in Silverman's experiments.

One kind is the control set, consisting of neutral words or pictures that have no particular psychological meaning in this context, such as a picture of a tree or the words "PEOPLE THINKING." The second, experimental set, is used to stimulate unconscious libidinal processes. The experimental set consists of words or pictures having aggressive, sexual, or fantasy content, such as a man stabbing a woman or the words "DESTROY MOTHER." These two kinds of stimuli are presented in varying orders (although a baseline control stimulus is always given first) and the subject is asked to describe each stimulus as it is presented.

The measure of psychodynamic activation is derived from the difference between response times for the control stimuli and the experimental stimuli. The effect of psychodynamic activation on behavior or symptoms is then observed, such as the expression of psychopathological symptoms in men with schizophrenia. Silverman has investigated the effects of activating pathology-inducing unconscious wishes in a wide range of psychologically disturbed individuals, and in many cases has achieved the expected results (Bornstein, 1990; Silverman, 1976).

In early studies using the subliminal psychodynamic activation method, Silverman tested specific psychoanalytic hypotheses regarding the causes of particular behaviors, such as the now outdated hypothesis that homosexuality is caused by an early experience of incest. In this experiment (Silverman et al., 1973), two groups of male homosexuals were exposed to subliminal messages intended to activate conflict over incestuous wishes. Self-report ratings made after this activation of conflict showed an increase in homosexual feelings and a decrease in heterosexual feelings.

In other research, Silverman and his colleagues manipulated subliminal activation conditions to

continued

---

detail. There is little question that empathy on the part of the therapist is an important ingredient in successful therapy. However, there is some risk that the expression of empathy, in the forms suggested by Rogers and his colleagues, might sound trite to clients today. There are many instances in movies and television in which such "feeling"-oriented talk is parodied in portrayals of psychotherapy. It might be difficult for clients in today's society to accept empathic statements as genuine if they have heard stereotyped versions of them in humorous contexts.

The proponents of humanistic theories saw their ideas as a radical departure from the traditional focus of psychology, which minimized the role of free will in human experience. These theorists also saw human behavior in much more positive terms and viewed psychopathology as the result of restricted growth potential. It is clear today that although humanistic theories have limitations and do not play a central role in the understanding of psychological disorder, their influence has been widespread and is felt in many indirect ways.

SUMMARY

1. Theories have the purpose of organizing the way that information is organized about personality and psychological disorder, although in practice most psychologists rely on more than one theoretical perspective.

2. The psychodynamic perspective emphasizes the unconscious determinants of behavior. Freud's psychoanalytic theory was the first organized personality theory, describing a hypothetical structure of personality and

show that relevant messages could arouse specific reactions in different groups of individuals. In this study, people with diagnoses of depression responded as predicted with heightened depression to subliminal messages concerning aggression but not to subliminal messages concerning incest (Silverman et al., 1976). Silverman's claims regarding the subliminal activation method have gone further than showing that activation of unconscious wishes could increase pathological behaviors or reactions. Subliminal messages could also alleviate distress. By subliminally presenting the phrase "MOMMY AND I ARE ONE," Silverman and his colleagues have reported that many types of psychological symptoms and troublesome behaviors could be alleviated, from cigarette smoking to the fear of insects. Silverman had theorized that this phrase would have wide-ranging therapeutic effects because it stimulates the universal unconscious fantasy for merger or oneness with another (Silverman & Weinberger, 1985).

Although Silverman's procedure is fascinating and would seem to have unlimited potential for testing Freud's many ideas, you can probably imagine that such a controversial approach would not go uncriticized. A comprehensive review of Silverman's research appeared in the *American Psychologist* in 1988 (Balay & Shevrin, 1988), challenging Silverman's claims regarding the technique's validity and disputing the value of the technique as a test of psychoanalytic theory. Some of these criticisms were based on concerns over the method such as various mechanics of the tachistoscopic procedure. Perhaps the most serious charge is that the "neutral" stimuli used as controls are not really neutral. For example, in the study of homosexual men, a control stimulus was a picture of two men talking with the verbal label "PEOPLE TALKING." Later responses made by the men in the study indicated that these stimuli aroused sexual imagery. Similarly, in a study on schizophrenic individuals, who might be expected to be sensitive to stimuli with potential paranoid connotations, the supposedly neutral phrase "PEOPLE ARE TALKING" led them to the association "People are talking about me." These problems limit the conclusions that can be made based on the difference between the experimental and control conditions. Further, in the case of activating merger fantasies with the "MOMMY AND I ARE ONE" condition, the purportedly neutral stimuli have been found to have negative effects on psychological symptoms.

More theoretically based criticisms focus on whether such generic effects of activating merger fantasies can truly capture the unique experience of each individual. Freudian psychoanalysis is based on very specific interventions aimed at particular features of the individual's psychodynamic conflicts.

The subliminal activation procedure has had only limited success in supporting the idea of unconscious conflict as the root of psychological disorder. On the positive side, the method has made it possible to establish that being presented with subliminally perceived messages has some type of effect on psychological symptoms. Still remaining unanswered is the question of whether these effects have captured the essence of psychoanalysis as originally conceived by Freud.

---

ways that parts of the personality interact with one another. According to Freud, humans seek gratification of their instinctual desires, but are restricted by having incorporated society's ethical standards for behavior. Healthy individuals are able to meet their instinctual desires without violating society's standards; psychological disorder involves an imbalance among the structures of personality resulting in various symptoms and difficulties in adjusting to society's restrictions. Individuals develop psychologically through a series of stages in which the various parts of the body emerge as most sensitive to sensual pleasure. Early in this process, children experience a phase of sexually desiring their opposite-sex parent. The way in which this phase, called the *Oedipus crisis,* is resolved is a major determinant of later psychological well-being.

3. Later psychodynamic theorists have revised Freud's theory to emphasize the individual's relationship to society in general, and have focused on important others as influences on personality development and psychological disorder. Theorists such as Adler and Horney proposed that by clinging to an idealized image of the self, the individual creates the potential for psychological distress. Jung regarded an imbalance between conscious actions and repressed unconscious components of the personality as the source of disorder. Object relations theorists consider severely disturbed parent–child relationships to be the root of psychological disorder.

4. The goal of traditional psychoanalysis is to bring into conscious awareness the repressed desires buried within the unconscious mind, using techniques

such as free association, dream analysis, and analysis of transference. Revisions of Freudian therapeutic approaches have focused more on the client's self-concept, and on correcting the psychological remnants of disturbed early parent–child relationships.

5. The humanistic perspective represented by Rogers and Maslow proposes that people have an inherent drive toward maximum realization of their fullest potential. Inhibition of this drive is at the root of psychological disorder, and is the result of a childhood in which the individual was made to feel insecure about his or her self-worth. According to Maslow, people can achieve the highest state of self-fulfillment, called *self-actualization*, only if their more mundane, everyday needs for security and safety are met. Rogers proposed that self-actualization occurs when the individual is fully in contact with the reality of his or her experiences.

6. According to Rogers, the course of therapy should be set by the client, who has the potential for change and growth, rather than be dictated by the therapist's goals and objectives; hence Rogers termed his therapy "client-centered." Rogers believed that psychological change is most likely to occur if the clinician conveys empathy and concern for the client, and also appears to be genuinely honest and at an optimal level of psychological functioning.

7. Research based on the humanistic perspective of Rogers and Maslow has focused on the self-concept, the importance of empathy in promoting positive outcomes of psychotherapy, and an understanding of self-actualization. Although therapy based on the humanistic perspective is most useful for people who are attuned to their subjective experiences and do not have serious psychological disorders, the principles of empathy and communication developed by client-centered therapists have been incorporated into a wide range of therapeutic approaches.

KEY TERMS

Psychodynamic perspective: the theoretical orientation in psychology that emphasizes unconscious determinants of behavior. p. 88

Id: the structure of personality that contains the sexual and aggressive instincts. p. 89

Pleasure principle: a motivating force oriented toward the immediate and total gratification of sensual needs and desires. p. 89

Primary process thinking: a loosely associated, idiosyncratic, and distorted cognitive representation of the world. p. 89

Ego: the structure of personality that gives the individual the mental powers of judgment, memory, perception, and decision-making, enabling the individual to adapt to the realities of the external world. p. 89

Reality principle: a motivational force that leads the individual to confront the constraints of the external world. p. 89

Secondary process thinking: the kind of thinking involved in logical and rational problem-solving. p. 89

Libido: an instinctual pressure for gratification of sexual and aggressive desires. p. 89

Superego: the structure of personality that includes the conscience and the ego-ideal; incorporates societal prohibitions and exerts control over the seeking of instinctual gratification. p. 90

Ego-ideal: the individual's personal model of all that is exemplary in life. p. 90

Psyche: the Greek word for mind. p. 90

Psychodynamics (literally, *dynamics of the mind*): the processes of interaction among personality structures that lie beneath the surface of observable behavior. p. 90

Defense mechanisms: protective efforts that defend the ego against anxiety. p. 90

Repression: a defense mechanism involving motivated forgetting. p. 90

Denial: a defense mechanism in which the reality of an event that unfavorably affected the person's ego is rejected. p. 90

Isolation: a defense mechanism involving separation of feelings from actions. p. 91

Undoing: a defense mechanism in which the ego attempts to restore the individual to the state that existed before a certain need was expressed or a behavior occurred. p. 91

Displacement: a defense mechanism involving the shifting of impulses from the target of those feelings to someone or something that is more acceptable. p. 91

Reaction formation: a defense mechanism that involves transforming a feeling or desire into its opposite. p. 91

Projection: a defense mechanism that involves attributing to someone else one's own unconscious feelings. p. 91

Rationalization: a defense mechanism that involves finding a more acceptable reason to mask the potentially threatening "real" reason for a behavior. p. 91

Regression: a defense mechanism that involves reverting to behaviors that were more acceptable or more rewarding in childhood. p. 92

Sublimation: a defense mechanism involving translation of unacceptable impulses into more acceptable actions. p. 92

Fixation: arrested development at a particular stage of psychosexual development attributable to excessive or inadequate gratification at that stage. p. 92

Oral-passive or **receptive phase:** a period of psychosexual development in which the infant's pleasure comes from nursing or eating. p. 92

Oral-aggressive phase: a period of psychosexual development in which the infant's pleasure is derived from gumming and biting anything the infant can get into the mouth. p. 92

Genitality: the ability to express sexual feelings in a mature way and in appropriate contexts, reached when individual is able to "work and love". p. 93

Archetypes: images common to all human experience, presumed by Jung to make up the deepest layer of the unconscious mind. p. 94

Object relations: the unconscious representations that a person has of important people in one's life. p. 96

Empathy: a sharing of another person's perspective. p. 96

Free association: a method used in psychoanalysis in which the client is instructed by the clinician to speak freely, saying whatever comes to mind. p. 97

Dream analysis: a method used in psychoanalysis in which the client is asked to tell the clinician the events of a dream, and to free associate to these events. p. 98

Transference: the carrying over toward the therapist of feelings that the client had toward parents or other significant people in the client's life. p. 98

Neutrality: the attitude taken by the clinician of not providing any information that would reveal the clinician's preferences, personal background, or reactions to the client's revelations in therapy. p. 98

Working through: a phase of psychoanalytic treatment in which the client is helped to achieve a healthier resolution of issues than had occurred in the client's early childhood environment. p. 98

Resistance: unconscious blocking of anxiety-provoking thoughts or feelings. p. 98

Penis envy: the presumed jealousy that females have of the genitals of males. p. 101

Attachment style: the way a person relates to a caregiver figure. p. 101

Humanistic: an approach to personality and psychological disorder that regards people as motivated by the need to understand themselves and the world and to derive greater enrichment from their experiences by fulfilling their unique individual potential. p. 103

Existential: a theoretical position in psychology that emphasizes the importance of fully appreciating each moment as it occurs. p. 103

Client-centered: an approach based on the belief held by Rogers that people are innately good and the potential for self-impovement lies within the individual. p. 103

Congruence: a match between the person's self-conception and the more objective reality of a person's experiences. p. 104

Fully-functioning: a state of optimal psychological health in which the individual has an accurate view of the self and experiences. p. 104

Incongruence: a mismatch between a person's perception of self and the more objective characteristics of the self. p. 104

Conditions of worth: conditions in which the child receives love only when certain demands of the parent are fulfilled. p. 104

Self-actualization: the maximum realization of the individual's potential for psychological growth. p. 104

Peak experience: a feeling of tremendous inner happiness, and of being totally in harmony with oneself and the world. p. 104

Hierarchy of needs: according to Maslow the order in which human needs must be fulfilled. p. 105

Deficit needs: needs that represent a state in which the individual seeks to obtain something that is lacking. p. 105

Q-sort procedure: a measurement technique that involves having the individual sort into piles a number of statements potentially descriptive of the person's self-concept. p. 107

Case Report: Keith Crampton

Keith Crampton, a 22-year-old high school dropout, was referred to me by a social worker following his arrest on charges of rape. This was just one of a series of crimes, and the first one since his arrest as a juvenile that led to a long jail sentence. Most of his crimes went undetected. When I asked Keith how he felt about his past actions, he lacked any remorse over the hurt that he has caused other people. He had no interest in receiving psychotherapy, and insisted he had no psychological problems.

The records about Keith's troubled behavior go back to his childhood. As a second-grader, Keith had already developed a reputation for deceit and petty thievery. He often initiated fights with his classmates for no apparent reason. Interventions by social workers, teachers, and school psychologists seemed to have no impact on Keith's behavior. His family history was one of neglect and abuse, as well as criminal behavior on the part of his father, who also had a history of alcohol abuse. Because of the problems experienced by his parents, Keith's childhood home environment was chaotic to the point where there were no rules, discipline, or expectations.

Sarah Tobin, PhD

5

FAMILY SYSTEMS, BEHAVIORAL, AND BIOLOGICAL PERSPECTIVES

After completing her evaluation of Keith, Dr. Tobin diagnosed him as having antisocial personality disorder, which involves a chronic pattern of criminal activity, aggressiveness, deceit, and irresponsibility accompanied by lack of appreciation for the magnitude of these crimes. (You will read more about this disorder in Chapter 6.) Why do you think that Keith's behavior is so callous and malicious? Throughout this chapter, we will look at how theorists working in the family systems, behavioral, and biological perspectives would answer this question.

After reading this chapter, you should be able to:

- Describe the family systems perspectives to understanding psychological disorder.
- Understand family therapy as an approach to treating psychological disorder, and the contributions by family systems perspectives to a variety of treatment approaches.
- Outline the principles of classical and operant conditioning within the behavioral perspective.
- Describe variants of classical behavioral theory that emphasize social and cognitive processes in the acquisition of behaviors.
- Understand the basics of behavioral therapy in which psychological disorders are treated by changing the individual's behavior, and cognitive-behavioral therapy in which emotional and behavioral change is brought about by changing the individual's thoughts.
- Know the basic structures and functions of the nervous system and the role of the brain in behavior.

- Comprehend the fundamentals of genetics and genetic research as a way of understanding psychological disorders.
- Describe methods of treatment based on biological interventions.

FAMILY SYSTEMS PERSPECTIVE

Several of the perspectives discussed in Chapter 4 view experiences within the family as contributors to adult personality and psychopathology. People like Rogers, Erikson, Skinner, and even Freud theorized about the role that the family plays in influencing the child's development of self-esteem and interpersonal relationships. However, these theories focus their attention on the child as the recipient of family influences rather than as a participant in family interactions. It is surprising that most psychological theories of abnormal behavior do not really focus specifically on the formative influence of the family. Consider the example of a woman who suffers from headaches for which, after thorough physical examination, no physiological cause can be found. A psychoanalytically oriented clinician may attribute these headaches to the woman's unconscious need to punish herself due to guilt over sexual impulses. By contrast, a clinician working from a family perspective would look into what happens in the family when the woman develops a headache (Keeney & Ross, 1985).

The family perspective was developed in the late 1960s within the emerging framework of systems theory (Haley, 1976a). This perspective is based on the underlying premise that the individual's personality is inseparable from the pattern of interactions and relationships within the family; in other words, the individual is part of a system. A clinician working in a family systems perspective regards the family member with the symptoms as the **identified patient**. This term implies that the symptoms reflect not something wrong with the individual, but something wrong with the family system. The identified patient happens to be the one who expresses these underlying disturbances in the family. This person may be a child or an adult, depending on the particular characteristics of the family. Treatment for the patient may be sought by other family members, who usually are not aware that the identified patient's difficulties stem from problems within the family.

As the family perspective has evolved over the last three decades, several orientations within the approach have emerged. These are not so much separate theories as varying ways of looking at family interactions and the factors that contribute to psychological disorder. Each orientation also carries with it a particular approach to therapy, but all share the characteristic that therapy is directed at the group of family members and their interactions, or **family dynamics**, rather than toward the individual with the symptoms. The three orientations we will discuss focus on communication patterns in the family, the structure of relationships within the family, and the system of interacting relationships within the family as a whole.

Communication Patterns

The development of the family perspective was given dramatic impetus by the work of anthropologist Gregory Bateson (1904–1980), who turned to the studies of families as part of his research on communication. Bateson and his colleagues, working together in the 1950s and early 1960s at the Mental Research Institute in Palo Alto, built a theoretical model based on the assumption that communication is the fundamental key to understanding human behavior. Further, communication takes place within a system that, like a computer system, operates according to various feedback loops. By operating on one part of the system, then, other parts are also affected. In humans, communication is the medium through which such systemic interactions occur (Watzlawick et al., 1967).

Based on observations of people with schizophrenia and their families, Bateson and his co-workers inferred that these families have a particular kind of communication de-

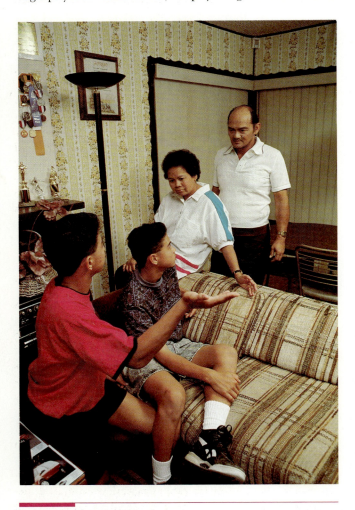

According to family systems theories, the cause of psychological disorder lies in family relationships.

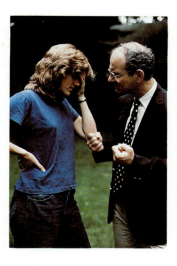

A father communicating double-bind messages to his daughter makes it difficult for her to figure out what he expects.

fect that contributes to the development of schizophrenia in the identified patient (Bateson et al., 1956). This defect results from repeated exposure to **paradoxical communication** within the family—messages that convey two contradictory meanings. For example, a mother communicates to her daughter the expectation that the daughter should be more independent. However, at the same time, the mother monitors and criticizes the daughter's every move. The daughter can never be sure whether or not her mother wants her to develop more independence. This form of communication is also called a *double bind*. The daughter is "caught" in the bind because she can never do the right thing in her mother's eyes. Ideally, children are exposed to clearer, less ambiguous messages so they can figure out what they need to do to ensure their parents' love and avoid their disapproval. When these patterns are severely disrupted, children have difficulty developing normal methods of giving and receiving communication. Although disturbed communication is no longer regarded as a tenable cause for schizophrenia, Bateson's focus on communication patterns within social groups set the stage for later family theorists to examine other forms of interaction and relationships within families, and to propose ways of introducing positive change in these systems (e.g., Watzlawick et al., 1974).

Relationship Structure

A second family systems approach focuses on the *structure* of the family as the source of difficulties. Salvador Minuchin (1922–   ) developed this theoretical approach after observing families in which the psychological disorder of one family member could be traced to deviant patterns of child and parent relationships (Minuchin, 1974, 1984). By altering these relationships, the symptoms of the identified patient could be alleviated.

The **structural approach** assumes that in normal families, parents and children have distinct roles, and there are boundaries between the generations. Parents have the roles of caring for and disciplining children, and giving them re-

sponsibility in accordance with their age. In a disturbed family, a child may take on the role of a parent and become a "caretaker" rather than the recipient of care. For example, in a family where the father is an alcoholic, the 10-year-old son may take on some of the father's responsibilities. Another problematic situation arises when a child forms an unusually close alliance with one of the parents, leaving the other parent out of the relationship.

Enmeshed families also experience problems; in these families, members are so closely involved in each other's lives that they have difficulties establishing relationships outside the family. Outsiders generally view them as eccentric. Minuchin, working with another family theorist, Jay Haley, believed that families must adapt to the developmental changes of their members, such as when children get older and leave home (Haley, 1976b, 1980). Presumably, when they fail to make these adaptations, one or more family members express the family's problems in their symptoms.

The Family as a System

A third view of the disturbed family comes from the *systemic approach* to family therapy, based on the work of therapists in Milan, Italy (Palazzoli et al., 1978). In this approach, the family is seen as an integrated system aimed at maintaining its own internal equilibrium. Families regulate their interactions so as to keep them at a stable level, much as a thermostat adjusts automatically to keep the temperature of a room constant. In a pathological family, stability is maintained at the expense of the identified patient. For example, a child who is creating problems in school may be inadvertently serving the function of keeping parents with an unhappy relationship from divorcing. As long as they have the child to worry about, their marital difficulties keep from reaching a crisis point.

Treatment

Each of the family systems approaches has developed its own approach, but all share the quality of involving in treatment as many members of the family as possible. In family therapy, the family is encouraged to try new ways of relating to each other or thinking about their problems (Hoffman, 1981). Often, the idea that the identified patient's symptoms could be the product of disturbed family interactions is a surprise, because everyone in the family assumes that the problems lie within the identified patient. This is not the last surprise that a family encounters in treatment. The therapist will probably use various measures intended to disturb and unbalance the system even further—techniques that are often unusual, even radical, departures from what most people regard as customary in therapy. In contrast to the psychoanalyst or client-centered therapist, the family therapist is usually very active.

The family therapist meets with the family, perhaps working with a co-therapist, and talks to one or more family members at a time. It is not unusual for the therapist to move around the room, sitting next to one family member for a period of time and then getting up to sit near another. These interventions may be used to draw attention to individual family members, or to establish an emotional alliance with a family member who appears to be resistant to the therapy process. At other times, the therapist may initiate a conversation between two family members and "coach" them as they talk to one another so that the family begins to see their relationship from the therapist's perspective. Often, family therapists conduct sessions in rooms with one-way mirrors so that colleagues can observe and comment with ideas and suggestions for improvements. Given their emphasis on the family as a system, family therapists work to avoid becoming so much a part of the system that they can no longer offer constructive interventions.

The family therapist often proposes ideas that on the surface may seem ridiculous, such as suggesting that the family engage in meaningless rituals together, or instructing the family to work hard to increase the level of the symptom in the identified patient. A worrying mother might, for example, be instructed to worry more during the week between sessions. In a **paradoxical intervention** such as this, when the symptoms are prescribed by the therapist, the interesting result is that the client has a more difficult time producing the symptoms spontaneously.

Returning to the case of Keith, a family therapist would focus on the dysfunctions of the family such as alcoholism and chaotic relationships. Furthermore, the therapist might interpret Keith's delinquent behavior as having served the function of keeping his parents interacting with each other. Once this pattern was established, it was difficult for Keith to break out of his pathological means of trying to keep his family together. The family therapist might try to restructure the relationships between Keith and his parents, and perhaps work with his parents on improving their relationship so that Keith would no longer be pressured to draw them together with his delinquent behavior.

Contributions of the Family Perspective

Since the late 1960s, and increasingly into the 1990s, clinicians have come to recognize the role of the family in maintaining abnormal behavior. From a critical perspective, though, the family systems approach is limited as a model for treating various psychological disorders. First, family treatment requires that the client be part of a family, or have a family who is willing to make the commitment to attend therapy sessions, conditions that cannot always be met. Second, increasing evidence on biological causes of serious psychological disorders such as schizophrenia challenge the position that such disorders could be acquired solely as the result of exposure to stressful family environ-

ments. Other factors outside the control of the family system are economic and social limitations. A family like Keith's with a delinquent child may be unable to solve the child's problems because the child is also affected by the neighborhood and community (Malcolm, 1978). Empirically, family systems approaches have been criticized on the grounds that reported studies supposedly demonstrating family therapy's effectiveness lack adequate controls, so that successful outcomes cannot be attributed to family therapy alone.

Despite these limitations, family therapy continues to be used in many clinical settings, and has proven particularly valuable in treating certain disturbances such as eating disorders (Minuchin et al., 1978; Strober & Humphrey, 1987). Furthermore, many clinicians recommend family therapy as a supplement to individual therapy. Even if the family has not played a central role in the problem, participation of family members in treatment can be valuable in supporting the individual through the difficult process of change.

BEHAVIORAL PERSPECTIVE

Behavioral psychologists resist elaborate speculations about the "whys" of behavior, preferring to look at the "whats." In looking for "what" behaviors to occur, behaviorists attempt to determine the functional relationships between events in the environment and the behaviors of the individual. Consistent with their emphasis on observable phenomena, behaviorists consider psychological disorders as behavioral responses that are controlled by the environment rather than conditions whose origins lie "within" the person. We begin with a review of the principles of classical and instrumental conditioning, principles that lie at the heart of the behavioral perspective on psychological disorder.

Classical Conditioning

The principles of classical conditioning are familiar to anyone who has ever owned a pet. When you open a can of dog food with an electric can opener, your dog might appear suddenly from another room as soon as the can opener begins to whir. The dog shows signs of eagerness well before the food is in the dish. At times when you use the electric can opener to open cans other than dog food, your dog also appears in the kitchen. On other occasions, when the dog has misbehaved, the scolding tone of your voice can result in your dog cowering and looking for a place to hide. The dog can tell by the tone of your voice that you are angry. It probably comes as no surprise to you that the same principles apply to human beings. Perhaps when you are hungry and see the "golden arches" of your favorite fast-food restaurant, you respond the way your dog does to the can opener.

The principles of classical conditioning, identified by Russian physiologist Ivan Pavlov (with white beard), are regarded today as the fundamental notions underlying a wide variety of emotional and behavioral reactions.

Or if while driving you see a police car with its lights flashing, your stomach turns and your heart races because you fear that you have been caught speeding.

Classical conditioning involves the connection between an originally neutral stimulus (electric can opener) and a naturally evoking stimulus (dog food) that produces an automatic reflexive reaction (eating readiness). This connection is formed through repeated pairings of the two kinds of stimuli. The neutral stimulus is called the **conditioned stimulus** because only after conditioning does it cause the response. The naturally evoking stimulus is called the **unconditioned stimulus**, because it produces the response before any conditioning takes place. The reflexive reaction (eating readiness), once it has become associated with the conditioned stimulus (can opener), is called the **conditioned response**. Prior to conditioning, this reflex is labeled the **unconditioned response**; in other words, no learning is necessary for a dog to jump up and down and salivate when presented with food.

You may be wondering what the connection is between salivating dogs and psychological disorder. The answer is that, according to classical conditioning principles, many emotions and behaviors are acquired through the pairing of neutral and emotion-provoking stimuli. Classical conditioning accounts for emotional reactions, such as the arousal of sexual desire when a person is exposed to a cologne worn by a previous lover, or the disgust a man feels when he sees a television advertisement for a brand of cold medicine that once made him nauseated.

As an explanation of psychological disorder, the classical conditioning paradigm accounts for the acquisition or learning through conditioning, of emotional reactions that interfere with a person's ability to carry out everyday tasks. For example, when 6-year-old Jerry is accidentally locked in a dark closet, he will probably become very upset the next time he needs something from that closet. His problem will become exacerbated through **generalization**, the expansion of learning from the original situation to one that is similar.

When Jerry enters an elevator on the following day, he responds with a level of panic similar to what he experienced in the closet, because the two stimuli (the closet and the elevator) are enclosed spaces. This kind of reaction, called **stimulus generalization**, takes place when a person responds in the same way to stimuli that share some common properties. **Discrimination** is the complementary related process in which learning becomes increasingly specific to a given situation. Discrimination would take place when the boy realizes that the elevator does not have the threatening potential of the dark, locked closet. Differentiating between two stimuli that possess similar but essentially different characteristics is called **stimulus discrimination**.

One of the best-known examples of conditioned fear was "Little Albert," an 11-month-old infant who was studied by John B. Watson (1878–1958), one of the most prominent early behaviorists. Watson and his associate, Rosalie Rayner, conducted an infamous set of experiments in which Albert was exposed to a loud noise while he petted a white rat. Their experiment represented a form of **aversive conditioning**, in which an aversive or painful stimulus (the noise) was paired with an initially neutral stimulus (the rat). Albert's conditioned fear of rats generalized to other white, furry objects.

John B. Watson is credited as the founder of behaviorism.

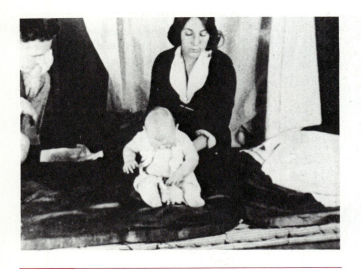

"Little Albert" was the subject of experiments conducted in the early 1900s by Watson and his associate Rosalie Raynor. No one knows what became of little Albert, but Watson's experiment is considered unethical by today's standards. © Archives of the History of American Pscychology.

This kind of experiment is now forbidden by ethical guidelines for research on human subjects. Watson's work has also been criticized on scientific grounds, in that various reports of his "experiments" on Albert would not stand up to hard scientific scrutiny by today's standards. For example, Albert acquired the response of putting his thumb in his mouth when frightened by the stimuli presented by Watson. Each time Albert did so, Watson removed the thumb. Albert's response of crying to the white furry objects may have been a reaction to having his thumb removed from his mouth rather than fear of the objects themselves (Samuelson, 1980). The conditioning of fear, then, may be more complicated than was implied by the behavioral approach of Watson.

Even though Watson's analysis may have been misguided, we can draw inferences from it regarding how people acquire irrational fears. You can probably think of instances when you were exposed to a similar kind of aversive conditioning. Perhaps you ate too much pizza and became ill shortly afterwards. The following week, when going by a pizzeria, you started to feel queasy. The pizza, previously a neutral or positive stimulus, has now acquired aversive meaning for you. This particular principle is very useful in certain forms of behavior therapy, as in the treatment of alcoholism. As you will see in Chapter 15, one form of treatment involves giving a person a drug that causes nausea when alcohol is consumed. The individual then learns to associate alcohol with nausea, and this, theoretically, should reduce the frequency of alcohol drinking.

Skinner's Model of Operant Conditioning

The term **operant conditioning** refers to a learning process in which an individual acquires a set of behaviors through reinforcement. In contrast to classical conditioning, oper-

ant conditioning involves the learning of behaviors that are not automatic. To illustrate, we will again use the example of a pet dog. Your dog not only comes running at the sound of the can opener, but also has probably learned a number of tricks or routines to gain attention or perhaps a dog biscuit. In other words, your dog "operates" on the environment to obtain certain rewards.

In operant conditioning, the learner tries to become proficient at performing behaviors that will lead to a positive outcome. Usually, the positive outcome is a reward such as attention, praise, or satisfaction of a biological need, but the "positive" outcome could also consist of the removal of an unpleasant or aversive circumstance. If your next-door neighbor's stereo is blasting, you may "operate" on the environment by making a phone call requesting that it be turned down. Your behavior results in the removal of an aversive stimulus.

The principles of operant conditioning were developed by B. F. Skinner who, along with Freud, is probably one of the most well-known names in psychology. Of course, Skinner's theory is diametrically opposed to Freud's, in its emphasis on observable behavior as the only appropriate subject matter for psychology. Like Freud, however, Skinner's ideas about behavior became the basis for a broad-ranging philosophy about human nature.

You probably learned Skinner's name in your introductory psychology class as the originator of operant conditioning. He developed the "Skinner box," a cage that contains a mechanism that delivers food pellets when the occupant pushes a lever. Using this device, Skinner taught pigeons a number of "tricks," including pecking out a tune on the xylophone and playing ping-pong. These antics proved useful for more serious purposes; the Skinner box was used to study a variety of fundamental processes involved in learning complex behaviors. Skinner moved considerably beyond the laboratory in his theories, with ideas that helped shape later advances in the field of childhood education and the treatment of psychologically disturbed individuals. Particularly noteworthy was Skinner's preference for the use of positive rewards in bringing about desirable changes in people rather than using punishment or other aversive techniques.

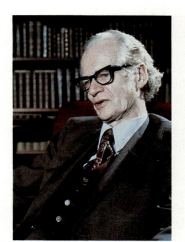

Burrhus Frederick Skinner developed the principles of operant conditioning. Throughout his career, Skinner devoted himself to the experimental manipulation of conditions as a way of studying the factors influencing behavior.

Ice cream is a primary reinforcer because it satisfies the primary need of hunger.

His view of Utopia, indeed, was one in which positive reinforcement was the main basis for promoting socialization and human development (Skinner, 1953).

Reinforcement is the principle that underlies Skinner's model of operant conditioning. The term "reinforce" means to "strengthen"; you can think of **reinforcement** as the "strengthening" of a behavior, increasing the likelihood that the behavior will be performed. You can probably recall many examples in which your own behavior was reinforced. Perhaps your friend told you how good a certain sweater looks on you. Soon after, you realized that you were wearing it more frequently. In technical terms, your friend's comment served as a positive reinforcer that increased the frequency of your sweater-wearing behavior. Extending this principle to psychological disorder, you can see how a disturbed behavior that is reinforced may become ingrained in a person. For example, an overprotective parent may be reinforcing a child's pathological dependency if every time the child expresses a minor fear, the parent consoles the child with hugs, kisses, and cookies.

As these examples imply, there can be many kinds of reinforcers. The ones that satisfy some biological need (hunger, thirst, relief from pain, sex) are called **primary reinforcers** because they are intrinsically rewarding. Behavior is also driven by **secondary reinforcers** which derive their value from association with primary reinforcers. Money is a good example of a secondary reinforcer because its value comes from the fact that it can be used to obtain primary reinforcers. As you will see later, some forms of behavior therapy use "tokens" as reinforcers, which are like money in that they can be used to purchase special treats or privileges.

Other kinds of secondary reinforcers do not have material value, but are reinforcing for other reasons. Praise, attention, and recognition are rewarding to us as adults because earlier in our lives they were associated with the pleasurable feelings of being fed and held by a parent. Over time, the attention and praise became rewarding in their own right. The value of secondary reinforcers extends beyond the family, in areas such as school, work, hobbies, and athletics. Secondary reinforcers can also be involved in the acquisition of various forms of abnormal behavior. For example, a hypochondriacal person who exaggerates the severity of normal physical signs may derive secondary reinforcement in the form of attention from family, friends, or health care professionals.

In operant, as in classical conditioning, reinforcement can have a pleasurable or unpleasurable effect. So far, our discussion has focused on **positive reinforcement**, in which a person repeats a behavior that leads to a reward. Sometimes, individuals operate on the environment to remove an unpleasant stimulus, as in the case of your request that a neighbor's stereo be turned down. The removal of the unpleasant stimulus constitutes what is called **negative reinforcement**.

It is easy to confuse negative reinforcement with the idea that a person is being penalized for engaging in a certain behavior. However, this is not accurate. **Punishment** involves the application of an aversive stimulus, such as scolding. The experience is intended to reduce the frequency of the behavior that preceded punishment. When a parent scolds a misbehaving boy, the presumption is that the scolding will cause the child to stop misbehaving. If you receive a speeding ticket, this punishment is intended to stop you from speeding in the future.

The purpose of negative reinforcement is to increase, not decrease, the frequency of the behavior that preceded it. For example, the parent of the misbehaving boy may tell him that as soon as he does what he is told, the scolding will stop. The example of the stereo illustrated the process of

Why does this woman find it hard to pull herself away from the slot machine? One factor is the variable ratio schedule of reinforcement, which strengthens her hope that a big win is about to come along.

negative reinforcement. Your behavior of calling the neighbor results in the cessation of the aggravating noise from the stereo. Negative reinforcement makes it more likely that you will repeat later the behavior that succeeded in removing the unpleasant stimulus. Behaviorists prefer negative reinforcement to punishment because research has shown that punishment has unpredictable effects on behavior. For example, a child who is spanked may rebel, learn to fear the parent, or even imitate the parent by being physically aggressive with peers and siblings.

You know from experience that reinforcers can influence your behavior even if they do not occur with great frequency. For example, it may take only one comment about your sweater to increase the frequency of your wearing it. Through research on operant conditioning with animals, behaviorists have found that the responses of an organism can be controlled by using **schedules of reinforcement** that determine when reinforcers are provided. Sometimes, particularly in the early stages of learning, the animal is given a reinforcer such as a food pellet every time the desired behavior is performed. As the response becomes established in the animal, the experimenter finds that it is not necessary to give the reinforcer every time. In fact, following a "partial" reinforcement schedule is often more effective in maintaining a behavior over time.

Gambling is the best example of a partial reinforcement schedule that maintains human behaviors over long periods of time at a high rate of responding. Gambling follows what is called a **variable ratio schedule of reinforcement**, because reinforcement occurs on an average of a certain number of times per response. People who use slot machines, for instance, are counting on the chance that if they put in enough coins, they will eventually hit the jackpot. Each time they win, this lures them into thinking that their next reinforcer is soon to follow, and they keep gambling. Slot machines are programmed to pay off on a certain ratio, but obviously the timing of the payoff is a matter of chance.

What happens if reinforcement stops? As you can imagine, in the absence of reinforcement, most learned behaviors have a tendency to diminish and finally cease. If you go to your favorite restaurant and find it is unexpectedly closed, you might return one or two more times, but eventually you will stop going there. **Extinction** is the technical term used to describe the cessation of behavior in the absence of reinforcement. In treating a behavior problem such as a girl who yells out answers in the classroom, the teacher might attempt to extinguish the behavior by ignoring the child, thereby withholding the reinforcer of attention. At the same time, the teacher would strengthen appropriate behaviors by attending to the child only when she raises her hand to answer a question.

We have discussed the learning of relatively simple behaviors. Most human behaviors are more complex. Take the example of a young child who is learning to say "daddy." At first, the child says "da." The parents respond favorably to this verbalization, and may even become quite excited, especially if it is the child's first word. They will respond even more favorably as the sound comes closer and closer to the word "daddy." According to behavioral theory, this process, called *shaping*, accounts for the learning of many complex behaviors, including language. **Shaping** refers to the process of providing reinforcement for behaviors that increasingly come to resemble a desired outcome. It is the method used by an animal trainer, for example, to teach a dolphin to jump through a hoop. The dolphin does not naturally perform this behavior, but is capable of doing so with the right incentives. The trainer establishes this "operant" behavior in stages until the desired response sequence is completely established.

Shaping is an important method in the treatment of certain behavior problems. As applied to psychological disorder, shaping would be used to help a woman to reduce her fear of heights by praising her each time she ventures higher up a flight of stairs.

Social Learning and Social Cognition

Perhaps you know parents of young children who object to their children watching the Saturday morning cartoons, claiming that the violence portrayed in these programs might lead the children to act in similarly destructive ways. What is the basis for their concerns? In all likelihood, they worry that their children will learn that violent behavior produces desirable outcomes, and that the children will act accordingly to get what they want. The process of acquiring new responses by imitating the behavior of another person, called **modeling**, has been studied by behaviorists who focus on **social learning**. Social learning theorists are interested in understanding how people develop psychological disorders through their relationships with others and through observation of other people. Some theorists within this perspective also focus on **social cognition**, the factors that influence the way people perceive themselves and others and form judgments about the causes of behavior. According to

Before public concern arose about the effects of television violence on children's behavior, Albert Bandura studied observational learning in the laboratory.

these perspectives, it is not only direct reinforcements that influence behavior, but indirect reinforcements that people acquire by watching others engaging in particular behaviors and seeing them being rewarded or punished.

According to the social learning theorist Albert Bandura (1925–   ), when you watch someone else being reinforced for a behavior, you receive **vicarious reinforcement**, because you identify with that person (called the "model") and put yourself in that person's place. When the model is reinforced, it is as if you are being reinforced as well. This kind of reinforcement is the underlying process through which advertisements have their effect. An actress in a hair product commercial is admired by other people in the

In Bandura's experiments, children observed an adult punching an inflated clown doll (top row). Later, they were more likely to behave aggressively when frustrated in their desire to play with attractive toys (bottom two rows). This experiment led to the formulation of a process that Bandura called "social" learning.

The process of vicarious reinforcement, according to social learning theorists, accounts for children acquiring the behaviors of adults.

commercial (attention is the reinforcement). The advertising agency hopes that women who watch this commercial will identify with the actress and feel as positively as she appears to be feeling. This positive feeling serves as vicarious reinforcement to the observer, who is more likely to buy the product with the expectation that if she uses it she will acquire the same rewards as the actress.

Social learning theory was considered revolutionary by behaviorists when first proposed, because it expanded the realm of influence of learning from direct consequences to the many indirect reinforcements that exist in life. Furthermore, social learning theory added the idea that people acquire "expectancies" for reinforcement as part of the learning process. This was a step in the direction toward a more cognitively oriented form of behavioral theory, which focuses on the role of thoughts and ideas in influencing behavior. Gradually, social learning theory has come to be known as social "cognitive" theory because of its increased focus on thought processes and how they influence overt behavior.

One important contribution of social learning theory has been to show how maladaptive behaviors are learned through observing other people engaging in these behaviors and seeing them receive rewards. For example, a man who is waiting to buy a concert ticket may forcefully push his way to the front of the line. If he succeeds, an observer may "learn" that it is acceptable and even beneficial to act selfishly and aggressively in such instances. Similar processes can account for the development of abusive behaviors in families. Parents who were abused as children are more likely to be physically violent with their own children. A boy who observes his father beating his mother may batter his own wife years later.

Bandura has also become known for his work on **self-efficacy**, the individual's perception of competence in various life situations. According to Bandura (1977, 1982, 1986), people will try harder to succeed in difficult tasks if they are confident that they can complete these tasks. The concept of self-efficacy can be applied to an understanding of motivation, self-esteem, and interpersonal relations. People who lack self-efficacy in a given situation can be trained to increase their confidence in their abilities to succeed and thus enhance their feelings of self-worth.

Cognitive-Behavioral Theory

When we began our discussion of behaviorism, we emphasized its focus on observable behaviors. It is true that behaviorists consider behavior the primary focus of their theories. However, it has become increasingly clear to some behaviorists that a theory that focuses only on observable behavior is limited, and that attention should be directed toward cognitive processes involved in personality and psychological disorder. **Cognitive-behaviorists** study thoughts and other unobservable processes that determine behavior. They recognize that emotions are the product of cognitive, or thought, processes.

You can gain some understanding of the cognitive-behaviorist perspective by reflecting on the common experience of talking yourself into a bad mood. Perhaps a friend told you he would call, and by the end of the day you haven't heard from him. You start to wonder whether maybe he really isn't interested in you. Now that you think about it, you begin to focus on the many times that people haven't returned your calls or followed through on other promises. Is it because there is something wrong with you? Such negative thoughts and questions about yourself can lead you to feel sad.

Three theorists are associated with the cognitive-behavioral perspective: Albert Ellis (1913–   ), Aaron Beck (1921–   ), and Donald Meichenbaum (1940–   ). All three emphasize the role of disturbed thinking processes in causing maladaptive behavior. For example, Beck (1976) and Beck et al., (1979) would describe depression arising from the failure of a friend to call as the result of "dysfunctional attitudes." For Ellis (1963) they would be "irrational beliefs," referring to your mistaken conclusion that because one friend does not call you, you are an unlikable person. Meichenbaum shares the view that people create their own unhappiness by having unduly negative thoughts about their situations.

The cognitive-behavioral perspective has been developed most comprehensively in the context of depression (Beck, 1991). Newer developments in cognitive-behavioral theory are also emerging as the theory is applied to a broader range of disorders such as anxiety disorders (Beck et al., 1985), personality disorders (Beck et al., 1990), and addictive behaviors (Marlatt & Gordon, 1985).

Beck was trained in psychiatry as a psychoanalyst. He became frustrated, though, by the length and expense of psychoanalysis, and by its failure as a treatment method. Based on his observations of depressed people in his work at the University of Pennsylvania hospital, Beck became convinced that their mood disturbances were the result of faulty thinking about themselves and their situations. He noted that people with depression often came to the wrong conclusions about events in their lives, blaming themselves unnecessarily, and often without realizing it.

Beck's approach falls within the tradition of the cognitive personality theory of George Kelly (1905–1967), which was based on the notion that personality is made up of a set of **personal constructs**, or ways of viewing the world and the self. Psychological disorder, Kelly proposed, occurs when these constructs fail to organize the individual's world (Kelly, 1955). The cognitive-behavioral theories we discuss in this section share Kelly's emphasis on the importance of thought processes in influencing people's emotions and behavior.

According to Beck, a pervasive feature of many psychological disorders is the existence of **automatic thoughts**—ideas so deeply entrenched that the individual is not even aware that they lead to feelings of unhappiness and discouragement. Automatic thoughts appear to arise spontaneously and are difficult to ignore. For example, in conversation with a friend, a person might start to think "What a boring person I am," or "That was a dumb thing to say," or "Why can't I be more clever and interesting?" Beck compared automatic thoughts to the "shoulds" described by Horney (see Chapter 4), which lead the person to try to achieve unrealistic goals of perfection. In the case of depression, automatic thoughts are inevitably followed by the emotion of sadness because these thoughts are so discouraging.

According to Beck's theory, automatic thoughts are the product of **dysfunctional attitudes**, a set of personal rules or values people hold that interfere with adequate adjustment. The sample items in Table 5-1 from the Dysfunctional Attitudes Scale give an idea of the range of beliefs that fall into this domain. The process leading to automatic thoughts begins with a dysfunctional attitude. Next, the person encounters an experience to which this dysfunctional attitude applies (being alone, asking a question, fail-

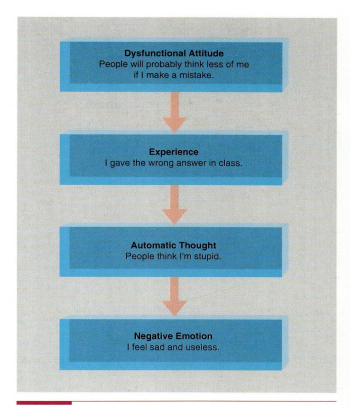

Figure 5-1

The relationships among dysfunctional attitudes, experiences, automatic thoughts, and negative emotions.

ing). The individual is then likely to interpret this experience in an excessively negative way, having been primed by the dysfunctional attitude to regard it as a negative reflection on the self.

Illogical processes of inference govern the way people with psychological disorders draw conclusions from their experiences. These processes are illustrated step by step in Figure 5-1. The steps in this example pertain to making a mistake in front of others, an event that almost everyone has experienced. People who are prone to depression begin with the assumption that mistakes are unacceptable and are a sign of personal failure. They are then primed to react far more negatively to making a mistake than people who do not hold this dysfunctional attitude. The subsequent automatic thought reflects having interpreted the mistake in these terms, and depression is a natural consequence of this belief.

In Chapter 10, we will see that depression-prone individuals make many other logical errors in their thinking, which contribute to the frequency of their negative automatic thoughts. In other psychological disorders, automatic thoughts of a different nature prevail. But whatever form of disorder is involved, the process through which negative emotions follow from these thoughts remains the central focus of cognitive-behavioral theory.

Ellis describes a linkage of cognitive and emotional processes in his "A-B-C" model, which proposes that

---

Table 5-1 Examples of Items from the Dysfunctional Attitudes Scale

1. It is difficult to be happy unless one is good looking, intelligent, rich, and creative.
2. People will probably think less of me if I make a mistake.
3. If a person asks for help, it is a sign of weakness.
4. If I fail partly, it is as bad as being a complete failure.
5. I am nothing if a person I love doesn't love me.
6. I should be upset if I make a mistake.
7. If I ask a question, it makes me look inferior.
8. Being isolated from others is bound to lead to unhappiness.
9. If someone disagrees with me, it probably indicates he does not like me.
10. If I do not do well all the time, people will not respect me.

Agreeing with these items indicates that the person holds dysfunctional attitudes.

Source: Weissman, (1978).

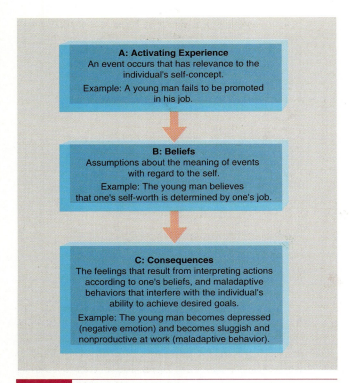

Figure 5-2 The A-B-C process in rational-emotive therapy A narrow focus on his job led this young man to overreact when he did not get the promotion he desired. A more rational belief is that a job is a part, but by no means all, of what determines one's self-worth. If the man's beliefs had been more rational, he would have reacted less extremely, and probably would be in a good position to receive a promotion at a later time.

people can make themselves either happy or miserable by the way they think about their experiences (see Figure 5-2). In this model, the "A" refers to "Activating Experience," the "B" to "Beliefs," and the "C" to "Consequences." According to Ellis, it is the "B"s that are often faulty or irrational, leading to lowered feelings of self-worth.

It is natural to feel sad when you fail at an important task, and people can be expected to have emotional ups and downs in reaction to external events. Psychological disorder develops when the individual's emotional reactions (such as rage, depression, worthlessness, anxiety, and self-pity) are extreme and when behavior becomes self-defeating as a result of these reactions. According to Ellis, these consequences occur because of **irrational beliefs**—views about the self and world that are unrealistic, extreme, and illogical. In many ways, they are comparable to Beck's notion of dysfunctional attitudes. Some examples of irrational beliefs are shown in Table 5-2.

According to Ellis (1987), emotional disturbance is a common feature of life and is perpetuated by processes such as those shown by the young man discussed in Figure 5-2. In many ways, Ellis agrees with the psychoanalytic position that neurotic misery is an integral feature of the human condition. According to Ellis, people create their own emotional disturbance by sticking rigidly to irrational musts

(what Ellis has called "musturbation") and then punishing themselves needlessly ("awfulizing"). They then engage in unnecessary self-pity ("I-can't-stand-it-itis") and refuse to admit that they need help. Rather than trying to change themselves, many people find ways to change their situations, such as seeking a divorce rather than learning what facets of their personalities contribute to marital distress. If we are to believe Ellis, it would seem that few people are ever really happy. On a more positive note, as we will see later, Ellis also offers some practical suggestions for how people can get out of the mess they create for themselves.

Treatment

Traditionally, behavior therapists focus on symptoms and are less concerned about the causes of those symptoms. According to the behavioral perspective, maladaptive behavior arises from faulty learning, and should be changed through corrective learning. The focus of behavior therapy is on specific tasks that client and therapist agree would lead to a desired goal, with therapy sessions structured around those tasks. Some of these tasks are performed by the client with the guidance of the therapist, other tasks by the client at home between therapy sessions.

Table 5-2 Examples of Irrational Beliefs as Described by Ellis

Ellis (1987) distinguishes between two types of irrational beliefs: those that are "obvious or blatant" and those that are "subtle or tricky." Each type is equally maladaptive, but the subtle beliefs are more difficult to change because their irrationality is harder to detect. See if you can recognize the difference as you read the following list:

1. Because I strongly desire to perform important tasks competently and successfully, I *absolutely must* perform them PERFECTLY WELL!

2. Because I strongly desire to perform important tasks competently and successfully, and because I REALLY TRY HARD to succeed at these tasks, I DESERVE to perform well and *absolutely must* perform that way!

3. Because I strongly desire to be approved by people I find significant, I *absolutely must* have their TOTAL AND PERFECT approval!

4. Because I strongly desire to be approved by people I find significant, and BECAUSE I AM A *SPECIAL KIND* OF PERSON, I *absolutely must* have their approval!

5. Because I strongly desire people to treat me considerately and fairly, and BECAUSE I AM UNUSUALLY WEAK AND UNABLE TO TAKE CARE OF MYSELF, people *absolutely must* treat me well!

6. Because I strongly desire people to treat me considerately and fairly, they *absolutely must* AT ALL TIMES *PERFECTLY* DO SO!

The obvious irrational thoughts are numbers 1, 3, and 6 and the rest are the subtle variety. Could you tell the difference? How many of them apply to you?

Source: Ellis, (1987).

In developing interventions, behavior therapists turn to the principles of both classical conditioning and operant conditioning, relying on mechanisms such as positive reinforcement, negative reinforcement, punishment, and extinction. To illustrate how a behavior therapist would approach treatment, consider the example of Bob, a waiter with a dreaded fear of fires, terrified that he might be burned even if he only lights a match. Bob's fear developed following a childhood experience in which the candles on his birthday cake burst into flame. In his job as a waiter, he must light candles when setting tables at night, and this sets off a strong fear reaction.

Bob has experienced an unfortunate kind of conditioning, in which something generally regarded as a relatively safe or "neutral" stimulus when properly controlled has become a dreaded conditioned stimulus. A behavior therapist treating Bob would focus on this particular problem rather than wonder whether Bob's personality as a child was characterized by uncertainty and reluctance to take risks. The therapist would note the pattern of Bob's bodily responses in the feared situation; changes in such processes as breathing and heartbeat provide important information about Bob's level of anxiety. These indications could be used to measure Bob's reactions during therapy.

A logical place to begin treatment would be to attempt to eliminate Bob's fear response to fire. How might this be accomplished? One method of treating such irrational fears is based on **counterconditioning**, the process of replacing an undesired response to a stimulus with an acceptable response. Counterconditioning is particularly effective when the new response is incompatible with the existing one. The assumption underlying counterconditioning is that if the undesired response was learned, it can be unlearned, and the acceptable response can be acquired through the same process.

Physician Joseph Wolpe (1915–   ) is regarded as the primary figure in the development of counterconditioning approaches. After classically conditioning cats to experience "anxiety" in a room in which they had been shocked, Wolpe developed methods to inhibit the anxiety by training them to associate the room with eating rather than shocks. From this experiment, Wolpe speculated that counterconditioning of anxiety could serve as a basis for a radically new therapy model. His insights (1958, 1973) have had a major impact on behavior therapy as it is practiced today.

In Bob's case, relaxation would be a desirable response to replace the undesirable response of fear, since he cannot be both anxious and relaxed at the same time. The therapist would train Bob in relaxation techniques and then reward him for showing a relaxation response instead of fear when presented with fire. Over time, the pairing of rewards with relaxation in the presence of the previously feared stimulus should establish the new response and reduce or eliminate the old one.

Table 5-3 Example of a Hierarchy Used in Systematic Desensitization

In the example used in the text, Bob is afraid of fire. The following list illustrates what Bob's desensitization hierarchy might look like, moving from the least to the most feared situation:

1. Looking at an unlit candle.
2. Watching a videotape of someone lighting a candle.
3. Watching someone else light a candle.
4. Holding a candle.
5. Holding a candle while someone else lights it.
6. Holding a matchbook.
7. Holding a cigarette lighter.
8. Preparing to light the match.
9. Striking the match.
10. Lighting a candle with the match.

A variant of counterconditioning is **systematic desensitization**, in which the therapist presents the client with progressively more anxiety-provoking images of stimuli while the client is in a relaxed state. This is considered to be a form of counterconditioning in that in each successive presentation, the therapist encourages the client to substitute the desired for the undesired response—relaxation rather than anxiety.

Systematic desensitization is used when a therapist believes that the client would be overwhelmed by having to confront the actual stimulus that has provoked the undesirable behaviors. For example, if Bob has a full-blown anxiety reaction at the sight of fire, it might be unwise to use counterconditioning because Bob would have difficulty relaxing under these circumstances. Instead, the therapist might expose Bob to the fire in gradual steps. Bob would first be taught to relax. Next, working with the therapist, Bob would develop a list or "hierarchy" of images associated with his fear, ranging from minimally feared situations to more troubling situations, and finally to the most intensely fearful situation of all (see Table 5-3). Then, the therapist would help Bob enter a relaxed state, and step-by-step would introduce images from the hierarchy. Ideally, Bob would be able to work his way up the hierarchy, becoming able to imagine himself in the most potentially upsetting scene without panicking. Anytime he indicated he was feeling anxious, though, the therapist would move him back down the hierarchy until Bob signaled that he felt relaxed again.

Between sessions, Bob might be instructed to practice self-relaxation exercises when he feels anxious. The therapist might also experiment with different ways of moving Bob through the hierarchy, either using actual exposure to the feared stimulus or having Bob imagine the stimuli in the hierarchy. As you will see in Chapter 7, systematic desensitization can be used in a variety of ways. Which method is used depends partly on the nature of the client's problem behavior and partly on which techniques have

An assertive style helps people in many situations. The television character Murphy Brown achieves results by making her opinions clear to her co-workers.

been demonstrated to be most effective for that particular behavior.

Another counterconditioning technique developed by Wolpe (1973) is **assertiveness training**, a method you might have heard about through the media. In assertiveness training, the client is taught to express justified anger rather than to be anxious and intimidated when other people are exploitative, unduly demanding, or disrespectful. As in counterconditioning, the underlying rationale is that a person cannot experience opposing emotions (anger and anxiety in this case). By strengthening the desired emotion (anger), the opposite emotion (anxiety) is unlearned in that situation. As an example, consider Janet, who is fearful of the most minor of unpleasant interactions with others. Regardless of how poorly she is treated by a store clerk, she cannot imagine speaking up to defend herself. Similarly, in more serious situations, such as being exploited by co-workers, she finds it impossible to stand up for her rights; instead, she submits to their demands that she take on their duties in addition to her own. In therapy, Janet would be taught effective communication methods that would lead to successful management of situations she previously found too threatening.

Contingency management techniques

Another category of behavioral therapy techniques uses a simple principle that many people follow in their daily lives: desired behavior can be established through rewards, and undesirable behavior can be eliminated by removing its rewards. **Contingency management** is a form of behavior therapy that involves this principle of rewarding a client for desired behaviors and not providing rewards for undesired behaviors. This treatment teaches the client to connect the outcome of the behavior with the behavior itself, so that a "contingency" or connection is established.

In everyday life, people use contingency management to stop smoking, to control their weight, to discipline their children, or to change many other behaviors. Some people turn to therapy if their own contingency management efforts have failed to change undesirable behaviors. A therapist can help monitor the client's behavior and suggest alternative ways to try to control it. A common form of contingency contracting used in psychiatric hospitals is the **token economy**, in which residents who perform desired activities earn plastic chips that can later be exchanged for some tangible benefit (Ayllon & Azrin, 1968).

Modeling and self-efficacy training

In the behavioral therapy methods we have discussed so far, clients directly experience reinforcement for actions that are carried out in the context of therapy. However, we

In a token economy, clients are given tangible rewards, or "tokens", that they exchange for desired activities or privledges.

have seen from Bandura's research that people can learn new behaviors vicariously. Bandura has in fact taken the principle of vicarious reinforcement and successfully applied it to behavioral therapy by exposing clients to videotapes or real-life models who are shown being rewarded for demonstrating the desired behaviors (Bandura, 1971). For example, a girl who is afraid of dogs might be shown a videotape of a girl happily petting a dog and playing ball with it. By seeing the videotape, the client develops the idea that playing with dogs can be fun and, more importantly, need not be dangerous.

Going one step further, the therapist might use **participant modeling**, a form of therapy in which the client is first shown a desired behavior and then guided through the behavior change with the help of the therapist. In treating the girl, the therapist might first play with the dog and then have the girl do the same while the therapist offers encouragement.

Another form of behavioral therapy relies on Bandura's concept of self-efficacy. According to Bandura, maladaptive behaviors such as irrational fears arise from the perception that one lacks the resources for handling a potentially threatening situation. If the client's feelings of self-efficacy are strengthened, then the client should be able to overcome the irrational fear (Bandura, 1991). Self-efficacy training can also be used to help a client overcome an undesired habit, such as in the case of a man who wants to quit smoking (Prochaska et al., 1983). A large component of therapy would focus on helping the man feel that he has the emotional strength to follow through on his wish to stop smoking. Once he believes that he has this strength, he will go a long way toward conquering his addiction.

Returning to the case of Keith, we see that from a behavioral perspective, there are many applicable principles of reinforcement and social learning. As you recall, his childhood was filled with learning experiences that could have led to his pattern of adult antisocial behavior. For example, he witnessed his father's alcoholism, he was the target of abuse and neglect, and his life was devoid of positive reinforcement. Further, he never learned to associate negative consequences with his misbehavior, because no rules or discipline were enforced in his house. An obvious goal of therapy would be to ensure that Keith learns to associate negative contingencies with his antisocial behaviors. However, this may be a difficult task, since being arrested has not succeeded in extinguishing Keith's pathological behavior. Peer counseling might be used to encourage Keith to identify with a more appropriate model. He might also be placed in a contingency management program aimed at increasing his prosocial behaviors, such as helping other people and showing respect for other people's belongings. Such a program would be intended to reverse Keith's past pattern of being rewarded for intimidating others and seeking gratification of his own needs at the expense of others.

We have tried to give you an idea of what behavioral therapy is about, but you should be aware that there are many more techniques that we did not cover here. A number of other techniques will be covered in later chapters, when we discuss their application to specific disorders. All of these methods rest on the assumption that the desired goal of therapy is a change in the client's behavior, and that this goal is best achieved by attempting to change the conditions in the person's life that maintain that behavior.

■ *Cognitive-behavioral therapy*

The principles of cognitive-behavioral therapy are straightforward and follow logically from the premise that dysfunctional emotions are the product of dysfunctional thoughts. You can get some insight into how cognitive-behavioral therapy works if you consider how you might counsel a friend who is feeling anxious over an upcoming exam or a class presentation. You might say something to your friend such as "Okay, what's the worst thing that could happen to you?", attempting to show that your friend's fears are unrealistic because the outcome will probably be less catastrophic than your friend imagines. You might also point out how well-prepared your friend is for the exam, so that there is little reason to believe that anything will go wrong. As another strategy, you might suggest something that your friend can think while taking the exam, such as "I can handle this," or "I know what I'm doing." Without making your friend feel foolish about being anxious, you would want to show your friend that there are alternative ways to handle the situation. Intuitively, then, you would be employing **cognitive restructuring**, one of the fundamental techniques of cognitive-behavioral therapy. In cognitive restructuring, the clinician attempts to alter the way the client views the self or the world, reframing negative ideas into more positive ones to encourage the development of more adaptive ways of coping with emotional difficulties.

In Beck's approach to cognitive-behavioral therapy, cognitive restructuring is the primary method used to alter the client's thoughts and thereby to change the client's emotions. Methods that the cognitive therapist uses include questioning, challenging, and making suggestions that the client can test in behavior outside the therapy session.

In a similar vein, the therapy of Ellis, developed in work at the Rational-Emotive Therapy Institute in New York City, involves a systematic attempt to dissuade clients from their irrational beliefs by showing them how mistaken they are, and to help clients arrive at more rational ways of thinking about themselves. In the case of the young man distraught over his failure to be promoted shown in Figure 5-2, Ellis would attempt to uncover the young man's irrational beliefs that are causing him to feel upset and are destroying his chances for future success. Ellis would try to show the young man that his focusing on a job as a source of self-worth is irrational. He might suggest that a more rational belief would be "It was disappointing not to get that promotion, but there are other rewards that I have in my life outside my work." Ellis might also try to show the young man that there are always other chances, and that all is not lost unless he mistakenly sabotages himself in his current job.

As with Beck's version of cognitive therapy, Ellis's rational-emotive therapy focuses on the client's thoughts, and puts far less emphasis on the relationship between the client and the therapist. This is very different from psychodynamic therapy, and completely unlike the client-centered therapist's communication of empathy in that Ellis repeatedly confronts the client's irrationality. Yet, Ellis maintains that the rational-emotive perspective is based on principles of humanistic psychology. How can we reconcile this paradox? According to Ellis, his theory, and the therapy which he prescribes, are more humanistic than most because they are based on the idea that people can control their own destinies rather than be driven by external stimuli (as in strict behaviorism) or by their instinctual drives (as in psychoanalysis). Rational-emotive therapy deals with the uniquely human qualities of thoughts, beliefs, and values (Ellis, 1973).

Meichenbaum agrees with Beck and Ellis that clients can be taught to control their dysfunctional emotions and behaviors by changing their thoughts about themselves and their situations. Meichenbaum goes beyond Beck and Ellis, though, to propose ways that clients can learn to prevent themselves from experiencing dysfunctional emotions, rather than wait until these emotions interfere with life. Working at the University of Waterloo in Ontario, Meichenbaum developed what he called **stress inoculation training**, a systematic stress management procedure that helps people prepare for difficult situations by anticipating them and practicing ways to control stress. The "inoculation" procedure is analogous to the way medical inoculation exposes the body to a small amount of the agent that causes the disease to promote the build-up of antibodies to fight the disease.

Stress inoculation training involves a series of techniques developed within the cognitive-behavioral framework, and proceeds through three phases. In the first, or conceptualization phase, an assessment is conducted to determine the nature of the client's problem behavior, the factors that seem to control the behavior, and the client's perception of what needs to be done to reduce the problem.

In the second phase, the client is taught a variety of methods for stress reduction, such as training in relaxation, problem-solving, and self-instruction. These techniques are practiced in preparation for the anticipated stressful event. Particularly important in terms of Meichenbaum's approach is the method of self-instruction or guided self-dialogue. In this procedure, the individual practices "coping self-statements" that are unique to the client and that can help control the client's reaction when silently repeated in the actual stressful situation (see Table 5-4).

The third phase of stress inoculation is application and follow-through. Here is where the "inoculation" feature of the technique comes most into play. The client is encouraged to use a variety of techniques to practice coping with the stressful situation by breaking it down into manageable units. These techniques include imagining the stressful situation, rehearsing it or role-playing it with the therapist, or

Table 5-4 Examples of Coping Self-Statements

I can work out a plan to handle this.
Stop worrying. Worrying won't help anything.
What are some of the helpful things I can do instead?
I'm feeling uptight—that's natural.
I can convince myself to do it.
One step at a time.
Look for positives; don't jump to conclusions.
As long as I keep my cool, I'm in control of the situation.
Things are not as serious as I make them out to be.
Time to take a slow, deep breath.
I can be pleased with the progress I'm making.
Don't try to eliminate stress entirely; just keep it manageable.

These are examples of statements that different clients have found helpful, but each individual would be encouraged to develop his or her own list. What self-statements might you use to combat stress? Make your own list and try them out the next time you confront a situation you feel you cannot handle.

Source: Meichenbaum, (1985).

watching the therapist demonstrate the appropriate behaviors in the situation. For example, a woman named Caroline feels stress when she must say "no" to someone. In stress inoculation training, Caroline might imagine herself being asked to do a favor, and would practice the coping self-statement "I can say 'no'; it may be difficult but I can do it." The therapist might role-play a situation in which Caroline is asked to do a favor and has to say "no," perhaps asking Caroline for various favors, ranging from large ones to which it is easy to say "no," to smaller ones that require greater effort for Caroline to decline.

In the last phase of treatment, clients are prepared for putting their training into action. Follow-up sessions might be scheduled for three-month periods after training ends, so that the therapist can monitor the client's progress and make any necessary adjustments. Helpful at this stage is instilling in the client the self-confidence for handling future stressful situations.

As an example of how cognitive-behavioral techniques might be applied to Keith's treatment, we will draw from Beck et al.'s (1990) detailed set of guidelines for the treatment of antisocial personality disorder. These authors have proposed a fascinating analysis of the cognitive underpinnings for this disorder, which is very difficult to treat (as you will see in the next chapter). Some of the beliefs that people such as Keith seem to hold include the following (paraphrased from Beck et al., 1990, p. 154):

1. Wanting something or wanting to avoid something justifies what I do.
2. My thoughts and feelings are accurate, because I have them.
3. I always make the right choice.
4. I know what I do is right because it feels right to me.

5. Other people's opinions are irrelevant unless they directly control what happens to me.

6. Bad things won't happen to me or if they do, they won't matter much.

These self-serving beliefs emphasize the immediate gratification that the individual seeks, and minimize the extent of future consequences, such as getting caught. In treating Keith, the therapist would systematically challenge these beliefs and would try to show Keith that it is to his advantage to change his behavior.

Contributions of the Behavioral Perspective

Perhaps the main appeal of the behavioral perspective is its relative simplicity and reliance on observable concepts. Behaviorists believe that you do not need to dig deeply into the unconscious mind to explain why people act the way they do, nor do you need to arrive at a philosophy regarding the ultimate goodness of human nature. Further, they assert that there is no need to grapple with difficult questions such as "What is personality?" and "What is abnormality?". Rather, the behavioral perspective employs a limited set of empirically based principles and circumvents sticky philosophical questions by not proposing complex structures that underlie behavior.

The very simplicity of the behavioral perspective is also its undoing, in the minds of many psychologists. The claims of Ellis aside, humanists contend that by restricting the definition of psychology to the study of behavior, behaviorists have failed to capture the complexity of human nature, and have portrayed free will as a negligible influence on humans compared to outside forces in the environment. Psychoanalysts argue that the de-emphasis on unconscious influences characteristic of behavioral approaches leaves out most of what is interesting and unique about human beings. Cognitive-behaviorists have come closest to satisfying both sets of criticism, in that they regard thought processes as worthy of studying (satisfying the humanist concerns) and propose that behavior can be influenced by unstated assumptions about the self (satisfying the psychoanalytic contentions). However, even the cognitive-behaviorists fail to provide an overall explanation of personality structure, restricting their observations to particular problem areas.

Although not comprehensive, the behavioral theories have a strong empirical base. Each of the major theoretical approaches has been grounded in research from its inception. The methods of therapy proposed by these theories have been tested in controlled studies (e.g., Bandura et al., 1974; Dobson, 1989; Ellis, 1957; Kanter, 1975; Meichenbaum, 1985; Moleski & Tosi, 1976; Paul, 1966; Shaw, 1977; Zettl & Hayes, 1987), and when such studies have failed to provide supportive evidence, the theory or proposed method of therapy has been adjusted accordingly. Clinicians using these methods can therefore feel relatively confident that they are employing a well-tested set of procedures relatively free of bias.

Even though a clinician may not adhere entirely to the behavioral model, most would recognize that certain behavioral strategies hold unique advantages. The incorporation of cognitive and social learning principles has helped the behavioral approach to gain increased acceptance, if not as the only form of therapy, then as an adjunct to more in-depth therapeutic efforts.

BIOLOGICAL PERSPECTIVE

You can appreciate the role of biology in psychological disturbance by considering some of your own experiences. How many times have you felt psychologically affected by something going on in your body? If you have been struck by influenza, you know how emotionally debilitating it can be. Factors that influence your nervous system, such as lack of sleep, drinking too much alcohol, or eating certain kinds of foods, can affect your mood and thinking.

Researchers are finding increasing evidence for the influence of physiological states on psychological phenomena such as emotions and cognitive processes. Each week, it seems, new evidence is reported for a link between disturbances in some aspect of bodily functioning and psychological disorder. The biological approach to understanding psychological disorder has become an exciting and promising area of research as new ways to understand the functions of the brain become available through scientific discoveries.

Researchers are also beginning to appreciate and gather data on another important way a person's psychological state can be affected by biology. Just as people inherit characteristics such as hair or eye color, they also inherit predispositions to developing certain disorders. It appears that some psychological disorders may be among these inheritable conditions. Thus, we divide our study of the biological perspective into two parts: the nervous system and genetics. Our description of the biological perspective will include a brief review of these concepts and their application to abnormal behavior.

The Nervous System and Behavior

Complex behaviors, thoughts, and emotions are the result of activities of the central nervous system (see Figure 5-3 on page 130). The **central nervous system** consists of the brain and the pathways of nerves going to and from the brain through the spinal cord. You can think of the central nervous system as a core information processing unit within the body, transmitting information regarding the body's current state to various decision-making centers, and then carrying these decisions back to the body as the basis for action. These activities occur at a rate of speed that exceeds even the most sophisticated computer, and involve millions of decisions every second participated in by trillions of cells.

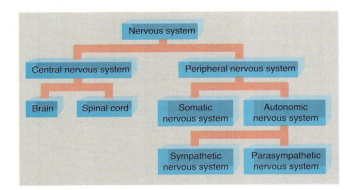

Figure 5-3   Schematic representation of the nervous system

The central nervous system communicates with two other networks in the **peripheral nervous system**. It is called peripheral because its pathways lie outside the brain and spinal cord. The two subdivisions are the *somatic nervous system* and the *autonomic nervous system*. In the **somatic nervous system**, information from outside and inside the body is brought to the central nervous system through sensory pathways which communicate information from the eyes, ears, and other senses. Instructions for action from the central nervous system are communicated through motor pathways in the somatic system, which give instructions to the muscles and certain glands. The autonomic nervous system controls various involuntary functions, such as digestion and the beating of the heart, which rarely enter into the sphere of the conscious thoughts and actions regulated by the central nervous system. We will discuss the autonomic nervous system in more detail later in the chapter.

To understand the fascinating results regarding the cause and treatment of psychological disorder that are being reported by researchers working in the biological perspective, we will examine the neuron and the synapse, and how they participate in the nervous system's overall functioning.

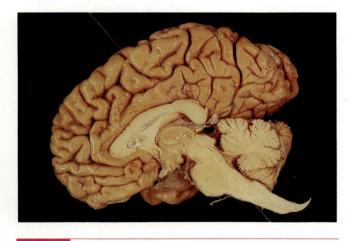

This model shows a mid-saggital view of the human brain.

■ *The Neuron and the Synapse*

The **neuron**, or nerve cell, is the basic unit of structure and function within the nervous system. The neuron's job is to transmit information. There are different types of neurons, but all possess the same parts, including the *cell body*, the *axon*, and *dendrites* (see Figure 5-4). The **cell body** houses the structures, found in all cells of the body, responsible for keeping the neuron alive. The **axon** is the section of the neuron that transmits information to other neurons. This information passes from fibers at the end of the axon

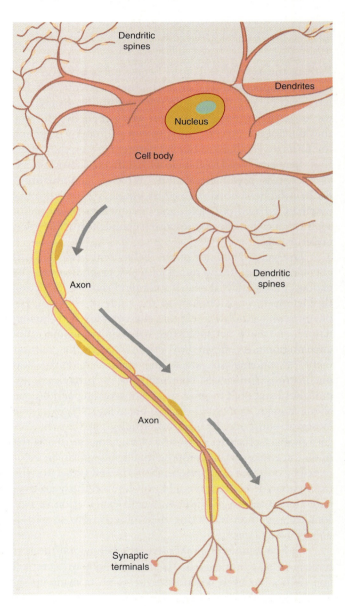

Figure 5-4   The Neuron   A typical neuron has a cell body, containing the cell's nucleus; dendrites, which receive impulses from other neurons; dendritic spines, which enlarge the receptive surface of the neuron; an axon, which transmits impulses through the neuron; and synaptic terminals, which communicate the impulses to other neurons.

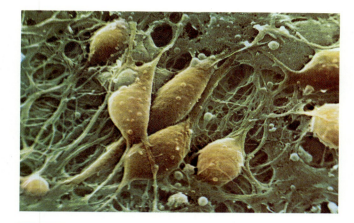

Magnification known as scanning electron micrograph affords a close-up view of neurons from the cerebral cortex. The colors shown are not real.

to the fibers on the **dendrites** of the neurons that receive the information. Spines along the length of the dendrites increase their effective surface area many thousand-fold.

Transmission of information throughout the nervous system takes place at **synapses**, points of communication between neurons. Electrical signals containing information are transmitted chemically across the synapse from one neuron to the next. Through this transmission, neurons form interconnected pathways along which information travels from one part of the nervous system to another. Most synapses involve information transmission from the axon of one neuron to the dendrites of another, since the dendrites comprise such a large surface area, but there are also axon–axon synapses, and axon–cell body synapses. As you can see from the photo, each neuron is surrounded by many others synapsing upon it, all over the surface of the neuron.

Synapses can have one of two effects—either "turning on" or "turning off" the neuron that receives the information. An **excitatory synapse** is one in which the message communicated to the receiving neuron makes it more likely to trigger a response. By contrast, an **inhibitory synapse** decreases the activity of the receiving neuron. At any given moment, the activity of a neuron, and whether it sends off a signal to the neurons in its pathway, depends on the balance between excitatory and inhibitory synapses. In this way, each neuron integrates information from all the signals feeding into it, and responds according to which of these signals are stronger.

Right now, as you read the words on this page, millions of electrochemical transmissions are taking place in your brain. What are these transmissions like? You might imagine something like the set of electrical wires that connect your stereo system. As the signal passes from one wire to another, the sound is transmitted until it finally reaches the speaker. The nervous system is like this, but with one important difference. There are no "hard-wire" connections between the neurons. The neurons do not touch. Instead, there is a gap at the point of juncture between neurons called the **synaptic cleft**. The transmission of information

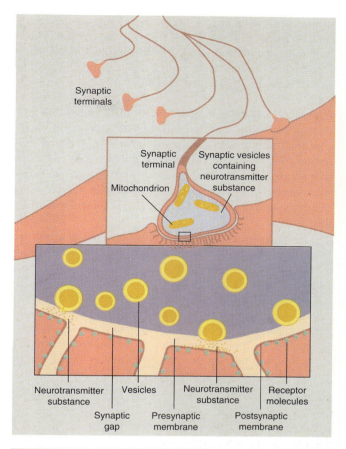

Figure 5-5
Neurotransmitters released across the synapse   Neurotransmitter molecules are carried to the presynaptic membrane in vesicles, which fuse with the membrane and release their contents into the synaptic gap. The neurotransmitters diffuse across the synapse and combine with receptor molecules in the postsynaptic membrane.

from the axon of one neuron to the dendrites of other neurons involves chemical and electrical activities occurring across the synaptic cleft. The fact that synapses do not involve direct connections will prove to be particularly important later, when we discuss how psychoactive medications affect the brain.

If information does not pass directly from neuron to neuron, how is it conveyed? The answer is that a chemical substance is released from the transmitting neuron into the synaptic cleft, where it drifts across the synapse and is absorbed by the receiving neuron. This substance is called a **neurotransmitter** (see Figure 5-5).

There are several kinds of neurotransmitters which differ in their chemical composition. Some of the more important ones are acetylcholine (ACh), gamma-aminobutyric acid (GABA), serotonin, dopamine, norepinephrine, and enkephalins. Some neurotransmitters are excitatory in that they increase the likelihood that the receiving neuron will trigger a response. Norepinephrine is generally considered to be an excitatory neurotransmitter, and a deficit in this substance is thought to be a causal factor in depression.

Other neurotransmitters, such as GABA, have an inhibitory effect when they pass through the synapse. This is how some tranquilizers work—by facilitating GABA activity which, in effect, "slows down" the nervous system. The enkephalins have received particular attention since the early 1980s because they have been recognized as the body's naturally produced painkillers. Abnormalities in other neurotransmitters are considered likely sources of some forms of abnormal behavior. Researchers have hypothesized that serotonin is involved in obsessive-compulsive behavior and that an excess of dopamine causes schizophrenic symptoms. Conversely, a dopamine deficit causes the symptoms of trembling and difficulty walking that are typical of Parkinson's disease.

You can see by these examples that neurotransmitters play a central role in affecting a variety of behaviors. Other disorders, particularly those that respond to medication, may someday be found to have their source in neurotransmitter imbalances. The potential that this approach offers to an understanding and treatment of psychological disorders cannot be over-emphasized, because it suggests relatively direct, simple interventions that can reduce the toll these disorders take on the quality of human life. However, it is unlikely that a "magic" cure will be found that, like penicillin for bacterial diseases, can eliminate a broad spectrum of serious mental disorders.

■ *The role of the brain in behavior*

Now that you have seen how neurons communicate information, let's move on to the big picture. How does the brain's functioning determine whether a person behaves abnormally? We will approach this question by taking a brief "tour" of the brain from the "bottom" to the "top," focusing particularly on those areas that seem most relevant to abnormal behavior.

The simplified representation of the central nervous system shown in Figure 5-6 shows where the major structures of the brain are located. In speaking of brain–behavior relationships, it is helpful to think of behavior along a continuum of "higher" to "lower," or higher-order to lower-order functions. Lower-order functions require little analysis or planning and cannot be easily controlled by the individual. Examples of lower-order functions are the perception of an object as round or the transmission of signals to the lungs to control breathing. Higher-order functions involve judgment and planning, and can be voluntarily controlled. Determining the best route to take to your destination is a higher-order behavior, as is reading or singing.

The higher-order functions are made possible by the activities of structures within the **cerebral cortex,** the thin covering of neural tissue (thinner than a pencil) surrounding the outer surface of the brain. The lower or more automatic functions are served by structures situated underneath and within the cerebral cortex. These **subcortical** structures operate much of the time as relay stations to prepare information for processing in the cerebral cortex

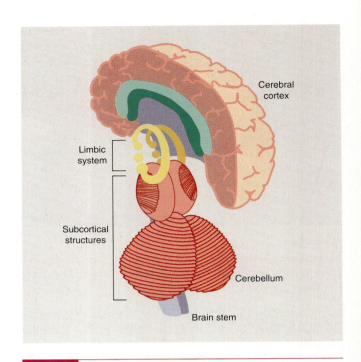

Figure 5-6   Diagram of the brain   This illustration shows the cerebral cortex and the internal structures that lie under it, including the limbic system, the cerebellum, and brain stem.

and to carry out the instructions given by the cerebral cortex for action by the muscles and glands.

The *brain stem* is the site of transition between the brain structures and the spinal cord. There are three structures within the brain stem: the *medulla oblongata, pons,* and *midbrain.* Running vertically to and through these structures is a diffuse collection of ascending and descending pathways called the **reticular formation.** This structure controls the level and direction of arousal of brain activity through excitation of certain pathways and inhibition of others. It is responsible for "consciousness" and is thought to be involved in dreams. Some of the other functions carried out by structures in this part of the brain include regulation and control of eye movements, facial muscles, sleep patterns, and adjustment of bodily position.

The **cerebellum** controls finely tuned voluntary movements. The ice skater or tightrope walker who performs elaborate balancing tricks is relying on the functioning of the cerebellum. Also involved in balance and motor control are the **basal ganglia,** a set of nuclei located deep within the brain. It is in the basal ganglia, specifically, that a dopamine deficiency can cause Parkinson's disease.

Because of its central role in many aspects of human behavior, the **hypothalamus** is the focus of extensive research attention. A tiny but crucial structure, it coordinates the activities of the central nervous system with systems involved in control of emotion, motivation, and bodily regulation. Parts of the hypothalamus control hunger, thirst, and sex needs. When stimulated, reward centers in the hypothalamus produce such pleasurable feelings that rats will spend long periods of time pushing electrode-connected levers that deliver excitation to these centers. There also are centers in the hypothalamus which, when stimulated, arouse a painful reaction. These motivational functions of the hypothalamus clearly influence human behavior. The hypothalamus is also involved in several other bodily control systems, integrating a wide range of thoughts, feelings, and bodily reactions. It is involved, for example, in responding to stress by controlling the individual's emotional state and the physiological arousal that accompanies stress.

The **limbic system** is a set of loosely connected structures that form a ring within the center portion of the brain. This system, which contains the hypothalamus, provides the neurological basis for the interaction between "rational" and "irrational" human behaviors. The limbic system also contains the **hippocampus**, which is responsible for the consolidation of short-term memory into long-term memory. Other limbic system structures called the *amygdala* and *septal area* are involved in control of emotional reactivity. Through its structures and pathways, the limbic system serves as the basis for integrating memory, learning, and motor behavior with the emotional states of pleasure, pain, and arousal.

The cerebral cortex covers the upper portions of the two halves of the brain. The two parts of the cerebral cor-

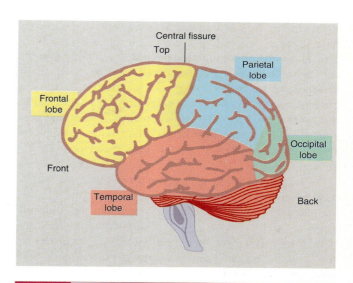

Figure 5-7 **The four lobes of the cerebral cortex**

tex—the **cerebral hemispheres**—are connected by a band of tissue called the **corpus callosum.** There is a degree of specialization between the two hemispheres, so that some functions are carried out by structures on the right side of the brain and others on the left. For example, language is typically carried out by left hemisphere structures in people who are right-handed.

The cerebral cortex has four major subdivisions: *parietal, temporal, occipital,* and *frontal lobes* (see Figure 5-7). Simply put, the **parietal lobe** is involved in the perception of bodily sensations such as touch; the **temporal lobe** is involved in speech and language; the **occipital lobe** in vision; and the **frontal lobe** in movement. The **prefrontal area** at the very front of the brain is responsible for abstract planning and judgment. The largest area of the cerebral cortex is made up of the **association cortex**, which synthesizes and integrates information from all over the brain.

■ *The autonomic nervous system*

Right now your body is attending to many functions that you are probably not even thinking about. Stop for a moment and feel your pulse. You are not consciously instructing your heart to beat, yet your pulse tells you that it is beating at approximately a rate of 60 times per minute. At the same time, your stomach is digesting your last meal. You are not controlling this process in the way that you would cause your right hand to move to turn the page. The automatic, involuntary processes that keep your body alive are controlled by the **autonomic nervous system**.

The two complementary functions of the autonomic nervous system are carried out by its two subdivisions: the *parasympathetic nervous system* and the *sympathetic nervous system*. The **parasympathetic nervous system** carries out the maintenance functions of the body when it is at rest, directing most of the body's activities to producing and storing energy to be used when the body is in action. After you eat, the parasympathetic nervous system takes over and

The cerebellum plays a crucial role in enabling this person to maintain her balance.

"instructs" the digestive system to begin to process what you have eaten.

The **sympathetic nervous system** is primarily responsible for mobilizing the body's stored resources when these resources are needed for energy-taxing activities. When you are in danger or when you are exercising, your sympathetic nervous system directs blood flow to the muscles and prepares you for action. Your heart pumps faster, your blood vessels constrict, and as a result your blood pressure increases.

The operation of both systems is coordinated by structures in the brain that receive and translate sensory information from inside and outside the body and transmit instructions through the spinal cord for the appropriate autonomic response. The hypothalamus plays a major role in this process, regulating many autonomic functions and communicating with other regions of the brain regarding the body's temperature, energy needs, and level of comfort or satisfaction.

■ *The endocrine system*

So far, we have focused on the role of the nervous system in behavior. The body's control processes are also maintained by hormones secreted by the glands in the **endocrine system** (see Figure 5-8). **Hormones** are chemicals that are released by the endocrine glands into the bloodstream. One major part of the endocrine system is controlled by the hypothalamus, which delivers hormones to the **pituitary gland**, sometimes called the "master" gland, located directly underneath the hypothalamus. This link between the endocrine system and the nervous system plays an important role in regulating many important behaviors relevant to feelings of psychological well-being and distress.

Hormones released by the pituitary gland stimulate the glands of the endocrine system to release a broad range of other hormones, including growth hormone, sex hormones, and cortisol, which is released by the adrenal gland and is involved in the body's response to stress. The endocrine system operates mainly on the principle of negative feedback. When the level of a hormone in the blood becomes too low, the hypothalamus sends a signal to the pituitary gland to stimulate the production of more of that particular hormone. One important exception to this negative feedback cycle is the onset of puberty, when sex hormones are released in large amounts.

Disturbances in the endocrine system can have widespread effects on behavior and health. For example, an excess of thyroid hormone can cause a person to become overexcitable, restless, and irritable. In contrast, a deficiency of thyroid hormone can cause a person to feel sluggish or depressed.

Genetic Influences on Behavior

One of the most exciting areas of investigation in recent years is the study of how people inherit predispositions to various physical and psychological disorders. It is now well established that certain diseases such as diabetes and heart disease run in families. Scientists have long suspected that there is a genetic basis for various psychological disorders, but only recently have they obtained significant evidence to confirm this hypothesis. For example, during the 1980s, it was demonstrated that relatives of people with mood disorders are much more likely to inherit a predisposition to developing these disorders themselves.

Why are some people predisposed to psychological disorder? The answer lies in an understanding of the mechanisms of genetic transmission. Here we will provide an overview of topics that will be covered in more depth in later chapters. As you will see throughout the text, some of these concepts and research methods have been instrumental in helping to solve the puzzle of what causes psychological disorder.

■ *Genetic inheritance*

The **gene** is the basic unit of heredity. Every cell in the body contains genes inherited from both parents, and these genes are responsible for transmitting inherited characteristics. Only a few genes are active in each cell, however. For example, in a neuron only certain genes are "turned on" to direct the cell to behave in a way specific to neurons.

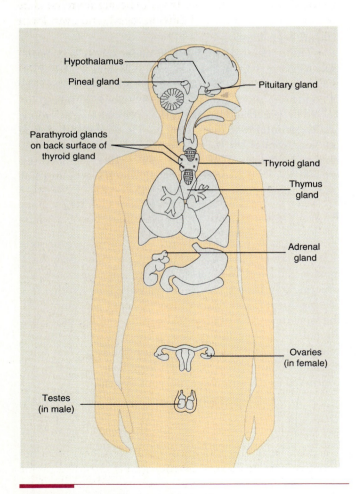

Figure 5-8   Organs in the endocrine system

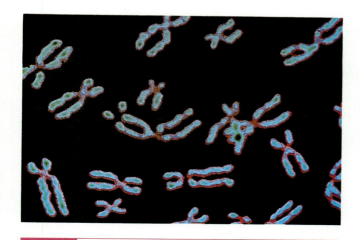

Normal human chromosomes.

Genes are often pictured as beads upon a string, making up a **chromosome** rather like a necklace. Chromosomes exist in a pair, with one chromosome contributed from each parent at conception. Human beings each have 23 pairs of chromosomes. Each of the "beads," or components of the chromosome, is made up of deoxyribonucleic acid (DNA) and protein. The DNA contains essential information that is coded in four units called the *nucleotides*. The sequence of these nucleotides is the code for the function of the gene. A typical gene has several thousand nucleotides arranged in pairs, each member of the pair being a contribution from one of the parents. The original set is duplicated millions of times as the egg develops into the adult so that every adult cell has equal contributions from mother and father.

It is amazing to think about how each cell of your body is made up of a combination of genes from your parents. As a result, many of your physical characteristics are determined by the genes that you inherited from your parents. Of course, factors such as height and weight also reflect the effects of environmental factors such as nutrition and lifestyle. It is difficult to trace exactly which characteristic came from which side of the family, because the inheritance patterns of many characteristics depend on a multitude of factors.

If it is puzzling to think about physical characteristics, you can imagine how complicated the issues are when considering the role of genetics in determining psychological qualities. Take the example of a young man who frequently loses his temper, a characteristic he shares with his father. Has the young man inherited the bad temper, or has he acquired it through observing his father? Researchers who study the causes of psychopathology grapple with questions such as these in trying to understand why people develop patterns of abnormal behavior. If psychological disorders are caused by genetic defects, then this should be reflected in patterns of family inheritance. Clearly, though, as our example shows, families are exposed to the same environment. They spend time together, share the same standard of living, see many of the same people, eat the same food, and have many of the same life experiences. How is it possible, then, to separate the influence of genetics from that of the environment in determining the cause of psychological dysfunction? Let's see how scientists have approached this question.

■ *Studies of genetic influence*

Most researchers begin the search for genetic causes by establishing that a particular disorder shows a distinct pattern of family inheritance. This process requires obtaining complete family histories from people who are identified as having symptoms of the disorder. Their genealogy must be traced in order to calculate the incidence of the disorder among blood relatives.

Another way to trace inherited causes of psychological disorders is to compare the **concordance rate**, or agreement ratios, between people diagnosed as having the disorder and their relatives. For example, a researcher may observe that out of a sample of 10 twins, the members of 6 pairs each have the same diagnosed psychological disorder. This would mean that, among this sample, there is a concordance ratio of .60 (6 out of 10). An inherited disorder would be expected to have the highest concordance between identical twins (whose genes are the same), somewhat lower rates between siblings and fraternal twins (who are no more alike genetically than siblings of different ages), and even lower rates among more distant relatives.

A more powerful way to determine whether a disorder has a genetic basis is through adoption studies. The most extensive evidence gathered from these studies comes from the Scandinavian countries, where complete records for the population are maintained by the government. Two types of adoptions are studied in this research. In the first, simply called an **adoption study**, researchers look at children whose biological parents have diagnosed psychological disorders but who are adopted by "normal" parents. In the second and rarer kind of adoption situation, called a **crossfostering study**, researchers look at children who are adopted by parents with psychological disorders but whose biological parents are psychologically healthy.

These kinds of studies enable researchers to draw powerful inferences about the relative contributions of biology and family environment to the development of psychological disorders. Take the example of a boy who is born to two seriously depressed parents but adopted by two parents with no diagnosed psychological disorder. If this child also develops serious depression later in life, it would make sense to infer that he was genetically predisposed. When researchers study many dozens of people in similar situations and observe a heightened incidence rate of psychological disorders among these children, they are able to draw these conclusions with a high degree of certainty. Conversely, consider the case of a girl born to parents with no diagnosed psychological disorder who is adopted, and at some later point her adoptive parents become psychologically disturbed. If she develops the adopting parents' psychological disorder, family environment would be one logical cause.

Treatment

Somatic therapies are the form of treatment that follow from the biological perspective. Some of these interventions are rather extreme, such as psychosurgery, discussed in Chapter 1. Less extreme, but also quite controversial, is electroconvulsive therapy (ECT) for the treatment of severe depression. Although the mechanisms through which ECT alleviates depression are not understood, it is thought that the passage of electrical current through the brain affects neurochemical transmission in such a way that a person's mood improves. Certainly the most common somatic intervention is medication. As we discuss many disorders later in the book, we will also describe the medications demonstrated to be effective in alleviating symptoms of these disorders.

In addition to these traditional somatic treatments, newer and more innovative approaches have been developed that do not involve directly changing a person's biological functioning with chemical, surgical, or electrical interventions. **Biofeedback** is a procedure that teaches people to monitor and control their autonomic responses, such as blood pressure, heart rate, skin conductance, and muscular tension. After biofeedback training, when people under stress become aware that their blood pressure is rising, they can use certain cognitive strategies to lower their blood pressure. Diet is another form of somatic treatment that is still considered outside the realm of traditional psychiatric interventions. However, researchers have demonstrated that by controlling a person's intake of certain kinds of foods or drinks, dramatic changes in psychological functioning can result. For example, removing caffeine from a person's diet may help to reduce anxiety. Even more radical, perhaps, are treatments involving meditation and exercise as ways of controlling psychological states.

These methods are not mutually exclusive, nor are they independent of psychological interventions. Increasingly, clinicians are beginning to propose treatment plans that address the client as a total person, with biological as well as psychological concerns.

At present, there is no treatment that follows directly from the genetic approach. However, as researchers explore methods of biotechnological and genetic engineering, such treatments, if not cures, may soon be discovered.

Contributions of the Biological Perspective

Biology, of course, is the foundation upon which all behavior is based. Ultimately, any psychological approach to abnormal behavior must consider the role of biology. Researchers have increasingly realized that many disorders that for decades had been explained in psychological terms may have biological components. In some cases, it is being recognized that the connection between biology and psychology is reciprocal. For example, when you are anxious, you can feel changes in your body such as increased heart rate and sweating. These changes can interfere with a number of psychological processes such as concentration. When you realize that you are having trouble concentrating, you can become even more anxious. Chronic anxiety, in turn, can cause physical changes that create long-standing health problems, and these can serve to increase already heightened levels of anxiety. Furthermore, researchers also have come to accept the notion that most forms of psychological disorder are caused by an interaction of "nature" and "nurture."

The case of Keith raises some fascinating questions concerning the role of biology in psychological disorders. Most people reading Keith's story would regard his troubled

In biofeedback, a person learns to regulate autonomic functions by attending to bodily changes registered on specialized recording instruments.

family life as a psychosocial or environmental cause of his antisocial personality. However, as you will discover in the chapter on personality disorders, antisocial personality disorder may have a biological component. Perhaps Keith inherited a predisposition to the disorder from his father. This knowledge may not alter the clinician's treatment plan, but it might provide the clinician with a perspective for understanding the development of Keith's disorder.

DEVELOPING A PERSPECTIVE: AN INTEGRATIVE APPROACH

Now that you have read about the major perspectives on abnormal behavior, you probably can see value in each of them. Certain facets of various theories may seem particularly useful and interesting to you. In fact, you may have a hard time deciding which approach is the "best." However, as we have said repeatedly, most clinicians select aspects of the various models rather than adhering narrowly to a single one. The needs of the client are viewed from multiple perspectives, and a treatment plan is developed that responds to these particular concerns. Some cases might involve focusing on the client's family, and others may call for more detailed analysis of the client's early development. One client may need more directive and educative work, while another client may benefit from support and nurturance. Similarly, in the course of therapy, components of several different models may come into play at different times. For example, a woman in long-term therapy with a psychodynamic focus might begin to experience symptoms of severe depression. At this point, the therapist might decide to incorporate cognitive-behavioral techniques aimed at relieving the client's depressive symptoms.

Our own preference is to adopt a flexible and integrative approach to understanding the causes of abnormal behavior. This means that we will view some disorders as stemming from a variety of potential causes, and regard others as best explained and treated by focusing on one of the available perspectives. This integrative perspective will be presented within each of the subsequent chapters. Follow our thinking as we attempt to bring together diverse perspectives regarding etiology and treatment.

SUMMARY

1. Family systems perspectives emphasize disturbances in the individual's role within the family as the cause of psychological disorder. Although different family systems theorists emphasize different aspects of family dynamics, all regard the individual as part of an interlocking web of relationships such that disturbances in one part of the system create dysfunctions elsewhere. Disturbed communication patterns are also regarded as contributing to psychological difficulties in the individual, who can develop a confused view of the self and the world by being subjected to conflicting and contradictory messages.

2. Family therapists use a variety of techniques to provoke change in a disturbed family system. The therapist takes an active role in working with various family members and encouraging them to view their relationships in a different way. Some forms of family intervention include the use of paradoxical interventions in addition to the use of one-way mirrors behind which colleagues can observe and offer intervention suggestions. Although family therapy is not as common as individual therapy, the principles of family dynamics have been widely incorporated into contemporary views of abnormal behavior.

3. Classical conditioning involves the pairing of an initially neutral stimulus with a stimulus that automatically provokes a reflexive response. This paradigm has been widely adopted as a model for the acquisition of dysfunctional emotional reactions. In operant conditioning, the individual acquires a complex volitional behavior through a process of shaping. By manipulating the types and schedules of reinforcement, researchers have been able to demonstrate different patterns of acquiring and maintaining new behaviors. Social learning theories account for the learning of new behaviors through observational processes. More cognitively oriented approaches within this perspective regard the acquisition of low feelings of self-efficacy as important contributors to personality and psychological disorders.

4. Behavior therapy refers to a wide range of techniques that focus primarily on treating psychological disorder by changing the individual's behavior. Techniques based on classical conditioning involve helping the individual to unlearn old, dysfunctional associations, and instead to learn new and more adaptive ones. Operant conditioning procedures are involved in contingency management, in which behavior change comes about through altering the reward structures that operate in the individual's life. In participant modeling, the individual learns through observation and guidance by the therapist to overcome the dysfunctional behavior. Self-efficacy training involves bolstering the individual's feeling of competence in overcoming problematic behaviors. In cognitive-behavioral therapy, the therapist attempts to help the individual change emotions and behaviors by altering thoughts through processes such as cognitive restructuring, in which a more positive perspective is placed on what was previously regarded as a negative situation.

5. The neuron is the basic unit of structure and function in the nervous system. Neurons communicate within the nervous system via synapses, gaps at the point of juncture across which neurotransmitters send chemical

messages. The nervous system is divided into the central nervous system and the peripheral nervous system. The central nervous system includes the brain and spinal cord. The brain is made up of various subcortical structures and the cerebral cortex. The peripheral nervous system includes the somatic nervous system, which is responsible for transferring information to and from the central nervous system, and the autonomic nervous system, which regulates automatic, involuntary behaviors. The four lobes of the cerebral cortex each regulate different aspects of complex behavior, and the association area synthesizes and integrates information from these areas.

6. The gene is the basic unit of inheritance. Chromosomes, on which genes are located, are found in pairs, with one from each parent. Researchers attempting to discover the role of heredity in influencing behavior and psychological disorder use a variety of strategies in studying families to separate the contributions of genetic inheritance and environmental influences. These methods include studies of family inheritance patterns, adoption studies, and cross-fostering studies.

7. Treatments within the biological perspective include somatic therapy such as electroconvulsive therapy and medications, as well as biofeedback, in which individuals learn to control their autonomic reactions.

KEY TERMS

Identified patient: a term used by family therapists to refer to the individual designated by the family as the focus of treatment, although family therapists are more likely to view the problem as lying with the whole family rather than limited to a single individual. p. 114

Family dynamics: the pattern of interrelationships among members of a family. p. 114

Paradoxical communication: messages that convey two contradictory meanings. p. 115

Structural approach: a way of looking at families that considers the roles of parents and children and the boundaries between the generations. p. 115

Enmeshed families: families in which the members are so closely involved in each other's lives that they lose perspective on the world outside the family. p. 115

Paradoxical intervention: a strategy in family therapy in which the therapist suggests the intentional enactment of a problem (such as arguing) with the usual outcome being that the family has difficulty producing the problem spontaneously. p. 116

Classical conditioning: the learning of a connection between an originally neutral stimulus and a naturally evoking stimulus that produces an automatic reflexive reaction. p. 117

Conditioned stimulus: a previously neutral stimulus that, after repeated pairings with the unconditioned stimulus, elicits a conditioned response. p. 117

Unconditioned stimulus: the stimulus that naturally produces a response without having been learned. p. 117

Conditioned response: an acquired response to a stimulus that was previously neutral. p. 117

Unconditioned response: a reflexive response that occurs naturally in the presence of the unconditioned stimulus without having been learned. p. 117

Generalization: the expansion of learning from the original situation to one that is similar. p. 117

Stimulus generalization: the process of learning to respond in the same way to stimuli that share common properties. p. 117

Discrimination: the process through which learning becomes increasingly specific to a given situation. p. 117

Stimulus discrimination: differentiating between two stimuli which possess similar but essentially different characteristics. p. 117

Aversive conditioning: a form of conditioning in which a painful stimulus is paired with an initially neutral stimulus. p. 117

Operant conditioning: a learning process in which an individual acquires a set of behaviors through reinforcement. p. 118

Reinforcement: the "strengthening" of a behavior. p. 119

Primary reinforcers: rewards that satisfy some biological need, making them intrinsically rewarding. p. 119

Secondary reinforcers: rewards that derive their value from association with primary reinforcers. p. 119

Positive reinforcement: the provision of rewards when certain behaviors are performed. p. 119

Negative reinforcement: the removal of aversive conditions when certain behaviors are performed. p. 119

Punishment: the application of an aversive stimulus. p. 119

Schedules of reinforcement: systems that determine when reinforcers are provided. p. 120

Variable ratio schedule of reinforcement: a schedule of reinforcement in which rewards occur on an average of a certain number of times per response. p. 120

Extinction: the cessation of behavior in the absence of reinforcement. p. 120

Shaping: a learning technique in which reinforcement is provided for behaviors that increasingly come to resemble a desired outcome. p. 120

Modeling: the learning of a new behavior by observing that of another person. p. 121

Social learning: a theoretical perspective that focuses on how people develop personality and psychological disorders through their relationships with others and through their exposure to the ways of others in their societies. p. 121

Social cognition: the factors that influence the way people perceive themselves and other people and form judgments about the causes of behavior. p. 121

Vicarious reinforcement: a form of learning in which a new behavior is acquired through the process of watching someone else receive reinforcement for the same behavior. p. 121

Self-efficacy: the individual's perception of competence in various life situations. p. 122

Cognitive-behaviorists: theorists who focus on observable behaviors as well as the thoughts that are assumed to underlie those behaviors. p. 122

Personal constructs: concepts or ways of viewing the world and the self. p. 123

Automatic thoughts: ideas so deeply entrenched that the individual is not even aware that they lead to feelings of unhappiness and discouragement. p. 123

Dysfunctional attitudes: a set of personal rules or values people hold that interfere with adequate adjustment. p. 123

Irrational beliefs: views about the self and world that are unrealistic, extreme, and illogical. p. 124

Counterconditioning: the process of replacing an undesired response to a stimulus with an acceptable response. p. 125

Systematic desensitization: a variant of counterconditioning that involves presenting the client with progressively more anxiety-provoking images while in a relaxed state. p. 125

Assertiveness training: a form of counterconditioning in which the individual is trained to replace intimidated with self-assertive behaviors. p. 126

Contingency management: a form of behavior therapy that involves the principle of rewarding a client for desired behaviors and not providing rewards for undesired behaviors. p. 126

Token economy: a form of contingency management in which a client who performs desired activities earns chips or tokens that can later be exchanged for tangible benefits. p. 126

Participant modeling: a form of therapy in which the client is first shown a desired behavior and then guided through the behavior change with the help of the therapist. p. 127

Cognitive restructuring: one of the fundamental techniques of cognitive-behavioral therapy in which clients are taught to reframe negative ideas into more positive ones. p. 127

Stress inoculation training: a systematic stress management procedure that helps people prepare for difficult situations by anticipating them and practicing ways to control stress. p. 128

Central nervous system: the part of the nervous system consisting of the brain and the pathways of nerves going to and from the brain through the spinal cord. p. 129

Peripheral nervous system: the part of the nervous system whose pathways lie outside the brain and spinal cord. p. 131

Somatic nervous system: the part of the nervous system in which information from outside and inside the body is brought to the central nervous system through sensory and motor pathways. p. 130

Neuron: the nerve cell; the basic unit of structure and function within the nervous system. p. 130

Cell body: the part of the cell that houses the structures responsible for keeping it alive. p. 130

Axon: the section of the neuron that transmits information to other neurons. p. 130

Dendrite: a section of the neuron that receives the information from other neurons. p. 131

Synapse: the point of communication between neurons. p. 131

Excitatory synapse: a synapse in which the message communicated to the receiving neuron makes it more likely to trigger a response. p. 131

Inhibitory synapse: a synapse in which the message communicated to the receiving neuron makes it less likely to trigger a response. p. 131

Synaptic cleft: the gap between two neurons at the point of synapse. p. 131

Neurotransmitter: a chemical substance released from the transmitting neuron into the synaptic cleft where it drifts across the synapse and is absorbed by the receiving neuron. p. 131

Cerebral cortex: the thin covering of neural tissue surrounding the outer surface of the brain. p. 132

Subcortical structures: parts of the brain that operate much of the time as relay stations to prepare information for processing in the cerebral cortex and to carry out the instructions given by the cerebral cortex for action by the muscles and glands. p. 132

Reticular formation: a diffuse collection of ascending and descending pathways that controls the level and direction of arousal of brain activity through excitation of certain pathways and inhibition of others. p. 132

Cerebellum: a part of the brain that controls finely tuned voluntary movements initiated by the cerebral cortex. p. 132

Basal ganglia: a set of nuclei located deep within the brain that are involved in balance and motor control. p. 132

Hypothalamus: a small structure in the brain that coordinates the activities of the central nervous system with systems involved in control of emotion, motivation, and bodily regulation. p. 132

Limbic system: a set of loosely connected structures that form a ring within the center portion of the brain, and that provides the neurological basis for the interaction between "rational" and "irrational" human behaviors. p. 133

Hippocampus: a limbic system structure responsible for the consolidation of short-term memory into long-term memory. p. 133

Cerebral hemispheres: the two halves of the cerebral cortex. p. 133

Corpus callosum: a band of tissue connecting the two halves of the cerebral cortex. p. 133

Parietal lobe: part of the cerebral cortex involved in the perception of bodily sensations such as touch. p. 133

Temporal lobe: part of the cerebral cortex involved in speech and language. p. 133

Occipital lobe: part of the cerebral cortex involved in visual perception. p. 133

Frontal lobe: the front portion of the cerebral cortex. p. 133

Prefrontal area: the area at the very front of the cerebral cortex responsible for abstract planning and judgment. p. 133

Association cortex: diffuse areas of the cerebral cortex which synthesize and integrate information from all over the brain. p. 133

Autonomic nervous system: the part of the nervous system that controls the automatic, involuntary processes that keep the body alive by regulating functions such as heartbeat and digestion. p. 133

Parasympathetic nervous system: part of the autonomic nervous system that carries out the maintenance functions of the body when it is at rest, directing most of the body's activities to producing and storing energy so that it can be used when the body is in action. p. 133

Sympathetic nervous system: part of the autonomic nervous system primarily responsible for mobilizing the body's stored resources when these resources are needed for energy-taxing activities. p. 134

Endocrine system: a bodily system composed of glands that produce hormones and secrete them into the bloodstream. p. 134

Hormones: chemicals that are released by the endocrine glands into the bloodstream, affecting the operation of a number of bodily organs. p. 134

Pituitary gland: sometimes called the "master" gland, a major gland in the endocrine system, located in the brain and under the control of the hypothalamus. p. 134

Gene: the basic unit of heredity. p. 135

Chromosome: structures found in each cell of the body that contain the genes and exist in a pair, with one chromosome contributed from each parent at conception. p. 135

Concordance rate: the percentage of people with the same disorder, usually calculated for biological relatives. p. 135

Adoption study: a method for studying genetic versus environmental contributions to a disorder by tracking the incidence of disorders in children whose biological parents have a disorder but whose rearing parents do not. p. 135

Crossfostering study: a method of comparing the relative effects of heredity and the environment, in which researchers study individuals who are adopted by parents with psychological disorders but whose biological parents are psychologically healthy. p. 135

Biofeedback: a procedure in which people are taught to monitor and control their autonomic responses, such as blood pressure, heart rate, skin conductance, and muscular tension. p. 136

Case Report: Harold Morrill

As I approached Harold Morrill in the waiting room, my eyes were drawn first to the two small gold earrings in his left ear. His appearance caught my attention in a few other ways as well. Perhaps it was his shaggy, unkempt look, or maybe I was struck by the fact that he appeared to be so much younger than the age—29 years—that was listed on his intake form.

Harold's initial description of his distress gave me a first glimpse into his confused state: "I feel lost and empty. I can't stand being alone, and yet I'm furious that people can't accept me for what I am. Sometimes, I just want to kill myself to make other people feel some of the pain that I feel all the time!" He followed this plaintive outcry by sharing with me his long history of emotional problems—a life that he characterized as filled with depression, anxiety, irritability, and uncontrollable anger. He spoke of the "emotional roller coaster" of his life that has left others, as well as himself, feeling bewildered.

When Harold spoke of his relationships, I found myself affected by the intensity of his interactions with others, both at work and in his personal life. In response to my inquiry about his numerous job changes, he described a series of bitter disputes with co-workers, most of which culminated in abrupt departures from jobs, either because Harold was fired or because he stormed out in anger. His intimate relationships were similarly unstable. Moving from partner to partner every few months, Harold had a long string of relationships, most of which ended because of Harold's violent outbursts and rageful interactions. In discussing his most recent lover, for instance, Harold told me with a seemingly gleeful tone of voice about the time he punctured the tires on her car in a fit of rage when she told him that she planned to take a vacation without him. Harold also described an experience during this particular incident that left him feeling a bit frightened that things were really getting out of control—he believed that a voice was telling him that his partner was a "she-demon who should be punished."

Although recognizing that desperate behaviors such as these had chased away previous lovers, Harold dreaded the pain of not being in an intimate relationship. Driven to panic and despair by these feelings of emptiness, Harold found himself rushing into new relationships with people who became instantaneously idealized in his mind. Each time, the infatuation quickly deteriorated into vicious animosity.

When I asked Harold about his sexual orientation, he described yet another issue that caused him confusion. He acknowledged that he was not sure whether his preference is for intimate relationships with men or with women and he explained his ambivalence by stating that the gender of his partner is less important than the person's ability to make a commitment to him.

After listening to Harold describe his chaotic and unsatisfying relationships, I became increasingly concerned about his ability to commit himself to a psychotherapy relationship. I also felt concerned about his capacity to act in abusive ways toward his therapist. My concerns intensified as Harold told me about his three prior experiences with psychotherapy, each of which he ended abruptly because of the "incompetence" of the professionals who were treating him. In response to my questions about whether he could make a commitment to long-term therapy, Harold tried to assure me that he was now "ready" to get the help he needed to become happier in life.

Sarah Tobin, PhD

6

PERSONALITY DISORDERS

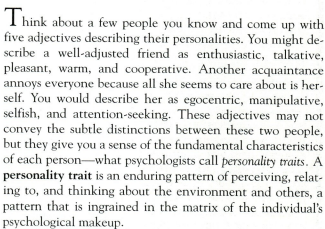

Think about a few people you know and come up with five adjectives describing their personalities. You might describe a well-adjusted friend as enthusiastic, talkative, pleasant, warm, and cooperative. Another acquaintance annoys everyone because all she seems to care about is herself. You would describe her as egocentric, manipulative, selfish, and attention-seeking. These adjectives may not convey the subtle distinctions between these two people, but they give you a sense of the fundamental characteristics of each person—what psychologists call *personality traits*. A **personality trait** is an enduring pattern of perceiving, relating to, and thinking about the environment and others, a pattern that is ingrained in the matrix of the individual's psychological makeup.

Personality disorders also are ingrained patterns of relating to other people, situations, and events, but with a rigid and maladaptive quality. For example, a young woman has a trait of affective instability: she tends to be moody and unpredictable. Although these traits are diagnostic of a personality disorder, the woman's behavior does not meet the other criteria for such a diagnosis. Her problem is not so maladaptive that it results in significant impairment in her functioning or excessive feelings of distress. By contrast, we saw that Harold's instability causes him considerable difficulty and unhappiness. Not only is he extremely unstable, but he seems to lack any other way of functioning emotionally. Because of the maladaptive nature of Harold's instability along with other features of his behavior, Harold would be regarded as having a personality disorder.

After reading this chapter, you should be able to:

- Define the characteristics of a personality disorder.

- Understand the nature of each of the personality disorders and the most current theories and treatments.

- Be able to compare the major theoretical approaches to understanding the personality disorders.

- Explain the major treatment approaches to the personality disorders, comparing psychodynamic and cognitive-behavioral perspectives.

- Understand the difficulties in everyday life that become problematic for people with personality disorders.

- Describe some of the proposed contributors in early childhood to the later development of personality disorders.

THE NATURE OF PERSONALITY DISORDERS

The personality disorders represent a collection of very diverse and complex patterns of behavior. The expression of psychological disturbance is quite different for each, yet the problems of these people are with them every day and in every interpersonal dealing. Whether in the form of excessive dependency, overwhelming fear of intimacy, intense worry, exploitative behavior, or uncontrollable rage, if their problems are left untreated, they will face a life filled with dissatisfaction. Their style of living and relating to others will only worsen as a vicious cycle becomes entrenched in which their disturbed personal style alienates others, resulting in the intensification of their problematic styles of relating. Because personality disorders involve the whole fabric of an individual's being, clinicians typically perceive them as being the most challenging of the psychological disorders to treat.

In considering the possibility that someone has a personality disorder, it is important to look at the person's overall life history. Have the person's problems played a long-term pervasive role throughout life? Or are they more circumscribed, perhaps related to a particular event or relationship? If the problems appear to be longstanding difficulties that go beyond the specifics of the particular situation, this person may very well have a personality disorder.

Take the example of a sensitive young woman who worries about whether the co-workers at her new job like her or not; she fears that they may be making critical comments about her work when she is out of the office. Assuming this to be a single incident, she would not be considered to have a personality disorder. By contrast, if the woman has a lifelong history of believing that others are talking about her, ridiculing her, or trying to harm her, this pattern would be considered rigid and maladaptive and would be regarded as indicative of a personality disorder.

The diagnosis of a personality disorder is particularly difficult because often the client is seeking treatment for other, more specific problems. For example, a severe depression can mask an underlying personality disorder. In one study of more than 200 patients who were hospitalized for serious depression, it was determined that at least 35 percent, and possibly as many as 75 percent, had personality disorders (Shea et al., 1987). Another diagnostic complication is that many personality disorders share similar features (Loranger et al., 1984; Morey, 1988). Because of these types of issues, the authors of *DSM-IV* have relied on large-scale empirical studies to help determine what changes are needed in the diagnostic criteria for these disorders (Widiger & Shea, 1991).

The two most extensively researched personality disorders are antisocial personality disorder and borderline personality disorder. For each of these disorders there is a

The woman talking may think her friends are ridiculing her. A lifelong pattern of suspicion toward others can be indicative of one of the personality disorders.

relatively specific set of theoretical perspectives and treatment approaches. Consequently, we will devote full sections to these two personality disorders. We will describe the remaining personality disorders, with the exception of one, in pairs that have a logical connection. There are so many personality disorders that it may initially be difficult to keep them straight. The pairings in this chapter should help you remember the distinguishing features of each disorder.

ANTISOCIAL PERSONALITY DISORDER

If you watch your local television news any night of the week, you will invariably hear about some shocking crime that has occurred that day. In many instances, the perpetrator has a long history of criminal behavior. When you hear such a story, you may wonder how a person with any sense of morality could have committed such a crime. Chances are that many of these criminals have **antisocial personality disorder** (Hare, 1983), which is characterized by lack of regard for society's moral or legal standards.

Characteristics of Antisocial Personality Disorder

Although you may never have heard the label "antisocial personality disorder," you may have heard of people called *psychopaths* or *sociopaths*, terms commonly used to refer to people with a pattern of traits that would currently be labeled antisocial personality disorder. For example, consider the case of the "Hillside Strangler," Kenneth Bianchi, who terrorized the people of southern California in the late 1970s by sexually assaulting and brutally murdering more than a dozen women and leaving their bodies strewn along highways. Or, recall the case of Ted Bundy, the serial killer, who was linked to the sexual assault and ruthless murder of several dozen women, yet was able to deceive people with his charming style. Both Bianchi and Bundy committed such brutal acts without concern for right or wrong, and without remorse for their deeds.

Most cases of antisocial personality disorder are far less extreme than Kenneth Bianchi or Ted Bundy, yet all share the characteristic of a lack of concern for what is right or wrong. People with this disorder wreak havoc in our society, and for this reason they have been the focus of a great deal of research. Antisocial personality disorder is disturbingly common, with an estimated prevalence of 5 percent of the adult males and 1 percent of the adult females in the United States (Robins et al., 1984).

Even if people with antisocial personality disorder never commit a serious crime, their lives are characterized by a long list of disreputable or manipulative behaviors. They lie, cheat, steal, fight, abuse alcohol and drugs, act promiscuously, and ignore family and job responsibilities. They behave in an impulsive, aggressive, and reckless manner, and show no remorse for the hurtful effects of their behavior. At times they may feign remorse, but even this is done with the intention of extricating themselves from a difficult situation. Some people with this disorder are "smooth talkers" who are able to get what they want by presenting themselves in a favorable light. For example, a man with this disorder may persuade others to give him money by using manipulative sales tactics, or he may play on their sympathy by convincing them that he is a victim of circumstances, and in the process get them to do something special for him.

It is important to distinguish between antisocial personality disorder and **adult antisocial behavior**, which refers to illegal or immoral behaviors such as stealing, lying, and cheating. It is only when such antisocial behaviors become longstanding characteristics that antisocial personality disorder would be considered an appropriate diagnosis.

As is the case with all personality disorders, the problematic characteristics of people with antisocial personality disorder are enduring in nature. That is, their problems begin in childhood and continue throughout most of their adulthood. As children, many of them have had serious problems with **impulse control**, the ability to restrain one's immediate needs or desires, and were regarded as having a conduct disorder (Loeber, 1990). Children with **conduct disorder**, as you will read in Chapter 13, get in trouble at home, in school, and in their neighborhoods. The more frequent and diverse the childhood antisocial acts are, the more likely the individual is to have a lifelong pattern of antisocial behavior in adulthood (Loeber, 1982). In moving toward *DSM-IV*, researchers have proposed adding trait-like diagnostic criteria for antisocial personality disorder to incorporate this evidence suggesting that long-standing personality dispositions drive people to seek a life of crime (Hare et al., 1991; Widiger et al., 1991).

Although the predictors in childhood of adult antisocial personality disorder seem relatively clear, the "careers" of these people are less well understood. Statistics show that the criminal activities of people with antisocial personality disorder seem to decrease when they reach the age of 40 (Hare et al., 1988), and that 94 percent of all serious crimes are committed by men under the age of 45 (U.S. Department of Commerce, 1989). Do older antisocial individuals experience "burnout," or have they just become more adept at avoiding detection? Or perhaps some of the more extreme cases are eliminated from the population because these people are killed or arrested in the course of their criminal activities. Most crime experts agree that with increasing age, people become mellower in this regard and are less likely to commit serious crimes (Shover, 1985).

Theories and Treatment

As you have just seen, antisocial personality disorder represents a deeply entrenched pattern of behavior with wide-ranging effects both on the individual and on people who come into contact with the individual. Here we will consider the most compelling explanations for the development of this personality disorder.

■ *Biological perspectives*

When you hear about a terrible crime such as a vicious mugging or ruthless murder, you probably don't presume that a biologically based disorder caused the perpetrator to commit this act. You may be surprised, then, to learn that there are a number of biological hypotheses of criminal behavior. There was tremendous excitement, for example, when researchers in the mid-1960s (Jacobs et al., 1965) made a discovery that they thought would explain what causes antisocial behavior. Some notorious criminals were found to have an extra Y (male) chromosome, causing an XYY pattern instead of the normal XY pair on chromosome 23. The extra chromosome was thought to be the cause of the criminals' brutally aggressive behaviors. This finding stimulated larger-scale research which ultimately failed to indicate a relationship between serious criminal behavior and the extra male chromosome (Witkin et al., 1977). Although this particular hypothesis was discredited, researchers have continued to pursue other biological causes and correlates of antisocial behavior.

A second biological hypothesis concerns the possibility that **testosterone**, the male sex hormone, is associated with the extent of a man's aggressive behavior (Olweus, 1987). However, it is difficult to determine, as you might imagine, whether higher testosterone is the cause or the result of heightened aggressiveness.

Various brain abnormalities are also cited as possible causes of antisocial personality disorder. These include defects in the frontal lobes of the cerebral cortex (Gorenstein, 1982), areas of the brain involved in planning future activities and in considering the moral implications of one's actions. Another potential source of defects is in the limbic system, which is involved in the control of aggressive behaviors. At one time, scientists were convinced that the **amygdala**, a part of the limbic system, played a role in causing the aggressive acts associated with antisocial behavior. Consequently, psychosurgery was recommended as a way of treating violent cases (O'Callaghan & Carroll, 1987).

Other biological approaches regard antisocial personality disorder as due to neuropsychological deficits in learning and attention. Hervey Cleckley (1950, 1976), a pioneering theorist in the field, wrote a fascinating clinical account reporting that people with this disorder are emotionally insensitive to events that others would regard as anxiety-provoking. Following along these lines, David Lykken (1957) found these individuals to be less physiologically reactive to aversive stimuli (electric shock). These findings, supported by later research (Patrick et al., 1990), would imply that people with antisocial personality disorder may not respond to threats of jail terms because they do not experience normal levels of anxiety. Interestingly, this abnormal pattern of responsiveness to threatening stimuli may explain why some people with antisocial personality

disorder are able to lie their way through a lie detector test without showing the increase in skin conductance that is taken as evidence of lying.

Further support for biological correlates of antisocial personality disorder comes from studies of electroencephalograms (EEGs). Criminals have slower alpha wave activity, indicating lower levels of arousal while awake (Itil, 1981; Mednick et al., 1987). This fundamental abnormality has two possible effects: under-arousal of the brain may contribute to a lower emotional reactivity in the individual, and criminals may be less able to learn from their experiences (Volavka, 1987).

If we move from these biological findings to a developmental understanding of antisocial personality disorder, we arrive at a new picture. These individuals may have neuropsychological limitations that impaired their ability as children to acquire the necessary socialization that leads ordinary people to follow cultural expectations. They did not learn how to stay out of trouble and to avoid the consequences that result from delinquent behavior. As adults, they continue this pattern, failing to modify their behavior in response to punishment (Buikhuisen, 1987).

If these neuropsychological abnormalities account for antisocial behavior, how is it that they develop in the first place? One possible cause is inheritance. It has been observed for decades that criminal behavior runs in families. As with other behaviors found to show such a pattern, scientists have questioned whether antisocial behavior is learned or is genetically acquired. We turn next to adoption studies and studies of family inheritance patterns used in the study of criminal behavior as clues to the understanding of the roots of antisocial personality disorder.

Studies of family inheritance patterns show that identical twins have a much higher concordance rate of criminal behavior (52 percent) than fraternal twins (22 percent) (Christiansen, 1977). However, some of the reason for the higher association could be that identical twins influence each other's behavior more than do fraternal twins (Carey, 1992).

Stronger evidence in favor of the genetic contribution to antisocial behavior comes from adoption studies. In a Danish study of more than 14,000 adoptions (Mednick et al., 1987), researchers found that the adopted male children of biological fathers with a criminal history had a higher crime rate than adopted sons whose fathers had no criminal record. Furthermore, the more longstanding the pattern of criminal behavior in the biological father, the greater the likelihood of criminal behavior in the adopted-away son. Given what appears to be an important role of genetics in determining criminal behavior, further research is needed to establish the link between genetic patterns of inheritance and abnormal psychophysiological reactivity.

■ *Psychological perspectives*

When we began our discussion of biological perspectives, we pointed out that few people would think of biology when they analyze the causes of criminal behavior. Rather,

they would focus on psychological factors, both as correlates and as causes of this personality disorder. Correlational research on factors related to antisocial personality disorder has focused on the presence of psychological problems in these people. For example, one group of researchers took a close look at a group of more than 500 people with antisocial personality disorder treated in Missouri mental health facilities during the 1970s, and found that approximately one-fourth of these people suffered from depression and anxiety (Weiss et al., 1983). Are these people depressed and anxious because of their personality disorder, or does their disorder result from emotional distress? Although this question cannot be answered by correlational research, the existence of a relationship between distress and antisocial personality disorder suggests that maybe not all individuals with this disorder are incapable of feeling remorse.

A more extensive line of research has focused on the factors in early life that may contribute to the development of antisocial personality disorder. One particular important factor seems to disharmony in the home. The landmark research in this area was a 30-year follow-up study of juvenile delinquents carried out by Lee Robins (1966). Although it is commonly assumed that children of divorce later develop problems because of a lack of adequate discipline, Robins found that it is not the event of divorce itself but disharmony between parents that preceded the child's development of antisocial behavior. Why might this be? According to Robins, the type of parents who are likely to argue excessively, especially fathers, may themselves have psychological difficulties, including antisocial tendencies.

In the research by Robins and others on the effect on a child of different kinds of child-rearing, inconsistent discipline appears to be especially problematic. When parents vacillate between unreasonable harshness and extreme laxity they send confusing messages to the child about what is right and what is wrong, or what is acceptable and what is unacceptable. Children with such parents fail to make a connection between their actions, bad or good, and the consequences (Buss, 1966).

Other discipline styles thought to predispose children to delinquency are excessive leniency and inattentiveness to children's misbehavior (McCord & McCord, 1959). Clearly, a parent who ignores or fails to deal with a child's misbehavior is setting the stage for later problems. One reason that discipline and rule enforcement are so important is that children feel more secure when their parents set limits for them. Even though the consequences may be difficult for the child to accept at the moment, it is nevertheless reassuring to know that parents are concerned about the child's well-being. In a related vein, children with parents who fail to show affection are prone to develop cold and

Researchers have been puzzled for decades about the causes of antisocial behavior.

distant relationships later in life. This kind of insensitivity breeds a personal style in which the exploitation of other people seems natural (Buss, 1966). Even more extreme are those parents who reject their children, a parental style that is frequently correlated with antisocial behavior (Eron & Huesmann, 1984; McCord & McCord, 1964).

Another common belief about people with antisocial personality disorder is that they come from impoverished backgrounds where people hold low-status jobs. Robert Merton, one of the most important sociologists of the twentieth century, has proposed that poverty leads some individuals to feel despondent over their inability to achieve what our society promotes as desirable material goals. Consequently, some of these individuals turn to a life of crime as a way of acquiring possessions (Merton, 1968). A number of researchers have reported results in support of the relationship between low social status and criminality (Gordon, 1976).

However, we might wonder whether antisocial behavior is the result of lower socioeconomic status or whether there are some mediating factors, such as education (McGarvey, et al., 1981). Children in lower-class environments typically have restricted access to high-quality schools, and they become trapped in the cycle of poverty. Forced to live in high-crime, inner-city neighborhoods, these children are recurrently exposed to negative influences. This does not mean, however, that poverty by itself causes a person to develop an antisocial personality disorder. In fact, you may be able to think of well-known individuals from the upper-middle class who have gained notoriety in recent years for their flagrantly antisocial behaviors, such as stock market fraud, tax evasion, and illegal banking practices. As Robins (1966) pointed out, criminal behavior is more likely to occur in families of any social class when the father is antisocial.

In considering theories on the cause of antisocial personality disorder, keep in mind that most studies are based, by necessity, on data from incarcerated individuals. Many people with antisocial personality disorder are able to avoid getting caught or prosecuted for their crimes. The remaining sample may be biased in some way toward the less "effective" criminals.

■ Treating antisocial personality disorder

From our discussion about antisocial personality disorder, you can probably conclude that people with this disorder do not change easily. For that matter, they are unlikely to seek professional help voluntarily. When they do see a clinician, it is because treatment is mandated by a court order. A clinician faced with treating such a client may have difficulty knowing what to believe, and whether the client has an ulterior motive. The client may be attempting to impress a judge or a probation officer of a serious intent to reform. Without giving up on the client or operating on the basis of preconceived biases, the clinician must be careful not to become unduly optimistic.

Tommy was the leader of a teenage street gang that was reputed to be the most vicious in the neighborhood. He grew up in a chaotic home atmosphere, his mother having lived with a series of violent men who were heavily into drug dealing and prostitution. At the age of 18, Tommy was jailed for the brutal mugging and stabbing of an elderly woman. This was the first in a long series of arrests for offenses ranging from drug trafficking to car thefts to counterfeiting. At one point, between jail terms, he met a woman at a bar and married her the next day. Two weeks later, he beat her when she complained about his incessant drinking and involvement with shady characters. He left her when she became pregnant, and refused to pay child support. From his vantage point now as a drug trafficker and leader of a child prostitution ring, Tommy shows no regret for what he has done, claiming that life has "sure given me a bum steer."

■ What behaviors of Tommy's would lead you to regard him as having antisocial personality disorder?

■ What does Tommy's lack of remorse suggest about his prospects for treatment?

Nevertheless, given the incorrigibility of people with antisocial personality disorder, how can a clinician achieve a satisfactory treatment goal? Experts contend that these people change their behavior only when they realize that what they have done is wrong (e.g., Lion, 1987). This realization can come about only when they begin to feel remorse for their hurtful behavior toward others. At this point they will begin to feel depressed and guilty. Thus, the goal of therapy, ironically, is not to get these individuals to feel better, but rather to feel worse about themselves and their situations. To accomplish this goal, the clinician must initially adopt a confrontational approach, showing ostensible disbelief for the client's presumed fabrications, and continually reflecting back to these clients the selfish and

In treating people with antisocial personality disorder, one strategy is to try to develop a sense of remorse in the individual for past criminal acts.

self-defeating nature of their behavior. Group therapy can be helpful in this process because the feedback from peers, who cannot be easily deceived, can have a forceful impact. When therapy successfully brings these clients to such powerful realization, feelings of hopelessness and despondency are likely to ensue. Keep in mind, though, that such a "positive" outcome is extremely difficult to achieve.

BORDERLINE PERSONALITY DISORDER

When you first see the term *borderline*, you may wonder what it means. Most of the other personality disorders have labels, such as *antisocial* or *paranoid,* that convey the essence of the disorder. What does it mean to be borderline? In current terminology, **borderline personality disorder** is characterized by a pervasive pattern of unstable mood, interpersonal relationships, and self-image. We will turn later to a more precise description of the symptoms of this disorder, but first let's look at how this diagnosis has evolved. As you will see, there has been considerable controversy among proponents of different theoretical traditions about what constitutes this disorder.

Characteristics of Borderline Personality Disorder

When the term *borderline* first became popular in psychiatry, it was used as a catchall for the most difficult and treatment-resistant of clients (Stern, 1938). These individuals were felt to be functioning somewhere at the "border" between neurosis and psychosis, on the fringes of schizophrenia (Knight, 1953). Despite the vagueness of the borderline concept, the term remained in use because it served to describe a certain subgroup of clients who did not seem to fit into the existing diagnostic categories. Efforts to clarify and define the nature of the disorder continued through the 1980s (Edell, 1987). Some researchers have maintained that borderline personality disorder is a variant of schizophrenia or mood disorder, or possibly a hybrid. The fact that it is regarded as a personality disorder reflects the predominant current understanding of the borderline condition as a separate entity from these disorders (McGlashan, 1983). However, the degree of overlap between borderline and other personality disorders remains to be specified (Gunderson & Zanarini, 1987).

You can get a sense of what a person with borderline personality is like from considering the qualities of the character Alex in the movie *Fatal Attraction*. If you saw the movie, you probably recall the very dramatic scene in which Alex became overwhelmingly distraught following a one-night sexual encounter and slashed her wrists at the moment her sexual partner was preparing to leave. In the weeks that followed, Alex obsessively pursued this man. Her intense emotionality and rage terrified him as well as the millions of moviegoers who sat in shock as she acted out many outrageous and disturbing behaviors (such as boiling the pet rabbit that belonged to the man's family). The intensity of this relationship, even one so brief, gives you a glimpse into a central characteristic of people with this disorder—their unstable interpersonal relationships (Modestin, 1987).

People with borderline personality disorder often experience a distinct kind of depression that is characterized by feelings of emptiness and variable negative emotionality (Westen, 1991). Although they rarely go so far as to harass other people, they tend to be deeply affected by interpersonal incidents that most other people would let pass. It is common for people with this disorder to form suddenly intense, demanding relationships with others, and for them to perceive other people as being "all good" or "all bad"—a phenomenon referred to as **splitting**. The inappropriate intensity of their relationships results in recurrent experiences of distress and rage. In fact, anger and hostility are enduring characteristics found in many people with this disorder (Gardner et al., 1991).

In addition to having disturbed relationships, people with borderline personality disorder are often confused about their own **identity**, or concept of "who" they are. Even after they have passed through the customary time of identity questioning in adolescence, they are unsure of what they want out of life and, at a deeper level, lack a firm grasp on their sense of self. This identity confusion may reach a point at which they become unclear about the boundaries between themselves and others. For example, in close relationships, they may have difficulty distinguishing between their own feelings and the feelings of the other person.

Other identity problems appear in the area of sexual orientation; these individuals may remain confused throughout life about whether they are homosexual or heterosexual, perhaps experimenting with a variety of partners. At times, their desperate pursuit of intimacy emerges from feelings of emptiness. They need someone else to make them feel complete. Being alone can be torture, and they will do almost anything to hold onto a relationship or maintain contact with other people.

Part of the search for stimulation through intimacy may also be attributable to chronic feelings of boredom. In order to fend off boredom these people may also engage in impulsive behaviors, including promiscuity, careless spending, reckless driving, binge eating, substance abuse, or shoplifting. Some individuals claim that the excitement from these activities makes them feel alive. Their moods are as unstable as their behavior. They may vacillate between extreme emotional states, one day feeling on top of the world, and the next feeling depressed, anxious, and irritable.

The extremes of feelings experienced by people with borderline personality disorder may drive them precipitously into a state of suicidal thinking and self-injurious behavior. Sometimes they are not intent on killing themselves, and their behavior—called **parasuicide** (Kreitman, 1977)—would be considered a gesture to get attention from family, a lover, or professionals. In other cases, they may hurt themselves with a knife or razor in an act of self-directed aggression (Simeon et al., 1992). Such behavior sometimes serves as a way of testing to see whether they are actually alive, a concept that most people take for granted but one that becomes a source of uncertainty for people with this disorder. The sight of blood and the physical pain is reassuring for them because it proves that their bodies have substance.

What is most striking to people who come into contact with individuals with borderline personality disorder is the fact that these people seem intensely angry much of the time. Even without provocation, they may fly into a fury. A seemingly innocent comment by a friend may cause them to lash out or seethe inwardly. Their rage may lead them to express physical violence against others.

Although people with this disorder are disturbed in many aspects of their functioning, most are able to manage the responsibilities of everyday life. Some are actually successful in various contexts (think of Alex in *Fatal Attraction*, who had a well-paid, important job). Yet, for many, there is a constant undercurrent of interpersonal conflict, and the risk that their unpredictability, dependency, and moodiness may drive their close ones away. At times, the demands of their lives may become overwhelming, and they fall into a transient psychotic-like state possibly characterized by delusional thinking. Such disruptions, if frequent enough, can lead them to require hospitalization.

Theories and Treatment

The seriousness of symptoms associated with borderline personality disorder and the fact that they often verge on being psychotic has led some investigators to pursue biological causes of the disorder. One group of researchers has found that relatives of people with this disorder are much more likely to have a history of borderline personality disorder or borderline-like disorders (Loranger et al., 1982), giving credence to the likelihood that genetics plays an important role. Researchers are also studying possible biological contributors to this disorder, and in the process are trying to identify physiological markers that would distinguish borderline personality disorder from mood disorders and schizophrenia. The search for these biological indices has focused on neuroendocrine functions and electrophysiological measures (Kutcher et al., 1987; Steiner et al., 1988). However, controversy exists over whether these measures can uniquely identify borderline personality disorder, because it is difficult to find people with this disorder who have no symptoms of another major clinical disorder.

Given what seems to be a fundamental disturbance in the identities of individuals with borderline personality disorder, psychological theories explaining its cause focus on problems in the early development of the self. Psychodynamic theorists such as Grinker (1979), Klein (1989),

Lisa is a 28-year-old account executive with a long history of interpersonal problems. At the office, her co-workers see her as being intensely moody and unpredictable. On some days she is pleasant and high-spirited, and on others she exhibits uncontrollable anger. Other people are often struck by her inconsistent attitudes toward her supervisors. She vacillates between idealizing them and devaluing them. For example, she may boast about the "brilliance" of her supervisor one day, only to follow with a burning criticism the next day. Her co-workers keep their distance from her because they have become annoyed with her constant demands for attention. She has also gained a reputation in the office for her promiscuous involvements with a variety of people, male and female. On several occasions she has been reprimanded for becoming inappropriately involved in the personal lives of her clients. One day, after losing one of her accounts, she became so distraught that she slashed her wrists. This incident prompted her supervisor to insist that Lisa obtain professional help.

- What would lead you to diagnose Lisa as having borderline personality disorder rather than a mood disorder such as depression?
- How does Lisa's disorder interfere with her ability to succeed at her profession?

Kernberg (1967), Masterson (1981), and Gunderson (1984) describe family conditions that seem linked to the later development of borderline pathology. It is thought that parents who fail to bolster the child's independent sense of self set the stage for a later lack of identity and sense of commitment to life goals. The child cannot develop a healthy "real" self that can form the basis for intimate, sharing, and committed relationships with others, or that can be creative, spontaneous, and assertive. Instead, the individual perceives other people in a distorted way, and builds a false self that is fused with these distorted perceptions of others (Masterson & Klein, 1989).

Abusive parenting is thought to be one cause of borderline personality disorder.

People with borderline personality disorder often have a difficult time with good-byes. Reluctant to end the session, such a client may bring up an "important" new issue, ignoring the therapist's cues that it is time to get up and leave.

Other possible causes of borderline personality disorder include early sexual, emotional, and physical abuse (Herman et al., 1989; Ogata et al., 1989; Westen et al., 1990). Serious neglect and inconsistency in parenting are also linked to the emergence of borderline symptoms. These conditions create a sense of insecurity in the child, who continually seeks comfort and reassurance but fails to find it. Millon (1987) contends that the deficient parenting that can give rise to this disorder may be exacerbated by the pressures of contemporary society that have placed a strain on families and individuals. Another possibility is that this pattern is perpetuated across generations, as the adult with borderline personality disorder who was abused as a child passes on this pattern of parenting to the next generation, who then become vulnerable to developing the disorder (Stone, 1990).

A cognitive-behavioral approach to understanding people with borderline personality disorder focuses on their maladaptive thoughts. According to Beck et al. (1990), people with this disorder have a tendency to dichotomize their thinking about themselves and other people—to think in terms of all or nothing. Such thinking could account for the individual's tendency to shift moods so readily and to use splitting in their relationships with others. If people are perceived as all good or all bad, when a person originally perceived as "good" fails to follow through on a promise, there is no middle ground and that person immediately becomes "bad." People with borderline personality disorder also apply this limited set of standards when evaluating themselves, and when they perceive themselves as falling short even on minor grounds, their entire self-evaluation is cast in a negative light. Finally, a low sense of self-efficacy related to their weak identity causes a lack of confidence in their decisions, low motivation, and inability to seek long-term goals.

Due to their volatility, inconsistency, and intensity, people with borderline personality disorder have difficulty remaining in therapy long enough to make progress. It is not uncommon for these individuals to become pathologically dependent on their therapist, and as a result to feel uncontrollably enraged when the therapist fails to live up to their idealizations. Consequently, therapists are watchful of their own emotional reactions, recognizing that these clients may evoke intense feelings of anger or helplessness. Furthermore, since these clients are prone to distort their relationship to the therapist, it is necessary to try to keep the client grounded in reality (Kernberg et al., 1989).

Some experts propose that therapists should confront the client's process of splitting, perhaps by pointing out the contradictory emotional responses that the client shows toward the therapist from session to session (Kernberg, 1984). Similarly, experts advise that the intensity of the client's responses to the therapist should be confronted in a gentle but firm manner. For example, a client may overreact to a therapist's vacation, misinterpreting it as abandonment. In response to the client's distortion, the therapist should attend to the client's distress but also make it clear that this vacation is routine and does not represent rejection.

Another crucial component of therapy is to provide a sense of stability and predictability. This includes consistency with regard to the scheduling of appointments and payment of fees. Clients with borderline personality disorder often try to manipulate these conditions, and the therapist must provide firm structure to keep the treatment on course. Similarly, the therapist must maintain very clear professional boundaries. These clients may try to become inappropriately involved in the personal life of the therapist, and so therapists must be particularly scrupulous about not encouraging such involvement. Finally, realizing that people with borderline personality disorder are at risk of hurting themselves through suicide attempts, drug abuse, or promiscuity, the therapist should help the client realize the self-destructive nature of these behaviors. These strategies for treating clients with this disorder are important regardless of the clinician's theoretical orientation (Waldinger, 1986).

Although clinicians agree on certain key facets of therapy for people with borderline personality disorder, controversy remains about whether to focus more on confrontive or supportive approaches (Gunderson, 1989). Some clinicians believe that the client's manipulative behavior can be held in check only by confrontation (Gunderson, 1984; Kernberg, 1975, 1984; Masterson, 1976; Masterson & Klein, 1989). When a client makes a derogatory remark about the therapist, for example, the therapist can use this opportunity to show the client the inappropriateness and destructiveness of misdirected anger. In contrast, other clinicians (Buie & Adler, 1982; Chessick, 1982) recommend a more supportive, nurturant technique. The therapist then would respond to the client's anger with statements of concern and understanding. This approach is based on the assumption that the client's disorder is the result of poor parenting, and that the therapist can provide a positive parental role. Carrying this supportive style a step further, some clinicians integrate supportive and cognitive-behavioral techniques to reduce the frequency of self-destructive acts (Linehan et al., 1991) and to improve the client's ability to handle feelings of anger and dependency (Linehan, 1987). In another integrative approach, cognitive-behavioral therapy can be combined with psychodynamic therapy (Westen, 1991); in this model, more emphasis is placed on interpretation than on simply providing support.

As an adjunct to psychological treatment of people with borderline personality disorder, some clinicians recommend medication. Depending on the individual's predominant symptoms, various medications have been tried, including antidepressants, antipsychotic drugs, lithium, and minor tranquilizers. These medications can alleviate some of the more distressing features of the disorder, but they must be prescribed with caution because of the possibility that the client might overdose or refuse to comply.

As you can see, both the symptoms and the treatment of people with borderline personality disorder are challenging and complex. In severe cases, successful treatment can be undertaken only in an inpatient setting. This is particularly true when clients are suicidal, experience psychotic-like episodes, or threaten harm to other people. The hospital can provide a safe and secure setting in which limits can be established and maintained. (Stone, 1990).

You can probably gather that treatment is a lengthy process, often taking years. Psychotherapy is further complicated by the fact that many people with this disorder also suffer from symptoms of other disorders such as a mood disorder or substance abuse. Clinicians treating these individuals face the challenge of trying to reconstruct a personality by establishing a therapeutic relationship aimed at correcting the individual's flawed early developmental history.

PARANOID PERSONALITY DISORDER

The term *paranoia*, as you have already learned, means suspiciousness, guardedness, and vigilance toward other people based on the belief that others intend harm. As you will see later in the book, paranoid thinking is present in various psychological disorders. Here we look at the personality disorder that is characterized by paranoia.

Characteristics of Paranoid Personality Disorder

People with **paranoid personality disorder** are extremely suspicious of others and are always on guard against potential danger or harm. Their view of the world is very narrowly focused, in that they seek to confirm their expectations that others will take advantage of them. This suspiciousness makes it virtually impossible for them to trust others. They refuse to take responsibility for their mistakes, and instead project blame onto others. If they are criticized, they become hostile. Although individuals with this disorder might be relatively successful in certain kinds of jobs requiring heightened vigilance, their emotional life tends to be isolated and constrained.

As you can imagine, the relationships of people with paranoid personality disorder are problematic. They keep other people at a distance because of irrational fears that others will harm them, and they are particularly sensitive to people in positions of power. For example, they may create a "paper trail" of their work, keeping records of everything in case they are ever accused of a mistake or impropriety.

A certain amount of paranoid thinking and behavior might be appropriate in some situations, such as in dangerous political climates where people must be on guard just to stay alive. However, people with paranoid personality disorder think and behave in ways that are unrelated to their environment.

Particularly frustrating to the relatives and acquaintances of these people is the fact that they refuse to seek professional help because they don't acknowledge the nature of their problem. In the unlikely event that they do seek therapy, their rigidity and defensiveness make it very difficult for the clinician to make inroads and work toward any kind of lasting change.

Theories and Treatment

Psychodynamic explanations of paranoid personality disorder see it as a style of viewing the world that is heavily reliant on the defense mechanism of projection, in which other people, rather than the self, are perceived as having negative or damaging motives (Shapiro, 1965). In contrast,

Anita is a computer programmer who constantly worries that other people will exploit her knowledge. She regards as "top secret" the new database management program she is writing. Even when she leaves the office at night, she fears that someone will sneak into her desk and steal her notes. Her distrust of others pervades all her interpersonal dealings. Even routine transactions in banks or stores are tainted by her suspicions that she is being cheated. Anita likes to think of herself as rational and able to make objective decisions; she regards her inability to trust other people as a natural reaction to a world filled with opportunistic and insincere corporate ladder climbers.

- How does Anita's sense of mistrust impair her relationships with others?
- What would lead you to think that Anita has a paranoid personality disorder rather than a form of psychosis involving paranoid symptoms?

cognitive-behavioral theorists (Beck et al., 1990) regard the person with paranoid personality disorder as someone who suffers from mistaken assumptions about the world. One researcher, using a novel approach of developing a computer simulation of the disorder, proposed that the paranoid individual views the world in terms of the dimensions of shame and humiliation and is primed to attribute mistakes and problems to other people (Colby, 1981). For example, consider the case of Martha, who read the wrong assignment for her biology course and subsequently failed her exam. Rather than attribute her error to her own failure to read the syllabus properly, Martha complained to her friends that it was her professor's fault for failing to remind the class of their reading list the week before the exam. She did not consider the possibility that her own inattentiveness caused the mistake and now uses this incident to prove her thesis that professors really have little regard for their students.

The cognitive-behavioral perspective of Freeman et al. (1990) incorporates these ideas but presents an alternate view, emphasizing the three basic mistaken assumptions held by people with paranoid personality disorder: "People are malevolent and deceptive," "They'll attack you if they get the chance," and "You can be OK only if you stay on your toes." The difficulty created by these assumptions is that they inevitably become proven by the behavior of others. Once you are primed to suspect other people's motives, you are likely to interpret what they do as proof. For instance, perhaps you believe that retail merchants deliberately take advantage of consumers. The next time a salesperson gives you the wrong change, you will interpret this not as a casual error but as confirmation of your fears. According to the cognitive-behavioral view, the third mistaken assumption, that people have to be vigilant to avoid being harmed, is related to feelings of low self-efficacy, leading paranoid people to believe that they cannot discern the harmful intentions of others and therefore must perpetually stay on guard.

The treatment of paranoid personality disorder that follows from the cognitive-behavioral perspective (Freeman et al., 1990) involves countering the client's mistaken assumptions in an atmosphere aimed at establishing a sense of trust. The therapist attempts to increase the client's feelings of self-efficacy so that the client feels able to handle situations without resorting to a defensive and vigilant stance. Since the client is likely to enter therapy feeling distrustful of the therapist, the therapist must allow the client to feel a part of the therapy process through collaboration. Other helpful interventions involve increasing the client's awareness of other points of view and helping the client to develop a more assertive approach to conflict with others. These increased interpersonal skills improve the quality of the client's interactions outside therapy and eventually contribute to disproving the client's mistaken assumptions.

SCHIZOID AND SCHIZOTYPAL PERSONALITY DISORDERS

The term *schizophrenia*, as discussed in Chapter 2, refers to a psychological disorder that causes the individual to experience severe disturbances in thought, affect, and behavior. Two personality disorders, *schizoid* and *schizotypal*, involve disturbances in personality that have schizophrenia-like qualities but do not take on the psychotic form seen in schizophrenia. As you will see in Chapter 12, researchers are studying the relationship between these personality disorders and schizophrenia. In fact, some researchers refer to these three disorders as **schizophrenia spectrum disorders**, implying that all three are on the same dimension of psychological disturbance and may somehow be related. For the present, we will describe the characteristics of these two personality disorders which share some aspects of the symptoms found in schizophrenia.

Characteristics of the Disorders

Schizoid personality disorder is characterized by an indifference to social relationships, as well as a very limited range of emotional experience and expression. Individuals with this disorder prefer to be by themselves rather than with others and they appear to lack any desire to be accepted or loved. They often seem vague about their purpose in life, and are indecisive and absentminded. As you might expect, they are perceived by others as being cold, reserved, withdrawn, and seclusive. Yet, the schizoid individual is unaware of, and typically insensitive to, the feelings and thoughts of others.

Many people with schizoid personality disorder manage to get through life by living and working in situations that involve minimal interactions with others. They prefer jobs in which they spend all of their work hours alone, such as long-distance truck driving. They may live in a single room where they guard their privacy and avoid any dealings with neighbors. Although they are not particularly distressed, or a risk to others, their self-imposed isolation and emotional constriction can be considered maladaptive. Nevertheless, people with schizoid personality disorder are not likely to seek psychotherapy. If they do enter therapy, perhaps for another psychological disorder such as a mood disorder or substance abuse, these people are difficult to treat because of their lack of interest in interpersonal relationships.

People with **schizotypal personality disorder** are regarded by others as being peculiar and even bizarre in the way they relate to others, the way they think, how they act, and even how they dress. Researchers have found that people with schizotypal personality disorder are more likely than those with schizoid personality disorder to show disturbances in thinking and behavior (Widiger et al., 1987). Their peculiar ideas may include magical thinking and beliefs in psychic phenomena such as clairvoyance or telepathy. They may have unusual perceptual experiences in the form of illusions. Though the content of their speech is not

Pedro, who works as a night security guard at a bank, likes his job because he can enter the private world of his thoughts without interruptions from other people. Even though his numerous years of service make him eligible for a daytime security position, Pedro has repeatedly turned down these opportunities because daytime work would require him to deal with bank employees and customers. Pedro has resided for more than 20 years in a small room at a rooming house. He has no television or radio, and he has resisted any attempts on the part of other house residents to involve him in social activities. He has made it clear that he is not interested in "small talk," and that he prefers to be left alone. Neighbors, co-workers, and even his own family members (whom he also avoids) perceive Pedro as a very peculiar person, who seems strikingly cold and detached. When his brother died, Pedro decided not to attend the funeral because he did not want to be bothered by all the "carrying on" and sympathetic wishes of relatives and others.

- To what extent might Pedro's eccentricity be due to his social isolation?
- If Pedro is not unhappy because of his self-imposed isolation, what would justify a diagnosis of schizoid personality disorder?

incoherent, it sounds strange to others. Their affect is inappropriate, and they are often suspicious of other people. Unable to enjoy pleasure, their lives are characterized by a sense of blandness that robs them of capacity for any kind of enthusiasm.

Theories and Treatment

The terms *schizoid* and *schizotypal* were originally meant to convey the notion that these personality disorders share some commonalities with schizophrenia. However, researchers disagree as to whether this is correct. Some believe that the symptoms of social isolation, eccentricity, peculiar communication, and poor social adaptation associated with the schizotypal personality disorder place it within the schizophrenic spectrum (Torgersen, 1985). According to this view, the symptoms of schizotypal personality disorder represent a **latent** form of schizophrenia. This would mean that people with schizotypal symptoms are vulnerable to developing a full-blown psychosis if exposed to difficult life circumstances that challenge their ability to maintain contact with reality. This position has received support from a 15-year follow-up study of people who met the criteria for schizotypal personality disorder, schizophrenia, and borderline personality disorder. At the end of the follow-up period, schizotypal individuals were functioning more like people diagnosed as having schizophrenia than like those with borderline personality disorder (McGlashan, 1986).

Other researchers regard schizotypal personality disorder and schizophrenia as having a genetic link but consti-

Odd behavior and appearance are characteristics of people with schizotypal personality disorder. Aimlessly wandering through town, this man appears absorbed in his own thoughts, unaware of what is going on around him.

Joe is a college junior who has devised an elaborate system for predicting which courses to take depending on the course number. He will not take a course with the number "5" in it because he believes that if he does so, he might have to "plead the Fifth Amendment." Rarely does he talk to people in his dormitory, believing that others are intent on stealing his term paper ideas. He has acquired a reputation for being "kind of flaky" because of his odd manner of dress, his reclusive tendencies, and his ominous drawings of sinister animals displayed on the door of his room. The sound of the nearby elevator, he claims, is actually a set of voices singing a monastic chant.

- How does Joe's lack of interest in social relations compare with the case of Pedro, who has a schizoid personality disorder?
- Why would Joe's odd behaviors constitute schizotypal personality disorder rather than a psychotic disorder?

tuting different disorders. (Baron et al., 1983; Kendler et al., 1981; Siever et al., 1990). In Chapter 12 we will discuss some intriguing research methods that have been used to study modes of genetic transmission. As you will see, many people with these disorders, as well as their relatives, show abnormal responses on specific physiological measures such as eye movements while scanning a visual display. Whether or not schizophrenia and schizotypal personality disorder are part of a continuum of the same disorder remains to be determined as more evidence on the similarities of long-term outcome and modes of genetic transmission becomes available (Siever et al., 1991).

The treatment of people with schizoid and schizotypal personality disorders is extremely difficult because they tend to be so inaccessible, both cognitively and emotionally. Their thinking is hard to follow, they may misinterpret what is said to them, and they lack the normal patterns of emotional responsiveness that play a role in human communications. The therapist must be careful to avoid setting unrealistically high goals for therapy, because progress with these individuals is likely to be slow and limited in scope (Stone, 1983). Most promising is an approach geared toward helping them clarify their communication skills and modify their isolated and eccentric behaviors (Freeman et al., 1990).

HISTRIONIC AND NARCISSISTIC PERSONALITY DISORDERS

Histrionic and narcissistic personality disorders include behaviors that involve excessive displays of emotion and egocentricity. People with these two disorders tend to be perceived by others as selfish, egotistical, unstable, and unreliable. Very little research has been done on either disorder, although some psychodynamic theorists such as Kohut have provided extensive analyses of the characteristics, de-

velopment, and treatment of people with narcissistic personality disorder.

Characteristics of the Disorders

Some people tend to be very dramatic in expressing themselves. When carried to an extreme, these tendencies form the basis for **histrionic personality disorder**. The term *histrionic* is derived from a Latin word meaning "actor." People with this disorder display theatrical qualities in their everyday behavior. They may put on a "show" of being overwhelmed with tears and sentimentality at the wedding of a distant relative. Similarly, they may greet an acquaintance at a party with ostentatious and attention-getting hugs and exclamations of affection. What differentiates people with this disorder from those who show appropriate emotionality is the fleeting nature of their emotional states and the fact that they show these excessive emotions for the effects on others rather than to express their feelings. This disorder is more commonly diagnosed in women, though it is not clear whether this is true because the disorder is more common in women, or because those assigning the label regard histrionic behaviors as stereotypically feminine.

People with histrionic personality disorder enjoy being the center of attention, and behave in whatever way necessary to ensure that this happens. Excessive concern with their own appearance may draw attention, but at times it may be so extreme that is makes them look ludicrous. Furthermore, they are likely to be seen as flirtatious and seductive, demanding the reassurance, praise, and approval of others, and becoming furious if they are rejected. They want immediate gratification of their wishes, and overreact to even minor provocations, usually in an exaggerated way such as by weeping or fainting. Although their relationships are superficial, they mistakenly assume them to be intimate, and refer to acquaintances as "dear" friends (Pfohl, 1991). These personality disturbances spread to the realm of cognitive function in that they usually lack analytic ability and perceive the world in broad, impressionistic terms.

You can imagine how such histrionic behaviors would cause others to keep their distance; being in a relationship

Trying to catch other people's attention is a common characteristic of people with histrionic personality disorder.

Lynnette is a 44-year-old high school teacher who is notorious for her outlandish behavior and inappropriate flirtatiousness. Several of her students have complained to the principal about her seductive behavior during individual meetings. She often greets students with overwhelming warmth and apparent concern over their welfare, leading some to find her appealing and engaging, but they invariably become disenchanted once they realize how shallow she is. To her colleagues, she brags about her minor accomplishments, making them sound like major victories. Yet, if she fails to achieve a desired objective, she sulks and breaks down into tears. She is so desperate for the approval of others that she will change her story to suit whomever she is talking to at the time. Because she is always creating "crises," and never reciprocates the concern of others, people have become immune and unresponsive to her frequent pleas for help and attention.

- How does Lynnette's behavior differ from that of Lisa, who was described as having borderline personality disorder?
- If you were a friend of Lynnette's how would you react to the dramatic style and behaviors characteristic of her historonic personality disorder?

Chad is a 26-year-old man who has been desperately trying to succeed in acting. However, he has only had minor acting jobs, and has been forced to support himself by working as a waiter. Despite his lack of success, he brags to others about all the roles that he rejects because they aren't good enough for him. Trying to make inroads into acting, he has been selfishly exploitative of any person whom he sees as a possible connection. He has intense resentment for acquaintances who have landed roles and devalues their achievements by commenting that they are just "lucky." Yet if anyone tries to give him constructive criticism on how to improve his presentation or his acting, Chad reacts with outrage, refusing to talk to the person for weeks. Because of what he regards as his "terrific" looks, he thinks he deserves special treatment from everyone. At the restaurant, he has recurrent arguments with his supervisor because Chad insists that he is a "professional" and that he should not have to demean himself by clearing dirty dishes from the tables. He annoys others because he always seeks compliments on his clothes, his hair, his intelligence, and his wittiness. So caught up with himself, he barely notices other people and is grossly insensitive to their needs and problems.

- How has Chad's self-absorption and grandiose sense of himself, characteristic of narcissistic personality disorder, caused problems in his life?
- Compare Chad's sense of self-importance with Lynnette's. In what ways are they similar? In what ways do they express their grandiosity differently?

with a person with a histrionic personality disorder can be exasperating and unsatisfying. The result, of course, is that people with this disorder have few, if any, close and reciprocal relationships.

People with **narcissistic personality disorder** have an unrealistic, inflated sense of their own importance, a trait known as **grandiosity**. The name of this disorder comes from the Greek legend of Narcissus, the youth who fell in love with his own reflection in the pond.

People with this disorder expect others to compliment them and gratify all their wishes and demands, yet they lack sensitivity to the needs of others. Because they perceive themselves as being so special, they feel that other people are unable to appreciate their special needs and problems. They possess excessive aspirations for their own lives and intense resentment for others whom they perceive as more successful, beautiful, or brilliant. They are preoccupied with and driven to achieve their own goals, and think nothing of exploiting others in order to do so. Despite their show of grand self-importance, they are often troubled by self-doubt. Relationships with others, whether social, occupational, or romantic, are distorted by the perception of other people as tools for self-gratification.

Narcissism is a common feature of other personality disorders, especially histrionic and borderline personality disorders, and it is estimated that as many as one-fifth of those with another personality disorder meet the diagnostic criteria for narcissistic personality disorder as well. Because of this high degree of overlap, researchers are currently working to refine the diagnostic criteria for both histrionic

and narcissistic personality disorder so that the two disorders are more clearly differentiated (Gunderson et al., 1991).

Theories and Treatment

In traditional psychoanalytic theory, the histrionic personality disorder is regarded as a variant of hysteria. Both are seen as the product of unresolved Oedipal conflicts (e.g., Abraham, 1927, 1948) whose symptoms can be accounted for by the person's overreliance on the defense mechanism of repression. Other psychoanalysts have emphasized a more cognitive basis for the histrionic individual's symptoms. According to these theorists, such symptoms result from an inability to focus on details or specifics; instead they use a global approach to understanding situations and problems (Shapiro, 1965). For example, the hysterical (or histrionic) cognitive style for figuring out a household budget would be to assume that there will "somehow" be a way to cover the week's expenses rather than to sit down with a calculator and a checkbook and arrive at an exact figure. This global approach to viewing problems leads not only to misfortune but to a tendency to speak in generalities and regard the world in superficial terms.

The cognitive-behavioral perspective on the histrionic personality disorder emphasizes some of these ideas regard-

ing the hysterical cognitive style and proposes that there are several mistaken assumptions that underlie the individual's approach to life (Freeman et al., 1990). One basic belief of the person with this disorder is that "I am inadequate and unable to handle life on my own," which leads to the next step of assuming that it is necessary to find someone else to make up this deficit (Millon, 1981). These individuals seek attention and approval through sex-role stereotyped patterns of hyperfemininity (for women) and hypermasculinity (for men) because they perceive these to be society's approved routes for acquiring the support they think they need.

Given the cognitive-behavioral position that emotions are a product of one's thoughts, it follows that the global nature of the histrionic individual's thinking style leads also to diffuse, exaggerated, and rapidly changing emotional states. These individuals' evaluation of people and situations is equally imprecise and subject to distortion, so that it is not surprising to find their opinions changing on a daily basis from one extreme to another.

Most theoretical attempts to understand the origins of the narcissistic personality disorder focus on difficulties in the individual's early development. The traditional Freudian approach has been to regard narcissism as the failure to progress beyond the early stages of psychosexual development. More current conceptualizations are focused on disturbances in the parent–child relationship. Every child needs to have reassurance and positive responses to accomplishments. When a parent fails to provide these acknowledgements, the child becomes insecure. This insecurity becomes expressed paradoxically in the form of an inflated sense of self-importance that can be understood as the individual's attempt to make up for what was missing in earlier life (Kohut, 1966, 1971). Lacking a firm foundation of a healthy self, these individuals develop a false self that is precariously based on grandiose and unrealistic notions about their competence and desirability (Masterson & Klein, 1989). Narcissistic personality disorder can be understood,

then, as the adult's expression of this childhood insecurity and need for attention.

To the psychodynamic explanation, the cognitive-behavioral perspective (Beck et al., 1990) adds that people with narcissistic personality disorder hold maladaptive ideas about themselves, including the view that they are special, exceptional people who deserve to be treated far better than ordinary humans. They lack insight or concern into the feelings of other people because they see themselves as above others. These beliefs hamper their ability to perceive their experiences realistically, and they encounter problems when their grandiose ideas about themselves clash with their experiences of failure in the real world.

Treatment of people with histrionic personality disorder based on psychodynamic principles involves the traditional focus on uncovering repressed conflicts regarding sexual impulses. The principles of cognitive-behavioral therapy lead to very different types of interventions (Freeman et al., 1990). Based on what you know of the theory so far, you can probably predict that the cognitive-behavioral therapist would attempt to help the client develop more articulate ways of approaching problems and situations. The therapist constantly works to focus the client on goals, and uses the session as a format for teaching the client how to think more precisely and objectively. By taking this approach, the therapist is modeling good problem-solving behavior while at the same time giving the client concrete help in dealing with various life issues. Clients can also be taught self-monitoring strategies to keep their impulsive tendencies in check. The improvement of interpersonal relationships is another important focus, and assertiveness training is seen as important tool in achieving this goal.

The psychodynamic approach to treating individuals with narcissistic personality disorder is based on the notion that they lacked early experiences of admiration for their positive qualities. Therapy is intended to provide a corrective developmental experience in which the therapist uses empathy to support the client's search for recognition and admiration, but at the same time attempts to guide the client toward a more realistic appreciation that no one is flawless. Somewhat paradoxically, the more the client is given recognition and support by the therapist, the more the client is helped to become less grandiose and self-centered (Kohut, 1971).

Cognitive-behavioral therapy for narcissistic personality disorder also is oriented toward reducing the client's grandiosity and enhancing the client's ability to relate to others. In working toward this goal, the therapist structures interventions that work with, rather than against, the client's self-aggrandizing and egocentric tendencies. Rather than try to convince the client to be less selfish, the therapist might try to show that there are better ways to reach important personal goals. At the same time, the therapist avoids giving into the client's demands for special favors and attention. By setting and following an agenda with clear treatment goals, the therapist may help the client learn how to set limits in other areas of life (Freeman et al., 1990).

A person with narcissistic personality disorder is preoccupied with appearance and extremely concerned about impressing others with his attractive and suave presentation.

AVOIDANT AND DEPENDENT PERSONALITY DISORDERS

Avoidant and dependent personality disorders represent extreme ends of the spectrum regarding attitudes toward relationships with other people. The avoidant individual stays away from other people, and in contrast, the dependent individual cannot have enough contact with others. Both types of individuals have difficulty establishing a balance between closeness and distance in their relations with others.

Characteristics of the Disorders

Most people feel some degree of shyness on occasion. Sometimes this is because they are entering an unfamiliar situation in which they do not know other people. They may be afraid of committing a social blunder and appearing foolish. But what if a person is always intimidated by social situations, fearful of any kind of involvement with others and terrified by the prospect of being publicly embarrassed? Such individuals may have **avoidant personality disorder**.

People with avoidant personality disorder refrain almost entirely from social encounters, especially avoiding any situation that contains the potential for personal harm or embarrassment, and they steer clear of novel activity that is not part of their usual everyday routine. Sometimes they imagine terrible calamities resulting from such activity and use this concern as a reason to avoid new situations. Their extreme sensitivity to rejection and ridicule makes them es-

pecially likely to interpret even innocent remarks as criticism. As a result, they tend to be loners. If they can be assured, however, of unconditional acceptance, they will enter into close and even intimate relationships.

You might think that this disorder is very similar to schizoid personality disorder. In both disorders, the person tends to stay away from intimate relationships. However, the person with the avoidant disorder truly desires closeness, and feels a great deal of emotional pain at the seeming inability to make connections with others. By contrast, the schizoid individual prefers to be alone, lacking a sense of distress about being uninvolved with others.

Unlike people with avoidant personality disorder, individuals with **dependent personality disorder** are strongly drawn to others. However, they have such an extreme neediness that they achieve the opposite of their desires. They feel inadequate to make even the most trivial decisions. For example, a man may feel incapable of picking out his clothes each day without consulting his mother. In more important spheres, he may rely on her to tell him what kind of job he should seek, whom he should date, and how he should plan his life.

Without others near them, people with dependent personality disorder feel despondent and abandoned. To avoid being disliked, they agree with other people's opinions even when they believe these opinions to be misguided. Sometimes they take on responsibilities that no one else wants in order to gain the approval and liking of others. If they are criticized, they feel shattered. They are likely to throw themselves wholeheartedly into relationships and therefore become devastated when relationships end. This extreme dependence causes them to worry ceaselessly about the possibility that they may be abandoned.

Although wanting to do so, a person with avoidant personality disorder cannot join in a lively conversation, due to the fear of saying something embarrassing.

Theories and Treatment

One of the most relevant theoretical perspectives on avoidant personality disorder was provided by Karen Horney (1945, 1950), whose theory we discussed in Chapter 4. According to Horney, the avoidant personality represents a "turning away from others." The avoidant individual expects to be rejected and criticized, and so turns away as a defense. Horney believed that if people can be made to feel more secure about their personal qualities and strengths, they can work toward establishing a better sense of their real self. This greater internal security will cause them to experience less anxiety regarding their interactions with others, and they will naturally find themselves becoming involved in intimate relationships.

Cognitive-behavioral approaches to avoidant personality disorder also regard the individual with this disorder as hypersensitive to rejection, due to childhood experiences of extreme criticism by parents (Beck et al., 1990; Freeman et al., 1990). According to this approach, the dysfunctional attitudes these individuals hold center around the core belief that they are flawed and unworthy of other people's regard. Because of their perceived unworthiness, they expect that people will not like them, and they therefore avoid getting close to others to protect themselves from what they believe to be inevitable rejection. Contributing to their dilemma are their distorted perceptions of experiences with others. Their sensitivity to rejection causes them to misinterpret seemingly neutral and even positive remarks. Hurt by this presumed rejection, they retreat inward, placing further distance between themselves and others.

Max is a delivery person for a large equipment corporation. His co-workers describe Max as a "loner" because he does not spend time in casual conversation and avoids going out to lunch. Little do they know that every day he struggles with the desire to interact with them, but is too intimidated to follow through. Recently, he turned down a promotion to become manager because he realized that the position would require a considerable amount of day-to-day contact with others. What bothered him most about this position was not just that it would require interaction with people, but also that he might make mistakes that would be noticed by others. Although he is 42 years old, Max has hardly ever dated. Every time he feels interested in a woman, he becomes paralyzed with anxiety over the prospect of talking to her, much less asking her for a date. When female co-workers talk to him, he blushes and nervously tries to end the conversation as soon as possible.

- Why would Betty be regarded as having a dependent personality disorder, instead of being a product of a society that once fostered dependency in women?
- How does Ken's behavior reinforce Betty's lack of assertiveness?

Betty has never lived on her own; even while a college student, 30 years ago, she commuted from home. She was known by her classmates as someone who was dependent on others. Relying on others to make choices for her, she did whatever her friends advised, whether it involved the choice of courses or the clothes she should wear each day. The week after graduation, she married Ken, whom she had dated all senior year. She was particularly attracted to Ken because his domineering style relieved her of the responsibility to make decisions. As she has customarily done with all the close people in her life, Betty goes along with whatever Ken suggests, even if she does not fully agree. She fears that he will become angry with her and leave her if she rocks the boat. Although she wants to get a job outside the home, Ken has insisted that she remain a full-time homemaker, and she has complied with his wishes. However, when she is home alone, she calls friends and desperately pleads with them to come over for coffee. The slightest criticism from Ken, her friends, or anyone else can leave her feeling depressed and upset for the whole day.

- How do the symptoms of Max's avoidant personality disorder compare with the isolation shown by Pedro, who had a schizoid personality disorder?
- What do you think is Max's potential to benefit from treatment?

Breaking through the negative cycle of avoidance is the main goal of cognitive-behavioral therapy. The client is helped to articulate the automatic thoughts and dysfunctional attitudes that are interfering with interpersonal relations. The client is encouraged to see the irrationality of these beliefs, but in a supportive atmosphere. These interventions are most successfully accomplished after the client has come to trust the therapist.

Individuals with dependent personality disorder have traditionally been regarded by psychodynamic theory as having become regressed or fixated at the oral stage of development because of parental overindulgence or parental neglect of dependency needs. Object relations theorists regard such individuals as being insecurely attached (West & Sheldon, 1988). Low self-esteem further contributes to their need to rely on others for guidance and support (Livesley et al., 1990).

A cognitive-behavioral approach to dependent personality disorder regards unassertiveness and anxiety over making independent decisions as resting at the heart of the disorder. Dependent individuals believe that they are inadequate and helpless, and therefore unable to tackle problems on their own. The natural solution for them is to find someone else who will "take care" of them and relieve them of the obligation to make independent decisions. Having arrived at this solution, they dare not act in assertive ways that might challenge the relationship's security.

Psychotherapy based on cognitive-behavioral principles involves providing structured ways for the client to

When waiting to meet a late-arriving friend, a person with dependent personality disorder may feel helpless, not knowing what to do.

practice increasing levels of independence in carrying out daily activities. The clinician also works with the client to identify actual areas of skill deficits and then to help the client acquire the necessary abilities. However, even as the therapist attempts to help the client in these ways, it is important for the therapist to avoid becoming an authority figure in the client's life. It would be counterproductive for the client to become as dependent on the therapist as on others in his or her life (Beck et al., 1990; Freeman et al., 1990).

OBSESSIVE-COMPULSIVE AND PASSIVE-AGGRESSIVE PERSONALITY DISORDERS

Obsessive-compulsive and passive-aggressive personality disorders share a common feature involving conflict over the issue of control. People with obsessive-compulsive personality disorder struggle continuously because of their overwhelming concern about neatness and the picayune details of everyday life. People with passive-aggressive personality disorder struggle with the appropriate expression of their anger. Individuals with these disorders have not learned how to take effective control over their lives, emotions, or interpersonal dealings.

Characteristics of the Disorders

You can probably think of instances in your own life when you have found it very difficult to make a decision. Perhaps you worried about the matter for days, going back and forth between two choices, somewhat tormented by the process of evaluating the pros and cons of each choice. Imagine what it would be like to go through life this way. People with **obsessive-compulsive personality disorder** constantly feel immobilized by their inability to make a decision. The word **obsessive** in this context has a different meaning from the way you will see it used in the next chapter when we discuss anxiety disorders. It is not that these people have specific thoughts that they are unable to get out of their minds (that is, obsessions); rather, their cognitive style has a worrying (or obsessive) quality to it. In addition to their inability to make a firm decision, people with obsessive-compulsive personality disorder are intensely perfectionistic and inflexible, attributes that are expressed in a number of maladaptive ways. In their striving for unattainable perfection, they become caught up in a worried style of thinking and their behavior is inflexible to the point of being rigid.

The disturbance of people with obsessive-compulsive personality disorder is also evident in how they act. They have an inordinate concern with neatness and detail, often to the point of losing perspective on what is important and what is not. This style is both irksome to others and inefficient for the individual with the disorder, because it makes it impossible to complete a project. Every single detail must come out just right, and by the time these details are handled, the person has run out of time or resources. Similarly, these individuals' daily lives are ruled by a fanatical concern with schedules. For example, they might refuse to start a meeting until the precise second that it is scheduled to begin or might insist on seating each person in a room according to alphabetical order. They are stingy with time and money, and tend to hoard objects even when these objects are worn out and worthless. The emotional expression of these people is held back, and they have few intimate relationships. Their intense involvement in their work contributes to this pattern, because they have little time for leisure or socializing. When they do interact with other people, they tend to be so rigid that they refuse to concede or compromise when there is disagreement. They may be regarded as excessively moralistic or prudish because of their narrow views on social, religious, and political issues.

It is important to keep in mind that there is a difference between the hard-working, well-organized person with high standards and a concern about getting a job done right and the person with an obsessive-compulsive personality disorder. People with this disorder are unproductive, and their pursuit of perfectionism is neurotic rather than constructive.

When you hear the term "passive-aggressive," you might wonder how it is that someone can be passive and aggressive at the same time. People with **passive-aggressive personality disorder** convey internal anger and hostile feelings in indirect ways. If you are angry with a friend who has let you down, you might express your disappointment directly to that person. By contrast, the person with a passive-aggressive personality disorder conveys anger and hostility in subtle but nevertheless hurtful ways. These feelings of anger and hostility develop without much provocation, and people with this disorder are often discontented. For example, if a woman feels that others are placing too many demands on her, she finds ways to avoid complying with these demands and rationalizes this as a way of "getting even" with the world. She may agree to a demand, such as picking

For as long as he can remember, Trevor has been preoccupied with neatness and order. As a child, his room was meticulously clean. Friends and relatives chided him for this excessive organization, such as his insistence that the toys in his toy closet be arranged by color and category. In college his rigid "housekeeping" regimens were a source of amazement and annoyance to his roommates. He was tyrannical in his insistence on keeping the room free from dust and clutter. Trevor has continued this pattern into his adult life. He is unhappy that he has not found a woman who shares his personal habits, but consoles himself by becoming immersed in his collection of rare record albums featuring music of the 1940s. Trevor, a file clerk, prides himself on never having missed a day of work regardless of health problems or family crises. However, he has not been able to qualify for a promotion, because his boss sees him as being overly attentive to details, thus slowing up the work of the office as he checks and rechecks everything he does. He enhances his sense of self-importance by looking for opportunities in the office to take control. For example, when his co-workers are planning a party, Trevor insists on coordinating the event down to the smallest detail, such as where the napkins will be placed on the table. Although occasionally appreciative of his efforts, his co-workers eventually find themselves annoyed by his rigidity even in such trivial matters.

- In assessing Trevor's behavior, where would you draw the line between careful attention to detail and obsessive-compulsive personality disorder?
- How does Trevor's behavior create problems in his personal and social life?

This woman has become annoyed waiting for an acquaintance who is late. A person with passive-aggressive personality disorder may keep others waiting as an indirect way of showing anger.

up a friend who needs a ride, and then fail to fulfill the commitment, either by coming late, forgetting it altogether, or picking up the friend but then taking a circuitous route causing unnecessary delay.

At first, other people might find it difficult to criticize the motivation of passive-aggressive people, because it may appear that these individuals are trying to be cooperative. When things go wrong, they say they were the victim of circumstances, yet secretly derive satisfaction by resisting the demands placed on them and asserting that they cannot be blamed when things do not work out.

As you can imagine, individuals with passive-aggressive personality disorder have very disturbed interpersonal relationships. They are seen as sulky, self-centered, unwilling to take their share of responsibility, insensitive to criticism, and self-righteous, as they put on a front of sincerely wanting to do the right thing for others. Further, their work relationships are strained by their attitude toward people in authority. In interactions with supervisors, they put on a guise of cooperation and compliance, while feeling resentful and critical. Rather than participate in a spirit of good will, they act out their anger by undermining a project or failing to follow through on directions.

Theories and Treatment

Freud believed that obsessive-compulsive and passive-aggressive styles were representative of fixation at or regression to the anal stage of psychosexual development. Psychodynamic thinking about these disorders has advanced somewhat from the time of Freud, with more attention being given to cognitive factors and prior learning experiences (e.g. Millon, 1981; Shapiro, 1965). Psychodynamic approaches to obsessive-compulsive personality disorder emphasize rigidity of thinking, conformity to external rules and regulations, devotion to routine, and a lack of apparent concern for human relations.

From the standpoint of cognitive-behavioral theory, people with this disorder are seen as having an unrealistic concern about being perfect and avoiding mistakes (Beck et al., 1990; Freeman et al., 1990). Their feelings of self-worth ride on their behaving in ways that conform to an abstract ideal of perfectionism, and if they fail to achieve that ideal (which inevitably, they must), they regard themselves as worthless. In this framework, obsessive-compulsive personality disorder is seen as based on a problematic way of viewing the self.

Passive-aggressive personality disorder is given less attention within the psychodynamic perspective, and traditionally is seen as a negativistic and oppositional style of relating to others (Millon, 1981). Within the cognitive-behavioral perspective (Beck et al., 1990; Freeman et al., 1990), passive-aggressive personality disorder is regarded as evolving from the belief that the open expression of anger would be dangerous. An individual with this disorder also mistakenly believes that others "should" know what the

Laura works as a cashier in a discount department store. She feels that the manager always expects her to work harder than the other cashiers. Every few weeks the manager asks her to tally up the receipts at the end of the day. Laura detests this task, but rather than tell this to the manager, she agrees to do it. Invariably, Laura's totals fail to add up properly and the manager has to stay at work an extra hour to correct the problem. Although Laura is annoyed when told to be more careful, she secretly enjoys the idea of her boss working late, trying to find her errors. At home, Laura takes a similar passively oppositional stance toward her parents. If one of her parents receives a telephone call, Laura often "forgets" to pass the message along. She "accidentally" drove her mother's car into a telephone pole when her mother asked her to take the family dog to the veterinarian. Laura disclaims any personal responsibility for these actions, pointing out instead how unlucky she is to suffer from such accidents and memory failures.

- What features of Laura's behavior would you regard as "aggressive"?
- How might Laura's life be less complicated if she could express her anger toward others in a more open fashion?

person wants in any given situation. Therefore, the passive-aggressive individual assumes that it is not necessary to ask for anything. But because the individual wishes to avoid conflict, the anger that results from violation of this assumption cannot be directly expressed and must be released in some other form.

To illustrate the pattern of thinking in passive-aggressive personality disorder, consider the case of Anthony, a sales representative who is irritated at his boss for not giving him a more lavish expense account, even though Anthony has never requested it. He feels that his boss should recognize that he needs to have more resources for entertaining his clients because, after all, Anthony is a rising young executive. Week after week, when it is clear that there is no increase in sight, Anthony indirectly retaliates by "absentmindedly" parking in the boss's space in the parking garage. From the cognitive-behavioral perspective, this behavior is seen as Anthony's translation of maladaptive thoughts into action.

Cognitive-behavioral treatment can be made more difficult by particular problems inherent in these two personality disorders. The person with the obsessive-compulsive personality disorder tends constantly to go over past actions and consider further ones in light of whether or not there is the danger of making a mistake. Cognitive-behavioral therapy, with its focus on examining the client's thought processes, may feed into this ruminative tendency. For the passive-aggressive individual, difficulties arise through the client's attempts to block or thwart the therapist's efforts. In both cases, a continued process by the therapist of focusing on the client's maladaptive thoughts can eventually lead to changes in these assumptions and in the behaviors that follow from them (Beck et al., 1990; Freeman et al., 1990). For the passive-aggressive individual, another strategy that may help to overcome the client's tendency to resist or sabotage treatment efforts is the paradoxical instruction to become more rather than less symptomatic. The client might be told, for example, to behave more stubbornly. In opposing this prescription, the client might actually become more cooperative (McCann, 1988).

CONTROVERSIAL PERSONALITY PATTERNS: SYNDROMES OR DISORDERS?

When *DSM-III-R* was being prepared in the mid-1980s, a great deal of debate centered on the possible inclusion of two personality disorders—*self-defeating personality disorder* and *sadistic personality disorder*. As *DSM-III-R* went to press, the decision was made to place these diagnoses in an appendix of the volume for diagnostic categories needing further study. In addition to the fact that relatively little systematized information had been collected about either of the diagnoses, several theoretical and political objections were raised, particularly regarding self-defeating personality disorder. Of particular concern was the complaint that self-defeating personality disorder is a diagnosis with sexist connotations. Let's look into this issue after clarifying the relevant terms.

Perhaps you have heard the terms *sadist* and *masochist*. A **sadist** is a person who derives pleasure from the infliction of pain or abuse on others. For example, a particularly harsh prison guard may be termed sadistic when ordering inmates to carry out demeaning tasks. Conversely, a **masochist** derives satisfaction or pleasure from being subjected to abuse or pain. The label *masochistic*, or the alternative *self-defeating*, may be used in referring to a person who does not seem to mind being exploited, but instead seems to welcome opportunities to be used, insulted, or thwarted. In Chapter 9, we will discuss two disorders in which the intertwining of sexuality and pain is a central feature—*sexual sadism* and *sexual masochism*. When the abuse of others or the solicitation of abuse are pervasive facets of the personality, the personality disorder diagnosis is considered.

Sadistic Personality Disorder

People with **sadistic personality disorder** act toward others in ways that are cruel and demeaning; their abusiveness takes place at home and at work, and may be physical, psychological, or both. They may be physically violent at home, beating spouse and children. Alternatively, the abuse may be more insidious, including the humiliation of others. People with these traits may be amused by and take a certain kind of pleasure in hearing about or observing the discomfort of others, or they may revel in frightening or upsetting others. Their pleasure may go further to become a morbid fascination with violence, weapons, or techniques of torture.

Self-Defeating Personality Disorder

People with **self-defeating personality disorder** act in ways that lead them to undermine themselves, be deprived of gratification, and suffer pain rather than pleasure. By making unfortunate life choices, they experience disappointment, failure, or abuse. Rather than seek help, they prefer to manage on their own, and may even go so far as to incite others to reject them or respond to them with anger. When such responses inevitably come their way, these individuals then feel hurt or humiliated.

Caught up in a vicious cycle of bringing distress upon themselves, these people seem driven to make any positive situation turn sour so that they will feel bad in the end. In the process, they usually create more problems for themselves. For example, a man working in a factory may repeatedly jeopardize his job by going out of his way to help co-workers finish their work on time, but at the cost of completing his own assignments. Perhaps the co-workers have not asked for such help; they may not even want it, but he seems driven to act in ways that will lead him to fail.

Controversy about this disorder arose in the mid-1980s when the Committee on Women of the American Psychiatric Association raised a number of objections, leading to its deletion from the official listing of psychiatric diagnoses in *DSM-III-R*. Their objections included the following:

1. It is a sex-biased diagnosis that would be applied almost exclusively to women;
2. It is based on outdated psychoanalytic theory;
3. It overlooks the fact that in our culture many behaviors that are fostered in women could be misinterpreted as being masochistic;
4. It describes many behaviors commonly associated with the experience of being victimized or abused;
5. It rests on the often faulty assumption that an individual has the opportunity to escape an abusive situation; and
6. It increases the likelihood that the victim, rather than the perpetrator of violence, will be seen as the disturbed individual (Kass et al., 1989).

We will see in subsequent years whether these two personality patterns, with their controversial histories, remain a part of the diagnostic system and hence are considered psychological disorders.

PERSONALITY DISORDERS: THE PERSPECTIVES REVISITED

Now that you have read about the wide variety of ingrained patterns represented in the personality disorders, you can

BIOLOGICAL	PSYCHODYNAMIC AND FAMILY	COGNITIVE-BEHAVIORAL
Biological vulnerability developing certain personality disorders such as antisocial, borderline, and schizotypal.	Borderline, narcissistic, avoidant, and dependent disorders are due to fundamental flaws in the structure of personality caused by disturbed parenting. Paranoid, histrionic, obssesive-compulsive, and passive-aggressive are the expression of defense mechanisms carried to an extreme. Antisocial due to faulty parenting and inconsistent discipline compounded by socioeconomic factors.	Each personality disorder is associated with dysfunctional attitudes that perpetuate the individual's symptoms and lead to difficulties in interpersonal relationships.
Treatment: Medications to relieve specific symptoms such as anxiety and depression.	**Treatment:** Restructuring of the individual's personality through intensive long-term psychotherapy.	**Treatment:** Cognitive restructuring to counter the individual's dysfunctional attitudes and behavioral interventions to alter dysfunctional patterns of interpersonal behavior.

appreciate that it is difficult to make general statements about the causes and treatment of this diverse group. Researchers continue to struggle with the issue of overlap among these disorders (Widiger, 1991), and without a clear set of guidelines to differentiate the disorders, clinicians are faced with the difficult job of arriving at definitive and distinct diagnoses.

As you have also seen, scientific knowledge is still severely limited about the causes of personality disorders. We can gain some insight, however, from looking at the results of research on normal personality development. Studies of infants have shown that even in the first months of life, the temperament of newborns is individualized. Infants may be placid and sociable, or irritable and unresponsive to intimacy. Is the whiny infant more likely to become a histrionic adult? Is the distancing child more likely to become schizoid? Researchers do not yet know enough about the connections between child and adult personality to draw firm conclusions about the personality disorders, but several long-term studies concur that characteristics evident early in life predict behavior patterns into the early years of adulthood (Caspi et al., 1987, 1988; Moss & Sussman, 1980). Although these studies do not address the question of whether it is biology or life experiences that account for temperamental consistency, other investigators are beginning to explore the contributions of genetic and environmental factors to long-term personality development (Plomin et al., 1990).

While researchers continue to probe the determinants of personality development, clinicians are faced with the job of treating people whose symptoms have endured over many years and have proved resistant to change. Given the

uncertainties regarding the causes and nature of these personality disorders, clinicians focus on more limited goals than bringing about total change, and instead focus their therapeutic efforts on the primary causes of the client's current distress. Although some clinicians follow a set of specific ideas about treatment, most individualize their treatment to respond to the particular problems of each client. For example, when treating a person with a dependent personality disorder, the clinician can help the client to understand the roots of this dependency, and then intervene in ways to reinforce autonomy. In contrast, when treating clients with avoidant personality disorder, the therapist focuses on helping the client to develop more satisfying interpersonal relations.

At times, the clinician may rely more on a particular theoretical perspective if it seems pertinent to the client's history and current symptoms. For example, when treating clients with borderline personality disorder, the approach recommended by some psychodynamic theorists may seem most appropriate. Even if the clinician does not identify strongly with this model, it might make sense to integrate relevant concepts from this approach into an overall treatment plan. Alternatively, the clinician may work within a cognitive-behavioral framework, focusing on the individual's behaviors and cognitive styles in an attempt to foster personality changes (Beck et al., 1990; Freeman et al., 1990). Even so, treatment of clients with personality disorders is often not successful in achieving substantial change (Andreoli et al., 1989).

Because of the chronic and persistent nature of personality disorders, as well as the difficulty in identifying their precise qualities, these disorders are likely to remain a challenging area for researchers and clinicians in the years ahead. It is also quite likely that the diagnostic criteria for these disorders, and even the names of these disorders, will undergo continued revision in future editions of the *DSM* as theorists and researchers continue to refine and elaborate their scientific base. In this process, we will gain not only a better understanding of this form of psychopathology, but perhaps a richer appreciation for the factors that contribute to normal personality growth and change through life.

SUMMARY

1. Personality disorders are rigid and maladaptive patterns of behavior that cause personal distress or interfere with a person's ability to lead a satisfying life. These disorders are regarded as ingrained in the individual's psychological make-up and are therefore very resistant to change.

2. Antisocial personality disorder involves a disregard for the laws and moral standards of society, and is often associated with criminal behavior. Biological theories have proposed that people with antisocial personality disorder differ physiologically from others in their ability to learn from the negative consequences of their behavior, and also differ in physiological arousal patterns. There is compelling evidence in support of genetic patterns of inheritance, but researchers have also been impressed by the fact that many antisocial individuals grew up in homes with inconsistent discipline, an impoverished standard of living, or an absent parent. Treatment of antisocial personality disorder is very difficult, mainly because of the lack of incentive on the part of the individual who has the disorder to seek help voluntarily. When such individuals do come to treatment, the clinician's goal is to help them develop an understanding of the hurtful effects of their antisocial behavior on others and in this way to establish a motivation for change.

3. Borderline personality disorder is characterized by a sense of self so poorly defined that the individual has a disturbed sense of identity at times bordering on psychosis. People with this disorder may have difficulty seeing themselves as separate individuals from others with whom they have established a relationship. They may vacillate from idealization to devaluation in the way they regard other people. They may be moody, and at times violent, possibly acting in ways that are harmful to themselves or others. Theoretical explanations of borderline personality disorder have focused on problems in the early development of the self. Psychodynamic theorists regard this disorder as resulting from inadequate parenting in which the individual was not nurtured as a separate, autonomous being. Building upon this notion, some researchers point out the prevalence of early life neglect and abuse as being linked to the development of this personality disorder later in life. From a cognitive-behavioral perspective, people with borderline personality disorder are regarded as holding unrealistic dichotomous views of themselves and others as either all good or all bad. Regarding treatment of people with borderline personality disorder, there is debate about whether to focus more on confrontational or supportive approaches. Most clinicians agree that therapy should provide a sense of stability and predictability, while helping the client establish a sense of identity and abandon self-destructive behaviors. Treatment of such individuals is difficult and challenging, sometimes requiring inpatient care.

4. Paranoid personality disorder involves the symptom of paranoia, in which the individual is suspicious, guarded, and vigilant toward other people based on the belief that others intend harm. Psychoanalytic explanations of paranoid personality disorder see it as a style of viewing the world that is heavily reliant on the defense mechanism of projection. Cognitive-behavioral theorists regard paranoid personality disorder as a product of mistaken assumptions; they assume that other people are potentially harmful, and that they themselves are unable to detect and manage mistreatment by others. This theoretical analysis would suggest an approach of countering the client's mistaken assumptions along with assertiveness training to improve the client's interactions with other people and break the negative cycle that reinforces the client's paranoid beliefs.

5. Schizoid and schizotypal personality disorders involve schizophrenic-like qualities but without the very disturbed thinking that characterizes schizophrenia itself. The schizoid individual has an aversion to close relationships, and usually leads an isolated and secluded lifestyle. The individual with schizotypal personality disorder has bizarre and unusual ways of reacting to others and viewing the world. Debate in the schizophrenia literature centers on whether these disorders are in fact variants of schizophrenia or whether they are separate disorders in their own right. Long-term studies and research on inheritance patterns of these disorders suggests that they might eventually be found to have a link to schizophrenia. Individuals with these personality disorders are difficult to treat because of their unresponsiveness to human interaction and their peculiar ways of thinking.

6. Histrionic personality disorder is characterized by excesses of emotionality, and narcissistic personality disorder by excesses of egocentrism. People with histrionic personality disorder tend to be very theatrical, as the name implies, and enjoy being the center of attention. Often they are flirtatious and seductive, but their involvement with others tends to be very superficial. Narcissistic individuals are self-centered and expect to be the focus of attention. Psychodynamic

(Summary continued on page 167)

Return to the Case

Harold Morrill

Harold's History

The story Harold told about his life helped me make sense of the turmoil of the past few years. The only child of middle-class parents, Harold spent much of his childhood seeking a compromise between his mother's demands that he stay "out of trouble" and his own desires to play and explore in his backyard and neighborhood. The words he used to describe his mother reflected the intensity of his feelings about her. Even relatively minor incidents were conveyed with terms that told me of his pained ambivalence toward her. She was a "bitch . . . always yelling at me for anything I did. She controlled my every move, yelled at me for playing too long with my friends, going too far from the house, leaving her home all alone. If I stayed in the backyard and near her, I was the good boy, and she would praise me and reward me with candy and cookies, but if I strayed for an hour, even when I was a teenager, she would yell down the street and humiliate me. Maybe it was her way of showing she loved me and worried about me, but it was a tough thing to deal with."

Harold's description of his father was certainly no more positive than that of his mother. He spoke of his resentment about the fact that his father was hardly ever home, and when he was there, he virtually ignored Harold. The message that his mother repeated so often to Harold haunts him to the present day. She told him that she needed him to be the "man of the house." According to Harold, this was his mother's rationalization for why she needed him to stay so close to her—he had "important responsibilities, after all."

Harold told me that during adolescence he desperately tried to flee the clutches of his mother. He became caught up in substance abuse, which seemed like his only chance "to escape." Introduced to the world of street drugs, Harold became involved in a promiscuous and dangerous lifestyle, as he became caught up in drug trafficking and petty thievery. He finally moved out of his mother's apartment to a squalid room in a boarding house, and hasn't spoken to his mother in over 5 years. Occasionally he sees his father, but is not interested in maintaining a relationship with him.

Throughout most of his 20s, Harold drifted from job to job, without any sense of purpose. He tried a few stints at college, but each time dropped out because the "teachers were such losers." Harold contended that his employment instability was due mostly to a series of health problems. He told me about three hospitalizations, each of which resulted from serious motorcycle accidents. He enumerated a long list of broken bones, concussions, and internal injuries he had sustained, and with a laugh in his voice commented, "You'd think I was trying to kill myself, wouldn't you?"

The arena of relationships has been a terribly unhappy one for Harold. Throughout adolescence and adulthood, he has moved from one relationship to another, abruptly walking out on people who have been unable to satisfy his insatiable demands for love and affection. As Harold described the many stormy relationships of his life, he found it difficult to acknowledge the possibility that he might have played some role in their failures.

Assessment

I had informed Harold that a psychological assessment battery would help me derive a clearer understanding of the nature of his problem. Initially he responded with an air of irritation, but he agreed to go through with it. This same ambivalence was evident throughout the testing sessions. At times he was cooperative and pleasant, but then became irascible and impatient a short while later.

Harold's IQ was above average, but his IQ score alone did not tell the whole story about Harold's intelligence. The variability among the *WAIS-R* subtest scores reflected the unevenness in his cognitive functioning, with impressive strengths on certain tasks (such as vocabulary) but notable deficits on others (such as comprehension). Harold's problem with comprehension tasks gave me a glimpse into his inadequate understanding of appropriate behavior in common situations. For instance, he responded to a question about why stoplights are needed by saying "so that people won't murder each other." Although the essence of Harold's response to this question suggested that he understood the issue, I was struck by the angry content of what he said and how he said it.

Harold's profile on the MMPI-2 revealed serious personality disorganization with some psychotic-like features. This impression was supported by his performance on the Rorschach test, in which he gave many unusual responses, describing images that are rarely reported by others who take the test. In the color cards, Harold saw fire, explosions, and bursts of

Harold Morrill continued

ammunition coupled with sadistic human destruction: "a grenade blowing up in the middle of a Sunday picnic." Themes of rage in the face of abandonment were particularly pronounced in Harold's TAT stories. People's moods were describe as changing suddenly and chaotically, and the plots of Harold's stories were similarly disorganized.

Diagnosis

Most striking about Harold's story is the chaos that has permeated most facets of his life. His relationships have been turbulent and unfulfilling, his emotions volatile, his behavior self-destructive and impulsive, and his sense of self seriously confused.

My initial interaction with Harold left me with a diagnostic impression about which I was fairly certain—that Harold had a borderline personality disorder. In part, my inference was based on his presenting problems and history, but I was also deeply affected by my own personal reactions to Harold. I found myself feeling sympathetic toward him at times, and at times feeling disturbed by his abusive responses to my efforts to understand and help him. I was tuning in to the process by which Harold was "splitting" in his dealings with me, at times complimenting me about my clinical skillfulness, but soon thereafter questioning my competence and ability to establish rapport with him.

My initial diagnostic hunch was confirmed as I considered the diagnostic criteria for borderline personality disorder. Harold had a history of unstable and intense interpersonal relationships in which he responded to people in dramatically different ways, vacillating between idealization and devaluation of anyone close to him. This was commonly intertwined with affective instability in which he felt tossed from one emotional state to another, feeling extremes of depression, anxiety, and irritability. At times, his mood would escalate into inappropriate and intense expressions of anger in the form of temper tantrums and victimizing behavior. At other times the anger would be self-directed and take the form of impulsive and self-destructive pursuits—such as reckless motorcycle driving, promiscuity, and drug abuse. Never really sure about his own identity, he wandered from lifestyle to lifestyle, from lover to lover, and from job to job, in a desperate attempt to fill the void that he painfully carried with him everywhere.

Axis I.   Rule out cocaine dependence.

Axis II.   Borderline personality disorder.

Axis III.   History of motorcycle injury that may include head trauma.

Axis IV.   Severity 2. Mildly stressful acute events and enduring circumstances.

Axis V.   Current Global Assessment of Functioning: 32. Highest Global Assessment of Functioning (past year): 32.

Case Formulation

My diagnosis of Harold seemed clear and accurate, in that he met the criteria for borderline personality disorder. But how did Harold develop this personality structure? By putting together the information from my interview, the psychological assessment, and Harold's history and current presenting problems, I was able to formulate hypotheses based on what clinicians and researchers know about this personality disorder.

When trying to understand the etiology of an individual's personality disorder, it is common to consider contributions of the family, both genetic and environmental. According to Harold, both his parents were "troubled people." We can see this disturbance in his mother's overprotective and anxious interactions with Harold and in his father's aloofness and emotional unavailability. Could the personality disturbances of his parents been transmitted genetically? Scientific understanding of this possibility remains limited, but it is reasonable to conclude that his parents' disturbance resulted in his growing up in an emotionally unhealthy home environment.

Looking at these issues more closely, we see a family system ripe for the development of a personality disorder. His father was distant, rejecting, and ineffective in moderating his wife's overcontrol of their son. Moreover, at a time when children need to be able to exercise some autonomy, Harold's mother was overly controlling. She punished him by withdrawing her love if he ventured away from her. The only way he could gain her love was by not leaving her in the first place. Harold's mother exerted similar pressure on him during his adolescence. Under these circumstances, Harold's ability to differentiate himself psychologically from his mother would have been impeded to an extreme degree, contributing to his current identity confusion.

Harold Morrill continued

Behavioral and systems perspectives help to augment this understanding of Harold's problems. For example, it is reasonable to imagine that Harold modeled his interpersonal relationships after the disturbed relationships he observed in his own life. Perhaps Harold "learned" negative attitudes about himself and inadequate strategies for coping with stresses, particularly those imposed upon him by his mother.

Harold's difficulties may also be seen as resulting from a disturbed family system in which an overinvolved mother formed a unit with Harold that excluded his father. Her overinvolvement continued into adolescence, a time when he should have been allowed to break away from the family. His descent into the world of street drugs could be seen as the result of his mother having placed him in an impossible situation of not being able to satisfy her and his own needs simultaneously. Perhaps he saw drugs as the only escape from this dilemma. In addition, Harold's inability to develop an adult identity reflects his mother's reluctance to let Harold grow up. He went on to substitute dependence on lovers for the pathological relationship with his mother.

Planning a Treatment

After my initial evaluation of Harold I was left with the impression that intervention should involve an attempt at a restructuring of his personality, while at the same time attending to his current stresses and self-defeating behaviors.

Outpatient psychotherapy was the recommended treatment for Harold. Had he been suicidal or more seriously self-destructive, I might have recommended that he admit himself to an inpatient treatment program. Sometimes inpatient treatment is beneficial when treating people with borderline personality disorder; this is especially true for those people who seem to need the security and stability of the milieu. Although I gave some consideration of this for Harold, his limited financial resources made hospitalization impossible.

Harold asked me if I would be his psychotherapist, stating that I was the "only person to seem to understand" his problems. Having treated a number of people with borderline personality disorder, I was alert to the probability that Harold's positive response involved idealization, commonly noted in people with this personality disorder. At the same time, I found myself feeling interested in treating Harold. There was something about him that affected me deeply. Perhaps I was moved by the belief that I could help him undertake major life changes. Some might call this a "rescue fantasy"—the notion that we as psychotherapists can rescue clients from the unhappiness that has become so much a part of their lives. With a bit of apprehension, and following a consultation with my colleagues about the wisdom of my treating Harold, I agreed to accept him into treatment and recommended that we schedule two sessions weekly for the first three months. I believed that the increased frequency of sessions would facilitate the development of rapport.

The treatment approach that I have found to be most effective in treating people like Harold involves an integration of psychodynamic and cognitive-behavioral approaches. Within the psychodynamic perspective, I planned an intense psychotherapy in which the pattern of Harold's early life relationships could be brought to the surface and re-examined. I was not so naive as to consider such an approach with Harold to be simple. I expected that his initial laudatory comments about my clinical expertise would very likely be replaced by devaluing critiques of my "incompetence." I was prepared for the likelihood that he would act and speak in provocative ways, perhaps testing me to see if I would angrily reject him, thereby proving that I wasn't really concerned about him. I knew that there was a considerable possibility that he would end treatment precipitously, and go to another therapist to whom he might describe me in very unflattering ways.

In addition to the psychodynamic framework, I thought that it would be wise to incorporate some cognitive-behavioral techniques with which Harold could learn appropriate styles of interacting with others, more constructive ways of perceiving himself, and more effective strategies for dealing with ordinary life stresses.

Outcome of the Case

To no one's surprise, including mine, Harold's treatment did not go very well. The first few months were difficult, and frankly fairly stressful for me. Harold became increasingly demanding of my attention and time, making emergency telephone calls on weekends, asking for extra sessions, and ruminating in therapy sessions about how frustrating it was not to be able to find out more about my personal life. One instance troubled me greatly. It took place

Harold Morrill continued

on a Friday afternoon as I was leaving my office, several hours after a session with Harold. As I got into my car, I noticed in the rearview mirror that Harold was sitting in his car across the parking lot, ostensibly ready to follow me home. Feeling both alarmed and angry, I walked over and spoke to Harold; he acknowledged that my hunch was correct, but became very angry with me when I pointed out the inappropriateness of this plan. When he didn't show up for either of our sessions the following week, there was part of me that felt greatly relieved. At the same time, I recognized my responsibility to reach out to Harold in a therapeutic manner, and so I decided to drop him a note urging him to come to our regularly scheduled session.

Harold returned to therapy, but his response to me remained troubling from that point on. His expressions of anger were more aptly characterized as rage, as he derided many of my efforts to help. By contrast, there were numerous times when he seemed responsive, and made temporary changes in his life that reflected a more healthy way of thinking and acting. We continued our therapy sessions for another year, during which our work could best be characterized as "rocky."

Another crisis unfolded when I informed Harold that I would be taking a three-week vacation several weeks hence. Once again, he failed to show up for our sessions, and once again I tried to reach out to him by urging him to resume therapy sessions. A week after I

mailed my letter to him, I received a disturbing phone call from the hospital emergency room physician informing me that Harold had taken an overdose of heroin, and wanted me to come to the emergency room located in the hospital where I was working. I went to see Harold and made arrangements for him to be admitted to the inpatient psychiatric unit. He told me how grateful he felt about my expression of concern, and how relieved he felt that our sessions would resume, this time on the inpatient unit. I wondered to myself whether I had been manipulated by him, but felt that the seriousness of his self-destructive behavior warranted inpatient treatment.

Harold remained on the unit for two weeks, and seemed to stabilize both physically and emotionally. However, in our session just prior to his discharge from the hospital, Harold angrily told me of his plans never to return to therapy with me. He stated that he wanted to find a therapist who would be "more giving" than I was. My efforts to work through this issue with Harold failed, and I never did see him again. Several months after our termination I read in the newspaper that Harold had been arrested and charged with high-speed driving while intoxicated. The photograph accompanying the newspaper story showed Harold staring into the camera with a knife-like intensity. I could see the rage in his eyes, yet at the same time I knew that underlying his rage were feelings of confusion, loneliness, and desperation.

theories regard these disorders as reflecting unresolved conflicts around sexuality. Both disorders are viewed within the cognitive-behavioral perspective as involving distorted ideas about the self and the world. People with histrionic personality disorder believe that they are unable to solve their own problems and that they require the assistance of others. They often attempt to obtain such help by putting on the guise of a stereotyped sex-role behavior. Narcissistic individuals regard themselves as privileged or entitled to special attention. Treatment of histrionic personality disorder based on cognitive-behavioral principles involves helping the client develop more articulate ways of approaching problems and situations. Narcissistic personality disorders would be treated from a psychodynamic perspective by giving the client a corrective developmental experience in an attempt to reverse

the presumably deficient responsiveness of parents to the individual's accomplishments as a child. From a cognitive-behavioral perspective, the therapist would work toward reducing grandiosity and enhancing the client's ability to relate to others.

7. Avoidant and dependent personality disorders represent two extremes of relating to people; the avoidant individual shuns contact with others and the dependent individual cannot survive without other people's help and support. The avoidant individual is understood within cognitive-behavioral theory as suffering from the mistaken belief that closeness to others inevitably brings criticism and rejection. Dependent individuals view themselves as lacking the skills they need to accomplish their goals, and as a result of years of relying on other people they may in fact lack certain abilities to handle problems and life tasks

independently. Psychodynamic approaches to this disorder emphasize disturbed attachment patterns that are theorized to date back to the individual's early relations in childhood with caregivers. Treatment of both disorders from the cognitive-behavioral perspective involves breaking through the negative cycles that perpetuate erroneous beliefs.

8. People with obsessive-compulsive and passive-aggressive personality disorders have conflicts regarding the issue of control. Obsessive-compulsive personality disorder involves an unreasonable concern about inconsequential details of life. The individual becomes set on rigid rules and routines, and is unable to make decisions without a great deal of vacillation and uncertainty. Passive-aggressive individuals experience a great deal of anger, but express their anger indirectly, usually causing considerable annoyance to other people. Contemporary psychodynamic theory does not offer much in the way of explaining these disorders, but the cognitive-behavioral perspective provides a useful explanation. According to the cognitive-behavioral perspective, people with obsessive-compulsive personality disorder fear the consequences of making a mistake, because their self-esteem hinges on seeing themselves as perfect. The symptoms of passive-aggressive personality disorder are seen, from this perspective, as due to a fear of being rejected if anger is expressed directly, combined with the belief that other people should be able to discern what the individual's needs and desires are. Treatment of both disorders involves focusing on the client's maladaptive thoughts. Treatment of obsessive-compulsive personality disorder from a cognitive-behavioral perspective can be successful if the therapist can avoid feeding into the client's ruminative tendencies. Passive-aggressive personality disorder is more difficult to treat, because the individual constantly thwarts the therapist's best efforts.

9. When the *DSM-III-R* was published, two controversial new categories of personality disorders were included: the sadistic and self-defeating personality disorders. These categories were suggested as areas needing further research, but even before *DSM-III-R* was published, they were the target of political and scientific criticism that they label the female victims of sexual and physical abuse as psychologically disturbed. It remains to be seen whether these disorders remain part of further *DSMs*.

10. As a general rule, the cognitive-behavioral and psychodynamic approaches offer the most viable and reasonable options for viewing personality disorders. Biological approaches seem to have less to contribute, although research on temperament and genetic contributions to personality suggest that these disorders may have a physical basis.

KEY TERMS

Personality trait: an enduring pattern of perceiving, relating to, and thinking about the environment and others. p. 141

Personality disorders: ingrained patterns of relating to other people, situations, and events with a rigid and maladaptive quality. p. 141

Antisocial personality disorder: a personality disorder characterized by a lack of regard for society's moral or legal standards. p. 143

Adult antisocial behavior: illegal or immoral behaviors such as stealing, lying, and cheating. p. 143

Impulse control: the ability to restrain the gratification of one's immediate needs or desires. p. 143

Conduct disorder: a development-related disorder that is the precursor in childhood of antisocial personality disorder. p. 143

Testosterone: the male sex hormone. p. 144

Amygdala: a structure in the limbic system of the brain involved in controlling aggressive behaviors. p. 144

Borderline personality disorder: a personality disorder characterized by a pervasive pattern of instability in mood, interpersonal relationships, and self-image. p. 147

Splitting: a tendency, common in people with borderline personality disorder, to perceive others as being all good or all bad, usually resulting in disturbed interpersonal relationships. p. 147

Identity: an individual's self-concept or sense of "who" one is. p. 147

Parasuicide: a suicidal gesture to get attention from loved ones or family. p. 147

Paranoid personality disorder: a personality disorder whose outstanding feature is that the individual is extremely suspicious of others and is always on guard against potential danger or harm. p. 150

Schizophrenia spectrum disorders: a term used by some researchers to characterize a continuum of disorders including schizophrenia, schizoid personality disorder, and schizotypal personality disorder. p. 151

Schizoid personality disorder: a personality disorder primarily characterized by an indifference to social relationships, as well as a very limited range of emotional experience and expression. p. 151

Schizotypal personality disorder: a personality disorder that primarily involves peculiarities and eccentricities of thought, behavior, appearance, and interpersonal style. People with this disorder may have peculiar ideas such as magical thinking and beliefs in psychic phenomena. p. 152

Latent: a state in which a disorder remains undetected but may subsequently become evident. p. 152

Histrionic personality disorder: a personality disorder characterized by exaggerated displays of emotional reactions, approaching theatricality, in everyday behavior. p. 153

Narcissistic personality disorder: a personality disorder primarily characterized by an unrealistic, inflated sense of self-importance and an inability to see the perspectives of other people. p. 154

Grandiosity: an exaggerated view of oneself as possessing special and extremely favorable personal qualities and abilities. p. 154

Avoidant personality disorder: a personality disorder whose most prominent feature is that the individual is desirous of, but fearful of, any involvement with other people and terrified at the prospect of being publicly embarrassed. p. 156

Dependent personality disorder: a personality disorder whose main characteristic is that the individual has an extreme neediness for other people, to the point of being unable to make any decisions or take independent action. p. 156

Obsessive-compulsive personality disorder: a personality disorder characterized by perfectionism and inflexibility. p. 158

Obsessive: a personal quality of being immobilized when having to make a decision followed by rumination after a decision has been made. p. 158

Passive-aggressive personality disorder: a personality disorder that is characterized primarily by angry feelings that are expressed indirectly rather than openly. p. 159

Sadist: a person who derives pleasure from the infliction of pain or abuse on others. p. 161

Masochist: a person who derives satisfaction or pleasure from being subjected to abuse or pain. p. 161

Sadistic personality disorder: a personality disorder, first introduced on an experimental basis in *DSM-III-R*, characterized mainly by a pervasive pattern of acting toward others in ways that are cruel and demeaning. p. 161

Self-defeating personality disorder: a personality disorder, first introduced on an experimental basis in *DSM-III-R*, in which the primary feature is a pervasive pattern of behaviors in which the individual's own best interests are undermined, gratification is avoided, and suffering is chosen over pleasure. p. 161

Case Report: Barbara Wilder

When Barbara Wilder first walked into the clinic on a snowy January afternoon, I was immediately struck by the look of fright and torment on her face. It was hard to believe that she was only 22 years old; her trembling voice and her anxiety-laden demeanor led me to think that she must be at least 10 years older. As she shuffled down the hallway toward my office, I even wondered if perhaps she was suffering from a medical problem that caused her to behave in ways that made her seem so much older.

Barbara began her story by telling me how the preceding 6 months had been "pure hell." It all began one evening when she was waiting in a crowded airport lounge to fly home to visit her parents, her first visit since starting her new job. All of a sudden she felt incredibly dizzy, and the words on the page of her paperback novel began to dance in front of her eyes. She felt a roaring sound in her ears and a sudden stabbing pain in her chest. Her heart was pounding wildly, and she broke out into a cold sweat. Her hands trembled uncontrollably. Just that day, Barbara had heard about the sudden death of a young woman due to a rare heart condition. As she struggled to overcome the choking sensation in her throat, she became convinced that she was about to die.

In what seemed to Barbara to be an absolute miracle, the woman next to her saw what was happening, and paramedics were rushed to the scene. Neither they nor the physicians who examined her could find anything physically wrong. Barbara was told that she was probably exhausted and that the airport lounge must have been too stuffy. She spent the night at the hospital and was released the next morning.

Barbara had to miss her visit to her parents, but her alarm about the incident gradually subsided. Two weeks later, though, the same thing happened again. She was shopping at the mall for a present for her roommate, who was to be married in a few days. Once again, a medical exam showed no physical abnormalities. Barbara began to suspect that the physicians were hiding something from her about the seriousness of her condition. Over the next several months, Barbara went from physician to physician, searching in vain for someone who would diagnose her illness and put her on a proper course of therapy. All they did, though, was advise her to get some rest. One physician prescribed a mild tranquilizer, but it offered her no relief from her attacks which became even more intense, occurring once every two weeks.

Little by little, Barbara found herself staying away from situations in which she would be trapped if she were to have an attack. She quit her job because she was terrified that she would have an attack in the elevator riding up to her office on the 26th floor. Eventually, Barbara became virtually a total recluse. She could not even walk out of her front door without feeling an overwhelming sense of dread. The only time she got out was when her former roommate, who was now married, came over to take Barbara to the grocery store or for a walk. It was at this friend's suggestion that Barbara sought help at the mental health clinic.

The picture was complete. I was dealing with a young woman who appeared to others for much of her early years as an individual who functioned quite well. Little did others realize, however, that within Barbara's hidden emotional life she was tremendously insecure and felt intensely dependent on others. When confronted with the challenging life transitions of her first job, she became caught up in a tempest of anxiety.

Sarah Tobin, PhD

7

ANXIETY DISORDERS

Everyone becomes anxious from time to time—an examination, a sporting match, a meeting with an important person, or concern over a new relationship can all create feelings of apprehension. Often a person's anxieties are about the future, whether it be long-term concerns over career or more immediate worries about a Saturday night date. Think about your own experiences involving anxiety. Perhaps you were so nervous while taking an examination that your mind went blank, or you were so "wound up" while playing in the basketball championship game that you missed the hoop in an easy shot. The anxiety of giving an oral presentation in class may have left you tongue-tied and embarrassed. As upsetting as any of these experiences may be, none would be considered abnormal functioning. They may have had benefits as well. You may have developed ways to calm yourself that you then found useful in other circumstances, or your anxiety may have energized you to overcome obstacles and perform more effectively. So in moderation, anxiety may actually serve some positive functions.

It is when anxiety reaches such an intense level that it interferes with a person's ability to function in daily life that it becomes a source of clinical concern. Imagine anxiety that is many times more intense and incapacitating than the instances we have mentioned—fear and apprehension so great that an individual enters into a panic state characterized by extreme physical and psychological reactions. Such an intense, irrational, and incapacitating experience is the basis of the **anxiety disorders**. These disorders are relatively common, affecting as many as 5 to 6 percent of the U.S. population every year (Weissman, 1988).

After reading this chapter, you should be able to:

- Define the fundamental qualities of the anxiety disorders.
- Understand the characteristics of the various anxiety disorders.
- Describe the biological approaches to understanding and treating anxiety disorders, including theories that focus on disturbances in neurotransmitters and specific brain pathways.
- Describe the cognitive-behavioral approaches to understanding and treating anxiety disorders, including theories that regard these disorders as the product of conditioned learning and those that focus on maladaptive thought processes.
- Contrast the major treatment approaches to anxiety disorders and understand how they can be integrated.

THE NATURE OF ANXIETY DISORDERS

Anxiety incorporates a wide range of physical and psychological responses. When you are anxious you feel that your stomach is "tied in knots," your heart beats more rapidly, you become flushed and sweaty, and your breathing becomes more frequent. People with anxiety disorders experience these reactions often and intensely, causing them to feel distressed and unable to function on a day-to-day basis. They tend to be **hypervigilant**—on edge and on guard against danger. As a result, they have difficulty feeling relaxed and comfortable in many situations.

In addition, people with anxiety disorders try to avoid contact with situations that cause them to feel anxious. As a result, they may miss opportunities to enjoy themselves or act in their own best interest. For example, people who are afraid to fly in airplanes limit their vacation plans and,

more seriously, may face job problems if their work requires air travel. People whose anxiety prevents them from leaving the house are even more disabled. The unpleasant experience of anxiety, and attempts to avoid anxiety, can complicate a person's life and interfere significantly with daily activities. It is perhaps because of the disabling nature of anxiety that prescription drugs for anxiety are among the most widely used in the United States (Gitlin, 1990; Zorc et al., 1991).

PANIC DISORDER

People with panic disorders experience **panic attacks**, periods of intense fear and physical discomfort in which they feel overwhelmed and terrified by a range of bodily sensations that cause them to feel as if they are losing control. These sensations include shortness of breath or the feeling of being smothered, hyperventilation, dizziness or unsteadiness, choking, heart palpitations, trembling, sweating, stomach distress, feelings of unreality, sensations of numbness or tingling, hot flashes or chills, chest discomfort, and fear of dying, "going crazy," or losing control. If you have ever had any of the symptoms of a panic attack, even to a small degree, you can imagine how upsetting it must be to someone who experiences a full-blown episode.

Characteristics of Panic Disorder

The diagnosis of **panic disorder** is made when panic attacks occur on a recurrent basis (at least four times within a month) or when the person has suffered weeks of apprehension and worry about the possibility of recurring attacks following a single episode. A fairly high percentage of the population, as many as nine percent, have experienced one

Sometimes anxiety can be so overwhelming that people feel unable to cope with the ordinary demands of life.

or more panic attacks by the time they reach adulthood. However, panic disorder is fairly uncommon, afflicting one to two percent of the population (Reiger et al., 1988).

Understandably, many people who have had a panic attack dread the possibility of having another one, fearing that a catastrophe will occur (Telch et al., 1989). They are especially concerned about having an attack when they are not in a position to find help on their own. One aspect of panic attacks that is so troubling to these individuals is their unpredictability. People who have panic attacks report that these attacks appear spontaneously, but they may sometimes be provoked by job or family difficulties (Mathews et al., 1981).

People with panic disorders learn to avoid places where they fear they may be trapped, such as elevators, crowded stores, or movie theaters. Often, such avoidance leads to symptoms of a related disorder, **agoraphobia**, which is the fear of being trapped or stranded without help if a panic attack occurs. A conversation with a neighbor on the street, a party, a limited-access highway, or a religious service may all be seen as situations of potential danger.

Because agoraphobic people become so fearful of panic attacks, they develop idiosyncratic personal styles and behaviors. For example, they may refuse to leave the house unless they are accompanied by someone who knows about their disorder. They go to extremes to avoid being in a crowd or going to an unfamiliar place. Even when they are not experiencing feelings of immediate danger, people with agoraphobia constantly worry about unexpectedly being put into what they perceive as risky situations. It is possible for people to experience agoraphobia without also having a panic disorder. Rather than fearing a panic attack, some agoraphobics fear that they will experience another type of misfortune such as vomiting in public.

Panic disorder, particularly panic disorder with agoraphobia, is more commonly diagnosed in women. When men develop panic disorder, they tend not to seek professional help, but try to cope with their symptoms by drinking alcohol (Chambless & Goldstein, 1982; Gorman & Liebowitz, 1986).

The course of panic disorder, when it goes untreated, is quite variable. For some individuals, years may go by with no panic attacks. Then suddenly, and without warning, an attack strikes. More typically, however, the disorder creates continuous problems for many years (Lelliott et al., 1987), with symptoms that are burdensome, severely limiting, and often unremitting (Pollack et al., 1990). People with panic disorder are also more vulnerable when faced with difficult life events that ordinarily cause non-anxious individuals to feel highly stressed (Roy-Byrne et al., 1986; Rapee et al., 1990). They have lower earning potential and less satisfactory relationships, and are likely to become depressed and may even become suicidal (Markowitz et al., 1989; Weissman, 1991).

Theories and Treatment

In trying to understand the causes of panic disorder and agoraphobia, researchers have tended to discuss both phenomena together, although some give more emphasis to one than the other. The available theories suggest that both disorders have psychological and physiological components, but it is unclear whether psychological factors cause physiological changes or vice versa.

Biological theories of panic disorder and agoraphobia postulate that the sensation of panic is triggered by changes in the body. These changes may be the result of an underlying biochemical abnormality that perhaps is inherited

(Sheehan, 1982). One prominent theory has focused on the role of *lactate* in contributing to panic attacks. **Lactate** is a chemical in the blood that normally produces no psychological problems; in fact, its production is stimulated by aerobic exercise such as running or swimming. According to the **lactate theory** of panic disorder, the intense anxiety experienced during a panic attack results from an increase of lactate in the blood. In studies testing the lactate theory, people diagnosed with panic disorder were injected with sodium lactate, causing them to experience symptoms reportedly similar to their routine panic attacks (Pitts & McClure, 1967; Liebowitz et al., 1984). Infusion of sodium lactate in people who do not have panic disorder does not produce this experience. From these results, researchers have concluded that people with panic disorder are hypersensitive to excess lactate in the blood, perhaps due to a neuroendocrine defect in the brain stem (Carr & Sheehan, 1984).

A second biological theory proposes that people with panic disorder have an excess of *norepinephrine* in the brain (Charney et al., 1990). Norepinephrine, a neurotransmitter, is activated when the individual is placed under stress or in a dangerous situation. This theory has been tested in ways similar to tests of the lactate theory. For example, when a drug that increases norepinephrine activity is administered to people with a history of panic disorder, they are more likely than people without the disorder to experience a panic attack.

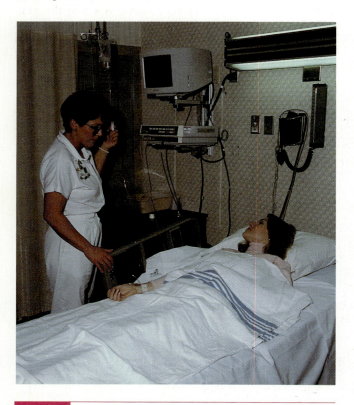

In an experiment to test the lactate theory of panic disorder, this woman is given an injection of sodium lactate to see if she will respond by having a panic attack.

Frieda is a 28-year-old former postal worker who sought treatment because of recurrent panic attacks that have led her to become fearful of driving. She has become so frightened about the prospect of having an attack on the job that she has asked for a medical leave. Although initially she would leave the house when accompanied by her mother, she now is unable to go out under any circumstances, and her family is concerned that she will become a total recluse.

■ How does Frieda's case illustrate the symptoms of panic disorder with agoraphobia compared to panic disorder without agoraphobia?

■ What role do you think Frieda's panic attacks played in her development of agoraphobia?

A third biological theory (Insel et al., 1984) proposes a defect in gamma-aminobutyric acid (GABA), a neurotransmitter with inhibitory effects on neurons. According to this theory, the anxiety experienced by people with panic disorders is due to underactivity of GABA. Neurons in subcortical parts of the brain involved in panic attacks become more active with less GABA to inhibit them.

Adding to whatever biological factors contribute to panic attacks are the **conditioned fear reactions** that may be set in motion when the panic attack first begins. These reactions involve an association of certain bodily sensations with memories of the last panic attack, and can cause a full-blown panic attack to develop even before measurable biological changes have occurred (Gorman & Liebowitz, 1986). Further, over time, the individual begins to anticipate the panic attack before it happens, leading to the avoidance behavior seen in agoraphobia (Klein, 1981). This possibility was tested in an intriguing study in which subjects with a history of agoraphobia with panic attacks were given an antianxiety medication to reduce unexpected panic attacks. With a decrease in the frequency of unexpected episodes of fear, these individuals were less likely to experience situational panic attacks and anticipatory anxiety (Rifkin et al., 1990).

Cognitive-behavioral factors, then, may interact with biological abnormalities in the development of panic disorder (Margraf et al., 1986). Some researchers have described these factors in terms of a "fear of fear" (Chambless & Goldstein, 1982) that builds upon itself in an ever-escalating cycle. The agoraphobic has become afraid of the situations in which fear or panic attacks have been elicited in the past, as well as the internal sensations of discomfort that occur during one of these attacks or fear episodes (Foa et al., 1984).

Given that biological factors play at least some role in causing panic disorder, many clinicians recommend treatment with medications. The most effective antianxiety medications are **benzodiazepines** (Davidson, 1990). These medications bind to receptor sites of GABA neurons which then become activated by this stimulation, leading to inhibition of the brain sites involved in panic attacks. Some commonly prescribed benzodiazepines are chlordiazepoxide (Librium), diazepam (Valium), chlorazepate (Tranxene), and alprazolam (Xanax). To be effective in treating panic disorders, these medications must be administered over at least 6 months, and possibly as long as a year (Ballenger, 1991).

Because these medications often lead to physiological or psychological dependence, clinicians have sought alternatives. Antidepressants have successfully been used (Roth et al., 1992), but these carry other risks when taken on a long-term basis (Noyes & Perry, 1990). Lastly, serotonin reuptake inhibitors such as fluoxetine (Prozac) have shown promise in the treatment of panic disorder (Paul, 1990). As useful as medications are in alleviating symptoms of panic, they are regarded as insufficient in the treatment of panic disorder. Combining medication with psychological treatment is regarded as important in treating the disorder (Klerman, 1992).

Most psychological interventions are based on some form of behavioral model (Barlow, 1988) and are intended to give the individual a sense of being able to control the attacks. In a form of counterconditioning, the client is instructed to hyperventilate intentionally and then to begin slow breathing, a response that is incompatible with hyperventilation. Following this training, the client can begin the slow breathing at the first signs of hyperventilation. This procedure teaches the client that it is possible to exert voluntary control over hyperventilation.

Relaxation training is another behavioral technique used in the treatment of panic disorder and agoraphobia. In this approach, which has been available for many years (Jacobsen, 1938), the client is systematically taught to alternate tensing and relaxing muscles all over the body, usually starting at the forehead and working downward to the feet. After training, the client should be able to relax the entire body when confronting a feared situation.

When an individual is agoraphobic, interventions similar to those used for other phobias can be adapted to the person's fear of public places (Barlow, 1988). Repeatedly exposing the individual to the feared situation reduces the "fear of fear" until the individual realizes that no harm will occur. A related treatment involves stimulating physiological symptoms resembling those that occur at the onset of a panic attack. With the guidance of the therapist, clients can learn to interpret these bodily changes without becoming panicked (Barlow, 1990) (see Research Focus).

SPECIFIC PHOBIAS

Everyone has fears or unpleasant responses to certain objects, situations, or creatures. Perhaps you shrink away from the sight of a spider, rodent, or snake. Or maybe looking down from a high place causes you to feel trembly and nauseated. Standing in a crowded hallway may lead you to feel uncomfortable, even a bit edgy, and you seek an open space. Such responses of discomfort or dislike, called **aversions**, are common and are not much of a cause for concern. However, if a person's response to one of these experiences is far out of proportion to the danger or threat posed by the stimulus, the person is considered to have a *phobia*. A **specific** (or **simple**) **phobia** is an irrational and unabating fear of a particular object, activity, or situation.

The University of Wisconsin football team practices a relaxation exercise to prepare for the anxiety of a game.

TESTING A MODEL OF PANIC

David Barlow is one of the nation's leading experts on the psychological aspects of anxiety disorders. In his cognitive-behavioral model of anxiety disorders (Barlow, 1988), he proposed that anxiety becomes an unmanageable problem for an individual through a vicious cycle. The cycle begins with the sensation of highly negative feelings (such as unpleasant bodily sensations in a panic attack), which in turn lead to the feeling that what is happening to the individual is unpredictable and uncontrollable. As these feelings increase in intensity, they draw the individual's attention like a magnet. The individual is now left awash in these unpleasant sensations and cannot do anything else except think about them. Faulty cognitions and misperception of cues both within the person's body and in the environment further contribute to the sensation of anxiety, as in the case of phobias.

The model proposed by Barlow has stimulated a growing body of research both in his clinic at the State University of New York at Albany and elsewhere throughout the world. We will focus here on one of these studies as reported by Barlow (1990)

because it provides a good illustration of his model of panic disorder with agoraphobia, and because it shows some of the principles of controlled research investigations described in Chapter 1.

In this research, Barlow tested a systematic exposure method of treating panic disorder with agoraphobia called *panic control treatment* or *PCT*. It is assumed that people with panic disorder have become overly sensitive to their internal bodily cues (heart palpitations, hyperventilation, dizziness) and also misinterpret these cues as signs of impending physical disaster. In PCT, the client is made to experience these cues *in vivo* (as by running up a flight of stairs) and through imagery. The client is also taught to use cognitive restructuring and other methods proposed by Beck

et al. (1985) to challenge faulty beliefs about anxiety. In the research, patients were assigned to one of four groups: (1) a waiting-list control who were assessed initially but did not receive treatment until 15 weeks later; (2) a group receiving PCT (exposure/cognitive); (3) a group taught to use relaxation when anxious or panicky; and (4) a group receiving a combination of methods (2) and (3). The results (shown in Figure 7-1) show that groups 2 and 4 improved the most and that relaxation training alone was no better than the waiting list control condition. The percentages of improvement were calculated on the basis of the total sample, including those who dropped out, and amounted to 79 percent in the exposure and cognitive group, 73 percent in the combined group, 40 percent in the relaxation group, and 33 percent in the waiting list control group.

A second study tested the effectiveness of psychological therapy as contrasted with medications. The combined therapy condition (cognitive-behavioral plus relaxation) was contrasted with groups receiving alprazolam (Xanax, an antianxiety medication) or a placebo administered in a double-blind fashion. A

Characteristics of Specific Phobias

You have probably heard the term "phobia" many times, perhaps in a humorous context. People with phobias go to great lengths to avoid contact with the target of their irrational fears. Usually the person is frightened about what will happen when the feared object is encountered. For instance, there is no real danger that a person will die of asphyxiation while sleeping in an adequately ventilated pup tent. A man with **claustrophobia** (fear of closed spaces), though, feels that he cannot even enter such a small space without becoming overwhelmed with a fear of suffocation. His anxiety is so intense that if he attempts to enter the tent he may feel panicky and breathless.

In some phobias, the stimulus itself is totally harmless unless improperly used, such as a bread knife. Take the case

of a woman who has a phobic response to knives because of their potentially harmful purpose. Or consider another individual who has a phobia not of a specific object, but of a situation; any situation that necessitates using math causes the person to feel upset and panicky. When a phobia is narrowly circumscribed to specific stimuli that are rarely encountered in the course of everyday life, it is unlikely that the individual will seek treatment. For example, a man's snake phobia is not particularly problematic for him because he resides in New York City and knows enough to avoid going to zoos and pet shops. People with phobias to objects or situations that are not easily avoided, such as elevators or bridges, are more likely to seek professional help.

Although many people experience phobic symptoms (Barlow, 1988), only about 5 to 10 percent of the adult population are diagnosed as having specific phobias (Myers et al., 1984). Some phobias can be traced back to childhood, fourth group was in a waiting-list control condition. After 15 weeks, patients in the alprazolam and therapy groups both improved more than did the patients in the placebo or waiting list groups. However, those in the therapy group rated themselves as having less intense symptoms, particularly on one key variable, shortness of breath.

In follow-up studies carried out 6 and 24 months after the original investigations, the long-term advantages of PCT were dramatically demonstrated. As shown in Figure 7-2, the exposure/cognitive group (PCT) were more likely to be panic-free than either the combined or relaxation groups. The combination of relaxation with PCT seemed, surprisingly, to interfere with the progress attributed to PCT alone.

This type of research is essential in establishing the validity of new treatment techniques. In terms of providing a perspective on the anxiety disorders, Barlow's work clearly supports the efficacy of cognitive-behavioral treatments and shows that even a disorder as pervasive and severe as panic disorder can be successfully treated.

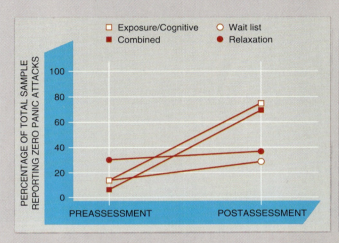

Figure 7-1
Percentage of total sample from Barlow (1990) reporting zero panic attacks after treatment.

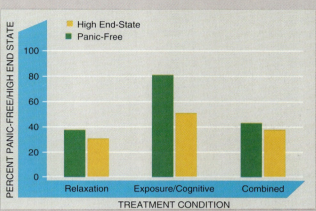

Figure 7-2
Panic-free and end-state (much improved or cured) status at 24-month follow-up in Barlow's (1990) research.

such as animal phobias (McNally & Steketee, 1985), blood-injury phobias (Marks, 1988), claustrophobia, and dental phobias (Öst, 1987). Most children do experience certain fears such as fear of the dark, of strangers, of death, and of imaginary creatures; however, most of these dissipate on their own (Emmelkamp, 1982).

Although the phobias that begin in childhood tend to be the most common, there are actually a wide variety of phobias and aversions that can afflict people. These include situations involving eating, flying in airplanes, recurrent nightmares, darkness, wind, thunderstorms and lightning, urinating away from home, body odor, balloons popping, whistling, wigs and false hair, and fabrics such as cotton, wool, velvet, and suede, peach skin, rubber, and buttons (Marks, 1987). Other, very rare, phobias are listed in Table 7-1 (on page 178). Some researchers have postulated that agoraphobia is actually a specific phobia (Craske, 1991).

Herbert is a 32-year old lawyer who sought treatment for his irrational fear of thunderstorms. He has had this phobia since the age of 4, and throughout life has developed various strategies for coping with his fear. Whenever possible, he avoids going outside when a storm is forecast. Not only will he stay within a building, but he will ensure that he is in a room with no windows and no electrical appliances. As his job has grown in responsibility, Herbert has found that he can no longer afford to take time off, and he has sought professional help for this fear that he knows is irrational.

■ What symptoms of Herbert's would lead you to conclude that he has a specific phobia?

■ Given that Herbert is afraid to leave the house if a storm is imminent, why would he not be regarded as having agoraphobia?

Table 7-1   List of Words Used to Describe Rare Phobias

Below are terms used to label various rare phobias. Although they are not part of any current diagnostic classification system, they illustrate the variety of phobias documented throughout history.

Word	Fear of
Ailurophobia	Cats
Antlophobia	Floods
Chionophobia	Snow
Dromophobia	Crossing streets, wandering about
Erythrophobia	The color red
Harpaxophobia	Robbers
Metallophobia	Metals
Osphreisiophobia	Body odors
Phasmophobia	Ghosts
Ponophobia	Work
Scopophobia	Being stared at
Theophobia	God
Triskaidekaphobia	The number 13

Source: Tuma & Maser, (1985).

Theories and Treatment

Speculation about the psychological causes of phobias goes back at least as far as the time of Freud. Although Freud did not initially consider phobias to be psychologically based, his later writings reflected his notion of phobias as psychological symptoms that served to defend the ego against anxiety. Around the same time that Freud was writing on the topic, behavioral psychologists were demonstrating in the laboratory that phobic behavior could be acquired through conditioning by animals and humans alike, leading to the conclusion that phobias resulted from maladaptive learning. Current conceptualizations add to this behavioral model the notion that the individual's thoughts also play a role in the acquisition and maintenance of specific phobias. One group of researchers has suggested that underlying the association between the feared situation and the response of anxiety is a memory that, when activated, sets off the fear response (Foa & Kozak, 1986).

Cognitive-behavioral theorists (Beck et al., 1985) view anxiety disorders such as specific phobias as rooted in and maintained by cognitive styles of the client. According to this view, phobic individuals have overactive "alarm systems" to danger and misinterpret stimuli they perceive as dangerous. Their perceptions are based on faulty inferences and overgeneralizations. For example, a 30-year-old man may experience a fear of dying that is triggered by an unexpected physical sensation. The man *interprets* the physical sensation as a sign of physical disease and becomes anxious; in this way, a chain reaction is set up. He then generalizes in such a way that everything looks dangerous. His attention

Climbing an outside staircase causes this man with acrophobia to feel panicky.

becomes stuck on potentially dangerous stimuli, and less attention is available to think rationally. Then he thinks that he is losing his mind and this makes matters worse.

Another theory incorporates biological and anthropological notions, proposing that people are biologically "prepared" to learn to fear anything that threatens survival of the species. This biological propensity might explain how people can so rapidly acquire irrational fears that are so resistant to extinction. Although this theory is controversial, it provides some interesting ideas for future research (McNally, 1987).

Specific phobias respond well to behavioral therapy because the symptoms are relatively easy to identify and the stimuli are limited to specific situations or objects. As illustrated in Table 7-2, behavioral treatments vary according to the nature of the client's exposure to the phobic stimulus (live or imagined) and the degree of intensity with which the stimulus is confronted (immediate full exposure or exposure in graduated steps).

Systematic desensitization, described in Chapter 5, rests on the premise that an individual can best overcome

Table 7-2   Variations of Behavioral Therapy of Phobias

Type of Exposure	Graduated	Suddenly Intense
Imagery	Systematic desensitization	Imaginal flooding
Live	Graded *in vivo*	Flooded *in vivo*

maladaptive anxiety by approaching feared stimuli gradually, while in a relaxed state. A therapist might decide, though, that systematic desensitization is either too time-consuming, impractical, or unnecessary. Consider the case of Florence, a medical student who sees a therapist in desperation one week before she starts an anatomy course. She has fainted on past occasions when watching videotapes of surgical procedures and is sure that she will make a fool out of herself in anatomy class. One week is not enough time to go through the systematic desensitization procedure. Furthermore, Florence's anxiety is not so severe as to be terrifying. Her therapist therefore decides to use a behavioral technique called **flooding**, in which the client is totally immersed in the sensation of anxiety rather than being more gradually acclimated to the feared situation. Florence's therapist chooses a variant of flooding called **imaginal flooding**, in which Florence listens to someone read several vivid descriptions of the dissections of human cadavers. Florence is told to imagine exactly what these scenes look like. Exposure to the threatening stimulus while in a safe context will condition her to confront the target of her phobia without feeling unduly anxious.

Both behavioral techniques described so far use imagery in conditioning the client to feel less anxious toward the phobic stimulus. The alternative to imagery, and one that is generally more effective (Emmelkamp, 1982), is

In systematic desensitization for snake phobia, clients progress through stages of approaching and holding the feared stimulus. They begin with the least threatening stimulus, such as a rubber snake, and gradually learn that they can actually handle a snake without being overwhelmed by fear.

actual exposure of the client to the feared object or situation until the client no longer feels anxious. Obviously this **in vivo** (from the Latin "in life" or "live") **method** requires that the therapist have ready access to the phobic stimulus. Florence's therapist could just as easily show her a surgical videotape as encourage her to imagine the sight of blood. However, if the client fears flying in an airplane, it would be impractical for the therapist to embark on *in vivo* treatment by accompanying the client on an airplane ride (although cases of such treatment are occasionally reported).

The *in vivo* method can be dangerous if it causes so much anxiety that the client's health is threatened. *In vivo* flooding is probably the most stressful of any of the treatments described; an alternative is a graded *in vivo* method involving a gradual exposure to increasingly anxiety-provoking stimuli. The graded methods usually employ encouragement on the part of the therapist or modeling by the therapist of the desired non-anxious response. In treating a client with fear of enclosed spaces, the therapist could go with him into smaller and smaller rooms. Seeing his therapist showing no signs of fear could lead a client to model the therapist's response. Praise offered to a client by his therapist could further reinforce the new response that a client is learning.

Positive reinforcement is implicit in all behavioral techniques. The therapist becomes both a guide and a source of support and praise for the successes of the client. It may also be useful for the therapist to incorporate some techniques from the cognitive perspective into the behavioral treatment, since maladaptive thoughts are often part of the client's difficulties. Cognitive-behavioral treatment focuses on teaching the client more adaptive ways of thinking about previously threatening situations and objects.

Cognitive restructuring, described in Chapter 5, can be used to help the client view the feared situation more rationally, such as challenging the client's irrational beliefs about the feared stimulus. For example, the therapist may show a man with an elevator phobia that the "disastrous" consequences he believes will result from riding in an elevator are unrealistic and exaggerated. The client can also be taught to "talk to himself" while in this situation, telling himself that his fears are ridiculous, that nothing bad will really happen, and that he will soon reach his destination.

In **thought stopping**, the individual learns to stop anxiety-provoking thoughts. In therapy, the client is instructed to alert the therapist when the anxiety provoking thought is present, and at this point the therapist yells "Stop!" Outside therapy, the client is instructed to verbalize a similar shout (in his or her thoughts) each time the anxiety provoking thought comes to mind.

Through stress inoculation, the client can be taught coping self-statements (Meichenbaum, 1985), another cognitive-behavioral method described in Chapter 5. The client prepares a list of statements that can be used when the feared situation is confronted, providing reassurance that the situation can be adequately managed. Examples of such statements are "I can cope with this," "It is irrational for me to feel so scared," "I've gotten through difficult situations before so I can get through this one," and "Don't think about my fear." These statements increase the individual's sense that the situation can be conquered.

Bolstering the client's sense of self-efficacy is a related therapy component (Bandura, 1986) that helps the client feel more confident about being able to manage the phobic stimulus. For example, Florence, whose blood-injury phobia we described earlier, could be taught through self-efficacy training to see herself as successfully handling her fears. She may observe or imagine observing someone else treating patients who are bleeding, using vicarious reinforcement to change her beliefs about her own ability to come close to a bleeding person. As Florence herself is put into actual situations with increased exposure to blood or injury, she can practice telling herself that she has the capability to cope with the situation, until she no longer experiences anxiety.

SOCIAL PHOBIA

Many people become nervous or jittery before getting up to speak in front of a group, appearing in a musical performance, or displaying athletic skills in a game or contest. People with **social phobia**, however, feel tremendous anxiety not only in these situations, but in virtually all situations where others might be observing them.

Characteristics of Social Phobia

People with social phobia have irrational concerns that something about their behavior will catch the attention of others and result in their being mocked or criticized. For example, when writing out a bank deposit slip, they worry that others may notice their trembling hands; when eating in a restaurant, they think that other people will laugh at the way they are holding their fork or swallowing their food. They also may fear that they will blush, sweat, drop something, choke on their food, or vomit (Marks, 1987). These fears evaporate when the individual is alone or unobserved; it is the *social* aspect of the situation that causes excessive anxiety. In addition to these specific fears about being observed, people with social phobia have low self-esteem and underestimate their talents and areas of competence (Uhde et al., 1991).

Social phobia can have effects similar to agoraphobia in that fears about public embarrassment may prevent the individual from leaving the house. However, the two disorders are psychologically distinct in that the anxiety experienced by people with social phobia is specific to certain situations, while agoraphobia tends to be more generalized. Even biological processes seem to differ between those who experience social phobia and those who suffer from panic disorder and agoraphobia (Uhde et al., 1991). For example, social phobics do not respond with panic attacks to sodium lactate infusions (Liebowitz et al., 1985).

Among the phobias, social phobia is second only to panic disorder in frequency, with a prevalence estimated at between 1.5 and 2 percent of the general population (Myers et al, 1984; Pollard & Henderson, 1988). The disorder is equally common in males and females and it usually becomes evident during adolescence (Marks, 1987). There appear to be two subtypes of social phobia: specific and generalized (Agras, 1990). Some individuals with social phobias have fears specific to given situations such as public speaking or performing a musical instrument in front of an audience. Others have a generalized avoidance of all social situations. In both cases, the individual's occupational and social functioning are impaired by the disorder. For example, people with musical talent might steer away from careers as musicians because of the anxiety engendered by their social phobia (Clark, 1989). About 90 percent of those suffering from social phobia experience impairment in occupational performance because of their emotional problems. For approximately half the people suffering from generalized social phobia, the problem becomes compounded when they seek relief by turning to alcohol (Turner et al., 1986).

Theories and Treatment

Although social fears and anxieties have existed throughout the ages, social phobia has only relatively recently been understood as a separate category of the anxiety disorders (Barlow, 1988). In 1966, Marks and Gelder (1966) first defined social phobia as a fear of performing certain behaviors in public. Later research has supported the idea that there is a unique quality to this set of anxieties. However, the picture is not quite so clear. More recently researchers have observed overlap between social phobia and avoidant personality disorder (Widiger, 1992).

As a means of understanding how social phobia develops, think about a time when you have been called upon to perform some action in public, such as hitting a baseball, delivering a speech, or giving a solo musical performance. Perhaps your hands were shaking and your heart was pounding as you prepared to go into the spotlight. You may have imagined the laughter or criticism of others if you made a mistake. Once you started performing the action, though, chances are that you forgot about these distractions and concentrated on doing the best job you possibly could.

According to one model of social phobia, people with this disorder are unable to take the step of shifting their attention away from anticipated criticism and onto their performance. While performing or speaking, they fear making a mistake and, because their concentration is impaired, they are likely to make that dreaded mistake. Their fears acquire a solid basis in experience each time this happens, and these people soon become phobic and avoidant of similar situations. Even if the individual manages to keep from making a mistake, the unpleasantness of the situation is so intense that it sets in motion a desire to avoid repetition.

Ted is a 19-year-old college freshman who reports that he is "terrified" at the prospect of speaking in class. His anxiety about this matter is so intense that he has enrolled in very large lecture classes, where he sits in the back of the room, slouching in his chair to make himself as "invisible" as possible. On occasion, one of his professors randomly calls upon students to answer certain questions. When this occurs, Ted begins to sweat and tremble. Sometimes he rushes from the classroom and frantically runs back to the dormitory for a few hours and tries to calm himself down.

- What symptoms would lead you to regard Ted as having social phobia?
- To what extent has Ted become caught up in a vicious cycle in which he avoids opportunities to confront anxiety-provoking situations?

The treatment of people with social phobia involves helping them learn more appropriate responses to the situations they fear. Behavioral and cognitive-behavioral techniques, such as those used to treat people with specific phobias, are particularly helpful in reaching this goal. Social phobics need to develop new ways of thinking about their interactions with others. Impressive treatment benefits have been achieved when techniques such as cognitive restructuring are combined with *in vivo* exposure (Butler et al., 1984; Clark & Agras, 1991; Heimberg & Barlow, 1988; Mattick et al., 1989). Another treatment approach involves social skills training, in which social phobics are taught methods for coping with interpersonal stress, so that they can feel more confident and comfortable in their interactions (Öst et al., 1984). In some severe cases, pharmacological treatment either in the form of antidepressant (Liebowitz et al., 1985) or antianxiety medication (Davidson et al., 1991) is warranted. But even in cases where medications are prescribed, cognitive-behavioral techniques have been recommended (Gelernter et al., 1991; Heimberg & Barlow, 1991).

GENERALIZED ANXIETY DISORDER

Sometimes anxiety is not associated with a particular object, situation, or event but seems to be a constant feature of a person's day-to-day existence. The diagnosis of **generalized anxiety disorder** is used to capture this category of anxiety-related experiences.

Characteristics of Generalized Anxiety Disorder

Generalized anxiety disorder is one of the more common anxiety disorders, affecting an estimated 2 to 8 percent of

People with generalized anxiety disorder have many worries and physical symptoms that prevent them from enjoying life.

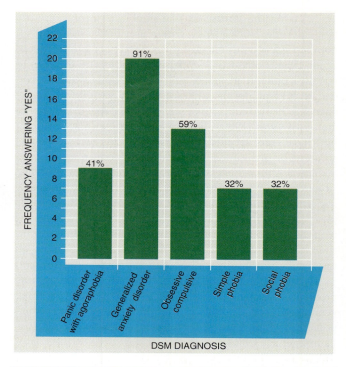

Figure 7-3
This graph shows the percentages of 22 patients from five anxiety disorder categories who answered "yes" when asked if they worry excessively about minor things (Sanderson and Barlow, 1990).

adults (Weissman, 1990b). People with this disorder feel anxious much of the time and suffer a number of symptoms, both physical and psychological. They may experience heart palpitations, sweating, trembling, fidgeting, restlessness, shortness of breath, dizziness, nausea, hot flashes or chills, frequent urination, or a lump in the throat. Their psychological symptoms include feelings of foreboding, worry, edginess, dread, difficulty concentrating, irritability, and trouble falling asleep.

Often, these bodily reactions, feelings, and thoughts have no direct connection with a discernible issue in the person's life. If the individual does verbalize specific fears or concerns, these are usually unrealistic and extend to several domains. (To be diagnosed as having this disorder, the individual must experience worry in two or more areas of life.) For example, a man may worry that his college-age son, who is in good health, will develop some life-threatening disease, and he may also be distraught by worries about going bankrupt even though his business is thriving. Both sets of worries are without grounds, yet he finds himself consumed with anxiety and distracted from his daily responsibilities.

Gina is a 32-year-old hairdresser who sought professional help for her longstanding feelings of anxiety. Though there are several concerns in her life such as the pressure of being a single parent and numerous financial problems, she does not see these specific issues as the cause of her anxiety. Most of the time she feels uncomfortable and tense, and sometimes her tension becomes so extreme that she begins to tremble and sweat. Her heart races and she becomes nauseated. She has consulted a variety of medical specialists, each of whom has been unable to diagnose a physical problem.

- What symptoms of Gina's would lead you to regard her as having generalized anxiety disorder?
- How would you distinguish Gina's disorder from panic disorder?

The kinds of worries experienced by people with generalized anxiety disorder are not just passing concerns; the diagnosis is only given in cases where a person has suffered from anxiety for more than 6 months. In fact, people with this disorder often state that there has been no time in their lives when they have not felt tense and anxious. They are seen by others as "worrywarts." Figure 7-3 provides statistics for people with various anxiety disorders who report that they worry excessively about minor concerns (Sanderson & Barlow, 1990).

You know from your own experience that when you are worried about something, it is difficult if not impossible to enjoy yourself. You can understand, then, that people with generalized anxiety disorder rarely are able to lead satisfying lives. Some researchers (Margraf et al., 1986) have suggested that generalized anxiety disorder should be categorized with panic disorder in light of the fact that some individuals who have generalized anxiety disorder develop panic disorder. However, there is evidence that the two disorders, although occasionally linked, are separate diagnostic entities. People with panic disorder, as discussed earlier, improve when treated with antidepressants; people with generalized anxiety disorder respond only to antianxiety medications (Klein, 1981). Evidence from epidemiological, family, and twin studies further supports the contention that they are separate disorders. (Weissman, 1990a). Nevertheless, the two disorders often co-occur, and can be difficult to separate clinically.

Theories and Treatment

Despite the fact that so many people suffer from this disorder, generalized anxiety disorder has not been extensively researched and there are relatively few explanations for how it develops. One possibility is that people with this disorder have a biological abnormality similar to that proposed to account for other anxiety disorders (Insel et al., 1984). It is also possible that generalized anxiety disorder might be a response to life stresses. One group of researchers found that over a one-year period, men who had experienced four or more unexpected negative life events (such as loss of a job) had a risk of generalized anxiety disorder that was nearly nine times greater than men reporting fewer stressful life events (Blazer et al., 1987).

It also appears that people with generalized anxiety disorder become easily distressed and worried by the minor nuisances or small disruptions of life. If something goes wrong in their day-to-day existence, such as car trouble, an argument with a co-worker, or a home repair problem, they magnify the extent of the problem and become unduly apprehensive about the outcome. Their attention shifts from the problem itself to their own worries, and as a result their concern becomes magnified. At the same time, they are less efficient in their daily tasks, and consequently develop more to worry about as more goes wrong for them. For whatever reason, once the anxiety is initiated, it begins to spiral out of control with worry piling upon worry (Barlow, 1988). Particularly damaging is the individual's lack of confidence in the ability to control or manage anxious feelings and reactions, as well as a lack of confidence in the ability to manage daily tasks effectively.

Although benzodiazepines and newer antianxiety drugs that are less habit-forming can effectively control many of the bodily symptoms associated with generalized anxiety disorder (Gitlin, 1990), clinicians are reluctant to prescribe such medications on a long-term basis. As an alternative, cognitive-behavioral methods can be used, and there is evidence that this form of therapy may be an effective treatment strategy without medication (Butler et al., 1991). In the cognitive-behavioral approach, clients are taught to recognize anxious thoughts, to seek more rational alternatives to worrying, and to take action to test out these alternatives (Beck et al., 1985). The emphasis is on breaking the cycle of negative thoughts and worries. Once this cycle is broken, the individual can develop a sense of control over the worrying behavior and become more proficient at managing and reducing anxious thoughts.

OBSESSIVE-COMPULSIVE DISORDER

If you have ever had a thought that you could not seem to force out of your consciousness, you have some insight into the experience of an obsession—a persistent and intrusive idea, thought, impulse, or image. Perhaps you could not seem to stop thinking about a particular concern, such as something hurtful that you said to a close friend. Thoughts about this concern may have distracted you from your studies or work. Multiply this experience hundreds of times in intensity and you will have a sense of what life is like for the person with true obsessions.

Many people with obsessions also struggle with compulsions. A compulsion is a repetitive and seemingly purposeful behavior performed in response to uncontrollable urges or according to a ritualistic or stereotyped set of rules.

To illustrate these phenomena, consider the example of a woman who has the nightmarish obsessive thought of using a knife to kill her children, a thought that she finds horrifying and totally out of character with the deep love that she feels toward them. She may develop a compulsive ritual to prevent herself from carrying out this obsessive thought, such as cleaning out the silverware drawer. The irrational concern over the possibility of harming her children constitutes the obsession that fuels her compulsion to clean the drawer. Following her cleaning of the drawer, she feels transient relief from her intense anxiety, only to have the anxiety erupt again shortly afterwards.

Characteristics of Obsessive-Compulsive Disorder

Obsessive-compulsive disorder is characterized by the experience of intrusive thoughts that the individual can alleviate only by engaging in patterns of rigid, ritualistic behaviors. The disorder is considered to be an anxiety disorder because anxiety is assumed to be the driving force behind the individual's thoughts and actions. Obsessive thoughts and compulsive ritualistic behaviors were once believed to serve an adaptive function in that they distract the individual from the original source of anxiety (Salzman & Thaler, 1981). However, this explanation has become outdated as it is increasingly recognized that the disorder greatly interferes with the individual's life and in fact may *cause* considerable anxiety (Rapoport, 1990). The obsessive

This woman has a compulsion that drives her to clean the dining room table several times a day because she fears that germs may contaminate and poison her food.

Table 7-3   Examples of Obsessions and Related Compulsions

OBSESSION:		COMPULSION:	
	A college student has the urge to shout out obscenities while sitting through lectures in his classes.		Keeping an eye on his watch, he bites his tongue every sixty seconds in order to ward off the inclination to shout out.
	A woman cannot get the thought out of her mind that she might accidentally leave her gas stove turned on, causing her house to explode.		Each day before leaving for work, she feels the irresistible urge to check the stove exactly 10 times.
	A 9-year-old boy worries incessantly that something terrible might happen to his mother while the family is sleeping.		On his way up to bed each night, he insists that he must climb the stairs according to a fixed sequence of three steps up, followed by two steps down in order to ward off danger.
	A young woman is continuously terrified by the image that cars might careen onto the sidewalk and run her down.		She feels that she must walk as far from the street pavement as possible, and always wear red clothes when in town so that she will be immediately visible to an out-of-control driver.
	A woman is tormented by the concern that she might inadvertently contaminate food as she cooks dinner for her family each night.		On a daily basis she sterilizes all cooking utensils in boiling water, scours every pot and pan before placing food in it, and wears rubber gloves while handling food.

thoughts and compulsive behaviors are usually inconsistent with the individual's conscious wishes, values, and personal style. They are time-consuming, irrational, and distracting, and the individual may strongly desire to stop them. Returning to the woman with the obsessive thoughts about harming her children, not only are her thoughts upsetting and distracting, but her needless cleaning of the drawers wastes time and energy.

The most common compulsive rituals involve washing, and are accompanied by obsessive thoughts about contamination. Checking compulsions associated with fears of future harm are also quite common (Marks, 1987). Table 7–3 contains examples of some other common obsessions and compulsions experienced by people with this disorder.

It is important to emphasize that obsessions are *not* fleeting thoughts, passing fancies, or reactions to particular situations. They are persistent and unpleasant, appear spontaneously, and are very difficult to control. Obsessions are different from matters that an individual may choose to become absorbed with and spend time thinking about. People occasionally use the word "obsessed" to refer to a hobby or pursuit that consumes their energy, time, and thought. For example, a young man's friends describe him as being "obsessed" with sports. He seems to think about sports all the time and can recall inconsequential facts from the past century of major sports. His thinking, however, lacks the driven, senseless, and unpleasant qualities associated with a clinical obsession.

Similarly, a compulsion is not the same as a behavior that is rigidly performed, because the compulsion is governed by a set of orders or instructions. For example, it would not be considered a compulsive behavior for a grocery clerk to follow a certain cashing-out procedure at the end of the shift. A compulsion would involve the clerk feeling internally driven to include certain ritualistic behaviors in the process, such as the need to touch the money only with her left hand, and to run to the lavatory to wash her hand every time she touches a $20 bill.

Another important distinction is between the obsessive-compulsive anxiety disorder and obsessive-compulsive personality disorder. The person with an obsessive-compulsive personality disorder is a rigid and inflexible worrier who does not engage in the extremely disturbed kinds of thinking and behaving that characterize

---

Mark is a 16-year-old high school student referred for treatment by his teacher, who became disturbed by Mark's irrational concern about the danger posed by an electrical outlet at the front of the classroom. Mark pleaded daily with the teacher to have the outlet disconnected to prevent someone from accidentally getting electrocuted while walking by it. The teacher told Mark that his concerns were unfounded, but he remained so distressed that he felt driven, when entering and leaving the classroom to shine a flashlight into the outlet to make sure that a loose wire was not being exposed. During classtime, he could think of nothing else but the outlet.

- What is Mark's obsession and what is his compulsion?
- How does Mark's behavior differ from that of a person with obsessive compulsive personality disorder?

people with obsessive-compulsive anxiety disorder. For example, a man with an obsessive-compulsive personality disorder may have a very rigid classification system for all of his books and become very upset if anyone puts a book back in the wrong place. By contrast, the person with a compulsion may feel driven to check the order of the books on the shelf many times a day to ensure that they have not somehow been moved. If anything interferes with his checking of the books, he feels a great deal of distress. As you can see, there is some relationship between these two disorders, but there are also some important differences.

Obsessive-compulsive disorder, which is found equally in males and females, is experienced by about 2 to 3 percent of the population at some point in their lives (Robins et al., 1984). This amounts to as many as 6 million people in the United States, with one-half to one-third of these people developing symptoms of the disorder by childhood or adolescence (Rapoport, 1990). Obsessive-compulsive disorder is debilitating and chronic. The symptoms of the disorder can be so bizarre and upsetting that they seem psychotic, and they often become the major focus of activity for the individual.

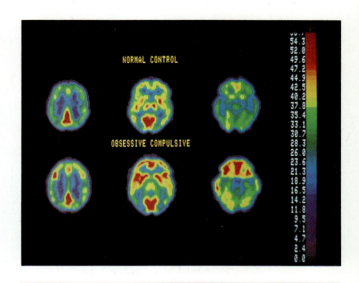

PET scans of the brains of people with obsessive-compulsive disorder show increased metabolic activity, as indicated by larger red areas in the caudate nucleus of the basal ganglia (bottom center) and frontal lobes (bottom right).

Theories and Treatment

Following Freud's theories about the unconscious causes of obsessive-compulsive disorder it was thought that this disorder was a form of neurosis involving defenses such as isolation, displacement, reaction formation, and undoing (Salzman & Thaler, 1981). However, treatment based on these theories proved to have limited effectiveness, and in time behavioral principles, which focused on removal of the symptoms, became increasingly popular (Jenike et al., 1986). These behavioral treatments were based on the general principle that the symptoms became established through their association with the relief of a momentary reduction of anxiety. The behavioral treatment methods include thought-stopping to reduce obsessional thinking along with exposure to situations that provoke the compulsive rituals or obsessions (Greist, 1990; Jenike et al., 1986). For the most part, little attention is given within the behavioral approach to the origins of the disorder in the individual's life; instead treatment is directed toward reducing the troubling compulsive behaviors and obsessive thoughts.

As a psychologically based theory and treatment, the behavioral approach has been shown to produce symptom relief for up to one year in approximately 75 percent of those treated. However, behavioral treatments fail to provide effective long-term relief of symptoms for the other 25 percent who enter treatment. Since many people with this disorder refuse to seek treatment at all, it is difficult to make accurate predictions about treatment effectiveness (Foa et al., 1985; Steketee et al.,1982).

A great deal of excitement has been generated in recent years about the use of medications in treating obsessive-compulsive disorder. In the mid-1970s, it was discovered that an antidepressant drug, clomipramine, had the unanticipated effect of reducing obsessions in depressed people. This led investigators to wonder about the possible effectiveness of clomipramine for treating nondepressed people suffering from obsessive-compulsive disorder. Extensive experimental tests of this drug yielded very encouraging results, as researchers began to hypothesize that, at least for some people, obsessive-compulsive disorder might have biological rather than psychological origins. Researchers noted that serotonin activity was reduced in people who responded favorably to clomipramine. From this it could be inferred that serotonin probably played a central role in causing the symptoms of this debilitating disorder (Rapoport, 1990).

Other evidence supporting a biological hypothesis began to fall into place. For example, a higher concordance rate was found to exist in monozygotic twins compared to dizygotic twins, supporting the hypothesis that genetics plays an important role in the development of this disorder (Turner et al., 1985). Brain abnormalities have also been found in people with obsessive-compulsive disorder. Since the late 1800s, it has been known that symptoms of obsessions and compulsions exist in people suffering from various neurological disorders including epilepsy, Parkinson's disease, and toxic lesions of the basal ganglia. More recently, a correlation has been found to exist between another disorder involving the basal ganglia (Syndenam's chorea), and obsessive-compulsive symptoms (Rapoport, 1989). Using high-technology brain-imaging techniques, researchers have found more specific links between dysfunction of these areas of the brain and symptoms of obsessive-compulsive disorder (Luxenberg et al., 1988). The results of PET scan studies have lent further support to these findings, and have also shown that there are abnormalities in the

Following a disaster such as the 1989 San Francisco earthquake, many victims struggle with immediate losses, anxiety, and long-lasting psychological problems such as post-traumatic stress disorder.

frontal lobes of the brain involved in the planning of bodily movement (see photograph).

These findings have led researchers to hypothesize that the repetitive compulsive motions of people with obsessive-compulsive disorder are caused by dysregulation of the control that normal people have over their movements (Baxter et al., 1987). Thus, these people have thoughts and actions that they literally cannot inhibit, although the brain structures involved in this process are, in essence, "working overtime," to try to control them.

Presently, treatment with clomipramine has proven to be the most effective biological treatment available for obsessive-compulsive disorder, especially when combined with behavior therapy (Jenike, 1990). Unfortunately, for some people, neither pharmacological nor psychotherapeutic interventions offer any relief. In such extreme cases, the radical intervention of psychosurgery may be used (Chiocca & Martuza, 1990; Tippin & Henn, 1982). This surgical procedure involves cutting neuronal tracts between the frontal lobe and a part of the limbic system. Studies have shown that among the small number of people who have been treated with psychosurgery, there is gradual improvement in the months following surgery (Perse, 1988). Although , as we have pointed out elsewhere, brain surgery is a radical intervention for psychological disorders, it is important to consider the alternative. The lives of some people with obsessive-compulsive disorder involve a daily battle with haunting thoughts and damaging behaviors that deprive them of even a moment's peace.

POST-TRAUMATIC STRESS DISORDER

A **traumatic experience** is a disastrous or extremely painful event that has severe psychological and physiological effects. Every day there are reports in the local, national, or world news of a tragedy or disaster. You may read or hear about a serious automobile accident, a train or airplane crash, a fire, or a major earthquake. In times of war, the news is filled with stories of lives being lost and people being injured. Violent events that affect individuals, such as being robbed, raped, or hurt in an accident, can also cause traumatic reactions.

Each traumatic event carries with it a toll of human suffering, as the survivors cope with the loss of close ones who were victims of the disaster, the loss of property when homes are destroyed, or the sense of personal violation after being assaulted or raped. Survivors must cope with the painful memories of the traumatic event, which often involve vivid images of seeing other people killed or seeing their own lives nearly ended. If you have ever had such an experience, or been close to someone who has, you must certainly be aware of how emotionally painful this process can be. Fortunately, most survivors of such disasters or traumatic events are able to return to a normal life after some period of adjustment ranging from days or months to a year or more. Others, however, don't seem to recover and develop **post-traumatic stress disorder** or **PTSD.**

Characteristics of Post-Traumatic Stress Disorder

People who suffer from PTSD continually reexperience a traumatic event or series of events although they desperately try to avoid reminders of the event. PTSD sufferers have a variety of physiological symptoms of anxiety such as trembling, inability to sleep, and hypersensitivity to noise. Anything associated with the traumatic event may provoke great emotional distress; even the anniversary of the event may stir up intense psychological and physical disturbance.

For example, a woman avoids driving by the site where her house burned to the ground several years ago, because she knows that even a fleeting reminder of the trauma will result in great psychological distress, nightmares, and physical symptoms of anxiety and dread. A wide range of events can lead to PTSD, but the most common include those pertaining to injury, loss of a loved one, participation in an atrocity, or exposure to grotesque death. Generally speaking, the greater the trauma, the greater the risk of developing PTSD (Davidson & Foa, 1991).

Following a traumatic life event, people go through a series of characteristic responses (Horowitz, 1986). The initial reaction to a traumatic life event is the **outcry phase**. During this phase, the person reacts with alarm and a strong emotion, such as fear or sadness. Sometimes people shriek or hit something during this phase. When the event involves the immediate threat of personal danger, such as in an earthquake, the outcry phase may not occur immediately because of the need to cope with the situation at hand. In such instances people may experience the outcry phase internally, or may find that the outcry takes place at a later time, perhaps in a safer place, when the imminent threat has passed.

The second series of reactions to a traumatic life event, the **denial intrusion phase** involves alternation between the experience of *denial*, or a distancing of oneself from the event, and *intrusion*, being tormented by disruptive thoughts and feelings about the event. The **denial phase** is characterized by a defensive reaction in which the individual insists that the event never happened, perhaps hoping that it was just a nightmare. Denial also includes acting in ways that create psychological distance from the trauma. During a denial phase the person becomes noticeably detached from other people and activities, staring blankly into space, ignoring help offered by others, feeling numb, and seeing the world as bleak. In extreme instances of denial, a person may try to escape into drugs, alcohol, or thrill-seeking activities such as auto racing.

After some period of time, anywhere from days to months, the event repeatedly intrudes into the person's consciousness. During this **intrusion phase** the individual becomes hypervigilant, overwhelmed by graphic and terrifying illusions and hallucinations (called **flashbacks**), nightmares, and unwanted thoughts about the event. The person is emotionally unstable, obsessed with the event, and afflicted with numerous physical irregularities such as a racing heartbeat or heavy sweating. Consider a young man, Gary, who was in a car accident that killed his friend. Gary had recurrent images of the scene of the fatal crash. When riding in cars, he was overreactive to every approaching car, repeatedly bracing himself for another imagined crash. He thought he could hear the voice of his deceased friend crying "Watch out!" For weeks following the accident, he repeatedly "saw" his friend's face when he tried to sleep. He could not get out of his mind the thought that he should have done something to prevent his friend's death.

In the 1980s, when the diagnosis of PTSD was added to the *DSM*, attention was drawn in the media to the psy-

Years after the Vietnam War ended and their physical wounds healed, many veterans were left tormented by the emotional scars of combat.

chological aftereffects of combat experienced by Vietnam War veterans. The Vietnam War was the most publicized, but certainly not the only, war to produce psychological casualties. Reports of psychological dysfunction following exposure to combat emerged after the Civil War; following World War I and World War II, there were numerous reports of psychological impairment described with such terms as "shell shock," "traumatic neurosis," "combat stress," or "combat fatigue." Estimates of PTSD incidence among Vietnam veterans are high, ranging from 19 to 30 percent of veterans exposed to low levels of combat to as high as 25 to 70 percent for veterans exposed to high levels. These percentages translate into an estimated 500,000 to 800,000 Americans. When the effects on their families are taken into account, the impact is even greater (Oei et al., 1990).

Theories and Treatment

Questions about human responses to trauma have plagued theorists for many years. According to Freud (1921), symptoms such as those found in the disorder currently labeled PTSD represent a flooding of the ego's defenses with uncontrollable anxiety originating from the intensity of experiences such as those involved in combat. The experiences themselves may be traumatic enough to cause this reaction, or they may trigger painful memories of earlier unresolved unconscious conflicts and cause anxiety to overflow as a result of an inability to keep these memories repressed (e.g., Lidz, 1946). For example, the experience of killing another person in battle may stimulate the emergence of previously repressed aggressive impulses. Anxiety over the expression of these impulses could trigger the stress reaction.

In recent years, an empirical understanding of PTSD has been gained through studies of Vietnam veterans. In trying to understand what aspects of the combat experience caused some of these soldiers to develop psychological disorder, researchers have noted that compared to other wars, there was little reported incidence of combat fatigue or combat stress during the war itself (Bourne, 1970). The emergence of psychological symptoms became more apparent after the veterans began to return home. In explaining this phenomenon, researchers have noted that the Vietnam War was not politically popular; when the veterans returned home, they were not given a hero's welcome. Some experts speculated that this lack of social support, rather than the combat experience itself, may have contributed to the development of the disorder (Sparr & Pankratz, 1983). Nevertheless, the degree of exposure to combat and violence also contributes to the likelihood that a war veteran will develop PTSD (Foy et al., 1987). Guilt over combat actions can also add to the veteran's distress (Hendin & Hass, 1991).

Experts remain perplexed about the fact that not all people exposed to the same conditions develop PTSD. One group of researchers attempted to understand the causes of individual differences in susceptibility to PTSD by evaluating pre-combat personality, intensity of combat experiences, and post-combat experiences and social support (Green et al., 1990). A number of fascinating results emerged from this research, illustrating the complex nature of the relationship between exposure to traumatic experiences and psychological disorder. Soldiers with various psychiatric diagnoses prior to combat, such as mood disorder or alcohol and drug abuse, were found to be more likely to get into situations in which they were exposed to grotesque combat experiences such as witnessing or participating in the mutilation of Vietnamese citizens. These veterans, in turn, were less likely to seek social support by talking to friends, and suffered more negative life events after their return home. Younger and less well-educated men, perhaps because of their lower rank in the military, were also exposed to more stressful combat experiences involving daily life threat. However, over and above any of these factors, the extent to which the individual was exposed to life-threatening risks on a daily basis proved to be the major contributor to the development of PTSD.

Although some researchers have suggested that PTSD is actually rare among Vietnam veterans (Helzer et al., 1987), it is important nonetheless to take seriously the mental health needs of people who appear to suffer from PTSD (Breslau & Davis, 1989). A particular need exists for treatment of substance abuse, a disorder to which veterans with PTSD are particularly vulnerable (McFall et al., 1991). With the current information available on the Vietnam War experience, mental health professionals were better prepared to develop strategies for helping veterans of the 1991 Desert Storm action cope with their return from active duty (Hobfall et al., 1991). These strategies may also generalize to fostering recovery in victims of other traumatic events.

Other important factors in determining reactions to a trauma include socioeconomic conditions and availability of resources in the community. People living in impoverished conditions in developing countries are at high risk for developing PTSD when disasters strike because of the lack of adequate mental health services (Lima et al., 1991). Even when mental health resources are available, however, PTSD victims may be too demoralized to seek treatment, as was noted in World War II holocaust survivors (Kuch & Cox, 1992).

Research on psychological and social factors provides some clues to understanding the development of PTSD, but biological factors also play a role. In evaluating the possible contribution of biology, some researchers have proposed that PTSD is the outcome of sustained hyperactivity of parts of the nervous system involved in preparing the body for danger, including the autonomic nervous system and subcortical pathways in the brain (ver Ellen & van Kammen, 1990). If indeed a person's nervous system remains more or less permanently "turned on" in preparing for danger, this would explain the ongoing state of hypervigilance seen in PTSD.

The behavioral approach proposes a two-factor model of conditioning to account for the development of reactions to trauma (Mowrer, 1947), and this model has been applied to an understanding of PTSD (Little & James, 1964). According to the behavioral model, classical conditioning accounts for how the PTSD victim acquires a conditioned fear to the stimuli that were present at the time of the trauma. After this learned association is formed, the individual experiences anxiety when these stimuli are present even in the absence of the traumatizing experience. The second factor in this model is avoidance learning. It becomes reinforcing for the individual to escape, at least in fantasy, from the traumatic event, and this reinforcement then strengthens the withdrawal reaction seen in PTSD victims.

More recently (Foa et al., 1989), cognitive-behavioral explanations of PTSD have incorporated the concept of how people's beliefs about a traumatic event influence how they cope with it. Beliefs that are likely to have a detrimental effect, and can ultimately lead to PTSD, include an attitude of excessive self-blame for events that are beyond any personal control, and guilt over the outcome of these events. Unsuccessful and damaging attempts by the individual to reduce the stress experienced in the aftermath of the event can also increase the risk for PTSD. Some of these problematic coping methods include prolonged avoidance of problems, blaming and lashing out at other people, adopting a cynical and pessimistic view of life, catastrophising or exaggerating the extent of current difficulties, isolating oneself socially, and abusing drugs and alcohol (Hobfall et al., 1991). In Chapter 17, we will look more closely at the role of coping in managing stress in daily life. In the case of PTSD, as in other dysfunctional reactions to stress, not only do inadequate coping strategies fail to reduce the stress of the traumatic life event, but they can actually result in an increase in the experience of stress (Lazarus, 1991).

Traditionally, the most effective treatments for PTSD involve a combination of "covering" and "uncovering" techniques. "Covering" techniques such as supportive ther-

Table 7–4

Table 7–4	ANXIETY DISORDERS: A SUMMARY CHART OF PERSPECTIVES	
DISORDER	COGNITIVE-BEHAVIORAL	BIOLOGICAL
Panic Disorder	A "fear of fear" leads people with agoraphobia to become afraid of developing a panic attack when symptoms are first evident. **Treatment:** Exposure to threatening situations while being cued to relax.	Excess blood lactate or level of norepi-norepinephrine leads to hyperarousal. **Treatment:** Medication.
Specific Phobia	Fears of specific objects or situations are due to individual's unrealistic thoughts about the object or situation. **Treatment:** Exposure to phobic objects or situations while being cued to relax or stop anxious thoughts; cognitive restructuring to encourage more rational thoughts and increase feelings of self-efficacy.	Biological preparedness to fear certain objects of situations is an adaptive evolutionary mechanism. **Treatment:** Medication.
Social Phobia	Fear of performing in front of others is due to exaggerated fear of criticism and embarrassment. **Treatment:** Exposure therapy, cognitive restructuring, and social skills training.	No specific explanation. **Treatment:** Medication.
Generalized Anxiety Disorder	Establishment of a worry cycle in which small anxieties and concerns become magnified. **Treatment:** Increasing confidence in the ability to control worrying with the goal of breaking the worry cycle.	Excess activity of GABA receptors. **Treatment:** Medication.
Obsessive-Compulsive Disorder	Obsessions and compulsions established through association with relief of anxiety. **Treatment:** Exposure and response prevention.	Excess activity of serotonin in the brain and overarousal of motor control centers in the brain. **Treatment:** Medication, and in extreme cases, psychosurgery.
Post-Traumatic Stress Disorder	Two-factor conditioning model; maladaptive ways of attempting to manage stress. **Treatment:** Coping methods to teach effective ways to reduce stress; flooding and desensitization.	Hyperarousal of subcortical brain structures involved in emotional reactivity. **Treatment:** Medication.

For the past 15 years, Steve has suffered from flashbacks in which he relives the horrors of his 9 months of active duty in Vietnam. These flashbacks occur unexpectedly in the middle of the day, and Steve is thrown back into the emotional reality of his war experiences. These flashbacks, and the nightmares he often suffers from, have become a constant source of torment. Steve has found that alcohol provides the only escape from these visions and from the distress he feels over his situation. Often, Steve ruminates about how he should have done more to prevent the deaths of his fellow soldiers, and feels that his friends, rather than he, should have survived.

- If Steve could be convinced that he did all he could to help his friends, how might this affect him?
- To what extent do you think Steve's flashbacks and nightmares are due to the emotional effects of stress rather than his alcohol use?

apy and stress management help the client seal over the pain of the trauma. They may also help the client reduce stress more effectively and in the process eliminate some of the secondary problems caused by the client's symptoms. For example, PTSD victims who isolate themselves from friends and family are cutting themselves off from social support, which is an important therapeutic agent. By learning alternate coping methods, clients can become better able to seek out this kind of support.

PTSD victims can also be taught to reduce stress by approaching their situations more rationally and by breaking their problems down into manageable units. A better balance between self-blame and avoidance can also be achieved. Individuals who feel excessively guilty for their role in the traumatic incident can learn to see that their responsibility was not so great as imagined. Conversely, those who feel that they have no control over what happens to them and avoid confronting problems can be helped to feel a greater sense of control and mastery over the course of their lives (Hobfall et al., 1991).

"Uncovering" techniques, which involve a reliving of the trauma, include the behavioral treatments of imaginal flooding and desensitization. As in the reduction of other forms of anxiety disorder, exposure of the PTSD victim to cues that bring back memories of the event in a graded fashion or in a situation in which the individual is taught simultaneously to relax can eventually lead to a breaking of the conditioned anxiety reaction. Other treatments such as psychodrama can also be useful in bringing to conscious awareness, under a controlled setting, repressed memories of the traumatic event.

The effectiveness of therapeutic techniques may vary according to the phase of the client's symptoms. Covering techniques are most helpful for clients who are suffering from intrusive images and memories of the trauma. During states of denial or numbness, uncovering techniques can be therapeutic (Fairbank & Nicholson, 1987), but they must be used with caution because they can provoke a worsening of the client's symptoms (Pitman et al., 1991). Medications can be used as an adjunct to help alleviate symptoms of anxiety, depression, and intrusive thoughts or nightmares (Friedman, 1988; Roth, 1988).

ANXIETY DISORDERS: THE PERSPECTIVES REVISITED

As you can see, anxiety disorders cover a broad spectrum of problems ranging from very specific, seemingly idiosyncratic responses to diffuse and undifferentiated feelings of dread. These disorders involve an intriguing intertwining of biological and psychological phenomena. Fortunately, relatively straightforward behavioral treatments are available that can successfully alleviate the symptoms of anxiety for many people who suffer from these disorders. The effectiveness of behavioral techniques can be enhanced with a number of other strategies that involve cognitive, insight-oriented, and psychopharmacological interventions. Knowledge gained from research on the causes and treatment of anxiety disorders can also have some practical benefits for the management of lesser difficulties. For example, if you encounter anxious discomfort when walking into an unfamiliar situation, you may want to try some of the cognitive-behavioral strategies we have discussed to help you gain confidence in your ability to control and manage your fears. Contemporary approaches to anxiety disorders are dominated by the behavioral and biological perspectives. Although traditionally, psychodynamic approaches were thought to provide an understanding of these disorders and a basis for treatment, these approaches are gradually being replaced as more empirical evidence is available on therapeutic effectiveness.

SUMMARY

1. Anxiety disorders are characterized by the experience of physiological arousal, apprehension or feelings of dread, hypervigilance, avoidance, and occasionally a specific fear or phobia. Anxiety is a common feature of human experience, so common that medications for treating anxiety are the most commonly prescribed drugs in the United States.

2. Panic disorder is characterized by frequent and recurrent panic attacks—intense sensations of fear and physical discomfort. This disorder, which afflicts an estimated 3 percent of the population, is often found in association with agoraphobia, the fear of being trapped or unable to escape if a panic attack occurs. Panic disorder is a very disabling condition, interfering significantly with the individual's ability to lead a productive and satisfying life. Cognitive-

behavioral understandings of panic disorder explain it as an acquired "fear of fear" in which the individual becomes hypersensitive to early signs of a panic attack, and fear of a full-blown attack leads the individual to become unduly apprehensive and avoidant of another attack. Treatment based on the cognitive-behavioral perspective involves methods such as relaxation training and *in vivo* or imaginal flooding as ways of breaking the negative cycle initiated by the individual's fear of having a panic attack. Biological explanations of panic disorder regard it as due to excess amounts of lactate or norepinephrine, substances that have been found to exist in higher levels in people with this disorder. An excess activity of GABA receptors is another possible cause of panic disorder. Benzodiazepines, antianxiety medications, can reduce the symptoms of panic disorder, but they can also be habit-forming. Clonidine is another medication that has been successfully used in the treatment of panic disorder, and does not have addictive qualities.

3. Specific phobias are fears of particular objects or situations. Although many people have phobic symptoms, the disorder is diagnosed among only 5 to 10 percent of the adult population. Examples of specific phobias include fear of airplanes, darkness, thunder, animals, blood and injury, heights, and enclosed spaces. Previous learning experiences and a cycle of negative, maladaptive thoughts are regarded by cognitive-behaviorists as the cause of specific phobias. Treatment based on the biological perspective involves medications. Treatments recommended by the cognitive-behavioral approach include flooding, systematic desensitization, imagery, *in vivo* exposure, and participant modeling, as well as procedures aimed at changing the individual's maladaptive thoughts, such as cognitive restructuring, coping self-statements, thought stopping, and increasing the sense of self-efficacy.

4. A social phobia is a fear of being observed by others acting in a way that will be humiliating or embarrassing. Social phobia can be a very disabling condition, often associated with drug or alcohol abuse. People with social phobias may not only fear performance in front of large audiences, but also may be fearful of performing even seemingly mundane activities in front of others such as eating or writing their name. Cognitive-behavioral approaches to social phobia regard the disorder as due to an unrealistic fear of criticism, a fear that causes people with the disorder to lose the ability to concentrate on their performance and instead to shift attention to how anxious they feel, which then causes them to make mistakes and therefore to become more fearful. Behavioral methods that provide *in vivo* exposure along with cognitive restructuring and social skills training seem to be the most effective in helping people with social phobias. Medication is the treatment recommended within the biological perspective for severe cases of this disorder.

5. People who are diagnosed as having generalized anxiety disorder have a number of worries that spread to various spheres of life, rather than having one specific fear or concern. They tend to worry about these matters on a frequent basis, and their worries are unrealistic. Estimates of the prevalence of this disorder in the adult population range from 2 to 8 percent. The cognitive-behavioral approach to generalized anxiety disorder emphasizes the unrealistic nature of these worries, and regards the disorder as a vicious cycle that feeds on itself as people with this disorder become worried not only about various life problems, but also about the fact that they worry. The theory emphasizes that these individuals' lack of confidence in their ability to control their worries is a major factor contributing to the disorder. Cognitive-behavioral treatment approaches recommend breaking the negative cycle of worrying by teaching the individual techniques that allow the individual to gain a sense that it is possible to control the worrying. Biological treatment emphasizes medications.

6. In obsessive-compulsive disorder, individuals develop obsessions, or thoughts they cannot rid themselves of, and compulsions, which are irresistible, repetitive behaviors. These thoughts and behaviors, which are usually inconsistent with the individual's personality and lifestyle cause the individual great unhappiness. A common obsession is the thought that one must avoid contact with all germs, and a related compulsion is hand-washing or other cleansing behaviors. These thoughts and behaviors are unrealistic, and they often take a ritualistic form. The hand-washing, for example, must be performed every 10 minutes and in a certain invariant pattern. The disorder affects approximately 2 to 3 percent of the adult U.S. population, with one-half to one-third of all cases originating during childhood or adolescence. A cognitive-behavioral understanding of obsessive-compulsive disorder regards the symptoms as the product of a learned association between anxiety and the thoughts or acts, which temporarily can produce relief from anxiety. A growing body of evidence supports a biological explanation of the disorder, with the most current research suggesting that it is associated with an excess of serotonin. Treatment with the drug clomipramine seems to have the greatest effectiveness, although cognitive-behavioral methods involving exposure and thought stopping may help to reduce the symptoms of the disorder.

7. In post-traumatic stress disorder, the individual is unable to recover from the anxiety associated with a traumatic life event, such as tragedy or disaster, an accident, or participation in combat. The aftereffects of the traumatic event include flashbacks, nightmares, and intrusive thoughts that alternate with attempts by the individual to deny that the event ever took place.

Research on Vietnam War veterans has shown a direct connection between severity of combat experience and the existence of PTSD symptoms, although it also appears that certain individuals are more vulnerable to being exposed to more severe experiences. For example, soldiers in Vietnam who had a diagnosed psychiatric disorder were more likely to become involved in atrocities, and these war experiences contributed to the development of PTSD when these soldiers returned home. Biological explanations of PTSD propose that victims of the disorder suffer from a permanent change in the nervous system following their exposure to life-threatening circumstances. The behavioral model proposes that conditioning and avoidance learning play roles in the acquisition and maintenance of PTSD. Cognitive-behavioral approaches regard the disorder as the result of negative and maladaptive thoughts about one's role in causing the traumatic events to happen, feelings of ineffectiveness and isolation from others, and a pessimistic outlook on life as a result of the experience. Cognitive-behavioral approaches attempt to teach PTSD victims new coping skills so that they can more effectively manage stress and reestablish social ties with others who can provide ongoing support. Effective treatments of people with PTSD have included a combination of "covering" techniques, such as supportive therapy and stress management and "uncovering" techniques such as imaginal flooding and desensitization.

KEY TERMS

Anxiety disorders: a group of disorders characterized by intense, irrational, and incapacitating fear and apprehension. p. 171

Hypervigilant: overly sensitive to sounds and sights in the environment. p. 172

Panic attack: a period of intense fear and physical discomfort accompanied by the feeling that one is being overwhelmed and is about to lose control. p. 172

Panic disorder: an anxiety disorder that is diagnosed when an individual has panic attacks on a recurrent basis or has constant apprehension and worry about the possibility of recurring attacks. p. 172

Agoraphobia: the fear of being trapped or stranded without help. p. 173

Lactate: a chemical in the blood whose level increases after physical exertion that is found to be higher in people with panic disorder. p. 174

Lactate theory: a theory of panic disorder proposing that the intense anxiety experienced during a panic attack results from an increase of lactate in the blood. p. 174

Conditioned fear reactions: acquired associations between an internal or external cue and feelings of intense anxiety. p. 174

Benzodiazepines: medications containing a chemical that can be instrumental in slowing down central nervous system reactions thought to contribute to anxiety. p. 174

Relaxation training: a behavioral technique used in the treatment of anxiety disorders that involves progressive and systematic patterns of muscle tensing and relaxing. p. 175

Aversions: responses of discomfort or dislike to a particular object or situation. p. 175

Specific (sometimes called simple) phobia: an anxiety disorder involving irrational and unabating fear of a particular object, activity, or situation. p. 175

Claustrophobia: fear of closed spaces. p. 176

Flooding: a behavioral technique in which the client is immersed in the sensation of anxiety by being exposed to the feared situation in its entirety. p. 179

Imaginal flooding: a behavioral technique in which the client is immersed through imagination in the feared situation. p. 179

In vivo method: a behavioral technique that involves placing the client in the actual situation in which the client experiences fear. p. 180

Thought stopping: a cognitive-behavioral method in which the client is taught to stop having anxiety provoking thoughts. p. 180

Social phobia: an anxiety disorder characterized by irrational and unabating fear that one's behavior will be scrutinized by others, causing the individual to feel embarrassed and humiliated. p. 180

Generalized anxiety disorder: an anxiety disorder characterized by anxiety that is not associated with a particular object, situation, or event but seems to be a constant feature of a person's day-to-day existence. p. 181

Obsessive-compulsive disorder: an anxiety disorder characterized by the experience of intrusive thoughts that the individual can alleviate only by engaging in patterns of rigid, ritualistic behavior. p. 183

Traumatic experience: a disastrous or extremely painful event that has severe psychological and physiological effects. p. 186

Post-traumatic stress disorder (PTSD): an anxiety disorder in which the individual experiences several distressing symptoms following a traumatic event such as reexperiencing the traumatic event, avoidance of reminders of the trauma, a numbing of general responsiveness, and increased arousal. p. 186

Outcry phase: the first reaction to a traumatic event in which the individual reacts with alarm accompanied by a strong emotion. p. 187

Denial/intrusion phase: reactions to a traumatic event involving alterations between denial, or a distancing of oneself from the event, and intrusion, being tormented by disruptive thoughts and feelings about the event. p. 187

Flashbacks: graphic and terrifying illusions and hallucinations associated with a traumatic event (as well as LSD use) which arise spontaneously. p. 187

Return to the Case

Barbara Wilder

Barbara's History

As Barbara shared her life history with me, the flow of her speech frequently was interrupted by sobs and pleas that I be patient with her. As Barbara's story unfolded, I came to understand how the emotional scars left by growing up in a dysfunctional family plagued her throughout childhood and adolescence.

Barbara was raised almost exclusively by her mother. Her father spent very little time at home, because he worked as a sales representative for a company that had branch offices spread across a three-state area. When he was home, he was almost always inebriated. Barbara's mother was very protective of her, restricting almost all social and after-school activities. Barbara remembers feeling somewhat resentful of her mother's strong control over her, but sees her mother's behavior as justified because "After all, she couldn't count on my father to help her, and besides, I was a pretty difficult kid and she didn't want me getting into trouble."

Barbara's father was known to have out-of-town affairs with women, and he was regarded by everyone as a failure in his job. However, these problems were never discussed openly. Barbara remembers being frightened of her father because when he was drinking he would get furious over even her slightest failure to respond instantly to his instructions. Usually, these instructions were unclear or contradictory, so she could not predict when he would yell at her and when he would be satisfied with her response. When she tried to apologize, he criticized her even more. Barbara learned that the best way to deal with him was to stay out of his way.

Barbara explained to me that it was not only her father who struggled with psychological impairment. Her mother had suffered for most of her adult years with an intense fear of leaving the house alone, and she was afflicted by deep depression related to her unhappy marriage. Going back a generation, Barbara's grandmother was considered by most people as peculiar because of her insistence on living the life of a recluse and acting in ways toward her husband that others considered domineering, bordering on sadistic. Barbara's maternal grandfather put up with the abuse, never complaining, always appearing to others as a quiet accommodating "gentleman." It was quite a shock to the whole community when at the age of 62 he asphyxiated himself and left a note filled with rage about his "miserable marriage."

In her senior year of high school, Barbara began to write away to a number of colleges for applications. It never occurred to her that her parents would object to her going to college, as long as she could support herself with a scholarship. Since Barbara's grades were excellent, she felt quite certain that she would earn some kind of financial aid. One day, her mother stopped Barbara as she was leaving the house, loaded with a stack of envelopes ready to mail. Barbara's mother asked her what she was doing, and when Barbara explained, her mother burst into tears. She told Barbara that it was time for them to have a talk. They sat down in the kitchen, and Barbara's mother poured forth what for Barbara was an amazing confession. Ever since Barbara was a child, it had been very important for her mother to have Barbara with her at home. That was why she found it so hard to let Barbara go out with her friends and do things after school. She said that Barbara's father had been so impossible that she was unhappy almost all the time. She couldn't even leave the house to run a simple errand unless she had Barbara with her. She begged Barbara not to go away to school, saying that she could not bear the thought of her leaving. Barbara was stunned. She did not realize how much she meant to her mother. There was no way she could even consider going away to school under these circumstances. Barbara threw away all her letters, and applied to the community college located 10 miles away from home.

After college Barbara took a job in an insurance company, where she became a top-notch typist and receptionist. When her boss was transferred to another city, he told Barbara that he wanted her to move also. She could enroll in the university and take courses there to complete her bachelor's degree, all at company expense. According to her boss, Barbara had a lot of potential to advance in a career if she had the proper training. Concerned about leaving her mother, Barbara asked her what she should do. Barbara's mother assured her that she would "manage somehow." Barbara made the move, and all seemed to be going well. She felt particularly lucky to have found a roommate with whom she shared many common interests, ideas, and feelings. They soon became inseparable. Sadly, things would not remain so serene for Barbara; the ghosts of unresolved conflicts and pain were to reappear and take the form of her current emotional crisis.

Barbara Wilder continued

Assessment

Although I had some reasonable hypotheses about the nature of Barbara's disorder, there were important gaps that needed to be filled in. Of particular concern was the possibility that Barbara might be suffering from a medical problem. It is not uncommon for people with certain neurological and cardiovascular diseases to experience the kind of psychological disturbance that afflicted Barbara. Yet, the physician who conducted the physical examination could find no physiological basis for what was going on with her. Could drugs or alcohol have been the cause? No. Barbara had never abused drugs, and she only occasionally drank alcohol in desperate attempts to calm herself down.

One of my colleagues gave Barbara a battery of psychological tests. By the time Barbara had been tested—one week after her first session with me—she had calmed down a bit. The psychologist described her as a "well-dressed and attractive young woman who looked self-conscious and nervous throughout the interview." There was nothing to suggest intellectual impairment or a personality disorder, but what was particularly noteworthy in the testing emerged from the projective techniques— themes of dependency, passive acquiescence to other people's demands, and discomfort in situations involving interpersonal conflict.

Diagnosis

The most striking feature of Barbara's presenting problems was the occurrence of what appeared to be panic attacks. After experiencing several of these on a frequent basis, Barbara could not leave her apartment because of her fears of having an attack in public.

I first considered Barbara's health history to determine whether her symptoms might be attributable to a physical disorder such as coronary artery disease, hypoglycemia, adrenal tumor, hyperthyroidism, withdrawal from substances such as barbiturates, or psychoactive substance-induced intoxication from caffeine or amphetamines. After ruling out these alternative conditions on the basis of the medical work-up, I felt confident in concluding that Barbara was suffering from an anxiety disorder involving panic attacks and agoraphobia. I focused my attention on Barbara's symptoms during the episodes that she described to me, which included experiences of dizziness, speeded-up heart rate, uncontrollable trembling, sweating, choking sensations, chest discomfort, and fear of dying. I was secure in the belief that these episodes constituted panic attacks, in that they involved sudden, unexpected periods of intense fear. Compounding the distress for Barbara was the fact that these panic attacks were accompanied by symptoms of agoraphobia.

Axis I. Panic Disorder with Agoraphobia

Axis II. Rule out Personality Disorder. Not Otherwise Specified.

Axis III. No physical disorders or conditions

Axis IV. Severity: 2. Acute events include recent move to a new job and city, away from parents. Enduring events include family tension and excessive demands from mother.

Axis V. Current Global Assessment of Functioning: 37. Highest Global Assessment of Functioning (past year): 83.

Case Formulation

What factors might have contributed to Barbara's developing such a troubling and incapacitating disorder? As I pondered this question I considered her genetic history as well as Barbara's family system. In evaluating genetic contributions my thoughts were drawn to the problems experienced by both her mother and her grandmother. Their problems had a ring of similarity to Barbara's, leading me to hypothesize that Barbara had inherited a biological propensity to develop panic attacks.

In reviewing information about Barbara's family, I thought of her stories of being so distraught about her father's frequent absences, and her resentment about her overcontrolling mother who could not protect her from the tyrannical ways of her unreliable and unpredictable father. Conflicts were not aired, and Barbara learned that the best way to get along with people was to do what they wanted or to stay out of their way. At a time when Barbara should have been allowed to begin her independent life, her mother made it virtually impossible for her to leave. When Barbara finally did leave her mother, she must have experienced considerable guilt, knowing how much her mother depended on her.

As her life went on, Barbara came to realize more and more that she could not please everyone. Perhaps her first panic attack grew out of this unresolvable conflict. Indeed, all of Barbara's early panic attacks were connected with some kind of emotional conflict in her life. The second attack occurred when Barbara was about to experience separation from the room-

Barbara Wilder continued

mate to whom she had become so attached. Other panic attacks occurred when Barbara was going to her office, a place that symbolized her abandonment of her mother. Although the panic attacks started in particular situations that had some link to an emotional conflict, they eventually generalized to all places outside Barbara's apartment. Barbara came to fear not the situations themselves, but the attacks, which caused her to experience an excruciating degree of pain, embarrassment, and terror.

Planning a Treatment

As I sat down to write up my treatment recommendations for Barbara, I thought immediately of my colleague, Dr. Herter, who in recent years has specialized in the treatment of people with anxiety disorders. By using a number of behavioral and cognitive-behavioral treatment techniques, Dr. Herter has treated many people with impressive results. I called Dr. Herter and explained the nature of Barbara's problem to her. As we spoke about this case, Dr. Herter put forth a treatment approach not commonly used by most other colleagues. She thought it would be a good idea for her to begin the therapy in Barbara's home, a nonthreatening context in which she could begin establishing a trusting alliance with Barbara. In time, Dr. Herter would introduce in vivo techniques and graded exposure training in which Barbara would be guided step-by-step through situations that more closely approximated those that had terrified her in the past. At the same time, Dr. Herter planned to work with her in restructuring her beliefs about her inability to control her panic attacks. Dr. Herter told me that as time went on, she might also incorporate assertiveness training.

Outcome of the Case

I had concurred with Dr. Herter's initial optimism about the likelihood that Barbara would show fairly quick improvement once treatment was begun. Barbara responded very positively to Dr. Herter's willingness to provide home-based therapy. During the first 3 weeks, which included 6 sessions, Dr. Herter took a comprehensive history of the problem and developed a relationship with Barbara that facilitated the initiation of behavioral techniques during the second phase. In the beginning of the second phase, Dr. Herter taught Barbara techniques that could be used to change the way she thought about panic-arousing situations. Bar-

bara was instructed to imagine herself conquering her fear and feeling a sense of increased self-esteem following her success. She became able to envision herself as competent in situations that previously had seemed so threatening. In the third phase, Dr. Herter accompanied Barbara outside her apartment to a nearby convenience store. Step-by-step, in the weeks that followed, Dr. Herter introduced situations that were increasingly more threatening, culminating in Barbara's successful trip to a crowded shopping mall unaccompanied by her therapist.

Along with conquering her fears of leaving home, Barbara also began to gain some insight into the connection between interpersonal conflicts and her panic attacks. Several weeks into treatment, Barbara reported that her mother was starting to telephone her more and more frequently. Barbara's mother had started to develop terrible headaches which made her incapable of doing anything for hours at a time. Although she did not ask directly, Barbara felt very strongly that her mother was hinting for Barbara to move back home. Barbara missed a session, something that was very unusual for her. Dr. Herter became concerned that Barbara was experiencing a relapse. A call to Barbara's apartment confirmed this. Barbara had experienced another panic attack during the week, and was unable to leave her apartment. The cognitive techniques she had practiced so faithfully had failed to work. Barbara had wanted to call Dr. Herter but felt too ashamed. After discussing this situation, Barbara was able to understand how this particular panic attack had been provoked by interpersonal conflict; this insight proved useful in motivating Barbara to resume and follow through with her treatment program.

In time Barbara's mother began making fewer demands on her, and Barbara was able to recover the gains she had made in individual therapy prior to the panic attack. Barbara and Dr. Herter continued to meet for another 6 months, during which time Barbara's progress was cemented. Soon after Barbara terminated with Dr. Herter she dropped me a note to thank me for the referral. In the note, she boasted about her success in overcoming the problem that had been so threatening and devastating for her. She explained how she had developed new ways of solving her problems, whether the problems pertained to possible panic attacks or to the difficulties she was likely to encounter in her relationship with her mother.

Case Report: Rose Marston

It was late on a Friday afternoon that I received a call from Dr. Thompson, one of the hospital's emergency room physicians, asking me to conduct an evaluation of Rose Marston, a 37-year-old woman who had become a frequent visitor to the emergency room with an array of physical problems. The story Dr. Thompson told me about Rose was similar to the histories he had presented to me on previous occasions about other problematic patients. I found myself completing some of his sentences as he described the frustrations felt by the emergency room staff in their dealings with Rose. Dr. Thompson had become convinced that Rose's recurrent "physical problems" were attributable to psychological rather than physical factors.

During the preceding year Rose had come to the emergency room on 15 occasions and each time complained about what seemed like serious medical problems. Extensive medical testing had been conducted and specialists had been consulted, but no diagnosable medical conditions had ever been confirmed. Her medical chart included complaints about gastrointestinal problems such as vomiting, nausea, and bloating; complaints of pain in her chest, back, joints, and hands; neurological symptoms including double vision and dizziness; and problems of irregular menstruation. On occasion she had fainted, and several times she could not get her legs to move, and was unable to walk.

Dr. Thompson shared with me his own distress about his most recent emergency room contact with Rose. Following one of Rose's customary enumerations of physical complaints, Dr. Thompson told Rose that he had come to believe that her problems were emotionally based, rather than medical in origin. Moments later Rose collapsed on the floor in the throes of what appeared to be an epileptic seizure. Upon resuming consciousness, Rose stated that she remembered nothing of what had just happened and, indeed, could not even recall how she got to the emergency room. When Dr. Thompson reviewed the situation with Rose, she became enraged and, with a voice that echoed through the corridors, yelled out, "I know that you wish I would go away. Maybe you'd be relieved if I'd just kill myself!" After calming down, Rose reluctantly agreed to take Dr. Thompson's recommendation to consult with me about her problems.

Rose approached our initial meeting with considerable skepticism. Her first words were, "I guess they've tried to convince you that I'm some kind of hypochondriac crackpot." I tried to assure Rose that my efforts to understand her would in great part be determined by what she had to tell me about her problems. Although I would ask for her permission to speak to the medical staff, I wanted her to know that I was committed to helping her find a way to feel better, both psychologically and physically. I tried tactfully to point out that people often develop physical problems when they are upset about something. Or, perhaps real physical problems become aggravated during times of stress. I could tell that she was cautious about speaking with me, but nevertheless she seemed willing to give it a try.

In our first session Rose told me the story of her many physical problems dating back to childhood. Although she was relatively healthy as a young girl, her parents often commented that when she did come down with a cold or flu, she would get "much sicker than other people." In fact, Rose's mother frequently had to stay home from work to nurse Rose back to health for conditions such as allergies. As Rose entered her teen years, her physical problems became a great source of distress. On numerous occasions she sought help from medical specialists, but routinely left these consultations feeling frustrated and misunderstood when physicians told her that they could not find the source of Rose's problems. Rose ultimately came to believe that she had unusual medical problems that physicians were unable to understand or treat.

Sarah Tobin, PhD

8

SOMATOFORM AND DISSOCIATIVE DISORDERS

In this chapter, we will discuss two sets of disorders, *somatoform disorders* and *dissociative disorders*, which involve the expression of conflict through radical, and sometimes bizarre, disturbances in behavior. These disorders have an important role in the history of abnormal psychology because they alerted the medical community of the 1800s to the role that psychological processes can play in causing otherwise unexplained symptoms. Recall our discussion in Chapter 1 about hysteria and how medical experts with training in neurology were confused and astounded by case after case of patients with mysterious "physical" symptoms that seemed to have no physical basis. Freud's insight that these physical symptoms could have a psychological basis led to a revolution in the understanding and treatment of many unusual disorders. Although somatoform and dissociative disorders are relatively uncommon in today's society, these disorders have not disappeared, and they remain one of the more fascinating areas of abnormal behavior.

After reading this chapter, you should be able to:

- ■ Define and identify the central characteristics of somatoform disorders, including conversion disorder, somatization disorder, body dysmorphic disorder, and hypochondriasis.
- ■ Distinguish among somatoform disorders, malingering, and factitious disorders.
- ■ Understand current theories regarding somatoform disorders and be able to compare the roles of learning, conflict, and stress in their development.
- ■ Contrast somatoform and dissociative disorders as alternative ways of reacting to psychological conflict.

- Define the central features of multiple personality disorder, understand the history of this diagnosis, and become familiar with current theories about the origins of this disorder.

- Recognize the main features of other dissociative disorders, including psychogenic amnesia, psychogenic fugue, and depersonalization disorder.

- Identify some of the factors that can contribute to an individual's development of a dissociative disorder and understand the methods of treatment most commonly used for these disorders.

SOMATOFORM DISORDERS

Imagine the following scenario. A classmate of yours, a star quarterback, wakes up one morning complaining that he is unable to move his hand. He then says in an oddly indifferent manner that the situation is very unfortunate because the game that he is scheduled to play that day would be a very important one for the team. He dismisses the problem as "bad luck." You may be perplexed at his lack of alarm but would nevertheless presume that there was something physically wrong with his hand. But might there be more to the story? Perhaps you are wondering whether your classmate's problem is "all in his head." Maybe he is very concerned about his performance in the game and is "faking" his injury. Or on a deeper level, perhaps his anxiety is so great that he does not consciously make the connection between his inability to move his hand and his worry about playing in the game.

Characteristics of Somatoform Disorders

Somatoform disorders include a variety of conditions in which psychological conflicts become translated into physical problems or complaints. The term *somatoform* comes from the Greek word *soma* meaning body. However, somatoform disorders are considered psychological rather than physical disorders because there is no physical abnormality that can explain the individual's bodily complaint. If your classmate's condition is due to a somatoform disorder, his dysfunctional hand will not produce abnormal responses on neurophysiological testing. In fact, the pain or stiffness he feels would probably not correspond to the symptoms of any known physical disorder.

■ *Conversion disorder*

As the example of the football player illustrates, psychological conflict may be converted into physical problems in some very dramatic ways. **Conversion disorder** involves this translation of unacceptable drives or troubling conflicts into physical symptoms. The essential feature of this disorder is an involuntary loss or alteration of a bodily function due to psychological conflict or need. The person is not intentionally producing the symptoms (as in facti-

tious disorder and malingering); however, a medical basis for the symptoms cannot be found, and it is assumed that the person is "converting" the psychological conflict or need into a physical problem.

In the mid-1800s, a French physician named Paul Briquet systematically described and categorized the symptoms of hysteria based on his review of more than 400 patients. In the latter part of the nineteenth century, the French neurologist Jean Martin Charcot used hypnosis to show that psychological factors play a role in the physical symptoms of hysteria. Under hypnosis, hysterical symptoms could be produced or removed at the suggestion of the hypnotist. A student of Charcot's, Pierre Janet, theorized that this difference between normal and hysterical people was due to the presence, in hysterics, of dissociated contents of the mind. These parts of the mind had become dissociated because of hereditary degeneration of the brain. The ideas and functions within the dissociated part of the mind took autonomous hold over the individual and created symptoms that appeared beyond the person's voluntary control. Hippolyte Marie Bernheim, another French neurologist, maintained that hypnotizability could be demonstrated in both normal and hysterical people.

The work of Janet and Bernheim attracted attention all over Europe, and Freud became fascinated with their ideas. Through contact with Janet and Bernheim, Freud eventually developed a radically different theory of hysteria in his work with Breuer in the 1890s. Freud called conversion disorder **hysterical neurosis**, implying that it is a form of reaction to anxiety ("neurosis") that involves a physical reaction.

The mechanism through which the symptoms of conversion disorder arise is still as much in dispute as it was in Freud's day. What is fascinating about conversion symptoms is the way in which they shed light on the relationship between psychological processes and the workings of the body. It is known that many physical disorders can be produced or aggravated by emotional problems that place undue demands on a part of the body or a particular organ system. Similarly, conversion symptoms are also the physical expression of a psychological disturbance, but the translation from "mind" to "body" occurs in a way that defies medical logic.

An intriguing feature of a conversion symptom is that once the symptom is moved from the realm of the psychological to the realm of the physical, it no longer poses a threat to the individual's peace of mind. The individual usually pays little attention to the symptom and dismisses it as minor, even though it may be incapacitating. This phenomenon is called **la belle indifference**, or the "beautiful" lack of concern, to indicate that the individual is not distressed by what might otherwise be construed as very inconveniencing physical problems. Once thought to be a criterion for diagnosing conversion disorder, la belle indifference is now regarded as an interesting but not defining aspect, seen in about one-third to one-half of clients with this disorder (Ford & Folks, 1985).

Anna O. (Bertha Pappenheim), who was one of psychotherapy's first "success stories," went on to become one of the founders of the modern social work movement. © The Granger Collection, New York.

Conversion symptoms fall into four categories, each involving mystifying and very different kinds of disturbances. **Motor disturbances** range from abnormal bodily movements, such as tremors, to paralysis. **Sensory disturbances** involve distortions of sensation as in the case of hearing loss, tunnel vision, or disturbances of skin sensation. **Symptoms simulating physical illness** involve conversions that mimic the actual symptoms of a physical disorder and make diagnosis very difficult. Lastly, **symptoms complicating physical illness** are those that complicate or delay physical recovery from a diagnosed physical disorder.

The most widely cited example of a conversion disorder was a young woman named "Anna O.," a central case in *Studies on Hysteria*, written by Freud and Breuer in 1893–1895. Shortly after the death of her father from a respiratory ailment, Anna developed a variety of physical abnormalities, including loss of appetite, severe cough, sleepiness during the day and insomnia at night, headaches, stiffness of the neck, muscular rigidity, and eye squints. Her body became paralyzed in ways that did not correspond to physiological causes. She suffered from visual hallucinations and temporary loss of consciousness. None of Anna's symptoms could be accounted for by physical diseases, and they disappeared when Anna was eventually able to talk with Breuer about her emotional conflicts .

Further understanding of conversion disorder came about as the result of observations made on the thousands of soldiers who developed combat stress ("shell shock," as it was called) during World War I. Combat stress, which occurs when a soldier can no longer face battle because of the emotional turmoil caused by participating in a war, can lead to a variety of physical complaints including heart problems, dizziness, or breathing difficulty. Unlike the conversion symptoms of Anna O., which Freud assumed to have an unconscious origin, the symptoms of combat stress appeared to result from external circumstances. More recently, one fascinating report was published that documented the loss of visual acuity as a conversion symptom in Cambodian refugees following years of imprisonment in communist labor camps (Rozée & Boemel, 1989).

A common circumstance involving conversion symptoms occurs when people have a real physical illness but respond in very dramatized ways. For example, during a physical examination, a very nervous and tense patient may faint, not because of physical weakness, but because of the anxiety associated with the situation. In another situation, a patient feels as though the physician is paying insufficient attention to the patient's problems; unconsciously, the patient's symptoms may worsen out of a hidden hope that the physician will become alarmed and attend more seriously to the patient's needs.

As you can imagine, it is very difficult for a mental health professional to diagnose conversion disorder. One danger in helping a person who shows conversion-like symptoms is that a real physical problem will be wrongly attributed to psychological causes. Obviously, if a serious physical disease exists, the client may not receive prompt medical attention. Indeed, as many as one-half of those who are diagnosed as having conversion disorders turn out years later to have had some physical illness not apparent when they were first seen for treatment (Ford & Folks, 1985).

■ *Somatization disorder*

Like conversion disorder, **somatization disorder** involves the expression of psychological issues through bodily problems that have no basis in a physiological dysfunction. The difference between somatization disorder and conversion disorder is that somatization disorder involves multiple and recurrent bodily symptoms rather than a single physical complaint. The individual seeks help from physicians, often several different ones simultaneously over the course of years, with seemingly exaggerated physical complaints. These symptoms can range throughout all parts of the body, and can sometimes be very dramatic. Examples of the kinds of symptoms found in people with somatization disorder include pain in the hands and feet, back pain, seizures, blurred vision, loss of voice, paralysis, amnesia, shortness of breath, difficulty swallowing, vomiting, chest pain, bloating, diarrhea, pain during sexual intercourse, and painful or irregular menstruation.

Somatization disorder was originally called Briquet's Syndrome, after the French physician who first described it in 1859. Briquet was intrigued by his observation that psychologically based physical symptoms could feel as real to the individual suffering from them as would the symptoms of a physical illness. The term *somatization* was proposed by Stekel (1943) to describe a physical manifestation of neurotic conflict, a concept similar to Freud's notion of conversion hysteria. Although the exact terminology may differ, the essential feature of somatization disorder is that it represents a broad set of bodily symptoms whose origin lies in the psychological domain.

In most cases, somatization disorder first appears during adolescence and progresses to a fluctuating, lifelong

Helen, a 29-year-old woman, is seeking treatment because her physician said there was nothing more he could do for her. When asked about her physical problems, Helen recited a litany of complaints, including frequent episodes when she cannot remember what has happened to her and other times when her vision is so blurred that she cannot read the words on a printed page. Helen enjoys cooking and doing things around the house, but she becomes easily fatigued and short of breath for no apparent reason. She often is unable to eat the elaborate meals she prepares because she either cannot swallow or feels nauseated. According to Helen's husband, their sexual relations have ebbed to the point where they have intercourse only about once a month, usually at his insistence. Helen complains of painful cramps during her menstrual periods and at other times says she feels that her "insides are on fire." Helen lives in a large old Victorian house, from which she ventures only infrequently "because I need to be able to lie down when my legs ache."

- How do Helen's symptoms correspond to the symptoms of somatization disorder?
- What circumstances in Helen's life might have contributed to her disorder?

course during which stressful events can cause episodic intensifications. Individuals with somatization disorder rarely go through a year without seeking medical treatment for some form of undiagnosable physical problem. These people go to extreme lengths, compulsively seeking medical and surgical procedures, in their efforts to get treatment for their vague and unsubstantiated physical problems (Ford, 1983). Not surprisingly, the disorder can cause significant work and social impairment.

Somatization disorder is relatively rare. Estimates of its prevalence in the general U.S. population are .23 percent in women and .02 percent in men (Swartz et al., 1991). Understandably, the disorder is more prevalent in medical settings, with rates reported in one study of 3 percent of men and 14 percent of women (deGruy et al., 1987). People with this disorder tend to be from lower socioeconomic classes, with relatively little education or psychological sophistication. Their family histories often include a home life lacking in emotional support and disturbed by alcoholic or antisocial problems on the part of one or both parents. These people generally experienced school problems during their youth, and in many cases they have records of delinquency. As they grew into adolescence, many were sexually promiscuous and married at a young age into unstable relationships with spouses who were substance abusers. Often, they themselves have a history of substance abuse problems (Ford, 1983).

Because they do not consider their difficulties to have an emotional cause, people with somatization disorder do not voluntarily seek psychotherapy. Only upon the insistence of a physician are they likely to do so, and even then, they make it clear to the psychotherapist that they feel misunderstood and that their physical problems have not been

adequately assessed. The therapist's job is to help the client draw the connections between physical problems and psychological conflicts. Even in the best of these therapies, however, the chances for success are slim.

In contrast to somatization disorder, **somatoform pain disorder** involves only the complaint of pain. As in the other somatoform disorders, no physical basis can be established for the individual's symptoms.

Brian complains of a constant toothache that at times is so severe that he spends the entire day flat on his back at home. He has visited numerous dentists, and no one can find any evidence of tooth decay, injury, or gum diseases that could account for Brian's pain. At 48 years old, Brian finds for the first time in his life that he is forced to stay home from work for more than a few days at a time. Brian has worked since the age of 19, beginning his career in merchandising as a shipping clerk for a large retail discount chain. He advanced to his current managerial position through what he regards as "smooth talking" and the determination to make something of himself in the business world.

- What symptoms does Brian have that fit the definition of somatoform pain disorder?
- Is there anything about Brian's symptoms that might lead you to suspect that he is faking them?

- *Body dysmorphic disorder*

Perhaps, like most people, you are self-conscious about some aspect of your body such as your height, your weight, your shape, the size of your nose, or something about your hair. If you confide in friends, they may tell you that they are also self-conscious about some feature of their bodies. In fact, many people have distorted negative concerns about their bodies (Thompson, 1990); for example, in one study of college students, as many as 70 percent of the group complained of some dissatisfaction with an aspect of their appearance (Fitts et al., 1989).

People with body dysmorphic disorder are not just dissatisfied, but are preoccupied, almost to the point of being delusional, with the idea that some part of their body is ugly or defective. They may believe that there is something wrong with the texture of their skin, that they have too much or too little facial hair, or that there is a deformity in the shape of their nose, mouth, jaw, or eyebrows. Other less frequent concerns of people with body dysmorphic disorder are that they have something wrong with the appearance of their feet, hands, breasts, or some part of the body other than the face. For the most part, the defects these people are concerned about are entirely imaginary. In other instances, there really is something abnormal about the body part, but the person's concern is grossly exaggerated.

Body dysmorphic disorder has been described in the psychiatric literature of different cultures for more than a century. Although the concerns of people with this disorder

Lydia is a 43-year-old woman who was referred to the mental health clinic by a local plastic surgeon. For the last 8 years, Lydia has visited plastic surgeons across the country to find one who will perform surgery to reduce the size of her hands, which she perceives as being "too fat." Until she has this surgery she will not leave her house without wearing gloves. The plastic surgeon concurs with Lydia's family members and friends that Lydia's perception of her hands is distorted and that plastic surgery would be inappropriate and irresponsible.

- What symptoms of Lydia's would lead you to regard her as having body dysmorphic disorder?
- In your opinion, would plastic surgery alleviate Lydia's suffering?

may sound trivial, the disorder can lead to very serious psychological difficulties including social isolation, work problems, unnecessary cosmetic surgery, and in severe cases depression and suicide (Phillips, 1991).

■ *Hypochondriasis*

Everybody has heard about "hypochondriacs," who run to physicians with every small ache or pain or every slight bodily abnormality. People with the somatoform disorder known as **hypochondriasis** believe or fear that they have a serious disease when, in fact, they are merely experiencing normal bodily reactions. For example, a stomachache that lasts for more than a day might lead a hypochondriacal woman to worry that she has an advanced case of stomach cancer. Or a recurrent headache might lead a hypochondriacal man to infer that he has a brain tumor. Even the most minor of bodily changes, such as itching skin, can unleash a

flurry of behavior directed at getting medical attention. To the dismay of people with hypochondriasis, medical tests fail to confirm their assumptions; nevertheless, they remain preoccupied with the possibility of disease. Approximately 4 to 5 percent of medical patients have hypochondriasis and they account for a disproportionate share of medical services (Barsky et al., 1992).

Unlike conversion disorder or somatization disorder, hypochondriasis does not involve extreme bodily dysfunction or unexplainable medical symptoms. Instead, hypochondriasis is an exaggeration or distortion of normal bodily occurrences. Further, unlike some of the disorders we have seen so far, a characteristic of hypochondriasis is the person's intense preoccupation with the perceived abnormality of functioning. Thus, people with hypochondriasis do not show *la belle indifference* experienced by some people with conversion disorders. In fact, a substantial proportion have accompanying symptoms of anxiety or depression (Barsky et al., 1992). Hypochondriacs become so alarmed about their symptoms that they appear to be on the verge of panic. No amount of reassurance from medical authorities can relieve their fears. Yet, these fears are not delusional, because the individual is aware of the possibility that the fears are unfounded or exaggerated.

People with hypochondriasis are the nemesis of many physicians because they persist in their claims that something is physically wrong with them, and their interpersonal style tends to be clinging and demanding. Other people who interact with hypochondriacs eventually respond in a similar fashion, feeling annoyed and drained by the hypochondriac's constant whining and complaining.

You may know a person who went through a transient period of hypochondriasis, possibly associated with an actual medical problem or a stressful event that occurred at

A hypochondriac may spend a small fortune on unnecessary medications to treat imagined bodily disorders.

Beth is a 48-year-old mother of two children, both of whom have recently moved away from home. Within the last year, her menstrual periods have become much heavier and more irregular. Seeking an explanation, Beth began to spend days and days reading everything she could find on uterine cancer. Although medical books specified menstrual disturbance as a common feature of menopause, one newspaper article mentioned the possibility of uterine cancer. She immediately made an appointment with her gynecologist, who tested her and concluded that her symptoms were almost certainly due to menopause. Convinced that her physician is trying to protect her from knowing the awful "truth," Beth has continued to visit one gynecologist after another in search of someone who will properly diagnose what she is certain is a fatal illness. Beth realizes that her concerns may be exaggerated, but as she points out "one can never be too sure at my age."

- How would you determine whether or not Beth's hypochondriasis is a transient response to her concerns about her aging body?
- What symptons differentiate Beth from a person who has somatization or conversion disorder?

the time. In fact, researchers have begun to distinguish this transient form of hypochondriasis (Barsky et al., 1990) from hypochondriasis as a somatoform disorder. Transient hypochondriasis may be part of an adjustment disorder (see Chapter 17) related to ongoing psychological stresses. Take the case of a young man who has just started a new job and becomes inordinately concerned that his gassy stomach may develop into an ulcer. Panic-stricken, he goes from doctor to doctor seeking confirmation of his fears. Over time, as his emotional stress abates, the physical concerns diminish as well. Transient hypochondriasis may also occur when a person has a real physical disorder (Yates, 1991). For example, a man who has suffered a heart attack may become excessively worried about his health to the point of calling the doctor several times a week for an emergency appointment.

One way to understand hypochondriasis is to regard it as a way for people who are uncomfortable about expressing psychological concerns to find a more acceptable reason to seek help. For example, a woman in her 60s, feeling lonely and isolated after the death of her husband, may become consumed with worries about her physical health yet never acknowledge the emotional stress associated with the loss of her spouse. This phenomenon, referred to as **masked depression**, is thought to exist in many cases of older persons who otherwise appear to be hypochondriacal (Blazer & Williams, 1980; Neshkes & Jarvik, 1987). They find it more acceptable to seek help for medical problems than to acknowledge their underlying sense of depression, because they have not been as acculturated to the idea of seeking psychological treatment as have younger generations of adults.

■ Conditions related to somatoform disorders

Somatoform disorders are different from **psychophysiological disorders**, a set of disorders we will discuss in Chapter 17 that involve real physical problems such as asthma, headaches, and ulcers. These conditions, unlike somatoform disorders, correspond to known medical problems.

In another condition that may resemble somatoform disorder, called **malingering**, individuals deliberately feign the symptoms of physical illness for an ulterior motive. Returning to the example of the quarterback with the paralyzed hand, we might consider the possibility that he has fabricated the complaint to avoid playing in a game his team is certain to lose. Another example of malingering would be a case in which a physical problem enables a person to obtain financial gain such as disability benefits.

In another phenomenon, **factitious disorder**, people feign symptoms or disorders, not for the purpose of any particular gain, but because of an inner need to maintain a sick role. The symptoms may be either physical or psychological, or may be a combination of both. Individuals with this disorder may neglect real physical problems with the intent of making their actual symptoms worsen (Kooiman, 1987). They relish the notion of being ill, and may go to great lengths either to appear ill or to make themselves sick.

An extreme version of factitious disorder with physical symptoms is **Munchausen's syndrome**, named after Baron von Munchausen, a retired German cavalry officer in the 1700s known for his "tall tales" (Asher, 1951). The term *Munchausen's syndrome* is used to describe chronic cases in which the individual's whole life becomes consumed with the pursuit of medical care. In some cases, individuals go beyond merely complaining about physical distress and inflict injury upon themselves in order to look "sick." For example, a person may inject saliva into his skin in order to produce abscesses, or a person who is allergic to penicillin may willingly accept an injection to induce a reaction. In other cases, individuals have sought surgery for supposed ailments such as back or stomach problems that the physician could

It is sometimes difficult to distinguish legitimate medical complaints from the fabrications of a person with factitious disorder.

not rule out through medical examination. These individuals present themselves as dramatically as possible, trying to create scenarios in which their illness plays a starring role. They may simulate a heart attack, appendicitis, kidney stone pain, or fevers of unknown origin. If they are not believed, however, they may become incensed and immediately seek medical help elsewhere, possibly flying all over the country to different medical centers where they can become the center of concern for their baffling diseases.

In factitious disorder with psychological symptoms, the individual feigns psychological problems such as psychosis or depression. In such cases the individual's symptoms tend to be vague and fail to correspond to any particular psychological disorder. However, such individuals tend to be suggestible, and take on new symptoms that a clinician inadvertently implies are commonly associated with the hypothesized psychological disorder.

At times, clinicians encounter an especially intriguing form of factitious disorder, in which a person induces physical symptoms in another person who is under that individual's care. For example, a mother may cause her young daughter to become sick, possibly by feeding her toxic substances, and go from physician to physician with this sick and helpless child. In such a case, the mother is using her

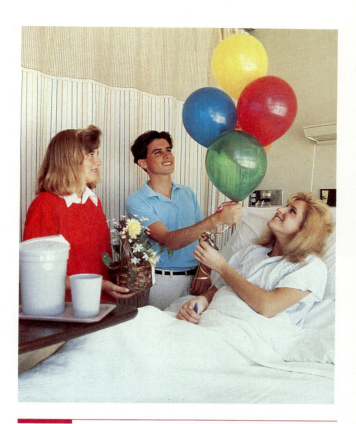

Might this kind of attention contribute to the maintenance of symptoms in a person with a conversion disorder?

daughter as an instrument to gain access to medical attention and concern. This syndrome, which has been reported only in women (Robins & Sesan, 1991), is referred to as *factitious disorder by proxy.*

Why would people exert such extreme effort to present themselves as being ill? In addition to wanting to be the center of attention, they seem to be motivated by a desire to be nurtured in the hospital setting or possibly have a masochistic wish to experience pain. Looking into the childhood backgrounds of these individuals, it appears that many were physically abused. Disease or some experience with the medical profession may also have figured into their childhood experiences, possibly setting the stage for them perceiving professional attention as positively reinforcing (Ford, 1983).

Theories and Treatment

Why would people "want" to be sick? To answer this question, it is perhaps helpful to look at what they gain. Psychologists talk about the *primary gain* and *secondary gain* associated with sickness. **Primary gain** refers to the avoidance of burdensome responsibilities because one is "disabled." Going back to the case of the football player, his primary gain is the avoidance of playing a game that entails high risk, both in terms of physical injury and loss of self-esteem. **Secondary gain** refers to the sympathy and attention that the sick person receives from other people. For

Linda is a 33-year-old janitor who had an accident at work one year ago when she slipped on a freshly mopped floor. Linda badly bruised her right knee, and since the accident she has been unable to bend her knee or to support her weight on that leg. Consequently, she has found it necessary to rely on crutches and even a wheelchair for mobility. Linda has undergone numerous medical assessments, but no physical bases for her problems have been found. Linda has been unable to work and has filed a worker's compensation claim that would provide disability benefits. Linda complains that this accident occurred at the worst possible time in her life, because her husband recently left her and she is concerned about her ability to support herself and her 2-year-old daughter. She is comforted by the thought that, if she were to be awarded disability benefits, she would have permanent financial security and would be able to remain home to take care of her daughter. She is distressed by her physician's doubt that she has a real physical disability, and she has vowed to find the "best orthopedic surgeon in the country" to find out what the problem is. If necessary, she will sue her employer and the worker's compensation insurance company to get her benefits.

- What conditions in Linda's life might lead you to suspect that she is malingering?
- Contrast Linda to Helen, who was described as having somatization disorder. How do their life circumstances differ and what features of their symptoms differentiate them?

example, the football player might be secretly gratified by the solicitous concern of his friends and teammates.

Many potential costs are involved in adopting the sick role, however. Lost or reduced wages can result from disability, and the incapacitation it causes may engender annoyance or anger, not sympathy, from others. However, people who take on the sick role find that more rewards than costs become available to them. Society also tends to make it more acceptable for people to receive care for a physical illness than for stress-related problems that seem to be more under voluntary control (Ford, 1983).

The psychodynamic explanation for somatoform disorders has its theoretical roots in the work of Freud. Freud's case of Anna O., which paints a classic picture of "hysteria," started Freud on his search for an understanding of unconscious processes. The Freudian view of hysteria was that an individual has become fixated at the Oedipal stage of development. In the case of Anna O., her father's death brought out her repressed Oedipal desires, and the only acceptable outlet for this energy was a disorder of her own body. The result of this conversion was that Anna did not have to cope with guilt over her sexual attraction to her father. Moreover, she obtained a great deal of secondary gain in the form of the attention she received from her physician. Classic psychoanalytic theory, then, regards the repression of unconscious conflicts, such as Anna O.'s, as the primary reason for somatoform disorders.

Combining the insights of several perspectives is an approach that regards somatoform disorders as due to an interplay of biological factors, learning experiences, emotional factors, and faulty cognitions (Kellner, 1990; Lipowski, 1988). According to this integrative approach, events in childhood set the stage for the later development of symptoms. As children, people with this disorder may have had parents who dealt with stress by complaining about various unfounded physical ailments. As adults, they are primed to react to emotional stress with physical complaints. Some of these complaints may have a basis in reality, in that stress can cause muscle tension in parts of the body such as the head, back, or gastrointestinal system. Although too subtle to show up on diagnostic tests, these symptoms of muscle tension create discomfort, and serve as a focus of attention and concern by the individual. A cycle is established in which concern over these physical sensations becomes magnified, creating more tension and leading to more distress. Reinforcing this process are the rewards the individual stands to gain from being sick, such as disability benefits or attention from friends and family members.

Most contemporary approaches to treating somatoform disorders involve exploration of a person's need to play the sick role and also consider the extent to which stressful events might enter into the picture. Behavioral techniques are also used, sometimes involving the cooperation of family members. If Anna O. were to be treated today, for example, her therapist might work with her family to change the reinforcers that maintain her sick role as well as try to help her through the stress associated with grieving for her father.

Irrespective of the specific therapeutic techniques that are employed, a supportive and trusting relationship between the therapist and the client with a somatoform disorder is very important. As was true for Rose Marston, whose case was presented at the outset of the chapter, a client may become upset if challenged by a disbelieving therapist regarding physical symptoms that seem very real and troubling.

Interestingly, the prognosis for recovery from conversion disorder is fairly good following treatment. In one study of 61 patients with the disorder, only a dozen still had their symptoms one year later (Hafeiz, 1980). In another study, half of the 50 patients with conversion disorder were symptom-free by the time of their discharge from the hospital (Folks et al., 1984). Those people most likely to recover are ones who develop the disorder precipitously in response to stress, and who were in good mental and physical health prior to the onset of their symptoms (Ford & Folks, 1985).

DISSOCIATIVE DISORDERS

As you have seen, somatoform disorders involve the bodily expression of conflict through a range of disorders involving varying degrees of disturbance and impact on a person's life. Dissociative disorders are far more extreme. These are disorders in which anxiety or conflict is so severe that part of the individual's personality actually becomes separated from the rest of conscious functioning. The individual experiences a temporary alteration in consciousness involving a loss of personal identity, decreased awareness of immediate surroundings, and odd bodily movements. Once the dissociation has occurred, the contents of the dissociated part become inaccessible to the rest of the client's conscious mind.

Psychologists have learned some fascinating clues to understanding normal personality functioning from studying individuals with dissociative disorders. We generally take for granted the idea that within one person's body there can exist only one personality. Dissociative disorders show that these assumptions about human nature do not apply to everyone.

Multiple Personality Disorder

Multiple personality disorder is a dissociative disorder in which one individual develops more than one self or personality. These personalities are referred to as **alters**, in contrast to the core personality, called the **host**. The disorder was made famous in novels and movies such as *Sybil* (Schreiber, 1973) and *The Three Faces of Eve* (Thigpen & Cleckley, 1957), each of which tells the fantastic but true story of a woman who had several distinct "personalities." In multiple personality disorder, each alter is a consistent and enduring pattern of perceiving, relating to, and thinking about the environment and the self.

Mark Peterson, a 31-year-old grocery worker from Oshkosh, Wisconsin, defends himself in court in November 1990, against a rape charge brought against him by Sarah, a woman with multiple personality disorder. He met 26-year-old "Franny" at a bar, and asked her for a date. Franny told Peterson about fun-loving 20-year-old "Jennifer" and reportedly, he summoned Jennifer and invited her to have sex with him. During intercourse, six-year-old "Emily" emerged; he reportedly told Jennifer to keep their activities secret from Sarah. But Franny and Emily told Sarah, who pressed charges against him. Although the jury voted to convict Peterson, the judge overturned the verdict on the grounds that the defense was not allowed to have Sarah examined by a psychiatrist before the trial.

■ *Characteristics of multiple personality disorder*

In classic cases of multiple personality disorder, there are at least two fully developed personalities that each have unique memories, behavior patterns, and social relationships; in other cases, there may be varying degrees of sharing among the personalities. The alters may be very discrepant, even opposites of each other. One may be reserved and another extremely extroverted. The separation between alters may be remarkably distinct. Two alters may have different social histories, physiological characteristics, and reactions to psychological tests. The various alters may be of either sex, of a different race or age, or from a different "family" than the other alters. One may be a child, another a teenager, and yet a third an adult. Each alter may have a separate set of clothes and may vary in physical presentation, including handedness, physical disabilities, and speech patterns.

The transition from one alter to another is usually sudden, triggered by psychosocial stress or some idiosyncratically salient stimulus. At any given moment, only one alter interacts with the external environment, although the others may actively perceive what is happening or influence what is going on. Most of the personalities have a sense of lost or distorted experiences of time. An alter may piece together memories to make up for unaccounted gaps, or an alter may have access to memories of the other alters.

Richard Kluft, a psychiatrist at the Institute of the Pennsylvania Hospital, has played a major role in disseminating information about multiple personality disorder in the scientific community. Kluft has described several key features of multiple personality disorder, including the nature of the personalities that reside within the same individual and their relationships to each other. The classic host personality, who seeks professional help, tends to be depressed, anxious, compulsively "good," masochistic, and moralistic. The most frequently seen alters include children, "protectors," "helpers," expressers of forbidden impulses, those based on lost loved ones, ones that carry lost memories or family secrets, avengers who express anger over past experiences of being abused, and defenders of the abusers (Kluft, 1984a).

As a way of refining and standardizing the diagnosis of multiple personality disorder, Canadian psychiatrist Colin Ross and his colleagues (Ross, 1989) developed the Dissociative Disorders Interview Schedule. Some of the key questions, reproduced in Table 8-1, give further insight into the nature of the symptoms associated with this disorder.

Table 8-1 Items from the Dissociative Disorders Interview Schedule

---

"Yes" responses to all questions would be rated in the direction of a high dissociative disorder score:

Have you ever walked in your sleep?
Did you have imaginary playmates as a child?
Were you physically abused as a child or adolescent?
Were you sexually abused as a child or adolescent? (Sexual abuse includes rape, or any type of unwanted sexual touching or fondling that you may have experienced.)
Have you ever noticed that things are missing from your personal possessions or where you live?
Have you ever noticed that there are things present where you live, and you don't know where they came from or how they got there? (e.g., clothes, jewelry, books, furniture.)
Do people ever come up and talk to you as if they know you but you don't know them, or only know them faintly?
Do you ever speak about yourself as "we" or "us"?
Do you ever feel that there is another person or persons inside you?
If there is another person inside you, does he or she ever come out and take control of your body?

Source: Ross, (1989)

One question commonly asked about multiple personality disorder is whether each alter has an awareness of the others. According to Kluft (1987b), the alters usually have some awareness of each other's experiences. In fact, different alters can have alliances, relationships, or ongoing antagonisms. One alter can go so far as to try to hurt or even kill another alter. However, the question of whether the boundaries among alters are actually this flexible has been controversial (Orne et al., 1984).

Multiple personality disorder gained a great deal of recognition in the 1980s, starting with the publication in 1980 of four major papers on the topic (Bliss, 1980; Coons, 1980; Greaves, 1980; Rosenbaum, 1980). That same year, the disorder was first included in the *DSM*, and was defined in such a way that it no longer was reserved for cases as extreme as those of Eve and Sybil. The diagnosis could now be applied in situations where a person experienced a disorganization of the self, and labeled discrepant experiences as due to the operation of separate individuals residing within the self. Along with this broadening of the definition came a proliferation of cases of multiple personality disorder to the point where it became referred to as an "epidemic" (Boor, 1982). More cases of this disorder were reported during one 5-year period in the 1980s than had been documented in the preceding two centuries (Putnam et al., 1986). Clinicians and researchers began to wonder whether this increase was due to the disorder's actually becoming more prevalent or whether it was an artificial phenomenon due to the broadening of the definition of the disorder.

Some maintain that the increase in reported prevalence of multiple personality is due to more accurate diagnosis of the disorder. Supporting this argument is the finding that in the cases of more than 300 people who ultimately were diagnosed as having this disorder, an average interval of almost 7 years had elapsed between their first seeking treatment and receiving the correct diagnosis. During that time, these individuals were given many other erroneous diagnoses including depression, "neurotic disorder," personality disorder, schizophrenia, "hysterical schizophrenia," substance abuse, bipolar disorder, and epilepsy (Putnam et al., 1986; Ross et al., 1989). In one extreme case, it took 23 years for the disorder to be diagnosed.

Although on one level it is shocking to see such cases of misdiagnosis, on another level the problems in diagnosis are understandable. Several lines of investigation link the disorder to epilepsy, schizophrenia, and somatoform disorder (Bliss, 1980; Devinsky et al., 1989; Kluft, 1987a). The problem of diagnosis may further be exacerbated by the facts that the symptoms of multiple personality disorder are not consistent over time, the individual may attempt to cover up the symptoms, and the dissociative symptoms may be mixed with a mood disturbance or a personality disorder. In some cases, the individual may have a high level of functioning in various areas of life, and the symptoms of multiple personality disorder may never even be suspected (Kluft, 1986). All of these factors contribute to underdiagnosis of multiple personality disorder.

On the other side of the debate are those researchers who maintain that the increase since 1980 in reported cases of this disorder is artifically inflated. Popular first-person characterizations of the disorder (e.g., Bass & Davis, 1988), media attention, and efforts by dedicated clinicians and people claiming to have had this disorder have all contributed to what is considered an inappropriate degree of emphasis on this rare but fascinating form of psychological disorder.

Some skeptics have raised the possibility that certain clients may actually be responding to their therapists' suggestion that their problems are attributable to multiple personality rather than more customary disorders such as depression or personality disorder. According to this view, some clients are highly suggestible and may pick up on cues from their therapist to construe their problems in terms of multiple personality disorder. According to this logic, over time they tell stories about alternate personalities and may actually develop behaviors that fit these different personalities (Orne et al., 1984; Simpson, 1989; Spanos et al., 1985).

Following the heightened publicity concerning multiple personality disorder, cases have also been reported of clients who deliberately fabricated the symptoms of the disorder. These cases of malingering may be due to the individual's seeking some external gain, such as being excused from responsibility for a crime. This occurred in the famous case of Kenneth Bianchi, the Hillside Strangler (see discussion in Chapter 6), who fabricated symptoms of multiple personality disorder as a way of avoiding criminal prosecution (Orne et al, 1984; Watkins, 1984). In cases of factitious disorder, the individual simply wants to be sick (Brick & Chu, 1991) and chooses to simulate the dramatic symptoms of multiple personality disorder.

In response to some of these controversies, the authors of *DSM-IV* have considered a more detailed and symptom-oriented list of criteria for multiple personality disorder. Most importantly, to fit this diagnosis the individual must have had the experience of **amnesia**, an inability to remember important personal information (Spiegel & Cardeña, 1991). Presumably, adding a more stringent condition would reduce the number of false diagnoses. (Ross et al., 1990).

✗ *Theories and treatment*

As children, most of us develop a sense of self through interactions with parents and peers, and in this process maintain a sense of continuity over time. In people with multiple personality disorder, this integration process goes awry. Such a fundamental defect must require a major disruption of normal developmental processes, and as researchers have found, the overwhelming majority of people with multiple personality disorder experienced severe abuse during childhood including physical torture and neglect, psychological traumatization, or very sadistic forms of sexual abuse (Coons et al., 1989; Ross et al., 1990; Terr, 1991; Wilbur & Kluft, 1989). The alters develop as a defense

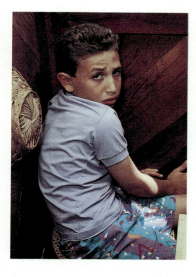

The terror of abuse drives some children into a dissociative state in which their fantasies provide them with an escape from the harsh realities of their lives.

personalities in response to their experiences of abuse (Kluft, 1984b).

Women outnumber men by a ratio of approximately 9 to 1 in instances of multiple personality disorder (Ross et al., 1989). This disparity between the genders is thought to reflect higher incidence of sexual abuse of girls, although boys are not free of victimization (Ross, 1989). Some researchers have reported that in many cases the parents of individuals who develop multiple personality disorder themselves suffered from the disorder; the abuse of the child may have taken place through the actions of a parent's alter personality (Braun, 1985).

What are the early signs of multiple personality disorder? Some clues to the incipient development of this disorder come from a small case study of four children. These children, even at the early age of 4, were already showing some of the symptoms of the disorder. They would become dazed or enter a trance-like state, and show marked changes in their personality, possibly swinging from being shy and reserved to being dominant and pushy. Their behavior was also variable in other domains including academic performance, physical skills, likes and dislikes, and even very identifiable characteristics such as handwriting. Often, these children would act out behaviors that were threatening to themselves and others, such as being self-injurious and suicidal, hurtful to others, truant, sexually precocious, and deceitful. Observations by people who knew these children were paralleled by the descriptions the children gave regarding their own behavior. The children talked about their imaginary playmates, their feelings of loneliness, and their confusion about time (Fagan & McMahon, 1984).

against the horror of such trauma, as the child escapes into a dissociative, self-hypnotic state filled with fantasy and thoughts of being someone else. Repeated exposure to experiences of victimization lead the child to enter this state more and more frequently. As this happens, the split-off dissociated parts of experience and memory develop independently, and the child's personality and sense of self fail to become integrated (Ross, 1989).

It is important to keep in mind that only a small percentage of traumatized children develop such dissociative disorders. Thus, although many people with multiple personality disorder have a history of abuse, the converse does not necessarily hold true. Researchers do not yet understand what makes these particular children vulnerable to developing this disorder. Some unknown factor, which could be either biological or psychological, seems to predispose a subset of traumatized children to develop multiple

The goal of therapy in multiple personality disorder is integration of the alters into a unified whole, with adequate coping strategies to enable the person to deal with the painful memories of the past and the stresses of current life

Hypnotherapy is often used in treating clients with dissociative disorders, such as multiple personality disorder, to help the client achieve an integrated personality.

without resorting to fragmentation (Wilbur & Kluft, 1989). The most commonly used treatment approach has involved techniques derived from psychoanalytic psychotherapy, often including **hypnotherapy**, in which the client is hypnotized and encouraged to recall painful past experiences while in a trance state (Kluft, 1984b). The various alters with their associated memories are brought out one by one and unified into a consistent whole. A separate treatment may be required for each of the alters, including the establishment of a positive working relationship with each. Because some of these alters may be abrasive and antagonistic, while others may be dependent and seductive, they each may respond differently to alternate interventions (Kluft, 1984b).

One danger in this process is that the clinician may inadvertently reinforce the client's expression of multiple alters by focusing attention on these alters. For example, a clinician who seems amazed and intrigued by a woman's multiple personality experience may be communicating to the client that she is very special because of these unusual experiences and that to hold onto her specialness, she should maintain and possibly expand her different alters.

In addition to hypnotherapy, cognitive-behavioral methods can be used to identify and change the dysfunctional attitudes held by people with multiple personality disorder (Caddy, 1985; Ross & Gahan, 1988). These attitudes, arising from the client's history of abuse, include the beliefs that different parts of the self are separate selves, that the victim is responsible for abuse, that it is wrong to show anger or defiance, that the host cannot handle painful memories, that one of the alters hates the parents (but the primary personality loves them), that the host must be punished, and that neither the self nor others can be trusted. According to Ross (1989), each of these core beliefs carries with it a set of assumptions that further guide the individual's behavior. Although countering these beliefs is not considered sufficient for treating multiple personality disorder, this process would seem to be an important component of an overall treatment plan.

Another aspect of cognitive-behavioral therapy that might be helpful is to bolster the individual's sense of self-efficacy through a process called *temporizing* (Kluft, 1989), in which the client controls the way that the alters make their appearance. This is accomplished through hypnosis, and gives the client coping skills to use when stress might precipitate a personality shift.

As more reliable information becomes available on multiple personality disorder, improved methods of treatment are certain to be developed (Dunn, 1992). Nevertheless, several factors contribute to difficulty in treating this disorder. First, this is a very broadly defined disorder that ranges from cases such as those of Sybil and Eve to people who show far less dramatic symptoms. Second, clinicians and researchers have ascertained that most people with this disorder also suffer from other psychological problems such as mood disorders or personality disorders. Third, it can be very difficult to repair the damage done by abuse and

Myra is a young single woman who works as a clerk in a large retail bookstore. She lives by herself, never goes out socially except to see her relatives, and dresses in a conservative manner that her associates ridicule as "prudish." At the age of 25, Myra says that she is "saving" herself sexually for marriage; yet, she seems totally uninterested in pursuing any close relationships with men. This brief summary describes Myra as she is known to her work acquaintances and family. There are, however, other alters residing within Myra's body, who go by other names and behave in ways that are totally incongruous with "Myra's" personality. "Rita" is flamboyant, outgoing, and uninhibited in her sexual passions. She has engaged in numerous love affairs with a variety of unsavory characters she picked up in nightclubs and discotheques. "Rita" is aware of "Myra," and regards her with extreme disdain. A third personality, "Joe," occasionally emerges from "Myra's" apartment. Dressed in a man's three-piece business suit, "Joe" goes downtown to do some shopping. According to "Joe," "Rita," is nothing but a "slut," who is heading for "big trouble someday." Myra's alters are oblivious to the details of her life.

- What factors in Myra's personal history might her therapist look for when trying to understand the basis of Myra's multiple personality disorder:?
- Can you see any relationship among the alters, and how do they relate to the host personality?

trauma that took place decades earlier in the client's life. Finally, consider what it must be like for the clinician to work with the individual with multiple personality disorder whose problems and style of presentation are so diverse and contradictory. Given all of these obstacles, you can see why it can take many years to reach the desired goal of personality integration (Kluft, 1989).

Other Dissociative Disorders

Multiple personality disorder is perhaps the most dramatic form of dissociative disorder, but the other forms can be equally compelling in terms of their impact on the individual's life and in terms of the way they challenge our understanding of mind–body relationships.

- *Psychogenic amnesia*

In **psychogenic amnesia**, sometimes called *dissociative amnesia*, the individual becomes unable to remember important personal details and experiences. This memory loss is not attributable to brain dysfunction associated with brain damage or drugs. Psychogenic amnesia is regarded as a dissociative disorder because it involves dissociating oneself from that part of one's personality that includes one's personal history.

Imagine how distressing it would be to experience psychogenic amnesia. You know how annoying it is to forget

An automobile accident can be so traumatizing that a person may forget events that happened only moments earlier.

something once in a while, such as an appointment, a fact on an examination, or an umbrella. But what if you were unable to recall your name, your address, your occupation, or anything about yourself? It would almost certainly transform your life into a nightmare. You might walk around aimlessly in a state of confusion and panic as you try to piece together your identity. The memories of ourselves over time are among the most important features of our sense of who we are. Without these memories, our identities become cloudy and confused.

Psychogenic amnesia is a rare disorder, yet it is the most common of the dissociative disorders (Nemiah, 1985). It received a great deal of attention following the two world wars, in which many individuals with combat-related trauma experienced amnesia (Kardiner & Spiegel, 1947; Lowenstein, 1991). More attention has been paid to the disorder in recent years as clinicians noted the fact that many people with amnesia had childhood histories of physical or sexual abuse (Coons et al., 1989).

There are four forms of psychogenic amnesia that vary according to the extent of the individual's memory loss. In **localized amnesia**, the most common form, the individual forgets all events that occurred during a specified time interval. Usually, this interval immediately follows a very disturbing event, such as a car accident, fire, or natural disaster. In **selective amnesia**, the individual fails to recall some, but not all, details of events that have occurred during a given period of time. The survivor of a fire may remember the ambulance ride to the hospital, but not having been rescued from the burning house. **Generalized amnesia** is a syndrome in which a person cannot remember anything at all from his or her past life. **Continuous amnesia** involves a failure to recall past events from a particular date, up to and including, the present time. For example, a war veteran may remember his childhood and youth until the time he entered the armed services, but may have forgotten everything that took place after his first tour of combat duty.

Psychogenic amnesia is very difficult for clinicians to diagnose because there are so many possible causes of memory loss. For example, as you will see in later chapters, amnesia can be caused by a physical dysfunction due to brain injury, psychoactive substance abuse, or epilepsy. Alternatively, other psychological disorders have symptoms that

In a daze, Norma entered the mental health crisis center, tears streaming down her face. "I have no idea where I live or who I am. Will somebody please help me?" The crisis team helped her search her purse, but could find nothing other than photograph of a blond-haired little girl. Norma appeared to be exhausted, and was taken to a bed where she promptly fell asleep. The crisis team called the local police to find out if there was a report of a missing person. As it turned out, the little girl in the photograph was Norma's daughter. She had been hit by a car in the parking lot of a shopping center. Although badly injured with a broken leg, the child was resting comfortably in the pediatrics ward of the hospital. Her mother, however, had disappeared. Norma had apparently been wandering around for several hours, leaving her wallet and other identifying papers with the hospital social worker in the emergency room. When Norma awoke, she was able to recall who she was and the circumstances of the accident, but remembered nothing of what had happened since.

■ How would a clinician determine that Norma is suffering from pschogenic amnesia rather than amnesia caused by physical injury?

■ What is the possible relationship between Norma's disorder and the circumstances surrounding her daughter's accident?

may cause the individual to appear amnestic. A person in a catatonic stupor who does not communicate may be construed to be amnestic. When the individual is questioned, though, it may be possible to elicit some information about the person's past.

As is the case for multiple personality disorder, a person might pretend to have amnesia in order to gain certain benefits or advantages. Clinicians usually try to rule out the possibility of malingering when evaluating symptoms of amnesia by being alert to hidden motivations for "forgetting." For example, a man who has committed a serious crime may claim that he remembers nothing of the incident or even who he is. You can understand how someone interviewing this man would be skeptical regarding his memory loss and would try to ascertain whether the amnesia is genuine or not. As in the other dissociative disorders, careful interviewing and history-taking is required in making this determination.

Psychogenic fugue

In all likelihood you have read newspaper accounts that document the fascinating story of a person who has found his way to a community far away from home with no idea of how he got there or who he is. Everyone is perplexed and intrigued by the dramatic features involved in this person's misfortune. Although such cases are rare, they capture the attention of the media because they seem so unbelievable. Many of the people in such stories are experiencing a **fugue**, a condition in which a person is confused about personal identity suddenly and unexpectedly travels to another

place. The person in a fugue state is unable to recall his or her own past history or identity and may assume a new identity. After the fugue state has passed, the individual has no recall of what took place during the fugue.

A fugue is rare and often passes quickly. The disorder is more likely to occur at certain times, such as during a war or following a natural disaster. Fugue states can also be precipitated by personal crises or extreme stress, such as financial problems, the desire to escape punishment (Spiegel & Cardeña, 1991), or a psychologically dangerous situation.

Bizarre things can occur while a person is in a fugue state. A man may act in ways that are uncharacteristic of his customary behavior, such as spending a lot of money, acting promiscuously, or even committing a crime. You can imagine that when this man returns to his normal identity, he would be shocked by what he did during his fugue state. Even in cases that involve less extreme behaviors during the fugue state, the consequences can be disturbing.

Depersonalization disorder

You may be able to think of a time when you had a feeling of being "unreal." Perhaps you had gone for a long period of time without sleep or food and you had the sensation that you were an outsider observing the movements of your body, as if in a dream. The phenomenon of depersonalization refers to alterations of mind–body perception ranging from detachment from one's experiences to the feeling that one has stepped out of one's body. Depersonalization experiences occur in normal people when they are placed under great stress or when they use mind-altering drugs, such as marijuana or LSD. In **depersonalization disorder**, however, distortions of mind–body perceptions hap-

George was an administrator at a small college in a rural town. He was a reliable worker, keeping mostly to himself and rarely discussing his personal life with his colleagues. All they knew about him was that he lived with his wife Judy and their two teenage children. Family life was quiet until one afternoon when Judy received a telephone call from George's secretary, asking if she knew George's whereabouts. He had not shown up at work in the morning, nor had he called in sick. The secretary was concerned that George might be very upset about the previous day's announcement by the college president that the college would be closing permanently at the end of the academic year. Judy was startled by the news because George had made no mention of it at dinner the evening before. George was not heard from for three weeks following the date of his mysterious disappearance. During that time, he traveled to Stanford University with the intention of applying for a position as a philosophy professor. One day he suddenly woke up in a California hotel room mystified about how he had gotten there.

- What symptoms of a psychogenic fugue were evident in George's behavior?
- What factors in George's life might have contributed to his symptoms?

Robert entered the psychiatrist's office in a state of extreme agitation, almost panic. He described the terrifying nature of his "nervous attacks" that began several years ago but have now reached catastrophic proportions. During these "attacks," Robert feels as though he is floating in the air, above his body, watching everything he does but feeling totally disconnected from his actions. He reports that he feels as if his body is a machine controlled by outside forces: "I look at my hands and feet and wonder what makes them move." Robert's thoughts are not delusions, though; he is aware that his altered perceptions are not normal. The only relief he experiences from his symptoms comes when he strikes himself with a heavy object until the pain finally penetrates his consciousness. His fear of seriously harming himself adds to his main worry that he is losing his mind.

- If you were Robert's therapist, how would you differentiate whether he is hallucinating or experiencing symptoms of depersonalization disorder?
- What differentiates Robert's symptoms from those of a panic attack?

Imagine what it would be like to be this man who suffers from depersonalization disorder and feels that he is in a dreamlike state observing his own actions.

pen repeatedly and without provocation by drugs. Periods of extreme stress, such as the time immediately following an accident, can also precipitate an episode of depersonalization in a vulnerable individual. Some experts have noted that the experience of depersonalization commonly follows a stressful event and emerges in the "calm following the storm" (Shader & Scharfman, 1989).

People with depersonalization disorder feel as though they are not "real," that their body is changing in shape or size, or that they are being controlled by forces outside of themselves, as if they were an automaton or robot. At times, the individual may experience episodes of "conversations" between an observing and participating self (Steinberg, 1991). Most people with this disorder are aware that something is wrong with them, and this awareness is a further source of distress. Yet, they may be reluctant to tell other people about their experiences out of fear that they will sound "crazy." Thus, they can feel quite alone and isolated from others as well as frightened about their loss of contact with reality.

The onset of depersonalization disorder usually occurs in adolescence or early adulthood. The disorder tends to be chronic, with remissions and exacerbations that are triggered by anxiety, depression, or stress.

Theories and Treatment

In addition to the role of early chronic abuse in the development of multiple personality disorder, such abuse can lead to other dissociative disorders (Terr, 1991). Other kinds of traumatic events can also result in dissociative experiences. Some of these experiences are transient, and others become more deeply engrained. If you recall our discussion of posttraumatic stress disorder in Chapter 7, you will remember the kinds of dissociative experiences reported in people who have been traumatized. People who have lived through terrifying experiences often talk about

their feeling of unreality and detachment, particularly in the period just following the trauma. Whether they have lived through a hurricane, a plane crash, or a physical assault, they are likely to experience altered states of consciousness. For example, researchers reported that more than half of those who were involved in an airplane crash said that they felt detached and estranged afterwards (Sloan, 1988). In another study, survivors of a series of devastating tornadoes spoke of feelings of detachment, loss of interest in everyday concerns, and diminished sexual drive (Madakasira & O'Brien, 1987). As you might imagine, when the trauma is longlasting, as in the case of war, the emotional impact can be tremendous, with enduring feelings of psychic numbing, detachment, and other dissociative symptoms (Bremmer et al., 1992; Feinstein, 1989; Solomon et al., 1989). It is still not known why some people are more vulnerable than others to the effects of trauma. Perhaps some people carry a biological vulnerability to major stressors that results in their developing dissociative disorders in response to trauma.

In treating individuals with dissociative disorders, therapists tread a fine line in helping the client uncover and eventually conquer the painful memories without pushing the client into a dissociative episode. One method used to accomplish this goal is to bring the client into a state of relaxation in which access to forgotten memories may be possible. In the case of fugue or amnesia, the first goal is to ascertain the person's identity and the second goal is to gain access to the experiences that caused the person to become amnestic. After access is obtained to the repressed memories, the goal then is to take the emotional charge out of these incapacitating memories of trauma that originally led the person into a dissociative state. This process can be very lengthy, requiring the use of more than one technique, and demanding a great deal of patience and skill on the part of the clinician.

A clinician might use hypnosis in treatment, alone in or in combination with certain relaxation-inducing drugs such as barbiturates (sodium amobarbital or sodium pentobarbital) which facilitate the recollection of emotionally charged memories (Linn, 1989). Depersonalization disorder has also been treated with medications, including antidepressants, antianxiety drugs, and barbiturates. Although some positive outcomes have been reported with the use of medication, the results are considered inconclusive due to lack of proper controls in the various research studies (Shader & Scharfman, 1989).

The dissociative disorders provide us with a unique opportunity to understand the complexity of the human mind and the very strange ways in which people respond to stressful life experiences. As fascinating as they are, it is important to keep in mind that these are very rare disorders and that, when they are encountered, they are very difficult to treat. Although current explanations rely heavily on psychological perspectives, it is possible that in the future more will be learned about a biological substrate for the development of these conditions.

SOMATOFORM AND DISSOCIATIVE DISORDERS: THE PERSPECTIVES REVISITED

Now that you have read about the somatoform and dissociative disorders, you should be able to understand why, historically, they were regarded as neuroses rather than psychoses. People with these disorders have experienced conflict or trauma during their lives, and these circumstances have created strong emotional reactions that could not be integrated into their memory, personality, and self-concept. The symptoms of somaticizing or dissociating represent not a loss of contact with reality, but a translation of these emotions into terms that are less painful to acknowledge than the original conflict or trauma.

This explanation has its origins in the psychodynamic principles of conflict and repression. However, contemporary researchers have moved well beyond these notions to an integration of the roles of trauma and stress in these disorders. It is now believed that actual, rather than imagined, trauma is the source of dissociative symptoms. Stress-related factors, not repressed sexuality, are currently regarded as central in understanding somatoform disorders. In addition, learning seems to play a strong role, particularly as individuals with these disorders develop secondary gain from their symptoms. Cognitive-behavioral explanations of the somatoform and dissociative disorders add to these understandings. Low feelings of self-efficacy, lack of assertiveness, and faulty ideas about the self can all serve as contributing factors to these disorders. For example, the belief that one must be sick in order to be worthy of attention is a dysfunctional attitude that could underlie a somatoform disorder. Similarly, faulty beliefs about the self and the role of the self in past experiences of trauma seem to be important cognitive factors in multiple personality disorders. Adding to these psychological components are the biological factors that may contribute to an individual's vulnerability to developing these maladaptive thoughts or susceptibility to trauma.

While researchers continue to explore possible causes of the somatoform and dissociative disorders, clinicians have been relying increasingly on treatment through hypnosis. At the same time, supportive therapy aimed toward gradual exploration of the role of stress or trauma in the individual's life seems to play an important role. Cognitive-behavioral methods of enhancing the individual's feelings of self-efficacy, assertiveness, and awareness of dysfunctional thinking patterns are also being incorporated into an integrative treatment approach.

Table 8–2	SOMATOFORM AND DISSOCIATIVE DISORDERS: A SUMMARY CHART OF PERSPECTIVES	
DISORDER	**PSYCHODYNAMIC**[1]	**BEHAVIORAL**
Somatoform disorders	Physical symptoms are an expression of sexual conflict that has become repressed.	Physical symptoms are maintained by primary and secondary gain.
	Treatment: Support and exploration of intrapsychic conflict.	**Treatment:** Change reinforcers associated with sick role.
DISSOCIATIVE DISORDERS	**PSYCHODYNAMIC**	**COGNITIVE-BEHAVIORAL**
Multiple personality disorder	Physical and sexual abuse during early development led the individual to "escape" by entering an altered personality or state of consciousness.	Victims of trauma or abuse developed dysfunctional beliefs about their role in contributing to their misfortune.
	Treatment: Hypnotherapy combined with support.	Bolster the individual's sense of self-efficacy and counter dysfunctional beliefs.
Other dissociative disorders	Traumatic events at any point in life can cause dissociative symptoms.	No relevant approaches.
	Treatment: Hypnosis or other relaxtion-inducing techniques to facilitate recall of emotionally charged memories.	

[1]The term "psychodynamic" is used loosely here, in that most current approaches incorporate supportive and hypnotic techniques.

Return to the Case

Rose Marston

Rose's History

I remember feeling surprised when Rose returned to see me for the second session we had scheduled. People with stories involving numerous undiagnosable medical problems rarely come back after the intake meeting with a mental health clinician. In our second session Rose told me a life story that gave me the basis for some reasonable hunches about the nature of her problems.

The older of two daughters, Rose grew up in the center of a city close to the factory where her father worked. Rose vividly remembers the day her younger sister Emily was born, 2 days after Rose's seventh birthday. All the excitement surrounding Rose's birthday celebration and the birth of a baby in the family abruptly deteriorated to emotional chaos when Rose's parents were informed, hours after the birth, that Emily had serious abnormalities. This bad news about Emily caused Rose to become extremely worried, particularly about her father, whose drinking problem was apparent to her even at her young age and had already threatened the stability of the family. With this added stress, Rose began to fear that he might drift further into his alcoholic ways.

In the years that followed, Rose's parents were forced to devote most of their attention to her disabled sister. Feeling obliged to help her parents, Rose spent all her available time tutoring her sister, playing with her, and protecting her from the jeers of neighborhood children. When I inquired about Rose's remarkable level of devotion to her sister, Rose confided that much of this was the result of Rose's intense feeling of guilt about being so much "luckier" than Emily. Tragically, Rose's sister died from heart trouble in her teenage years. Prior to this, Rose had planned to go to college and become a special education teacher, but her attempts to carry out this ambition were hampered after her sister's death by a series of unexplainable illnesses and ailments, none of which were very serious but which caused her to drop out of college.

After leaving college, Rose took a job as a cosmetics consultant in a department store, but she had to quit after a short time due to her nagging and incapacitating physical symptoms. Because of her inability to work, Rose had recently applied for disability benefits from the government, and told me that she lives from day to day in dread that she may be denied these benefits.

When I inquired about intimate relationships in her life, Rose became ostensibly uncomfortable as she told me about her "lousy batting average" with men. Citing a long list of brief relationships, Rose explained that these relationships generally fell apart because her physical problems constantly got in the way. Recurrently frustrated by the lack of sympathy on the part of the men whom she had met, Rose concluded that she is "probably better off without them."

Assessment

Although the information provided to me by both Dr. Thompson and Rose gave me the basis for a diagnostic hypothesis, I was intrigued by the unconscious factors within Rose that might relate to her problems. Rose, who had submitted to countless medical tests in the past, was open to the psychological assessment that I recommended. She did express some reservations about the validity of any kind of tests, pointing out that the dozens of medical tests she had taken had been unable to pinpoint any of her problems.

Psychological testing showed Rose to be a bright woman, with an IQ in the above-average range. Her cognitive functioning was consistent across the subscales of the *WAIS-R*, although she did show some evidence of difficulties in breaking down a problem into component parts and in understanding social situations. Rose's *MMPI-2* profile was predictable, with elevations on Scales 1 (Hypochondriasis), 2, (Depression), and 3 (Hysteria), suggesting the likelihood that Rose defends against depression by using denial and by dwelling on possible physical problems.

TAT responses showed Rose to have a highly romanticized, superficial view of intimate relationships with many unrealistic "happy endings" to her stories. There was also a strong element of jealousy in the relationships between female figures. On the Rorschach test, Rose's first few responses were quite creative and potentially very rich in content, but she seemed unable to sustain this high level of production and quickly reverted to simple images. Throughout testing, Rose complained frequently of various physical complaints that made it necessary to interrupt testing. What struck me as odd about this was the fact that Rose seemed to develop a physical symptom just at the point of becoming immersed in the assessment tasks.

Rose Marston continued

Diagnosis

As I worked toward confirming a diagnosis, my thoughts understandably focused on Rose's lengthy history of unsubstantiated medical complaints. Although I am reluctant to conclude that any person's medical complaints are without physical basis, the evidence supporting the assumption of a psychological, rather than medical, basis was substantial. For a brief moment I considered the possibility that Rose might be malingering. But for what gain? I did not believe that she wanted to be "sick" just to collect disability benefits—Rose's problems and complaints pre-dated any concern about financial support. Might Rose be a hypochondriac? Certainly some facets of her story might lead to such a diagnosis, but there was a major difference. Rose truly believed she was suffering from physical diseases. It was my sense that even though her problem was psychologically rooted, the discomfort and incapacitation that Rose suffered was very real to her. Her lengthy list of recurrent bodily complaints and chronic pursuit of medical help for conditions that lacked any medical basis led me to diagnose Rose as having somatization disorder.

Axis I. Somatization Disorder.
Axis II. Deferred. Rule out Histrionic Personality Disorder.
Axis III. No diagnosable physical disorders or conditions.
Axis IV. Severity: 2 (Mild). Longstanding isolation and impaired interpersonal relationships.
Axis V. Current Global Assessment of Functioning: 70. Highest Global Assessment of Functioning (past year): 70.

Case Formulation

Rose's history was similar to that of the few other people with somatization disorder whom I had seen in my clinical practice. She was an individual with a long history of medical complaints, which had provided her with a good deal of secondary gain. As I thought about the possible origins of this psychological disorder, I was struck by the fact that her physical complaints first developed after the death of her younger sister, an event that Rose described as devastating. It is my sense that Rose struggled with guilt about being more intelligent, capable, and healthier than her sister. By taking over a parental role in relation to her sister, perhaps Rose was able to relieve some of this guilt. An-

other result of her sister's physical problems was that Emily was favored with more attention from her parents, who naturally had to turn more of their time and energy to the disabled sister. Feeling guilty as she did toward her sister, it was difficult for Rose to acknowledge any of the jealous feelings she quite understandably harbored. Thus, early in life Rose had to cope with powerful feelings of guilt and jealousy, and given her youth she turned to the immature defense of denial. Had Rose's sister survived her illness, Rose might very well have learned to express her feelings in a more mature fashion. However, her sister's death cut this process off prematurely. Indeed, when her sister died, Rose's physical symptoms began. One hypothesis about the cause of the symptoms at this time was that Rose identified with her sister and took on symptoms that bore a superficial resemblance to those that characterized Emily's fatal medical problems. The symptoms also incapacitated Rose so that she could have a legitimate reason not to live up to her own potential. By punishing herself she could, at an unconscious level, resolve her guilt over having been more capable and healthier than her sister, and at the same time having been ineffective in saving her.

Rose's symptoms also served a function in the family. For years, Rose's parents had turned all their energies as a couple toward caring for their disabled child. This allowed them to deflect their attention away from their own marital problems centered around her father's alcoholism. With the death of their ill child, a substitute was needed to serve a similar function in the marriage. Perhaps Rose's symptoms served, in this sense, as unconscious compliance with the needs of her parents. Additionally, Rose's symptoms gave her secondary gain in the form of attention and concern from her parents, reactions that she had not gotten from them for many, many years.

Planning a Treatment

My decision to accept Rose into psychotherapy was made with some ambivalence. I was well aware of the low odds for success, yet at the same time I was touched by Rose's willingness to give therapy a chance. From the outset she acknowledged her skepticism about the utility of psychotherapy, particularly in light of her belief that her medical problems were genuine. At the same time, she acknowledged that she might derive some benefit if we directed our

Return to the Case

Rose Marston continued

attention to the management of stress in her life. I agreed that this should be a component of the treatment, but I also felt that a broad, integrative therapy was necessary. It was my belief that for Rose's life to change for the better, psychotherapy would have to focus on some of the unconscious conflicts underlying her symptoms, the secondary gain she has received as reinforcement, and the problems in Rose's current family life that have maintained her disorder.

I recommended individual outpatient psychotherapy on a weekly basis; however, I also realized that individual psychotherapy for people with such problems is usually insufficient. Ideally, they should be seen in multiple contexts including group therapy and family therapy, as well as vocational counseling. Rose agreed to participate in a therapy group with another therapist and a group of seven clients dealing with life stresses in general, and problems with close relationships more specifically. As for family therapy, she told me emphatically that her father would not agree to any kind of professional "intrusion."

Outcome of the Case

In the initial weeks of therapy, Rose tried to redirect my attention away from psychological concerns to her somatic complaints. Gently but firmly I tried to make it clear that our work must focus on emotional rather than medical matters, but Rose was not receptive to my efforts. After a few sessions, she began to question openly the value of therapy, and 2 weeks later she announced that she had found a "cure" for her symptoms and was going to discontinue therapy. A friend had told Rose about a new technique of pain management through hypnosis, and Rose was sure that it would be just right for her.

Several months later, I received a note from the emergency room staff informing me that Rose had been admitted to the psychiatric unit following a suicide attempt involving an overdose of pain medication. She told the physician that she was looking for a way to escape her physical problems and pains. After a brief hospital stay, Rose was released from inpatient care and agreed to resume psychotherapy.

In her second round of therapy, Rose made some progress in terms of coming to understand the psychological causes of her symptoms. However, Rose's denial of conflict was firmly entrenched, and she never seemed very convinced of the connection between her physical problems and the difficulties in her emotional life. Whatever gains Rose started to make were wiped out when she had a car accident and required a series of minor operations. Rose phoned me several months later, to say that she would not be returning for psychotherapy. She explained that she would not have time, because the physical problems she had sustained in the accident would require many months of intensive medical care and rehabilitation. I was somewhat at a loss for words, but refrained from wondering aloud about whether Rose had finally achieved what she had come to desire for so long—clearly diagnosable medical problems and the attention that would accompany these problems.

SUMMARY

1. Somatoform disorders involve the expression of psychological conflict in physical symptoms that have no medical basis. In conversion disorder, individuals can show motor disturbances, sensory disturbances, symptoms that simulate physical illness, or symptoms that complicate physical illness. People with conversion disorder show a curious lack of concern over their apparent physical problems. Somatization disorder similarly involves the experience of physical symptoms that lack a medical basis. In somatization disorder, however, these symptoms are widespread and involve several bodily systems. Somatoform pain disorder is diagnosed when an individual's only symptom is pain that has no medical basis. Body dysmorphic disorder is an undue concern about the appearance of part of one's body that goes far beyond ordinary self-consciousness. Hypochondriasis is the fear that one has a serious disease, a fear that is unfounded in that the individual has no physical abnormality. People with hypochondriasis misinterpret the normal signs and functions of the body as signs of illness.

2. Somatoform disorders are distinct from psychophysiological disorders, in which there are measurable

physical abnormalities. In malingering, the individual fabricates physical symptoms for the purpose of achieving some kind of gain or benefit, and in factitious disorder, the individual becomes sick because of an inner need to maintain a sick role.

3. Theories about somatoform disorders emphasize the role of conflict, learning, and stress. Important concepts in understanding these disorders are primary and secondary gain, the advantages that people consciously or unconsciously hope to gain from their presumed physical symptoms. These advantages are not generally the cause of the disorder, but they contribute to its maintenance. Most understandings of somatoform disorders regard them as the product of conflict or stress in the individual's life which, instead of being expressed through emotional outlets, takes a physical route of expression. A supportive therapeutic relationship in which the therapist takes care not to reward unduly the individual's somatic symptoms is seen as the most effective method of treatment.

4. Like somatoform disorders, dissociative disorders involve the indirect expression of psychological conflict. In contrast to somatoform disorders, dissociative disorders involve expressing this conflict through the dissociation, or separation, of part of the individual's personality, memory, or both. The symptoms of dissociative disorders tend to be more bizarre and extreme than the symptoms of somatoform disorder.

5. Multiple personality disorder is a dissociative disorder in which one individual develops other personalities, called *alters*. Famous cases of multiple personality disorder, such as Eve and Sybil, illustrate extreme forms of the disorder, in which the alters maintain distinct separations. Current conceptualizations of the disorder are that it may involve less clear-cut boundaries among alters, with communication possible among them, or among them and the main personality, or host. Clinicians and researchers debate the incidence of the disorder and the authenticity of reported cases. However, there is agreement that the disorder is an extreme reaction to abuse in childhood. By escaping into the personalities of the alters, the individual avoids confronting the pain and trauma of the abuse. Treatment for multiple personality disorder focuses on integrating the alters into the host, primarily through hypnosis and supportive psychotherapy.

6. Psychogenic amnesia is a form of memory loss due to psychological processes, particularly a traumatic or stressful life circumstance. In a psychogenic fugue, the individual enters an altered state of consciousness and engages in behaviors that cannot be remembered at a later point. Depersonalization disorder is an extreme form of the more common experience of depersonalization in which an individual experiences the self as unreal or as a machine.

7. Dissociative disorders are understood as extreme reactions to trauma or stress in individuals who have a physiological vulnerability. The most common treatment methods involve hypnotherapy or medications that allow the individual to relax, and in this relaxed state, to gain access to the repressed memories of trauma.

KEY TERMS

Somatoform disorders: a variety of conditions in which psychological conflicts become translated into physical problems or complaints. p. 198

Conversion disorder: a somatoform disorder involving the translation of unacceptable drives or troubling conflicts into physical symptoms. p. 198

Hysterical neurosis: a term used by Freud to describe conversion disorder, implying that it is a reaction to anxiety. p. 198

La belle indifference: lack of concern by the individual with a conversion disorder over what might otherwise be construed as very disturbing physical problems. p. 198

Motor disturbances: abnormal bodily movements ranging from minor tremors to paralysis, which in conversion disorder are psychogenic. p. 199

Sensory disturbances: abnormal sensory processing ranging from abnormalities to loss of functioning in one of the senses; in conversion disorder, these disturbances are psychogenic. p. 199

Symptoms simulating physical illness: symptoms of conversion disorder that mimic the actual symptoms of a physical disorder. p. 199

Symptoms complicating physical illness: physical symptoms that complicate or delay physical recovery from a diagnosed physical disorder; in conversion disorder these symptoms are psychogenic.p. 199

Somatization disorder: a somatoform disorder in which multiple and recurrent bodily symptoms, which lack a physiological basis, are the expression of psychological issues. p. 199

Somatoform pain disorder: a somatoform disorder in which the only symptom is pain that has no physiological basis. p. 200

Hypochondriasis: a somatoform disorder characterized by the misinterpretation of normal bodily functions as signs of serious disease. p. 201

Masked depression: excessive concern with physical health that "masks" or covers an underlying state of dysphoria. p.202

Psychophysiological disorders: a set of physical disorders that are caused by or exacerbated by stress. p. 202

Malingering: the fabrication of physical or psychological symptoms for some ulterior motive. p. 202

Factitious disorder: a disorder in which people feign symptoms or disorders not for the purpose of any particular gain, but because of an inner need to maintain a sick role. p. 202

Munchausen's syndrome: an extreme form of factitious disorder in which the individual goes to great lengths to maintain a sick role. p. 202

Primary gain: the relief from anxiety or responsibility due to the development of physical or psychological symptoms. p. 203

Secondary gain: The sympathy and attention that the sick person receives from other people. p. 203

Multiple personality disorder: a dissociative disorder in which one individual develops more than one self or personality. p. 204

Alters: the alternative personalities that develop in an individual with multiple personality disorder. p. 204

Host: the central personality of the individual with multiple personality disorder. p. 204

Hypnotherapy: a method of therapy in which hypnosis is used for various purposes such as helping a person recall repressed memories. p. 208

Psychogenic amnesia (sometimes called **dissociative amnesia**): an inability to remember important personal details and experiences that is not attributable to brain dysfunction. p. 208

Localized amnesia: inability to remember all events that occurred in a specific time period. p. 209

Selective amnesia: inability to remember some, but not all, events that occurred in a specified time period. p. 209

Generalized amnesia: inability to remember anything from one's past life. p. 209

Continuous amnesia: inability to recall past events from a particular date up to, and including, the present time. p. 209

Fugue (sometimes called **dissociative** or **psychogenic fugue**): a dissociative condition in which a person, confused about personal identity, suddenly and unexpectedly travels to another place, and is unable to recall the past. p. 210

Depersonalization disorder: a dissociative disorder in which the individual experiences recurrent and persistent episodes of depersonalization. p. 210

Case Report: Scott Boyden

When I first read the note on the intake form indicating that Scott Boyden had been ordered by the court to obtain psychotherapy for his sexual molestation of a child, I felt a sense of uneasiness as I prepared to meet him in the intake interview. The words on the form were blunt and startling: "Pedophile. . .raped a 10-year-old boy. Court-ordered treatment." Perhaps I was struck and troubled by the fact that a tragedy of such proportions could be reduced to a few terse phrases. At the same time, I was aware of the difficult issues involved in treating pedophiles, many of whom are resistant to change and regress to their molesting behavior. I knew that I would not be Scott's therapist, because it was clinic policy to assign such cases to Dr. Stephanie Draper, a staff psychologist with expertise in treating sex offenders. My task was to conduct an intake evaluation and psychological assessment to assist Dr. Draper in formulating an appropriate treatment plan for Scott.

In my first meeting with Scott, he was ostensibly uncomfortable. Using words like "humiliated" and "mortified" Scott tried to describe his deep feelings of distress about his uncontrollable urges to seduce young boys. A 46-year-old married man, Scott was the devoted father of two young daughters. He feared he would lose his job as a bank teller following his arrest for child molestation.

When I asked Scott to tell me the details of his sexual episodes, he began to cry, and only after a long delay could he summon the words to tell me what had happened. Scott had often volunteered his time to take disadvantaged youths on overnight camping trips to a state park. While sleeping in the tent one night he became overwhelmed with sexual desire and began to fondle the genitals of one of the boys. Scott covered the boy's mouth to prevent him from screaming, and he mounted the child in an attempt at anal intercourse. In terror the young boy managed to scream, causing an adult in a nearby tent to rush over and witness what was taking place.

When I asked Scott if anything like this had ever happened before, his immediate response was denial, but I sensed that he was not telling me the truth. Gazing at the floor, Scott once again began to weep, and in his weeping I could hear the hint of stories involving other seductions. As he struggled to regain his composure, he proceeded to tell me that on many previous camping trips, he had fondled boys who were sleeping in his tent, but they had always remained asleep and Scott had never attempted intercourse before.

Scott's wife knew nothing of his problem, although he had struggled with these urges since adolescence. Up until a few years ago, he had limited himself to sexual fantasies and masturbation about being sexually intimate with young boys. However, when he placed himself in the situation of being so close to sleeping youngsters, the urges became irresistible.

By the end of the intake hour with Scott I felt drained. I realized that at least one more session would be needed to gather information about Scott's history before proceeding to the psychological testing. The images of the boys who had been exploited were intertwined with the tormented face of this middle-aged man. His problem had been one of longstanding duration, and had become so enmeshed with his psychological and sexual functioning that only an extreme form of intervention could provide any hope of altering this tragic life course. I sensed that Scott's honesty about the nature and duration of his problem was rooted in his desperate wish to escape from the shackles of this nightmarish struggle.

Sarah Tobin, PhD

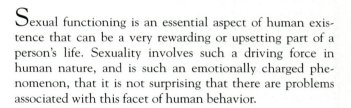

9

SEXUAL DISORDERS

Sexual functioning is an essential aspect of human existence that can be a very rewarding or upsetting part of a person's life. Sexuality involves such a driving force in human nature, and is such an emotionally charged phenomenon, that it is not surprising that there are problems associated with this facet of human behavior.

After reading this chapter, you should be able to:

- Understand the issues involved in defining "abnormal" sexual behavior.
- Define a paraphilia and be familiar with various forms of this disorder, including exhibitionism, fetishism, frotteurism, pedophilia, sexual sadism, sexual masochism, transvestic fetishism, and voyeurism.
- Compare theoretical perspectives regarding paraphilias.
- Define a gender identity disorder and understand the relevant theories and treatment.
- Understand the nature of sexual dysfunctions in terms of the sexual response cycle and become familiar with the variety of disorders in this category, including hypoactive sexual desire disorder, sexual aversion disorder, female sexual arousal disorder, male erectile disorder, orgasmic disorder, premature ejaculation, and sexual pain disorders.
- Contrast theoretical perspectives concerning sexual dysfunctions, including biological and psychological approaches.

WHAT IS ABNORMAL SEXUAL BEHAVIOR?

How would you define abnormal sexual behavior? Look at the following list of sexual activities. On a scale of 1 to 10, with 1 being normal and 10 being abnormal, how would you rate each of these activities?

- Self-stimulation of genitals
- Making love in a place other than a bedroom
- Slapping, biting, pinching, or scratching one's partner
- Tying up or holding down one's partner
- Having heterosexual intercourse with the female on top
- Having anal intercourse
- Reading or looking at pornography
- Putting honey, whipped cream, wine, or other edibles on one's partner
- Having sex in a kneeling position
- Having one partner undress the other
- Wearing sexy bedroom clothing
- Kissing, licking or sucking each other's genitals
- Having intercourse with an anonymous stranger

What criteria did you use in labeling any of these behaviors "abnormal"? For some people, all of these behaviors would be considered abnormal, and for others none would be. In and of themselves, these behaviors are not considered to represent psychological disturbance. For the sake of our discussion, we assume that a sexual behavior is a psychological disorder if (1) it causes harm to other people or (2) it causes distress for the individual. According to the first criterion, sexual molestation of a child is clearly a psychological disorder. According to the second criterion, a distressing aversion to sexuality is a psychological disorder. But what about those cases in which the individual finds a behavior pleasurable that society regards as unacceptable or deviant? As you will see in this chapter, the distinction between normal and abnormal in the sexual domain of behavior is complicated and far from clear.

In evaluating the normality of a given sexual behavior, the context is extremely important, as are customs and mores, which change over time. Many attitudes and behaviors related to sex have changed since the 1970s (Spees, 1987). For example, the kinds of magazines and videos featuring explicit sexual behavior that are commonplace in the 1990s would have been grounds for arrest in most American communities just 20 years ago.

For most of the twentieth century, surprisingly little factual evidence was available about sexual disorders because of such restrictive social attitudes. Much changed in the 1960s and 1970s, partly as a result of the dramatic and candid accounts of human sexual behavior generated by the world-renowned experts on human sexuality, William Masters and Virginia Johnson (1966, 1970), whom you will read about later in the chapter. In part as a result of their pioneering efforts, researchers in the 1970s and 1980s began to apply various theoretical perspectives to understanding human sexual functioning and its variations. We will begin our discussion of sexual disorders by looking at those variations that traditionally have been considered "deviant."

Sexually provocative magazines have become so much a part of American culture that few eyebrows are raised by the fact that they are displayed side-by-side with mainstream publications.

PARAPHILIAS

The term **paraphilia** (*para* meaning deviation and *philia* meaning attraction) literally means a deviation involving the object of a person's sexual attraction. Paraphilias are recurrent, intense sexual urges and sexually arousing fantasies focused on nonhuman objects, the suffering or humiliation of oneself or one's partner, or children or other nonconsenting persons.

The key feature of a paraphilia is psychological dependence on the target of desire such that the individual is unable to feel sexual gratification unless this target is present in some form. This is a long-term condition; a person who has a fleeting whim or daydream about an unusual sexual practice would not be regarded as having a paraphilia. People with paraphilias find themselves recurrently compelled to think about or carry out their unusual behavior and cannot achieve sexual fulfillment in any other way. Even if they do not actually fulfill their urges or fantasies, they are obsessed with these to the point of suffering considerable personal distress. A paraphilia can become so strong and compelling that it can make the individual lose sight of any goals other than the achievement of sexual fulfillment.

To illustrate these points, compare the two examples of Brian, who has a paraphilia, and Charles, who does not. Brian is extremely upset by his preoccupation with the sight and smell of women's leather gloves, is tormented by his intense arousal when he sees women wearing gloves, and can achieve sexual fulfillment only if his partner is wearing gloves. Brian would be considered to have a paraphilia (namely, fetishism). Conversely, Charles finds it sexually stimulating when his girlfriend wears high heels to bed, but it is not necessary for her to wear these in order for him to be stimulated to orgasm. His attraction seems a little "kinky" to him, but not really very unusual. Charles does not have a paraphilic disorder. Such distinctions are important to keep in mind as you read about the paraphilias.

Except for sexual sadism and sexual masochism, almost all reported cases of paraphilia are males. Information about the incidence of paraphilias is limited, primarily because people with these disorders are so ashamed or embarrassed that they rarely seek psychological help. The extent to which paraphilias exist may be inferred indirectly by considering the large commercial market in pornographic magazines, movies, and objects sold in adult book stores and through the mail.

Exhibitionism

In **exhibitionism**, a person has intense sexual urges and arousing fantasies involving the exposure of genitals to a stranger. The sight of shock or fear in the onlooker is arousing to the exhibitionist, who actually does not expect a sexual reaction. Some exhibitionists have the fantasy, however, that the onlooker will become sexually aroused.

Exhibitionists take pleasure in the shock value of their behavior.

Typically, the exhibitionist is a male, and the victim a female (child or adult). Although the exhibitionist's behavior does not ordinarily cause physical pain or involve the use of force on a victim to commit sexual acts, there are exceptions, and the exhibitionist can become violent if the desired responses in the victim are not obtained (Masters et al., 1982). In some cases, the exhibitionist does not experience sexual gratification from exposing himself but instead feels a brief period of exaltation followed shortly by feelings of disgust, shame, and embarrassment (Witzig, 1968).

In trying to understand why people would become so compulsively driven to display their genitals, it is useful to consider early developmental experiences having to do with analogous situations. In some cases of exhibitionism, a man has had a childhood experience in which he was sexually aroused while displaying himself and excited by the distress that his inappropriate behavior caused in other people. Over time, repetition of this behavior becomes reinforcing to such an extent that it becomes like an addiction for the person. In fact, exhibitionists often prefer this form of behavior to sexual intercourse because they have come to associate intense feelings of sexual gratification with the display of their genitals to alarmed strangers (Money, 1984).

Some researchers think that exhibitionistic behavior may have a biological basis resulting, perhaps, from a loss of the higher-order control in the nervous system that usually inhibits the overt expression of sexual behavior. According to this view, derived from the field of sociobiology, men are genetically programmed to engage in sexual display behaviors while trying to attract a woman in much the way that the male peacock spreads its feathers in mating. Some biological anomaly causes exhibitionists to express sexual

Ernie is in jail for the fourth time in the last 2 years for public exposure. As Ernie explained to the court psychologist who interviewed him, he has "flashed" much more often than he has been apprehended. In each case he has chosen as his victim an unsuspecting teenage girl, and he jumps out at her from behind a doorway, a tree, or a car parked at the sidewalk. He has never touched any of these girls, instead fleeing the scene after having exposed himself. On some occasions he masturbates immediately after the exposure, fantasizing that his victim was swept off her feet by his sexual prowess and pleaded for him to make love to her. This time, seeing that his latest victim responded by calling the police to track him down, Ernie felt crushed and humiliated by an overwhelming sense of his own sexual inadequacy.

- Why do you think Ernie chooses teenage girls as his victims?
- Might there be a connection between Ernie's feelings of sexual inadequacy and his engaging in exhibitionistic behaviors?

display behaviors in this aberrant way (Fedora et al., 1986). Perhaps this behavior enhances their feelings of masculinity and power, especially as the shock value of their behavior is so strong and easily observed in the victim.

The most effective treatment of exhibitionists relies on learning principles such as counterconditioning or aversive conditioning. The connection between sexual pleasure and the exhibitionistic behavior must be unlearned, either through creating new associations between sexuality and appropriate stimuli or through causing the person to associate pain and embarrassment instead of pleasure with exhibitionistic behavior. For example, the therapist might use **covert conditioning**, a behavioral method in which the client is instructed by the therapist to imagine a great deal of shame when his acquaintances observe him engaging in his exhibitionist behaviors. In an extreme version of this kind of treatment, the exhibitionist is required to expose himself and masturbate in front of a group of treating professionals, who confront him throughout the session and insist that he describe his experience. The session is repeated several times, and over time the exhibitionistic behavior ceases completely (Wickramasekera, 1976).

Fetishism

A **fetish** is a strong, recurrent sexual attraction to an object. People with the paraphilia of **fetishism** are preoccupied with some object, and they become dependent on this object for achieving sexual gratification, actually preferring it over sexual intimacy with a partner. It is difficult to estimate how common fetishism is, because fetishists are unlikely to seek treatment for their disorder, but one estimate based on psychiatric discharge records over a 20-year period

placed the incidence at less than 1 percent (Chalkley & Powell, 1983).

The most common fetishistic objects are ordinary items of clothing such as underwear, stockings, shoes, and boots. Some fetishes involve very specific attractions, such as a man who is obsessed with brown boots lined with fur. Reports in the psychiatric literature have described cases, all of them males, involving a wide range of fetishes for objects such as rubber items, leather objects, diapers, safety pins, amputated limbs, foreskin, and hair (Wise, 1985). Some fetishists are obsessed with body parts, a variant of fetishism called **partialism** because the person is interested solely in sexual gratification from a specific part of another person's body.

A fetishist becomes sexually excited by fondling or wearing the fetishistic object while masturbating. He may become sexually excited by smelling the object, rubbing against it, or having his sexual partner wear it during sexual encounters. In some cases, the fetishist may not even desire to have intercourse with the partner, preferring instead to masturbate with the fetishistic object. Some fetishists engage in bizarre behavior such as anal insertion of the object, sucking it, rolling in it, burning it, or cutting it into pieces.

In the case of fetishes, it is important to keep in mind the difference between what is considered "normal" sexual behavior and what would be considered deviant. Fantasies and behaviors that occasionally enhance a person's sexual excitement are different from the ritualistic preoccupations seen in true fetishism (Wise, 1985). Fetishism involves a compulsive kind of behavior that seems beyond the control of the individual, and it can be the source of considerable distress.

Fetishism appears to develop in a way similar to exhibitionism in that early life experiences result in a connection between sexual excitation and a fetishistic object. As the person grows older, he becomes conditioned to associate sexual gratification with the object rather than with another person. Presumably, fetishists prefer baby-related objects such as diapers, crib sheets, or rubber diaper pants because of the association from childhood between pleasurable genital feelings and the touching of these objects (Gosselin & Wilson, 1980). To test this learning hypothesis (in experiments that would be regarded as unethical by today's standards), one group of researchers reported that they could condition male subjects to acquire a fetish (Rachman, 1966; Rachman & Hodgson, 1968). In one of these studies, men were shown pictures of nude or scantily dressed women (unconditioned stimulus) paired with pictures of fur-lined boots (conditioned stimulus). A special apparatus was used to measure the men's erectile response. After repeated pairings of the pictures of women and boots (and other footwear), the men became aroused by the pictures of footwear alone (conditioned stimulus). You may be wondering whether the researchers in this study sent the men away to pursue their newly acquired fetishistic interests. The answer is that they did not; extinction was achieved by repeatedly showing the shoes and boots without the pictures of

For several years Tom has been breaking into cars and stealing boots or shoes, and he has come close to being caught on several occasions. Tom takes great pleasure in the excitement he experiences each time he engages in the ritualistic behavior of procuring a shoe or boot and going to a secret place to fondle the shoe and masturbate. In his home, he has a closet filled with dozens of women's shoes, and he chooses from this selection the particular shoe with which he will masturbate. Sometimes he sits in a shoe store and keeps watch for women trying on shoes. After a woman tries on and rejects a particular pair, Tom scoops the pair of shoes from the floor and takes them to the register, explaining to the clerk that the shoes are a gift for his wife. With great eagerness and anticipation, he rushes home to engage once again in his masturbatory ritual.

- If Tom's fetishistic behavior did not involve the act of stealing, do you believe that it should be considered a psychological disorder?
- If Tom were arrested, should he be sent to prison for a crime, or ordered to participate in therapy for a psychological disorder?

women. Over time, the men lost interest in these objects which no longer had sexual associations.

As controversial as this study was, it provides a model for the treatment of fetishes, and researchers have established that extinction and other behavioral methods are effective treatment strategies. One technique is aversion therapy, in which the individual is subjected to punishment such as taking a vomit-inducing drug or being hypnotized in order to feel nauseated while masturbating with the fetishistic object.

Orgasmic reconditioning is another behavioral method geared toward a relearning process (Kilman et al., 1982). In this procedure, developed by Davison (1968) for treating paraphilias, an individual is instructed to arouse himself with a fantasy of the unacceptable object, then masturbate while looking at an appropriate sexual stimulus such as a picture of an adult partner. If his arousal decreases he may return to the fantasy of the unacceptable object, but he should only attain orgasm while focusing on the acceptable stimulus. In time the individual relies less and less on the unacceptable object for sexual excitement, and increasingly on the desired sexual stimulus.

Frotteurism

The term **frotteurism** is derived from the word *frottage*, which means to masturbate by rubbing against another person. A **frotteur** has recurrent, intense sexual urges and sexually arousing fantasies of rubbing against or fondling another person. The target of the frotteur is not a consenting partner, but a stranger. While rubbing against or touching his victim, the frotteur fantasizes that they are involved in a close intimate relationship. As a means of avoiding detection, he has to act quickly and be prepared to run before his victim realizes what is happening.

As you would expect, frotteurs seek out crowded places such as buses or subways where they can pick out an unsuspecting victim. The scenario usually involves the selection of a victim whom the frotteur rubs up against until he ejaculates. Customarily, it is a very brief encounter and the victim is unaware of what has just taken place.

A crowded subway provides an opportunity for the frotteur to become sexually excited by rubbing against other people.

> Bruce, who works as a delivery messenger in a large city, rides the subway all throughout the day. He thrives on the opportunity to ride crowded subways where he becomes sexually stimulated by rubbing up against unsuspecting women. Having developed some cagey techniques, Bruce is often able to take advantage of women without their comprehending what he is doing. As the day proceeds his level of sexual excitation grows, so that by the evening rush hour he targets a particularly attractive woman and only at that point in the day allows himself to reach orgasm.
>
> - If the women who are the targets of Bruce's behavior are unaware of what he is doing, why does his behavior qualify as a paraphilia?
> - What therapeutic techniques might be used to help Bruce replace his paraphilia with more normal sexual behavior?

As with other paraphilias, learning theory provides a useful model for understanding the development of frotteurism. According to this view, at some point in the frotteur's life, this behavior was acquired through a pleasurable, perhaps inadvertent experience, and each repetition of the behavior provides additional reinforcement. Treatment involves an unlearning of these associations through such methods as extinction and covert conditioning.

Pedophilia

You have probably read media accounts of cases involving the sexual abuse of children. These cases involve a very heinous form of paraphilia called **pedophilia**, a term derived from the Latin *pedo* (child), in which an adult's sexual urges are directed toward children. Perpetrators have been known to submit children to grotesque and horrifying forms of victimization, at times kidnapping children and holding them in submissive captivity for months or even years at a time. Although these extreme cases are rare, the prevalence of child sexual abuse is disturbingly high in the United States. Estimates are that as many as 10 to 15 percent of children and adolescents are sexually victimized a least once during their early developmental years, with twice as many girls as boys being victims (Mrazek, 1984). The vast majority of pedophiliacs are male, and approximately 75 percent of them choose girls as their victims; only a very small percentage are indiscriminate in their choice of the gender of their victim (Langevin, 1983). The disturbance is usually so deeply ingrained in the character of pedophiles that they are likely to return to their victimizing behavior, even following periods of incarceration or treatment (Furby et al., 1989).

- ### Characteristics of pedophilia

Although pedophiles all are attracted to children, there is a great deal of variability in their sexual preferences and behavior. Some do not act out their impulses but have disturbing fantasies and inclinations to molest children. Those people who do act on their pedophilic impulses are known to commit such acts as undressing the child, touching the child's genitals, coercing the child to participate in oral-genital activity, or attempting vaginal or anal intercourse.

Researchers have used various systems to distinguish varieties of pedophiles. A particularly useful one (Lanyon, 1986) involves the distinction among **situational molesters**, **preference molesters**, and **child rapists**. Situational molesters have a normal history of sexual development and interests, and as adults are primarily interested in relationships with other adults. However, in certain contexts, such as during a stressful time, they are overcome by a strong impulse to become sexual with a child. Rather than feeling relieved after the incident, though, situational molesters feel distress. For the preference molester, pedophilic behavior is ingrained into his personality and lifestyle, and he has a clear preference for children, especially boys. He will marry only out of convenience to be near children or as a cover for his disorder. The preference molester sees nothing wrong with his behavior, and if anything he feels that society is too critical of what he regards as simply a variant of sexual expression. The child rapist is a violent child abuser whose behavior is an expression of hostile sexual drives.

Growing evidence suggests that sexual victimization in childhood leads to many difficulties later in life. Female survivors of sexual victimization are likely to have a variety of psychological problems including multiple personality disorder (described in Chapter 8), low self-concept, vulnerability to further abuse, sexual dysfunctions, substance abuse, difficulty in trusting others, and depression (Alexander & Lupfer, 1987; Becker et al., 1986; Browne & Finkelhor, 1986).

Public attention about pedophilia heightened during the 1980s, in large part because of the publicity surrounding the most expensive and longest criminal prosecution in U.S. history—the McMartin Preschool trial. In 1984, seven

Peggy McMartin Buckey and her son, Raymond Buckey, were not convicted in the McMartin Preschool molestation trial, but the case helped raise the level of public concern about pedophilia.

people connected with the McMartin Preschool in Manhattan Beach, California, were indicted on charges that as many as 100 children, some as young as 2 years old, might have been sexually molested at the school over a 10-year period. The trial focused public awareness on the reports of child pornography and abuse as month after month, over a 6-year period, stories appeared in the media about the legal proceedings. Ultimately, the case was declared a mistrial. Nevertheless, the proceedings brought to the public's attention the possibility that otherwise trusted adults could lure vulnerable and frightened children to participate in sexual acts.

During the 1980s, attention was also drawn to the problem of child sex rings in which children are victimized by adults seeking power and financial rewards. Reports were published of children being forced or enticed with drugs or alcohol into sexual acts such as mutual masturbation, sodomy, sadism, exhibitionism, degradation, and humiliation (Burgess et al., 1984; Cozolino, 1989).

With pedophilia becoming more widely recognized, it is clear that the problem extends beyond these publicized cases. There are thousands of instances of pedophilia, and most often the molesters are respectable, otherwise law-abiding people who have an existing relationship with the child, such as being a neighbor, coach, teacher, clergy, or family friend (Lanyon, 1986).

■ *Theories and treatment*

In seeking explanations of pedophilia, researchers have debated the role of power versus sexual gratification as a motivation. Nicholas Groth, an influential author in this area, wrote that needs other than sexual drives are the more powerful influences on pedophilic behavior (Groth, 1979). Such motivations include the desire to overpower someone, to overcome loneliness, and to act out aggressive impulses.

Other researchers, notably David Finkelhor, maintain that sexuality is indeed an important component of pedophilia and that the sexual nature of the offense must be considered when attempting to explain its causes. Finkelhor and his associates (Browne & Finkelhor, 1986; Finkelhor & Araji, 1986) have developed a comprehensive model that analyzes the contributions of emotional reactions, sexual arousal, and socialization to the pedophile's behavior.

First, Finkelhor assumes that the pedophile finds it gratifying to have sexual relations with a child because it is emotionally congruent with the pedophile's needs. The pedophile is emotionally immature, has low self-esteem, seeks to dominate others, is narcissistic, and believes that men should be dominant in sexual relationships. Second, the pedophile becomes sexually aroused by children, perhaps because he was victimized as a child and became conditioned to feel aroused by sexual activity between adults and children. It is estimated that 40 percent of pedophiles were physically abused as children, and 56 percent were sexually abused (Barnard et al., 1985). Third, the pedophile experiences emotional blockage; he cannot relate sexually and emotionally to adults. Finally, the pedophile does not re-

Shortly following his marriage, Kirk began developing an inappropriately close relationship with Amy, his 8-year-old stepdaughter. It seemed to start out innocently when he took extra time to give her bubble baths and backrubs. But after only 2 months of living in the same house, Kirk's behavior went over the boundary of common parental physical affection. After his wife left for work early each morning, Kirk invited Amy into his bed on the pretext that she could watch cartoons on the television in his bedroom. Kirk would begin stroking Amy's hair and gradually proceed to more sexually explicit behavior, encouraging her to touch his genitals saying that it would be "good" for her to learn about what "Daddy's" are like. Confused and frightened, Amy did as she was told. Compliance to his demands was reinforced by Kirk's threats that if Amy told anyone about their secret, he would deny everything and she would be severely beaten. This behavior continued for more than 2 years until one day Kirk's wife returned home unexpectedly and was horrified at what she saw.

■ Would Kirk be regarded as a situational or a preference molester?
■ How is Kirk's pedophilic behavior likely to affect Amy when she becomes an adult?

spond to the process of socialization that inhibits this behavior in most adults. Poor impulse control, alcoholism, and personal stress may lead a man to act in these inappropriate ways toward children.

The chances for treatment success are not very high, and at present the most effective intervention available involves the use of behavioral techniques similar to those used to treat fetishists. The point of these procedures is to replace the pedophile's attraction to a child as a sexual target with an appropriate adult object. For example, while masturbating using his customary fantasies of sexual activity with a child, the pedophile is instructed to replace the child image with an adult image as he approaches the point of orgasm. Other behavioral techniques involve principles of aversive conditioning; with the stimulus of a child's picture or image, the pedophile masturbates beyond the point of orgasm such that the experience becomes both physically and emotionally unpleasant. Alternatively, the pedophile might be instructed to talk about his sexual practices to an "audience" who criticize and deride him. The behavioral techniques are intended not only to extinguish the inappropriate behavior and replace it with appropriate sexual behavior, but also to reinforce socially acceptable ways of relating to other adults (Turner, 1989).

When such behavioral treatments are being used, the pedophile's level of arousal may be measured with a penile plethysmograph, an instrument that measures the blood flow in the penis and hence objectively registers the degree of a man's erection. This procedure, called *phallometry*, is an accurate technique for determining pedophilic responses in males (Freund & Blanchard, 1989), and can be used for diagnosis and research purposes or to provide an objective assessment of the effectiveness of treatment.

Biological treatments are also used for treating pedophilia, but they are controversial and are not necessarily effective. Some of these methods have also been tried with rapists and other sex offenders. The most common physiological intervention involves administering the female hormone progesterone to reduce the pedophile's sex drive by effectively lowering his level of testosterone. There are drawbacks to this method, however, because it involves potentially dangerous physical side effects and also lowers the pedophile's ability to respond to appropriate sexual partners. If the drug does have beneficial effects, it might lead the individual to conclude prematurely that he is "cured" so that he needs no further treatment (Freund, 1980). Further, lowered levels of testosterone do not necessarily lower sexual arousal responses to children; a firmly established sexual response pattern may be independent of testosterone levels (Cooper, 1987).

The most radical physiological interventions are those that involve surgery. These procedures would only be considered when the individual has been untreatable through less drastic measures. Castration, or removal of the testes, is performed to eliminate testosterone production and thereby reduce the man's sex drive. Although this procedure would seem to be the most effective because of its irreversibility, it is still possible for the man to be sexually aroused, and to have intercourse or masturbate. Because of its limited effectiveness, this method is rarely employed in the United States. Although it was widely used in the 1960s in European countries for sex offenders, most of these countries have resorted to other alternatives such as the administration of drugs (Marshall et al., 1991).

A second surgical procedure is psychosurgery involving *hypothalamotomy*, or destruction of the ventromedial nucleus of the hypothalamus. This procedure is intended to change the individual's sexual arousal patterns by targeting the source of these patterns in the central nervous system. Hypothalamotomies have been used most frequently in Germany, but with limited effectiveness. Apart from the ethical issues involved in this procedure, there is also the problem that the destruction of brain tissue can have unintended side effects in adversely affecting intellectual and emotional functioning (Marshall et al., 1991). Another significant problem with physiological methods is that even if they do decrease the pedophile's sex drive, they do not eliminate his sexual preference for children (Langevin, 1983).

Once again, keep in mind that these surgical procedures are very rare and represent extreme forms of intervention. But it is also important to consider why these alternatives are even regarded as viable methods of treatment. The men for whom these treatments are recommended are incorrigible individuals who have callously and repeatedly exploited and seriously harmed vulnerable individuals. Even though it is difficult for some people to understand or support the use of such radical interventions in modern society, it is also disturbing to consider the alternatives, which may include life imprisonment as the only means of preventing these men from repeating their offenses against children.

Sexual Masochism and Sexual Sadism

The term **masochism** comes from the name of the nineteenth-century Austrian writer Leopold Baron von Sacher-Masoch (1921). A *masochist* is someone who seeks pleasure from being subjected to pain. The term **sadism** comes from the name of the eighteenth-century French author Marquis de Sade, who wrote extensively about obtaining sexual enjoyment from inflicting cruelty. The psychiatric terms *sadism* and *masochism* were coined by Krafft-Ebing (1840-1903), a German physician who pioneered the scholarly approach to understanding the broad range of human sexual behavior in his book *Psychopathia Sexualis* (1886, 1950).

Sexual masochism is a disorder marked by an attraction to situations in which sexual gratification is achieved by having painful stimulation applied to one's own body either alone or with a partner. Men and women with this disorder achieve sexual satisfaction by such means as binding with cloth or ropes, injuring the skin with pins or knives, or administering electric shocks. Some sexual masochists do not act on their fantasies, but feel recurrent urges, and may feel distressed by the power of these urges.

Sexual sadism is the converse of sexual masochism, in that it involves deriving sexual gratification from activities or urges to harm another person. The sadist is excited by seeing or imagining another's pain. In contrast to sexual masochism, which does not require a partner, sexual sadism clearly does require a partner for the enactment of sadistic fantasies.

People with these disorders may alternate playing sadistic and masochistic roles. In some sexual activities one of the partners acts in a very submissive role and begs to be hurt and humiliated. In other activities, the partners re-

Sadists and masochists seek each other out in a subculture that is characterized by a fascination with the interweaving of pain and sex.

verse the roles such that the same person now acts as the inflictor of pain and dominates the interaction. The term **sadomasochist** is used when referring to people who derive pleasure from both inflicting and receiving pain.

The specialized nature of their sexual activities and their desire to meet other people with similar preferences lead some sadomasochistic individuals to join organizations designed to cater to their needs, such as the Till Eulenspiegel Society in New York City or the Janus Society in San Francisco (Weinberg & Kamel, 1983). In a survey of sadomasochists who were members of such a society, researchers found the most prevalent sadistic sexual interests to be spanking, master-slave relationships, bondage, humiliation, and restraint. Less common were the infliction of pain, whipping, verbal abuse, stringent bondage, and enemas and other toilet-related activities. Interestingly, women and men reported similar levels of interest in most of these behaviors, with somewhat higher percentages of women indicating interest in bondage, wearing erotic lingerie, and verbal abuse (Breslow et al., 1985). In another study (Weinberg et al., 1984), researchers observed the behaviors of sadomasochists in bars, clubs, parties, and bathhouses. They found that sadomasochistic behaviors cover a wide spectrum ranging from emotional and psychological abuse to the infliction of very serious and, at times, life-threatening pain. Some people act out dramatic scenarios, such as being led around on a collar and leash and ordered to act like a submissive puppy who may be spanked for slight misbehaviors.

Activities such as cutting, bondage, pricking, or shocking can be dangerous, and this danger adds to the excitement felt by sadomasochists. Even more extreme, however, is oxygen deprivation by strangling, wearing a mask or plastic bag, or ingesting a nitrate gas that causes asphyxiation. This type of activity is usually accompanied by fantasies of near escapes from death; however, such fantasies sometimes become reality when the limits are pushed too far (Hazelwood et al., 1983).

One avenue to understanding sexual sadism and sexual masochism is to consider the role that punishment and discipline played in the early lives of people with these disorders. Presumably, some unfortunate connection was formed such that sexual excitation came to be associated with the experience of pain or chastisement. The attention they received in the process of being disciplined may have been the only caretaking received from otherwise negligent parents. Even a beating was preferable to being ignored, leading to a later sexual preference for masochism. Another scenario involves the pairing of physical punishment with subsequent parental cuddling and reassurance, leading to the association of pain with love (Gosselin & Wilson, 1980). Sadists, conversely, may be driven by a wish to conquer others the way they were controlled early in life by harsh parental figures. The fact that sadists and masochists may switch roles complicates this analysis, but it is possible that the need for cooperating partners drives their reversal of sexual roles.

For a number of years Ray has insisted that his wife Jeanne submit to his demeaning and abusive sexual behavior. In the early years of their relationship, Ray began to ask Jeanne if she would acquiesce to his sadistic wishes that she be tied to the bed during intercourse and scream as if she were being hurt. As time went on, Ray became consumed with pornography involving the abuse of women, and he insisted that Jeanne act out his fantasies, which became more and more demeaning toward her. Their sexual activities now involve him whipping her while she is handcuffed, and ultimately submitting her to rough intercourse. Despite the hurtful level of pain that Ray directs toward Jeanne, she seems to have no desire to leave Ray, nor does she object to what goes on between them in their sexual encounters.

- Do you think Jeanne has become masochistic and actually prefers this form of sexual encounter to more customary sexual intimacy, or is she a woman who has been victimized by a controlling and frightening man?
- If Ray and Jeanne both consent to this form of sexual activity, why would it be considered a paraphilia?

Most sadists and masochists do not seek professional help. In fact, the vast majority have no interest in changing their behaviors. They come to the attention of professionals when their behavior results in physical injury or when they become distressed over the dissolution of a relationship with a partner. For the small number of people who spontaneously seek help and wish to change their sadistic or masochistic behaviors, group and individual therapy focusing on behavioral principles of conditioning and reinforcement has been found most effective (Marcotte, 1989).

Transvestic Fetishism

A syndrome found only in males is **transvestic fetishism**, in which a man has an uncontrollable craving to wear a woman's clothes (called cross-dressing) as his primary means of achieving sexual gratification. This sexual gratification has a compulsive quality to it such that, like other fetishes, it can consume a tremendous amount of the individual's emotional energy. Cross-dressing is often accompanied by masturbation or fantasies in which the man imagines that he is the object of other men's attraction to him as a woman. When he is not cross-dressed, he looks like a typical man, and he may be sexually involved with a woman. In fact, the definition of this disorder implies that the man sees himself as a man and is heterosexual in orientation (Stoller, 1971).

There is a wide range of transvestic behaviors. Some men put on only a single item of women's clothing such as underwear, often surreptitiously under their masculine clothing. Others have complete wardrobes and while alone

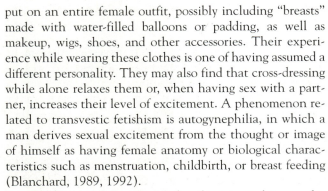

Unlike transsexuals, people with transvestic fetishism do not seek to change their assigned sex; rather, they are driven to cross-dress for sexual gratification.

With no knowledge of her history, it would be difficult to guess that the British model Tula was biologically male at birth.

put on an entire female outfit, possibly including "breasts" made with water-filled balloons or padding, as well as makeup, wigs, shoes, and other accessories. Their experience while wearing these clothes is one of having assumed a different personality. They may also find that cross-dressing while alone relaxes them or, when having sex with a partner, increases their level of excitement. A phenomenon related to transvestic fetishism is autogynephilia, in which a man derives sexual excitement from the thought or image of himself as having female anatomy or biological characteristics such as menstruation, childbirth, or breast feeding (Blanchard, 1989, 1992).

It is important to note that homosexual men who make themselves up as women are not transvestic fetishists because they are generally not dressing this way to gain sexual satisfaction. They do not have the same sense of compulsion that transvestic fetishists have. Rather, cross-dressing for some homosexual men has more to do with their participation in a subculture that they find inviting.

Individuals who develop transvestic fetishism often begin cross-dressing in childhood or adolescence. They may have been forced to wear girl's clothes as a form of humilia-

tion or to fulfill a parental fantasy that they were actually girls. Over time, the cross-dressing behavior seems to take on a life of its own, perhaps pleasurable at first but ultimately compulsive in nature. This behavior is not without conflict, and in fact transvestic fetishists go through phases in which they destroy or give away all feminine clothing, swearing that they will give up this activity (Prince & Bentler, 1972).

Relatively few transvestic fetishists seek professional help, and when they do it as a consequence of another psychological problem such as depression (Croughan et al., 1981). Because of the great reluctance on the part of these men to abandon cross-dressing behavior, not many interventions have been effective.

When these men do become distressed enough to seek help, it is usually attributable to their lack of control over their behavior rather than the cross-dressing itself. Consequently, therapists focus on helping the individual develop a sense of control rather than extinguishing the behavior altogether. When a person is motivated to change, therapists use behavioral methods already described in the treatment of other paraphilias such as a aversive conditioning,

tracted to members of both sexes. Constancy of sexual orientation is typical but not universal; some people change over time and circumstance.

Characteristics of Gender Identity Disorders

A **gender identity disorder** is a discrepancy between an individual's assigned sex and gender identity. People with gender identity disorders experience a strong and persistent identification with the other gender. You may have heard the more commonly used term **transsexualism**, which also refers to this phenomenon in which a person has an inner feeling of belonging to the other sex. Some people with gender identity disorders wish to live as members of the other sex, and act and dress accordingly. Unlike individuals with transvestic fetishism, these people do not derive sexual gratification from cross-dressing.

A girl with gender identity disorder may refuse to acknowledge that she possesses a girl's body and instead insist that she will grow a penis. This rejection of her female sex may express itself in various behaviors, such as standing while she urinates, and refusal to have anything to do with normative feminine behavior or dress. Similarly, a boy with gender identity disorder may disdain the fact that he is a male with a penis. He may have an aversion to wearing pants or playing traditionally masculine games and instead be attracted to more traditionally feminine clothing and toys.

Distress over their assigned sex is usually evident before children with gender identity disorder reach their fourth birthday. Gender identity disorder persists from childhood into adulthood, as the individual struggles with a feeling of ongoing inappropriateness about being male or female along with recurrent fantasy or behavior of cross-dressing.

It is difficult to identify whether a person with gender identity disorder has a homosexual or heterosexual sexual orientation. For example, the transsexual individual whose body is female and whose gender identity is male would reject the label of homosexual just because of an attraction to females. Rather, this person would insist on being called heterosexual because the object of sexual desire is the "other sex." To deal with this issue, clinicians specify the gender of those to whom people with gender identity disorder are attracted: males, females, both, or neither.

Theories and Treatment

The causes of gender identity disorders are not well understood. Although some theorists contend that these disorders are rooted in early experiences and family relationships, most current theory points to the importance of biology in setting the stage for the development of such disorders. For example, it has been demonstrated that some girls who display stereotypically masculine behaviors were exposed to androgen-like hormones during fetal development, and this finding gives credence to the notion that there may be neuroendocrine underpinnings of certain gender behaviors (Ehrhardt & Baker, 1974; Money & Ehrhardt, 1972). It is probable that many individuals who develop gender identity disorders have biological predispositions or vulnerabilities present at birth. Add to this certain psychosocial experiences in early life and the stage is set for the development of confusion and discomfort regarding one's assigned sex (Lothstein, 1983).

Clinicians usually approach therapy with gender disordered clients in ways similar to treating clients who are very dissatisfied with their lives. They are helped to understand the causes of their distress, focusing on possible biological and psychosocial origins. But more importantly, the clinician works in a supportive way to help the individual try to learn how to live with these feelings and experiences (Braunthal, 1981).

A small minority of gender disordered individuals seek sex reassignment surgery; for these people the term "transsexual" is appropriate in that they are crossing over to the other sex, and in this process will confront several complex issues. First, these procedures are available at only a few medical facilities and can cost between $50,000 and $100,000. Second, surgeons who carry out these procedures insist that the individual complete a lengthy course of psychotherapy and a comprehensive psychological assessment prior to being accepted for surgery. Along with this, the individual must have lived as a member of the other sex during the evaluation period; this would include changes in legal

Dale describes himself as a woman living in a man's body. His memories back to the age of 4 are of feeling discomfort with his assigned gender. As a young child, he was often mistaken for a girl because his mannerisms, style of play, and clothes were stereotypically feminine. He was glad he had an ambiguous name, and throughout adolescence he would lead others to believe that he really was a girl. Schoolmates teased him at times, but he was not bothered by this because he took pride in his feminine attributes. Dale's parents became increasingly alarmed, and sent him to a psychologist when he was 15 years old. The psychologist recognized that Dale had a gender identity disorder, and she explained to Dale that he could not pursue sex reassignment surgery until adulthood, because a surgeon would insist on Dale having the maturity and life experience necessary for making such a dramatic decision. At the age of 25, Dale is about to follow through on his wish to have the body of a woman and is going to a Gender Dysphoria clinic at a major medical school.

■ How does Dale's gender identity disorder differ from that of a man who suffers from transvestic fetishism?"
■ What aspects of Dale's case would make him an acceptable candidate for sex reassignment surgery?

name, clothing, and self-presentation. Third, and perhaps most significant, the surgery is very complicated and the physical results are never perfect. Female-to-male transsexuals cannot expect to have a penis that looks or functions normally. For example, a constructed penis may require artificial inflation in order to become erect. Although the male-to-female surgery is less complicated, there are still some risks such as the possibility of the constructed vagina closing up following surgery. Hormonal supplements are needed to facilitate the change and maintain secondary sex characteristics of the new gender. Finally, although surgery changes a person's genitals, it cannot give a person the childbearing capability of the newly acquired gender.

After this brief description of some of the complications sex reassignment surgery entails, you are probably wondering what happens to people who undergo this radical form of treatment. Is this procedure worth the pain, expense, and emotional upheaval involved? In answering this question, it is important to keep in mind that prior to surgery, true transsexuals characteristically describe themselves as extremely unhappy, complaining that they are "trapped" in the body of the wrong gender. They feel that they cannot have a fulfilling life until this mistake is corrected. Their sexual adjustment prior to the surgery is unsatisfactory, and they may feel that their situation can only improve.

Researchers who have studied the effects of sex reassignment surgery have found contradictory outcomes in the post-operative psychological adjustment of transsexuals, with reports varying on the success of the surgery in alleviating distress and problems in sexual functioning. Some researchers report a number of cases of poorer post-surgical adjustment, or at best no change. In a few cases, post-operative transsexuals have sought a reversal of the operation because of their unhappiness (Lindemalm et al., 1986). However, other researchers have found that the majority of these individuals show psychological improvement following the surgery (Abramowitz, 1986; Mate-Kole et al., 1988; Pauly & Edgerton, 1986; Roberto, 1983).

The level of improvement in these peoples' lives depends on a number of factors. Satisfaction is usually greater when the transition is from female-to-male rather than the converse. People who are better adjusted prior to the surgery are more likely to experience a favorable outcome assuming that they are satisfied with the results of surgery and have no trouble being accepted as a person of their newly assumed gender (Kuiper & Cohen-Kettenis, 1988). The strength of the individual's commitment and identification as a member of the other sex prior to surgery is important as well, because this provides the motivation and determination to carry through with the procedures. It is clear that a thorough psychological assessment is needed in order to evaluate whether the individual is appropriate for this surgery (Beatrice, 1985).

SEXUAL DYSFUNCTIONS

The disorders we will discuss in this section are very different from the paraphilias and disorder of gender identity in that they are not considered deviant behaviors, and they involve no victimization of others. The term **sexual dysfunction** refers to an aberration or abnormality in an individual's sexual responsiveness and reactions. Although precise prevalence figures are not known, it is believed that sexual dysfunctions, particularly in milder forms, are relatively common, with estimates of various disorders ranging from 2 percent to 35 percent (Cole, 1985).

Sexual dysfunctions are defined by the individual, often in terms of an intimate relationship and almost invariably in the context of cultural expectations and values about what constitutes normal sexual functioning. There is no one "correct" pattern of sexual activity; what one individual considers dysfunctional may be regarded as healthy and normal by another. An important factor discriminating normal behavior from dysfunctional behavior is whether or not a person feels distressed. This is a critical notion to keep in mind as you read about each of the disorders in this section.

Another feature of sexual dysfunctions that will become evident as you read the clinical descriptions and case histories is that sometimes sexual dysfunctions are signs or symptoms of problems in a person's life that do not directly pertain to sexuality. For example, a person who is very upset about job-related stresses or family problems may develop sexual performance problems. At times, people are not even aware of the connection between the sexual problem and other life stresses. On the other hand, some sexual problems are more clearly connected to problems within a particular

After an initial evaluation, Dale was told that he would need to begin a presurgery evaluation process that would last for at least a year and a half. During this time, he would live publicly as a woman. This would involve dressing as a woman, changing all documentation that referred to him as a male (such as voting records, credit card applications, and driver's license). He would have to enter psychotherapy to evaluate his psychological health and readiness for surgery. Lastly, Dale would have to begin taking hormones that would cause him to develop female secondary sex characteristics. After completing the evaluation process, Dale would be able to enter the next phase of the sex reassignment process in which his physical characteristics would start to be transformed.

- If you were Dale's therapist, what kinds of questions would you ask in an effort to determine whether or not Dale should be accepted for sex reassignment surgery?
- What do you think that Dale should tell other people in his life about his decision to change his sex?

William Masters and Virginia Johnson brought the discussion of human sexual functioning and dysfunctions into the open.

relationship, or to experiences in the person's past in which the foundation of a sexual problem was established.

In our discussion of sexual dysfunctions most of the attention is focused on problems experienced by individuals in the realm of heterosexual functioning. In fact, most of the literature on the topic has been exclusively focused on heterosexuals. Although our discussion refers to disturbances in heterosexual functioning, it is important to realize that homosexuals can also be affected by these disorders.

To understand sexual dysfunctions, it is helpful to gain a perspective on the factors that contribute to healthy sexual functioning. Masters and Johnson (1966, 1970), in their pioneering research on human sexuality, attempted to gain insight into sexual behavior by systematically observing the sexual responses of men and women under controlled laboratory conditions. This research gained wide publicity and served to dispel many myths regarding sexuality. For example, their observational studies of women provided more or less definitive proof that there is no physiological difference between vaginal and clitoral orgasms. This finding vindicated those who had disagreed with Freud's vigorous assertions that they differ. Not only did Masters and Johnson provide a more scientific basis for understanding sexual dysfunctions, but they also took a more humanistic approach to these disorders, treating them, insofar as possible, in the context of the interpersonal relationships in which they often develop.

The work of Masters and Johnson is not without its flaws, however. One criticism is that the laboratory setting they used was too artificial to provide a valid indicator of sexual functioning in naturalistic settings. Other criticisms are based on the selectivity of the sample. Think about whether you would want to volunteer to be a subject in this kind of research. Every aspect of a subject's sexual responses was monitored via electrophysiological recording devices, devices that obviously would be quite intrusive and uncomfortable. Even more to the point, the subjects in this research had to be willing to allow themselves to be observed in the sexual act by a team of male and female researchers. People who are modest about their sexuality would obviously refrain from volunteering for such research. In the case of couples who were treated for sexual dysfunctions, and whose progress was then documented in the second volume in the series, it was clear that these couples were highly motivated to undergo the effort and expense of the therapy process. They also had to be willing to subject themselves to disclosure of highly personal details about their lives and sexual idiosyncrasies. Masters and Johnson have also been criticized for what some regard as a sex bias in some of their diagnostic criteria that tends to pathologize women regarding the phenomenon of orgasmic dysfunction (Wakefield, 1987). Despite these limitations, the work of Masters and Johnson has received widespread recognition and is used as the foundation for understanding the sexual dysfunctions.

Masters and Johnson identified four phases of the sexual response cycle: arousal, plateau, orgasm, and resolution. During the arousal stage, the individual's sexual interest heightens, and the body prepares for sexual intercourse (vaginal lubrication in the female and the penile erection in the male). Sexual excitement continues to build during

Table 9-2 Phases of Human Sexual Response Cycle and Associated Disorders

SEXUAL DESIRE

	Male	Female
Normal response	Interest in sexual activity	Interest in sexual activity
Sexual dysfunctions	Desire disorder, sexual aversion disorder	Desire disorder, sexual aversion disorder

SEXUAL AROUSAL

	Male	Female
Normal response	Penile erection	Lubrication and swelling of vagina
Sexual dysfunctions	Male erectile disorder	Female sexual arousal disorder

ORGASM

	Male	Female
Normal response	Feeling of inevitability of orgasm followed by rhythmic contractions of prostate and urethra and expulsion of semen	Rhythmic contractions of vagina and uterus
Sexual dysfunctions	Inhibited male orgasm, premature ejaculation	Inhibited female orgasm

the plateau phase, and during the orgasm phase the individual experiences muscular contractions in the genital area that are associated with intense sensations of pleasure. The resolution phase is a period of return to a physiologically normal state. People differ in their typical patterns of sexual activity in that some people progress more readily through the phases and others progress at a slower pace. Not every sexual encounter necessarily involves all phases, either; an individual may, for example, become sexually aroused but not have an orgasm.

Sexual dysfunctions are associated with the arousal and orgasm phases, as well as with a person's overall level of sexual desire (see Table 9-2). Some people with sexual dysfunctions have little or no interest in sex, others experience a delay in a particular phase of sexual arousal or do not become aroused at all. Others may become highly aroused, but are unable to experience the sexual release of orgasm. Still other people proceed too rapidly through the phases from arousal to orgasm, and in the process feel that the en-

counter lacks the emotional meaning associated with a more relaxed approach to sexual relations. In some cases, an individual's partner may feel distressed over what feel like unacceptable deviations from a desired pattern of activity. Yet other sexual dysfunctions are the result of the experience of pain rather than pleasure during a sexual encounter.

You may wonder where to draw the line between ordinary day-to-day variations in human sexual responsiveness and the pattern of psychological disorder represented by a sexual dysfunction. Sexual dysfunctions involve persistent and recurrent symptoms. To illustrate this point, consider two examples. Six weeks after the birth of her third child, Heather finds that she cannot regain her former interest in having sexual relations with her husband. At her sister's advice, Heather and her husband take a 5-day vacation during which the baby will be cared for by Heather's sister. Although she still experiences occasional fatigue that dulls her sexual appetite, she has regained her previous interest in sexual activity. Heather does not have a disorder because her symptoms are temporary and nonrecurrent. Treatment would not necessarily be indicated other than the common-sense advice given by her sister.

Contrast Heather's situation with that of Christine, whose desire for sexual relations with her husband has dwindled for the last 5 years until it is now very infrequent. Christine eventually seeks treatment when she realizes that unless things change, her husband will give up on her and find sexual gratification elsewhere. Christine's loss of sexual desire has been persistent and is considered dysfunctional.

Tensions about minor sexual problems can escalate to a point where they become a major cause of distress in a relationship.

It is important to realize that at times other psychological problems are the basis of sexual difficulties. For example, abnormally low sexual desire in someone who is depressed would not be considered grounds for diagnosing a sexual dysfunction but instead would be regarded as part of the depression.

It is also important to keep in mind that sexual dysfunctions can be physically as well as psychologically based, and that often there is an interaction between physical and psychological factors. Many people with sexual dysfunctions, and even some professionals treating them, are quick to conclude that all sexual problems must be emotionally caused; they fail to consider that a sexual problem may be associated with physical disease, medication, or general level of health.

One final point about sexual dysfunctions is that sexual problems can begin fairly innocuously but then develop into into something more serious because of anxiety about the problem. For example, a man who has too much to drink at a party experiences difficulty getting an erection in bed with his partner, and he becomes worried. This concern may impair his performance the next time he is sexually intimate, making it even more difficult the time after that. This process may soon escalate into a dysfunction. Masters and Johnson use the term **spectatoring** to refer to the experience in which the individual feels unduly self-conscious during sexual activity, as if evaluating and monitoring the sexual encounter.

Hypoactive Sexual Desire Disorder

The individual with **hypoactive sexual desire disorder** has an abnormally low level of interest in sexual activity. The individual neither seeks out actual sexual relationships, imagines having them, nor has the wish for a more active sex life. According to Masters et al. (1982), most people with this disorder develop problems as the result of other psychological difficulties such as depression, prior sexual trauma, poor body image or self-esteem, interpersonal hostility, or relationship power struggles. In some cases, the disorder may develop as a means of coping with a preexisting sexual dysfunction. For example, a man who lacks ejaculatory control may lose interest in sex because of embarrassment and anxiety about his problem.

Sexual Aversion Disorder

Sexual aversion disorder is characterized by an active dislike of intercourse or related sexual activities. The individual may be interested in sex and may enjoy sexual fantasies, but is repulsed by the act of genital contact with another person. People with sexual aversion disorder are distressed by the disdain they feel about sexual behavior, and they find themselves feeling lonely and resistant to entering into intimate relationships. If already in a close relationship, they

With the pressures of managing a full-time advertising job and raising 3-year-old twins, Carol says that she has "no time or energy" for sexual relations with her husband Bob. However, her lack of involvement in sexual activity does not simply reflect lack of available opportunity. In the last 6 months, Carol has taken on a number of optional extra assignments that keep her busy at home, well into the late hours of the night. Even though she can afford to buy clothing for her twins, she insists on sewing for them herself, usually on weekend evenings. She also plans elaborate dinner parties for Bob's associates and refuses to hire professional help with the cooking. She recently joined a community theater group, an activity that keeps her out late at night at least once a week. When Carol first began to embark on this frenetic pace of activity, Bob took pride in her "superwoman" skills. After a while, though, he became discouraged by her constant refusals to have sex and her statements that she had lost interest in sex. He began to think that perhaps Carol was taking on all these added responsibilities because she wanted to avoid sexual intimacy. What was especially puzzling to him was that on the rare occasions that they did engage in sexual intercourse, Carol truly seemed responsive and achieved orgasm without any apparent difficulty.

■ To what extent might Carol's hypoactive sexual desire be due to relationship problems?
■ How would you account for the discrepancy between Carol's enjoyment of intercourse and her avoidance of sexual intimacy with Bob?

can encounter discord with their partner because of their disturbed reaction to the prospect of sexual intercourse.

Masters et al. (1982) specify four primary causes of this disorder: (1) severely negative parental sex attitudes, (2) a history of sexual trauma such as rape or incest, (3) a pattern of constant sexual pressuring by a partner in a long-term relationship, and (4) gender identity confusion in men. In the typical case, the individual has sexual activity only once or twice a year, if that often, and this is a source of strain in a long-term monogamous relationship.

Female Sexual Arousal Disorder

Women with **female sexual arousal disorder** experience persistent or recurrent inability to attain or maintain the normal lubrication response of sexual excitement during the arousal phase of sexual activity, or else they find themselves unable to feel sexual excitement or pleasure during sexual activity. The desire for sexual activity remains present, though, and some women with female sexual arousal disorder are able to have orgasms, especially when their clitoris is stimulated intensely, as with a vibrator. It is during normal intercourse that their bodies become unresponsive

Frustrated by unsatisfying attempts at sexual intercourse, partners can feel hurt and rejected.

and they do not experience the normal physiological reaction of vaginal lubrication. Consequently, penetration by a man's penis may cause considerable discomfort, and possibly pain (Kaplan, 1986).

Male Erectile Disorder

Male erectile disorder involves recurrent partial or complete failure to attain or maintain an erection during sexual activity or a persistent lack of a subjective sense of sexual

Brian is 19 years old and has been dating the same woman for more than a year. This is his first serious relationship and the first person with whom he has been sexually intimate. During the past 6 months they have frequently tried to have intercourse, but each time they have become frustrated by Brian's inability to maintain an erection for more than a few minutes. Every time this happens Brian becomes very upset, despite his girlfriend's efforts to reassure him that things will work out better next time. He fears he is "impotent" and will never be able to have a normal sex life.

- To what extent do you think that Brian's erectile dysfunction is caused by anxiety over his sexual performance?
- How do you think Brian might try to resolve this problem?

excitement and pleasure during sexual activity. The term "impotence" was formerly used in referring to this disorder, but this term is now considered objectionable and inappropriate.

Like women who experience female sexual arousal disorder, men with erectile disorder retain their interest in sex. Some men can ejaculate with a flaccid penis, although their level of pleasure is markedly less intense than they would experience with an erection. Because of the emotional distress and embarrassment caused by their erectile difficulty, men with this disorder may avoid sex with a partner altogether. A distinction is made between men with *primary erectile dysfunction*, who have never had an erection, and those with *secondary erectile dysfunction*, who develop problems after some period of normal functioning (Karacan et al., 1978).

Female Orgasmic Disorder

Inability to achieve orgasm, or distressing delay in achievement of orgasm, constitutes the disorder called **female orgasmic disorder** (also called **inhibited female orgasm** or **anorgasmia**). Some women are inorgasmic in all situations, and for others the problem is situational. Perhaps they are able to reach orgasm by means of self-stimulation, or maybe with a partner engaging in sexual behaviors other than intercourse.

For many years women with inhibited female orgasm and female sexual arousal disorder were labeled with the offensive and inappropriate term "frigid." In understanding this disorder, it is important to understand that the female orgasm spans a range of experiences. Kaplan (1986) describes how at one extreme are a small number of women who can achieve orgasm merely by engaging in erotic fantasies, stimulation of the breasts, or kissing. Then there are the approximately 20 percent to 30 percent who are able to reach orgasm through intercourse alone, without direct stimulation of the clitoris. Then there is a group of women who can reach orgasm during intercourse, but only if assisted by manual stimulation of the clitoris. Next are those women who are unable to reach orgasm with a partner, but who are able to stimulate themselves to the point of orgasm. At the far end of the continuum are the approximately 8 percent of women who have never had an orgasm at all. Kaplan points out that the demarcation between "normal" and "pathological" on this continuum is debatable, although most clinicians would regard the last two groups as sexual dysfunctions.

Male Orgasmic Disorder

Male orgasmic disorder, also known as **inhibited male orgasm**, involves a specific difficulty in the orgasm stage. As with its female counterpart, this disorder may be generalized or situational. Men with *generalized orgasmic disorder* find it impossible to reach orgasm in any situation, whereas men with *situational orgasmic disorder* have difficulty in certain situations such as intercourse but not during masturbation. The most common complaint of men with this disorder is that, though fully aroused during intercourse, they find it impossible to reach orgasm with a partner at the point of desired release.

This disorder spans a range from very mild situational delays in ejaculating to total inability to reach orgasm. At the mild end of the spectrum are those men who take an exceptionally long time before they ejaculate. Then there is a group of men who require added stimulation either from a partner or themselves in order to reach orgasm. Next on the continuum are those men who find it possible to reach orgasm only when alone during masturbation. At the far extreme are those men who find it impossible to reach orgasm regardless of the situation. In each of these cases, psychological distress results from the man's concern over the problem or from interpersonal difficulties that emerge in his close relationship.

Premature Ejaculation

The man with **premature ejaculation** reaches orgasm in a sexual encounter long before he wishes to, perhaps even prior to penetration. The man is distressed because when he ejaculates prematurely, it is without an experience of satisfaction. The male with premature ejaculation enjoys sexual intimacy and is attracted to his partner, but as soon as he reaches a certain point of excitement loses control. Usually premature ejaculation occurs with all his partners, because the problem is that he has not learned voluntary control over his ejaculatory reflexes. (Kaplan, 1986). Responses to this problem vary from those men who are mildly distressed by it to those men and their partners who are severely distressed by the problem and are unable to develop other mutually satisfying lovemaking patterns.

Sexual Pain Disorders

Sexual pain disorders, which involve the experience of pain during intercourse, are diagnosed as either *dyspareunia* or

Shirley is a 31-year-old single woman who has attempted to have sex with many different men over the past 10 years. Despite her ability to achieve orgasm through masturbation, she has found herself unable to tolerate penetration during intercourse. In her own mind she feels a sense of readiness, but her vaginal muscles inevitably tighten up and her partner is unable to penetrate. It is clear to Shirley that this problem has its roots in her childhood when she was sexually abused by an older cousin, an event that she realizes was traumatic for her. Although she recognizes that she should seek professional help, Shirley is too embarrassed and has convinced herself that the problem will go away if she can find the right man who will understand her problems.

- Do you agree that Shirley's problems could be cured by finding a sensitive and caring partner?
- What do you think the connection is between Shirley's childhood experiences and her current vaginismus?

vaginismus. **Dyspareunia**, which affects both males and females, involves recurrent or persistent genital pain before, during, or after sexual intercourse. **Vaginismus**, which only affects females, involves recurrent or persistent involuntary spasms of the outer muscles of the vagina. Ordinarily a sexually aroused woman experiences a relaxing of the vaginal muscles, but the woman with vaginismus experiences a closing of the muscles such that penetration is impossible or painful. Many women with vaginismus experience similar muscle spasms in response to any attempt at vaginal penetration, including attempts to insert tampons. In some cases, physicians must use anesthesia in order to perform a pelvic examination (Kaplan, 1986).

Theories and Treatments

Because there are many possible reasons for sexual dysfunctions, the same problem in two different people might have two very different causes. Take the example of inhibited male orgasm. One man may suffer from this problem because of conflicts he has about physical intimacy; another man's problem may be the result of a physical disorder such as diabetes. Researchers now recognize that some sexual disorders result from physical problems, some from psychological problems, and others from an interaction between the two. Thus, psychological factors may come into play with disorders that are physiologically based once the disorder has become established. In the example of the man with diabetes, you can imagine the emotional turmoil that might result from his sexual difficulty. Even knowing that it is physically based may not be particularly reassuring and might in fact cause other psychological problems such as depression. Keeping in mind that most sexual dysfunctions arise from a complicated set of factors and interactions, let's now turn to the major theoretical approaches for understanding these disorders.

- ### Biological perspective

As important as psychological processes are to sexuality, sexuality is very much a physiological function. Consequently, it should come as no surprise that physical problems can cause or aggravate sexual difficulties. Yet, people suffering from sexual problems do not customarily turn first to physiological explanations. In recent years, attention has increasingly been given to the fact that sexual functioning is very sensitive to bodily processes such as illness, medication, diet, and even sleep. For most people, sexuality is far from their minds when they are sick with a cold or the flu. On the other hand, you are also probably aware that some physical experiences can enhance sexuality. For example, a glass of wine makes some people feel more relaxed and open to sexual intimacy. In trying to understand the causes of a person's sexual dysfunction, it is important first to conduct a comprehensive assessment of physical factors.

Various illnesses and diseases have direct connections to sexual problems. Some are quite obvious, such as a urinary infection, but others are not so evident and can involve a wide range of bodily systems such as neurological and cardiovascular disorders, liver or kidney disease, hormonal abnormalities, brain tumors, or hypothalamic-pituitary problems. Specific problems associated with the male and female reproductive organs can also cause sexual dysfunctions. For example, dyspareunia in women can be the result of inadequate vaginal lubrication which might result, in turn, from a glandular disorder. Menstrual abnormalities can contribute to changes in the uterus which make it very sensitive to the contractions that occur during orgasm. A man's dyspareunia might result from some kind of anatomical abnormality such as foreskin tightness. Painful orgasms in men might be attributable to a variety of conditions that can affect the genital region.

These examples are just some of the many physical factors that can contribute to sexual functioning problems. But sexual problems can result from factors other than illnesses and physical abnormalities. It is now known that many chemical substances, both medications and illicit drugs, affect sexual functioning. Earlier, we mentioned the example of alcohol as an enhancer of sexual interest. However, alcohol in excess depresses sexual responsivity. Amphetamines and cocaine produce similar phenomena but as the result of different drug actions. Both of these drugs stimulate dopamine and norepinephrine activity. A man taking large amounts of cocaine may feel sexually aroused due to the stimulating effects of dopamine activity, but experience erectile and orgasm problems as the result of stimulation of norepinephrine activity (Crenshaw & Goldberg, 1989).

Medications used in the treatment of physical and psychological disorders can also interfere with sexual functioning. For example, medications that have vasoconstrictive

Sex therapy often helps couples resolve their sexual problems and focus on the more pleasurable aspects of the relationship.

effects, which are used for treating hypertension, reduce the amount of blood supply to the genitals, causing a man taking these medications to experience erectile difficulties. For some medications, the connection between the drug's effects and sexual dysfunction is not so obvious. Take the example of tricyclic antidepressants, which have been found to interfere with sexual functioning. These drugs depress the activity of the parasympathetic nervous system which is involved in sexual arousal (Crenshaw & Goldberg, 1989). Unfortunately, many physicians fail to consider such side effects, or to warn their patients. They face the dilemma of wanting to use a medication that is therapeutically effective for the patient's medical problem but risking the difficulties that this medication may create for the patient's sex life.

Of all the sexual dysfunctions, treatment of male erectile dysfunction involves the most extreme forms of intervention ranging from the prescription of medication to fairly extensive surgery. Here, we will take an in-depth look at these somatic treatments following a discussion of some of the possible causes of this disorder.

An important change has taken place in scientific understanding of male erectile dysfunction in the last 20 years. In 1970, Masters and Johnson claimed that virtually all (95 percent) men with erectile dysfunction had psychological problems such as anxiety and job stress, boredom with long-term sexual partners, and other relationship difficulties. During the 1970s and 1980s, researchers arrived at very different conclusions as a result of new and more sophisticated assessment devices sensitive to the presence of physiological abnormalities.

Recent research provides estimates that more than half of erectile dysfunction is attributable to physical problems of a vascular, neurological, or hormonal nature. Furthermore, in many cases, physical and psychological difficulties interact in producing this disorder (Melman et al., 1988). Other researchers have pointed out the many ways in which erectile functioning is sensitive to physiological changes. In addition to certain drugs and alcohol, cigarette smoking has also been shown to cause erectile difficulties. In one study, it was demonstrated that men who were smokers had less of a response to pictures of erotic stimuli than did nonsmokers (Gilbert et al., 1986). It is ironic in a way that cigarettes and alcohol are often associated with male virility and potency in advertising, considering that both substances actually inhibit male sexual response. Other physical conditions that can limit male erectile ability include cardiovascular difficulties and neurological disorders (Segraves & Schoenberg, 1985).

The distinction between physical and psychological causes of erectile dysfunction is more than of just academic interest, because treatment hinges upon what is regarded as the primary cause. If a man's erectile problems are due to psychological factors, individual or couples therapy would be recommended. When the cause of erectile dysfunction is found to be physical, one of several somatic interventions may be used. The most invasive treatment is surgical implantation of a penile prosthesis such as a rod or inflatable device. The inflatable device has the advantage of being adjustable, and has a higher post-surgical success rate than the rod (Mohr & Beutler, 1990). Another somatic treatment is an arterial bypass operation, which is intended to correct problems due to vascular disease or blockage of the arteries leading to the penis. Alternatively, an injection of vasodilator medication into the penis may be used in order to induce an erection (Szasz et al., 1987). Specially designed vacuum devices are also occasionally recommended, especially for men whose problems are the result of vascular insufficiency (Nadig et al., 1986).

You can imagine that these treatments for erectile dysfunction, though they may be effective, have great psychological impact on the individual and his sexual partner. Each of these treatments is intrusive in some way and can interfere with spontaneous and comfortable intimacy. Furthermore, when a man is having erectile difficulties, the heightened attention being placed on his performance by both himself and his partner may inadvertently increase his anxiety and interfere with the beneficial effects of the somatic treatment (Mohr & Beutler, 1990).

The other sexual dysfunctions do not have such clear-cut means of resolution. The clinician looks for possible physical causes and treatment routes and in some cases is able to recommend an effective medical intervention. For example, in cases involving side effects from medications, attempts may be made to find substitutes that do not complicate sexual functioning. In cases where a person is suffering from a physical disorder, treatment of this disorder would optimally resolve the sexual dysfunction. However, keep in mind that some medical problems are not easily treated. For example, a neurological impairment that results in sexual dysfunction may be incurable; consequently, the sexual problems will remain. In these instances, therapists may recommend other psychological interventions that are geared toward helping the individual develop alternative forms of sexual expression.

■ *Psychological perspective*

For many people, the whole topic of sexuality is steeped in mystery and misinformation. In evaluating complaints of sexual dysfunction, clinicians first determine whether the individual has a reasonable understanding of the normal range of sexual behavior. For example, a man may complain of premature ejaculation because of his inability to sustain arousal for more than an hour. Or a woman may be frustrated by her inability to have multiple orgasms in a single sexual encounter. For these people, an educative approach that provides them with accurate information may be all that is needed.

Presently, methods for treating sexual dysfunctions rely upon conceptual models that incorporate physical, educative, attitudinal, intrapsychic, and interpersonal factors. Most therapists treating clients with sexual dysfunctions rely at least in part upon the methods developed by Masters and Johnson (1970). These methods typically focus on the couple's sexual behavior patterns and less upon personality and relationship issues. Masters and Johnson conceptualized much of the difficulty involved in sexual dysfunctions as due to spectatoring, and hence their treatment methods are attempts to reduce anxiety over sexual performance. For example, a man who is worried about losing his erection during intercourse may become so obsessed with his performance that he loses touch with the sexual experience itself. This objectification of the experience begins to interfere with his sexual arousal, and consequently, he actually does lose his erection. His worst fears are then confirmed, and he approaches his next sexual encounter with increased anxiety. (Barlow, 1986, 1988; Heimberg & Barlow, 1991).

The treatment approach recommended by Masters and Johnson has several components. A primary objective is to refocus the individual's attention from anxiety over performance to the sensual pleasures of close physical contact with one's partner. Also important is the need for the couple to communicate clearly to each other what their sexual wishes are. To achieve these two goals Masters and Johnson recommend that couples use **sensate focus**. This method of treatment involves having the partners take turns stimulating each other in nonsexual but affectionate ways at first, and then gradually progressing over a period of time toward genital stimulation. During the sensate focus exercise, individuals are instructed to focus on their own sensations rather than the partner's needs. During the early stage of treatment, intercourse is specifically forbidden, a fact that might seem surprising given that this is a method of "sex" therapy. The premise behind this prohibition is that by eliminating the option of a couple having intercourse, neither partner feels pressured to perform, thereby eliminating the potential for failure. Further, the couple can learn to stimulate each other in a variety of new ways that they may never have tried before, and in the process improve their communication about sex.

Originally, Masters and Johnson insisted that couples come to their St. Louis clinic for a 2-week treatment program in which they would be free from distractions and able to concentrate on the development of more satisfying sexual behaviors. Since the 1970s, their techniques have been adapted by numerous clinicians and have been modified so that the couple can practice between sessions in the privacy of their own home and over a longer period of time. More recently, sex therapists have taken a somewhat more moderate stand on the issue of whether intercourse prohibition is absolutely necessary; instead they recommend that a decision regarding this matter be made on the basis of an individualized assessment of each couple (Lipsius, 1987).

An important aspect of sex therapy is the assumption that it take place with a sexual partner. Sometimes a partner is unwilling to participate, and in other instances the person may have a sexual dysfunction but not be in an intimate relationship. Although some therapists have recommended the use of surrogate partners who have sexual relations with the client for treatment purposes, this method is quite controversial (Wolfe, 1978).

Numerous other behavioral methods have evolved from the work of Masters and Johnson. For example, for treating premature ejaculation, the **squeeze technique** and the **stop-start** masturbatory procedures have been recommended. For couples using the squeeze technique, the partner is instructed to stimulate the man's penis during foreplay and squeeze it when he indicates that he is approaching orgasm. This delays the ejaculatory response and in turn shows the man that he may indeed have more control over ejaculation than he had previously thought possible. In the stop-start procedure (Semans, 1956), either the man or his partner stimulates him to sexual excitement, and as he approaches the point of orgasmic inevitability, stimulation is stopped. He regains his composure and stimulation is resumed and stopped repeatedly. With recurrent exercising of this procedure, the man develops greater control over his ejaculatory response.

For women, behavioral techniques have been developed in addition to sensate focus to help treat dysfunctions such as orgasmic disorder and vaginismus. A woman who feels frustrated because of her inability to reach orgasm may be instructed to begin a masturbation program (Heiman & LoPiccolo, 1988) in which she moves through a series of steps beginning with bodily exploration, progressing through masturbatory orgasm, and culminating in sexual intercourse while her partner stimulates her genitals manually or with a vibrator. A woman with vaginismus would be instructed to penetrate her vagina with small prelubricated cylindrical objects (called dilators) while in a relaxed state. Gradually, she would use dilators that are larger in circumference and that ultimately approximate the size of a penis. This approach is based on the theory that as she grows more comfortable with this experience, her muscles will become reconditioned to relax rather than constrict during intercourse.

As you read about these behavioral methods, you may wonder whether more is involved than just learning new sexual responses. Although some sexual dysfunctions can be successfully treated by a circumscribed behavioral intervention, most sexual problems are multifaceted and require an approach that incorporates attention to relational and in-

trapsychic factors. This integrative approach was advocated by Helen Singer Kaplan, another well-known specialist in the treatment of sexual problems (Kaplan, 1974, 1979, 1983). Kaplan recognized that many sexual problems are the result of intrapsychic conflicts and that the successful treatment of the problem necessitates exploration of the conflict and its roots. Inhibited orgasm could be associated with intrapsychic problems such as a strict religious upbringing, strongly suppressed hostility, mixed feelings about one's partner, or unconscious conflicts about sex.

For both men and women, cultural expectations can be translated into sexual difficulties as men feel they must be "masculine" to perform adequately in the sexual relationship and women feel they must accept the "feminine" role of passivity and dependence. Disparities between the individual's personal preferences and these cultural norms can create conflict and thus inhibit the individual's sexual functioning. The challenge for the therapist working with such individuals is to focus treatment both on the source of their conflict and on the unsatisfactory sexual behaviors. Therapists using Kaplan's approach usually limit the exploration of the conflict to the extent needed to resolve the sexual problem while recommending certain sexual exercises and changes in sexual patterns that are geared toward more sexual intimacy.

When treating people with sexual dysfunctions, it is important to determine whether the sexual problem is the reflection of a relationship gone sour (LoPiccolo & Stock, 1986). If the therapist determines that the relationship is really the source of the trouble, then trying to treat the sexual problem while ignoring the difficulties between the partners is fruitless. The therapist would instead focus initially on improving communication between the partners and then move on to a sexual focus only when improved communication has been established.

As sensible and legitimate as the process of sex therapy appears, it does have some problems. For example, imagine yourself sharing very intimate details about your sexuality with a stranger. Most people would find this embarrassing enough to prevent them from seeking professional help. Thus, when considering the effectiveness of sex therapy methods, you must take into account that the samples who have been studied are not representative of the population at large. The literature is filled with astounding claims of success in treating people with sexual dysfunctions, but these claims should be evaluated with considerable caution. Not only are the samples select, but the outcome measures are often poorly defined and the follow-up intervals too short to determine if the treatment had lasting effects (Cole, 1985).

Even if the success rates are not as high as some claim, sex therapy techniques have opened up new treatment opportunities for many people whose difficulties would never have received attention otherwise. Furthermore, the widespread publicity associated with these techniques has made it much easier for people seeking self-help treatments to find resources and suggestions for dealing with their problems on their own.

| Table 9-3 | SEXUAL DISORDERS: A SUMMARY CHART OF PERSPECTIVES |

	BIOLOGICAL	PSYCHOLOGICAL
Paraphilias	Genetic, hormonal, or neuroendocrine abnormalities that predispose individual to develop abnormal "lovemaps". **Treatment:** Administration of hormones. Surgery such as castration or hypothalamotomy in extreme cases for treating pedophilia.	Early experiences in which sexuality becomes associated with aberrant objects or situations. **Treatment:** Behavioral treatments such as counterconditioning, aversive therapy, extinction, orgasmic reconditioning.
Gender Identity Disorders	Neuroendocrine disorder with origins in prenatal development. **Treatment:** Sex reassignment surgery.	Early life psychoscial experiences in a person who is biologically predisposed. **Treatment:** No relevant treatments.
Sexual Dysfunctions	Physiological conditions secondary to illness or drugs. **Treatment:** Treatment of medical problems, cessastion or replacement of drugs. Surgery for erectile dysfunction.	Anxiety over performance. Relationship difficulties. History of past trauma. **Treatment:** Behavioral techniques such as sensate focus, squeeze or stop-start methods, accompanied by non-behavioral treatment such as exploration of relationship difficulties.

SEXUAL DISORDERS: THE PERSPECTIVES REVISITED

The sexual disorders constitute three discrete sets of difficulties involving varying aspects of sexual functioning and behavior. Although there are many unanswered questions concerning their causes, the behavioral perspective appears to hold the most promise as an explanation for how most of these diverse problems are acquired. Similarly, behavioral treatments of sexual disorders can be applied to the paraphilias and sexual dysfunctions. However, the biological perspective has important applications as well, particularly to the gender identity disorders and the treatment of erectile dysfunction. Further, the exploration of personal history and relationship difficulties through insight-oriented and couples therapy seems to be an important adjunct to both the behavioral and biological approaches to treatment.

Interest in understanding and treating sexual disorders has a relatively recent history in the field of abnormal psychology. Even in this short time, though, there have been significant advances made. We can expect these advances to continue as researchers and clinicians gain greater insight into the roles of biology and learning in these fascinating and often troubling conditions.

SUMMARY

1. Sexual behaviors vary so widely from person to person and sexuality can be expressed in such a broad range of ways that it is difficult to define what is "abnormal" in this domain. For definitional purposes, a behavior is regarded as reflecting a sexual disorder if it causes harm to other people or causes the individual to experience distress. There was little scientific information about sexuality until the late 1960s, when Masters and Johnson began their pioneering investigations in the laboratory documenting the physiological changes associated with the human sexual response cycle. These investigations helped pave the way for a more open approach in society toward discussing human sexuality and toward understanding sexual disorders.

2. A paraphilia is a sexual disorder in which the individual has recurrent, intense sexual urges and sexually arousing fantasies focused on nonhuman objects, on

emotional or physical pain, or on children or other nonconsenting persons. The sexual attraction toward these objects becomes so fixed and rigid that the individual is unable to achieve sexual gratification without the particular object or situation, and the need for these objects can be so strong that it becomes an all-consuming passion.

3. In exhibitionism, the sexual urges involve the exposure of one's genitals to strangers. In fetishism, the person is preoccupied with an object upon which the individual comes to depend for sexual gratification, preferring this object over sexual intimacy with a partner. Frotteurism is a disorder in which the individual achieves sexual gratification from rubbing against the body of an unsuspecting victim. Early learning experiences are commonly associated with the acquisition of paraphilias. Researchers have also speculated about the possibility that some paraphilic behaviors may result from a loss of higher-order control in the nervous system that usually inhibits the overt expression of sexual behavior.

4. In pedophilia, an adult (usually a male) develops a preference for sexual activity with children. Three types have been delineated: situational molesters, preference molesters, and child rapists. Many pedophiles were themselves abused sexually as children, and current theories of pedophilia emphasize the factors of learning, stress, faulty socialization, and personality traits. Although pedophiles are very difficult to treat, behavioral interventions appear to have promise, as do cognitive-behavioral methods. Biological interventions, including castration, psychosurgery, and hormonal treatments, have all been tried with varying success. Because of the extreme nature of these interventions and lack of consistent effectiveness, they are not considered treatments of choice.

5. Sexual masochism involves deriving sexual gratification from having pain and humiliation inflicted onto oneself; sexual sadism involves the converse behavior of deriving pleasure from causing others to experience emotional or psychological pain. Often, these two disorders occur together in the same individual, a condition described as sadomasochism. Transvestic fetishism is a form of fetishism in which the individual has an uncontrollable craving to dress in woman's clothing in order to derive sexual gratification. Usually the individual is a heterosexual male who finds it sexually stimulating to dress in women's clothes. In voyeurism, the individual is compelled by sexual urges to observe strangers in an unclothed state or having sexual intercourse.

6. Paraphilias are currently understood as reflecting the effects of a biological predisposition in conjunction with early learning experiences that reinforce the association between sexual pleasure and exposure to the paraphilic object. Treatment, in turn, most often fol-lows a behavioral or cognitive-behavioral model in which the individual learns to associate nonparaphilic objects with sexual gratification.

7. A gender identity disorder involves a discrepancy between the individual's biological or assigned sex and his or her gender identity, or internal feelings of being male or female. An individual who experiences this discrepancy, sometimes referred to as transsexualism, feels intense distress and is inclined to act and dress like a person of the other sex. Theoretical explanations of gender identity disorder emphasize biological vulnerability combined with early learning experiences. Therapy with these individuals is focused on helping the client to understand the nature and possible origins of the disorder and to learn to live with the feelings of discomfort and distress associated with their assigned sex. In extreme cases, the individual may undergo sex reassignment surgery, a complicated and expensive procedure that does not guarantee positive results.

8. Sexual dysfunctions differ from the paraphilias in that they include behaviors that would not be regarded as deviant and do not involve victimization or harm. They are, however, associated with considerable distress for the individuals who experience their symptoms. Sexual dysfunctions are associated with sexual desire as well as the arousal and orgasm phases. The sexual dysfunctions involve more than a minor diminution of interest or lack of sexual responsiveness; they are persistent and recurrent phenomena that cause the individual distress. These dysfunctions may begin as relatively minor aberrations but become more problematic for the individual because of the heightened self-consciousness about sexual performance that such aberrations may cause.

9. In hypoactive sexual desire disorder, the individual has a chronically low level of interest in sexual activity. In sexual aversion disorder, the individual feels repelled by sexual activity to the point of actively avoiding sexual contact with others. In female sexual arousal disorder, a woman's body does not go through the normal physiological changes associated with the arousal phase of the sexual response cycle, and she may experience discomfort during intercourse. Women with this disorder may become unable to become aroused psychologically as well, although they may be able to have orgasms by means other than sexual intercourse. Male erectile disorder is a dysfunction in which the man is unable to attain or maintain an erection during sexual activity. The embarrassment and distress he feels may lead him to avoid having sex with a partner.

10. In female orgasmic disorder, the woman is unable to have an orgasm, either in all situations or while having intercourse. A similar difficulty can afflict men with male orgasmic disorder. Premature ejaculation is

a sexual disorder involving the orgasmic phase in men. Because they ejaculate before they wish to, these men feel distressed about their inability to control their sexual response. Another category of sexual dysfunctions is sexual pain disorders, which include dyspareunia (painful intercourse) and vaginismus (inability to relax the muscles surrounding the vagina).

11. The causes of sexual dysfunctions incorporate a range of physical factors, including illness and disease. A variety of substances, including alcohol, medications, illicit drugs, and even cigarettes can also inhibit an individual's sexual functioning. Anxiety, particularly anxiety over sexual performance (a phenomenon referred to as spectatoring), can add to these physical causes or may serve as a cause of sexual dysfunctions in its own right. Treatment of sexual disorders includes a wide range of physiological interventions, such as penile implants for males with erectile disorders, or behavioral and cognitive-behavioral interventions that focus on reducing the individual's level of anxiety about sexual functioning. Several specific therapies have also been developed for particular disorders, including the squeeze and stop-start techniques for premature ejaculation, and the technique of sensate focus for individuals with a variety of other dysfunctions. In sensate focus, the couple is instructed to proceed gradually from nongenital pleasuring through various stages toward more satisfying sexual intimacy. When treating people with sexual dysfunctions, it is important to determine whether the sexual problem is the reflection of other emotional problems, either in one of the individuals or in the relationship; in such cases, therapy must first focus on the emotional problem.

KEY TERMS

Paraphilia: a sexual deviation involving recurrent, intense sexual urges and sexually arousing fantasies focused on nonhuman objects, on emotional and physical pain or on children, or other nonconsenting persons. p. 221

Exhibitionism: a paraphilia in which a person has intense sexual urges and arousing fantasies involving the exposure of genitals to a stranger. p. 221

Covert conditioning: a behavioral intervention in which a client is instructed by the therapist to imagine a highly negative experience when engaging in an undesirable behavior. p. 222

Fetish: a strong, recurrent sexual attraction to an object, upon which a person is dependent for achieving sexual gratification. p. 222

Fetishism: a paraphilia in which the individual is preoccupied with an object and depends on this object rather than sexual intimacy with a partner for achieving sexual gratification. p. 222

Partialism: a variant of fetishism in which the person is interested solely in sexual gratification from a specific part of another person's body. p. 222

Orgasmic reconditioning: a behavioral intervention geared toward, a relearning process in which the individual associates sexual gratification with appropriate stimuli. p. 223

Frotteurism: a paraphilia in which the individual masturbates by rubbing against an unsuspecting stranger. p. 223

Frotteur: a person with the paraphilia of frotteurism. p. 223

Pedophilia: a paraphilia in which an adult's sexual urges are directed toward children. p. 224

Situational molester: a pedophiliac who has a normal history of sexual development and interests but who will, in certain contexts, be overcome by a strong impulse to become sexual with a child. p. 224

Preference molester: a pedophiliac for whom children are preferred sexual partners. p. 224

Child rapist: a violent child abuser whose behavior is an expression of hostile sexual drives. p. 224

Sexual masochism: a paraphilia marked by an attraction to situations in which sexual gratification is achieved by having painful stimulation applied to one's own body. p. 226

Sexual sadism: a paraphilia in which sexual gratification is derived from activities or urges to harm another person. p 226

Sadomasochist: a person who derives pleasure from both inflicting and receiving pain. p. 227

Transvestic fetishism: a paraphilia in which a man has an uncontrollable craving to dress in women's clothing in order to derive sexual gratification. p. 227

Voyeur: a person with the paraphilia of voyeurism. p. 229

Voyeurism: a paraphilia in which the individual has a compulsion to derive sexual gratification from observing the nudity or sexual activity of others. p. 229

Lovemap: the representation of an individual's sexual fantasies and preferred practices. p. 230

Gender identity: the individual's self-perception as a male or female. p. 230

Assigned sex (or **biological sex):** the sex of the individual that is recorded on the birth certificate. p. 230

Gender role: the behaviors and attitudes a person has that are indicative in one's society of maleness or femaleness. p. 230

Sexual orientation: the degree to which a person is erotically attracted to members of the same or opposite sex. p. 230

Gender identity disorder: a discrepancy between an individual's assigned sex and gender identity, involving a strong and persistent identification with the other gender. p. 231

Transsexualism: a term sometimes used to refer to gender identity disorder, specifically pertaining to individuals choosing to undergo sex reassignment surgery. p. 231

Sexual dysfunction: an aberration or abnormality in an individual's sexual responsiveness and reactions. p. 232

Spectatoring: the experience in which the individual feels unduly self-conscious during sexual activity, as if evaluating and monitoring the sexual encounter. p. 235

Hypoactive sexual desire disorder: a sexual dysfunction in which the individual has an abnormally low level of interest in sexual activity. p. 235

Sexual aversion disorder: a sexual dysfunction characterized by an active dislike of intercourse or related sexual activities. p. 235

Female sexual arousal disorder: a sexual dysfunction characterized by a persistent or recurrent inability to attain or maintain the normal physiological and psychological arousal responses during sexual activity. p. 235

Male erectile disorder: a sexual dysfunction marked by a recurrent, partial, or complete failure to attain or maintain an erection during sexual activity or a persistent lack of a subjective sense of sexual pleasure during sexual activity. p. 236

Female orgasmic disorder (also called **inhibited female orgasm** or **anorgasmia):** a sexual dysfunction in which a woman experiences problems in having an orgasm during sexual activity. p. 236

Male orgasmic disorder (or **inhibited male orgasm):** a sexual dysfunction in which a man experiences problems having an orgasm during sexual activity. p. 237

Premature ejaculation: a sexual dysfunction in which a man

Return to the Case

Scott Boyden

Scott's History

In our second intake session, Scott told me some of the details of his life history, which enabled me to gain a perspective on how an otherwise normal man would have acquired such a serious disorder.

As is so common in the story of adults who abuse children, Scott himself was an abused child. The form of his abuse was primarily physical abuse inflicted upon him by his father, who beat him frequently because he was so "slow to catch on to anything." Scott's mother was a quiet woman who told Scott there was nothing she could do to intervene because Scott's father was so unreasonable. It was true that Scott was not an "A" or even a "B" student in school, mainly because he had difficulty concentrating on his work. Rather than try to help Scott, his father only came down harder on him when his report card failed to live up to expectations. With a smirk on his face, Scott pointed out the irony that his father was a dedicated volunteer in many social organizations, yet was so cruel to Scott.

The cruelty his father directed toward Scott was compounded by the very different approach taken with Scott's two brothers. It seemed to Scott that the other two were spared their father's abuse by virtue of Scott's "taking the rap" for them. If anything, they were inordinately treated to favorable attention. Later in life, the other two sons were to become partners in the father's furniture store, while Scott was left to his own resources to make his way in the world.

Starting from the time Scott was in high school, his main ambition in life, apart from finding a good job after graduation, was to help young boys in trouble and set them onto the "right path." Unfortunately, before he knew what was happening, Scott found himself drawn to sexual intimacy with young boys. Struggling with these impulses and fantasies during late adolescence, Scott had naively hoped that if he got married, his sexual preoccupation with young boys would disappear.

Assessment

It was Dr. Draper's preference to have the results of a comprehensive psychological assessment before planning a treatment, because pedophilia takes various forms and emerges for many different reasons. An understanding of the role of pedophilia in the conscious and unconscious realms of an individual's personality can facilitate a more effective treatment. A standard battery of psychological tests was supplemented by several specialized assessment techniques. Scott was administered the WAIS-R, the MMPI-2, the Rorschach, and the TAT. In addition, Scott was given specialized sexual assessment inventories pertaining to functioning and preferences.

Scott's IQ fell in the average range, with his performance IQ much higher than his verbal IQ, and with a pattern of subscale scores suggesting an inability to temper impulses with more cautious reflection. Scott seems to be oblivious to socially acceptable behaviors, and is more prone to acting on his own desires rather than taking the needs of others into consideration. On the MMPI, Scott responded in the direction of appearing guarded and suspicious, possibly because of concern over how the scores would be used in court proceedings. The responses he produced to the Rorschach indicated impulsivity and a restricted ability to fantasize. Both of these tendencies could lead to his acting upon his immediate needs without considering the consequences of his actions. His TAT stories contained themes of victimization, but there was also denial of interpersonal problems. Most of the TAT stories had unrealistic "happily ever after" endings, suggesting a naive and unfounded optimism.

The sexual assessment inventories confirmed Scott's preference for sex with young boys, almost to the exclusion of any other sexual acts. Sexual intercourse with adults was a behavior that he tolerated to maintain harmony with his wife, but he lacked any interest or desire in such activities. Scott was not interested in sexual intimacy with adult males, and in fact, found the notion of such activities to be repulsive.

Diagnosis

It was clear to me that Scott met the diagnostic criteria for pedophilia in that he has had recurrent intense sexual urges and fantasies involving sexual activity with children which he has acted upon.

Axis I.   Pedophilia, same sex, exclusive type, severe.
Axis II. Deferred.
Axis III. No medical diagnosis
Axis IV. Severity: 1. No acute events or enduring circumstances that could be relevant to the disorder.

Scott Boyden continued

Axis V. Global Assessment of Functioning in the past year: 48. Serious symptoms as well as serious impairment in social functioning due to the disorder

Case Formulation

What would prompt a man, who holds his own daughters so close to his heart, to exploit children in order to satisfy his own cravings? Questions such as this are deeply perplexing. There are no clear answers, but as I reviewed some of the facts about Scott's life experiences, I began to develop a rudimentary understanding of what might account for his developing along this path of deviance.

As a youngster, Scott was subjected to very harsh treatment by his father and a not-so-benign neglect by his mother. Scott could not live up to his father's unrealistic expectations of him, and consequently was labeled a "failure." This label remained with him and eventually resulted in Scott's being left out of the favorable situation his younger brothers were to enjoy in the father's business. Although he managed to achieve a degree of material success and respect in the community, Scott still longed for his father's approval and felt outraged at having been made to feel so worthless. He suppressed these powerful feelings through the very immature and fragile defense of denial. Scott's poor ability to hold his impulses in check led Scott to act on the sexual desires he felt toward the boys he was ostensibly aiming to help. At the same time, Scott's childlike view of himself caused him to identify with these boys so that he did not see them as any different from himself. One remaining piece in the puzzle of Scott's disorder concerned the possibility that he was sexually abused as a child. People with Scott's disorder often have a background of sexual abuse.

Planning a Treatment

In evaluating the context in which Scott's treatment should take place, Dr. Draper and I concluded that outpatient care made sense. In some cases of pedophilia, inpatient care is warranted if there is concern that the individual may continue victimizing children. Scott's mode of exploitation was limited to specific situations, which would obviously have to be avoided from that point forward. Dr. Draper agreed to accept Scott into her treatment program, which consisted of intensive individual and group psychotherapy.

Augmenting Scott's psychotherapy would be his participation in an aversion therapy program aimed toward reducing and eventually eliminating his sexual responsiveness to children.

Outcome of the Case

Scott responded to the aversion therapy offered by the sex offenders program, with minimal sexual arousal to stimuli involving young boys by the end of the 10-week treatment program. In his individual psychotherapy sessions, the story was much more complicated. Initially, Scott was eager to impress Dr. Draper by showing what a "good patient" he was. However, Scott revealed very little about himself, talking mostly in vague, superficial, and clichéd terms. Gradually, Scott began to make more progress in individual psychotherapy. What emerged from his individual sessions was his recollection of having been sexually abused by a neighbor, a "good friend" of his father. Scott felt afraid and guilty and had never told anyone. By talking about this incident with Dr. Draper, Scott was able to gain some insight into his own behavior with young boys as a repetition of the pattern that had been enacted with him in his childhood.

Scott's legal difficulties were not as great as they might have been. In judicial proceedings on the matter, a compromise was reached in which Scott was given a 6-month prison sentence and placed on 5 years probation and required to participate in a sex offenders treatment program. Of course, he was ordered to refrain from participating in any situations with young children in which private interactions might take place.

Scott continued in therapy for that 2-year period, but immediately after terminating with Dr. Draper, Scott moved his family to another state to "start a new life." He felt that the rumors about his child molestation would always haunt him and his family, and relocation was the only hope Scott had of putting those rumors behind him.

reaches orgasm well before he wishes to, perhaps even prior to penetration. p. 237

Dyspareunia: a sexual dysfunction affecting males and females that involves recurrent or persistent genital pain before, during, or after sexual intercourse. p. 238

Vaginismus: a sexual dysfunction that involves recurrent or persistent involuntary spasms of the musculature of the outer part of the vagina. p. 238

Sensate focus: a method of treatment for sexual dysfunctions that involves having the partners take turns stimulating each other in nonsexual but affectionate ways at first, then gradually progressing over a period of time toward genital stimulation. p. 240

Squeeze technique: a method of treatment for premature ejaculation in which the partner is instructed to stimulate the man's penis during foreplay and squeeze it when he indicates that he is approaching orgasm. p. 241

Stop-start procedure: a method of treatment for premature ejaculation in which the man or his partner stimulates him to sexual excitement, and as he approaches the point of orgasmic inevitability, stimulation is stopped. When this procedure is repeated over time, the man can bring his orgasmic response under greater control. p. 241

Case Report: Janice Butterfield

When I returned Janice's phone call to schedule our initial appointment, I heard a faint, slow-paced voice on the other end of the phone. Immediately, the diagnostic hunch of depression flashed through my thoughts. Janice told me that she had been referred to me by her personal physician, Dr. Hampden, who felt that Janice needed professional help in dealing with her depression.

My impressions of Janice on the phone were confirmed upon first meeting her. Sadness was written across her face, and her lethargic bodily movements conveyed the impression that she must be older than her stated age of 35. Thin and pale, with eyes that appeared puffy from crying, Janice described herself as a "hopeless loser" who had no reason for living. Janice explained that she had been overcome by frequent and uncontrollable feelings of sadness. She had been sleeping poorly for weeks, had no interest whatsoever in eating, and had become so lethargic that she could hardly find the energy to walk.

Janice shared with me the fact that not only was she upset about her condition, but that her husband was "reaching the end of his rope." He had been complaining more and more about her neglect of household responsibilities, her insensitivity to their 8-year-old daughter, and her lack of interest in being affectionate and sexually intimate with him. Even Janice seemed distressed by the fact that she was spending most of each day clothed in her bathrobe and slippers, staring aimlessly at the walls.

Apparently Janice had been suffering with these symptoms for about 6 months, but she had refused to follow her husband's urging that she get professional help. She was here now, on the advice of Dr. Hampden, because she had tried to kill herself. Her suicide attempt was certainly more than a gesture, and it seemed to me that she was intent on taking her life. She told me how she had locked herself in the garage with the car running, very much believing that she would die. It was only because her husband had left work early that day that he found her in time.

Interactions with depressed people are usually stressful for therapists, and this stress intensifies when the client has been suicidal. I knew that my work with Janice would be challenging; nevertheless, I was hopeful that I might play some role in relieving her despair.

Sarah Tobin, PhD

10

MOOD DISORDERS

It is a common experience to feel happy and energized at times and sad and apathetic at other times. Everyone experiences periodic mood fluctuations, and thinking about your own variations in how you feel can give you insight into the nature of mood disorders.

The disorders presented in this chapter are far more painful and disruptive than the relatively normal day-to-day variations in mood. In mood disorders that involve elation, a person may lose control, doing wild and bizarre things. In mood disorders that involve serious depression, as in the case of Janice, the pain and hurt may cause a person to become virtually immobilized and suicidal.

After reading this chapter, you should be able to:

- Define the nature of mood disorders, and understand the major categories of these disorders.
- List the characteristics of major depressive episodes, the subtypes of depressive disorders, and gain an appreciation for the variants in the experience of depression.
- Contrast dysthymia with other forms of depression.
- List the characteristics of disorders involving alternations in mood, including bipolar disorder and cyclothymia.
- Describe and contrast the main ideas from the biological, psychodynamic, behavioral, cognitive-behavioral, and interpersonal perspectives regarding mood disorders.
- Summarize the forms of treatment proposed by each of the major theoretical perspectives for mood disorders.

THE NATURE OF MOOD DISORDERS

A mood disorder involves a disturbance in a person's emotional state or mood. People can experience one of two types of mood disorder: *depressive* and *bipolar*. The primary characteristic of depressive disorders is that the individual feels overwhelming **dysphoria**, or sadness. The primary characteristic of bipolar disorders is the experience of mood at the opposite "pole," in the form of **euphoria**, or elation. The term "bipolar" is used because many, although not all, individuals with bipolar disorders experience fluctuations between the "two poles" of sadness and elation.

DEPRESSIVE DISORDERS

Although many people experience depressive symptoms, with estimates ranging from 13 to 20 percent of the population, a far smaller percentage of the population have these symptoms to such a degree that they are diagnosed with a depressive disorder. **Major depression**, which at some time afflicts 1.9 to 3.5 percent of the population, involves acute, but time-limited, episodes of depressive symptoms. The risk of a person's developing any form of major depression at some point in life is about 6 percent in the United States (Regier et al., 1988). In other words, 6 out of every 100 people will develop this disorder at some point in life. **Dysthymia**, which afflicts a similar number of people, involves a less intense, but more long-lasting, experience of depression (Blazer et al., 1988).

Major Depression

Think of a time in your life when something very sad or tragic happened to you and you felt overwhelmed with feelings of unhappiness, loss, or grief. Try to recall what those feelings were like and how despondent you were. As painful as this experience was, you probably could see the connection between the tragic event and your feelings and you probably recovered after a period of time. What if these feelings just hit you without any obvious cause, or what if you could not overcome your sense of loss? If you were to experience unremitting feelings of hopelessness, fatigue, worthlessness, and suicidality, these feelings would be comparable to those of a person suffering from a **major depressive episode**. Such episodes last for at least 2 weeks during which time the individual suffers a variety of symptoms related to a dysphoric mood, such as feeling sad, losing interest or pleasure in ordinary activities, having difficulty concentrating, feeling guilty or worthless, contemplating suicide, and experiencing changes in eating or sleeping habits, energy level, and psychomotor activity. Major depressive episodes vary in their severity, from mild forms that include only a few symptoms to severe forms that involve psychotic features.

■ *Characteristics of major depressive episodes*

The emotional symptoms of a major depressive episode involve a dysphoric mood whose intensity far outweighs the ordinary vicissitudes of everyday life. Physical signs of a major depressive episode are called **somatic**, or bodily, symptoms. Lethargic and listless, the person may experience *psychomotor retardation*, a slowing down of bodily movement. Alternatively, some depressed people show the opposite sign, *psychomotor agitation*, giving their behavior a frenetic quality. Eating disturbances are common, as the individual deviates from usual appetite patterns, either avoiding food or overindulging. People experiencing a depressive episode also show a significant change in their sleeping patterns, either sleeping more than usual or suffering from **insomnia**, an inability to sleep.

People in a major depressive episode also experience cognitive symptoms reflecting an intensely negative self-view expressed in the form of low self-esteem and feelings that they deserve to be punished. They become tyrannized by guilt as they dwell unrelentingly on past mistakes. Such negativity leads many people to look for escape—by thinking about or actually committing suicide.

Anxiety frequently accompanies depression, and although the two disorders are thought of as distinct, there is growing evidence of a sizeable percentage (10 to 13 percent) of the population with symptoms of both anxiety and depression (Blazer et al., 1988; Eaton et al., 1989; Murphy, 1990). People who fall into this mixed anxiety-depression group do not have severe enough symptoms to be diagnosed as having either a depressive or an anxiety disorder; however they are deeply disturbed individuals who are impaired in their everyday lives, finding it difficult to enjoy life and feeling chronically tense or on edge (Clark & Watson, 1991). If placed under stress, they are at risk for developing an anxiety or depressive disorder (Katon & Roy-Byrne, 1991).

In the throes of a depressive episode, this woman probably feels that life is not worth living.

Variants of depression

People who suffer from major depression commonly fall into one of two subclassifications—*melancholic* and *seasonal*. People with **melancholic depression** lose interest in most activities (including ones that normally are enjoyable), have more severe depressive symptoms in the morning (compared to the rest of the day), and suffer loss of appetite or weight. People with **seasonal depression** develop depressive symptoms at about the same time each year, usually for about 2 months, but then they return to normal functioning. As you will see later, observation of people with seasonal depression has led some researchers to propose that their depression is caused by an alteration in biological rhythms linked to seasonal variations in amount of daylight.

Depression has been a major focus of attention in the mental health field for centuries. Since ancient Roman times, those treating depression have attempted to make clear distinctions among various subtypes. The melancholic type, described above, has long been thought of as **endogenous depression**, and is seen as primarily caused by biological factors. In contrast, nonendogenous or **reactive depression** has been thought of as precipitated by stressful events. The symptoms experienced by people with reactive depression tend to be less psychotic and involve fewer bodily reactions and more cognitive symptoms. These individuals are also relatively more responsive to psychotherapy than are people with endogenous depression.

The delineation between endogenous and reactive depression is still being debated, but researchers have found some interesting differences between people with each type in terms of number of stressful life events and cognitive reactions to these events (Robins et al., 1990). People with reactive depression have usually had more stressful life

Men and women in U.S. society are socialized to express emotions in different ways. At the funeral of a child, a mother may feel more freedom to express her grief openly, while the father suppresses his grief.

events in their recent past. Compared to people with endogenous depression, whose disorder may be more biologically determined, individuals with reactive depression are more likely to hold dysfunctional attitudes that cause them to view the world in an unduly negative way (Peselow et al., 1990).

Sex and age differences in depression

Major depression is a relatively common psychological disorder. Out of every 100 people, between 8 and 12 men and between 20 and 26 women will develop this disorder at some point in life (Weissman et al., 1986). As you can see, women are about twice as likely to be diagnosed with major depression as are men, a sex difference that has not been observed in children (Carlson & Cantwell, 1982). The sex difference in adults has been a source of controversy. Some researchers have interpreted this sex difference as reflecting biological differences between men and women (Weissman & Klerman, 1985). Another explanation focuses on the effect of gender role socialization, which encourages women to become more focused on their emotions and therefore more likely to be in touch with their depression. Men, in contrast, are seen as socialized to express their depression in more action-oriented, behavioral ways (Nolen-Hoeksema, 1987). For example, because of gender-based socialization patterns, a woman may react to a disappointment, such as having a close friend move away, by crying, thinking about how much she misses her friend, and talking to her family about how sad she is. By contrast, a man may transform his unhappiness into a fast ride on the highway, a rough game of handball, or increased involvement in his work. Along similar lines, some researchers regard sex differences in the diagnosis of depression as due to differences in help-seeking behavior, with women being more likely to seek professional help.

Jonathan is a 37-year-old construction worker who was brought to the psychiatric facility by his wife. Although Jonathan has been functioning normally for the past several years, he suddenly became severely disturbed and depressed. At the time of admission, Jonathan was agitated, dysphoric, and suicidal, even going so far as purchasing a gun to kill himself. He had lost his appetite and had developed insomnia during the preceding 2 weeks. He had become hypersensitive in his dealings with neighbors, co-workers, and family, insisting that others were being overly critical of him. This was the second such episode in Jonathan's history, the first having occurred 5 years earlier following the loss of his job due a massive layoff in his business.

- What symptoms of major depression are shown in Jonathan's behavior?
- What information would you need in order to determine whether Jonathan's depression is endogenous or reactive in nature?

The symptoms and patterns of depression also tend to vary somewhat according to age. Estimates of the prevalence in children range from 2 percent (Kashani & Simonds, 1979) to 10 percent (McKnew et al., 1983). Although children are less likely to be suicidal, they do experience depressive symptoms similar to those experienced by adults (Kazdin, 1989). The statistics for depression are not what many people might expect. Adults under the age of 40 are three times more likely to have an initial episode of major depression than are those over the age of 40 (Coryell, 1992a). What happens when people grow older? Researchers have found that the experience of depression among people over 65 is common (27 percent), yet surprisingly, only a very small percentage (0.8 percent) suffer from major depression (Blazer, 1987a).

For both young and old, the symptoms of depression may be expressed in a disguised fashion, with children perhaps expressing their distress by misbehaving in school or complaining about physical problems (Carlson & Cantwell, 1980). Elderly persons may express their depressed feelings through concerns about their health (Blazer & Williams, 1980; Gaylord & Zung, 1987).

■ Course of the disorder

In trying to define the course of major depression, researchers have come to realize that depression is a very heterogeneous disorder with many possible courses. Approximately half of those who have only a single episode never have another major depressive episode (Belsher & Costello, 1988). Among those who do suffer from repeated episodes, the future course of the disorder may take one of several forms. About 20 percent of those who are chronically depressed experience recurrent and severe depressive episodes. Chronic depression may be exacerbated by the life disrup-

tions caused by depressive episodes (Cassano et al., 1983). Chronic depression may also be maintained by a ruminative pattern of preoccupation with symptoms (Nolen-Hoeksema, 1991). Yet, there are people who are able to carry on normal lives between their depressive periods though it is likely that they will remain fearful that at any unexpected moment the depression may resurface.

Researchers have identified a number of factors that seem to contribute to patterns of depressive episodes. The longer a person goes without a relapse, the less likely it is that a relapse will occur. People who are predisposed to having recurrent depressions are those who have a history of past depressive episodes, the experience of recent stress, and minimal social support (Belsher & Costello, 1988; Blazer et al., 1992).

The timing and pattern of episodes seem to run consistently in families, in that relatives of people who develop major depression early in adulthood and show recurrent symptoms have a substantial risk of developing major depressive disorders (Bland et al., 1986). This form of inherited depression may, then, represent a more biologically caused and serious form of the disorder.

What seems clear from the literature on depression is that the experience of a single major depressive episode warrants careful attention. Even if someone seems to recover from a depressive episode, that person still is at risk of having another. Consequently, some researchers have recommended that immediate action should be taken when a person who has suffered a previous episode starts to show signs of a recurrence. Most people would probably rather forget about a past period of unhappiness in their lives, or might be inclined to deny the possibility that an episode will recur. Without overreacting, the individual should seek help at the first signs of a return of the depression.

This woman's chronic depression interferes with her ability to concentrate and study for an exam.

Dysthymia

Not all forms of depression involve the severe symptoms that we have discussed. For some people depression involves sadness that is not so deep or intense as a major depressive episode. Keep in mind that we are not talking about normal blue moods that everyone experiences from time to time, but a more serious depression. During the 1980s the term *dysthymia* was used in reference to these less severe forms of depression, but its use was limited to chronic cases in which the depression had lasted for at least 2 years. Recently, however, a trend has developed toward viewing dysthymia as a disorder that may be brief in duration, appearing either in a single episode or recurrent episodes (American Psychiatric Association, 1991).

People with dysthymia suffer from some of the same kinds of symptoms as people with major depressions, such as appetite disturbance, sleep disturbance, low energy or fatigue, low self-esteem, poor concentration, decision-making difficulty, and feelings of hopelessness. However, they do not experience as many symptoms, nor are these symptoms as severe. Some people with dysthymia do have a periodic worsening of their symptoms and may develop major depression. Some dysthymic individuals also have an additional substance abuse disorder because they use drugs or alcohol excessively in misguided attempts to reduce their chronic feelings of depression and hopelessness. Hospitalization is uncommon for these people, except in those cases where the depression leads to a suicide attempt.

> Miriam is a 34-year-old community college professor, who for the past 3 years has had persistent feelings of depressed mood, inferiority, and pessimism. Her appetite is low and she struggles with insomnia. During waking hours she lacks energy and finds it very difficult to do her work. She fails to fulfill many of her responsibilities, and for the past 3 years has received consistently poor teacher evaluations. Getting along with her colleagues has become increasingly difficult, and consequently she spends most of her free time alone in her office, sitting aimlessly behind her desk.
>
> - How do Miriam's symptoms of dysthymia differ from those of a person with major depression?
> - To what extent do Miriam's symptoms lead her to create situations that worsen her depression?

DISORDERS INVOLVING ALTERNATIONS IN MOOD

For some individuals, a mood disorder takes the form of extreme elation or euphoria. There are two forms of mood disorders in which alternations in mood are the primary

Composer Robert Schumann's bipolar disorder was reflected in the dramatic alternating styles of his music—some pieces filled with wild energy, others subdued and melancholic. Despite his success as a composer, he and his musician wife, Clara, suffered greatly because of the torment created by his disorder.

characteristic. **Bipolar disorder** involves an intense and very disruptive experience of heightened mood, called a **manic episode**, possibly alternating with major depressive episodes. **Cyclothymia** involves a less intense vacillation between states of euphoria and dysphoria.

Bipolar Disorder

Think of a time when you felt unusually energetic and happy. You felt "on top of the world." Excitement filled your emotions and intense energy rushed through your body. During such episodes, you may have been able to go without your customary amount of sleep or meals, and you may have had the vigor to accomplish some remarkable task. You were "charged up" or "hyped," and you felt great. You may have maintained this heightened energy level for several days, but then suddenly crashed, perhaps becoming exhausted or even a bit depressed. Experiences such as these, but in an extreme form, constitute the basis for manic episodes.

People with bipolar disorder can become hyperagitated and irritable. They may develop exaggerated views of their own importance, such as directing traffic, unaware of the inappropriateness of their behavior.

People who have manic episodes, even if they have never had a depressive episode, are diagnosed as having *bipolar disorder,* a term that has replaced *manic-depression* in the psychiatric nomenclature. From what you know about the more commonly used term, manic-depression, you would probably expect that a bipolar disturbance would involve mood swings. The term "bipolar" does imply that there are two poles, mania and depression. However, not all people with bipolar disorder shows signs of depression. The assumption underlying the diagnostic term is that at some point in time people with this disorder will become depressed.

Throughout history, a number of well-known people have been reputed to experience wide swings in their moods. Particularly notable are certain musical composers whose music is regarded by some as reflecting alternations in their moods. For example, G. F. Handel, Hector Berlioz, Robert Schumann, and Gustav Mahler described states of mind that would now be considered symptoms of bipolar disorder. Berlioz, who wrote the "Symphonie Fantastique" and other compositions, saw his two moods as passionate and morose. Schumann, a composer of piano and vocal music, published pieces that contrasted two characteristic styles: one impulsive and high-spirited, and the other melancholic and inwardly gazing. Schumann died in an insane asylum from self-starvation at the age of 46. Gustav Mahler, a Viennese composer who actually consulted with Freud for help with his psychological problems, also showed symptoms of bipolar disorder. When he was 19 years old, he wrote to a friend: "Much has happened within me since my last letter; I cannot describe it. Only this: I have become a different person. I don't know whether this new person is better; he certainly is not happy. The fires of a supreme zest for living and the most gnawing desire for death alternate in my heart, sometimes in the course of a single hour."

Who can say how the disorder these musical geniuses struggled with affected their creativity? Did their manic episodes inspire bouts of creative energy? Did their depressed states lead them to periods of inactivity? What about the content of what they wrote? Was their music light, frenetic, and high-spirited when they were in a manic state, and somber when they were depressed? Musicologists are reluctant to draw connections between a composer's productions and the composer's state of mind. No one will ever know exactly how the disorder affected these composers' works, but it is fascinating to think about the possibility (DeAngelis, 1989).

Many people picture a manic individual as one who is outgoing, alert, full of creative energy, witty, and self-confident. To a large extent this is true. However, the experience of a manic episode is far more complicated. The positive feelings involved are unreasonably positive to such an extent that these people become irrational. Their optimism is unwarranted, and their apparent creativity often is nonproductive. There is also a down side to a manic episode: the euphoria may suddenly turn into extreme irritability, even aggressiveness and hostility, especially if other people thwart their unrealistic and grandiose plans. The suggestion that they obtain professional help is greeted with annoyance and anger.

In contrast to major depression, bipolar disorder is relatively rare. Less than one percent of the U.S. population is likely to be diagnosed as having bipolar disorder at some point in life. Bipolar disorder is equally prevalent in males and females, most commonly first appearing in people in their 20s (Robins et al., 1984). However, a sizeable number of cases also arise in those over the age of 50 (Weissman et al., 1986).

Isabel is a 38-year-old realtor who for the past week has shown signs of uncharacteristically outlandish behavior. This behavior began with Isabel's development of an unrealistic plan to create her own real estate "empire." Within 3 days she had put deposits on seven houses, together valued at over $3,000,000 although she had no financial resources to finance even one of them. She went without sleep or food for 3 days, spending most of her time at her computer developing far-fetched financial plans. She made several visits to local banks, where she had been known and respected, and "made a scene" with each loan officer who expressed skepticism about her plan. In one instance she angrily pushed over the banker's desk, yanked his phone from the wall, and screamed at the top of her lungs that the bank was keeping her from earning a multimillion dollar profit. The police were summoned and they brought her to the psychiatric emergency room, from which she was transferred for intensive evaluation and treatment.

- Which of Isabel's behaviors are symptoms of a manic episode?
- How would you distinguish Isabel's manic outburst from a realistic response to frustration over having her plan thwarted?

The experience of a manic episode can be as exhilarating as a ride on a roller coaster. Sometimes people in these states don't want the manic ride to end.

Differences between bipolar disorder and major depression also exist in terms of predisposing factors. Major depression is more common among people in lower socioeconomic classes, and bipolar disorder among those in upper socioeconomic classes. Researchers have also found that people who are married or involved in long-term close relationships are less prone to develop major depression than those who are unattached. However, divorced people seem to be more frequently represented in the population of people with bipolar disorder (Weissman et al., 1986), perhaps because their irritability and tendency to make poor decisions during manic episodes contribute to interpersonal difficulties and strains on a marriage. Another contrast between major depression and bipolar disorder is in the personalities of people with these disorders. People who become depressed often had personalities prior to their illness characterized as insecure, lethargic, introverted, overly sensitive, unassertive, dependent, and obsessional. In contrast, people who develop bipolar disorder had been seen as having normal personalities; when the disorder surfaces, it seems to come out of the blue.

The average duration of a manic episode is 3 months, but with professional treatment a person may improve within 3 weeks. There is considerable variability in frequency of manic episodes and in the extent to which these episodes alternate with depressive episodes. Not everyone fits the stereotypic image of someone who swings back and forth between depression and mania. It is possible for a person to have several bouts of depression before ever becoming manic. Others may have several manic episodes prior to becoming depressed. The interval between episodes also varies, with some people having several episodes in a single year, while others may go for a decade without problems. Some people experience what is called *rapid cycling*, with frequent alternations between manic and depressive episodes (American Psychiatric Association, 1991; Coryell et al. 1992b; Dunner, 1979).

There are some intriguing indications that the mood swings of people with bipolar disorder vary with seasons of the year. Similar to people with depression, people with bipolar disorder are more susceptible to depression during the fall and winter months (Akiskal & Mallya, 1987).

Cyclothymia

Everyone experiences mood changes, but the mood shifts exhibited by people with cyclothymia are unusually dramatic and recurrent, though not as intense as those experienced by people with bipolar disorder. People with cyclothymia experience chronic vacillations in mood ranging from dysphoria to **hypomania**, milder symptoms of mania. This disorder generally begins in a person's 20s. The symptoms may not be apparent at first, but over time, individuals with this disorder notice that their moods fluctuate dramatically. The hypomania is never severe enough to be diagnosed as a manic episode, and the dysphoria is never severe enough to be diagnosed as a depressive episode. Still, their lives are disrupted by the destabilizing effects of this disorder on their sense of well-being.

Larry is a 32-year-old bank cashier who has sought treatment for his mood variations, which date back to the age of 26. For several years, co-workers, family, and friends have repeatedly told him that he is very "moody." He acknowledges that his mood never feels quite stable. He goes through some periods of feeling depressed and lethargic and others of feeling excited and invigorated. During his depressive periods, his confidence, energy, and motivation are very low. During his hypomanic periods, he willingly volunteers to extend his work day and to undertake unrealistic challenges at work. On weekends, he acts in promiscuous and provocative ways, commonly sitting outside his apartment building making seductive comments and gestures to women walking by. Transitions between mood states are often quite abrupt and unpredictable. Within moments a high-spirited exchange with a customer might suddenly turn into a hostile encounter that causes Larry to enter into a depressive period lasting several weeks.

- How do Larry's symptoms of cyclothymia differ from those of Isabel, who has bipolar disorder, and Miriam, who is dysthymic?
- What aspects of Larry's symptoms might contribute to his experiencing distress in his daily life?

THEORIES AND TREATMENTS OF MOOD DISORDERS

As you have seen, mood disorders range from ones that are chronic and debilitating to very brief yet disruptive experiences. Most theories about mood disorders have focused on

Because of the purity of genetic linkage and the care with which they keep marriage and birth records, the Amish have been interesting subjects for genetic researchers.

depression, with relatively little attention given to mania outside the biological perspective. Furthermore, psychological theories of depression tend to focus on reactive forms of depression or dysthymia rather than on the endogenous form of major depression, which is increasingly seen to be biologically determined.

Biological Perspectives

■ *Theory*

From our discussion so far, you are already aware that biology is connected in an important way to mood disorders. On the very simplest level, mood disorders cause physical changes such as disturbances of appetite and sleep patterns. More complex is the effect of biological processes on feelings of depression and elation.

GENETICS   The most compelling evidence supporting a biological model of mood disorders involves the role of genetics. Family studies provide some, although not conclusive, evidence in support of genetic contributions to such disorders. In families where one parent has a mood disorder,

approximately 30 percent of the children are at risk of developing a disorder themselves. When both parents have a mood disorder, between 50 and 75 percent of the children will also develop a mood disorder (Gershon, 1983).

Studies of twins provide further evidence for the role of genetics in determining mood disorder. The concordance rates in **dizygotic twins** (nonidentical or fraternal), who have the same level of genetic relationship as other siblings, vary between 15 and 20 percent. This means that in a fraternal twin pair, if one twin has a mood disorder, the odds are approximately 1 in 5 that the other twin will also have a mood disorder. However, in **monozygotic** (identical) **twins**, who share the same genetic inheritance, the concordance rate more than triples, reaching as high as 67 percent (Torgersen, 1986; Wender et al., 1986).

Further evidence for genetic contributions to mood disorders comes from a very large longitudinal study of people with mood disorders sponsored by the National Institute of Mental Health (Rice et al., 1987). This study, which was carried out in five prestigious psychiatric facilities in the country, provides some of the most thoroughly documented family prevalence data on mood disorders. Of the 955 **probands** (people with symptoms of the disorder—in this case, mood disorder) in the sample, 612 had relatives who were willing to be interviewed as part of the study. This group was comprised of 2225 people, including parents, siblings, children, and spouses. On the basis of family interviews, the researchers were able to estimate the prevalence of mood disorders among these relatives. Of the relatives of probands with major depression, 1 percent showed symptoms of this same disorder. The family prevalence for probands with bipolar disorder was five times higher.

These statistics on the family histories of people with bipolar disorder are consistent with smaller-scale studies and the initial findings of researchers (Egeland et al., 1987) who looked at a small, inbred sect of Old Order Amish people in Lancaster, Pennsylvania. This group of researchers was particularly interested in studying the Amish because of the purity of their genetic lineage. All 15,000 people in this society were descended from 30 couples who originally moved there in the early 1700s. The Amish kept careful genealogical records, so that it was evident how each member of the society was related to every other member. Other important factors such as drug or alcohol use that could confound the results could be ruled out because of the strict religious tenets of this community. By looking at medical records and conducting surveys of the population, the researchers identified 32 families in which at least one family member had bipolar disorder. One large extended family included 3 of these 32 family units identified as having a member with bipolar disorder. Of the 81 members in this extended family, 5 had major depression and 14 were diagnosed as having bipolar disorder. The researchers then went on to look for the precise nature of the genetic link and found evidence for an abnormality on chromosome 11. These findings were initially regarded as exciting new clues in the search for genetic contributions to mood disorders.

The excitement over these findings was, however, short-lived. In reanalyzing the data, the researchers found it necessary to retract the claim that they had discovered the gene responsible for bipolar disorder (Kelsoe et al., 1989). Some of this reanalysis included the addition of new members to the study, changing the statistical evidence slightly, but not significantly. More damaging to the original results was information that the researchers could not have figured into the calculations—namely, the change in illness status of 2 of the family members. One of these members developed bipolar disorder, but the other suffered a major depressive disorder. This evidence was enough to lower the statistics in favor of a defect on chromosome 11 to the level of no greater than chance. Subsequent research has cast further doubt on the possibility of a defect on this chromosome as a cause of bipolar disorder (Nöthen et al., 1992).

What would have made the finding regarding the Amish so important is the fact that chromosome 11 is located on the gene involved in the production of dopamine, a neurotransmitter thought to be involved in mood disorders. As in research on other disorders thought to have genetic causes, which you will read about in later chapters, the research on the Amish demonstrates that no easy answers exist to complex questions regarding gene–environment interactions in the causation of psychological disorders.

Adoption studies have also been used to study the effects of genetics versus environment on mood disorders. For example, Mendlewicz and Rainer (1977) found that 31 percent of individuals who were adopted and later developed mood disorders had biological parents with this type of disorder, whereas only 2 percent of the adoptees who did not have mood disorders had a biological parent with a mood disorder. Researchers in a later study (Wender et al., 1986) looked at the biological and adoptive relatives of adoptees, including not only parents but siblings and half-siblings. Adoptees with major depression had an 8-times-greater likelihood of having relatives with a history of depression than were the matched controls, adoptees who had no psychiatric diagnosis. Another impressive statistic from this study was the finding that the suicide rate was 15 times higher among the biological relatives of adoptees with a mood disorder.

Taking these findings together, you can see why researchers have become so interested in evaluating the role of genetics in determining whether people will develop a mood disorder. However, it is important to point out that genetics is not the whole story. After all, some relatives of mood-disordered individuals, including identical twins, do not develop mood disorders. This tells us that life experiences must also play a role in determining whether a person develops a mood disorder. Genetic inheritance is undoubtedly an important factor in the cause of mood disorders, but it is by no means the exclusive cause.

BIOCHEMICAL   The mechanisms that genetically predispose high-risk people to become depressed or have manic episodes are still unknown. At present, the most widely held biological theories focus on some altered features of neurotransmitter functioning as the cause of mood disorders. Because scientists cannot directly observe the actions of neurotransmitters in the human brain, research in this area must involve studies of animals and observations of people who take certain types of drugs.

The earliest theory along these lines was the **catecholamine hypothesis** (Schildkraut, 1965), which asserts that a relative shortage of norepinephrine (a catecholamine) causes depression, and an overabundance of norepinephrine causes mania. Although this hypothesis has been discredited, it is important to understand how it was developed and what it proposed. The catecholamine hypothesis emerged from several lines of observation of people's reactions to medications that affect this neurotransmitter's functioning. For example, clinical evidence suggested that people who take certain antihypertensive medications become depressed (Petrie et al., 1982), presumably because the drug's action depletes the levels of norepinephrine and other catecholamines. In contrast, certain antidepressant medications work by making catecholamines more available to postsynaptic neurons.

To understand the processes described by the catecholamine hypothesis, it is necessary to review a few basic facts about what happens at the synapse. The main elements involved in the synapse are the *presynaptic neuron* and the *postsynaptic neuron*. Neurotransmitters are released from the presynaptic neuron into the synaptic cleft. These chemical substances disperse in this area and migrate to the postsynaptic neuron, where they interact with receptors on that receiving neuron's surface. This interaction with the receptors causes changes in the postsynaptic neuron (either an increased or decreased likelihood of triggering a response). The catecholamine hypothesis proposed that in people with depression, less of the catecholamine neurotransmitters are available to the postsynaptic neurons. The catecholamines were thought to be either broken down into inert substances or absorbed back into the presynaptic neuron before being taken up by the postsynaptic neuron. Depression would be the expression of a deficiency of these catecholamines, most notably norepinephrine, which is an excitatory neurotransmitter that activates behavior.

An alternative to the catecholamine hypothesis is the *indolamine hypothesis* (Glassman, 1969). You might guess from the similarity of these terms that these substances are similar in structure, and indeed they are both considered to be biogenic *amines*, chemical substances whose molecular structure includes a particular amino group. The *monoamines* comprise one group of biogenic amines, and include catecholamines (norepinephrine and dopamine) and indolamines (such as serotonin). According to the **indolamine hypothesis**, a deficiency of serotonin contributes to the behavioral symptoms of depression. The processes causing a deficiency of serotonin are thought to be similar to those causing norepinephrine deficits.

These monoamine deficit hypotheses provided an important breakthrough in the biological understanding of

The dim days of winter cause people with seasonal depression to be particularly prone to dysphoric moods.

mood disorders, however, they are now considered far too simplistic. One problem with such theories is the fact that antidepressant medications do not have their effects immediately, as would be the case if a rise in the catecholamine level were enough to alleviate depression. These medications typically take at least 2 weeks to become therapeutically effective, yet we know that they change neurochemical transmission in less than a day. Secondly, the observation that antihypertensive medications cause depression by altering catecholamine activity has been called into question by a study of medical claims among a sample of over 4,000 adults in which no relationship was found between the use of these medications and the clinical diagnosis of depression (Bright & Everitt, 1992).

More recent biochemical theories of depression focus on alterations in the postsynaptic neurons, specifically the receptors on these neurons that respond to the presence of neurotransmitters in the synapse (Heninger & Charney, 1987; Reisine, 1981). One theory proposes that depressed people are hypersensitive to norepinephrine levels, and that biochemical changes in their brain have decreased this abnormal sensitivity through a process called **down-regulation**. The ameliorative effects of antidepressant drugs are not that they simply increase the availability of norepinephrine, but that they allow the beta receptors to become more responsive to the neurotransmitter. At the same time, antidepressants may also work by stimulating, or *up-regulating*, alpha noradrenergic receptors. Changes in the alpha receptors may play an important role in triggering an adaptive response in the beta receptors.

Other biological theories posit neurophysiological and neuroendocrine abnormalities as causes of depression (Thase et al., 1985). In attempting to discover the role of neurophysiological abnormalities in causing mood disorders, researchers have focused on the sleep disturbances known to afflict people with mood disorders. Electroencephalograms (EEGs) have shown that depressed individuals experience abnormal lateralization of brain activity, an altered distribution of REM sleep, and an abbreviated period of time between falling asleep and the onset of the first REM period (Thase et al., 1992b).

In addition to disturbance in sleep activity, people with mood disorders show evidence of different daily rhythms from that of most people. Many depressed people find themselves waking up much earlier than they wish to, but are unable to get back to sleep despite fatigue. Seasonal variations are another factor, with depression being more commonly reported in the fall and winter, and the rate of mania being highest in the spring.

Various research projects on mood disorders have focused on the role of abnormalities in daily rhythms and on pathological desynchronization of bodily rhythms. For example, it has been thought that daily bodily rhythms might be disorganized in severely depressed individuals, possibly because of these people's increased sensitivity to changes in sunlight. In fact, some people with bipolar disorders show an exaggerated response to bright light in the production of the hormone *melatonin*. Melatonin is secreted by a section of the brain called the *pineal gland*, which receives input from the retina. Some interesting research by Lewy and his associates has shown that providing more light to depressed people actually relieves some of their depression (Lewy, 1987; Lewy et al., 1987). Furthermore, these researchers pinpointed a possible biological marker for bipolar disorder by studying the responses of people with this disorder to interruptions of darkness during the night. People in this study were exposed to fluorescent light for one hour in the middle of the night while their level of melatonin was monitored. Those individuals with bipolar disorder showed a dramatic suppression of their melatonin levels after the light exposure; most of the normal controls had no diminution of melatonin production (Lewy et al., 1985). It is fascinating to think that such a simple indicator could someday be used as a biological test of vulnerability to developing this disorder.

Neuroendocrine research has pointed out an important relationship between hormonal activity and the experience of depression. Researchers have focused on the body's production of **cortisol**, a hormone involved in the mobilization of the body's resources in times of stress. Ordinarily, people given a steroid called *dexamethasone* suppress their production of cortisol for at least one day after this drug is administered. The measurement of their cortisol levels during this period is called, naturally enough, the **dexamethasone suppression test** or **DST**. When people with endogenous depression take the DST, they do not show the suppression response (Carroll, 1982). These results provide further support for the role of biological factors in mood disorders, particularly endogenous depression. In addition, the fact that depressed people show this abnormal response may provide the basis someday for a precise biological method to assess mood disorders and a person's predisposition to developing these disorders. Unfortunately, at present the test is imprecise, because people with other disorders also show an abnormal response to the DST (Thase et al., 1985).

Although the role of biology in mood disorders is still incompletely understood, multiple lines of research seem to converge in pointing to some biological contribution to the causes and symptoms of mood disorders. Particularly compelling are the research findings in the area of genetics. As we discuss other theoretical contributions to the understanding of mood disorders, keep in mind the interaction among biological, psychological, and social factors. Regardless of what precipitates a depression, depressed people experience biological changes. Any intervention must address the individual's physical as well as psychological state.

■ *Treatments*

In light of the strong support for biological influences on mood disorders, it should come as no surprise that somatic treatments are often used in treating people with these disorders. Antidepressant medication is the most common form of somatic treatment for people who are depressed, and lithium carbonate (lithium) is the most widely used medication for people who have bipolar disorder. The two major forms of antidepressants are tricyclic antidepressants and monoamine oxidase inhibitors (MAOIs).

Tricyclic antidepressants derive their name from the fact that they have a 3-ring chemical structure. These medications, with market names such as Elavil and Tofranil, are effective in alleviating depression particularly in those people who suffer from some of the more common biological symptoms such as disturbed appetite and sleep. Although the exact process by which tricyclic antidepressants work still remains unclear, it is known that these medications alter the balance of biogenic amines by increasing their ac-

tivity (McNeal & Cimbolic, 1986). This increase is the outcome of medication causing more excitatory neurotransmitters to be available at the synapse. The medication blocks the premature reuptake of amines back into the presynaptic neuron before they can have their excitatory effects on the postsynaptic neuron. The antidepressant effect of MAOIs is thought to be due to their inhibiting action on the enzyme *monoamine oxidase*, which converts the biogenic amines such as norepinephrine and serotonin into inert substances so that they cannot excite the postsynaptic neuron. Thus, both forms of medication are thought to have their effect by changing the chemical environment in the synaptic cleft.

Antidepressant medications take time to work; a period of 2 to 6 weeks may be needed before the client's symptoms begin to lift. Once the depression has subsided, the client is customarily instructed to remain on the medication for 4 or 5 additional months, and those with a history of recurrent, severe depressive episodes may need to stay on tricyclics for a longer time. However, long-term use of these medications carries certain risks because of possible side effects involving the cardiovascular system. Further, even though tricyclics are the most effective pharmacological intervention for treating depression, they are not completely effective for everyone. In other cases, different somatic interventions may be necessary (Schatzberg, 1992).

MAOIs are also effective in treating depression, and are particularly therapeutic in treating individuals who are suffering from anxiety, particularly in the form of panic attacks. MAOIs are as effective in treating depression as tricyclics, but they have many more side effects, particularly if the client eats certain foods such as herring, cheese, beer, or chocolate, or uses such drugs as cocaine, amphetamines, or allergy medications. The combination of a MAOI and any of these substances can result in a hypertensive crisis, with symptoms including a dangerous rise in blood pressure, severe headache, chest pain, fever, and vomiting. However, MAOIs may be the only recourse for treating people either with bipolar disorder during depressive episodes (Thase et al., 1992a), or those with major depression who do not respond to tricyclics (Thase et al., 1991).

The traditional treatment for the manic symptoms of bipolar disorder is lithium carbonate, referred to as lithium. Regarded as the miracle drug of the 1970s, lithium helped thousands of people who previously could find no relief from the disruptive symptoms of mania. Lithium is a salt, found in small amounts in drinking water. When used medically, this natural substance replaces sodium in the body. The psychopharmacological effect of this medication is to calm the manic individual by decreasing the catecholamine levels in the nervous system.

People who have frequent manic episodes, such as two or more a year, are advised to remain on lithium continuously as a preventative measure. The drawback to such a recommendation is that even though lithium is a natural substance in the body, it can have dangerous side effects, such as mild central nervous system disturbances,

Prozac: Wonder Drug of the 90s?

During each of the recent decades, one or another medication has become used on a widespread basis and has been hailed as a revolutionary medication that would change psychiatric treatment forever. For example, in the 1960s, Thorazine was heralded as the medication that would end institutionalization of people with psychotic disorders. In the 1970s, Lithium was regarded as the ultimate treatment for mania. Valium also became widely used at this time for helping people fend off symptoms of anxiety. While all of these drugs have had their share of success in benefitting psychologically distressed people, there have also been some problems associated with their use. It soon became evident that Thorazine was not a cure for schizophrenia, but just a treatment for some of the symptoms of this disorder. Lithium is effective when used in its recommended dose, but manic individuals are typically reluctant to take a medication that lowers their elevated moods. The abuse of Valium, as you prob-

ably know, became a national scandal; its indiscriminate use led to millions of people becoming dependent on this drug to resolve everyday life stresses. Furthermore, each of these medications, even when used properly, has side effects, some of them very serious which were not understood completely when the drugs were first introduced.

Prozac (fluoxetine) is the latest psychotropic medication to make a big splash. This antidepressant, which was introduced in the late 1980s, has accounted for nearly half a billion dollars in annual sales and is presently being prescribed more than any other antidepressant medication. Part of the reason for the large sales figure is its high price relative to the other antidepressants; because of its effectiveness and relatively minor side effects, people have been willing to pay this price. In addition to being therapeutically effective for people suffering from depression, Prozac has also worked in alleviating obsessive-compulsive symptoms.

You may be wondering what is in this miracle drug. Actually, it is not that different in its actions from the tricyclic antidepressants. Prozac is unique, however, in that it targets its effects on only one of the catecholamines—serotonin—rather than the broader range of neurotransmitters acted upon by the tricyclics. Like these other medications, Prozac usually takes some weeks for its effects to be felt.

Similar to the miracle drugs of previous decades, there is a risk associated with Prozac's precipitous rise in use. There have been some anecdotal reports of troubling side effects including suicidality and dangerous impulsivity (Steiner, 1991; Teicher et al., 1990). However, in a large-scale controlled study of more than 1,000 people with major depressive disorder, researchers concluded that there was no basis for alarm regarding the prescription of Prozac (Fava & Rosenbaum, 1991).

gastrointestinal upsets, or more serious cardiac effects. Because of these side effects, many people who experience manic episodes are reluctant or even unwilling to take lithium on a continuous basis. Furthermore, because lithium interferes with the "highs" associated with bipolar disorder, manic individuals may be reluctant to take the medication, craving the good feelings that accompany escalation into the manic episode. By the time a full-blown episode develops, these individuals may have become so grandiose that they refuse to acknowledge that they even have a problem. Those taking lithium face a difficult choice regarding whether or not to remain on maintenance doses of the drug. On the one hand, side effects must be considered. On the other hand, not taking the medication puts them at considerable risk of having another episode (Suppes et al., 1991). Some people are encouraged by their therapists to participate in *lithium groups*, which are offered to clients who use the medication on a regular basis. In these groups, members provide support to each other regarding the importance of staying on the medication. Education regarding the side effects of lithium also plays an important role in this process.

In addition to lithium, other medications have been successfully used in treating bipolar disorder. For example, carbamazine (Tegretol), an anticonvulsant medication, is effective particularly for treating people in acute states of mania (Small et al., 1991).

For some mood-disordered clients, pharmacological interventions either do not work or are considered to be too slow to treat a severe, life-threatening disorder. Particularly in cases involving incapacitating depression, the clinician may recommend electroconvulsive therapy (ECT). Although ECT is the most powerful somatic treatment for

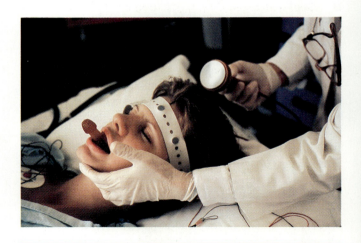

As this woman is prepared for ECT, precautions are taken to prevent injury. She is administered muscle relaxants, and a device is inserted into her mouth to prevent her from biting her tongue.

major depression, it is the least commonly used because of adverse connotations associated with this treatment and concern about short-term and long-term side effects. If you saw the movie *One Flew over the Cuckoo's Nest*, you will probably never forget the dramatic presentation of the misuse of ECT. Indeed, negative attitudes toward ECT are due mainly to historical misuse of this procedure as punishment rather than treatment. Today ECT continues to be administered because it has been shown to be a life-saving treatment for severely depressed people for whom medications alone are ineffective.

ECT is usually given six to eight times, once every other day until the person's mood returns to normal. The person undergoing the treatment is given anesthesia to reduce discomfort, a muscle relaxant, oxygen, and medication to help control heart rhythm. The lowest voltage needed to induce a convulsion is delivered to the client's head for less than a second. This is followed 2 to 3 seconds later by a *tonic phase* lasting 10 to 12 seconds, during which all muscles in the body under voluntary control undergo involuntary contractions. Lastly, there is a *clonic phase* consisting of 30 to 50 seconds of convulsions, which appear more like a slight bodily tremor because of the muscle relaxant. A few minutes later, the individual emerges from the anesthesia, alert, without pain, and without recollection of what just transpired.

One aspect of ECT that troubles some clinicians and clients is the fact that no one understands why ECT works. Most current hypotheses center on ECT-induced changes in neurotransmitter receptors and in the body's natural opiates. As for side effects, the primary complaints of clients following an ECT trial are short-term memory loss and confusion, which disappear within 2 weeks of the final treatment. No permanent brain damage or memory loss is known to result from ECT (Calev et al., 1991). ECT has also been found to be particularly effective in treating depressed people who also suffer from panic disorder (Figiel et al, 1992).

Less well-tested than medication or ECT is the treatment of depression by light therapy, which would be most appropriate for those individuals whose depression follows the seasonal pattern. Exposing depressed individuals to special lights, either white (Kripke et al., 1992; Terman et al., 1989) or green (Oren et al., 1991), during the winter has been shown to alleviate their symptoms. Another less known but promising somatic treatment is sleep deprivation. Some people who do not respond well to medications improve when deprived of sleep for a period of 36 hours. This sleep deprivation has the surprising effect of increasing the efficacy of antidepressant medications for some people (Leibenluft & Wehr, 1992).

Although the thought of somatic interventions such as medication and ECT may be viewed unfavorably by some, for many people these treatments have provided effective and sometimes life-saving help. In and of themselves, though, these treatments are regarded by most therapists as insufficient. Consequently, individual, family, or group psychotherapy is typically recommended as an adjunct to help the individual understand both the etiology of the disorder and strategies for preventing recurrences. Let's turn now to the contributions of the various perspectives that address these psychological issues.

Psychodynamic Perspectives

Early psychoanalytic theories of mood disorders reflected themes of loss and feelings of rejection. The later psychodynamic theories have replaced some of these ideas, but have retained a focus on inner psychic processes as the basis for mood disturbances.

■ *Theory*

One of the first psychoanalytic theorists, Karl Abraham (1911, 1968), focused on the notion that depression is triggered by a reaction to loss. Freud (1917) took Abraham's ideas and expanded them in what has become a central paper in psychoanalysis, "Mourning and Melancholia." However, the reaction to loss involved in depression is not a straightforward expression of grief or sadness. Instead, the loss is felt at an unconscious level in a way that causes the person to feel a combination of guilt and abandonment. In other words, guilt may arise in response to mixed feelings that the depressed person had about the other, but when that other person is gone, a sense of emptiness is experienced.

Themes of loss are prominent in object relations approaches to depression, such as those of the well-known British psychoanalyst John Bowlby. Based on his research and writings on the topic of early life losses, Bowlby (1980) developed some interesting notions of the ways in which depression can result from experiences of separation and loss. He has also pointed out how people can become depressed when they are raised by parents who fail to provide them with a stable and secure relationship or who repeatedly convey to them that they are inadequate, unlovable, or incompetent. Jules Bemporad (1985) also focused on

Neglectful parents can leave a child feeling unlovable.

deficient parenting as a cause of depression. According to Bemporad, in childhood the individual begins to build up a false sense of self in an attempt to feel loved by others. As an adult, the depressed person tends to form relationships in which the partner becomes overvalued and heavily relied upon for support. Should the partner die, end the relationship, or become detached, the depressed person becomes overwhelmed with feelings of inadequacy and loss.

The connection between early parental loss and later mood disorder has not been supported by empirical evidence (Crook & Eliot, 1980; Landerman et al., 1991); however, psychoanalytic emphasis on parental neglect or failure to acknowledge a child's worth continue to inform current theories and treatment for mood disorders.

Psychoanalytic explanations of mania are similar to those of depression. In this view, mania is seen as a defense mechanism by which an individual staves off feelings of inadequacy, loss, and helplessness. Presumably, people develop feelings of grandiosity and elation or become hyperenergetic as an unconscious defense against sinking into a state of gloom and despair.

■ *Therapy*

Clinicians use psychodynamic therapy techniques in working with clients for whom unconscious conflict is presumed to play an important role in initiating or maintaining the mood symptoms. The psychodynamically based short-term psychotherapies developed by David Malan (1979) and Peter Sifneos (1979) choose a specific focus for the psychotherapeutic intervention and last from 3 to 12 months. Both forms of short-term psychotherapies rely on the relationship between the client and therapist as a vehicle of change, as the therapist focuses on one specific feature of the client's "transference" onto the therapist. For instance, take the case of Celia, a depressed individual who is convinced that she is a "loser" and that no one likes her. The short-term psychotherapy may be focused on the way Celia's relationship with the therapist reflects her assumption about how others feel toward her. Even at her first therapy session, this issue makes itself manifest as Celia tells her therapist that it would probably be better for him not to treat her because she would not be worth his time and energy. The therapist would explore with Celia why she feels this way, and how this feeling contributes to her depression.

Other short-term psychotherapies may focus on one specific life concern that the client believes has contributed to the depression. Once this issue is resolved, the therapy ends. Rather than attempt to change the underlying personality structure of the client, short-term dynamic psychotherapy is designed to alleviate the client's symptoms and to help the client understand that certain ways of interacting with people have contributed to the experience of depression. Over a number of years, as the individual participates in repeated short-term therapies, it is likely that more enduring change will eventually come about. Each therapy

remains a self-contained unit, though, intended to help the client achieve growth and relief from unhappiness.

Behavioral Perspectives

Most depressed people act and speak in ways that make their depression fairly obvious. Their bodily movements and verbal expression seem slowed down, and they have a negative and pessimistic perspective. It is this slowing of responsiveness and lack of a positive outlook that form the main targets of behavioral approaches to depression.

■ *Theory*

Early behavioral theories of depression (e.g., Lazarus, 1968; Skinner, 1953) regarded the symptoms of the disorder as the result of a reduction in positive reinforcements. Depressed people, according to this view, withdraw from life because they have no incentives to be more active. Consider the example of a formerly successful athlete who suffers an injury. Lacking the positive reinforcement of the athletic successes to which he has become accustomed, he might retreat into a depressive state.

Another source of depression might be deficient social skills that cause the person to behave in ways that interfere with more satisfying interpersonal relationships (Lewinsohn & Shaw, 1969). Without the reinforcements derived from other people's interest and concern, the individual is likely to become depressed and stay depressed. In time, the depressed person may derive a certain amount of secondary gain from being depressed—escape from responsibility such as work and family commitments may be reinforcement for remaining depressed.

As you might imagine, the early behavioral theories are now regarded as too superficial to explain the complex experience of depression. However, the idea that depressed people's poor social skills might contribute to their unhappiness is one that interpersonal theorists have found to be very important, as we will discuss later.

More recently, behavioral theories have focused on more complex processes as explanations for depression, including a focus on stressful life events as influencing the onset of depression (Wing & Bebbington, 1985). This focus is based on the findings of many researchers who have studied the relationship between people's emotional adjustment and the events that occur in their lives. Stressful events can prompt a number of emotional reactions in people's lives. Traumatic experiences have the potential to provoke posttraumatic stress disorder, while events involving loss, such as widowhood, can instigate a major depressive episode (Bruce et al., 1991; Zisook & Shuchter, 1991) and lead to years of psychological distress (Nuss & Zubenko, 1992; Thompson et al, 1991).

According to the behavioral model, stressful events disrupt the individual's ability to carry out important and relatively automatic behavior patterns (Hoberman & Lewinsohn, 1985). These patterns, called *scripts*, can include

A parent who suddenly loses a spouse may have trouble adjusting to the doubling of household and family responsibilities, leading to depression and despondency.

such routine activities as getting dressed in the morning and going to work. Disruptions in these scripted activities, which may result from relatively minor nuisances or from major traumatic life events, cause the person to become upset. The important factor determining whether a person will become depressed is the extent to which the individual's scripts are interfered with by the circumstances or event.

As an example of how disruptions in scripts can lead to depression, consider the case of a woman who becomes widowed. She has not only lost a close relationship but also must make vast changes in her day-to-day life. Her life becomes less predictable, and her responsibilities are doubled. In this behavioral formulation of depression, such an interruption of a person's daily life patterns results in a loss of positive reinforcements (the loss of a close relationship) and also makes the person feel more self-conscious in carrying out activities that are unfamiliar to her. For example, when she goes to a restaurant, she feels awkward and embarrassed at the fact that she is sitting alone, or when she goes to the bank for the first time to discuss her financial situation, she feels uncomfortable and afraid of making a mistake in front of the bank personnel.

The increased self-awareness that accompanies a disruption of scripted behavior leads the person to become more self-critical, to take responsibility for negative outcomes, and to withdraw from others. Behaviors, cognitions, emotions, and interpersonal relationships become those of a depressed person.

Although the revised behavioral position is too limited to explain all forms of depression, it provides a reasonable explanation for some kinds of reactive depression. Further, as you will see later in the textbook when we discuss adjustment disorders, the impact of stressful life events

may be partly attributed to their negative effect on how people cope with daily pressures and responsibilities.

One important variant of the behavioral approach to depression is the **learned helplessness model**, which proposes that depressed people have come to view themselves as incapable of having an effect on their environment. Perhaps in your introductory psychology course you studied the phenomenon of *learned helplessness*, a term coined by psychologist Martin Seligman (Maier & Seligman, 1976). In their controversial and disturbing experiments, Seligman and his co-workers studied the conditioning of fear and escape learning in dogs. They placed a group of dogs in a cage where they could not escape from an electrical apparatus when subjected to electric shock. A warning light preceded each administration of shock. Next, the dogs were placed in a chamber where they could escape shock by jumping over a partition if they did so when the warning light was presented. Seligman had originally hypothesized that the dogs would immediately jump over the partition to escape the painful consequences. To his surprise, rather than escape, the dogs lay down "helplessly" until the experimenter finally turned off the shock. In contrast, a group of dogs that had never been subjected to inescapable shock took the normal action of jumping across the partition once they learned that this escape route was available.

You can imagine what this experiment must have entailed, and why it is so controversial. Today, such research would be heavily criticized because of the inhumanness of subjecting animals to inescapable shock. However, Seligman and his colleagues felt it was necessary to document the universality of this phenomenon.

Naturally, Seligman and his co-workers were interested in the applicability of the learned helplessness phenomenon to humans. Of course, they could not present humans with the same kind of stimuli that were applied to the animals. Instead, they conditioned helplessness in humans (college students) by presenting them with uncontrollable noise delivered through earphones. When given the opportunity to turn off the noise, the conditioned helplessness group failed to do so and instead listened passively to the noise (Hiroto, 1974). In addition to responding this way to a physiological stimulus, humans showed the same response to a cognitive task. When they were confronted with unsolvable cognitive problems such as anagrams, college students gave up attempting to find solutions when given new problems that could be solved (Hiroto & Seligman, 1975). Perhaps you have felt this way when taking a particularly hard exam, and know the feeling of "giving up" because it does no good to keep trying.

So what does this have to do with depression? According to Seligman's initial explanation, depressed people are showing behavioral symptoms of learned helplessness in their apathy and passivity. They show these symptoms in response to prior experiences in which they were made to feel powerless to control their destiny. Almost as soon as Seligman proposed this connection, his position was criticized as being an overly simplistic translation from animal data to clinical problems in humans. One important limitation of the original explanation of depression was that it did not account for the fact that depressed people blame themselves for their failures. If they feel powerless to control the outcome of what happens to them, how could they blame themselves? Seligman and his group modified their theory to take this factor into account, developing the "revised formulation" of the learned helplessness theory (Abramson et al., 1978; Peterson & Seligman, 1984).

The revised version of the learned helplessness theory takes into account the role of **attributions**, explanations that people make of the things that happen to them. For example, if your stereo is stolen, you might attribute this to the fact that you forgot to lock your room before you left for the evening. In the revised learned helplessness model, Abramson et al. (1978) proposed that exposure to situations inducing helplessness (traumatic or negative life events) leads depressed people to attribute their powerlessness to a lack of personal resources, to see this situation as unremitting, and to see their powerlessness as extending to every aspect of their lives. The model labels these attributions as "internal, stable, and global." By contrast, nondepressed people attribute their problems to situations outside their control (external attributions), see their problems as temporary (not stable), and regard them as fairly specific to the situation (not global).

Returning to the example of the stolen stereo, a depressed woman would see the theft as being typical of her stupidity in failing to lock the door, would regard the theft as part of an overall life pattern, and would see her carelessness as something that causes her grief in many situations. A nondepressed woman would attribute blame to the unsavory people lurking about her dorm, instead of seeing the theft as her own fault. She also would view the theft as an isolated incident in her life, and would regard it as atypical of the other things that happen to her. The kinds of attributions made by depressed people, according to later work on learned helplessness theory, render these individuals particularly vulnerable to feelings of hopelessness when confronted with negative life events (Metalsky et al., 1987).

Although the learned helplessness theory has some interesting facets, the theory is limited in its utility as an explanation of why people become depressed or stay depressed. Specifically, depression is a broad-spectrum disorder that ranges from mild yet chronic dysphoria to intense but episodic despair. Much of the research in this area would lead one to think that all depressed people are alike. As you know from reading about dysthymia and major depression, these are different disorders which vary in their symptoms and causes. Another problem with the revised learned helplessness theory of depression is that the research evidence used to support it relies on samples of people who would not be considered clinically depressed but rather mildly dysphoric (e.g., Alloy & Abramson, 1979).

■ *Therapy*

Behavioral therapy of depression begins with a careful assessment of the frequency, quality, and range of activities and social interactions in the client's life. The clinician then implements a treatment involving a combination of changing the client's environment, teaching the client certain social skills, and making it more pleasant for the client to seek out activities that help restore a proper mood balance. Specific reinforcements might be found from among activities that the client enjoyed in a nondepressed state.

Education is an essential component of behavioral intervention. Depressed clients often set unrealistic goals and then are unable to implement behaviors to reach these goals. Regular homework assignments are given in order to produce gradual behavior changes and increase the probability of successful performance. Contracting and self-

In behavioral interventions, clients are given homework assignments that encourage them to engage in more pleasurable activities.

reinforcement procedures are also incorporated. For example, every time the client follows through on initiating a social activity, reward should follow. Such rewarding may consist of self-congratulatory statements or may involve more concrete behaviors such as having a favorite snack. If these procedures do not succeed, the behavioral therapist moves toward more extensive didactic instruction, modeling, coaching, role-playing and rehearsal, and "real world" trials.

Cognitive-Behavioral Perspectives

Think of a time when you have been depressed, and try to recall the reasons for your depression. Perhaps you lost a close friend, or you felt pessimistic about your future. Maybe you misinterpreted something that someone said to you, which caused you to feel bad about yourself. Cognitive-behavioral approaches propose that serious mood changes can result from events in our lives or from our perceptions of events.

■ *Theory*

According to the cognitive-behavioral perspective, people develop depressive disorders if they have been sensitized by early experiences to react in a particular way to a particular kind of loss or stressful event. Depressed people react to stressful experiences by activating a set of thoughts that Beck (1967) called the **cognitive triad**: a negative view of self, world, and the future. Beck proposed that once activated, this depressive way of viewing self, the world, and the future (called a depressive *schema*) perpetuates itself through a cyclical process (Derry & Kuiper, 1981). For example, perhaps you have known someone who is always negative in her thinking. Even if something good happens to her, she manages to see the down side of the situation. What is happening, according to theorists such as Beck, is that she interprets every situation in terms of her schema which prevents her from seeing anything but problems, hopelessness, and her own inadequacy. Because she is so negative, her views of herself and her situations can never be influenced in a favorable way by circumstances and, indeed, it is likely that her negative outlook will prevent her from having more positive experiences. People become bored and irritated with her and eventually give up trying to involve her in social activities. Thus, the cycle of depression is perpetuated.

Adding to the cycle of depressive thinking are **cognitive distortions**, errors that depressed people make in the way they draw conclusions from their experiences (Beck et al., 1979; Beck & Weishaar, 1989). These cognitive distortions involve the application of illogical rules such as arbitrary inferences, jumping to conclusions, overgeneralizing, and taking a detail out of context. These rules make the depressed person ascribe negative meanings to past and present events and to make gloomy predictions about the future. The person is probably not even specifically aware of having these thoughts because they have become such a constant feature of the individual's existence. The situation is comparable to what you might experience if you were sitting for a long time in a room with a noisy air conditioner. You do not actually notice how noisy the room is until someone else walks in and comments on it. Similarly, it takes a specific effort to isolate and identify automatic thoughts when they have become such permanent fixtures in the person's consciousness. Some examples of cognitive distortions are shown in Table 10-1.

Contributing further to the unhappiness of depressed people, according to Beck, is the content of their thought. Depressed people feel sad because they believe they have been deprived of something that is important to them, and this perceived loss implies a threat to self-esteem. Further, depressed people are convinced that they are responsible for the loss. Their dysfunctional attitudes cause them to assume that they are worthless and helpless, and that their efforts

Table 10-1   Examples of Cognitive Distortions

Overgeneralizing:	If it's true in one case, it applies to any case that is even slightly similar. Example: "I failed my first English exam so I am probably going to fail all of them."
Selective abstraction:	The only events that matter are failures, deprivation, etc. Example: "Even though I won the election for sorority president, I'm not really popular because not everyone voted for me."
Excessive responsibility:	I am responsible for all bad things, failures, etc. Example: "My one strike-out in the baseball game caused our team to lose."
Assuming temporal causality:	If it has been true in the past, then it's always going to be true. Example: "My last date was a wipe-out; next week's is probably going to be a dud, too."
Self-references:	I am the center of everyone's attention—especially my bad performances. Example: "My wrong answer in class was noticed by everyone, and I'm sure they all thought I was an idiot."
Catastrophizing:	Always think of the worst; it's most likely to happen to you. Example: "The squeak in my new car is sure evidence that I've bought a lemon."
Dichotomous thinking:	Everything is either one extreme or another (black or white, good or bad). Example: "Everything about this college is crummy—the students, the professors, the dorms, and the food."

Source: Adapted from Beck et al., 1979, p. 261

are doomed to fail. They distort any experience, including a positive one, so that it fits in with this generalized belief (Beck et al., 1979). They cannot learn from any experiences that challenge their beliefs because their initial perception of those experiences, particularly in the interpersonal realm, is distorted and unrealistic (Safran, 1990a).

■ *Therapy*

Cognitive-behavioral therapy involves a short-term, structured approach that focuses on the client's negative thoughts and includes suggestions for activities that will improve the client's daily life. This technique involves an active collaboration between the client and the therapist and is oriented toward current problems and their resolution.

The cognitive-behavioral approach incorporates (1) didactic work, (2) cognitive restructuring, and (3) behavioral techniques. *Didactic work* involves explaining the theory to the client—teaching the client how depression results from faulty thinking. *Cognitive restructuring* (Sacco & Beck, 1985) involves a multi-step approach. First, the client needs to identify and monitor dysfunctional automatic thoughts. Second, the client needs to recognize the connection between thoughts, emotions, and behavior. Third, the client must evaluate the reasonableness of the automatic thoughts. Fourth, the client must learn how to substitute more reasonable thoughts for the dysfunctional automatic thoughts. Finally, the client must identify and alter dysfunctional assumptions. In other words, the therapist attempts to break down the maladaptive thinking patterns that underlie the depressed individual's negative emotions.

Behavioral techniques, comprising the third part of the cognitive-behavioral approach, rest on the assumption that behavior change is needed in order to identify and alter dysfunctional cognitions. Behavioral methods include (1) pleasure prediction experiments, (2) weekly activity schedules, and (3) graded task assignments. Pleasure prediction experiments involve planning an activity, predicting how much pleasure it will produce, and then observing how much it actually does produce. Such an exercise can help a depressed client see that he or she is mistaken about gloomy predictions. The weekly activity schedule helps the client to monitor activities on an hour-by-hour basis, with the goal of showing the client that it is not true that he or she "never accomplishes anything." The client is asked to rate mastery and pleasure of each activity. If the client really is inactive, then activities are planned hour-by-hour for each day of the week. Graded task assignments involve identifying a goal that the client wishes to attain but thinks is impossible, breaking the goal into simple component tasks, and helping the client experience the success of accomplishing a task, however simple.

Interpersonal Theory

As we have already discussed, the depressed person's interactions with other people often play an important role either in causing or maintaining a dysphoric mood. Recall our discussion of family systems perspectives in Chapter 5. Within this perspective, mood disorders are viewed as symptomatic of problems in the family system as a whole. Interpersonal theorists are also interested in mood disorder as a function of disturbed relationships, but their perspec-

According to the interpersonal theory of depression, poor social skills can contribute to a cycle of disturbed relationships that worsen the individual's experience of depression.

tive differs from the family systems perspective in that it focuses on social deficiencies as comprising the central core of the individual's unhappiness.

■ Theory

Some depressed people have had lifelong difficulties in their interactions with other people. Consider the case of a 40-year-old man who for most of his life has acted in abrasive ways that alienate others. As the years go by, he becomes increasingly saddened by the fact that he has no friends and realizes that it is unlikely that he will ever have a close relationship. For depressed people like this man whose social skills are so deficient (Marx et al., 1992), a cycle is created as their constant pessimism and self-deprecation make other people feel guilty (Folkman & Lazarus, 1986) and depressed (Howes et al., 1985). As a result, other people respond in unhelpful ways with criticism and rejection (Coyne, 1976; Joiner et al., 1992), further reinforcing the depressed person's negative view of the world (Coyne & Gotlib, 1983). Particularly problematic for the depressed person are disturbed intimate relationships and social isolation (Barnett & Gotlib, 1988).

Expanding on these ideas, Myrna Weissman and Gerald Klerman and their associates have developed a model of understanding mood disorders that integrates virtually all of the perspectives we have discussed so far, and places particular emphasis on disturbed social functioning (Klerman, et al., 1984). This theory incorporates the ideas of behavioral psychologists who focus on the poor social skills of the depressed individual, but it goes one step further in looking at the origins of the depressed person's fundamental problems.

Rooted in the interpersonal approaches of Adolph Meyer (1957) and Harry Stack Sullivan (1953a; 1953b), and the attachment theory of John Bowlby, this theory takes into consideration early life experiences that set the stage for intimacy and personal happiness later in life. Meyer was known for his psychobiological approach to abnormal behavior, emphasizing how psychological problems might represent an individual's misguided attempts to adapt to the psychosocial environment. He believed that physical symptoms can also develop in association with psychological distress. Sullivan, whose theory was discussed in Chapter 4, characterized abnormal behavior as a function of impaired interpersonal relationships, including deficiencies in communication. Each of these theories could apply to a variety of psychological disorders, but Bowlby's theory, with its specific focus on disturbed attachment bonds in early childhood as the cause of unhappiness later in life, is particularly relevant to depression.

Interpersonal theory connects the ideas of these psychoanalytic theorists with the behavioral and cognitive-behavioral theorists in the following way. A person's failure in childhood to acquire the skills needed to develop satisfying intimate relationships leads to a sense of despair, isolation, and resulting depression. Once a person's depression is established, it is maintained by poor social skills and impaired communication that lead to further rejection by others. Re-

active depressions in adulthood may arise when the individual suffers a stressful life event such as the end of a relationship or death of a significant other. After the depressive symptoms begin, they may become perpetuated by the maladaptive social skills that the individual develops. For example, a man whose wife dies may become so distraught over an extended period of time that he alienates his friends and family members. In time, a vicious cycle becomes established in which his behavior causes people to stay away, and because he is so lonely, he becomes even more difficult in his interactions with others. Although the individual circumstances differ in each case, it is this cycle of depression, lack of social interaction, and deterioration of social skills that interpersonal theory regards as the core problem of depression.

■ Therapy

Therapy following from the interpersonal theory adheres to a set of guidelines derived from an empirical base. Therapists who use interpersonal therapy are continuously evaluating its efficacy according to these guidelines. Interestingly, interpersonal therapy involves many of the techniques that most therapists probably use spontaneously, but it frames these techniques in a systematic approach, including manuals to guide therapists in their application of the method (Rounsaville et al., 1988).

Interpersonal therapy is divided into three broad phases. The first phase involves assessing the magnitude and nature of the individual's depression using quantitative assessment measures. Interview methods are also used to determine the factors that precipitated the current episode. At that point, depending on the type of depressive symptoms the individual shows, treatment with antidepressant medications is considered.

In the second phase, the therapist and the client collaborate in formulating a treatment plan that focuses on the primary problem. Typically these problems are related to grief, interpersonal disputes, role transitions, and problems in interpersonal relationships stemming from inadequate social skills. The treatment plan is then carried out, with the methods varying according to the precise nature of the client's primary problem. In general, these methods involve a combination of encouraging self-exploration, providing support, educating the client in the nature of depression, and providing feedback on the client's ineffective social skills.

The last phase is the termination phase, during which the therapist and the client review progress and lay out future goals. Frequently, in connection with the research goals of interpersonal therapy, a one-year follow-up is conducted to evaluate long-term effectiveness. In addition to attending to the treatment needs of the depressed person, clinicians recognize that the partner of a depressed person needs clinical attention (Halgin & Lovejoy, 1991). Feeling neglected, emotionally isolated, and anxious, partners are at risk of becoming depressed themselves in the absence of support and understanding.

A groundbreaking study funded by the National Institute of Mental Health explored the controversy over the relative effectiveness of medications compared with psychotherapy in the treatment of depression (Elkin et al., 1989). In this study, 250 people at six different sites were randomly assigned to one of four treatment groups: (1) interpersonal psychotherapy, (2) cognitive-behavioral therapy, (3) tricyclic antidepressant medication, and (4) placebo. In both placebo and antidepressant drug conditions, which were conducted in a double-blind fashion, participants met weekly for 20 to 30 minutes with a therapist who monitored their progress and provided them with support. To assure consistency across sites and therapists in the way that the treatments were administered, the researchers developed a standardized manual describing the underlying theory of the approach the therapists were to use, the general strategies to be adopted, and suggested ways to deal with specific problems.

The study continued for 16 weeks, and the outcomes of the four treatments were compared using a variety of clinical indices including clinician and self-report ratings of de-

INTERPERSONAL THERAPY FOR DEPRESSION

pression and other psychological symptoms. The outcomes of treatment differed depending on the severity of the client's initial level of depression. As you can see from Figure 10-1, on the depression rating scale, people with less severe depression benefitted nearly equally from medication and from either of the two psychotherapy conditions. For the more severely depressed, though, interpersonal therapy was equivalent in effectiveness to medications, but cognitive-behavioral therapy was not. This finding did not hold true on all measures and all analyses, as can be seen from Figure 10-2, which shows the results in terms of the Global Adjustment Scale (Axis V of the *DSM*). In this figure, the less severely depressed people showed

equivalent results with all forms of treatment, including the condition involving the placebo drug plus clinical management. Surprisingly, clinical contact alone (the placebo condition) seemed to have therapeutic value for these people. For those individuals who were severely depressed, the nature of the intervention did make a difference, and medications plus support proved to be more effective than the psychotherapies.

Left unanswered in this study were questions regarding the long-term effectiveness of the four treatments and the effectiveness of medication plus psychotherapy. The long-term effects are continuing to be investigated and the findings show encouraging support. Depressed people whose therapy included a consistent interpersonal focus were symptom-free for up to 2 years after the end of treatment (Frank et al., 1991). If these gains continue to be maintained, it would suggest that the combination of medication plus psychotherapy using the interpersonal approach can be very effective in helping people with severe depression.

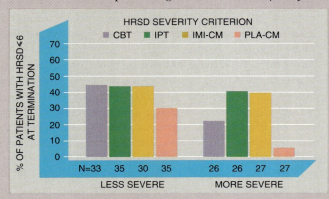

Figure 10-1
Comparison of Hamilton Rating Scale Depression (HRSD) scores of cognitive-behavioral therapy (CBT) interpersonal psychotherapy (IPT), imipramine hydrochloride plus clinical management (IMI-CM), and placebo plus clinical management (PLA-CM) in research by Elkin et al., 1989. Percentages are for all subjects, including those who dropped out before receiving treatment.

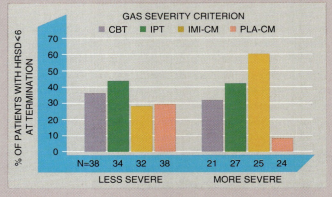

Figure 10-2
Comparison of Global Assessment Scale (GAS) scores of cognitive-behavioral therapy, interpersonal psychotherapy, imipramine plus clinical management, and placebo plus clinical management in research by Elkin et al., 1989. Percentages are for all subjects, including people who dropped out before receiving treatment.

Table 10–2   MOOD DISORDERS: A SUMMARY CHART OF PERSPECTIVES

BIOLOGICAL	PSYCHODYNAMIC	
Family incidence and adoption studies show evidence of genetic inheritance. Studies of biochemical abnormalities focus on serotonin and norepinephrine, altered biorhythms, and hormonal disturbances. **Treatment:** Depression—Antidepressants (e.g., tricyclics and MAOIs); exposure to light, sleep deprivation; ECT for extreme cases. Bipolar disorder—Medication (e.g., lithium).	Loss of a loved one stimulates feelings of conflict and guilt that turn inward; separation and loss in early childhood sensitizes the individual to later experiences of loss and leads to development of low self-esteem. **Treatment:** Short-term dynamically based psychotherapy that focuses on the client's feelings through analysis of transference.	
BEHAVIORAL	COGNITIVE-BEHAVIORAL	INTERPERSONAL
Decrease of positive reinforcers. Disruption of automatic routines resulting from change in life circumstances leads to distress and heightened self-consciousness. Learned helplessness. **Treatment:** Change the client's environment to provide more positive reinforcement; teach social skills.	Cognitive triad causes individual to have low self-esteem and a pessimistic outlook. Dysfunctional attitudes maintain these negative thoughts as individual cannot take in new, positive information about the self. **Treatment:** Counter the client's negative outlook by showing more logical ways of interpreting experiences. Provide assignments to help the client develop more positive experiences outside therapy.	Deficits in social skills cause the individual to have more negative interpersonal experiences, which perpetuate a cycle of loneliness, inability to obtain social support, and heightened depression. **Treatment:** Self-exploration, support, education about the nature of depression and help in improving interpersonal skills.

MOOD DISORDERS: THE PERSPECTIVES REVISITED

As you learned about each of the perspectives on mood disorders, you probably saw features that you felt were convincing, only to read on and find another approach that seemed equally compelling. This is because each approach has something valuable to offer in the way of understanding and treating mood disorders. You are probably wondering how a clinician goes about determining the techniques to tap when treating clients with mood disorders. For the most part, clinical decisions are based on the nature of the individual's problems. For example, a client having a manic episode would probably be started immediately on medication such as lithium, and this treatment would be supplemented by psychotherapy. A depressed client who has suffered a recent loss would be treated with psychotherapy; medication would be unlikely. How does the clinician make these decisions? Many clinicians have preferences for one form of treatment over another, but in addition to these prefer-

ences, they turn to the latest research findings to guide them in developing treatment plans responsive to each client's needs.

Much of what you have read should lead you to conclude that biology is an important contributor to mood disorders. Consequently, you may expect that somatic treatment approaches would be the most effective. Many experts in the field of depression would agree. However, as we have pointed out, medication alone has its limitations and in some instances may not be as effective as psychotherapy (review Research Focus).

It is encouraging to see the substantial progress being made in the understanding and treatment of mood disorders. Given the relatively high prevalence of these disorders, such progress will obviously have a broad impact on many individuals and on society as a whole. Furthermore, the understanding gained from research on mood disorders is likely to enrich science's knowledge about the functioning of the brain and the role of genetics in human behavior. In the coming years, you will no doubt read and hear about many more advances in this heavily researched area.

Janice Butterfield

Janice's History

Janice's voice quavered as she recounted the story of her life. The tears that streamed down her face were constant reminders for me of her inner pain. The oldest daughter in a family of three girls, Janice described a harmonious family life during her early years that took a very sad turn when her father passed away when she was 14 years old. Prior to that unhappy date, Janice's mother had been a charming and energetic woman who devoted herself to the family. Everything changed dramatically following the death of Janice's father, when her mother became extremely withdrawn and uninvolved with her children. A few months later Janice's mother was hospitalized for the first of several episodes of serious depression.

During each of her mother's hospitalizations, Janice was required to take over much of her mother's household responsibilities. This pattern of heavy family responsibility remained on Janice's shoulders for her remaining years in high school. Upon graduation, Janice realized that she couldn't leave home because of her mother's reliance on her, so she enrolled in a local community college and earned a degree in business administration. She continued to play an important role in caring for her two younger sisters until they left home.

Janice stayed on with her mother and worked as a buyer for a local clothing store. She fell in love with a man named Jed, whom she had met at a church-sponsored function. Jed asked her to marry him, but she insisted that her mother needed her at home and that she could not possibly leave her. Several years later, Janice's mother became terminally ill. Janice nursed her until her death. Janice was so distraught over her mother's death that she could not return to work for 6 months. The death was particularly traumatic for Janice because it left her without a living parent. By this time, Janice was 30 years old. Jed had not yet gotten married, and he again proposed to her. Janice accepted and they were married.

Janice explained that during the early years of her marriage she felt happy and energetic. She had taken some of the insurance money acquired after her mother's death and began her own consulting firm. During the first 6 months of her marriage, Janice worked long hours at the office and managed her household. Two years later, Janice gave birth to a girl. Although she had intended to keep working after her baby was born, she acquiesced to her husband's request that she sell the business so she could be a full-time homemaker. She agreed to go along with this plan, but harbored resentment about this matter.

Assessment

Although it was evident to me that Janice was depressed, I felt that psychological testing would provide me with some insight into her mood disorder. On each of the tests that Janice took, she showed evidence of deep sadness and discontent. Janice's MMPI-2 profile was that of a person suffering from serious depression and obsessional thinking. Rorschach and TAT responses reflected themes of emotional constriction, guilt, depression, and anxiety. On the WAIS-R, Janice's lethargy resulted in her receiving a performance IQ in the below average range, in contrast to her verbal IQ which was well above average.

Diagnosis

The prominence of Janice's mood disturbance led me to feel certain that she was suffering from a serious form of depression. She showed no psychotic symptoms, nor was there any history of a manic episode. I was able to rule out dysthymia as a diagnosis because of the relative brevity of her disturbance. All signs pointed to a diagnosis of Major Depressive Disorder—depressed mood, diminished interest in ordinary activities, appetite disturbance, sleep disturbance, psychomotor retardation, fatigue, feelings of worthlessness and guilt, poor concentration, and suicidality.

Axis I.   Major Depression.
Axis II. No evidence of personality disorder.
Axis III. No physical disorders or conditions.
Axis IV. Severity: 1. No acute events or enduring circumstances that may be relevant to the disorder.
Axis V.   Current Global Assessment of Functioning: 45. Highest Global Assessment of Functioning (past year): 90.

Case Formulation

In reviewing Janice's story in my attempt to understand why she would have become so severely depressed, my attention was first drawn to the fact that her mother had also suffered from serious depression. Genetic factors, of course, have been shown to play an important role in the etiology of mood disorders. But I also felt that there was more to Janice's story that warranted consideration. Specifically, she had experienced several major shifts in her life

Return to the Case

Janice Butterfield continued

within the past 5 years. First, the death of her mother was felt by Janice as a painful loss, even though she had contrasting feelings of elation as she came to realize that she was freed from her mother's excessive demands. She felt a great deal of conflict about her mixed feelings regarding her mother's death. Any sense of relief that she felt in this regard caused her to feel guilty. The chain of disturbance continued yet another step, in that her guilt led Janice to berate herself for not having been more attentive to her mother.

Events within Janice's current family added further emotional stress to an already fragile level of emotional functioning. As Janice's daughter reached toddlerhood, Janice's conflict around the issue of mother–daughter relationships was reactivated. Furthermore, her husband's demands that she become a full-time homemaker affected her self-esteem in that she was thwarted from fulfilling her career aspirations. I wondered whether her feelings of inadequacy, listlessness, and unhappiness were a turning-inward of the resentment she felt toward her husband. She saw suicide as her only escape from the unsatisfying trap of her life.

Planning a Treatment

As with all cases involving a serious suicide attempt, Janice needed to be hospitalized, even if only for a brief period of time for the purpose of continued evaluation and mood stabilization. She remained in the hospital for 3 weeks. Following her discharge I continued to see her weekly in individual psychotherapy for a year.

My approach with Janice was multipronged. Several factors about her current functioning and family history led me to the conclusion that antidepressant medication was warranted. Specifically, she was in a deep state of depression involving both psychological and biological processes. In addition, the fact that her mother had a mood disorder suggested to me that Janice was biologically predisposed to depression, and therefore biological intervention should be considered as a component of the treatment plan.

Regarding psychological intervention, I chose a combination of cognitive-behavioral and psychodynamically based techniques in my individual therapy, augmented by couples therapy provided by one of my colleagues.

I felt that cognitive-behavioral techniques would be effective in helping Janice to reduce the frequency of her depressive thoughts and to develop appropriately assertive interpersonal styles. In addition, I felt that Janice needed to explore her feelings about her mother to gain some insight into the ways in which unresolved mother-daughter issues had interfered with her own happiness. Lastly, couples therapy was needed so that Janice and Jed could begin working on some of the problems in their relationship, in particular, how he had stood in the way of Janice's feeling a greater sense of fulfillment in her professional life.

Outcome of the Case

During her stay in the hospital, Janice's mood improved as the antidepressant medication began to take effect. By the time she was ready to return home, she was feeling much more capable of handling her responsibilities.

In therapy, Janice learned to identify the ways in which her thinking was distorted and self-blaming, and to replace these thoughts with healthier ones. We focused on Janice's becoming more assertive, and this helped her to become better able to express her needs. In time, Janice came to see how the conflicts she had harbored all these years about this relationship had seriously interfered with her achievement of happiness. Early in our work together, Janice came to the conclusion that she would seek a part-time job, an idea with which I concurred. It seemed to me that Janice needed a context other than her family in which to derive improved feelings of self-worth.

In couples therapy, Janice and Jed each worked on developing clearer styles of communication. Jed came to recognize that his wife's depression was related to her loss of power in their relationship. Reluctantly he began to accede to her requests for greater independence outside the home and more influence in their relationship. When he saw that these changes correlated with Janice's improved psychological functioning, he began to understand the impact of his behavior not only on Janice, but on the whole family system.

As I think back upon my work with Janice, I feel a certain sense of satisfaction. When I first met Janice, she had just been rescued from a serious suicide attempt. Her self-esteem had been severely damaged, and her ability to live life as a happy and fulfilled person seemed only a remote possibility. That picture changed dramatically. Our work together, combined with the couples therapy, helped bring this woman from a period of despair to a state of fulfillment.

SUMMARY

1. The essential feature of mood disorders is a disturbance in the individual's emotional state or mood. There are two main categories of mood disorders: depressive and bipolar. Depressive disorders involve a dysphoric or sad mood, and bipolar disorders involve alternations in mood from dysphoria to euphoria. One qualification in the distinction between these disorders is that a person who has had a manic episode is regarded as having bipolar disorder whether or not a depressive episode has ever been experienced. Each type of mood disorder may occur in an intense, but time-limited, fashion, as is the case for major depressive disorder and bipolar disorder. Dysthymia and cyclothymia are less intense but more chronic mood disorders.

2. Major depression is characterized by depressive episodes in which the individual suffers a variety of somatic and psychological symptoms related to dysphoric mood. The somatic symptoms include lethargy, psychomotor agitation or retardation, appetite disturbances, and disruption of sleeping patterns. The psychological symptoms of depression include feelings of worthlessness and low self-esteem, intense and unreasonable guilt, and preoccupation with suicide. Anxiety frequently accompanies depression, and recent research is pointing to the possibility of a group of people with symptoms involving a mixture of anxiety and depression. There are two variants of major depression: melancholic and seasonal. In contrast to endogenous depression, which may be biologically based, there is reactive depression which is thought to develop in response to a traumatic loss or a stressful life event. Depression is more common in women than men. People vary in the number and frequency of depressive episodes they experience, and some might have only one in their entire lives. Although dysthymia is less intense than major depression, it involves chronic feeling of sadness.

3. Some mood disorders involve alternations in mood in which individuals feel uncharacteristically elated at times, and depressed at other times. Bipolar disorder involves an intense and very disruptive experience of heightened mood, called a manic episode. Many, although not all, people with bipolar disorder experience episodes of severe depression. People with cyclothymia experience recurrent mood shifts, but these shifts are not as intense as those of bipolar disorder.

4. Biological theories of mood disorders focus on genetic influences, as suggested by data on family inheritance patterns of mood disorders, twin studies, and adoption studies. Biochemical explanations of mood disorders have included the catecholamine hypothesis, which concerns the neurotransmitter norepinephrine, and the indolamine hypothesis, which proposes that serotonin abnormalities are the cause of mood disorders. More recent approaches propose that mood disorders are the result of down-regulation by neurons in response to excess amounts of norepinephrine in the central nervous system. Disturbances in sleep and biorhythms have led some researchers to suggest that mood disorders are the result of faulty responses in the body to daily variations in the cycle of light and dark. Biological treatments currently in use include tricyclic antidepressants and monamine oxidase inhibitors (MAOIs) for depression, and lithium carbonate for bipolar disorders. In severe cases when all other forms of treatment fail, the individual may be treated with electroconvulsive therapy (ECT). Newer forms of treatment include light therapy and sleep-deprivation therapy.

5. From the psychodynamic perspective, mood disorders are explained in terms of the experience of loss combined with guilt or ambivalence over the loss. Object relations theorists focus on deficiencies in early parenting that lead to faulty views of the self as the cause of depression. Bipolar disorder, according to psychodynamic theory, represents a reaction formation to feelings of inadequacy, loss, and helplessness. The grandiose and elated feeling of bipolar disorder are seen as defenses against sinking into gloom and despair. Psychodynamic therapy, oriented toward resolving these issues, focuses on transference conflicts in the therapeutic relationship as a way of helping the individual cope with feelings of loss and low self-worth.

6. Behavioral theories of depression originally regarded the disorder as due to a lack of positive reinforcement in the individual's life, but more recently have focused on stressful life events as causing depression by disrupting the individual's "scripts," or customary routines, and leading to heightened self-consciousness. The learned helplessness model, a variant of the behavioral model, proposes that depressed individuals have lost a sense of the ability to control the events in their lives and unrealistically attribute their misfortunes to their own failings. Behavior therapy involves increasing the amount of positive reinforcement the individual experiences through the prescription of assignments that change the client's environment, teach social skills, and strive toward mood balance.

7. According to the cognitive-behavioral theory of depression, individuals become depressed because of an inadequate feeling of self-esteem that perpetuates the cognitive triad of viewing themselves, the world, and their future in a negative way. Depressed people make cognitive errors, called cognitive distortions that cause them to draw faulty inferences from their experiences. They hold dysfunctional attitudes that lead them to form automatic thoughts whose content result in the experience of negative emotions such as worthlessness, helplessness, feelings of deprivation,

and low self-esteem. Cognitive-behavioral therapy uses cognitive restructuring and the behavioral method of assigning tasks that are intended to produce positive outcomes. Cognitive-behavioral therapy attempts to break down the maladaptive thinking patterns that underlie the depressed individual's negative emotions.

8. The interpersonal theory of depression is based on the premise that depressed people have deficient ways of relating to others that cause others to reject them. These experiences of rejection then further reinforce their low self-esteem. Interpersonal theorists have suggested exploring the origins of the depressed person's problem. Looking into early life experiences surrounding intimacy and personal happiness is one technique. Interpersonal therapy combines social skill training with cognitive-behavioral techniques according to a specific set of guidelines designed to facilitate the empirical evaluation of the therapy's effectiveness. Treatment plans commonly employ the encouragement of self-exploration, provide support, educate the client about the nature of depression, and provide feedback on ineffective social skills.

KEY TERMS

Dysphoria: the emotion of sadness. p. 250

Euphoria: the emotion of elation. p. 250

Major depression: a mood disorder in which the individual experiences acute, but time-limited, episodes of depressive symptoms. p. 250

Dysthymia: a mood disorder involving chronic depression of a less intensity than major depression. p. 250

Major depressive episode: a period in which the individual suffers a variety of psychological and physical symptoms related to a dysphoric mood. p. 250

Somatic symptoms: bodily disturbances or complaints. p. 250

Insomia: an inability to sleep. p. 250

Melancholic depression: a form of depression in which the individual loses interest in most activities, has more severe depressive symptoms in the morning, and suffers loss of appetite or weight. p. 251

Seasonal depression: a form of depression in which the individual has varying symptoms according to time of year, with symptoms usually developing during the same months every year. p. 251

Endogenous depression: a variant of depression primarily caused by biological factors. p. 251

Reactive depression: a variant of depression thought of as precipitated by stressful events. p. 251

Bipolar disorder: a mood disorder involving manic episodes, intense and very disruptive experiences of heightened mood, possibly alternating with major depressive episodes. p. 253

Manic episode: a period of euphoric mood. p. 253

Cyclothymia: a mood disorder that, compared with bipolar disorder, involves a less intense vacillation between states of euphoria and dysphoria. p. 253

Dizygotic twins: nonidentical or fraternal twins who are related to the same degree as other siblings. p. 255

Monozygotic twins: identical twins who share the same genetic inheritance. p. 255

Probands: a term used in genetic research to refer to people who have the symptoms of a particular disorders. p. 255

Catecholamine hypothesis: a hypothesis that asserts that a relative shortage of norepinephrine (a catecholamine) causes depression, and an overabundance of norepinephrine cause mania. p. 257

Indolamine hypothesis: a hypothesis that proposes that a deficiency of serotonin causes depression. p. 257

Down-regulation: a biochemical process that results in a decreased sensitivity of receptors to a neurotransmitter that is present in excess amounts in the nervous system. p. 258

Cortisol: a hormone involved in the mobilization of the body's resources in times of stress. p. 259

Dexamethasone suppression test (DST): a method of testing neuroendocrine functioning by injecting the individual with dexamethasone, which in normal individuals results in the suppression of cortisol. p. 259

Learned helplessness model: a behavioral approach to depression that proposes that depressed people have come to view themselves as incapable of having an effect on their environment. p. 263

Attributions: explanations that people make of the things that happen to them. p. 264

Cognitive triad: a negative view of self, world, and the future. p. 265

Cognitive distortions: errors that depressed people make in the way they draw conclusions from their experiences. p. 265

Case Report: David Marshall

David Marshall was 22 years old when his parents brought him to the psychiatric unit of the hospital. The look of torment on David's face was mirrored in the eyes of both his father and his mother who, with pain in their voices, described the horror of the preceding several days. Listening to but a few of David's unintelligible comments led me to guess that he was in a psychotic state. His parents explained that for the past 2 days David had been uttering a string of bizarre statements, such as "You can't stop me from my mission! Zoroaster is coming to save us all!" As David's parents struggled to tell me the story, David continued to interrupt with loud, dramatic assertions that he had a mission to "protect humankind from the evil force of 'thools,' creatures from the planet Dortanus."

With an air of threat in his voice, David warned his parents and me that anyone who stood in the way of his destiny might be at great risk. Mr. and Mrs. Marshall sat by quietly, allowing me to assess the severity of David's problem as he told me the story of how he had been chosen as a special envoy for Zoroaster, an alien god with an "intergalactic message of salvation." In response to my questioning, David told me that he had been informed of this special assignment by way of television commercials targeted especially at him, and also by "the voice of Zoroaster" which spoke to him at two o'clock each afternoon. At that point, his parents interjected that "in preparation for his mission," David had hoarded a roomful of spray cans to be used to break through the ozone layer in order to save the world from destruction.

I soon realized that because of David's disordered state of mind and disruptive behavior, he would be unable to give me accurate information about his current state or a clear sense of important experiences in his life. Consequently, I asked to meet privately with his parents to collect some of this very important information—a request that provoked a moment of rage from David. Warning me that they were "part of a plot" to suppress his message, he stormed out of the room and then bolted from the hospital. I was somewhat startled at the Marshall's apparent lack of response to David's departure. Mr. Marshall explained that scenes like this took place every day. Sometimes David disappeared for a few days, but he always returned home, primarily because he wished to return to the private enclave of his room.

The Marshalls described David's deterioration during the course of his late adolescent years. David failed every course during the first semester of his first year in college due to the fact that he spent most of his time alone in his dormitory room listening to rock music. After flunking out of college, David returned home, where he spent his time reading science fiction and esoteric religious writings. Mrs. Marshall noted that other oddities in his behavior became apparent around that time; she told of how David would often attract attention on the street because of his peculiar bodily movements and postures. For example, he would gaze heavenward, begin to wave his hand in a kind of spraying motion, and laugh with a sinister tone. Mrs. Marshall wept as she commented, "If only we had asked for help then, maybe David wouldn't have gotten so bad."

Sarah Tobin, PhD

11

CHARACTERISTICS OF SCHIZOPHRENIA AND RELATED PSYCHOTIC DISORDERS

The disorders we will discuss in this chapter include ones that afflict people like David, and are commonly referred to as falling in the category of *psychosis*. As you will discover in this chapter, there are a number of important differences among the forms of psychotic disorders, but they share the central feature of a severe disturbance in the individual's experience of reality about the world and the self. People with psychotic disorders may have difficulty thinking or speaking in a coherent manner and may be tortured by vivid images or voices.

Psychotic episodes are among the most frightening and tormenting of human experiences. But even more frightening, perhaps, is their apparent uncontrollability. The distress of people going through psychotic episodes is made worse by the fear and aversion such behaviors create in other people. It is difficult for the ordinary person not to be repulsed by the eccentricities and strange ramblings of people in a psychotic state. Because people with psychotic disorders are so often rejected by others, they frequently are isolated and have little opportunity to interact with other people.

After reading this chapter, you should be able to:

- Describe the central features of psychotic disorders, including schizophrenia and schizophrenia-like conditions.
- Be familiar with the incidence of schizophrenia, its effects on the individual, and its history.
- Understand the symptoms of schizophrenia.
- Recognize the phases, types, and dimensions of schizophrenia.

- Describe the symptoms of schizophrenia-like disorders, including brief reactive psychosis, schizophreniform disorder, schizoaffective disorder, delusional disorders, and induced psychotic disorder.
- Understand how each schizophrenia-like disorder compares to schizophrenia and be familiar with current theories and treatments for these disorders.

SCHIZOPHRENIA

Have you ever seen a man on the street muttering to himself, gesturing oddly, and acting as though he is hearing voices that no one else can hear? You may have wondered what was wrong with him. Although these behaviors can be associated with a number of conditions, including drug reactions, in many cases they are symptoms of a form of psychosis called *schizophrenia,* which afflicts approximately one percent of the population (Regier et al, 1988; Robins et al., 1984). **Schizophrenia** is a disorder with a range of symptoms involving disturbances in content of thought, form of thought, perception, affect, sense of self, motivation, behavior, and interpersonal functioning. Although only a small percentage of the population is afflicted with this disorder, it translates into large amounts of resources needed to care for people with this disorder. Estimates of the percentage of clients treated at mental health facilities who have a diagnosis of schizophrenia range from 12 to 21.5 percent. Within psychiatric hospital settings, this number rises to almost 40 percent (NIMH, 1986; Rosenstein et al., 1989).

As the deinstitutionalization movement has taken hold, however, the burden of care has shifted increasingly to families. It was estimated, for example, that in 1985, the average family with a schizophrenic member spent nearly $4,000 and 798 hours in providing care, amounting to a total dollar cost of almost $12,000 per year (McGuire, 1991). As you read about this disorder, you will see further that its symptoms are frightening and distressing to those who experience them, and also to these individuals' families and friends.

The disorder that we currently call schizophrenia was first identified as a disease by a French physician, Benedict Morel (1809–1873), and was systematically defined by the German psychiatrist Emil Kraepelin (1856–1926). **Dementia praecox**, as it was called, was thought to be a degeneration of the brain (*dementia*) that began at a relatively young age (*praecox*) and ultimately led to disintegration of the entire personality. Kraepelin believed that the hallucinations, delusions, and bizarre behavioral disturbances seen in people with schizophrenia could ultimately be traced to a physical abnormality or disease.

Challenging Kraepelin's views that dementia praecox was a disease of the brain was the Swiss psychologist Eugen Bleuler (1857–1939). Bleuler (1911) proposed a dramatic change in both the name and the understanding of the disorder. Abandoning the term *dementia praecox,* Bleuler maintained that a more appropriate name of the disorder

Eugen Bleuler coined the term "schizophrenia" to refer to what he regarded as the core of the disorder—the splitting of normal psychological functions.

was *schizophrenia,* a term that incorporated ideas central to Bleuler's understanding of the disorder. Literally, schizophrenia was intended to refer to a *splitting* (schiz) or lack of integration among the individual's psychological functions of perceptions, thoughts, emotions, and behavior. In characterizing the symptoms of the disorder, Bleuler described four fundamental features which are still commonly referred to as *Bleuler's Four A's:*

1. *Association*—disorders of thought (as might be evident through rambling and incoherent speech).
2. *Affect*—disorder of the experience and expression of emotion (for example, inappropriate laughter in a sad situation).
3. *Ambivalence*—the inability to make or follow through on decisions.
4. *Autism*—the tendency to maintain an idiosyncratic style of egocentric thought and behavior.

Influenced by his contemporary, Sigmund Freud, Bleuler also looked for unconscious determinants of the symptoms of these patients. Unlike Kraepelin, Bleuler characterized schizophrenia as not always following a deteriorating course.

Bleuler had a significant influence on American psychiatry's views of schizophrenia as a diagnosis that could apply to a wide variety of people showing signs of disturbed thought and behavior. In fact, the early diagnostic manuals, such as *DSM-I* and *DSM-II*, included definitions of the disorder that are very broad and encompass many forms of psychotic behavior or psychotic-like behavior. These definitions were so broad, however, that far too many people were diagnosed as having schizophrenia even when they did not demonstrate any of the more dramatic symptoms now associated with the disorder. Disagreeing with Bleuler's broad characterization of schizophrenia was a German psychiatrist, Kurt Schneider (1887–1967), who introduced the idea that for the diagnosis of schizophrenia to be made, certain "first-rank" symptoms would have to be documented

(1959). For example, a person might hear voices that are commenting on the person's actions, or believe that thoughts are inserted into the person's mind by an outside agent.

First-rank symptoms are now recognized to be present in disorders other than schizophrenia such as certain forms of mood disorder, so Schneider's ideas about using them as the sole diagnostic indicators of schizophrenia are no longer considered valid. However, Schneider's thinking laid the foundation for more precision in the diagnosis of schizophrenia. In fact, at the time when American psychiatry was adopting Bleuler's rather broad definition of schizophrenia, European mental health professionals were basing their diagnostic system on the more narrow criteria suggested by Schneider. This discrepancy became apparent through studies that revealed that schizophrenia was diagnosed twice as frequently in the United States as in Great Britain for individuals who had the same symptoms (Leff, 1977).

By the time *DSM-III* was published, American psychiatry had moved away from Bleuler's general criteria toward the more restrictive definition based on Schneider's first-rank symptoms. *DSM-III-R* restricted the criteria even further, so that only a fraction of those who would have been diagnosed as having schizophrenia in the 1960s would now meet the criteria for this disorder. Interestingly, American mental health professionals working on the *DSM-IV* recognized the need to broaden *DSM-III-R*'s diagnostic criteria to include symptoms that are not overtly psychotic (Frances et al., 1990).

Symptoms of Schizophrenia

As you can see, considerable controversy exists over the precise definition of schizophrenia. Although the disorder has been the subject of thousands of research studies during the past century, experts on schizophrenia cannot come to a consensus about its exact symptoms and characteristics. Researchers and clinicians are now recognizing that this is because schizophrenia is a complex and multifaceted disorder, and it can take one of many forms in different individuals (Andreasen, 1987). If any kind of generality can be made, it is that the essence of schizophrenia lies in a cluster of symptoms that represent disturbances in the way an individual thinks, perceives, acts, and relates to others.

■ *Disturbance of thought content*

What would you think if a friend told you that articles in the campus newspaper were referring to him in a disguised fashion? For example, suppose he shows you the personals section of the college newspaper and points out 12 ads that he claims refer to something about him. He is sure that one or more other people are trying to seduce him but are disguising it by using a variety of names. At first you might think that he is kidding, or you might wonder whether he could be right. In all likelihood you would conclude that his claim is outlandish and you might be troubled

by his resistance to recognizing the absurdity of his assertion. If your friend were to persist, perhaps expanding his claims to even more outrageous levels such as believing that the songs on the radio were further attempts to seduce him, you would certainly conclude that he was suffering from delusions.

Delusions, or deeply entrenched false beliefs, are the most common disturbance of thought content associated with schizophrenia. As we discussed in Chapter 3, there are many kinds of delusions. They occur in association with schizophrenia as well as with other disorders such as mood disorders and disorders of cognitive impairment. Examples of delusions include delusions of reference, persecution, grandeur, poverty, self-accusation, control, nihilism, and infidelity. Other delusions pertain to irrational beliefs about one's thought processes, such as the belief that thoughts can be broadcast, inserted, or withdrawn from the mind by some external person or force. Somatic delusions involve bizarre erroneous beliefs about the workings of the body; for instance, a young man with schizophrenia may believe that his brain is being eaten by termites. No attempt by others can succeed in convincing him that he is mistaken.

■ *Disturbance of style of thought, language, and communication*

The cognitive processes of people with schizophrenia can be so disorganized and dysfunctional that their thinking lacks cohesiveness and logic. The way they express their ideas in thought and language can be grossly distorted to the point of incomprehensibility. It is extremely perplexing for other people attempting to communicate with a person who has a thought disorder (Rutter, 1985). In the following excerpt from an interview with a schizophrenic individual you can get a sense of disturbed thought:

Interviewer:	Why do you think people believe in God?
Patient:	Um, because making a do in life. Isn't none of that stuff about evolution guiding, isn't true anymore now. It all happened a long time ago. It happened in eons and eons and stuff they wouldn't believe in him. The time that Jesus Christ people believe in their thing people believed in, Jehovah God that they didn't believe in Jesus Christ that much.
Interviewer:	Um, what do you think about current political issues like the energy crisis?
Patient:	They're destroying too many cattle and oil just to make soap. If we need soap when you can jump into a pool of water, and then when you go to buy your gasoline, m-my folks always thought they should, get pop but the best thing to get, is motor oil, and, money. May-may as well go there

and, trade in some, pop caps and, uh, tires, and tractors to grup, car garages, so they can pull cars away from wrecks, is what I believed in. So I didn't go there to get no more pop when my folds said it. I just went there to get a ice-cream cone, and some pop, in cans, or we can go over there to get a cigarette . . . (Andreasen, 1986, p. 477).

You may recall from our discussion of the mental status examination in Chapter 3 that several forms of disturbed cognitive processes are associated with schizophrenia. Some commonly noted cognitive disturbances are incoherence, loose associations, neologisms, blocking, and poverty of content of speech. You may want to reread the excerpt just presented to see which cognitive disturbances are evident in the dialogue of this person (see Table 3-4).

Some instances of disturbed communication are not so dramatic; instead the person speaks in a peculiar way and uses awkward or pompous sounding speech. For example, when casually asked about the weather, the person may say, "It is an auspicious day for a feast on the grass, but the cumulus meanderings above us seem oh so ominous." In addition, the speech may have odd intonations and the individual may lack the usual expressiveness and gestures common to everyday talk. Even in what they write, they may use language so stilted and formal that it sounds artificial. In some extreme cases the individual may be mute, saying nothing for hours or days, or speaking in such a terse manner that others cannot understand what is being communicated.

■ Disturbances in perception: hallucinations

Have you ever had the experience as you were falling asleep of "hearing a voice" and thinking it was real? Perhaps you sat up in bed and responded. Upon realizing that no one was there, you might have just laughed to yourself. The mind often plays such tricks immediately before we fall asleep. But what if these voices, which no one else heard, were part of your everyday existence? What if you were hearing the voice of an angry man telling you to hit someone sitting across from you, or if you heard someone telling you how stupid or unattractive you are? Certainly you would be upset and frightened, and it might be a struggle for you to resist the commands.

Hallucinations, another distressing symptom of schizophrenia, are false perceptions involving any of the five senses. Although hallucinations do not correspond to actual stimuli, they seem very "real" to the person with schizophrenia. Hallucinations are not under voluntary control by the individual, but occur spontaneously despite the individual's attempts to ward them off. Such images, which may be frightening and painful, occur without any warning and obviously become very disruptive. Take the example of a man with schizophrenia who is recurrently taunted by voi-

Sometimes auditory hallucinations involve negative and upsetting comments about a person or a command to engage in some behavior that may be bizarre or threatening.

ces stating, "I am following you. I am watching you. You are under my control." Think of how disturbed you would be if your were alone in your room and suddenly heard these words spoken with such vehemence and clarity that you were convinced that another person must be there with you.

■ Disturbance of affect

People with schizophrenia often express their emotions in ways that seem abnormal to others. For most people, **affect** is consistent with emotional state. If you see someone smiling, you assume that person is feeling happy. People are accustomed to "reading" the cues provided by the affect of other people. This channel of communication is often missing when people speak with an individual who has schizophrenia, making it difficult for others to know how to react. Imagine you are talking to an acquaintance who giggles as she tells you about her recent bereavement. Chances are you will feel very uncomfortable, and over time you may avoid her if she continues to express her emotions so oddly. In a similar way, people with schizophrenia are shunned by others, who find being around them a confusing and uncomfortable experience.

■ Psychomotor disturbance

Sometimes people with schizophrenia move in odd and disturbing ways. For example, a man may suddenly slam his arm down in a sharp cutting action, perhaps in response to some form of hallucination. Whatever the precipitant, the behavior looks odd to other people. Alternatively, he may gesture in some odd fashion or grimace in a way that strikes others as strange. At times a person with schizophrenia may show signs of a catatonic disturbance, in the form of either stupor, rigidity, or excitement. *Catatonic stupor* is a state of being unresponsive to external stimuli, possibly to

What would you think if you were participating in a serious conversation in which one person unexpectedly broke out laughing? Such inappropriate affect is found in some people with schizophrenia.

A stiff and bizarre posture characterizes catatonic rigidity.

the point of being unaware of one's surroundings. *Catatonic rigidity* involves stiffened posturing of the body and resistance to efforts to be moved. Just as extreme is *catatonic excitement*, which involves apparently purposeless and repetitive bodily movements.

■ *Disturbed interpersonal relating ability*

You have seen that many people with schizophrenia have difficulties in relating to others because of their inability to regulate affect and because of peculiarities in their thinking and behavior. As a result, other people may avoid them, and an important source of contact with reality is lost. Imagine what it would be like for you to find that other people do not want to talk to you and even go out of their way to avoid you. Over time you would lose a sense of how to interact in appropriate ways with other people. Of course, not all people with schizophrenia are disturbed by social rejection; some actually prefer a life of isolation. Regardless of whether or not the individual wants to be left alone, social isolation usually triggers a vicious cycle of impairment in relational style; over time, the socially disturbed and isolated person is likely to be rejected and to retreat further into a world of fantasy and delusion.

■ *Disturbance in sense of self*

Most of us take for granted the continuity of our own identity over time. You know that you are the same person you were 10 years ago, even though you are also aware of many changes you have experienced since then. People with schizophrenia often express perplexity concerning their identity over a much shorter range of time, not just

from year to year, but from day to day and even moment to moment. They may not be sure who inhabits their body or even whether or not their body is really "theirs." Most of us occasionally ponder the meaning of our existence when we are in a philosophical mood. But a person with schizophrenia may be continually preoccupied with existential questions. These **disturbances in the sense of self** may range from expressing confusion about who one is to actual delusional thinking in which the individual believes that he or she is under the control or even part of some external person or force.

Staring intensely might cause other people to feel uncomfortable and avoid a person so that, over time, the person becomes isolated and even less capable of appropriate interactions with others.

■ *Disturbance of motivation*

People with schizophrenia may find themselves unmotivated either because of a lack of drive or interest in following through on a course of action or because of overwhelming ambivalence regarding possible choices. When such a disturbance of motivation is accompanied by confused or obsessive thoughts, these people become virtually incapacitated to the point of being immobilized.

Phases of Schizophrenia

To be diagnosed as having schizophrenia, an individual must show signs of disturbance for at least 6 months, including an **active phase** in which psychotic symptoms are present. Experts have debated about the minimum duration for this active phase. In *DSM-III-R*, the active phase was specified as lasting at least a week, although some have proposed that a month should be considered the minimum duration (American Psychiatric Association, 1991). The active phase does not usually appear without warning signs. Most, but not all, cases involve a **prodromal phase**—a period prior to the active phase during which the individual shows progressive deterioration in social and interpersonal functioning. The types of changes shown during this phase can include social withdrawal, inability to work productively, eccentricity, poor grooming, inappropriate emotionality, the development of peculiar thought and speech, unusual beliefs, odd perceptual experiences, and diminishment of initiative and energy. For many people, the active phase of symptoms is followed by a **residual phase** in which there are continuing indications of disturbance evidenced by the same kinds of behaviors that characterize the prodromal phase. Symptoms such as delusions or peculiar speech may remain during the residual phase, but these symptoms are usually not as intense and disruptive as they were during the active phase. As you will see when we discuss the process-reactive dimension of schizophrenia, the phases may vary according to the individual's particular constellation of schizophrenic symptoms.

Types of Schizophrenia

Although we speak of "schizophrenia" as a single disorder, it is really quite diverse, taking on dramatically different forms from individual to individual. Not every person with a diagnosis of schizophrenia shows all of the symptoms we described. For example, for some people paranoid delusions are the most prominent symptoms, but for others, delusions may be completely absent.

■ *Catatonic schizophrenia*

When the prominent symptom in schizophrenia pertains to bizarre or unusual bodily movements, the person is likely to be diagnosed as having **catatonic schizophrenia**.

Maria is a 19-year-old college freshman who has been psychiatrically hospitalized for more than a month. For days prior to her admission, and for the weeks since her arrival in the hospital, Maria has been mute. Rigidly posturing her body and staring at the ceiling, she spends most of the day in a trancelike state that seems impenetrable. Her family and college acquaintances have been mystified. In trying to sort out why and when she began showing such odd behavior, the only incident that could be recalled was Maria's ranting and raving, just prior to going into the catatonic state, that one of her professors was a "demon."

■ What type of catatonic behavior is shown by Maria's staring and mutism?
■ Given Maria's current symptoms, what is suggested by her behavior of the preceding week?

You will recall from our earlier discussion the different ways in which catatonic behavior is displayed. People with catatonic schizophrenia show a variety of catatonic symptoms ranging from immobility and stupor to frenetic stereotyped bodily movements.

Convinced that assassins are in close pursuit, a person with paranoid schizophrenia might stay barricaded behind a heavily locked door.

Joshua is 43-year-old man who can be found daily standing near the steps of a local bank on a busy street corner. Every day he wears a Yankees baseball cap, a yellow T-shirt, worn-out hiking shorts, and orange sneakers. Rain or shine, day in and day out, Joshua maintains his "post" at the bank. Sometimes he can be seen "conversing" with imaginary people. Without provocation he sobs miserably, and at other times he explodes in shrieks of laughter. Police and social workers keep taking him to shelters for the homeless, but Joshua manages to get out and be back on the street before he can be treated.

- What behaviors shown by Joshua suggest that he has disorganized schizophrenia?
- Have you ever seen a person like Joshua and wondered why he or she behaved that way?

Sometimes a schizophrenic person becomes so impaired that hospitalization is necessary.

Disorganized schizophrenia

Disorganized schizophrenia is characterized by a combination of symptoms that include being incoherent, making loose associations, showing inappropriate affect, and behaving in a grossly disorganized manner. Even the person's delusions and hallucinations, when present, lack any coherent theme. Individuals whose disorders fall into this category are noticeably odd in their behavior and appearance and usually have serious impairment in work and other social contexts.

Paranoid schizophrenia

The essential feature of **paranoid schizophrenia** is preoccupation with one or more bizarre delusions or with auditory hallucinations that are related to a particular theme of being persecuted or harassed. People with paranoid schizophrenia, compared to people with other forms of schizophrenia, are older at the onset of their symptoms, function at higher levels prior to developing the disorder, and are more likely to recover. Their symptoms develop rapidly and appear intermittently over the first 5 years of their illness (Fenton & McGlashan, 1991a).

Esther is a 31-year-old unmarried woman who lives with her elderly mother. A belief that the outside air is filled with radio waves that will insert evil thoughts into her head keeps Esther from leaving the house. The windows in her bedroom are "protected" with aluminum foil that "deflects the radio waves." She often hears voices that comment on these radio signals. For example, one comment was the slow, deep voice of an elderly man who angrily stated, "We're going to get these thoughts into your head. Give up your fight!"

- What behaviors of Esther's would lead you to consider her as having paranoid schizophrenia?
- How do Esther's symptoms differ from those of a person with paranoid personality disorder?

You may be wondering how paranoid schizophrenia differs from paranoid personality disorder, which we discussed in Chapter 6. The primary difference lies in the fact that people with paranoid schizophrenia experience a range of psychotic symptoms, such as delusions and hallucinations. Although the thinking of a person with a paranoid personality disorder may at times border on being delusional, this would be a transient phenomenon.

Undifferentiated schizophrenia

In some people with schizophrenia, the symptom picture is mixed, and the clinician cannot classify the disorder into one of the types just discussed. A diagnosis of **undifferentiated schizophrenia** is used when a person shows a complex of schizophrenic symptoms such as delusions, hallucinations, incoherence, or disorganized behavior, but does not meet the criteria for the paranoid (systematic

Bruce, a 24-year-old maintenance worker, is considered "peculiar" by almost everyone he meets. He has a "strange" look in his eyes, and he commonly mumbles to himself as if he were holding a conversation with someone. The words he uses sometimes sound like those of a foreign language, but no one else can understand them. At times he stares out the window for hours, and barks angrily at anyone who disturbs him. It seems as though he is lost in a world of fantasy, but he nevertheless manages to keep up with his custodial duties.

- What symptoms of various types of schizophrenia are evident in Bruce who has a diagnosis of undifferentiated schizophrenia?
- In light of the fact that Bruce is able to function in a job, do you feel that he should be urged to get professional help or simply be left alone?

> Three years after her third hospitalization for schizophrenia, Joyce's condition seems to have reached a point of stability. She has a set routine for taking her antipsychotic medications; for checking in regularly at the Center for Independent Living, which supervises her work placement in a glove factory; and for visiting with her sister and family. Joyce, a somewhat overweight 45-year-old woman, shows only occasional signs of the illness that at one time had totally incapacitated her. She still sometimes becomes preoccupied with the idea that her former mother-in-law is sending her invisible poisoned envelopes in the mail. At other times, she cannot stop herself from pacing the floor. These symptoms never last very long, though, and she is soon able to resume her daily schedule without being unduly distressed.
>
> ■ What warrants referring to Joyce as a person with residual schizophrenia?
> ■ Do you think that Joyce should be receiving psychotherapeutic treatment?

bizarre delusions), catatonic (abnormalities of movement), or disorganized (disturbed or flat affect) types of schizophrenia.

■ *Residual schizophrenia*

Some people who have previously been diagnosed as having schizophrenia no longer have prominent psychotic symptoms but still show some lingering signs of the disorder. Although they are not delusional, hallucinating, incoherent, or disorganized, they may retain some symptoms such as emotional blunting, social withdrawal, eccentric behavior, or illogical thinking. These individuals would be diagnosed as having **residual schizophrenia**.

Dimensions of Schizophrenia

In addition to the types of schizophrenia we have just discussed, researchers have been exploring other ways of categorizing the varieties of schizophrenia. As you consider the descriptions of the types of schizophrenia, you can readily see how very different paranoid schizophrenia is from catatonic schizophrenia. However, many clinicians and researchers feel that the current categories fail to capture the essential dimensions underlying individual differences in symptoms (Hemsley, 1987). Instead, they prefer ways of thinking about schizophrenia that focus on the presence or absence of dramatic symptoms (such as bizarre hallucinations, delusions, and prominent thought disorder) as well as on the course of the disorder over time. All of these attempts to classify types of schizophrenia represent efforts by the scientific community to gain a better grasp on understanding the causes of this disorder. Researchers hope that the discovery of the best classification scheme will ultimately lead to clues about the disorder's causes.

■ *Positive-negative dimension*

The idea of a need to distinguish between two fundamentally different categories of schizophrenia goes back to the original views of Kraepelin, who implied that there were two kinds of symptoms associated with the disorder. Kraepelin spoke of one kind as being more dramatic and observable, and the other as being marked by deficit, such as loss of the ability to experience pleasure. This distinction was made more explicit by Bleuler, and continued to be used by clinicians for the next half-century until it was replaced by a broader definition of schizophrenia. New evidence for the validity of Kraepelin's formulation began to emerge in the early 1980s, with the publication of work by Thomas Crow (Crow, 1980, 1985) on the distinction between what he called *Type I* and *Type II* schizophrenia. These categories were differentiated based on the nature of the symptoms as well as a number of other characteristics related to the course of the disorder and response to treatment. The kinds of symptoms that distinguish these groups were called *positive* and *negative*.

Why are these symptoms referred to in this way? One way to think of the difference is in terms of deviation from a baseline of normal functioning. **Positive symptoms** are exaggerations or distortions of normal thoughts, emotions, and behavior; **negative symptoms** involve an absence or reduction compared to baseline functioning. Looking at Table 11-1, you can begin to see why this distinction is referred to as *positive-negative*. Symptoms such as *anhedonia* (lack of pleasure), apathy, and poverty of speech are *negative* in the sense that they represent losses or deficits in normal functioning. In contrast, delusions and hallucinations, called *positive*, are very dramatic, bizarre, and compelling. As you can imagine, it is much easier to diagnose schizophrenia when positive symptoms are present; negative symptoms are more ambiguous. You may notice that many of the positive symptoms are those that characterize paranoid schizophrenia. In fact, some experts have proposed that paranoid schizophrenia be renamed *schizophrenia, positive type* (American Psychiatric Association, 1991).

You should be aware that there is considerable debate in the research community about the validity and utility of the positive-negative subtype distinction (Carpenter et al., 1988). It is often difficult to form a clear-cut diagnosis according to the distinction between positive and negative symptoms (Andreasen et al., 1990). Many people with a diagnosis of schizophrenia fall into a "mixed" category, meaning that they have both positive and negative symptoms. However, the positive-negative distinction has held up in a number of investigations as a reliable basis for predicting the long-term outcome of schizophrenia (Fenton & McGlashan, 1991b; Pogue-Geile & Harrow, 1987).

What about the person who only has negative symptoms of schizophrenia such as apathy, anhedonia, attentional impairment, and other deficits in functioning? Some researchers and clinicians believe that such an individual

Table 11-1 Characteristics of Positive and Negative Subtypes of Schizophrenia

DISTINGUISHING FEATURE	POSITIVE SUBTYPE "TYPE I"	NEGATIVE SUBTYPE "TYPE II"
Types of symptoms	Hallucinations. Delusions. Thought disorder. Bizarre or disorganized behavior.	Poverty of speech. Poverty of content of speech. Affective flattening. Anhedonia. Asociality. Avolition. Apathy. Attentional impairment.
Onset	Acute.	Insidious.
Course	Exacerbations and remissions.	Chronic.
Response to treatment	Favorable response to neuroleptics.	Poor response to neuroleptics.
Intellectual impairment	Minimal.	Significant.
Brain abnormalities	Increased dopamine receptors. Abnormalities in parts of the limbic system.	Enlarged ventricles. Frontal lobe abnormalities. Normal CT scans.
Social functions	History of exacerbations and remissions. Normal social functioning between episodes.	Poor social functioning.

might have schizophrenia, yet might not meet the very narrow criteria that were listed in *DSM-III-R* (Andreasen & Flaum, 1990). One prominent team of researchers at Yale University has suggested retaining the original subtypes of paranoid, undifferentiated, disorganized, catatonic, and residual, because these continue to make clinical and empirical sense (McGlashan & Fenton, 1991). To these subtypes would be added the diagnosis of simple schizophrenia, which would be used to refer to people who show only negative symptoms (McGlashan & Fenton 1991, 1992). Ironically, this brings the diagnostic nomenclature back to where it was when *DSM-II* was in use and when schizophrenia was broadly defined in the tradition of Bleuler, a definition that many thought was far too vague and general (Andreasen, 1989). However, the weight of the evidence currently appears to support the reinstatement of negative symptoms in the diagnosis of schizophrenia.

■ *Process-reactive dimension*

Another dimension differentiates kinds of schizophrenia by how the symptoms emerge. Recall our discussion about the prodromal phase, a period of gradual deterioration prior to the active phase involving obvious symptoms. Perhaps you have heard of a person who acts normally one day only to wake up the following day in a state of psychosis. Does this person have the same disorder as the individual who goes through a prodromal phase of weeks or months? These two examples represent points on a dimen-

sion called *process versus reactive* (Garmezy, 1970). As the terms imply, **process** refers to the gradual appearance of the disorder over time, and **reactive** indicates that some precipitant provoked the onset of symptoms. These two types also differ in their **premorbid functioning**, the period prior to the onset of symptoms. People with the process form of schizophrenia are more likely to show signs of maladjustment before diagnosable symptoms become apparent, in contrast to people with reactive schizophrenia, who appear normal until their symptoms develop.

Researchers and clinicians began to use the process-reactive delineation in the 1950s, because they believed that this was an important indicator of the likelihood that a person with the diagnosis of schizophrenia would recover. People with the process form of schizophrenia were thought to have a much poorer chance of recovering, and their illness was considered to be much more deeply ingrained. In contrast, reactive schizophrenia was regarded as developing in response to some upsetting life event such as the death of a loved one; presumably, the healing process of time would enable the individual to return to normal functioning.

Although the process-reactive distinction became very popular from the 1950s to the 1980s, considerable controversy exists over the value of this dimension (Harrow & Westermeyer, 1987; Herron, 1987). Originally, the distinction was intended to help clinicians and researchers understand the etiology and prognosis of schizophrenia in different people. However, as we pointed out earlier, the

The difference in the experiences of this woman and this man captures the distinction between positive and negative symptoms of schizophrenia. The woman's hallucinations and bizarre delusions are positive symptoms. The man's flat affect and apathy are negative systems.

diagnosis of schizophrenia that had evolved by the 1980s was much narrower than that of the 1950s. Thus, many people who were diagnosed as having schizophrenia and fit the reactive definition would no longer be regarded as even having schizophrenia if they were diagnosed today. For

example, a previously normal young man who is admitted to the hospital with disturbing delusions, hallucinations, and bizarre thoughts and behavior following some traumatic event would not currently be diagnosed with schizophrenia, although such a label may well have been applied to him 20 years ago. The process-reactive distinction has therefore lost some of its relevance, because a person with "reactive" onset would probably now be regarded as having some other disorder such as a personality disorder, a mood disorder, or brief reactive psychosis, which we will discuss later in this chapter. One possible compromise is a suggestion that impairment in premorbid social functioning be added as a third category to the positive-negative subtype dimension (Lenzenweger et al., 1991). This strategy would combine the more generally supported positive versus negative symptom distinction with an important aspect of the process versus reactive distinction. There would then be three categories of people with schizophrenia: those with positive symptoms, those with negative symptoms, and those with poor premorbid functioning characterized by impaired personal and social relationships.

The Course of Schizophrenia

There is no single route that schizophrenia takes in the lives of people who become afflicted with the disorder. You have just read about two proposed ways of differentiating forms of schizophrenia, one that involves different kinds of symptoms and another that pertains to the development of the disorder. Both these dimensions involve differences in onset and outcome of the disorder.. Some people suffer the symptoms of schizophrenia for a relatively brief portion of their lives, following which they return to normal functioning. For others the course involves chronic impairment (Carpenter & Strauss, 1991) particularly if they have negative symptoms (Mueser et al, 1991). Still others contend with intense episodic outbreaks of symptoms. Researchers do not yet understand why the course of this disorder is so variable and why one person recovers and another remains permanently impaired. One question that has arisen is whether such individuals are actually suffering from the same disorder. As we said earlier, it is possible that in the decades to come these disorders will be recognized as separate entities.

According to current estimates, about 20 percent of people diagnosed with schizophrenia recover (Breier et al., 1991; Carone et al., 1991). Using less stringent criteria for recovery, other researchers report more optimistic statistics, with estimates of improvement or recovery ranging from one-half to two-thirds (Harding et al., 1987). It is important to note, though, that however recovery is defined, it does not necessarily constitute a "cure," since the individual still may feel vulnerable about the possibility of the illness returning (Rund, 1990).

What about those people who do not recover? As you can imagine, their lives are profoundly affected by their disorder. The symptoms of schizophrenia interfere with many aspects of daily life, particularly social interactions (Wiedl & Schöttner, 1991). Loneliness and depression are commonly reported long-term problems experienced by people with schizophrenia during phases of remission (Guze et al., 1983; Herz & Melville, 1980). Mortality statistics show that people with schizophrenia have higher rates of suicide, death by violence, and even cardiovascular problems than age-matched adults in the general population (Allebeck, 1989). The life of a person with chronic schizophrenia often takes unpredictable and unwanted turns as a consequence of the illness (Bleuler, 1978). The symptoms may recede for a period of time only to return with a vengeance that destroys whatever hopes the schizophrenic person may have had that the illness was in remission.

OTHER PSYCHOTIC DISORDERS

At one time the diagnosis of schizophrenia was applied so broadly to people with a wide range of maladaptive behaviors that the majority of people living in institutions were labeled with this diagnosis. One of the most troubling facets of the overuse of this diagnosis was the corresponding notion that once a person was diagnosed as having schizophrenia, that person was doomed to carry that label for life. Even for people with only brief psychotic symptoms, clini-

cians mistakenly assumed that schizophrenia would subsequently lie dormant beneath the surface, waiting to burst out again in the form of new symptoms at any time. Many clinicians advised clients who had shown psychotic symptoms to take antipsychotic medication for life to prevent their symptoms from recurring. This situation began to change during the 1970s, in part because researchers discovered a group of disorders that shared some but not all symptoms with schizophrenia.

The schizophrenia-like disorders share three common features: (1) each is a form of psychosis representing a serious break with reality; (2) none of them is considered to be caused by disorder of cognitive impairment; and (3) mood disturbance is not a primary symptom. Each disorder has aspects similar to certain features of schizophrenia, but each is distinguished from schizophrenia by other components of the disorder, such as presumed cause and course. Further, each of the schizophrenic-like disorders has a different set of proposed causes, symptom picture, and recommended course of treatment.

Brief Reactive Psychosis

You may be able to think of a time when someone you knew was so upset he felt like he was "losing his mind." Perhaps his reaction was so severe that he was described as having a "nervous breakdown," a common term that is actually a

CRITICAL ISSUE

Do People Recover from Schizophrenia?

For many years it was thought that once people were diagnosed as having schizophrenia, recovery was impossible. Even if no symptoms followed a psychotic episode, many clinicians presumed that schizophrenia was in "hiding," waiting to resurface unexpectedly. The term "in remission" was used to describe a person who previously had been diagnosed as having schizophrenia but did not currently suffer from the symptoms. You can imagine how this label and its underlying expectations could doom a person's entire life.

Contemporary views of schizophrenia are much more optimistic about the long-term outcome of the disorder. This change has occurred gradually over the past two decades, as a result of more rigorous research methods and more precise definitions of what constitutes schizophrenia. In studying recovery from schizophrenia, researchers have first had to grapple with the issue of what constitutes

"recovery." Does recovery mean just staying out of the hospital with no recurrent psychotic episodes or does the term imply also returning to normal levels of social functioning? In an ideal sense, recovery would involve both of these factors. However, in reality, the situation is far more complex.

Let's take a look at each aspect of recovery separately. Staying out of the hospital may have more to do with social or insurance factors than with the presence of an incapacitating disorder. Regarding the recurrence of a psychotic episode, we must consider what length of time to use as a criterion for a person to be considered no longer at risk. For example, is a year of being free from psychosis a long enough period for researchers to regard the individual as "recovered"? Or should the interval be 2, 3, or perhaps 5 years? Finally, consider the question of the return to normal functioning. Many people who were diagnosed as having schizo-

phrenia do not return to a completely "normal" existence but are able to carry out many everyday activities, including some form of employment. A woman living in a group home for people with psychological disorders may work at a community day treatment center in a very nondemanding job such as assembling wooden toys. Whether or not she is counted in the "recovered" category may vary from researcher to researcher. Many of these issues are common to concerns in other outcome research, but in the case of schizophrenia they have particular relevance because of the severely debilitating nature of this disorder. Researchers acknowledge that the phenomenon of recovery must be very broadly defined in view of these complications, but they agree that the essence of recovery involves lack of symptoms and a return to social and occupational functioning.

For some people, personal stresses reach such intensity that they develop brief reactive psychosis, with transient symptoms that resemble those of schizophrenia.

misnomer; the person's nerves do not really break down. The correct term would be **brief reactive psychosis**. When some people face overwhelming stress they develop psychotic symptoms and are given this diagnosis. This disorder is characterized by a sudden onset of psychotic symptoms that are time-limited, lasting anywhere from a few hours to a month. These symptoms usually appear after some stressful event or set of events, and eventually the person returns to normal functioning. The stress may be something that others would clearly recognize as being serious, like the death of a spouse or a house fire, but, in some instances the stress may not be so dramatic (e.g., academic or, financial problems). Some individuals become briefly psychotic, without any apparent stressor. For these cases, the term acute psychotic disorder has been proposed (American Psychiatric Association, 1991).

For a relatively short period of time, the person in the midst of a brief reactive psychosis or acute psychotic disorder may appear to have schizophrenia because of symptoms such as delusions, hallucinations, thought disorder, and bizarre behavior. However, such disorders are markedly different because they are time-limited. The individual does not embark upon a deteriorating course, but typically recovers and returns to a normal state of functioning.

Brief reactive psychosis is thought to be determined by psychological rather than biological factors, although it is possible that certain people may be biologically predisposed to develop this disorder when faced with considerable psychological stress. Most people have adequate resources for dealing with difficulties and anxiety. When these customary defenses fail, or when a crisis is unusually stressful, a person may begin to "fall apart."

The notion of reactive psychosis was popular in European psychiatry as a way of accounting for stress-related reactions following traumatic life events. As we mentioned earlier, most forms of psychotic behavior had been thought of in American psychiatric circles as representing schizophrenia. In the late 1960s, *DSM-II* incorporated the diagnosis of reactive psychosis, on the basis of many clinical reports that people could develop psychotic symptoms following stressful events. Currently, some controversy exists over whether true psychosis can develop in response to stress without any predisposing condition such as a mood or personality disorder (Munoz et al., 1987). In other words, some experts believe that it is unlikely that a person who shows psychotic symptoms after a stressful life event was psychologically healthy prior to the onset of symptoms. Alternatively, some researchers have argued that the diagnosis is not used enough and that the criteria for it should be broadened (Jauch & Carpenter, 1988). At the present time, clinicians continue to use this diagnosis for those cases in

Anthony is a 22-year-old senior at a prestigious small college. His family has traditionally held high standards for Anthony, and his father had every expectation that his son would go on to enroll at Harvard Law School. Anthony felt intensely pressured as he worked day and night to maintain a high grade point average, while diligently preparing for the national examination for admission to law schools. His social life became devoid of any meaningful contact. He even began skipping meals because he did not want to take time away from studying. On the day that Anthony received the scores for the law school admission exam, he was devastated because he knew that his scores were too low to get into any good law school. He began crying uncontrollably, wandering around the dormitory hallways screaming obscenities, and telling people that there was some "plot" on the part of the college dean to keep him from getting into law school. After 2 days of this behavior, Anthony's resident advisor convinced him to go to the infirmary, where his condition was diagnosed and treated. After a week of rest and some medication, Anthony returned to normal functioning and was able to assess his academic situation more rationally.

- What factors in Anthony's life appear related to his development of brief reactive psychosis?
- Which of Anthony's symptoms are also found in schizophrenia?

which severe symptoms emerge in individuals not otherwise considered psychotic.

Treatment of brief reactive psychosis usually consists of a combination of medication and psychotherapy. Short-term use of antianxiety or antipsychotic medication is often needed to help the individual return to normal functioning. The nature of the psychological intervention depends on the nature of the stressor, when one is evident. Sometimes, the disturbance can be reduced by removing the person from the stressful situation. At other times, this may not be possible. In either case, effective psychotherapy integrates support, education, and the development of insight regarding the determinants of the person's disturbed reaction.

Schizophreniform Disorder

The term *schizophreniform* means that a disorder takes the form of schizophrenia but is somehow different. People with **schizophreniform disorder** have psychotic symptoms that are essentially the same as those found in schizophrenia, except for the duration and chronic nature of the symptoms. The symptoms of schizophreniform disorder usually last longer than those of brief reactive psychosis, but not so long that the person would be diagnosed as having schizophrenia. Specifically, active symptoms usually last from 1 to 6 months. If the symptoms last longer than 6 months, then the diagnosis of schizophrenia is more likely.

Biology appears to play a prominent role in determining whether a person will develop schizophreniform disorder. For example, it has been found that people with this disorder have unusually large brain ventricles (DeLisi et al., 1991), a phenomenon also observed in people with schizophrenia. Another suggestion of a link to schizophrenia is the finding of similar patterns of brain activity during a cognitive task as measured by a PET scan (Rubin et al., 1991). A biological explanation for schizophreniform disorder is also suggested by the fact that relatives of people with this disorder have a higher likelihood of having the disorder. Researchers are working to sort out the significance of these strands of evidence supporting a biological explanation; they are also trying to understand the ways in which schizophreniform disorder is related to schizophrenia. We will return to this subject in the next chapter.

Regarding treatment, most people with schizophreniform disorder need medication to help bring their symptoms under control. For some, the symptoms will go away spontaneously, but the behavior of people with schizophreniform disorder is usually so disturbed that family and friends insist on an intervention. Most commonly antipsychotic medication is prescribed, particularly for the acute phase of the disorder. Other treatments include lithium or antianxiety medications. In cases where the individual is dangerously out of control, electroconvulsive therapy can offer quick improvement. Because people with this disorder function normally when not experiencing a psychotic

At the time that Edward developed a psychological disorder, he was 26 years old and worked for a convenience store chain. Although always regarded by family and friends as unusual, he had not experienced psychotic symptoms. This all changed as he grew more and more disturbed over the course of several months. His mother thought that he was just "stressed out" because of his financial problems, but Edward did not seem concerned about such matters. He gradually developed paranoid delusions and became preoccupied with reading the Bible. What brought his disturbance to the attention of his supervisors was an incident in which he submitted an order to the district office for 6000 loaves of bread. He scribbled at the bottom of the order form the words "Jesus will multiply the loaves." When questioned about this inappropriate order, Edward lost control, ranting and raving, insisting that his superiors were plotting to keep him from fighting world hunger. Paranoid themes and bizarre behaviors also surfaced in Edward's dealings with his wife and children. Following 2 months of increasingly disturbed behavior, Edward's boss referred him for a psychiatric evaluation. With rest and relatively low doses of antipsychotic medication, Edward returned to normal functioning after a few weeks of hospitalization.

- How do Edward's schizophreniform symptoms differ from those of schizophrenia?
- What differentiates Edward's disorder from brief reactive psychosis?

episode, most clinicians prefer to reduce and discontinue medication after some period of time.

Psychotherapy can also be beneficial to people with this disorder. Initially the therapist works to help the individual regain control, but eventually the focus shifts to possible causes of the disorder.

Schizoaffective Disorder

A major controversy pertains to the issue of whether schizophrenia and mood disorders are mutually exclusive disorders that have no overlap or whether there are some people with symptoms of both disorders. Bleuler believed that the diagnosis of schizophrenia should take precedence, regardless of how severe a client's mood disturbance might be. Many clinicians and researchers have moved away from this position, insisting that some individuals have symptoms that are both schizophrenic and affective in nature. In such cases, the diagnosis of **schizoaffective disorder** is used. Because schizoaffective disorder is an imprecise diagnosis, it has been difficult to determine its incidence and prevalence.

Debate has focused on whether schizoaffective disorder is a variant of schizophrenia, with similar etiology or whether it should be regarded as a mood disorder. In reviewing the evidence on both sides of the issue, Nancy Andreasen, a world expert in the field, concluded that the term *schizoaffective disorder* most probably refers to a combination of schizophrenic and mood disorder symptoms that cannot clearly be separated (Andreasen, 1987). Researchers studying individuals during a 5-year period following hospitalization for schizoaffective disorder have found that these individuals attain somewhat better overall posthospital functioning than people with schizophrenia, somewhat poorer functioning than bipolar manic patients, and much poorer functioning than people who had been diagnosed with unipolar depression. Because poor outcome is apparently associated with the presence of schizophrenia-like psychotic symptoms during the active phase of the disorder, these researchers concluded that schizoaffective disorder is not just a variant of mood disorder (Grossman et al., 1991). In a related vein, retrospective studies of people discharged from a psychiatric hospital over a 25-year period also indicated that the more schizophrenic the symptom picture, the worse the outcome was among people with schizoaffective disorder (McGlashan & Williams, 1990).

The disagreement over whether schizoaffective disorder is a valid psychiatric diagnosis has muddied the theoretical explanations of the disorder. Those researchers who maintain that schizoaffective disorder is a variant of schizophrenia rely on theories of schizophrenia. Similarly, for researchers who regard the disorder as primarily a mood disturbance, theories of mood disorders are seen as pertinent.

Clinicians are sometimes reluctant to use the diagnosis of schizoaffective disorder because it has no systematic treatment protocol. Pharmacological intervention for people with this diagnosis usually involves a trial-and-error approach that may include lithium, antidepressants, and antipsychotic medication either alone or in various combinations. For the most part, antipsychotic medication is combined with lithium for clients with manic symptoms, and with antidepressants for clients who are depressed. Psychotherapy obviously needs to be individualized for each client with this diagnosis. The psychotherapist must be prepared to deal with abrupt symptom changes and with the client's unpredictable feelings and behaviors.

Delusional Disorders

Some individuals who otherwise function adequately have a single striking psychotic symptom—delusional thinking. They do not show the other symptoms that would make a diagnosis of schizophrenia or mood disorder an appropriate one. Their delusions are systematized and prominent, but lack the bizarre quality commonly found in schizophrenia. In fact, it is sometimes initially difficult for others to determine whether these people are delusional, because they can be quite convincing and coherent in the expression of their beliefs. However, with continued contact, most people are able to discern that the beliefs of a person with a delusional disorder are very strange.

There are five subtypes of delusional disorder. People with **erotomania** have a delusion that another person, usually of great prominence, is deeply in love with them. In some cases, symptoms of mood disorder, such as depression or mania, may also be present (Rudden et al., 1990). For example, an otherwise healthy woman may be firmly convinced that a famous talk show host is in love with her, and that he communicates secret love messages to her in his monologue each night. **Grandiose delusional disorder** is characterized by the delusion that one is an extremely important person. For example, a man may believe that he is the Messiah, waiting for a sign from heaven to begin his active ministry. **Jealous delusional disorder** is characterized

Delusions of grandeur are characterized by a belief that one is a prominent or famous figure. This woman parades down the street with gestures indicative of a belief that she is Jesus Christ.

by the delusion that one's partner is being unfaithful. For example, a man may be mistakenly convinced that his wife is having an affair, and may construct a set of "evidence" of routine domestic events (such as an unexplained charge on the phone bill) to "prove" her infidelity. People with **persecutory delusional disorder** believe that they are being persecuted. For example, a woman may believe that she is the object of a government plot, and she may misconstrue the most insignificant of events as evidence that she is a target for assassination. People with **somatic delusional disorder** believe that they have some dreaded disease or that they are dying. Their adherence to such a belief is extreme and incorrigible. For example, a woman may believe that her teeth are turning to chalk and that this deterioration process will then lead to the deterioration of her skull.

Induced Psychotic Disorder

Induced psychotic disorder is a disorder in which one or more people develop a delusional system as a result of a close relationship with a psychotic person who is delusional. Typically two people are involved in this disorder, and the term *folie a deux* (folly of) is applied to the couple. Occasionally, three or more people or the members of an entire family are involved (Glassman et al., 1987).

Unlike schizophrenia, which develops with no apparent external provocation, induced psychotic disorder develops in the context of an intimate relationship in which there is a history of pathological dependence. The nonpsy-

chotic person gets caught up in the delusional system of the psychotic person and becomes equally consumed by the irrational belief. If the two separate, the previously

Julio and Carmen, both in their 30s, had been dating for 6 months. Having met at the accounting office where they both worked, they kept their intimate relationship a secret from co-workers at Julio's insistence. With Julio being the dominant partner in the relationship, and Carmen correspondingly submissive, the couple kept exclusive company with each other. Most of their conversation centered around Julio's unwavering belief, which Carmen had come to share, that other people at their office did not like them and that several people wanted them fired. The two of them often stayed after work to search the desks and files of co-workers for evidence that would support Julio's notion. The slightest comment directed toward either of them was construed as evidence of this plot. On the rare occasions when they talked to co-workers, they immediately recorded the conversation in a secret log book. They refused to use the office computer because they were convinced that it was programmed to keep tabs on them. Eventually, both lost their jobs, but not for the reasons they had constructed. Their odd behaviors aroused so much suspicion that the office routine was disrupted and they had to be let go.

■ What symptoms of induced psychotic disorder are evident in the case of Carmen and Julio?
■ If Carmen were not in a relationship with Julio, do you think that she would have other serious psychological problems?

In induced psychotic disorder, a nonpsychotic person becomes drawn into the delusional system of a psychotic person. This phenomenon usually occurs in a close relationship, such as between two sisters.

nonpsychotic person will very likely return to normal functioning and thinking.

This disorder is very rare. In the few instances that it is diagnosed, it is usually found among members of the same family, with the most common cases involving two sisters. This is followed in frequency by mother/child, father/child, and husband/wife combinations. Occasionally it is found between two friends or lovers. Approximately one-fourth of the submissive partners suffer from some form of physical disability, which may contribute to their dependence on the dominant member of the pair.

Induced psychotic disorder is explained primarily from a psychological perspective. The dominant person in these pairs feels desperately isolated from others due to numerous psychological problems. This person seeks out another person who can serve as an ally. The dependent person usually needs the dominant person for some reason, such as safety, financial security, or emotional support, and is therefore willing to surrender to the delusions of the dominant member.

People with induced psychotic disorder rarely seek treatment because they do not perceive themselves as being disturbed. Occasionally, relatives or friends of the submissive partner urge this person to get professional help. Effective intervention involves separating the two people, at which point the submissive person sometimes becomes more open to rational discussion of the disturbed relationship. At that point, therapy can focus on personal issues that seem related to this person's vulnerability to being dominated. The therapist would explore ways to bolster the client's self-esteem in order to prevent recurrence.

LOOKING AHEAD

By this point you have probably developed some sense of how disruptive and debilitating schizophrenia and related disorders can be. Imagine how you would feel if someone you love started to lose control of thought processes, behavior, sensations, and affect. You would certainly be deeply affected and concerned. You would probably try to understand the reasons for such changes in this individual, and you would very likely want to look for ways that the person could be helped. In the next chapter we will discuss the current state of knowledge about this baffling disorder, and will present the treatment approaches that are currently regarded as most effective.

SUMMARY

1. The disorders covered in this chapter include conditions commonly referred to as *psychoses*, whose central feature is a severe disturbance in the individual's experience of reality about the world and the self.

2. Schizophrenia is a psychotic disorder with a range of symptoms involving disturbances in content of thought, form of thought, perception, affect, sense of self, motivation, behavior, and interpersonal functioning. Schizophrenia afflicts about one percent of the population. Although this is a small percentage, this number reflects a significant amount of resources needed to

Table 11-2 Summary of Schizophrenia and Schizophrenia-Like Disorders

Disorder	Types of Symptoms[1]	Types or Dimensions
Schizophrenia	Delusions. Cognitive disturbances. Hallucinations. Flat or inappropriate affect. Psychomotor disturbance. Social withdrawal. Disturbed sense of self. Lack of motivation.	Types: Catatonic Disorganized Paranoid Undifferentiated Residual Dimensions: Positive-negative Process-reactive
Brief reactive psychosis	Psychotic symptoms precipitated by stress and lasting for short period of time (a month or less).	
Schizophreniform disorder	Psychotic symptoms that last from 1 to 6 months.	
Schizoaffective disorder	Schizophrenic symptoms combined with symptoms of mood disorder.	
Delusional disorder	Psychosis characterized by the single symptom of delusional thinking.	Types: Erotomania Grandiose Jealous Persecutory Somatic
Induced delusional disorder	Development of a delusional system within a close relationship with a delusional person.	

[1]Not all symptoms are found in all cases of these disorders; symptoms given here provide examples of the types of symptoms often observed.

care for people with the disorder. Beyond the cost to society of caring for people with schizophrenia is the emotional and social toll the disorder takes on its sufferers, whose chances for normal life are often severely hampered.

3. The disorder currently called schizophrenia was first systematically described by Kraepelin, who referred to it as *dementia praecox* and regarded it as a brain disease. Bleuler challenged this position and described schizophrenia as a psychological disorder caused by a splitting or lack of integration among the functions of the mind. Bleuler described psychological symptoms to be used in diagnosing the disorder, criteria that form the basis for current approaches to diagnosis. These features are called "Bleuler's four As," which are association (disorder of thought), affect (inappropriate emotion), ambivalence (inability to make decisions), and autism (egocentric thought and behavior). Like Freud,

Bleuler believed that schizophrenia had its origins in disturbed unconscious processes. Although Bleuler's contributions aided tremendously in the diagnosis of schizophrenia, his definitions were considered far too broad. Schneider further refined the diagnosis of schizophrenia by narrowing the definition to include documentation of "first-rank symptoms."

4. To be diagnosed as having schizophrenia, an individual must show behavioral disturbances for a 6 month period, during which there is at least a week of an active phase of psychotic symptoms. The active phase is usually preceded by a prodromal phase, and followed by a residual phase.

5. There are five types of schizophrenia. Catatonic schizophrenia is characterized mainly by bizarre motor behaviors. In disorganized schizophrenia, the individual shows a variety of symptoms ranging from cognitive to motor disturbance. Paranoid schizophrenia is characterized by

paranoid delusions or other psychotic symptoms that have a theme of persecution. People with undifferentiated schizophrenia show a mixture of symptoms that do not clearly fall into the other categories. Finally, residual schizophrenia is the diagnosis used to characterize people who no longer show active symptoms of the disorder but still behave in disturbed ways.

6. In addition to categorizing the types of schizophrenia, researchers have attempted to define dimensions of schizophrenia that would reflect fundamental aspects of the disorder. The positive-negative dimension refers to the range of positive and negative symptoms of the disorder, with positive symptoms including hallucinations and delusions and negative symptoms including apathy and withdrawal. This dimension has become increasingly important in the theoretical understanding of schizophrenia. The process-reactive dimension distinguishes between an insidious version of the disorder (process dimension) and a version that represents a reaction to significant life stresses or trauma (reactive dimension). People with reactive schizophrenia have a much better chance of recovering than people with process schizophrenia.

7. Other disorders also involve a serious break with reality. Brief reactive psychosis is defined as a period of psychotic symptoms lasting less than a month, usually in reaction to a stressful life event. In schizophreniform disorder the symptoms can last anywhere from 1 to 6 months. Schizoaffective disorder constitutes a mixture of schizophrenic and mood disorder symptoms.

8. Delusional disorders are characterized by the single prominent symptom of delusional thinking and include: erotomanic, grandiose, jealous, persecutory, and somatic. In erotomania, the individual mistakenly believes that he or she is loved by someone else, often a famous person. Grandiose delusional disorder involves delusions of greatness. Jealous delusional disorder is characterized by delusions that one's lover is unfaithful, and persecutory delusional disorder by delusions of being the target of persecution. In somatic delusional disorder, the delusions concern bizarre ideas about one's body or health.

9. Induced delusional disorder involves the development of delusions by an individual through the influence of another person or group. Although the influence of someone else provokes the disorder, the individual usually has personal qualities that make him or her vulnerable to the other person's delusional ideas.

10. Antipsychotic medications and supportive psychotherapy are the treatments most often used for treating schizophrenia-like disorders. In the case of schizoaffective disorder, antidepressants or lithium may be used in conjunction with antipsychotic medications.

KEY TERMS

Schizophrenia: a disorder with a range of symptoms involving disturbances in content of thought, form of thought, perception, affect, sense of self, motivation, behavior, and interpersonal functioning. p. 276

Dementia praecox: the term coined by Kraepelin to describe what is currently known as schizophrenia. According to Kraepelin this condition involved a degeneration of the brain that began at a young age and ultimately led to a degeneration of the entire personality. p. 276

Affect: the outward expression of an emotion. p. 278

Disturbances in the sense of self: perplexity about one's identity expressed in disturbances ranging from confusion about who one is to delusional thinking in which the individual believes that he or she is in under the control or even part of some external person or force. p. 279

Active phase: a period in the course of schizophrenia in which psychotic symptoms are present. p. 280

Prodromal phase: a period in the course of schizophrenia prior to the active phase of symptoms during which the individual shows progressive deterioration in social and interpersonal functioning. p. 280

Residual phase: a period in the course of schizophrenia, following the active phase, in which there are continuing indications of disturbance, evidenced by the same kinds of behaviors that characterize the prodromal phase, most notably, impaired social and interpersonal functioning. p. 280

Catatonic schizophrenia: a form of schizophrenia characterized by a variety of catatonic symptoms. p. 280

Disorganized schizophrenia: a form of schizophrenia characterized by a combination of symptoms involving thought, communication, and behavior, and lacking any consistent theme. p. 281

Paranoid schizophrenia: a form of schizophrenia characterized by preoccupation with one or more bizarre delusions or with auditory hallucinations that are related to a particular theme of being persecuted or harassed. p. 281

Undifferentiated schizophrenia: a form of schizophrenia characterized by a complex of schizophrenic symptoms such as delusions, hallucinations, incoherence, or disorganized behavior, that does not meet the criteria for other types of schizophrenia. p. 281

Residual schizophrenia: a form of schizophrenia in which people who have previously been diagnosed as having schizophrenia, but who no longer have prominent psychotic symptoms, do have some remaining symptoms of the disorder such as emotional blunting, social withdrawal, eccentric behavior, or illogical thinking. p. 282

Positive symptoms: symptoms of schizophrenia involving exaggerations or distortions of normal thoughts, emotions, and behavior. p. 282

Negative symptoms: symptoms of schizophrenia involving an absence or reduction of thoughts, emotions, and behaviors compared to baseline functioning. p. 282

Process: a term used to refer to the gradual appearance of schizophrenia over time; contrasts with reactive. p. 283

Reactive: a term used to refer to the development of schizophrenia in response to a precipitant that provokes the onset of symptoms; contrasts with process. p. 283

Premorbid functioning: the period prior to the onset of the individual's symptoms. p. 283

Brief reactive psychosis: a disorder characterized by the sudden onset of psychotic symptoms that are limited to a period of less than a month, and which develop in response to a stressful event or set of events. p. 286

Schizophreniform disorder: a disorder characterized by psychotic symptoms that are essentially the same as those found in schizophrenia, except for the duration and chronic nature of the symptoms; specifically, symptoms usually last from 1 to 6 months. p. 287

Schizoaffective disorder: a psychotic disorder characterized by symptoms associated with both schizophrenia and mood disorder. p. 287

Erotomania: a psychotic disorder in which the individual has a delusion that another person, usually of great prominence, is deeply in love with him or her. p. 288

Grandiose delusional disorder: a psychotic disorder in which the individual has delusions of being an extremely important person. p. 288

Jealous delusional disorder: a psychotic disorder characterized by the delusion that one's partner is being unfaithful. p. 288

Persecutory delusional disorder: a psychotic disorder in which the individual has delusions of persecution. p. 289

Somatic delusional disorder: a psychotic disorder in which the individual believes he or she has a dreaded or terminal disease. p. 289

Induced psychotic disorder: a psychotic disorder in which one or more people develop a delusional system as a result of a close relationship with a psychotic person who is delusional. p. 289

Continuation of Case: David Marshall

Three days after my initial meeting with the Marshalls, during which David had darted from the hospital moments before being admitted, Mr. and Mrs. Marshall brought David back to the hospital. This time we took security precautions to prevent David from leaving again and made arrangements to have him involuntarily admitted. The events of the preceding few days had left the Marshalls feeling exhausted and deeply upset about David's poor judgment and bizarre behavior. They explained to me that David had not returned home the night following our last meeting. The Marshalls had become alarmed, because the weather had turned very cold and snowy. They knew that it was unlikely for David to seek shelter anywhere other than his own room. Consequently, they decided to notify the police, who organized a search of the area around David's home.

Two nights passed without David being found, but finally, in the early morning hours, the police located him. With the help of police dogs, David was tracked down deep in the woods a mile from the Marshall home. Perched on a rock, sitting in a lotus position, David was staring at the tops of the trees and speaking in a loud voice, apparently conversing with his "friends in the planets." He seemed unaffected by the dire weather conditions despite his lightweight clothing and oblivious to the small group of searchers who tried to speak to him. Offering no resistance, he acquiesced to their request that he follow them to their nearby vehicle. As David spoke to his rescuers, it was clear that he believed that they were sent from Zoroaster, and that it was his duty to adhere to their wishes. Moments after David was returned to his home, Mr. Marshall called for an ambulance to take David back to the psychiatric hospital.

Sarah Tobin, PhD

12

THEORIES AND TREATMENT OF SCHIZOPHRENIC DISORDERS

The mysterious nature and frightening consequences of schizophrenia have made it a central focus of research in abnormal psychology. The disorder that intrigued Kraepelin almost a century ago remains a source of fascination to scholars and practitioners today. Because the nature of the disorder is so puzzling, much controversy has been generated in the quest for explanations.

After reading this chapter, you should be able to:

- Describe the problems involved in researching the causes of schizophrenia.
- Understand the biological perspectives regarding schizophrenia, including differences in brain structure and function as well as genetic explanations of the disorder.
- Describe psychological perspectives on schizophrenia, including family systems, psychodynamic, and behavioral explanations.
- Define the vulnerability model and show how it combines biological and psychological perspectives.
- Explain contemporary approaches to treating people with schizophrenia, including biological and psychological treatments.

UNDERSTANDING SCHIZOPHRENIA

In the previous chapter, we tried to give you a basic grasp of the nature of schizophrenia. We now turn our attention to explanations of how schizophrenia develops and how people with this disorder are treated. As you prepare to read about views that may sound technical and theoretical, it is important to keep in mind that schizophrenia involves a disruptive and heartbreaking set of symptoms. Many people, when they hear about schizophrenia, think about a problem that happens only to other people, not to anyone they know. But, as you will discover as you proceed through life, schizophrenia touches the lives of millions of people—possibly someone in your own life. The plight of people with schizophrenia was stated well by William Carpenter, a prominent researcher (1987, p. 3): "[T]his illness strikes at the very heart of what we consider the essence of the person. Yet, because its manifestations are so personal and social, it elicits fear, misunderstanding, and condemnation in society instead of sympathy and concern."

A review of the past century of research on schizophrenia shows us that despite major advances in our understanding of this disorder, we remain sadly ignorant about its essence and causes. Starting with the most fundamental issue, it is surprising that experts still lack a reliable and valid set of diagnostic criteria for schizophrenia. When researchers attempt to identify the causes of this disorder, their job is made far more difficult by this lack of specificity. The problems are compounded by the fact that the research on the causes of schizophrenia goes back over several decades, a period over which the definition of schizophrenia evolved from a very vague, broad concept to a specific and narrow set of criteria. Many people who were diagnosed as having schizophrenia in 1960 would not meet the criteria for the disorder in the 1990s. Furthermore, it is difficult to evaluate results of studies from the 1960s, because the people with "schizophrenia" who were studied comprised such a diverse group.

Some researchers have addressed these definitional problems by reanalyzing data from early studies using present-day criteria. Unfortunately, even this approach does not provide a solution because the definition of schizophrenia still varies from researcher to researcher. As a way of dealing with these differences in definitions, many researchers decided to look at a broad cluster of associated conditions related to schizophrenia, called the schizophrenic spectrum disorders. This term refers to schizophrenic-like conditions ranging from some of the personality disorders (e.g., schizoid and schizotypal) to certain psychotic disorders (e.g., schizophreniform and schizoaffective).

Theories accounting for the origin of schizophrenia have traditionally fallen into two categories: biological and psychological. In the first part of this century, a debate raged between proponents of both sides. More recently, researchers have begun to accept that both biology and experience interact in the determination of schizophrenia. Having given up the hope of finding a simple explanation for the causes of schizophrenia, researchers have begun to build complex theoretical models that incorporate multiple factors (e.g., Nuechterlein, 1987). These models are based on the concept of **vulnerability**, proposing that individuals have a biologically determined predisposition to developing schizophrenia, but the disorder develops only when certain environmental conditions are in place. As we look at each of the contributions to a vulnerability model, keep in mind that no single theory contains the entire explanation.

BIOLOGICAL PERSPECTIVES

Biological explanations of schizophrenia have their origins in the writings of Kraepelin, who thought of schizophrenia as a disease caused by a degeneration of brain tissue. Kraepelin's ideas paved the way for later investigation of factors such as brain structure, biochemical processes, and genetics, all of which are now recognized as contributing to an individual's biological vulnerability to schizophrenia.

Differences in Brain Structure and Function

Interest in possible brain abnormalities in people with schizophrenia goes back to the first scientific attempts to understand schizophrenia in the nineteenth century. Some of the early efforts to examine the brains of these individuals were very crude and imprecise, because they could only be examined after the person died. It has only been in the latter part of the twentieth century that sophisticated techniques have been developed to enable researchers to study the living brain. The technologies of computerized tomography (CT or CAT scan) and magnetic resonance imaging (MRI) have enabled researchers in schizophrenia to take a picture of the brain and to analyze that picture quantitatively.

One of the most consistent discoveries using these new brain imaging methods was that the brains of people with schizophrenia have enlarged ventricles (the cavities within the brain that hold cerebrospinal fluid) (Zipursky et al., 1992). Researchers have speculated that ventricular enlargement is caused by decreases in dopamine in brain areas near these ventricles (Iacono et al., 1988). Ventricular enlargement is often accompanied by **cortical atrophy**, a wasting away of brain tissue (Shelton & Weinberger, 1986). Furthermore, in one 2-year follow-up study larger ventricle size during the first schizophrenic episode was correlated with poorer outcome (DeLisi et al., 1992). These findings would seem to support Kraepelin's belief that schizophrenia is a process of brain degeneration. However, as you might imagine, the findings are more complicated than they first appeared. People with other psychological dysfunctions including mood disorders, organic disorders, and chronic alcoholism also show enlarged brain ventricles (Meltzer, 1987). Researchers have since discovered, though, that people with schizophrenia have enlarged third ventricles, whereas ventricular enlargement occurs elsewhere in people with schizophreniform disorder, bipolar disorder, and major depression.

Apart from the lack of clear findings, studies of total brain size or volume are inherently limited in the information they can provide about the organic basis for schizophrenia. The particular psychological symptoms shown by people with this disorder must surely be accounted for by changes more specific than a reduction in the amount of brain tissue (Shelton et al., 1988). It became clear to investigators, then, that they had to look with more precision at changes in various parts of the brain if they were to make progress in discovering the organic basis for this disorder. To do so, they took advantage of positron emission tomography (PET) which, as you will recall from Chapter 3, monitors brain metabolic activity to gather information on alterations in brain function. Together with CT and MRI techniques, these measures have produced a number of hypotheses about the changes in the brain that play a role in causing the behavioral abnormalities seen in people with schizophrenia.

The primary areas of the brain that show abnormalities on various brain imaging techniques include the frontal and prefrontal cortex, the basal ganglia, and parts of the limbic system including the hippocampus and amygdala (Buchsbaum, 1990; Kirkpatrick & Buchanan, 1990). Deficits in these areas are thought to underlie disturbances associated with schizophrenia in thoughts and perceptions, attention, planning and execution of organized behavior, and the regulation of motivation.

How are changes in the brain connected to the symptoms of schizophrenia? Answering this question is one of the greatest challenges that researchers in this area have faced. In investigating this issue, researchers have found greater support for the positive-negative (Type I-Type II) subtype distinction, discussed in Chapter 11. Smaller frontal lobes (Andreasen et al., 1986; Brown & White, 1991) and limbic system structures (Kirkpatrick & Buchanan, 1990) are thought to relate to the negative or Type II subtype of schizophrenia. Presumably, these abnormalities are what underlie the flattened affect and low level of motivation shown by people with the negative symptoms of schizophrenia. Another intriguing suggestion in this regard is the idea that the negative symptoms of schizophrenia are due to a failure in the genetic program through which one hemisphere of the brain becomes dominant (Crow, 1990). Brain dominance affects many facets of behavior including speech and communication. It is fascinating to think that some of the symptoms of schizophrenia may somehow be intertwined with the asymmetry of the brain.

Yet another path in the search for brain–behavior connections has been followed by researchers investigating the role of neurotransmitters, particularly dopamine. According to what is called the **dopamine hypothesis**, the delusions, hallucinations, and attentional deficits shown by people with schizophrenia can be attributed to an overactivity of neurons that communicate with each other via the transmission of dopamine (Carlsson, 1988; Meltzer, 1987). This hypothesis emerged from two related lines of evidence. The first was the observation that antipsychotic drugs work to reduce the frequency of hallucinations and delusions by blocking dopamine receptors. The second line of evidence was that certain drugs that are biochemically related to

dopamine, such as amphetamines, increase the frequency of psychotic symptoms.

When the dopamine hypothesis was introduced, it was heralded as a breakthrough in accounting for the more bizarre and puzzling symptoms of schizophrenia. For a time, it was thought that the hypothesis might provide the ultimate explanation for this mysterious disorder. Gradually, though, as with most explanations of schizophrenia, original enthusiasm has been tempered by later findings. In the case of the dopamine hypothesis, later studies have added complexity to what was originally a very simple idea. After the dopamine hypothesis was proposed, researchers attempted to verify it by comparing the levels of dopamine metabolites in the spinal fluid and blood of people with schizophrenia with the levels found in normal controls. To their dismay, researchers found no differences between these two groups in the levels of dopamine metabolites (Widerlov, 1988). As it turned out, there were important differences not in the *total* amount of dopamine but in the amount of dopamine associated with different brain areas. So, while the average levels of dopamine metabolites were equivalent, the relative amounts in various areas differed markedly. Findings about the relative differences in dopamine activity in different parts of the brain have given researchers a handle for explaining why people with schizophrenia can have positive and negative symptoms at the same time. It has been suggested that low prefrontal dopamine activity causes negative symptoms, and excessive dopamine activity in subcortical areas results in positive symptoms (Davis et al., 1991).

In studies of people with schizophrenia, the amount of dopamine activity does seem related to the nature of their symptoms. People with Type I schizophrenia have higher levels of dopamine, and those with Type II have lower dopamine activity (Pickar et al., 1990). As more evidence emerges, this refined version of the dopamine hypothesis may provide not only an explanation for the biochemical basis of schizophrenia, but also more support for the Type I-Type II or positive-negative subtype distinction.

Genetic Explanations

Evidence in support of genetic contributions to schizophrenia vulnerability comes from studies based on family patterns of inheritance. As you will recall from our discussion in Chapter 5, genetic contributions are studied in several ways. Schizophrenia researchers have used three kinds of studies in their attempt to assess the contributions of genetics: family and twin studies, adoption studies, and studies of biological markers.

■ *Family and twin studies*

Family patterns of individuals afflicted with schizophrenia provide convincing evidence in favor of a biological (on page 298) explanation. The information in Figure

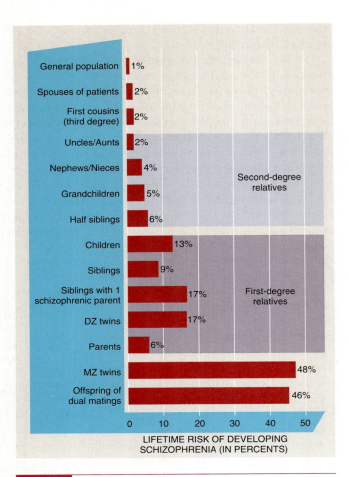

General population — 1%
Spouses of patients — 2%
First cousins (third degree) — 2%
Uncles/Aunts — 2%
Nephews/Nieces — 4%
Grandchildren — 5%
Half siblings — 6%

Second-degree relatives

Children — 13%
Siblings — 9%
Siblings with 1 schizophrenic parent — 17%
DZ twins — 17%
Parents — 6%
MZ twins — 48%
Offspring of dual matings — 46%

First-degree relatives

0   10   20   30   40   50
LIFETIME RISK OF DEVELOPING
SCHIZOPHRENIA (IN PERCENTS)

FIGURE 12–1
Grand average risks for developing schizophrenia, compiled from the family and twin studies conducted in European populations between 1920 and 1987; the degree of risk correlates highly with the degree of genetic relatedness.
Source: Gottesman (1991)

12–1 shows clearly that the closer a relative is to an individual with schizophrenia, the greater the concordance in the incidence of the disorder. As you can see, identical twins have the highest concordance and the more distant the genetic relationship, the smaller the concordance rate.

Studies such as these, which report a higher incidence rate of the disorder among genetically linked family members, obviously are flawed in that the researchers have not been able to rule out the effects of a shared family environment. In other words, the high concordance rate may be attributable to genetics or to the fact that family members live in the same home. Studies on the concordance rate of schizophrenia between identical twins fail to separate these two influences. In addition to looking at the data from identical twins reared together, then, researchers also need to examine evidence from identical twins reared apart, but such cases are infrequent. Based on the few cases that have been reported, there is an impressive concordance rate of 64 percent (Gottesman & Shields, 1982). Keep in mind, though, that even this design has possible confounds;

specifically, the question needs to be addressed regarding the reasons why twins would have been separated and reared apart. Was there some problem in the family that led to the drastic action of separating identical twins?

Another way to tackle the question of looking at twin data is to consider the discordant identical twin pairs in which one twin has schizophrenia and the other does not. If genetics is a major determinant, then the child of a non-schizophrenic twin should still be at risk for developing the disorder. In fact, this is precisely what researchers have found. The rates of schizophrenia or a schizophrenia-like psychosis were found to be roughly equal in the offspring of nonaffected twins and in children of twins with schizophrenia (McGue & Gottesman, 1989). This finding suggests that the twins who did not develop schizophrenia transmitted the risk of this disorder as part of their genetic endowment to their offspring. Researchers do not know why, though, the original nonschizophrenic member of the twin pair did not show symptoms of schizophrenia. If these people were carrying the genetic endowment for schizophrenia, what factors protected them from developing the disorder and how were these factors different from the influences on their identical siblings?

These more refined twin studies provide a number of intriguing clues in support of genetic explanations, then, but still leave many unanswered questions. Because of the limitations in twin studies, researchers have turned to the powerful design of the adoption study, which provides a "natural experiment" in which genetic and environmental factors can be independently assessed because the child is separated from the biological parents.

■ *Adoption studies*

In the typical adoption study, researchers track the incidence of schizophrenia in children who are raised by non-schizophrenic parents but whose biological parents do have schizophrenia. In those cases where the child is separated from the parents early in life, the confounding role of family environment is removed. Cross-fostering is another and more rare form of adoption study involving the less likely circumstance of a child whose biological parents have no disorder but who is adopted by a parent who has a schizophrenic spectrum disorder.

Both types of adoption paradigms were used in a series of Danish adoption studies begun in the 1960s. These studies were performed by a team of researchers from the United States who went to Denmark in their search for the best available information on adoption and patterns of mental disorder (Kety et al., 1968). Because of the comprehensive birth, adoption, and health records kept by the Danish government, this country was ideal for the study. The relatively homogeneous and stable population of Denmark provided further advantages for conducting this kind of research.

There have been many reports based on the Danish studies since the mid-1960s. These reports first included information only from the registers of Copenhagen, but later

Table 12–1 Summary of Danish Adoption Studies

Form of Schizophrenia	Site of Study	Adoption Status[1] Index	Adoption Status[1] Controls
Chronic schizophrenia (definite or probable)	Copenhagen only	5.2%	0%
	Denmark	5.8%	0.9%
Latent schizophrenia	Copenhagen only	8.6%	2.2%
	Denmark	12.5%	0.9%

[1]Incidence of disturbance in biological relatives.
Source: Based on Kety (1988).

were expanded to include the entire country of Denmark. In the original Copenhagen investigation, 34 people with diagnoses falling into the schizophrenic spectrum were identified from the adoption records of almost 5500 individuals. These 34 people, called the *index adoptees*, were matched with a sample of *control adoptees* who did not have a psychiatric disorder but matched the index adoptees on other important characteristics. The various investigations involved in this research included numerous attempts to provide refined and accurate estimates of the incidence of schizophrenia and schizophrenic spectrum disorders in the biological relatives of the index versus the control adoptees. In addition, other studies based on this investigation specifically examined the prevalence of schizotypal personality disorder and other related conditions in order to determine the role of genetics in the entire range of schizophrenic-like mental disorders.

The Danish adoption studies were very complex, and they were made even more complicated by the fact that definitions and diagnoses of schizophrenia changed so radically over the two decades of the investigation. We have summarized a report by Seymour Kety (1988) in Table 12–1, which provides representative results from this long series of studies. This table includes the incidence of schizophrenia ("definite" and "probable" cases) among the relatives of the index adoptees (who developed schizophrenia) compared to the relatives of the control adoptees (free of schizophrenia but matched with the index adoptees on other important characteristics). As you can see, the rates of chronic schizophrenia (5.2 to 5.8 percent) in the biological relatives of index adoptees are far higher than the rates in the relatives of control adoptees (0 to .9 percent). A similar pattern is shown in comparing cases of the disorder currently called schizotypal personality disorder (which was once referred to with labels such as latent schizophrenia). These statistics provide very compelling support for the role of genetics. Yet, as you will soon see, they do not tell the whole story.

Further clues to solving the genetics–environment puzzle come from results of the cross-fostering adoption study. Recall that a cross-fostering study involves identifying children whose biological parents did not have schizophrenia but whose rearing parents did. The researchers conducting the schizophrenia cross-fostering studies sought such individuals, again, from the Danish adoption register. By scanning the records from all of Denmark, Paul Wender and his co-workers (1974) were able to find a total of 38 individuals who were "cross-fostered." These 38 people were compared with a group of 79 adoptees, who had normal biological and rearing parents, and with a third group of 69 "index adoptees" similar to those in the Kety studies (their biological parents had a schizophrenic spectrum disorder and their rearing parents were normal). The design of this study is outlined in Table 12–2. In looking at Wender's results, first compare the group with a biological predisposition to schizophrenia (the index adoptees) with the other two groups whose parents did not have schizophrenia. This comparison addresses the question already studied by Kety and his associates in their traditional adoption studies. If the index adoptees have higher rates of schizophrenia than the people in the other two groups, then genetics plays a role independent of the environment. As you can see from the results displayed in the table, the researchers found this to be true. The rate of 18.8 percent for the index adoptees group is obviously far higher than the rate in either of the other two groups. The number is also higher than the number reported by Kety, but this discrepancy is probably

Table 12–2 Results of Cross-Fostering Studies

Group	Diagnosis of Parent Biological	Diagnosis of Parent Rearing	Rate of Schizophrenic Spectrum Disorders
Index adoptees	Schizophrenic spectrum	Free to vary	18.8%
Control adoptees	No diagnosis	Free to vary	10.7%
Cross-fostered	No diagnosis	Schizophrenic spectrum	10.1%

Source: Wender et al., (1974)

accounted for by differing definitions of the schizophrenic spectrum.

The next comparison to note is between the control adoptees and the cross-fostered adoptees. This comparison tests the hypothesis that family environment can contribute to the child's developing schizophrenia independently of genetic inheritance. If this hypothesis is correct, then the cross-fostered group (normal biological parent/schizophrenic rearing parent) should have a higher rate of schizophrenic spectrum disorders than the control adoptees (normal biological parent/normal rearing parent). This, as you can see, was not the case. The rate of schizophrenic spectrum disorders in the cross-fostered group was almost the same as the rate in the control adoptees. The researchers concluded from this finding that the family environment was far less significant than biological predispositions in making an individual vulnerable to developing schizophrenia.

Once again, however, the answer is not this straightforward. Data from subsequent research have suggested that the environment is more prominent in the genetics–environment equation than was once thought. Interactive models of genetic and environmental influences have received growing support from studies with more refined methodologies than the original Danish adoption studies; in more recent studies, researchers have been able to specify and control for many more factors related to the circumstances of adoption and the later family environment of the adopted child. The largest of these studies is currently being carried out by a team of researchers led by Pekka Tienari in Finland.

Tienari and his colleagues undertook the massive effort of tracking down the childbirth records of almost 20,000 women who had been diagnosed as having schizophrenia or paranoid psychosis, spanning almost a 20-year period and including the entire country of Finland. From this very large population, Tienari and his associates were able to identify a total of 171 women who had given their children up for legal adoption within the first 4 years of the child's life. A sample of 184 children of these women made up the index adoptees (children whose biological mother had schizophrenia). The ages of these index adoptees ranged from 5 to 57 years. The initial identification of records took place between 1969 and 1978, and at the same time, researchers identified a control sample of adoptees whose parents had no psychiatric history. Upon their initial entry into the study, the index adoptees and their families were given extensive measurements including family assessments and individual assessments of the parents of index offspring. The families were also contacted by telephone from 5 to 7 years after their first assessment, and then were retested in 1982–1984. At that time, 112 index adoptees and 135 control adoptees were available for study. Interviews and assessments were also conducted on 85 of the biological mothers of the index adoptees. Thus, the study included a longitudinal analysis of the mental status of the adoptees, as well as continued assessments of the biological mothers and the environments in which the adoptees were reared.

Positive family relationships are an important protective function for children who are biologically vulnerable to schizophrenia.

The results of research by Tienari and his colleagues (1987) provide some tantalizing evidence about the interaction between the individual's biological inheritance and the family's home environment in determining schizophrenia. One set of findings confirms what Kety and his collaborators demonstrated in the Danish studies. The rate of schizophrenia in the index adoptees (whose biological mothers were schizophrenic) was 7 percent, compared to a rate of 1.5 percent in the control adoptees (those who had non-schizophrenic parents). The second set of findings provides dramatic evidence, though, for the role of the home environment. Of the 112 index adoptees, 49 grew up in homes that were rated as healthy or only mildly disturbed. None of these offspring, despite their genetic predisposition, developed a psychotic disorder. In contrast, of the 43 index adoptees who grew up in very disturbed home settings, a high percentage (37 percent) developed severe psychiatric problems. This is a very surprising outcome in light of the compelling support for a genetic model provided by the Danish studies. What protects these genetically predisposed individuals from developing schizophrenia? Another way to look at the issue is to consider what takes place in a disturbed family environment that brings out the disorder in people with comparable genetic predispositions. Al-

Margarita is a 22-year-old engineering student who has shown mild signs of disturbance for several years. Ever since high school, her classmates have regarded her as being somewhat peculiar. She kept secret the fact that her mother has been repeatedly hospitalized for schizophrenia, making the excuse that her mother needed to take frequent business trips. During her senior year in college, Margarita began displaying some of the same symptoms shown by her mother. In particular, she developed paranoid delusions, believing that the cafeteria people were serving her poisoned food, following the orders of the president of the United States. She also had auditory hallucinations, hearing voices making derogatory comments about her while she sat in class. Her professors turned her papers back because they were incoherent and bizarre; the papers were filled with neologisms, sentence fragments, and references to the president's plot to kill her. When Margarita went home for spring break, her father became alarmed about her behavior, seeing the signs of disturbance in Margarita that he had seen so often in his wife.

- What information would a clinician need to determine whether or not Margarita is suffering from schizophrenia?
- What role might genetics play in contributing to the development of Margarita's condition?

though the Finnish study has yet to provide answers to these questions, other research on the offspring of mothers with schizophrenia has provided some clues.

■ *Studies of biological markers*

Working on the assumption that schizophrenia is genetically influenced, researchers have sought to develop a mathematical model that would explain how the disorder is passed from generation to generation. To understand contemporary genetic approaches to schizophrenia, consider the case of eye color, which follows **simple mendelian genetics**, a straightforward pattern of inheritance in which observed traits are explained completely by the pattern of dominant and recessive genes. In terms of this model, brown (represented by "B") is a dominant characteristic and blue ("b") is recessive. A person with the Bb combination will have brown eyes; blue eyes reflect a bb genetic inheritance. The difference between schizophrenia and eye color is that monozygotic twins always have the same eye color but, as you know, they do not have perfect concordance for schizophrenia. Genetic epidemiological studies have been used to test the mendelian explanation and have found that it is simplistic. Researchers have moved on, then, to more complex explanations.

Most prominent among the alternate genetic models for schizophrenia is the **multi-factorial polygenic threshold** model (Gottesman, 1991; Gottesman et al., 1987). Researchers who hold to this model maintain that several genes with varying influence are involved in the transmission of schizophrenia. The vulnerability for schizophrenia is

actually a continuum from low to high, depending on the combination of genes that the individual inherits. The symptoms of schizophrenia are produced when the accumulation of genetic and environmental factors exceeds a certain threshold value. Most contemporary researchers agree that this model provides a better explanation for the actual patterns of family incidence than does the single gene model or others based on simpler proposed mechanisms of genetic inheritance.

Researchers trying to understand the specific mechanisms involved in such a complex model of genetic transmission have found it helpful to study measurable characteristics whose family patterns parallel the pattern of schizophrenia inheritance, called **biological markers**. Investigators attempting to identify biological markers have experimented with a variety of psychophysiological measures thought to reflect some of the attentional deficits observed in people with schizophrenia. Through decades of refinement in theory and technique, researchers have identified a relatively small number of possible markers that have promise for eventually serving to indicate which individuals have an inherited vulnerability for the disorder.

Two measures stand out as particularly important in the search for biological markers: *sustained attention* and *smooth pursuit eye movements* (Erlenmeyer-Kimling & Cornblatt, 1987). Laboratory measures of **sustained attention** involve having the person being tested make a response when a certain target stimulus is displayed. This target stimulus is presented along with other stimuli at unpredictable intervals. For instance, the subject may be instructed to push a button whenever the letter "A" appears from among a series of letters presented individually for very brief periods of time (on the order of milliseconds). This is a tedious task that requires constant vigilance in order to receive a high score. The task can also be made more complex by adding other demands, such as requiring that the button be pushed only if the letter "A" is preceded by the letter "Q." Typically, people with schizophrenia do very poorly on these tasks, especially when the demands of

Studying attentional defects in people with schizophrenia, a researcher records the time it takes to react to stimuli presented on the screen.

the task are increased so that the individual's cognitive capacities are stretched to their limits. More to the point, the biological relatives of people with schizophrenia also show deficits on the more complex version of the sustained attention task.

The second biological marker, disturbance in **smooth pursuit eye movements**, is measured by having subjects visually follow a target, such as a small point of light on a dark background, while their eye movements are closely monitored with recording devices. In contrast to normal individuals, people with schizophrenia show irregular pursuit of a moving target along with many interruptions by extraneous eye movements. This abnormality in the smooth pursuit function is also shown by first-degree relatives of people with schizophrenia. Following the initial report of this finding (Holzman et al., 1974), subsequent studies were conducted to determine whether this abnormal pattern of eye movements was in fact specific to schizophrenia. Results of this research (Holzman, 1987) have confirmed the original conclusions with findings of a much higher percent of abnormalities among people with schizophrenia (65 percent) and their biological relatives (40 percent) compared to nonschizophrenic people (8 percent) or relatives of people with other psychological disorders (14 percent). Through a series of carefully controlled studies, researchers have been able to rule out competing explanations, such as lower motivation or the effects of drugs, for the poorer performance of people with schizophrenia and their relatives (Holzman & Matthysse, 1990). Researchers using eye movements as biological markers have also found support for the concept of a complex genetic model underlying the inheritance of schizophrenia (Clementz et al., 1992; Iacono et al., 1992).

In their search for markers, researchers have also followed the trail of another well-documented experience of people with schizophrenia—namely that they have a difficult time screening out irrelevant sensory stimuli (McGhie & Chapman, 1961). For example, when you are watching a movie in a theater, you would probably be oblivious to the background noise made by the air-conditioning system. In contrast, a person with schizophrenia might feel bombarded by the air-conditioning noise and be unable to concentrate on anything else. Researchers have thought that this abnormal reaction to stimuli might reflect an underlying brain abnormality that could be translated into a laboratory measure. With such a measure, investigators could then look at the differences among groups of people with schizophrenia, people with other mental disorders, biological relatives, and normal controls.

The measure that researchers decided to use, the **event related potential (ERP)**, assesses the electrical activity of the brain when a person is exposed to certain sensory stimuli. When the investigators looked at the ERPs of people who have schizophrenia, they discovered a pattern that seemed to confirm the reports about an inability to screen out irrelevant stimuli. Specifically, when people with schizophrenia listened through earphones to successive pairs of clicking noises, their brains responded just as much to the

second stimulus as they did to the first. In contrast, people without schizophrenia become conditioned so that their brains responded with less brain wave activity to the second stimulus. This response is called **sensory gating**, a term that alludes to the notion that most people "shut the gate" on their sensory processing with repeated presentation of the same stimulus. Going back to the example of the person sitting in the movie theater, the brain of the person with schizophrenia fails to "shut the gate" on the repeated stimulation provided by the air conditioner noise. Such a deficiency is showing up as a biological marker in a number of studies (e.g., Freedman et al., 1987; Holzman & Matthysse, 1990).

Using abnormal eye tracking as a biological marker, Philip Holzman and his associates have developed an intriguing genetic model of schizophrenia. According to this model (Holzman & Matthysse, 1990), a genetic predisposition is inherited through the combined effect of several genes. This predisposition is thought to be a form of disease process that can affect different parts of the central nervous system. The individual with this predisposition may develop schizophrenia, eye movement dysfunction, or both, depending on where in the central nervous system the disease process takes hold.

Other marker studies using biochemical measures involve more explicit attempts to determine where the genes for schizophrenia are located on human chromosomes. These studies involve **genetic mapping**, a process currently used by researchers studying a variety of diseases thought to have a hereditary basis. When you pause and reflect on what this research involves, the implications are widespread. This research may eventually lead to an unlocking of the fundamental secrets of life itself. Researchers attempting to map areas of human genes begin this amazing enterprise by studying the family distribution of characteristics that appear to be inherited together with the symptoms of the disorder under study. We touched briefly on this method in the discussion of mood disorders in Chapter 10.

Genetic mapping has been extensively applied in schizophrenia research. One very exciting but unfortunately unfounded hypothesis emerged from the study of some very obvious physical characteristics, primarily facial appearance and head shape, in a family where a young man and his uncle shared these abnormalities in addition to symptoms of schizophrenia (Bassett, 1989). Interestingly, the researcher did not begin her work by searching for people with schizophrenia who also had physical abnormalities. It was only after noting the somewhat unusual appearance of a young man hospitalized for schizophrenia and then later finding out that he resembled his uncle, who also had schizophrenia, that the researcher began to track down this specific genetic abnormality. By using sophisticated laboratory methods, the investigator was in fact able to identify a defect on chromosome 5, and her finding generated excitement that the locus of the schizophrenia "gene" had been discovered. Although one other research group corroborated this finding (Sherrington et al., 1988), the enthusiasm

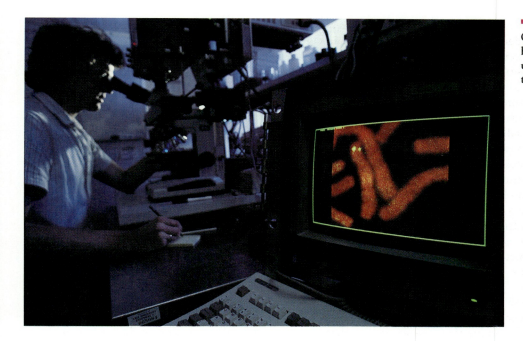

Genetic researchers map the human genome in their attempts to unravel the mysteries of genetic transmission of schizophrenia.

proved to be premature—other researchers found no such defects on that particular chromosome (Hallmayer et al., 1992; Kennedy et al., 1988; St. Clair et al., 1989). Similarly, researchers were unable to confirm that a genetic defect underlies dopamine receptor abnormalities in people with schizophrenia (Moises et al., 1991).

This pattern of initial enthusiasm, followed by failure to substantiate the findings in other research laboratories, is unfortunately all too common in schizophrenia research. However, as the diagnosis for the disorder and the laboratory methods for analyzing genetic material advance, researchers are optimistic that greater agreement will be reached in the search for genetic mechanisms.

■ *The unique case of the Genain quadruplets*

Drawing on many of the concepts, research findings, and theoretical models involved in biological explanations of schizophrenia is one investigation that surely must stand alone in the annals of psychiatric literature—the long-term follow-up study of the Genain quadruplets. You will surely appreciate the value of this study given what you have learned so far about the intricate relationships between genetics and environmental factors, whose effects have proven so difficult to separate in understanding the causes of schizophrenia.

The Genain quadruplets are four women born in the early 1930s who share an identical genetic makeup. Their life stories are truly fascinating in and of themselves, because their situation is so rare, but even more compelling is the fact that each woman developed symptoms of schizophrenia starting in her 20s. The disorder was to remain with these women for their entire adult lives, although as they have entered later adulthood, their symptoms have changed in severity. Fortunately for the sake of schizophrenia research, the quadruplets were intensely studied over almost

the entire course of the disorder, and extensive information is available about their family history and life events in adulthood. Analyses of these data have not yet provided the answers that might be hoped for, but they have suggested many intriguing new hypotheses about the dynamic interplay among the influences of family inheritance, early childhood experiences, and the unpredictable course of chronic psychological disturbance over the years of adulthood.

The Genain quadruplets provided researchers with a unique opportunity to study the role of genetics in the development of schizophrenia. Would you be able to tell from this photograph which of the sisters developed the most severe psychotic symptoms in adulthood?

The name "Genain" is actually a pseudonym that stands for "dreadful genes," and the first names (also pseudonyms) of the quadruplets were derived from the names of the research institute that sponsored much of the investigation, the National Institute of Mental Health (NIMH). The four women were named, accordingly, Nora, Iris, Myra, and Hester, in order of birth, with Nora being the "first-born" and Hester being the "youngest." Nora was also the first to be hospitalized for schizophrenia (at the age of 21), followed by Iris, 7 months later. The remaining two sisters were diagnosed as having schizophrenia when they all entered the NIMH for study in 1955. Prior to that time, Hester had shown clear symptoms of a psychotic disorder, but Myra had no psychotic symptoms until this hospitalization. Myra was also the only one to marry, and she bore two sons. All four sisters spent the majority of their adult years living in their mother's home when they were not institutionalized in a state hospital.

What makes the study of these women so interesting is the fact that although they are concordant with regard to the existence of schizophrenia, they differed in the disorder's degree of severity and its course over the decades of the study. Such differences have provided ample room for speculation about the relative contributions of genetics and life experiences as causes of the disorder.

In the original report of the study (Rosenthal, 1963), different patterns of life stresses were given as explanations for the divergence in diagnoses among the four women. For example, Hester was generally regarded as the least competent sister, and worse, was labeled a "sex maniac" and a "moron" by her parents. Iris, although physically more comparable to Nora and Myra, was paired with Hester, and these two were treated as the less capable pair throughout their childhood and adolescence. In their teens, both were in fact submitted to a surgical procedure on their genitals by the family physician who thought they needed a cure for their excessive masturbation. Nora and Myra were given a great deal of favorable attention by their parents. Despite the fact that the two pairs were treated so differently, Mrs. Genain insisted that she always treated the four sisters "identically." Not only did she communicate contradictory and confusing messages, but the pressure to conform became a dynamic that impeded the growth of the healthier sisters. Myra, for example, had never shown evidence of psychotic symptoms prior to her hospitalization for the study at NIMH. Was she inappropriately cast into the mold of the schizophrenia diagnosis by her own wish to conform or by the staff's intention to treat her equally with her sisters? Or, was she truly schizophrenic, and her symptoms for some reason lay dormant for another 20 years? These differing life stress factors might have pushed the sisters into differing degrees of disturbance.

Other stresses, however, were similar for all four sisters. One was the extreme interest generated by their uniqueness, causing them and their hometown to be the focus of media attention and publicity despite Mrs. Genain's considerable efforts to keep her daughters out of the public lime-

light. Ironically, in the process of trying to protect her daughters, Mrs. Genain may have pushed them into their own fantasy worlds and out of touch with reality. Mrs. Genain's goal was to allow her daughters to lead normal lives, but the outcome was just the opposite. The stresses of such influences as the pressure to conform, the attention directed toward them by the media, and their mother's desire to protect them might have interacted with the differences created by the "pairings" into the more and less competent twosomes.

In the 1981 follow-up, the sisters were extensively tested over a 3-and-a-half month period, with and without medication, on eye movement and continuous performance tests, CT scans, PET scans, dopamine activity, and other measures of brain function, personality, and intelligence. As a group, the four performed as would be expected on many of these tests, and their scores were very similar, reflecting their identical genetic endowment. One important exception was the CT scans, which showed no signs of ventricular enlargement in any of the four women. Across many of the tests, though, the sisters differed in their relative degree of impairment. The most dramatic difference was in their response to being taken off the neuroleptic medications that they were all receiving. Myra and Iris deteriorated less than the other two sisters, and they were eventually able to leave the hospital medication-free. In this regard, then, Myra and Iris had now become the better functioning pair. This represented a switch from the earlier line-up of Nora and Myra being the more intact two sisters.

The question arises once again: Why, given the same genetic endowment, would there be any differences in schizophrenic symptoms, much less shifts over the course of adulthood in the relative degree of impairment within the foursome? The answer to this question, according to the investigators, lies in considering the interactive effects of environmental stress with brain abnormalities that predispose the individual to developing the attentional and other processing deficits that can trigger symptoms of schizophrenia. Nora and Hester, the first and last born, were more likely to have suffered brain damage during delivery; Iris and Hester were the sisters who received the most negative treatment as children and teenagers. The order of relative impairment, then, corresponds to the interaction of these factors (see Table 12-3). Myra, according to this reasoning, would

Table 12–3 The Relative Contributions of Stress and Brain Damage in the Genain Quadruplets

| | | Environmental Stress | |
		Low	High
Brain Damage	Low	Myra	Iris
	High	Nora	Hester

Source: Based on Mirsky & Quinn, (1988).

have been the most advantaged because she was low on both factors; Hester, in contrast, was high on both factors and therefore suffered the most. With genetics a constant factor, then, differences in the expression of schizophrenic symptoms may be accounted for by a combination of biological and psychological forces (Mirsky & Quinn, 1988). It is important to be cautious about placing too much emphasis on the role of Mrs. Genain's behavior as a cause of schizophrenia in her daughters.

What makes the Genain study so important is not only the control over genetic factors that it provided, but also the fact that these variant patterns were discovered only after an extensive period of follow-up. These results could not have been detected by one-time assessments. This is an important fact to keep in mind when reading the literature on schizophrenia, much of which is based on short-term assessments.

PSYCHOLOGICAL PERSPECTIVES

Although the biological explanation can indicate who is constitutionally vulnerable to schizophrenia, that approach is insufficient for explaining who will *develop* schizophrenia. There is certainly more to the process of acquiring schizophrenia than mere biology. Consequently, we must turn to psychological explanations to help fill out the picture.

Family Systems Perspective

Researchers working within the family systems perspective focus their attention on the "system" of roles, interactions, and patterns of communication in the family environment in which the person with schizophrenia grew up. In studies on modes of communication and behavior within families with a schizophrenic member, researchers attempt to document deviant patterns of communication and inappropriate ways that parents interact with their children. These disturbances in family relationships are thought to lead to the development of defective emotional responsiveness and cognitive distortions fundamental to the psychological symptoms of schizophrenia.

One psychoanalytic idea related to the family systems perspective was the notion of the **schizophrenogenic mother** (Fromm-Reichmann, 1948). This idea gained favor among professionals in the mid-twentieth century, and although it has since been rejected (Hirsch & Leff, 1975), it influenced much of the research that took place in the decades to follow both within the psychoanalytic and family systems perspectives. According to this view, schizophrenia can be induced in a child through a mothering style characterized by confusing kinds of communication, overintrusiveness, and devaluation of the child's sense of self-worth. Observational studies of family interactions have

since shown that it was unreasonable to hold the mother responsible for causing schizophrenia in the child. Instead, family systems theorists proposed that disturbance in the entire set of relationships contributes to the child's development of the disorder.

Observational research on families yielded another hypothesis that for many years had an important influence on theories of psychosocial causes of schizophrenia. According to the **double-bind hypothesis** (Bateson et al., 1956), the schizophrenic individual develops faulty communication and thinking processes through years of being exposed to conflicting messages from other family members. As we explained in Chapter 5, the "double-bind" is created when the parent makes it impossible for the child to behave in a way that avoids disapproval. Bateson described a compelling example of a double-bind in the case of a young man who was greeted by his mother in the hospital following his recovery from an acute schizophrenic episode. He enthusiastically threw his arms around her; when she stiffened, he withdrew. His mother then chided him that he should not be so easily embarrassed and afraid of his feelings. Becoming extremely upset, the young man could stay with her only a few minutes more and when she left the hospital, he had to be calmed by the staff (Bateson et al., 1956). If you were placed in this kind of situation, you can imagine how confused you would feel because nothing you did would be right. Further, in the double-bind situation, the child is implicitly prohibited from pointing out the incompatible messages being communicated by the parent. When repeated many times and in many contexts, the double-bind style of communication can understandably cause a great deal of confusion in the thoughts and feelings of the child.

Intrigued by the possibility that disturbed communication in the family may lie at the root of schizophrenia, researchers working within the family systems perspective went on to identify several other problematic communication styles within families of people with schizophrenia. These researchers contended that the parents of children with schizophrenia often give vague, indefinite, and fragmented messages lacking in direction (Singer & Wynne, 1963). This style of communication causes the child to feel unclear about what the parent intends and makes it likely that the child will become emotionally paralyzed. Another important concept tested in family observational research was that abnormal patterns of dominance or power within the family set the stage for the child's development of schizophrenia. These abnormal patterns include leaving the child out of family decision-making processes (Mishler & Waxler, 1975) and failing to establish clear boundaries between parental roles and those of the child. For example, a child may become "parentified" by a parent who expects the child to take an inordinate amount of responsibility within the family system. For a young child, this excessive responsibility can feel very burdensome and confusing.

When these ideas regarding disturbed family relationships were placed under the scrutiny of careful empirical study, they were found to be lacking as adequate explana-

Many people with schizophrenia have difficulty readjusting to their families after a period of hospitalization. According to the theory of expressed emotion, returning to a family that is highly critical increases the chances that a relapse of the disorder will occur.

tions for the development of schizophrenia. In part, this might have been due to the fact the original hypothesis emerged from clinical observations. Clinicians approach their evaluation of family interactions with a somewhat biased eye. The clinician knows that the family has produced a child with schizophrenia, which may color the assessment of the family's communication patterns. In addition, the clinician who works with a family in which a member has schizophrenia is dealing with a family under stress. Their interaction patterns may have been altered from what they were prior to the advent of the child's disorder. When families are studied more objectively, and in ways that minimize these biases, the results fail to bear out the intuitive belief that family disturbances lead to the child's symptoms of schizophrenia. It is now recognized that disturbed family communication is not a sole cause of schizophrenia but that they can trigger symptoms of schizophrenia in a child who has inherited or acquired a biological vulnerability to the disorder.

Other researchers have approached the issue of disturbed family relationships from a very different perspective by trying to predict outcome or recovery in adults who have been hospitalized for schizophrenia. Instead of regarding a disturbed family as the cause of schizophrenia, these researchers began to view the family as a potential source of stress in the environment of the person who is trying to recover from a schizophrenic episode. Relatives of affected individuals were interviewed in an attempt to measure the emotional quality of the home environment. A scale of **expressed emotion** (or **EE**) was developed that provided an index of the degree to which family members speak in ways that reflect criticism, hostile feelings, and emotional overinvolvement or overconcern with regard to the schizophrenic individual. Initial research results supported this

theory when it was observed that people recovering from hospitalization for schizophrenia who return to families high in EE were more likely to suffer a relapse than people who returned to low-EE families. These results, originally reported on a British sample, were replicated in southern California, obviously a very different locale (Brown et al., 1972; Leff & Vaughn, 1981; Vaughn et al., 1984; Vaughn & Leff, 1976). However, the excitement dwindled when researchers in Germany, Australia, and Great Britain failed to find an effect of EE on relapse rates (Dulz & Hand, 1986; MacMillan et al., 1986; Parker, et al., 1988).

Contemporary views of family influences on the development of schizophrenia seem to be moving in the direction of looking for protective factors that can maintain the adaptive functioning of those who are predisposed to the disorder. In part, this change in direction was stimulated by a backlash against the EE findings which, like the schizophrenogenic mother hypothesis, lays the blame for the disorder on family members. It is now recognized that families of schizophrenic individuals must cope with a heavy burden themselves in caring for their disturbed relative. Further, as you will see later in this chapter in our discussion of research on high-risk children, a disturbed child can be both a product of and a contributor to family disturbance. A disturbed child alters the interaction of family members in a way that would most likely not occur if the child had no psychological problems. Placed under greater stress by a socially difficult child, parents may experience chronic conflict and tension that in turn aggravate the child's problem, setting in motion a vicious cycle. To interrupt this cycle, and to help relatives of people with schizophrenia, researchers have turned to preventive models that emphasize protection in vulnerable individuals and coping methods for overburdened family members (Strachan, 1986).

Psychodynamic Perspective

The main contribution of the psychodynamic perspective is in Sullivan's work on orienting clinicians to the potential meaning of the distorted perceptions and communications expressed by the individual with schizophrenia. Based on Freudian theory, Sullivan looked for the unconscious meanings of the symptoms of the disorder such as hallucinations and delusions. He eventually came up with his own theory, in which he proposed that people with schizophrenia have acquired deficient communication patterns as the result of extreme anxiety-producing experiences in infancy. Presumably, such experiences early in life interfere with the normal development of personality and cognitive functioning. According to this view, the individual grows up physically, but mentally regresses to the level of the young child in thoughts, feelings, and behavior, resulting in the person's acting and thinking in ways that are deemed by others to be psychotic.

Empirical research has not supported these psychodynamic notions. Nevertheless, Sullivan's work has achieved a great deal of respect because he showed clinicians that schizophrenic communication may not be as devoid of meaning as it might otherwise sound.

Behavioral Perspective

Proponents of behavioral theories emphasize the role of learning as a cause of schizophrenia. These theories were first proposed in the 1960s as a radical alternative to biological explanations of the disorder. The behavioral theorists were impressed by evidence from early experiments showing that people with symptoms of schizophrenia could, through proper reinforcements, behave in socially appropriate ways. If the schizophrenic behaviors could be unlearned, these theorists reasoned, the same behaviors could have been acquired through a learning process.

But what type of learning process could account for the acquisition of behaviors that stray so far from the norm? These theorists proposed that individuals first acquire the symptoms of schizophrenia through a failure to learn how to direct their attention to important cues in social interactions. Presumably, this faulty learning process begins during childhood. The child's lack of attentiveness might result from the experience of punishment by other people; it becomes more rewarding for the child to retreat to an inner world of thoughts and fantasies. The child has no incentive to pull away from this idiosyncratic universe because the reality of the outside world is so unpleasant. Another possibility is that the adults in the child's environment are cold and withholding. Not only might this precipitate the child's retreat into an inner world, but also the adult's behavior provides no reinforcement for the child to become emotionally expressive or to exhibit socially appropriate behavior. In either case, the child's behaviors start to acquire a quality that

Robert, a 28-year-old former television sportscaster, lost his job after many months of psychological deterioration that culminated in overt psychosis. Problems became apparent shortly after Robert's promotion to a network-level position with heavy responsibilities. Co-workers noticed that Robert's hygiene had begun to deteriorate, his ideas were peculiar, and his emotions volatile and inappropriate. Robert's symptoms reached a point where it was clear that he could no longer work and he was fired. His behavior was not just eccentric, but bizarre, and in his conversations with others he seemed to be responding to voices. When asked about these voices, his responses were incomprehensible. No one knew Robert's history, and the fact that he grew up in a house where his schizophrenic grandmother caused major emotional upheaval throughout Robert's childhood. Although Robert's mother was not schizophrenic herself, she was regarded by most people as eccentric and reclusive. Taking on a high-pressure job proved to be too much for Robert to bear.

- To what extent did Robert's exposure to high stress lead to the development of his psychotic symptoms?
- Based on what you know about Robert's functioning prior to developing a psychological disorder, what do you think the chances are that he will recover?

sets the child apart from others. Eventually, this child comes to be labeled "odd" or "eccentric" by other children, parents, and teachers (Ullmann & Krasner, 1975). This **labeling** may eventually lead to the individual's being called "schizophrenic"—and a vicious cycle is begun. Once labeled, the individual acts in ways that conform to this label (Scheff, 1966).

When hospitalized and labeled as schizophrenic, the individual is further drawn into a pattern of maladaptive behaviors. In mental hospitals, disturbed behaviors may be

A gradual retreat from other people can be one of the first signals that a child is at risk for developing schizophrenia.

inadvertently reinforced. For example, nursing staff may be content to let a disturbed individual sit quietly and hallucinate in a corner, but react negatively to the individual's assertiveness in requesting more attention. If staff members fail to reinforce socially appropriate behavior, the clients have no incentive to act in ways that others would perceive as normal. Further, to the extent that the atmosphere in many psychiatric hospitals lacks adequate stimulation, the clients have nothing to distract them from their idiosyncratic and disturbed ways of thinking. They may also receive rewards for maintaining the sick role—what we described in Chapter 8 as secondary gain. According to the behavioral perspective, all of these circumstances lead to a situation in which the individual's schizophrenic symptoms are maintained and worsened. To reverse the process, behaviorists suggest that the dysfunctional symptoms be unlearned through staff's reinforcement of normal behaviors.

When these ideas were first proposed, clinicians responded enthusiastically. Behaviorists suggested ways that people with a disorder considered to be chronically incapacitating could have their symptoms alleviated without the need for extensive insight-oriented therapy or risky medications. As we have seen so many times, initial optimism about this approach faded as some of its limitations became evident. However, even those who do not accept the behavioral explanation of the origins of schizophrenia have come to agree that reinforcement can affect the expression of schizophrenic symptoms.

VULNERABILITY MODELS

The concept of vulnerability to schizophrenia was introduced by a well-known psychologist, Paul Meehl (1962), in a presidential address to the American Psychological Association on the challenges faced by schizophrenia researchers. Meehl proposed ideas on the issue of genetics versus environmental contributions that were to have profound influence on schizophrenia research for the rest of the century. According to Meehl, people who inherit a schizophrenic gene acquire a neural defect that forms the basis for their personality structure. As a result, they are more vulnerable to becoming psychotic in response to certain circumstances. Meehl proposed that genetics is a necessary, but not sufficient condition, for the development of schizophrenia. Through these ideas, Meehl opened the door to in-depth studies of the complex and puzzling interactive relationship between genes and the environment as causes of schizophrenia.

Meehl's proposal set the stage for the next decade of research and theory on the causes of schizophrenia. One of the more influential models to surface during this time was the **diathesis-stress model**, a proposal that people are born with a predisposition (or diathesis) that places them at risk for developing the disorder. Presumably this vulnerability is genetic, although some theorists have proposed that the vulnerability may also be acquired due to certain early life

events such as traumas, diseases, birth complications, and even family experiences (Zubin & Spring, 1977). People with this vulnerability were thought to possess it as an enduring trait, and therefore they always would be at risk for developing a full-blown psychosis if exposed to certain extremely stressful life experiences. When the stress passes, the individual can once again return to normal functioning, even without psychiatric interventions.

The diathesis-stress model has proved helpful in focusing attention on factors such as stress and the relationship between psychiatric disorders and life events. This model spurred other researchers to develop a new approach to studying schizophrenia: the **high-risk design**. In this type of research, investigators follow the lives of children who are considered to be at risk for developing schizophrenia because they have a biological parent with the disorder. This design was first used in Denmark in 1962 by Sarnoff Mednick and his associates (Mednick & Schulsinger, 1968) and has since been used by a number of other investigators in the United States (Watt et al., 1984). The reason that researchers are so interested in this group lies in the fact that children of parents with schizophrenia have a much greater likelihood of developing schizophrenia than children with normal parents. Children with one schizophrenic parent have a 12 percent risk over their lifetime of becoming schizophrenic, in contrast to a rate of 1 to 2 percent in the general population. If both parents have schizophrenia, the lifetime risk to the offspring jumps dramatically to rates of between 35 and 46 percent (Erlenmeyer-Kimling et al., 1982). The children of people with schizophrenia, then, are important to study because of their statistically greater chance of developing the disorder, although as you can see by the numbers, most of them will not.

By studying high-risk children prior to an age when they would be expected to show signs of schizophrenia, researchers hope to discover what distinguishes the subgroup of those who actually develop schizophrenia from those who lead lives free of symptoms. Researchers have also looked at other kinds of comparison groups such as the children of people with other forms of psychiatric disorders, children who show behavioral signs of disturbance even though their parents are normal, and normal control groups of children. In all of these studies, a **longitudinal research design** is used, in which the children are followed up over a period of years or decades. The advantage of this strategy is that the researchers can observe the evolution of the disorder in the subgroup of those who are destined to develop its symptoms. Information can be gathered that is far more accurate than would be possible from retrospective studies, which rely on people's memories from the distant past and which may be biased because the individual in question is known to have later developed schizophrenia.

Research on high-risk children has provided some of the most compelling evidence in favor of complex vulnerability models for the development of schizophrenia. A child who shows early signs of disturbance is more difficult to parent, especially by adults who themselves are psychologically

A mother who has a history of hospitalization for schizophrenia struggles every day to exert some control over her son. His difficult behaviors increase her own stress, making her less able to provide him with appropriate care and attention.

troubled. A high-risk child, then, is not just a passive participant in a stressful home environment but is an active player in whatever disturbances can arise. Consider the case of Brandon, the 8-year-old son of a schizophrenic woman. He shows a number of problem behaviors at home, in school, and with peers. These behaviors would make him a difficult child to raise under any circumstances, but especially so for a parent who may lack the psychological resources to cope with him. Brandon's mother, for example, fails to provide a good model of how to relate to other people because she herself is withdrawn and apathetic. Not only that, but she feels overwhelmed when Brandon is loud and offensive to other people, and this further exacerbates Brandon's misbehaviors. You can see how a vicious cycle becomes established in which his behaviors provoke greater disturbance in his mother, and her disturbance aggravates his difficulties. It is quite likely that Brandon's abnormal behaviors have their origins, at least in part, in his genetic vulnerability to schizophrenia. And you can see that this vulnerability might be a factor in raising the stress he experiences from his home environment. The end result is that Brandon's vulnerability is increased even more because of the particular combination of his own genetic predisposition and his mother's disturbed parenting style.

High-risk children also face another form of environmental stress if their parents have overt psychological disturbance. When parents are hospitalized or separated as a result of their own disorder, the child's life can be thrown into turmoil. Further, when the parent is home and has psychotic symptoms such as delusions and hallucinations, the impact on a child can be frightening and confusing.

Research on high-risk children has revealed that they show more signs of disturbance compared to control children, but that some of the stresses in the home are not unique to children whose parents have schizophrenia. Children whose parents have other major psychological disorders are also likely to have serious emotional and behavioral difficulties. The fact that schizophrenia is not unique in this regard presents a serious challenge to the diathesis-stress model of schizophrenia. Furthermore, the kinds of behavioral, emotional, and social difficulties shown by high-risk children may not necessarily mean that the child is doomed to develop schizophrenia. These childhood signs of disturbance, such as disturbed interpersonal functioning, are not equivalent to the adult form of schizophrenia (Sameroff et al., 1987). Even among those children who would seem most likely to develop schizophrenia, many never do. Some factor or factors must be involved that protect these vulnerable individuals from progressing to the point of showing overt signs of psychosis (Weintraub, 1987). Are these protective factors biological or experiential? As yet, this question has no definitive answer.

CONTEMPORARY APPROACHES TO TREATMENT

The vulnerability model we have just discussed implies that schizophrenia has no single cause. Although a particular theory may appear to be dominant, treatment must be based on a multifaceted approach that incorporates various theoretical components. Current comprehensive models of care include biological treatments, behavioral training programs, family therapy, and rehabilitation programs.

Biological Treatments

In the 1950s, effective medication was introduced for treating the symptoms of schizophrenia. This breakthrough was to have massive impact on the mental health system. Recall our discussion from Chapter 1 about how the advent of antipsychotic medications helped to spur on the deinstitutionalization movement. The fact that the most debilitating symptoms of psychosis could be controlled, at least to some extent, meant that hundreds of thousands of people could be treated on an outpatient basis rather than be confined and under constant supervision.

Prior to the 1950s, somatic interventions involved much more invasive treatments, the most extreme being the prefrontal lobotomy, in which neural tracts connecting the prefrontal lobes to the thalamus were severed. Although this kind of surgery helped to reduce aggressive behaviors in people suffering from hallucinations and delusions, lobotomies also had many unfavorable outcomes including a significant loss of motivation, creativity, and cognitive functions. With the advent of antipsychotic medication in the 1950s, the procedure was all but abandoned.

Electroconvulsive therapy (ECT) also was widely used several decades ago for relieving the symptoms of schizophrenia. The seizures produced by electric charges were intended to reduce the intensity of psychotic symptoms. Like psychosurgery, ECT has fallen out of favor in the United States, but it continues to be used in Great Britain for treating people with acute symptoms, particularly those involving catatonic phenomena (Weiner & Coffey, 1988).

As with other somatic treatments for schizophrenia, antipsychotic medications were discovered indirectly. In fact, they were developed through a most improbable route—in the formulation of antihistamines, drugs used for the treatment of allergies and asthma. Antihistamines were unexpectedly found to have a calming effect on people, and some physicians had the insight that if the sedative power of these medications were increased, perhaps they could be useful in treating disorders in people who seemed to be severely agitated. Chlorpromazine (marketed under the trade name Thorazine), the first antipsychotic medication, was initially used to sedate surgery patients (Deniker, 1970), and the sedating qualities of this medication led to its use for treating people who were grossly disturbed and agitated.

There are now several categories of antipsychotic medication, also called *major tranquilizers* or **neuroleptics** from the French, meaning that which "takes the neuron" (Gitlin, 1990). In addition to their sedating qualities, neuroleptics function to reduce the frequency and severity of psychotic symptoms. These medications are extremely effective in treating acute forms of schizophrenia, as was shown almost 30 years ago in large-scale investigations comparing the effectiveness of neuroleptics to placebos (Cole et al., 1964; Goldberg et al., 1965). There are differences among the neuroleptics in the dosage needed to achieve therapeutic effects, ranging from *low-potency* medications which require large dosages to *high-potency* medications which require comparatively smaller dosages. The low-potency class includes medications such as chlorpromazine (Thorazine) and thioridazine (Mellaril); middle-potency drugs include trifluoperazine (Stelazine) and thiothixine (Navane); high potency drugs include haloperidol (Haldol) and fluphenazine (Prolixin). A highly agitated patient would be more likely to have a low-potency medication prescribed because these tend to be more sedating than the high-potency drugs. For a patient who is less agitated, the high-potency drugs may be preferable but they do carry the risk of more serious side effects.

The most commonly used antipsychotic medications work to reduce psychotic thinking by blocking dopamine receptors. In other words, these medications contain chemical substances that become attached to the sites on the neuron that would ordinarily respond to the neurotransmitter dopamine. This action has two behavioral results, one therapeutic and the other unintended and troublesome. The therapeutic result is reduced frequency and intensity of psychotic symptoms, as the dopamine receptors are deactivated in sections of the brain that affect thoughts and feelings. On the negative side are consequences that can greatly interfere with the individual's movements and endocrine function. People taking such medications may suddenly experience symptoms such as uncontrollable shaking,

muscle tightening, and involuntary eye movements. What is happening biochemically to cause these side effects? Dopamine is accumulating because it is not being taken up by neurons whose receptor sites have been blocked by the drug. As the dopamine level rises, the neurons in other areas of the brain that control motor movements are thrown into dysregulation. Interestingly, people with Parkinson's disease, a movement disorder that is caused by an insufficiency of dopamine, are treated with a medication that enhances dopamine activity. From what you know so far, you should not be surprised by the fact that a commonly reported side effect of this anti-Parkinsonian medication is psychotic-like behavior and thinking.

One of the most troubling effects from long-term use of neuroleptics is an irreversible neurological disorder called **tardive dyskinesia**, which affects 10 to 20 percent of people who take neuroleptics for a year or more. People with tardive dyskinesia experience uncontrollable movements in various parts of their bodies, including the mouth, tongue, lips, fingers, arms, legs, and trunk. As you can imagine, these involuntary movements can seriously impair the person's ability to walk, breathe, eat, and talk, to say nothing of how embarrassing it is to be seen in this state.

A more recently introduced antipsychotic medication that does not cause the side effects commonly associated with other neuroleptics is clozapine (Clozaril), a medication that has a different biochemical mode of action from the neuroleptics. Clozapine has been enthusiastically welcomed by the 10 to 20 percent of people with schizophrenia whose symptoms were untouched by other antipsychotic medications. Research studies have shown that clozapine is significantly more effective and has fewer side effects than chlorpromazine (Thorazine) (Claghorn et al., 1987). Unfortunately, the use of clozapine involves a very serious health risk. A very small number of these people taking clozapine have developed agranulocytosis, a medical condition in which a person's bone marrow stops producing white blood cells. Such a condition is very serious because it leaves an individual vulnerable to infection, and can consequently be the indirect cause of death. Because of this alarming possibility, prescription of this medication has been limited to a small group of people for whom other medications have been unsuccessful. Those taking clozapine must be closely monitored for any signs of agranulocytosis (Kane et al., 1988).

Although antipsychotic medications have proven to be of tremendous benefit for treating the positive symptoms of schizophrenia, it is important to keep in mind that these medications do not cure the disorder. In fact, the negative symptoms such as low motivation, social difficulties, and isolation do not change as a function of these medications (Gitlin, 1990). One dilemma that health care providers face when recommending antipsychotic medication is whether or not people with schizophrenia should continue to be maintained on full doses of these medications when they are not experiencing the overt positive symptoms of the disorder. Clinicians must weigh the benefits and costs of any treatment, particularly one with side effects as potentially serious as those associated with antipsychotic medication. A reasonable compromise used with a client who is being closely monitored involves reduction or cessation of medication during periods of good functioning, and reintroduction or increase in medication when signs of disturbance reappear (Gitlin, 1990; Herz et al., 1982).

Behavioral and Family Treatments

Although effective in relieving some of the symptoms of schizophrenia, biological treatments do not cure the disorder, nor do they necessarily alleviate the distressing effects of the disorder on the individual's life. For this reason, clinicians also rely on psychological interventions for helping people with schizophrenia. The most common interventions are those derived from the behavioral and family systems perspectives.

Behavioral treatments are based on the assumption that a large part of the difficulty faced by many people with schizophrenia is due to their having acquired a number of bizarre and maladaptive behavior patterns. The focus in these treatments is on the particular symptoms of the individual that interfere with social adjustment and functioning. For example, consider Aimee, a woman whose paranoid delusions have caused her to respond to other people in ways that alienate them. She turns away when others start a conversation with her, acting in a cold and distant manner that discourages them from getting to know her. Her therapist might help Aimee to develop the more socially appropriate behaviors of responding pleasantly to others and even, perhaps, initiating conversations herself. Aimee might also be a member of a therapy group comprised of individuals with similar difficulties. The therapist would work with the group as a whole to encourage each member to develop more appropriate interpersonal behaviors.

Cognitive-behavioral treatments can also be applied in individual psychotherapy. The client can be taught to detect the early signs of a relapse, to take a more positive approach to evaluating the ability to cope with daily problems, and to develop a broader range of ways to handle emotional distress and anxiety (Wasylenki, 1992).

Several approaches within the behavioral model have been widely used in treating people with schizophrenia. In a token economy (Ayllon & Azrin, 1965), individuals are rewarded with plastic chips called "tokens" for acting in socially appropriate ways (see Table 12-4). They either do not earn tokens or must forfeit them when they display inappropriate behaviors. The tokens can be used by the individual to acquire special privileges or opportunities. Over time, the expectation is that the new behaviors will become habitual and not dependent on being reinforced by tokens.

Consider the case of a hospitalized woman with schizophrenia who has very poor personal hygiene and grooming. Her therapist might use a token economy system to encourage her to develop appropriate hygiene. For each privilege that she wishes to "purchase," she must cash in a fixed num-

Table 12–4 Example of Token Economy Used in Treating a Person with Schizophrenia

Earn tokens for the following behaviors:
    Eat with proper utensils.
    Brush hair in the morning.
    Keep clothing on during the day.
    Answer when spoken to.
    Participate in therapeutic activities.
Lose tokens for the following behaviors:
    Shout at other people.
    Take off clothes in public.
    Eat with hands.
    Refuse to participate in therapeutic activities.

ber of tokens. She may need 10 tokens to go on a weekend pass, or 2 tokens to go to the hospital snack shop. Taking a daily shower may earn her 2 tokens, and combing her hair may be worth 1 token. The incentive to have these privileges would presumably be strong enough to motivate her to engage in appropriate grooming behaviors. Eventually these behaviors become established and are reinforcing in their own right so that the tokens are no longer necessary. Additionally, the attention and praise she receives when she earns each token can add to the reinforcement value of the tokens themselves. In this process, she learns to value such positive attention, making it more likely that she will work to maintain her grooming skills.

Social skills training is another behavioral intervention that, like token economy, makes the achievement of a desirable outcome or reinforcement dependent on the individual's carrying out a desirable behavior. The types of behaviors that are the focus of social skills training are those

In social skills training, the client receives feedback from others as a way of learning appropriate responses in social interactions.

involved in interpersonal situations (Liberman et al., 1985). People with schizophrenia often speak or act in ways that others regard as abnormal. In social skills training, an individual's inappropriate behaviors are identified and targeted, and reinforcement becomes dependent on the individual's acting in more socially acceptable ways. For example, a disturbed individual may speak with an unusual tone or voice volume, move in peculiar ways, stare at others, or fail to maintain appropriate distance when speaking to people. In social skills training, the therapist provides feedback to the individual about the inappropriateness of each of these behaviors. Such feedback may be given in the context of role-playing exercises, direct instruction, or a group setting in which participants are encouraged to comment openly on each other's behaviors. Using the feedback of others, the individual learns to behave in more appropriate ways until such behavior becomes virtually automatic (Bellack et al., 1989).

Milieu therapy is another approach to intervention that involves social processes as a tool for changing the individual's behavior. In this approach, all staff and clients in a treatment setting work as a therapeutic community to promote positive functioning in the clients. Members of the community participate in group activities ranging from occupational therapy to training classes. Clients are encouraged to work with and spend time with other residents, even when leaving on passes. Decisions are made by the entire community, sometimes involving an executive council with elected members from units of the treatment setting. Every staff person, whether a therapist, nurse, or paraprofessional, takes part in the overall mission of providing an environment that supports positive change and appropriate social behaviors. The underlying idea behind milieu therapy is that the pressure to conform to conventional social norms of behavior discourages the individual with schizophrenia from expressing problematic symptoms. The "normalizing" effects of such an environment are intended to help the individual make a smoother and more effective transition to community life.

Although milieu therapy is an important component of many hospital and community-based programs, systematic investigation reveals that a social learning approach combining token economy and social skills training is a more effective prescription for inpatient treatment of people with schizophrenia. In one very influential study (Paul & Lentz, 1977), these behavioral methods were contrasted with milieu therapy. The social learning treatment proved to be more effective as a means of promoting positive change in the hospital setting as well as greater adaptation to community life outside the institution.

The social learning method is also effective for people living outside institutions when used in the context of family therapy. In fact, researchers who compared the effectiveness of individual therapy interventions with family therapy interventions found that behavioral family therapy had clear advantages and more long-lasting effects (Falloon et al., 1985). These researchers went to the homes of people

Groups such as Schizophrenics Anonymous provide a setting in which people with this disorder can obtain support and understanding from people who know first-hand how torturous the symptoms can be.

who had been discharged from the hospital with diagnoses of schizophrenia, and they trained family members to employ a structured problem-solving method in which they defined collectively some problem, considered various solutions, and agreed on a detailed solution plan. In those cases where families were deficient in interpersonal communication, family members were trained in communication skills. In cases where conflict, anxiety, or depression were evident in any family member, specific behavioral strategies were provided. The people in this group were compared with a group who were treated in a clinic and given individual psychotherapy oriented toward teaching them coping skills for maintaining themselves in the community. After 9 months of treatment, the family-managed individuals showed markedly different patterns of functioning from those in the other group in that they had fewer relapses, less intense symptoms, and fewer hospitalizations. Most impressively, the family-managed individuals were able to hold onto their gains through the second year of the study. By the end of the study, the researchers claimed that half of those in the family-managed group showed no psychiatric disorders, whereas the individually treated people still showed high rates of disturbance.

People with schizophrenia definitely require professional help, but not all help must come from a professional source. Indeed, professional treatment will be ineffective unless the schizophrenic person wishes to be assisted, and works collaboratively with the clinician in developing adaptive styles of living. Schizophrenic persons often find themselves overwhelmed by a world that is confusing and threatening. Tapping internal resources often seems difficult if not impossible. Sometimes assistance can be obtained from others who are similarly distressed. The book *On Our Own* (Chamberlin, 1978) laid out a very compelling statement urging psychiatric patients to join forces to meet needs that the psychiatric establishment was regarded as incapable of fulfilling. During the 1980s, many self-help groups were organized throughout the United States.

Started by former psychiatric patients who have felt alienated from society, these groups have served a monumental function in helping formerly institutionalized and currently distressed psychiatric patients adapt to the demands of society.

In addition to self-help, people with schizophrenia must often turn to family members and loved ones for support as they struggle to contend with the stormy forces within themselves and the pressures of the outside world. E. Fuller Torrey, a respected psychiatrist, has played a major role in teaching family members how to be supportive and helpful. His book *Surviving Schizophrenia* (1988) is an invaluable guide to understanding and helping those suffering from the debilitating symptoms of this disorder.

Comprehensive models of treatment coordinate services provided in the hospital setting with those available in the community. In this model, inpatient hospital-based programs are regarded as "asylums" (Wasow, 1986) where the individual can seek refuge during acute episodes of the illness. Such an approach avoids the institutionalized existence that historically characterized the long-term treatment of people with schizophrenia. The ideal program focuses on rehabilitation, maximizing the individual's chances of maintaining an independent life outside the hospital (Talbott & Glick, 1986).

SCHIZOPHRENIA: THE PERSPECTIVES REVISITED

Schizophrenia is a disorder that has mystified people for centuries, although it is only within the last 100 years that the disorder has had a name. As researchers attempt to gain a scientific understanding of the disorder, clinicians, family members, and afflicted individuals seek ways to cope on a daily basis with its many widespread effects.

As we approach the twenty-first century, relatively few conclusions about the causes of schizophrenia are evident. One fact does stand out, however—people do not develop schizophrenia solely as the result of troubled childhoods. It is clear that biology plays a central role, although the precise nature and extent of biological causes remain unclear. We know that there are differences in brain structure and functioning in people with schizophrenia compared with others. We also know that people with schizophrenia have a high likelihood of having relatives with this disorder, and the closer the relative the greater the rate of concordance. Scientists have delineated specific biological markers that have assisted them in their efforts to understand which factors and genes are implicated in the acquisition of this disorder.

Even through few would contest the central role of biological factors in determining schizophrenia, we know that biology cannot tell the whole story. Events happen in the life of the person predisposed to schizophrenia that trigger the disorder. Twin studies show us that environmental factors must play some role; otherwise, identical twins would have a 100 percent concordance rate for this disorder. But what are those factors in life that make one more vulnerable to schizophrenia? Numerous studies of early life relationships have failed to pinpoint a causal connection between faulty parenting and the development of this disorder. What does seem clear is the fact that certain stresses might set off the disorder, and a disturbed cycle sets in. Faced with an unusual child, parents become more tense, and this increased

Table 12–5	SCHIZOPHRENIA: A SUMMARY CHART OF PERSPECTIVES		
BIOLOGICAL	FAMILY SYSTEMS	PSYCHODYNAMIC	BEHAVIORAL
Cortical atrophy and enlarged brain ventricles suggesting degenerative process. Excess of dopamine activity. Genetic models propose multigenetic basis for inheritance. Vulnerability model proposes interactive set of causes.	Disturbed family communication patterns and faulty parenting, cause symptoms to develop. Overly harsh and intrusive families increase risk of suffering a relapse.	Deficient communication patterns are result of anxiety-producing experiences during infancy; hallucinations and delusions are symbolic expressions of unconscious conflicts.	Maladaptive behaviors learned through reinforcement and failure of the individual to learn to respond appropriately to social cues. Once learned these behaviors become self-perpetuating.
Treatment: Neuroleptic medications.	**Treatment:** Group therapy for family members to help them cope with their ill relatives and teach effective communication skills.	**Treatment:** Symptoms are interpreted as expressions of symbolic unconscious conflict.	**Treatment:** Token economy, social skills training, milieu therapy, and teaching of coping methods.

Return to the Case

David Marshall

David's History

In part because they were so upset about David, Mr. and Mrs. Marshall found it difficult to remember many details about his early years. In response to my initial questions about his childhood, the Marshalls responded that he was a "normal kid." However, upon probing they recalled that he was a very "quiet boy who kept most things to himself." David's subdued style stood in sharp contrast to the liveliness of his brother Michael, who was a year older. When I asked about the family environment during David's early years, Mr. Marshall stated, with a tone of embarrassment in his voice, that their marital relationship had been fairly "stormy" during those years, and that they had come close to divorce when David was about 2 years old. With the help of marital therapy they worked things out over the course of a year.

In recalling David's childhood personality, Mrs. Marshall pointed out an interesting contrast with his adolescent years, in that he was an exceptionally neat and clean child. She remembered how he would become very angry if for some reason he was unable to take his 7 PM bath. By the time he was in his late teens, however, David's finicky habits had changed entirely. He went without washing for several days at a time, and would do so only at the insistence of his mother, who practically had to drag him into the shower. Mrs. Marshall said that she never would have believed that her formerly clean son would one day have greasy hair, shoddily pulled into a pony tail, unwashed for weeks at a time.

The Marshalls told me of their dismay and horror as they witnessed the almost total incapacitation of a young man who was once healthy and intelligent. They spoke of the impact on their own lives, as they had come to worry about the safety of having such a disturbed young man living with them. I asked them to elaborate regarding this concern, and Mr. Marshall told me about David's nightly rituals in his room. With his door shut and locked, David each night lit two dozen candles as part of a "communication exercise with Zoroaster." Any use of fire by a man so disturbed was worrisome; the proximity of burning flames to the many spray cans in David's room increased his parents' alarm even further.

Moving on to a discussion of family history, the Marshalls told me that the only relevant bit of information that came to mind was the fact that Mrs. Marshall's sister had a long history of psychological problems, and had been hospitalized three times because of she had "crazy beliefs, heard voices, and acted very strange."

Assessment

In light of David's severe disturbance, psychological testing was not viable. My assessment of David was therefore limited to a 30-minute mental status examination, in which his delusions and hallucinations were remarkable. Regardless of the question being asked, most of David's responses focused on his beliefs about Zoroaster and the aliens. His disorientation was apparent in his responses indicating that his name was "Brodo," that the date was the "36th of Fruen" in the "year of the next heaven, 9912," and that he was being held in a prison by the enemies of Zoroaster. After giving these answers, David began to laugh in the sinister way described by his mother, and then waved his arms high over his head in the spraying motion to which she also had referred. He then stopped, as if he heard something, and looked at his watch. The time was 11 AM. Muttering to himself, "It's too early," he seemed to go off into a reverie. At that point, I concluded that David was hearing voices. When I asked him if this was the case, he said it was not a voice, but a message telling him what he must do next to proceed on his mission. Further questioning at this point revealed David's beliefs about his secret mission and the daily messages he had been receiving from the television set. I asked David to carry out some simple calculations, which he did adequately, and to copy some simple geometric figures. In the process of doing so, he began to write elaborate equations all over the piece of paper, and to draw pictures of what he called "hollow soft forms." He asked me if I knew the difference between these and "hollow hard forms," which he illustrated on another sheet of paper. These drawings consisted of squiggles and letter-like symbols that apparently contained a great deal of meaning to David, but made no sense to others. Despite my best efforts to communicate with David in a logical and clear manner, I felt thwarted in my attempt to get David to tell me anything about himself other than his delusional concerns.

Diagnosis

As I evaluated David's personal history and current symptoms, all signs pointed to a diagnosis of schizophrenia. In terms of personal history, David was in the age group during which

David Marshall continued

schizophrenia most commonly surfaces, and he had a biological relative with a disorder suggestive of schizophrenia. Of course, neither of these two facts would have been sufficient to conclude that David was suffering from schizophrenia. The course and the symptoms of his disorder provided the most telling evidence.

David was a young man with a progressively worsening course of functioning. He had deteriorated markedly from his high school years in his academic performance, personal habits, and interpersonal relations. During the years preceding his hospitalization, David had become increasingly symptomatic.

David's symptoms were those of a person with psychosis. He had delusions, hallucinations, loosening of associations, and bizarre behaviors. He was impaired in most areas of everyday functioning, living a life of social isolation, behaving in a bizarre and idiosyncratic manner, and failing to take care of himself even in regard to personal hygiene.

As for the particular kind of schizophrenia with which David was suffering, the most tenable diagnosis was Undifferentiated Type. I assigned this diagnosis because David was not prominently paranoid in his delusions, nor was he catatonic or prominently disorganized in his symptom presentation.

Axis I. Schizophrenia, Undifferentiated Type.

Axis II. Deferred.

Axis III. No physical disorders or conditions.

Axis IV. Severity: 1. No acute events or enduring circumstances that may be relevant to the disorder.

Axis V. Current Global Assessment of Functioning: 30. Highest Global Assessment of Functioning (past year): 45.

Case Formulation

There was little question about the fact that David Marshall had schizophrenia. But what caused this tragic set of symptoms to unfold in a young man who as a child was nothing other than a quiet and reserved boy? What took place in his biology and psychology that caused the transition from shyness to schizophrenia over the course of his adolescent years? As I tried to answer these questions, my thoughts were drawn to the important biological fact that David's aunt was in all likelihood schizophrenic. The significance of this one fact, of course, lies

in the current understanding of the critically important role played by genetics in the etiology of this disorder. At the same time, experts know that biological predisposition is generally regarded as insufficient in determining whether or not a person will develop schizophrenia. Consequently, I turned to David's personal history for clues.

Throughout his early life, David was reticent and withdrawn compared to his active and outgoing brother. On the one hand, David's behavior made him a target of scrutiny in his parents' attempts to find out what he was feeling and thinking. On the other hand, David's parents clearly devoted most of their attention to his older brother, communicating to David the message that they really were less concerned with his well-being. I also wondered about the impact on David of the discord between his parents during the early years of his life.

Planning a Treatment

The plan that I implemented for David took into account the need for decisive intervention over the short-term, and continued treatment for the years ahead. I realized that even when his psychotic symptoms were under control, he would have residual problems requiring monitoring and treatment. David's parents concurred with me that his overt psychotic symptoms needed to be brought under control, and that this could best be accomplished by medication. But would David take the medication voluntarily? Much to the surprise of David's parents, he did agree to give it a try. His decision to comply led me to wonder whether David, on some level, had come to recognize the seriousness of his problem and had become more willing to accept help.

I recommended that David remain in the hospital for 3 months, during which time he could be stabilized on his medication and the two of us could develop a working relationship. Ideally, we would continue to meet on an outpatient basis following his discharge. Our therapeutic work would center on several tasks. First, I wanted to help David to develop some understanding of his disorder and the importance of his maintaining an ongoing relationship with a mental health professional. Second, I wanted to help him to develop coping strategies to be used in his everyday life. He needed to learn how to care for himself and work to begin leading a more normal life.

During the initial weeks of David's hospitalization, the antipsychotic medication began to

David Marshall continued

reduce the severity of his symptoms. As he became more lucid, he was able to carry on conversations without the intrusion of ideas about Zoroaster and a secret mission of saving the world. David told me of the despair he experienced about his symptoms, and how incapable he felt of ever getting anywhere in his life. Gradually, David interacted more with other patients on the unit, though his preference was clearly to stay in his room alone, listening to rock music. At first, this preference for being alone caused his parents some distress, and they wondered whether he was really getting better or not. However, I felt less concerned, because his behavior seemed markedly different from his actions prior to his hospitalization. It was clear to me that David cherished his privacy, and that being alone did not necessarily mean that he had become lost in a delusional world.

After David had stabilized and his symptoms were under control, he and I talked about discharge from the hospital. I recommended to David that, instead of returning home, he should take up residence in a halfway house. He rejected this idea outright on the grounds that such facilities do not afford much privacy. We arrived at a compromise that involved his returning home but attending a day treatment program for at least 6 months. In such a program David would be supervised in his daily activities, would have some opportunity to socialize, and would be able to take part in vocational training. I agreed to continue seeing him in weekly psychotherapy sessions.

Outcome of the Case

Following David's discharge from the hospital, he moved back home and followed my recommendation that he participate in the hospital's day treatment program, where he thrived with the support of the treatment staff. As I might have predicted, he remained a withdrawn young man, who could feel content sitting alone in a corner thinking. To the relief of his parents, David agreed to continue taking his medication, despite the fact that he complained about minor hand tremors.

After 12 months in the day treatment program, the treatment staff decided that David was ready for a trial run in a real job. He was placed in a position at a library, where he shelved books. He liked this job because it involved so little contact with the public, and there was an orderliness about it which he found comforting. After a few months David's excellent performance was noted by his supervisor, and he received a small promotion to a job at the circulation desk, which involved more contact with the public. This proved to be a mistake. The stress of exposure to many people over the course of the day was too much for David to handle, and within 2 weeks he had decompensated into a full-blown psychotic episode.

After a short hospital stay, in which he was restabilized on his medications, David returned to the day treatment program, where he remained for another 6 months. By this time, there was an opening in a group home, and David was finally able to move out of his parents' house. He now lives in this setting, and has gone back to his former job at the library.

I have continued to see David over these past few years, but our sessions at present are scheduled only once a month, a frequency that seems most comfortable for David. Although we have worked together for more than 4 years, I have never gotten a clear message from David that he values our work or that he even cares about coming to psychotherapy. Nevertheless, it has become part of his life routine, and I hold onto the belief that our work together has played some role in his remaining relatively healthy for this long period.

familial tension can lead to a worsening of the child's disturbance.

Although current understanding of the causes of schizophrenia remains incomplete, scientists continue to look for ways to alleviate its symptoms. Biological approaches, particularly in the form of medication, provide the most effective route to symptom improvement. It is important to keep in mind that medication does not cure the disorder, but only treats the symptoms. Furthermore, this treatment is not without its costs. Worrisome side effects are associated with the use of antipsychotic medications, and clinicians face difficult dilemmas as they help schizophrenic individuals weigh the costs and the benefits of pharmacological interventions.

Just as biology is insufficient as an explanation for the disorder, medication is an incomplete intervention for treating people with schizophrenia. Individualized treatment plans range from tightly structured, institutionally affiliated programs to periodic psychotherapy that is provided when needed. Generally, those who are incapacitated by the disorder require comprehensive and permanent treatment and support. But there are also many thousands of people with schizophrenia who function adequately in the world, and have only occasional need for active intervention, when their psychotic symptoms flare up.

Despite the inadequacy of current knowledge about this disorder, the tremendous gains made during the past decade are certainly cause for optimism. New research techniques have provided scientists with access to the human brain, where many of the secrets of this perplexing disorder lie. Refinements in genetic research have also provided hope that scientists soon will come to grips with the issue of why some relatives develop schizophrenia while others do not. In light of the speed of recent advances, it is possible that within a decade we will look back to the 1990s with disbelief about the limited state of our knowledge.

SUMMARY

1. Interpreting the existing research on the causes of schizophrenia is made complicated by the fact that the diagnostic criteria for the disorder have changed so drastically from the 1960s to the present day. To deal with this problem, researchers in the 1980s began to move toward the idea of studying schizophrenia spectrum disorders, which include the range of disorders that have schizophrenia-like symptoms such as disturbed thought, mood, and behavior.

2. Theories on schizophrenia have traditionally fallen into two categories: biological and psychological. While these theories contribute greatly to an understanding of schizophrenia, neither one is sufficient to provide a complete explanation. Researchers working within the biological perspective have based their approach on Kraepelin's belief that schizophrenia is caused by a degenerative brain disease. Through sophisticated technological brain imaging procedures, researchers have demonstrated that certain brain abnormalities are associated with schizophrenia, including cortical atrophy, enlarged ventricles, and deficits in a variety of brain areas involved in cognitive, attentional, and motivational functions. Interpreting these abnormalities is complicated by the fact that people with other psychological disorders also show enlarged ventricles. Although not a solution to this problem, some researchers have proposed that another way to look at the findings is to compare Type I and Type II schizophrenia. People with Type I schizophrenia may have an overactive dopamine neurotransmitter system that is responsible for their hallucinations, delusions, and accentuated motor behaviors. In contrast, people with Type II schizophrenia symptoms seem to show more evidence of brain degeneration and possibly differences in the development of brain hemisphere dominance that underlie their attentional deficit, lack of motivation, and withdrawal. These findings add support to the concept that there may be two subtypes of schizophrenia, each having different biological correlates. In addition, this analysis suggests a clarification of the disputed dopamine hypothesis in that an altered dopamine system may account for one type of schizophrenia but not the other.

3. Evidence in favor of a genetic explanation of schizophrenia has accumulated from studies on family inheritance patterns, adoption, and biological markers. Family studies have reliably shown that the incidence of schizophrenia is higher in biological relatives of people with the disorder, with a concordance rate among monozygotic twins of 48 percent. Adoption studies add more weight to this evidence, because they rule out the influence of a shared environment among biological relatives living together. In a large-scale adoption study carried out in the 1960s in Denmark, researchers found that the rates of chronic schizophrenia in the biological relatives of index adoptees were far higher than the rates in the relatives of control adoptees. A cross-fostering study on a much smaller sample provided similar evidence in favor of the role of genetics in that people whose biological parents had a diagnosis of schizophrenia were more likely to develop the disorder themselves whether or not their adoptive parents also had a diagnosis of schizophrenia. These findings have also been extended to schizophrenia spectrum disorders. More recent adoption studies that have taken place in Finland suggest a larger role of the environment, however, providing further support for interactive models of genetic and environmental factors. These findings suggest that a deficient family environment may not create a schizophrenic child, but a favorable environment may prevent the disorder's development in a child who is genetically prone to the disorder.

4. One genetic model for schizophrenia that seems to hold the most potential is the multi-factorial polygenic threshold model, which states that many genes are involved in the transmission of schizophrenia. When the genetic and environmental factors reach a certain threshold, schizophrenic symptoms are produced. Studies using biological markers have helped to gain greater understanding of the genetic model for the transmission of schizophrenia. Two important biological markers, both of which have been found to be abnormal in schizophrenic people and their close relatives, are sustained attention and smooth eye pursuit movements. Genetic models can be developed by using these tasks to study relatives with varying degrees of relatedness to people with schizophrenia. Event-related potential (ERP) is another assessment procedure used in this research. People with schizophrenia, and their relatives, show a deficit in the ability to tune out irrelevant stimuli (sensory gating). Genetic mapping has provided further insight into possible genetic links to schizophrenia.

5. The Genain quadruplets have been studied intensively since their development of schizophrenic symptoms in the 1950s when they were in their 20s. By following the Genains over their adult years, researchers have determined that although genetics played a role in their development of the disorder, this was not the total answer. Each sister showed varying degrees of severity and course of schizophrenia, as well as varying responses on tests involving eye movement, CT and PET scans, dopamine activity, brain function, personality, and intelligence. Environmental explanations had to be sought to account for these differences shown among the four women. An interactive model combining biological (brain damage) and psychological (environmental stress) factors seemed to account best for the development of symptoms in these women over the course of their adult lives.

6. Contemporary psychological perspectives to schizophrenia have their origins in the work of Fromm-Reichmann, who believed that the disorder was caused by disturbed interpersonal relationships in childhood. Specifically, she proposed the idea of the schizophrenogenic mother, who, was thought to create a schizophrenic child by virtue of a combination of overintrusiveness, devaluation, and confusing communications patterns. This idea gained some acceptance in the 1950s and 1960s through the work of family systems researchers who proposed that disturbances in family interaction and communication patterns were related to the symptoms of schizophrenia. Specifically, these researchers maintained that a double-bind communication pattern could lead a child to develop a communication disorder that eventually became transformed into schizophrenia. These ideas concerning family origins of schizophrenia were largely discredited by controlled observational research in the late 1960s and 1970s, in which no differences could be found between families with a schizophrenic child and families with normal children. Another proposal put forth in the 1970s was that a highly critical and overintrusive family environment could increase the individual's risk for relapse once he or she had been hospitalized for schizophrenia. This idea of a family's expressed emotion as an influence on schizophrenia was also found to be insufficient, although it has been recognized that a supportive family atmosphere can serve a protective function in an individual who has already been diagnosed as having schizophrenia. In contemporary family approaches to schizophrenia, emphasis is placed on helping family members cope with the disorder rather than in assigning a causative role to the family's interaction pattern in the development of the disorder.

7. The psychodynamic perspective, like the family systems perspective, holds that schizophrenia is caused by deficiencies in the individual's early parenting. Specifically, Sullivan hypothesized that people with schizophrenia acquired abnormal communication patterns as the result of extreme anxiety-producing experiences in infancy. The delusions and hallucinations of people with schizophrenia are also interpreted in terms of their potential symbolic meaning. Although the psychodynamic perspective has little credence among contemporary researchers, it has proven helpful to clinicians in pointing to the possible meaning of their client's disturbed communication.

8. According to the behavioral perspective, schizophrenia represents a maladaptive behavior pattern acquired in childhood through a deficit in attention toward socially relevant cues. As a child, the individual found it more rewarding to fantasize than to face the unpleasant reality of a world that was either punitive or cold and withholding. Once labeled as "odd" by peers, parents, and teachers, the child finds it difficult to escape from a vicious cycle that eventually escalates and leads to hospitalization. In the institution, the individual receives little incentive for behaving in socially appropriate ways, and sinks deeper into a retreat of schizophrenic thinking and behaviors. The secondary gain of maintaining the sick role further reduces the individual's likelihood of changing. Although support for the behavioral model has faded in view of biological evidence, researchers and clinicians agree that labeling and reinforcement are useful concepts in understanding symptoms of schizophrenia.

9. The vulnerability model combines several features of the major theoretical perspectives to schizophrenia. According to this model, which has emerged from the diathesis-stress model, people who develop schizophrenia have acquired a biological predispositon in the form of their genetic inheritance. These people are especially vulnerable to deficient parenting or other environmental stresses that can trigger the development of schizophrenia. If these environmental factors are present to a sufficient degree, the individual will develop the disorder, and it they are not, the individual will grow normally into adulthood. Support for the vulnerability model has come from research on high-risk children who have a biological parent with the disorder and are statistically more likely to develop schizophrenia over the course of their lifetimes. This research has shown that in childhood, high-risk individuals show more behavioral abnormalities than do their low-risk peers, but no more so than children whose parents have other forms of psychological disorder.

10. Before the advent of antipsychotic medications, biological treatments for schizophrenia involved electroconvulsive therapy and radical somatic treatments such as prefrontal lobotomies. Lobotomies are rarely used today, as they can produce disturbing effects such as loss of motivation, creativity, and cognitive functions; ECT is used primarily in the treatment of severe depression. Neuroleptic or antipsychotic medications are now the primary form of biological interventions.

The antipsychotic and sedating effects of these drugs are attributed to their blocking of dopamine receptors. The high-potency medications that are prescribed to very agitated clients have serious side-effects, including tardive dyskinesia, an irreversible neurological disorder involving uncontrollable bodily movements. Lower-potency medications are available for less severely agitated clients and carry less of a long-term risk. Another alternative medication is clozapine, which reduces psychotic symptoms in some people for whom neuroleptics have been ineffective. Although there are fewer side-effects, serious health risks are sometimes involved in its use. Behavioral methods are widely used in treating people with schizophrenia. Cognitive-behavioral therapy can help people with schizophrenia cope with their symptoms and reduce their distress. Token economies are used in institutional settings to replace inappropriate behaviors with appropriate behaviors that contribute to the normalization of the individual, such as good grooming and table manners. Social skills training, another behavioral method, involves reinforcing clients for interacting with others, such as regulating their expression of affect to fit the situation. In milieu therapy, the entire group of staff and clients work as a therapeutic community to facilitate appropriate social behaviors in a range of interactions and settings. Although milieu therapy can be beneficial, researchers have demonstrated greater effectiveness using a combination of token economy and social skills training. Self-help and family-oriented organizations have emerged around the country as a way to help people with schizophrenia and their families cope with the symptoms of the disorder and share ways of dealing with their feelings of alienation from society. These organizations are particularly important given the deinstitutionalization movement, which resulted in large numbers of people with schizophrenia moving from institutions into the community. Family-oriented organizations work to help members reduce social skills conflicts, anxiety and depression, and promote healthy communication skills. It is increasingly recognized that people with schizophrenia need comprehensive treatment approaches that coordinate hospital and community services.

KEY TERMS

Vulnerability: when used in the context of psychological disorders, a biologically based predispostion to developing a particular disorder when certain environmental conditions are in place. p. 296

Cortical atrophy: a wasting away or deterioration of tissue in the cerebral cortex of the brain. p. 296

Dopamine hypothesis: a biological explanation for schizophrenia which proposes that delusions, hallucinations, and attentional deficits result from overactivity of neurons that communicate with each other via the transmission of dopamine. p. 297

Simple mendelian genetics: inheritance of a characteristic that is controlled by a single gene which is either in dominant or recessive form. p. 301

Multi-factorial polygenic threshold: a model to explain the relationship between genetic and environmental contributions to schizophrenia proposing that several genes with varying influence are involved in the transmission of schizophrenia. p. 301

Biological markers: measurable characteristics, such as smooth pursuit eye movement, whose patterns parallel the inheritance of a disorder. p. 301

Sustained attention: a biological marker that is measured by having a subject make a response when a certain target stimulus is displayed; people with schizophrenia and their relatives typically do poorly on this task. p. 301

Smooth pursuit eye movements: a biological marker that is measured by having subjects follow a visual target; people with schizophrenia and their relatives have been found to show irregular pursuit of a moving target with many interruptions by extraneous eye movements. p. 302

Event related potential (ERP): a measure of the electrical activity of the brain when a person is exposed to certain sensory stimuli or "events," researchers have found that people with schizophrenia have difficulty screening out irrelevant stimuli. p. 302

Sensory gating: the closing down of sensory processing with repeated presentation of the same stimulus. p. 302

Genetic mapping: the attempt by biological researchers to identify the characteristics controlled by each gene. p. 302

Schizophrenogenic mother: an outdated concept referring to the hypothesis that a certain kind of mothering style, characterized by confusing communication, could produce a schizophrenic child. p. 305

Double-bind hypothesis: a notion that the schizophrenic individual develops faulty communication and thinking processes through years of being exposed to conflicting messages from other family members. p. 305

Expressed emotion (or EE): an index of the degree to which family members speak in ways that reflect criticism, hostile feeling, and emotional overinvolvement or overconcern with regard to the schizophrenic individual. p. 306

Labeling: a social process in which an individual is designated as having a certain disease or disorder, and once given this label the individual acts in ways that conform to this label. p. 307

Diathesis-stress model: predisposition (or diathesis) that places people at risk for developing a disorder, if exposed to certain extremely stressful life experiences. p. 308

High-risk design: a research method in which investigators follow the lives of children who are considered to be at risk for developing schizophrenia because they have a biological parent with the disorder. p. 308

Longitudinal research design: a method of study in which the same individuals are repeatedly studied over a period of years or decades. p. 308

Neuroleptics: a category of medications used to reduce the frequency and intensity of psychotic symptoms. p. 310

Tardive dyskinesia: an irreversible neurological disorder which affects 10 - 20 percent of people who take neuroleptics for a year or more; this disorder involves uncontrollable movements in various parts of the body, including the mouth, tongue, lips, fingers, arms, legs, and trunk. p. 310

Social skills training: a form of behavioral treatment that identifies and targets inappropriate behaviors and reinforces socially acceptable behavior. p. 311

Milieu therapy: the provision of a therapeutic environment on a 24-hour basis in an inpatient psychiatric facility. p. 312

Case Report: Jason Newman

Janet and Malcolm Newman could no longer deny that their 8-year-old-son, Jason, had a problem. Neighbors had complained for years, each of his classroom teachers had urged the Newmans to get help for him, and most of their relatives had explicitly conveyed their concern about Jason's behavior during each family gathering.

There was tension in Mrs. Newman's voice as she described her years of struggling with Jason's problems. Although he was a quiet child during his infancy, things began to change right around Jason's first birthday. As soon as he began walking, Jason became a "terror." In describing a day at home with Jason, Mrs. Newman said she often felt as though she were locked up with an unmanned motorcycle that roared through the house, wrecking everything in its path. Although I had heard many descriptions of hyperactive children, the words chosen by Janet Newman had tremendous power, leaving me with the sense that this was an exhausted and exasperated parent.

Mrs. Newman frequently used the term "hyper" in describing her son. Jason was a fidgeter, always squirming in his seat, frequently jumping up and running around regardless of whether they were in church, at a movie, or having dinner at home. Jason was a constant source of aggravation to his playmates because he caused trouble regardless of what they were playing. Even in the simplest of games, such as basketball, Jason would break the rules, steal the ball from other children, refuse to wait his turn, or intentionally provoke others to a point where all the children on the playground would yell at him and tell him to go home.

Mrs. Newman had lost count of the number of special teacher conferences to which she had been summoned. In every meeting the story was the same. Jason was not paying attention in school; he disrupted virtually every classroom activity; he threw things at other children; he played tricks on the teachers; and he talked out loud even during quiet reading time. Each of Jason's teachers had observed that Jason was clearly bright, but they could not get him to do his assignments, either for classroom activities or homework. Even when Jason had completed his homework, he would usually lose it on his way to school, along with his books and pencils. The teachers had developed several intervention plans that included behavioral strategies, but the effectiveness of these attempts was limited. As Mr. Newman admitted, "We never followed through with the plan when Jason was home, so I guess that's why he hasn't changed very much."

The Newmans then proceeded to explain what prompted them finally to seek professional help for Jason. Apparently his behavior had gotten so out of control that he was risking the safety of others. At school one day during the previous week, Jason had been caught setting fires. Having taken a box of wooden matches from home, Jason took the matches into the boys' lavatory, ignited a roll of toilet paper and some paper towels, and threw a lit match into the waste basket. The smoke detector set off the school fire alarm, and everyone was evacuated. This was the final straw for the school principal, who called the Newmans and made it clear that Jason could not return to school until a professional treatment plan was in place.

After finishing with the Newmans, I asked Jason to meet with me for 15 minutes alone. This was a difficult session, but it gave me the opportunity to experience first-hand the impact of Jason's behavior on others. He answered some of my questions, ignored others, and often abruptly changed the topic. I did get the sense that Jason was upset about his lack of friends. He told me that his teachers were "boring," and that he would rather stay home and practice basketball because he wanted to play big league basketball when he grew up. After 15 minutes with Jason, I could understand the ambivalence that clearly characterized his own mother's response to him. He was an attractive child with some very endearing qualities. At the same time, he engaged in many annoying behaviors that made even brief interactions with him feel exhausting.

Sarah Tobin, PhD

13

DEVELOPMENT-RELATED DISORDERS

Disorders that begin in childhood, because they strike so early, are of great concern to the adults who have a role in the child's life. Some of the disorders that we will discuss in this chapter are present at birth, and others develop in the early years of life.

Imagine what it would be like if, as a parent, you faced problems like Jason's on a daily basis. You would probably feel a great deal of personal distress as you struggled to deal with his needs. The emotional burden of having a disturbed child can indeed be great for those who are close to the child, and the pain experienced by the atypical child can last throughout life. Some cases of disturbance are so serious that even the best efforts to bring these children into the mainstream of society have limited positive impact (Wallander & Hubert, 1987). Consequently, some children face slim chances that they will have a normal life when they grow into adulthood (Clarke & Clarke, 1988). Fortunately, children have become a focus of mental health research within recent years, and there is promise that many people with conditions that formerly created life-long difficulties can be successfully treated (Casey & Berman, 1985).

After reading this chapter, you should be able to:

- Discuss the issues involved in defining and diagnosing development-related disorders.
- Define mental retardation, recognize the forms of mental retardation, and understand some of its more common causes and modes of prevention.
- Understand the nature of autism, its primary features, the unusual nature of autistic savant syndrome, theories to explain autism, and current modes of treatment.

- Define the types of specific developmental disorders, be familiar with their impact on the lives of children and adults who have these disorders, and understand current theories and methods of treatment.
- Describe the three types of disruptive behavior disorder, their similarities and differences, and current ways of thinking about and treating these disorders.
- Recognize the anxiety disorders of childhood and adolescence, the forms these disorders take, and the theories and treatments used to approach these disorders.
- Distinguish among other disorders of childhood in the areas of eating, motor behavior, elimination, speech, identity, and attachment.

INTRODUCTORY ISSUES

As you read about the conditions we describe in this chapter, you may wonder at times why they would be considered psychological disorders. For example, different types of learning disabilities, as well as mental retardation, are given psychiatric diagnoses. Some would contend that it is inappropriate to include these conditions in a list of psychiatric disorders. Along related lines, some so-called "disorders" may actually represent developmental aberrations rather than psychiatric abnormalities. For example, you will read about a disorder called *oppositional defiant disorder*, which involves a pattern of disruptive and uncooperative behavior. Perhaps you will question whether a boy who commonly loses his temper, argues with his parents, refuses to obey rules, acts in annoying ways, swears, and lies should be diagnosed with a psychiatric disorder. You may be concerned about the long term ramifications of being labeled so early in one's life.

At some point in your life you may come into close contact with children very much like those you will read about. Many people bear children with problems, and others teach or coach or supervise such children. After learning

Most children are stubborn at times, but chronically difficult behavior becomes a source of distress and burden to parents.

about these disorders, you should be able to gain sensitivity to the complex issues involved in diagnosing and treating children with psychological problems. Imagine how you would feel if you were told that your child is hyperactive and needs medication. You might feel relieved, or you might feel insulted and angry. Because of the intensity of feelings involved as well as the long-term importance of diagnostic and treatment decisions, the issues we discuss here are not simply theoretical and abstract; they have a great deal of personal relevance.

MENTAL RETARDATION

In recent years, you may have noticed some workers in stores and restaurants who seem intellectually disabled. For example, you may have heard a person who is bagging groceries at a supermarket described as "retarded"; this person may in fact have a condition referred to as *mental retardation*. **Mental retardation** is a condition, present from childhood, characterized by significantly below-average general intellectual functioning (an IQ of less than 65 to 75). Approximately 1 percent of the population have mental retardation, and the condition is more common in males. Mental retardation is a broad term that encompasses several gradations of intellectual and adaptive capabilities. These gradations are reflected in the categorization system developed by the American Association of Mental Deficiency and incorporated into the psychiatric nomenclature.

In addition to their intellectual deficits, people with mental retardation have significant impairments in various facets of their ability to adapt to everyday life. They may lack social skills and judgment, have difficulty communicating, and be impaired in their ability to care for themselves. Consequently, they may have to depend on others for their personal care and well-being.

The variations within the population of mentally retarded individuals are summarized in Table 13–1. In this table you can see the common social and academic capabilities at each level of retardation.

Theories and Treatments

Mental retardation may be caused by an inherited condition or by an event or illness during the course of development at any point from conception through adolescence. Some inherited forms of mental retardation can result from defective genes that are passed along to the child at the time of conception. Phenylketonuria, Tay-Sachs disease, and Fragile X Syndrome are specific genetic disorders known to cause mental retardation. Infants born with **phenylketonuria (PKU)** fail to produce an enzyme necessary for normal development. **Tay-Sachs disease** is a metabolic disorder, most commonly found in descendants of Eastern European Jews, that causes neural degeneration and

Table 13-1   Classification of Mental Retardation by IQ Scores and Behavioral Competencies

Degree of Retardation	IQ Range	BEHAVIORAL COMPETENCIES	
		Preschool (0–5)	School Age (6–18)
Mild	50/55–69	Can develop social and communication skills; minimal retardation in sensory–motor area; often not distinguished until later ages.	Can learn academic skills up to sixth grade; can be guided toward social conformity.
Moderate	35/40–50/55	Can talk or learn to communicate; poor social awareness; fair motor skills; profits from self-help skill training; requires some supervision.	Can profit from training in social and occupational skills; unlikely to progress beyond second-grade level; some independence in familiar places possible.
Severe	20/25–35/40	Poor motor development and minimal language skill; generally cannot profit from training in self-help; little communication.	Can learn to talk or communicate; can be trained in elemental self-help skills; profits from systematic habit training.
Profound	Under 20 or 25	Gross retardation, with minimal capacity for functioning in sensory–motor areas; requires intense care.	Some motor development present; may respond to very limited range of training in self-help.

Source: Crnic, (1988).

early death, usually before the age of 4. **Fragile X syndrome**, which is more common in men and derives its name from the fact that it is transmitted through the X chromosome, is associated with severe forms of retardation, as well as speech and other communication difficulties.

Some forms of inherited disorders are not transmitted through the parents' genes, but begin as the result of an accident in chromosomal formation during conception. These

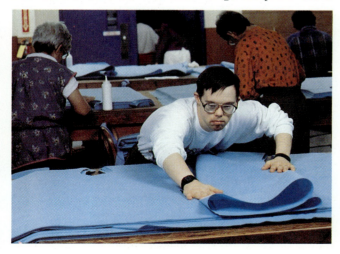

If given the opportunity, people with Down syndrome can lead productive lives with beneficial results for society and the individual.

forms of mental retardation occur as the result of random mutations that alter the structure of the chromosomes of the developing offspring. **Down syndrome** is the most well-known of these forms of mental retardation. People with Down syndrome have a very characteristic facial structure and one or more physical handicaps and abnormalities. Their average life expectancy is briefer than average, although during the last 60 years it has risen from a maximum of 9 years to more than 30 years. In fact, one-quarter of people with Down syndrome now live to be 50 years old, although the health picture for those living to this age is not a good one. Nearly all who live this long develop brain changes resembling those of Alzheimer's disease (see Chapter 14), suggesting a link between these two disorders (Oliver & Holland, 1986). The problems of longer life span in people with Down syndrome go beyond physical deterioration; a large percentage of those who live beyond the age of 20 suffer from major depression. The longer life span of people with Down syndrome is due in great part to changes in societal policies and concerns which have brought about improvements in therapeutic and educational interventions. With longer life expectancy for people with Down syndrome, society will also face new challenges for helping these people lead productive and healthy lives (Fryers, 1986).

A large category of environmental hazards comprises the second major cause of mental retardation. During prenatal development, the fetus is at risk of being harmed

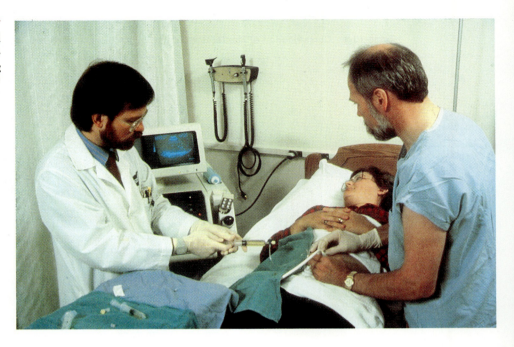

Amniocentesis is a procedure used to detect chromosomal abnormalities in a developing fetus, providing important diagnostic information.

through exposure to certain drugs or toxic chemicals, maternal malnutrition, or infections in the mother during critical phases of fetal development. For example, it has been determined that mothers who contract rubella ("German measles") during the first 3 months of pregnancy are likely to have retarded children. Problems during the baby's delivery that can cause retardation include infections, **anoxia** (loss of oxygen leading to brain damage), or injury to the brain. Premature birth can also be associated with mental retardation. After birth and all during childhood, mental retardation can result from diseases, head injuries caused by accidents or child abuse, or from exposure to toxic substances such as lead or carbon monoxide.

Exposure to cigarette smoke during prenatal development and in the early years of the child's life is one potential risk factor that can adversely affect the child's cognitive development (Naeye & Peters, 1984; Sexton et al., 1990). Unfortunately, many children are exposed to this risk. A government survey reported that about one-half of the nation's children are exposed to cigarette smoke at some time during gestation or in the first 5 years of life. Although the effects on IQ were not determined objectively in this study, parents who smoked were twice as likely to rate their children as having fair to poor physical health (Overpeck & Moss, 1991).

Fetal alcohol syndrome (FAS), another condition associated with mental retardation, has received widespread attention since it was identified in 1973 (Jones & Smith, 1973). This condition, which results from the pregnant woman consuming large amounts of alcohol on a regular basis, consists of a number of physical and behavioral abnormalities, including mental retardation. Estimates of how many children are born with fetal alcohol syndrome vary widely, from an estimated nationwide incidence of 3 to 9 for every 100,000 births (Chavez et al., 1989) to a much higher

rate of almost 2 infants for every 1999 live births (Abel & Sokol, 1987). These estimates vary according to the groups who are sampled; the rates are much higher among Native Americans and African Americans than among middle-class whites (NIAAA, 1991).

Children with fetal alcohol syndrome are destined to suffer a life of problems from which they may never fully recover. At birth they are deficient in weight and length, and remain abnormally small throughout their lives. Their IQ is usually in the mildly retarded range, and although some have normal IQs, others are severely retarded. Many have a characteristic appearance, including a small head; short, slanty eye slits with droopy eyelids; a "cross-eyed" look; a short nose and a long upper lip; a short jaw; and a narrow forehead (Sokol & Clarren, 1989). In addition, they com-

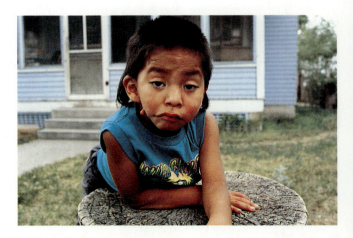

The face of a child with fetal alcohol syndrome is a graphic image of the deforming effects of alcohol on physical development. Less apparent from looking at his face is fetal alcohol syndrome's debilitating impact on cognitive and emotional functioning.

monly have abnormalities of the heart, genitals, kidneys, and nervous system.

Throughout their childhood, individuals with FAS suffer from a number of cognitive deficiencies as well as lack of coordination, impulsiveness, and impairments in speech and hearing—deficits which can persist into adulthood (Streissguth et al., 1991). The severity and nature of the individual's dysfunction depends on the stage in fetal development in which the mother ingested alcohol and the amount of alcohol intake (Ernhart et al., 1987). At present, it is not clear how much alcohol a mother may consume without harming the fetus (NIAAA, 1991a). Even relatively moderate amounts of alcohol during pregnancy can result in lower birth weight and higher risks of infant mortality.

Researchers have come to realize, then, that the developing individual is quite vulnerable to toxic influences such as alcohol and is also very much in need of adequate nutrition and nurturance. In addition to the harmful effects of substances such as drugs and alcohol on the developing fetus's intellectual and physical development, a host of other factors during childhood have been identified that impair normal development and can play a causative role in mental retardation. Undernutrition in the early years, particularly the first year of life, can cause mental retardation, leading to long-term deficits in cognitive and behavioral functions. Poor prenatal care or grossly inadequate and inattentive parenting also can contribute to **failure to thrive**, a condition in which the child does not grow physically and mentally at a normal rate (Lozoff, 1989).

Now that we have identified some causes of mental retardation, let's look at how people with this condition are helped to function in daily life at their maximal level of ability. For many years, people with mental retardation were placed in institutions for their entire lives. Even as recently

as 15 years ago, it was quite rare to see a mentally retarded person on the street, working in a store, or going to a movie. This situation has changed as a result of a social movement called **mainstreaming**, which advocates fully integrating people with mental and physical disabilities into society. The Education for All Handicapped Children Act (P.L. 94-142), passed in 1975, helped to propel this movement by mandating the inclusion of children with physical

Juanita is a 5-year-old girl with Down syndrome. Her mother was 43 when she and her husband decided to start their family. Because of her age, Juanita's mother was advised to have an amniocentesis during her pregnancy to check for any abnormalities in the chromosomal makeup of the developing fetus. Juanita's mother was shocked and distressed when she was given the test results. By the time Juanita was born, her parents were prepared for what to expect in terms of the child's appearance, behavior, and possible medical problems. Fortunately, Juanita needed no special medical attention. Her cognitive development, as expected, was much slower than that of a normal infant. She has been walking since the age of 18 months, but she is still fed by her parents, wears a diaper, cannot talk, and plays with toys meant for infants and small toddlers. Her measured IQ is 46, but she is making progress in her ability to communicate because of her parents' commitment to enrich her life as much as possible. Juanita is an affectionate, happy child and seems to want to develop the skills her parents are encouraging her to learn.

- As a parent of Juanita's, how would you have reacted to her birth?
- Would you recommend that Juanita be placed in a public school, or would you favor her receiving specialized training?

and mental handicaps into ordinary school classrooms with special assistance geared to their particular needs. Another related piece of legislation, The Developmentally Disabled Assistance and Bill of Rights Act, also furthered the deinstitutionalization of mentally retarded people by requiring that they be treated in the least restrictive setting possible. In other words, a mentally retarded person should live in a group home rather than a hospital if the group home would be sufficient for the individual's care.

Although no cure exists for mental retardation, the intellectual and physical development of the mentally retarded person can be enriched through early intervention. The symptoms of Fragile X Syndrome, for example, can be ameliorated with certain diet supplements (Bregman, et al., 1987). It is also possible to train people with mental retardation in many skills needed to live in a productive way in society. Intervention can produce gains in a person's ability to perform tasks requiring motor skills and eye-hand coordination. People with mental retardation can also be helped to speak and use language appropriately, and to acquire social skills needed to interact with others. Their cognitive abilities can also be enhanced, and they can even show IQ improvements (Gibson & Harris, 1988).

Behavioral interventions are perhaps the most useful in producing motor, language, social, and cognitive gains. Parents can also be included in this process. They can be taught to reward a child for appropriate behaviors and to respond negatively to inappropriate behaviors. Family-based interventions can also provide parents with a context within which to discuss family problems and issues associated with a special needs child. Such interventions can be an important source of support for people who otherwise have few places to turn for help and understanding.

To show how a combined behavioral-family approach might work, consider the case of parents of a retarded daughter who are reluctant to take her out of the house, even to go grocery shopping. When they do, she pulls things off the shelves, cries when food items are taken away from her, and sits in the aisle refusing to get up. A behavioral approach to treating the problem would involve training parents to respond immediately with verbal reprimands to undesirable behaviors and to provide positive reinforcement for desirable ones. They might be instructed to yell forcefully when the child sits in the aisle, and to provide the child with touch and praise when the child acts appropriately (Crnic & Reid, 1989).

Because of increased public awareness, more attention is being given to prevention of the physical disorders that lead to mental retardation. The most straightforward form of prevention is involved in the early detection of PKU. Every child who is born in a hospital is tested immediately after delivery for this disorder. If the baby tests positively, steps are taken to correct the disorder by means of a special diet. The other genetic causes of mental retardation, however, cannot be reversed.

In contrast to genetically caused mental retardation, many environmentally caused forms of mental retardation can be prevented. In recent years societal attempts have been made to teach people ways to improve conditions of prenatal development and to make the birth process safer. For example, alcoholic beverage containers and cigarette packages are now labeled with cautions about the relationship between alcohol during pregnancy and birth defects, and public education campaigns have urged pregnant women to avoid contact with people with infectious diseases such as rubella, and to attend to their health during the crucial months of pregnancy.

Important technological advances have brought about improved conditions for childbirth, with more effective measures for preventing oxygen deprivation during the

Public legislation in 1975 set a federal mandate for children with mental retardation to be integrated into regular classrooms in the public schools.

birth process. Furthermore, parents are being alerted to the importance of protecting children from head injuries; for example, bicycle helmets, children's car seats, and automobile seatbelts are being advocated to avoid potentially debilitating traumas to the brain.

AUTISM

Most people can think of someone they know or have seen with mental retardation but many have never encountered a person with autism. **Autism** is a developmental disorder that involves a massive impairment in an individual's ability to communicate and relate emotionally to others. To help you get a feel for the nature of autism, try to put yourself in the following situation. Imagine yourself sitting in a rocking chair and staring at a nearby clock, rocking in synchrony to the movement of the pendulum. You might become absorbed by the clock's movements and become lost in a hypnotic-like-state, perhaps oblivious to anything else in the room. Think of what it would be like to go through your entire life in such a state of detachment, and you will have some small sense of the experience of autism.

Characteristics of Autism

Starting in infancy, people with autism show an unresponsiveness to other people that characterizes much of their later existence. As infants, they struggle in resistance to the cuddling or tickling of a parent. Unlike normal babies, who smile when they are happy or in response to an adult's laughter, the autistic child remains aloof and unresponsive. Although there are variations among children with autism, they share a fundamental difficulty in forming emotional bonds with family members and other children (Shapiro et al., 1987). Rather than becoming attached to people, children with autism become attached to inanimate objects such as household appliances, and may play with these for hours at a time. To the extent that they do interact with people, they lack emotion and sensitivity. Their verbal communication consists of very unusual speech which may at times be inappropriately loud, monotonous, or high-pitched. Furthermore, the content of what they say sounds strange to other people. For example, they may confuse pronouns such as "I" and "you," saying "You am hungry." Their speech is often characterized by **echolalia**, an echoing of words or phrases that they hear. In response to your question, "What is your name?" the person might say "Your name, your name, your name." In less severe cases, the person with autism may be able to use speech normally, but is unable to maintain a normal conversational exchange, instead speaking incessantly in a monologue.

In addition to their speech being disturbed, people with autism behave in unusual ways. They may shake their arms, spin around repetitively, rock back and forth, or engage in harmful, self-damaging behavior such as head-banging. Regressive behaviors are very common, such as temper tantrums, childish expressions of anger, and soiling of clothes by defecating or urinating. They usually adhere to rigid rituals in their daily routines, and may become very disturbed at the slightest change. For example, when opening a can of soda, a boy with autism may insist that the tab be at a particular position, and if it is not, refuse to drink the soda.

Autism is evident during infancy or childhood and continues throughout the individual's life, taking one of a number of forms varying in symptoms and severity. About one-third show fair to good adjustment, overcoming the more severe features of the disorder and even leading relatively normal lives (Rumsey et al., 1985; Rutter, 1970). The majority, however, are unable to live independently as adults. The disorder is rare, affecting 2 to 4 out of every 10,000 people, and is more common in males (Folstein & Rutter, 1988).

Autistic Savants

In an extremely unusual variant of this disorder, called *autistic savant syndrome* (alternatively called *idiot savant*), the individual possesses, in addition to a severe handicap, an extraordinary skill of some kind, such as the ability to perform extremely complicated numerical operations (for example, correctly telling which day of the week a date thousands of years away would fall on) (Treffert, 1988). Some autistic savants have exceptional musical talents such as the remarkable case of one savant who, at the age of 6 months, could hum complex operatic arias (Treffert, 1989). The autistic savant syndrome was dramatized in the movie *Rainman*, in which the central character had an astounding mathematical ability as well as an incredible knowledge of baseball trivia.

Another example of an autistic savant was described by the neurologist and author Oliver Sacks (1987) in his fascinating book *The Man Who Mistook His Wife for a Hat*. José, a 21-year-old man "said to be hopelessly retarded" (p. 214), was interviewed by Sacks (1987). The following exchange occurred after Sacks handed José a pocket watch and instructed him to draw it (this was an informal measure that Sacks invented to help gather a sense of the patient's "character" as well as neurological data):

> 'He's an idiot,' the attendant broke in. 'Don't even ask him. He don't know what it is—he can't tell time. He can't even talk. They say he's 'autistic,' but he's just an idiot.' José turned pale, perhaps more at the attendant's tone than at his words—the attendant had said earlier that Jose didn't use words (pp. 214 and 215).

Not only did José understand the instructions, but he proceeded to draw a faithful as well as artistically interesting reproduction of the watch. The same exercise was repeated with a picture of a canoe on a pond and one of a trout taken from a magazine that Sacks had in his office. In both cases,

José produced a drawing, from memory, that was more dramatic and alive than the original. José was demonstrating the rare but well-documented ability shown by some autistic savants to remember an incredible amount of detail from a visual display.

Sacks maintains that the isolated area of proficiency shown by a person like José with autistic savant syndrome is too often regarded by clinicians as a neurological aberration rather than as the expression of a creative personality. He maintains that treatment may increase the individual's overall adaptation to the world, but at the same time may flatten out this high peak of unique ability. In José's case, the treatment involved placing him in a special ward and giving him the "job" of printing ward notices by hand, a job that did not nearly match his artistic potential. As Sacks sadly commented, "For, as the stars stand, he will probably do nothing, and spend a useless, fruitless life, as so many other autistic people do, overlooked, unconsidered, in the back ward of the state hospital" (p. 232).

Autism or Childhood Schizophrenia?

In reading about autism, it is possible that some of the symptoms may cause you to think of schizophrenia. You may even ask why the disorder is not called "childhood schizophrenia." The fact is that these are two substantially different disorders both in terms of course and symptoms. Schizophrenia is very rare among children, and its symptoms are distinguishable from autism even by the untrained observer. For example, autistic children usually show disturbed interpersonal relating ability from the earliest months of life in contrast to schizophrenic children who, prior to developing schizophrenic symptoms, are often smiling, responsive, affectionate babies, who like being picked up and prefer being in the company of other people. Unlike autistic children, most children who develop schizophrenia are interested in and curious about their environment (Cantor, 1988), and while mental retardation is fairly common among autistic children, this is not the case among schizophrenic children. As they grow into adulthood, people with autism continue to have different symptoms and act in ways that are markedly different from what is observed in people with schizophrenia.

Theories and Treatment

The earliest psychological explanations of autism focused on psychodynamic processes as being at the root of the disturbance in the child's attachment to the parents (e.g., Bettelheim, 1967; Kanner, 1943). The term "refrigerator mother" was used to describe the cold and detached type of parenting theorized to create an autistic child. In the 1970s, psychologists shifted to a more cognitive explanation of autism, regarding it as a disorder of language, attention, and perception (e.g., Rutter, 1984). Psychologists trying to understand the puzzling nature of autism still disagree as to whether the disorder reflects a fundamental deficit in social and emotional functioning (Hobson, 1989). Many theorists still believe that people become autistic because they lack an innate ability to form emotional bonds with others, beginning with their parents. This lack of emotional attachment leads the individual to develop serious flaws in the ability to relate socially to others. Conversely, according to cognitive explanations (Baron-Cohen, 1988), autism is the result of a cognitive impairment that prevents the individual from developing appropriate ways to communicate with others through language. A third possibility, that autism is the result of a deficit in symbolization, would suggest that people develop this disorder because they lack the ability to form inner representations of their world, both social and intellectual (Yirmiya & Sigman, 1991).

As psychologists debate these issues, biologists look for underlying causes in the biochemistry of the brain. The idea that autism is biologically caused is supported by ample evidence that autism shows a pattern of familial inheritance (Smalley et al., 1988). Siblings of children with autism are more likely to develop this disorder or to show other signs of cognitive problems such as language delay (Silliman et al., 1989). Further evidence in support of genetic factors comes from the finding that the concordance rate is much higher in monozygotic than dizygotic twins, both in the development of autism and in cognitive deficits (Folstein & Rutter, 1988).

When researchers looked at the EEG patterns of people with autism, they found heightened brain wave activity, suggesting higher levels of arousal. On a related note, people with autism have an increasing likelihood with age of developing epileptic seizures. Some autistic individuals also fail to show the age-related decrease in the neurotransmitter serotonin that occurs in normal people (Ritvo & Freeman, 1984). Finally, the brains of people with autism appear to have structural abnormalities; CT scans show that some individuals with autism have larger ventricular spaces in the brain (Rosenbloom et al., 1984). In another study using magnetic resonance scans, 14 out of 18 autistic individuals showed evidence of underdeveloped portions of the cerebellum (Courchesne et al., 1988).

Although it is evident that neurological differences exist between autistic and normal individuals, the basis for these differences is not clear. It is possible that there are different subtypes of autism, with different causes and with distinct patterns of neurological deficits.

Environmental causes of autism have also been theorized. A significant number of autistic children had birth complications or were products of high-risk pregnancies in which the mothers were over the age of 35. Possibly some undiagnosed traumatic event occurs at birth and results in the abnormal development of the child's nervous system (Tsai & Stewart, 1983). Another possible cause is exposure by the mother, while pregnant, to viral infections such as rubella (Ritvo & Freeman, 1984).

According to the behavioral perspective, the primary issue is not what causes autism, but what can be done to reduce the frustration and the emotional distance between the child and parents created by the child's symptoms. A cycle becomes established in which the parents find it difficult to interact positively with the child who recoils from their touch or their attempts to establish emotional warmth. Some experts have raised the possibility that the child's self-injurious behaviors can be understood in terms of reinforcement principles. It could be that these behaviors are maintained by attention from adults or by the escape they provide from situations that the child finds even more aversive (Ross & Carr, 1980).

Clinicians who treat autistic children focus on five specific goals (Rutter, 1985). First, treatment should facilitate normal development in language, cognition, and socialization. Behavioral interventions are most effective in meeting this goal; for example, parents or caretakers may be instructed to use reinforcement strategies either in the form of reward or punishment. Second, the child is helped to develop new learning skills that will give the child some experiences of success in problem-solving; for example, the child might be taught to break down a large problem such as getting dressed into smaller tasks that the child can accomplish. This is an important aspect of treatment, because when frustrated, the child is likely to regress to problem behaviors such as rocking and head-banging. Third, the clinician attempts to introduce small changes into the child's environment. Over time, these changes have the cumulative effect of reducing the child's extreme dependence on a particular routine or set of environmental cues. Fourth, the clinician makes concerted efforts to reduce maladaptive behaviors such as tantrums, aggression, and soiling. Fifth, the clinician is sensitive to the family's distress and works to strengthen the family's ability to understand and cope with the special needs of the autistic child.

A number of specific behavioral strategies are used to accomplish these treatment goals. *Self-control procedures*, *relaxation training*, and *covert conditioning* are three methods that incorporate cognitive therapy with behavioral principles (Baron et al., 1988). Lovaas (1977, 1981, 1987), an expert in the field, has proposed behavioral treatments that attempt to eliminate all odd behaviors, including those that involve self-harm. At the same time, clinicians can teach autistic children appropriate eye contact and responsiveness to instructions as necessary preconditions for other therapeutic and educational interventions. This program targets undesirable behaviors and then reduces them through operant conditioning methods of positive reinforcement, extinction, negative reinforcement, and in some cases, punishment.

Take the example of a young boy who is being aggressive toward other people and engaging in disruptive behaviors such as shouting. The staff might be told to ignore the child (extinction), thereby withdrawing the attention that has presumably served to reinforce his engaging in these behaviors. At the same time, the child would be given positive reinforcement for engaging in desirable behaviors such as social interaction and appropriate playing with toys. If extinction does not produce results, the child may be removed from the play area and sent to a "time-out" room. For more resistant and dangerous behaviors, such as head-banging, the child may be given verbal punishment (a loud "no") or even more extreme, a slap on the thigh. The important point about this kind of treatment is that the consequence of the child's behavior occurs very soon after the behavior is performed. *Shaping* is another operant principle that is used in this procedure, involving positive

Teaching appropriate interpersonal behavior to children with autism requires patience and skill.

reinforcement for behaviors that increasingly approximate the desirable target behaviors. A child who cannot sit still in a chair must be rewarded first for sitting before the therapist can move on to more complex interactive skills.

It is important to realize that in order for these behavioral programs to be effective, they must be carried out intensively for a long period of time, beginning early in the child's life (less than 4 years of age). In a long-term follow-up of a research project begun in 1970, Lovaas (1987) reported that a high rate of success was achieved only after years of 40-hour per week treatment. Almost one-half of the children treated with this intensive program went on to achieve normal intellectual and educational functioning by the time they reached first grade. This success rate is particularly striking in light of the fact that improvement was shown by only 2 percent of the control group (who were treated for 10 hours or less per week).

In recent years, experts in this field have formulated interventions involving peer relationships based on the belief that autistic children can derive some very important benefits from appropriate interactions with other children. In this approach, normal or mildly handicapped children are taught how to interact with autistic children. This situation approximates a more normal type of social environment, where children typically serve a powerful role in the modification of a peer's behavior. In contrast to interventions in which adults provide the reinforcement, peer-mediated interventions have the advantage of allowing children to carry on with their ordinary activities without the interruption of adults (Newsom & Rincover, 1989).

One behavioral technique that is the subject of considerable controversy involves aversive conditioning using stimuli that produce pain (see Critical Issue). In this method, the autistic individual experiences very harsh consequences for behaving in dangerous ways. These consequences go beyond slapping, including, for example,

Brian is a 6-year-old child being treated at a residential school for emotionally handicapped children. As an infant, Brian did not respond well to his parents' efforts to play with and hold him. His mother noticed that his whole body seemed to stiffen when she picked him up out of his crib. No matter how much she tried, she could not entice Brian to smile. When she tried to play games by tickling his toes or his touching his nose, he averted his eyes and looked out the window. It was not until Brian was 18 months old that his mother first realized that his behavior reflected more than just a quiet temperament—that he in fact was developing abnormally. Brian never did develop an attachment to people, but instead clung to a small piece of wood that he carried with him everywhere. His mother often found Brian rocking his body in a corner, clinging to this piece of wood. It was Brian's language, though, that finally indicated the presence of serious disturbance. At an age when most children start to put together short sentences, Brian was still babbling incoherently. His babbling did not sound like that of a normal infant. He would repeat the same syllable over and over again, usually the last syllable of something that was just said to him, in a high-pitched, monotone voice. Perhaps the most bizarre feature of Brian's "speech" was that it was not directed at the listener. Brian seemed to be communicating in a world of his own.

- What behaviors of Brian's would lead you to regard him as having autism?
- What are the prospects for Brian's being able to benefit from therapy aimed at helping him relate normally to other people?

electric shock and hosing with cold water. The justification for these measures rests on the premise that the child will encounter greater harm by continuing to engage in self-

CRITICAL ISSUE

Pros and Cons of Aversive Treatment for Autism

In recent years, methods for controlling self-injurious behaviors of autistic people have caused considerable controversy. These treatments are used with autistic individuals who bang their heads, bite themselves, pull their hair, and harm themselves in other ways. The most controversial form of these treatments is aversive therapy, which consists of severe punishments including spanking, pinching, application of "white noise," and cold showers. The most extreme aversive treatment involves the use of a *restrained time-out station*. In this station, which is approximately the size of a telephone

booth, the autistic person is restrained for a 15-minute period during which he receives aversive stimuli consisting of a stream of water vapor which is sprayed into his face. During this process, his legs are bound together and shackled to a counter, his head is covered with a helmet, and thick foam is placed over his eyes. His hands, also bound to a counter, are placed close to a button so that he can press to stop the stream of water vapor. This procedure may sound totally inhumane to you, and many people have fought hard to prohibit such treatments. However, the strongest proponents of

aversive treatment are the family members who see the dramatic improvements in their autistic relatives. For example, one mother said, "I'd rather have my son get punished and get aversives than act like an animal the rest of his life. . . . He used to have 70 to 80 tantrums a day. It's the only way to go with John. He's excellent now," (*Boston Globe*, December 1, 1986). Parents have felt so strongly about the positive impact of these methods that they went to court to keep the state from closing schools that used aversive treatment (*New York Times*, November 19, 1985).

damaging behaviors than would be incurred by the relatively brief application of a painful stimulus.

Medication to treat autism is also being investigated, based on the assumption that the disorder results from a biochemical disturbance. Fenfluramine is a medication that reduces serotonin levels and has been found to alleviate symptoms of hyperactivity and stereotypic behaviors in autistic children. Not all autistic children respond to this type of medication; those with higher IQ scores seem to show the most improvement (du Verglas et al., 1988).

Given the complexity and seriousness of autism, it is clear that its treatment requires a comprehensive program of intervention. This program must involve work with the family, peers, and the schools as well as the disturbed individual. In addition, some kind of institutional placement may be required at least until the more dangerous behaviors are brought under control.

SPECIFIC DEVELOPMENTAL DISORDERS

Perhaps you know someone who has a "block" about math. Even simple calculations cause this person to feel frustrated. Or you may have a classmate who has trouble reading and needs special assistance with course assignments. In extreme forms, these conditions may reflect a **specific developmental disorder**, a delay or deficit in some particular area of functioning, such as academic skills, language and speech, or motor coordination.

You may be wondering why a person's difficulty with math or reading would be regarded as a psychological disorder. This is actually a very controversial issue. Some clinicians feel it is inappropriate to include learning difficulties in a classification system designed for diagnosis of psychological disorders. The rationale for including these conditions is that they are often associated with emotional distress and they may seriously interfere with the person's everyday life and social relationships (Rourke, 1988; Wallander & Hubert, 1987). For example, a boy who is having difficulty completing his eighth-grade homework assignments because of a reading disorder will probably feel ashamed and anxious. Over time, these emotions will have a cumulative impact on the boy's self-esteem and sense of well-being.

Characteristics of Specific Developmental Disorders

Specific developmental disorders are reportedly found in slightly over 4 percent of school-aged children. This statistic represents more than two times the number reported at the time of the passage of the Education for All Handicapped Children Act in 1975 (U.S. Department of Education, 1985). The increase in reported prevalence concerns some specialists in the field, who point to disparities from state to state in the criteria for diagnosis of particular learning disorders. Take the case of a boy who was considered "learning disabled" in his school because he was underachieving. Some might question whether this is an

Table 13-2   Famous People Who Had Problems in School

Sir Winston Churchill (1874–1965)
Described as a "dull youth" by his father, who thought he would not be able to make a living, this legendary British statesman was also seen as hyperactive in childhood. Although he enjoyed history and literature, he refused to study Latin, Greek, or math, and repeatedly failed his school exams.

Charles Darwin (1809–1882)
As a child, he was told by his father that he cared for nothing but "shooting, dogs, and rat-catching." Darwin failed in his medical studies and marked time in college until he took the trip on the *H.M.S. Beagle* that changed his life.

Thomas A. Edison (1874–1931)
In school, Edison's performance was so poor that his headmaster warned that he "would never make a success of anything." His mother helped him learn to read, and he soon began inventing.

Albert Einstein (1879–1955)
Einstein's parents feared that he was retarded because of his delayed speech and language development. His school performance on all subjects except mathematics was dismal, and he failed his college entrance exams. While in the process of developing his relativity theory, he had trouble holding down a job.

Henry Ford (1863–1947)
A poor reader in school, Ford always preferred working with machines. He achieved early prowess in fixing tools and building waterwheels and steam engines.

Sir Isaac Newton (1642–1727)
Described as an "idler" and "mechanical dabbler," Newton proved to be so inefficient that he could not even run the family farm. A poor student, he suddenly came to life after a fight with a bully motivated him to advance himself.

Source: Adapted from Wallace et al., (1980).

appropriate use of the term or whether the boy might have other difficulties that are contributing to his poor school performance, such as family problems. Because of situations such as this, there is a clear need for care in the delineation of criteria for what constitutes a learning disability (Chalfant, 1989).

■ *Learning disorders*

A **learning disorder** is a delay or deficit in an academic skill. Learning disorders are evident in three areas, each associated with a given academic skill—mathematics, writing, and reading. In **mathematics disorder**, the individual has difficulty with mathematical tasks and concepts. A school-age child with this disorder may have problems understanding subtraction, recognizing an addition sign, copying numbers correctly, or learning multiplication tables. An adult with this disorder might be unable to balance a checkbook because of difficulty performing simple mathematical calculations. In a **disorder of written expression**, the individual's writing is characterized by poor spelling, grammatical or punctuation errors, and disorganization of paragraphs. This characteristic obviously creates serious problems for children in many academic subjects. For adults, this disorder can be very embarrassing and inconvenient, perhaps limiting the person's range of job opportunities. **Reading disorder**, commonly called *dyslexia*, is a form of learning disorder in which the individual omits, distorts, or substitutes words when reading, and reads in a slow, halting fashion. The child's ability to make progress in a variety of school subjects is inhibited by this inability to read. Similarly, adults with dyslexia face embarrassment and restrictions in the type of employment for which they may qualify.

Adolescence is the peak time during which adjustment, behavioral, and emotional problems associated with learning disorders are evident. In the more severe cases the learning deficits may persist into adulthood, but many associated psychological difficulties subside by the 30s (Spreen, 1988). In fact, there are some extremely famous people who overcame a childhood learning disorder, such as Albert Einstein, Thomas Edison, Woodrow Wilson, Nelson Rockefeller, Winston Churchill, Charles Darwin, General George Patton, and John Kennedy (see Table 13-2). On the other hand, a learning disorder is not a matter to be taken lightly, and it can have serious lifelong consequences.

■ *Speech and language disorders*

Think of how frustrated you may have felt when you were trying to communicate an idea that others could not seem to understand, or when others could not comprehend your slurred speech because you were too exhausted to be articulate. These innocent examples can give you a glimpse into the experience of an individual with disturbances in speech and language, but they cannot convey the pain and frustration experienced by people who confront situations on a daily basis in which they cannot understand the words of others or in which their own words cannot be understood by other people.

Expressive language disorder is a specific developmental disorder that is characterized by obvious problems of verbal expression. Children with this disorder differ from others their own age in their ability to express themselves; this may be evident in language style that includes limited and faulty vocabulary, speaking short sentences with simplified grammatical structures, omitting critical words or phrases, or putting words together in peculiar order. A person with this disorder may, for example, always use the present tense, referring to activities of the previous day by saying, "I have a good time yesterday." In contrast, **receptive language disorder** is an inability to understand certain kinds of words or phrases, such as directions, or in more severe forms, basic vocabulary or entire sentences. Even simple directions such as being told to take the "third door on the right" might confuse an individual with this disorder. Typically this disorder also involves a disturbance in expressive language.

The expressive difficulties of some people are characterized not by their ability to understand or express language, but by difficulties specific to speech. A person with **phonological disorder** misarticulates, substitutes, or omits speech sounds. As children, mispronunciations may be regarded as "cute," such as when a child says "pesgeti" for "spaghetti." However, children who have chronic speech problems usually encounter academic difficulties, and as they grow into adulthood this disorder can be publicly embarrassing, as when the person says "tree" for "three." In **cluttering**, the individual speaks in quick bursts, making it impossible for other people to understand what is being said. **Stuttering** involves a disturbance in the normal fluency and patterning of speech that is characterized by such verbalizations as sound repetitions or prolongations, broken words, blocking out sounds, word substitutions to avoid problematic words, or words expressed with an excess of tension. **Voice disorder** involves speech that is characterized by abnormalities in pitch, loudness, tone, or resonance that interferes with the person's normal functioning in academic and social situations.

The long-term effects of speech and language disorders can be serious. In one study, 44 percent of children with speech and language disorders were found to have psychiatric diagnoses such as anxiety disorders. When the children in this study were followed up 4 to 5 years after first being evaluated, the incidence of psychiatric problems had risen to 60 percent. The problems identified in the follow-up included mood disorders and several disorders of childhood you will read about shortly, such as attention deficit disorder, oppositional/conduct disorder, and adjustment disorders (Baker & Cantwell, 1987).

■ *Motor skills disorders*

The primary form of motor skill disorder is **developmental coordination disorder**. The child with this disorder is clumsy and unable to complete certain age-related tasks such as tying shoelaces, fastening zippers, and assembling puzzles. Such a person might be regarded with annoyance by parents and friends because of accident-proneness. Whether it is breaking the dish on which lunch is served, or falling down a flight of stairs, the individual can never seem to do anything "right."

Theories and Treatments

Just as there are many forms of specific developmental disorders, there are a number of possible causes, most of them neurological in nature. The most popular explanations of specific developmental disorders focus on abnormalities in the brain (Brown & Aylward, 1987). It is believed that damage to various brain sites responsible for the affected functions has occurred during fetal development, at birth, or in early childhood. This damage, which may be genetically caused, the result of head trauma, or a consequence of disease, results in a deviation from normal brain development.

For example, in normal development, one hemisphere of the brain becomes dominant. For most people, the dominance is in the left hemisphere (and they correspondingly will be right-handed). Children with certain kinds of specific developmental disorders, in contrast, are thought to develop mixed brain dominance in the process of early development.

Difficulty in integrating information from the different brain areas involved in vision, speech, and language comprehension is another possible source of certain kinds of specific developmental disorders. For example, a child who has an impaired ability to remember sequences of letters or words may have difficulties in comprehending speech. An 8-year-old child should be able to remember the following sentences: "Joe asked his mother to take him to see the cows in the barn. Luis carved a handsome statue out of wood with his sharp knife." However, an 8-year-old child with auditory memory problems would most likely confuse the sequence of events while forgetting most of the details. As you can imagine, deficits in the central nervous system that result in impaired cognitive processing can result in serious social and emotional disturbance (Rourke, 1988).

The school environment is usually the primary site of treatment for specific developmental disorders. A treatment plan is designed by an interdisciplinary team consisting of various professionals such as a school psychologist, a special education teacher, the classroom teacher, a speech language therapist, and possibly a neurologist. Typically, these children require more structure, fewer distractions, and presentation of new material that uses more than one sensory modality at a time. For example, the child may be taught science concepts through oral presentation combined with hands-on laboratory experience. Perhaps most important, it is essential to build on the child's strengths so that the child can feel a sense of accomplishment and increased self-esteem (Aylward et al., 1987).

DISRUPTIVE BEHAVIOR DISORDERS

Think back to your days in grade school and try to recall children in your class who were regarded by your teachers and classmates as a constant nuisance. Perhaps they were so restless that they could not stay seated, or perhaps they were always getting into fights and causing trouble. It is quite possible that they had one of the disruptive behavior disorders that we will discuss in this section.

Characteristics of Disruptive Behavior Disorders

Disruptive behavior refers to persistent negative behavior patterns that usually incite caretakers or peers to respond with anger, impatience, punishment, or avoidance (Loeber, 1990). There are three kinds of disruptive behavior disorders: *attention-deficit hyperactivity disorder, conduct disorder,* and *oppositional defiant disorder.*

■ *Attention-deficit hyperactivity disorder (ADHD)*

You have probably known children who seem to have a very difficult time paying attention. They may be easily distracted, have trouble following the rules of a game, and jump from one activity to another. Associated with their difficulties in paying attention, these children are restless, over-talkative, and likely to behave in troublesome ways that annoy other people. Such children, if their difficulties are sufficiently serious, may be diagnosed as having **attention-deficit hyperactivity disorder (ADHD)**. Children with this disorder have a great deal of trouble finishing what they start, and their school work is disorganized, messy, and careless. They are very impulsive and they fail to wait their turn in class, instead blurting out answers to questions. When given instructions, they cannot follow through. Because of their inattention and impulsiveness, they often have accidents. In addition to the cognitive and behavioral aspects of the disorder, these children usually have low self-esteem, poor frustration tolerance, and unstable mood. Their peer relationships are strained because they are so irritating, aggressive, and intense. Consequently, they have few friends (Whalen & Henker, 1985).

Interestingly, experts in this field have noted that some children with ADHD are able to concentrate with remarkable intensity on certain tasks that interest them. With the advent of the Nintendo video game craze in the late 1980s, both parents and experts began to notice with astonishment that children who could not sit still in any other situation stayed glued to their video games for hours at a time. This led psychologists to recognize that a child with ADHD can actually be very attentive if the task if sufficiently appealing (Barkley, 1989).

The recognition that a child has ADHD usually occurs fairly early in the child's life. Before entering school, children with ADHD are usually regarded as "difficult" by their parents, relatives, and friends. When they enter school,

High energy levels often cause hyperactive children to behave in ways that seem out of control.

their erratic and disruptive behavior leads to further problems because it impedes their academic performance and social interactions (Ross & Ross, 1982).

It is estimated that from 1 to 5 percent of all children have some degree of ADHD, with the prevalence rate of those seeking treatment five to ten times higher in boys than girls (Barkley, 1981; Weiss, 1990). ADHD typically persists throughout childhood and into adolescence (Brown & Borden, 1986; Weiss & Hechtman, 1986), and a significant proportion of these troubled children encounter problems with the law during their adolescent years (Gittelman et al., 1985). One researcher found that boys who were rated by their teachers as having attention problems were more likely to be arrested by the time they reached late adolescence. This outcome was particularly likely for boys with low IQs and alcoholic fathers (Wallander, 1988). Girls with ADHD seem to show different patterns of behavior associated with the attentional deficit, namely depression, lower self-esteem, and cognitive impairment (Berry et al., 1985). ADHD, then, is a potentially very serious childhood disorder with long-term ramifications. As you will see later, many researchers and clinicians have attempted to gain an understanding of its cause and treatment.

Joshua's mother has just had a conference with her son's teacher, who related that Joshua, age 7, has been extremely restless and distractible in class. Every few minutes he is out of his desk, exploring something on a bookshelf or looking out the window. When in his seat, he kicks his feet back and forth, drums his fingers on the table, shifts around, and generally keeps up a constant high level of movement. He may ask to go to the bathroom three times in an hour. He speaks very quickly, and his ideas are poorly organized. During recess, Joshua is aggressive and violates many of the playground rules. Joshua's mother corroborated the teacher's description of Joshua with similar stories about his behavior at home. Although Joshua is of normal intelligence, he is unable to sustain concentrated attention on any one activity for more than a few minutes.

- What features of Joshua's behavior would suggest that he has ADHD?
- Do you think Joshua could improve his behavior if he were better disciplined?

Bert, a 16-year-old high school dropout, was arrested for the third time in a 2-year period. All three crimes involved thefts of small equipment from people's homes, such as stereos, videocassette recorders, and home computers. Acting alone and without a weapon, Bert was caught in each case when he tried to sell the stolen goods. As he described his actions in each crime, Bert expressed defiance and showed a complete lack of remorse. To the contrary, he bragged about how often he had gotten away with similar crimes.

- What characteristics of Bert's case point to a diagnosis of conduct disorder?
- Do you think that the case of Bert should be handled by the legal system or the mental health system?

A related condition, *attention deficit disorder (ADD)* is also characterized by attention deficit and impulsivity, but not by the heightened motor activity involved in hyperactivity. This is an important diagnostic distinction, but one that is rarely made in the literature. Consequently, we will treat the terms synonymously in our discussion of theories and treatment.

■ *Conduct disorder*

You can pick up any newspaper and find stories about teenage gang wars, juvenile delinquency, and other forms of crime among youth involving muggings, sexual assault, and drugs. Often, a focus of these stories is that the perpetrators are relatively young children. Statistics tell of dramatic increases in the number of young people involved in serious crimes. For example, between the years 1975 and 1985, the number of juveniles in custody because of delinquent and criminal behavior increased 35 percent (U.S. Dept. of Justice, 1989). Many of the youths involved in these criminal activities have **conduct disorder**, the precursor in childhood of antisocial personality disorder.

The behaviors of conduct disordered youth violate the rights of others and society's norms or laws. Their delinquent behaviors include stealing, truancy from school, running away from home, lying, fire-setting, breaking and entering, physical cruelty to people and animals, sexual assault, and mugging. These youths, who often abuse drugs or alcohol, may act alone or in groups. When caught, they deny their guilt, shift blame onto others, and lack remorse about the consequences of their actions.

Conduct disorder usually begins before puberty. Its incidence is estimated at about 9 percent for males and 2 percent for females, but there is a wide range of severity. For example, mild cases of conduct disorder might involve pranks, insignificant lying, or group mischief. Severe forms of conduct disorder, which are less frequent, include behaviors that seriously harm other people.

What happens to children with conduct disorder? Do they become hardened criminals, or do they "grow out" of the disorder as they develop through adolescence? This question was addressed in a classic study by the prominent researcher Lee Robins (1966), who followed into adulthood children who were seen at a child guidance clinic. Over the 30-year course of the study, the aggressive and antisocial children were found to be more likely to have serious problems as adults than were children with anxiety disorders such as fears and phobias. Furthermore, the more severe the antisocial behavior was during childhood, the more likely it was that the individual encountered serious problems in adulthood such as marital difficulties, reduced occupational and economic opportunities, impoverished social relationships, heavy alcohol use, and poor physical health. Only one in six of the original sample was completely free of psychological disorder as adults; over one-quarter had antisocial personality disorder.

■ *Oppositional defiant disorder*

Most children go through periods of negativism and mild defiance, particularly in adolescence, and most parents complain of occasional hostility or argumentativeness in their children. But what if such behaviors are present most of the time? In all likelihood, a parent of a child like this would conclude that the problem is more than a passing mood of irritability or a transient noncompliance with household rules. There are, of course, variations among children in the degree to which they are negative and oppositional, and it is well-known that many adolescents react negatively to authority. The child or adolescent is diagnosed as having **oppositional defiant disorder**, however, when these rebellious kinds of behaviors are prominent, last for more than 6 months, and cause significant family or school problems. This disorder is much more extreme than the typical childhood or adolescent rebelliousness, and it is more than a "phase." Youths with this disorder repeatedly lose their temper, argue, use foul language, refuse to do what

Mindy, at age 13, has changed in the last year from a relatively reserved and socially isolated young teenager to what her father now calls "a little tramp." Apart from her behavior, which includes staying out late at night visiting the college dormitories in town and cutting most of her classes during the day in school, Mindy's looks suggest those of a much older and street-wise adolescent. Mindy dyed her hair orange, wears heavy makeup, and dresses in provocative clothes. The more her parents tell Mindy to behave and dress like a "normal" girl, the more Mindy seems driven to defy them.

- What would make you think that Mindy has oppositional defiant disorder rather than conduct disorder?
- What kind of intervention might redirect Mindy from her oppositional behavior pattern?

they are told, and deliberately annoy other people. They are touchy, resentful, belligerent, spiteful, and self-righteous. Rather than seeing themselves as the cause of their problems, they blame circumstances or other people. Some young people who behave in this way are more oppositional with their parents than with outsiders, but most have problems in every sphere. To the extent that their behavior interferes with their school performance and social relationships, they lose the respect of teachers and friendship of peers. These losses can make them feel inadequate and depressed.

Oppositional defiant disorder typically becomes evident between the ages of 8 and 12. Preadolescent boys are more likely to develop this disorder than girls of the same age, but after puberty it tends to be equally common in males and females. Some youths with this disorder may develop mood disorders or passive-aggressive personality disorder. In some cases oppositional defiant disorder progresses to conduct disorder; in fact, most children with conduct disorder have had histories of oppositional defiance when they were younger, though not all children with oppositional defiant disorder progress to the more serious disruptive behaviors associated with conduct disorder (Loeber et al., 1991).

Theories and Treatments

The search for what causes a child to develop a disruptive behavior disorder is complicated by the many different definitions and diagnostic criteria associated with this group of disorders, and by the difficulty of separating environmental from biological influences on children's development. In our discussion of theories and treatments, we will focus on ADD and ADHD, as these disorders have received the greatest research attention.

The attentional deficit in ADD and the hyperactivity associated with ADHD suggest that these conditions may involve some underlying abnormality of brain development that involves cognitive functions (Werry et al., 1987). Reflecting this idea, ADHD was formerly termed *minimal brain dysfunction*. Because of the relatively high prevalence of these disorders and their long-term effects on individuals and costs to society, a great deal of effort has been devoted to understanding how these disorders develop.

Perhaps spurred on by the fact that relatives of people with ADHD have a much higher rate of this disorder (Biederman et al., 1987; Faraone et al., 1991), investigators have tried to find possible biological causes. For example, altered patterns of glucose metabolism have been found among adults with a history of childhood-onset ADHD, with lower activity in the frontal cortex, the part of the brain involved in controlling attention and motor activity (Zametkin et al., 1990). Neuropsychological testing has corroborated the physiological evidence of frontal lobe deficits (Barkley, 1989).

A variety of factors have been suggested as contributing to the neurological deficit underlying ADHD, including genetics, birth complications, acquired brain damage, exposure to toxic substances, and infectious diseases. Perhaps it is not a single factor, but some combination of several factors that leads to the development of this disorder (Barkley, 1989; Weiss, 1990). Further, there may be subtypes of ADHD depending on whether it co-occurs with other disorders, such as mood or anxiety disorders, learning disabilities, or conduct or oppositional defiant disorder. Each of these subtypes seems to have different patterns of family inheritance, risk factors, neurobiology, and responses to drugs (Biederman et al., 1991).

As important as biology is, it does not tell the whole story of why certain children develop ADHD. Turning to psychological contributions, we see that children with ADHD are more likely to have grown up in a disturbed family environment and to have more failure experiences in school. Might these conditions contribute in some way to attentional deficits and behavioral problems? There is also a question of how much the child's disorder contributes to these family and school problems. It is more difficult to raise a child with ADHD than a normal child, and the stress placed on the family by the child's presence could very well lead to family disturbances. Similarly, experiences of failure in school can be seen as the result, rather than the cause, of attentional disturbances.

Experts currently believe that ADHD has a biological basis, but that its expression is triggered by certain stressful environmental conditions. Once ADHD becomes manifest, the child's adjustment to family and school is further complicated by attentional and behavioral difficulties, often drawing parents and other adults into a cycle of negative interactions in which the adult becomes more controlling and the child feels more and more devalued (Du Paul et al., 1991). Early intervention, then, is crucial in reducing the degree of disturbance in the child's life and increasing the child's attentional capacity.

Biological theories of ADHD have also been supported by observations of the therapeutic effects of certain medica-

Parents face a difficult decision about whether or not to medicate a hyperactive child. Medication helps to alleviate the symptoms of hyperactivity, but it may have undesirable side effects.

tions on children with ADHD. Since these drugs work on such a large proportion of children with ADHD, it is reasoned that there must be a neurophysiological basis for the disorder. Oddly enough, the medications that help these children calm down are stimulants. Methylphenidate (Ritalin), the most commonly prescribed stimulant for the treatment of ADHD, successfully improves the child's attentional control, impulse control, ability to work on a task without interruption, and academic productivity (Barkley, 1989; Murray, 1987). Teachers and parents report that when hyperactive children are placed on stimulants, they are less disruptive and noisy; even their handwriting seems to improve.

No one knows exactly why this medication works, yet its effects are so dramatic that researchers have focused on the neurophysiological mechanisms of its action in hyperactive children. A number of hypotheses have emerged out of this research, most of them involving catecholamine neurotransmitters (Zametkin & Rapoport, 1987). Some people are understandably concerned about side effects associated with stimulant use in children. For example, some children on the medication have trouble sleeping and have a reduced appetite. More serious side effects involve the development of uncontrollable bodily twitches and verbalizations, as well as temporary growth suppression. Stimulants are not effective in treating all ADHD children, and some who are unresponsive to methylphenidate seem to benefit from treatment with tricyclic antidepressants (Pliszka, 1987).

Put yourself in the place of parents trying to decide whether to follow the recommendation of putting a hyper-

active child on medications that have worrisome side effects. In agreeing to go along with such a recommendation, parents are hoping that the benefits of the child's improved attentional control and decreased hyperactive behavior will make such a choice worthwhile. Experts in this field (Barkley, 1989) believe that the benefits clearly outweigh the costs, in that children who feel more in control of themselves tend to be happier, more academically successful, and more socially appropriate. Further, they are more likely to have positive interactions with their parents (Danforth et al., 1991), because the medications make it more likely that they will comply with their parents' requests.

The behavioral approach is also widely used in understanding and treating ADHD. Many children with ADHD do not respond to stimulant medication treatment; others have only mild forms of the disorder, or have parents who object to the use of medications for treating their children. Behavioral techniques are based on the assumption that hyperactivity is a learned behavior that can be unlearned through appropriate methods of reinforcement, teaching of self-control, and changes in the environment. Work with a child might involve using self-reinforcement to encourage the child to regulate behaviors such as settling into a task, delaying gratification, maintaining self-motivation, and monitoring progress toward goals (Whalen et al., 1985). Implicit in the behavioral approach is the notion that the family must be directly involved in reducing the child's disruptive behaviors. Family members can be taught to use behavioral methods. Coordinating these efforts with comparable intervention by classroom teachers, improves the odds for helping the child to gain better self-control (Barkley, 1989).

Disagreement has existed among researchers about whether or not there is a connection between ADHD and conduct disorder. There is a high co-occurrence of these disorders, with a range of from 30 to 50 percent of children with one disorder having symptoms of the other (Biederman et al., 1991). Whatever connection exists between these disorders may be accounted for by a pattern that becomes established early in a child's life. Children with ADHD typically have problems getting along with others and following rules; perhaps these difficulties lead them to be seen as troublemakers, a role that becomes deeply engrained over time. Furthermore, they become frustrated by their inability to focus their attention on tasks in school, and they act out this frustration in the classroom and at home. They compensate for their failure in school by attempts to gain attention in the misguided belief that "showing off" will bring them admiration from their classmates. This attention-getting behavior initiates an unfortunate cycle that becomes part of their character; over time they may develop serious conduct problems such as substance abuse and academic underachievement, and may suffer low self-esteem (DuPaul et al., 1991; Windle, 1990).

However, some researchers would argue that the two disorders are distinct entities, and that the hyperactive child's difficulty in attending differs from the deliberate

A hyperactive child on the playground is likely to antagonize peers because of out of control behavior.

"bad" behavior shown by the conduct-disordered child (Biederman et al., 1991). In fact, research has shown that some children develop conduct disorder independently of attentional deficits, with conduct problems resulting from factors such as poor socialization and the reinforcement of their negative behaviors by others in their surroundings. Many of these children come from homes in which violence, substance abuse, and criminal activity is common. They imitate the aberrant behavior of their parents and siblings and may even be encouraged to do so. This disturbance in the home is often mirrored in peer relationships; frequently, these children have friends who engage in comparable negativistic behaviors. Socialization by the group or street gang may further reinforce antisocial patterns established in the home. Not every child who grows up in a disturbed family setting or neighborhood develops a conduct disorder, however, and the question remains as to why some children are particularly vulnerable to developing such disorders (Hinshaw, 1987).

Clinicians have been frustrated for decades in their attempts to develop effective treatment programs for conduct-disordered youth. Traditional psychotherapy is ineffective, and attempts to work with the family are often compromised by severe problems such as alcoholism and abuse that typify the home environment of these children. A combination of behavioral, cognitive, and social learning approaches appears to be the most useful strategy in working with conduct-disordered youths. The goal of treatment is to help the child learn appropriate behaviors such as cooperation and self-control and to unlearn problem behaviors such as aggression, stealing, and lying. Therapy focuses on reinforcement, behavioral contracting, modeling, and relaxation training, and may take place in the context of peer therapy groups and parent training (Herbert, 1987). Sadly, many interventions with conduct-disordered youth are ini-

tiated during adolescence, a developmental point that some experts in this field consider to be too late. Behavioral interventions that have been shown to be relatively effective are those that are begun in preadolescence, when the problematic behaviors of these youths can still be modified (McMahon & Wells, 1989).

ANXIETY DISORDERS OF CHILDHOOD OR ADOLESCENCE

Every child experiences anxiety. If you think back to your own childhood, you can probably remember times of feeling nervous or fearful. Perhaps you felt apprehensive on the first day of school or extremely shy when you first met a new playmate. These are common childhood reactions. For some children, though, anxiety becomes a very powerful and disruptive force. They cannot leave the house without panicking, they cling to their parents, they are mute with strangers, or they worry obsessively about being hurt. In this section, we will discuss the three types of conditions that comprise childhood anxiety disorders: *separation anxiety disorder*, *avoidant disorder*, and *overanxious disorder*.

Characteristics of Anxiety Disorders of Childhood or Adolescence

■ *Separation Anxiety Disorder*

From the moment of birth, the infant's cries evoke caregiving behavior in adults. As infants develop in the first year of life, they become more sophisticated in the ways they keep their parents and other important adults nearby to care for them, as they become able to reach, crawl, grasp, and use verbal utterances to communicate their needs. At the same time, children begin to develop a psychological attachment to their parents and become distressed when their parents are not present (Ainsworth, 1989). Although most children maintain a strong attachment to their parents, there is a change around the age of 18 months, when they become less distressed at separation (Emde et al., 1976). However, a small percentage of children do not overcome the experience of separation anxiety, but go on to develop symptoms of **separation anxiety disorder**. For example, Jennie wavers briefly and then skips happily into the classroom of her day care center when her father drops her off in the morning. In contrast, Emily is terrified about being left by her parents for any period of time.

Children like Emily experience severe reactions when confronted with the prospect of being apart from their parents. They become upset and often physically ill when facing a normal separation such as a parent's leaving for work

Four weeks have gone by since the beginning of the school year, and 8-year-old Kira has not yet attended a full day of school. Each morning she pleads with her mother to let her stay home, some days complaining of stomachaches and other days saying she feels so weak she fears that she will faint on her walk to school. Kira's parents are perplexed by her behavior because she did well in school during second grade and had a circle of good friends. On the few days that she has ventured to school, Kira has insisted that the school nurse call home to report her health problem of the day. While at home, Kira becomes alarmed if her mother runs downtown to do an errand, and insists that she be allowed to come along. Even sleep time is disturbed; Kira frequently wanders into her parents' bedroom in the middle of the night complaining of fears that someone might break in and harm her. Concern about Kira's problems has prompted her mother to ask the school guidance counselor to help develop some plan of intervention for Kira and the family.

- How do Kira's symptoms of separation anxiety disorder compare to those of an adult with agoraphobia or panic disorder with agoraphobia?
- Should Kira's mother be understanding or should she insist that Kira stop acting like a "baby"?

Five-year-old Megan has always been painfully shy. Her parents have sought treatment for her because Megan's shyness has taken on much more serious proportions since she entered kindergarten. The teacher reports having found Megan hiding in the janitor's closet after disappearing from class. Megan's mother has tried to get her to socialize with neighborhood children, but Megan stubbornly resists all such efforts. Last week, Megan's mother drove her to a classmate's birthday party. When her mother tried to leave Megan at the party, Megan clung to her mother's legs, screaming for her to stay. Because of Megan's extreme fear of strangers, her parents are unable to leave her with a baby-sitter. The last time they tried, Megan locked herself in the bathroom and would not come out until her parents promised to stay home and send the sitter away. Megan's behavior has caused considerable tension between her parents. They also feel guilty about their resentment of Megan's manipulative behavior.

- How are Megan's symptoms of avoidant disorder different from the behavior a normal, shy child?
- If Megan's problems are untreated, what might happen to Megan when she grows to adulthood?

or the child's going to a relative's house for a visit. Some may refuse to sleep overnight at a friend's house, or go to camp or school. They fear that something terrible will happen to them or to their parents during the period of separation, such as being attacked by an animal. Even going to sleep may represent a traumatic separation. They may insist that a parent stay with them until they fall asleep or may plead to sleep in their parents' bed. When not with an attachment figure, they become panicky, miserable, homesick, socially withdrawn, and sad. They are also demanding, intrusive, and in need of constant attention. Sometimes they cling so closely to a parent that they will not let the parent out of their sight.

This disorder usually becomes evident by the time a child is of school age. It persists for years, although there may be extended periods when the child's separation anxiety diminishes. It is equally common in boys and girls.

■ *Avoidant disorder of childhood or adolescence*

If you have ever baby-sat, you are probably familiar with the child who reacts fearfully to new people. Toddlers, in particular, are likely to show signs of stranger anxiety when meeting a new baby-sitter for the first time. For example, 2-year-old Daniel initially acts in a very shy manner but then quickly warms up to a new baby-sitter. At the other extreme is 6-year-old Sam, who shrinks from contact with every new person, including children his own age.

Children like Sam have **avoidant disorder**, an anxiety disorder of childhood that causes the child to refrain from contact with unfamiliar people. Even seemingly innocuous

encounters with strangers cause them to become withdrawn, timid, and embarrassed. They cling to the people they know, relying on them for comfort. At times their clinging behavior is extreme, and they become whiny and demanding. These children are similar to adults with avoidant personality disorder, in that they actually have a strong need for social involvement. Their excessive stranger anxiety, however, prevents them from following through on this desire for interaction.

Avoidant disorder is usually apparent from a very early age, although it does not become a major problem until a child enters school. A child may develop this disorder in response to a stressful event, such as some major loss. Perhaps a close relative becomes ill or dies, the family moves, or the child loses a pet. Some children seem to improve naturally, either through a change in their environment or through encouragement to take risks by their parents. However, other children seem to get worse, and without treatment they become increasingly isolated, depressed, and at times suicidal. By the time they reach adulthood, they may develop a personality disorder.

■ *Overanxious disorder*

All children experience anxiety as a natural part of growing up, but children with **overanxious disorder** become so incapacitated by worrying that they are unable to get through a day without obsessing over some unrealistic concern. Unlike other children whose worries may come and go, these children have anxieties that are unrelenting. In fact, for this disorder to be diagnosed, the child must have been chronically anxious for at least 6 months. Some of the concerns of these children include anxious worrying

Martin is only 7 years old, but he appears much older because of the habitual worried expression on his face. He is extremely conscientious, tidy in his grooming and personal habits, and concerned about the impressions he makes on others. Virtually unable to make any kind of decision (such as how to spend his allowance money), Martin spends literally hours trying to resolve imaginary social problems. Typically, he will spend several days worrying whether he hurt someone else's feelings by something he said. Sometimes his anxieties keep him awake for hours past his bedtime. He worries constantly, too, about his school performance. He demands that his parents practice his weekly multiplication tables with him even when it is clear that he knows the material by heart. Martin's parents, both of whom have demanding and high-level jobs, are concerned that he feels an undue pressure to excel so that they will accept him.

- Do you think that Martin has overanxious disorder, or is his behavior an expectable reaction to living in a home environment with two high-achieving and competitive parents?
- How does Martin's behavior differ from the symptoms of the other anxiety disorders of childhood?

about ordinary events of daily life such as what clothes to wear, where to sit on the school bus, whether they will be scolded by a teacher, or whether they might be injured in gym class. Sometimes their anxiety is so intense that they may feel physically sick, suffering from headaches, stomachaches, nausea, or dizziness. In addition to their generalized worries regarding many features of their lives, they also are likely to dwell on particular situations in which their competence may be tested. For example, they may fret all week over the Friday morning spelling bee in their class. Adding to their constant worrying is their tendency to be perfectionistic, and as a result, they are plagued by self-doubt. If something should go wrong in their lives, such as a family crisis, their worrying intensifies. Unfortunately for many of these children, their anxiety disorder persistrs into adulthood.

Theories and Treatment

As you know, anxiety is an experience that involves both physical and psychological reactions. Recalling our discussion from Chapter 7, where we explored anxiety disorders in adults, it is important to consider both of these factors in trying to explain and treat the anxiety disorders of childhood. When looking at the biological component of anxiety, investigators have turned to sources of information such as familial patterns and responsiveness to antianxiety medication. As is the case in other areas of research, familial patterns provide information about the possible role of genetics.

The existence of separation anxiety disorder in children has been linked to higher rates of panic disorder in parents (Weissman et al., 1984). What is the relevance of this finding to the genetics of separation anxiety? Adults with panic disorder seem to have been more likely to experience symptoms of separation anxiety when they were children (Gittelman & Klein, 1985). Thus, the fact that parents of children with separation anxiety showed symptoms of this disorder as children points to a possible genetic link. These findings suggest further that there is a continuation into adulthood of the child's experience of anxiety, although it takes a different form. Presumably, these two disorders are different manifestations of the same core problem.

Many questions remain unanswered concerning the connection between anxiety disorders of childhood and adulthood. The current thinking by one renowned specialist is that further research will probably verify the patterns of family inheritance and the relationship between childhood and adult anxiety disorders (Barlow, 1988). It has been proposed that anxiety disorders of childhood be listed in the same section of the *DSM* as other anxiety disorders; this would be comparable to the handling of mood disorders and schizophrenia, disorders which do not have separate entries for instances involving children (American Psychiatric Association, 1991).

Although biological research suggests a genetic component to anxiety disorders of childhood, learning also plays an important role. Children, like adults, respond to threatening situations with feelings of edginess, fear, and discomfort. It is possible that temperamental differences that are rooted in biology cause some children to experience heightened reactivity to these kinds of situations. From the psychodynamic and family systems perspectives, anxiety disorders are seen as the result of children being held back and failing to learn how to negotiate the normal developmental tasks of separating from parents.

The primary task of the clinician is to help the child gain control over anxiety-provoking situations. As with most childhood disorders, behavioral treatments have been demonstrated to be particularly effective (Weisz et al., 1987). Behavioral techniques used for treating fears and anxieties in children include systematic desensitization, prolonged exposure, and modeling. Contingency management and self-management are also useful in teaching the child to react more positively and competently to a fear-provoking situation. These various behavioral techniques may be applied either individually or in combinations. For example, a child with separation anxiety disorder may be taught relaxation techniques along with cognitive strategies for thinking more positively about separation. Medications are sometimes used, but their effectiveness has not been clearly demonstrated (Barrios & O'Dell, 1989).

Regardless of the specific modality, at some point parents become involved in the child's treatment. Family therapists give the greatest emphasis to the role of parents in helping the anxious child, but therapists from all perspectives recommend that treatment involve the family.

DISORDER	BIOLOGICAL	BEHAVIORAL AND COGNITIVE-BEHAVIORAL	FAMILY SYSTEMS
Mental retardation	Genetic inheritance. Environmental hazards. Alcohol or substance abuse in mother. Inadequate nutrition. Illness.	No relevant theory.	No relevant theory.
	Treatment: Prevention through early detection, prenatal education, and medical care.	**Treatment:** Teaching of social and living skills.	**Treatment:** Work with families to provide support and teach behavioral interventions.
Autism	Genetic inheritance. Abnormal brain activity. Birth complications. High-risk pregnancies. Illness.	Socioemotional defect. Cognitive impairments. Defective symbolization ability. Self-injurious behaviors reinforced by attention.	Cold and detached style of mothering.
	Treatment: Medications (eg., fenfluramine).	**Treatment:** Teach problem-solving skills. Increase behavioral flexibility. Reduce frequency of maladaptive behaviors through reinforcement. Self-control, covert conditioning, relaxation training. Peer reinforcement. Aversive conditioning.	**Treatment:** Family support and education.
Specific developmental disorders	Genetic inheritance. Exposure to toxic substances. Infectious diseases.	No relevant theory.	No relevant theory.
	Treatment: No relevant treatment.	**Treatment:** Integrative treatment in which child is given more structure in the classroom, presentation of new material in multiple modalities, and more opportunities to develop positive self-esteem.	**Treatment:** No relevant treatment.

DISORDER	BIOLOGICAL	BEHAVIORAL AND COGNITIVE-BEHAVIORAL	FAMILY SYSTEMS
Disruptive behavior disorders (ADHD and conduct disorder)	ADHD: Genetic inheritance. Abnormalities in frontal lobes of the brain. Birth complications.	ADHD: Hyperactivity is learned behavior maintained through reinforcement. Conduct Disorder: Negative behaviors reinforced by others in child's surroundings.	ADHD: Disturbed family environment as well as failure experiences in school. Conduct Disorder. Family environment in which violence, substance abuse, and criminal activity is common.
	Treatment: ADHD: Stimulant medication which paradoxically calms the child. Tricyclic antidepressants.	**Treatment: ADHD:** Teach child self-reinforcement to on-task behavior, self-control, delayed gratification, self-motivation, and monitoring of progress toward goals. Conduct disorder: Reinforcement, behavioral contracting, modeling, and relaxation training, perhaps in context of peer groups.	**Treatment: ADHD:** Family members taught to use behavioral methods to reduce disruptive behaviors at home. Conduct disorder: parent training of behavioral methods.
Anxiety disorders	Genetic inheritance.	Fears acquired through learning.	Family interaction patterns impede development of independence in the child.
	Treatment: Antianxiety medications.	**Treatment:** Systematic desensitization. Exposure. Modeling. Contingency management. Self-management.	**Treatment:** Work with family to facilitate separation process.

OTHER DISORDERS THAT ORIGINATE IN CHILDHOOD

A variety of other somewhat miscellaneous disorders exist that originate in childhood and are either overcome by the time the individual reaches adulthood or become a permanent aspect of the individual's functioning. These disorders are fairly rare, but they can severely impair the individual's social functioning and level of well-being.

Childhood Eating Disorders

Pica is the recurrent eating of inedible substances such as paint, string, hair, animal droppings, and paper. A child may, for example, dump out the cereal from its box and chew the cardboard instead of eating the food inside. Another form of eating disorder is **rumination disorder of infancy**, in which the child regurgitates food after it has been swallowed and then either spits it out or re-swallows it.

Tic Disorders

A **tic** is a rapid, recurring involuntary movement or vocalization. Examples of motor tics include eye blinking, facial twitches, and shoulder shrugging. Vocal tics include coughing, grunting, snorting, uttering obscenities (Called **coprolalia**), and clicking. One example is **Tourette's disorder**, a chronic combination of movement and vocal tics. The individual may repeatedly make facial grimaces accompanied by the involuntary shouting of vulgarities.

Elimination Disorders

Children with elimination disorders have not, in colloquial terms, become "toilet-trained," long past the time when they were physiologically capable of maintaining continence and using the toilet properly. In **functional encopresis**, the child has bowel movements either in clothes or in some other inappropriate place. In **functional enuresis**, the child urinates in clothes or in bed after the age when the child is expected to be continent.

Reactive Attachment Disorder

Reactive attachment disorder is a severe disturbance in the individual's ability to relate to others, usually due to grossly inadequate care during the early years of life. The individual may be unresponsive to others, apathetic, and prefer to be alone rather than interact with friends or family.

Stereotypy/Habit Disorder

The voluntary repetition of nonfunctional behaviors such as body-rocking, head-banging, and teeth-grinding constitutes **stereotypy/habit disorder**. This behavior can potentially be very damaging to the individual's physical well-being.

Elective Mutism

In **elective mutism**, the individual consciously refuses to talk. Sometimes this mutism is accompanied by oppositional or avoidant behavior.

DEVELOPMENT-RELATED DISORDERS: THE PERSPECTIVES REVISITED

Now that you have read about the various forms of childhood disorders, you can appreciate our opening comments about the complexities involved in diagnosing and treating children. Perhaps you have also gained some insight into how painful it is for parents and teachers to see a child afflicted with such troubling problems. You can also understand the dilemmas faced by the adults in a child's life about the best course of action to follow in making treatment decisions.

In some ways, the disorders of childhood are like a microcosm of all abnormal psychology. In fact, there is considerable debate among researchers and clinicians about whether separate diagnostic categories should exist for children in the area of schizophrenia and depression. The question of overlap between childhood and adult forms of psychological disorder is one that is likely to remain unresolved for some time as researchers continue to explore whether these really are separate entities.

Questions might also be raised about the origin of a child's referral for psychological evaluation or treatment. A parent's reporting of a child's "symptoms" may be a cry for help from an overburdened parent of a normal but "difficult" child, or the reflection of a disturbance that lies outside the child and instead within the parent, the family, the school, or the larger social milieu. Nevertheless, when children experience these symptoms, they are real and painful, and a legitimate cause of concern. If they are not seriously treated, the problems can accompany the child into adulthood, causing many years of prolonged unhappiness. Because of the relationship between early life difficulties and later adjustments, researchers are actively pursuing a number of intriguing leads for understanding and intervening in the disorders of childhood.

SUMMARY

1. Although development-related disorders are considered part of the psychiatric nomenclature, clinicians have debated the appropriateness of regarding them as psychological disorders. Some of these disorders, such as mental retardation or learning disabilities, do not involve "abnormal" behavior, and others, such as oppositional defiant disorder, may represent developmental aberrations. By regarding these as psychological disorders, professionals may inappropriately label children with these conditions as deviant, creating further adjustment difficulties for the individual.

2. Mental retardation is a condition present from childhood characterized by below-average intellectual functioning. In addition to their intellectual deficits, people with mental retardation have impairments in their ability to adapt to everyday life. There are four categories of mental retardation depending on the severity of impairment of the individual's IQ: mild, moderate, severe, and profound. The causes of mental retardation include genetic disorders, birth complications, prematurity, head injury, exposure to toxins, and viral infections. Heavy alcohol use by the mother while pregnant can lead to fetal alcohol syndrome. (Summary continued on p. 345.)

Jason Newman

Jason's History

Jason accompanied his parents to the second intake session, although he appeared very unhappy about being brought along. First I met with all three of them, but later in the session I discussed Jason's history alone with Mr. and Mrs. Newman, and then I spent some time alone with Jason. I started my discussion with the Newmans by asking them to tell me a bit about themselves and their marriage, so that I would have a context within which to understand Jason. I told the Newmans that in the initial meetings, before having a grasp of Jason's problem, it was not clear whether or not I would continue as the clinician for this case following the intake. I explained that in some instances family therapy is sufficient, and if that was the case here, I could serve as the family therapist. However, in other cases a specialist in child treatment is needed, in which case another therapist would be recommended. At first, Mr. Newman expressed reservations about telling me all the details of the case without assurance that I would be the clinician, but in response to Mrs. Newman's urgings, he agreed to go along. They proceeded to share with me the pain and distress of the past 7 years.

Although only 8 years old, Jason had suffered for most of his life from an inability to control his behavior. He had antagonized every important person in his life time and time again. The older of two children, Jason had a 7-year-old sister, Anna, who showed none of the disturbance that was so much a part of Jason.

Jason's father was 34 years old; he owned and managed a small but successful local card store, where 32-year-old Mrs. Newman worked as a part-time salesperson while the children were in school. The Newmans had been married for 10 years, and they had been relatively happy prior to the onset of Jason's problems. For the past 7 years, however, the tension between Mr. and Mrs. Newman had intensified greatly. From what I could tell, it seemed as though Mr. Newman had denied the seriousness of Jason's problems, usually minimizing the troubles by making comments such as, "He's just a typical boy." Alternatively, Mr. Newman would blame teachers for not having enough structure in the classroom.

As Jason's problems grew, Mr. Newman spent less and less time at home, contending that it was necessary to devote his energy to the family business. Thus, Mrs. Newman often felt isolated. She tried to turn to her friends, but over time she began to sense that they did not want to maintain the relationship, because they also found it difficult to interact with Jason. Mrs. Newman told me how she prayed every day that Jason would become normal. She knew he was an intelligent and attractive child, but had become detested by acquaintances and dreaded by teachers.

Assessment

In light of the fact that Jason had recently taken an IQ test in school, it was not necessary to repeat intelligence testing. The report received from the school psychologist indicated that Jason's IQ, as assessed with the *WISC-III*, placed him in the above-average range of intelligence for both verbal and performance IQ. I felt that it would be helpful to have some quantitative data about Jason's behavioral problems, however, so I asked his parents to complete a child behavior checklist and some other scales that could be completed by Jason's teachers. Both assessment instruments confirmed the picture that Mr. and Mrs. Newman had conveyed in our discussions. Jason's scores were those found in hyperactive children. For example, on the Conners scale, Jason received scores that were more than a full standard deviation above the mean of the subscales of Learning Problems, Impulsivity-Hyperactivity, and the Hyperactivity Index.

Diagnosis

There was little question in my mind that Jason met the criteria for attention-deficit hyperactivity disorder. His current behaviors and his long history of behavioral disturbance made such a conclusion fairly obvious. Everyone involved with Jason concurred with this diagnosis—parents, teachers, and mental health professionals.

Axis I. Attention-deficit hyperactivity disorder.

Axis II. None.

Axis III. No physical disorders or conditions.

Axis IV. Severity: 1. No acute events or enduring circumstances that may be relevant to the disorder.

Axis V. Current Global Assessment of Functioning: 55. Highest Global Assessment of Functioning (past year): 55.

Case Formulation

Although in all likelihood biological factors played an important role in Jason's problem, there was certainly more to the picture. Jason's

Return to the Case

Jason Newman continued

disruptive behavior was serving some function both at home and in school. Perhaps, somewhat unconsciously, Jason was trying to seek attention by means of his disruptive and annoying behaviors. Feeling unable to control his own behavior or thoughts, Jason became increasingly hurt by his lack of friends, but at the same time he felt incapable of modifying his behavior in positive directions. His failure to obtain the nurturance that he craved led Jason to an escalation of his behavior that culminated in the dangerous fire-setting at school.

Jason's problem was not one limited to his behavior alone; it had become a family problem and a school problem, and required intervention in both contexts.

Planning a Treatment

Focusing first on Jason, I recommended that he be seen in individual therapy by Dr. Clara Hill, a child psychiatrist highly regarded for her expertise in treating hyperactive children. My recommendation was based on two assumptions. First, I believed that Jason would benefit from medication. Second, I felt that Jason would respond positively to the idea that he would have his own private therapist, who would spend time alone with him each week. Regarding Mr. and Mrs. Newman, I suggested that they meet with Dr. Hill's colleague, a psychologist named Dr. Albert Kennedy, who would develop a contingency management program that could be implemented both at home and in school. Dr. Kennedy had ample experience with hyperactive children, and he was respected by the local school administrators and teachers for the interventions he had developed for other children. Dr. Kennedy would also meet with Mr. and Mrs. Newman on a regular basis to help them through the process and to give them an opportunity to work on their own relationship, focusing on the ways in which Jason's problem had so deeply affected both of them.

Outcome of the Case

Two years have passed since I first evaluated Jason, and the news so far has been promising. Jason was started on Ritalin shortly after being seen by Dr. Hill, and the changes in his behavior were dramatic and quick. He settled down both at school and at home in ways that caused everyone who knew him to sigh with relief. Of course, he did not turn from urchin to angel overnight. In fact, he continued to be provocative and somewhat disruptive at times, but rarely to the extreme of his pre-treatment days. Mr. and Mrs. Newman learned from Dr. Kennedy the importance of being swift with repercussions for inappropriate behavior and of rewarding positive changes. Through meetings with the Newmans and consultations with school staff, Dr. Kennedy developed a comprehensive intervention program that was consistent and clear. Dr. Hill informed me that after 6 months of weekly sessions with Jason, she reduced the frequency to bimonthly and then monthly meetings. At the point of each reduction in frequency, Jason's disruptive behaviors flared up temporarily, but in time he settled back into his routine.

I was relieved to learn of Jason's progress, and felt confident that his prognosis could now be considered improved. It is difficult to know, however, what scars will remain with this boy from the turbulent years that preceded his treatment. I am hopeful that Jason's positive personality traits will serve as resources to help him continue to grow, unburdened by the hurts of his childhood years.

Inadequate nutrition, medical care, and parenting can lead to failure to thrive, another cause of mental retardation. The federally mandated mainstreaming of mentally retarded children has led to their integration in public schools and into society overall. Individuals with mental retardation can be helped by behavioral and family interventions that are designed to help them function more effectively in the community. There is increasing emphasis on prevention of mental retardation through early detection of genetic abnormalities, the provision of adequate prenatal care, and attempts to prevent head injury and other conditions that can interfere with the child's normal intellectual development.

3. Autism is a massive deficit in the individual's ability to communicate and relate emotionally to others. This disorder begins during infancy as a general unresponsiveness and continues during childhood as a resistance to closeness with people and an attachment to inanimate objects. Children with autism may make strange sounds and engage in odd, even self-damaging, motor behaviors such as head-banging. They may also develop ritualistic behaviors. In an unusual variant of autism, called *autistic savant syndrome,* the individual

becomes exceptionally talented at a particular skill, such as drawing, or develops an encyclopedic knowledge of a specific subject. Autism differs from childhood schizophrenia in that the child with schizophrenia is responsive and curious about the environment and mental retardation is not common. Autism is understood as a cognitive disorder of language, attention, and perception with a neurological basis that is perhaps acquired through genetic inheritance, through diseases during the mother's pregnancy, or an accident during delivery. Current approaches to treating autism focus on behavioral methods involving reinforcement that can help to reduce the emotional distance between parents and child created by the child's symptoms, and to reduce the frequency of self-injurious behaviors shown by the autistic child. The child can also learn skills that will promote successful problem-solving experiences and flexibility in adapting to new situations. However, these behavioral treatments, even though they are not aimed at cure, must be lengthy and intense if they are to have a significant impact on the child's life.

4. There are a variety of specific developmental disorders that involve a delay or deficit in some area of functioning, including academic skills, language and speech, and motor coordination. These disorders can interfere with the child's ability to make progress in school and in social situations, and for adults, can interfere with occupational success and social adjustment. Neurological impairments are thought to be at the root of these disorders. Treatment for specific developmental disorders occurs in the schools, and involves a multidisciplinary approach designed by special education teachers, school psychologists, specialized therapists, and parents. One focus of treatment involves building on the child's strengths so the child can feel a sense of self-esteem and accomplishment.

5. Disruptive behavior disorders include attention-deficit hyperactivity disorder (ADHD), conduct disorder, and oppositional-defiant disorder. These disorders share the quality of involving behaviors that include persistent negative behavior patterns that interfere with the goals or activities of others. In attention-deficit hyperactivity disorder, the child is extremely restless, impulsive, and inattentive. Conduct disorder, which is more prevalent in males, is the childhood version of antisocial personality disorder, and often precedes the later development of antisocial behaviors. Some of the delinquent behaviors associated with conduct disorder are stealing, truancy from school, breaking and entering, sexual assault, and drug and alcohol abuse. In oppositional-defiant disorder, the individual is negative and uncooperative beyond the point of mere stubbornness or adolescent rebelliousness and can be resentful and self-righteous, externalizing blame onto others. In their attempts to understand ADHD,

researchers have come to see the disorder as developing in children who have a biological vulnerability and who are placed under a high degree of environmental stress. Treatment for ADHD includes medications, particularly a stimulant medication that paradoxically serves to calm the hyperactive child. However, side effects of this medication can be serious, and the treatment not always effective, so clinicians have sought alternative treatments. Behavioral treatments are also very helpful, particularly when implemented by family members in the child's home. In behavioral treatment, the child would be taught methods of self-reinforcement to regulate on-task behavior, self-motivation, and self-monitoring of progress toward goals. Conduct disorder is highly resistant to treatment, but there are greater chances for success if interventions are begun before the child becomes an adolescent. The most useful strategies involve reinforcement, behavioral contracting, modeling, and relaxation training in the context of peer therapy, groups, and parent training. Researchers debate whether ADHD is related to conduct disorder.

6. The anxiety disorders of childhood and adolescence include separation anxiety disorder, avoidant disorder, and overanxious disorder. In separation anxiety disorder, the child is abnormally fearful of being apart from the parents, becoming panicky and perhaps even physically ill when away from a caregiver. Avoidant disorder involves fearfulness toward strangers taken to the extreme. Children with this disorder refrain from contact with strangers, clinging to the people they know out of timidity and embarrassment. A child with overanxious disorder is an excessive worrier, a perfectionist, and full of self-doubts. Researchers have attempted to establish connections between childhood and adult anxiety disorders, and they do appear to have some relationship. The cause of childhood anxiety disorders is seen as an interaction between genetic predispositions and learning experiences that cause the child to associate the unpleasant emotions of anxiety with particular situations. Treatment that follows the behavioral model seems to be most effective, including methods that help adults, such as desensitization. In addition, contingency management and self-management help the child form new connections between feared situations and more positive emotions.

7. Other childhood disorders include disorders of eating, such as pica and rumination disorder, tic or motor disorders, elimination disorders, reactive attachment disorder, stereotypy/habit disorder; and elective mutism. Each of these disorders has its own unique symptom pattern and each can be very distressing to the child who suffers from them as well as parents and other family members.

KEY TERMS

Mental retardation: a condition, present from childhood, characterized by significantly below-average general intellectual functioning (an IQ of less than 65 to 75). p. 322

Phenylketonuria (PKU): a disorder of infancy characterized by failure to produce an enzyme necessary for normal development that causes mental retardation. p. 322

Tay-Sachs disease: a metabolic disorder that causes neural degeneration and early death, usually before the age of 4. p. 322

Fragile X syndrome: a defect transmitted through the X chromosome that leads to a severe form of mental retardation and serious speech and communication difficulties. p. 323

Down syndrome: a form of mental retardation caused by abnormal chromosomal formation during conception. p. 323

Anoxia: the cutting off of oxygen supply to the body, potentially causing brain damage. p. 324

Fetal alcohol syndrome (FAS): a condition associated with mental retardation in a child whose mother consumed large amounts of alcohol on a regular basis while pregnant. p. 324

Failure to thrive: a condition in which the child does not grow physically and mentally at a normal rate caused by poor prenatal care or grossly inadequate and inattentive parenting. p. 325

Mainstreaming: a governmental policy intended to integrate fully into society people with mental and physical disabilities. p. 325

Autism: a massive impairment in an individual's ability to communicate and relate emotionally to others. p. 327

Echolalia: an echoing of words or phrases. p. 327

Specific developmental disorder: a delay or deficit in some particular area of functioning, such as academic skills, language and speech, or motor coordination. p. 331

Learning disorder: a delay or deficit in an academic skill—mathematics, writing, or reading. p. 322

Mathematics disorder: a learning disorder in which the individual has difficulty with mathematical tasks and concepts. p. 332

Disorder of written expression: a learning disorder in which the individual's writing is characterized by poor spelling, grammatical or punctuation errors, and disorganization of paragraphs. p. 332

Reading disorder (dyslexia): a learning disorder in which the individual omits, distorts, or substitutes words when reading, and reads in a slow and halting fashion. p. 332

Expressive language disorder: a specific developmental disorder characterized by a limited and faulty vocabulary, speaking short sentences with simplified grammatical structures, omitting critical words or phrases, or putting words together in peculiar order. p. 333

Receptive language disorder: a specific developmental disorder in which the individual is unable to understand certain kinds of words or phrases such as directions, or in more severe forms, basic vocabulary or entire sentences. p. 333

Phonological disorder: a specific developmental disorder in which the individual misarticulates, substitutes, or omits speech sounds. p. 333

Cluttering: a specific developmental disorder in which the individual speaks in quick bursts, making it impossible for other people to understand what is being said. p. 333

Stuttering: a specific developmental disorder in which the individual suffers a disturbance in the normal fluency and patterning of speech that is characterized by such verbalizations as sound repetitions or prolongations, broken words, blocking on sounds, word substitutions to avoid problematic words, or words expressed with an excess of tension. p. 333

Voice disorder: a specific developmental disorder in which the individual's speech is characterized by abnormalities in pitch, loudness, tone, or resonance. p. 333

Developmental coordination disorder: the primary form of motor skill disorder, in which the individual has difficulty carrying out simple motor activities, appearing clumsy and uncoordinated. p. 333

Attention-deficit hyperactivity disorder (ADHD): a disruptive behavior disorder of childhood characterized by difficulty in maintaining attention and restlessness of motor activity. p. 334

Conduct disorder: a behavior disorder of childhood that involves recurrent malicious behavior that is the precursor of antisocial personality disorder. p. 335

Oppositional defiant disorder: a disruptive behavior disorder of childhood that is characterized by undue hostility, stubbornness, strong temper, belligerence, spitefulness, and self-righteousness. p. 335

Separation anxiety disorder: an anxiety disorder of childhood characterized by difficulty in separating from caregivers. p. 338

Avoidant disorder: an anxiety disorder of childhood that causes a child to refrain from contact with unfamiliar people. p. 339

Overanxious disorder: an anxiety disorder of childhood characterized by anxiety so incapacitating that the child is unable to get through a day without obsessing over some unrealistic concern. p. 339

Pica: the recurrent eating of inedible substances such as paint, string, hair, animal droppings, and paper. p. 342

Rumination disorder of infancy: a development-related disorder in which the child regurgitates food after it has been swallowed and then either spits it out or re-swallows it. p. 342

Tic: a rapid, recurring, involuntary movement or vocalization. p. 345

Coprolalia: the involuntary uttering of obscenities. p. 345

Tourette's disorder: a development-related disorder involving a chronic combination of movement and vocal tics. p. 345

Functional encopresis: a development-related disorder in which the child is incontinent of feces and has bowel movements either in clothes or in some other inappropriate place. p. 345

Functional enuresis: a development-related disorder in which the child is incontinent of urine and urinates in clothes or in bed after the age when the child is expected to be continent. p. 345

Reactive attachment disorder: a development-related disorder in which the individual has a severe disturbance in the ability to relate to others and is unresponsive to people, is apathetic, and prefers to be alone rather than interact with friends or family. p. 346

Stereotypy/habit disorder: a development-related disorder in which the individual voluntarily repeats nonfunctional behaviors such as rocking or head-banging that can potentially be damaging to the individual's physical well-being. p. 346

Elective mutism: a disorder originating in childhood in which the individual consciously refuses to talk, sometimes accompanying this refusal by oppositional or avoidant behavior. p. 346

Case Report: Irene Heller

Irene Heller is a 67-year-old retired school-teacher, brought to the mental health clinic by her son, Jonathan. Before leaving my office to meet Irene, I was buzzed on the intercom by the receptionist who told me that my 2 o'clock client was "causing a stir in the waiting room." Apparently, Irene was yelling at her son that he had no business taking her to the clinic. As tactfully as I could, I interrupted Irene and invited her and Jonathan to my office. Rather belligerently, she barked, "Mind your own business," but to my surprise she did get up from her chair and follow me down the hallway.

Upon entering my office, Irene launched into a monologue trying to convince me that nothing was wrong with her. Fortunately, she sat quietly as Jonathan told a markedly different story. According to Jonathan, his mother had changed over the past few years from being an intellectually alert, vibrant, and active person who loved teaching into a forgetful, easily distracted, unhappy individual. She suffered distinct memory problems as well, often unable to recall what a person had said just moments earlier.

When I asked Jonathan what had prompted him to bring his mother for professional attention at this particular time, he explained that his visit to me followed months of struggle during which he saw his mother changing in some alarming ways. Recent events finally made it clear that action had to be taken. Jonathan had been expecting his mother to visit his family in their new home. When she failed to show up at the appointed time, he telephoned her and received an indignant response from his mother accusing him of trying to trick her.

Apparently, Irene had gone to his former residence, ostensibly oblivious to the fact that he had moved nearly two months ago. Despite his insistence that he had reminded her of his new address just the day before, Irene claimed to have no recollection and insisted that he must be trying to free himself from any obligations to her. The following day, Irene called Jonathan as if nothing unusual had taken place between the two of them. Clearly, she had forgotten all the turmoil that had taken place less than 24 hours ago.

As Jonathan talked about his mother's slow but relentless deterioration, he explained how her loss of memory was accompanied by increasingly disruptive and uncharacteristic behaviors. For example, one day Jonathan was called by the manager of a local department store who complained that Irene was roaming aimlessly through the store muttering the phrase "a stitch in time, a stitch in time." When the manager asked if he could be of help, Irene began to yell obscenities at him and tried to assault him. As the manager attempted to take her to the office, she screamed "Murderer! Take your hands off me!" In anguish and embarrassment, Jonathan rushed to the store to find his mother sobbing quietly in a corner of the office. Although occasional peculiar events involving his mother had occurred during the year, none were this extreme. Jonathan had downplayed each one until it became obvious that Irene needed professional attention.

Sarah Tobin, PhD

14

ORGANIC DISORDERS INVOLVING COGNITIVE IMPAIRMENT

What would you think if someone in your life began acting in the ways that Irene Heller did? Like Mrs. Heller's son, you might first assume that she was suffering from an emotional problem, possibly related to an upsetting event in her life. Few people think to consider that a person's behavioral difficulties might be caused by brain damage or a disease that affects the nervous system. Yet, as you will learn in this chapter, there are many ways in which neurological disorders can cause people to experience major changes in their intellectual functioning, mood, and perceptions. You will also see that a variety of physical conditions can cause cognitive impairments through damage to the central nervous system.

After reading this chapter, you should be able to:

- Understand the defining features of organically based cognitive impairments.
- Describe the characteristics of delirium.
- Contrast organically based amnestic disorders with psychogenic amnesia.
- List the symptoms of dementia.
- Describe the characteristics of Alzheimer's disease, including incidence, brain changes, and phases of dementia associated with this disease.
- Compare Alzheimer's disease to dementias produced by other organic disorders and by depression.
- Understand the issues involved in the diagnosis of Alzheimer's disease.
- Describe and compare theoretical perspectives for understanding and treating Alzheimer's disease.

THE NATURE OF COGNITIVE IMPAIRMENT DISORDERS

The term **organic**, in the context of psychological disorders, has traditionally been used to refer to physical damage or dysfunction that affects the integrity of the brain. The brain disorder, in turn, is thought to be responsible for a particular pattern of behavioral, cognitive, and emotional disturbance. Correspondingly, the term organic disorders has been used to describe psychological disorders that are due to brain damage or disease, with the primary feature of these disorders consisting of a disturbance of cognitive functioning involving judgment, language, thought, speech, memory, orientation, perception, or attention. Although clinicians continue to use the term *organic* (Lipowski, 1990), researchers have suggested that the formal name for the group of disorders characterized by this set of symptoms be changed to the more descriptive term of **cognitive impairment disorders** (Spitzer et al., 1992).

The move away from the term *organic* is based on the premise that many other psychological disorders also have their origins in brain dysfunction. For example, as you read in Chapter 12, researchers now recognize that schizophrenia has a strong biological basis, and could therefore be regarded as organic. Even though schizophrenia involves thought disorder and impaired intellectual functioning, it is not considered a cognitive impairment disorder, because cognitive impairment is not the primary feature of schizophrenia (Popkin et al, 1989; Tucker et al., 1990).

Most people are unaware of the fact that very strange experiences such as hallucinations and delusions can be caused by physical abnormalities. Imagine what you would think if a friend was experiencing bizarre hallucinations. Unless you are familiar with the various symptoms of organic disorders involving cognitive impairment, your first thought might be that your friend was experiencing a psychological disorder such as a brief reactive psychosis. In fact, various physically based syndromes exist that mimic schizophrenia, mood disorders, and personality disorders. People can develop delusions, hallucinations, mood disturbances, and extreme personality changes through abnormalities in the body resulting from disease, reactions to medication, or exposure to toxic substances. People with disorders involving the brain are frequently found to be suffering from depression either due to the disabling effects of the illness or as a result of physiological changes that underlie both the physical and psychological abnormalities (McNamara, 1991). As you will see in Chapter 15, drugs and alcohol can also cause a person to think, feel, and act in ways that mimic serious psychological disturbances.

You can imagine how difficult it must be to differentiate symptoms that are associated with a psychological disorder from those arising in response to a physical disorder. Fortunately, this process has been facilitated by advances in neuropsychological assessment and the development of new technologies to assess brain structure and function (see Chapter 3). But even in an age of sophisticated diagnostic technology, it is sometimes very difficult for clinicians to determine whether a person's psychological problems are attributable to organic factors. Consider the case of Flora, a 59-year-old woman who had been hospitalized many times for what appeared to be bipolar disorder. Her symptoms included suicide attempts, extreme belligerence toward her family, and grandiose beliefs about herself. Only after several psychiatric hospitalizations was it determined, by an astute clinician, that Flora's symptoms were caused by an endocrine disorder. After only a few weeks of treatment, Flora's medical condition improved and her "psychiatric" symptoms diminished.

Another physical disorder with symptoms that appear to be psychological in nature is **epilepsy**, a neurological condition that involves recurrent bodily seizures with associated changes in EEG patterns. Because people with epilepsy may sometimes act in ways that strike others as being odd, or even psychotic, they may mistakenly be regarded as having a psychological disorder. Epilepsy has been misunderstood for centuries, and many people with this condition have suffered from society's lack of understanding about epilepsy and discrimination against those suffering with this condition. Some very famous people have been afflicted with epilepsy, including Russian author Fyodor Dostoevsky.

Epilepsy is classified into two groups according to the extent of brain involvement in the seizure: one type involves generalized seizures and the other involves partial or focal seizures (Solomon & Masdeu, 1989). People who experience generalized convulsive seizures are stricken by what are called *grand-mal* seizures during which they lose consciousness, stop breathing for a brief period, and undergo uncontrollable bodily jerking. Following the seizure, they feel drowsy and confused. Another form of generalized seizure consists of a *petit-mal* seizure in which the individual experiences a temporary loss of consciousness, possibly accompanied by rhythmic movements of the lips, mouth, head, and eyelids, but does not undergo the full-body spasms that occur with grand-mal seizures.

In contrast to generalized seizures, some people experience partial or focal seizures involving abnormal EEG patterns that are localized in a cortical or subcortical region of one cerebral hemisphere. Of particular interest to our discussion here are those seizures that arise from the temporal lobe or nearby limbic areas, because these seizures result in symptoms that have the appearance of being psychological disturbances. For example, people with this condition, called *temporal lobe epilepsy*, may experience a number of symptoms such as increased fear, mood swings, inappropriate affect, bursts of anger, illusions or hallucinations, altered thought processes, and bizarre behavior. A small percentage of people with temporal lobe epilepsy undergo a disturbing period of psychotic-like behavior that can last from moments to as long as a few days following a seizure. Interestingly, the symptoms of anxiety and depression are more frequently observed in people with left compared with right temporal lobe dysfunction (Hermann et al., 1991).

You can see that without careful and precise diagnosis, it would be possible to overlook an organic condition such as epilepsy or endocrine disease, and mistakenly treat an individual with such a disorder as suffering solely from emotional disturbance.

DELIRIUM

The term *delirious* is one you have probably heard many times, possibly as a description for someone who is in a state of uncontrolled excitement. Or perhaps you have personally experienced delirium in a different form while in the grips of a high fever or following an injury. You may have awakened from your sleep not knowing where you were or what time it was. Family members may have been perplexed by your inability to respond to them in conversation. Perhaps you had some strange thoughts or perceptions that you later realized were hallucinations. If you have ever had such an experience, you know first-hand how a bodily disturbance can result in an altered state of consciousness accompanied by bizarre symptoms.

Delirium involves a temporary state in which a person's thoughts, level of consciousness, speech, memory, orientation, perceptions, and motor patterns are very confused, unstable, or otherwise grossly disturbed. In addition to these visible signs of delirium, there may also be severe dysfunction of the autonomic nervous system. The delirious individual may experience delusions, illusions, or hallucinations, as well as emotional disturbances such as anxiety, euphoria, or irritability. As you can imagine, such symptoms are dramatic and frightening, both for the person who is suffering from them and for anyone who might be observing. Delirium can involve some serious medical risks, including permanent brain damage, and it is therefore im-

Jack is a 23-year-old carpenter who was brought to the emergency room by his co-workers a few hours after he fell from a 30-foot ladder at the work site. Although Jack was not ostensibly injured, it was obvious to Jack's co-workers that something was wrong. When they asked Jack questions about whether he was hurt, he repeatedly responded with the nonsensical answer, "The hammer's no good." Jack's co-workers were startled and perplexed by his bizarre suggestions that they were trying to steal his tools, and by his various paranoid sounding remarks. Grabbing at things in the air, Jack insisted that objects were being thrown at him. Jack couldn't remember the names of anyone at the site; in fact, he was unsure of where he was at the time. Initially he resisted the attempts of his co-workers to take him to the hospital, because of his concern that they had formed some plot to harm him.

- How would a clinician determine whether or not Jack's delirium is due to head trauma?
- If you were one of Jack's co-workers, how would you react to his changes in behavior?

portant that this condition be accurately diagnosed so that emergency measures can be taken.

Delirium is caused by a change in the metabolism of the brain, and usually reflects something abnormal occurring in the body. Perhaps the individual has suffered brain damage from a head injury, drug addiction, high fever, or some other medical problem. A person of any age can be afflicted with delirium, but it is more common among medically hospitalized elderly patients (Johnson et al., 1990; Liptzin et al., 1991), probably because they are more prone to falls and are more likely to have undergone surgery, experiences that can provoke a state of delirium.

Although the syndrome has no typical course, it follows some general trends. Delirium is typically characterized by a fairly rapid onset and brief duration, developing over a short period of time or, at most, over a few days. However, some individuals do show a slower, more subtle manifestation of symptoms. Over the course of a day, a delirious individual may experience a variety of emotional disturbances such as anxiety, fear, depression, irritability, euphoria, and apathy. These emotions can fluctuate considerably, and symptoms may vary by time of day, diminishing in the morning and worsening during sleepless nights or in the dark. Distinct neurological deficits are not usually detected when a person with delirium is tested, but abnormal bodily movements, such as tremor or shaking, are often evident. Also, signs of autonomic nervous system disturbance are often present, such as tachycardia (rapid heartbeat), sweating, flushed face, dilated pupils, and elevated blood pressure. Rarely does delirium last for more than a month. The individual either naturally recovers, is effectively treated, develops a progressive neurological deficit, or dies from the underlying physical condition.

A person in a state of delirium experiences numerous cognitive, emotional, and behavioral disturbances. Elderly, medical hospital patients are particularly prone to delirium.

AMNESTIC DISORDERS

As you have learned from our discussion of psychogenic amnesia in Chapter 8, there are instances in which some people lose their memory because of psychological reasons. But there are biological causes for loss of memory as well; such conditions are referred to as **amnestic disorders**. People with amnestic disorders are unable to recall events of the recent past or to register new memories. Two forms of amnesia are possible in amnestic disorders. People with **retrograde amnesia** have lost their memories for events prior to the physical problem that caused the amnesia. In **anterograde amnesia**, people lose the ability to learn or remember events taking place after the damage has occurred.

This inability to incorporate recent events into memory or to recall important information can be very disturbing, because the individual loses a sense of personal identity. The individual may try to cover up the social problems caused by memory loss through denial or confabulation, the fabrication of facts or events to fill a memory void. However, these tactics cannot compensate for the feeling of a lack of connectedness with one's own daily and past experiences.

The most common cause of amnestic disorder is chronic alcohol use, as you will see in Chapter 15. Some other conditions that can lead to amnestic disorder include head trauma, brain tumors, tubercular meningitis, post-encephalitis, neurosurgery, loss of oxygen (anoxia), stroke, and herpes simplex (Kopelman, 1987). Regardless of the specific condition that has caused the amnesia, the effect of memory loss is due to some form of damage to the subcortical regions of the brain responsible for consolidating and retrieving memories.

This disorder is uncommon, but in those people who are stricken, it is usually chronic and unremitting. Whether or not a person recovers from amnestic disorder depends on what caused it in the first place. In most cases, the individual never does recover fully.

DEMENTIA

It is a sad and disturbing experience to encounter someone who seems to have lost control of thought and behavior because of a physical condition. If you have ever visited a nursing home, you may have observed elderly people who seemed to be very confused and forgetful, speaking in peculiar or incomprehensible manner, and seemingly detached from everything going on around them. Many people mistakenly think that cognitive impairment caused by brain deterioration only happens to elderly people. However, this condition, known as *dementia*, also afflicts many people with AIDS, and is sometimes the first clue that a person has this deadly disease (Perry, 1990).

The diagnosis of dementia involves a thorough physical and psychological assessment to evaluate symptoms such as aphasia, apraxia, and memory loss.

Harvey is a 57-year-old music teacher in a public high school. While bicycling to work one day, he was struck by a car and was rushed to the emergency room. In addition to having a broken leg, Harvey had suffered a head injury and was unable to remember anything that had happened during the preceding 2 weeks. Furthermore, he had no idea how old he was, where he was born, or whether he was married. This lack of ability to remember his personal past was a source of great distress to Harvey. By contrast, Harvey had no trouble remembering the ambulance ride to the hospital or the name of the emergency room physician who first examined him. Following a 3-day hospital stay, Harvey was transferred to a rehabilitation facility for 3 months, where memory therapy helped him to learn mnemonic strategies for recalling important information.

- ■ What type of amnesia does Harvey appear to be suffering from?
- ■ If Harvey were to receive psychotherapy, what issues might the clinician focus on with him?

Dementia is a form of cognitive impairment involving generalized progressive deficits in a person's memory and learning of new information, ability to communicate, judgment, and motor coordination. In addition to experiencing cognitive changes, people with dementia undergo changes in their personality and emotional state. As you might guess, such disturbances in how a person thinks and acts are certain to wreak havoc in that person's ability to work and interact normally with other people. The term *dementia* comes from the Latin words *de*, meaning *out of*, and *mens*, meaning *mind*. You can see why the term, whose literal meaning is to be out of one's mind, is used to describe this disorder.

The main cause of dementia is profuse and progressive brain damage. A variety of physical disorders can cause this condition, including brain tumors, infectious disorders such as HIV, and neurological disease. Dementias are found in people of all ages, including children. In this chapter, we will focus on Alzheimer's disease, the leading cause of dementia resulting from factors other than substance abuse.

Characteristics of Dementia

The symptoms of dementia may begin as mild forgetfulness, only slightly noticeable and annoying. However, if the underlying brain disorder that causes the dementia cannot be treated, the person's symptoms will become increasingly obvious and distressing. As the condition of people with dementia worsens, so also does their capacity for caring for themselves, for staying in touch with what is going on around them, and for living a normal life.

■ *Memory loss*

The first sign of dementia is generally a slight memory impairment. In fact, a common but insensitive joke made by many people whose memory occasionally falters is that they must have Alzheimer's. However, the memory impairment of people with dementia is no laughing matter. As their disease progresses, they are able to remember less and less until they reach a point of being incapable of retaining any new information. As time goes on they become unable to remember even the basic facts about themselves and their lives.

■ *Aphasia*

The term **aphasia** refers to a loss of the ability to use language. Aphasia is caused by damage to the brain's speech and language area, and this damage influences the production and understanding of language. Such damage also disrupts the neural networks connecting these areas to other parts of the brain (Damasio, 1992). Two forms of aphasia are *Wernicke's aphasia* and *Broca's aphasia*, both named after the people who discovered them. In **Wernicke's aphasia**, the individual is able to produce words, but has lost the ability to comprehend them, so that these verbalizations

have no meaning. The aphasia also causes loss of comprehension for sentences spoken by others. In his powerful book *The Shattered Mind*, Harvard neurologist Howard Gardner provided an example of his interviews with a Wernicke's aphasia patient:

> "What brings you to the hospital?" I asked the 72-year-old retired butcher four weeks after his admission to the hospital.
>
> "Boy, I'm sweating. I'm awful nervous, you know, once in a while I get caught up, I can't mention the tarripoi, a month ago, quite a little, I've done a lot well, I impose a lot, while, on the other hand, you know what I mean, I have to run around, look it over, trebbin and all that sort of stuff." (p. 68).

In contrast to Wernicke's aphasia, the person with **Broca's aphasia** has a disturbance of language production but intact comprehension abilities. In other words, the individual knows the rules of sentence construction and can grasp the meaning of language, but is unable to produce complete sentences; verbal production is reduced to the fundamental communication of content with all modifiers left out. Again, an example from Gardner (1974) illustrates what it is like to talk to a person with Broca's aphasia. The following is an excerpt from an interview with David Ford, a 39-year-old Coast Guard radio operator who was recovering from a stroke that affected the left side of his brain.

> I asked Mr. Ford about his work before he entered the hospital.
>
> "I'm a sig . . . no . . . man . . . uh, well, . . . again." These words were emitted slowly and with great effort. The sounds were not clearly articulated; each syllable was uttered harshly, explosively, in a throaty voice . . . .
>
> "Let me help you," I interjected. "You were a signal . . ."
>
> "A sig-nal man . . . right," Ford completed my phrase triumphantly.
>
> "Were you in the Coast Guard?"
>
> "No, er, yes, yes . . . ship . . . Massachu . . . chusetts . . . Coastguard . . . years." He raised his hands twice, indicating the number "nineteen."
>
> "Oh, you were in the Coast Guard for nineteen years."
>
> "Oh . . . boy . . . right . . . right," he replied.
>
> "Why are you in the hospital, Mr. Ford?"
>
> Ford looked at me a bit strangely, as if to say, Isn't it patently obvious? He pointed to his paralyzed arm and said, "Arm no good," then to his mouth and said "Speech . . . can't say . . . talk, you see," . . . (pp. 60–61).

In contrast to this forced and hesitant speech pattern, Mr. Ford had no difficulty naming the days of the week, counting to 20, and reciting the Pledge of Allegiance to the United States flag. This disparity between the naming of objects and the use of grammatical terms is a classic sign of Wernicke's aphasia.

■ *Apraxia*

A person with **apraxia** has lost the ability to carry out coordinated bodily movements that could previously be performed with no difficulty. This impairment is not due to physical weakness or abnormal muscle tone, but rather is due to brain deterioration. Gardner (1974) gave the example involving a request to Mr. Ford that he pretend to blow out a match, but all Mr. Ford was capable of doing was making a loud sputtering sound. He was also unable to produce a cough upon command. It was not that Mr. Ford was incapable of blowing out the match or coughing, but rather his dysfunctional brain impaired his capacity to perform these tasks when instructed to do so.

■ *Agnosia*

The term **agnosia** refers to the inability to recognize familiar objects or experiences, despite the ability to perceive their basic elements. The following excerpt from Sack's book *The Man Who Mistook His Wife for a Hat* (1987) describes a person with visual agnosia. This dysfunction is very unusual, but it serves as an excellent illustration of how a dementing condition can radically alter the individual's everyday life and relationships with others.

> Dr. P. was a musician of distinction, well-known for many years as a singer, and then, at the local School of Music, as a teacher. It was here, in relation to his students, that certain strange problems were first observed. Sometimes a student would present himself and Dr. P. would not recognize him; or, specifically, would not recognize his face. The moment the student spoke, he would be recognized by his voice. Such incidents multiplied, causing embarrassment, perplexity, fear—and, sometimes, comedy. . . [In the middle of the neurological examination he seemed] to have decided that the examination was over and started to look around for his hat. He reached out his hand and took hold of his wife's head, tried to lift it off, to put it on. He had apparently mistaken his wife for a hat! His wife looked as if she was used to such things (pp. 8 and 11).

Senile Dementia of the Alzheimer's Type (Alzheimer's Disease)

A common fear that many people have is that, as they get older, they will lose control of their mental functioning and become "senile." This fear is largely unfounded, since only a very small percentage of elderly people become afflicted with the form of dementia known as Alzheimer's disease, or senile dementia of the Alzheimer's Type. The term "senile" in this context refers to "old," but the term has taken on the unfortunate connotation that being old means being mentally incompetent. Although the odds are low that a person will develop Alzheimer's disease, when it does strike, the disorder initiates an irreversible process of mental deterioration.

Alzheimer's disease was first reported in 1907 by a German psychiatrist and neuropathologist, Alois Alzheimer, who documented the case of a 51-year-old woman complaining of poor memory and disorientation to time and place (Alzheimer, 1907, 1987). Eventually, the woman be-

Elderly people are often victims of the stereotype that they are prone to developing senile dementia. However, the majority of elderly people are in good physical and psychological health and are able to enjoy productive lives.

came depressed and began to hallucinate. She showed the classic cognitive symptoms of dementia including loss of language and lack of recognition of familiar objects, as well as an inability to perform voluntary movements. Alzheimer was unable to explain this process of deterioration until after she died. Upon autopsy, he found that most of the tissue in this woman's cerebral cortex had degenerated. By examining brain tissue under a microscope, Alzheimer also found that individual neurons had degenerated and formed abnormal clumps of neural tissue. Although there is still no explanation for what causes the process of brain deterioration that forms the core of this disease, the term *Alzheimer's disease* has come to be associated with this severe cerebral atrophy as well as the characteristic microscopic changes in brain tissue.

INCIDENCE OF THE DISORDER   The incidence of Alzheimer's disease is estimated to be approximately 6 percent of the over-65 population (Cohen, 1988), with women having higher rates than men (Jorm et al., 1987). Although only a small percentage of elderly people develop this disorder, the actual numbers of people potentially affected by Alzheimer's disease has increased as the number of people in the over-65 population has grown (see Figures 14–1 and 14–2). In the last few decades, there has been a dramatic rise in the percent of the U.S. population who are over 65—from 8 percent in 1950 to 12 percent in 1987 (U.S. Bureau of the Census, 1975; U.S. Department of Commerce, 1989). By the time current college-age individuals are in their 60s, they will make up nearly one-quarter of the entire U.S. population (U.S. Bureau of the Census, 1989). Current estimates of the incidence of Alzheimer's indicate a rise from approximately 3 million people over the age of 65 with the disorder in 1980 to more than 10 million by the year 2050 (Evans, 1990).

Adding to the magnitude of the problem is the fact that Alzheimer's disease is more common among people

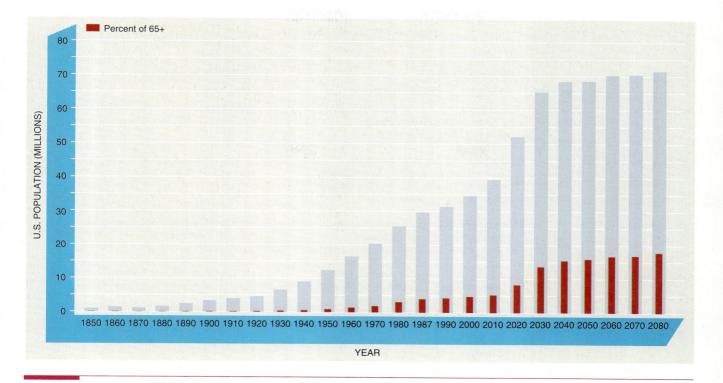

Figure 14-1
Census projection showing aging of population
Source: U.S. Bureau of the Census (1975, 1989); U.S. Department of Commerce (1989).

over the age of 85. Estimates of the number of people older than 85 who have this disease range from 20 percent (Jarvik, 1988) to almost 50 percent (Evans et al., 1989). This is precisely the part of the population expected to show the greatest increase in size in the next half-century. As this oldest segment of the population grows, many chronic diseases, including Alzheimer's, will become significant public health problems.

BRAIN CHANGES   Three characteristic changes are seen in the autopsied brains of people with Alzheimer's. The first is the formation of **neurofibrillary tangles**, in which the cellular material within the cell bodies of neurons becomes replaced by densely packed, twisted protein *microfibrils*, or tiny strands. The second change is the development throughout the cortex of **senile plaques**, which are clusters of dead or dying neurons mixed together with fragments of protein molecules. The third change involves **granulovacuolar degeneration**, in which clumps of granular material accumulate within the cell bodies of neurons and result in the abnormal functioning of these neurons. The cause and significance of these abnormal developments in the brain are not understood, but it seems clear that their existence plays some role in the deterioration of functioning seen in the afflicted individual's behavior.

STAGES   Alzheimer's disease progresses in stages that are marked by progressive deterioration of cognitive functioning along with changes in personality and interpersonal relationships. As you can see from Table 14–1 (on page

354), the behavioral symptoms of dementia due to Alzheimer's disease are memory loss, disorientation, decline of judgment, deterioration of social skills, and extreme changeability or flatness of affect. These symptoms evolve over time, but their rate of progress varies from person to person (Teri et al., 1990). Other psychological symptoms include agitation, wandering, hallucinations, delusions, aggressiveness, insomnia, demandingness, and an inability to adapt to new routines or surroundings (Ham, 1990).

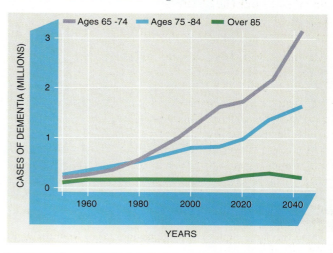

Figure 14-2
Proportion of population with dementia
Source: Cook-Deegan & Whitehouse (1987).

Table 14-1 Phases of Dementia

Stage	Cognitive Deficits	Personality Changes
Forgetfulness	Forgetting where one has placed familiar objects and names but no objective deficits in work or social situations.	Appropriate concern with mild forgetfulness.
Early confusional	Getting lost in going to familiar place; co-workers and family notice forgetfulness of names and words; poor reading comprehension; inability to concentrate.	Denial of memory problems, but anxiety accompanies symptoms of forgetfulness and confusion.
Late confusional	Decreased knowledge of current events; forgetting of one's personal history; decreased ability to travel or handle finances.	Very obvious use of denial regarding memory problems. Flattening of affect and withdrawal from challenging situations.
Early dementia	Inability to recall some important features of current life such as address, telephone number, or names of grandchildren; inability to recall some personal facts such as the name of one's high school. Some disorientation with regard to time or date.	No assistance needed for toileting or eating but may have difficulty choosing proper clothing.
Middle dementia	May occasionally forget name of spouse; largely unaware of all recent events and experiences and many events of past life. Unaware of surroundings, and season of year, but can distinguish familiar from unfamiliar people.	Totally dependent on spouse or caregiver for survival. Many personality and emotional changes, including becoming delusional, obsessive, and anxious. Fails to follow through on intentions due to forgetfulness.
Late dementia	Loss of all verbal abilities. Incontinent of urine and requires toileting and feeding. Loss of basic psychomotor skills, including ability to walk.	Complete deterioration of personality and social skills; individual is almost totally unresponsive to all but the simplest form of communication.

Source: Adapted from Reisberg, (1983).

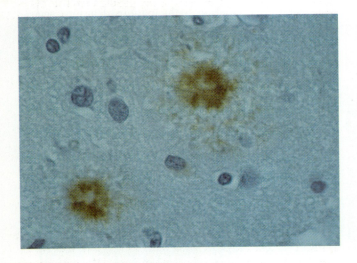

These two large circles are senile plaques taken from the brain of a patient with Alzheimer's disease. Each has a central core of amyloid protein surrounded by a circle of deteriorated neurons. Scientists believe that these amyloid deposits might hold the secrets to the ravaging effects of Alzheimer's disease on the brain.

The progression from early to late dementia in people with Alzheimer's usually occurs over a 5- to 10-year period, ending in death through the development of complicating diseases such as pneumonia. If psychotic symptoms such as hallucinations and delusions are present in the early phase of the disorder, this may be predictive of early cognitive decline (Rubin, 1990).

■ *Conditions and diseases with symptoms that can resemble Alzheimer's*

It is important to keep in mind that diseases other than Alzheimer's can cause dementia. In fact, dementia can also develop in response to prolonged exposure to substances such as industrial chemicals, intense fumes from house paint, styrene used in plastics manufacturing, and petroleum-distilled fuels. People who work with these substances can experience a variety of cognitive and physical problems such as memory impairment, slow reaction time, reduced dexterity, poor concentration, irritability, fatigue, and headaches. Their memory, learning, and attentional abilities can become impaired, and they may have difficulty with abstract concepts.

Dementia can also result from nutritional deficiencies. Severely undernourished people are prone to developing folate deficiency, which can lead to progressive cerebral atrophy. If the deficiency is not counteracted by dietary improvements, the individual can become depressed and show various cognitive impairments such as poor memory and abstract reasoning. Many chronic heavy users of alcohol develop a thiamine deficiency which leads to an organic disorder known as Korsakoff's syndrome, which we will discuss in Chapter 15.

Sometimes dementia associated with physical disorders and toxic reactions can be reversed if the person receives prompt and appropriate medical treatment. However, if no intervention is made for a treatable dementia in the early stages, the brain damage tragically becomes irreversible. The more widespread the structural damage to the brain, the lower the chances that the afflicted person will ever regain lost functions.

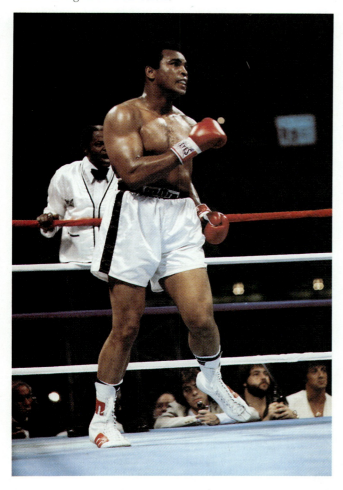

Muhammad Ali's medical condition highlights the fact that people of any age can develop neurological disorders. Ali suffers from Parkinson's disease, which involves tremors, slowness of movement, muscle rigidity, and balance difficulty. Some have speculated that the severe beatings Ali suffered in his final matches were due to his inability to move quickly (Hauser, 1991).

PHYSICAL DISEASES   **Pick's disease** is a relatively rare degenerative disease that affects the frontal and temporal lobes of the cerebral cortex. In addition to suffering memory problems, people with this disorder become socially disinhibited, acting inappropriately and impulsively; at other times they may act apathetic and unmotivated. In contrast to the sequence of changes shown by people with Alzheimer's disease, people with Pick's disease undergo personality alterations before they begin to suffer memory problems. The cause of Pick's disease is unknown, but there is some evidence that it is hereditary (Chui, 1989).

Parkinson's disease involves neuronal degeneration of the basal ganglia, subcortical structures that control the person's motor movements. Deterioration of diffuse areas of the cerebral cortex may also occur. Parkinson's disease is usually progressive, with the most striking feature of the disorder involving various motor disturbances. At rest, the person's hands, ankles, or head may shake involuntarily. The person's muscles become rigid, and it is difficult to initiate movement, a symptom referred to as **akinesia**. A general slowing of motor activity, known as **bradykinesia**, also occurs, as does a loss of fine coordination. The individual's face appears expressionless and speech becomes stilted, losing its normal rhythmic quality. People with Parkinson's disease walk with a slowed, shuffling gait; they have difficulty starting to walk and, once started, difficulty in stopping. In addition to these motor abnormalities, they show signs of cognitive deterioration such as slowed scanning on visual recognition tasks, diminished conceptual flexibility, and slowing on motor response tests. They have difficulty producing words on tests that demand verbal fluency. However, many cognitive functions, such as attention, concentration, and immediate memory remain intact. Because of the tremendous frustration that they usually feel about their deteriorating physical abilities, many people with this disorder suffer from decreased self-esteem and become depressed (Knight et al., 1988; Starkstein & Robinson, 1991).

In **Huntington's disease**, there is widespread deterioration of subcortical brain structures and parts of the frontal cortex that control motor movements. The corpus callosum, which connects the two halves of the brain, also degenerates. Huntington's disease is a hereditary condition whose symptoms first appear in adulthood, sometimes as early as the age of 20. The disease was once called Huntington's "chorea" (from the Greek *choreia*, meaning to dance) because of the prominence of involuntary spasmodic and often tortuous movements that ultimately become profoundly disabling. Huntington's disease also causes cognitive and personality disturbances (Caine & Shoulson, 1983). People with this disorder have difficulty completing tasks that require speed or mental tracking, that lack familiarity and structure, and that require complex perceptions or responses. In terms of personality changes, people with Huntington's disease can become irritable, anxious, emotionally unpredictable, impaired in their social judgment, and aggressively or sexually impulsive. Depression also

Jacqueline du Pré was regarded as one of the most gifted and promising young cellists in the world when, at the age of 26, she began to experience difficulty fingering and bowing the cello. She soon discovered that these symptoms were the first signs of progressive multiple sclerosis. Tragically, this disease ended her career and eventually led to her death in 1987 at the age of 42.

frequently accompanies this disabling illness (Mindham et al., 1985). Because of these symptoms, the disorder may be incorrectly diagnosed as schizophrenia or a mood disorder even if the sufferer has had no prior history suggestive of schizophrenia. Yet, at the same time, people with Huntington's disease can also appear apathetic because of their decreasing ability to plan, initiate, or carry out complex activities. Their movement disorder gets in the way of sustained performance of any kind of behavior, even maintaining an upright posture, and eventually most become bedridden. It is thought that loss of neurons that contain the inhibitory neurotransmitter GABA may play a role in the degenerative process underlying this disease (Heuser et al., 1991).

Multiple sclerosis is a progressive neurological disease that begins during early adulthood and involves deterioration of the fatty insulation around nerve fibers (the *myelin sheath*), and the subsequent forming of plaques around the areas of myelin degeneration. This disease process disrupts the normal transmission of electrochemical impulses from neuron to neuron. People with this disease experience weakness or loss of limb control, uneven or unrhythmic speech, eye muscle problems causing double vision, loss of sphincter control, and numbness of sensation. It is also common for people with multiple sclerosis to experience cognitive impairments such as memory deterioration (McIntosh-Michaelis et al., 1991). As the disease progresses, the individual may undergo mood changes, including depression and preoccupation with physical disabilities or, conversely, denial of physical problems. Further into the disease, the individual can become emotionally changeable, irritable, and highly distractible.

The disease known as **normal pressure hydrocephalus** results from obstruction of the flow of cerebral spinal fluid (CSF) so that this fluid begins to build up within the ventricles of the brain. As the ventricles enlarge to accommodate the fluid increase, CSF pressure returns to normal. Scarring from a previous injury or infection, or abnormalities such as hemorrhage or tumor are common causes of this disease. The main area of the brain damaged in this process is the midbrain reticular formation, leading to a variety of problems including disorientation, confusion, decreased attention span, and mental and motor slowing. Incontinence and gait disturbances are two characteristic symptoms of this disorder. The individual may become depressed about these handicapping impairments, because self-awareness is retained until late in the progress of disease. In later stages the disorder resembles Alzheimer's disease, and at that point it is incurable; however, in the early stages it can be reversed by a relatively straightforward neurosurgical procedure.

In addition to these specific diseases, dementia can result from various other medical conditions. For example, infectious diseases such as neurosyphillis, encephalitis, tuberculosis meningitis, or localized infections in the brain can result in dementia. People who experience kidney failure may suffer symptoms of dementia caused by a toxic accumulation of substances that the kidneys cannot cleanse from the blood. People who develop certain kinds of brain tumors also experience cognitive impairments and other symptoms of dementia.

Dementia can also result from anoxia, oxygen deprivation to the brain, which may occur during surgery under general anesthesia or may result from carbon monoxide poisoning. Anoxia can have severe effects on many brain functions, because neurons quickly die if they are deprived of oxygen. Because neurons do not replace themselves, the loss of a significant number of neurons can lead to permanent impairments in such functions as new learning ability, attention, concentration, and tracking, and in tendencies to concrete thinking. The emotional effects of brain damage due to anoxia can include affective dulling and disinhibition as well as depression. The person's ability to plan, initiate, and carry out activities can be drastically reduced.

Another possible cause of dementia is cardiovascular disease affecting the supply of blood to the brain. Such a condition is called **vascular dementia**. At one time it was thought that arteriosclerosis ("hardening of the arteries") was the major cause of Alzheimer's disease. It was then found that the degenerative changes in the brains of people with Alzheimer's disease were very different from changes due to vascular illness. Vascular dementia is caused by the death of selected groups of neurons in the cerebral cortex when clusters of capillaries in the brain are cut off by *infarctions*, acute forms of circulatory disease. Myocardial infarction is the technical term for what is commonly referred to as a "heart attack." The dementia caused by multiple infarctions in the brain is due to a series of minor strokes that cut off the blood supply to different regions of the cortex.

Vascular dementia may resemble dementia due to Alzheimer's disease in some ways, but vascular dementia involves a pattern of cognitive functioning distinctly different from Alzheimer's. The typical clinical picture of vascular dementia is of certain cognitive functions remaining intact and others showing significant loss. This pattern is called

In diagnosing a person thought to have Alzheimer's disease, clinicians use a variety of approaches, including psychological testing. A primary focus of such testing includes evaluation of the individual's cognitive functions with particular attention to memory.

patchy deterioration, because the losses occur in patches or selected areas. Another unique feature of vascular dementia is that it shows a stepwise deterioration in intellectual functioning: a cognitive function that was relatively unimpaired is suddenly lost or severely deteriorates. This is in contrast to the gradual pattern shown by a person with Alzheimer's disease. While vascular dementia is still in its early stages, treatment of hypertension and vascular disease may prevent further progression of cognitive losses.

Diagnosis of vascular dementia can be aided by CT scanning, which reveals evidence of areas of hemorrhage or infarction. An electroencephalogram may also reveal useful information, such as focal abnormalities not evident in Alzheimer's. The absence of these findings cannot be used to rule out the diagnosis, though, because brain lesions must be at least one millimeter in size to be visible on a CT scan. Unfortunately, as with Alzheimer's disease, there are no clear behavioral patterns shown on psychological testing to facilitate accurate diagnosis of vascular dementia.

You can see, then, that a variety of physical conditions can cause dementia in addition to Alzheimer's disease.

Some of these conditions are reversible, such as folate deficiency, and if treated promptly, the individual can be spared an unnecessary, painful, and ultimately fatal decline.

DEPRESSION   It might surprise you to learn that many depressed people have cognitive symptoms that mimic those apparent in the early stages of Alzheimer's disease. These cognitive changes constitute a condition known as **pseudodementia**, or false dementia (Caine, 1981; Wells, 1979). It is estimated that between 10 and 20 percent of depressed elderly persons have such symptoms (Reynolds et al., 1988). Complicating the situation is the fact that depression may also co-exist with Alzheimer's disease (Merriam et al., 1988), particularly during the early to middle phases when the individual is aware of the onsent of the disorder and is still cognitively intact enough to realize the deterioration that lies ahead. It has also been suggested that there exists a depressive dementia which involves disturbances of mood and cognition, and is due to underlying neurobiological disease (Emery & Oxman, 1992).

Clinicians who are treating a cognitively impaired depressed person are faced with the difficult task of trying to determine whether an individual's depression is caused by Alzheimer's disease or whether an individual's cognitive impairment is caused by depression. It is important to distinguish between pseudodementia and Alzheimer's disease, because the symptoms of depression can be successfully treated. Several indicators can help in the process of differentiating depression from dementia. Depressed individuals are more keenly aware of their impaired cognition, and frequently complain about their faulty memory, although at present it is believed that there is no physical basis for their complaints. In contrast, the individual with Alzheimer's tries to hide or minimize the extent of impairment or explain it away when the loss cannot be concealed. As the disorder progresses, people with Alzheimer's disease lose awareness of the extent of their cognitive deficits and may even report improvement as they lose their capacity for critical self-awareness. The order of symptom development also differs between people with Alzheimer's and depressed individuals. In depressed elderly people, mood changes precede memory loss; the reverse is true for people with Alzheimer's disease.

People with pseudodementia can also be distinguished by the nature of their symptoms, which follow the classic pattern seen in people with major depression. The depressed person is anxious, has difficulty sleeping, shows disturbed appetite patterns, and experiences suicidal thoughts, low self-esteem, guilt, and lack of motivation. People with dementia, in contrast, experience unsociability, uncooperativeness, hostility, emotional instability, confusion, disorientation, and reduced alertness. People with pseudodementia also are likely to have a history of prior depressive episodes which may have gone undiagnosed. Their memory problems and other cognitive complaints have a very abrupt onset compared with people with dementia, who suffer a more slowly developing downward course (Wells, 1979). Another clue to detecting the difference between Alzheimer's and pseudodementia may be found by exploring the individual's recent past to determine whether a stressful event has occurred that may have precipitated the onset of depression.

■ *Diagnosis of Alzheimer's disease*

Because of the importance of early diagnosis to rule out treatable dementias, researchers and clinicians have devoted significant energy and attention to the development of behavioral tests for diagnosing Alzheimer's disease in its initial stages. An erroneous diagnosis would be a fatal mistake if the person had a dementia that would have been reversible if the proper treatment had been applied when the symptoms first became evident. Similarly, if the individual had a disorder with a nonorganic basis, a crucial opportunity to intervene would have been missed.

Regrettably, no valid indicators currently exist for the certain diagnosis of Alzheimer's disease in its early stages. A definitive diagnosis of Alzheimer's disease can only be made after the person has died by studying microscopic changes in brain tissue. Because biopsies of the brain are dangerous and impractical, the best that can be done for a living person with the symptoms of dementia is to administer a variety of clinical and neurological tests and to infer a diagnosis of Alzheimer's if no other specific cause can be determined.

Various strategies have been attempted to improve on this imprecise and unsatisfactory method of diagnosis. In the 1970s, CT scanning was used to detect structural lesions capable of producing the patient's symptoms of cognitive deterioration. This method showed that brain atrophy and hydrocephalus (expansion of the ventricular space in the brain) associated with advanced dementia of all types could be diagnosed easily. However, there was nothing specific in the CT pattern that would uniquely identify Alzheimer's disease (Jagust et al., 1987). PET scans became available as diagnostic measures in the late 1970s, using radioactive tracers specific for brain metabolism and blood flow (Budinger, 1987). These newer tests were advantageous because of their greater sensitivity to changes in the brain at earlier stages of the disease. In the early 1980s, these methods led to the discovery of a particular pattern of metabolic defects that was specific to Alzheimer's disease. So far, however, this method is not regarded as definitive enough to be used as a sole indicator for the presence of Alzheimer's. Similarly, the hope that MRI could detect brain abnormalities associated with Alzheimer's disease has failed to meet with success (Kumar et al., 1992).

Another approach to diagnosing dementia combines neurological and neuropsychological evaluations, using cognitive measures along with measures of brain metabolism (Foster et al., 1984). Still other experimental approaches rely on purely psychological methods, involving identification of abnormalities in the cognitive processes of memory and learning (Weingartner et al., 1987) or performance on neuropsychological tests (Storandt, 1990). These kinds of tests have promise, but they are still far from satisfactory.

Several aspects of performance on cognitive tests, however, can at least serve to make the important distinc-

tion between dementia and pseudodementia (Lezak, 1983). Depressed people are able to use language properly, and they can remember new information over a delayed period of time even when their immediate recall is impaired. Depressed individuals make errors of *omission* (not answering questions), while demented individuals make errors of *commission* (making up answers just to be able to say something). Performance by depressed people on drawing and construction tasks may be careless, shabby, or incomplete as a result of apathy, low energy level, and poor motivation, but with enough time and encouragement they may make a recognizable and often fully adequate response. In contrast, people with Alzheimer's show signs of aphasia, apraxia, or agnosia, and severe impairment on drawing and constructional tasks. They make virtually no appropriate response or make a fragment of a response that may be distorted by perseverations despite their obvious efforts to do as asked.

Currently, the most common practice for diagnosing Alzheimer's disease is to use a specialized form of the mental status examination (see Table 14–2). Some of the deficits shown by people with Alzheimer's disease on this type of mental status examination include circumstantiality, perseveration, and lack of richness and detail in descriptions of objects, people, and events. Various activities of daily life such as using the telephone, mailing a letter, using money,

---

Table 14–2 Mental State Measure Used to Assess Alzheimer's Disease

Questions to assess orientation:
What is the (year) (season) (date) (day) (month)?
Where are we: (state) (county) (town) (hospital) (floor)?

Assessment of memory for new information:
Name 3 objects: 1 second to say each. Then ask the patient all 3 after you have said them. Give 1 point for each correct answer. Then repeat them until he or she learns all 3.
Count trials and record.

Attention and calculation:
Serial 7s (subtracting 7 from 100 serially). 1 point for each correct answer. Stop after 5 answers. Alternatively spell "world" backwards.

Memory recall:
Ask for the 3 objects repeated above. Give 1 point for each correct answer.

Language:
Name a pencil, and watch.
Repeat the following "No ifs, ands, or buts."
Follow a 3-stage command:
  "Take a paper in your right hand, fold it in half, and put it on the floor."
Read and obey the following:
  CLOSE YOUR EYES
Write a sentence.
Copy design (2 intersecting pentagons).

Assessment of level of consciousness:

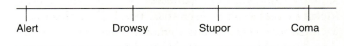

| Alert | Drowsy | Stupor | Coma |

Source: Folstein et al., (1975).

---

grocery shopping, grooming, and eating are also assessed (Lowenstein et al., 1989). At present, though, evidence of deficits in these aspects of functioning is not regarded as sufficient for a diagnosis of Alzheimer's disease.

A period of inpatient observation can also aid in the diagnosis of Alzheimer's disease. This method provides an opportunity to observe the individual in a variety of contexts and under a variety of cognitive and behavioral demands. For instance, people who recall things while in a hospital despite complaints of memory loss are unlikely to be suffering from dementia. On the other hand, disorientation during the nighttime hours, inappropriate grooming, difficulty learning new tasks in occupational therapy, and repeated confusion about medication may point to the likelihood of Alzheimer's disease.

■ Theories and treatments

All theories regarding the cause of Alzheimer's disease focus on biological abnormalities involving the nervous system. Other theoretical perspectives, however, can offer insight into understanding the impact of the disease on the individual's life and relationships with others.

One prominent biological theory proposes that the primary disturbances involved in Alzheimer's disease are in the acetylcholine neurotransmitter system, which is thought by many experts to be involved in processes of learning and memory (Coyle et al., 1983). According to this view, people with Alzheimer's disease have insufficient amounts of **choline acetyltransferase (CAT)**, which is essential for the synthesis of acetylcholine. As work in this area continues, researchers are also attempting to link changes at the biochemical level with the characteristic neurofibrillary tangles, senile plaques, and granulovacuolar degeneration that are associated with Alzheimer's disease (Geula & Mesulam, 1989). Whether these changes precede or follow changes at the biochemical level has yet to be discovered. Particularly important in understanding the symptoms of Alzheimer's disease is the fact that many of the biochemical and structural changes found in the brains of people with this disorder are in the area of the *hippocampus*, a structure in the limbic system involved in memory and learning of new information (Chui, 1989). It has been suggested that changes in this area of the brain may play a role in causing the cognitive deficits associated with Alzheimer's disease (Martin et al., 1987).

Another line of biological research has focused on diminished levels of cortical metabolism found in the temporoparietal region of the brains of people with Alzheimer's disease. This area of the brain plays an important role in language and cognitive functions. These metabolic changes could reflect an actual abnormality in glucose metabolism or simply normal metabolism occurring in fewer neurons because of a loss of tissue in this part of the brain (Jagust et al., 1987). Abnormal EEG patterns have also been detected in this area of the brain (Rice et al., 1990). If the abnormality in glucose metabolism is a primary effect of the disease, then this could suggest a possible mechanism for the degeneration of brain tissue caused by Alzheimer's.

THE TEMPORAL LOBE IN ALZHEIMER'S DISEASE

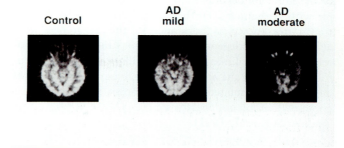

Pictured here are PET scans of the brains of a normal control subject, an individual in the early stages of Alzheimer's disease (AD mild), and one in the later stages of the disease (AD moderate). Darker areas reflect lower brain activity. The brain of the normal control shows normal levels of activity; the AD mild brain shows decreased activity in the temporal lobe; and the brain of the individual with more advanced Alzheimer's shows a more severe decrease in brain activity.

Evidence from studies of the incidence of Alzheimer's among family members suggests that genetic factors may play a role in causing the disorder (Breitner et al., 1986a, 1986b). Relatives of people with Alzheimer's are three times as likely as others to develop this disease (Jarvik, 1988). Other suggestive evidence of genetic factors is the fact that there is an increased risk of Down syndrome within families of people who develop Alzheimer's at a relatively young age. Furthermore, Alzheimer's disease commonly develops in people with Down syndrome who survive into their 30s and 40s (Turkel & Nusbaum, 1986). Interestingly, the brain deficits of people with Alzheimer's resemble those of people with Down syndrome; in both disorders the areas of the brain that involve learning and memory are particularly affected (Schapiro & Rapoport, 1988). In the late 1980s, a good deal of excitement was generated by the possibility that an Alzheimer gene is located on chromosome 21, the same chromosome that plays a part in Down syndrome (St. George-Hyslop et al., 1987). However, as was the case in the search for chromosomal defects in schizophrenia and bipolar disorder, the solution to the Alzheimer's puzzle was not to come so easily. Other teams of researchers using a different sample of families were unable to establish a link between Alzheimer's and the marker on chromosome 21 (Roses et al., 1990; Schellenberg et al., 1988). If there is a genetic contribution to the disease, the pattern of inheritance is more complicated than was originally thought.

There is some exciting evidence on the horizon concerning the role of ß-amyloid protein, a substance known to form the core of senile plaques. Some researchers have suggested that a genetic defect causes the high accumulation of a ß-amyloid protein found throughout the brain in people with Alzheimer's (Behrouz et al., 1991; Joachim & Selkoe, 1989; Kosik, 1992). It is unclear whether accumulation of this protein is the cause of senile plaques, or whether it is the outcome of neural degeneration in the cortex. To find answers to this question, researchers injected the ß-amyloid protein into the brains of laboratory rats and observed neural degeneration similar to that found in people with Alzheimer's. Further, by injecting another neurotransmitter known as "substance P," the researchers were able to halt the degeneration process. The ß-amyloid protein may also be linked to neurofibrillary tangles; the neurons surrounding the areas where the ß-amyloid protein was deposited accumulated a protein known as *tau*, which is contained in neurofibrillary tangles (Marx, 1991, citing Yankner & Kowall, 1991).

Applying some of the latest genetics technology, several teams of researchers working independently pursued this line of investigation by inserting genes that produce ß-amyloid protein or precursors of this protein into mouse brains (Kawabata et al., 1991; Quon et al., 1991; Wirak et al., 1991). The mice were reported to develop plaques, tangles, and degeneration of neurons in the hippocampus and cortex, conditions that strongly resembled those found in humans with Alzheimer's. These findings were taken as providing strong evidence of a genetic cause of Alzheimer's disease. However, the picture is far more complicated; suspicions regarding the validity of some of the findings have been raised and suggest that at least some of these data were mistaken (Jucker et al., 1992; Marx, 1992; Wirak et al., 1992). While this controversy is likely to continue for some time to come, evidence of abnormally high levels of amyloid protein in an individual's brain may eventually serve as an early diagnostic test for the disease (Bissette et al., 1991).

You may have heard about another theory that proposed that a toxic accumulation of aluminum in the cells of the brain causes Alzheimer's (Schiffman, 1986; Ward, 1986). This controversial theory gained a great deal of media attention in the 1980s. According to this view, aluminum, a trace element in the environment, enters the brain through the nasal passages and damages the cortex, beginning with the olfactory cortex. It was even thought that aluminum pots and pans might be implicated in causing Alzheimer's. Aluminum is thought to be an important toxin because abnormal accumulations of it are often found inside neurons that have neurofibrillary tangles. Further, increased aluminum levels have been found in autopsies of the brains of people who had the disease. The support for this theory, however, is mixed.

The cause of Alzheimer's will ultimately be found by researchers working within the biological perspective, but until then, there is no hope of finding a cure for the disorder. Even when a cure is discovered, though, there will be a need to apply other theoretical perspectives to understanding the concerns of people with Alzheimer's. From a psychological perspective, when the disease is in its early stages, the individual is likely to experience emotional distress and depression over cognitive symptoms such as memory loss (Reifler et al., 1987), and this distress can contribute significantly to whatever cognitive decline can be attributed to the disease itself. People with Alzheimer's disease are also likely to experience symptoms of other psychological disorders, including psychotic symptoms, anxiety,

disturbed behaviors such as wandering and aggressiveness, and sleep disorders; these symptoms can occur early in the progression of the disease (Eisdorfer et al., 1992).

Although experts in the field of Alzheimer's have not yet succeeded in explaining the causes of this disorder, they have made impressive advances in understanding the social and familial impact of this condition. Particularly impressive has been work pertaining to the emotional toll on the family.

Put yourself in the place of a person responsible for caring for a family member with Alzheimer's disease. Imagine what it would be like to care for a person whose behavior is at times unpredictable and bizarre, or who cannot remember an action taken only moments earlier. The burden is tremendous, and those close to the afflicted person are certain to be deeply affected (Chenoweth & Spencer, 1986; George & Gwyther, 1986; Pearlin et al., 1990; Zarit et al., 1986). (See Table 14–3.) Partners of people with Alzheimer's face a dramatic redefinition of their intimate relationship as they assume the role of caregivers (Wright, 1991). They are likely to find themselves emotionally drained, exacerbating their own problems with aging (Vitaliano et al., 1991). For example, researchers have found that older men, many of whom have not been socialized to be caregivers, are likely to become depressed when faced with caring for wives with Alzheimer's disease (Schulz & Williamson, 1991).

But emotional strain is not limited just to the spouse. Adult children are also deeply affected, and may become depressed and anxious themselves (Dura et al., 1991). Relationships between siblings can become strained if the primary caregiver feels resentful that other siblings are not contributing enough to the care of their parent (Lerner et al., 1991). Such perceptions may arise, in part, from the caregiver's expecting greater help from siblings than the sib-

Caring for an elderly friend or relative can be emotionally difficult and taxing, particularly for older people who themselves have health problems.

lings are able or willing to provide. To the extent that such a conflict exists, the stress on the caregiver is greatly increased (Strawbridge & Wallhagen, 1991). Whether spouse or child, the individual who serves as the primary caregiver is likely to take on the major share of the responsibility for the family member with Alzheimer's disease without the help of members of the extended family (Baum & Page, 1991). At the same time, many afflicted elderly individuals are sensitive to the effects of their illness on family members and wish to avoid being a burden.

Feelings of guilt, obligation, and frustration are likely to reverberate throughout the family system when a family member develops Alzheimer's. These feelings become heightened as the disease progresses to more advanced stages and the question of institutionalization begins to be considered. As much as family members wish to avoid mov-

A visit to an elderly friend or relative in a nursing home often benefits both the older person and the visitor.

ing their relative to a nursing home, this step becomes almost inevitable (Lieberman & Kramer, 1991). Caregivers must then cope with even more guilt because they feel as though they are abandoning their parent or spouse. At the same time, they must contend with the high cost that institutionalization usually entails. When family members feel that they are not doing a good job in their helping role, they are especially prone to feeling depressed (Townsend et al., 1989).

As demoralizing as the situation may sound, there may actually be some positive aspects of caring for relatives with Alzheimer's (Shulz et al., 1990). It may be emotionally rewarding to see the relative respond positively to the caregiver's efforts, or for the caregiver to feel supported by other family members and friends (Kinney & Stephens, 1989).

Although we can be certain that Alzheimer's disease is not rooted in maladaptive learning, the behavioral approach can nevertheless provide a framework for understanding how certain inappropriate behaviors are maintained. For example, the attention associated with the enactment of certain behaviors may reinforce the likelihood that the afflicted individual will continue to engage in these behaviors. On a practical level, behavioral approaches provide a structure for analyzing the maladaptive behaviors of the individual and devising an appropriate plan for carrying out the activities of daily life.

Although Alzheimer's is based on a biological disease process, much can be gained by drawing upon what the other approaches have to offer regarding the ways in which those who are afflicted can be helped. Because no medical cure exists for Alzheimer's disease, treatment efforts are directed toward maintaining the individual as long as possible at his or her current level of functioning. Various services are available within the community, including diagnostic and medical assessment programs, counseling, support groups, financial planning assistance, and home care services (Coyne, 1991). Many institutions that care for elderly persons offer day care services so that caregivers can work outside the home. Long-term facilities may also offer respite services, allowing caregivers to leave their relatives in the care of the institution for a period of several days to a few weeks while the caregivers take needed breaks or vacations. These programs, which involve short stays or daily care within the institution can make the ultimate transition to institutional living easier for Alzheimer's patients and for those who care for them.

Researchers have desperately sought a cure for Alzheimer's, but at present only some minor symptomatic relief is available. A number of medications have been used on an experimental basis, but none to date have provided anything approaching significant results (Satlin & Cole, 1988). These medications include vasodilators or metabolic enhancers that increase the blood flow to the brain and that affect neurotransmission and the metabolism of neurons. Choline-based substances also may be used to increase the activity of acetylcholine (Wecker, 1990).

Based in part on medical research that began with studies on laboratory animals in the 1970s, various methods of preventing the disease have attained a certain amount of popularity. As researchers began to focus their attention on CAT deficiencies, there was increased interest in lecithin, a natural substance that promotes the manufacturing of CAT in the nervous system. Controlled studies of drugs containing lecithin, however, failed to show any preventative or treatment effects (Becker & Giacobini, 1988). More recently, researchers have been experimenting with a drug called *tetrahydroaminoacridine* (or *tacrine*), which decreases the activity of *cholinesterase*, an enzyme that breaks down acetylcholine in the nervous system. After some initial enthusiasm about the beneficial effects of tacrine on cognitive functioning (Summers et al., 1986), a set of negative findings shattered the hope that these drugs could reverse or minimize the effects of Alzheimer's disease on memory dysfunction (Chatellier & Lacomblez, 1990; Gauthier et al., 1990; Weinstein et al., 1991).

More success has been achieved in using medications to treat other symptoms, such as depression, in the early phases of the disorder (Teri et al., 1991). Neuroleptics are used to treat the symptoms of paranoid thinking, hallucinations, and agitation that sometimes accompany Alzheimer's. Benzodiazepines can be given to treat agitation as well as anxiety. Although these medications can be useful, they must be administered with great care (Satlin & Cole, 1988; Teri et al., 1991), particularly in light of the fact that the rate at which drugs are metabolized is slower in elderly persons than in younger adults, possibly leading to more toxic side effects in elderly people with Alzheimer's.

Although psychodynamic theory presents no pertinent explanations for causes of Alzheimer's or effective intervention for those who are afflicted, insight-oriented therapy can be helpful in treating close ones. As you can imagine, the emotional reactions of loved ones are usually intense and conflict-laden. Perhaps they feel guilty or angry about the circumstances relating to the severe disturbance being experienced by a spouse, parent, or loved one. Psychodynamic techniques can offer the clinician the means for exploring some of these feelings (Rose & DelMaestro, 1990).

In line with the behavioral perspective's emphasis on maladaptive behaviors rather than on disease processes, behavior therapists attempt to maximize the individual's ability to adapt to the environment, by focusing on dressing, bathing, cooking, and social skills. Disruptive behaviors (such as wandering or incontinence) that make it hard for caregivers to manage the individual (Burton et al., 1992) can be reduced through carefully designed behavioral assessment and training programs (Hussian, 1981; Teri & Lewinsohn, 1986). Similarly, assessment of the reinforcements the individual is receiving for engaging in excessively dependent behaviors can form the basis for a behavioral management program that rewards independence (Sperbeck & Whitbourne, 1981).

Cognitive-behavioral interventions can also be used to treat depression associated with Alzheimer's, perhaps by encouraging a client to think less about the distressing impact of memory impairment, and to focus more productively on ways of compensating for memory problems. The therapist might also work with the client to provide a structured environment and simplified routines that are not so reliant on well-functioning memory (Teri & Gallagher-Thompson, 1991). Cognitive-behavioral therapy may also be helpful in alleviating depression in family members. For example, a wife may hold the belief that she is the only person capable of providing care for her husband. By framing this belief as a dysfunctional attitude, a therapist may be able to help the wife to take advantage of services offered by other caregivers, at least occasionally (Lewin & Lundervold, 1990).

In incorporating a family systems perspective into treatment, some clinicians use an intergenerational approach, in which family members of all generations are brought into therapy. One aim of this kind of therapy could be to give the family members with primary responsibility an opportunity to air frustrations and concerns about having to cope with the difficult, almost overwhelming, task of caring for their relative. Family members would also be encouraged to work together on solutions to the many practical problems faced in caring for a person with dementia. Therapy may proceed over the course of a number of years, tailored to the particular developmental stage of the family and to the current needs of the family member with the disorder.

As sensible as family therapy and family support groups may seem, they are not widely used (Coyne et al., 1990). There are a number of reasons for this underutilization, including a lack of knowledge and familiarity with mental health services and lack of time because the caregiving role is so demanding. To overcome these problems, telephone information and referral services have been developed that provide emotional support along with useful knowledge about Alzheimer's (Coyne, 1991). These services can include peer networks, where caregivers can talk to other caregivers (Goodman & Pynoos, 1990). Computer networks are also being developed, including an electronic encyclopedia in which caregivers can find information about Alzheimer's disease, the experience of caregiving, clinical care, and local services. Through this network, people can

Some elderly people are able to take advantage of computer networks that provide information and support for relatives of Alzheimer's patients.

leave and respond to messages and questions regarding the care of their relatives with Alzheimer's (Brennan et al., 1991). Families can also obtain information in more traditional ways, such as through self-help books that are widely available in paperback form (e.g., Mace & Rabins, 1991).

You can see, then, that although the prospect of Alzheimer's is frightening and painful for all individuals involved, a number of interventions are available. Until a cure for the disorder is found, however, clinicians must be content to see their gains measured less as progress toward a cure and more as success in prolonging the period of maximum functioning for the individual and the individual's family.

ALZHEIMER'S DISEASE: THE PERSPECTIVES REVISITED

The cognitive impairments associated with organic disorders are, by definition, best understood from a biological perspective. However, the biological perspective has not yet produced a viable treatment for one of the most devastating of these disorders, Alzheimer's disease. Until a cure is found, individuals and their families whose lives are touched by the disease must be willing to try a variety of approaches to alleviate the suffering caused by Alzheimer's. Many research programs are currently underway to explore strategies for reducing the stress placed on caregivers. Some of these approaches involve innovative, high-technology methods, such as computer networks; others take the more traditional approach of providing emotional support to afflicted individuals and their families. The application of cognitive-behavioral and other methods of therapy to helping people cope with Alzheimer's represents another useful approach. It seems that the bottom line in all this research on understanding and treating those affected by Alzheimer's disease is that it is not necessary for psychologists to wait until biomedical researchers discover a cure. Much can be done to improve the quality of life for people suffering from Alzheimer's and to maintain as long as possible their functioning and their dignity.

Table 14–4	ALZHEIMER'S DISEASE: A SUMMARY CHART OF PERSPECTIVES		
BIOLOGICAL	**FAMILY SYSTEMS**	**BEHAVIORAL**	**COGNITIVE-BEHAVIORAL**
Acetylcholine deficiencies. Deterioration of temperoparietal region of the brain. Genetic defect possibly linked in unknown way to excess of ß-amyloid protein. Accumulation of trace elements such as aluminum.	Primary caregiver is placed under heavy stress by responsibility of caring for Alzheimer's patient; this stress can have an impact on the family system.	Some dysfunctional behaviors maintained by attention and reinforcement.	Beliefs about personal incompetence can cause worsening of cognitive functioning; dysfunctional beliefs of caregivers add to their sense of burden.
Treatment: Medications to treat associated conditions such as depression and psychotic symptoms; no treatments available to slow process of brain deterioration although efforts have been made to develop choline enhancers and vasodilators to improve brain functioning.	**Treatment:** Respite and family support groups and other forms of group support for family members.	**Treatment:** Reinforcement contingencies to maximize independent behavior for as long as possible and to reduce the frequency of disruptive behaviors.	**Treatment:** Depression in early stages can be treated by examining and challenging dysfunctional beliefs; family members can be helped to view their responsibilities in a more realistic manner.

Return to the Case

Irene Heller

Irene's History

In order to put together a picture of Irene Heller's life history, I had to rely on her as well as Jonathan for details. For parts of the story, she was coherent and accurate in her recall. For other parts, however, she left out pieces of information which Jonathan had to fill in. Fortunately, Jonathan had collected a considerable amount of information about his mother from relatives and from Irene's friends. When he joined in telling the story, his voice was filled with sadness.

Irene grew up in a poor family in a small mining town in the Appalachians. Despite the family's poverty, she went away to a state university and upon graduation was offered a fellowship to pursue a doctorate in mathematics, an unusual opportunity for a woman in the 1930s. However, Irene declined the fellowship because she met and fell in love with Jonathan's father and they decided to get married. The couple had three sons in short succession. After the birth of their third child, Irene's husband became caught up in gambling and drinking, eventually leaving his wife and moving across the country, never to be heard from again.

Over the years Irene managed to get by, struggling as a poorly paid teacher. All three boys did well academically, going on to college and successful careers, one in New York City and the other two in the same city as Irene. By the time she retired from teaching, she had gained enormous respect from the people in her community, from her fellow teachers, and from the many students she helped through her role as teacher and advisor. She had accumulated a large enough pension to allow her to fulfill her life's dream of being able to travel, pursue her interests in gardening and needlework, and "just plain relax." However, her deterioration over the course of the past year had made those plans impossible.

Jonathan repeatedly noted that the onset of his mother's problems seemed to coincide with her retirement. He had come to recognize that her problems were far more serious than adjustment difficulties, but he couldn't help wondering how much the major life change had stirred up something that was waiting to happen. When I asked Jonathan to be specific in his description of his mother's problems, he discussed her memory difficulties, her poor judgment, and her inappropriate behaviors.

Assessment

Irene agreed to take a battery of tests, and I referred her to Dr. Furcolo, the staff neuropsychologist. Dr. Furcolo's report indicated that Irene had moderate cognitive deficits, including the inaccurate naming of objects, poor performance on tests of abstract reasoning and verbal fluency, disorientation as to time and place, and impairment of recent memory. Her intellectual abilities were relatively intact on scales of well-learned abilities measured in a familiar format and on scales of immediate memory recall not requiring any encoding processes. In contrast, she performed poorly on intelligence test scales involving unfamiliar, abstract, speed-dependent tasks that strained her capacity for attention and learning. Irene showed no signs of a psychotic disorder, nor did she suffer from specific symptoms of depression. Her symptoms appeared to have had a gradual onset and to have progressed over at least a 2-year period. Irene's annoyance when she described her past symptoms reinforced my impression, and Dr. Furcolo's, that her irritability was related to frustration over her declining mental faculties.

In a case such as Irene's, where there is a strong likelihood of physical involvement, a comprehensive medical workup is necessary, including laboratory tests and brain imaging. Irene agreed to my recommendation that she enter the hospital for 3 days of testing. The test results showed that her endocrine and metabolic functioning were normal, and there was no evidence of excessive alcohol or substance use. Irene's EKG, blood pressure, cerebral angiography (X-ray of cerebral blood vessels), and measure of cerebral blood flow showed no evidence of cardiovascular or cerebral-vascular abnormalities. The CT scan revealed some atrophy and enlargement of ventricles, but there was no evidence of focal lesions or trauma. Her EEG pattern showed some evidence of slowing, but no evidence of focal abnormalities.

Diagnosis

It was my assumption that Irene was suffering from more than just emotional problems related to her retirement. The medical workup and the nature of her symptoms pointed to a physically based disorder involving dementia; specifically, all signs pointed to a diagnosis of Senile Dementia of the Alzheimer Type.

Return to the Case

Irene Heller continued

Axis I.   Senile Dementia of the Alzheimer Type.
Axis II. Deferred.
Axis III. Alzheimer's disease.
Axis IV. Severity: 1. No acute events or enduring circumstances that may be relevant to the disorder. (Note: Irene's retirement occurred over 1 year ago, so it is not rated on this scale.)
Axis V.   Current Global Assessment of Functioning: 28. Highest Global Assessment of Functioning (past year): 60.

Case Formulation

I formed the diagnosis of Senile Dementia of the Alzheimer Type for this 67-year-old retired schoolteacher after extensive medical and neuropsychological testing and observation on an inpatient unit by an interdisciplinary team of professionals. Irene had been suffering from the symptoms of dementia for an undetermined period of time, possibly as long as 2 years, when she apparently first noted symptoms of long-term memory loss and difficulty registering new information into short-term memory. Although Irene's retirement occurred around the time when her symptoms first were appearing, it is likely that the retirement was not the cause of the onset of the disorder. It did not appear that retirement in and of itself posed a stress to Irene, who was looking forward to spending her time in travel and other leisure pursuits.

Planning a Treatment

Irene's dementia was sufficiently advanced so that a return to her home without any supervision or assistance was out of the question. I consulted with Mary Lyon, the hospital's social worker, about the options that were available locally for Irene. Ms. Lyon recommended that Irene move into an apartment complex that provided supervised living arrangements for elderly people. The income from the sale of her house plus her retirement pension would give her the financial resources to live in a reasonably large and comfortable apartment without the responsibilities of owning a home. In addition to helping arrange Irene's residential needs, Ms. Lyon consulted with Irene, Jonathan, and me about treatment options. We all agreed that a multidisciplinary treatment team was needed, including a psychologist, a social worker, and a counselor from the local Council on Aging. Particular attention was needed to help Irene develop methods of self-care and independent living.

Outcome of the Case

It has been more than 3 years since my consultation with Irene and her son. Sadly but predictably, matters have not improved in Irene's life. She initially moved into a supervised apartment and attended a day program at a local nursing home, but her deterioration was rapid and unyielding. After only 6 months, it was necessary for her to move into a nursing home, because she repeatedly endangered herself by carelessly disposing of matches and by wandering out of her apartment at night, and getting lost.

In a recent note I received from Jonathan, he explained how impaired his mother had become. Although she had some good days, in which they could converse satisfactorily, on most days she seemed unaware that he was her son. Jonathan ended his note with the expression of a faint hope that science might find some of the answers to this tragic disease.

SUMMARY

1. A group of disorders exists whose primary characteristic is cognitive impairment due to some type of brain damage or disease. These disorders have traditionally been referred to as *organic disorders*, reflecting the fact that they clearly have biological causes. Schizophrenia and other disorders may also have biological causes, but these are not viewed as being comparable to the organic changes that cause cognitive impairment disorders. Further, although other disorders such as schizophrenia may involve cognitive impairment, this impairment is not the primary characteristic. Another important consideration is the fact that other disorders caused by brain damage or disease may result in changes in mood or personality as their primary symptom.

2. *Delirium* is a disorder characterized by gross disturbances in the individual's thoughts, level of consciousness, speech, memory, orientation, perceptions, and motor patterns. Delusions, hallucinations, and emotional disturbances may also occur in delirium. Delirium is a temporary state, usually having a rapid onset, and is caused by a change in brain metabolism due to an abnormality somewhere in the body. The outcome of delirium depends on the underlying cause. If it

reflects a progressive neurological process, it is unlikely the individual will recover, and it is possible that the person will die as a result of the disease.

3. In amnesia, the individual suffers a loss of memory for past events and experiences. Chronic alcohol use is the most common form of organically caused amnesia. Retrograde amnesia is a term used to describe amnesia in which events prior to the organic disorder cannot be recalled. Anterograde amnesia involves a loss of the ability to learn or remember events that happen after the damage has occurred.

4. Dementia is a severe and progressive form of cognitive impairment caused by a gradual and invasive process of brain deterioration. Individuals with dementia experience memory loss as well as one or more symptoms involving problems with language (aphasia), or motor functioning (apraxia), and recognition of familiar objects (agnosia). Wernicke's aphasia involves an inability to comprehend words. Although the person can produce words, these words have no meaning to the person. Broca's aphasia is a loss of the ability to produce language, although the person's ability to comprehend the language of others remains intact.

5. A number of conditions can cause dementia in people of all ages, but the most common is Alzheimer's disease, which is most prevalent among people over the age of 65. Alzheimer's disease is found in approximately 6 percent of the over-65 population, but its incidence is estimated to be 20 to 50 percent among those over the age of 85. Because the over-85 population is rapidly growing, the number of people with Alzheimer's will rise dramatically by the middle of the twenty-first century unless a cure is found.

6. Three characteristic changes in neurons are associated with Alzheimer's disease: neurofibrillary tangles, senile plaques, and granulovacuolar degeneration. The cause of these changes is not yet known, but is seems clear that they play a role in the cognitive impairments associated with Alzheimer's. The symptoms of Alzheimer's progress in phases which typically end in death between 5 and 10 years after the symptoms initially appear.

7. Other diseases can cause symptoms that mimic Alzheimer's, including Pick's disease, Parkinson's disease, Huntington's disease, multiple sclerosis, normal pressure hydrocephalus, brain tumors, anoxia, kidney failure, and vascular dementia. Some of these diseases are reversible if treated in their initial stages, so accurate early diagnosis is essential. Depression and other psychological disorders can also cause symptoms similar to those of Alzheimer's disease. The pattern of cognitive impairment associated with depression is referred to as *pseudodementia*.

8. Although accurate early diagnosis of Alzheimer's is essential, no reliable physical or psychological tests currently exist that can produce a diagnosis with certainty until after the person has died and the brain tissue can be examined. Among the diagnostic measures used have been brain imaging techniques, mental status examinations, and neuropsychological testing. Differences between pseudodementia and Alzheimer's can be fairly reliably established through psychological testing.

9. The most widely accepted theories of Alzheimer's disease come from the biological perspective. Prominent among these theories is the hypothesis that a deficiency of acetylcholine is the cause of memory defects associated with Alzheimer's. Another theory focuses on the lower metabolic rate observed in the temporal lobe of the brain, an abnormality that could account for language deficits in people with the disorder. Genetic factors seem to play a role as well. In the early 1990s it was thought that the "Alzheimer's gene" had been found, but it appears now that the genetic contributions to Alzheimer's are more complex. Current research efforts appear most promising with regard to the β-amyloid protein, a substance known to form the core of senile plaques. An excess amount of this protein could trigger the neural degeneration that results in senile plaques. Less probable is the theory that Alzheimer's results from excess aluminum reaching the brain through the nasal passages.

10. Even though Alzheimer's disease is biologically caused, other theoretical perspectives have much to offer in the way of assessing the impact of this disorder and offering interventions. A psychological perspective is useful for understanding the emotional distress experienced early in the disorder as well as the later-evolving symptoms of psychosis, anxiety, wandering, aggressiveness, and sleep disorders. The family systems perspective considers the impact of Alzheimer's on the family members of the afflicted individual. The family is invariably affected in a number of significant ways by the disorder, because the care of the person with Alzheimer's typically falls on the spouse or the children, who experience considerable stress. Feelings of guilt and burden are likely to have an impact throughout the family system, particularly when the decision to institutionalize the afflicted family member becomes necessary. A behavioral perspective to understanding Alzheimer's focuses on the reinforcements that maintain dysfunctional and disruptive behaviors in the afflicted individual.

11. No biological treatment currently exists that can slow down or reverse the degenerative processes associated with Alzheimer's disease. Although researchers have experimented with medications that stimulate the production of CAT, and others that increase the oxygen supply to the brain, none of these have proven effective either in slowing or reversing brain changes. The best that can be hoped for is that the individual's other psychological or medical symptoms can be alleviated so that the individual's functioning is maintained at a

stable level for as long as possible. A variety of community and institutional services can help family members through this long and difficult process, including respite and day care services, counseling, peer groups, and telephone and computer networks offering information and support services. Alzheimer's patients and family members can also benefit from insight-oriented supportive therapy. Behavioral treatments can be used to maintain the individual's autonomy for as long as possible, and to reduce the frequency of disruptive behaviors. The depression associated with Alzheimer's and the strain experienced by family members can also be alleviated by cognitive-behavioral therapy.

12. There is no question that Alzheimer's disease brings tragedy to those older people and their families whose lives are touched by it. However, many strategies can benefit family members and afflicted individuals until a cure for the disorder is found. By taking advantage of the approaches offered by the various perspectives, people can reduce at least some of the suffering associated with Alzheimer's.

KEY TERMS

Organic: a term that, when used in the context of psychological disorders, refers to physical damage or dysfunction that affects the integrity of the brain. p. 350

Cognitive impairment disorders: a set of disorders due to brain damage or disease that involves loss or deterioration of cognitive abilities including judgment, language, thought, speech, memory, orientation, perception, or attention. p. 350

Epilepsy: a neurological condition that involves recurrent bodily seizures with associated changes in EEG patterns. p. 350

Delirium: a condition in which a person's thoughts, level of consciousness, speech, memory, orientation, perceptions, and motor patterns are very confused, unstable, or otherwise grossly disturbed. p. 351

Amnestic disorder: a cognitive impairment disorder involving inability to recall events of the recent past or to register new memories. p. 352

Retrograde amnesia: a loss of memories for events prior to the physical damage that caused the amnesia. p. 352

Anterograde amnesia: a loss of ability to learn or remember events taking place after the physical damage that caused the amnesia has occurred. p. 352

Dementia: a form of cognitive impairment involving generalized progressive deficits in a person's memory and learning of new information, ability to communicate, judgment, and motor coordination. p. 353

Aphasia: a loss of the ability to use language. p. 353

Wernicke's aphasia: a form of aphasia in which the individual is able to produce language, but has lost the ability to comprehend so that these verbal productions have no meaning. p. 353

Broca's aphasia: a form of aphasia that involves disturbance of language production, but intact comprehension abilities. p. 353

Apraxia: a loss of the ability to carry out coordinated bodily movements that could previously be performed without difficulty. p. 353

Agnosia: the inability to recognize familiar objects or experiences, despite the ability to perceive their basic elements. p. 354

Neurofibrillary tangles: a characteristic of Alzheimer's disease in which the material within the cell bodies of neurons becomes filled with densely packed, twisted protein microfibrils, or tiny strands. p. 355

Senile plaque: a characteristic of Alzheimer's disease in which clusters of dead or dying neurons become mixed together with fragments of protein molecules. p. 355

Granulovacuolar degeneration: a characteristic of Alzheimer's disease in which clumps of granular material accumulate within the cell bodies of neurons and result in the abnormal functioning of these neurons. p. 355

Pick's disease: a relatively rare degenerative disease that affects the frontal and temporal lobes of the cerebral cortex. p. 357

Parkinson's disease: a disease involving the degeneration of neurons in the subcortical structures that control motor movements. p. 357

Akinesia: a motor disturbance in which a person's muscles become rigid and it is difficult to initiate movement. p. 357

Bradykinesia: a motor disturbance involving a general slowing of motor activity. p. 357

Huntington's disease: a hereditary condition that can begin as early as a person's 20s involving a widespread deterioration of the subcortical brain structures that control motor movements, along with the motor areas in the frontal cortex. p. 357

Multiple sclerosis: a neurological disease that involves deterioration of the fatty insulation around nerve fibers. p. 358

Normal pressure hydrocephalus: a neurological disorder that involves obstruction of the flow of cerebral spinal fluid (CSF) so that the fluid begins to build up within the ventricles of the brain. p. 358

Vascular dementia: a form of dementia resulting from a vascular disease that causes deprivation of the blood supply to the brain. p. 358

Pseudodementia: literally *false dementia*, referring to an apparent loss of cognitive abilities due to depression. p. 359

Choline acetyltransferase (CAT): an enzyme that is essential for the synthesis of acetylcholine. p. 361

ß-amyloid protein: a substance known to form the core of senile plaques. p. 361

Case Report: Carl Wadsworth

One morning our receptionist gave me a message to call Dr. Elaine Golden, the director of residency training in the medical school, about a special client she needed to discuss with me. I called her back as soon as I found a free moment that afternoon. Dr. Golden told me that she was looking for a psychotherapist to treat one of the physicians in the surgical residency program. It was not unusual for physicians in training to be referred for treatment of depression or anxiety, but neither of those problems afflicted 31-year-old Dr. Carl Wadsworth. Rather, his problem involved an intense addiction to cocaine, a problem that had been brought to Dr. Golden's attention by Carl's wife, Anne. Increasingly alarmed about what was happening to Carl, she had urged him to seek help. Although he was reluctant at first, Carl eventually acquiesced to Anne's wishes and asked Dr. Golden to assist him in getting professional attention for his addiction.

I explained to Dr. Golden that Carl would have to request a consultation directly, so she handed the phone to Carl. With an urgency in his voice, Carl pleaded that I see him as soon as possible. We set up an intake appointment for later that day.

When first meeting Carl Wadsworth, I was struck by the fact that he seemed so young and unsure of himself. Yet, his face was marked by a gaunt and haggard look, suggesting that he was run down, perhaps to the point of exhaustion. My suspicions were confirmed. With a tremulous voice he told me the painful story of his seduction by cocaine and its eventual grasp over his whole life. He acknowledged that the problem had become so serious that he was at risk of destroying his family and ruining his career, realizations that had become startlingly

apparent to him when Anne, pregnant with their second child, told Carl that she would divorce him if he did not obtain professional help.

Carl explained that when he first began using cocaine one year ago, he fully believed that he could control his use and maintain it as a harmless pastime. Predictably, though, Carl began to rely on the drug more and more heavily. Money problems began to accumulate, and rather than attribute these to the expense of his cocaine habit, he blamed them on his inadequate salary. It became necessary to draw on the family bank account in order to pay the household bills. Carl soon began to spend more and more time away from home. Telling Anne that he was at work, he spent hours each day seeking ways to pick up extra cash. At the hospital his work had become sloppy, and Dr. Golden let him know that he was at risk of being dismissed from the hospital. His patients were complaining to the nursing staff about his abrupt and insensitive manner.

As we talked about the changes in Carl's professional behavior, I could see that he was becoming increasingly distraught, and when I asked him about his family life, he fought to hold back tears. He explained how much he loved his wife and daughter, but that he found himself losing control in his interactions with them. He had become irritable and impatient with them, and occasionally so angry that he came close to physical violence.

At the time Carl first came to see me, he was a professional in serious trouble. He was accurate in his perception that his personal life and his career were on the line, and that immediate attention was needed.

Sarah Tobin, PhD

15

SUBSTANCE-RELATED DISORDERS

We live in a society where the use of mind-altering substances has become a central part of our culture. Pick up any popular magazine or watch a football game on television and you are certain to come across enticing messages that show fun-loving, attractive people using alcohol or cigarettes. These legal drugs represent only a small fraction of *psychoactive substances* that are ingested by Americans each day. As you will see, both legal and illegal drugs affect all sectors of the population, including well-educated and professional people such as Carl.

After reading this chapter, you should be able to:

- Define the nature of a psychoactive substance and the concepts of intoxication, withdrawal, and tolerance, and be able to understand the issues involved in defining substance abuse and dependence.
- Describe the patterns of alcohol use in the United States, and the risks associated with alcohol use, as well as the short- and long-term effects of alcohol on the nervous system and the rest of the body.
- Compare the biological and psychological perspectives as approaches to understanding and treating alcohol dependence.
- Describe how stimulants, including amphetamines, cocaine, and caffeine affect the nervous system and behavior.
- Understand how marijuana affects the brain and be aware of concerns over its long-term effects on behavior.
- Describe the effects of hallucinogens and be familiar with their long-term risks.

- Understand the nature of opioid dependence and the brain mechanisms that underlie its effects.
- Describe the effects of sedative-hypnotic and antianxiety drugs.
- Compare biological and psychological approaches to substance abuse, and be able to describe the difficulties in treating disorders associated with dependence.

THE NATURE OF SUBSTANCE ABUSE AND DEPENDENCE

A **psychoactive substance** is a chemical that alters a person's mood or behavior by being smoked, injected, drunk, inhaled, or swallowed in pill form. Because psychoactive substances are so much a part of everyday life, most people take them for granted. A glass of wine at dinner, a cup of coffee in the morning, a beer or two at a party, a sleeping pill at night—none of these may seem particularly unusual or troublesome. Although the majority of people are able to regulate their use of such psychoactive substances, many drugs pose high risks to the individual. It is estimated that about 4 out of every 100,000 deaths in the United States are directly due to drug use, and this figure does not include deaths due to drug-related causes such as accidents and homicides (USDHHS, 1992). When accidents are taken into account, this figure rises substantially. The combination of heightened risk of accidents along with the deleterious effects of alcohol on health have led statisticians to estimate that a minimum of 3 out of every 100 deaths in the United States can be attributed to alcohol-related causes (USDHHS, 1990).

Behaviors Associated with Substance-Related Disorders

Let's first turn our attention to the ways in which psychoactive substances affect human behavior. Although each substance has specific effects that depend on its chemical composition and effects on the brain or body, it is helpful to have an overview of how substances in general can change behavior.

■ Behavioral effects

In all likelihood you have heard the term *intoxicated,* possibly used in the phrase driving while intoxicated. **Intoxication** refers to the experience of altered behaviors due to the accumulation of a psychoactive substance in the body. In the case of alcohol intoxication, the individual experiences impaired judgment and attention, slurred speech, abnormal eye movements, slowed reflexes, unsteady walking, and changeable moods. By contrast, intoxication following the ingestion of amphetamines is quite different, involving

For some people, the sight of the addictive substance causes intense cravings that make quitting seemingly impossible.

the experience of accelerated bodily functioning as well as perspiration or chills. Did you know that you can even become intoxicated from drinking coffee? People who drink a great amount of any caffeinated beverage are likely to experience a number of troubling bodily sensations including nervousness, twitching, insomnia, and agitation.

In addition to the effects that follow the ingestion of psychoactive substances, there are also psychological and physical changes that occur when some substances are discontinued, reactions which are referred to as **withdrawal**. Withdrawal takes different forms according to the actual psychoactive substance involved. If anyone in your life has quit smoking after prolonged use, you have very likely observed the anxiety and irritability that so commonly accompanies nicotine cessation; these are signs of nicotine withdrawal. People taking substances with higher potency can undergo such severe psychological and physical withdrawal symptoms that they need medical care.

Tolerance, which is related to withdrawal, refers to the extent to which the individual requires larger and larger amounts of the substance in order to achieve its desired effects or feels less of its effects after using the same amount of the substance. A businessman, for example, may find that the six-pack of beer that he has drunk every night after work no longer relaxes him the way it used to and that he now needs to drink at least two six-packs to achieve the same level of comfort. You will see as you read this chapter that tolerance can develop in different ways; in some instances tolerance is caused by changes in the body's metabolism of the drug, and in others it results from the way the drug affects the nervous system.

■ Patterns of use

When does a person's *use* of psychoactive substances become *abuse?* When does a person's *need* for psychoactive substances reach the point of dependency and become an addiction? These are questions that researchers and clini-

Would you guess that this is an experimental laboratory? Researchers at the University of Washington designed this "BAR-LAB" (Behavioral Alcohol Research Laboratory) as a way of investigating the psychological aspects of alcohol dependence.

cians have struggled with for decades. Currently, **substance abuse** is defined as the use of a drug in a way that creates significant problems for a person in daily life; perhaps the person is driving while intoxicated, or the substance use is causing problems at work, school, or home. The main feature of abuse, then, is a pattern of behavior in which the individual continues to use psychoactive substances even when it is clear that such behavior entails significant risks or creates problems in living. For example, a college professor may insist on having three martinis at lunch despite the fact that this interferes with her ability to teach her afternoon seminar. She is abusing alcohol, because she is drinking despite the fact that doing so impairs her work. In contrast, her husband occasionally has a glass of beer late in the day, but at other times has a can of soda. Her husband would not be regarded as an abuser.

The notion of substance abuse carries with it no implication that the individual is addicted to the drug. Continuing with the example of the three-martini professor, we must ask to what extent she "needs" to have those drinks in order to get through the day. If she has gotten to a point of reliance on this form of drinking, she would be considered to be dependent on alcohol. **Dependence** involves a psychological and often physical need for a substance. The line between abuse and dependence is not clear, however, and researchers continue efforts to delineate these phenomena (Nathan, 1991).

Experts also struggle to understand the differential roles played by psychological and physiological factors in defining dependence or tolerance to a substance. In other words, to what extent is a given person's dependence on a substance psychological and to what extent is it physiological in nature? Physiological or physical dependence involves a set of changes in the body's tissues in response to continued intake of a substance. Psychological dependence

is a condition in which a drug or alcohol produces a craving that requires periodic or continuous administration of the drug to produce pleasure or avoid discomfort. This distinction is difficult to make, since both physical and psychological dependence characterize addiction and may be inseparable at the cellular level. (Koob & Bloom, 1988).

ALCOHOL

Alcohol, perhaps more than any other psychoactive substance, has touched the lives of most people. You may be related to an alcoholic, or you may have had personal struggles with alcohol yourself. Researchers have found that nearly 43 percent of the population has had exposure to alcoholism in the family. More specifically, approximately 18 percent of all adults in the United States have lived with an alcoholic at some time during their childhood; nearly 38 percent have at least one blood relative who is or was an alcoholic or problem drinker; and 9 percent have been married to an alcoholic (Schoenborn, 1991). In addition to the emotional burden of contending with alcoholism in the family, millions of people have learned first-hand that alcohol abuse or dependence can disrupt one's life. It is estimated that 10 percent of the adults in the United States—or 15 million people—abuse or are dependent on alcohol (Williams et al., 1989). When asked if they have had an alcohol-related problem within the past 12 months, such as job or school impairment, 15.4 percent of the population 12 years of age and older admit that they have (NIAAA, 1991b).

If you are one of the millions of people whose lives have been affected by having grown up in a family with an alcoholic parent, you may have heard of a phenomenon that has received a great deal of media attention during the past decade—the notion that as a result of a disturbed family life, the offspring of alcoholic parents commonly carry certain personality styles into adulthood that impair their functioning. Janet Woititz (1983) refers to these individuals as *adult children of alcoholics* (ACOAs). Woititz's book helped to start the "Children of Alcoholics" movement, from which thousands of groups have emerged across the country where people with comparable experiences meet to explore the impact on their lives of having been raised by an alcoholic parent. Woititz enumerated more than a dozen traits that she has observed in children of alcoholics. For example, Woititz asserts that because of their chaotic and unpredictable home life during childhood, these people go through life having a difficult time knowing what "normal" is. They are unable to have fun, and they have difficulty establishing intimate relationships. Further, according to Woititz, they tend to feel different from other people, act impulsively, lie, and desperately seek approval and attention. The increasing recognition given to the problems shared by children of alcoholics has helped many people gain self-understanding. A certain danger exists, though, whenever specified personality traits are applied to many diverse people. It is all too easy to over-identify with this list of traits and to believe that all of them apply to you as an individual (Logue et al., 1992).

Another concept related to ACOA is *codependency* (Whitfield, 1989), the need for the alcoholic's spouse or partner to control the alcoholic's behavior. Like ACOAs, people who are codependent become so focused on the feelings or behavior of others that they ignore their own needs and feelings. Furthermore, their preoccupation is thought to become an addiction. Codependence is seen in the partners of a variety of chemically dependent people, and is associated with depression (O'Brien & Gaborit, 1992).

In addition to the emotional problems that alcohol-related disorders create for individuals and families, there is a huge economic price tag for alcoholism. This cost includes payment for medical treatment for conditions associated with alcoholism, lost work time, loss of human life, and treatment of children with fetal alcohol syndrome. Estimates of the yearly cost of alcohol abuse in the United States in the late 1980s ranged from $86 billion (Rice et al., 1990) to $136 billion, with projections as high as $150 billion by the year 1995 (USDHHS, 1990).

Even occasional use of alcohol is associated with many risks. Most striking perhaps is the fact that alcohol is estimated to be responsible for more than half of the fatal automobile accidents in this country (Kanas, 1988). Alcohol also plays a significant role in other types of accidents. For example, intoxicated pedestrians are four times more likely than nonintoxicated pedestrians to be hit by a car, and alcohol increases the risks of accidental drownings, falls, fires, and burns (Hingson & Howland, 1987; Howland & Hingson, 1987, 1988). When intoxicated people are involved in an accident, they are more likely to suffer serious physical trauma (Anda et al., 1988).

The effects of alcohol have crept into countless facets of life, placing innumerable people at risk of harm, danger, or violence. For example, researchers have found that almost two-thirds of husbands who abused their wives were drinking when they were violent (NIAAA, 1987), a fact that has brought a great deal of social attention to the alarming relationship between alcohol and wife battering (Atwood, 1991; Collins, 1989; Randall, 1991).

The Effects of Alcohol on the Body

People consume alcohol, in part, because they want to achieve an altered mood and state of awareness. Before ex-

The unpredictability and dysfunctional behavior of an alcoholic parent or spouse create tension and insecurity for all family members.

amining the long-term effects of chronic alcohol use, we will look first at its immediate effects on the user and the mechanisms thought to be responsible for these effects.

■ *Immediate effects*

In small amounts, alcohol has sedating effects, leading to feelings of warmth, comfort, and relaxation. In larger amounts, alcohol may lead the drinker to feel more outgoing, self-confident, and disinhibited. In part, the extent to which people actually experience these mood changes depends on their expectations (Critchlow, 1986) and whether they are alone or with others (Sher, 1985). Contrary to popular depictions of alcohol as an enhancer of sexual arousal and potency, alcohol diminishes the male sexual response, as measured by penile erection (Briddell & Wilson, 1976). Interestingly, however, most men believe that alcohol increases their sexual responsiveness, and when they anticipate consuming alcohol they can actually become sexually aroused (Newlin, 1987).

Some people stop drinking when they have achieved the positive mood they were seeking from alcohol. If an individual continues to drink, though, the effects of alcohol as a **depressant** drug become more apparent, as feelings of sleepiness, uncoordination, dysphoria, and irritability set in. Excessive drinking affects a person's vital functions, and can be fatal. Of particular concern is the mixture of alcohol with other drugs, including both medications and illicit substances. Because alcohol is a depressant, combining it with a depressant drug causes **potentiation**—an intensified effect that is greater than the effect of either substance alone.

What accounts for the mood-altering effects of alcohol? To find the answer to this question, researchers have investigated the changes in the brain that accompany alcohol intake. It is known that alcohol enters neurons in the brain from the bloodstream, but the changes caused by this process are not well understood. For decades scientists believed in the *membrane hypothesis*, a speculation that alcohol molecules change the structure of the neural membrane in nonspecific ways that lower its overall reactivity to stimulation (Chin & Goldstein, 1977). More recently, scientists have begun to investigate the effects of alcohol on specific neurotransmitters that play a role in the inhibition of central nervous system activity. One possibility is that alcohol activates or enhances the inhibitory activity of GABA receptors, the same receptors that are involved in actions of benzodiazepines such as diazepam (Valium) (Suzdak et al., 1988). Such changes would account for the sedating effects of alcohol. Researchers have also studied the effects of alcohol on *glutamate*, an amino acid that serves as an excitatory neurotransmitter in the brain. Alcohol may inhibit a receptor for glutamate, and in the process reduce the excitatory activity of this substance (Lovinger et al., 1989). Changes in the receptor for glutamate could provide an explanation for some of the deleterious effects of alcohol on memory and learning (Lister et al., 1987).

The rate at which alcohol is absorbed into the bloodstream depends in part on the rate at which it is consumed, the concentration of alcohol in the particular beverage, and whether the beverage is carbonated or not. The rate of alcohol absorption also depends on individual characteristics, including a person's metabolism rate, or the rate at which the body converts nutrients to energy (in this case, the "nutrient" is alcohol).

The rate at which alcohol is metabolized determines how long the person will continue to experience the effects of alcohol. The average person metabolizes alcohol at a rate of one-third of an ounce of 100 percent alcohol per hour, which is equivalent to an ounce of whiskey per hour.

An environmental disaster in 1989 involving the *Exxon Valdez* oil tanker was an example of alcohol's potential to lead a person to cause severe harm. The captain of the tanker was found to be intoxicated while on duty, and his mistaken judgment resulted in a massive oil spill that necessitated a multimillion dollar cleanup.

Apart from the physiological determinants of the effects of alcohol, there are different personal responses to alcohol. So-called "experienced drinkers" have learned strategies to conceal the fact that they have had too much to drink (Benton et al., 1982). They also have developed tolerance, which leads to an increased rate of alcohol metabolism in their bodies. Consequently, when consuming the same amount of alcohol, heavy alcohol users do not develop blood alcohol levels that are as high as those of people who drink less heavily.

Following a bout of extensive intake of alcohol, a person is likely to experience an *abstinence syndrome,* colloquially referred to as a "hangover." The symptoms of hangover include nausea and vomiting, tremors, extreme thirst, headache, tiredness, irritability, depression, and dizziness. The extent of a person's hangover depends on how much alcohol was consumed and over what period of time. There is no cure for a hangover other than to wait for the body to recover. Metabolism rate also affects the duration of a person's hangover.

■ Long-term effects

Alcohol affects almost every organ system in the body either directly or indirectly. Long-term, heavy users of alcohol pay a high price for their consumption in terms of a serious risk of damage to the brain, liver, pancreas, heart, and immune system (USDHHS, 1990).

In part, the reason for alcohol's harmful long-term effects may be attributed to the factor of tolerance. The more a person consumes, the more alcohol that person needs to achieve the desired impact. This means that the heavy user's intake of alcohol constantly increases over time, leading to the potential for more bodily damage. As we will see later, scientists are attempting to understand the biochemical changes associated with long-term heavy alcohol use as a way of comprehending the factors leading to tolerance and dependence.

Long-term use of alcohol can lead to permanent brain damage, with symptoms of dementia, blackouts, seizures, hallucinations, and damage to the peripheral parts of the nervous system (Miller & Gold, 1987). Two forms of dementia are associated with long-term, heavy alcohol use: *Wernicke's disease* and *Korsakoff's syndrome.* **Wernicke's disease** is an acute condition involving delirium, eye movement disturbances, difficulties in movement and balance, and deterioration of the peripheral nerves to the hands and feet. The cause of Wernicke's disease is not alcohol itself, but a thiamine deficiency due to the deleterious effects of alcohol on the metabolism of nutrients, as well as an overall pattern of poor nutrition. Adequate thiamine intake can reverse Wernicke's disease. By contrast, **Korsakoff's syndrome** is a permanent form of dementia in which the individual develops retrograde and anterograde amnesia, leading to an inability to remember recent events or learn new information. People who develop Wernicke's disease are likely to develop Korsakoff's syndrome (Reuler et al., 1985). It has been suggested that both disorders represent the same underlying disease process, with Wernicke's being the acute form and Korsakoff's being the chronic form of the disorder (Thomson et al., 1987). The chances of recovering from Korsakoff's syndrome are less than one in four, and about one-quarter of those who suffer from this disorder require permanent institutionalization.

In recent years, there has been some attention given to the possibility that moderate alcohol consumption—one or two drinks a day—over a person's life can help prevent cardiovascular disease (Klatsky, 1987; Lange & Kinnunen, 1987; Stampfer et al., 1988). This conclusion is based on the fact that alcohol has some beneficial effects such as preventing blood clotting. As interesting as such findings are, they are not without controversy. Some researchers (Shaper et al., 1987) contend that even though light drinkers have relatively lower levels of heart disease, this group also has other noteworthy characteristics: a lower proportion of smokers, people with lower blood pressure, and fewer manual laborers. So, might these other factors be more central to the prevention of heart disease than alcohol consumption? Regardless of whether or not moderate alcohol consumption is beneficial, it is clear that regular heavy intake of alcohol has a deadly effect on the heart, destroying the heart muscle and interferring with the rhythmic beating of the heart. Heavy alcohol use is also associated with chronic high blood pressure, deficient blood circulation to the heart, and cerebrovascular disorders (Lange & Kinnunen, 1987).

Death from long-term, heavy alcohol use is often associated with liver disease. Most chronic alcohol users develop *fatty liver,* a condition characterized by abnormal changes in the blood vessels in the liver. This condition develops in 90 to 100 percent of heavy drinkers, and may be a precursor to *cirrhosis,* a degenerative disease that results in progressive and irreversible liver damage. Cirrhosis is the ninth leading cause of death in the United States and is one of the primary factors associated with death due to chronic alcohol use (USDHHS, 1992).

Alcohol also causes a number of harmful changes in the gastrointestinal system, including inflammation of the esophagus and stomach lining, a slowing down of smooth muscle contractions throughout the gastrointestinal tract, and pancreatitis. These conditions can be quite painful, and they also can cause serious nutritional deficiencies including, as mentioned above, Korsakoff's syndrome. Many chronic heavy users of alcohol become malnourished because of poor eating habits associated with frequent drinking. Further complications arise from fasting and from a diet that is deficient in zinc, leading to a decrease in the activity of **alcohol dehydrogenase (ADH)**. This zinc-containing enzyme breaks alcohol down into fatty acids, carbon dioxide, and water, which are then absorbed by the body's tissues. With less ADH, alcohol enters the bloodstream, where it produces more toxic effects throughout the body. Women are more vulnerable to the effects of alcohol because of their lower amounts of ADH, leading to the dispersion of greater amounts of undigested alcohol throughout the body's tissues (Frezza et al., 1990).

The list of deleterious effects of alcohol goes on and on. Chronic alcohol consumption lowers a person's bone strength, and puts the individual at risk for developing chronic muscle injury due to atrophy and a bone-weakening disease called *osteoporosis*. Alcohol can increase a person's risk of developing various forms of cancer, a risk that grows if the individual also smokes cigarettes. A reduction in the functioning of the immune system, which helps fight off cancer as well as infectious diseases, appears to play a role in the deteriorative process. Because of the effects of alcohol on the immune system, people carrying the AIDS virus who drink heavily are more likely to accelerate the disease's progression. And finally, abrupt withdrawal of alcohol after chronic usage can result in a number of symptoms including severe hangover, sleep disturbances, profound anxiety, tremulousness, sympathetic hyperactivity, psychoses, seizures, and even death (USDHHS, 1990).

Patterns of Alcohol Use and Abuse

Alcohol abuse and dependence are widespread in the United States, and although the amount of alcohol consumed per person has declined from the late 1970s to the late 1980s (NIAAA, 1991; see Figure 15–1), alcohol is the drug most widely used by Americans, with an estimated 83 percent of the population over age 12 reporting the use of alcohol within the previous year, and 51.2 percent within the previous month (NIAAA, 1991). Indeed, most of the decline in alcoholic beverage consumption during the decade of the 1980s was due to a decrease in consumption

of hard liquor; beer and wine consumption remained steady during this period (see Figure 15–2 on page 378). Of the 15 million Americans who abuse or are dependent on alcohol, approximately two-thirds are men (Williams et al., 1989), with the highest incidence of alcohol abuse and dependence being among men between the ages of 18 and 29 years.

Among high school seniors, whose drug use has been surveyed every year since 1975, the patterns of current and occasional heavy drinking have decreased fairly steadily since the early 1980s, reaching a new low in 1988 (Johnston et al., 1989). The percentages are still distressingly high, however, with reports of 64 percent of high school seniors having used alcohol within the past 30 days, and slightly more than one-third being "heavy drinkers," having taken five or more drinks in one sitting within the past two weeks. Almost all (92 percent) reported having tried alcohol.

Alcohol Dependence: Theories

Despite the well-known negative effects of alcohol, people still continue to drink. But why is it that some individuals progress from occasional or social drinking to the point at which their drinking gets out of control? In this section we will turn our attention to current explanations.

■ *Biological perspectives*

Major advances have been made in the past two decades in understanding the important role that biology plays in determining whether a person becomes dependent

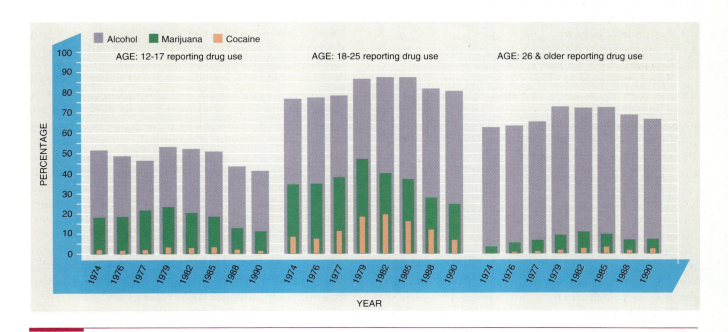

Figure 15–1
Drug and alcohol use by people 12 and older in the U.S. population between the years 1974 and 1990.
SOURCE: NIAAA (1990).

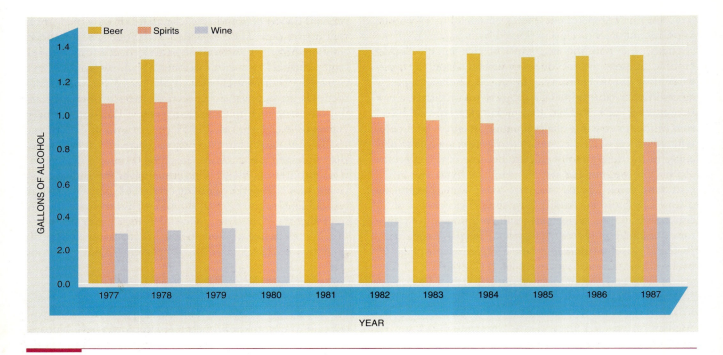

Figure 15–2
Estimated per capita consumption of types of alcohol in the U.S. population between the years 1977 and 1987
Source: NIAAA (1989).

on alcohol, with impressive advances in the areas of genetics and biochemistry.

The common belief that alcoholism runs in families was given scientific credence in studies published during the 1970s (Cotton, 1979), and further research has con-

Rhona is a 55-year-old homemaker, married to a successful builder. Every afternoon she makes herself the first of a series of daiquiris. Many evenings she has passed out on the couch by the time her husband arrives home from work. Rhona lost her driver's license a year ago after being arrested three times on charges of driving while intoxicated. Although Rhona's family has urged her to obtain treatment for her disorder, she denies that she has a problem because she can "control" her drinking. The mother of three grown children, Rhona began to drink around the age of 45 when her youngest child left for college. Prior to this time, Rhona kept herself extremely busy through her children's extra-curricular activities. When she found herself alone every afternoon, she took solace in having an early cocktail. Over a period of several years, the "cocktail" developed into a series of five or six strong drinks. Rhona's oldest daughter lately has begun to insist that something be done for her mother. She does not want to see Rhona develop the fatal alcohol-related illness that caused the premature death of her grandmother.

■ Would you consider Rhona's pattern of alcohol use to be alcohol abuse or dependence?
■ What factors in her life may be contributing to Rhona's use of alcohol?

firmed and clarified this conclusion (Devor & Cloninger, 1989). Genetics researchers have determined that there is a higher concordance of alcohol dependence between identical twins than between fraternal twins (Hrubec & Omenn, 1981; Kaij, 1960; Pickens et al., 1991), particularly for males (McGue et al., 1992). As we have pointed out in the context of other psychological disorders, twin studies provide important evidence in favor of genetic contributions, but it is important when reviewing the findings of twin studies to address the possibility that effects might be due to the fact that twins share the same experiences. In the case of alcohol abuse and dependence, researchers have regarded the sharing of experiences as particularly important, because continued contact between twins might lead one twin to be induced to drink by the other. In one ingenious study of the entire population of male twins between the ages of 24 and 49 in Finland (over 5600 men), it was found that identical twins had more social contact than fraternal twins, so that the higher concordance in alcohol consumption among identical twins could very well result from their spending more time together. However, when this factor of shared experiences was ruled out, there still remained a higher concordance of drinking patterns between identical twins than between fraternal twins (Kaprio et al., 1987). Similar findings have been obtained in a study of female twins in Australia (Heath et al., 1989).

Evidence of family inheritance also comes from studies of parents and children. The sons of alcoholics are four times more likely to become alcoholic than are the sons of nonalcoholic parents, and based on adoption studies, the risk to children seems to exist regardless of whether or not they were raised by their biological alcoholic parents (Cloninger et al., 1981; Goodwin, 1985).

Having established that there is a reasonably strong genetic influence on the development of alcoholism, researchers have tried various approaches to identifying biological markers that would predict whether an individual with a family history of alcoholism will develop the disorder. In one approach, nonalcoholic children of alcoholics were compared with nonalcoholic individuals who had no family history of alcoholism. Both groups were then given alcohol followed by physiological and behavioral tests to see if the children of alcoholics showed abnormal responses to alcohol. Children of alcoholics experienced less of a subjective reaction to alcohol than children of nonalcoholics (Lex et al., 1988; Schuckit & Gold, 1988), implying that children of alcoholics are genetically predisposed to require more alcohol intake to experience its psychological effects.

In a second biological marker approach, children of alcoholics and controls are compared on psychophysiological measures on which alcoholic individuals have been found to perform abnormally. For example, when subjects are given a cognitive task, such as discriminating between visual stimuli, there is usually a large positive brain wave (termed the *P300 wave*) that occurs about 300 milliseconds after the stimuli are presented. Even when abstinent, alcohol-dependent people show a lowering of the P300 wave (Porjesz et al., 1987). A similar pattern of responding is shown by the children of alcoholic fathers, but not in the children of nonalcoholic fathers. Amazingly, this pattern was identified in boys as young as 7 years old, none of whom had ever used alcohol or drugs (Begleiter et al., 1987), suggesting a powerful genetically based difference in brain functioning. As the search continues for genetic markers for alcoholism, investigators are exploring a variety of other behavioral and electrophysiological measures, including hormone responses, balance, mood, and decreases in cognitive and psychomotor performance (Moss et al., 1989; Schuckit, 1987; Schuckit et al., 1987). If this research continues to provide encouraging results, then it could have major implications for early identification of individuals biologically prone to alcohol dependence (Nathan, 1986).

Researchers working on biochemical explanations of alcohol dependence are exploring the possibility that alcohol causes changes in neurotransmitters leading to the behavioral manifestations of dependence. The most likely systems involve GABA, serotonin, and dopamine neurotransmitters. In the case of GABA, it is known that when alcohol is taken over a long period of time, it reduces the inhibition of neurons in the GABA pathways. This long-term inhibition can cause convulsive discharges in the hippocampus of the brain and could contribute to the convulsions associated with alcohol withdrawal (Miles & Wong, 1987; Ueha & Kuriyama, 1991).

A deficiency in serotonin is also regarded as a possible cause of increased alcohol consumption. As you will see later, drugs that increase the amount of available serotonin are being tested as medications to control alcohol dependence. However, the reason that these drugs work is not well understood, and they may owe their effects to mechanisms outside the serotonin system (Amit et al., 1991). Conversely, an *excess* in dopamine is associated with increased alcohol consumption. It is thought that dopamine mediates the activity of the reward centers of the brain in the limbic system and serves to maintain alcohol-seeking behavior (Kornetsky et al., 1988; Tabakoff & Hoffman, 1988). Researchers are currently seeking an "alcohol" gene that influences dopamine receptors (Blum et al., 1990; Comings et al., 1991). Failure to confirm the original reports of discovery of such a gene (Bolos et al., 1990; Gelernter et al., 1991; Turner et al., 1992) makes it clear that more research is needed to determine whether linkages exist between genetic and biochemical causes of alcohol dependence.

■ *Psychological perspectives*

Psychologists have recognized the need to incorporate biological factors into an explanation of alcohol dependence and have therefore proposed an integrative **biopsychosocial model** that proposes an integration of biological, psychological, and sociocultural factors in explaining why some people develop alcoholism (Donovan, 1988; Institute of Medicine, 1990; Schall et al., 1992; Zucker & Gomberg, 1986). This model originated in part from a review of six major longitudinal studies in which individuals were followed from childhood or adolescence to adulthood, the time when most individuals who become alcohol dependent make the transition from social or occasional alcohol use to dependence (Zucker & Gomberg, 1986). The individuals most likely to become alcohol-dependent in adulthood had a history of childhood antisocial behavior, including aggressive and sadistic behavior, trouble with the law, rebelliousness, lower achievement in school, completion of fewer years of school, and more truancy. They also showed a variety of behaviors possibly indicative of some type of early neural dysfunction, including nervousness and fretfulness as infants, hyperactivity as children, and poor physical coordination. These characteristics may reflect a genetically based vulnerability that, when combined with environmental stresses, leads to the development of alcohol dependence.

The extent to which biological and psychological or experiential factors influence the development of alcohol dependence may also vary from person to person. Cloninger (1987) has proposed that two subtypes of alcoholism exist which differ in the extent to which genetic and environmental factors play a role. People with Type 1 alcoholism, which usually develops after the age of 25, have a hereditary predisposition to becoming alcohol-dependent, but their drinking behavior is more strongly influenced by environmental factors. These individuals try to control their drinking, feel guilty and afraid of becoming alcohol-dependent, and worry about the effects of their drinking on other people. As you might guess, these people are more receptive to treatment. By contrast, people who develop Type 2 alcoholism are more heavily influenced by genetic factors. They are more commonly males who develop problems before the age of 25. Feeling compelled to seek out new and exciting experiences, and not concerned about the consequences of their actions, they engage in high-risk behaviors that often get them in trouble with the law.

Moving into a more specific understanding of the psychological processes involved in the transition from social drinking to dependence, G. Alan Marlatt and his associates developed the **expectancy model**, which focuses on cognitive-behavioral and social learning perspectives (Marlatt et al., 1988; Stacy et al., 1990). According to this view, people acquire the belief that alcohol will reduce stress, make them feel more competent socially, physically, and sexually, and will give them feelings of pleasure. These experiences can develop as early as seventh and eighth grade (Christiansen et al., 1989); watching others enjoy alcohol and then having first-hand pleasurable and anxiety-reducing experiences sets up these expectations (Barrett, 1985). Reinforcements, then, both vicarious and direct, establish a pattern of alcohol consumption that leads to the physiological processes of tolerance and predisposition to withdrawal symptoms.

Concepts central to the expectancy model are self-efficacy and coping. Self-efficacy, as you will recall from Chapter 5, refers to an individual's perception that he or she has the ability to meet the challenges of a difficult situation. The concept of coping, as used in the cognitive-behavioral model, refers to the strategies that an individual uses to reduce the perception of a threat or danger. In the case of the expectancy model, these cognitive factors, along with the individual's ideas or expectations about the effects of alcohol, presumably play a role in determining whether or not an individual will relapse to problem drinking. An assessment inventory based on the model is shown in Table 15–1.

The expectancy model describes a series of reactions that occur when an alcohol-dependent individual attempts to remain abstinent. Consider the contrasting cases of Marlene, who has been successful in remaining abstinent, and Edward who has been unsuccessful. Both Marlene and Edward encounter high-risk situations such as a party where other people are consuming alcohol. Marlene is able to abstain from drinking at the party because she has learned how to cope with such situations, and she feels capable of carrying through with her intention not to drink alcohol. Each successful episode of abstinence reinforces her sense of self-efficacy, causing her to feel more capable of abstaining in subsequent situations. By contrast, unsuccessful individuals lack a satisfactory coping response. It is not the actual consumption of alcohol that leads to a relapse, but the individual's interpretation of the act of drinking as a sign of loss of self-control. So, when Edward enters a high-risk situation, his low sense of self-efficacy results in his feeling incapable of staying away from alcohol. A compelling expectation that alcohol will have a positive mood-altering effect adds to his low sense of self-efficacy and leads him to take that fateful first drink. The positive sensations pro-

According to the expectancy model of alcohol dependence, people who are trying to remain abstinent may struggle when faced with situations that cause them to question their ability to control their drinking.

duced by the alcohol further weaken Edward's resolve, but cognitive factors enter at this point in the process as well. By having violated the self-imposed rule of remaining abstinent, he now is subject to what is called the **abstinence violation effect**, a sense of loss of control over one's behavior that has an overwhelming and demoralizing effect (see Figure 15–3). Convinced more than ever of having a fatal weakness of self-control, Edward's self-efficacy is further eroded and a downward spiral is initiated that eventually ends in renewed alcohol dependence.

Alcohol Dependence: Treatment

The search for effective treatment of alcohol dependence has proven to be a difficult and challenging process. Alcohol use is so much a part of Western culture that many people who abuse or are dependent on alcohol do not realize that their behavior is problematic. There are no legal sanctions against the use of alcohol other than a minimum drinking age; in fact, endorsements of drinking as a socially acceptable behavior appear in countless advertisements (Sigvardsson et al., 1985). Little consideration is given to the down side of alcohol consumption, namely, that it can involve a serious disorder. Nor is a great deal of attention given to the fact that alcohol-related disorders are treatable.

The majority of alcohol dependent individuals do not seek treatment voluntarily. Of the estimated 15 million Americans who abuse or are dependent on alcohol, less than 10 percent receive treatment (NIAAA/NIDA, 1989). Most people with alcohol problems have a remarkable capacity for denial, insisting to themselves and others that their alcohol consumption is not really a problem (Massella, 1991).

Table 15–1 Sample Items from Expectancy-Based Assessment Measures

The *Inventory of Drinking Situations* is used to determine which situations represent a high risk for the alcohol-dependent individual. Each item is rated according to the following scale: "I DRANK HEAVILY—Never, Rarely, Frequently, Almost Always." The items on the *Situational Confidence Questionnaire* (Annis, 1984b) match the *Inventory of Drinking Situations,* but each item is rated on the scale of "I WOULD BE ABLE TO RESIST THE URGE TO DRINK HEAVILY," with ratings in percentages ranging from Not at All Confident (0 percent) to Very Confident (100 percent).

The scale each item represents is shown in parentheses.

(Intrapersonal Determinants)
When I felt that I had let myself down. (Negative emotional state)
When I would have trouble sleeping. (Negative physical state)
When I felt confident and relaxed. (Positive emotional state)
When I would convince myself that I was a new person now and could take a few drinks. (Testing personal control)
When I would remember how good it tasted. (Urges and temptations)

(Interpersonal Determinants)
When other people treated me unfairly. (Social rejection)
When pressure would build up at work because of the demands of my superior. (Work problems)
When I felt uneasy in the presence of someone. (Tension)
When I had an argument with a friend. (Family/friends problems)
When I would be out with friends and they would stop by for a drink. (Social pressure to drink)
When I would be out with friends "on the town" and wanted to increase my enjoyment. (Social drinking)
When I wanted to heighten my sexual enjoyment. (Intimacy)

Source: Annis, (1984a).

■ *Biological treatments*

Biological treatments of alcohol dependence consist of medications that are used for a variety of alcohol-related problems. Some medications are used to control symptoms of co-existing disorders (Liskow & Goodwin, 1987); for example, benzodiazepines can manage the symptoms of withdrawal and prevent the development of **delirium tremens**, a physical condition consisting of autonomic nervous system dysfunction, confusion, and possible seizures. Other antianxiety drugs, and also antidepressants, can also be of use in treating co-existing psychological disorders, and may help reduce the individual's dependence on alcohol by alleviating symptoms of anxiety and depression that can foster the need for alcohol.

Other medications used to treat alcohol dependence are much more ambitious in their intent, aiming to counter the presumed brain changes associated with drinking behavior in order to eliminate the individual's desire to consume alcohol. These drugs have their effect by stimulating various neurotransmitter systems that produce biochemical changes in the brain. The GABA system is one logical target for interventions, because it is implicated in both the short- and long-term changes in the brain associated with

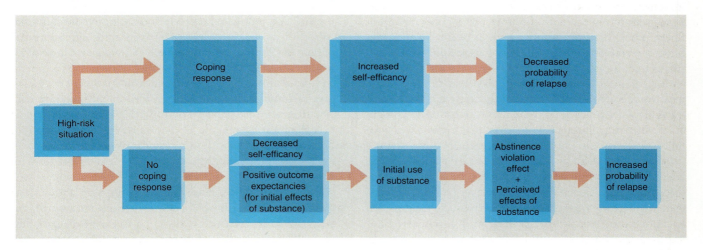

Figure 15–3 A cognitive-behavioral model of the relapse process
Source: Marlatt & Gordon (1985).

alcohol intake. Agents that interact with GABA receptors in the brain have been shown to reduce alcohol intoxication and consumption in laboratory animals (Suzdak et al., 1986). However, the results of interventions with humans given *acamprosate*, a drug that acts on the GABA system, are less encouraging (Lhuintre et al., 1990). Somewhat more favorable outcomes have been achieved with *citalopram*, a medication that inhibits the uptake of serotonin, raising the available level of serotonin in the nervous system (Naranjo et al., 1987). *Buspirone,* a medication used in treating anxiety disorders, also appears to reduce alcohol consumption in dependent individuals through its effects on serotonin uptake (NIAAA, 1990). Medications that decrease the amount of effective dopamine in the brain also seem to have promise as ways to reduce alcohol dependence and consumption (Borg, 1983). As researchers continue to find out more about the brain mechanisms involved in alcohol dependence, the development of medications to combat this disorder will no doubt progress as well.

Another category of medications used to treat alcohol dependence consists of those that are intended to produce a strongly aversive physiological reaction when a person drinks. This method relies on an aversive conditioning process in which the unpleasant reaction to alcohol provoked by the medication causes the individual to form a negative association to alcohol intake, providing a strong disincentive for drinking. The medication used in this form of treatment is **disulfiram**, known popularly as *Antabuse*. Disulfiram inhibits **aldehyde dehydrogenase (ALDH)**, an enzyme that, along with ADH, is responsible for metabolizing alcohol. When ALDH is inhibited, the level of blood acetaldehyde, a toxic substance, rises and within 30 minutes the individual experiences a severe physical reaction lasting for as long as one hour. Depending on the amount of alcohol in the body, this reaction includes headache, hot flushed face, chest pain, weakness, sweating, thirst, blurred vision, confusion, rapid heart rate and palpitations, a drop in blood pressure, difficulty breathing, nausea, and vomiting. Interestingly, the combined effects of alcohol and disulfiram were discovered quite by accident when two researchers investigating disulfiram became ill at a cocktail party (Institute of Medicine, 1990).

If the logic behind the use of disulfiram is correct, you may wonder why any other type of therapy would be needed for alcohol dependence. Yet, the results of controlled studies on disulfiram's effectiveness are not that clear-cut; it promotes abstinence in only about 60 percent of those who use it (Sereny et al., 1986). In addition, the 60 percent success rate is achieved only under strict supervision. To be effective, the medication must be taken every day. Without a method of guaranteeing compliance, the success rates with disulfiram are lower (Fuller et al., 1986). Another limitation is that because of the intensity of the physical reaction it provokes, disulfiram is not prescribed for individuals with cardiovascular problems, cirrhosis, or diabetes, disorders that are common among chronic alcohol users.

Before leaving the topic of pharmacological treatments for alcohol dependence, it is important that we point out that such treatments are controversial. Criticism rests on what some perceive as an irony—using one form of substance to eliminate abuse of another form of substance.

■ *Psychological treatments*

The administration of disulfiram in treating alcohol dependence is a biological intervention, but as you can see, it relies heavily on behavioral principles of aversive conditioning. It is not an ideal aversive stimulus however, because its effects are not immediate. Other behavioral methods use an aversive conditioning model in which something unpleasant, such as a mild electric shock, occurs in direct association with alcohol consumption during a treatment session. Again, although this approach appears to have obvious merit, and has been used for more than 50 years, its effectiveness rate—approximately 50 percent abstinent one year after treatment—is not regarded by most experts as high enough to counter the objections about its safety (Cannon et al., 1988).

In the **cue exposure method** (Rankin et al., 1983), another behavioral approach, the individual is given a priming dose of alcohol that initiates the craving for more alcohol. At that point, the individual is urged to refuse further alcohol. Each successive treatment constitutes an extinction trial that is intended to reduce craving.

An alternative to approaches aimed at replacing positive associations to alcohol with aversive ones is **relapse prevention therapy**, a treatment method based on the expectancy model. Built into the model is the assumption that alcohol-dependent individuals invariably become faced with the temptation to have a drink and at some point fail to follow through with the desire to abstain. What happens at that point is crucial (Marlatt et al., 1988). According to the notion of the abstinence violation effect, if the lapse is seen as a sign of weakness, or character flaw, this will damage the individual's sense of self-efficacy so severely that the possibility of future abstinence seems out of the question. If, instead, the individual can learn to interpret the drinking episode as a single incident that was unfortunate but not a permanent failing, the individual's self-efficacy can remain intact and a relapse can be prevented (Annis, 1990).

In relapse prevention, the individual is taught decision-making abilities that make it possible to analyze a high-risk situation and determine which coping skills would work best to prevent a relapse. Skill training can also be used to help individuals learn how to express and receive positive and negative feelings, how to initiate contact, and how to reply to criticism (Oei & Jackson, 1982). For example, consider the case of a woman named Sheila, who knows that going to a party will put her in a high-risk situation. For years Sheila had come to believe that she needed alcohol in such situations so that she could "loosen up," thereby appearing more likable and lively. Now that she is trying to maintain abstinence, she can make alternative plans prior to going to a party that will prepare her with coping skills, such as staying away from the bar and asking a friend to keep her glass full with a nonalcoholic beverage. Cognitive

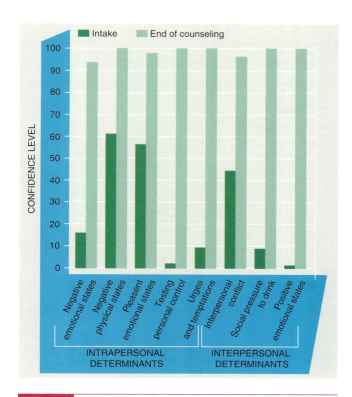

Figure 15–4
Situational Confidence Questionnaire profile before and after alcohol treatment
Source: Annis (1988).

Central to the Alcoholics Anonymous movement are the meetings. Members describe their experiences with alcohol dependence, hoping to inspire others to resist the omnipresent temptations of the addiction.

restructuring would help her to interpret high-risk situations more productively. If she believes that it is necessary to have alcohol in order to be popular and lively, she can learn to reframe this belief so that she can see that people like her even if she is not high on alcohol. Maintenance is an important part of the treatment approach as well, and Marlatt thus emphasizes the need for continued therapeutic contacts, social support from friends and family, and changes in lifestyle to find alternate sources of gratification. Sheila would need to keep in periodic contact with her therapist, to find new friends and seek help from her family, and to find other ways to socialize, such as joining a health club. Skill training and the development of alternate coping methods can also be combined with behavioral techniques, such as cue exposure (Marlatt, 1990).

The goal of relapse prevention cannot be achieved in one step, but requires a graded program that exposes the individual to high-risk situations in greater and greater increments. At each step, the individual is encouraged by the therapist to draw inferences from successful behavior that will reinforce feelings of self-efficacy. A comparison of self-efficacy evaluations of a client before and after treatment based on this model is shown in Figure 15–4.

The relapse prevention model is relatively new, and is growing in popularity, although it requires more testing before it will be recommended on a widespread basis. For example, the self-efficacy training program we have just described (Annis & Davis, 1988) proved to yield only a 29

percent abstinence rate after 6 months. The results obtained from this model are more favorable when amount of alcohol consumption, rather than absolute abstinence, is used as the criterion of treatment effectiveness (Solomon & Annis, 1990). As this model receives continued testing and elaboration, more data will be available to judge its effectiveness.

■ *Alcoholics Anonymous*

While biologists and psychologists continue to explore treatment approaches based on scientific models of alcohol dependence, one intervention model, whose roots are in spirituality rather than science, continues to be used on a widespread basis: *Alcoholics Anonymous,* or AA. This movement was founded in 1935 by Bill W., a Wall Street stockbroker, and Dr. Bob, a surgeon from Akron, Ohio, and from these humble beginnings has grown to worldwide proportions. A 1987 survey conducted by the organization determined that there were an impressive 1.5 million persons in 73,000 AA groups throughout the world (AA World Services, 1987). This survey also revealed that two-thirds of AA members are men, and most are in the age range of 31 to 50. Along with growth in the numbers of AA participants has been a general acceptance and recognition of the value of this approach (Bradley, 1988; Robinson & Henry, 1979), and it is a component of the majority of treatment programs in the United States (Boscarino, 1980).

Table 15–2 The Twelve Steps of Alcoholics Anonymous

The twelve steps to recovery form the heart of the Alcoholics Anonymous program. AA members strive to pass through each step, and once they have, they maintain a commitment to helping new members, a process called *twelfth-stepping.*

1. We admitted we were powerless over alcohol—that our lives had become unmanageable.
2. Came to believe that a Power greater than ourselves could restore us to sanity.
3. Made a decision to turn our will and our lives over to the care of God *as we understood Him.*
4. Made a searching and fearless moral inventory of ourselves.
5. Admitted to God, to ourselves, and to another human the exact nature of our wrongs.
6. Were entirely ready to have God remove all these defects of character.
7. Humbly asked God to remove our shortcomings.
8. Made a list of all persons we had harmed, and became willing to make amends to them all.
9. Made direct amends to such people wherever possible, except when to do so would injure them or others.
10. Continued to take personal inventory, and when we were wrong, promptly admitted it.
11. Sought through prayer and meditation to improve our conscious contact with God *as we understand Him*, praying only for knowledge of His will for us and the power to carry that out.
12. Having had a spiritual awakening as the result of these steps, we tried to carry this message to alcoholics and to practice these principles in all our affairs.

Source: Adapted from Maxwell, (1984). Original form is copyrighted, Alcoholics Anonymous, 1939.

The standard recovery program in AA involves a strong commitment to participate in AA-related activities, with the most important component being the AA meeting. Every AA meeting begins with an introduction of members, who state their first name, followed by the statement "I am an alcoholic." This ritual is the basis for the name of the movement, "Alcoholics Anonymous," meaning that members never consider themselves not to be alcoholics, and that they are not required to divulge their identities. During the meeting, one or two members tell their stories—how they developed drinking problems, the suffering their drinking caused, the personal debasement they may have experienced as they lied and cheated, and finally how they "hit bottom" and began to turn around their drinking patterns and their lives. They describe how they were introduced to AA and how AA has helped them recover, and also give advice on how to negotiate the 12 steps to recovery that form the heart of AA's philosophy (see Table 15–2). The second component of AA is the constant availability of another member, called a *sponsor,* who can provide support and advice during times of crisis when the urge to drink becomes overpowering. Round-the-clock hotlines staffed by AA volunteers also help to make such assistance continuously available.

The fundamental approach to understanding alcohol dependence fostered by AA is that alcoholism is an illness that prevents those who have it from controlling their drinking. If the alcoholic does succumb to temptation and goes on a binge, this is attributed within the AA model not to a moral failing, but to a biological process. A second tenet of AA is that alcoholics are never cured; they are "recovering." The goal of AA treatment is total abstinence. According to the AA philosophy, one drink is enough to send the individual back into a state of alcohol dependence.

An offshoot of AA was formed in the early 1950s for relatives and friends of people with alcohol dependence. Called *Al-Anon,* to distinguish it from AA, this movement provides a setting for people who are close to alcoholics and require support in coping with the problems caused by alcoholism in their lives. A later movement, called *Al-A-Teen,* is specifically designed for teenagers whose lives have been affected by alcoholism in the family. As we mentioned earlier, there are also groups for children of alcoholics, which focus on the psychological problems that result from growing up in a family with an alcoholic parent.

Millions of people credit AA for their sobriety; in addition, proponents of AA cite glowing outcome figures that, if correct, would make it the most successful approach to treating alcohol dependence. However, it is important to be aware of the fact that no well-controlled studies have been conducted to support the claims of AA's effectiveness (Trice & Staudemeier, 1989). According to AA's 1987 survey, the average length of abstinence is slightly over 4 years; 29 percent have been abstinent for more than 5 years, 38 percent from 1 to 5 years, and 33 percent for less than a year. However, these figures are based on a biased sample, since the individuals who responded to the survey were more likely to remain involved in the program and the dropouts who failed to benefit from AA were not sampled. A further bias in such figures stems from the fact that less than 20 percent of those who are referred to AA actually attend meetings (Institute of Medicine, 1990).

Nevertheless, AA does work for some individuals in promoting abstinence, particularly when combined with other treatment programs (Emrick, 1987). What lessons can researchers and clinicians learn from AA? We can see from the elements involved in this program that it shares common approaches with cognitive-behavioral methods.

The alcohol dependent individual is encouraged to avoid self-blame for failures and to develop alternative coping skills, both features of the expectancy model (Marlatt et al., 1988). In the case of AA, though, alcohol is regarded as a disease. This relegates the control over drinking to an outside force, rather than to the individual's powers of self-control (Brickman et al., 1982). Similarly, in AA, the individual is encouraged to use coping skills that rely on seeking help from outside the self rather than from within. Perhaps these features appeal to certain kinds of individuals, who regard their lives as determined by external forces, and this is why AA works for some people, but not all. The expectancy model, with its emphasis on internal coping strategies that draw on personal resources, perhaps appeals to individuals who view themselves as being in control of their fate. Both approaches, however, share the element of recommending continued contact with the treatment provider. They also include an emphasis on social support, one of the most striking elements in the AA model.

All alcohol treatment programs, however, share the major limitation of having an appeal and being effective only with those who are motivated to change. Without that motivation, neither drugs nor the most elaborate psychological treatment strategy will have a lasting impact (Miller, 1985).

STIMULANTS

You have probably had the experience on many occasions of wishing you could be more alert and energetic. You may have sought a "pick-me-up" such as a cup of coffee. Caffeine is just one of a category of drugs called **stimulants**—substances that have an activating effect on the central nervous system. The stimulants associated with psychological disorders are amphetamines, cocaine, caffeine, and nicotine. These differ in their chemical structure, their specific physical and psychological effects, and their potential danger to the user. Because of these differences, we will discuss separately each of the major stimulant drugs.

Amphetamines

Amphetamines, (sometimes called "speed," "bennies" or "uppers") are stimulants that cause a range of psychological effects depending on the amount, method, and duration of use as well as the specific form of the drug that is taken. In moderate amounts taken orally, amphetamines cause feelings of euphoria, increased confidence, talkativeness, and energy. Taken intravenously, more powerful effects are experienced. Immediately after injection, the user feels enhanced energy and self-confidence as well as a surge or "rush" of extremely pleasurable sensations that is described by users as similar to orgasm. Continued use of amphetamines at the high doses that produce these powerful effects can cause a person to appear psychotic with accompanying delusions and hallucinations. Chronic use can lead to amphetamine-induced psychosis, even after long periods of abstinence.

Amphetamines have some legitimate medical uses, although even these have become a matter of concern in the medical profession. For example, amphetamines have long been used as appetite suppressants for people trying to lose weight, but because of the likelihood of dependence developing, they have fallen into disfavor. As we described in Chapter 13, amphetamines have also been used to treat hyperactive children because of their paradoxical effect of calming an over-excited child. However, medications that do not have the habit-forming quality of amphetamines are now being substituted for this purpose. Another major medical application of amphetamines has been in the treatment of people with narcolepsy, a disorder that causes uncontrollable sleepiness.

The psychological effects of amphetamines reflect their action on the central and autonomic nervous systems of enhancing the action of norepinephrine, an excitatory neurotransmitter. The results of increased sympathetic nervous system activity include increased blood pressure and heart rate, nausea, sweating, dilated pupils, blurred vision, reduced blood flow to internal organs, and heightened blood flow to muscles involved in movement. It is this stimulation of the nervous system that accounts for the excitability as well as the psychotic-like symptoms observed in people who take large amounts of amphetamines for prolonged periods of time. The effects of amphetamines on appetite are due to the suppression of the appetite centers in the hypothalamus. The reduced need for sleep in people who take amphetamines is the result of the stimulating effect of these drugs on the reticular activating formation, the brain center responsible for sleep and wakefulness.

One reason that amphetamines become a problem for users is that people quickly build up tolerance. For example, people who use them for dieting find that after a certain period (sometimes 4 to 6 weeks), they must use higher doses to maintain the same appetite suppressant effect. At that point, they usually have become dependent on the drug's mood-altering results. Tolerance to amphetamines also extends to psychological effects. In order to achieve the same "high," long-term users must take greater doses of the drug. A debate exists about whether amphetamines cause physical dependence, but most researchers agree that these drugs are psychologically addictive.

Although it is rare for an overdose of amphetamines to result in death, many medical problems can occur, such as stroke, heart irregularity, kidney failure, temporary paralysis, circulatory collapse, seizures, and even coma. **Stimulant psychosis** is a condition that can develop from chronic abuse or can appear with one very large dose of amphetamines. An individual experiencing stimulant psychosis develops paranoid delusions, and may have tactile hallucinations as well, such as feeling that bugs are crawling on the skin. People in this state may have little control over their behavior; feeling terrified or out of control, they may act in violent or self-destructive ways.

When people discontinue amphetamines after heavy usage, they exhibit withdrawal symptoms that include profound depression, extreme hunger, craving for the drug, exhaustion, and disturbed sleep. These symptoms can last for 2 weeks or more, and some residual problems may last for a year.

The route to amphetamine dependence can occur in one of two ways: through medical abuse or through street abuse. In medical abuse, the individual begins taking amphetamines for a medical reason, such as to reduce weight or to treat fatigue, increasing the dose as tolerance develops, and obtaining the drug by seeking multiple or refillable prescriptions. Efforts to stop taking the drug result in an increase of the symptoms it was intended to reduce, leading the individual to increase dosages to harmful levels. Street abusers take amphetamines for the deliberate purpose of altering their state of consciousness, perhaps in alternation with depressants. An even more dangerous mode of amphetamine use involves taking the drug in "runs" of continuous ingestion for 2 to 4 days. This pattern of abuse is most likely to result in problems of withdrawal and psychosis (Schuckit, 1989).

Cocaine

Cocaine (also called "coke," "gold dust," and "snow") became the drug of choice for recreational users during the 1980s, and spread to every segment of the population (Adams et al., 1987; Washton & Gold, 1987). Among people between the ages of 18 and 25, the most common users of cocaine, the rates of lifetime use skyrocketed from 9.1 percent in 1972 to a peak of 28.3 percent in 1982. In 1985

Catherine is a 23-year-old salesperson who tried for 3 years to lose weight. Her physician prescribed amphetamines, but cautioned her about the possibility that she might become dependent on them. She did begin to lose weight, but she also discovered that she liked the extra energy and good feelings caused by the diet pills. When Catherine returned to her doctor after having lost the desired weight, she asked him for a refill of her prescription to help her maintain her new figure. When he refused, Catherine asked around among her friends until she found the name of a physician who was willing to accommodate her wishes for ongoing refills of the prescription. Over the course of a year, Catherine has developed a number of psychological problems including depression, paranoid thinking, and irritability. Despite the fact that she realizes that something is wrong, she feels driven to continue using the drug.

- Would you regard Catherine as dependent on amphetamines? Why?
- What kind of personality traits would you expect to find in a person who has such limited control over both eating behavior and substance dependence?

This harmless-looking powder is the highly addictive substance crack cocaine. Many contend that the widespread availability of this drug is at the root of many contemporary social problems.

alone, 12 million Americans used cocaine (Kozel & Adams, 1986). Since 1985, however, the percent of the population who has used cocaine and **crack cocaine** (a crystallized, inexpensive form of street cocaine that is usually smoked) has been steadily decreasing, to an estimated 7.3 million in the year 1990, which represents 3.6 percent of the population over 12 years old (NIAAA, 1991). Nevertheless, a significant proportion of the population struggles with cocaine dependence, and social problems created by the crime associated with crack dealing have become nothing short of a national emergency. Its use in the inner cities has led to what some see as urban anarchy and devastation. Countless numbers of "crack babies," the offspring of addicted mothers, are themselves born with an addiction. Even children who are not addicted suffer neglect and abuse inflicted by crack-addicted parents (Inciardi, 1990).

The decreases nationwide in the use of cocaine and crack cocaine that took place in the late 1980s may be attributed, in part, to changes in the perception of the nature of cocaine. Whereas it was once thought of as a relatively harmless substance that the user can easily control (Washton et al., 1988), cocaine is now viewed more accurately as a highly dangerous and addictive drug. By 1990, more than 70 percent of Americans had come to view occasional use of cocaine and other high-potency drugs as involving a great risk, and 90 percent considered regular use to be outright dangerous (NIAAA, 1991).

Cocaine has a fascinating history that dates back thousands of years. In the United States, its popular use can be traced to the late 1800s, when it was marketed as a cure for everything from fatigue to malaria. A major drug company, Parke-Davis, sold tablets, sprays, and cigarettes that contained cocaine. Coca-Cola was developed in the 1880s, and its stimulating mixture of cocaine and caffeine made it a popular beverage. The cocaine was eliminated from Coca-Cola in 1905.

In the early 1900s, as the use of cocaine continued to spread, authorities in medicine and government began to

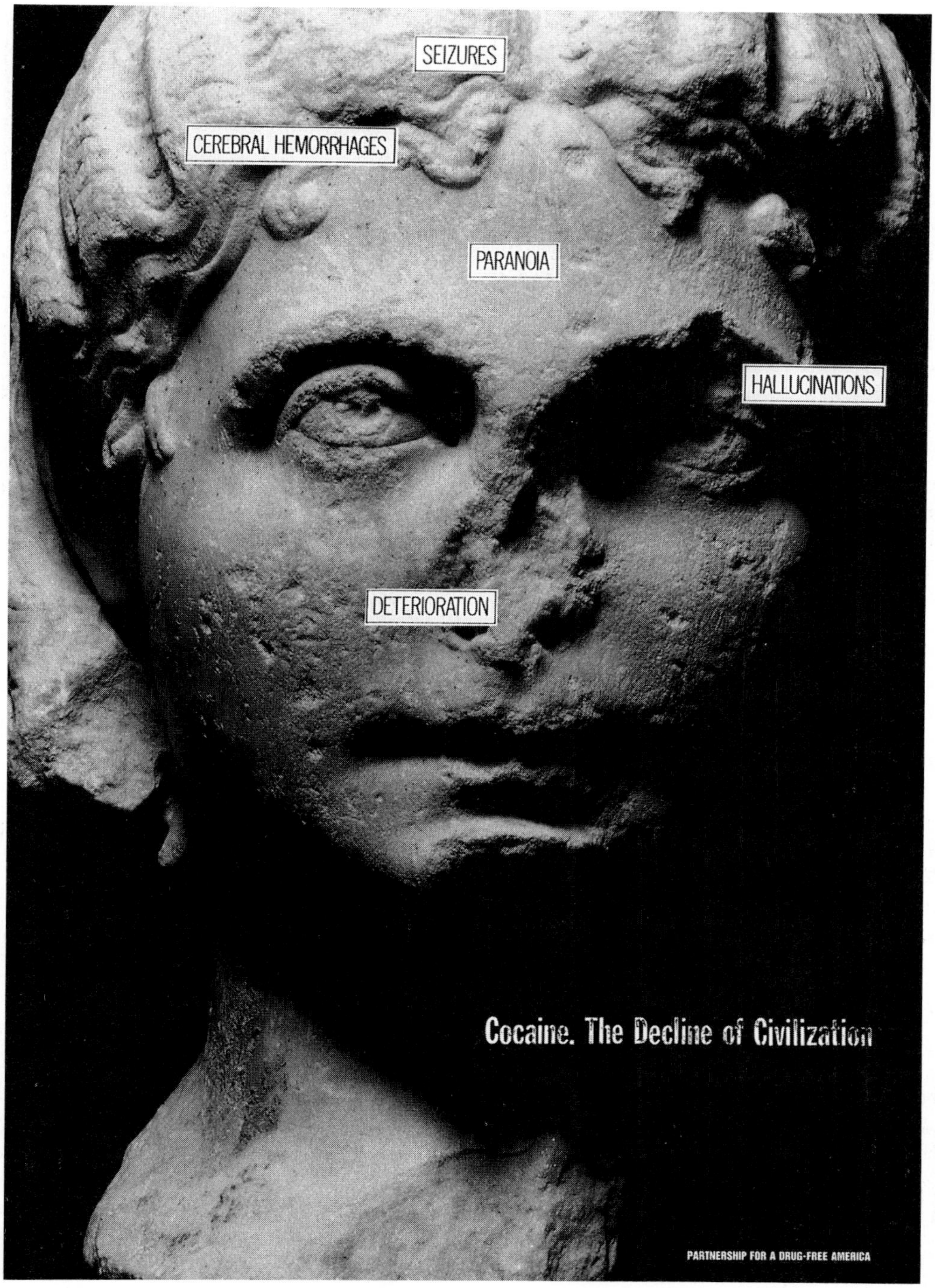

SEIZURES

CEREBRAL HEMORRHAGES

PARANOIA

HALLUCINATIONS

DETERIORATION

Cocaine. The Decline of Civilization

PARTNERSHIP FOR A DRUG-FREE AMERICA

Aggressive advertising is being used to bring public attention to the dangers of cocaine use.

question the medicinal value of the drug and the potential harm it could cause. Reports of addiction, death, and associated crime circulated throughout the United States, resulting in legislation prohibiting interstate shipment of cocaine-containing products. Government controls continued to tighten on the distribution of cocaine for medicinal purposes until it was banned. The drug then became so expensive and difficult to obtain that its use sharply declined for several decades.

During the 1960s and 1970s, a resurgence of cocaine use occurred, because the drug became inaccurately perceived once again as relatively harmless (Smith, 1986). The crack form of cocaine became available on a widespread basis in the 1980s (Siegel, 1982). It appears now that the pendulum is once again swinging toward decreased use of cocaine, including crack cocaine.

Compared to amphetamines, the stimulating effects of cocaine are shorter but much more intense. The strongest effects are experienced within the first 10 minutes after administration, and quickly subside. In moderate doses, cocaine leads to feelings of euphoria, sexual excitement, potency, energy, and talkativeness. At higher doses, users may experience symptoms similar to those of amphetamine psychosis, in which they become delusional, hallucinate, and feel confused, suspicious, and agitated. Their paranoid delusions tend to include suspicions that the police or drug dealers are about to apprehend them or that others who are nearby plan to attack them and steal their cocaine. They may have illusory experiences, perhaps misinterpreting an unexplained noise or misperceiving an object in ways that coincide with their delusional thinking. They may also hallucinate that bugs or foreign objects are on their skin and try desperately to scratch off these objects (Brady et al., 1991). Violence is a common part of the scenario; these people may become dangerously out of control and lash out at others, including those who are closest to them (Amaro et al., 1990).

Needless to say, the psychotic-like states that result from cocaine use are distressing and even terrifying. Between one-half and two-thirds of chronic cocaine users seen in treatment experience these symptoms, and these symptoms are more intense and appear earlier in a cocaine binge in long-term, heavy users (Brady et al., 1991; Satel et al., 1991a). When the effects of cocaine wear off, the user "comes down" or "crashes," experiencing symptoms of depressed mood, sleep disturbance, agitation, craving, and fatigue (Gawin & Kleber, 1986). Chronic heavy users experience these symptoms intensely for up to 3 or 4 days, and for a month afterward still feel some effects of withdrawal (Satel et al., 1991b; Weddington et al., 1990). During these periods, many users reach out to the anxiety-relieving effects of sedatives or alcohol (Gawin & Ellinwood, 1988), and in the process develop a secondary problem of alcohol abuse or dependence (Rounsaville et al., 1991).

In addition to the powerful addictive effects of cocaine, this substance poses a significant danger to a person's vital functions of breathing and blood circulation. With the widespread use of cocaine in the United States during the mid-1980s, the number of fatal cocaine overdoses increased nine times. Although the number of emergency room visits due to cocaine overdose decreased by 1990 (NIDA, 1991), the risks to the chronic user are nevertheless significant. These risks are the result of cocaine's actions as a stimulant to the central nervous system and the sympathetic nervous system, and as a local anesthetic. Cocaine acts simultaneously to increase the sympathetic nervous system stimulation to the heart and to anesthetize the heart muscle so that it is less able to contract and pump blood. During a binge, the individual seeks an ever-greater high by taking in more and more cocaine, leading to higher and higher blood levels of the drug. At these levels, the pumping of the heart becomes impaired, and the heart becomes unable to contract to force blood into the arteries. Also, at high levels, there is a paradoxical effect on the way cocaine is eliminated from the blood. Rather than being eliminated in higher amounts, as you might expect, the elimination rate actually is reduced, further contributing to a rise in cocaine blood levels. Other calamitous changes in the heart also occur during a binge: oxygen can be cut off to the heart muscle, further impairing its ability to contract, and changes in the electrophysiological functioning of the heart lead to irregular rhythms (NIDA, 1991). Cocaine may produce the effect of *kindling*, through which the user develops convulsions because the brain's threshold for seizures has been lowered by repeated exposure to cocaine (Kosten & Kosten, 1991).

Although cocaine produces many harmful side effects, many users are blindly driven in their pursuit of the euphoria associated with a cocaine high. The drug produces this high, it is thought, by blocking the reuptake by neurons of the excitatory neurotransmitters norepinephrine, dopamine,

Actor and comedian John Belushi, shown here in the movie *Animal House*, died tragically from a cocaine overdose. Throughout much of his career, Belushi abused cocaine, claiming that it infused him with the energy and creativity he needed to perform.

Table 15–3 Sample Items from the *Cocaine Abuse Assessment Profile: Addiction/Dependency Self-Test*

Each item receives a "yes" or "no" answer; a "yes" counts toward a positive cocaine abuse score.

1. Do you tend to use whatever supplies of cocaine you have on hand, even though you try to save some for another time?
2. Do you go on cocaine binges for 24 hours or longer?
3. Do you need to be high on cocaine in order to have a good time?
4. Does the sight, thought, or mention of cocaine trigger urges and cravings for the drug?
5. Do you feel guilty and ashamed of using cocaine and like yourself less for doing it?
6. Have your values and priorities been distorted by cocaine use?
7. Do you tend to spend time with certain people or go to certain places because you know that cocaine will be available?
8. Do you hide your cocaine use from "straight" friends or family because you're afraid of their reactions?
9. Have you become less involved in your job or career due to cocaine use?
10. Do you worry about whether you are capable of living a normal and satisfying life without cocaine?

Source: By A. Maxwell, from *The Alcoholics Anonymous Experience* © 1984 by McGraw-Hill and reprinted by permission of the publisher.

and serotonin, leading to higher levels of these substances in the central nervous system. Effective increases of these substances in the brain, particularly dopamine, lead to heightened activity of the sympathetic nervous system and stimulation of pleasure reward centers in the brain (Cooper & Wise, 1980; Koob & Bloom, 1988). In laboratory animals such changes in dopamine lead to self-stimulatory behavior, repetitive actions, hyperactivity, and sexual excitation (Kozel & Adams, 1985). In humans, a similar process accounts for the behaviors associated with the positively reinforcing effects of cocaine. These effects, along with the factor of tolerance, lead users to seek higher and higher dosages of the drug.

As biological researchers attempt to understand the physiological mechanisms responsible for cocaine dependence, clinicians have tried to develop psychological measures sensitive to the behavioral aspects of this disorder. The questions on the *Cocaine Abuse Assessment Profile* shown in Table 15-3 provide a good example of the factors that clinicians look for in assessing signs of the disorder.

How do people become cocaine-dependent? We have already seen that cocaine possesses positive reinforcing qualities that can explain why people become dependent on the drug. But might there also be some factors that predispose certain individuals to be more likely to pursue the experience of a cocaine high? One intriguing possibility comes from the finding that more than one-third of a sample of cocaine-dependent adults had histories of attention-deficit hyperactivity disorder during childhood, or in some cases, continuing into adulthood. Recall from our discussion in Chapter 13 that amphetamines are commonly used to treat children with ADHD. With this fact in mind, researchers have speculated that this past history of stimulant use might predispose individuals to seek cocaine in adulthood. Along these lines, it has also been suggested that some adults may use cocaine as a way to treat their own symptoms of attention deficit disorder (Rounsaville et al., 1991).

Caffeine

Caffeine is a drug that has been used or at least tried by virtually everyone. Over 85 percent of the adults in the United States ingest caffeine on a daily basis, with an average intake of about 200 milligrams per day, or about one cup of coffee (Gilbert, 1984). Even though you may not be a coffee drinker, you almost certainly have had chocolate candy or caffeinated soft drinks. You may even have taken caffeine without knowing it. Caffeine is an ingredient in many prescription and nonprescription medications, including headache remedies and diet pills.

Although you may not think of caffeine as a psychoactive substance, it has a number of effects on mood and alertness (Hughes et al., 1992; Schuckit, 1989) through its activation of the sympathetic nervous system. Even half a cup of coffee can bring about slight improvements in mood, alertness, and clarity of thought; however, as the amount of caffeine ingested on one occasion increases (up to three to four cups of coffee), symptoms of anxiety and irritability similar to those seen in amphetamine use begin to appear. After four to six cups of coffee, the individual can develop symptoms that resemble those of a panic attack, and may experience overstimulation, anxiety, dizziness, ringing in the ears, feelings of derealization, visual hallucinations, and confusion. People who are susceptible to panic attacks may experience these symptoms even after consuming relatively small amounts of caffeine.

You might think that only large quantities of caffeine at one time can bring on physical symptoms, but in fact regular consumption of two to three cups a day can lead to a variety of unpleasant reactions including restlessness, nervousness, excitement, insomnia, flushed face, increased urination, digestive disturbances, muscle twitching, rambling thought or speech, abnormal heart rhythms, inexhaustibility, and psychomotor agitation. A person who drinks up to six cups of coffee a day on a regular basis may develop

Some young people feel that they can achieve social acceptance by agreeing with those who pressure them to try drugs. Researchers have found that marijuana users are much more likely to abuse other substances as well.

delirium. Over the course of years of such heavy consumption, the individual may develop medical conditions such as high blood pressure, rapid and irregular heartbeat, increased respiration rate, and peptic ulcers.

Again, we ask the question—if we know caffeine has so many negative physical and psychological effects, why do most of us consume it regularly? Laboratory research provides impressive evidence about the reinforcing value of caffeine. A subject in an experiment who is given the option of pulling a lever for the reward of a small amount of coffee will pull the lever as many as 2500 times in a row (Hughes et al., 1992). Would you do the same? Perhaps you think you wouldn't, but what if that was the only way you could obtain caffeine? Part of the reason that many people continue to consume caffeine is that they experience unpleasant withdrawal symptoms upon cessation. Caffeine withdrawal symptoms include headache, decreased arousal, fatigue, anxiety, nausea, muscle tension, and irritability. These symptoms, which occur even among moderate caffeine users, appear as soon as 12 hours after caffeine deprivation, peak at 20 to 48 hours, and last at least one week (Griffiths & Woodson, 1988).

MARIJUANA

Marijuana, (also called "grass," "pot," and "weed") is the most widely used illegal drug in the country. By 1990, close to one-third of the U.S. population over the age of 12, or 66.5 million people, had tried marijuana at some point in their lives, and of these, more than one-fifth had used it more than 100 times. Although the percentage of people using marijuana dropped during the 1980s, it remains more popular than all other illegal substances. And although the drop in numbers is encouraging from a public health standpoint, some of the statistics are still of concern (NIDA, 1991). Marijuana users are far more likely than nonusers to use alcohol, cigarettes, and other illicit drugs. The age of first use has become lower in recent years, with usage among teenagers not nearly the rare event it was three decades ago.

What accounts for the relative popularity of marijuana? Two factors seem to be of central importance. First, only 40 percent of Americans surveyed by NIDA regarded trying marijuana as harmful—a far smaller number than those who perceive cocaine use to be risky. Second, marijuana is the most widely available illegal drug.

Marijuana has been used for more than 4,000 years in many cultures throughout the world (Schuckit, 1989). The active drug in marijuana, delta-9-tetrahydrocannabinol (THC), comes from *Cannabis sativa*, a tall, leafy, green plant that thrives in warm climates. The more sunlight the plant receives, the higher the percent of active THC it produces. Marijuana comes from the dried leaves of the plant, and hashish, containing a more potent form of THC, comes from the resins of the plant's flowers. The marijuana or hashish that reaches the street is never pure THC, but always has other substances, such as tobacco, mixed in with it. Synthetic forms of THC are used for medicinal purposes such as treating asthma and glaucoma, and reducing nausea in cancer patients undergoing chemotherapy.

The most common way to take marijuana is to smoke it, but it can also be eaten or injected intravenously. When it is smoked, the peak blood levels are reached in about 10 minutes, but the subjective effects of the drug do not become apparent for another 20 to 30 minutes. The effects of intoxication last for 2 to 3 hours, but the metabolites of THC may remain in the body for 8 or more days.

People take marijuana in order to alter their perceptions of their environment and their bodily sensations. The actual quality and intensity of the experience depends on the purity and form of the drug, on how much is ingested, and, importantly, on what the user's expectations are about the drug's effects. At moderate doses the psychological effects include relaxation and an experience of time "slowing down," a heightened intensity of sensual and sexual enjoyment, hunger, and a greater awareness of stimuli in the surroundings. Thoughts can become more focused on internal experiences and perceptions, but the user's short-term memory and ability to follow instructions can also become impaired (Wu et al., 1988). Some people report that marijuana causes them to feel suspicious and paranoid. At high doses, some people have visual hallucinations accompanied by paranoid delusions (Edwards, 1983); these experiences are more likely to occur in people with a prior psychiatric disorder (e.g., Andreasson et al., 1987; Weller & Halikas, 1985).

Most of the acute effects of marijuana use are reversible, but when taken over long periods of time, marijuana can have a number of adverse effects (Schuckit, 1989). Nasal and respiratory problems such as those encountered by tobacco smokers can develop, including chronic sinus inflammation, bronchial constriction, breathing difficulty, and loss of lung capacity. After years of heavy marijuana use, as with all forms of smoking, the risk of cancer and cardiovascular disease increases. Marijuana has also been shown to have negative effects on reproductive functioning. Men who use the drug regularly have a lower sperm count and are more likely to produce defective sperm, and women may experience delayed ovulation. It has been claimed that a pregnant woman's use of marijuana may also interfere with fetal development (Nahas, 1984), but these effects have been challenged (Smith & Asch, 1987).

You may have heard it said that people who are long-term marijuana users experience memory loss, motivational reduction, and depression. However, it is not clear whether marijuana causes such psychological deficits or whether, long-term heavy users may have had problems *before* they began using the drug. Perhaps they were depressed and amotivational, and were drawn to marijuana use as an attractive form of relief from their personal distress (Schuckit, 1989).

One of the more disturbing effects of marijuana use is increased risk of accidents. In one study, it was reported that up to 17 percent of drivers involved in fatal car accidents tested positively for marijuana (Fortenberry et al., 1986). Similarly, in another study involving airline pilots, it was shown that impaired judgment lasts for as long as 24 hours following marijuana intake (Yesavage et al., 1985).

Since the boom of marijuana use in the 1970s, researchers have been pursuing the causes for its effects on the user as well as its long-term risks. The short-term memory impairment that occurs with marijuana use has been related to decreased rates of acetylcholine activity in the hippocampus (Deadwyler et al., 1990; Domino, 1981). THC also affects other areas of the limbic system, which could account for its subjective time-lengthening effects, changes in

Gary, a 22-year-old man, has lived with his parents since dropping out of college 3 years ago midway through his freshman year. Gary was an average student in high school, and although popular, was not involved in many extracurricular activities. When he entered college, Gary became interested in the enticing opportunities for new experiences, and he began to smoke marijuana casually with his roommates. However, unlike his roommates, who limited their smoking to parties, Gary found that a nightly "hit" helped him relax. He started to rationalize that it also helped him study, because his thinking was more creative. As his first semester went by, he gradually lost interest in his studies, preferring to stay in his room and listen to music while getting high. He realized that it was easy to support his habit by selling marijuana to other people in the dorm. Although he convinced himself that he was not really a dealer, Gary became one of the primary suppliers of marijuana on campus. When he received his first-semester grades, he did not feel particularly discouraged about the fact that he had flunked out. Rather, he felt that he could benefit from having more time to himself. He moved home and hooked up with some local teenagers who frequented a nearby park and shared drugs there. Gary's parents have all but given up on him, having become deeply discouraged by his laziness and unproductivity. They know that he is using drugs, but they feel helpless in their efforts to get him to seek professional help. They have learned that it is better to avoid discussing the matter with Gary, because vehement arguments always ensue.

- Do you think Gary's personality was a strong factor in the development of his marijuana use, or was he more influenced by the college environment?
- What advice would you give Gary's parents to help them cope with the situation?

emotionality, and decreases in motivation. Marijuana is also thought to have pain-alleviating properties, and researchers are seeking the existence of a "marijuana receptor" in the brain to determine if a THC-like substance is a naturally occurring pain reliever in the brain (Howlett et al., 1988). Efforts are even underway to isolate and clone the gene that would produce such marijuana receptors (NIDA, 1991). The field of marijuana research is an active one, and as investigations continue, debate will likely persist regarding whether or not it is a harmful substance.

HALLUCINOGENS

The drugs that fall into the category of **hallucinogens** cause abnormal perceptual experiences in the form of illusions or hallucinations, usually visual in nature. Hallucinogens come in a number of forms, as both naturally occurring and synthetic substances. The most frequently used hallucinogens are lysergic acid diethylamide (LSD), psilocybin

The use of hallucinogenic drugs in the late 1960s was associated with a psychedelic culture involving "flower children," who expressed themselves through eccentric art forms such as body painting.

(found in hallucinogenic mushrooms), dimethyltryptamine (DMT), mescaline (peyote), dimethoxymethylamphetamine (DOM or STP, which stands for "serenity, tranquility, and peace"), methylene dioxymethamphetamine (MDMA), and phecyclidine (PCP). Although the mechanism of their action is not known, it is thought that hallucinogens alter serotonin activity throughout the entire brain, from the brain stem to the cortex (Schuckit, 1989).

LSD (which is also known as "acid," "blue dots," and "cube") was discovered accidentally in a pharmaceutical laboratory in the late 1930s, when a scientist named Albert Hoffman was working with a fungus that was absorbed into his skin, causing him to have a hallucinogenic experience. A few days following his first experience, he thought he would take a small amount to study the effects. This "small" amount was actually many times larger than what is now known to be a sufficient dose to trigger hallucinations, and Hoffman suffered intense and frightening effects. He reported thinking that he was losing his mind, that he was outside his own body, and that time was standing still. Everything around him seemed distorted, and he became terrified of what he saw—experiences now known to be typical effects of LSD ingestion. As reports of this powerful drug spread through the scientific community, researchers wondered whether LSD could be used to understand the symptoms of schizophrenia, which the drug seemed to mimic. This gave rise to a new theory of schizophrenia, but it was later determined that the LSD actions are quite different from those occurring in people with schizophrenia. It was also thought that by using LSD as an adjunct to psychotherapy, the individual's ego defenses could be broken down. In the 1960s, LSD became the central component of a nationwide drug "culture," started by two former Harvard professors, Timothy Leary and Richard Alpert (Alpert now calls himself Baba Ram Dass). Many of the "flower chil-

dren" of the 1960s celebrated the effects of LSD in art, music, and theater.

LSD is an extremely potent psychoactive drug. After ingesting LSD, which us usually taken orally, the user experiences dizziness, weakness, and various physiological changes that lead to euphoria and hallucinations. This experience can last from 4 to 12 hours, with the "high" depending on a number of factors such as the dose, the individual's expectations, prior drug experiences, the setting, and any past psychiatric history. People who use LSD for prolonged periods of time may experience flashbacks, or spontaneous hallucinations, delusions, or disturbances in mood. These symptoms may appear months or even years after the person has stopped taking the drug altogether and may be triggered by stress or by the taking of a milder drug such as marijuana (Schuckit, 1989).

Candace is a 45-year-old artist who used LSD for a number of years because she felt they enhanced her paintings and made them more visually exciting. Although she felt she knew the amount of LSD she could handle, she was caught off guard on one occasion, when the dose she took was unexpectedly potent. She began sweating, her vision became blurred, she became uncoordinated, and she was shaking all over. Paranoid and anxious, Candace ran out of her studio and into the street ranting incoherently. She was picked up by the police and brought to an emergency room where she was given antipsychotic medication.

- Given that Candace claims to have been using LSD to enhance her artwork, would you regard her as dependent on the drug?
- What hazards does Candace face from her long-term use of LSD?

Other hallucinogens differ from LSD in various ways, although they all stimulate visual and sometimes auditory hallucinations. Psilocybin (hallucinogenic mushrooms), in low doses, produces relaxation and feelings of euphoria. PCP, also called "angel dust," "rocket fuel," and "purple," has very unpredictable effects when smoked. In low doses, it acts as a depressant, and the user feels effects similar to alcohol intoxication. Larger doses cause distorted perceptions of self and the environment, sometimes causing users to become aggressive and irrational, even violent. Unlike LSD, PCP can precipitate a temporary psychotic state with symptoms that are virtually indistinguishable from those of schizophrenia. Through a combination of effects on the autonomic nervous system, PCP can also produce severely toxic, life-threatening effects including coma, convulsions, and high blood pressure, progressing to severe brain damage with psychotic symptoms (Schuckit, 1989). Some very disturbing cases have been reported of PCP users becoming so disoriented that they died as a result of accidental falls, drowning, or self-inflicted injuries.

Currently LSD use is relatively uncommon; in a 1990 survey only one percent of Americans over the age of 12 indicated that they had used hallucinogens in the past year. This relatively small incidence of hallucinogen use appears to reflect the perception of most people that these drugs involve a good deal of risk. However, usage by teenagers is higher, with 2.4 percent of those between the ages of 12 and 17 acknowledging hallucinogen use within the past year. Given the many risks associated with its use, there are disturbing implications of the fact that so many teenagers have exposed themselves to these powerful drugs (NIDA, 1991).

OPIOIDS

For much of this century, when people spoke of drug abuse, they were referring to an addiction to *opioids*. Opioids were not regulated by the U.S. government until the 1930s, and they were commonly found in patient medicines issued without prescriptions. Opioids are also called **narcotics**, a term referring to the category of drugs that includes the naturally occurring derivatives of the opium poppy: opium, morphine, and codeine. Other narcotics, such as heroin, are semisynthetic in that they are produced by slight chemical alterations in the basic poppy drug. People who abuse opioids do so for the intensely pleasurable physical sensations and the feelings of euphoria they provide. These drugs also have strong pain-relieving properties.

The use of heroin (also called "brown," "H," and "smack") reached a peak in the 1970s, when approximately 1 percent of the 18 to 25-year-old population was using this drug. Today's youth are one-half as likely to use heroin than the youth of the 1970s. One possible deterrent to heroin use among younger people has been a fear of contracting AIDS by sharing needles (Kozel & Adams, 1986). There are, however, some disturbing reports that heroin use is once again on the rise (Treaster, 1992).

Jimmy is a 38-year-old homeless man who has been addicted to heroin for the past 10 years. He began to use the drug at the suggestion of a friend who told him it would help relieve the pressure Jimmy was feeling from his unhappy marriage and financial problems. In a short period of time, he became dependent on the drug and got involved in a theft ring in order to support his habit. Ultimately he lost his home and ended up moving to a shelter, where he was assigned to a methadone treatment program.

- How similar is Jimmy's drug "career" to the experiences of other heroin users?
- What role do you think the stresses in Jimmy's life played in the development of his addiction?

Among those who started using heroin in the 1970s, many continue to be addicted (Maddux & Desmond, 1981; NIDA, 1991). The life of the heroin addict is filled with desperate attempts to pay for this very expensive addiction through crimes including theft, drug sales, and prostitution (Nurco et al., 1985).

Opioids create their effects by mimicking the action of the body's naturally occurring pleasure-producing and analgesic substances in the nervous system. The **enkephalins** and **endorphins**, as they are called, are produced by the brain in a self-protective way when the body is afflicted by pain. These neurotransmitters bind to neurons that produce pleasurable sensations when stimulated, the same phenomenon that occurs during vigorous, physical exercise (Koob & Bloom, 1988).

Users of opioids develop tolerance to these drugs, become physically dependent on them, and experience intense withdrawal when they stop taking them. Within 12 hours of the last dose, the individual starts to experience physical discomfort such as runny nose, tearing of the eyes, sweating, and yawning. For the next day or two, the indi-

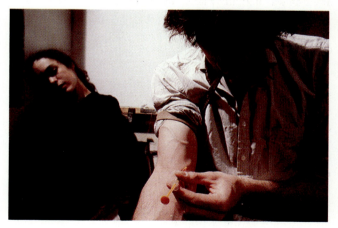

The life of a heroin addict is filled with the daily pursuit to satisfy irresistible cravings. In addition to ravaging their bodies through drug abuse, heroin addicts face the risk of contracting AIDS by sharing needles.

vidual goes into a state of restless sleep, and at that time starts to show other signs of withdrawal including dilated pupils, loss of appetite, gooseflesh, tremor, and back pain. Craving and emotional irritability accompany these physical changes, and in the latter phases of withdrawal (up to one week after the last dose), the individual experiences insomnia, incessant yawning, flu-like symptoms of weakness and gastrointestinal discomfort, and muscle spasms. The acute symptoms are disabling and can be so severe as to be life-threatening. The person feels extremely depressed and possibly suicidal. For a period as long as a year after the last dose, other physiological abnormalities remain including a decrease in respiratory efficiency, an increase in blood pressure, and a sense of vague discomfort that may propel the individual into another episode of heroin use (Schuckit, 1989).

SEDATIVE-HYPNOTICS AND ANTIANXIETY DRUGS

Sedative-hypnotics and antianxiety drugs include a wide range of substances that share the property of inducing relaxation, sleep, tranquility, and reduced awareness of the environment. They are commonly referred to as "downers." All have recognized medical value and are manufactured by pharmaceutical companies; therefore, they are not illegal. However, because these drugs have high potential for abuse, much tighter federal controls have been placed on them since the 1970s. We will discuss *sedative-hypnotics*, a class of drugs comprised of both barbiturate and nonbarbiturate substances. The term **sedative** refers to the calming effect of these drugs on the central nervous system, and the term **hypnotic** refers to their sleep-inducing qualities. We will also look at antianxiety medications as abusive substances.

Barbiturate Sedative-Hypnotics

The barbiturates most frequently abused are ones whose effects persist for several hours at a time, including secobarbital (Seconal), pentobarbitol (Nembutal), amobarbital (Amytal), butabarbitol (Butisol), and combinations of these substances, amobarbital and tuinal. (The street names for these drugs are "blue heavens," "blue devils," "blue angels," "goofballs," and "rainbows"). People who use these substances recreationally are seeking a dulling of consciousness similar to the effects of alcohol use. In low doses, these drugs give a feeling of calm and sedation. At the same time, the individual also feels a sense of increased outgoingness, talkativeness, and euphoria. In higher doses, these barbiturates produce sleep. The sedative effects of barbiturates are due to their action on the GABA and benzodiazepine receptors in the brain (Schoch et al., 1985).

Barbiturates are used medically as anesthetics, anticonvulsants, and sleeping pills. Users find that they quickly become tolerant to the drug, and they must take larger and

What begins as a seemingly harmless use of barbiturates to induce sleep can quickly become a serious problem of dependence and abuse.

larger doses to achieve the desired effects. In the process, they risk accidental suicide due to respiratory failure. Many users also risk death by combining alcohol with these drugs. Alcohol potentiates the effects of barbiturates, and since both kinds of drugs are depressants, the combination can prove fatal. Tolerant users also find that they become physiologically dependent on barbiturates. If they try to stop taking the drug, they experience a withdrawal very similar to that found in people who have become dependent on alcohol.

Nonbarbiturate Sedative-Hypnotics

The most frequently used drug in the category of nonbarbiturate sedative-hypnotics is methaqualone, once marketed as Quaalude. The popularity of this drug, (popularly termed "Lude") can be attributed to the mistaken notion that it is an aphrodisiac or "love drug." When these drugs were introduced in the 1970s, it was thought that they would be nonaddictive and safe substitutes for the barbiturates. They were originally intended to resolve some of the side effects of barbiturate sedative-hypnotics such as sleep disturbances and the feelings of morning-after "hangovers" (Schuckit, 1989). However, it was soon found that the nonbarbiturates have equally addicting effects. They have since been withdrawn from medical use because of their high abuse potential and because nonaddictive substitutes are now available.

Users of methaqualone report that the "high" they experience is more pleasant than that achieved from barbiturate use because there is less of a "knock-out" effect. The feeling that users desire is total dissociation from their physical and mental selves, loss of inhibitions, and greater euphoria during sexual encounters. This latter effect is an illusion, because in reality the user's sexual performance is impaired. Tolerance and dependence develop in ways similar to that for barbiturate use.

Another group of nonbarbiturate medications, sold over-the-counter, are used to induce sleep. The most common brands are NyTol and Sominex. These are actually antihistamines whose efficacy in inducing sleep is variable from person to person.

Antianxiety Medications

The antianxiety medications include diazepam (Valium), clonazepam (Clonopin), chlordiazepoxide (Librium), flurazepam (Dalmane), and temazepam (Restoril). These medications are used specifically to treat anxiety, although they do have other medical uses. They are the most widely prescribed of all medicines. It is only in recent years that the extent of legal abuse of antianxiety medications has become evident. At one time prescriptions for these medications were open-ended; that is, they were given without limits placed on the length of time they could be taken. It was a common misconception that tolerance and dependence did not develop. However, many users found that they had in fact become addicted to these medications. As this phenomenon became more widely known, the federal government placed tighter controls on these substances. The notoriety associated with the tightened controls also focused attention on the use of antianxiety medications as recreational drugs.

Abusers of antianxiety medications seek the sense of calm and relaxation that these substances produce, and over time many increase their intake and become addicted. People who use them for more than a year almost always have withdrawal symptoms when they stop. These symptoms include restlessness, irritability, insomnia, muscle tension, and occasionally other bodily sensations such as weakness, visual problems, and various aches and pains.

They may have troubling nightmares and become hypersensitive to light and sound.

SUBSTANCE ABUSE AND DEPENDENCE: GENERAL TREATMENT ISSUES

In biological treatments of dependence on psychoactive substances other than alcohol, concepts similar to those used in treating alcohol dependence have been applied. For example, blocking agents such as naltrexone (used for heroin dependence) have been administered that prevent the positively reinforcing consequences of the drug. Such approaches have been tried with cocaine, heroin, and sedative hypnotics; however, as in the case of disulfiram for alcohol dependence, these pharmacological treatments alone are not sufficient. The individual must be motivated to comply with such treatment.

Perhaps more successful than blocking or aversive medications has been the provision of **methadone** for heroin addicts. Methadone is a synthetic opioid that produces a safer and more controlled reaction than heroin. When taken daily and in large enough doses, methadone helps prevent the psychological craving for heroin and also blocks its euphoria-producing effects. Unlike heroin, methadone does not interfere with the individual's ability to work and carry out a normal life in the community. A large number of studies on the effectiveness of methadone dating from the mid-1960s (Dole & Nyswander, 1967) to the 1980s (Ball & Corty, 1988) testify to its importance in treating heroin dependence.

A biological focus is also involved in **detoxification treatment** programs, which are intended to minimize the physiological changes associated with withdrawal as the

In methadone treatment programs, addicts are given methadone, a synthetic substance that is less harmful than heroin and presumably allows them to return to normal functioning.

individual goes through the difficult early stages of abstinence. In a detoxification program, the individual is medically monitored and treated throughout the entire withdrawal process. These biological treatments play an important role in breaking the cycle of drug dependence and its associated disorganization of the person's life. When individuals are able to achieve abstinence, they can experience dramatic improvements in their ability to function normally in society, which in turn help further to reinforce abstinence (Kosten et al., 1988).

Comprehensive treatment programs that involve a multifaceted approach to reducing substance dependence seem to hold the greatest potential for successful interventions (Pickens & Fletcher, 1991). Many of the more successful programs in existence today are historically linked to Synanon, a residential treatment approach founded in 1958 based in large part on the philosophy of Alcoholics Anonymous. Other programs based on the same concept are Daytop Village and Phoenix House.

These comprehensive programs rely on the concept of the **therapeutic community** (DeLeon, 1985) in which non-professional staff, who are themselves recovering addicts, help residents become resocialized to a drug-free lifestyle. An important component of the therapeutic community is the staff's continuous confrontation of drug problems that the residents attempt to deny or minimize. Individual and group counseling are also provided, and there is a strong emphasis on self-help; residents are encouraged to share their experiences in small groups and through their daily interactions. Vocational rehabilitation is also used to provide job skills and to offer an opportunity to develop improved feelings of self-esteem. Following from the relapse prevention model, other elements of successful treatment rely on the cognitive-behavioral perspective, including increasing the motivation for abstinence, developing coping skills, finding social support, and reducing the associations of drug-related cues with positive rewards (Finney & Moos, 1992; Hall et al., 1991).

As appealing as such a comprehensive treatment program may sound, the question remains as to whether such treatments are effective. Here again, as in the field of alcohol dependence, the results are less than encouraging. Although any individual who is sufficiently motivated to participate in treatment for substance dependence may in fact be able to maintain abstinence or, at least, reduce intake of the drug, most abusers never enter treatment. It is estimated that more than one-half of intravenous drug abusers have never been in treatment, because either they lack the incentive to change, they are unable to pay for treatment, or they do not want their drug problem exposed to others. Further, of those who manage to enter treatment, 50 percent secretly continue to use illicit drugs, 80 percent eventually drop out of the program, and about 50 percent of those who complete treatment relapse within 3 years (Pickens & Fletcher, 1991). Over the 12-year period of one

follow-up study of opioid users who had sought treatment, a significant number (39 percent) were still using opioids, and 25 percent were using alcohol as a substitute (Simpson & Sells, 1990).

These very discouraging statistics highlight the frustrating nature of substance abuse as a problem for individuals and for society. The ostensibly voluntary nature of substance dependence makes it hard for people who are not substance abusers to understand why it is not possible for abusers to stop at will. A well-known anti-drug campaign has proposed that people should "just say no" to drugs. Although this is an important message to youth who are tempted to experiment with drugs, saying no to drugs may not be so easy for those who have become dependent upon them. Clinicians working with substance abusers know that the treatment of drug dependence is an extremely complicated process requiring extensive commitment on the part of the client, sensitivity on the part of the clinician, and support from family members.

SUBSTANCE ABUSE AND DEPENDENCE: THE PERSPECTIVES REVISITED

It is clear that the biochemical mechanisms involved in the brain's responses to substance intake play a primary role in determining a drug's effects on physical and psychological functioning. However, it is also clear that these physiological factors interact with psychological influences to produce patterns of dependence in drug users. Although each substance involves unique biochemical patterns of responsiveness, there appear to be similarities across drugs in the factors involved in developing dependence. Marlatt, whom we discussed in the context of understanding and treating alcohol dependence, based the development of the expectancy model on the assumption that similar processes underlie all the addictions, including alcohol, other psychoactive substances, compulsive eating, and cigarette smoking.

In formulating a general model of psychoactive substance dependence, we can start with the proposition that for a drug to have a high addictive potential, the receptors to which the drug binds in the nervous system must somehow play a role in causing a subjective sense of pleasure or relief from a state of distress. Once the pattern of reinforcement has been established, biochemical changes in the brain produce a long-term pattern of dependence, with the associated symptoms of tolerance and withdrawal. Adding to these physiological–behavioral mechanisms are cognitive expectations that the user has regarding the effects of the substance. In cases where the user attempts to achieve abstinence, the ability to do so also depends on perceived feelings of self-efficacy, and whether the user feels able to control the pattern of substance abuse.

Table 15–4	SUBSTANCE RELATED DISORDERS: A SUMMARY CHART OF PERSPECTIVES	
SUBSTANCE	BIOLOGICAL	OTHER PERSPECTIVES
Alcohol	Genetic factors suggested by familial patterns, twin and adoption studies, and psychophysiological marker studies. Biochemical explanations focus on GABA, dopamine, and serotonin neurotransmitters.	Integrates biological predispositions to alcoholism along with life history and sociocultural factors. Research on Type 1–Type 2 alcoholism suggests differing contributions of genetic and environmental factors in different forms of alcoholism. Cognitive expectations about alcohol, coping skills, self-efficacy, and interpretation of lapses further influence development of dependence in vulnerable individuals.
	Treatments: Medications to block alcohol's effects or to create aversive associations between alcohol use and unpleasant physical reactions. Other medications ameliorate psychological symptoms such as anxiety and depression, and control withdrawal symptoms.	**Treatments:** Behavioral therapy, including covert sensitization and cue exposure. Relapse prevention model based on cognitive-behavioral model to build coping skills and Self-help programs such as Alcoholics Anonymous emphasize similar processes, but regard alcoholism as a disease outside a person's control.
Other Psychoactive Substances Amphetamines	Stimulant action due to effects on norepinephrine which stimulates the sympathetic nervous system. Tolerance quickly develops. Dependence may occur in an individual using the drug for medical purposes.	Psychological dependence develops along with physical dependence.
Cocaine	Blocks the reuptake of dopamine leading to increased levels of this neurotransmitter in the brain and associated stimulation of pleasure reward centers.	Positive reinforcement caused by stimulation of pleasure centers in brain along with increased tolerance lead users to seek higher and higher dosages of cocaine.
Caffeine	Activates the sympathetic nervous system.	Positive reinforcement maintains caffeine dependence.
Marijuana	Active substance, delta-9-THC, is thought to bind with "marijuana receptors" in the brain.	People attracted to marijuana may be depressed and amotivational and drawn to marijuana to relieve their personal distress.
Hallucinogens	Serotonin activity is altered throughout the entire brain.	Positive stimulation of a "high" causes user to feel sense of expanded consciousness.
Opioids	Produce pleasurable effects by binding to opiate receptors in the brain and simulating the effects of enkephalins and endorphins.	Inability to maintain abstinence occurs as a result of craving for the drug and a desire to relieve painful withdrawal symptoms.

Table 15–4   SUBSTANCE RELATED DISORDERS: SUMMARY CHART (CONTINUED)

SUBSTANCE	BIOLOGICAL	OTHER PERSPECTIVES
Sedative-hypnotics and anti-anxiety drugs	Sedative effects of barbiturates produced by actions on GABA and benzodiazepine receptors. **Treatment**: Administering medications that block the effects of the drug, produce aversive consequences, or (in the case of heroin) simulate the drug's effect. Detoxification used to help individual overcome withdrawal symptoms.	Relief from anxiety is reinforcing and dependence develops from a need to avoid withdrawal symptom **Treatment**: Therapeutic communities emphasize processes of mutual support, confrontation of denial, and resocialization to a drug-free lifestyle. Cognitive-behavioral interventions which build coping skills, feelings of self-efficacy, and social support, and attempt to remove positive associations to drug use.

SUMMARY

1. A psychoactive substance is a chemical that alters a person's mood or behavior when it is ingested. When people become intoxicated with a psychoactive substance, their behavior is altered by an accumulation of the substance in the body. Signs of withdrawal often follow intoxication. During withdrawal, the individual experiences physical and psychological symptoms that can sometimes include frightening and life-threatening changes. People who are chronic users of psychoactive substances often develop tolerance, a condition in which more and more of the substance is needed to obtain the desired effect (or less effects are experienced when the same amount is taken). Tolerance can occur either through changes in the body's metabolism or through the drug's effects on the nervous system.

2. Substance abuse consists of using alcohol or drugs in excessive amounts, such that the individual's health or safety is threatened and problems are created in daily life. The point at which substance abuse becomes dependence is debated by researchers and clinicians, but it is generally agreed that dependence involves a pattern of tolerance to the substance along with withdrawal when the drug is discontinued. Another important and controversial distinction is made between psychological and physiological or physical dependence. Psychological dependence is regarded as the subjective sense of craving for the substance, and physiological dependence involves an altered state of the body's cells, which have adapted to continued intake of the substance.

3. Problems with alcohol use affect a large percentage of people in the United States, including people who have problems themselves and people who are related to alcohol-dependent individuals. Some of the emotional problems that children of alcohol-dependent parents face have been the focus of attention of the Adult Children of Alcoholics (ACOA) movement. Alcohol is costly in economic as well as human terms, with estimates of yearly expenses related to alcohol use ranging up to $136 billion. The number of deaths due to alcohol-related illness and accidents is estimated to be a minimum of 3 out of every 100.

4. In small amounts, alcohol has sedating effects, and in larger amounts, it can help the user feel less inhibited and more socially adept. As alcohol is taken in larger and larger amounts, its function as a depressant becomes more apparent, and the individual becomes sleepy, uncoordinated, dysphoric, and irritable. Many factors influence the subjective and physiological effects of alcohol on the individual, including the drinker's expectations, the setting, the drinker's metabolism rate, and the rate and form of alcohol intake. Following extensive alcohol use, a person may experience an abstinence syndrome, or "hangover," which includes symptoms of nausea, vomiting, headache, tiredness, irritability, depression, and dizziness. The short-term effects of alcohol appear to be attributable to alcohol's effects of increasing the inhibitory activity of the GABA neurotransmitter system, and also possibly to decreasing the excitatory activity of glutamate. There are many harmful effects of long-term alcohol use, including forms of dementia such as Wernicke's disease and Korsakoff's syndrome, cardiovascular disease, cirrhosis of the liver, damage to the gastrointestinal system, osteoporosis, muscle damage, a heightened risk of cancer, and reduced immune functioning.

(Summary continued on p. 400.)

Return to the Case

Carl Wadsworth

Carl's History

After meeting with Carl for an initial intake session, I asked him to return 2 days later so that I could take some additional history. When Carl returned for our second meeting, he seemed relieved and said that acknowledging the fact that he had a problem was tremendously comforting to him. I explained to Carl that I wanted to get a clearer picture of his life history, and he proceeded to tell the story that would later help me understand how he had gotten to this point of desperation.

An only child, Carl grew up in a small midwestern town where his father was a well-loved and respected "family doctor." Carl's father had himself been the son of a physician, and it was generally assumed by his parents all through Carl's childhood that Carl would carry on the family tradition. This meant that Carl had to devote himself entirely to his schoolwork, since math and science did not come easily to him. In college, he became desparate and repeatedly sought out help from his classmates. After he entered medical school, this pattern of dependence continued, and he would find one or two older students who would help him through his exams, lab work, and hospital duties because they felt sorry for him. Even though Carl felt guilty about his reliance on others, he contended that it was necessary because his parents would be crushed if he failed. In his third year of medical school Carl met Anne, a nurse at the medical school, whom he married after a few months of dating. Shortly after their marriage, Anne became pregnant, and they mutually agreed that she would stay home and care for their baby after the birth.

Assessment

The only psychological test that I administered to Carl was the *MMPI-2*. The diagnostic picture seemed fairly clear to me, but I usually find it helpful to have the quantitative data provided by the *MMPI-2* to formulate my treatment recommendations. Carl's profile was that of a man struggling with dependency issues and having a propensity for acting out, particularly when confronted with difficult or demanding situations. It was not surprising to see that Carl scored very highly on indicators of addiction proneness.

Diagnosis

Carl's Axis I diagnosis was clear. Carl was using heavy amounts of cocaine; he had begun to undermine successful life pursuits in his attempt to satisfy his cravings; cocaine use was interfering with his work and family life; and he had become more and more withdrawn from others as he compulsively pursued satisfaction for his cravings. As apparent as the diagnosis of cocaine dependence was, this single diagnostic label could not tell the whole story. It was apparent to me that Carl also had a personality disorder, a style of functioning that led him to become overly reliant on other people, defining himself according to the wishes of his parents and passing through life's hurdles by becoming pathologically dependent on others.

Axis I.   Cocaine Dependence.
Axis II. Dependent Personality Disorder.
Axis III. Deferred.
Axis IV. Severity: 3. Family and work stresses.
Axis V.   Current Global Assessment of Functioning: 50. Serious symptoms or impairment are likely. Highest Global Assessment of Functioning (past year): 7. Some mild difficulty in functioning.

Case Formulation

What would lead a young man to risk such a promising career and potentially happy family life just to get high on cocaine? Obviously there is no simple explanation for why Carl could have become so compulsively involved in a world of drugs. Looking back to Carl's youth, I saw a boy growing up in a family where intense pressure to become a doctor not only determined his career choice, but also set the stage for his becoming reliant on others in order to reach his goal. It was as if Carl had absorbed a message from his father that a medical career was the only acceptable option, and his failure to achieve such a goal would result in rejection. Desperate to avoid this, Carl resorted to any means necessary to succeed, rationalizing that his dependence on others was necessary for the good of other people. As the pressures of medical training mounted and his own feelings of inadequacy grew, Carl sought out someone on whom to rely. His marriage to Anne probably was more of an expression of his need for a caretaker than an expression of love and mutuality. As time went by, Anne could not save Carl from his own feelings of low self-esteem, so he felt compelled to find something that would make him feel better about himself. Unfortunately, that something was cocaine, an insidious substance that would delude Carl into

Carl Wadsworth continued

believing that he was happy, competent, and successful.

Planning a Treatment

Carl Wadsworth had both immediate and long-term treatment needs. First and foremost, his cocaine dependence required aggressive intervention. I knew that my recommendation would not be enthusiastically received by Carl, but I felt that a 4-week inpatient stay would be required in order for him to receive the multi-disciplinary attention that a severe substance abuse problem requires. As I expected, Carl raised a number of concerns about interruption of his medical training, disruption of his family life, and one other concern that was at the heart of Carl's objections—what would other people think? In response, I impressed on Carl the seriousness and the urgency of his problem. I also convinced him that this was a good time for him to begin to work on being more honest with other people. Initially, Carl took offense at this observation, but he soon began to see my point. The long-term plan would involve intensive psychotherapy, probably lasting at least a year following his discharge from the substance abuse treatment program. I pointed out to Carl that he needed to come to grips with the issues in his life that led him to this pathetic situation; he also needed to develop autonomy and an improved sense of self-esteem. Perhaps he could begin to set his own goals in life; perhaps he could tap his own inner resources to achieve those goals; and perhaps he could develop new cognitive strategies that would result in his feeling better about himself. All this would require intensive confrontational psychotherapy.

Outcome of the Case

Carl did follow through on my recommendations, although initially it seemed to me that his compliance was dictated by a fear of being expelled from residency training. Upon entering the center, Carl was not completely prepared for the rigor and vigilance shown by the staff in preventing the patients from gaining access to drugs. He made unsuccessful attempts to obtain cocaine, and he was confronted very harshly on this behavior by other patients and staff. The harshness of the confrontation apparently awakened Carl to the depth of his problem; this proved to be a major turning point for Carl on his road to recovery.

By the time of his discharge, Carl had shown a good deal of psychological growth and was prepared to move to the next step of treatment: intensive psychotherapy. Carl was referred to a psychologist who specializes in treating professionals with substance abuse problems. A part of Carl's treatment involved participation in weekly meetings of a local group of physicians who had similar problems with substance abuse. The changes in Carl over the course of a year were dramatic. By the time his second child was born, Carl's priorities had evolved to a point where he was able to recognize the centrality of his wife and children in his life. At work, he consciously devoted effort to resuming a bedside manner with patients that, a few years earlier, had engendered a great deal of respect from others. Carl began to think in more constructive ways, looking for solutions to life's problems rather than escape, and feeling that he had the personal competence to work toward these solutions.

As I recall the case of Carl Wadsworth, I think of a man who was on the verge of self-destruction. Had he not encountered an understanding supervisor who responded to his crisis with firm insistence that he get help, I fear that Carl's fate would have been tragic.

5. Alcohol is the most widely used drug in the United States. Patterns of alcohol use show that of the 15 million Americans who abuse or are dependent on the substance, the majority (approximately two-thirds) are men, particularly those between the ages of 18 and 29. However, alcohol-related problems also exist in other populations. Although the percentage of high school-seniors who report occasional or heavy alcohol use has been declining since 1975, a significant proportion are regular drinkers, and almost all high school seniors have tried alcohol.

6. Patterns of family inheritance and evidence from twin and adoption studies suggest that there is an inherited component to alcohol dependence. Further evidence of genetic contributions comes from biological marker studies in which sons of alcoholics show patterns of EEG and subjective responses to alcohol similar to alcoholics. Researchers are exploring the biochemical mechanisms of alcohol dependence, and are focusing their attention on the GABA, serotonin, and dopamine systems. There are also efforts underway to find an "alcoholism gene" that would account for

abnormalities in biochemical processes in the brains of alcoholics.

7. Psychological explanations of alcohol dependence focus on life history, experiential factors, and socio-cultural influences, but also integrate these factors with genetic and biological mechanisms in what is called the *biopsychosocial model*. Research on the transition from adolescent to adult drinking patterns suggests that some individuals with strong genetic predispositions to becoming alcohol-dependent show early signs of antisocial behavior and lack of close relationships with others. A proposed distinction between Type 1 and Type 2 differentiates groups of people according to the role of genetic versus environmental causes of alcohol dependence. The *expectancy model* focuses on cognitive-behavioral and social learning factors involved in psychological dependence. According to this model, individuals become dependent on alcohol and are unable to abstain from its use because they hold positive expectations about alcohol's effects, have low self-efficacy regarding their ability to control their drinking, and misinterpret lapses in their attempt to remain abstinent as further evidence of their lack of self-control, a phenomenon referred to as the abstinence violation effect.

8. Biological treatments of alcohol dependence involve different types of medications that serve different functions in helping alcoholics recover. The first set of medications are benzodiazepines, used to manage withdrawal symptoms and prevent delirium tremens. Other antianxiety and antidepressant medications reduce co-existing symptoms associated with alcohol dependence. The third category of medications, all of which are in the experimental stage, produce changes in the brain intended to reduce the desire for alcohol through stimulation of neurotransmitters such as GABA, serotonin, and dopamine. The fourth category of medications are used in combination with principles of aversive conditioning and are intended to produce an association between alcohol and a set of unpleasant, even violent, bodily reactions. Disulfiram (Antabuse) is the most well-known of these medications.

9. Psychological treatments of alcohol dependence use behavioral or cognitive-behavioral methods to help individuals control their drinking. The more behaviorally oriented approaches are based on techniques similar to those involved in the use of disulfiram, namely, to break the individual's positive associations to alcohol use and replace these with aversive associations. In one variant of the behavioral method that relies on principles of extinction, the cue exposure method, the individual is given a small dose of alcohol and urged not to have more. Cognitive-behavioral methods based on the expectancy model, called *relapse prevention*, focus on the user's expectations about the effects of alcohol, the situational factors that affect drinking behavior, and feelings of self-efficacy regard-

ing the ability to control relapses. Individuals are given homework assignments in which they become increasingly exposed to high-risk situations and practice abstinence. They are encouraged to view their lapses as unfortunate, but not as proof of their inability to control their drinking. To be effective, this form of treatment requires a long-term program of maintenance therapy.

10. Alcoholics Anonymous, a self-help movement started in the mid-1930s, provides a set of guidelines that have been widely adopted in alcohol treatment programs. Through a series of "twelve steps," alcohol-dependent individuals learn to regard their drinking behavior as a disease that can never be cured, and that can be controlled only by total commitment to maintaining abstinence. Social support and frequent meetings in which members share their experiences with alcohol form a fundamental aspect of treatment. The efficacy of Alcoholics Anonymous has been questioned, because relatively few alcohol-dependent individuals enter this form of treatment and survey results are biased because dropouts are not included in the statistics. However, Alcoholics Anonymous appears to work for many individuals, especially when combined with other treatment methods and for those who regard their behavior as controlled by factors outside their personal control, such as fate or spirituality.

11. Amphetamines are stimulants that cause feelings of euphoria, increase confidence, talkativeness, and energy. Continued use at high doses can cause a person to appear psychotic. Amphetamines have been used in medical contexts as appetite suppressants, but because of the likelihood of dependence developing, they have fallen into disfavor. The psychological effects of these drugs reflect their action on the central and autonomic nervous systems of enhancing the action of norepinephrine. Users quickly build a tolerance to amphetamines and easily become dependent on them. Many medical problems can result from amphetamine use, and withdrawal is experienced following cessation.

12. Although all stimulant drugs are of concern, the use of cocaine and crack cocaine (a crystallized form of cocaine) has generated the greatest cause for alarm in recent years. During the 1980s cocaine became the drug of choice for recreational users. Compared to amphetamines, the stimulating effects of cocaine are shorter but more intense, with the strongest effects being felt within the first 10 minutes after administration. Cocaine causes feelings of euphoria, sexual excitement, potency, energy, and talkativeness. At higher doses, users may experience symptoms similar to those of amphetamine psychosis. When the effects of cocaine wear off the user "crashes," experiencing symptoms of depressed mood, sleep disturbance, agitation, craving and fatigue. In addition to powerful addictive effects, cocaine poses a danger to a person's vital functions of breathing and blood circulation. Despite serious risks,

cocaine addicts are driven in their pursuit of the euphoria associated with a cocaine high. The drug produces this high by blocking the reuptake by neurons of the excitatory neurotransmitters norepinephrine, dopamine, and serotonin, leading to higher levels of these substances in the central nervous system; the result is stimulation of pleasure reward centers in the brain.

13. Caffeine is a drug used or tried by almost everyone, with 85 percent of adults reporting daily intake. Low doses of caffeine produce alertness and clarity of thought due to an activation of the sympathetic nervous system. High doses can create anxiety and irritability, and even dizziness, visual hallucinations, and confusion. Two to three cups of coffee a day can lead to a variety of reactions, including restlessness, nervousness, insomnia, and agitation. Over the course of many years, heavy consumers can develop serious medical problems such as high blood pressure, and ulcers. The withdrawal symptoms associated with caffeine include headache, fatigue, nausea, and irritability.

14. Marijuana, the most widely used illegal drug in the United States, contains the ingredient delta-9-THC. At moderate doses, this substance causes the user to experience a pleasurable sense of relaxation, but at higher doses it can lead to visual hallucinations and paranoid delusions. There are a number of documented medical effects of long-term marijuana use, but the extent to which chronic users experience negative psychological effects is unclear. Researchers are attempting to find a "marijuana receptor" in the brain that accounts for THC's effects.

15. Hallucinogens are psychoactive substances that cause the user to have abnormal perceptual experiences in the form of illusions and hallucinations. These drugs appear to have their effects through actions on the level of serotonin in the brain. There are a number of serious effects of chronic hallucinogen use, perhaps the most disturbing of which are flashbacks, in which the individual has hallucinations without having taken the drug.

16. Opioids, including heroin and morphine, are chronically addictive substances, and users often remain dependent for 20 years or more. These drugs owe their addictive potential in large part to the high degree of euphoria they create as well as the extremely unpleasant physical withdrawal symptoms and strong sense of craving they create when drug use is stopped. The effect of opioids has been attributed to their role in stimulating the activity of opioid receptors in the brain which naturally respond to enkephalins and endorphins, the brain's pain-killing substances. These drugs are very dangerous because they can lead to death from overdose.

17. Sedative-hypnotics and antianxiety drugs give users feelings of calm, relaxation, and sleepiness. However, after taking the drug for more than a year, if they try to discontinue, users experience withdrawal symptoms involving anxiety, irritability, insomnia, and other disturbing bodily sensations. The effects of barbiturates are due to their interaction with GABA and benzodiazepine receptors. All of these drugs have high addictive potential, and when used for medical purposes must be carefully monitored.

18. In formulating a general model of substance abuse and dependence, the role of biological factors appears to be central; most psychoactive substances trigger changes in the body that lead to the development of tolerance and withdrawal. These drugs also appear to stimulate neurotransmitters in the brain involved in positive reward, and therefore their use is highly reinforcing. There is also some indication that some individuals have a genetic predisposition to becoming dependent on certain substances. The person's positive expectations about the effects of a substance, lack of coping skills for handling high-risk situations, and feelings of low self-efficacy over controlling substance use areadditional cognitive-behavioral factors that can propel the individual into an unremitting pattern of dependence.

19. Evidence is discouraging regarding the long-term effectiveness of substance abuse treatment programs in helping chronic users to maintain abstinence and avoid relapses. Few users are motivated to enter treatment, and once they do, there is a strong temptation to obtain drugs illicitly or to drop out of the program altogether. The most successful treatment programs are comprehensive therapeutic communities in which clients are resocialized to a drug-free lifestyle and taught new job and coping skills.

KEY TERMS

Psychoactive substance: a chemical that alters a person's mood or behavior by being drunk, smoked, inhaled, swallowed in pill form, or directly injected. p. 372

Intoxication: the experience of altered behaviors due to the accumulation of a psychoactive substance in the body. p. 372

Withdrawal: physical and psychological changes that accompany discontinuation of a psychoactive substance. p. 372

Tolerance: the extent to which the individual requires larger and larger amounts of the substance in order to achieve its desired effects or feels less of its effects after using the same amount of the substance. p. 372

Substance abuse: a pattern of psychoactive substance use said to occur when an individual's health or safety is threatened and problems are created in daily life. p. 373

Dependence: a psychological and often physical need for a psychoactive substance. p. 373

Depressant: a psychoactive substance that causes depression of central nervous system activity. p. 375

Potentiation: the combination of effects of two or more psychoactive substances such that the total effect is greater than the effect of either substance alone. p. 375

Wernicke's disease: an acute condition, associated with long-term, heavy alcohol use, involving delirium, eye movement disturbances, difficulties in movement and balance, and deterioration of the peripheral nerves to the hands and feet. p. 376

Korsakoff's syndrome: a permanent form of dementia associated with long-term alcohol use in which the individual develops retrograde and anterograde amnesia, leading to an inability to remember recent events or learn new information. p. 376

Alcohol dehydrogenase (ADH): a zinc-containing enzyme that breaks alcohol down into fatty acids, carbon dioxide, and water. p. 377

Biopsychosocial model: a model that proposes an integration of biological, psychological, and sociocultural factors in explaining why some people develop alcoholism. p. 379

Expectancy model: an approach to alcohol dependence that focuses on expectancies of alcohol as pleasure producing and anxiety-reducing, reinforcement, and tolerance. p. 380

Abstinence violation effect: a concept associated with the expectancy model referring to a sense of loss of control over one's ability to refrain from engaging in an addictive behavior. p. 380

Delirium tremens: a physical condition consisting of autonomic nervous system dysfunction, confusion, and possible seizures associated with alcohol withdrawal. p. 381

Disulfiram: known popularly as Antabuse, a medication used in the treatment of alcoholism that inhibits aldehyde dehydrogenase (ALDH) and causes severe physical reactions when combined with alcohol. p. 382

Aldehyde dehydrogenase (ALDH): an enzyme that is involved in metabolizing alcohol. p. 382

Cue exposure method: a behavioral approach to alcohol treatment in which the individual is given a priming dose of alcohol that initiates the craving for more alcohol; the person is then urged to refuse further alcohol. p. 382

Relapse prevention therapy: a treatment method based on the expectancy model, in which individuals are encouraged not to view lapses from abstinence as signs of certain failure. p. 382

Stimulants: psychoactive substances that have an activating effect on the central nervous system. p. 385

Stimulant psychosis: a condition involving delusions or hallucinations that develops from chronic use of amphetamines, or with one very large dose of amphetamines. p. 385

Crack cocaine: a crystallized form of cocaine. p. 386

Hallucinogens: psychoactive substances that cause the user to experience abnormal perceptual experiences in the form of illusions or hallucinations, usually visual in nature. p. 391

Narcotics: a term referring to the category of opioid drugs that includes the naturally occurring derivatives of the opium poppy: opium, morphine, and codeine. p. 393

Enkephalins: natural painkilling substances produced by the brain that can produce pleasurable sensations. p. 393

Endorphins: natural painkilling substances produced by the brain that can produce pleasurable sensations. p. 393

Sedatives: psychoactive substances that have a calming effect on the central nervous system. p. 394

Hypnotics: psychoactive substances that are used as sleep medications. p. 394

Methadone: a synthetic opioid that produces a safer and more controlled reaction than heroin and is used in treating heroin addiction. p.395

Detoxification treatment: the managing of an individual's withdrawal symptoms through the difficult early stages of abstinence. p. 395

Therapeutic community: a concept developed in treating substance abuse in which individuals are resocialized to a drug-free lifestyle through a multi-faceted approach. p. 396

Case Report: Neil Gorman

When I read the weekend emergency admission log on Monday morning, I was perplexed by the entry next to Neil Gorman's name: "22-year-old white male; depression and suicidal ideation because of gambling problems." It is unusual for problem gamblers to seek professional help and extremely rare for them to be hospitalized. Although I was very experienced in conducting assessments of depressed individuals, I felt a bit unsure about how to evaluate the role of gambling in an individual's depression. My preliminary concerns subsided once I heard Neil's story.

When I first met Neil, I was struck by several things about him. As he walked into my office, his shuffling gait and sad demeanor reflected his depression. I was struck by the many scars that marked his face and neck—apparently the residual signs of severe acne. Neil's response to my inquiry about his current problems was a sheepish recitation of self-denigrating comments about how stupid he was not to have realized how out of control his gambling had gotten. Not only had Neil lost every penny during these past 2 years, but he had incurred debts so large that it would be many years before he would be able to pay them off.

Neil's deepening addiction to gambling had begun with relatively innocent forays into gambling as a teenager and culminated in financial disaster during his early 20s. With each card game, with each new bet, Neil had become increasingly desperate in his attempt to fulfill his fantasy of "winning big" and being able to erase the dozens of debts he had accumulated. Realizing that the odds were more and more against him, Neil reached a point of feeling that suicide was the only way out. His wife, Beverly, became increasingly aware of the seriousness of his depression and insisted he go to the hospital.

Neil's story was certainly a sad one. He was a relatively young man who had created a problem for himself that had no easy solution. His financial situation was bleak and his emotional state desperate. Helping this man overcome the tragic crisis he had created in his life would be a tremendous challenge.

Sarah Tobin, PhD

16

DISORDERS OF SELF-CONTROL

You have probably had experiences in which you felt an uncontrollable impulse to do something that you later regretted. Perhaps you yelled at a driver who cut you off in traffic, and maybe you even fantasized about physically confronting the person. There may have been other times when you binged on junk food to the the point of feeling sick. Or perhaps, as in the case of Neil's compulsive gambling, you have gotten carried away at a racetrack or in a poker game, feeling unable to resist going after a bigger win. Such experiences are relatively common; however, some people go to extremes, engaging in these behaviors repetitively and compulsively, and feeling tormented by their inability to control themselves. In this chapter we will discuss disorders that are characterized by a seeming inability to resist the urge to engage in certain unacceptable and harmful behaviors.

After reading this chapter, you should be able to:

- Define an impulse control disorder.
- Describe the features of disorders of impulse control, including kleptomania, pathological gambling, pyromania, sexual impulsivity, trichotillomania, and intermittent explosive disorder.
- Understand current theories and treatments for the disorders of impulse control.
- Describe the eating disorders of anorexia nervosa and bulimia nervosa.
- Understand current theories and treatments of eating disorders.

IMPULSE CONTROL DISORDERS

Many of the self-control disorders involve disturbances in the ability to regulate an **impulse**—an urge to act. People with **impulse control disorders** act on certain impulses involving some potentially harmful behavior that they cannot resist. Impulsive behavior in and of itself is not necessarily harmful; in fact, we all act impulsively upon occasion. Usually our impulsive acts have no ill effects, but in some instances they may involve risk. Consider the following two examples. While walking through a clothing store, a young woman decides on the spur of the moment to charge an expensive sweater which is over her budget; she may regret her decision later, but few serious consequences will result. Were she to use all her financial resources to buy an expensive sports car, the consequences would be considerably more serious. Neither of these situations is as threatening as that of another woman, who invites a man she has just met at a singles bar to her apartment where they have unprotected sex—a behavior that puts her at serious risk. People with impulse control disorders repeatedly engage in behaviors that are potentially harmful, feeling unable to stop themselves, and experiencing a sense of desperation if they are thwarted from carrying out their impulsive behavior.

Impulse control disorders have three essential features. First, people with these disorders are unable to stop from acting on impulses that are harmful to themselves or others. Some people attempt to fight their impulses and others give in when they feel the urge to act. The act can be spontaneous or planned. Second, before they act on their impulse, people with these disorders feel pressured to act, experiencing tension and anxiety that can only be relieved by following through on their impulse. Some people with these disorders experience a feeling of arousal that they liken to sexual excitement. Third, upon acting on their impulse, they experience a sense of pleasure or gratification, also likened to the release of sexual tension.

Individuals with impulse control disorders are not usually conflicted at the moment of choosing to engage in the behavior. Conflict, regret, and remorse, if they do occur, appear afterwards.

Kleptomania

You may have heard the term *kleptomaniac* used to describe a person who shoplifts or takes things from other people's houses. People with the impulse control disorder called **kleptomania** do not take things on a whim or out of economic necessity, but because they are driven by persistent urges to steal.

■ *Characteristics of kleptomania*

If you thought that a kleptomaniac was someone driven to acquire possessions, it may surprise you to learn that people with this impulse control disorder are driven by the desire to steal, not the desire to have. The main motivation for their behavior is an urge to release tension. The act of stealing provides this release and gives the kleptomaniac a temporary thrill, even though the individual regards the urge to steal as unpleasant, unwanted, intrusive, and senseless. Kleptomaniacs steal just about anything, although the most common objects include food, clothes, jewelry, cosmetics, records, toys, pens and paper, and, in some cases, money. While most kleptomaniacs steal from a store or workplace, for some the behavior is limited to stealing from a particular person, perhaps someone about whom they feel

People with kleptomania are less interested in what they steal than in the act of stealing itself.

Gloria is a 45-year-old well-dressed and attractive executive with a comfortable salary and a busy lifestyle. For the past few years, she has been under considerable stress and has worked long hours as the result of reorganizations in her company. As a teenager, Gloria occasionally took small, inexpensive items such as hair barrettes and nail polish from the drug store, even though she could well afford to pay for them. Lately, Gloria has started shoplifting again. This time, her behavior has an intensity that she cannot control. During her lunch hour, Gloria often visits one of the large department stores near her office building, walks around until she finds something that catches her eye, and then slips it into her purse or pocket. Although she has sworn to herself that she will never steal again, every few days she finds the tension so great that she cannot stay out of the stores.

- What characteristics differentiate Gloria's behavior from that of an ordinary shoplifter?
- What events in Gloria's life could have triggered her recent bout of kleptomania?

intense feelings of attraction or jealousy. Keep in mind that it is not the intrinsic value of these objects that motivates the kleptomaniac to steal, but rather the act of stealing itself. In fact, most kleptomaniacs are perplexed about what to do with their acquired items. Some hoard the objects, as in the case of a woman whose closet was overflowing with thousands of inexpensive plastic combs and brushes taken over the course of several years. Others give away the items, or may even throw them in the trash. This lack of interest in the stolen items is the main feature that differentiates a typical shoplifter or burglar from a kleptomaniac.

■ *Theories and treatments*

Although kleptomania is a fascinating psychological disorder, it has received relatively little attention from researchers, perhaps because relatively few cases come to professional attention except for those referred to forensic psychologists. Clinicians usually become aware of a person's kleptomania only when the individual is in treatment for some other psychological problem such as an anxiety disorder, psychoactive substance abuse, eating disorder, or mood disorder. (Bradford & Balmaceda, 1983; McElroy et al., 1991). The fact that most kleptomaniacs seen in a clinical context also suffer from another psychological disorder raises some interesting questions. Is it possible that kleptomanic behavior is a symptom of some other disorder, possibly biologically caused? With this possibility in mind, some researchers have speculated that a serotonin deficiency might underlie kleptomania, an idea that is supported by the fact that the medication fluoxetine (Prozac), which increases serotonin in the nervous system, has been found to reduce kleptomanic behavior (McElroy et al., 1991).

In addition to pharmacological interventions, behavioral treatments are also used to help individuals control

their urge to steal. In covert sensitization, the client is instructed to conjure up aversive images during the act of stealing (Glover, 1985). For example, a kleptomaniac may be instructed to conjure up disgusting images, such as vomit, when the compulsion to steal is emerging. Alternatively, the client may be instructed to use thought-stopping techniques, in which dramatic internal cries to resist thinking about the stealing behavior serve to prevent the person from following through on the urge.

Pathological Gambling

Gambling is a common feature of everyday life. Even if you do not consider yourself a "gambler," you have probably bought a raffle ticket, scratched off the disk on a game card in a cereal package, sent a card in the mail to a sweepstakes contest, bet on your home team, or wagered a dollar with a friend that your answer to a test question was correct. Perhaps you have been to a gambling casino, where you played the slot machines or sat at the blackjack table for an hour or two. If you have had any of these experiences, you know

Many pathological gamblers get started through rather harmless ventures, such as a neighborhood poker game. Most people gamble recreationally with no ill effects; by contrast, pathological gamblers get caught up in a cycle that they are unable to control.

how thrilling it can be to see your bet pay off. People who are troubled by **pathological gambling** have an urge to gamble that is much stronger than that of the average person, and often end up spending their entire lives in pursuit of big wins.

■ *Characteristics of pathological gambling*

During the late 1980s the sports world was taken by the story that one of the leading baseball figures of all time, Pete Rose, had been betting thousands of dollars a day on baseball games. Admitting his guilt, Rose publicly acknowledged that he was unable to control his gambling, despite his realization that this would lead to his banishment from baseball. Pete Rose's problem brought attention to a disorder with which few Americans had been familiar.

Pathological gamblers feel unable to resist the betting impulse. Obsessed with a desire to gamble, they spend their money recklessly and engage in extreme behaviors such as lying, cheating, and stealing in a effort to fuel their habit. If for some reason they are prevented from gambling, they become restless and irritable. Some pathological gamblers try desperately to stop but find themselves unable to resist, deceiving themselves and others that if they can just recoup their losses, they will stop—a dream that never comes true. In the process, their family and work lives deteriorate as financial and legal problems resulting from their losses overtake them. Some pathological gamblers become so distraught by feelings of hopelessness that they contemplate or even commit suicide. You can evaluate your own propensity for this problem by considering how you would respond to questions from the South Oaks Gambling Screen(Lesieur & Blume, 1987) shown in Table 16-1.

It is easy to be oblivious to the prevalence and seriousness of pathological gambling unless the problem has personally touched your life. Statistics show, however, that

Table 16-1 Sample Items from the South Oaks Gambling Screen

Respondents indicate "yes" or "no" to the following questions. Of the 20 questions on the scale, a total of 5 or more "yes" responses indicates that a person is at risk for being a compulsive gambler.

1. Did you ever gamble more than you intended to?
2. Have you ever felt guilty about the way you gamble or what happens when you gamble?
3. Have you ever felt like you would like to stop gambling but didn't think you could?
4. Have you ever hidden betting slips, lottery tickets, gambling money, or other signs of gambling from your spouse, children, or other important people in your life?
5. Have you ever borrowed from someone and not paid them back as a result of your gambling?

Other questions concern how the respondent obtained the money to pay for gambling; these sources include borrowing cash from banks, loan companies, credit unions, or loan sharks, cashing in stocks or bonds, passing bad checks, and selling personal or family property.

Source: Lesieur & Blume, (1987).

recent growth of the number of people who have this disorder has been dramatic; thus the possibility of encountering someone with this problem at some point in your life may be greater than you think. Pathological gambling is becoming a serious problem in U.S. society; it is estimated that this disorder affects from 1 to 4 million adults (Nadler, 1985), or 3 percent of the adult population, with a greater proportion of men than women having this problem (Volberg & Steadman, 1988). Some experts believe that the increasing incidence of pathological gambling is directly related to the tremendous growth of legalized gambling enterprises. For example, state lotteries became tremendously popular during the 1980s, as did off-track betting; furthermore, the availability of casino gambling on the East Coast enticed many people who otherwise would not have had access to this form of gambling. In 1987, Americans legally bet almost $184 billion, an eleven-fold increase in little more than a decade (Gambino & Stein, 1989); in a mere 4 years the figure had risen to approximately $286 billion (Finch, 1991).

In addition to the destructive effects of pathological gambling on the individual's life, this behavior erodes the well-being of families. In an unusual survey of spouses (mostly wives) attending a national meeting of Gam-Anon (an organization analogous to Al-Anon), a number of serious problems were identified in the families of pathological gamblers, leading the vast majority to regard themselves as "emotionally ill" (Lorenz & Shuttlesworth, 1983). Many of these spouses had resorted to dysfunctional coping behaviors such as excessive drinking, smoking, under- or overeating, and impulsive spending. Almost half of these women reported that they had experienced emotional, verbal, or physical abuse, and 12 percent said they had at-

When Pete Rose was discovered to be a pathological gambler, Americans were shocked that a national hero would ruin his reputation with what appeared to be senseless behavior.

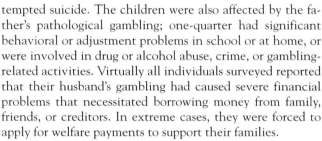

As many states have turned to legalized betting as a way to generate revenues, more people than ever have become part of the gambling culture.

The dream of another big win propels pathological gamblers into a life in which gambling becomes an all-consuming passion.

tempted suicide. The children were also affected by the father's pathological gambling; one-quarter had significant behavioral or adjustment problems in school or at home, or were involved in drug or alcohol abuse, crime, or gambling-related activities. Virtually all individuals surveyed reported that their husband's gambling had caused severe financial problems that necessitated borrowing money from family, friends, or creditors. In extreme cases, they were forced to apply for welfare payments to support their families.

Clearly, although U.S. society presents many opportunities for gambling, not everyone who gambles becomes a pathological gambler. How does such a seemingly harmless pastime develop into a compulsive, self-destructive pattern? According to the late psychiatrist Robert L. Custer, who in 1974 established the first clinic for treatment of pathological gambling in the United States, a person becomes a pathological gambler through a series of stages in which gambling progresses from a relatively harmless sport to a total focus of life (Custer, 1982). In the first stage, the individual is simply a recreational gambler who enjoys gambling as a social activity. The person's behavior, at this point, is indistinguishable from the gambling patterns shown by ordinary individuals who stop when they begin to lose, or set a time or spending limit on their gambling. Movement into the next stage, which is the beginning of a pathological gambling pattern, occurs when the individual begins to start winning. At this point, the gambler starts to gain an identity as a "winner," and the more often that success is encountered in gambling, the more this identity becomes reinforced.

During the early winning stage, the individual gains gambling skills, making it possible to enhance whatever luck is experienced with greater knowledge of the various strategies involved in winning. If at this point the person encounters a **big win**, a gain of large amounts of money in one bet, the gambler becomes propelled into a pattern of addiction which inevitably becomes almost impossible to

break. This event is so reinforcing, both financially and psychologically, that the individual becomes possessed with the need to reexperience it. The gambler is now convinced of the possession of unique good fortune and gambling skills, and starts to make riskier and more expensive bets. However, inevitably the luck does not hold out, and the person begins to lose. Whatever money was gained from the big win disappears as the losses begin to outweigh the gains. Keeping the person going is the fictitious belief that if the big win could only be repeated, all troubles would be over. The gambler even may promise to stop after landing

Wayne is a 22-year-old auto mechanic, a father of two, married to a factory worker. Two years ago, he went to the local race track with a friend who showed him how to bet on horses. To his surprise, Wayne made some good bets and came home with a $50 profit. Buoyed by his success, he made repeated trips to the track and, in time, began taking days off from work to bet on the races. On one of these occasions, Wayne won $5000. This made him feel extremely proud of his betting expertise, and convinced him that he had special skills at picking the right horse. Even though he was losing many of his bets, he now felt certain that his winnings would more than compensate. He had a feeling of self-confidence that, for once in his life, he was a success. To keep up his image, Wayne started to make larger and larger bets on long-shots that failed to pay off. As his losses accumulated into the tens of thousands of dollars, he grew panicky and felt driven to bet even more.

- What factors do you think were the primary contributors to Wayne's moving from being a recreational gambler to becoming a pathological gambler?
- Do you think that Wayne experienced any pleasure in gambling once he began to lose?

another large win. At this point, the individual begins to "chase" or bet more and more to recoup earlier losses. As the desperation mounts, the individual is fully launched into an intensive and all-consuming enterprise. And precisely because of this desperation, the gambler suffers a loss of judgment and bets unwisely.

In the doomed search for another big win, a cycle becomes established in which the pathological gambler has periodic wins that maintain an unreasonable optimism, but these gains never erase the debt, because for every win experienced, continued gambling leads to heavier losses. In time, the gambler's physical, psychological, and financial resources are depleted and the person considers drastic action such as suicide, running away, or embarking on a life of crime.

■ *Theories and treatments*

We have just seen the stages that are thought to lead from recreational to pathological gambling. These stages seem to involve some of the same factors that play a role in alcohol and drug addiction, in that the individual continually seeks pleasure from a behavior that, although leading to trouble, possesses strong reward potential. The perpetual pursuit of the big win is much like the alcohol-dependent person's search for stimulation and pleasurable feelings through alcohol use, though there are some significant differences between the two. Spending money in not inherently pleasurable as is taking a psychoactive substance; also, gamblers are not reinforced during every gambling venture, whereas alcoholics do receive reinforcement each time they drink (Rachlin, 1990).

Despite these differences, both alcohol dependence and pathological gambling are addictive behaviors, and researchers continue to explore why many pathological gamblers also have substance abuse disorders (McCormick et al., 1987). Perhaps this connection rests on the fact that like some substance abusers, pathological gamblers are looking for sensations that are new and exciting (Blaszczynski et al., 1986). Gamblers easily become bored (Rosenthal, 1986) and crave excitement, what they call "being in action." They are excited by the risk of losing as well as by the thrill of winning—experiences that add to the reinforcing value of gambling.

In addition to a proneness to addiction, what other factors account for certain people becoming pathological gamblers? Several interesting personality characteristics are common to pathological gamblers; for example, male gamblers tend to be compulsive and antisocial; women with this disorder are more commonly dependent, submissive, and passive-aggressive (Peck, 1986). Pathological gamblers are also narcissistic and aggressive (Dell et al., 1981), looking to succeed through unconventional means (Taber et al., 1986). In the survey of Gam-Anon members (Lorenz & Shuttlesworth, 1983), the wives' descriptions of their husbands also provided some interesting insight into the personality of the pathological gambler. Almost all of the wives said they saw their husbands as liars who were irresponsible, uncommunicative, insincere, and impulsive.

In addition to these personality characteristics, it has been suggested that a large number of pathological gamblers suffer from mood disorders; in fact, there is mounting evidence that points to pathological gambling as related to mood disorder (McElroy et al., 1992). Researchers investigating the possible role of biological factors in pathological gambling have come across some interesting characteristics in people with this disorder. For example, pathological gamblers show more norepinephrine activity (Roy et al., 1988) and a greater likelihood of EEG abnormalities (Goldstein et al., 1985) than comparison subjects.

Interestingly enough, pathological gamblers believe that they are in control of the random aspects of gambling (Dickerson & Adcock, 1987). For example, when playing slot machines, pathological gamblers switch machines regularly, taking time to examine a slot machine before playing on it. They carefully study facets of the machine that are unnoticed by others, such as the machine's position in a row of slot machines or how the handle feels. Mistakenly convinced that they can control the probabilities that affect the outcome of their bets, they develop grandiose ideas that lead them to become convinced of their ultimate success.

In some instances, an individual's pathological gambling may be sustained by a disturbed marital relationship. The husband's gambling may allow his wife to blame marital conflicts on her husband's gambling rather than on her own problems. Or, a husband may inadvertently urge his wife to bet if he shares her false optimism that she will magically have a big win (Gaudia, 1987). Even if a nongambling spouse attempts to break away from the marriage, this may be made difficult by the gambler's threats or false promises. In the survey of Gam-Anon spouses, wives of pathological gamblers indicated that they had difficulty carrying through on their intent to withhold money from their husbands, and although more than three-quarters of them had indicated their desire to break out of the marriage, many remained with their spouses because they loved them and hoped they would improve. Interestingly, almost one-fifth of the wives in this study came from families in which a parent had been a pathological gambler (Lorenz & Shuttlesworth, 1983).

Like individuals who are alcohol dependent, pathological gamblers deny the extent of their difficulties and tend not to seek treatment. When they do, it is out of desperation, feeling that they have no choice because of serious financial, legal, and family problems. Even then, they must be confronted with the grave nature of their gambling problem. This approach is used in groups such as Gamblers Anonymous where members penetrate the walls of denial among each other (Franklin & Ciarrocchi, 1987).

Behavioral methods similar to techniques for treating alcohol dependence are the most commonly used. In aversive conditioning, the most frequently used behavioral method, the individual receives an unpleasant but not painful electric shock to the fingers after reading a series of phrases about gambling (McConaghy et al., 1983). For the *in vivo* exposure method, the individual is taken by the therapist to a gambling casino or club but allowed only to watch and not to gamble. Another method, which appears to have the greatest long-term effectiveness (McConaghy et al., 1991), is *imaginal desensitization*. In this form of treatment, clients are told to imagine scenes in which they feel tempted to gamble and to relax as they imagine each successive behavior involved in this particular scene. The desensitization in this procedure is comparable to that used in treating people with phobias, in that the individual learns to substitute the usual response to this situation with a new response that replaces the problem behavior. By substituting relaxation for arousal in these situations, they learn to avoid becoming distressed when not allowed to gamble, and come to recognize that they have the ability to control their addiction.

Pyromania

The sight of fire is fascinating to many people. If a building is on fire, most passersby stop and watch while it is brought under control. Candles and fireplaces are commonly regarded as backdrops to a romantic or intimate evening. For

The lure of a fire proves to be so fascinating for the pyromaniac that the urge to start fires is irresistible.

the very small percentage of the population who have the impulse control disorder called **pyromania**, fascination with fire goes beyond this normal degree of interest and becomes a compulsive and dangerous urge to set fires deliberately.

■ Characteristics of pyromania

As is true with all impulse control disorders, people with pyromania cannot restrain themselves from acting on strong and compelling urges; in this case the urges involve the intense desire to prepare, set, and watch fires. Before the fire, these people become tense and aroused, and upon setting the fire they experience intense feelings of pleasure, gratification, or relief. Their behavior is not motivated by financial or criminal motives, as in the case of an arsonist who reaps monetary gain through insurance fraud.

Pyromania is a rare disorder; even among fire starters, only 2 to 3 percent would be considered to be pyromaniacs (Crossley & Guzman, 1985). As with pathological gambling, pyromania is more common in males, with most showing the first signs of a pathological interst in fire during childhood (Jacobson, 1985). In numerous cases, sexual arousal has been reported to play a role in compulsive firesetting behavior (e. g., Bourget & Bradford, 1987; Quinsey et al., 1989), pointing to the possibility that in some cases pyromania might actually be appropriately regarded as a paraphilic, fetishistic behavior. However, little systematic research has been conducted to confirm this notion.

■ Theories and treatments

Most individuals with pyromania are afflicted with one or more other problems or disorders, and in most cases the disorder is rooted in childhood problems and firesetting behavior. In efforts to understand how patterns of uncontrollable firesetting begin, and in an attempt to develop early intervention programs, researchers have conducted extensive studies of firesetting in children, who set two out of every five fires (Wooden, 1985). A firesetting child does not necessarily grow up to become a pyromaniac; firesetting behavior among children and adolescents emerges from various sets of issues. Wooden (1985) delineated four types of childhood firesetters: curious youngsters who accidentally start fires while playing with matches, older problem-ridden youth who seem to be crying out for attention and help, delinquents who use fire to act out against authority, and a group with severe psychological disturbance who go on to chronic firesetting in adulthood. Among these extreme cases, Wooden delineated two personality types: the *impulsive neurotic* and the *borderline psychotic*. The impulsive neurotic is impatient, almost hyperactive, and prone to destruction and thievery. The borderline psychotic experiences mood swings, intense anger, numerous phobias, and a proneness toward violence. One of the most famous cases of an individual who engaged in this extreme form of firesetting behavior was David Berkowitz, the confessed "Son of

Floyd, a 32-year-old man, developed an intense fascination with fires and fire-fighting equipment as a child. By the time he reached adolescence, he had begun to set abandoned buildings on fire because he found the experience to be exhilarating and sexually exciting. After graduating from high school, he applied to be a firefighter for the city, but was denied a position because his psychological profile showed that he had difficulty controlling destructive impulses. He moved to a small town where he knew he could join the volunteer fire brigade without any questions. However, since such a small town had few fires, Floyd deliberately began to set fires himself. At first, no one noticed anything unusual about the increase in the number of fires that had occurred since Floyd joined the department. After watching Floyd's reaction to the fires, though, the fire chief began to suspect that it was Floyd who was setting the fires.

- What behaviors shown by Floyd during a fire might have led the fire chief to suspect that Floyd had pyromania?
- Why would Floyd not be considered an arsonist?

Sam" serial murderer who was reported to have set more than 2000 fires in New York City during a 3-year period in the mid-1970s.

Other research on children who get caught up in recurrent firesetting behavior tells us more about how these children differ from their peers (Kolko & Kazdin, 1988, 1989a, 1989b). Firesetting children have a compelling attraction to and curiosity about fire, which commonly develops as a result of their observation and modeling of adult firesetting behavior. They know more about what it takes to get fires started, and they usually have an impressive knowledge of combustible materials. In addition, family issues, particularly those pertaining to discipline, are influential factors. Parents of firesetting children are more likely to use unpredictable disciplinary styles ranging from harsh discipline to ineffective mild punishment (Kolko & Kazdin, 1989a). Child–parent relationships are commonly characterized by inconsistency, emotional disturbance, and abuse, resulting in the development of conduct-disordered behavior including firesetting (Lowenstein, 1989).

The possibility of biological contributions to pyromania is suggested by research showing lower levels of serotonin and norepinephrine in people with this disorder (Roy et al., 1988; Virkkunen et al., 1987).

Most individuals with pyromania avoid treatment, so clinicians are likely to see only those who are caught and are ordered to obtain professional help. People who are apprehended for serious firesetting are sent either to prison or to a psychiatric hospital, depending on the circumstances of their arrest and the ensuing legal proceedings. Ideally, some form of treatment will be provided regardless of the placement of the firesetter.

As there is little information on biological treatments, the most commonly employed psychological intervention for pyromania relies on behavioral principles. The most well-known of these is the *graphing technique*, initially developed for treating children who engage in firesetting (Bumpass, 1989). In following this method, the clinician and client construct a graph that corresponds to the individual's history of behaviors, feelings, and experiences associated with firesetting. Presumably, a visual presentation of the chronological history of this behavior enables the client to become aware of cause–effect relationships, and to become attuned to signals that the compulsion to set fires is about to strike. In response to the signal, the individual can substitute more appropriate ways to discharge tension. This technique has been effective in helping many individuals stop their firesetting, but it is only the preliminary component of a therapy that should then focus on developing more insight into this dangerous behavior.

Sexual Impulsivity

People with **sexual impulsivity** are unable to control their sexual behavior, engaging in frequent and indiscriminate sexual activity. This disorder has gained widespread attention since the early 1980s, largely through the publication of a book called *Out of the Shadows: Understanding Sexual Addiction* by Carnes (1983).

■ *Characteristics of sexual impulsivity*

Sexual impulsivity is sometimes referred to as *compulsive sexuality* or *sexual addiction*, but these terms are misnomers (Barth & Kinder, 1987), because the main feature of the disorder involves neither a true compulsion nor an addiction, but rather a lack of control over sexual impulses. People with this disorder are preoccupied with sex, feeling uncontrollably driven to seek out sexual encounters which they later regret. This drive is similar to that reported in other disorders of self-control, involving a state in which the individual is transfixed by the need for sex. Often, sexual impulsivists engage in many sexual encounters in a brief period of time, even at the risk of disease or arrest.

As is true for other disorders of impulse control, the uncontrollable behavior of sexual impulsivists interferes with their ability to carry out normal social and occupational roles. They feel a great deal of distress about their behavior, and following sexual encounters they are likely to feel dejected, hopeless, and ashamed. Although a few sexual impulsivists are consumed by the constant need to masturbate, most seek out partners, usually people they do not know and do not remain involved with any longer than the anonymous sexual encounter.

The most detailed investigation of sexual impulsivity was conducted with a male homosexual and bisexual sample (Quadland, 1985). In this group, sexual impulsivists averaged more than 29 partners per month and more than

2000 different sexual encounters over their lifetimes. They frequently sought sex in public settings and used alcohol or drugs with sex, and they typically had a history of few long-term relationships.

■ *Theories and treatments*

The most tenable explanations for the development of sexual impulsivity incorporate elements of family systems

Raj is a 24-year-old clerk who lives alone in an apartment in a large city. A loner since high school, Raj nevertheless is intensely preoccupied with the pursuit of sex. At work, he constantly thinks about each person he meets as a potential sexual partner. Recurrently on his mind are plans to find new places where he can have sex. On a typical day, Raj goes to a pornographic movie theater during his lunch hour where he seeks to have oral sex activities with as many different men as he can find. On his way home from work, he often stops at a highway rest area where he once again seeks anonymous sex partners. During the weekend he frequents singles bars, where he usually succeeds in picking up women. Although he continues to involve himself in these sexual activities, Raj is quite distressed by his behavior. Guilt and negative feelings about himself cause him to feel depressed, and even suicidal at times. However, his behavior seems to him to be beyond his control. Although he has thought of obtaining professional help, he is too embarrassed to admit his problem to anyone.

■ How does Raj's sexual impulsivity differ from the behavior of a person with a paraphilia?

■ In what ways are Raj's symptoms similar to those of people with other impulse control disorders?

and behavioral theory. Sexual impulsivity can result from either unduly restrictive attitudes toward sex or as a result of neglect and abuse in the family (Coleman, 1987). Families with extremely restrictive outlooks on sexuality foster guilt with regard to pleasure-seeking behaviors. The child becomes secretive and anxious about his or her developing sexuality. One reaction to this emotional atmosphere is to develop sexual dysfunctions, such as sexual aversion disorder. At the other extreme, the child may react by acting out in sexual ways. The more the parents attempt to repress the child's sexuality, the more the child is driven to engage secretly in sexual pursuits. By the time such children have grown into adolescence, sexual pursuit has become an uncontrollable part of their lives.

In cases of childhood neglect and abuse, the abused child feels sad and lonely, and looks to sex as a temporary relief from emotional pain. The unhappy child comes to associate sexuality with escape from a neglecting or abusing family member. Because sexual gratification is such a powerful reinforcement, it is very difficult to break the association between escape from unhappiness and sexual release. In time, the child learns to rely on sexuality and other mind-numbing activities such as overeating or substance abuse. As an adult, such an individual can become addicted to drugs or alcohol as well as sex (Schwartz & Brasted, 1985.

It is possible that some cases of sexual impulsivity are caused by abnormally high levels of testosterone that lead the individual to become hypersexual (Berlin & Meinecke, 1981; Gagne, 1981). Clearly, given the role of physiology in sexual response, biological factors are important to consider in understanding cases of sexual impulsivity.

Treatment for sexual impulsivity involves a combination of components derived from insight-oriented, behavioral, and family systems approaches. Insight-oriented therapy focuses on bringing to the surface the individual's underlying conflicts that motivate the behavior. These conflicts include resolving nonsexual problems through sexual means, needing reassurance, and feeling insecure about one's sex role (Weissberg & Levay, 1986). Behavioral techniques include aversive covert conditioning, in which the individual is trained to associate unpleasant images with inappropriate sexual behavior (McConaghy et al., 1985). Other techniques include behavioral contracting, substitution of alternative forms of activity, and methods to bolster the individual's low self-esteem (Schwartz & Brasted, 1985). The inclusion of family or couples therapy is important for clients whose excessive sexual behavior occurs in the context of long-term close relationships. This approach focuses on improving the communication between the client and the client's partner and restructuring their relationship to correct dysfunctional patterns of interaction that are enacted in the sexual domain (Sprenkle, 1987).

In cases involving sexual victimization of other people, antiandrogenic medication is sometimes used to reduce the individual's testosterone level. This method involves some of the same concerns that are present in the treatment of sex offenders (see Chapter 9).

As with other disorders involving impulse control, group therapy seems to be useful in the treatment of sexual impulsivity (Quadland, 1985). The elements of a successful group approach include peer support, confrontation, and availability of an alternate social network.

Trichotillomania

The urge to pull out one's hair, which becomes a compulsion in people with the rare disorder called **trichotillomania**, may seem bizarre and far removed from the realm of everyday human behavior. In our culture, many women are self-conscious about facial hair and go to some trouble to remove it. However, for some people the act of hair-pulling develops a compulsive quality, causing them to become so preoccupied with pulling out their hair that they are oblivious to the fact that they may actually be marring their appearance.

■ *Characteristics of trichotillomania*

Like people with other disorders of impulse control, the person with trichotillomania experiences an increasing sense of tension which is temporarily relieved by the act of hair-pulling. This problem occurs most often among women and girls, usually beginning in childhood or adolescence (Muller, 1987). People with this disorder feel unable to resist the urge to pull hair, regardless of the fact that their behavior results in bald patches and in lost eyebrows, eyelashes, armpit hair, and pubic hair. In extreme cases, some individuals swallow the hair after they have pulled it out, risking the danger that it will solidify in the stomach or intestines.

Trichotillomania often goes undetected because those suffering from the irresistible urge to pull out their own hair usually deny their behavior.

Despite physical evidence suggesting intentional hair pulling, people with this disorder tend to deny that they are engaging in the behavior. But still, they cannot resist the urges to pluck their hair. As a result, dermatologists rather than mental health professionals are typically the ones who discover the disorder. The usual scenario involves a parent bringing the child to the dermatologist because of the child's mysterious hair loss. Upon examination, the dermatologist may notice many short, broken hairs around the bald areas on the skin, indicating the hairs have been plucked. In other cases it is not a dermatological concern that brings clinical attention, but some other psychological problem; people with trichotillomania also tend to have mood, anxiety, substance abuse, and eating disorders

For most of her childhood and adolescence, 15-year-old Janet lived a fairly isolated existence with no close friends. Although Janet never discussed her unhappiness with anyone, she often felt very depressed and hopeless. As a young child, Janet secretly lay in bed on many nights tugging at her hair. Over time, this behavior increased to the point where she would pluck the hair, strand by strand, from her scalp. Typically, she would pull out a hair, examine it, bite it, and either throw it away or swallow it. Because her hair was thick and curly, her hair loss was not initially evident, and Janet kept it carefully combed to conceal the bald spots. One of her teachers noticed that Janet was pulling her hair in class, and in looking closer, she saw these patches on Janet's head. She referred Janet to the school psychologist, who called Janet's mother and recommended professional help.

■ What connection might there be between Janet's unhappiness and her hair-pulling behavior?

■ What clues might be used to differentiate Janet's disorder from a medically caused loss of hair?

(Christenson et al., 1991), and may come to the attention of a clinician because of one of these problems.

Although relatively few cases of trichotillomania have been officially recorded, this disorder is apparently more common than clinicians realized even as recently as the 1970s. At that time, approximately 8 million Americans were estimated to have the disorder (Azrin & Nunn, 1978). During the late 1980s, discussion of the topic appeared in newspaper articles and on talk shows, resulting in many more people coming forward to acknowledge that they suffered from this problem. Interestingly, in one experimental study comparing different treatment methods, the subjects were obtained when they called the National Institute of Mental Health after seeing the disorder described on the ABC television program *20/20* (Swedo et al., 1989).

■ *Theories and treatments*

Trichotillomania is an intriguing disorder that is not well understood, although proponents of the major models have put forth some hypotheses about why this behavior would begin and become so resistant to change. Proponents of the biological perspective have suggested that trichotillomania is a variant of obsessive-compulsive disorder. This notion is supported by the facts that in both disorders behavior is driven by anxiety or tension, and that people with both disorders respond to various medications, including lithium (Christenson et al., 1991) and antidepressants (Pollard et al., 1991), particularly clomipramine, an antidepressant that reduces obsessional symptoms (Swedo et al., 1989). While medications are effective in reducing hair-pulling behavior, their long-term effectiveness has not yet been demonstrated; furthermore, people are understandably reluctant to take medication for years when effective psychological interventions are available.

From a psychological perspective, trichotillomania is seen as originating in disturbed parent–child relationships; an upset child who feels neglected, abandoned, or emotionally overburdened may resort to this behavior in an attempt to gain attention or to derive a disturbed form of gratification (Krishnan et al. 1985). Although this is a tenable hypothesis, it does not explain why the behavior becomes so firmly established and maintained. From a behavioral perspective this pattern develops because the individual learns to associate hair-pulling behavior with relief from tension.

Behavioral treatments for people with trichotillomania fall into five categories: enhanced awareness of the behavior, reinforcement, aversive conditioning, relaxation or hypnotic techniques, and substitution with other behaviors (Ratner, 1989). In procedures geared toward enhancing awareness, the individual is encouraged to become more consciously attentive to hair-pulling behavior; this can be accomplished by keeping a record of each incident, by talking aloud about the behavior while pulling out hairs, or by asking family members to point out times when the individual is engaging in the behavior. By heightening awareness of the habit, it is assumed that the individual will develop the ability to stop the behavior before the occurrence of a hair-pulling episode.

Reinforcement techniques follow those used with any behavior a person is working to extinguish; for example, praising the individual for successful abstinence from the behavior or for improved appearance due to cessation of hair-pulling can strengthen the individual's resolve to change this behavior. Aversive techniques may involve instructing the individual to administer some unpleasant stimulus at the point of awareness of the behavior, perhaps snapping a taut rubber band worn around the wrist as punishment for hair-pulling (Stevens, 1984).

Although general relaxation techniques have not been particularly effective in helping people stop hair-pulling, more specific techniques involving hypnosis have shown promise. Effective hypnotic methods are those aimed at increasing awareness of the habit, sensitivity to the unpleasant aspects of this behavior, and the individual's feelings of personal self-control (Ratner, 1989).

Another behavioral technique involves the substitution of a more acceptable behavior such as hand-clenching for the hair-pulling (Tarnowski et al., 1987). This approach is based on the idea that if the individual is doing something that is physically incompatible with hair-pulling each time the urge arises, this more acceptable behavior will aid in the extinction of the less desirable behavior of hair-pulling. Moving beyond straight behavioral techniques to those involving cognitive-behavorial principles, some experts urge the individual to initiate inner dialogues in order to provide a warning of situations in which the behavior is likely to occur (Ratner, 1989).

Intermittent Explosive Disorder

As is true for the other disorders of impulse control, **intermittent explosive disorder** involves an inability to hold back an urge that other people experience but have no serious problem restraining. The urge, in this case, is to express strong angry feelings and associated violent behaviors.

■ *Characteristics of intermittent explosive disorder*

The behaviors found in people with intermittent explosive disorder are occasional bouts of extreme rage in which the individual becomes assaultive or destructive without serious provocation. During these episodes, these people can cause serious physical harm to themselves, other people, and property. While in the midst of an episode, they feel as if they are under a spell, and some have even used terms that suggest that it is like a seizure state. Just prior to the outburst, they may feel an impending sense that something is about to happen, an experience that has been compared to the *aura*, or anticipatory state, that people with epilepsy experience prior to a seizure. Between episodes, people with intermittent explosive disorder show no signs

A sudden eruption of rage causes people with intermittent explosive disorder to lose control over what they say and do.

of being unusually impulsive or temperamental. This rare disorder is more common among men, some of whom are imprisoned for their destructive or assaultive behavior. Women with this disorder are more likely to be sent to a mental health facility for treatment.

■ Theories and treatments

Many features of intermittent explosive disorder suggest that biological factors play an important determining role, possibly in combination with environmental factors (Hamstra, 1986). For example, as we noted earlier, people with this disorder report an aura experience just prior to their outbursts similar to that of people with epilepsy. However, epilepsy does not account for this impulse control disorder (Leicester, 1982), so there must be other explanations. In one study, people diagnosed with intermittent explosive disorder were found to have abnormal patterns of insulin secretion (Virkkunen, 1986). Lower levels of serotonin and norepinephrine have also been reported (Linnoila et al., 1983; Virkkunen et al., 1989). Other features supporting a biological explanation are the unpredictability of the out-

Ed, a 28-year-old high school teacher, has recently had unprovoked violent outbursts of aggressive and assaultive behavior. During these episodes, Ed throws whatever objects he can get his hands on and yells profanities. He soon calms down, though, and feels intense regret for whatever damage he has caused, explaining that he didn't know what came over him. In the most recent episode, he threw a coffeepot at another teacher in the faculty lounge, inflicting serious injury. After the ambulance had taken the injured man to the hospital, Ed's supervisor called the police.

■ What differentiates Ed, who has intermittent explosive disorder, from a person with antisocial personality disorder?

■ What medical conditions should Ed be tested for?

bursts and the apparent lack of externally precipitating events.

Because of the belief that biology plays a central role in causing this disorder, clinicians have looked to somatic treatments (Mattes, 1985), usually augmented by behavioral interventions. In recommending medications for this disorder, clinicians turn to those used in treating aggression (Lion, 1989). For example, benzodiazepines have been used to reduce explosive behaviors in people with certain personality disorders. Medications that alter norepinephrine metabolism, including lithium and a category of medications called *beta blockers*, can also reduce aggressive behaviors (Eichelman, 1988).

EATING DISORDERS

The psychological meaning of food extends far beyond its nutritive powers. It is common for people to devote many hours and much effort to choosing, preparing, and serving food. In addition to physical dependence on food, humans have strong emotional associations with food. Hungry people feel irritable and unhappy; by contrast, a good meal can cause people to feel contented and nurtured.

For some people, food takes on inordinate significance, and they find themselves becoming enslaved to bizarre and unhealthy rituals around the process of eating. People with eating disorders struggle to control their disturbed attitudes and behaviors regarding food and, to the distress of those who are close to them, many put their lives at risk. We will look at two disorders associated with eating: *anorexia nervosa* and *bulimia nervosa*. Although they are distinct disorders, there are important similarities in the ways that they are understood. Consequently, we will combine our discussion of the theories and treatments of these disorders.

Characteristics of Anorexia Nervosa

Although many people in Western society diet to lose weight at some point in their lives (Polivy & Herman, 1987), people with the eating disorder **anorexia nervosa** carry the wish to be thin to an extreme, developing an intense fear of becoming fat that leads them to diet to the point of emaciation. This fear of becoming fat is a central feature of assessment techniques used for diagnosing anorexia nervosa (see Table 16–2). In addition to extreme dieting, anorexic individuals engage in various behaviors geared toward weight loss such as abusing laxatives or diet pills and becoming compulsive exercisers. Some people with this disorder regularly force themselves to **purge**, or rid themselves of whatever they have just eaten. The starvation associated with anorexia nervosa causes a number of physical abnormalities such as menstrual disturbance, dry and cracking skin, slowed heartbeat, reduced gastrointestinal activity, and muscular weakness (Kaplan & Woodside,

Table 16–2 Items from the Goldfarb Fear of Fat Scale

_____	My biggest fear is of becoming fat.
_____	I am afraid to gain even a little weight.
_____	Becoming fat would be the worst thing that could happen to me.
_____	If I eat even a little, I may lose control and not stop eating.
_____	Staying hungry is the only way I can guard against losing control and becoming fat.

Source: Agras, (1991).

1987). Some people with this disorder go to such extremes that they actually die from the medical complications resulting from starvation.

The word _anorexia_ literally means _without appetite,_ a somewhat misleading term in light of the fact that loss of appetite is not the key feature of this disorder, at least not initially. On the contrary, people with this disorder are very interested in eating and having normal appetites, although they have difficulty reading their hunger cues. Some anorexic individuals go to great lengths to prepare high-calorie meals and baked goods for other people, taking great delight in their handling of food as they prepare it. Others develop compulsive rituals involving food. For example, they may hide food around the house, eat meals in a ritualistic fashion, and take many hours to eat a small portion of food. Aware of how unusual such behaviors will seem to others, they go to extremes to conceal their eccentric eating habits.

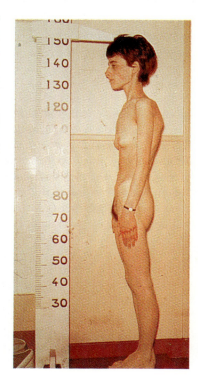

Despite their emaciated state, people with anorexia nervosa have such a distorted body image that they believe themselves to be overweight. The ravaging effects of starvation jeopardize the health of these individuals, placing some of them at risk of death.

Lorraine is an 18-year-old first-year college student who, since leaving home to go away to school, has been losing weight steadily. Initially, Lorraine wanted to lose a few pounds, thinking this would make her look sexier. She stopped eating at the cafeteria because they served too many starchy foods, choosing instead to prepare her own low-calorie meals. Within 2 months, she was obsessed with dieting and exercise and had developed the bizarre notion that she was grossly overweight. She had stopped menstruating and her weight had dropped from 110 to 80 pounds. When Lorraine went home for Thanksgiving break, her parents were so alarmed that they insisted she go for professional help.

■ What behaviors of Lorraine's are symptoms of anorexia nervosa?

■ What role do you think the stresses of college adjustment played in Lorraine's development of this eating disorder?

Body image disturbance is a core feature of anorexia nervosa. In fact, family members of people with this disorder are recurrently frustrated as they attempt to convince these individuals that, despite their belief that they are fat, they are actually horrendously thin. As anorexics look in the mirror, they see an obese person rather than the skin and bones so evident to everyone else.

Estimates of the prevalence of this disorder range from a low of .1 to .7 percent (Strober, 1991) to a high of 1 to 3 percent of the U.S. population (Andersen, 1983), with the disorder being strikingly more prevalent among females, and most commonly developing during adolescence.

Characteristics of Bulimia Nervosa

People with the eating disorder known as **bulimia nervosa** alternate between the extremes of eating large amounts of food in a short time, and then forcing themselves to get rid of the recently consumed food, either by vomiting or other extreme actions. Episodes of overeating are known as **binges**; during a binge, the person keeps eating even after reaching a point of feeling full, and stops only when a point of extreme physical discomfort is reached. Binges are carried out in secret, and may occur from a few times a month to many times a day. After a binge episode is over, bulimics try to pay for their overindulgence by purging themselves of the food they have eaten through methods such as severely limiting their further intake of food, causing themselves to vomit, taking laxatives, diuretics, or diet pills, or exercising vigorously. This cycle of binging and purging becomes self-perpetuating; the binges result from hunger caused by extremely rigid restrictions on food intake. After a binge, the individual feels compelled by guilt to try to remove what-

A person with bulimia would think nothing of sitting down to eat a collection of high-fat high-carbohydrate foods. Following a binge on such food, a bulimic is likely to purge by vomiting.

Cynthia is a 26-year-old dance teacher. Ever since adolescence, Cynthia has struggled with her weight. A particular problem for Cynthia has been her love of high-calorie carbohydrates. She regularly binges on a variety of sweets and then forces herself to vomit. Over the years, Cynthia has developed a number of physical problems from the frequent cycles of binging and purging. She recently went to her physician, complaining of severe stomach cramps that had bothered her for several weeks.

■ What physical symptoms in addition to stomach cramps might signal to Cynthia's physician that she has bulimia?
■ How does Cynthia's disorder differ from Lorraine's?

ever weight was gained through any means possible. The hunger that inevitably follows such misguided efforts sets the cycle in motion again.

Although some people have both anorexia and bulimia, two critical features distinguish these disorders. The first is body image. People with anorexia nervosa have very distorted perceptions of their body size. Even when close to a chronic state of starvation, anorexics see themselves as overweight. This is not the case for the individual with bulimia, who although having an exaggerated concern with weight, has a normal body image. The second difference is the amount of weight that the individual has lost. People with anorexia weigh significantly below the norm for height and build, whereas people with bulimia have weight that is average or above average.

Although according to the strict criteria of the disorder, only a small percentage of the population suffers from bulimia (1 to 2 percent of high school and college women and .2 percent of college men), a disturbingly large percentage of young people have some symptoms of this disorder (5 to 15 percent of adolescent girls and young adult women)

(Carlat & Camargo, 1991; Herzog et al., 1991). Perhaps someone you know has struggled with the potentially devastating and unhealthy behaviors associated with bulimia.

Many medical complications commonly develop in individuals with bulimia. The most serious of these problems involve life-threatening complications associated with purging. For example, the medication ipecac syrup, which is used to induce vomiting in people who have swallowed a poisonous substance, has severe toxic effects when taken regularly and in large doses by people with eating disorders. These effects occur throughout the gastrointestinal, cardiovascular, and nervous systems. Toxic effects can also result from the laxatives, diuretics, and diet pills used by bulimics to induce weight loss. Some bulimics also engage in harmful behaviors such as using enemas, regurgitating and then rechewing their food, or overusing saunas in efforts to lose weight. In addition to the effects of dehydration caused by binging and purging, the bulimic individual runs the risk of permanent gastrointestinal damage, fluid retention in the hands and feet, destruction of the heart muscle or collapse of the heart valves, and possibly even ventricular enlargement in the brain (Mitchell et al., 1991).

Other medical complications of bulimia cause discomfort but do not pose as great a risk, such as finger callouses (from using the finger to induce vomiting), swollen salivary glands, tooth erosion (from frequent vomiting), and bleeding on the face or inside the mouth. Some of these symptoms can serve as signals to others that the individual has bulimia (Kaplan & Woodside, 1987).

Theories and Treatments of Eating Disorders

Eating disorders have been examined from a wide variety of perspectives (Tobin, 1991), ranging from classic psychoanalytic theories to explanations based on biochemical abnormalities. Food is important to us for sociocultural, psychological, and biological reasons. In seeking explana-

Ads for weight-loss control systems are intended to lead people, especially women, to believe that they can become attractive by consuming a specialized diet product.

tions for why people develop eating disorders, experts have investigated each of these sets of factors.

Let's begin by looking at the sociocultural influences on people's attitudes toward eating and diet (Striegel-Moore et al., 1986). Society's idealization of thinness leads many adolescent girls to equate beauty with a slim figure. As an adolescent girl matures, she reads magazines, talks to her friends, and watches television and movies, repeatedly confronting the glamorization of thinness. Through vicarious reinforcement, she is likely to adopt the belief that if she can achieve the goal of being slender, she will be rewarded with attention, praise, admiration, and financial success. Perhaps because of this idealization of thinness, it is common in our culture for dieting to become well-established among girls as young as 9 years old (Hill et al., 1992). As significant as sociocultural factors are in affecting the development of eating disorders, though, the overwhelming majority of adolescents do not develop these disorders. Certainly there are other contributors to this problem.

Moving from the broad societal perspective to individual factors, experts in this area have focused their attention on the role of family experiences in the development of eating disorders. Family systems theorists have proposed that some girls develop anorexia nervosa in an effort to assert their independence (Minuchin et al., 1978). Perhaps girls who feel that their families are standing in the way of their becoming autonomous develop aberrant eating patterns as a way to become separated from their parents (Bruch, 1982). Other disturbances in the family may also contribute to the development of eating disorders, including a family that is chaotic, incapable of resolving conflict, unaffectionate and lacking in empathy (Strober & Humphrey, 1987).

At the more personal level of emotional functioning, many young people with eating disorders are afflicted with a great deal of inner turmoil and pain, and turn to food for comfort and a feeling of being nurtured. For some, the pursuit involves a desperate expression of their unresolved feelings of dependency on their parents (Bornstein & Greenberg, 1991); others are tormented by feelings of guilt as they struggle to achieve an identity that is separate from what they feel their parents want for them (Friedman, 1985). A great deal of attention has been given in recent years to the striking correlation between early struggles with eating disorders and the subsequent development of borderline personality disorders (Kennedy et al., 1990)—a connection that suggests that these individuals have some fundamental difficulties in the development of identity that goes back to early relationships with parents.

Proponents of the biological perspective view eating disorders as resulting from biochemical abnormalities that possibly have genetic links. Researchers have observed that eating disorders tend to run in families and that mood disorders are far more common in families of people with eating disorders (Strober, 1991). Recalling our discussion of the strong genetic influences in the acquisition of mood disorders, you can understand why researchers are intrigued by the possibility that the two disorders might be somehow intertwined and passed along from one generation to the next.

Researchers have also been fascinated by the fact that deficient production of norepinephrine and serotonin is found in people with anorexia and bulimia. Serotonin, in particular, seems to play a role in the regulation of feelings of hunger or satiety; according to some theorists, a deficiency of serotonin is related to feelings of hunger (leading to binging), and an excess is related to feelings of fullness (leading to anorexia) (Kaye & Weltzin, 1991). As we know, norepinephrine and serotonin deficiences are also theorized to underlie mood and compulsive disorders, and since many people with bulimia or anorexia have one of these disorders (Mitchell et al., 1991), it seems natural to suggest that a similar biochemical abnormality may be responsible for eating disorders. Further support for this proposal comes from the observations that people with mood disorders often suffer from change in appetite, that disorders of the endocrine system often involve changes in mood, and that people with bulimia are subject to depression (Kaye & Weltzin, 1991).

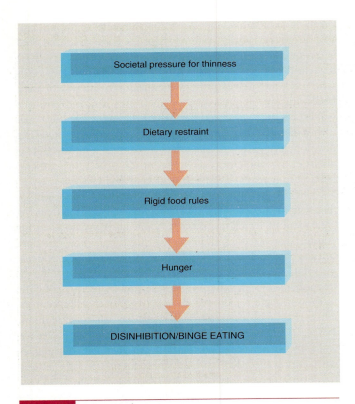

tinely necessary in treating people with eating disorders, regardless of how effective medications may be in symptom relief. In therapy using cognitive-behavioral techniques (Fairburn, 1981, 1988), the client is taught to use self-monitoring to keep track of food intake, including binging and purging. The client is also instructed to eat balanced meals, and to try to eat foods that the individual previously was afraid to eat because they were perceived as fattening. Cognitive restructuring is also used to help change the client's distorted body image and beliefs about food. The concept of relapse prevention, as described in Chapter 15, is also incorporated into the cognitive-behavioral approach (Johnson et al., 1987). In the study shown in Figure 16–2, this combination of medication and cognitive-behavioral therapy was found to reduce binging by as much as 80 percent (see Figure 16–2).

Group therapy can also be helpful in the treatment of eating disorders. In psychodynamically oriented groups, the

Figure 16–1

A cognitive-behavioral model of bulimia   The bulimic incorporates society's attitudes toward thinness and translates them into extreme restraints and rigid rules about how much and what kinds of foods to eat. However, as hunger inevitably builds, the bulimic is thrown into an episode of binge eating, violating these inflexible and maladaptive rules about food. Source: American Journal of Psychiatry, Volume 149, pp. 82–87, 1992. Copyright © 1992, the American Psychiatric Association. Reprinted by permission.

From a cognitive-behavioral perspective, the eating disorder of bulimia emerges when the individual's incorporation of society's beliefs about thinness leads the individual to adopt a set of rules and restrictions regarding food. In the case of bulimia these rules break down when the individual becomes hungry, and a binge pattern is set in motion (Agras, 1991; see Figure 16–1).

Given the multiple perspectives on the causes of eating disorders, it follows that effective treatment requires a combination of approaches. Medications are frequently used because of their dramatic and often life-saving effects. For example, fluoxetine (Prozac) has been shown to reduce the symptoms of anorexia (Kaye et al., 1991) and bulimia, presumably by increasing the available levels of serotonin in the brain (Hollander et al., 1992). Antidepressants have also been used because of the theorized role of depression in bulimia, and because these medications reduce eating disorder behaviors while they are being administered. Early in the 1980s, MAO inhibitors began to be used in treating bulimia (Walsh et al., 1984); however, these medications have many undesirable side effects, and their long-term effectiveness has not been successfully demonstrated (Walsh, 1991).

Experts know that some form of psychotherapy is rou-

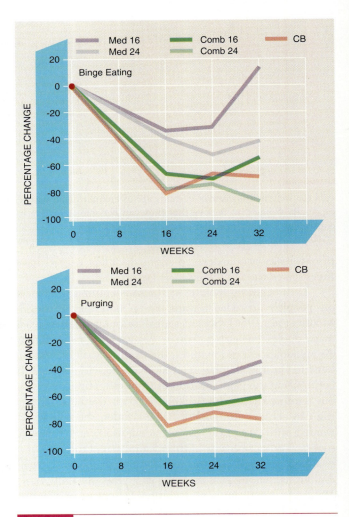

Figure 16–2

Changes in binge eating and purging in bulimic individuals   These graphs show the results of treatment with medications for 16 or 24 weeks, with cognitive-behavioral therapy, or with a combination of both. Follow-up occurred at 32 weeks. Source: Agras et al. (1992).

DISORDER	BIOLOGICAL	PSYCHOLOGICAL
Kleptomania	People with kleptomania have other disorders, suggesting common biological origins relating to serotonin deficiency. **Treatment:** Medications such as fluoxetine which increase available serotonin.	Stealing becomes reinforced because it reduces anxiety. **Treatment:** Covert sensitization and thought stopping to reduce frequency of stealing.
Pathological Gambling	Pathological gambling may be related to mood disorders, suggesting a biological link. Brain abnormalities may exist, such as increased norepinephrine and abnormal EEG activity. **Treatment:** No relevant treatments.	Gambling becomes established as a search for the positive reinforcement experienced during a big win. People with certain personality traits may be more prone to addiction. Disturbed family relationships contribute to gambling patterns. **Treatment:** Aversive conditioning, *in vivo* exposure, imaginal desensitization.
Pyromania	Lower levels of serotonin and norepinephrine. **Treatment:** No relevant treatments.	Fascination with fire combined with unpredictable discipline by parents sets early predisposition to fire-starting. **Treatment:** Graphing technique, in which the individual records behaviors, feelings, and experiences associated with firesetting.
Sexual impulsivity	Abnormally high levels of testosterone may contribute to hyper-sexuality. **Treatment:** Antiandrogenic medication to reduce testosterone levels.	Unduly restrictive parenting or neglect and abuse lead child to rebel or to seek sex as an escape. Sexuality becomes associated with relief and escape from loneliness. **Treatment:** Insight-oriented therapy to discuss nonsexual conflict. Behavioral methods of aversive therapy and covert conditioning, behavioral contracting, substitution of alternate forms of activity, and methods to bolster self-esteem. Family or couples therapy to improve communication.
Trichotillomania	Link to obsessive-compulsive disorder suggests a biological connection.	Disturbed parent-child relationships lead child to seek gratification or attention by hair-pulling, which becomes reinforcing.

DISORDER	BIOLOGICAL	PSYCHOLOGICAL
Trichotillomania (con't)	**Treatment:** Lithium and antidepressants, particularly clomipramine.	**Treatment:** Enhanced awareness of the behavior, reinforcement, aversive conditioning, relaxation or hypnotic techniques, and substitution with other behaviors.
Intermittent Explosive Disorder	Biological causes suggested by reports of aura experiences and abnormal insulin secretion. **Treatment:** Benzodiazepines and medications that alter norepinephrine activity.	No relevant theory. **Treatment:** Behavioral interventions used to augment somatic treatment.
Eating Disorders	Possible genetic contributions. Deficient levels of norepinephrine and serotonin **Treatment:** Fluoxetine and antidepressant medications.	Sociocultural influences lead women to value thinness. Dysfunctional patterns within the family limit the child's development of independence or involve high levels of conflict or lack of empathy. Related to family systems perspective. Struggles with parents in gaining independence interfere with the development of identity. Rigid beliefs about weight and food dominate the person's life. **Treatment:** Self-monitoring, cognitive restructuring, and relapse prevention. Improving self-esteem and relationships.

focus is placed on the symbolism of food and eating (Brotman et al., 1985). In cognitive-behavioral groups, clients are helped to reformulate the way they think about eating and are given practical help in changing their eating behaviors (Garner & Bemis, 1982). As is true with other types of self-help groups, groups for people with eating disorders provide support and help participants develop perspective by sharing their experiences with similarly troubled people.

Finally, in an interesting new approach, the method of interpersonal therapy developed for treating depression has been successfully applied to the treatment of bulimia. In this approach, no specific attempt is made to change the bulimic's eating behavior; instead, therapy focuses on helping the client cope with stress in interpersonal situations and feelings of low self-esteem. By intervening in these domains, interpersonal therapy helps improve the client's mood, reducing the reliance on food as a means of coping with negative feelings (Agras, 1991).

DISORDERS OF SELF-CONTROL: THE PERSPECTIVES REVISITED

In this chapter we have discussed several disorders that involve people's struggles in controlling their behavior. Some of these disorders represent behaviors that, in moderation, are not problematic. Nothing is wrong with dieting, gambling, or having sexual interests. It is also normal to lose one's temper on occasion. However, when these behaviors are carried to an extreme, they can become a source of distress to the individual and to others. In contrast, fire-starting and stealing are outside the realm of what society regards as acceptable behavior, because these actions violate the rights of others. Regardless of the degree or acceptability of the behavior, the main issue in understanding these disorders is that the individual feels powerless to control the impulse to act.

Return to the Case

Neil Gorman

Neil's History

I was curious to hear Neil's story, and to learn how such a young man had gotten himself into so much trouble. What life experiences and personality factors might have brought him to a point of financial ruin and emotional devastation? In discussing his current situation, Neil explained that he had recently lost his job as a handyman at a large apartment complex. Although he was upset about being unemployed, he was happy to get away from the work of a handyman. Neil had come to hate this job because it was unchallenging and tedious, but he had held onto it because there were so few alternatives for a person lacking a college education. He had been married to Beverly, a waitress, for 4 years and they had two young children, both under the age of 3. Although they had managed to get by financially prior to the onset of Neil's gambling problem, Neil often felt frustrated by his inability to afford some of the nice things in life that his friends seemed to have.

Neil grew up in a working-class family, the youngest of three boys. He described his childhood as being filled with feelings of being neglected by parents and disliked by teachers. Never succeeding at anything in which he could take pride, Neil's lack of self-confidence grew more oppressive as he proceeded through his teenage years. Compounding his low self-esteem was the onset of severe acne, which caused him to feel continuously embarrassed and to avoid close relationships. Neil recalled how his social life consisted of poker games with a handful of other high school acquaintances. In a short period of time, Neil came to realize that he was actually very good at poker, and his reputation spread around town. Because of the limited financial resources of everyone who played, the monetary gains were never particularly great for Neil, but the emotional significance of this successful endeavor was tremendous.

Upon graduation from high school, Neil's poker friends went their own way, leaving him feeling abandoned and alone. Two weeks after finishing high school, he met Beverly, and they dated for a few months and decided to get married. At first, Beverly was amused by Neil's interest in gambling. She was also impressed by how lucky he seemed to be. Neil told me how pleased he was when Beverly got excited about one of his wins. Even a $5 win on an instant lottery ticket would bring a big reaction from Beverly; little did she know how desperate Neil had become for those positive responses. He felt

gratified not only by the money, but also by the emotional rewards that ensued from a win. Of course, there was also the downside—the losses. The pain of even a minor loss would disrupt him for days, propelling him into a frenzied state of attempting to recover whatever he had lost by making another bet.

Serious trouble started for Neil when he and Beverly took a trip to Atlantic City for their third anniversary. This was Neil's first exposure to big-time gambling, and he was excited over the prospect of showing his wife how clever he was at gambling. One night at the blackjack table, Neil had a streak of good fortune and ended up with a couple of thousand dollars in his pocket. Beverly was thrilled with his winnings, and urged him to quit while he was ahead. Neil reassured Beverly that everything would be fine and he continued to gamble. The next day his luck ran out and he started losing. The more he lost, the more panicky he became. Without telling his wife, he began to draw money from their bank account at one of the nearby automatic teller machines. Finally, Beverly was able to convince Neil to return home.

Although Neil promised her that he would never do anything so stupid again, he still felt driven to recoup his losses and to go for a big win. Secretly, he sought out a local bookie and started placing large bets with money that he borrowed from various sources, including relatives, friends, and banks. This went on for many months, and Neil was able to pay back some of his debts through his winnings. However, he was consumed by the dream of becoming rich through his gambling, and he began to take larger and larger risks. This became a full-time occupation, and Neil was let go from his job because of too many missed days. As his losses mounted, Neil became despondent and began talking to Beverly about killing himself, so that at least she would have some life insurance money to support herself and the children.

Assessment

The case of Neil Gorman seemed fairly clear. I did not feel the need to conduct a comprehensive psychological testing; consequently I limited testing to the *MMPI-2*. Neil's profile on this test was like that of most people with serious gambling problems—indicating low tolerance for frustration and low self-esteem. What was most troubling, however, was Neil's elevated score on the depression subscale. I wondered about the

Neil Gorman continued

extent to which his depression was a longstanding problem or more reflective of his current state of despair associated with his financial problems. My conclusion was that both characterological and situational factors were at play. For years Neil had been suffering from low self-esteem and associated depressive symptoms; his recent crisis served to deepen his feelings of despair ultimately leading him to consider taking his own life.

Diagnosis

There was little question in my mind that Neil met the criteria for a diagnosis of pathological gambling. Preoccupied with gambling, Neil had formed a vicious pattern in which he felt the need to gamble increasing amounts of money in order to achieve his desired level of excitement. When he was not gambling, he felt restless and anxious. Rather than being discouraged by financial losses, Neil would return to the games as he desperately "chased" big wins. He became caught up in lying to his wife, jeopardizing the welfare of his family, and relying on others to bail him out of his horrendous financial problems.

Axis I: Pathological Gambling.
Axis II: No diagnosis.
Axis III: No significant medical problems.
Axis IV: Psychosocial stressors; 3. Loss of job, financial hardship.
Axis V: Current Global Assessment of Functioning: 50. Highest Global Assessment of Functioning (past year): 70

Case Formulation

Neil felt chronically unsure about his own competence, attractiveness, and intelligence, and he undertook desperate measures in an effort to compensate for his perceived inadequacies. His marriage to Beverly helped him feel better about himself for a while, but in time he felt the need to impress her. Having gambled since adolescence, Neil looked to this pursuit as an opportunity to succeed. He fantasized that his winnings would prove to his wife and to himself that he could be a big shot. These were mostly daydreams until Neil and Beverly traveled to Atlantic City, the first time in his life when he was faced with the prospect of big-time gambling. After his big win at the blackjack table, he became hooked. The fact that Beverly was initially so pleased with Neil's winnings encouraged him, and although she soon expressed her disapproval, Neil kept hoping that if he won more money she would be even more impressed with him. After Beverly convinced Neil to return home, his secret gambling became more intense and he placed himself in serious financial jeopardy. His depression and suicidal thinking

---

A number of the disorders we have covered in this chapter cause considerable harm to other people in addition to the client. Even if the client does not recognize a need for treatment, interventions may be mandated by legal authorities or may be insisted on by family members. Unfortunately, the nature of these disorders makes it particularly difficult for these individuals to seek help, and even when they do, to seize control over their behavior.

As researchers attempt to gain an understanding of these disorders of self-control, which until recently were given little systematic attention, a formulation is emerging that places these disorders into an "affective spectrum." This spectrum includes mood disorders, obsessive-compulsive disorder, substance abuse disorders, eating disorders, and anxiety disorders (McElroy et al., 1992). According to this formulation, the disorders of self-control belong on the affective spectrum because they share commonalities with the other affective spectrum disorders in terms of symptoms, hypothesized biological mechanisms, and treatments. As researchers continue to explore these

links, we can look forward to improved understanding of these mysterious and disabling psychological phenomena.

SUMMARY

1. An impulse control disorder is a disturbance in the ability to regulate one's urges to act. People with impulse control disorders continue to engage in behaviors that can be harmful to themselves or others, feeling driven to do so and becoming desperate if they cannot carry through with their desires. After acting on their impulses, they feel a sense of relief.

2. A kleptomaniac is a person who is driven to steal items, not for their material value, but for the thrill and relief from tension that stealing provides. They are disinclined to seek treatment, and those who do see a clinician typically have other psychological disorders for which they are seeking treatment. The

Neil Gorman continued

were extreme reactions to the financial losses and the assaults on his self-esteem resulting from these losses.

Planning a Treatment

It was clear to me after my intake session with Neil that he should be treated by a professional who was knowledgeable about this particular form of addictive behavior. In looking for a clinician with this kind of expertise, I was surprised to learn that the problem was more common than I had realized—so common, in fact, that weekly meetings of Gamblers Anonymous were taking place at a nearby community center. In addition, a local social worker named Miguel Carreira had an active treatment program for people who struggled with pathological gambling. Neil remained in the hospital for 3 days. During this time we ruled out suicide risk and made arrangements for follow-up treatment. Prior to his discharge, Neil attended his first Gamblers Anonymous meeting, and he returned to the unit expressing a great sense of relief. He felt that finally he had reason to hope that this monster that had tormented him could now be expelled from his life.

Neil's new therapist told me that Neil's treatment program would involve a commitment to active participation in GA, as well as individual and couples therapy for at least 3

months. Mr. Carreira explained that Neil would also be referred to an employment and career counselor, so that he could begin laying out plans for a more satisfying career.

Outcome of the Case

A year after my brief intervention with Neil Gorman I was pleasantly surprised to receive a New Year's card from his wife thanking me for helping get Neil back on track. His treatment with Mr. Carreira and his participation in GA had apparently helped Neil to change dramatically. Not only had he stayed away from gambling completely, but he had also taken some important steps toward developing a more fulfilling career. He had enrolled in an auto mechanics program at the local technical college, which offered him on-the-job-training. With the help of Mr. Carreira, he had worked out a plan with the bank in which his loans would be repaid over a 5-year period by means of payroll deductions.

The couples therapy had helped Neil to realize that it made no sense for him to use gambling in an attempt to feel better about himself or to impress Beverly. Instead he could derive improved self-esteem and respect from Beverly through his commitment to a new, healthier course of personal growth.

---

medication fluoxetine has been shown to reduce kleptomanic behavior; behavioral methods such as covert sensitization and thought-stopping are also used with the goal of breaking the positive association that has formed between stealing and tension relief.

3. Gambling, which has become a common feature of daily life, poses a serious risk to those individuals who are likely to become pathological gamblers. Often, the path from recreational to pathological gambling occurs through a set of phases, with the most important transformation taking place when the person has a "big win." Pathological gambling is then maintained by the gambler's desire to repeat this highly positive experience. This disorder has become more common with the growth of the legalized betting industry. Some of the psychological conditions associated with pathological gambling include a cluster of certain personality traits, depression, and inaccurate cognitions about gambling and payoff conditions. In psychological treatment of gambling, methods comparable to

those of Alcoholics Anonymous are used; the individual can present his or her problems to Gamblers Anonymous (GA) group and receive the support, help, and confrontation of people who have been through similar experiences. Behavioral methods, such as those used in treating addiction, have also proved helpful. Gambling involves many psychosocial and economic issues that decrease the person's ability to take a simple route to cure, however.

4. People with pyromania have an unrestrained urge to set fires, and this behavior provides them with a release from tension. This dangerous behavior, which poses a serious risk to others, is not well understood. It appears to originate in childhood, as the child develops an attraction to and curiosity about fires in the context of a family characterized by inconsistent and disturbed parenting styles. Those who are caught are usually ordered to get professional help, but the disorder is very resistant to change. The most commonly used method is the graphing technique.

5. People with sexual impulsivity have frequent, uncontrollable urges to have sex, and when these urges occur, they seek any available sexual partner. Little scientific information exists on this disorder. Theories regarding its causes emphasize the role of early family dynamics and learning. People with this disorder typically grew up in families characterized either by restrictive attitudes toward sex or by the experience of neglect and abuse. Sexual activity provided either a way of reacting against overly restrictive parenting guidelines or a way of seeking comfort and escape from an unhappy family setting. Biological explanations emphasize the role of hormonal abnormalities such as heightened levels of testosterone. Insight-oriented therapy involves bringing to the surface the conflicts that underlie the behavior. Behavioral and cognitive-behavioral techniques include aversive covert conditioning, behavioral contracting, and self-esteem enhancement. Family approaches focus on improving the client's ability to communicate with the client's partner and on correcting dysfunctional patterns that are enacted in the sexual domain. In extreme cases involving abuse of others, hormonal therapy may be administered. Group therapy, involving peer support and confrontation may also be recommended.

6. In trichotillomania, the individual is driven to pull or pluck out bodily hair, an act that provides a relief from tension, even though the individual may be very distressed by the disorder. Although this disorder is not common, it has received increased attention in the past decade and is beginning to be a focus of research. People with this disorder are usually first seen by dermatologists rather than mental health professionals because they deny they have a problem with hair-pulling. From a biological perspective, trichotillomania is understood as a variant of obsessive-compulsive disorder, and both disorders have been shown to respond to the same medications. Behavioral methods involving principles of extinction or substitution of alternate responses for hair-pulling have also proved useful, as have aversive conditioning and relaxation. In a cognitive-behavioral approach, the individual initiates self-dialogues as a warning to control the impulse in situations where hair-pulling is likely to occur.

7. Intermittent explosive disorder involves the inability to control impulses to lash out in fierce anger, often involving physically as well as verbally aggressive behaviors. A connection is thought to exist between these uncontrollable aggressive behaviors and physical abnormalities, but this link has not yet been established. Medications such as benzodiazepines and those that alter norepinephrine activity seem to be effective in reducing explosive behaviors as have behavioral interventions.

8. People with eating disorders, most of whom are females, develop problematic attitudes and behaviors with regard to food. In anorexia nervosa, individuals become obsessed with the idea of thinness; no matter how emaciated they become, they remain convinced that they are fat. In bulimia nervosa, the individual maintains a normal weight, but does so through alternating between the extremes of binging and purging. Both types of eating disorders involve serious medical complications that can prove fatal. These disorders are distressing both to the individual with the disorder and to the person's family. There are multiple perspectives on understanding eating disorders, with many theorists emphasizing the role of socialization in Western culture, which idealizes thinness in women. Within the family, a number of abnormalities in dynamics have been identified as possible contributors to eating disorders, including parents who make it difficult for their children to assert their independence, and conflicted, chaotic, or indifferent family relationships. Biological theories focus on possible genetic contributions, the linkages between eating disorders and mood disorders, and a possible link between these psychological difficulties and altered norepinephrine and serotonin activity. From a cognitive-behavioral perspective, eating disorders emerge when the individual's incorporation of social beliefs about thinness leads the person to adopt rigid dietary restrictions. In the case of bulimia, hunger makes the individual unable to adhere to these rules, leading to a pattern of binge eating. Biological treatment of eating disorders has involved the use of fluoxetine, which acts on the serotonin system, and antidepressant medications. Cognitive-behavioral techniques help to maintain long-term abstinence and reduction of binging by incorporating self-monitoring, cognitive restructuring, and principles of relapse prevention. Group therapy can also be useful, providing peer support and helping clients develop a perspective on their disorder. Interpersonal therapy, which focuses on improving the individual's relationships with others and building self-esteem, is also proving to have positive benefits even though the treatment does not focus specifically on eating behaviors.

KEY TERMS

Impulse: an urge to act. p. 406

Impulse control disorders: psychological disorders in which people act on certain impulses involving some potentially harmful behavior that they cannot resist. p. 406

Kleptomania: an impulse control disorder that involves the persistent urge to steal. p. 406

Pathological gambling: an impulse control disorder involving the persistent urge to gamble. p. 408

Big win: a gain of large amounts of money in one bet which propels the pathological gambler into a pattern of uncontrollable gambling. p. 409

Pyromania: an impulse control disorder involving the persistent and compelling urge to start fires. p. 411

Sexual impulsivity: a condition in which people feel uncontrollably driven to seek out sexual encounters and engage in frequent and indiscriminate sexual activity. p. 412

Trichotillomania: an impulse control disorder involving the compulsive persistent urge to pull out one's own hair. p. 414

Intermittent explosive disorder: an impulse control disorder involving an inability to hold back urges to express strong angry feelings and associated violent behaviors. p. 415

Anorexia nervosa: an eating disorder involving an intense fear of becoming fat that leads people to engage in various behaviors geared to weight loss. p. 416

Purge: to eliminate food through unnatural methods such as vomiting or excessive use of laxatives. p. 416

Bulimia nervosa: an eating disorder involving the alternation between the extremes of binging and purging. p. 417

Binge: the ingestion of large amounts of food during a short period of time, even after reaching a point of feeling full, and stopping only when a point of extreme physical discomfort is reached. p. 417

Case Report: Maria Nunez

There are few sadder events in the work of a clinician than intervening with a person who has attempted suicide. For me, the stress is compounded when the suicide attempt involves a young person. So I was understandably affected when I received word that I was being assigned a new client named Maria Nunez, an 18-year-old woman who had tried to kill herself the night before by ingesting a bottle of sleeping pills. I knew all too well how difficult my initial encounter with Maria would be because of many experiences with people following suicide attempts.

As I entered the hospital room, the faces of several suicide attempters flashed through my thoughts. The scene was very much the same—medical equipment engulfing the patient, a caring relative sitting apprehensively beside the bed, and a hospital staffer vigilantly nearby. Maria herself was very groggy, apparently knowing where she was, but wishing that she were elsewhere, perhaps home, perhaps dead. I'm sure my discomfort was evident as I introduced myself and struggled to offer a solicitous comment to Maria and to her mother.

Two days later, when Maria was transferred to the short-term psychiatric unit, I reintroduced myself and held my first session with her. Still in anguish, Maria initially had a very difficult time conversing with me. Her speech and movements reflected her despair. The frequent appearance of tears in her eyes corresponded to the feelings of sadness and hopelessness she shared with me. Despite my alarm about the depth of Maria's depression, I was able to feel some small amount of hope because she was able to talk about how she felt and offer some insight into how things had gotten so bad in her life.

Sarah Tobin, PhD

17

REACTIONS TO LIFE STRESS

Think of the times in your life when you were "stressed out." What strategies did you use to cope? Most people have a repertoire of adaptive mechanisms that enables them to cope with the stress that arises in their lives. **Stress** is the feeling that one's resources are inadequate to meet the demands of a situation. For example, if you are studying for three examinations in the same week, and you receive news from home that a relative is ill, you may feel overwhelmed and unable to manage your troubled emotions. The stress in this situation is your perception of being overwhelmed. What follows from this perception are a number of psychological and physiological reactions. You might feel depressed, anxious, physically exhausted, or even sick. These are typical reactions to stress, and for most people they pass in time. In some cases, however, the reactions to stress are extremely severe and do not readily abate.

In this chapter, we will discuss a diverse group of disorders that can be conceptualized as reactions to stress. Some of these disorders involve physical changes in response to stress and others involve adjustment to changes in life circumstances. Post-traumatic stress disorder, which may seem to fit logically with other reactions to stress, was discussed in Chapter 7 because it is regarded as an anxiety disorder by most experts. We will begin this chapter looking at another extreme reaction to life stress—suicide—which can be regarded as a deadly failure to cope with the stress in one's life.

After reading this chapter, you should be able to:

■ Describe the characteristics of people who commit suicide and the perspectives on which current theories and treatments are based.

- Define an adjustment disorder and understand theories of stress and coping that help explain why people respond differently to distressing events and circumstances.
- Understand the nature of psychophysiological conditions and how stress and emotions can relate to physical disease.
- Describe the area of behavioral medicine and how it is relevant to the treatment of psychophysiological conditions.
- Understand the major categories of sleep disorders and current ways of treating them, including ways to manage mild sleep disturbances.
- Describe the conditions that can serve as a focus of attention or treatment that are not considered psychological disorders.

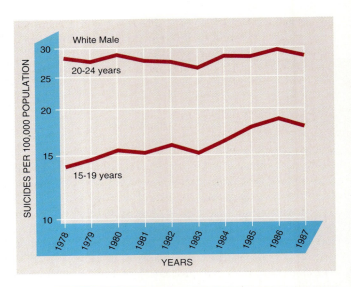

Figure 17–1 Death rates for suicide among white males 15–24 years, 1978–1987

SUICIDE

Imagine what it must take for a person to become so despondent that suicide seems to be the only possible course of action. People who reach this point feel that they lack the resources to cope with their problems. In some cases, a suicide attempt is said to be a "call for help." For example, a young man may swallow 20 aspirin tablets and then telephone his mother to tell her what he has done—a phone call that reflects his ambivalence about dying and his desire to be helped. Many people who attempt to commit suicide do so out of the conviction that the only way they can get help from others is by taking desperate actions. Rather than follow through on the act, they communicate their suicidal intent early enough so that they can be rescued.

Although some people respond to overwhelming stress by taking the drastic action of killing themselves by means of a dramatic single act such as hanging or shooting, there are other forms of self-inflicted, life-terminating behaviors (Farberow, 1980). Some people deal with their stress by engaging in behaviors that are ultimately self-destructive. A young woman may ignore dietary restrictions for treating her diabetes and as a result, frequently suffer from insulin shock. Similarly, a man who has been diagnosed with lung cancer may persist in smoking two packs of cigarettes a day. Or perhaps an unhappy adolescent goes out and drives recklessly after every argument with his parents. Although these reactions to stress are not actual suicide attempts, these behaviors can have fatal consequences.

Who Commits Suicide?

Each year almost 30,000 Americans kill themselves; this number represents an average of 12 out of every 100,000 people (USDHHS, 1991). The suicide rate varies considerably by age, gender, and race. The highest suicide rate is for white men over the age of 85—66 per 100,000—(USDHHS, 1988) although the rate for nonwhite elderly men and women is increasing (Manton et al., 1987). Another group at heightened risk for suicide are men between the ages of 15 to 24, among whom the suicide rate has been steadily growing over the last 30 years (NCHS, 1990). In fact, during the mid-1980s, suicide had become the second leading cause of death for men in this age group (CDC, 1985). Looking more closely at this group, researchers have found that the rate is much higher for those between the ages of 20 and 24 than for 15- to 19-year olds. However, the gap is narrowing, as suicides among white males between the ages of 15 and 19 have begun to rise dramatically (NCHS, 1990) (see Figure 17–1).

Irrespective of age, men are more likely than women to commit suicide. Women make more suicide attempts but do not carry these through to completion as often as men do. When race is considered, white men are much more likely than nonwhite men to commit suicide. Married people commit suicide less frequently than unmarried people, leading some researchers to conclude that marriage acts as a protective factor against suicide. This is especially true for men (Klerman, 1987).

No formal diagnostic category in the *DSM* specifically applies to people who attempt suicide, although most of these people are seriously depressed, suffering from a mood disorder such as major depression or dysthymia. However, it is important to recognize that sometimes suicidal behavior is associated with other disorders as well, such as schizophrenia, somatoform disorders, or anxiety disorders (Winokur et al., 1988). Panic disorders, in particular, have been linked to suicidality; some panic-stricken individuals become so terrified that they perceive this drastic measure as the only route of escape (Anthony & Petronis, 1991; Johnson et al., 1990;

Weissman et al., 1989). Suicidality is also a prominent feature in some personality disorders. Recall our discussion in Chapter 6 of people with borderline personality disorder, among whom suicidal gestures and attempts are common.

Why Do People Commit Suicide?

As we have just pointed out, people who commit suicide often have one of a range of psychological disorders, so it is difficult to formulate general statements about its causes. However, several general theories of suicide have been proposed, with one of the most well-known being the theory of the French sociologist Emile Durkheim (1897, 1952). A principal reason for suicide, according to Durkheim, is *anomie*, or a feeling of alienation from society. Another popular explanation was provided by Edwin Shneidman, a prominent researcher, who views suicide as an attempt at interpersonal communication. According to Shneidman, people who attempt suicide are trying to communicate frustrated psychological needs to important people in their lives (Shneidman, 1984, 1985).

In the late 1980s, suicide theories began to focus more on the phenomena of depression and stress as causes. According to Aaron Beck and his co-workers, people who feel hopeless about their lives are at the highest risk for suicide (Beck et al., 1983). What may tip the balance from depression to hopelessness is the perception of insurmountable stress. Among depressed individuals, suicide is more likely for people who have suffered from stressful life events, particularly those events that are uncontrollable and involve loss of social support such as death of a spouse (Slater & Depue, 1981).

The nature of the stressful events that can precipitate feelings of hopelessness varies across the life span. Adoles-

A sense of hopelessness is one of the strongest predictors of suicide.

Following the suicide of an adolescent, high school students are often brought together by counselors to talk about their feelings. Such discussions are important to help teenagers cope with their sense of loss and to reduce the likelihood that they will see suicide as a way out of their problems.

cents may commit suicide because of feelings of marginality in a society that is focused on adults and their accomplishments. With technological advances in the labor market, there is also greater pressure to compete, leaving fewer jobs for younger workers who do not have the required training. A society-wide increase in self-destructive behaviors, such as drug and alcohol use, is also regarded as a possible influence on adolescent suicides (Curran, 1987). Further, from an individual perspective, when a young person commits suicide, the event does not usually take place in an otherwise happy and healthy existence. Adolescent males at high risk for suicide are more likely to have either a mood disorder, a family history of mood disorder, a history of prior suicide attempts, or a substance abuse problem (Brent et al., 1988). One study reported that more than 90 percent of adolescents who had attempted suicide met the diagnostic criteria for depressive disorders (Chabrol & Moron, 1988).

Increasing concern has arisen during the past decade about the role of "copy-cat" suicides, and in fact imitation of peers who have committed suicide accounts for an increasing number of adolescent suicides (Chiles et al.,

1985). Studies have shown that news stories and movies about suicide have a dramatic effect on youth (Gould & Shaffer, 1986; Phillips & Carstensen, 1986), and peers who are close to a suicide victim, especially those who witness the suicide, are at particularly high risk (Berman, 1987).

It is unclear what accounts for the fact that such a disproportionately large number of people in their early 20s commit suicide. One possibility is that after reaching the age of 21, men in particular feel a heightened societal pressure to start on the path toward success in their careers and to establish a family life. Those who commit suicide regard their situations as hopeless, feeling pessimistic and powerless to reach their goals (Peck, 1987).

For older adults, economic concerns and illness may produce the kind of stress that leads a person to consider suicide. Those who are physically ill or isolated are also at higher risk for suicide (Rich et al., 1991).

Apart from these psychosocial factors that contribute to suicide, there are also some important leads from the biological perspective. Researchers have found genetic patterns of suicidality, including higher rates of concordance between identical (13.2 percent) compared to fraternal (.7 percent) twins (Roy et al., 1991)—a link that adoption studies have shown cannot be attributed to environmental factors. Because of these startling findings, clinicians and researchers routinely ask about instances of suicide among one's relatives (Klerman, 1987), knowing that a family history of suicide statistically increases the risk of suicide.

Another fascinating line of biological inquiry has focused on anatomical and physiological differences between suicide completers and controls. For example, autopsies of suicide completers have provided evidence of abnormalities in brain neurotransmitter systems. In one study, suicide victims had lower concentrations of GABA in the hypothalamus (Korpi et al., 1988), and other researchers found indicators of lower serotonin activity in the nervous systems of suicide completers compared to people who died for other reasons (Brown et al., 1982). These findings are particularly impressive in that lower serotonin was associated with suicide regardless of the victim's psychiatric diagnosis.

Predicting and Preventing Suicide

Although suicide statistics are alarming, they nevertheless reflect a low incidence in the population. When a clinician is attempting to evaluate whether a particular client is at high risk for committing suicide, this low probability must be factored into the assessment, because it means that few people are likely to carry through with a suicidal wish. Nevertheless, clinicians tend to err on the conservative side, and if there is any chance that a client is suicidal, all precautions are taken to ensure the client's safety.

Various methods are available to improve the odds of predicting whether a given client presents a serious suicide risk. First, an assessment is made of the individual's suicidal

Some powerful means of suicide are shown here.

intent and *lethality*. **Suicidal intent** refers to how committed a person is to dying. A person who is highly committed to dying would be regarded as having a high degree of suicide intent. In contrast, a person who is ambivalent in the wish to die would be regarded as having lower suicidal intent. **Suicidal lethality** refers to the dangerousness of the person's intended method of dying. Some examples of highly lethal methods include combining high doses of barbiturates with alcohol, hanging, shooting oneself, and jumping from high places. Methods that would be low in lethality include taking over-the-counter medications or making superficial cuts on one's wrist.

Suicidal intent and lethality are usually linked, but not always, and both factors must be considered when evaluating a person who is suicidal. One way to aid in assessing suicidality is to ask the individual if he or she has a "plan"; a carefully worked out plan is usually a very worrisome indicator. Consider the example of a woman who is convinced that she wants to die and chooses a method that would clearly be lethal, such as heavy overdosing on barbiturates. She figures out a way to obtain the drugs and sets a time and place where she can carry out her act without being interrupted. This is a carefully worked out plan, indicating a high risk of attempting suicide.

Many suicidal people are willing to tell others about their intentions, but may find that other people become uncomfortable and are reluctant to discuss their concerns. There is a common misconception that asking a person if he or she is suicidal might suggest the idea to the individual. Many people unfortunately conclude that it might be better to avoid the topic, and even go so far as to ignore warning signs.

Even if a person denies suicidal intent, behavioral clues can provide indications of a person's level of suicidality. For example, a depressed young man who gives away his stereo and mementos and puts his financial affairs in order might be preparing to end his life. However, it is easy to mistake the normal emotional and behavioral instability associated with puberty for signs of suicidality (Curran, 1987). Changes in mood, declining grades, recklessness, substance abuse, a giving up of former interests, and stormy relationships are frequently cited as suicide risk signs, but are common experiences of adolescence, particularly during the early teen years.

As you have probably realized by this point, each potential suicide involves a unique set of factors. For example, a teenage girl who is upset about her poor academic performance is quite different from an individual with a long history of bipolar disorder and multiple past suicide attempts. Clinicians must evaluate a range of factors such as the individual's age, gender, race, marital status, health, and family history; however, experienced clinicians know that these risk factors can be used only as guides rather than as conclusive evidence of suicidality.

Suicidal behavior is treated in many contexts, including suicide hotlines, hospital emergency rooms, mental health clinics, and inpatient psychiatric facilities. The treatments offered in these settings vary considerably in their scope and depth. Cutting across the varying intervention contexts are two basic strategies for treating suicidal individuals: providing social support and helping these individuals regain a sense of control over their lives.

The need to provide social support is based upon the idea that when an individual is suicidal, he or she feels very alone; having other people around reduces that sense of isolation. Professionals follow through on this idea by establishing a formal connection to the suicidal individual by way of a "contract." This contract is a two-way agreement in which the client promises to contact the clinician upon experiencing suicidal impulses. The clinician, in turn, agrees to be available in the event of such a crisis. If a client will not agree to these conditions, the clinician is likely to consider having the client hospitalized.

Cognitive-behavioral techniques can be used to help the individual gain control over suicidal feelings. Using these procedures, the client is helped to think of alternative ways of dealing with stress. The client might also be encouraged to consider reasons for living and to shift the focus

Providing comfort and support to a depressed person can help that person see alternatives to suicide.

away from death to life. In any case, it is important for the client to be given the opportunity to talk about suicidal feelings in order to develop some perspective on the situation and a sense of control (Boyer & Guthrie, 1985).

Despite the popularity and widespread development of suicide hotlines throughout the United States, researchers have found that the presence of a suicide hotline in a community does not necessarily reduce that locality's suicide rate. The reason seems to be, at least in part, that many suicidal people don't call these services when they are at highest risk. Also, callers who are under the influence of psychoactive substances or who have serious emotional difficulties do not respond as well to the assistance provided by such services. However, people who do seek help from crisis intervention centers are likely to receive life-saving services. The effectiveness of crisis intervention also depends, of course, on the quality of services provided. Some of the more effective strategies for suicide intervention are summarized in Table 17–1 (on page 434).

ADJUSTMENT DISORDERS

When upsetting events occur, some kind of emotional or behavioral disturbance is considered expectable and understandable. For example, the divorce of one's parents can lead a person to feel distressed and unable to concentrate. For most people who go through this sort of experience, the

Table 17–1 Telephone Strategies for Suicide Intervention

Assess Lethality
The first step in telephone intervention is to evaluate the caller's potential for self-harm. The following areas should be addressed:

- Ask about a *plan*: "Do you have a plan?" "How are you going to kill yourself?" The answers to these questions should be evaluated in terms of the individual's lethality.
- Find out about *history* of suicide attempts: "Have you ever tried to commit suicide before?" "What methods did you use?" "How often have you attempted to kill yourself?" People who have made previous attempts are at higher risk.
- Evaluate the person's *resources:* "Do you have any friends?" "Is help available from clergy or acquaintances?" "How do you usually cope with stress?" The availability of external and internal resources reduces the individual's suicide risk.
- Determine degree of *isolation:* "Do you live alone?" "Is there anyone at home now?" "Do you feel lonely?" The more isolated the person feels, the higher the risk.
- Rate the degree of current life *stresses:* "What kind of stresses have you experienced lately?" "Have you lost anyone close to you?" Suicide often follows stressful life experiences.
- Evaluate *other relevant factors* such as ambivalence, level of distress, attempts to mask suicidal intent, the possibility that the individual has already acted, temporal factors (suicides are more frequent on weekends and Monday mornings), the presence of delusional thinking, hopelessness, and possible risk to other people.

Interventions
After assessing lethality, the next step is to intervene. Contact with the caller must be maintained at all costs through the development of a helping relationship. This is especially important because, unlike face-to-face contact, the client can easily terminate the intervention.

- Allow for *ventilation* of feelings: Let the caller talk about painful emotions and distress. This might include anger directed at the helper, which the helper must tolerate.
- Reassure the caller of your *availability:* Restate your willingness to listen when the caller complains that no one cares.
- Reinforce *positive responses:* Support any statements made by the caller that reflect attempts to obtain help, see things in a more positive light, or take constructive action.
- *Avoid superficial restating* of negative statements: If a caller says "I'm upset about losing my job," it is not particularly useful for the helper to say "You sound upset about losing your job." Instead, it is better to offer problem-solving statements that provide the caller with a sense of direction and hope. In this example, it would be better for the helper to say "What steps could you take to find a new job?"
- Provide *alternative avenues* of expression: Give the caller suggestions for other methods of coping with distress such as continuing to talk with the helper, relying on previously used coping strategies, and seeking social support.
- *Acknowledge* the person's distress: Take the caller's concerns seriously while avoiding simplistic reflective statements. The helper can recognize the caller's obvious feelings of despair with statements such as "The fact that you are calling here shows how unhappy you are but that you are also willing to allow yourself to be helped."
- Negotiate a *"no-suicide"* contract: Urge the caller to agree not to engage in self-destructive behavior. The contract should specify a time period and spell out contingencies in case the caller feels a mounting urge to act self-destructively.
- Explore *lethality:* Talk about the caller's lethality at the moment whenever it seems appropriate in the conversation.
- *Avoid nontherapeutic* interactions: Do not express hostility, sarcasm, impatience, or indifference. Do not let yourself be drawn into power struggles in the form of arguing with the caller.

Source: Adapted from Neville & Barnes, (1985).

period of extreme unhappiness abates, and they go on with their lives. However, some people experience such a depth of disturbance that they become seriously impaired in their daily functioning. A college student may become irresponsible and totally uninterested in prior activities, dropping out of school, quitting a job, and starting to drink heavily. Such a reaction falls outside the normal expectable limits as a response to an upsetting life event and would be considered an *adjustment disorder.*

Characteristics of Adjustment Disorders

An **adjustment disorder** is a reaction to one or more changes in a person's life that is more extreme than would

normally be expected under the circumstances. The reaction can persist for 6 months, or perhaps longer, and results in significant impairment or distress for the individual.

Adjustment disorders manifest themselves in several forms: emotional reactions such as anxiety and depression, disturbances of conduct, physical complaints, social withdrawal, or disruptions in work or academic performance. For example, a woman may react to the loss of her job by developing a variety of somatic symptoms, including headaches, backaches, and fatigue. A man may respond to a diagnosis of a serious illness by becoming reckless, self-destructive, and financially irresponsible. In these cases, the individual's reaction can be temporally linked to the occurrence of the stressor. Moreover, the reactions are considered out of proportion to the nature of the stressful experience.

Adjustment disorders are extremely common in college students (Arnstein, 1983), many of whom face stressors for which they may not have developed the necessary coping skills. When pressures of new life experiences such as intimate relationships, career decisions, and family problems at home arise, some people feel ill-equipped to manage the multiple demands placed upon them, and need professional attention.

Even exciting events in one's life, such as starting college, can be so stressful for some individuals that they develop an adjustment disorder.

Theories and Treatments

In trying to understand why some people develop adjustment disorders, it may be useful for you to recall stressful experiences in your own life and how you successfully dealt with them. For example, when disappointed over the breaking up of a relationship or the loss of a job, you may have felt saddened and upset, but in time you came to terms with the loss. Consider what went on in your own emotions, thoughts, and behavior that enabled you to cope with this stressor. Perhaps you talked with other people and received helpful support from them. Or maybe you involved yourself in activities that bolstered your fragile emotions. You may have gone through a period of intense sadness, but gradually you began to resume a more positive outlook on life. In contrast, think of an event in your life when you did not manage stress as effectively. Consider the style of feeling, thinking, and acting that characterized your response. You may have felt distraught and despondent. You may have lost all perspective and believed that your life was totally ruined by this event. Your reactions may have included self-destructive behaviors, such as substance abuse, dropping out of school, or becoming socially withdrawn. What accounts for the difference between the adaptive and maladaptive responses to these stressful events? This is the question that researchers in the area of stress and coping are attempting to answer.

Several explanations have been proposed to account for differences in people's reactions to stressors. Some of these probably would seem quite obvious to you. Perhaps the most reasonable place to start is by looking at the nature of the events themselves. For example, the death of a relative would seem to be more stressful than problems at work. In fact, a large body of research exists showing a relationship between the magnitude of stressful life events and health outcomes, both mental and physical (Cohen, 1988). The Social Readjustment Rating Scale (Holmes & Rahe, 1967), shown in Table 17–2 (on page 436), is the measurement instrument primarily used in this research, and by reading it you can obtain a sense of the variations in severity of life stressors.

Researchers have also found, however, that it is not just the event itself but the way it is interpreted that determines its impact. The death of a spouse may be viewed by one person as a horrible calamity and by another person as distressing but not devastating. Further, the context of the event plays a role in determining its impact. If the death of a spouse follows a long, debilitating terminal illness, the survivor may feel a sense of relief. The individual's internal capacities are yet another set of influences on the impact of a stressful event. Some people are particularly susceptible to stress for a variety of reasons, including biological, personality, and cognitive vulnerabilities (Cohen & Edwards, 1989). Finally, external resources can influence a person's interpretation of a stressful event; for example, the availability of a social network and material resources can make stressful situations more tolerable (Cohen & Wills, 1985).

Table 17–2 Social Readjustment Rating Scale

Holmes and his colleagues (Holmes & Holmes, 1970; Holmes & Rahe, 1967; Rahe & Arthur, 1978) have developed the Social Readjustment Rating Scale (SRRS), an objective method for measuring the cumulative stress to which an individual has been exposed over a period of time. This scale measures life stress in terms of "life change units" (LCU) involving the following events.

Events	Scale of Impact	Events	Scale of Impact
Death of spouse	100	Change in responsibilities at work	29
Divorce	73	Son or daughter leaving home	29
Marital separation	65	Trouble with in-laws	29
Jail term	63	Outstanding personal achievement	28
Death of close family member	63	Wife begins or stops work	26
Personal injury or illness	53	Begin or end school	26
Marriage	50	Change in living conditions	25
Fired at work	47	Revision of personal habits	24
Marital reconciliation	45	Trouble with boss	23
Retirement	45	Change in work hours or conditions	20
Change in health of family member	44	Change in residence	20
Pregnancy	40	Change in schools	20
Sex difficulties	39	Change in recreation	19
Gain of new family member	39	Change in church activities	19
Business readjustment	39	Change in social activities	18
Change in financial state	38	Small mortgage or loan	17
Death of close friend	37	Change in sleeping habits	16
Change to different line of work	36	Change in number of family get-togethers	15
Change in number of arguments with spouse	35	Change in eating habits	15
		Vacation	13
High mortgage	31	Christmas	12
Foreclosure of mortgage or loan	30	Minor violations of the law	11

For people who had been exposed in recent months to stressful events that added up to an LCU score of 300 or above, these investigators found the risk of developing a major illness within the next 2 years to be very high, approximately 80 percent.

Source: Adapted from Holmes & Rahe, (1967).

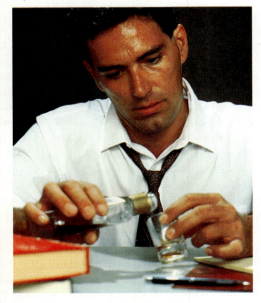

People who use emotion-focused coping strategies often resort to escape through drugs or alcohol to handle the stress in their lives.

Coping is the process through which people reduce stress. There are two primary means of coping with stressful events (Lazarus & Folkman, 1984). One is to change something about the situation that makes it stressful. This coping strategy is called *problem-focused,* because it involves doing something that addresses the situation. The other coping method is called *emotion-focused.* In emotion-focused coping, a person does not change anything about the situation itself, but instead tries to improve the feelings about the situation. "Thinking positively" is one emotion-focused coping method that people use to make themselves feel better under stressful conditions. Avoidance is another emotion-focused strategy. This coping method is similar to the defense mechanism of denial, in which the individual refuses to acknowledge that a problem or difficulty exists. In extreme form, avoidance as a coping strategy can involve escape into drugs or alcohol and can lead to additional problems in the person's life. Examples of these coping strategies are shown in Table 17–3.

Which coping style is more effective depends on the stress-provoking situation. In some cases, particularly when there is nothing one can do about a problem, it is probably

Table 17–3 Sample Items from the Ways of Coping Questionnaire

The Ways of Coping Questionnaire assesses the strategies that people use to manage internal or external demands in a stressful encounter. In research using this questionnaire, Susan Folkman and Richard Lazarus and their associates found that people use a variety of these coping methods in any one stressful encounter. As you read about the eight types of coping listed below, think of a recent stressful situation that you confronted and consider which styles characterized your way of managing the stress. Then think of which of these coping styles repeatedly characterize your method of handling stress.

Confrontive Coping:
I tried to get the person responsible to change his or her mind.
I stood my ground and fought for what I wanted.

Planful Problem-Solving
I knew what had to be done, so I doubled my efforts to make things work.
I made a plan of action and followed it.

Distancing
I went on as if nothing had happened.
I didn't let it get to me—refused to think about it too much.

Self-Control
I tried to keep my feelings to myself.
I kept others from knowing how bad things were.

Seeking Social Support
I talked to someone who could do something concrete about the problem.
I accepted sympathy and understanding from someone.

Accepting Responsibility
I criticized or lectured myself.
I realized I brought the problem on myself.

Escape-Avoidance
I wished that the situation would go away or somehow be over with.
I tried to make myself feel better by eating, drinking, smoking, using drugs or medication, etc.

Positive Reappraisal
I changed or grew as a person in a good way.
I found new faith.

Two of these scales (Confrontive Coping and Planful Problem-Solving) reflect problem-focused coping strategies which are directed primarily at changing something about the situation to make it less stressful. Four of the scales (Distancing, Self-Control, Accepting Responsibility, and Positive Reappraisal) reflect emotion-focused coping. Seeking Social Support serves both emotion- and problem-focused functions.

Source: Adapted from Folkman & Lazarus, (1988).

best to feel as good about it as possible. Consider the case of a woman who broke her ankle while ice skating; dealing with the stress may become more tolerable if she reframes the temporary disability as an opportunity to slow down her hectic life. When the situation is more controllable, problem-focused coping is more adaptive (Folkman et al., 1986). For example, a man who is refinancing his mortgage may become very upset because the interest rates suddenly rise. Rather than save money, he stands to lose thousands of dollars. Problem-focused coping would involve developing alternative financial plans to resolve his monetary problems.

Coping strategies can play an important role in determining whether or not an individual will suffer an adjustment disorder. A person with poor coping skills is much more likely to develop the emotional distress and behavioral problems that characterize adjustment disorders. In contrast, an individual who is able to manage stress will emerge from the stressful situation with fewer adverse consequences. It is also important to note that stress does not always have negative consequences. Some people thrive on higher levels of activation and find that the accompanying stress actually energizes them (DeLongis et al., 1988). Consider people you know who perform much more effectively when they are very busy and are facing deadlines.

Clinicians treating people with adjustment disorders usually direct efforts toward supporting the individual through the period of crisis, and try to bolster the individual's coping skills for handling stress. Because the adjustment disorders involve such a wide range of reactions, treatments must be individualized for every client. The client who is extremely anxious requires strategies for managing tension. Relaxation techniques and involvement in constructive distractions are particularly effective for this purpose. A person who is extremely depressed benefits from support and cognitive restructuring.

Regardless of the specific form of the adjustment disorder, early intervention is very important, because it reduces immediate distress and also reduces the likelihood of the problem becoming chronic. Brief therapy is considered the treatment of choice. For example, a client suffering from an adjustment disorder may be seen once a week for approximately 12 weeks with a focus specifically on the current problem or stress (Horowitz, 1986).

In treating people with adjustment disorders, clinicians try to alleviate distress but not at the cost of long-term growth in the client. For example, it would be all too easy to limit treatment to the prescription of antianxiety medication for a person suffering from an adjustment disorder characterized by anxiety. This method risks depriving the client of the opportunity to develop the coping strategies and resources needed to manage anxiety in everyday life.

PSYCHOPHYSIOLOGICAL CONDITIONS

In addition to the emotional toll of stress, many people suffer physical consequences when they are under duress. You may have heard the expression "stress can kill." A growing body of research is bearing out this claim. For example, Eysenck (1988), on the basis of studying more than 4000 people over a 10-year period, showed a strong link between stress and mortality.

Stress and Physical Illness

In your own life you have probably noticed connections between stress and physical illness. On the day of a big examination you may have had an upset stomach. At another time you may have taken an arduous trip somewhere and developed a throbbing headache. People with certain chronic physical conditions find that during times of pressure, their health takes a turn for the worse. For example, a woman with asthma may become more symptomatic at the end of the semester when she faces many deadlines, or a student may find that at times of stress his acne flares up.

In the *DSM*, the term *psychological factors affecting physical condition* has been used to refer to situations in which a person's physical problems are temporally linked to a stressful event. For the sake of simplicity, we refer to these conditions by the traditional term, **psychophysiological**. Among the physical problems that can be triggered by psy-

Brenda is the manager at a large discount chain store. She faces tremendous pressures to maintain high sales, particularly on the weekends when there are special store promotions. For the past year, she has suffered from severe headaches which make it nearly impossible for her to concentrate on her job. She has visited many health practitioners such as headache clinics and acupuncture specialists, but none of these has given her long-term relief.

- ■ What relationship seems to exist between Brenda's headaches and the intensification of her job pressures?
- ■ How does Brenda's psychophysiological condition differ from the condition of a person with a somatoform disorder?

When people are under stress, they often suffer physical symptoms such as headaches.

chological stressors are eating disorders, headaches, heart pains or spasms, painful menstruation, sacroiliac pain, skin problems, rheumatoid arthritis, rapid heartbeat, breathing irregularity or difficulty, ulcers, nausea, vomiting, and frequency of urination. As you can see from this partial listing, any bodily system can be involved. Further, a person's health-related behaviors can also affect the risk of developing certain diseases. Cigarette smoking, poor diet, and substance abuse can all make a person more vulnerable to physical illness (Stoudemire & Hales, 1991).

Psychophysiological conditions were at one time referred to as *psychosomatic disorders*, and conditions such as asthma and rheumatoid arthritis were treated with insight-oriented psychotherapy or psychoanalysis. However, that term has been abandoned because of evidence disproving the notion that such physical problems are "in the person's head" (Moran, 1991). In psychophysiological disorders, the individual experiences real physical symptoms; what makes them significant within a mental health context is the fact that these symptoms are connected to psychological stressors. The psychological factors have either initiated, aggravated, or perpetuated a medical disease or a physical problem.

Theories and Treatments

Why is it that when you have an important examination, you experience physical symptoms such as upset stomach or headache? Perhaps you have automatically assumed that a connection exists between the stressful event and your physical reaction; such reactions are so common that people rarely question why they occur. Once you stop and think about it, though, you may realize that these reactions are not easily explained. In struggling with this issue, scientists have developed a large body of research on the relationship between bodily and psychological problems.

Within the realm of psychophysiological disorders, the new field of **psychoneuroimmunology** is beginning to pro-

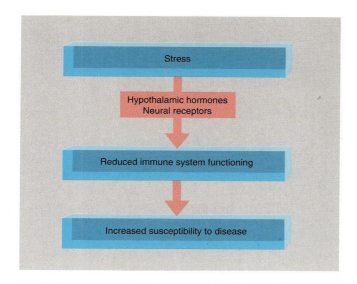

Figure 17–2
Relationships among stress, immune functioning, and disease

vide answers to some of the complex questions regarding the nature of the mind–body relationship (Vollhardt, 1991). This imposing term refers to the study of connections among psychological stress, nervous system functioning, and the immune system.

As shown in Figure 17–2, a stressful event can initiate a set of reactions within the body that lower the body's resistance to disease. These reactions can also aggravate the symptoms of a chronic stress-related physical disorder. The current understanding of these relationships is that stress stimulates hormones regulated by the hypothalamus, and these hormones lower the activity of the immune system (Rabin et al., 1989). With less protection, the body is less

resistant to fighting off infection, allergens, and the more serious intruders such as carcinogens. Nervous system reactions also alter immune system functioning through nerve endings in parts of the body involved in the immune system, such as the lymph nodes, thymus, and spleen. These processes appear to account for a wide range of physical disorders, including bronchial asthma, allergic rhinitis, rheumatoid arthritis, ulcerative colitis, and cancerous conditions such as leukemia and lymphomas (Schleifer et al., 1986).

People under stress also tend to have poorer health habits, possibly smoking more, drinking more alcohol, eating less nutritious meals, or getting less sleep. In a state of stress, most people are more susceptible to becoming sick, possibly due to an increased vulnerability to infectious diseases. They turn to other people for support, and ironically, their increased social interaction with others also increases their exposure to viruses and infectious agents. Some people in states of stress seek out sexual intimacy, possibly indiscriminately and with inadequate attention to safe sex practices. If stressed individuals become sick, regardless of the cause, they are less likely to comply with recommended treatment, putting themselves at even greater physical risk (Cohen & Williamson, 1991).

Researchers have also investigated the effect on bodily functions when a person inhibits expression of emotions. In David McClelland's research on exam stress described in the Research Focus, students high in power motivation were especially stressed because they felt unable to control the outcome of the situation. Their power motivation was, in this sense, suppressed.

In a similar vein, attempts to understand cancer have focused on the role of emotional suppression that characterizes a certain personality style (Greer & Watson, 1985).

RESEARCH FOCUS

HOW TAKING EXAMS CAN MAKE YOU SICK

Have you ever gotten sick after an important exam? Was it a coincidence, or do you think it might have been related to the stress of taking the exam? Researchers have tried to assess this issue through scientific methods. They have studied stress responses in students taking exams and have related these responses to their immune function. David McClelland and his associates were particularly interested in students who had high motivation to achieve power or control over their environment. These students would be especially likely to view an important exam as stressful because they felt that they would see the outcome as beyond their control.

Bodily excretions (saliva and urine) of these students were assessed after an examination to measure the concentration of. norepinephrine, an index of arousal of the sympathetic

nervous system. The activity of the immune system was also measured after the examination. Norepinephrine inhibits immune system functioning, and as was found in these studies, the students with higher norepinephrine levels also had lower immune responses. In short, when you interpret a situation (such as an exam) as stressful, your body responds with greater sympathetic arousal, preparing you for "fight or flight." After the exam is over, you become more vulnerable to infection because your immune system is still functioning at an impaired level (McClelland, 1985; McClelland, Davidson, & Saron, 1985).

The *cancer prone* personality, also called *Type C*, is an individual who suppresses emotional expression, especially anger, and tends to be highly compliant and conforming. According to this proposal, when a person becomes emotionally aroused, the sympathetic nervous system reacts with heightened activity. Expressing emotion is an important outlet for this activation, and failure to express emotion causes the body to remain in a state of heightened activation. As shown in Figure 17–2, this state is unhealthy because high levels of arousal of the sympathetic nervous system reduce the efficiency of the immune system—leading to the greater risk of developing cancer. Critics have argued, though, that there is more impressive evidence in support of the role of psychosocial factors as contributing to the progression of cancer. Specifically, people who become depressed after being diagnosed as having cancer or who lack social support to help them cope with their disease seem to be at higher risk for continued progression of the disease (Levenson & Bemis, 1991).

If emotional suppression is unhealthy, it would seem reasonable to conclude that the expression of emotion is beneficial to one's physical and mental well-being. It is a common belief that you should "get it off your chest" when you feel unhappy or upset. Research connecting emotional expression with immune system functioning is bearing out this belief. In a series of innovative experiments, Pennebaker and his colleagues (summarized in Pennebaker & Susman, 1988) showed that actively confronting one's emotions arising from an upsetting or traumatic event can have long-term health benefits. For example, writing about a distressing experience facilitates coping and contributes to physical health. In one study, college freshmen were assigned to write about the experience of coming to college, and a control group of students were instructed to write about superficial topics. The different kinds of writing had dramatic effects. Although those who wrote about their college adjustment experiences reported higher levels of homesickness than the control subjects, they made fewer visits to physicians. By the end of the year, the experimental subjects were doing as well or better than the control subjects in terms of grade point average and the experience of positive moods. From this study, the researchers concluded that the confrontation of feelings and thoughts regarding a stressful experience can have long-lasting positive effects, even though the initial impact of such confrontation may be disruptive (Pennebaker et al., 1990).

Along similar lines, emotions can also affect the cardiovascular system. For example, think of a time when you felt furious over a minor inconvenience. Perhaps you became angry about having to stand in line at the bank, and you felt what seemed like a rise in your blood pressure. If this happens to you once in a while, it probably has no serious consequence for your health. However, if you frequently feel a sense of impatience, irritability, or pressure to get something done in a hurry, you may be at risk for developing heart problems. This pattern of being hard-driving, competitive, impatient, cynical, suspicious of others, and easily irritated is called *Type A* (see Table 17–4). Converging evidence from several large studies points to the higher risk that people with Type A behavior patterns have of developing hypertension and associated heart problems (e.g., Barefoot et al., 1987). The sympathetic nervous systems of Type A people are in a state of almost constant activation, and this results in *hypertension*, or chronically high blood pressure. The kinds of diseases that can result from hypertension include coronary heart disease, cerebral atherosclerosis ("hardening" of the blood vessels in the brain), and atherosclerosis in other parts of the body, all of which can be life-threatening medical problems. For some Type A individuals, the effects are not so gradual, but rather can result in sudden cardiac death (Kamarck & Jennings, 1991).

Because people with Type A behavior patterns are more impatient and edgy much of the time, it is not surprising that they routinely engage in high-risk behaviors such as reckless driving or that they react with vehement anger when mildly provoked. For these reasons, people with Type A behavior patterns are also more likely to have fatal accidents, or to die from violent causes (Suls & Sanders, 1988).

Because psychophysiological disorders comprise such a vast array of physical problems, no single treatment model exists. For most of these disorders, treatment addresses both the physical and the psychological needs of the client. Narrow medical approaches for treating psychophysiological disorders have traditionally relied on drugs or surgery. However, during the past two decades clinicians have increasingly realized that medical treatments alone are insufficient. New health behaviors must also be introduced and reinforced.

Psychologists have collaborated with physicians in developing an interdisciplinary approach to psychophysiological disorders known as **behavioral medicine** (Gentry, 1984). Behavioral medicine techniques are rooted in behavioral theory, and use learning principles to help the client gain psychological control over unhealthy bodily reactions. Clients are taught to take responsibility for their health, to

For a person with a Type A behavior pattern minor frustrations, such as a traffic jam, can evoke a storm of outrage with accompanying physical and psychological disturbance.

Table 17–4 Are You Type A?

The Jenkins Activity Survey assesses the degree to which a person has a coronary-prone personality and behavior pattern. People with high scores, referred to as *Type A,* tend to be competitive, impatient, restless, aggressive, and pressured by time and responsibilities. In the items below, you can see which responses would reflect these characteristics:

Do you have trouble finding time to get your hair cut or styled?
—   Never
—   Occasionally
—   Almost always

Has your spouse or friend ever told you that you eat too fast?
—   Yes, often
—   Yes, once or twice
—   No, never

How often do you actually "put words in the person's mouth" in order to speed things up?
—   Frequently
—   Occasionally
—   Almost never

Would people you know well agree that you tend to get irritated easily?
—   Definitely yes
—   Probably yes
—   Probably no
—   Definitely no

How often do you find yourself hurrying to get to places even when there is plenty of time?
—   Frequently
—   Occasionally
—   Almost never

At work, do you ever keep two jobs moving forward at the same time by shifting back and forth rapidly from one to the other?
—   No, never
—   Yes, but only in emergencies
—   Yes, regularly

initiate and maintain health-producing behaviors, and to terminate unhealthy ones. They are taught to "read" their bodies in order to be alert to unhealthy bodily processes, and to take action to avoid or modify circumstances in which they are likely to become sick. In some instances behavioral medicine techniques have completely replaced the use of somatic interventions. For example, people with chronic backaches or tension headaches have been successfully treated with biofeedback and training in relaxation techniques (Blanchard, 1987). Such patients are taught to monitor early signs of mounting tension and to initiate steps to avert the further development of pain. These steps include learning various emotion- and problem-focused coping strategies, such as leaving a stressful situation or reframing one's perspective on a situation that is inescapable.

Drawing on the research linking the Type C personality style to cancer proneness, clinicians have developed treatments for cancer that focus on confrontation and emotional expression. For example, cancer patients are taught ways to vent their emotions when they would otherwise have suppressed their feelings of anger. Meditation techniques are also used to facilitate relaxation. In addition, cancer patients are taught to use imagery as a means of acti-

vating their immune system in "fighting" the cancer cells (Lerner & Remen, 1987). Of course, few people would argue that these methods should replace conventional medical treatment of cancer, but the psychological techniques are thought to be an important adjunct.

Successful treatment of people whose physical problems are associated with the Type A behavior pattern integrates education, training in coping strategies, and behavioral interventions (Roskies et al., 1989). The educational component teaches clients to understand coronary problems and the relationship between these problems and Type A behavior. The coping strategies include relaxation training and cognitive restructuring techniques. For example, instead of responding to a line at the bank with anger, a person would be taught to relax. Imaging is used as a behavioral intervention. The client is instructed to imagine a troublesome situation and to practice adaptive coping strategies for managing stress in that situation. Through behavior modification, individuals are given opportunities to rehearse more adaptive behaviors when provoked (Nunes et al., 1987).

There are, of course, individual differences in susceptibility to the physical toll of stress and stressful emotions. As

Exercise can help relieve potentially harmful effects of stress on the body.

we pointed out earlier, some people seem to thrive on stress and find that it improves5 their emotional state. In the physical realm, there is also evidence that some "hardy" individuals are able to avoid the potentially harmful physical effects of stress. For example, studies on business executives, who are exposed on a daily basis to high levels of stress, have identified a subgroup who do not suffer from the typical stress-related diseases seen in other executives. The hardy executives remain healthy because they have a sense of commitment, challenge, and control regarding their work. In addition to this buffering effect of personality against stress, these executives also are protected against illness by regular exercise and a strong social network (Kobasa et al., 1985). Similar research has shown that aerobic exercise has stress-ameliorating effects on police officers, whose work is among the most stressful of any occupation (Norris et al., 1990). This research has clear implications for psychological interventions. Even though hardiness cannot be easily instilled, people can be encouraged to exercise and to take advantage of available social supports to help offset the harmful effects of stress on the body.

Individuals can help themselves manage the physical consequences of stress in many different ways. In your own life, think of changes in your behavior that could make you more resistant to the harmful effects of everyday stress. Do you wait until the last minute to begin important projects? If you do, you are probably setting yourself up to experience pressures that could be avoided. Do you put yourself in situations where you are likely to feel resentful, powerless, and frustrated? Perhaps there are things you can do to heighten your sense of control. Do you keep your emotions bottled up? Everyone does to a certain extent, but if you consistently internalize feelings of anger and tension, you are putting yourself at a health risk. Asking questions such as

these can help you identify your unhealthy behavioral patterns and prompt you to look for ways to change.

SLEEP DISORDERS

Everyone occasionally has trouble sleeping, but such problems seldom become major sources of concern. When sleep disturbances do persist for more than several days, they can become a source of problems during waking hours. Over time, the emotional toll of sleep problems becomes greater as a person's fatigue builds and coping abilities decrease. It is at this point that a sleep disturbance can take on the proportions of a sleep disorder.

Characteristics of Sleep Disorders

Sleep disorders involve disturbances in the amount, quality, or timing of sleep, or abnormal events that occur while a person is sleeping or falling asleep. To be considered a psychological disorder, a disturbance in sleep must be chronic and must not be attributable to a physical problem. In addition to sleep disorders, people may experience other disturbances in their sleep that, though transitory, can cause considerable distress and disruption. We will look at these temporary sleep disturbances first.

■ *Transient sleep disturbances*

Transient sleep disturbances affect almost everyone at some point in life. College students often complain about sleeping difficulties. However, most sleep difficulties in college students, although distressing, are brief in duration and are associated with specific situations (Giesecke, 1987). In your own experience, you can probably remember a time when you had an important examination, job interview, or work deadline, and you felt that it was important to be well-rested. This heightened pressure to get a good night's sleep may actually have interfered with your ability to relax enough to sleep well.

■ Dyssomnias

The category of sleep disorders referred to as **dyssomnias** include disturbances in the amount, quality, or timing of sleep. People with a dyssomnia can suffer from one of three kinds of sleep problems: too much sleep, too little sleep, or disturbances in the scheduling or patterning of sleep.

INSOMNIA   Many people say they have *insomnia* after an occasional sleepless night. As a psychological disorder, **insomnia**, or chronic difficulty obtaining enough sleep, can take various forms. A person suffering from insomnia may have difficulty falling asleep, may awake frequently during the night, or may even have a full night's sleep but not feel rested in the morning. For example, a man may fall asleep readily each night, but awaken at 3 A.M. and be unable to get back to sleep. In contrast, a woman may take 2 or 3 hours to drop off to sleep at night. A third person may sleep a full 8 hours every night, but wake up feeling exhausted. All three people would be regarded as suffering from insomnia. In practice, however, it is often difficult to distinguish among these forms of insomnia, and some researchers have used electrophysiological measures to improve diagnostic accuracy (Reynolds et al., 1991).

HYPERSOMNIA   Feeling an excessive need for sleep can be just as disturbing to the individual as the inability to sleep. People with **hypersomnia** never feel rested, and be-come very sleepy during the day even after they rest sufficiently at night. A small proportion of people with this disorder have extreme difficulty awakening in the morning. Not only does hypersomnia make it difficult for a person to keep a job, but it interferes greatly with social relationships. Other people become annoyed by a person who is constantly sleepy.

SLEEP–WAKE SCHEDULE DISORDER   You have probably heard of or experienced "jet lag"—the feeling you have after airplane travel to a different time zone that your body is on a different time schedule than that shown by the clock. **Sleep–wake schedule disorder** is essentially the same condition, but in chronic form. People with this disorder suffer from a mismatch between their bodily sleep rhythms and the demands of their environment. As you might expect, people who work on rotating shifts are at risk for developing this disorder. These workers tend to fall asleep on the job and are more accident-prone during nonwork hours (Moore-Ede & Richardson, 1985). By the time they become accustomed to one schedule, it is time for them to switch to another, and they never fully adjust to the changes.

■ Parasomnias

Sometimes abnormal events occur during sleep or as a person is awakening. An individual may have nightmares, wake up screaming, or sleepwalk. When such behaviors become recurrent and disruptive, they are considered symptomatic of the category of disorders known as **parasomnias**.

In general, parasomnias are more common in children than in adults. For example, as many as 15 percent of all children experience single episodes of sleepwalking, and

The night seems interminable to insomniacs, who toss and turn, desperately craving the solace of deep sleep.

Repeated nightmares that can be recalled in terrifying detail plague people with dream anxiety disorder.

approximately 5 percent are afflicted by one of the parasomnias. Most children outgrow these disorders by early adolescence. If the disorder begins in adulthood, it has a more chronic course.

DREAM ANXIETY DISORDER   An ordinary nightmare is a disturbing experience that often remains on the person's mind until the next day, but not usually for much longer. People with **dream anxiety disorder** experience nightmares on a repeated basis. They wake up from sleep, quickly become alert, and have a detailed recall of frightening dreams. They are very distressed by the dream itself or by the disturbance in their sleep.

Chronic nightmare sufferers have a number of unpleasant psychological problems during their waking hours, including heightened levels of anxiety, depression, somatization, paranoia, and occasional bizarre thinking (Berquier & Ashton, 1992). Although it cannot be concluded whether frequent nightmares cause these problems, or whether psychological difficulties follow from the experience of having nightmares, it is clear that nightmares have adverse psychological associations.

It is important for you to realize that the experience of nightmares does not necessarily mean that a person has a psychological disorder. Most people have occasional nightmares, particularly following some stressful event in their lives. Shortly after the San Francisco earthquake, a team of prominent researchers investigated the incidence of nightmares among undergraduates at two colleges in the area and compared the frequency of earthquake-related nightmares with those reported by students living in Arizona. Not surprisingly, given the severity of the trauma to which they were exposed, slightly over one-quarter of the San Francisco area students reported having an earthquake-related nightmare within three weeks after the earthquake; only 3 percent of Arizona students reported such nightmares in the same period (Wood et al., 1992).

SLEEP TERROR DISORDER   People with **sleep terror disorder** repeatedly have the upsetting experience of waking up suddenly and in a panic from a sound sleep. This experience is different from waking up from a bad dream in that sleep terror disorder involves a set of distressing physical sensations in addition to the psychological experience of fear. These physical reactions include sweating, racing heartbeat, and gasping for breath. It is difficult to calm a person who wakes in such a state because for several minutes, the person is totally confused and disoriented. Surprisingly, people who have these frightening sleep experiences do not remember them in the morning, a feature that distinguishes sleep terror from dream anxiety disorder.

SLEEPWALKING DISORDER   Sleepwalking is a fascinating and frightening condition. Many stories, and even a well-known opera, have been written about the odd behavior of sleepwalkers. Perhaps you have heard stories about yourself or a relative who walked around the house or did something humorous while in a sound state of sleep. Single instances of sleepwalking are relatively common, particularly in children, and they usually have no serious consequences. People who repeatedly sleepwalk are diagnosed as having **sleepwalking disorder**.

Most people think of the sleepwalker as a person who stares blankly and appears to be out of touch with the environment. This image accurately conveys the essential features of this disorder. Not only are sleepwalkers unresponsive to other people and to attempts to awaken them, but they forget what happens during their sleepwalking episodes. In rare instances, sleepwalkers may commit violent acts for which they have no recall after they awaken.

One particularly interesting case of sleepwalking (Oswald & Evans, 1985) involved just such a scenario. A 14-year-old boy was staying overnight at his aunt's house and at 2 A.M. the boy walked into the kitchen, took a knife, and stabbed his 5-year-old cousin, severely injuring her. The boy denied any memory of the stabbing, but he remembered finding himself downstairs with the knife and then, when he heard commotion, running out of the house. The stabbing appeared to the family to be inexplicable. His parents, relatives, and schoolteachers gave a picture of a nonaggressive, healthy boy, who was fond of his cousin, and was happy staying with his aunt. The psychiatrist who evaluated the boy determined that he had no reason to want to harm his cousin. There was no family history of sleepwalking, but the boy was said to have talked in his sleep.

The only explanation that seemed plausible was that the boy was acting out in a dream his anger toward his friends. Apparently the boy had quarreled with his friends on the afternoon prior to the stabbing, and as a consequence he felt angry and depressed all evening. The court allowed his plea to be changed from guilty to not guilty based on the legal argument that "the sleeping mind cannot form an intent."

In addition to the legal implications of this case, it illustrates a number of important features about sleepwalking. Sleepwalkers commonly carry out complicated acts such as eating, unlocking doors, and walking around the house.

Most sleepwalkers forget what they did while they were asleep. Furthermore, their behavior while asleep does not necessarily correspond to their customary waking behavior. A relatively calm person, for example, may act in aggressive ways when sleepwalking.

Theories and Treatments

Given that sleep is a physiological function, it makes sense that there should be physical explanations of the sleep disorders. In insomnia, hyperarousal of the sympathetic nervous system that accompanies anxiety may interfere with the brain's ability to enter a sleep state. Hypersomnia, in contrast, may be associated with feelings of depression. In this disorder, the connection appears to be insufficient arousal of the sympathetic nervous system. The parasomnias have physical components as well. The symptoms of sleep terror disorder and sleepwalking disorder occur during the slow-wave phases of the sleep cycle. In contrast, the nightmares of dream anxiety disorder occur during REM sleep (Vela-Bueno et al., 1987). The fact that all three disorders are more frequent in children than in adults suggests some connection with changes in brain-wave rhythms during childhood. Furthermore, these sleep disorders tend to run in families (Simonds & Parraga, 1982).

Sleep disorders can also be caused by neurological conditions such as *narcolepsy* and *sleep apnea* (breathing interruptions during sleep) (Fry, 1985). Other bodily conditions can also affect sleep, including diseases or the effects of drugs and alcohol. In the psychological sphere, emotions such as depression, anxiety, and anger can affect one's ability to sleep (Soldatos & Kales, 1982).

A common pattern of psychologically-based sleep disturbance is that a person's worry about sleep leads to a vicious cycle in which anxieties about sleep interfere with the ability to fall and stay asleep. The person may toss and turn, watching the clock, becoming increasingly anxious as the nighttime hours pass. Worrying that the sleep struggle may repeat itself and may cause another restless night. If this continues for several nights, the bedroom becomes associated with the unpleasant experience of sleeplessness, and a disturbed sleeping cycle becomes established.

In attempting to understand the psychological causes of sleep disorders, some researchers have focused on the correlations between sleep disorders and other psychological disorders. In the case of sleep terror disorder, the sleep disturbance may be a variant of an anxiety disorder. Supporting this notion is the fact that antianxiety medication is often effective in the treatment of night terrors (Carlson et al., 1982). Sleepwalkers, in contrast, tend to have more explosive, hypomanic, and aggressive personality traits (Kales et al., 1980). One commonality between the two types of disorders, however, is that both sleep terror and sleepwalking disorders respond to hypnosis (Hurwitz et al., 1991).

In many cases, sleep disorders can be treated with behavioral methods. On the simplest level, just teaching a

Table 17–5 Steps to Improve Your Sleep

How to Facilitate Good Sleeping Habits
1. Exercise during the day but avoid strenuous exercise just before bedtime.
2. Avoid taking daytime naps.
3. Do not take caffeine within 6 hours of bedtime and, if necessary, do not take caffeine at all.
4. Try not to get too upset if you do lose sleep.
5. Evaluate your sleep on how refreshed you feel rather than on the number of hours you have slept. If you feel refreshed when you awaken, you have probably gotten enough sleep.
6. Do not use your bed for stressful activities such as study or work.
7. Establish a regular sleep cycle. Go to bed and get up at approximately the same time each day.
8. Look for ways to reduce daily stresses that may be interfering with your sleep.

Bedtime Hints
1. Engage in restful activities such as reading, listening to music, or taking a relaxing bath at the end of the day.
2. Avoid heavy alcohol intake before going to bed.
3. If you are having trouble falling asleep, drink some warm milk. This time-tested remedy works because warm milk contains L-tryptophan, an amino acid that promotes sleep. Over-the-counter medications should be avoided. Even though they make you drowsy, they do not induce sleep. Prescription drugs should be a last resort.
4. Do not lie awake in bed for more than 15 minutes if you are unable to sleep. It is better to get out of bed and find something to do that relaxes you such as light reading.
5. Use relaxation techniques such as thinking of peaceful scenes and meditating.

Source: Adapted from Giesecke (1987).

person the good sleep habits shown in Table 17–5 can be sufficient to treat insomnia. Sleep–wake schedule disorder is treatable by establishing a more regular schedule. Similarly, sleep disorders in children can be effectively managed without large scale intervention by explaining to parents that these disorders are usually outgrown (Fry, 1985). More elaborate behavioral methods for treating sleep disorders include deep-muscle relaxation, biofeedback, and cognitive techniques of self-control (Alley, 1983; Barowsky et al., 1990). Clients can also benefit from learning how to manage the stress in their lives that is contributing to their sleep problems (Kirmil-Gray et al., 1985).

Various other methods are also available in treating sleep disorders. One recent innovation involves the use of bright light in the treatment of clients suffering from a combination of sleep and mood disorders (Lewy, 1987). This procedure readjusts the client's disturbed circadian rhythm (the body's clock) that is interfering with normal sleep patterns. In extreme cases, medications may be used. Because many sleep-altering drugs, such as sedative-hypnotics, have addictive qualities or other serious side effects, they are

Table 17–6 Examples of Conditions Not Attributable to a Psychological Disorder That Are a Focus of Attention or Treatment (V Codes)

Condition	Example
Academic Problem	A 9-year-old boy is brought to the school psychologist because his grades have taken a dramatic downturn.
Borderline Intellectual Functioning	The unit manager at the institution for developmentally disabled people refers a 28-year-old retarded woman to a psychologist for help with her difficulty in following daily routines.
Adult Antisocial Behavior	A 21-year-old college student is evaluated by the jail counselor after being arrested for selling cocaine on campus.
Childhood or Adolescent Antisocial Behavior	Because of repeated stealing from a local department store, a 14-year-old boy is referred to a child psychologist.
Malingering	A college sophomore goes to the student mental health clinic requesting permission for a late withdrawal from his statistics class (which he had already been failing) with the obviously fabricated story that he is depressed over his parent's separation.
Noncompliance with Medical Treatment	A psychologist is called in by a physician to consult with a diabetic patient who recurrently puts her health at risk by failing to comply with the designated medical regimen.
Marital Problem	A couple in their late 20s seek professional help because of their recurrent problems with misunderstandings and poor communication.
Parent–Child Difficulties	Following a year-long set of disagreements over their adolescent son's staying out all night, taking the car without permission, and spending money frivolously, the boy's parents insist that the young man participate in family therapy.
Other Specified Family Circumstances	Because of repeated physically assaultive fighting between a 12-year-old boy and his 11-year-old brother, a family seeks professional intervention.
Other Interpersonal Problems	A 28-year-old man seeks professional consultation to assist him in dealing with some very obnoxious and upsetting co-workers.
Uncomplicated Bereavement	Following the death of her husband, a 72-year-old woman goes to a psychologist to help her deal with the loss and make some decisions about her future.
Occupational Problem	A 35-year-old man goes to see a vocational counselor to get help in deciding on a change of career because of his dissatisfaction with his current job.
Phase of Life Problem or Other Life Circumstance Problem	To help her deal with her difficult adjustment to college, a young woman sees a mental health counselor for a few sessions until she feels calmer.

Many people seek out professional help for reasons other than psychological disorders. For example, those seeking a change of career sometimes consult professionals for vocational testing and counseling.

considered the treatment of last resort. Furthermore, although these drugs may have positive short-term effects, they have less long-term efficacy compared to behavioral methods (McClusky et al., 1991).

CONDITIONS NOT ATTRIBUTABLE TO A PSYCHOLOGICAL DISORDER THAT ARE A FOCUS OF ATTENTION OR TREATMENT

There are many instances when clients seek help for problems that are not technically considered psychological disorders. Often, these problems represent temporary disturbances precipitated by stressful life events.

In some cases, clients seeking help for these kinds of problems also have a psychological disorder. However, the focus of their current presenting problem is not related to their disorder.

Table 17–7   REACTIONS TO LIFE STRESS : A SUMMARY CHART OF PERSPECTIVES

DISORDER	BIOLOGICAL	PSYCHOLOGICAL
Suicide	Genetic inheritance of suicidality. Lower concentrations of GABA and serotonin in the brain.	Suicidality caused by factors such as alienation, attempts to communicate distress, and feelings of hopelessness, depression and stress. **Treatment**: Careful assessment of suicidal intent and lethality, combined with efforts to provide social support and to restore sense of control.
Adjustment disorders	Stressful life events can predispose a person to physical illness. **Treatment**: In extreme cases, temporary use of medications to alleviate symptom distress, but not at the expense of psychological growth of the client.	Life events and the perception of situations as overwhelming cause stress. Adjustment disorders result when coping efforts are unsuccessful. **Treatment**: Provide support during periods of crisis; teach coping strategies used to manage stress focused either on changing one's emotions or changing the situation.
Psychophysiological conditions	Psychoneuroimmunology regards psychophysiological conditions as reflecting the influence of stress on the nervous system and the immune system; stress can also reduce the quality of the person's health habits. **Treatment**: Medical treatment for somatic problems.	Behavior patterns, such as Type A and Type C, can influence vulnerability to physical disorders, such as cardiovascular disease and cancer. **Treatment**: Behavioral medicine teaches clients ways to reduce the symptoms of psychophysiological disorders through behavioral and cognitive-behavioral methods such as relaxation, biofeedback, coping skills, training, education, exercise, and imagery techniques; specific treatments offer help to people with Type A and Type C behavior patterns in changing their responses to stress.
Sleep disorders	Neurological abnormalities, substance abuse, diseases. Dyssomnias caused by altered sympathetic nervous system activity. Parasomnias caused by abnormal brainwave activity. **Treatment**: Light therapy; sedative hypnotics	Emotions such as depression, anxiety, and anger can interfere with sleep. Certain sleep disorders due to negative expectations about sleep which create a vicious cycle of worry and impaired sleep. **Treatment**: Behavioral and cognitive-behavioral methods can be used to help clients establish regular sleeping patterns and break out of the cycle caused by worry over sleep. Relaxation, biofeedback, and stress management.

Return to the Case

Maria Nunez

Maria's History

My first meeting with Maria following her transfer to the psychiatric unit was tense for both of us. I was aware of my own feelings of awkwardness as I began discussing her suicide attempt, and Maria's discomfort in discussing the matter was dramatically evident as well.

I asked Maria to share with me the story of her life, with particular attention to those experiences that would have led her to the extreme of trying to commit suicide. Maria started her story by telling me that she had no friends—a lifelong painful experience for Maria. She recounted how, as a child, she had spent most days alone, never understanding what it was about her that stood in the way of close friendships. Even as a grade school child, she studied long hours and tried desperately to excel in her academic pursuits, knowing that she was trying to fill the painful void caused by her lack of friends. Maria and her family took pride in her good grades, but Maria constantly wondered why her teachers never responded to her with the same enthusiasm that they showed with other children. Along those same lines, Maria was painfully aware of an emotional distance between her parents and herself for all of her life. Never understanding the causes for this coldness, she came to blame herself for being defective in some way.

Grade school blurred into high school, and little changed in Maria's life. She earned good grades, but she felt lonely and isolated. During the fall of Maria's senior year in high school, she became interested in George, a varsity basketball player. She felt that George liked her, and was thrilled when he asked her out for a date. They went out a few times, and Maria assumed that they were going steady. She began to read into George's conversation that he was thinking about committing himself to a long-term relationship with her. Maria's thoughts were filled with wishes and fantasies that they would someday marry. When George pressured her to have sex, she consented, although she felt unready and confused about making this choice. The next day Maria saw George flirting with one of her classmates at the mall, and she felt devastated. In the days that followed she was unable to study or eat; as her depression deepened, Maria concluded that she was unlovable and had no reason to go on living. Suicide seemed to be the only means of escape from her fate.

Assessment

Because of the depth of Maria's depression, I felt that it was inadvisable and unnecessary to administer formal psychological testing. In addition to my interview I conducted a mental status examination, and in my report noted several features of Maria's thoughts and behavior that are reflective of depression. Maria's lethargic movements and slow speech corresponded to her descriptions of her mood as "extremely low." There were no signs of psychotic behavior or thought, although her thinking had an obsessional quality in that she repeatedly returned to a discussion of her feelings about George—thoughts which she could not get out of her mind. Maria's level of insight regarding her current plight was fairly good, although she had some initial difficulty seeing a possible connection between lifelong personality and family problems and her recent drastic reaction to a stressful life event. Despite this limited level of understanding, Maria seemed motivated to make some changes so that she could manage her feelings about this recent crisis as well as develop better coping strategies in general.

Diagnosis

As I considered Maria's lifelong problems and recent history, it was evident to me that she suffered from problems on both Axes I and II. In other words, recent life stresses resulted in significant adjustment problems leading to her suicide attempt. However, there was more to the diagnostic picture than recent adjustment difficulties. Maria had a lifelong history of personality disturbance in which she craved to be close to others but felt terrified about the prospect of taking action to attain such closeness.

As for Maria's Axis I diagnosis, she was struggling to adjust to recent life stresses, and her response was characterized by deep depression. She desperately sought to fit into the social scene of her high school, and saw George as a way to gain acceptance. Investing an inordinate amount of fantasy and hope in him, she was cast into a suicidal depression when her dreams failed to come true.

Maria's lifelong personality was that of an individual whose everyday experience was a dramatized conflict between yearning to be close to other people, yet paralyzed by the prospect of initiating any social contact. Upon finally reaching a point at which she could feel

Maria Nunez continued

some minor degree of hope, she was cast into a suicidal depression when her fantasy was shattered.

Axis I.   Adjustment Disorder with Depressed Mood.

Axis II.   Avoidant Personality Disorder.

Axis III. Recovery from barbiturate overdose.

Axis IV.   Severity of psychosocial stressors: 2. Failed relationship.

Axis V.   Current Global Assessment of Functioning: 5. Highest Global Assessment of Functioning (past year): 57.

Case Formation

Maria's story affected me deeply. Perhaps it was being brought back to the crises of my own adolescence, or perhaps it was the pain in her eyes that upset me so greatly. Whatever the cause of my intense response, I was aware that Maria's pain had existed for much longer than just the past few weeks. This was a young woman whose emotional affliction had permeated her childhood and adolescence. The distance between Maria and her parents from an early age had left her ill-equipped to develop close relationships during adolescence, and her extreme sensitivity to possible criticism had kept her from exposing herself to situations where she could learn, through experience, appropriate ways of interacting with her peers.

Maria misinterpreted George's interest as representing a romantic commitment on his part, leading her to allow herself to become sexually involved with him. She had unrealistically hoped that this relationship would save her from a life of isolation. When her hopes were crushed, she lacked the coping resources to manage her distress. She was too ashamed to turn to her parents for help and perceived them as being too preoccupied to respond. Internalizing her distress resulted in her deep feelings of despondency and hopelessness—feelings so painful that she saw no way out except suicide.

Planning a Treatment

A suicide attempt as serious as Maria's always entails a stay in the hospital, so there was no question that this would be necessary for Maria. In fact, I recommended that she remain in the hospital for a month, so that the treatment staff would have sufficient time to help her restabilize physically and emotionally. I agreed to continue as Maria's therapist, proba-

bly out of a hope that I might be able to rescue her from the unhappy fate to which she apparently felt doomed. I conducted intense psychotherapy with Maria in the hospital, seeing her three times a week for that month. After 10 days or so, Maria's depression had lifted dramatically. She formed a solid working alliance with me, and she began to develop some caring relationships with other patients on the unit.

Combining supportive and exploratory techniques, I was able to get to some of the issues that had plagued Maria for years—her feelings of being unloved and unlovable, her fear of closeness with others, and her low self-esteem. At the same time, I knew that Maria had to develop more effective coping strategies to deal with the stresses of everyday life as well as the pressures of moving from adolescence into adulthood.

Outcome of the Case

I saw Maria for 2 years following her discharge from the hospital. In many ways the therapy seemed to help Maria tremendously. Yet, I frequently wondered how successful we were in changing some of the basic personality styles that impaired her so greatly. I was confident that Maria's depression had lifted and that she was coping much more effectively than she had during her adolescent years. But I knew that Maria continued to feel pained by her discomfort in approaching other people, her awkwardness in social situations, and her perceptions of herself as interpersonally inadequate. Although I didn't feel that our work was complete, it was Maria's decision to terminate the therapy. Maria told me that she wanted to start a new life, in another part of the country; she believed that without the burdens of other people's expectations, she would be freed up to act in ways that might shock those who were close to her. I recall feeling a great deal of ambivalence about Maria's plan, but I also felt that maybe she was right. In our last session both of us became a bit tearful as she hugged me, thanked me for helping her, and said goodbye. Several years have passed, and I have not heard from Maria, although I have thought of her often.

A special category in the DSM system (called **V Codes**) is used to apply to situations when professional treatment is sought for conditions not technically considered disorders. As you can see from Table 17–6, these conditions cover a broad range of concerns. They include problems for which people would seek help on their own, as well as situations in which treatment is recommended by others. Perhaps you or someone you know has been troubled by one of these conditions. Many people are able to resolve these difficulties themselves, but for some, professional psychological assistance is beneficial.

REACTIONS TO LIFE STRESS: THE PERSPECTIVES REVISITED

In this chapter, we have looked at a range of reactions to stressful or difficult circumstances in life. Some are considered psychological "disorders," and others are considered part of the expectable reactions that people have to significant life changes. Although these conditions range in intensity and quality, they share the component of stress as a precipitant. As we have emphasized, stress is a feature of an individual's perception, not an inherent quality of a life event or circumstance. Further, the perception of an event or life change as stressful can sometimes lead to a cyclical process, in which the perception of stress leads a person to make decisions, take actions, or interpret future situations in ways that can exacerbate the initial set of problems.

All of the disorders we have discussed in this chapter involve reactions to stress, but it should be evident to you that stress is also a factor in other psychological disorders. Stressful events can heighten the risk of relapse for a person with schizophrenia, or can lead a person prone to panic disorder to consider suicide. The dissociative disorders, which are thought to be triggered by traumatic events in childhood, can also be regarded as reactions to stress, as can post-traumatic stress disorder. We should also be aware that the stress management techniques outlined in this chapter can be useful in helping people with a variety of disorders to manage stress-related problems in an adaptive way.

The many connections between psychological and physiological manifestations of stress also point to the importance of the biological perspective. Finally, from the standpoint of the cognitive-behavioral approach, the idea that stress is a function of a person's perceptions of a situation follows directly from the notion that people's emotions are a function of their thoughts. It would seem that the concepts of stress and coping integrate many features of the theoretical perspectives to understanding and treating psychological disorders.

SUMMARY

1. Suicide is the most extreme reaction to the perception of stress, occurring when a person feels there is no other recourse. In some cases, suicides represent a call for help. Approximately 12 out of every 100,000 Americans commit suicide each year, with the highest rate among white men over the age of 85. Another group at high risk are men between the ages of 15 to 24, with higher rates among the 20- to 24-year-olds. At all ages, men are more likely than women to complete a suicide, and whites have a higher suicide rate than nonwhites.

2. In trying to understand why a person would take the drastic action of committing suicide, theorists have pointed to psychosocial influences, social alienation, depression, hopelessness, and stressful life events. There may also be biological influences on suicidal behavior, as indicated by a pattern of familial transmission and physiological abnormalities found in the brains of suicidal individuals.

3. The prediction of suicide is complicated by the low rate of suicide in the general population, but certain guidelines can be used to help a clinician assess a client's suicidality. Clinicians try to evaluate both the suicidal intent and the lethality of a client's plan, and also consider factors such as age, gender, and ethnicity in determining whether a person is at high risk. Many people ignore, or do not properly read, the warning signs of suicide. Suicide prevention is based on two principles: providing social support and helping the individual regain a sense of control over his or her life. The formation of a "contract" can be very helpful in implementing both of these principles. Cognitive-behavioral methods that provide clients with alternate ways of managing stress are also helpful. Suicide prevention telephone services have also been found to be life-saving, but only if these services are used.

4. Adjustment disorders include a wide range of emotional, physical, and behavioral reactions that are more extreme than would normally be expected under the circumstances. Whether or not a person develops such a disorder following a life change is theorized to be a function of how the individual perceives that change. A person is said to be experiencing stress when a life change or event is perceived as overwhelming; this perception depends on the individual's internal and external resources. Stress can be reduced through a variety of coping methods, but the two main coping strategies are *problem-focused* and *emotion-focused*. Problem-focused coping involves doing something that addresses the situation; in emotion-focused coping the person tries to improve feelings about the situation. In treating people with adjustment disorders, clinicians provide support and attempt to bolster their coping skills in a way that will help clients develop more successful methods for managing future stress.

5. Psychophysiological conditions include a broad range of physical disorders that are connected in some way

to the individual's experience of stress. In explaining why people develop these conditions, researchers have developed the field of psychoneuroimmunology, in which reactions to stress are seen as triggering changes in the nervous and immune systems that increase a person's susceptibility to disease. Researchers have investigated the effect on bodily functions when a person inhibits expression of emotions, and have found that people who express their emotional reaction to a stressful event experience physical as well a mental health benefits. In another line of research, a connection has been made between the Type A personality style and cardiovascular disease; people with Type A personality are in a state of almost constant activation, and this results in hypertension. In the emerging field of behavioral medicine, clinicians use techniques rooted in behavioral theory to help clients gain control over unhealthy bodily reactions. Treatment recommendations include steps that individuals can take to improve their health and reduce their risk of developing stress-related diseases. Even the treatment of cancer sometimes includes techniques that incorporate emotional expression, meditation, and the use of imagery.

6. Sleep disorders include chronic disturbances in the individual's sleep pattern or sleep-related behaviors that are not attributable to a physical problem. In the dyssomnias, individuals either are unable to sleep in sufficient amounts (insomnia), sleep too much (hypersomnia), or cannot adjust their body's daily rhythm to the demands of their environment (sleep-wake schedule disorder). Parasomnias include a range of recurrent and disruptive abnormal sleep behaviors, such as nightmares (dream anxiety disorder), panicky awakenings from sleep (sleep terror disorder), and sleepwalking. In the psychological sphere, depression, anxiety, and anger can cause sleep disorders. Biological factors are involved in sleep disorders, but the individual's expectations about sleep also play an important role. When people develop concerns about their sleep patterns, this worry can become a vicious cycle that is difficult to break. Sleep disorders can be treated with antianxiety medication, with behavioral techniques that include relaxation and biofeedback, and with light therapy, which attempts to reset a disturbed circadian rhythm.

7. Conditions not attributable to a psychological disorder that are a focus of treatment or attention are referred in the DSM as V codes. These conditions include academic problems, borderline intellectual functioning, antisocial behavior, noncompliance with medical treatment, family and other interpersonal problems, bereavemen, occupational problems, and difficulties associated with the person's phase of life.

KEY TERMS

Stress: the feeling that one's resources are inadequate to meet the demands of a situation. p. 429

Suicidal intent: how committed a person is to taking his or her own life. p. 432

Suicidal lethality: the dangerousness of a suicidal person's intended method of dying. p. 432

Adjustment disorder: a reaction to one or more changes in a person's life that is more extreme than would normally be expected under the circumstances. p. 434

Coping: the process through which people reduce stress. p. 436

Psychophysiological condition: a physical problem that reflects a connection between psychological and physiological processes. p. 438

Psychoneuroimmunology: the study of connections among psychological stress, nervous system functioning, and the immune system. p. 438

Behavioral medicine: an interdisciplinary approach to psychophysiological disorders rooted in learning theory. p. 440

Dyssomnias: disturbances in the amount, quality, or timing of sleep. p. 443

Insomnia: a form of dyssomnia characterized by chronic difficulty obtaining enough sleep. p. 443

Hypersomnia: a form of dyssomnia in which the individual never feels rested, and becomes very sleepy during the day, even after sufficient rest at night. p. 443

Sleep-wake schedule disorder: a form of dyssomnia in which the individual suffers a mismatch between bodily sleep rhythms and the demands of the environment. p. 443

Parasomnias: sleep disorders characterized by the recurrent experience of abnormal events during sleep. p. 443

Dream anxiety disorder: a parasomnia in which the individual has nightmares on a repeated basis. p. 443

Sleep terror disorder: a parasomnia in which the individual repeatedly has the upsetting experience of waking up suddenly and in a panic from a sound sleep. p. 444

Sleepwalking disorder: a parasomnia in which the individual recurrently sleepwalks. p. 444

V codes: a set of problems that may come to the attention of a clinician, but that are not technically considered psychological disorders. p. 450

GLOSSARY

The first chapter in which the term is introduced appears in parentheses at the end of each entry.

Abstinence violation effect: a concept associated with the expectancy model referring to a sense of loss of control over one's ability to refrain from engaging in an addictive behavior. (15)

Active phase: a period in the course of schizophrenia in which psychotic symptoms are present. (11)

Adjustment disorder: a reaction to one or more changes in a person's life that is more extreme than would normally be expected under the circumstances. (17)

Adoption study: a method for studying genetic versus environmental contributions to a disorder by tracking the incidence of disorders in children whose biological parents have a disorder but whose rearing parents do not. (5)

Adult antisocial behavior: illegal or immoral behaviors such as stealing, lying, and cheating. (6)

Affect: an individual's outward expression of an emotion. (3)

Agnosia: the inability to recognize familiar objects or experiences, despite the ability to perceive their basic elements. (14)

Agoraphobia: a condition often associated with panic disorder involving fear of being trapped or stranded without help. (7)

Akinesia: a motor disturbance in which a person's muscles become rigid and it is difficult to initiate movement. (14)

Alcohol dehydrogenase (ADH): a zinc-containing enzyme that breaks alcohol down into fatty acids, carbon dioxide, and water. (15)

Aldehyde dehydrogenase (ALDH): an enzyme that is involved in metabolizing alcohol. (15)

Alters: the alternative personalities that develop in an individual with multiple personality disorder. (8)

Amnestic disorder: a cognitive impairment disorder involving inability to recall events of the recent past or to register new memories. (14)

Amygdala: a structure in the limbic system of the brain involved in controlling aggressive behaviors. (6)

Analog observation: a form of behavioral assessment that takes place in a setting or context specifically designed for observing the target behavior. (3)

Anorexia nervosa: an eating disorder involving an intense fear of becoming fat that leads people to engage in various behaviors geared to weight loss. (16)

Anoxia: the cutting off of oxygen supply to the body, potentially causing damage to the brain. (13)

Antecedents: events preceding a specified behavior that are identified in a behavioral assessment. (3)

Anterograde amnesia: a loss of ability to learn or remember events taking place after the physical damage that caused the amnesia has occurred. (14)

Antisocial behavior: illegal or immoral behaviors such as stealing, lying, and cheating. (6)

Antisocial personality disorder: a personality disorder characterized by a lack of regard for society's moral or legal standards. (6)

Anxiety disorders: a group of disorders characterized by intense, irrational, and incapacitating fear and apprehension. (7)

Aphasia: a loss of the ability to use language. (14)

Apraxia: a loss of the ability to carry out coordinated bodily movements that could previously be performed with no difficulty. (14)

Archetypes: images common to all human experience, presumed by Jung to make up the deepest layer of the unconscious mind. (4)

Assertiveness training: a form of counterconditioning in which the individual is trained to replace intimidated with self-assertive behaviors. (5)

Assessment: the evaluation of a client's psychological or physical status. (3)

Assigned sex (or **biological sex**): the sex of the individual that is recorded on the birth certificate. (9)

Association cortex: diffuse areas of the cerebral cortex which synthesize and integrate information from all over the brain. (5)

Asylum: a place of refuge or safety; originally used to describe a psychiatric facility that later came to have negative connotations. (1)

Attachment style: in research based on object relations theory, a pattern of behavior shown by a young child toward a caregiver figure. (4)

Attention-deficit hyperactivity disorder (ADHD): a disruptive behavior disorder of childhood characterized by difficulty in maintaining attention and restlessness of motor activity. (13)

Attributions: explanations that people make of the things that happen to them; a concept applied in the revised version of the learned helplessness theory of depression. (10)

Auditory hallucination: the false perception of a sound. (3)

Autism: a pervasive developmental disorder involving massive impairment in an individual's ability to communicate and relate emotionally to others. (13)

Automatic thoughts: in cognitive-behavioral theory of depression, ideas so deeply entrenched that the individual is not even aware that they lead to feelings of unhappiness and discouragement. (5)

Autonomic nervous system: the part of the nervous system that controls the automatic, involuntary processes that keep the body alive by regulating functions such as heart beat and digestion. (5)

Aversions: responses of discomfort or dislike to a particular object or situation. (7)

Aversive conditioning: a form of conditioning in which a painful stimulus is paired with an initially neutral stimulus. (5)

Avoidant disorder: an anxiety disorder of childhood that causes a child to refrain from contact with unfamiliar people. (13)

Avoidant personality disorder: a personality disorder whose most prominent feature is that the individual is desirous of, but fearful of any involvement with other people and terrified at the prospect of being publicly embarrassed. (6)

Axon: the section of the neuron that transmits information to other neurons. (5)

ß-Amyloid protein: a substance known to form the core of senile plaques. (14)

Basal ganglia: a set of nuclei located deep within the brain that are involved in balance and motor control. (5)

Base rate: the frequency of a disorder's occurence in the general population. (2)

Baseline: the period in which a subject is observed prior to being given treatment for the purpose of documenting frequency of the target behavior. (1)

Behavioral assessment: a number of measurement techniques based on objective recording of the individual's behavior. (3)

Behavioral checklists and inventories: behavioral assessment devices in which the client checks off or rates whether or not certain events or experiences have transpired. (3)

Behavioral interviewing: a specialized form of interviewing in which the clinician asks for information on the behavior under consideration as well as what preceded and followed that behavior. (3)

Behavioral medicine: an interdisciplinary approach to psychophysiological disorders rooted in learning theory. (17)

Behavioral self-report: a method of behavioral assessment in which the individual provides information about the frequency of particular behaviors. (3)

Benzodiazepines: medications that can be instrumental in slowing down central nervous system reactions thought to contribute to anxiety. (7)

Big win: a gain of large amounts of money in one bet which propels the pathological gambler into a pattern of uncontrollable gambling. (16)

Binges: in bulimia, the ingestion of large amounts of food during a short period of time, even after reaching a point of feeling full, and stopping only when a point of extreme physical discomfort is reached. (16)

Biofeedback: a procedure in which people are taught to monitor and control their autonomic responses, such as blood pressure, heart rate, skin conductance, and muscular tension. (5)

Biological markers: measurable characteristics, such as smooth pursuit eye movement, whose patterns parallel the inheritance of a disorder. (12)

Biopsychosocial model: a model that proposes an integration of biological, psychological, and sociocultural factors in explaining why some people develop alcoholism. (15)

Bipolar disorder: a mood disorder involving manic episodes, intense and very disruptive experiences of heightened mood, possibly alternating with major depressive episodes. (2)

Blood pressure: the resistance offered by the arteries to the flow of blood as it is pumped from the heart, a measure used to derive information about an individual's psychological functioning. (3)

Borderline personality disorder: a personality disorder characterized by a pervasive pattern of instability in mood, interpersonal relationships, and self-image. (6)

Bradykinesia: a motor disturbance involving a general slowing of motor activity. (14)

Brain electrical activity mapping (BEAM)™: a procedure in which electrodes are attached to a person's head to measure brain activity, a computer analyzes the information about the wave patterns, and then constructs a multicolored pattern of brain activity. (3)

Brief reactive psychosis: a disorder characterized by the sudden onset of psychotic symptoms that are limited to a period less than a month, and which develops in response to a stressful event or set of events. (11)

Broca's aphasia: a form of aphasia that involves disturbance of language production, but intact comprehension abilities. (14)

Bulimia nervosa: an eating disorder involving the alternation between the extremes of binging and purging. (16)

Case formulation: an analysis of the client's development and the factors that might have influenced the client's current psychological status. (2)

Case study: an intensive study of a single person described in detail. (1)

Catatonia: motor disturbances in a psychotic disorder not attributable to physiological causes. (3)

Catatonic schizophrenia: a form of schizophrenia characterized by a variety of catatonic symptoms. (11)

Catecholamine hypothesis: a hypothesis that asserts that a relative shortage of norepinephrine (a catecholamine) causes depression, and an overabundance of norepinephrine causes mania. (10)

Cell body: the part of the cell that houses the structures responsible for keeping it alive. (5)

Central nervous system: the part of the nervous system consisting of the brain and the pathways of nerves going to and from the brain through the spinal cord. (5)

Cerebellum: a part of the brain that controls finely tuned voluntary movements initiated by the cerebral cortex. (5)

Cerebral cortex: the thin covering of neural tissue surrounding the outer surface of the brain. (5)

Cerebral hemispheres: the two halves of the cerebral cortex. (5)

Child rapist: a violent child abuser whose behavior is an expression of hostile sexual drives. (9)

Choline acetyltransferase (CAT): an enzyme that is essential for the synthesis of acetylcholine. (14)

Chromosome: structures found in each cell of the body that contain genes and exist in a pair, with one chromosome contributed from each parent at conception. (5)

Classical conditioning: the learning of a connection between an originally neutral stimulus and a naturally evoking stimulus that produces an automatic reflexive reaction. (5)

Claustrophobia: fear of closed spaces. (7)

Client: a person seeking psychological treatment. (2)

Client-centered: an approach based on the belief held by Rogers that people are innately good and the potential for self-improvement lies within the individual. (4)

Clinical psychologist: a mental health professional with training in the behavioral sciences who provides direct service to clients. (2)

Cluttering: a specific developmental disorder in which the individual speaks in quick bursts, making it impossible for other people to understand what is being said. (13)

Cognitive-behaviorism: a theoretical perspective that focuses on observable behaviors as well as the thoughts that are assumed to underlie those behaviors. (5)

Cognitive distortions: in cognitive-behavioral theory, used to refer to errors that depressed people make in the way they draw conclusions from their experiences. (10)

Cognitive impairment disorders: a set of disorders due to brain damage or disease that involve loss or deterioration of cognitive abilities including judgment, language, thought, speech, memory, orientation, perception, or attention. (14)

Cognitive restructuring: one of the fundamental techniques of cognitive-behavioral therapy in which clients are taught to reframe negative ideas into positive ones. (5)

Cognitive triad: in cognitive-behavioral theory, the negative view of self, world, and the future held by a depressed individual. (10)

Commitment: the involuntary placement of an individual into a psychiatric facility. (2)

Community mental health centers (CMHC): out-patient clinics that provide psychological services on a sliding fee scale to serve individuals who live within a certain geographic area. (2)

Competency to stand trial: a determination of whether an individual is psychologically capable of testifying on his or her own behalf in a court of law. (2)

Compulsion: a repetitive and seemingly purposeful behavior performed in response to uncontrollable urges or according to a ritualistic or stereotyped set of rules. (3)

Computerized axial tomography (CAT or CT): a measure that provides an image of the brain by means of a computerized combination of many thousands of separate x-rays taken from different vantage points or axes through a person's head. (3)

Concordance rate: in genetic research, the percentage of people with the same disorder, usually calculated for biological relatives. (5)

Conditioned fear reactions: in behavior theory, the acquired associations between an internal or external cue and feelings of intense anxiety. (7)

Conditioned response: in behavior theory, the acquired response to a stimulus that was previously neutral. (5)

Conditioned stimulus: in behavior theory, the stimulus that, after conditioning, elicits the unconditioned response. (5)

Conditions of worth: in Rogerian theory, the conditions in which the child receives love only when certain parental demands are fulfilled. (4)

Conduct disorder: a disruptive behavior disorder of childhood that involves recurrent malicious behavior that is the precursor of antisocial personality disorder. (6)

Congruence: in Rogerian theory, a match between the person's self-conception and the more objective reality of a person's experiences. (4)

Consequences: events following a specified behavior that are identified in a behavioral assessment. (3)

Contingency management: a form of behavior therapy that involves the principle of rewarding a client for desired behaviors and not providing rewards for undesired behaviors. (5)

Continuous amnesia: inability to recall past events from a particular date up to, and including, the present time. (8)

Control group: the group of subjects who do not receive the "treatment" thought to influence the behavior under study. (1)

Conversion disorder: a somatoform disorder involving the translation of unacceptable drives or troubling conflicts into physical symptoms. (8)

Coping: the process through which people reduce stress. (17)

Coprolalia: the involuntary uttering of obscenities. (13)

Corpus callosum: a band of tissue connecting the two halves of the cerebral cortex. (5)

Correlation: an association, or co-relation, between two variables. (1)

Cortical atrophy: a wasting away or deterioration of tissue in the cerebral cortex of the brain. (12)

Cortisol: a hormone involved in the mobilization of the body's resources in times of stress. (10)

Counterconditioning: in behavior therapy, the process of replacing an undesired response to a stimulus with an acceptable response. (5)

Covert conditioning: a behavioral intervention in which a client is instructed by the therapist to imagine a highly negative experience when engaging in an undesirable behavior. (9)

Crack cocaine: a crystallized form of cocaine. (15)

Cross-fostering study: a method of comparing the relative effects of heredity and the environment, in which researchers study individuals who are adopted by parents with psychological disorders but whose biological parents are psychologically healthy. (5)

Cue exposure method: a behavioral approach to alcohol treatment in which the individual is given a priming dose of alcohol that initiates the craving for more alcohol; the person is then urged to refuse further alcohol. (15)

Cyclothymia: a mood disorder that, compared with bipolar disorder, involves a less intense vacillation between states of euphoria and dysphoria. (10)

Day treatment program: a structured program in a community treatment facility that provides activities similar to those provided in a psychiatric hospital. (2)

Decision tree: a strategy used for the purpose of diagnosis, consisting of a series of simple yes/no questions that guide the clinicians in ruling in or out various psychological disorders. (2)

Defense mechanisms: in psychoanalytic theory, protective efforts that defend the ego against anxiety. (4)

Deficit needs: in Maslow's theory, needs that represent a state in which the individual seeks to obtain something that is lacking. (4)

Deinstitutionalization movement: the release of psychiatric patients into community treatment sites as a result of dramatic changes in public policy. (1)

Delirium tremens: a physical condition consisting of autonomic nervous system dysfunction, confusion, and possible seizures associated with alcohol withdrawal. (15)

Delirium: a condition in which a person's thoughts, level of consciousness, speech, memory, orientation, perceptions, and motor patterns are very confused, unstable, or otherwise grossly disturbed. (14)

Delusion: a deeply entrenched false belief that is not consistent with the client's intelligence or cultural background. (3)

Demand characteristics: the expectations of people in an experiment about what is going to happen to them or the proper way to respond. (1)

Dementia: a form of cognitive impairment involving generalized progressive deficits in a person's memory and learning of new information, ability to communicate, judgment, and motor coordination. (14)

Dementia praecox: the term coined by Kraepelin to describe what is currently known as schizophrenia; according to Kraepelin this condition involved a degeneration of the brain that began at a young age and ultimately led to a degeneration of the entire personality. (11)

Dendrite: a section of the neuron that receives the information from other neurons. (5)

Denial: in psychoanalytic theory, a defense mechanism in which the reality of an event that unfavorably affected the person's ego is rejected. (4)

Denial/intrusion phase: reactions to a traumatic event involving alterations between denial, or a distancing of oneself from the event, and intrusion, being tormented by disruptive thoughts and feelings about the event. (7)

Dependence: a psychological and often physical need for a psychoactive substance. (15)

Dependent personality disorder: a personality disorder whose main characteristic is that the individual has an extreme neediness for other people, to the point of being unable to make any decisions or take independent action. (6)

Dependent variable: the variable whose value is the outcome of the experimenter's manipulation of the independent variable. (1)

Depersonalization: an altered experience of the self ranging from feeling that one's body is not connected to one's mind to the feeling that one is not real. (3)

Depersonalization disorder: a dissociative disorder in which the individual experiences recurrent and persistent episodes of depersonalization. (8)

Depressant: a psychoactive substance that causes depression of central nervous system activity. (15)

Detoxification treatment: the managing of an individual's withdrawal symptoms through the difficult early stages of abstinence. (15)

Developmental coordination disorder: the primary form of motor skill disorder, in which the individual has difficulty carrying out simple motor activities, appearing clumsy and uncoordinated. (13)

Deviation IQ: an index of intelligence derived from comparing the individual's score on an intelligence test with the mean score for that individual's reference group. (3)

Dexamethasone suppression test (DST): a method of testing neuroendocrine functioning by injecting the individual with dexamethasone, which in normal individuals results in the suppression of cortisol. (10)

***Diagnostic and Statistical Manual of Mental Disorders* (DSM):** a book published by the American Psychiatric Association that contains standard terms and definitions of the various psychological disorders. (2)

Diathesis-stress model: a theoretical model which proposes that a predisposition (or diathesis) places people at risk for developing a disorder if exposed to certain extremely stressful life experiences. (12)

Differential diagnosis: the process of systematically ruling out alternative diagnoses. (2)

Discrimination: in behavior theory, the process through which learning becomes increasingly specific to a given situation. (5)

Disorder of written expression: a learning disorder in which the individual's writing is characterized by poor spelling, grammatical or punctuation errors, and disorganization of paragraphs. (13)

Disorganized schizophrenia: a form of schizophrenia characterized by a combination of symptoms involving disturbed thought, communication, and behavior, lacking any consistent theme. (11)

Displacement: in psychoanalytic theory, a defense mechanism involving the shifting of impulses from the target of those feelings to someone or something that is more acceptable. (4)

Disturbances in the sense of self: perplexity about one's identity expressed in disturbances ranging from confusion about who one is to delusional thinking in which the individual believes that he or she is under the control of, or even part of, some external person or force. (11)

Disulfiram: known popularly as Antabuse, a medication used in the treatment of alcoholism that inhibits aldehyde dehydrogenase (ALDH) and causes severe physical reactions when combined with alcohol. (15)

Dizygotic twins: non-identical or fraternal twins who are related to the same degree as other siblings. (10)

Dopamine hypothesis: a biological explanation for schizophrenia which proposes that delusions, hallucinations, and attentional deficits result from overactivity of neurons that communicate with each other via the transmission of dopamine. (12)

Double-bind hypothesis: a notion based in family systems theory which proposed that the schizophrenic individual develops faulty communication and thinking processes due to years of being exposed to conflicting messages from other family members. (12)

Double-blind technique: an experimental procedure in which neither the person giving the treatment nor the person receiving the treatment has knowledge of whether the subject is in the experimental or control group. (1)

Down-regulation: a biochemical process that results in a decreased sensitivity of receptors to a neurotransmitter that is present in excess amounts in the nervous system. (10)

Down syndrome: a form of mental retardation caused by abnormal chromosomal formation during conception. (13)

Dream analysis: a method used in psychoanalysis in which the client is asked to tell the clinician the events of a dream, and to free associate to these events. (4)

Dream anxiety disorder: a parasomnia in which the individual has nightmares on a repeated basis. (17)

Duty to warn: the clinician's responsibility to notify a potential victim of a client's harmful intent toward that individual. (2)

Dysfunctional attitudes: in cognitive-behavioral theory, a set of personal rules or values people hold that interfere with adequate adjustment. (5)

Dyspareunia: a sexual dysfunction affecting males and females that involves recurrent or persistent genital pain before, during, or after sexual intercourse. (9)

Dysphoria: the emotion of sadness. (10)

Dysphoric mood: unpleasant feelings such as sadness or irritability. (3)

Dyssomnias: disturbances in the amount, quality, or timing of sleep. (17)

Dysthymia: a mood disorder involving chronic depression of less intensity than major depression. (10)

Echolalia: an echoing of words or phrases. (13)

Ego: in psychoanalytic theory, the structure of personality that gives the individual the mental powers of judgment, memory, perception, and decision-making, enabling the individual to adapt to the realities of the external world. (4)

Ego-ideal: in psychoanalytic theory, the individual's personal model of all that is exemplary in life. (4)

Elective mutism: a disorder originating in childhood in which the individual consciously refuses to talk, sometimes accompanying this refusal by oppositional or avoidant behavior. (13)

Electrocardiogram (ECG): a measure of electrical impulses that pass through the heart. (3)

Electroconvulsive therapy (ECT): the application of electrical shock to the head, for the purpose of inducing therapeutically effective seizures. (1)

Electrodermal response (also called **Galvanic Skin Response** or **GSR**): minor electrical changes in the skin that result from sweating. (3)

Electroencephalogram (EEG): a measure of changes in the electrical activity of the brain. (3)

Electromyography (EMG): a measure of electrical activity of the muscles. (3)

Elevated mood: mood that is more cheerful than average. (3)

Empathy: a sharing of another person's perspective. (4)

Empirical criterion keying: a method of constructing a test in which an item is included on a scale if it empirically differentiates between groups of people. (3)

Endocrine system: a bodily system composed of glands that produce hormones and secrete them into the bloodstream. (5)

Endogenous depression: a subtype of depression primarily caused by biological factors. (10)

Endorphins: natural painkilling substances produced by the brain that can produce pleasurable sensations. (15)

Enkephalins: natural painkilling substances produced by the brain that can produce pleasurable sensations. (15)

Enmeshed families: in family systems theory, families in which the members are so closely involved in each other's lives that they lose perspective on the world outside the family. (5)

Epilepsy: a neurological condition that involves recurrent bodily seizures with associated changes in EEG patterns. (14)

Erotomania: a psychotic disorder in which the individual has a delusion that another person, usually of great prominence, is deeply in love with him or her. (11)

Euphoria: the emotion of elation. (10)

Euphoric mood: a state in which the individual feels an exaggerated sense of happiness, elation, and excitement. (3)

Event related potential (ERP): a measure of the electrical activity of the brain when a person is exposed to certain sensory stimuli or "events"; researchers have found that people with schizophrenia have difficulty screening out irrelevant stimuli. (12)

Excitatory synapse: a synapse in which the message communicated to the receiving neuron makes it more likely to trigger a response. (5)

Exhibitionism: a paraphilia in which a person has intense sexual urges and arousing fantasies involving the exposure of genitals to a stranger. (9)

Existential: a theoretical position in psychology that emphasizes the importance of fully appreciating each moment as it occurs. (4)

Expectancy model: an approach to alcohol dependence that focuses on expectancies of alcohol as pleasure-producing and anxiety-reducing, reinforcement, and tolerance. (15)

Experimental group: the group of subjects who receive the "treatment" thought to influence the behavior under study. (1)

Experimental method: the process used in scientific research of altering or changing the conditions to which subjects are exposed and observing the effects of this manipulation on the behavior of the subjects. (1)

Expressed emotion (or EE): a measure used in research on schizophrenia that assesses the degree to which family members speak in ways that reflect criticism, hostile feelings, and emotional overinvolvement or overconcern with regard to the schizophrenic individual. (12)

Expressive language disorder: a specific developmental disorder characterized by a limited and faulty vocabulary, speaking short sentences with simplified grammatical structures, omitting critical words or phrases, or putting words together in peculiar order. (13)

Extinction: in behavioral theory, the cessation of behavior in the absence of reinforcement. (5)

Factitious disorder: a disorder in which people feign symptoms or disorders not for the purpose of any particular gain, but because of an inner need to maintain a sick role. (8)

Failure to thrive: a condition in which the child does not grow physically and mentally at a normal rate caused by poor prenatal care or grossly inadequate and inattentive parenting. (13)

Family dynamics: the pattern of interrelationships among members of a family. (5)

Family history: information gathered in a psychological assessment regarding the sequence of major events in the lives of the client's relatives, including those who are closest to the client as well as more distantly related family members. (3)

Family therapy: psychological treatment in which the therapist works with the family. (2)

Female orgasmic disorder (also called **inhibited female orgasm** or **anorgasmia**): a sexual dysfunction in which a woman experiences problems in having an orgasm during sexual activity. (9)

Female sexual arousal disorder: a sexual dysfunction characterized by a persistent or recurrent inability to attain or maintain the normal physiological and psychological arousal responses during sexual activity. (9)

Fetal alcohol syndrome (FAS): a condition associated with mental retardation in a child whose mother consumed large amounts of alcohol on a regular basis while pregnant. (13)

Fetish: a strong, recurrent sexual attraction to an object, upon which a person is dependent for achieving sexual gratification. (9)

Fetishism: a paraphilia in which the individual is preoccupied with an object and depends on this object, rather than sexual intimacy with a partner, for achieving sexual gratification. (9)

Fixation: in psychoanalytic theory, arrested development at a particular stage of psychosexual development attributable to excessive or inadequate gratification at that stage. (4)

Flashbacks: graphic and terrifying illusions and hallucinations associated with a traumatic event (as well as LSD use) which arise spontaneously. (7)

Flat affect: the virtual lack of emotional expression, as in speech that is monotonous or a face that is immobile. (3)

Flexible interview: a set of open-ended questions that are aimed at determining the client's reasons for being in treatment, symptoms, health status, family background and life history. (3)

Flooding: a behavioral technique in which the client is immersed in the sensation of anxiety by being exposed to the feared situation in its entirety. (7)

Fragile X syndrome: a defect transmitted through the X chromosome that leads to a severe form of mental retardation and serious speech and communication difficulties. (13)

Free association: a method used in psychoanalysis in which the client is instructed by the clinician to speak freely, saying whatever comes to mind. (4)

Frontal lobe: the front portion of the cerebral cortex. (5)

Frotteur: a person with the paraphilia of frotteurism. (9)

Frotteurism: a paraphilia in which the individual masturbates by rubbing against an unsuspecting stranger. (9)

Fugue: (sometimes called **dissociative** or **psychogenic fugue**): a dissociative condition in which a person, confused about personal identity, suddenly and unexpectedly travels to another place, and is unable to recall the past. (8)

Fully-functioning: in Rogerian theory, a state of optimal psychological health in which the individual has an accurate view of the self and experiences. (4)

Functional encopresis: a development-related disorder in which the child is incontinent of feces and has bowel movements either in clothes or in some other inappropriate place. (13)

Functional enuresis: a development-related disorder in which the child is incontinent of urine and urinates in clothes or in bed after the age when the child is expected to be continent. (13)

Gender identity: the individual's self-perception as a male or female. (9)

Gender identity disorder: a discrepancy between an individual's assigned sex and gender identity, involving a strong and persistent identification with the other gender. (9)

Gender role: the behaviors and attitudes a person has that are indicative in one's society of maleness or femaleness. (9)

Gene: the basic unit of heredity. (5)

Generalization: in behavioral theory, the expansion of learning from the original situation to one that is similar. (5)

Generalized amnesia: inability to remember anything from one's past life. (8)

Generalized anxiety disorder: an anxiety disorder characterized by anxiety that is not associated with a particular object, situation, or event but seems to be a constant feature of a person's day-to-day existence. (7)

Genetic mapping: the attempt by biological researchers to identify the characteristics controlled by each gene. (12)

Genitality: in psychoanalytic theory, the ability to express sexual feelings in a mature way and in appropriate contexts, reached when an individual is able to "work and love". (4)

Global Assessment of Functioning (GAF): Axis V of the *DSM*, a scale that rates the individual's overall level of psychological health. (2)

Grandiose delusional disorder: a psychotic disorder in which the individual has delusions of being an extremely important person. (11)

Grandiosity: an exaggerated view of oneself as possessing special and extremely favorable personal qualities and abilities. (6)

Granulovacuolar degeneration: a characteristic of Alzheimer's disease in which clumps of granular material accumulate within the cell bodies of neurons and result in the abnormal functioning of these neurons. (14)

Group therapy: psychological treatment in which the therapist facilitates discussion among a group of several clients who talk together about their problems. (2)

Gustatory hallucination: the false perception of a taste. (3)

Halfway house: a community treatment facility designed for deinstitutionalized clients coming out of a hospital who are not yet ready for independent living. (2)

Hallucination: a false perception, not corresponding to the objective nature of stimuli present in the environment. (3)

Hallucinogens: psychoactive substances that cause the user to experience abnormal perceptual experiences in the form of illusions or hallucinations, usually visual in nature. (15)

Hierarchy of needs: according to Maslow, the order in which human needs must be fulfilled. (4)

High-risk design: a research method in which investigators follow the lives of children who are considered to be at risk for developing a disorder because they have a biological parent with the disorder. (12)

Hippocampus: a limbic system structure responsible for the consolidation of short-term memory into long-term memory. (5)

Histrionic personality disorder: a personality disorder characterized by exaggerated displays of emotional reactions, approaching theatricality, in everyday behavior. (6)

Hormones: chemicals that are released by the endocrine glands into the bloodstream, affecting the operation of a number of bodily organs. (5)

Host: the central personality of the individual with multiple personality disorder. (8)

Humanistic: an approach to personality and psychological disorder that regards people as motivated by the need to understand themselves and the world and to derive greater enrichment from their experiences by fulfilling their unique individual potential. (4)

Huntington's disease: a hereditary condition that can begin as early as a person's 20s involving a widespread deterioration of the subcortical brain structures that control motor movements, along with the motor areas in the frontal cortex. (14)

Hypersomnia: a form of dyssomnia in which the individual never feels rested, and becomes very sleepy during the day even after sufficient rest at night. (17)

Hypervigilant: a state of being overly sensitive to sounds and sights in the environment. (7)

Hypoactive sexual desire disorder: a sexual dysfunction in which the individual has an abnormally low level of interest in sexual activity. (9)

Hypnotherapy: a method of therapy in which hypnosis is used for various purposes such as helping a person recall repressed memories. (8)

Hypnotics: psychoactive substances that are used as sleep medications. (15)

Hypnotism: a method of using suggestion to induce a trance state. (1)

Hypochondriasis: a somatoform disorder characterized by the misinterpretation of normal bodily functions as signs of a serious disease. (8)

Hypothalamus: a small structure in the brain that coordinates the activities of the central nervous system with systems involved in control of emotion, motivation, and bodily regulation. (5)

Hypothesis formation process: the stage of research in which the researcher generates ideas about cause-effect relationships between the behaviors under study. (1)

Hysteria: a disorder in which psychological problems become expressed in physical form. (1)

Hysterical neurosis: a term used by Freud to describe conversion disorder, implying that it is a reaction to anxiety. (8)

Id: in psychoanalytic theory, the structure of personality that contains the sexual and aggressive instincts. (4)

Identified patient: a term used by family therapists to refer to the individual designated by the family as the focus of treatment, although family therapists are more likely to view the problems as lying with the whole family rather than limited to a single individual. (5)

Identity: an individual's self-concept or sense of "who" one is. (6)

Identity confusion: a lack of clear sense of who one is, ranging from confusion about one's role in the world to actual delusional thinking. (3)

Illusion: misperception of a real object. (3)

Imaginal flooding: a behavioral technique in which the client is immersed through imagination in the feared situation. (7)

Impulse: an urge to act. (16)

Impulse control: the ability to restrain the gratification of one's immediate needs or desires. (6)

Impulse control disorders: psychological disorders in which people act on certain impulses involving some potentially harmful behavior that they cannot resist. (16)

***In vivo* observation:** a form of behavioral assessment in which the individual is observed in the natural context where the target behavior occurs. (3)

***In vivo* exposure:** a behavioral technique that involves placing the client in the actual situation in which the client experiences fear. (7)

Inappropriate affect: an inconsistency between the person's expression of emotion and the context or the content of what is being said. (3)

Incongruence: in Rogerian theory, a mismatch between a person's perception of self and the more objective characteristics of the self. (4)

Independent variable: the variable whose level is adjusted or controlled by the experimenter. (1)

Individual psychotherapy: psychological treatment in which the therapist works on a one-to-one basis with the client. (2)

Indolamine hypothesis: a hypothesis that proposes that a deficiency of serotonin causes depression. (10)

Induced psychotic disorder: a psychotic disorder in which one or more people develop a delusional system as a result of a close relationship with a psychotic person who is delusional. (11)

Informed consent: the client's statement of understanding about the potential risks and benefits of therapy, confidentiality and its limits, and the expected length of therapy. (2)

Inhibitory synapse: a synapse in which the message communicated to the receiving neuron makes it less likely to trigger a response. (5)

Insanity defense: the argument presented by a lawyer acting on behalf of the client that because of the existence of a mental disorder, the client should not be held legally responsible for criminal actions. (2)

Insomnia: a form of dyssomnia characterized by chronic difficulty obtaining enough sleep. (10)

Intelligence quotient: a method of quantifying performance on an intelligence test, originally calculated according to the ratio of a person's tested age to that person's chronological age, and changed in the 1960 revision of the Stanford-Binet to the deviation IQ. (3)

Intermittent explosive disorder: an impulse control disorder involving an inability to hold back urges to express strong angry feelings and associated violent behaviors. (16)

Intoxication: the experience of altered behaviors due to the accumulation of a psychoactive substance in the body. (15)

IQ: an abbreviation of the term intelligence quotient. (3)

Irrational beliefs: in cognitive-behavioral theory, views about the self and world that are unrealistic, extreme, and illogical. (5)

Irresistible impulse: a legal defense claiming that because of the presence of a psychological disorder, the individual is unable to inhibit actions that he or she feels compelled to carry out. (2)

Isolation: in psychoanalytic theory, a defense mechanism involving separation of feelings from actions. (4)

Jealous delusional disorder: a psychotic disorder characterized by the delusion that one's partner is being unfaithful. (11)

Kleptomania: an impulse control disorder which involves the persistent urge to steal. (16)

Korsakoff's syndrome: a permanent form of dementia associated with long-term alcohol use in which the individual develops retrograde and anterograde amnesia, leading to an inability to remember recent events or learn new information. (15)

La belle indifference: lack of concern by the individual with a conversion disorder over what might otherwise be construed as very disturbing physical problems. (8)

Labeling: a social process in which an individual is designated as having a certain disease or disorder, and once given this label the individual acts in ways that conform to this label. (12)

Lactate: a chemical in the blood whose level increases after physical exertion that is found to be higher in people with panic disorder. (7)

Lactate theory: a theory of panic disorder proposing that the intense anxiety experienced during a panic attack results from an increase of lactate in the blood. (7)

Latent: a state in which a disorder remains undetected but may subsequently become evident. (6)

Learned helplessness model: a behavioral theory applied to depression that proposes that depressed people have come to view themselves as incapable of having an effect on their environment. (10)

Learning disorder: a delay or deficit in an academic skill—mathematics, writing, or reading. (13)

Least restrictive alternative: a treatment setting that provides the fewest constraints on the client's freedom. (2)

Libido: in psychoanalytic theory, an instinctual pressure for gratification of sexual and aggressive desires. (4)

Limbic system: a set of loosely connected structures that form a ring within the center portion of the brain, and that provides the neurological basis for the interaction between "rational" and "irrational" human behaviors. (5)

Localized amnesia: inability to remember all events that occured in a specified time period. (8)

Longitudinal research design: a method of study in which the same individuals are repeatedly studied over a period of years or decades. (12)

Lovemap: according to John Money, the representation of an individual's sexual fantasies and preferred practices that is formed early in life. (9)

Magnetic resonance imaging (MRI) (sometimes called **nuclear magnetic resonance** or **NMR**): a scanning procedure that uses magnetic fields and radio-frequency pulses to construct an image. (3)

Mainstreaming: a governmental policy intended to integrate fully into society people with mental and physical disabilities. (13)

Major depression: a mood disorder in which the individual experiences acute, but time-limited, episodes of depressive symptoms. (10)

Major depressive disorder: a mood disorder characterized by a consistently sad mood along with other bodily symptoms. (2)

Major depressive episode: a period in which the individual suffers a variety of psychological and physical symptoms related to a dysphoric mood. (10)

Male erectile disorder: a sexual dysfunction marked by a recurrent, partial, or complete failure to attain or maintain an erection during sexual activity or a persistent lack of a subjective sense of sexual pleasure during sexual activity. (9)

Male orgasmic disorder (or inhibited male orgasm): a sexual dysfunction in which a man experiences problems having an orgasm during sexual activity. (9)

Malingering: the fabrication of physical or psychological symptoms for some ulterior motive. (8)

Manic episode: a period of euphoric mood. (10)

Masked depression: excessive concern with physical health that "masks" or covers an underlying state of dysphoria. (8)

Masochist: a person who derives satisfaction or pleasure from being subjected to abuse or pain. (6)

Mathematics disorder: a learning disorder in which the individual has difficulty with mathematical tasks and concepts. (13)

Medical model: the view that abnormal behaviors result from physical problems and should be treated medically. (1)

Melancholic depression: a form of depression in which the individual loses interest in most activities, has more severe depressive symptoms in the morning, and suffers loss of appetite or weight. (10)

Mental retardation: a condition, present from childhood, characterized by significantly below-average general intellectual functioning (an IQ of less than 65 to 75). (13)

Mental status examination: a focused way to provide a snapshot of the client's current functioning in the areas of behavior, orientation, content of thought, thinking style and language, affect and mood, perceptual experiences, sense of self, motivation, intelligence, and insight. (3)

Mesmerized: derived from the name Mesmer, used to refer to a state of heightened suggestibility brought about by the words and actions of a charismatic individual. (1)

Methadone: a synthetic opioid that produces a safer and more controlled reaction than heroin and is used in treating heroin addiction. (15)

Milieu therapy: the provision of a therapeutic environment on a 24-hour basis in an inpatient psychiatric facility. (2)

Modality: the form in which psychotherapy is offered. (2)

Modeling: in social learning theory, the learning of a new behavior by observing that of another person. (5)

Monozygotic twins: identical twins who share the same genetic inheritance. (10)

Mood: a person's experience of emotion, the way the person feels inside. (3)

Moral treatment: the philosophy that people can, with the proper care, develop self-control over their own disturbed behaviors. (1)

Motor behavior: how a person moves; may refer to fine movements such as handling small objects or large movements involved in walking. (3)

Motor disturbances: abnormal bodily movements ranging from minor tremors to paralysis, which in conversion disorder are psychogenic. (8)

Multiaxial system: a multidimensional classification and diagnostic system that summarizes a variety of relevant information about an individual's physical and psychological functioning. (2)

Multi-factorial polygenic threshold: a model to explain the relationship between genetic and environmental contributions to schizophrenia proposing that several genes with varying influence are involved in the transmission of schizophrenia. (12)

Multiple baseline approach: a research design involving the observation of different dependent variables in the same person over the course of treatment, or observing the behavior as it occurs under different conditions. (1)

Multiple personality disorder: a dissociative disorder in which one individual develops more than one self or personality. (8)

Multiple sclerosis: a neurological disease that involves deterioration of the fatty insulation around nerve fibers. (14)

Munchausen's syndrome: an extreme form of factitious disorder in which the individual goes to great lengths to maintain a sick role. (8)

Narcissistic personality disorder: a personality disorder primarily characterized by an unrealistic, inflated sense of self-importance and an inability to see the perspectives of other people. (6)

Narcotics: a term referring to the category of opioid drugs that includes the naturally occurring derivatives of the opium poppy: opium, morphine, and codeine. (15)

Negative reinforcement: in behavioral theory, the removal of aversive conditions when certain behaviors are performed. (5)

Negative symptoms: symptoms of schizophrenia involving an absence or reduction of thoughts, emotions, and behaviors compared to baseline functioning. (11)

Neurofibrillary tangles: a characteristic of Alzheimer's disease in which the material within the cell bodies of neurons becomes filled with densely packed, twisted protein microfibrils, or tiny strands. (14)

Neuroleptics: a category of medications used to reduce the frequency and intensity of psychotic symptoms. (12)

Neurometrics: the measurement and analysis of brain activity. (3)

Neuron: the nerve cell; the basic unit of structure and function within the nervous system. (5)

Neuropsychological assessment: a process of gathering information about a client's brain functioning on the basis of performance on psychological testing. (3)

Neurosis: a nontechnical term referring to behavior involving symptoms that are distressing to an individual and are recognized by that person as unacceptable; sometimes used to characterize certain psychological disorders considered to be less severe than psychosis. (2)

Neurotransmitter: a chemical substance released from the transmitting neuron into the synaptic cleft where it drifts across the synapse and is absorbed by the receiving neuron. (5)

Neutrality: the attitude taken by the clinician of not providing any information that would reveal the clinician's preferences, personal background, or reactions to the client's revelations in therapy. (4)

Normal mood or **euthymic mood:** mood that is neither unduly happy nor sad, but shows day to day variations within a relatively limited range. (3)

Normal pressure hydrocephalus: a neurological disorder that involves obstruction of the flow of cerebral spinal fluid (CSF) so that the fluid begins to build up within the ventricles of the brain. (14)

Object relations: in psychodynamic theory, the unconscious representations that a person has of important people in one's life. (4)

Observation: the stage of research in which the researcher watches and records the behavior of interest. (1)

Obsession: an unwanted repetitive thought or image that invades a person's consciousness. (3)

Obsessive: a personal quality of being immobilized when having to make a decision followed by rumination after a decision has been made. (6)

Obsessive-compulsive disorder: an anxiety disorder characterized by the experience of intrusive thoughts that the individual can alleviate only by engaging in patterns of rigid, ritualistic behavior. (7)

Obsessive-compulsive personality disorder: a personality disorder characterized by perfectionism and inflexibility. (6)

Occipital lobe: part of the cerebral cortex involved in visual perception. (5)

Olfactory hallucination: the false perception of a smell. (3)

Operant conditioning: in behavioral theory, a process in which an individual acquires a set of behaviors through reinforcement. (5)

Oppositional defiant disorder: a disruptive behavior disorder of childhood that is characterized by undue hostility, stubbornness, strong temper, belligerence, spitefulness, and self-righteousness. (13)

Oral-aggressive phase: in psychoanalytic theory, a period of psychosexual development in which the infant's pleasure is derived from gumming and biting anything the infant can get into the mouth. (4)

Oral-passive or **receptive phase:** in psychoanalytic theory, a period of psychosexual development in which the infant's pleasure comes from nursing or eating. (4)

Organic: a term that, when used in the context of psychological disorders, refers to physical damage or dysfunction that affects the integrity of the brain. (14)

Orgasmic reconditioning: a behavioral intervention geared toward a relearning process in which the individual associates sexual gratification with appropriate stimuli. (9)

Orientation: a person's awareness of time, place, and identity. (3)

Outcry phase: the first reaction to a traumatic event in which the individual reacts with alarm accompanied by a strong emotion. (7)

Overanxious disorder: an anxiety disorder of childhood characterized by anxiety so incapacitating that the child is unable to get through a day without obsessing over some unrealistic concern. (13)

Panic attack: a period of intense fear and physical discomfort accompanied by the feeling that one is being overwhelmed and is about to lose control. (7)

Panic disorder: an anxiety disorder that is diagnosed when an individual has panic attacks on a recurrent basis or has constant apprehension and worry about the possibility of recurring attacks. (7)

Paradoxical communication: in family systems theory, messages that convey two contradictory meanings. (5)

Paradoxical intervention: a strategy in family therapy in which the therapist suggests the intentional enactment of a problem (such as arguing) with the usual outcome being that the family has difficulty producing the problem spontaneously. (5)

Paranoid personality disorder: a personality disorder whose outstanding feature is that the individual is extremely suspicious of others and is always on guard against potential danger or harm. (6)

Paranoid schizophrenia: a form of schizophrenia characterized by preoccupation with one or more bizarre delusions or with auditory hallucinations that are related to a particular theme of being persecuted or harassed. (11)

Paraphilia: a sexual deviation involving recurrent, intense sexual urges and sexually arousing fantasies focused on nonhuman objects, or emotional or physical pain, or on children or other nonconsenting persons. (9)

Parasomnias: sleep disorders characterized by the recurrent experience of abnormal events during sleep. (17)

Parasuicide: a suicidal gesture to get attention from loved ones or family. (6)

Parasympathetic nervous system: part of the autonomic nervous system that carries out the maintenance functions of the body when it is at rest, directing most of the body's activities to producing and storing energy so that it can be used when the body is in action. (5)

Parietal lobe: part of the cerebral cortex involved in the perception of bodily sensations such as touch. (5)

Parkinson's disease: a disease involving the degeneration of neurons in the subcortical structures that control motor movements. (14)

Partialism: a variant of fetishism in which the person is interested solely in sexual gratification from a specific part of another person's body. (9)

Participant modeling: in social learning theory, a form of therapy in which the client is first shown a desired behavior and then guided through the behavior change with the help of the therapist. (5)

Passive-aggressive personality disorder: a personality disorder that is characterized primarily by angry feelings that are expressed indirectly rather than openly. (6)

Pathological gambling: an impulse control disorder involving the persistent urge to gamble. (16)

Peak experience: in Maslow's theory, a feeling of tremendous inner happiness, and of being totally in harmony with oneself and the world. (4)

Pedophilia: a paraphilia in which an adult's sexual urges are directed toward children. (9)

Penis envy: in psychoanalytic theory, the presumed jealousy that females have of the genitals of males. (4)

Percentile score: the percent of those who score below a certain number on a test. (3)

Peripheral nervous system: the part of the nervous system whose pathways lie outside the brain and spinal cord. (5)

Persecutory delusional disorder: a psychotic disorder in which the individual has delusions of persecution. (11)

Personal history: information gathered in a psychological assessment regarding important events and relationships in areas of the client's life such as school performance, peer relationships, employment and health. (3)

Personal constructs: in Kelly's cognitive personality theory, concepts or ways of viewing the world and the self. (5)

Personality disorders: ingrained patterns of relating to other people, situations, and events, with a rigid and maladaptive quality. (6)

Personality trait: an enduring pattern of perceiving, relating to, and thinking about the environment and others. (6)

Phenylketonuria (PKU): a disorder of infancy characterized by failure to produce an enzyme necessary for normal development that causes mental retardation. (13)

Phonological disorder: a specific developmental disorder in which the individual misarticulates, substitutes, or omits speech sounds. (13)

Pica: the recurrent eating of inedible substances such as paint, string, hair, animal droppings, and paper. (13)

Pick's disease: a relatively rare degenerative disease that affects the frontal and temporal lobes of the cerebral cortex. (14)

Pituitary gland: sometimes called the "master" gland, a major gland in the endocrine system, located in the brain and under the control of the hypothalamus. (5)

Placebo condition: the condition used in experimental research in which people are given an inert substance or treatment that is similar in all other ways to the experimental treatment. (1)

Pleasure principle: in psychoanalytic theory, a motivating force oriented toward the immediate and total gratification of sensual needs and desires. (4)

Population: the entire group of individuals sharing a particular characteristic. (1)

Positive reinforcement: in behavioral theory, the provision of rewards when certain behaviors are performed. (5)

Positive symptoms: symptoms of schizophrenia involving exaggerations or distortions of normal thoughts, emotions, and behavior. (11)

Positron emission tomography (PET) scan: a measure of brain activity in which a small amount of radioactive sugar is injected into an individual's bloodstream, following which a computer measures the varying levels of radiation in different parts of the brain and yields a multi-colored cross-sectional image. (3)

Post-traumatic stress disorder (PTSD): an anxiety disorder in which the individual experiences several distressing symptoms following a traumatic event such as re-experiencing the traumatic event, avoidance of reminders of the trauma, a numbing of general responsiveness, and increased arousal. (7)

Potentiation: the combination of effects of two or more psychoactive substances such that the total effect is greater than the effect of either substance alone. (15)

Preference molester: a pedophiliac for whom children are preferred sexual partners. (9)

Prefrontal area: the area at the very front of the cerebral cortex responsible for abstract planning and judgment. (5)

Premature ejaculation: a sexual dysfunction in which a man reaches orgasm well before he wishes to, perhaps even prior to penetration. (9)

Premorbid functioning: the period prior to the onset of the individual's symptoms. (11)

Primary gain: the relief from anxiety or responsibility due to the development of physical or psychological symptoms. (8)

Primary process thinking: in psychoanalytic theory, a loosely associated, idiosyncratic, and distorted cognitive representation of the world. (4)

Primary reinforcers: in behavioral theory, rewards that satisfy some biological need, making them intrinsically rewarding. (5)

Principal diagnosis: the disorder that is considered to be the primary cause for the individual's seeking professional help. (2)

Probability: the odds or likelihood that an event will happen. (1)

Probands: a term used in genetic research to refer to people who have the symptoms of a particular disorder. (10)

Process: a term used to refer to the gradual appearance of schizophrenia over time (contrasts with reactive). (11)

Prodromal phase: a period in the course of schizophrenia prior to the active phase of symptoms during which the individual shows progressive deterioration in social and interpersonal functioning. (11)

Prognosis: a client's likelihood of recovering from a disorder. (2)

Projection: in psychodynamic theory, a defense mechanism that involves attributing to someone else one's own unconscious feelings. (4)

Projective test: a technique in which the test-taker is presented with an ambiguous item or task and asked to respond by providing his or her own meaning or perception. (3)

Pseudodementia: literally false dementia, referring to an apparent loss of cognitive abilities due to depression. (14)

Psyche: the Greek word for mind. (4)

Psychiatrist: a medical doctor (M.D.) with advanced training in treating people with mental disorders. (2)

Psychoactive substance: a chemical that alters a person's mood or behavior by being drunk, smoked, inhaled, swallowed in pill form, or directly injected. (15)

Psychoanalysis: a theory and system of practice that relies heavily on the concepts of the unconscious mind, inhibited sexual impulses, early development, and the use of the "free association" technique and dream analysis. (1)

Psychoanalytic model: an approach that seeks explanations of abnormal behavior in the workings of unconscious psychological processes. (1)

Psychodynamic perspective: the theoretical orientation in psychology that emphasizes unconscious determinants of behavior. (4)

Psychodynamics (literally, **dynamics of the mind**): the processes of interaction among personality structures that lie beneath the surface of observable behavior. (4)

Psychogenic amnesia (sometimes called **dissociative amnesia**): an inability to remember important personal details and experiences that is not attributable to brain dysfunction. (8)

Psychological testing: a broad range of measurement techniques, all of which involve a process of having people provide scorable information about their psychological functioning. (2)

Psychometrics: literally means "measurement of the mind", reflecting the goal of finding the most suitable tests for psychological variables under study. (3)

Psychoneuroimmunology: the study of connections among psychological stress, nervous system functioning, and the immune system. (17)

Psychophysiological condition: a physical problem that reflects a connection between psychological and physiological processes. (17)

Psychophysiological disorders: a set of physical disorders that are caused by or exacerbated by stress. (8)

Psychophysiological processes: physiological processes that have a clear relationship with psychological functioning. (3)

Psychosis: a nontechnical term used to describe various forms of behavior involving loss of contact with reality. (2)

Psychosurgery: a form of brain surgery, the purpose of which is to reduce psychological disturbance. (1)

Psychotherapy: the treatment of abnormal behavior through psychological techniques. (1)

Punishment: in behavioral theory, the application of an aversive stimulus. (5)

Purge: in eating disorders, eliminating food through unnatural methods such as vomiting or excessive use of laxatives. (16)

Pyromania: an impulse control disorder involving the persistent and compelling urge to start fires. (16)

Q-sort procedure: a measurement technique that involves having the individual sort into piles a number of statements potentially descriptive of the person's self-control. (4)

Rationalization: in psychoanalytic theory, a defense mechanism that involves finding a more acceptable reason to mask the potentially threatening "real" reason for a behavior. (4)

Reaction formation: in psychoanalytic theory, a defense mechanism that involves transforming a feeling or desire into its opposite. (4)

Reactive: a term used to refer to the development of schizophrenia in response to a precipitant that provokes the onset of symptoms (contrasts with process). (11)

Reactive attachment disorder: a development-related disorder in which the individual has a severe disturbance in the ability to relate to others and is unresponsive to people, apathetic, and prefers to be alone rather than interact with friends or family. (13)

Reactive depression: a variant of depression thought of as precipitated by stressful events. (10)

Reactivity: in behavioral theory, change in a person's behavior in response to knowledge that he or she is being observed. (3)

Reading disorder (dyslexia): a learning disorder in which the individual omits, distorts, or substitutes words when reading, and reads in a slow and halting fashion. (13)

Reality principle: in psychoanalytic theory, a motivational force that leads the individual to confront the constraints of the external world. (4)

Receptive language disorder: a specific developmental disorder in which the individual is unable to understand certain kinds of words or phrases such as directions, or in more severe forms, basic vocabulary or entire sentences. (13)

Regression: in psychoanalytic theory, a defense mechanism that involves reverting to behaviors that were more acceptable or more rewarding in childhood. (4)

Reinforcement: in behavioral theory, the "strengthening" of a behavior. (5)

Relapse prevention therapy: a treatment method based on the expectancy model, in which individuals are encouraged not to view lapses from abstinence as signs of certain failure. (15)

Relaxation training: a behavioral technique used in the treatment of anxiety disorders that involves progressive and systematic patterns of muscle tensing and relaxing. (7)

Reliability: the consistency of measurements or diagnoses. (2)

Representativeness: the extent to which a sample adequately reflects the characteristics of the population from which it is drawn. (1)

Repression: in psychoanalytic theory, a defense mechanism involving motivated forgetting. (4)

Residual phase: a period in the course of schizophrenia, following the active phase, in which there are continuing indications of disturbance, evidenced by the same kinds of behaviors that characterize the prodromal phase, most notably, impaired social and interpersonal functioning. (11)

Residual schizophrenia: a form of schizophrenia in which people who have been previously diagnosed as having schizophrenia, but who no longer have the prominent psychotic symptoms, do have some remaining symptoms of the disorder such as emotional blunting, social withdrawal, eccentric behavior, or illogical thinking. (11)

Resistance: in psychoanalytic theory, unconscious blocking of anxiety-provoking thoughts or feelings. (4)

Reticular formation: a diffuse collection of ascending and descending pathways that controls the level and direction of arousal of brain activity through excitation of certain pathways and inhibition of others. (5)

Retrograde amnesia: a loss of memories for events prior to the physical damage that caused the amnesia. (14)

Rumination disorder of infancy: a development-related disorder in which the child regurgitates food after it has been swallowed and then either spits it out or reswallows it. (13)

Sadist: a person who derives pleasure from the infliction of pain or abuse on others. (6)

Sadistic personality disorder: a personality disorder, first introduced on an experimental basis in *DSM-III-R*, characterized mainly by a pervasive pattern of acting toward others in ways that are cruel and demeaning. (6)

Sadomasochist: a person who derives pleasure from both inflicting and receiving pain. (9)

Sample: a selection of individuals from a larger group. (1)

Schedules of reinforcement: in behavioral theory, systems that determine when reinforcers are provided. (5)

Schizoaffective disorder: a psychotic disorder characterized by symptoms associated with both schizophrenia and mood disorder. (11)

Schizoid personality disorder: a personality disorder primarily characterized by an indifference to social relationships, as well as a very limited range of emotional experience and expression. (6)

Schizophrenia: a disorder with a range of symptoms involving disturbances in content of thought, form of thought, perception, affect, sense of self, motivation, behavior, and interpersonal functioning. (11)

Schizophrenia spectrum disorders: a term used by some researchers to characterize a continuum of disorders including schizophrenia, schizoid personality disorder, and schizotypal personality disorder. (6)

Schizophreniform disorder: a disorder characterized by psychotic symptoms that are essentially the same as those found in schizophrenia, except for the duration and chronic nature of the symptoms; specifically, symptoms usually last from 1 to 6 months. (11)

Schizophrenogenic mother: an outdated psychoanalytic concept referring to the hypothesis that a certain kind of mothering style, characterized by confusing communication, could produce a schizophrenic child. (12)

Schizotypal personality disorder: a personality disorder that primarily involves peculiarities and eccentricities of thought, behavior, appearance, and interpersonal style. People with this disorder may have peculiar ideas such as magical thinking and beliefs in psychic phenomena. (6)

Seasonal depression: a form of depression in which the individual has varying symptoms according to time of year, with symptoms usually developing during the same months every year. (10)

Secondary gain: the sympathy and attention that the sick person receives from other people. (8)

Secondary process thinking: in psychoanalytic theory, the kind of thinking involved in logical and rational problem-solving. (4)

Secondary reinforcers: in behavioral theory, rewards that derive their value from association with primary reinforcers. (5)

Sedatives: psychoactive substances that have a calming effect on the central nervous system. (15)

Selective amnesia: inability to remember some, but not all, events that occurred in a specified time period. (8)

Self-actualization: in humanistic theory, the maximum realization of the individual's potential for psychological growth. (4)

Self-defeating personality disorder: A personality disorder, first introduced on an experimental basis in *DSM-III-R*, in which the primary feature is a pervasive pattern of behaviors in which the individual's own best interests are undermined, gratification is avoided, and suffering is chosen over pleasure. (6)

Self-efficacy: in social cognitive theory, the individual's perception of competence in various life situations. (5)

Self-monitoring: in behavioral assessment, a self-report technique in which the client keeps a record of the frequency of specified behaviors. (3)

Self-report clinical inventory: a psychological test with standardized questions having fixed response categories that the test-taker completes independently, "self"-reporting the extent to which the responses are accurate characterizations. (3)

Senile plaque: a characteristic of Alzheimer's disease in which clusters of dead or dying neurons become mixed together with fragments of protein molecules. (14)

Sensate focus: a method of treatment for sexual dysfunctions that involves having the partners take turns stimulating each other in nonsexual but affectionate ways at first, then gradually progressing over a period of time toward genital stimulation. (9)

Sensory disturbances: abnormal sensory processing ranging from abnormalities to loss of functioning in one of the senses; in conversion disorder, these disturbances are psychogenic. (8)

Sensory gating: the closing down of sensory processing with repeated presentation of the same stimulus. (12)

Separation anxiety disorder: an anxiety disorder of childhood characterized by difficulty in separating from caregivers. (13)

Sexual aversion disorder: a sexual dysfunction characterized by an active dislike of intercourse or related sexual activities. (9)

Sexual dysfunction: an aberration or abnormality in an individual's sexual responsiveness and reactions. (9)

Sexual impulsivity: a condition in which people feel uncontrollably driven to seek out sexual encounters and engage in frequent and indiscriminate sexual activity. (16)

Sexual masochism: a paraphilia marked by an attraction to situations in which sexual gratification is achieved by having painful stimulation applied to one's own body. (9)

Sexual sadism: a paraphilia in which sexual gratification is derived from activities or urges to harm another person. (9)

Sexual orientation: the degree to which a person is erotically attracted to members of the same or other sex. (9)

Shaping: a learning technique in which reinforcement is provided for behaviors that increasingly come to resemble a desired outcome. (5)

Simple mendelian genetics: inheritance of a characteristic that is controlled by a single gene which is either in dominant or recessive form. (12)

Single-subject design: an experimental procedure in which one person at a time is studied in both the experimental and control conditions. (1)

Situational molester: a pedophiliac who has a normal history of sexual development and interests but who will, in certain contexts, be overcome by a strong impulse to become sexual with a child. (9)

Sleep terror disorder: a parasomnia in which the individual repeatedly has the upsetting experience of waking up suddenly and in a panic from a sound sleep. (17)

Sleep-wake schedule disorder: a form of dyssomnia in which the individual suffers a mismatch between bodily sleep rhythms and the demands of the environment. (17)

Sleepwalking disorder: a parasomnia in which the individual recurrently sleepwalks. (17)

Smooth pursuit eye movements: a biological marker that is measured by having subjects follow a visual target; people with schizophrenia and their relatives have been found to show irregular pursuit of a moving target with many interruptions by extraneous eye movements. (12)

Social cognition: the factors that influence the way people perceive themselves and other people and form judgments about the causes of behavior. (5)

Social learning: a theoretical perspective that focuses on how people develop personality and psychological disorders through their relationships with others and through their exposure to the ways of others in their societies. (5)

Social norm: a standard for acceptable behavior that is established in a given society or culture. (1)

Social phobia: an anxiety disorder characterized by irrational and unabating fear that one's behavior will be scrutinized by others, causing the individual to feel embarrassed and humiliated. (7)

Social skills training: a form of behavioral treatment that identifies and targets inappropriate behaviors and reinforces socially acceptable behavior. (12)

Somatic delusional disorder: a psychotic disorder in which the individual believes he or she has a dreaded or terminal disease. (11)

Somatic nervous system: the part of the nervous system in which information from outside and inside the body is brought to the central nervous system through sensory and motor pathways. (5)

Somatic symptoms: bodily disturbances or complaints. (10)

Somatization disorder: a somatoform disorder in which multiple and recurrent bodily symptoms, which lack a physiological basis, are the expression of psychological issues. (8)

Somatoform disorders: a variety of conditions in which psychological conflicts become translated into physical problems or complaints. (8)

Somatoform pain disorder: a somatoform disorder in which the only symptom is pain that has no physiological basis. (8)

Specific developmental disorder: a delay or deficit in some particular area of functioning, such as academic skills, language and speech, or motor coordination. (13)

Specific (or simple) phobia: an anxiety disorder involving irrational and unabating fear of a particular object, activity, or situation. (7)

Spectatoring: the experience in which the individual feels unduly self-conscious during sexual activity, as if evaluating and monitoring the sexual encounter. (9)

Splitting: a tendency, common in people with borderline personality disorder, to perceive others as being all good or all bad, usually resulting in disturbed interpersonal relationships. (6)

Squeeze technique: a method of treatment for premature ejaculation in which the partner is instructed to stimulate the man's penis during foreplay and squeeze it when he indicates that he is approaching orgasm. (9)

Standardized interview: a highly structured series of assessment questions, with a predetermined wording and order. (3)

Statistical average: the arithmetical mean on a given measure, calculated by dividing the sum of all scores by the number of people who are measured. (1)

Stereotypy/habit disorder: a development-related disorder in which the individual voluntarily repeats nonfunctional behaviors such as rocking or head-banging that can potentially be damaging to the individual's physical well-being. (13)

Stimulant psychosis: a condition involving delusions or hallucinations that develops from chronic use of amphetamines, or with one very large dose of amphetamines. (15)

Stimulants: psychoactive substances that have an activating effect on the central nervous system. (15)

Stimulus discrimination: in behavioral theory, differentiating between two stimuli which possess similar but essentially different characteristics. (5)

Stimulus generalization: in behavioral theory, the process of learning to respond in the same way to stimuli that share common properties. (5)

Stop-start procedure: a method of treatment for premature ejaculation in which the man or his partner stimulates him to sexual excitement, and as he approaches the point of orgasmic inevitability, stimulation is stopped. When this procedure is repeated over time, the man can bring his orgasmic response under greater control. (9)

Stress: the feeling that one's resources are inadequate to meet the demands of a situation. (17)

Stress inoculation training: in cognitive-behavioral theory, a systematic stress management procedure that helps people prepare for difficult situations by anticipating them and practicing ways to control stress. (5)

Structural approach: in family systems theory, a way of looking at families that considers the roles of parents and children and the boundaries between the generations. (5)

Stuttering: a specific developmental disorder in which the individual suffers a disturbance in the normal fluency and patterning of speech that is characterized by such verbalizations as sound repetitions or prolongations, broken words, blocking on sounds, word substitutions to avoid problematic words, or words expressed with an excess of tension. (13)

Subcortical structures: parts of the brain that operate much of the time as relay stations to prepare information for processing in the cerebral cortex and to carry out the instructions given by the cerebral cortex for action by the muscles and glands. (5)

Sublimation: in psychoanalytic theory, a defense mechanism involving translation of unacceptable impulses into more acceptable actions. (4)

Substance abuse: a pattern of psychoactive substance use said to occur when an individual's health or safety is threatened and problems are created in daily life. (15)

Suicidal intent: how committed a person is to taking his or her own life. (17)

Suicidal lethality: the dangerousness of a suicidal person's intended method of dying. (17)

Superego: in psychoanalytic theory, the structure of personality that includes the conscience and the ego-ideal; incorporates societal prohibitions and exerts control over the seeking of instinctual gratification. (4)

Sustained attention: a biological marker that is measured by having a subject make a response when a certain target stimulus is displayed; people with schizophrenia and their relatives typically do poorly on this task. (12)

Sympathetic nervous system: part of the autonomic nervous system primarily responsible for mobililizing the body's stored resources when these resources are needed for energy-taxing activities. (5)

Symptoms complicating physical illness: physical symptoms that complicate or delay physical recovery from a diagnosed physical disorder; in conversion disorder these symptoms are psychogenic. (8)

Symptoms simulating physical illness: symptoms of conversion disorder that mimic the actual symptoms of a physical disorder. (8)

Synapse: the point of communication between neurons. (5)

Synaptic cleft: the gap between two neurons at the point of synapse. (5)

Syndrome: a collection of symptoms that together form a definable pattern. (2)

Systematic desensitization: in behavioral theory, a variant of counterconditioning that involves presenting the client with progressively more anxiety-provoking images while in a relaxed state. (5)

Tactile hallucination: the false perception of sensation or movement. (3)

Tardive dyskinesia: an irreversible neurological disorder which affects 10–20 percent of people who take neuroleptics for a year or more; this disorder involves uncontrollable movements in various parts of the body, including the mouth, tongue, lips, fingers, arms, legs, and trunk. (12)

Target behavior: in behavioral assessment, a behavior of interest or concern. (3)

Tay-Sachs disease: a metabolic disorder that causes neural degeneration and early death, usually before the age of 4. (13)

Temporal lobe: part of the cerebral cortex involved in speech and language. (5)

Testosterone: the male sex hormone. (6)

Therapeutic community: a concept developed in treating substance abuse in which individuals are resocialized to a drug-free lifestyle through a multi-faceted approach. (15).

Thought disorder: a disturbance in the way the person thinks or uses language. (3)

Thought stopping: a cognitive-behavioral method in which the client is taught to stop having anxiety provoking thoughts. (7)

Tic: a rapid, recurring, involuntary movement or vocalization. (13)

Token economy: in behavioral theory, a form of contingency management in which a client who performs desired activities earn chips or tokens that can later be exchanged for tangible benefits. (5)

Tolerance: the extent to which the individual requires larger and larger amounts of a psychoactive substance in order to achieve its desired effects or feels less of its effects after using the same amount of the substance. (15)

Tourette's disorder: a development-related disorder involving a chronic combination of movement and vocal tics. (13)

Transference: a notion rooted in psychoanalytic theory which refers to the carrying over toward the therapist of feelings that the client had toward parents or other significant people in the client's life. (4)

Transsexualism: sometimes used to refer to gender identity disorder, specifically pertaining to individuals choosing to undergo sex reassignment surgery. (9)

Transvestic fetishism: a paraphilia in which a man has an uncontrollable craving to dress in women's clothing in order to derive sexual gratification. (9)

Traumatic experience: a disastrous or extremely painful event that has severe psychological and physiological effects. (7)

Trephining: a treatment in prehistoric times, presumably for the purpose of curing psychological disorder, by drilling a hole in the skull. (1)

Trichotillomania: an impulse control disorder involving the compulsive persistent urge to pull out one's own hair. (16)

Unconditioned response: in behavioral theory, a reflexive response that occurs naturally in the presence of the unconditioned stimulus without having been learned. (5)

Unconditioned stimulus: in behavioral theory, the stimulus that naturally produces the response without having been learned. (5)

Undifferentiated schizophrenia: a form of schizophrenia characterized by a complex of schizophrenic symptoms such as delusions, hallucinations, incoherence, or disorganized behavior, that does not meet the criteria for other types of schizophrenia. (11)

Undoing: in psychoanalytic theory, a defense mechanism in which the ego attempts to restore the individual to the state that existed before a certain need was expressed or a behavior occurred. (4).

V codes: a set of problems that may come to the attention of a clinician, but that are not technically considered psychological disorders. (17)

Vaginismus: a sexual dysfunction that involves recurrent or persistent involuntary spasms of the musculature of the outer part of the vagina. (9)

Validity: the extent to which a diagnosis or rating accurately and distinctly characterizes a person's psychological status. (2,3)

Variable: a dimension along which people, things, or events differ. (1)

Variable ratio schedule of reinforcement: in behavioral theory, a schedule of reinforcement in which rewards occur on an average of a certain number of times per response. (5)

Vascular dementia: a form of dementia resulting from a vascular disease that causes deprivation of the blood supply to the brain. (14)

Vicarious reinforcement: in behavioral theory, a form of learning in which a new behavior is acquired through the process of watching someone else receive reinforcement for the same behavior. (5)

Visual hallucination: the false visual perception of objects or persons. (3)

Voice disorder: a specific developmental disorder in which the individual's speech is characterized by abnormalities in pitch, loudness, tone, or resonance. (13)

Voyeur: a person with the paraphilia of voyeurism. (9)

Voyeurism: a paraphilia in which the individual has a compulsion to derive sexual gratification from observing the nudity or sexual activity of others. (9)

Vulnerability: when used in the context of psychological disorders, a biologically based predisposition to developing a particular disorder when certain environmental conditions are in place. (12)

Wernicke's aphasia: a form of aphasia in which the individual is able to produce language, but has lost the ability to comprehend so that these verbal productions have no meaning. (14)

Wernicke's disease: an acute condition associated with long-term, heavy alcohol use, involving delirium, eye movement disturbance, difficulties in movement and balance, and deterioration of the peripheral nerves to the hands and feet. (15)

Withdrawal: physical and psychological changes that accompany discontinuation of a psychoactive substance. (15)

Working through: a phase of psychoanalytic treatment in which the client is helped to achieve a healthier resolution of issues than had occurred in the client's early childhood environment. (4)

REFERENCES

Abel, E. L., & Sokol, R. J. (1987). Incidence of fetal alcohol syndrome and economic impact of FAS-related anomalies. *Drug and Alcohol Dependence, 19,* 51–70.

Abraham, K. (1911/1968). Notes on the psychoanalytic investigation and treatment of manic-depressive insanity and allied conditions. In K. Abraham, *Selected papers of Karl Abraham.* New York: Basic Books.

Abraham, K. (1927/1948). Manifestations of the female castration complex. In D. Bryan & A. Strachey (Trans.), *Selected papers of Karl Abraham.* London: Hogarth Press.

Abramowitz, S. I. (1986). Psychosocial outcomes of sex reassignment surgery. *Journal of Consulting and Clinical Psychology, 54,* 183–189.

Abramson, L. Y., Seligman, M. E. P., & Teasdale, J. D. (1978). Learned helplessness in humans: Critique and reformulation. *Journal of Abnormal Psychology, 87,* 49–74.

Achenbach, T. M., & Edelbrock, C. (1983). *Manual for the child behavior checklist and revised child behavior profile.* Burlington: University of Vermont, Department of Psychiatry.

Adams, E. H., Gfroerer, J. C., Rouse, B. A., & Kozel, N. J. (1987). Trends in prevalence and consequences of cocaine use. *Advances in Alcohol and Substance Abuse, 6*(2), 49–71.

Adler, A. (1931/1958). *What life should mean to you.* (Alan Porter, Ed.). New York: Capricorn.

Agras, W. S. (1990). Treatment of social phobias. *Journal of Clinical Psychiatry, 51*(10, Suppl.), 52–55.

Agras, W. S. (1991). Nonpharmacologic treatment of bulimia nervosa. *Journal of Clinical Psychiatry, 52*(Suppl. 10), 29–33.

Agras, W. S., Rossiter, E. M., Arnow, B., Schneider, J. A., Telch, C. F., Raeburn, S. D., Bruce, B., Perl, M., & Koran, L. M. (1992). Pharmacologic and cognitive-behavioral treatment for bulimia nervosa: A controlled comparison. *American Journal of Psychiatry, 149,* 82–87.

Ainsworth, M. D. S. (1989). Attachments beyond infancy. *American Psychologist, 44,* 709–716.

Ainsworth, M. D. S., Blehar, M., Waters, E., & Wall, S. (1978). *Patterns of attachment.* Hillsdale, NJ: Erlbaum.

Akiskal, H. S., & Mallya, G. (1987). Criteria for the "soft" bipolar spectrum: Treatment implications. *Psychopharmacological Bulletin, 23,* 68–73.

Alcoholics Anonymous World Services (1987). *AA membership survey.* New York: Author.

Alexander, P. C., & Lupfer, S. L. (1987). Family characteristics and long-term consequences associated with sexual abuse. *Archives of Sexual Behavior, 16,* 235–245.

Allebeck, P. (1989). Schizophrenia: A life-shortening disease. *Schizophrenia Bulletin, 15,* 81–89.

Alley, P. M. (1983). Helping individuals with sleep disturbances: Some behavior therapy techniques. *Personnel and Guidance Journal, 61,* 606–608.

Alloy, L. B., & Abramson, L. Y. (1979). Judgment of contingency in depressed and nondepressed students: Sadder but wiser? *Journal of Experimental Psychology: General, 108,* 441–485.

Alzheimer, A. (1907/1987). About a peculiar disease of the cerebral cortex. (L. Jarvik & H. Greenson, Trans.). *Alzheimer's Disease and Associated Disorders, 1,* 7–8.

American Psychiatric Association (1987). *Diagnostic and statistical manual of mental disorders* (3rd. ed.–rev.). Washington, D.C.: American Psychiatric Association.

American Psychiatric Association (1991). *DSM-IV Options Book.* Washington, DC: Author.

Amit, A., Smith, B. R., & Gill, K. (1991). Serotonin uptake inhibitors: Effects on motivated consummatory behaviors. *Journal of Clinical Psychiatry, 52*(12, Suppl.), 55–60.

Anastasi, A. (1988). *Psychological testing* (6th ed.). New York: Macmillan.

Anda, R. F., Williamson, D. F., & Remington, P. L. (1988). Alcohol and fatal injuries among US adults. *Journal of the American Medical Association, 260,* 2529–2532.

Andersen, A. E. (1983). Anorexia nervosa and bulimia: A spectrum of eating disorders. *Journal of Adolescent Health Care, 4,* 15–21.

Andreasen, N. C. (1986). Scale for the assessment of thought, language, and communication (TLC). *Schizophrenia Bulletin, 12,* 473–481.

Andreasen, N. C. (1987). The diagnosis of schizophrenia. *Schizophrenia Bulletin, 13,* 9–22.

Andreasen, N. C. (1989). The American concept of schizophrenia. *Schizophrenia Bulletin, 15,* 519–531.

Andreasen, N. C., & Flaum, M. A. (1990). Schizophrenia and related psychotic disorders. *Hospital and Community Psychiatry, 41,* 954–956.

Andreasen, N. C., Flaum, M., Swayze, V. W., II, Tyrrell, G., & Arndt, S. (1990). Positive and negative symptoms of schizophrenia: A critical reappraisal. *Archives of General Psychiatry, 47,* 615–621.

Andreasen, N. C., Scheftner, W., Reich, T., Hirschfeld, R. M., Endicott, J., & Keller, M. B. (1986). The validation of the concept of endogenous depression. *Archives of General Psychiatry, 43,* 246–251.

Andreasson, S., Allebeck, P., Engstrom, A., & Rydberg, U. (1987). Cannabis and schizophrenia: A longitudinal study of Swedish conscripts. *Lancet, 2,* 1483–1486.

Andreoli, A., Gressot, G., Aapro, N., Tricot, L., & Gognalons, M.Y. (1989). Personality disorders as a predictor of outcome. *Journal of Personality Disorders, 3,* 307–320.

Annis, H. M. (1984a). *Inventory of drinking situations: Short form.* Toronto: Addiction Research Foundation.

Annis, H. M. (1984b). *Situational confidence questionnaire: Short form.* Toronto: Addiction Research Foundation.

Annis, H. M. (1990). Relapse to substance abuse: Empirical findings within a cognitive-social learning approach. *Journal of Psychoactive Drugs, 22,* 117–124.

Annis, H. M., & Davis, C. S. (1988). Self-efficacy and the prevention of alcoholic relapse: Initial findings from a treatment trial. In T. B. Baker & D. Cannon (Eds.), *Assessment and treatment of addictive disorders* (pp. 88–112). New York: Praeger.

Anthony, J. C., & Petronis, K. R. (1991). Panic attacks and suicide attempts. *Archives of General Psychiatry, 48,* 1114.

Arend, R., Gove, F. L., & Sroufe, L. A. (1979). Continuity of individual adaptation from infancy to kindergarten: A predictive study of ego-resiliency and curiosity in preschoolers. *Child Development, 50,* 950–959.

Arnstein, R. L. (1983). Survey of DSM-III use. *Journal of American College Health, 32,* 110–113.

Asher, R. (1951). Munchausen's syndrome. *Lancet, 1,* 339–341.

Atwood, J. D. (1991). Domestic violence: The role of alcohol. *Journal of the American Medical Association, 265,* 460.

Avery, D., & Winokur, G. (1977). The efficacy of electroconvulsive therapy and antidepressants in depression. *Biological Psychiatry, 12,* 507–523.

Ayllon, T., & Azrin, N. H. (1965). The measurement and reinforcement of behavior of psychotics. *Journal of the Experimental Analysis of Behavior, 8,* 357–383.

Ayllon, T., & Azrin, N. H. (1968). *The token economy: A motivational system for therapy and rehabilitation.* Englewood Cliffs, NJ: Prentice-Hall.

Aylward, E. H., Brown, F. R., III, Lewis, M. E. B., & Savage, C. R. (1987). Planning for treatment of learning disabilities and associated primary handicapping conditions. In F. R. Brown, III & E. H. Aylward (Eds.), *Diagnosis and management of learning disabilities: An interdisciplinary approach* (pp. 127–146). Boston: College Hill.

Azrin, N. H., & Nunn, R. G. (1978). *Habit control in a day.* New York: Simon & Schuster.

Baker, L., & Cantwell, D. P. (1987). A prospective psychiatric follow up of children with speech/language disorders. *Journal of the American Academy of Child and Adolescent Psychiatry, 26,* 546–553.

Balay, J., & Shevrin, H. (1988). The subliminal psychodynamic activation method: A critical review. *American Psychologist, 43,* 161–174.

Ball, J. C., & Corty, E. (1988). Basic issues pertaining to the effectiveness of methadone maintenance treatment. In C. G. Leukefeld & F. M. Tims (Eds.), *Compulsory treatment of drug abuse: Research and clinical practice* (pp. 178–191). Washington, DC: U.S. Government Printing Office.

Ballenger, J. C. (1991). Long-term pharmacologic treatment of panic disorder. *Journal of Clinical Psychiatry, 52*(Suppl. 2), 18–23.

Bandura, A. (1971). Psychotherapy based upon modeling principles. In A. E. Bergin & S. L. Garfield (Eds.), *Handbook of psychotherapy and behavior change* (pp. 653–708). New York: Wiley.

Bandura, A. (1977). Self-efficacy: Toward a unifying theory of behavioral change. *Psychological Review, 84,* 191–215.

Bandura, A. (1982). Self-efficacy mechanism in human agency. *American Psychologist, 37,* 122–147.

Bandura, A. (1986). *Social foundations of thought and action: A social cognitive theory.* Englewood Cliffs, NJ: Prentice-Hall.

Bandura, A. (1991). Human agency: The rhetoric and the reality. *American Psychologist, 46,* 157–162.

Bandura, A., Adams, N. E., & Beyer, J. (1977). Cognitive processes mediating behavioral change. *Journal of Personality and Social Psychology, 35,* 125–139.

Bandura, A., Jeffery, R. W., & Wright, C. L. (1974). Efficacy of participant modeling as a function of response induction aids. *Journal of Abnormal Psychology, 83,* 56–64.

Barefoot, J. C., Siegler, I. C., Nowling, J. B., Peterson, B. L., Haney, T. L., & Williams, R. B., Jr. (1987). Suspiciousness, health, and mortality: A follow-up study of 500 older adults. *Psychosomatic Medicine, 49,* 450–457.

Barkley, R. A. (1981). *Hyperactive children: A handbook for diagnosis and treatment.* New York: Guilford Press.

Barkley, R. A. (1989). Attention deficit-hyperactivity disorder. In E. J. Mash & R. A. Barkley (Eds.), *Treatment of childhood disorders* (pp. 39–72). New York: Guilford Press.

Barlow, D. H. (1986). Causes of sexual dysfunction: The role of anxiety and cognitive interference. *Journal of Consulting and Clinical Psychology, 54,* 140–148.

Barlow, D. H. (1988). *Anxiety and its disorders: The nature and treatment of anxiety and panic.* New York: Guilford Press.

Barlow, D. H. (1990). Long-term outcome for patients with panic disorder treated with cognitive-behavioral therapy. *Journal of Clinical Psychiatry, 51*(12, Suppl. A), 17–23.

Barnard, J. W., Robbins, L., Newman, G., & Hutchinson, D. (1985). Differences found between rapists, child molesters. *Psychiatric News, 20,* 34–35.

Barnett, P. A., & Gotlib, I. H. (1988). Psychosocial functioning and depression: Distinguishing among antecedents, concomitants, and consequences. *Psychological Bulletin, 104,* 97–126.

Baron, M., Gruen, R., Asnis, L., & Kane, J. (1983). Familial relatedness of schizophrenic and schizotypal states. *American Journal of Psychiatry, 140,* 1437–1442.

Baron, M. G., Groden, J., & Cautela, J. R. (1988). Behavioral programming. In G. Groden & M. G. Baron (Eds.), *Autism: Strategies for change* (pp. 49–73). New York: Gardner Press.

Baron-Cohen, S. (1988). Social and pragmatic deficits in autism: Cognitive or affective? *Journal of Autism and Developmental Disorders, 18,* 379–402.

Barowsky, E. I., Moskowitz, J., & Zweig, J. B. (1990). Biofeedback for disorders of initiating and maintaining sleep. *Annals of the New York Academy of Sciences, 602,* 97–103.

Barrett, R. J. (1985). Behavioral approaches to individual differences in substance abuse: Drug-taking behavior. In M. Galizio & S. Maisto (Eds.), *Determinants of substance abuse treatment: Biological, psychological, and environmental factors* (pp. 125–175). New York: Plenum Press.

Barrett-Lennard, G. T. (1962). Dimensions of therapist response as causal factors in therapeutic change. *Psychological Monographs, 76* (43, Whole No. 562).

Barrios, B. A. (1988). On the changing nature of behavioral assessment. In A. S. Bellack & M. Hersen (Eds.), *Behavioral assessment: A practical handbook* (3rd ed., pp. 3–41). New York: Pergamon.

Barrios, B., & Hartmann, D. P. (1986). The contributions of traditional assessment: Concepts, issues, and methodologies. In R. O. Nelson & S. C. Hayes (Eds.), *Conceptual foundations of behavioral assessment* (pp. 81–110). New York: Guilford Press.

Barrios, B. A., & O'Dell, S. L. (1989). Fears and anxieties. In E. J. Mash & R. A. Barkley (Eds.), *Treatment of childhood disorders.* New York: Guilford Press.

Barsky, A. J., Wyshak, G., & Klerman, G. L. (1990). Transient hypochondriasis. *Archives of General Psychiatry, 47,* 746–752.

Barsky, A. J., Wyshak, G., & Klerman, G. L. (1992). Psychiatric comorbidity in *DSM-III-R* hypochondriasis. *Archives of General Psychiatry, 49,* 101–108.

Barsky, A. J., Cleary, P. D., Wyshak, G., Spitzer, R. L., Williams, J. B. W., & Klerman, G. L. (1992). A structured diagnostic interview for hypochondriasis: A proposed criterion standard. *Journal of Nervous and Mental Disease, 180,* 20–27.

Barth, R. J. & Kinder, B. N. (1987). The mislabeling of sexual impulsivity. *Journal of Sex and Marital Therapy, 13,* 15–23.

Bass, E., & Davis, L. (1988). *The courage to heal: A guide for women survivors of child sexual abuse.* New York: Harper & Row.

Bassett, A. S. (1989). Chromosome 5 and schizophrenia: Implications for genetic linkage studies. *Schizophrenia Bulletin, 15,* 393–402.

Bateson, G. D., Jackson D. D., Haley J., & Weakland J. (1956). Toward a theory of schizophrenia. *Behavioral Science, 1,* 251–264.

Baum, M., & Page, M. (1991). Caregiving and multigenerational families. *The Gerontologist, 31,* 762–769.

Baxter, L. R., Phelps, N. E., Mazziotta, J. C., Guze, B. H., Schwartz, J. M., & Selin, C. E. (1987). Local cerebral glucose metabolic rates in obsessive-compulsive disorder: A comparison with rates in unipolar depression and normal controls. *Archives of General Psychiatry, 44,* 211–218.

Beatrice, J. (1985). A psychological comparison of heterosexuals, transvestites, preoperative transsexuals, and post operative transsexuals. *Journal of Nervous and Mental Disease, 173,* 358–365.

Beck, A. T., Steer, R. A., Kovacs, M., & Garrison, B. (1985). Hopelessness and eventual suicide: A 10-year prospective study of patients hospitalized with suicidal ideation. *American Journal of Psychiatry, 142,* 559–563.

Beck, A. T. (1967). *Depression: Clinical, experimental, and theoretical aspects.* New York: Harper & Row.

Beck, A. T. (1976). *Cognitive therapy and the emotional disorders.* New York: International Universities Press.

Beck, A. T. (1987). *Beck Depression Inventory*. San Antonio, TX: Psychological Corporation.

Beck, A. T. (1991). Cognitive therapy: A 30-year retrospective. *American Psychologist, 46*, 368–375.

Beck, A. T., Emery, G., & Greenberg, R. L. (1985). *Anxiety disorders and phobias: A cognitive perspective.* New York: Basic Books.

Beck, A. T., Freeman, A., and Associates (1990). *Cognitive therapy of personality disorders.* New York: Guilford Press.

Beck, A. T., Rush, A. J., Shaw, B. F., & Emery, G. (1979). *Cognitive therapy of depression: A treatment manual.* New York: Guilford Press.

Beck, A. T., & Weishaar, M. (1989). Cognitive therapy. In A. Freeman, K. M. Simon, L. E. Beutler, & H. Arkowitz (Eds.), *Comprehensive handbook of cognitive therapy* (pp. 21–36). New York: Plenum Press.

Beck, J. C. (1987). The potentially violent patient: Legal duties, clinical practice, and risk management. *Psychiatric Annals, 17*, 695–699.

Becker, J. V., Skinner, L. J., Abel, G. G., & Cichon, J. (1986). Level of postassault sexual functioning in rape and incest victims. *Archives of Sexual Behavior, 15*, 37–49.

Becker, R. E., & Giacobini, E. (1988). Mechanisms of cholinesterase inhibition in senile dementia of the Alzheimer type: Clinical, pharmacological and therapeutic aspects. *Drug Development Research, 12*, 163–195.

Begleiter, H., Porjesz, B., Rawlings, B., & Eckardt, M. (1987). Auditory recovery function and P3 in boys at high risk for alcoholism. *Alcohol, 4*, 315–321.

Behrouz, N., Defossez, A., Delacourte, A., & Mazzuca, M. (1991). The immunohistochemical evidence of amyloid diffuse deposits as a pathological hallmark in Alzheimer's disease. *Journal of Gerontology: Biological Sciences, 46*, B209–212.

Bellack, A. S., Morrison, R. L., & Mueser, K. T. (1989). Social problem solving in schizophrenia. *Schizophrenia Bulletin, 15*, 101–116.

Belsher, G., & Costello, C. G. (1988). Relapse after recovery from unipolar depression: A critical review. *Psychological Bulletin, 104*, 84–96.

Bemporad, J. R. (1985). Long-term analytic treatment of depression. In E. E. Beckham & W. R. Leber (Eds.), *Handbook of depression: Treatment, assessment, and research* (pp. 82–99). Homewood, IL: Dorsey Press.

Bender, L. (1938). *A visual motor Gestalt test and its clinical use* (Research Monograph No. 3). New York: American Orthopsychiatric Association.

Ben-Porath, Y. S., & Butcher, J. N. (1989). Psychometric stability of rewritten MMPI items. *Journal of Personality Assessment, 53*, 645–653.

Benton, A. L. (1974). *The Visual Retention Test: Clinical and experimental applications* (4th ed.). New York: Psychological Corporation.

Benton, R. P., Banks, W. P., & Bolger, R. E. (1982). Carryover of tolerance in alcohol in moderate drinkers. *Journal of Studies on Alcohol, 43*, 1137–1148.

Bergin, A. E., & Jasper, L. G. (1969). Correlates of empathy in psychotherapy: A replication. *Journal of Abnormal Psychology, 74*, 477–481.

Bergin, A. E., & Strupp, H. H. (1972). *Changing frontiers in the science of psychotherapy.* New York: Aldine-Atherton.

Berlin, F. S., & Meinecke, C. F. (1981). Treatment of sex offenders with antiandrogenic medication: Conceptualization, review of treatment modalities, and preliminary findings. *American Journal of Psychiatry, 138*, 601–607.

Berman, A. L. (1987). Adolescent suicide: Clinical consultation. *Clinical Psychologist, 40*, 87–90.

Bernay, T., & Cantor, D. W., (Eds.), (1986). *The psychology of today's women: New psychoanalytic visions.* Hillsdale, NJ: Analytic Press.

Bernheim, K. F., Lewine, R. R. J., & Beale, C. T. (1982). *The caring family: Living with chronic mental illness.* New York: Random House.

Berry, C. A., Shaywitz, S. E., & Shaywitz, B. A. (1985). Girls with attention deficit disorder: A silent minority? A report on behavioral and cognitive characteristics. *Pediatrics, 76*, 801–809.

Bettelheim, B. (1967). *The empty fortress.* New York: Free Press.

Bibring, E. (1965). The mechanism of depression. In P. Greenacre (Ed.), *Affective disorders* (pp. 13–48). New York: International Universities Press.

Biederman, J., Munir, K., Knee, D., Armentano, M., Autor, S., Waternaux, C., & Tsuang, M. (1987). High rate of affective disorders in probands with attention deficit disorders and in their relatives: A controlled family study. *American Journal of Psychiatry, 144*, 330–333.

Biederman, J., Newcorn, J., & Sprich, S. (1991). Comorbidity of attention deficit hyperactivity disorder with conduct, depressive, anxiety, and other disorders. *American Journal of Psychiatry, 148*, 564–577.

Bissette, G., Smith, W. H., Dole, K. C., Crain, B., Ghanbari, H., Miller, B., & Nemeroff, C. B. (1991). Alterations in Alzheimer's disease-associated protein in Alzheimer's disease frontal and temporal cortex. *Archives of General Psychiatry, 48*, 1009–1012.

Blanchard, E. B. (1987). Long-term effects of behavioral treatment of chronic headache. *Behavior Therapy, 18*, 375–385.

Bland, R. C., Newman, S. C., & Orn, H. (1986). Recurrent and nonrecurrent depression: A family study. *Archives of General Psychiatry, 43*, 1085–1089.

Blashfield R. K. (1984). Diagnostic reliability. In R. K. Blashfield (Ed.), *The classification of psychopathology: Neo-Kraepelinian and quantitative approaches* (pp. 84–109). New York: Plenum Press.

Blaszczynski, A. P., Wilson, A. C., & McConaghy, N. (1986). Sensation seeking and pathological gambling. *British Journal of Addiction, 81*, 113–117.

Blazer, D., Hughes, D. C., & George, L. K. (1987a). The epidemiology of depression in an elderly community population. *The Gerontologist, 27*, 281–287.

Blazer, D., Hughes, D. C., & George, L. K. (1987b). Stressful life events and the onset of a generalized anxiety syndrome. *American Journal of Psychiatry, 144*, 1178–1183.

Blazer, D., Schwartz, M., Woodbury, M., Manton, K. G., Hughes, D., & George, L. K. (1988). Depressive symptoms and depressive diagnoses in a community population. *Archives of General Psychiatry, 45*, 1078–1084.

Blazer, D., & Williams, C. D. (1980). Epidemiology of dysphoria and depression in an elderly population. *American Journal of Psychiatry, 137*, 439–444.

Blazer, D., Hughes, D. C., & George, L. K. (1992). Age and impaired subjective support: Predictors of depressive symptoms at one-year follow-up. *Journal of Nervous and Mental Disease, 180*, 172–178.

Bleuler, E. (1911). *Dementia praecox oder gruppe der schizophrenien. [Dementia praecox or the group of schizophrenias].* Leipzig: F. Deuticke.

Bleuler, M. (1978). *The schizophrenic disorders: Long-term patient and family studies* (S. M. Clemens, Trans.). New Haven: Yale University Press.

Bliss, E. L. (1980). Multiple personalities: A report of 14 cases with implications for schizophrenia and hysteria. *Archives of General Psychiatry, 37*, 1388–1397.

Blomhoff, S., Seim, S., & Friis, S. (1990). Can prediction of violence among psychiatric inpatients be improved? *Hospital and Community Psychiatry, 41*, 771–775.

Blos, P. (1967). The second individuation of adolescence. *The Psychoanalytic Study of the Child, 22*, 162–186.

Blum, K., Noble, E. P., Sheridan, P. J., Montgomery, A., Ritchie, T., Jagadeeswaran, P., Nogami, H., Briggs, A. H., & Cohn, J. B.

(1990). Allelic association of human dopamine D$_2$ receptor gene in alcoholism. *Journal of the American Medical Association, 263,* 2055–2060.

Bolos, A. M., Dean, M., Lucas-Derse, S., Ramsburg, M., Brown, G. L., & Goldman, D. (1990). Population and pedigree studies reveal a lack of association between the dopamine D$_2$ receptor gene and alcoholism. *Journal of the American Medical Association, 264,* 3156–3160.

Boor, M. (1982). The multiple personality epidemic: Additional cases and inferences regarding diagnosis, etiology, dynamics, and treatment. *Journal of Nervous and Mental Disease, 170,* 302–304.

Borg, V. (1983). Bromocriptine in the prevention of alcohol abuse. *Acta Psychiatrica Scandinavica, 68,* 100–110.

Bornstein, R. F. (1990). Critical importance of stimulus unawareness for the production of subliminal psychodynamic activation effects: A meta-analytic review. *Journal of Clinical Psychology, 46,* 201–210.

Bornstein, R. F., & Greenberg, R. P. (1991). Dependency and eating disorders in female psychiatric patients. *Journal of Nervous and Mental Disease, 179,* 148–152.

Boscarino, J. (1980). A national survey of alcoholism treatment centers in the United States: A preliminary report. *American Journal of Drug and Alcohol Abuse, 7,* 403–413.

Boston Globe, Dec. 1, 1986. Court test gets underway today for aversive therapy. p. 53.

Bourget, D., & Bradford, J. (1987). Fire fetishism, diagnostic and clinical implications: A review of two cases. *Canadian Journal of Psychiatry, 32,* 459–462.

Bourne, P. G. (1970). *Men, stress, and Vietnam.* Boston: Little, Brown.

Bowlby, J. (1980). *Attachment and loss: Volume III: Loss: Sadness and depression.* New York: Basic Books.

Boyer, J. L., & Guthrie, L. (1985). Assessment and treatment of the suicidal patient. In E. E. Beckham & W. R. Leber (Eds.), *Handbook of depression: Treatment, assessment, and research* (pp. 606–633). Homewood, IL: Dorsey Press.

Bradford, J., & Balmaceda, R. (1983). Shoplifting: Is there a specific psychiatric syndrome? *Canadian Journal of Psychiatry, 28,* 248–254.

Bradley, A. M. (1988). Keep coming back: The case for a valuation of Alcoholics Anonymous. *Alcohol Health and Research World, 12,* 192–199.

Brady, K. T., Lydiard, R. B., Malcolm, R., & Ballenger, J. C. (1991). Cocaine-induced psychosis. *Journal of Clinical Psychiatry, 52,* 509–512.

Braun, B. G. (1985). The transgenerational incidence of dissociation and multiple personality disorder: A preliminary report. In R. P. Kluft (Ed.), *Childhood antecedents of multiple personality disorder* (pp. 167–196). Washington, DC: American Psychiatric Press.

Braunthal, H. (1981). Working with transsexuals. *International Journal of Social Psychiatry, 27,* 3–11.

Bregman, J. D., Dykens, E., Watson, M., Ort, S. I., & Leckman, J. F. (1987). Fragile X syndrome: Variability of phenotypic expression. *Journal of the American Academy of Child and Adolescent Psychiatry, 26,* 463–471.

Breier, A., Schreiber, J. L., Dyer, J., & Pickar, D. (1991). National Institute of Mental Health longitudinal study of chronic schizophrenia: Prognosis and predictors of outcome. *Archives of General Psychiatry, 48,* 239–246.

Breitner, J. C. S., Folstein, M. F., & Murphy, E. A. (1986a). Familial aggregation in Alzheimer dementia: I. A model for the age-dependent expression of an autosomal dominant gene. *Journal of Psychiatric Research, 20,* 31–43.

Breitner, J. C. S., Murphy, E. A., & Folstein, M. F. (1986b). Familial aggregation in Alzheimer dementia: II. Clinical genetic implications of age-dependent onset. *Journal of Psychiatric Research, 20,* 45–55.

Bremner, J. D., Southwick, S., Brett, E., Fontana, A., Rosenheck, R., & Charney, D. S. (1992). Dissociation and posttraumatic stress disorder in Vietnam combat veterans. *American Journal of Psychiatry, 149,* 328–332.

Brennan, P. F., Moore, S. M., & Smyth, K. A . (1991). Computer-Link: Electronic support for the home caregiver. *Advances in Nursing Science, 13,* 14–27.

Brent, D. A., Perper, J. A., Goldstein, C. E., Kolko, D. J., Allan, M. J., Allman, C. J., & Zelenak, J. P. (1988). Risk factors for adolescent suicide. *Archives of General Psychiatry, 45,* 581–588.

Breslau, N., & Davis, G. C. (1989). Chronic posttraumatic stress disorder in Vietnam veterans. *Harvard Mental Health Letter, 5,* 3–5.

Breslow, N., Evans, L., & Langley, J. (1985). On the prevalence and roles of females in the sadomasochistic subculture: Report of an empirical study. *Archives of Sexual Behavior, 14,* 303–317.

Breuer, A., & Freud, S. (1985/1982). *Studies in hysteria.* (J. Strachey, Ed. and Trans., with the collaboration of A. Freud). New York: Basic Books.

Brick, S. S., & Chu, J. A. (1991). The simulation of multiple personalities: A case report. *Psychotherapy, 28,* 267–272.

Brickman, P., Rabinowitz, V. C., Karuza, J., Coates, D., Cohn, E., & Kidder, L. (1982). Models of helping and coping. *American Psychologist, 37,* 368–384.

Briddell, D. W., & Wilson, G. T. (1976). Effects of alcohol and expectancy set on male sexual arousal. *Journal of Abnormal Psychology, 85,* 225–234.

Bright, R. A. & Everitt, D. E. (1992). ß-blockers and depression: Evidence against an association. *Journal of the American Medical Association, 267,* 1783–1787.

Brotman, A. W., Alonso, A., & Herzog, D. B. (1985). Group therapy for bulimia: Clinical experience and practical recommendations. *Group, 9,* 15–23.

Brown, F. R., III, & Aylward, E. H. (1987). *Diagnosis and management of learning disabilities: An interdisciplinary approach.* Boston: College Hill Press.

Brown, G. L., Goodwin, F. K., & Bunney, W. E. (1982). Human aggression and suicide: Their relationship to neuropsychiatric diagnoses and serotonin metabolism. In B. T. Ho, J. C. Schoolar, & E. Usdin (Eds.), *Serotonin in biological psychiatry: Advances in biochemical psychopharmacology* (Vol. 34, pp. 287–304). New York: Raven Press.

Brown, G. W., Birley, J. L. T., & Wing, J. K. (1972). Influence of family life on the course of schizophrenic disorders: A replication. *British Journal of Psychiatry, 121,* 241–258.

Brown, R. T., & Borden, K. A. (1986). Hyperactivity at adolescence: Some misconceptions and new directions. *Journal of Clinical Child Psychology, 15,* 194–209.

Browne, A., & Finkelhor, D. (1986). Impact of child sexual abuse: A review of the research. *Psychological Bulletin, 99,* 66–77.

Bruce, M. L., Kim, K., Leaf, P. J., & Jacobs, S. (1991). Depressive episodes and dysphoria resulting from conjugal bereavement in a prospective community sample. *Americal Journal of Psychiatry, 147,* 608–611.

Bruch, H. (1982). Anorexia nervosa: Therapy and theory. *American Journal of Psychiatry, 139,* 1531–1538.

Buchsbaum, M. S. (1990). The frontal lobes, basal ganglia, and temporal lobes as sites for schizophrenia. *Schizophrenia Bulletin, 16,* 379–389.

Budinger, T. F. (1987). New technologies for noninvasive imaging in aging and dementia. In G. G. Glenner & R. J. Wurtman (Eds.), *Advancing frontiers in Alzheimer's disease research* (pp. 175–199). Austin: University of Texas Press.

Buie, D., & Adler, G. (1982). The definitive treatment of the borderline personality. *International Journal of Psychoanalysis, 9,* 51–87.

Buikhuisen, W. (1987). Cerebral dysfunctions and persistent juvenile delinquency. In S. A. Mednick, T. E. Moffitt, & S. A. Stack (Eds.), *The causes of crime: New biological approaches* (pp. 168–184). Cambridge: Cambridge University Press.

Bumpass, E. (1989). Pyromania. In T. B. Karasu (Ed.), *Treatment of psychiatric disorders* (pp. 2468–2473). Washington, DC: American Psychiatric Association.

Burgess, A. W., Hartman, C. R., McCausland, M. P., & Powers, P. (1984). Response patterns in children and adolescents exploited through sex rings and pornography. *American Journal of Psychiatry, 141*, 656–662.

Burton, L. C., German, P. S., Rovner, B. W., Brant, L. J., & Clark, R. D. (1992). Mental illness and the use of restraints in nursing homes. *The Gerontologist, 32*, 164–170.

Buss, A. H. (1966). *Psychopathology*. New York: Wiley.

Butcher, J. N. (Ed.). (1987). *Computerized psychological assessment: A practitioner's guide*. New York: Basic Books.

Butcher, J. N. (1990). *MMPI-2 in psychological treatment*. New York: Oxford University Press.

Butcher, J. N., Graham, J. R., Dahlstrom, W. G., & Bowman, E. (1990). The MMPI-2 with college students. *Journal of Personality Assessment, 54*, 1–15.

Butler, G., Cullington, A., Munby, M., Amies, P., & Gelder, M. (1984). Exposure and anxiety management in the treatment of social phobia. *Journal of Consulting and Clinical Psychology, 52*, 642–650.

Butler, G., Fennell, M., Robson, P., & Gelder, M. (1991). Comparison of behavior therapy and cognitive behavior therapy in the treatment of generalized anxiety disorder. *Journal of Consulting and Clinical Psychology, 59*, 167–175.

Butterfield, F. (1985, November 19). School's use of physical punishment as therapy is challenged. *New York Times*, p. A20.

Caddy, G. P. (1985). Cognitive behavior therapy in the treatment of multiple personality. *Behavior Modification, 9*, 267–292.

Caine, E. D. (1981). Pseudodementia. *Archives of General Psychiatry, 38*, 1359–1364.

Caine, E. D., & Shoulson, I. (1983). Psychiatric syndromes in Huntington's disease. *American Journal of Psychiatry, 140*, 728–733.

Calev, A., Nigal, D., Shapira, B., Tubi, N., Chazan, S., Beh-Yehuda, Y., Kugelmass, S., & Leher, B. (1991). Early and long-term effects of electroconvulsive therapy and depression on memory and other cognitive functions. *Journal of Nervous and Mental Disease, 179*, 526–533.

Cannon, D. S., Baker, T. B., Gino, A., & Nathan, P. E. (1988). Alcohol aversion therapy: Relationship between strength of aversion and abstinence. In T. B. Baker & D. Cannon (Eds.), *Assessment and treatment of addictive disorders* (pp. 205–237). New York: Praeger Press.

Cantor, S. (1988). *Childhood schizophrenia*. New York: Guilford Press.

Caplan, L. (1984). *The insanity defense and the trial of John W. Hinkley, Jr.* Boston: David R. Godin.

Carey, G. (1992). Twin imitation for antisocial behavior: Implications for genetic and family environment research. *Journal of Abnormal Psychology, 101*, 18–25.

Carlat, D. J., & Camargo, C. A. (1991). Review of bulimia nervosa in males. *American Journal of Psychiatry, 148*, 831–843.

Carlson, C. R., White, D. K., & Turkat, I. D. (1982). Night terrors: A clinical and empirical review. *Clinical Psychology Review, 2*, 455–468.

Carlson, G. A., & Cantwell, D. P. (1980). Unmasking masked depression in children and adolescents. *American Journal of Psychiatry, 137*, 445–449.

Carlson, G. A., & Cantwell, D. P. (1982). Suicidal behavior and depression in children and adolescents. *Journal of the American Academy of Child Psychiatry, 21*, 361–368.

Carlsson, A. (1988). The current status of the dopamine hypothesis of schizophrenia. *Neuropsychopharmacology, 1*, 179–186.

Carnes, P. (1983). *Out of the shadows: Understanding sexual addiction*. Minneapolis: Compcare Publications.

Carone, B. J., Harrow, M., & Westermeyer, J. F. (1991). Posthospital course and outcome in schizophrenia. *Archives of General Psychiatry, 48*, 247–253.

Carpenter, W. T. (1987). Approaches to knowledge and understanding of schizophrenia. *Schizophrenia Bulletin, 13*, 1–7.

Carpenter, W. T., Heinrichs, D. W., & Wagman, A. M. I. (1988). Deficit and nondeficit forms of schizophrenia: The concept. *American Journal of Psychiatry, 145*, 578–583.

Carpenter, W. T., & Strauss, J. S. (1991). The prediction of outcome in schizophrenia IV: Eleven-year follow-up of the Washington IPSS cohort. *Journal of Nervous and Mental Disease, 179*, 517–525.

Carr, D. B., & Sheehan, D. V. (1984). Panic anxiety: A new biological model. *Journal of Clinical Psychiatry, 45*, 323–330.

Carroll, B. J. (1982). The dexamethasone suppression test for melancholia. *British Journal of Psychiatry, 140*, 292–304.

Casey, R. J., & Berman, J. S. (1985). The outcome of psychotherapy with children. *Psychological Bulletin, 98*, 388–400.

Caspi, A., Elder, G. H., Jr., & Bem, D. J. (1987). Moving against the world: Life-course patterns of explosive children. *Developmental Psychology, 23*, 308–313.

Caspi, A., Elder, G. H., Jr., & Bem, D. J. (1988). Moving away from the world: Life-course patterns of shy children. *Developmental Psychology, 24*, 824–831.

Cassano, G. B., Maggini, C., & Akiskal, H. S. (1983). Short-term subchronic and chronic sequelae of affective disorders. *Psychiatric Clinics of North America, 6*, 55–57.

Cattell, R. B., & IPAT Staff (1986). *The 16 personality factor questionnaire*. Palo Alto, CA: IPAT.

Centers for Disease Control (1985). *Suicide surveillance 1970–1980*. Atlanta: U.S. Department of Health and Human Services, Public Health Service, Violent Epidemiology Branch, Center for Health Promotion and Education.

Chabrol, H., & Moron, P. (1988). Depressive disorders in 100 adolescents who attempted suicide. *American Journal of Psychiatry, 145*, 379.

Chalfant, J. C. (1989). Learning disabilities: Policy issues and promising approaches. *American Psychologist, 44*, 392–398.

Chalkley, A. J., & Powell, G. (1983). The clinical description of forty-eight cases of sexual fetishism. *British Journal of Psychiatry, 142*, 292–295.

Chamberlin, J. (1978). *On our own*. New York: Hawthorn Books.

Chambless, D. L., & Goldstein, A. J. (Eds.). (1982). *Agoraphobia: Multiple perspectives on theory and treatment*. New York: Wiley.

Chapman, A. H. (1976). *Harry Stack Sullivan: The man and his work*. New York: Putnam.

Charney, D. S., Woods, S. W., Nagy, L. M., Southwick, S. M., Krystal, J. H., & Heninger, G. R. (1990). Noradrenergic function in panic disorder. *Journal of Clinical Psychiatry, 51*(12, Suppl. A.), 5–11.

Chatellier, G., & Lacomblez, L. (1990). Tacrine and lecithin in senile dementia of the Alzheimer type: A multicentre trial. *British Journal of Medicine, 300*, 495–499.

Chavez, G. F., Cordero, J. F., & Becerra, J. E. (1989). Leading major congenital malformations among minority groups in the United States, 1981–1986. *Journal of the American Medical Association, 261*, 205–209.

Chenoweth, B., & Spencer, B. (1986). Dementia: The experience of family caregivers. *The Gerontologist, 30*, 267–272.

Chessick, R. (1982). Intensive psychotherapy of a borderline patient. *Archives of General Psychiatry, 39*, 413–419.

Chiles, J. A., Strosahl, K. D., McMurtray, L., & Linehan, M. M. (1985). Modeling effects on suicidal behavior. *Journal of Nervous and Mental Disease, 173*, 477–481.

Chin, J. H., & Goldstein, D. B. (1977). Drug tolerance in bio-membranes: A spin label study of the effects of ethanol. *Science, 196*, 684–685.

Chiocca, E. A., & Martuza, R. L. (1990). Neurosurgical therapy of the patient with obsessive-compulsive disorder. In M. A. Jenike, L. Baer, & W. E. Minichiello (Eds.), *Obsessive compulsive disorders: Theory and management* (2nd ed.). Chicago: Yearbook Medical Publishers.

Chodorow, N. (1978). *The reproduction of mothering.* Berkeley: University of California Press.

Christiansen, B. A., Smith, G. T., Roehling, P. V., & Goldman, M. S. (1989). Using alcohol expectancies to predict adolescent drinking behavior after one year. *Journal of Consulting and Clinical Psychology, 57*, 93–99.

Christenson, G. A., Popkin, M. K., Mackenzie, T. B., & Realmuto, G. M. (1991). Lithium treatment of chronic hair pulling. *Journal of Clinical Psychiatry, 52*, 116–120.

Christiansen, K. O. (1977a). A review of studies of criminality among twins. In S. A. Mednick & K. O. Christiansen (Eds.), *Biosocial bases of criminal behavior* (pp. 45–88). New York: Gardner Press.

Christiansen, K. O. (1977b). A preliminary study of criminality among twins. In S. A. Mednick & K. O. Christiansen (Eds.), *Biosocial bases of criminal behavior* (pp. 89–108). New York: Gardner Press.

Chui, H. C. (1989). Dementia: A review emphasizing clinico-pathologic correlation and brain-behavior relationships. *Archives of Neurology, 46*, 806–814.

Claghorn, J., Honigfeld, G., Abuzzahab, F. S., Wans, R., Steinbook, R., Tuason, V., & Klerman, G. (1987). The risks and benefits of clozapine versus chlorpromazine. *Journal of Clinical Psychopharmacology, 7*, 377–384.

Clark, D. B., (1989). Performance-related medical and psychological disorders in instrumental musicians. *Annals of Behavioral Medicine, 11*, 28–34.

Clark, D. B., & Agras, W. S. (1991). The assessment and treatment of performance anxiety in musicians. *American Journal of Psychiatry, 148*, 598–605.

Clark, L. A., & Watson, D. (1991). Tripartite model of anxiety and depression: Psychometric evidence and taxonomic implications. *Journal of Abnormal Psychology, 100*, 316–336.

Clarke, A. M., & Clarke, A. D. (1988). The adult outcome of early behavioural abnormalities. *International Journal of Behavioral Development, 11*, 3–19.

Cleckley, H. M. (1976). *The mask of sanity* (5th ed.). St. Louis: Mosby.

Clementz, B. A., Grove, W. M., Iacono, W. G., & Sweeney, J. A. (1992). Smooth-pursuit eye movement dysfunction and liability for schizophrenia: Implications for genetic modeling. *Journal of Abnormal Psychology, 101*, 117–129.

Cloninger, C. R. (1987). Neurogenic adaptive mechanisms in alcoholism. *Science, 236*, 410–416.

Cloninger, C. R., Bohman, M., & Sigvardsson, S. (1981). Inheritance of alcohol abuse. *Archives of General Psychiatry, 38*, 861–868.

Cohen, G. D. (1988). *The brain in human aging.* New York: Springer.

Cohen, L. S. (1988). *Life events and psychological functioning: Theoretical and methodological issues.* Newbury Park, CA: Sage.

Cohen, S. (1984). The hallucinogens and the inhalants. *Psychiatric Clinics of North America, 7*, 681–688.

Cohen, S., & Edwards, J. R. (1989). Personality characteristics as moderators of the relationship between stress and disorder. In R. W. J. Neufeld (Ed.), *Advances in the investigation of psychological stress* (pp. 235–283). New York: Wiley.

Cohen, S., & Williamson, G. M. (1991). Stress and infectious disease in humans. *Psychological Bulletin, 109*, 5–24.

Cohen, S., & Wills, T. A. (1985). Stress, social support, and the buffering hypothesis. *Psychological Bulletin, 98*, 310–357.

Colby, K. M. (1981). Modeling a paranoid mind. *The Behavioral and Brain Sciences, 4*, 515–560.

Cole, J. O., Goldberg, S. C., & Klerman, G. L. (1964). Phenothiazine treatment in acute schizophrenia. *Archives of General Psychiatry, 10*, 246–261.

Cole, N. J. (1985). Sex therapy—A critical appraisal. *British Journal of Psychiatry, 147*, 337–351.

Coleman, E. (1987). Sexual compulsivity: Definition, etiology, and treatment considerations. *Journal of Chemical Dependency Treatment, 1*, 189–204.

Collins, J. J., (1989). Alcohol and interpersonal violence: Less than meets the eye. In N. A. Weiner & M. E. Wolfgang (Eds.), *Pathways to criminal violence* (pp. 49–67). Newbury Park, CA: Sage.

Collins, J. J., Jr. (1981). Alcohol use and criminal behavior: An empirical, theoretical, and methodological overview. In J. J. Collins, Jr. (Ed.), *Drinking and crime: Perspectives on the relationships between alcohol consumption and criminal behavior* (pp. 288–316). New York: Guilford Press.

Comings, D. E., Comings, B. G., Muhleman, D., Dietz, G., Shahbahrami, B., Tast, D., Knell, E., Kocsis, P., Baumgarten, R., Kovacs, B. W., Levy, D. L., Smith, M., Borison, R. L., Evans, D. D., Klein, D. N., MacMurray, J., Tosk, J. M., Sverd, J., Bysin, R., & Flanagan, S. D. (1991). The dopamine D2 receptor locus as a modifying gene in neuropsychiatric disorders. *Journal of the American Medical Association, 266*, 1793–1800.

Coons, P. M. (1980). Multiple personality: Diagnostic considerations. *Journal of Clinical Psychiatry, 41*, 330–336.

Coons, P. M., Bowman, E. S., Pellow, T. A., & Schneider, P. (1989). Post-traumatic aspects of the treatment of victims of sexual abuse and incest. *Psychiatric Clinics of North America, 12*, 325–335.

Cooper, A. J. (1987). Sadistic homosexual pedophilia treatment with cyproterone acetate. *Canadian Journal of Psychiatry, 32*, 738–740.

Cooper, J. E., Kendell, R. E., Gurland, B. J., Sharpe, L., Copeland, J. R. M., & Simon, R. (1972). *Psychiatric diagnoses in New York and London.* New York: Oxford University Press.

Cooper, M. L., Russell, M., Skinner, J. B., Frone, M. R., & Mudar, P. (1992). Stress and alcohol use: Moderating effects of gender, coping, and alcohol expectancies. *Journal of Abnormal Psychology, 101*, 139–152.

Corcoran, K. & Fischer, J. (1987). *Measures for clinical practice: A source book.* New York: Free Press.

Coryell, W., Endicott, J., & Keller, M. (1992a). Major depression in a nonclinical sample: Demographic and clinical risk factors for first onset. *Archives of General Psychiatry, 49*, 117–125.

Coryell, W., Endicott, J., & Keller, M. (1992b). Rapidly cycling affective disorder: Demographics, diagnosis, family history, and course. *Archives of General Psychiatry, 49*, 126–131.

Costa, P. T., Jr., & McCrae, R. R. (1985). *The NEO-PI.* Odessa, FL: Psychological Assessment Resources.

Cotton, N. S. (1979). The familial incidence of alcoholism: A review. *Journal of Studies on Alcohol, 40*, 89–116.

Courchesne, E., Yeung-Courchesne, R., Press, G. A., Hesselink, J. R., & Jernigan, T. L. (1988). Hypoplasia of cerebellar vermal lobules VI and VII in autism. *New England Journal of Medicine, 318*, 1349–1354.

Coyle, J. T., Price, D. L., & DeLong, M. R. (1983). Alzheimer's disease: A disorder of cortical cholinergic innervation. *Science, 219*, 1184–1190.

Coyne, A. C. (1991). Information and referral service usage among caregivers for dementia patients. *The Gerontologist, 31*, 384–388.

Coyne, A. C., Meade, H. M., Petrone, M. E., Meinert, L. A., & Joslin, B. L. (1990). The diagnosis of dementia: Demographic characteristics. *The Gerontologist, 30*, 339–344.

Coyne, J. C. (1976). Depression and the response of others. *Journal of Abnormal Psychology, 85*, 186–193.

Coyne, J. C., & Gotlib, I. H. (1983). The role of cognition in depression: A critical appraisal. *Psychological Bulletin, 94*, 472–505.

Cozolino, L. J. (1989). The ritual abuse of children: Implications for clinical practice and research. *Journal of Sex Research, 26*, 131–138.

Craske, M. G. (1991). Phobic fear and panic attacks: The same emotional states triggered by different cues? *Clinical Psychology Review, 11*, 599–620.

Crenshaw, T. L., & Goldberg, J. P. (1989). Drug therapy. In T. S. Karasu (Ed.), *Treatment of psychiatric disorders* (Vol. 3, pp. 2343–2359). Washington, DC: American Psychiatric Association.

Critchlow, B. (1986). The powers of John Barleycorn: Beliefs about the effects of alcohol on social behavior. *American Psychologist, 41*, 751–764.

Crits-Cristoph, P. (1992). The efficacy of brief dynamic psychotherapy: A meta-analysis. *American Journal of Psychiatry, 149*, 151–158.

Crnic, K. A., & Reid, M. (1989). Mental retardation. In E. J. Mash & R. A. Barkley (Eds.), *Treatment of Childhood Disorders* (pp. 247–285). New York: Guilford Press.

Crook, T., & Eliot, J. (1980). Parental death during childhood and adult depression: A critical review of the literature. *Psychological Bulletin, 87*, 252–259.

Crossley, T., & Guzman, R. (1985). The relationship between arson and pyromania. *American Journal of Forensic Psychiatry, 3*, 39–44.

Croughan, J. L., Saghir, M., Cohen, R., & Robins, E. (1981). A comparison of treated and untreated male cross-dressers. *Archives of Sexual Behavior, 10*, 515–528.

Crow, T. J. (1980). Molecular pathology of schizophrenia: More than one disease process? *British Medical Journal, 280*, 66–68.

Crow, T. J. (1985). The two-syndrome concept: Origins and current status. *Schizophrenia Bulletin, 11*, 471–486.

Crow, T. J. (1990). Temporal lobe asymmetries as the key to the etiology of schizophrenia. *Schizophrenia Bulletin, 16*, 433–443.

Curran, D. K. (1987). *Adolescent suicidal behavior*. Washington, DC: Hemisphere.

Custer, R. L. (1982). An overview of compulsive gambling. In S. Kieffer (Ed.), *Addictive Disorders Update*. New York: Human Sciences Press.

Damasio, A. R. (1992). Aphasia. *New England Journal of Medicine, 326*, 531–539.

Danforth, J. S., Barkley, R. A., & Stokes, T. F. (1991). Observations of parent-child interactions with hyperactive children: Research and clinical implications. *Clinical Psychology Review, 11*, 703–727.

Davidson, J. R. T. (1990). Continuation treatment of panic disorder with high-potency benzodiazepines. *Journal of Clinical Psychiatry, 51*(12, Suppl. A), 31–37.

Davidson, J. R. T., & Foa, E. B. (1991). Diagnostic issues in posttraumatic stress disorder: Considerations for the *DSM-IV*. *Journal of Abnormal Psychology, 100*, 346–355.

Davidson, J. R. T., Ford, S. M., Smith, R. D., & Potts, N. L. S. (1991). Long-term treatment of social phobia with clonazepam. *Journal of Clinical Psychiatry, 52*(11, Suppl.), 16–20.

Davis, K. L., Kahn, R. S., Ko, G., & Davidson, M. (1991). Dopamine in schizophrenia: A review and reconceptualization. *American Journal of Psychiatry, 148*, 1474–1486.

Davison, G. C. (1968). Elimination of a sadistic fantasy by a client-controlled counter-conditioning technique: A case study. *Journal of Abnormal Psychology, 73*, 84–90.

Deadwyler, S. A., Heyser, C. J., Michaelis, R. C., & Hampson, R. E. (1990). The effects of delta-9-THC on mechanisms of learning and memory. In *Neurobiology of drug abuse: Learning and memory* (NIDA Research Monograph Series 97, pp. 79–93). (DHHS Publication No. ADM 90-1677). Washington, DC: U.S. Government Printing Office.

DeAngelis, T. (1989, January). Mania, depression and genius. *APA Monitor*, pp. 1, 24.

Dear, M. J., & Wolch, J. R. (1987). *Landscapes of despair: From deinstitutionalization to homelessness*. Cambridge: Polity Press.

deGruy, F., Crider, J., Hashimi, D. K., Dickinson, P., Mullins, H. C., & Troncale, J. (1987). Somatization disorder in a university hospital. *Journal of Family Practice, 25*, 579–584.

DeLeon, G. (1985). The therapeutic community: Status and evolution. *International Journal of the Addictions, 20*, 823–844.

DeLeon, G., & Schwartz, S. (1984). Therapeutic communities: What are the retention rates? *American Journal of Drug and Alcohol Abuse, 10*, 267–284.

DeLisi, L. E., Hoff, A. L., Schwartz, J. E., Shields, G. W., Halthore, S. N., Gupta, S. M., Henn, F. A., & Anand, A. (1991). Brain morphology in first-episode schizophrenic-like psychotic patients: A quantitative magnetic resonance imaging study. *Biological Psychiatry, 29*, 159–175.

Dell, L. J., Ruzicka, M. F., & Palisi, A. T. (1981). Personality and other factors associated with the gambling addiction. *International Journal of the Addictions, 16*, 149–156.

DeLongis, A., Folkman, S., & Lazarus, R. S. (1988). The impact of daily stress on health and mood: Psychological and social resources as mediators. *Journal of Personality and Social Psychology, 54*, 486–495.

Deniker, P. (1970). Introduction of neuroleptic chemotherapy in psychiatry. In F. Ayd & B. Blackwell (Eds.), *Discoveries in biological psychiatry*. Philadelphia: Lippincott.

DeRogatis, L. (1975). *Symptom Check List-90-Revised*. Towson, MD.: Clinical Psychometric Research.

Derry, P. A., & Kuiper, N. A. (1981). Schematic processing and self-reference in clinical depression. *Journal of Abnormal Psychology, 90*, 286–297.

Deutsch, A. (1949). *The mentally ill in America* (2nd ed.). New York: Columbia University Press.

Devinsky, O., Putnam, F., Grafman, J., Bromfield, E., & Theodore, W. H. (1989). Dissociative states and epilepsy. *Neurology, 39*(6), 835–840.

Devor, E. J., & Cloninger, C. R. (1989). Genetics of alcoholism. *Annual Review of Genetics, 23*, 19–36.

Dickerson, M., & Adcock, S. (1987). Mood, arousal, and cognitions in persistent gambling: Preliminary investigation of a theoretical model. *Journal of Gambling Behavior, 3*, 3–15.

Dinnerstein, D. (1976). *The mermaid and the minotaur: Sexual arrangements and human malaise*. New York: Harper.

Dobson, K. S. (1989). A meta-analysis of the efficacy of cognitive therapy for depression. *Journal of Consulting and Clinical Psychology, 57*, 414–419.

Dole, V. P., & Nyswander, M. E. (1967). Rehabilitation of the street addict. *Archives of Environmental Health, 14*, 477–480.

Domino, E. F. (1981). Cannabinoids and the cholinergic system. *Journal of Clinical Pharmacology, 21*, 249S–255S.

Donovan, D. M. (1988). Assessment of addictive behaviors: Implications of an emerging biopsychosocial model. In D. M. Donovan & G. A. Marlatt (Eds.), *Assessment of addictive behaviors* (pp. 3–48). New York: Guilford Press.

Dulz, B., & Hand, I. (1986). Short-term relapse in young schizophrenics: Can it be predicted and affected by family (CFI), patient and treatment variables? In M. J. Goldstein, I. Hand, & K. Hahlweg (Eds.), *Treatment of schizophrenia* (pp. 59–75). New York: Springer-Verlag.

Dunn, G. E. (1992). Multiple personality disorder: A new challenge for psychology. *Professional Psychology: Research and Practice, 23*, 18–23.

Dunner, D. L. (1979). Rapid cycling bipolar manic depressive illness. *Psychiatric Clinics of North America, 2,* 461–467.

DuPaul, G. J., Guevremont, D. C., & Barkley, R. A. (1991). Attention deficit-hyperactivity disorder in adolescence: Critical assessment parameters. *Clinical Psychology Review, 11,* 231–245.

Dura, J. R., Stukenberg, K. W., & Kiecolt-Glaser, J. K. (1991). Anxiety and depressive disorders in adult children caring for demented parents. *Psychology and Aging, 6,* 467–473.

Durkheim, E. (1897/1952). *Suicide: A study in sociology* (J. A. Spaulding & C. Simpson, Trans.). London: Routledge and Kegan Paul.

du Verglas, G. B., Banks, S. R., & Guyer, K. E. (1988). Clinical effects of fenfluramine on children with autism: A review of the research. *Journal of Autism and Developmental Disorders, 18,* 297–308.

Eagle, M. N. (1984). *Recent developments in psychoanalysis.* New York: McGraw-Hill.

Eaton, W. W., Dryman, A., Sorenson, A., & McCutcheon, A. (1989). *DSM-III* major depressive disorder in the community: A latent class analysis of data from the NIMH Epidemiologic Catchment Area Programme. *British Journal of Psychiatry, 155,* 48–54.

Edell, W. S. (1987). Relationship of borderline syndrome disorders to early schizophrenia on the MMPI. *Journal of Clinical Psychology, 43,* 163–176.

Edwards, G. (1983). Psychopathology of a drug experience. *British Journal of Psychiatry, 143,* 509–512.

Egeland, J. A., Gerhard, D. A., Pauls, D. L., Sussex, J. N., Kidd, K. K., Allen, C. R., Hostetter, A. M., & Housman, D. E. (1987). Bipolar affective disorders linked to DNA markers on chromosome 11. *Nature, 325,* 783–787.

Ehrhardt, A. A., & Baker, S. W. (1974). Fetal androgens, human central nervous systems differentiation, and behavior sex differences. In R. C. Friedman, R. M. Richart, & R. L. VandeWiele (Eds.), *Sex differences in behavior* (pp. 33–51). New York: John Wiley & Sons.

Eichelman, B. (1988). Toward a rational pharmacotherapy for aggressive and violent behavior. *Hospital and Community Psychiatry, 39,* 31–39.

Eisdorfer, C., Cohen, D., Paveza, G. J., Ashford, J. W., Luchins, D. J., Gorelick. P. B., Hirschman, R. S., Freels, S. A., Levy, P. S., Semla, T. P., & Shaw, H. A. (1992). An empirical evaluation of the Global Deterioration Scale for staging Alzheimer's disease. *American Journal of Psychiatry, 149,* 190–194.

Elkin, I., Shea, M. T., Watkins, J. T., Imber, S. D., Sotsky, S. M., Collins, J. F., Glass, D. R., Pilkonis, P. A., Leber, W. R., Docherty, J. P., Fiester, S. J., & Parloff, M. B. (1989). National Institute of Mental Health treatment of depression collaborative research program: General effectiveness of treatments. *Archives of General Psychiatry, 46,* 971–982.

Ellis, A. (1957). Outcome of employing three techniques of psychotherapy. *Journal of Clinical Psychology, 13,* 344–350.

Ellis, A. (1973). *Humanistic psychotherapy.* New York: McGraw-Hill.

Ellis, A. (1982). *A guide to personal happiness.* North Hollywood, CA: Wilshire Books.

Ellis, A. (1987). The impossibility of achieving consistently good mental health. *American Psychologist, 42,* 364–375.

Emde, R. N., Gaensbauer, T. J., & Harmon, R. J. (1976). *Emotional expressions in infancy: A biobehavioral study.* New York: International Universities Press.

Emery, V. L. & Oxman, T. E. (1992). Update on the dementia spectrum of depression. *American Journal of Psychiatry, 149,* 305–317.

Emmelkamp, P. M. G. (1982). *Phobic and obsessive-compulsive disorders.* New York: Plenum Press.

Emrick, C. D. (1987). Alcoholics Anonymous: Affiliation processes and effectiveness in treatment. *Alcoholism (NY), 11,* 416–423.

Endicott, J., & Spitzer, R. L. (1978). A diagnostic interview: The schedule for affective disorders and schizophrenia. *Archives of General Psychiatry, 35,* 837–844.

Erdelyi, M. H. (1985). *Psychoanalysis: Freud's cognitive psychology.* New York: Freeman.

Erikson, E. H. (1963). *Childhood and society* (2nd ed.). New York: Norton.

Erlenmeyer-Kimling, L., & Cornblatt, B. (1987). High-risk research in schizophrenia: A summary of what has been learned. *Journal of Psychiatric Research, 21,* 401–411.

Erlenmeyer-Kimling, L., Cornblatt, B., Friedman, D., Marcuse, Y., Rutschmann, J., Simmens, S., & Devi, S. (1982). Neurological, electrophysiological, and attentional deviations in children at risk for schizophrenia. In F. A. Henn & H. A. Nasrallah (Eds.), *Schizophrenia as a brain disease* (pp. 61–98). New York: Oxford University Press.

Ernhart, C. B., Sokol, R. J., Martier, S., Moron, P., Nadler, D., Ager, J. W., & Wolf, A. (1987). Alcohol teratogenicity in the human: A detailed assessment of specificity, critical period, and threshold. *American Journal of Obstetrics and Gynecology, 156,* 33–39.

Eron, L. D., & Huesmann, L. R. (1984). The control of aggressive behavior by changes in attitudes, values, and the conditions of learning. In R. J. Blanchard & D. C. Blanchard (Eds.), *Advances in the study of aggression* (pp. 139–173). New York: Academic Press.

Evans, D. A., Funkenstein, H. H., Albert, M. S., Scherr P. A., Cook, N. R., Chown, M. J., Hebert, L. E., Hennekens, C. H., & Taylor, J. O. (1989). Prevalence of Alzheimer's disease in a community of population of older persons: Higher than previously reported. *Journal of the American Medical Association, 262,* 2551–2556.

Evans, D. A., Scherr, P. A., Cook, N. R., Albert, M. S., Funkenstein, H. H., Smith, L. A., Hebert, L. E., Wetle, T. T., Branch, L. G., Chown, M., Hennekens, C. H., & Taylor, J. O. (1990). Estimated prevalence of Alzheimer's disease in the United States. *Milbank Quarterly, 68,* 267–289.

Exner, J. E. (1974). *The Rorschach: A comprehensive system.* New York: Wiley.

Eysenck, H. J. (1952). The effects of psychotherapy: An evaluation. *Journal of Consulting Psychology, 16,* 319–324.

Eysenck, H. J. (1959). Review of the Rorschach. In O. K. Buros (Ed.), *The fifth mental measurements yearbook* (pp. 276–278). Highland Park, NJ: Gryphon Press.

Eysenck, H. J. (1967). *The biological basis of personality.* Springfield IL: Charles C. Thomas.

Eysenck, H. J. (1988). Personality, stress and cancer: Prediction and prophylaxis [Special issue: Stress and health]. *British Journal of Medical Psychology, 61,* 57–75.

Fagan, J., & McMahon, J. J. (1984). Incipient multiple personality in children. *Journal of Nervous and Mental Disease, 172,* 25–36.

Fava, M., & Rosenbaum, J. F. (1991). Suicidality and fluoxetine: Is there a relationship? *Journal of Clinical Psychiatry, 52,* 108–111.

Fairbank, J. A. & Nicholson, R. A. (1987). Theoretical and empirical issues in the treatment of post-traumatic stress disorder in Vietnam veterans. *Journal of Clinical Psychology, 43,* 44–55.

Fairburn, C. G. (1981). A cognitive-behavioral approach to the management of bulimia nervosa. *Psychological Medicine, 11,* 701–707.

Fairburn, C. G. (1988). The current status of psychological treatments for bulimia nervosa. *Journal of Psychosomatic Research, 32,* 635–645.

Falloon, I. R., Boyd, J. L., McGill, C. W., Williamson, M., Razani, J., Moss, H. B., Gilderman, A. M., & Simpson, G. M. (1985). Family management in the prevention of morbidity of schizophrenia. *Archives of General Psychiatry, 42,* 887–896.

Faraone, S. V., Biederman, J., Keenan, K., & Tsuang, M. T. (1991). A family-genetic study of girls with DSM-III attention deficit disorder. *American Journal of Psychiatry, 148,* 112–117.

Farber, I. E. (1975). Sane and insane–constructions and misconstructions. *Journal of Abnormal Psychology, 84,* 589–620.

Farberow, N. L. (Ed.). (1980). *The many faces of suicide: Indirect self-destructive behavior.* New York: McGraw-Hill.

Fedora, O., Reddon, J. R., & Yeudall, L. T. (1986). Stimuli eliciting sexual arousal in genital exhibitionists: A possible clinical application. *Archives of Sexual Behavior, 15,* 417–427.

Feinstein, A. (1989). Posttraumatic stress disorder: A descriptive study supporting DSM-III-R criteria. *American Journal of Psychiatry, 146,* 665–666.

Finch, P. (1991, July 29). Confessions of a compulsive high-roller. *Business Week,* pp. 78–79.

Finkelhor, D., & Araji, S. (1986). Explanations of pedophilia: A four factor model. *Journal of Sex Research, 22,* 145–161.

Finney, J. W., & Moos, R. H. (1992). The long-term course of treated alcoholism: II. Predictors and correlates of 10-year functioning and mortality. *Journal of Studies on Alcohol, 53,* 142–153.

Fischer, P. J., & Breakey, W. R. (1991). The epidemiology of alcohol, drug, and mental disorders among homeless persons. *American Psychologist, 46,* 1115–1128.

Fisher, S., & Greenberg, R. P. (1977). *The scientific credibility of Freud's theory and therapy.* New York: Basic Books.

Fitts, S. N., Gibson, P., Redding, C. A., & Deiter, P. J. (1989). Body dysmorphic disorder: Implications for its validity as a DSM-III-R clinical syndrome. *Psychological Reports, 64,* 655–658.

Foa, E. B., & Kozak, M. J. (1986). Emotional processing of fear: Exposure to corrective information. *Psychological Bulletin, 99,* 20–35.

Foa, E. B., Steketee, G. S., & Ozarow, B. J. (1985). Behavior therapy with obsessive-compulsives: From theory to treatment. In M. Mavissakalian, S. M. Turner, & L. Michelson (Eds.), *Obsessive-compulsive disorder: Psychological and pharmacological treatment* (pp. 49–129). New York: Plenum Press.

Foa, E. B., Steketee, G., & Rothbaum, B. O. (1989). Behavioral/cognitive conceptualizations of post-traumatic stress disorder. *Behavior Therapy, 20,* 155–176.

Foa, E. B., Steketee, G. S., & Young, M. C. (1984). Agoraphobia: Phenomenological aspects, associated characteristics, and theoretical considerations. *Clinical Psychology Review, 4,* 431–457.

Folkman, S., & Lazarus, R. S., (1986). Stress processes and depressive symptomatology. *Journal of Abnormal Psychology, 93,* 107–113.

Folkman, S., & Lazarus, R. S., (1988). Coping as a mediator of emotion. *Journal of Personality and Social Psychology, 54,* 466–475.

Folkman, S., Lazarus, R. S. Gruen, R. J., & DeLongis, A. (1986). Appraisal, coping, health status, and psychological symptoms. *Journal of Personality and Social Psychology, 50,* 571–579.

Folks, D. G., Ford, C. V., & Regan, W. M. (1984). Conversion symptoms in a general hospital. *Psychosomatics, 25,* 285–295.

Folstein, S. E., & Rutter, M. L. (1988). Autism: Familial aggregation and genetic implications. *Journal of Autism and Developmental Disorders, 18,* 3–30.

Ford, C. V. (1983). *The somatizing disorders—Illness as a way of life.* New York: Elsevier Biomedical.

Ford, C. V., & Folks, D. G. (1985). Conversion disorders: An overview. *Psychosomatics, 26,* 371–383.

Fortenberry, J. C., Brown, D. B., & Shevlin, L. T. (1986). Analysis of drug involvement in traffic fatalities in Alabama. *American Journal of Drug and Alcohol Abuse, 12,* 257–267.

Foster, N. L., Chase, T. N., Mansi, L., Brooks, R., Fedio, P., Patronas, N. J., & DiChiro, G. (1984). *Annals of Neurology, 16,* 649–654.

Foster, S. L., Bell-Dolan, D. J., & Burge, D. A. (1988). Behavioral observation. In A. S. Bellack & M. Hersen (Eds.), *Behavioral assessment: A practical handbook* (3rd ed., pp. 119–160). New York: Pergamon.

Foy, D. W., Carroll, E. M., & Donahoe, C. P., Jr. (1987). Etiological factors in the development of PTSD in clinical samples of Vietnam combat veterans. *Journal of Clinical Psychology, 43,* 17–27.

Frances, A., Pincus, H. A., Widiger, T. A., Davis, W. W., & First, M. B. (1990). DSM-IV: Work in progress. *The American Journal of Psychiatry, 147,* 1439–1448.

Frankl, V. (1963). *Man's search for meaning.* New York: Simon & Schuster.

Franklin, J., & Ciarrocchi, J. (1987). The team approach: Developing an experimental knowledge base for the treatment of the pathological gambler. *Journal of Gambling Behavior, 3,* 60–67.

Freedman, R., Adler, L. E., Gerhardt, G. A., Waldo, M., Baker, N., Rose, G. M., Drebing, C., Nagamoto, H., Bickford-Wimer, P., & Franks, R. (1987). Neurobiological studies of sensory gating in schizophrenia. *Schizophrenia Bulletin, 13,* 669–678.

Freeman, A., Pretzer, J., Fleming, B., & Simon, K. M. (1990). *Clinical applications of cognitive therapy.* New York: Plenum Press.

Freud, A. (1936/1966). *The ego and the mechanisms of defense.* (rev. ed.). In *The writings of Anna Freud* (Vol. 2). New York: International Universities Press.

Freud, S. (1900/1953). The interpretation of dreams. In J. Strachey (Ed. and Trans.), *The standard edition of the complete psychological words of Sigmund Freud* (Vols. 4 and 5). London: Hogarth.

Freud, S. (1901/1960). The psychopathology of everyday life. In J. Strachey (Ed. and Trans.), *The standard edition of the complete psychological works of Sigmund Freud* (Vol. 6). London: Hogarth.

Freud, S., (1905/1953). *Three essays on the theory of sexuality.* In J. Strachey (Ed. and Trans.), *The standard edition of the complete psychological works of Sigmund Freud* (Vol. 7). London: Hogarth.

Freud, S. (1911/1958). Formulations of the two principles of mental functioning. In J. Strachey (Ed. and Trans.), *The standard edition of the complete psychological works of Sigmund Freud* (Vol. 12). London: Hogarth.

Freud, S. (1913/1958). Totem and taboo. In J. Strachey (Ed. and Trans.), *The standard edition of the complete psychological works of Sigmund Freud* (Vol. 13). London: Hogarth.

Freud, S. (1913–15/1963). Further recommendations in the technique of psychoanalysis. In S. Freud, *Therapy and technique* (P. Rieff, Ed.). New York: Collier.

Freud, S. (1917). Mourning and melancholia. In J. Strachey (Ed. and Trans.), *The standard edition of the complete psychological works of Sigmund Freud* (Vol. 14, pp. 151–169). London: Hogarth.

Freud, S. (1921). *Introduction to psychoanalysis of war neurosis.* London: Institute of Psychoanalytic Press.

Freud, S. (1923/1961). The ego and the id. In J. Strachey (Ed. and Trans.), *The standard edition of the complete psychological works of Sigmund Freud* (Vol. 19). London: Hogarth.

Freud, S. (1925/1959). An autobiographical study. In J. Strachey (Ed. and Trans.), *The standard edition of the complete psychological works of Sigmund Freud* (Vol. 20). London: Hogarth.

Freud, S. (1926/1959). Inhibitions, symptoms and anxiety. In J. Strachey (Ed. and Trans.), *The standard edition of the complete psychological works of Sigmund Freud* (Vol. 20). London: Hogarth.

Freud, S. (1930/1961). Civilization and its discontents. In J. Strachey (Ed. and Trans.), *The standard edition of the complete psychological works of Sigmund Freud* (Vol. 21). London: Hogarth.

Freud, K. (1980). Therapeutic sex drive reduction. *Acta Psychiatrica Scandinavica, 62,* 5–37.

Freund, K., & Blanchard, R. (1989). Phallometric diagnosis of pedophilia. *Journal of Consulting and Clinical Psychology, 57,* 100–105.

Frezza, M., DiPadova, C., Pozzato, G., Terpin, M., Baraona, E., & Lieber, C. S. (1990). High blood alcohol levels in women: The role of decreased gastric alcohol dehydrogenase activity and first-pass metabolism. *New England Journal of Medicine, 322,* 95–99.

Friedman, M. (1985). Survivor guilt in the pathogenesis of anorexia nervosa. *Psychiatry, 48,* 25–39.

Friedman, M. J. (1988). Toward rational pharmacotherapy for posttraumatic stress disorder: An interim report. *American Journal of Psychiatry, 145,* 281–285.

Fromm-Reichmann, F. (1948). Notes on the development of treatment of schizophrenics by psychoanalytic psychotherapy. *Psychiatry, 11,* 263–273.

Fry, J. M. (1985). Sleep disorders. *Medical Aspects of Human Sexuality, 19,* 104–124.

Fryers, T. (1986). Survival in Down's syndrome. *Journal of Mental Deficiency Research, 30,* 101–110.

Fuller, R. K., Lee, K. K., & Gordis, E. (1988). Validity of self-report in alcoholism research: Results of a Veterans Administration cooperative study. *Alcoholism: Clinical and Expermental Research, 12,* 201–205.

Fuller, R. K., Branchey, L., Brightwell, D. R., Derman, R. M., Emrick, C. D., Iber, F. L. James, K. E., Lacoursiere, R.B., Lee, K. K., Lowenstam, I., Maany, I., Neiderhiser, D., Nocks, J. J., & Shaw, S. (1986). Disulfiram treatment of alcoholism: A Veterans Administration cooperative study. *Journal of the American Medical Association, 256,* 1449–1455.

Furby, L., Weinrott, M. R., & Blackshaw, L. (1989). Sex offender recidivism: A review. *Psychological Bulletin, 105,* 3–30.

Gagne, P. (1981). Treatment of sex offenders with medroxyprogesterone acetate. *American Journal of Psychiatry, 138,* 644–646.

Gambino, B., & Stein, S. (1989). The problem gambler among clinical populations. *Compulsive Gambling Newsletter, 2,* 1–8.

Gardner, D. L., Leibenluft, E., O'Leary, K. M., & Cowdry, R. W. (1991). Self-ratings of anger and hostility in borderline personality disorder. *Journal of Nervous and Mental Disease 179,* 157–161.

Gardner, H. (1974). *The shattered mind: The person after brain damage.* New York: Vintage Books.

Garfield, S. (1984). Methodological problems in clinical diagnosis. In H. E. Adams & P. B. Sutker (Eds.), *Comprehensive handbook of psychopathology* (pp. 27–44). New York: Plenum Press.

Garfield, S. L., & Kurtz, R. (1976). Clinical psychologists in the 1970s. *American Psychologist, 31,* 1–9.

Garmezy, N. (1970). Process and reactive schizophrenia: Some conceptions and issues. *Schizophrenia Bulletin, 2,* 30–67.

Garner, D. M., & Bemis, K. M. (1982). A cognitive-behavioral approach to anorexia nervosa. *Cognitive Therapy and Research, 6,* 123–150.

Gaudia, R. (1987). Effects of compulsive gambling on the family. *Social Work, 32,* 254–526.

Gauthier, S., Bouchard, R., Lamontagne, A., Bailey, P., Bergman, H., Ratner, J., Tesfaye, Y., Saint-Martin, M., Bacher, Y., Carrier, L., Charbonneau, R., Clarfield, A. M., Collier, B., Dastoor, D., Gauthier, L., Germain, M., Kissell, C., Krieger, M., Kushnir, S., Masson, H., Morin, J., Nair, V., Neirinck, L., & Suissa, S. (1990). Tetrahydroaminoacridine-lecithin combination treatment in patients with intermediate-stage Alzheimer's disease. *New England Journal of Medicine, 322,* 1272–1276.

Gawin, F. H., & Ellinwood, E. H., Jr. (1988). Cocaine and other stimulants: Actions, abuse, and treatment. *New England Journal of Medicine, 318,* 1173–1182.

Gawin, F. H., & Kleber, H. D. (1985). Cocaine use in a treatment population: Patterns and diagnostic distinctions. In N. J. Kozel

& E. H. Adams (Eds.), *Cocaine use in America: Epidemiologic and clinical perspectives.* (pp. 182–192). NIDA Research Monograph Series 61. DHHS publication number (ADM) 85–1414. Washington DC: U.S. Government Printing Office.

Gawin, F. H., & Kleber, H. D. (1986). Abstinence symptomatology and psychiatric diagnosis in cocaine abusers: Clinical observations. *Archives of General Psychiatry, 43,* 107–113.

Gay, P. (1988). *Freud: A life for our time.* New York: Norton.

Gaylord, S. A., & Zung, W. W. K. (1987). Affective disorders among the aging. In L. L. Carstensen & B. A. Edelstein (Eds.), *Handbook of clinical gerontology* (pp. 76–95). New York: Pergamon.

Gelernter, C. S., Uhde, T. W., Cimbolic, P., Arnkoff, D. B., Vittone, B. J., Tancer, M. E., & Bartko, J. J. (1991). Cognitive-behavioral and pharmacological treatments of social phobia: A controlled study. *Archives of General Psychiatry, 48,* 938–945.

Gelernter, J., O'Malley, S., Risch, N., Kranzler, H. R., Krystal, J., Merikangas, K., Kennedy, J. L., & Kidd, K. K. (1991). No association between an allele at the D_2 dopamine receptor gene (DRD2) and alcoholism. *Journal of the American Medical Association, 266,* 1801–1807.

Gentry, W. D. (1984). *Handbook of behavioral medicine.* New York: Guilford.

George, L. K., & Gwyther, L. P. (1986). Caregiver well-being: A multidimensional examination of family caregivers of demented adults. *The Gerontologist, 26,* 253–259.

Gershon, E. S. (1983). The genetics of affective disorders. In L. Grinspoon (Ed.), *Psychiatry update* (pp. 434–457). Washington, DC: American Psychiatry Press.

Geula, C., & Mesulam, M. (1989). Special properties of cholinesterases in the cerebral cortex of Alzheimer's disease. *Brain Research, 498,* 185–189.

Gibson, D., & Harris, A. (1988). Aggregated early intervention effects for Down's syndrome persons: Patterning and longevity of benefits. *Journal of Mental Deficiency Research, 32,* 1–17.

Giesecke, M. E. (1987). The symptom of insomnia in university students. *Journal of American College Health, 35,* 215–221.

Gilbert, D. G., Hagen, R. L., & D'Agostino, J. A. (1986). The effects of cigarette smoking on human sexual potency. *Addictive Behaviors, 11,* 431–434.

Gitlin, M. J. (1990). *The psychotherapist's guide to psychopharmacology.* New York: Free Press.

Gittelman, R., & Klein, D. F. (1985). Childhood separation and adult agoraphobia. In A. H. Tuma & J. D. Maser (Eds.), *Anxiety and the anxiety disorders.* Hillsdale, NJ: Erlbaum.

Gittelman, R., Mannuzza, S., Shenker, R., & Bonagura, N. (1985). Hyperactive boys almost grown up. *Archives of General Psychiatry, 42,* 937–947.

Glassman, A. (1969). Indoleamines and affective disorder. *Psychosomatic Medicine, 31,* 107–114.

Glassman, J. N. S., Magulac, M., & Darko, D. F. (1987). Folie a famille: Shared paranoid disorder in a Vietnam veteran and his family. *American Journal of Psychiatry, 144,* 658–660.

Glosser, G., & Friedman, R. B. (1991). Lexical but not semantic priming in Alzheimer's disease. *Psychology and Aging, 6,* 522–527.

Goldberg, S. C., Klerman, G. L., & Cole, J. O. (1965). Changes in schizophrenic psychopathology and ward behaviour as a function of phenothiazine treatment. *British Journal of Psychiatry, 111,* 120–133.

Golden, C. J., Purisch, A. D., & Hammeke, T. A. (1985). *Luria-Nebraska neuropsychological battery: Forms I and II.* Los Angeles: Western Psychological Association.

Goldstein, L., Manowitz, P., Nora, R., Swartzburg, M., & Carlton, P. (1985). Differential EEG activation and pathological gambling. *Biological Psychiatry, 20,* 1232–1234.

Goodman, C. C., & Pynoos, J. (1990). A model telephone information and support program for caregivers of Alzheimer's patients. *The Gerontologist, 30*, 399–403.

Goodwin, D. W. (1985). Alcoholism and genetics: The sins of the fathers. *Archives of General Psychiatry, 42*, 171–174.

Gordon, R. A. (1976). Prevalence: The rare datum in delinquency measurement and its implicaitons for the theory of delinquency. In M. W. Klein (Ed.), *The juvenile justice system* (pp. 201–284). Beverly Hills, CA: Sage.

Gorenstein, E. E. (1982). Frontal lobe functions in psychopaths. *Journal of Abnormal Psychology, 91*, 368–379.

Gorman, J. M., & Liebowitz, M. R. (1986). Panic and anxiety disorders. In A. M. Cooper, A. J. Frances, & M. H. Sacks (Eds.), *The personality disorders and neuroses* (pp. 325–337). New York: Basic Books.

Gosselin, C., & Wilson, G. (1980). *Sexual variations.* New York: Simon & Schuster.

Gottesman, I. I. (1991). *Schizophrenia genesis: The origins of madness.* New York: Freeman.

Gottesman, I. I., McGuffin, P., & Farmer, A. E. (1987). Clinical genetics as clues to the "real" genetics of schizophrenia. *Schizophrenia Bulletin, 13*, 23–47.

Gottesman, I. I., & Shields, J. (1982). *Schizophrenia: The epigenetic puzzle.* Cambridge: Cambridge University Press.

Gough, H. G. (1987). *California personality inventory—revised.* Palo Alto, CA: Consulting Psychologists Press.

Gould, M. S., & Shaffer, D. (1986). The impact of suicide in television movies: Evidence of imitation. *New England Journal of Medicine, 315*, 690–694.

Goyette, C. H., Conners, C. K., & Ulrich, R. F. (1978). Normative data on Revised Conners Parent and Teacher Rating Scales. *Journal of Abnormal Child Psychology, 6*, 221–236.

Graham, J. R. (1990). *MMPI-2: Assessing personality and psychopathology.* New York: Oxford University Press.

Greaves, G. B. (1980). Multiple personality: 165 years after Mary Reynolds. *Journal of Nervous and Mental Disease, 168*, 577–596.

Green, B. L., Grace, M. C., Lindy, J. D., Gleser, G. C., & Leonard, A. (1990). Risk factors for PTSD and other diagnoses in a general sample of Vietnam veterans. *American Journal of Psychiatry, 147*, 729–733.

Greenberg, J. R., & Mitchell, S. A. (1983). *Object relations in psychoanalytic theory.* Cambridge, MA: Harvard University Press.

Greer, S., & Watson, M. (1985). Towards a psychobiological model of cancer: Psychological considerations [Special issue: Cancer and the mind]. *Social Science and Medicine, 20*, 773–777.

Greist, J. H. (1990). Treating the anxiety: Therapeutic options in obsessive compulsive disorder. *Journal of Clinical Psychiatry, 51*(11, Suppl.). 29–34.

Grinker, R. R., Sr. (1979). Diagnosis of borderlines: A discussion. *Schizophrenia Bulletin, 5*, 47–52.

Grosse, D. A., Wilson, R. S., & Fox, J. H. (1990). Preserved word-stem-completion priming of semantically encoded information in Alzheimer's disease. *Psychology and Aging, 5*, 304–306.

Grossman, L. S., Harrow, M., Goldberg, J. F., & Fichtner, C. G. (1991). Outcome of schizoaffective disorder at two long-term follow-ups: Comparisons with outcome of schizophrenia and affective disorders. *American Journal of Psychiatry, 148*, 1359–1365.

Groth, N. (1979). *Men who rape.* New York: Plenum Press.

Groth-Marnat, G. (1990). *Handbook of psychological assessment* (2nd ed.). New York: Wiley.

Grove, W. M., Andreasen, N. C., McDonald-Scott, P., Keller, M. B., & Shapiro, R. W. (1981). Reliability studies of psychiatric diagnosis: Theory and practice. *Archives of General Psychiatry, 38*, 408–413.

Gunderson, J. G. (1984). *Borderline personality disorders.* Washington, DC: American Psychiatric Press.

Gunderson, J. G. (1989). Borderline personality disorders. In American Psychiatric Association Task Force on Treatments of Psychiatric Disorders (Eds.), *Treatments of psychiatric disorders* (Vol. 3, pp. 2749–2759). Washington, DC: American Psychiatric Association.

Gunderson, J. G., Ronningstam, E., & Smith, L. E. (1991). Narcissistic personality disorder: A review of data on DSM-III-R descriptions. *Journal of Personality Disorders, 5*, 167–177.

Gunderson, J. G., & Zanarini, M. C. (1987). Current overview of the borderline diagnosis. *Journal of Clinical Psychiatry, 48* (8, Suppl.), 5–11.

Gutheil, T. G., & Appelbaum, P. S. (1982). *Clinical handbook of psychiatry and the law.* New York: McGraw-Hill.

Guze, S. B., Cloninger, C. R., Martin, R. M., & Clayton, P. J. (1983). A follow-up and family study of schizophrenia. *Archives of General Psychiatry, 40*, 1273–1276.

Hafeiz, H. B. (1980). Hysterical conversion: A prognostic study. *British Journal of Psychiatry, 136*, 548–551.

Haley, J. (1976a). A history of a research project. In C. E. Sluzki & D. C. Ransom (Eds.), *The double bind: The foundation of the communicational approach to the family* (pp. 59–104). New York: Grune & Stratton.

Haley, J. (1976b). *Problem-solving therapy.* New York: Harper.

Haley, J. (1980). *Leaving home.* New York: McGraw-Hill.

Halgin, R. P., & Lovejoy, D. W. (1991). An integrative approach to treating the partner of a depressed person. *Psychotherapy, 28*, 251–258.

Hall, S. M., Wasserman, D. A., & Havassy, B. E. (1991). Relapse prevention. In R. W. Pickens, C. G. Leukefeld, & C. R. Schuster (Eds.), *Improving drug abuse treatment.* (NIDA Research Monograph No. 106, pp. 279–292). (DHHS Publication No. ADM 91–1754). Washington, DC: U. S. Government Printing Office.

Halstead, W. C., (1947). *Brain and intelligence: A quantitative study of the frontal lobes.* Chicago: University of Chicago Press.

Ham, R. J. (1990). Alzheimer's disease and the family: A challenge of the new millenium. In T. Zandi & R. J. Ham (Eds.), *New directions in understanding dementia and Alzheimer's disease* (pp. 3–20). New York: Plenum Press.

Hamstra, B. (1986). Neurobiological substrates of violence: An overview for forensic clinicians. *Journal of Psychiatry and Law 14*, 349–374.

Harding, C. M., Brooks, G. W., Ashikaga, T., Strauss, J. S., & Breier, A. (1987). The Vermont longitudinal study of persons with severe mental illness, 1: Methodology, study sample, and overall status 32 years later. *American Journal of Psychiatry, 144*, 718–726.

Hare, R. D. (1978). Electrodermal and cardiovascular correlates of psychopathy. In R. D. Hare & D. Schalling (Eds.), *Psychopathic behaviour: Approaches to research* (pp. 107–143). Chichester, England: Wiley & Sons.

Hare, R. D. (1983). Diagnosis of antisocial personality disorder in two prison populations. *American Journal of Psychiatry, 140*, 887–890.

Hare, R. D., Hart, S. D., & Harpur, T. J. (1991). Psychopathy and the *DSM-IV* criteria for antisocial personality disorder. *Journal of Abnormal Psychology, 100*, 391–398.

Hare, R. D., McPherson, L. M., & Forth, A. E. (1988). Male psychopaths and their criminal careers. *Journal of Consulting and Clinical Psychology, 56*, 710–714.

Harrow, H., & Westermeyer, J. F. (1987). Process-reactive dimension and outcome for narrow concepts of schizophrenia. *Schizophrenia Bulletin, 13*, 361–368.

Hatfield, A. B. (no date). *Coping with mental illness in the family: A family guide.* Washington: National Alliance for the Mentally Ill.

Hathaway, S. R., & McKinley, J. C. (1989). *The Minnesota multiphasic personality inventory-2.* Minneapolis: University of Minnesota Press.

Hauser, T. (1991). *Muhammad Ali: His life and times.* New York: Simon & Schuster.

Hazelwood, R. R., Deitz, P. E., & Burgess, A. W. (1983). *Autoerotic fatalities*. Lexington, MA: Lexington Books.

Heath, A. C., Jardine, R., & Martin, N. G. (1989). Interactive effects of genotype and social environment on alcohol consumption in female twins. *Journal of Studies on Alcohol, 50*, 38–48.

Heiman, J. R., & LoPiccolo, J. (1988). *Becoming orgasmic: A sexual and personal growth program for women*. New York: Prentice-Hall.

Heimberg, R. G., & Barlow, D. H. (1988). Psychosocial treatments for social phobia. *Psychosomatics, 29*, 27–37.

Heimberg, R. G., & Barlow, D. H. (1991). New developments in cognitive-behavioral therapy for social phobia. *Journal of Clinical Psychiatry, 52* (11, Suppl.), 21–30.

Helzer, J. E., Robins, L. N., & McEvoy, L. (1987). Post-traumatic stress disorder in the general population: Findings of the epidemiologic catchment area survey. *New England Journal of Medicine, 317*, 1630–1634.

Hemsley, D. R. (1987). An experimental psychological model for schizophrenia. In H. Häfner, W. F. Gattaz, & W. Janzarik (Eds.), *Search for the causes of schizophrenia* (Vol. 1, pp. 179–188). Berlin: Springer-Verlag.

Henden, H. & Haas, A. P. (1991). Suicide and guilt as manifestations of PTSD in Vietnam combat veterans. *American Journal of Psychiatry, 148*, 586–591.

Heninger, G. R., & Charney, D. S. (1987). Mechanism of action of antidepressant treatments: Implications for the etiology and treatment of depressive disorders. In H. Y. Meltzer (Ed.), *Psychopharmacology: The third generation of progress* (pp. 535–544). New York: Raven.

Herbert, M. (1987). *Conduct disorders of childhood and adolescence* (2nd ed.). Chichester: Wiley.

Herman, J., Perry, J. C., & van der Kolk, B. A. (1989). Childhood trauma in borderline personality disorder. *American Journal of Psychiatry, 146*, 490–495.

Hermann, B. P., Seidenberg, M., Haltiner, A., & Wyler, A. R. (1991). Mood state in temporal lobe epilepsy. *Biological Psychiatry, 30*, 1205–1218.

Herron, W. G. (1987). Evaluating the process-reactive dimension. *Schizophrenia Bulletin, 13*, 357–368.

Herz, M. I., & Melville, C. (1980). Relapse in schizophrenia. *American Journal of Psychiatry, 137*, 801–805.

Herz, M. I., Szymanski, H. V., & Simon, J. C. (1982). Intermittent medication for stable schizophrenic outpatients: An alternative to maintenance medication. *American Journal of Psychiatry, 139*, 918–922.

Herzberg, F., Mausner, B., & Snyderman, B. B. (1959). *The motivation to work*. New York: Wiley.

Herzog, D. B., Keller, M. B., Lavori, P. W., & Sacks, N. R. (1991). The course and outcome of bulimia nervosa. *Journal of Clinical Psychiatry, 52* (Suppl. 10), 4–8.

Heuser, I. J. E., Chase, T. N., & Mouradian, M. M. (1991). The limbic-hypothalamic-pituitary-adrenal axis in Huntington's disease. *Biological Psychiatry, 30*, 943–952.

Hill, A. J., Oliver, S., & Rogers, P. J. (1992). Eating in the adult world: The rise of dieting in childhood and adolescence. *British Journal of Clinical Psychology, 31*, 95–105.

Hingson, R., & Howland, J. (1987). Alcohol as a risk factor for injury or death resulting from accidental falls: A review of the literature. *Journal of Studies on Alcohol, 48*, 212–219.

Hinshaw, S. P. (1987). On the distinction between attentional deficits/hyperactivity and conduct problems/aggression in child psychopathology. *Psychological Bulletin, 101*, 443–463.

Hiroto, D. S. (1974). Locus of control and learned helplessness. *Journal of Experimental Psychology, 102*, 187–193.

Hiroto, D. S., & Seligman, M. E. P. (1975). Generality of learned helplessness in man. *Journal of Personality and Social Psychology, 31*, 311–327.

Hirsch, S. R., & Leff, J. P. (1975). *Abnormalities in parents of schizophrenics: A review of the literature and an investigation of communication defects and deviances*. New York: Oxford University Press.

Hoberman, H. M., & Lewinsohn, P. M. (1985). The behavioral treatment of depression. In E. E. Beckham & W. R. Leber (Eds.). *Handbook of depression: Treatment, assessment, and research* (pp. 39–81). Homewood, IL: Dorsey Press.

Hobfall, S. E., Spielberger, C. D., Breznitz, S., Figley, C., Folkman, S., Lepper-Green, B., Meichenbaum, D., Milgram, N. A., Sandler, I., Sarason, I., & van der Kolk, B. (1991). War-related stress: Addressing the stress of war and other traumatic events. *American Psychologist, 46*, 848–855.

Hobson, R. P. (1989). Beyond cognition: A theory of autism. In G. Dawson (Ed.), *Autism: New perspectives on diagnosis, nature and treatment* (pp. 22–48). New York: Guilford Press.

Hoffman, J. A. (1984). Psychological separation of late adolescents from their parents. *Journal of Counseling Psychology, 31*, 170–178.

Hoffman, L. (1981). *Foundations of family therapy*. New York: Basic Books.

Hollander, E., Mullen, L. S., Carrasco, J. L., DeCaria, C. M., & Stein, D. J. (1992). Symptom relapse in bulimia nervosa and obsessive compulsive disorder after treatment with serotonin antagonists. *Journal of Clinical Psychiatry, 53*, 28.

Holmes, T. H., & Rahe, R. H. (1967). The social readjustment rating scale. *Journal of Psychosomatic Research, 11*, 213–218.

Holzman, P. S. (1987). Recent studies of psychophysiology in schizophrenia. *Schizophrenia Bulletin, 13*, 49–75.

Holzman, P. S., & Matthysse S. (1990). The genetics of schizophrenia: A review. *Psychological Science, 1*, 279–286.

Holzman, P. S., Proctor, L. R., Levy, D. L., Yasillo, N. J., Meltzer, H. Y., & Hurt, S. W. (1974). Eye-tracking dysfunctions in schizophrenic patients and their relatives. *Archives of General Psychiatry, 31*, 143–151.

Horney, K. (1945). *Our inner conflicts*. New York: Norton.

Horney, K. (1950a). *Neurosis and human growth*. New York: Norton.

Horney, K. (1950b). *The neurotic personality of our time*. New York: Norton.

Horowitz, M. J. (1986). Stress response syndromes: A review of posttraumatic and adjustment disorders. *Hospital and Community Psychiatry, 37*, 241–249.

Howes, M. J., Hokanson, J. E., & Loewenstein, D. A. (1985). Induction of depressive affect after prolonged exposure to a mildly depressed individual. *Journal of Personality and Social Psychology, 49*, 1110–1113.

Howland, J., & Hingson, R. (1987). Alcohol as a risk factor for injuries or death due to fires and burns: Review of the literature. *Public Health Reports, 102*, 475–483.

Howland, J., & Hingson, R. (1988). Issues in research on alcohol in nonvehicular unintentional injuries. *Contemporary Drug Problems*, Spring, 95–106.

Howlett, A. C. Johnson, M. R. Melvin, L. S. & Milne, G. M., (1988). Nonclassical cannabinoid analgetics inhibit adenate cyclase: Development of a cannabinoid receptor model. *Molecular Pharmacology, 33*, 297–302.

Hrubec, A., & Omenn, G. S. (1981). Evidence of genetic predisposition to alcoholic cirrhosis and psychosis: Twin concordance for alcoholism and its end points by zygosity among male veterans. *Alcoholism (NY), 5*, 207–215.

Hurwitz, T. D., Mahowald, M. W., Schenck, C. H., Schluter, J. L., & Bundlie, S. R. (1991). A retrospective outcome study and review of hypnosis as treatment of adults with sleepwalking and sleep terror disorder. *Journal of Nervous and Mental Disease, 179*, 228–233.

Hussian, R. A. (1981). *Geriatric psychology: A behavioral perspective*. New York: Van Nostrand Reinhold.

Iacono, W. G., Bassett, A. S., & Jones, B. D. (1988). Eye tracking dysfunction is associated with partial trisomy of chromosome 5 and schizophrenia. *Archives of General Psychiatry, 45,* 1140–1141.

Iacono, W. G., Moreau, M., Beiser, M., Fleming, J. A. E., & Lin, T. Y. (1992). Smooth-pursuit eye tracking in first-episode psychotic patients and their relatives. *Journal of Abnormal Psychology, 101,* 104–116.

Insel, T. R., Ninan, P. T., Aloi, J., Jimerson, D. C., Skolnick, P., & Paul, S. M. (1984). A benzodiazepine receptor-mediated model of anxiety. *Archives of General Psychiatry, 41,* 741–750.

Institute of Medicine (1990). *Broadening the base of treatment for alcohol problems.* Washington, DC: National Academy Press.

Jacobs, P. A., Brunton, M., & Melville, M. M. (1965). Aggressive behavior, mental subnormality, and the XYY male. *Nature, 208,* 1351–1352.

Jacobson, E. (1938). *Progressive relaxation.* Chicago: University of Chicago Press.

Jacobson, R. R. (1985). Child firesetters: A clinical investigation. *Journal of Child Psychology and Psychiatry, 26,* 759–768.

Jagust, W. J., Budinger, T. F., Reed, B. R., & Colina, M. (1987). Single-photon emission computed tomography in the clinical evaluation of dementia. In G. G. Glenner & R. J. Wurtman (Eds.), *Advancing frontiers in Alzheimer's disease research* (pp. 217–233). Austin: University of Texas Press.

Janofsky, J. S., Spears, S., & Neubauer, D. N. (1988). Psychiatrists' accuracy in predicting violent behavior on an inpatient unit. *Hospital and Community Psychiatry, 39,* 1090–1094.

Jarvik, L. F. (1988). Aging of the brain: How can we prevent it? *The Gerontologist, 6,* 739–747.

Jauch, D. A., & Carpenter, W. T. (1988). Reactive psychosis II: Does DSM-III-R define a third psychosis? *The Journal of Nervous and Mental Disease, 176,* 82–86.

Jenike, M. A. (1990). Approaches to the patient with treatment-refractory obsessive compulsive disorder. *Journal of Clinical Psychiatry, 51* (2 Suppl.), 15–21.

Jenike, M. A., Baer, L., & Minichiello, W. E. (Eds.). (1986). *Obsessive compulsive disorders.* Littleton, MA: PSG Publishing.

Joachim, C. L., & Selkoe, D. J. (1989). Minireview: Amyloid protein in Alzheimer's disease. *Journal of Gerontology: Biological Sciences, 44,* B77–B82.

John, E. R., Prichep, L. S., Fridman, J., & Easton, P. (1988). Neurometrics: Computer-assisted differential diagnosis of brain dysfunction. *Science, 239,* 162–169.

Johnson, C., Connors, M. E., & Tobin, D. L. (1987). Symptom management of bulimia. *Journal of Consulting and Clinical Psychology, 55,* 668–676.

Johnson, J., Weissman, M. M., & Klerman, G. L. (1990). Panic disorder, comorbidity, and suicide attempts. *Archives of General Psychiatry, 47,* 805–808.

Johnson, J. C., Gottlieb, G. L., Sullivan, E., Wanich, C., Kinosian, B., Forciea, M. A., Sims, R., & Hogue, C. (1990). Using DSM-III criteria to diagnose delirium in elderly general medical patients. *Journal of Gerontology: Medical Sciences, 45,* M113–M119.

Johnson, L. D., O'Malley, P. M., & Bachman, J. G. (1989). *Drug use, drinking, and smoking: National survey results from high school, college, and young adult populations, 1975–1988* (DHHS Publication No. ADM 89–1638). Rockville, MD: Alcohol, Drug, Abuse, and Mental Health Administration.

Joiner, T. E., Jr., Alfano, M. S., & Metalsky, G. I. (1992). When depression breeds contempt: Reassurance seeking, self-esteem, and rejection of depressed college students by their roommates. *Journal of Abnormal Psychology, 101,* 165–173.

Jones, A., & Crandall, R. (1986). Validation of a short index of self-actualization. *Personality and Social Psychology Bulletin, 12,* 63–73.

Jones, E. (1953). *The life and work of Sigmund Freud: The formative years and the great discoveries.* New York: Basic Books.

Jones, K. L., & Smith, D. W. (1973). Recognition of the fetal alcohol syndrome in early infancy. *Lancet, 2,* 999–1001.

Jorm, A. F., Korten, A. E., & Henderson, A. S. (1987). The prevalence of dementia: A quantitative integration of the literature. *Acta Psychiatrica Scandinavica, 76,* 465–479.

Jucker, W., Walker, L. C., Martin, L. J., Kitt, C. A., Kleinman, H. K., Ingram, D. K., & Price, D. L. (1992). Age-associated inclusions in normal and transgenic mouse brain. *Science, 255,* 1443–1445.

Jung, C. G. (1916). General aspects of dream psychology. In H. Read, M. Fordham, & G. Adler (Eds.), *The collected works of C. G. Jung.* Vol. 8, pp. 237–280. Princeton, NJ: Princeton University Press.

Jung, C. G. (1961). *Memories, dreams, reflections* (A. Jaffe, Ed.). New York: Pantheon.

Jung, C. G. (1936/1959/1969). The archetypes and the collective unconscious. In *The collected works of C. G. Jung* (Vol. 9). Princeton, NJ: Princeton University Press.

Kafka, M. P. (1991). Successful antidepressant treatment of nonparaphilic sexual addictions and paraphilias in men. *Journal of Clinical Psychiatry, 52,* 60–65.

Kahn, M. (1991). *Between therapist and client: The new relationship.* New York: W. H. Freeman.

Kaij, L. (1960). *Studies on the etiology and sequels of abuse of alcohol.* Lund, Sweden: University of Lund.

Kales, A., Soldatos, C. R., Caldwell, A. B., Kales, J. D., Humphrey, F. J., III, Charney, D. S., & Schweitzer, P. K. (1980). Somnambulism: Clinical characteristics and personality patterns. *Archives of General Psychiatry, 37,* 1406–1410.

Kamarck, T., & Jennings, J. R. (1991). Biobehavioral factors in sudden cardiac death. *Psychological Bulletin, 109,* 42–75.

Kanas, N. (1988). Psychoactive substance use disorders: Alcohol. In H. H. Goldman (Ed.), *Review of general psychiatry* (2nd. ed., pp. 286–298). Norwalk, CT: Appleton and Lange.

Kane, J., Honigfeld, G., Singer, J., Meltzer, H., & The Cloraril Collaborative Study Group (1988). Clozapine for the treatment-resistant schizophrenic. *Archives of General Psychiatry, 45,* 789–796.

Kanner, L. (1943). Autistic disturbances of affective contact. *Nervous Child, 2,* 217–250.

Kanter, J. S. (1984). *Coping strategies for relatives of the mentally ill,* (2nd ed.). Washington, DC: National Alliance for the Mentally Ill.

Kaplan, A. S., & Woodside, D. B. (1987). Biological aspects of anorexia nervosa and bulimia nervosa. *Journal of Consulting and Clinical Psychology, 55,* 645–653.

Kaplan, H. S. (1974). *The new sex therapy* (Vol. 1). New York: Brunner/Mazel.

Kaplan, H. S. (1979). *Disorders of sexual desire: The new sex therapy* (Vol. 2). New York: Brunner/Mazel.

Kaplan, H. S. (1983). *The evaluation of sexual disorders: Psychological & medical aspects.* New York: Brunner/Mazel.

Kaplan, H. S. (1986). Psychosexual dysfunctions. In A. M. Cooper, A. J. Frances, & M. H. Sacks (Eds.), *The personality disorders and neuroses* (pp. 467–479). New York: Basic Books.

Kaprio, J., Koshenvuo, M., Langinvainio, H., Romanov, K., Sarna, S., & Rose, R. J. (1987). Genetic influences on use and abuse of alcohol: A study of 5638 adult Finnish twin brothers. *Alcoholism (NY), 11,* 349–356.

Karacan, I., Salis, P. J., & Williams, R. L. (1978). The role of the sleep laboratory in diagnosis and treatment of impotence. In R. L. Williams & I. Karacan (Eds.), *Sleep disorders: Diagnosis and treatment* (pp. 353–382). New York: Wiley.

Kardiner, A., & Spiegel, H. (1947). *War stress and neurotic illness* (2nd ed.) New York: P. E. Hoeber.

Karon, B. P. (1978). Projective tests are valid. *American Psychologist, 33,* 764–765.

Karson, S., & O'Dell, J. W. (1987). Computer-based interpretation of the 16PF: The Karson Clinical Report in contemporary practice. In J. W. Butcher (Ed.), *Computerized psychological assessment: A practitioner's guide* (pp. 198–217). New York: Basic Books.

Kashani, J., & Simonds, J. F. (1979). The incidence of depression in children. *American Journal of Psychiatry, 136,* 1203–1205.

Kass, F., Spitzer, R. L., Williams, J. B. W., & Widiger, T. (1989). Self-defeating personality disorder and DSM-III-R: Development of the diagnostic criteria. *American Journal of Psychiatry, 146,* 1022–1026.

Katon, W., & Roy-Byrne, P. P. (1991). Mixed anxiety and depression. *Journal of Abnormal Psychology, 100,* 337–345.

Kawabata, S., Higgins, G. A., & Gordon, J. (1991). Amyloid plaques, neurofibrillary tangles and neuronal loss in brains of transgenic mice overexpressing a C-terminal fragment of human amyloid precurso protein. *Nature, 354,* 476–478.

Kaye, W. H., & Weltzin, T. E. (1991). Neurochemistry of bulimia nervosa. *Journal of Clinical Psychiatry, 52* (10, Suppl.), 21–28.

Kaye, W. H., Weltzin, T. E., Hsu, L. K. G., & Bulik, C. M. (1991). An open trial of fluoxetine in patients with anorexia nervosa. *Journal of Clinical Psychiatry, 52,* 464–471.

Kazdin, A. E. (1989). Childhood depression. In E. J. Mash & R. A. Barkley (Eds.), *Treatment of childhood disorders* (pp. 135–166). New York: Guilford Press.

Keeney, B. P., & Ross, J. M. (1985). *Mind in therapy: Constructing systemic family therapies.* New York: Basic Books.

Kellner, R. (1990). Somatization: Theories and research. *Journal of Nervous and Mental Disease, 178,* 150–160.

Kelly, G. A. (1955). *The psychology of personal constructs* (Vols. 1 and 2). New York: Norton.

Kelsoe, J. R., Ginns, E. I., Egeland, J. A., Gerhard, D. S., Goldstein, A. M., Bale, S. J., Pauls, D. L., Long, R. T., Kidd, K. K., Conte, G., Housman, D. E., & Paul, S. E. (1989). Reevaluation of the linkage relationship between chromosome 11p loci and the gene for bipolar affective disorder in the Old Order Amish. *Nature, 342,* 238–243.

Kendler, K. S., Gruenberg, A. M., & Strauss, J. S. (1981). An independent analysis of the Copenhagen sample of the Danish adoption study of schizophrenia, II.: The relationship between schizotypal personality disorder and schizophrenia. *Archives of General Psychiatry, 38,* 982–984.

Kennedy, J. L., Giuffra, L. A., Moises, H. W., Cavalli-Sforza, L. L., Pakstis, A. J., Kidd, J. R., Castiglione, C. M., Sjogren, B., Wetterberg, L., & Kidd, K. K. (1988). Evidence against linkage of schizophrenia to markers on chromosome 5 in a northern Swedish pedigree. *Nature, 336,* 167–170.

Kennedy, S. H., McVey, G., & Katz, R. (1990). Personality disorders in anorexia nervosa and bulimia nervosa. *Journal of Psychiatric Research, 24,* 259–269.

Kernberg, O. F. (1967). Borderline personality organization. *Journal of the American Psychoanalytic Association, 15,* 641–685.

Kernberg, O. F. (1975). *Borderline conditions and pathological narcissism.* New York: Jason Aronson.

Kernberg, O. F. (1984). *Severe personality disorders: Psychotherapeutic strategies.* New Haven: Yale University Press.

Kernberg, O. F., Selzer, M. A., Koenigsberg, H. W., Carr, A. C., & Applebaum, A. H. (1989). *Psychodynamic psychotherapy of borderline patients.* New York: Basic Books.

Kety, S. S. (1988). Schizophrenic illness in the families of schizophrenic adoptees: Findings from the Danish national sample. *Schizophrenic Bulletin, 14,* 217–221.

Kety, S. S., Rosenthal, D., Wender, P. H., & Schulsinger, F. (1968). The types and prevalence of mental illness in the biological and adoptive families of adopted schizophrenics. In D. Rosenthal & S. S. Kety (Eds.), *The transmission of schizophrenia.* (pp. 345–362) New York: Pergamon.

Kilmann, P. R., Sabalis, R. F., Gearing, M. L., Bukstel, L. H., & Scovern, A. W. (1982). The treatment of sexual paraphilias: A review of outcome research. *Journal of Sex Research, 18,* 193–252.

Kinney, J. M., & Stephens, M. A. P. (1989). Hassles and uplifts of giving care to a family member with dementia. *Psychology and Aging, 4,* 402–408.

Kirkpatrick, B., & Buchanan, R. W. (1990). The neural basis of the deficit syndrome of schizophrenia. *The Journal of Nervous and Mental Disease, 178,* 545–553.

Kirmil-Gray, K., Eagleston, J. R., Thoresen, C. E., & Zarcone, V. P. (1985). Brief consultation and stress management treatments for drug-dependent insomnia: Effects on sleep quality, self-efficacy, and daytime stress. *Journal of Behaviorial Medicine, 8,* 79–99.

Klatsky, A. L. (1987). The cardiovascular effects of alcohol. *Alcohol and Alcoholism, 22* (Suppl. 1), 117–124.

Klein, D. F. (1981). Anxiety reconceptualized. In D. F. Klein & J. Raskin (Eds.), *Anxiety: New research and changing concepts* (pp. 235–263). New York: Raven Press.

Klein, M. (1964). *Contributions to psychoanalysis.* New York: McGraw-Hill.

Klein, R. (1989). Introduction to disorders of the self. In J. F. Masterson & R. Klein (Eds.), *Psychotherapy of the disorders of the self: The Masterson approach.* New York: Brunner/Mazel.

Klerman, G. L. (1987). Clinical epidemiology of suicide. *Journal of Clinical Psychiatry, 48,* 33–38.

Klerman, G. L., Weissman, M. M., Rounsaville, B. J., & Chevron, E. S. (1984). *Interpersonal psychotherapy of depression.* New York: Basic Books.

Kluft, R. P. (1984a). An introduction to multiple personality disorder. *Psychiatric Annals, 14,* 19–24.

Kluft, R. P. (1984b). Aspects of the treatment of multiple personality disorder. *Psychiatric Annals, 14,* 51–55.

Kluft, R. P. (1986). High functioning multiple personality disorders. *Journal of Nervous and Mental Disease, 174,* 722–726.

Kluft, R. P. (1987a). First-rank symptoms as a diagnostic clue to multiple personality disorder. *American Journal of Psychiatry, 144,* 293–298.

Kluft, R. P. (1987b). The simulation and dissimulation of multiple personality disorder. *American Journal of Clinical Hypnosis, 30,* 104–118.

Kluft, R. P. (1989). Playing for time: Temporizing techniques in the treatment of multiple personality disorder. *American Journal of Clinical Hypnosis, 32,* 90–98.

Knight, R. (1953). Borderline states. *Bulletin of the Menninger Clinic, 17,* 1–12.

Knight, R. G., Godfrey, H. P. D., Shelton, E. J. (1988). The psychological deficits associated with Parkinson's disease. *Clinical Review, 8,* 391–410.

Kobasa, S. C.O., Maddi, S. R., Puccetti, M. C., & Zola, M. A. (1985). Effectiveness of hardiness, exercise and social support as resources against illness. *Journal of Psychosomatic Research, 29,* 525–533.

Kohut, H. (1966). Forms and transformations of narcissism. *Journal of the American Psychoanalytic Association, 14,* 243–272.

Kohut, H. (1971). *The analysis of the self.* New York: International Universities Press.

Kohut, H. (1984). *How does analysis cure?* New York: International Universities Press.

Kolko, D. J., & Kazdin, A. E. (1988). Prevalence of firesetting and related behaviors among child psychiatric patients. *Journal of Consulting and Clinical Psychology, 56,* 628–630.

Kolko, D. J., & Kazdin, A. E. (1989a). Assessment of dimensions of childhood firesetting among patients and nonpatients: The firesetting risk interview. *Journal of Abnormal Child Psychology, 17,* 157–176.

Kolko, D. J., & Kazdin, A. E. (1989b). The children's firesetting interview with psychiatrically referred and nonreferred children. *Journal of Abnormal Child Psychology, 17,* 609–624.

Koob, G. F., & Bloom-, F. E. (1988). Cellular and molecular mechanisms of drug dependence. *Science, 242,* 715–723.

Kooiman, C. G. (1987). Neglected phenomena in factitious illness: A case study and review of literature. *Comprehensive Psychology, 28,* 499–507.

Kopelman, M. D. (1987). Amnesia: Organic and psychogenic. *British Journal of Psychiatry, 150,* 428–442.

Kornetsky, C., Bain, G. T., Unterwald, E. M., & Lewis, M. J. (1988). Brain stimulation reward: Effects of ethanol. *Alcoholism: Clinical and Experimental Research, 12,* 609–616.

Korpi, E. R., Kleinman, J. E., & Wyatt, R. J. (1988). GABA concentrations in forebrain areas of suicide victims. *Biological Psychiatry, 23,* 109–114.

Koss, M. P., & Butcher, J. N. (1986). Research on brief psychotherapy. In S. L. Garfield & A. E. Bergin (Eds.), *Handbook of psychotherapy and behavior change* (3rd ed., pp. 157–212). New York: Wiley.

Kosten, T. R., Rounsaville, B. J., & Kleber, H. D. (1988). Antecedents and consequences of cocaine abuse among opioid addicts: A 2.5 year follow-up. *Journal of Nervous and Mental Disease, 176,* 176–181.

Kozel, N. J., & Adams, E. H. (1985). *Cocaine use in America: Epidemiologic and clinical perspectives* (pp. 221–226). NIDA Research Monograph Series 61. DHHS publication number (ADM) 85–1414. Washington DC: U.S. Government Printing Office.

Kozel, N. J., & Adams, E. H. (1986). Epidemiology of drug abuse: An overview. *Science, 234,* 970–974.

Krafft-Ebing, R. V. (1950). *Psychopathia sexualis.* New York: Pioneer Publications.

Kreitman, N. (Ed.). (1977). *Parasuicide.* New York: John Wiley & Sons.

Kripke, D. F., Mullaney, D. J., Klauber, M. R., Risch, S. C., & Gillin, J. C. (1992). Controlled trial of bright light for nonseasonal major depressive disorders. *Biological Psychiatry, 31,* 119–134.

Kris, E. (1952). *Psychoanalytic explorations in art.* New York: International Universities Press.

Krishnan, K. R. R., Davidson, J. R. T., & Guajardo, C. (1985). Trichotillomania—A review. *Comprehensive Psychiatry, 26,* 123–128.

Kuiper, B., & Cohen-Kettenis, P. (1988). Sex reassignment surgery: A study of 141 Dutch transsexuals. *Archives of Sexual Behavior, 17,* 439–457.

Kumar, A., Yousem, D., Souder, E., Miller, D., Gottlieb, G., Gur, R., & Alavi, A. (1992). High-intensity signals in Alzheimer's disease without cerebrovascular risk factors: A magnetic resonance imaging evaluation. *American Journal of Psychiatry, 149,* 248–250.

Kurtz, R. R., & Grummon, D. L. (1972). Different approaches to the measurement of therapist empathy and their relationship to therapy outcomes. *Journal of Consulting and Clinical Psychology, 39,* 106–115.

Kutcher, S. P., Blackwood, D. H. R., St. Clair, D., Gaskell, D. F., & Muir, W. G. (1987). Auditory P300 in borderline personality disorder and schizophrenia. *Archives of General Psychiatry, 44,* 645–650.

Laing, R. D. (1959). *The divided self.* New York: Penguin.

Laing, R. D. (1964). Is schizophrenia a disease? *International Journal of Social Psychiatry, 10,* 184–193.

Lange, L. G., & Kinnunen, P. M. (1987). Cardiovascular effects of alcohol. *Advances in Alcholism and Substance Abuse, 6,* 47–52.

Langevin, R. (1983). *Sexual strands: Understanding and treating sexual anomalies in men.* Hillsdale, NJ: Lawrence Earlbaum Associates.

Lanyon, R. I. (1986). Theory and treatment of child molestation. *Journal of Consulting and Clinical Psychology, 54,* 176–182.

Lazarus, A. A. (1968). Learning theory and the treatment of depression. *Behaviour Research and Therapy, 6,* 83–89.

Lazarus, R. S. (1991). *Emotion and adaptation.* New York: Oxford University Press.

Lazarus, R. S., & Folkman, S. (1984). *Stress, appraisal, and coping.* New York: Springer.

Leff, J. (1977). International variations in the diagnosis of psychiatric illness. *British Journal of Psychiatry, 131,* 329–338.

Leff, J., & Vaughn, C. (1981). The role of maintenance therapy and relatives' expressed emotion in relapse of schizophrenia: A two-year follow-up. *British Journal of Psychiatry, 139,* 102–104.

Leicester, J. (1982). Temper tantrums, epilepsy, and episodic dyscontrol. *British Journal of Psychiatry, 141,* 262–266.

Leigh, G., & Skinner, H. A. (1988). Physiological assessment. In D. M. Donovan & G. A. Marlatt (Eds.), *Assessment of addictive behaviors* (pp. 112–136). New York: Guilford Press.

Lelliott, P. T., Marks, I. M., Monteiro, W. O., Tsakiris, F., & Noshirvani, H. (1987). Agoraphobics 5 years after imipramine and exposure: Outcome and predictors. *Journal of Nervous and Mental Disease, 175,* 599–605.

Lenzenweger, M. F., Dworkin. R. H., & Wethington, E. (1991). Examining the underlying structures of schizophrenic phenomenology: Evidence for a three-process model. *Schizophrenia Bulletin, 17,* 515–524.

Lerner, M., & Remen, R. N. (1987). Tradecraft of the Commonweal Cancer Help Program. *Advances, 4,* 11–25.

Lerner, M. J., Somers, D. G., Reid, D., Chiriboga, D., & Tierney, M. (1991). Adult children as caregivers: Egocentric biases in judgments of sibling contributions. *The Gerontologist, 31* 746–755.

Lesieur, H. R., & Blume, S. B. (1987). The South Oaks Gambling Screen (SOGS): A new instrument for the identification of pathological gamblers. *American Journal of Psychiatry, 144,* 1184–1188.

Levenson, J. L., & Bemis, C. (1991). The role of psychological factors in cancer onset and progression. *Psychosomatics, 32,* 124–132.

Lewin, L. M., & Lundervold, D. A. (1990). Behaviorial analysis of separation-individuation conflict in the spouse of an Alzheimer's disease patient. *The Gerontologist, 30,* 703–705.

Lewinsohn, P. M., & Shaw, D. (1969). Feedback about interpersonal behavior as an agent of behavior change: A case study in the treatment of depression. *Psychotherapy and Psychosomatics, 17,* 82–88.

Lewy, A. J. (1987). Treating chronobiologic sleep and mood disorders with bright light. *Psychiatric Annals, 17,* 664–669.

Lewy, A. J., Nurnberger, J. I., Wehr, T. A., Pack, D., Becker, L. E., Powell, R. L., & Newsome, D. A. (1985). Supersensitivity to light: Possible trait marker for manic-depressive illness. *American Jouranal of Psychiatry, 142,* 725–727.

Lewy, A. J., Sack, R. L., Miller, S., & Hoban, T. M. (1987). Antidepressant and circadian phase-shifting effects of light. *Science, 235,* 352–354.

Lex, B. W., Lukas, S. E., Greenwald, N. E., & Mendelson, J. H. (1988). Alcohol-induced changes in body sway in women at risk for alcoholism: A pilot study. *Journal of Studies on Alcohol, 49,* 346–356.

Lezak, M. D. (1983). *Neuropsychological assessment.* New York: Oxford University Press.

Lhuintre, J. P., Moore, N. D., Tran, G., Steru, L., Langrenon, S., Daoust, M., Parot, P., Ladure, P., Libert, C., Boismare, F., & Hillemand, B., (1990). Acamprosate appears to decrease alcohol intake in weaned alcoholics. *Alcohol and Alcoholism, 25,* 613–622.

Liberman, R. P., Massel, H. K., Mosk, M. D., & Wong, S. E. (1985). Social skills training for chronic mental patients. *Hospital and Community Psychiatry, 36,* 396–403.

Lidz T. 1975. The origin & treatment of schizophrenic disorders. Hutchinson: London.

Lidz, T. (1946). Nightmares and combat neuroses. *Psychiatry, 9*, 37–49.

Lieberman, M. A., & Kramer, J. H. (1991). Factors affecting decisions to institutionalize demented elderly. *The Gerontologist, 31*, 371–374.

Liebowitz, M. R., Fyer, A. J., Gorman, J. M., Dillon, D., Appleby, I. L., Levy, G., Anderson, S., Levitt, M., Palij, M., Davies, S. O., & Klein, D. F. (1984). Lactate provocation of panic attacks: I. Clinical and behaviorial findings. *Archives of General Psychiatry, 31*, 764–770.

Liebowitz, M. R., Fyer, A. J., Gorman, J. M., Dillon, D., Davies, S., Stein, J. M., Cohen, B. S., & Klein, D. F. (1985). Specificity of lactate infusions in social phobia versus panic disorders. *American Journal of Psychiatry, 142*, 947–950.

Liebowitz, M. R., Schneier, F. R., Hollander, E. W., Welkowitz, L. A., Saoud, J. B., Feerick, J., Campeas, R., Fallon, B. A., Street, L., & Gitow, A. (1991). Treatment of social phobia with drugs other than benzodiazepines. *Journal of Clinical Psychiatry, 52* (11, Suppl.), 10–15.

Lima, B. R., Pai, S., Santacruz, H., & Lozano, J. (1991). Psychiatric disorders among poor victims following a major disaster: Armero, Colombia. *Journal of Nervous and Mental Disease, 179*, 420–427.

Lindemalm, G., Korlin, D., & Uddenberg, N. (1986). Long-term follow-up of "Sex Change" in 13 male to female transsexuals. *Archives of Sexual Behavior, 15*, 187–210.

Linehan, M. (1987). Dialectical behavior therapy for borderline personality disorder: Theory and method. *Bulletin of the Menninger Clinic, 51*, 261–276.

Linehan, M., Armstrong, H. E., Suarez, A., Allmon, D., & Heard, H. L. (1991). Cognitive-behavioral treatment of chronically parasuicidal borderline patients. *Archives of General Psychiatry, 48*, 1060–1064.

Linn, L. (1989). Psychogenic amnesia. In T. B. Karasu (Ed.), *Treatments of psychiatric disorders* (pp. 2186–2190). Washington, DC: American Psychiatric Association.

Linnoila, M., Virkkunen, M., Scheinin, M., Nuutila, A., Rimon, R., & Goodwin, F. K. (1983). Low cerebrospinal fluid 5-hydroxyindoleacetic acid concentration differentiates impulsive from nonimpulsive violent behavior. *Life Sciences, 33*, 2609–2614.

Lion, J. R. (1978). Outpatient treatment of psychopaths. In W. H. Reid (Ed.), *The psychopath* (pp. 286–300). New York: Brunner Mazel.

Lion, J. R. (1989). Intermittent explosive disorder. In T. B. Karasu (Ed.), *Treatment of psychiatric disorders* (pp. 2473–2476). Washington, DC: American Psychiatric Association.

Lipowski, Z. J. (1988). Somatization: The concept and its clinical application. *American Journal of Psychiatry, 145*, 1358–1368.

Lipowski, Z. J. (1990). Is "organic" obsolete? *Psychosomatics, 31*, 343–344.

Lipsius, S. H. (1987). Prescribing sensate focus without proscribing intercourse. *Journal of Sex and Marital Therapy, 13*, 106–116.

Liptzin, B., Levkoff, S. E., Cleary, P. D., Pilgrim, D. M., Reilly, C. H., Albert, M., & Wetle, T. T. (1991). An empirical study of diagnostic criteria for delirium. *American Journal of Psychiatry, 148*, 454–457.

Liskow, B. I., & Goodwin, D. W. (1987). Pharmacological treatment of alcohol intoxication, withdrawal and dependence: A critical review. *Journal of Studies on Alcohol, 48*, 356–370.

Lister, R. G., Eckardt, M. J., & Weingartner, H. (1987). Ethanol intoxication and memory: Recent developments and new directions. In M. Galanter, H. Begleiter, R. Deitrich, D. Goodwin, E. Gottleib, A. Paredes, M. Rothschild, D. Van Theil (Eds.), *Recent developments in alcoholism* (Vol. 5, pp. 111–127). New York: Plenum Press.

Little, J. C., & James, B. (1964). Abreaction of conditioned fear after 18 years. *Behavioral Research and Therapy, 2*, 59–63.

Lively, W. J., Schroeder, M. L., & Jackson, D. N. (1990). Dependent personality disorder and attachment problems. *Journal of Personality Disorders, 4*, 131–140.

Locke, B. Z., & Regier, D. A. (1985). Prevalence of selected mental disorders. In *Mental health, United States, 1985* (pp. 1–6). Washington, DC: U.S. Government Printing Office.

Loeber, R. (1982). The stability of antisocial and delinquent child behavior: A review. *Child Development, 53*, 1431–1446.

Loeber, R. (1990). Development and risk factors of juvenile antisocial behavior and delinquency. *Clinical Psychology Review, 10*, 1–41.

Loeber, R., Lahey, B. B., & Thomas, C. (1991). Diagnostic conundrum of oppositional defiant disorder and conduct disorder. *Journal of Abnormal Psychology, 100*, 379–390.

Loewenstein, R. J. (1991). Psychogenic amnesia and psychogenic fugue: A comprehensive review. *Annual Review of Psychiatry, 10*, 223–247.

LoPiccolo, J., & Stock, W. E. (1986). Treatment of sexual dysfunction. *Journal of Consulting and Clinical Psychology, 54*, 158–167.

Loranger, A. W., Oldham, J. M., Russakoff, L. M., & Susman, V. (1984). Structured interviews and borderline personality disorder. *Archives of General Psychiatry, 41*, 565–568.

Loranger, A. W., Oldham, J. M., & Tulis, E. H. (1982). Familial transmission of *DSM-III* borderline personality disorder. *Archives of General Psychiatry, 39*, 795–799.

Lorenz, V. C., & Shuttlesworth, D. E. (1983). The impact of pathological gambling on the spouse of the gambler. *Journal of Community Psychology, 11*, 67–76.

Lothstein, L. M. (1983). *Female-to-male transsexualism: Historical, clinical, and theoretical issues*. Boston: Routledge & Kegan Paul.

Lovaas, O. I. (1977). *The autistic child: Language development through behavior modification*. New York: Irvington.

Lovaas, O. I. (Ed.). (1981). *Teaching developmentally disabled children*. Baltimore: University Park Press.

Lovaas, O. I. (1987). Behavioral treatment and normal educational and intellectual functioning in young autistic children. *Journal of Consulting and Clinical Psychology, 55*, 3–9.

Lowenstein. D. A., Amigo, E., Duara, R., Guterman, A., Hurwitz, D., Berkowitz, N., Wilkie, F., Weinberg, G., Black, B., Gittelman, B., & Eisdorfer, C. (1989). A new scale for the assessment of functional status in Alzheimer's disease and related disorders. *Journal of Gerontology: Psychological Sciences, 44*, P114–P121.

Lowenstein, L. F. (1989). The etiology, diagnosis and treatment of the fire-setting behavior of children. *Child Psychiatry and Human Development, 19*, 186–194.

Lovinger, D. M., White, G., & Weight, F. F. (1989). Ethanol inhibits NMDA-activated ion current in hippocampal neurons. *Science, 243*, 1721–1724.

Lozoff, B. (1989). Nutrition and behavior. *American Psychologist, 44*, 231–236.

Lubin, B., Larsen, R. M., Matarazzo, J. D., & Seever, M. (1985). Psychological test usage patterns in five professional settings. *American Psychologist, 40*, 857–861.

Luborsky, L. (1984). *Principles of psychoanalytic psychotherapy: A manual for supportive-expressive treatment*. New York: Basic Books.

Luxenberg, J. S., Swedo, S. E., Flament, M. F., Friedland, R. P., Rapoport, J., & Rapoport, S. I. (1988). Neuroanatomical abnormalities in obsessive-compulsive disorders detected with quantitative X-ray computed tomography. *American Journal of Psychiatry, 145*, 1089–1093.

Lykken, D. I. (1957). A study of anxiety in the sociopathic personality. *Journal of Abnormal and Social Psychology, 55*, 6–10.

MacDonald, M. (1981). *Mystical bedlam: Madness, anxiety, and healing in seventeenth-century England*. New York: Cambridge University Press.

Mace, N. L., & Rabins, P. V. (1991). *The 36-hour day: A family guide to caring for persons with Alzheimer's disease, related dementing illness, and memory loss in later life.* Baltimore, MD: Johns Hopkins Press.

MacMillan, J. F., Gold, A., Crow, T. J., Johnson, A. L., & Johnstone, E. C. (1986). The Northwick Park Study of first episodes of schizophrenia: IV. Expressed emotion and relapse. *British Journal of Psychiatry, 148,* 133–143.

Madakasira, S., & O'Brien, K. F. (1987). Acute posttraumatic stress disorder in victims of a natural disaster. *Journal of Nervous and Mental Disease, 175,* 286–296.

Maddux, J. F., & Desmond, D. P. (1981). *Careers of opioid users.* New York: Praeger.

Maher, W. B., & Maher, B. A. (1985a). Psychopathology: I. From ancient times to the eighteenth century. In G. A. Kimble & K. Schlesinger (Eds.), *Topics in the history of psychology* (Vol. 2, pp. 251–294). Hillsdale, NJ: Lawrence Erlbaum.

Maher, W. B., & Maher, B. A. (1985b). Psychopathology: II. From the eighteenth century to modern times. In G. A. Kimble & K. Schlesinger (Eds.), *Topics in the history of psychology* (Vol. 2, pp. 295–329). Hillsdale, NJ: Lawrence Erlbaum.

Mahler, M. (1971). A study of the separation-individuation process and its possible application to borderline phenomena in the psychoanalytic situation. *Psychoanalytic Study of the Child, 26,* 403–424.

Mahler, M., Bergman, A., & Pine, F. (1975). *The psychological birth of the infant: Symbiosis and individuation.* New York: Basic Books.

Mahler, M., & Gosliner, B. (1955). On symbiotic child psychosis: Genetic, dynamic and restitutive aspects. *Psychoanalytic Study of the Child, 10,* 195–212.

Mahler, M. S., & McDevitt, J. B. (1982). Thoughts on the emergence of the sense of self, with particular emphasis on the body self. *Journal of the American Psychoanalytic Association, 30,* 827–848.

Maier, S. F., & Seligman, M. E. P. (1976). Learned helplessness: Theory and evidence. *Journal of Experimental Psychology: General, 105,* 3–46.

Malan, D. H. (1979). *Individual psychotherapy and the science of psychodynamics.* Boston: Butterworth.

Malcolm, J. (1978, May 15). A reporter at large: The one-way mirror. *The New Yorker,* pp. 39–114.

Manderscheid, R. W., & Sonnenschein, M. A. (Eds.), (1990). *Mental health, United States, 1990.* Washington DC: US Government Printing Office.

Manton, K. G., Blazer, D. G., & Woodbury, M. A. (1987). Suicide in middle age and later life: Sex and race specific life table and cohort analyses. *Journal of Gerontology, 42,* 219–227.

Marcotte, D. B. (1989). Sexual sadism and sexual masochism. In T. S. Karasu (Ed.), *Treatment of psychiatric disorders* (Vol. 1, pp. 647–655). Washington, DC: American Psychiatric Association.

Margraf, J., Ehlers, A., & Roth, W. T. (1986). Biological models of panic disorder—A review. *Behavior Research and Therapy, 24,* 553–567.

Markowitz, J. S., Weissman, M. M., Ouellette, R., Lish, J. D., & Klerman, G. L. (1989). Quality of life in panic disorder. *Archives of General Psychiatry, 46,* 984–992.

Marks, I. M. (1987). *Fears, phobias, and rituals: Panic, anxiety, and their disorders.* New York: Oxford University Press.

Marks, I. M. (1988). Blood-injury phobia: A review. *American Journal of Psychiatry, 145,* 1207–1213.

Marks, I. M., & Gelder, M. G. (1966). Different ages of onset in varieties of phobias. *American Journal of Psychiatry, 111,* 561–573.

Marlatt, G. A. (1990). Cue exposure and relapse prevention in the treatment of addictive behaviors. *Addictive Behaviors, 15,* 395–399.

Marlatt, G. A., Baer, J. S., Donovan, D. M., & Kivlahan, D. R. (1988). Addictive behaviors: Etiology and treatment. *Annual Review of Psychology, 39,* 223–252.

Marlatt, G. A., & Gordon, J. R. (1985). *Relapse prevention: Maintenance strategies in addictive behavior change.* New York: Guilford Press.

Marshall, W. L., Jones, R., Ward, T., Johnston, P., & Barbaree, H. E. (1991). Treatment outcome with sex offenders. *Clinical Psychology Review, 11,* 465–485.

Martin, E. M., Wilson, R. S., Penn, R. D., Fox, J. H., Clasen, R. A., & Savoy, S. M. (1987). Cortical biopsy results in Alzheimer's disease: Correlation with cognitive deficits. *Neurology, 37,* 1201–1204.

Marx, E. M., Williams, J. M. G., & Claridge, G. C. (1992). Depression and social problem solving. *Journal of Abnormal Psychology, 101,* 78–86.

Marx, J. (1991). New clue found to Alzheimer's. *Science, 253,* 857–858.

Marx, J. (1992). Major setback for Alzheimer's models. *Science, 255,* 1200–1202.

Masling, J. (Ed.). (1983). *Empirical studies of psychoanalytical theories* (Vol. 1). Hillsdale, NJ: Analytic Press.

Maslow, A. (1954/1970). *Motivation and personality.* New York: Harper & Row.

Maslow, A. H. (1962). *Toward a psychology of being.* Princeton, NJ: Van Nostrand.

Maslow, A. (1971). *The farthest reaches of human nature.* New York: Viking.

Massella, J. D. (1991). Intervention: Breaking the addiction cycle. In D. C. Daley & M. S. Raskin (Eds.), *Treating the chemically dependent and their families* (pp. 79–99). Newbury Park, CA: Sage Publications.

Masson, J. M. (1985). *The assault on truth: Freud's suppression of the seduction theory.* New York: Penguin.

Masters, W. H., & Johnson, V. E. (1966). *Human sexual response.* Boston: Little Brown.

Masters, W. H., & Johnson, V. E. (1970). *Human sexual inadequacy.* Boston: Little, Brown.

Masters, W. H., Johnson, V. E., & Kolodny, R. C. (1982). *Human sexuality.* Boston: Little, Brown.

Masterson, J. F. (1976). *Psychotherapy of the borderline adult.* New York: Brunner/Mazel.

Masterson, J. F. (1981). *The narcissistic and borderline disorders: An integrated developmental approach.* New York: Brunner/Mazel.

Masterson, J. F., & Klein, R. (Eds.). (1989). *Psychotherapy of the disorders of the self.* New York: Brunner/Mazel.

Matarazzo, J. D. (1972). *Wechsler's measurement and appraisal of adult intelligence.* Baltimore, MD: Williams & Wilkins.

Matarazzo, J. D. (1986). Computerized clinical psychological test interpretations. *American Psychologist, 41,* 14–24.

Mate-Kole, C., Freschi, M., & Robin, A. (1988). Aspects of psychiatric symptoms at different stages in the treatment of transsexualism. *British Journal of Psychiatry, 152,* 550–553.

Mathews, A. M., Gelder, M. G., & Johnston, D. W. (1981). *Agoraphobia: Nature and treatment.* New York: Guilford Press.

Mattes, J. A. (1985). Metoprolol for intermittent explosive disorder. *American Journal of Psychiatry, 142,* 1108–1109.

Mattrick, R. P., Peters, L., & Clarke, J. C. (1989). Exposure and cognitive restructuring for social phobia: a controlled study. *Behavior Therapy, 20,* 3–23.

May, R. (1983). *The discovery of being: Writings in existential psychology.* New York: Norton.

McCann, J. T. (1988). Passive-aggressive personality disorder: A review. *Journal of Personality Disorders, 2,* 170–179.

McClelland, D. C. (1980). Motive dispositions: The merits of operant and respondent measures. In L. Wheeler (Ed.), *Review of personality and social psychology* (Vol. 1). Beverly Hills, CA: Sage Publications.

McClelland, D. C., Davidson, R. J., & Saron, C. (1985). Stressed power motivation, sympathetic activation, immune function, and illness. *Advances, 2,* 42–52.

Mishler EG & Waxler 1975 The sequential patterning of interaction in normal & schizophrenic families. Family Process 14, 17-50

McClelland, D. C., Ross, G., & Patel, V. (1985). The effect of an academic examination on salivary norepinephrine and immunoglobulin levels. *Journal of Human Stress, 11*, 52–59.

McClusky, H. Y., Milby, J. B., Switzer, P. K., Williams, V., & Wooten, V. (1991). Efficacy of behavioral versus triazolam treatment in persistent sleep-onset insomnia. *American Journal of Psychiatry, 148*, 116–121.

McConaghy, N., Armstrong, M. S., & Blaszczynski, A. (1985). Expectancy, covert sensitization and imaginal desensitization in compulsive sexuality. *Acta Psychiatrica Scandanavica, 72*, 176–187.

McConaghy, N., Armstrong, M. S., Blaszczynski, A., & Alcock, C. (1983). Controlled comparison of aversive therapy and imaginal desensitization in compulsive gambling. *British Journal of Psychiatry, 142*, 366–372.

McConaghy, N., Blaszczynski, A., & Frankova, A. (1991). Comparison of imaginal desensitization with other behavioural treatments of pathological gambling: A two- to nine-year follow-up. *British Journal of Psychiatry, 159*, 390–393.

McCord, W., & McCord, J. (1959). *Origins of crime.* New York: Columbia University Press.

McCord, W., & McCord, J. (1964). *The psychopath: An essay on the criminal mind.* New York: Van Nostrand Reinhold.

McCormick, R. A., Russo, A. M., Ramirez, L. F., & Taber, J. I. (1984). Affective disorders among pathological gamblers seeking treatment. *American Journal of Psychiatry, 141*, 215–218.

McCormick, R. A., Taber, J., Kruedelbach, N., & Russo, A. (1987). Personality profiles of hospitalized pathological gamblers: The California Personality Inventory. *Journal of Clinical Psychology, 43*, 521–527.

McElroy, S. L., Hudson, J. I., Pope, H. G., Jr., Keck, P. E., Jr., & Aizley, H. G. (1992). The *DSM-III-R* impulse control disorders not elsewhere classified: Clinical characteristics and relationship to other psychiatric disorders. *American Journal of Psychiatry, 149*, 318–327.

McElroy, S. L., Pope, H. G., Jr., Hudson, J. I., Keck, P. E., Jr., & White, K. L. (1991). Kleptomania: A report of 20 cases. *American Journal of Psychiatry, 148*, 652–657.

McFall, M. E., Mackay, P. W., & Donovan, D. M. (1991). Combat-related PTSD and psychosocial adjustment problems among substance abusing veterans. *Journal of Nervous and Mental Disease, 179*, 33–38.

McGarvey, B., Gabrielli, W. F., Bentler, P. M., & Mednick, S. A. (1981). Rearing, social class, education, and criminality: A multiple indicator model. *Journal of Abnormal Psychology, 90*, 354–364.

McGhie, A., & Chapman, J. S. (1961). Disorders of attention and perception in early schizophrenia. *British Journal of Medical Psychology, 34*, 102–116.

McGlashan, T. H. (1983). The borderline syndromes: II. Is it a variant of schizophrenia or affective disorder? *Archives of General Psychiatry, 40*, 1319–1323.

McGlashan, T. H., (1986). The Chestnut Lodge follow-up study: III. Long-term outcome of borderline personalities. *Archives of General Psychiatry, 43*, 20–30.

McGlashan, T. H., & Fenton, W. S. (1991). Classical subtypes for schizophrenia: Literature review for *DSM-IV. Schizophrenia Bulletin, 17*, 609–632.

McGlashan, T. H., & Williams, P. V. (1990). Predicting outcome in schizoaffective psychosis. *Journal of Nervous and Mental Disease, 178*, 518–520.

McGue, M., & Gottesman, I. I. (1989). Genetic linkage in schizophrenia: Perspectives from genetic epidemiology. *Schizophrenia Bulletin, 15*, 453–464.

McGue, M., Pickens, R. W., & Svikis, D. S. (1992). Sex and age effects on the inheritance of alcohol problems: A twin study. *Journal of Abnormal Psychology, 101*, 3–17.

McGuire, T. G. (1991). Measuring the economic costs of schizophrenia. *Schizophrenia Bulletin, 17*, 375–388.

McIntosh-Michaelis, S. A., Roberts, M. H., Wilkinson, S. M., Diamond, I. D., McLellan, D. L., Martin, J. P., & Spackman, A. J. (1991). The prevalence of cognitive impairment in a community survey of multiple sclerosis. *British Journal of Clinical Psychology, 30*, 333–348.

McKnew, D. H., Jr., Cytryn, L., & Yahraes, H. (1983). *Why isn't Johnny crying? Coping with depression in children.* New York: W. W. Norton.

McMahon, R. J., & Wells, K. C. (1989). Conduct disorders. In E. J. Mash & R. A. Barkley (Eds.), *Treatment of childhood disorders* (pp. 73–132). New York: The Guilford Press.

McNally, R. J. (1987). Preparedness and phobias: A review. *Psychological Bulletin, 101*, 283–303.

McNally, R. J., & Steketee, G. S. (1985). Etiology and maintenance of severe animal phobias. *Behavioural Research and Therapy, 23*, 431–435.

McNamara, M. E. (1991). Psychological factors affecting neurological conditions: Depression and stroke, multiple sclerosis, Parkinson's disease, and epilepsy. *Psychosomatics, 32*, 255–267.

McNeal, E. T., & Cimbolic, P. (1986). Antidepressants and biochemical theories of depression. *Psychological Bulletin, 99*, 361–374.

Mednick, S. A., Gabrielli, W. F., Jr., & Hutchings, B. (1987). Genetic factors in the etiology of criminal behavior. In S. A. Mednick, T. E. Moffitt, & S. A. Stacks (Eds.), *The causes of crime: New biological approaches* (pp. 74–91). Cambridge: Cambridge University Press.

Mednick, S. A., & Schulsinger, F. (1968). Some premorbid characteristics related to breakdown in children with schizophrenic mothers. In D. Rosenthal & S. S. Kety (Eds.), *The transmission of schizophrenia* (pp. 267–291). New York: Pergamon Press.

Mednick, S. A., Volavka, J., Gabrielli, W. F., & Itil, T. M. (1981). EEG as a predictor of antisocial behavior. *Criminology, 19*, 219–229.

Meehl, P. E. (1956). Wanted—A good cookbook. *American Psychologist, 11*, 263–272.

Meehl, P. E. (1962). Schizotaxia, schizotypy, schizophrenia. *American Psychologist, 17*, 827–838.

Meichenbaum, D. (1985). *Stress inoculation training.* New York: Pergamon Press.

Melman, A., Tiefer, L., & Pederson, R. (1988). Evaluation of first 406 patients in urology department based center for male sexual dysfunction. *Urology, 32*, 6–10.

Meltzer, H. Y. (1987). Biological studies in schizophrenia. *Schizophrenia Bulletin, 13*, 77–111.

Mendlewicz, J., & Rainer, J. D. (1977). Adoption study supporting genetic transmission in manic-depressive illness. *Nature, 268*, 327–329.

Merriam, A. E., Aronson, M. K., Gaston, P., Wey, S., & Katz, I. (1988). The psychiatric symptoms of Alzheimer's disease. *Journal of the American Geriatrics Society, 36*, 7–12.

Merton, R. K. (1968). *Social theory and social structure.* New York: Free Press.

Metalsky, G. I., Halberstadt, L. J., & Abramson, L. Y. (1987). Vulnerability to depressive mood reactions: Toward a more powerful test of the diathesis-stress and causal mediation components of the reformulated theory of depression. *Journal of Personality and Social Psychology, 52*, 386–393.

Meyer, A. (1957). *Psychobiology: A science of man.* Springfield, IL: Charles C. Thomas.

Miles, R., & Wong, R. K. S. (1987). Latent synaptic pathways revealed after tetanic stimulation in the hippocampus. *Nature, 329*, 724–726.

Miller, N. S., & Gold, M. S. (1987). The diagnosis and treatment of alcohol dependence. *New England Journal of Medicine, 84*, 873–879.

Miller, W. R. (1985). Motivation for treatment: A review with special emphasis on alcoholism. *Psychological Bulletin, 98*, 84–107.

Millon, T. (1981). *Disorders of personality DSM-III: Axis II.* New York: Wiley.

Millon, T. (1987). On the genesis and prevalence of the borderline personality disorder: A social learning thesis. *Journal of Personality Disorders, 1,* 64–82.

Millon, T. (1991). Classification in psychopathology: Rationale, alternatives, and standards. *Journal of Abnormal Psychology, 100,* 245–261.

Mindham, R. H. S., Steele, C., Folstein, M. F., & Lucas, J. (1985). A comparison of the frequency of major affective disorder in Huntington's disease and Alzheimer's disease. *Journal of Neurology, Neurosurgery, and Psychiatry, 48,* 1172–1174.

Miner, J. B. (1983). The unpaved road from theory: Over the mountains to application. In R. H. Kilmann, K. W. Thomas, D. P. Slevin, R. Nath, & S. L. Jerrell (Eds.), *Producing useful knowledge for organizations* (pp. 37–68). New York: Praeger.

Minuchin, S. (1974). *Families and family therapy.* Cambridge, MA: Harvard University Press.

Minuchin, S. (1984). *Family kaleidoscope.* Cambridge, MA: Harvard University Press.

Minuchin, S., Rosman, B. L., & Baker, L. (1978). *Psychosomatic families: Anorexia nervosa in context.* Cambridge, MA: Harvard University Press.

Mirin, S. M., & Weiss, R. D. (1986). Affective illness in substance abusers. *Psychiatric Clinics of North America, 9,* 503–514.

Mishara, B. L., & Kastenbaum, R. (1980). *Alcohol and old age.* New York: Grune & Stratton.

Mishler, E. G., & Waxler, N. E. (1975). The sequential patterning of interaction in normal and schizophrenic families. *Family Process, 14,* 17–50.

Mitchell, J. (1974). *Psychoanalysis and feminism.* New York: Pantheon.

Mitchell, J. E., Specker, S. M., & deZwaan, M. (1991). Comorbidity and medical complications of bulimia nervosa. *Journal of Clinical Psychiatry, 52,* (Suppl. 10), 13–20.

Mochly-Rosen, D., Chang, F. H., Cheever, L., Kim, M., Diamond, I., & Gordon, A. S. (1988). Chronic ethanol causes heterologous desensitization of receptors by reducing alphas messenger RNA. *Nature, 333,* 848–850.

Modestin, J. (1987). Quality of interpersonal relationships: The most characteristic DSM-III BPD criterion. *Comprehensive Psychiatry, 28,* 397–402.

Mohr, D. C., & Beutler, L. E. (1990). Erectile dysfunction: A review of diagnostic and treatment procedures. *Clinical Psychology Review, 10,* 123–150.

Moises, H. W., Gelernter, J., Guiffra, L. A., Zarcone, V., Wetterberg, L., Civelli, O., Kidd, K. K., Cavalli-Sforza, Grandy, D. K., Kennedy, J. L., Vinogradov, S., Mauer, J., Litt, M., & Sjögren, B. (1991). No linkage between D_2 dopamine receptor gene region and schizophrenia. *Archives of General Psychiatry, 48,* 643–647.

Moleski, R., & Tosi, D. J. (1976). Comparative psychotherapy: Rational-emotive therapy versus systematic desensitization in the treatment of stuttering. *Journal of Consulting and Clinical Psychology, 44,* 309–311.

Monahan, J. (1981). *The clinical prediction of violent behavior.* Washington, D.C.: U.S. Government Printing Office.

Monahan, J. (1984). The prediction of violent behavior: Toward a second generation of theory and policy. *American Journal of Psychiatry, 141,* 10–15.

Money, J. (1984). Paraphilias: Phenomenology and classification. *American Journal of Psychotherapy, 38,* 164–179.

Money, J., & Ehrhardt, A. (1972). *Man and woman, boy and girl.* Baltimore, MD: Johns Hopkins University Press.

Moore-Ede, M. C., & Richardson, G. S. (1985). Medical implications of shift work. *Annual Review of Medicine, 36,* 607–617.

Moran, M. G. (1991). Psychological factors affecting pulmonary and rheumatologic diseases: A review. *Psychosomatics, 32,* 14–23.

Morey, L. C. (1988). Personality disorders in DSM-III and DSM-III-R: Convergence, coverage, and internal consistency. *American Journal of Psychiatry, 145,* 573–577.

Morgan, C. D., & Murray, H. A. (1935). A method for investigating fantasies: The Thematic Apperception test. *American Medical Association Archives of Neurology and Psychiatry, 34,* 289–306.

Morganstern, K. P. (1988). Behavioral interviewing. In A. S. Bellack & M. Hersen (Eds.), *Behavioral assessment: A practical handbook* (3rd ed., pp. 86–118). New York: Pergamon.

Moskowitz, J. A. (1980). Lithium and lady luck: Use of lithium carbonate in compulsive gambling. *New York State Journal of Medicine, 80,* 785–788.

Moss, H. A., & Susman, E. J. (1980). Longitudinal study of personality development. In J. Kagan & O. G. Brim, Jr. (Eds.), *Constancy and change in development* (pp. 530–595). Cambridge, MA: Harvard University Press.

Moss, H. B., Yao, J. K., & Maddock, J. M. (1989). Responses by sons of alcoholic fathers to alcoholic and placebo drinks: Perceived mood, intoxication, and plasma prolactin. *Alcoholism (NY), 13,* 252–257.

Mowrer, O. H. (1947). On the dual nature of learning—A reinterpretation of "conditioning" and "problem-solving". *Harvard Educational Review, 17,* 102–148.

Mrazek, F. J. (1984). Sexual abuse of children. In B. Lahey & A. E. Kazdin (Eds.), *Advances in child clinical psychology* (Vol. 6, pp. 199–215). New York: Plenum Press.

Mueller, J., Kiernan, R. J., & Langston, J. W. (1988). The mental status examination. In H.H. Goldman (Ed.), *Review of general psychiatry* (2nd ed., pp. 193–207). Norwalk, CT: Appleton & Lange.

Mueser, K. T., Douglas, M. S., Bellack, A. S., & Morrison, R. L. (1991). Assessment of enduring deficit and negative symptom subtypes in schizophrenia. *Schizophrenia Bulletin, 17,* 565–582.

Muller, S. A. (1987). Trichotillomania. *Dermatology Clinics, 5,* 595–601.

Munley, P. H., & Zarantonello, M. M. (1990). A comparison of MMPI profile types with corresponding estimated MMPI-2 profiles. *Journal of Clinical Psychology, 46,* 803–811.

Munoz, R. A., Amado, H., & Hyatt, S. (1987). Brief reactive psychosis. *Journal of Clinical Psychiatry, 48,* 324–327.

Murphy, G. E. (1984). The prediction of suicide: Why is it so difficult? *American Journal of Psychotherapy, 38,* 341–349.

Murphy, H. A., Hutchinson, J. M., & Bailey, J. S. (1983). Behavioral school psychology goes outdoors: The effect of organized games on playground aggression. *Journal of Applied Behavior Analysis, 16,* 29–35.

Murphy, J. (1990). Diagnostic comorbidity and symptom co-occurrence: The Stirling County Study. In J. D. Maser & C. R. Cloninger (Eds.), *Comorbidity of mood and anxiety disorders* (pp. 153–176). Washington, DC: American Psychiatric Press.

Murray, H. A. (1938). *Explorations in personality.* New York: Oxford University Press.

Murray, H. A. (1943). *Thematic Apperception Test manual.* Cambridge, MA: Harvard University Press.

Murray, J. B. (1987). Psychophysiological effects of methylphenidate (Ritalin). *Psychological Reports, 61,* 315–336.

Myers, B. A., & Pueschel, S. M. (1991). Psychiatric disorders in persons with Down syndrome. *The Journal of Nervous and Mental Disease, 179,* 609–613.

Myers, J. K., Weissman, M. M., Tischler, C. E., Holzer, C. E., III, Orvaschel, H., Anthony, J. C., Boyd, J. H., Burke, J. D., Jr., Kramer, M., & Stoltzman, R. (1984). Six-month prevalence of psychiatric disorders in three communities. *Archives of General Psychiatry, 41,* 959–967.

Nadig, P. W., Ware, J. C., & Blumoff, R. (1986). Noninvasive device to produce and maintain an erection-like state. *Urology, 27,* 126–131.

Nadler, L. B. (1985). The epidemiology of pathological gambling: Critique of existing research and alternative strategies. *Journal of Gambling Behavior, 1,* 35–50.

Naeye, R. R., & Peters, E. C. (1984). Mental development of children whose mothers smoked during pregnancy. *Obstetrics and Gynecology, 64,* 601–607.

Nahas, G. G. (1984). Pharmacologic and epidemiologic aspects of alcohol and cannabis. *New York State Journal of Medicine, 84,* 599–604.

Naranjo, C. A., Sellers, E. M., Sullivan, J. T., Woodley, D. V., Kadlec, K., & Sykora, K. (1987). The serotonin uptake inhibitor citalopram attenuates ethanol intake. *Clinical Pharmacology and Therapeutics, 41,* 266–274.

Nash, M. R., & Lynn, S. J. (1986). Child abuse and hypnotic ability. *Imagination, Cognition, and Personality, 5,* 211–218.

Nathan, P. E. (1986). Some implications of recent biological findings for the behavioral treatment of alcoholism. *Behavior Therapist, 9,* 158–161.

Nathan, P. E. (1991). Substance use disorders in the *DSM-IV. Journal of Abnormal Psychology, 100,* 356–361.

National Center for Health Statistics (NCHS). (1990). *Health United States, 1989* (DHHS Publication No. PHS 90-1232). Hyattsville, MD: Public Health Service.

National Institute on Alcohol Abuse and Alcoholism (NIAAA). (1987). *Sixth Special Report to the U.S. Congress on Alcohol and Health from the Secretary of Health and Human Services.* Rockville, MD: Author.

National Institute on Alcohol Abuse and Alcoholism (NIAAA). (1988). *National Household Survey on Drug Abuse: Main findings 1985* (DHHS Publication No. ADM 88-1586). Rockville, MD: Author.

National Institute on Alcohol Abuse and Alcoholism (NIAAA). (1989). *Apparent per capita alcohol consumption: National, state, and regional trends, 1977–1987* (Surveillance Report No. 13). Rockville, MD: Author.

National Institute on Alcohol Abuse and Alcoholism (NIAAA). (1991a). Fetal alcohol syndrome. *Alcohol Alert,* No. 13, 1–4.

National Institute on Alcohol Abuse and Alcoholism (NIAAA). (1991b). *National Household Survey on Drug Abuse: Main findings 1990* (DHHS Publication No. ADM 91–1788). Rockville, MD: Author.

National Institute on Drug Abuse (NIDA). (1991). *NIDA Notes,* 6(3).

National Institute on Drug Abuse and National Institute on Alcohol Abuse and Alcoholism (NIDA and NIAAA). (1989). *Highlights from the 1987 National Drug and Alcoholism Treatment Unit Survey (NDATUS).* Rockville, MD: Authors.

Nebes, R. D., & Brady, C. B. (1990). Preserved organization of semantic attributes in Alzheimer's disease. *Psychology and Aging, 5,* 574–579.

Nemiah, J. C. (1985). Janet redivivus: The centenary of *L'automatisme psychologique. American Journal of Psychiatry, 146,* 1527–1529.

Neshkes, R. E., & Jarvik, L. F., (1987). Affective disorders in the elderly. *Annual Review of Medicine, 38,* 445–456.

Neville, D., & Barnes, S. (1985). The suicidal phone call. *Journal of Psychosocial Nursing and Mental Health Services, 23,* 14–18.

Newlin, D. B. (1987). Alcohol expectancy and conditioning in sons of alcoholics. *Advances in Alcohol and Substance Abuse, 6,* 33–57.

Newman, J. P., Patterson, C. M., & Kosson, D. S. (1987). Response perseveration in psychopaths. *Journal of Abnormal Psychology, 96,* 145–148.

Newsom, C., & Rincover, A. (1989). Autism. In E. J. Mash & R. A. Barkley (Eds.), *Treatment of childhood disorders* (pp. 286–346). New York: Guilford Press.

Nigg, J. T., Lohr, N. E., Westen, D., Gold, L. J., & Silk, K. R. (1992). Malevolent object representations in borderline personality disorder and major depression. *Journal of Abnormal Psychology, 101,* 61–67.

Nolen-Hoeksema, S. (1987). Sex differences in unipolar depression: Evidence and theory. *Psychological Bulletin, 101,* 259–282.

Nolen-Hoeksema, S. (1991). Responses to depression and their effects on the duration of depressive episodes. *Journal of Abnormal Psychology, 100,* 569–582.

Norcross, J. (1992). (Ed.). *Handbook of eclectic psychotherapy.* New York: Brunner/Mazel.

Norcross, J. C., & Prochaska, J. O. (1988). A study of eclectic (and integrative) views revisited. *Professional Psychology: Research and Practice, 19,* 170–174.

Norris, R., Carroll, D., & Cochrane, R. (1990). The effects of aerobic and anaerobic training on fitness, blood pressure, and psychological stress and well-being. *Journal of Psychosomatic Research, 34,* 367–375.

Norton, G. R., Dorward, J., & Cox, B. J. (1986). Factors associated with panic attacks in nonclinical subjects. *Behavior Therapy, 17,* 239–252.

Nöthen, M. M., Erdmann, J., Körner, J., Lanczik, M., Fritze, J., Fimmers, R., Grandy, D. K., O'Dowd, B. & Propping, P. (1992). Lack of association between dopamine D_1 and D_2 receptor genes and bipolar affective disorder. *American Journal of Psychiatry, 149,* 199–201.

Noyes, R., Jr., & Perry, P. (1990). Maintenance treatment with antidepressants in panic disorder. *Journal of Clinical Psychiatry, 51*(12, Suppl. A), 24–30.

Nuechterlein, K. H. (1987). Vulnerability models for schizophrenia: State of the art. In H. Häfner, W. F. Gattaz, & W. Janzarik (Eds.), *Search for the causes of schizophrenia* (Vol. 1, pp. 297–315). Berlin: Springer-Verlag.

Nunes, E. V., Frank, K. A., & Kornfeld, D. S. (1987). Psychologic treatment for the Type A behavior pattern and for coronary heart disease: A meta-analysis of the literature. *Psychosomatic Medicine, 48,* 159–173.

Nurco, D. N., Ball, J. C., Shaffer, J. W., & Hanlon, T. E. (1985). The criminality of narcotic addicts. *Journal of Nervous and Mental Diseases, 173,* 94–102.

Nuss, W. S. & Zubenko, G. S. (1992). Correlates of persistent depressive symptoms in widows. *American Journal of Psychiatry, 149,* 346–351.

O'Brien, P. E. & Gaborit, M. (1992). Codependency: A disorder separate from chemical dependency. *Journal of Clinical Psychology, 48,* 129–136.

O'Callaghan, M. A. J., & Carroll, D. (1987). The role of psychosurgical studies in the control of antisocial behavior. In S. A. Mednick, T. E. Moffitt, & S. A. Stack (Eds.), *The causes of crime: New biological approaches* (pp. 312–328). Cambridge: Cambridge University Press.

O'Connor v. Donaldson, 95 S.Ct. 2486 (1975).

Ober, B. A., Shenaut, G. K., Jagust, W. J., & Stillman, R. C. (1991). Automatic semantic priming with various category relations in Alzheimer's disease and normal aging. *Psychology and Aging, 6,* 647–660.

Oei, T. P. S., & Jackson, P. R. (1982). Social skills and cognitive behavioral approaches to the treatment of problem drinking. *Journal of Studies on Alcohol, 43,* 532–547.

Oei, T. P. S., Lim, B., & Hennessy, B. (1990). Psychological dysfunction in battle: Combat stress reactions and posttraumatic stress disorder. *Clinical Psychology Review, 10,* 355–388.

Ogata, S., Silk, K. R., Goodrich, S., Lohr, N. E., Westen, D., & Hill, E. (1990). Childhood abuse and clinical symptoms in borderline personality disorder. *American Journal of Psychiatry, 147,* 1008–1013.

Oliver, C., & Holland, A. J. (1986). Down's Syndrome and Alzheimer's disease: A review. *Psychological Medicine, 16,* 307–322.

Olweus, D. (1987). Testosterone and adrenaline: Aggressive anti-social behavior in normal adolescent males. In S. A. Mednick, T. E. Moffitt, & S. A. Stack (Eds.), *The causes of crime: New biological approaches* (pp. 263–282). Cambridge: Cambridge University Press.

Oren, D. A., Brainard, G. C., Johnston, S. H., Joseph-Vanderpool, J. R., Sorek, E., & Rosenthal, N. E. (1991). Treatment of seasonal affective disorder with green light and red light. *American Journal of Psychiatry, 148,* 509–511.

Orne, M. T., Dinges, D. F., & Orne, E. C. (1984). On the differential diagnosis of multiple personality in the forensic context. *International Journal of Clinical and Experimental Hypnosis, 32,* 118–169.

Öst, L-G., Jerremalm, A., & Johansson, J. (1984). Individual response patterns and the effects of different behavioral methods in the treatment of social phobia. *Behaviour Research and Therapy, 22,* 697–708.

Öst, L-G. (1987). Age of onset in different phobias. *Journal of Abnormal Psychology, 96,* 223–229.

Oswald, I., & Evans, J. (1985). On serious violence during sleep walking. *British Journal of Psychiatry, 147,* 688–691.

Overpeck, M. D., & Moss, A. J. (1991). Children's exposure to environmental cigarette smoke before and after birth. *Advance Data, 202,* 1–12.

Palazzoli, M., Boscolo, L., Cecchin, G., & Prata, G. (1978). *Paradox and counterparadox: A new model in the therapy of the family in schizophrenic transaction.* New York: Jason Aronson.

Park, C. C., & Shapiro, L. N. (1976). *You are not alone: Understanding and dealing with mental illness: A guide for patients, families, doctors, and other professionals.* Boston: Little, Brown.

Parker, G., Johnston, P., & Hayward, L. (1988). Parental "expressed emotion" as a predictor of schizophrenic relapse. *Archives of General Psychiatry, 45,* 806–813.

Parker, K. (1983). A meta-analysis of the reliability and validity of the Rorschach. *Journal of Personality Assessment, 47,* 227–231.

Parker, K. C. H., Hanson, R. K., & Hunsley, J. (1988). MMPI, Rorschach, and WAIS: A meta-analytic comparison of reliability, stability, and validity. *Psychological Bulletin, 103,* 367–373.

Patrick, C. J., Cuthbert, B. N., & Lang, P. J. (1990). Emotion in the criminal psychopath: Fear imagery. *Psychophysiology, 27*(Suppl. 4A), S55.

Paul, G. L. (1966). *Insight vs. desensitization in psychotherapy: An experiment in anxiety reduction.* Stanford: Stanford University Press.

Paul, G. L., & Lentz, R. J. (1977). *Psychosocial treatment of chronic mental patients: Milieu versus social-learning programs.* Cambridge, MA: Harvard University Press.

Pauly, I. B., & Edgerton, M. T. (1986). The gender identity movement: A growing surgical-psychiatric liaison. *Archives of Sexual Behavior, 15,* 315–329.

Pearlin, L. I., Mullan, J. T., Semple, S. J., & Skaff, M. M. (1990). Caregiving and the stress process: An overview of concepts and their measures. *The Gerontologist, 30,* 583–591.

Peck, C. P. (1986). A public mental health issue: Risk taking and compulsive gambling. *American Psychologist, 41,* 461–465.

Peck, D. L. (1987). Social-psychological correlates of adolescent and youthful suicide. *Adolescence, 22* 863–878.

Pennebaker, J. W., Colder, M., & Sharp, L. K. (1990). Accelerating the coping process. *Journal of Personality and Social Psychology, 58,* 528–537.

Pennebaker, J. W., & Susman, J. R. (1988). Disclosure of traumas and psychosomatic processes. [Special issue: Stress and coping in relation to health and disease]. *Social Science and Medicine, 26,* 327–332.

Perry, S. W., (1990). Organic mental disorders caused by HIV: Update on early diagnosis and treatment. *American Journal of Psychiatry, 147,* 696–710.

Perse, T. (1988). Obsessive-compulsive disorder: A treatment review. *Journal of Clinical Psychiatry, 49,* 48–55.

Persson, G., & Nordland, C. L. (1985). Agoraphobics and social phobics: Differences in background factors, syndrome profiles and therapeutic response. *Acta Psychiatrica Scandinavica, 71,* 148–159.

Peselow, E. D., Robins, C., Block, P., Barouche, F., & Fieve, R. R. (1990). Dysfunctional attitudes in depressed patients before and after clinical treatment and in normal control subjects. *American Journal of Psychiatry, 147,* 439–444.

Peterson, C., & Seligman, M. E. P. (1984). Causal explanations as a risk factor for depression: Theory and evidence. *Psychological Review, 91,* 347–374.

Petrie, W. M., Maffucci, R. J., & Woosley, R. L. (1982). Propranolol and depression. *American Journal of Psychiatry, 139,* 92–94.

Pfohl, B. (1991). Histrionic personality disorder: A review of available data and recommendations for DSM-IV. *Journal of Personality Disorders, 5,* 150–166.

Phillips, D. P., & Carstensen, L. L. (1986). Clustering of teenage suicides after television news stories about suicide. *New England Journal of Medicine, 315,* 685–689.

Phillips, K. A. (1991). Body dysmorphic disorder: The distress of imagined ugliness. *American Journal of Psychiatry, 148,* 1138–1149.

Pickar, D., Breier, A., Hsiao, J. K., Doran, A. R., Wolkowitz, O. M., Pato, C. N., Konicki, P. E., & Potter, W. Z. (1990). Cerebrospinal fluid and plasma monoamine metabolites and their relation to psychosis. *Archives of General Psychiatry, 47,* 641–648.

Pickens, R. W., & Fletcher, B. W. (1991). Overview of treatment issues. In R. W. Pickens, C. G. Leukefeld, & C. R. Schuster (Eds.), *Improving drug abuse treatment* (NIDA Research Monograph No. 106, pp. 1–19). (DHHS Publication No. ADM 91–1754). Washington, DC: U.S. Government Printing Office.

Pickens, R. W., Svikis, D. S., McGue, M., Lykken, D. T., Heston, L. L. & Clayton, P. J. (1991). Heterogeneity in the inheritance of alcoholism. *Archives of General Psychiatry, 48,* 19–28.

Pitman, R. K., Altman, B., Greenwald, E., Longpre, R. E., Macklin, M. L., Poiré, R. E., & Steketee, G. S. (1991). Psychiatric complications during flooding therapy for posttraumatic stress disorder. *Journal of Clinical Psychiatry, 52,* 17–20.

Pitts, F. N., Jr., & McClure, J. N., Jr. (1967). Lactate metabolism in anxiety neurosis. *New England Journal of Medicine, 277,* 1329–1336.

Pliszka, S. R. (1987). Tricyclic antidepressants in the treatment of children with attention deficit disorder. *Journal of the American Academy of Child and Adolescent Psychiatry, 26,* 127–132.

Plomin, R., Lichtenstein, P., Pedersen, N. L, McClearn, G. E., & Nesselroade, J. R. (1990). Genetic influence in life events during the last half of the life span. *Psychology and Aging, 5,* P25–P30.

Pogue-Giele, M. F., & Harrow, M. (1987). Negative symptoms in schizophrenia: Longitudinal characteristics and etiological hypotheses. In P. D. Harvey & E. F. Walker (Eds.), *Positive and negative symptoms of psychosis* (pp. 94–123). Hillsdale, NJ: Lawrence Erlbaum.

Polivy, J., & Herman, C. P. (1987). Diagnosis and treatment of normal eating. *Journal of Consulting and Clinical Psychology, 55,* 635–644.

Pollack, M. H., Otto, M. W., Rosenbaum, J. F., Sachs, G. S., O'Neil, C., Asher, R., & Meltzer-Brody, S. (1990). Longitudinal course of panic disorder: Findings from the Massachusetts General Hospital Naturalistic Study. *Journal of Clinical Psychiatry, 51*(12, Suppl. A), 12–16.

Pollard, C. A., & Henderson, J. G. (1988). Four types of social phobia in a community sample. *Journal of Nervous and Mental Disease, 176,* 440–445.

Pollard, C. A., Ibe, I. O., Krojanker, D. N., Kitchen, A. D., Bronson, S. S., & Flynn, T. M. (1991). Clomipramine treatment of trichotillomania: A follow-up report on four cases. *Journal of Clinical Psychiatry, 52*, 128–130.

Popkin, M. K., Tucker, G., Caine, E., Folstein, M., & Grant, I. (1989). The fate of organic mental disorders in *DSM-IV, 30*, 438–441.

Porjesz, B., Begleiter, H., Bihari, B., & Kissin, B. (1987). Event-related brain potentials to high incentive stimuli in abstinent alcoholics. *Alcohol: An International Biomedical Journal, 4*, 283–287.

Prince, V., & Bentler, P. M. (1972). Survey of 504 cases of transvestism. *Psychological Reports, 31*, 903–917.

Prochaska, J. O., & DiClemente, C. C. (1983). Stages and processes of self-change of smoking: Toward an integrative model of change. *Journal of Consulting and Clinical Psychology, 51*, 390–395.

Prochaska, J. O. (1982). *Systems of psychotherapy: A transtheoretical analysis.* Pacific Grove, CA: Brooks/Cole.

Putnam, F. W., Guroff, J. J., Silberman, E. K., Barban, L., & Post, R. M. (1986). The clinical phenomenology of multiple personality disorder: Review of 100 recent cases. *Journal of Clinical Psychiatry, 47*, 285–293.

Quadland, M. C. (1985). Compulsive sexual behavior: Definition of a problem and an approach to treatment. *Journal of Sex and Marital Therapy, 11*, 121–132.

Quinsey, V. L., Chaplin, T. C., & Upfold, D. (1989). Arsonists and sexual arousal to fire setting: Correlation unsupported. *Journal of Behaviour Therapy and Experimental Psychiatry, 20*, 203–209.

Quon, D., Wang, Y., Catalano, R., Scardina, J. M., Murakami, K., & Cordell, B. (1991). Formation of B-amyloid protein deposits in brains of transgenic mice. *Nature, 18*, 239–241.

Rabin, B. S., Cohen, S., Ganguli, R., Lysle, D. T., & Cunnick, J. E. (1989). Bidirectional interaction between the central nervous system and immune system. *Critical Reviews in Immunology, 9*, 279–312.

Rachlin, H. (1990). Why do people gamble and keep gambling despite heavy losses? *Psychological Sciences, 1*, 294–297.

Rachman, S. (1966). Sexual fetishism: An experimental analog. *Psychological Record, 16*, 293–296.

Rachman, S., & Hodgson, R. J. (1968). Experimentally induced "sexual fetishism" replication and development. *Psychological Record, 18*, 25–27.

Randall, T. (1991). Reply to "Domestic violence: The role of alcohol." *Journal of the American Medical Association, 265*, 460–461.

Rankin, H., Hodgson, R., & Stockwell, T. (1983). Cue exposure and response prevention with alcoholics: A controlled trial. *Behaviour Research and Therapy, 21*, 435–446.

Rapee, R. M., Litwin, E. M., & Barlow, D. H. (1990). Impact of life events on subjects with panic disorder and on comparison subjects. *American Journal of Psychiatry, 147*, 640–644.

Rapoport, J. L. (1989, March). The biology of obsessions and compulsions. *Scientific American*, pp. 83–89.

Rapoport, J. L. (1990). The waking nightmare: An overview of obsessive compulsive disorder. *Journal of Clinical Psychiatry, 51*(11, Suppl.), 25–28.

Ratner, R. A. (1989). Trichotillomania. In T. B. Karasu (Ed.), *Treatment of psychiatric disorders* (pp. 2481–2486). Washington, DC: American Psychiatric Association.

Rauschenberger, J., Schmitt, N., & Hunter, J. E. (1980). A test of the need hierarchy concept by a Markov model of change in need strength. *Administrative Science Quarterly, 25*, 654–670.

Regier, D. A., Boyd, J. S., Burke, J. D., Rae, D. S., Myers, J. K., Kramer, M., Robins, L. N., George, L. K., Karno, M., & Locke, B. Z. (1988). One-month prevalence of mental disorders in the United States. *Archives of General Psychiatry, 45*, 977–986.

Reifler, B. V., Larson, E., & Teri, L. (1987). An outpatient geriatric psychiatry assessment and treatment service. *Clinics in Geriatric Medicine, 3*, 203–210.

Reisberg, B. (1983). Clinical presentation, diagnosis, and symptomatology of age-associated cognitive decline and Alzheimer's disease. In B. Reisberg (Ed.), *Alzheimer's disease* (pp. 173–187). New York: Free Press.

Reisine, T. (1981). Adaptive changes in catecholamine receptors in the central nervous system. *Neuroscience, 6*, 1471–1502.

Reuler, J. B., Girard, D. E., & Cooney, T. G. (1985). Wernicke's encephalopathy. *New England Journal of Medicine, 312*, 1035–1039.

Reynolds, C. F., III, Hoch, C. C., Kupfer, D. J., Buysse, D. J., Houck, P. R., Stack, J. A., & Campbell, D. W. (1988). Bedside differentiation of depressive pseudodementia from dementia. *American Journal of Psychiatry, 145*, 1099–1103.

Reynolds, C. F., III, Kupfer, D. J., Buysse, D. J., Coble, P. A., & Yeager, A. (1991). Subtyping *DSM-III-R* primary insomnia: A literature review by the *DSM-IV* work group on sleep disorders. *American Journal of Psychiatry, 148*, 432–438.

Rhoads, J. M. (1989). Exhibitionism and voyeurism. In T. S. Karasu (Ed.), *Treatment of psychiatric disorders* (Vol. 1, pp. 670–673). Washington, DC: American Psychiatric Association.

Rice, D. M., Buchsbaum, M. S., Starr, A., Auslander, L., Hagman, J., & Evans, W. J. (1990). Abnormal EEG slow activity in left temporal areas in senile dementia of the Alzheimer's type. *Journal of Gerontology: Medical Sciences, 45*, M145–M151.

Rice, D. P., Kelman, S., Miller, L. S., & Dunmeyer, S. (1990). *The economic costs of alcohol and drug abuse and mental illness: 1985.* San Francisco: Institute for Health and Aging.

Rice, J., Reich, T., Andreasen, N. C., Endicott, J., Van Eerdewegh, M., Fishman, R., Hirschfeld, R. M. A., & Klerman, G. L. (1987). The familial transmission of bipolar illness. *Archives of General Psychiatry, 44*, 441–447.

Rich, C. L., Warsradt, G. M., Nemiroff, R. A., Fowler, R. C., & Young, D. (1991). Suicide, stressors, and the life cycle. *American Journal of Psychiatry, 148*, 524–527.

Rifkin, A., Pecknold, J. C., Swinson, R. P., Ballenger, J. C., Burrows, G. D., Noyes, R., Dupont, R. L., & Lesser, I. (1990). Sequence of improvement in agoraphobia with panic attacks. *Journal of Psychiatric Research, 24*(1), 1–8.

Ritvo, E. R., & Freeman, B. J. (1984). A medical model of autism: Etiology, pathology and treatment. *Pediatric Annals, 13*, 298–305.

Roazen, P. (1974). *Freud and his followers.* New York: New American Library.

Roazen, P. (1976). *Erikson: The power and limits of a vision.* New York: Free Press.

Roberto, L. G. (1983). Issues in diagnosis and treatment of transsexualism. *Archives of Sexual Behavior, 12*, 445–473.

Robins, C. J., Block, P., & Peselow, E. D. (1990). Endogenous and nonendogenous depression: Relations to life events, dysfunctional attitudes and event perceptions. *British Journal of Clinical Psychology, 29*, 201–207.

Robins, L. N. (1966). *Deviant children grow up: A sociological and psychiatric study of sociopathic personality.* Baltimore: Williams & Wilkins.

Robins, L. N., Helzer, J. E., Croughan, J. L., & Ratcliff, K. S. (1981). The National Institute of Mental Health Diagnostic Interview Schedule. *Archives of General Psychiatry, 38*, 381–389.

Robins, L. N., Helzer, J. E., Weissman, M. M., Orvaschel, H., Gruenberg, E., Burke, J. D., Jr., & Regier, D. A. (1984). Lifetime prevalence of specific psychiatric disorders in three sites. *Archives of General Psychiatry, 41*, 949–958.

Robins, P. M., & Sesan, R. (1991). Munchausen syndrome by proxy: Another women's disorder? *Professional Psychology: Research and Practice, 22*, 285–290.

Robinson, D., & Henry, S. (1979). Alcoholics Anonymous in England and Wales: Basic results from a survey. *British Journal of Alcohol and Alcoholism, 13,* 36–44.

Rogers, C. R. (1951). *Client-centered therapy: Its current practice implications, and theory.* Boston: Houghton Mifflin.

Rogers, C. R. (1959(. A theory of therapy, personality, and interpersonal relationships as developed in the client-centered framework. In S. Koch (Ed.), *Psychology: A study of a science* (Vol. 3, pp. 184–256). New York: McGraw-Hill.

Rogers, C. R. (1961). *On becoming a person.* Boston: Houghton Mifflin.

Rogers, C. R. (1963). The concept of the fully functioning person. *Psychotherapy: Theory, Research and Practice,* 17–26.

Rogers, C. R., & Dymond, R. F. (Eds.). (1954). *Psychotherapy and behavior change.* Chicago: University of Chicago Press.

Rose, J. M., & DelMaestro, S. G. (1990). Separation-individuation conflict as a model for understanding distressed caregivers: Psychodynamic and cognitive case studies. *The Gerontologist, 30,* 693–697.

Rosenbaum, M. (1980). The role of the term schizophrenia in the decline of diagnoses of multiple personality. *Archives of General Psychiatry, 37,* 1383–1385.

Rosenbloom, S., Campbell, M., George, A. E., Kricheff, I. I., Taleporos, E., Anderson, L., Reuben, R. N., & Korein, J. (1984). High resolution CT scanning in infantile autism: A quantitative approach. *Journal of the American Academy of Child Psychiatry, 23,* 72–77.

Rosenhan, D. L. (1973). On being sane in insane places. *Science, 179,* 250–258.

Rosenstein, M. J., Milazzo-Sayre, L. J., & Manderscheid, R. W. (1989). Care of person with schizophrenia: A statistical profile. *Schizophrenia Bulletin, 15,* 45–57.

Rosenthal, D. (Ed.). (1963). *The Genain quadruplets: A case study and theoretical analysis of heredity and environment in schizophrenia.* New York: Basic Books.

Rosenthal, R. J. (1986). The pathological gambler's system of self-deception. *Journal of Gambling Behavior, 2,* 108–120.

Roses, A. D., Pericak-Vance, M. A., Clark, C. M., Gilbert, J. R., Yamaoka, L. H., Haynes, C. S., Speer, M. C., Gaskell, P. C., Hung, W. Y., Trofatter, J. A., Earl, N. L., Lee, J. E., Alberts, M. J., Dawson, D. V., Bartlett, R. J., Siddique, T., Vance, J. M., Conneally, P. M., & Heyman, A. L. (1990). Linkage studies of late-onset familial Alzheimer's disease. In R. J. Wurtman, S. Corkin, J. H. Growdon, & E. Ritter-Walker (Eds.), *Advances in neurology: Vol. 51. Alzheimer's disease* (pp. 185–196). New York: Raven.

Roskies, E., Seraganian, P., Oseasohn, R., Smilga, C., Martin, N., & Hanley, J. A. (1989). Treatment of psychological stress responses in healthy Type A men. In R. W. J. Neufeld (Ed.), *Advances in the investigation of psychological stress* (pp. 284–304). New York: Wiley.

Ross, A. O., & Carr, E. G. (1980). Childhood disorders. In A. E. Kazdin, A. S. Bellack, & M. Hersen (Eds.), *New perspectives in abnormal psychology* (pp. 376–395). New York: Oxford.

Ross, C. A., & Gahan, P. (1988). Cognitive analysis of multiple personality disorder. *American Journal of Psychotherapy, 42,* 229–239.

Ross, C. A., Miller, S. D., Reagor, P., Bjornson, L., Fraser, G. A., & Anderson, G. (1990). Structured interview data on 102 cases of multiple personality disorder from four centers. *American Journal of Psychiatry, 147,* 596–601.

Ross, D. M., & Ross, S. A. (1982). *Hyperactivity: Current issues, research, and theory* (2nd ed.). New York: Wiley.

Roth, W. T. (1988). The role of medication in post-traumatic therapy. In F. M. Ochberg (Ed.), *Post-traumatic therapy and victims of violence* (pp. 39–56). New York: Brunner/Mazel.

Roth, W. T., Margraf, J., Ehlers, A., Haddad, J. M., Maddock, R. J., Agras, W. S., & Taylor, C. B. (1992). Imipramine and alprazo-lam effects on stress test reactivity in panic disorder. *Biological Psychiatry, 31,* 35–51.

Rounsaville, B. J., Anton, S. F., Carroll, K., Budde, D., Prusoff, B. A., & Gawin, F. (1991). Psychiatric diagnoses of treatment-seeking cocaine abusers. *Archives of General Psychiatry, 48,* 43–51.

Rounsaville, B. J., O'Malley, S., Foley, S., & Weisman, M. M. (1988). Role of manual-guided training in the conduct and efficacy of interpersonal psychotherapy for depression. *Journal of Consulting and Clinical Psychology, 56,* 681–688.

Rourke, B. P. (1988). Socioemotional disturbances of learning disabled children. *Journal of Consulting and Clinical Psychology, 56,* 801–810.

Roy, A., Adinoff, B., Roehrich, L., Lamparski, D., Custer, R., Lorenz, V., Barbaccia, M., Guidotti, A., Costa, E., & Linnoila, M. (1988). Pathological gambling: A psychobiological study. *Archives of General Psychiatry, 45,* 369–373.

Roy, A., Segal, N. L., Centerwall, B. S., & Robinette, C. D. (1991). Suicide in twins. *Archives of General Psychiatry, 48,* 29–32.

Roy-Byrne, P. P., Geraci, M., & Uhde, T. W. (1986). Life events and the onset of panic disorder. *American Journal of Psychiatry, 143,* 1424–1427.

Rozée, P. D., & Van Boemel, G. (1989). The psychological effects of war trauma and abuse on older Cambodian refugee women. *Women and Therapy, 8,* 23–50.

Rubin, E. H. (1990). Psychopathology of senile dementia of the Alzheimer's type. In R. J. Wurtman, S. Corkin, J. H. Growdon, & E. Ritter-Walker (Eds.), *Advances in neurology: Vol. 51, Alzheimer's disease* (pp. 53–59). New York: Raven.

Rubin, P., Holm, S., Friberg, L., Videbech, P., Andersen, H. S., Bendsen, B. B., Stromso, Larsen, J. K., Lassen, N. A., & Hemmingsen, R. (1991). Altered modulation of prefrontal and subcortical brain activity in newly diagnosed schizophrenia and schizophreniform disorder. *Archives of General Psychiatry, 48,* 987–995.

Rudden, M., Sweeney, J., & Frances, A. (1990). Diagnosis and clinical course of erotomanic and other delusional patients. *American Journal of Psychiatry, 147,* 625–628.

Rumsey, J. M., Rapoport, J. L., & Sceery, W. R. (1985). Autistic children as adults: Psychiatric, social, and behavioral outcomes. *Journal of the American Academy of Child Psychiatry, 24,* 465–473.

Rund, B. R. (1990). Fully recovered schizophrenics: A retrospective study of some premorbid and treatment factors. *Psychiatry, 53,* 127–139.

Rutter, M. (1970). Autistic children: Infancy to adulthood. *Seminars in Psychiatry, 2,* 435–450.

Rutter, M. (1975). *Helping troubled children.* New York: Penguin.

Rutter, M. (1984). Psychopathology and development: II. Childhood experiences and personality development. *Australian and New Zealand Journal of Psychiatry, 18,* 314–327.

Rutter, M. (1985). The treatment of autistic children. *Journal of Child Psychology and Psychiatry, 26,* 193–214.

Sacco, W. P., & Beck, A. T. (1985). Cognitive therapy of depression. In E. E. Beckhan & W. R. Leber (Eds.), *Handbook of depression: Treatment, assessment, and research* (pp. 3–38). Homewood, IL: Dorsey Press.

Sacher-Masoch, R. V. (1835–95). *Venus in furs.* (Fernanda Savage, Trans.). Private printing.

Sacks, O. (1987). *The man who mistook his wife for a hat, and other clinical tales.* New York: Harper & Row.

Sadavoy, J., & Leszcz, M. (1987). *Treating the elderly with psychotherapy: The scope for change in later life.* Madison, CT: International Universities Press.

Safran, J. D. (1990). Towards a refinement of cognitive therapy in light of interpersonal theory: I. Theory. *Clinical Psychology Review, 10,* 87–105.

Salzman, L., & Thaler, F. H. (1981). Obsessive-compulsive disorders: A review of the literature. *American Journal of Psychiatry, 138,* 286–296.

Sameroff, A., Seifer, R., Zaax, M., & Barocas, R. (1987). Early indicators of developmental risk: Rochester longitudinal study. *Schizophrenia Bulletin, 13,* 383–394.

Samuelson, F. (1980). J. B. Watson's Little Albert, Cyril Burt's twins, and the need for a critical science. *American Psychologist, 35,* 619–625.

Sanderson, W. C., & Barlow, D. H. (1990). A description of patients diagnosed with DSM-III-R generalized anxiety disorder. *Journal of Nervous and Mental Disease, 178,* 588–591.

Satel, S. L., Price, L. H., Palumbo, J. M., McDougle, C. J., Krystal, J. H., Gawin, F., Charney, D. S., Heninger, G. R., & Kleber, H. D. (1991). Clinical phenomenology and neurobiology of cocaine abstinence: A prospective inpatient study. *American Journal of Psychiatry, 148,* 1712–1716.

Satel, S. L., Southwick, S. M., & Gawin, F. H. (1991). Clinical features of cocaine-induced paranoia. *American Journal of Psychiatry, 148,* 495–498.

Satlin A., & Cole, J. O. (1988). Psychopharmacologic interventions. In L. F. Jarvik & C. H. Winograd (Eds.), *Treatments for the Alzheimer patient.* New York: Springer.

Sayers, J. (1991). *Mothers of psychoanalysis.* New York: Norton.

Schall, M., Kemeny, A., & Maltzman, I. (1992). Factors associated with alcohol use in university students. *Journal of Studies on Alcohol, 53,* 122–136.

Schapiro, M. B., & Rapoport, S. I. (1988). Alzheimer's disease in premorbidly normal and Down's syndrome individuals: Selective involvement of hippocampus and neocortical associative brain regions. *Brain Dysfunction, 1,* 2–11.

Schatzberg, A.F. (1992). Recent developments in the acute somatic treatment of major depression. *Journal of Clinical Psychiatry, 53,* 20–25.

Scheff, T. J. (1966). *Being mentally ill: A sociological theory.* Chicago: Aldine.

Schellenberg, G. D., Bird, T. D., Wijsman, E. M., Moore, D. K., Boenke, M., Bryant, E. M., Lampe, T. H., Nochlin, D., Sumi, S. M., Deeb, S. S., Beyreuther, K., & Martin, G. M. (1988). Absence of linkage of chromosome 21q21 markers to familial Alzheimer's disease. *Science, 241,* 1507–1510.

Schiffman, S. S. (1986). The nose as a port of entry for aluminosilicates and other pollutants: Possible role in Alzheimer's disease [Special Issue: Controversial topics on Alzheimer's disease: Intersecting crossroads]. *Neurobiology of Aging, 7,* 576–578.

Schildkraut, J. J. (1965). The catecholamine hypothesis of affective disorders: A review of supporting evidence. *American Journal of Psychiatry, 122,* 509–522.

Schleifer, S. J., Scott, B., Stein, M., & Keller, S. E. (1986). Behavioral and developmental aspects of immunity. *Journal of the American Academy of Child Psychiatry, 26,* 751–763.

Schneider, K. (1959). *Clinical psychopathology.* New York: Grune & Stratton.

Schoch, P., Richards, J. G., Haring, P., Takacs, B., Stahli, C., Staehelin, T., Haefely, W., & Mohler, H. (1985). Co-localization of GABA $_A$ receptors and benzodiazepine receptors in the brain shown by monoclonal antibodies. *Nature, 314.* 168–171.

Schoenborn, C. A. (1991). Exposure to alcoholism in the family: United States, 1988. Advance data from vital and health statistics, No. 205. Hyattsville, MD: National Center for Health Statistics.

Schreiber, F.R. (1973). *Sybil.* Chicago: Henry Regnery.

Schuckit, M. A. (1987). Biological vulnerability to alcoholism. *Journal of Consulting and Clinical Psychology, 55,* 301–308.

Schuckit, M. A. (1989). *Drug and alcohol abuse: A clinical guide to diagnosis and treatment* (3rd ed.). New York: Plenum Medical Book.

Schuckit, M. A., & Gold, E. O. (1988). A simultaneous evaluation of multiple markers of ethanol/placebo challenges in sons of alcoholics and controls. *Archives of General Psychiatry, 45,* 211–216.

Schuckit, M. A., Gold, E., & Risch, C. (1987). Serum prolactin levels in sons of alcoholics and control subjects. *American Journal of Psychiatry, 144,* 854–859.

Schuckit, M. A., Zisook, S., & Mortola, J. (1985). Clinical implications of DSM-III diagnoses of alcohol abuse and alcohol dependence. *American Journal of Psychiatry, 142,* 1403–1408.

Schulz, R., Visintainer, P., & Williamson, G. M. (1990). Psychiatric and physical morbidity effects of caregiving. *Journal of Gerontology: Psychological Sciences, 45,* P181–P191.

Schulz, R., & Williamson, G. M. (1991). A 2-year longitudinal study of depression among Alzheimer's caregivers. *Psychology and Aging, 6,* 569–578.

Schwartz, G. E. (1982). Testing the biopsychosocial model: The ultimate challenge facing behavioral medicine. *Journal of Consulting and Clinical Psychology, 50,* 1040–1053.

Schwartz, M. F., & Brasted, W. S. (1985). Sexual addiction. *Medical Aspects of Human Sexuality, 19,* 103, 106–107.

Segraves, R. T., & Schoenberg, H. W. (Eds.). (1985). *Diagnosis and treatment of erectile disturbances.* New York: Plenum Medical Book Company.

Seligman, M. E. P. (1975). *Helplessness: On depression, development, and death.* San Francisco: W.H. Freeman.

Semans, J. H. (1956). Premature ejaculation: A new approach. *Southern Medical Journal, 49,* 353–361.

Sereny, G., Sharma, V., Holt, J., & Gordis, E. (1986). Mandatory supervised Antabuse therapy in an outpatient alcoholism program: A pilot study. *Alcoholism (NY), 10,* 290–292.

Sexton, M., Fox, N. L., & Hebel, J. R. (1990). Prenatal exposure to tobacco: II. Effects on cognitive functioning at age three. *International Journal of Epidemiology, 19,* 72–77.

Shader, R. I., & Scharfman, E. L. (1989). Depersonalization Disorder. In T. B. Karasu (Ed.), *Treatments of psychiatric disorders* (pp. 2217–2222). Washington, D.C.: American Psychiatric Association.

Shaper, A. G., Phillips, A. N., Pocock, S. J., & Walker, M. (1987). Alcohol and ischaemic heart disease in middle aged British men. *British Medical Journal, 294,* 733–737.

Shapiro, D. (1965). *Neurotic styles.* New York: Basic Books.

Shapiro, D. (1986). The Insanity Defense Reform Act of 1984. *Bulletin of the American Academy of Forensic Psychology, 1,* 1–6.

Shapiro, T., Sherman, M., Calamari, G., & Koch, D. (1987). Attachment in autism and other developmental disorders. *Journal of the American Academy of Child and Adolescent Psychiatry, 26,* 480–484.

Shaw, B. F. (1977). Comparison of cognitive therapy and behavior therapy in the treatment of depression. *Journal of Consulting and Clinical Psychology, 45,* 543–551.

Shea, M. T., Glass, D. R., Pilkonis, P. A., Watkins, J., & Docherty, J. P. (1987). Frequency and implications of personality disorders in a sample of depressed outpatients. *Journal of Personality Disorders, 1,* 27–42.

Sheehan, D. V. (1982). Current concepts in psychiatry: Panic attacks and phobias. *The New England Journal of Medicine, 307,* 156–158.

Shelton, R. C., Karson, C. N., Doran, A. R., Pickar, D., Bigelow, L. B., & Weinberger, D. R. (1988). Cerebral structural pathology in schizophrenia: Evidence for a selective prefrontal cortical defect. *American Journal of Psychiatry, 145,* 154–163.

Shelton, R. C., & Weinberger, D. R. (1986). X-ray computed tomography studies in schizophrenia: A review and synthesis. In

H. A. Nasrallah & D. R. Weinberger (Eds.), *The neurology of schizophrenia* (pp. 207–250). Amsterdam: Elsevier Science.

Sher, K. J. (1985). Subjective effects of alcohol: The influence of setting and individual differences in alcohol expectancies. *Journal of Studies on Alcohol, 46,* 137–146.

Sherrington, R., Brynjolfsson, J., Petursson, H., Potter, M., & Dudleston, K., Barraclough, B., Wasmuth, J., Dobbs, M., & Gurling, H. (1988). Location of the susceptibility locus for schizophrenia on chromosome 5. *Nature, 336,* 164–167.

Shimamura, A. P., Salmon, D. P., Squire, L. R., & Butters, N. (1987). Memory dysfunction and word priming in dementia and amnesia. *Behavioral Neuroscience, 101,* 347–351.

Shneidman, E. S. (1985). *Definition of suicide.* New York: Wiley.

Shneidman, E. S. (1984). Aphorisms of suicide and some implications for psychotherapy. *American Journal of Psychotherapy, 38,* 319–328.

Shneidman, E. S. (1985). Ten commonalities of suicide and their implications for response. *Crisis, 7,* 88–93.

Shostrom, E. L. (1974). *Manual for the Personal Orientation Inventory.* San Diego: EdITS/Educational & Industrial Testing Service.

Shover, N. (1985). *Aging criminals.* Beverly Hills, CA: Sage Publications.

Shulman, B. (1985). Cognitive therapy and the individual psychology of Alfred Adler. In M. J. Mahoney & A. Freeman (Eds.), *Cognition and psychotherapy* (pp. 243–258). New York: Plenum Press.

Siegel, R. K. (1982). Cocaine smoking. *Journal of Psychoactive Drugs: A Multidisciplinary Forum, 14,* 271–359.

Siever, L. J., Bernstein, D. P., & Silverman, J. M. (1991). Schizotypal personality disorder: A review of its current status. *Journal of Personality Disorders, 5,* 178–193.

Siever, L. J., Silverman, J. M., Horvath, T. B., Klar, H., Coccaro, E., Keefe, R. S. E., Pinkham, L., Rinaldi, P., Mohs, R. C., & Davis, K. L. (1990). Increased morbid risk for schizophrenia-related disorders in relatives of schizotypal personality disordered patients. *Archives of General Psychiatry, 47,* 634–640.

Sifneos, P. E. (1979). *Short-term dynamic psychotherapy, evaluation, and technique.* New York: Plenum Press.

Sifneos, P. E. (1981). Short-term anxiety provoking psychotherapy: Its history, technique, outcome, and instruction. In S.H. Budman (Ed.), *Forms of brief therapy* (pp. 45–81). New York: Guilford Press.

Sigvardsson, S., Cloninger, C. R., & Bohman, M. (1985). Prevention and treatment of alcohol abuse: Uses and limitations of the high risk paradigm. *Social Biology, 32,* 185–194.

Silliman, E. R., Campbell, M., & Mitchell, R. S. (1989). Genetic influences in autism and assessment of metalinguistic performance in siblings of autistic children. In G. Dawson (Ed.), *Autism: Nature, diagnosis, and treatment* (pp. 225–229). New York: Guilford Press.

Silverman, L. H. (1976). Psychoanalytic theory: "The reports of my death are greatly exaggerated." *American Psychologist, 31,* 621–637.

Silverman, L. H., Bronstein, A., & Mendelsohn, E. (1976). The further use of the subliminal psychodynamic activation method for the experimental study of the clinical theory of psychoanalysis: On the specificity of the relationship between symptoms and unconscious conflicts. *Psychotherapy: Theory, Research and Practice, 13,* 2–16.

Silverman, L. H., Kwawer, J. S., Wolitzky, C., & Coron, M. (1973). An experimental study of aspects of the psychoanalytic theory of male homosexuality. *Journal of Abnormal Psychology, 82,* 178–188.

Silverman, L. H., & Silverman, D. K. (1964). A clinical experimental approach to the study of subliminal stimulation: The effects of a drive-related stimulus upon Rorschach responses. *Journal of Abnormal and Social Psychology, 69,* 158–172.

Silverman, L. H., & Weinberger, J. (1985). Mommy and I are one: Implications for psychotherapy. *American Psychologist, 40,* 1296–1308.

Simeon, D., Stanley, B., Frances, A., Mann, J.J., Winchel, R., & Stanley, M. (1992). Self-mutilation in personality disorders: Psychological and biological correlates. *American Journal of Psychiatry, 149,* 221–226.

Simon, R. J., & Aaronson, E. E. (1988). *The insanity defense: A critical assessment of law and policy in the post-Hinckley era.* New York: Praeger.

Simonds, J. F., & Parraga, H. (1982). The parasomnias: Prevalence and relationships to each other and to positive family histories. *Hillside Journal of Clinical Psychiatry, 4,* 25–38.

Simpson, M. (1989). Multiple Personality disorder. *British Journal of Psychiatry, 155,* 565.

Simpson, D. D., & Sells, S. B. (1990). *Opioid addiction and treatment: A 12-year follow-up.* Malabar, FL: Robert E. Krieger.

Singer, M. T., & Wynne, L. C. (1963). Differentiating characteristics of parents of childhood schizophrenics, childhood neurotics, and young adult schizophrenics. *American Journal of Psychiatry, 120,* 234–243.

Skinner, B. F. (1953). *Science and human behavior.* New York: Free Press.

Skolnick, A. (1986). Early attachment and personal relationships across the life course. In P. B. Baltes, D. L. Featherman, & R. M. Lerner (Eds.), *Life-span development and behavior.* (Vol. 7, pp. 173–206). Hillsdale, NJ: Erlbaum.

Slater, J., & Depue, R. A. (1981). The contribution of environmental events and social support to serious suicide attempts in primary depressive disorder. *Journal of Abnormal Psychology, 90,* 275–285.

Sloan, P. (1988). Post-traumatic stress in survivors of an airplane crash-landing: A clinical and exploratory research intervention. *Journal of Traumatic Stress, 1,* 211–229.

Small, J. G., Klapper, M. H., Milstein, V., Kellams, J. J., Miller, M. J., Marhenke, J. D., & Small, I. F. (1991). Carbamazepine compared with lithium in the treatment of mania. *Archives of General Psychiatry, 48,* 915–921.

Smalley, S. L., Asarnow, R. F., & Spence, M. A. (1988). Autism and genetics: A decade of research. *Archives of General Psychiatry, 45,* 953–961.

Smith, C. G., & Asch, R. H. (1987). Drug abuse and reproduction. *Fertility and Sterility, 48,* 355–373.

Smith, D. E. (1986). Cocaine-alcohol abuse: Epidemiological, diagnostic and treatment considerations. *Journal of Psychoactive Drugs, 18,* 117–129.

Sokol, R. J., & Clarren, S. K. (1989). Guidelines for use of terminology describing the impact of prenatal alcohol on the offspring. *Alcoholism: Clinical and Experimental Research, 13,* 597–598.

Soldatos, C. R., & Kales, A. (1982). Sleep disorders: Research in psychopathology and its practical implications. *Acta Psychiatrica Scandinavica, 65,* 381–387.

Solomon, K. E., & Annis. H. M. (1990). Outcome and efficacy expectancy in the prediction of post-treatment drinking behaviour. *British Journal of Addiction, 85,* 659–665.

Solomon, S. (1985). Application of neurology to psychiatry. In H. I. Kaplan & B. J. Sadock (Eds.), *Comprehensive textbook of psychiatry* (4th ed., pp. 146–156). Baltimore: Williams & Wilkins.

Solomon, S., & Masdeu, J. C. (1989). Neuropsychiatry and behavioral neurology. In H. I. Kaplan & B. J. Sadock (Eds.), *Comprehensive textbook of psychiatry* (5th ed., pp. 217–240). Baltimore: Williams & Wilkins.

Solomon, Z., Mikulincer, M., & Benbenishty, R. (1989). Combat stress reaction: Clinical manifestations and correlates. *Military Psychology, 1,* 35–47.

Spanos, N. P., Weekes, J. R., & Bertrand, L. D. (1985). Multiple personality: A social psychological perspective. *Journal of Abnormal Psychology, 94*, 362–376.

Sparr, L., & Pankratz, L. D. (1983). Factitious posttraumatic stress disorder. *American Journal of Psychiatry, 140*, 1016–1019.

Spees, E. R. (1987). College students' sexual attitudes and behaviors, 1974–1985: A review of the literature. *Journal of College Student Personnel, 28*, 135–140.

Spencer, G. (1989). *Projections of the population of the United States, by age, sex, and race: 1988 to 2020 (U.S. Bureau of the Census, Current Population Reports, Series P-25, No. 1018)* Washington, DC: U.S. Government Printing Office.

Sperbeck, D. J., & Whitbourne, S. K. (1981). Dependency in the institutional setting: A behavioral training program for geriatric staff. *The Gerontologist, 21*, 268–275.

Spiegel, D., & Cardeña, E. (1991). Disintegrated experience: The dissociative disorders revisited. *Journal of Abnormal Psychology, 100*, 366–378.

Spitzer, R. L. (1975). On pseudoscience in science, logic in remission, and psychiatric diagnosis: A critique of D.L. Rosenhan's 'On Being Sane in Insane Places.' *Journal of Abnormal Psychology, 84*, 442–452.

Spitzer, R.L., First, M.B., Williams, J.B.W., Kendler, K., Pincus, H.A., & Tucker, G. (1992). Now is the time to retire the term 'organic mental disorders.' *American Journal of Psychiatry, 149*, 240–244.

Spitzer, R. L., Williams, J. B. W., & Gibbon, M. (1989). *Structured clinical interview for DSM-III-R (SCID)*. New York: New York State Psychiatric Institute.

Spitzer, R. L., Williams, J. B. W., & Skodol, A. E. (1980). *DSM-III: The major achievements and an overview. American Journal of Psychiatry, 137*, 151–164.

Spitzer, R. L., Williams, J. B. W., & Gibbon, M. (1987). *Structured clinical interview for DSM-III-R (SCID)*. New York: New York State Psychiatric Institute.

Spreen, O. (1988). Prognosis of learning disability. *Journal of Consulting and Clinical Psychology, 56*, 836–842.

Sprenkle, D. H. (1987). Treating a sex addict through marital sex therapy. *Family Relations, 36*, 11–14.

Sroufe, L. A., Fox, N. E., & Pancake, V. R. (1983). Attachment and dependency in developmental perspective. *Child Development, 54*, 1615–1627.

St. Clair, D. M., Blackwood, D., Muir, W., Baillie, D., Hubbard, A., Wright, A., & Evans, H. J. (1989). No linkage of chromosome 5q11-q13 markers to schizophrenia in Scottish families. *Nature, 339*, 305–309.

St. George-Hyslop, P. H., Tanzi, R. E., Polinsky, R. J., Haines, J. L., Nee, L., Watkins, P. C., Myers, R. H., Feldman, R. G., Pollen, D., Drachman, D., Growdon, J., Bruni, A., Foncin, J. F., Salmon, D., Frommelt, P., Amaducci, L., Sorbi, S., Piacentini, S., Stewart, G. D., Hobbs, W. J., Conneally, P. M., & Gusella, J. F. (1987). The genetic defect causing familial Alzheimer's disease maps on chromosome 21. *Science, 235*, 885–890.

Stacy, A. W., Widaman, K. F., & Marlatt, G. A. (1990). Expectancy models of alcohol abuse. *Journal of Personality and Social Psychology, 58*, 918–928.

Stampfer, M. J., Colditz, G. A., Willette, W. C., Speizer, F. E., & Hennekens, C.H. (1988). A prospective study of moderate alcohol consumption and the risk of coronary disease and stroke in women. *New England Journal of Medicine, 319*, 267–273.

Starkstein, S. E., & Robinson, R. G. (1991). Dementia of depression in Parkinson's disease and stroke. *Journal of Nervous and Mental Disease, 179*, 593–601.

Stein, D. M., & Lambert, M. J. (1984). Telephone counseling and crisis intervention: A review. *American Journal of Community Psychology, 12*, 101–126.

Steinberg, M. (1991). The spectrum of depersonalization: Assessment and treatment. *Annual Review of Psychiatry, 10*, 223–247.

Steiner, M., Links, P. S., & Korzekwa, M. (1988). Biological markers in borderline personality disorders: An overview. *Canadian Journal of Psychiatry, 33*, 350–354.

Steiner, W. (1991). Fluoxetine-induced mania in a patient with obsessive-compulsive disorder. *American Journal of Psychiatry, 148*, 1403–1404.

Stekel, W. (1943). *The interpretation of dreams: New developments and technique*. New York: Liveright.

Steketee, G., Foa, E. B., & Grayson, J. B. (1982). Recent advances in the behavioral treatment of obsessive-compulsives. *Archives of General Psychiatry, 39*, 1365–1371.

Stephenson, W. (1953). *The study of behavior: Q-technique and its methodology*. Chicago: University of Chicago Press.

Stern, A. (1938). Psychoanalytic investigation of and therapy in the border line group of neuroses. *Psychoanalytic Quarterly, 7*, 467–489.

Stern, D. N. (1985). *The interpersonal world of the infant: A view from psychoanalytic and developmental psychology*. New York: Basic Books.

Stevens, M. J. (1984). Behavioral treatment of trichotillomania. *Psychological Reports, 55*, 987–990.

Stoller, R. J. (1971). The term "transvestism." *Archives of General Psychiatry, 24*, 230–237.

Stone, A. (1990). *The fate of borderline patients: Successful outcome and psychiatric practice*. New York: Guilford Press.

Stone, M. H. (1983). Psychotherapy with schizotypal borderline patients. *Journal of the American Academy of Psychoanalysis, 11*, 87–111.

Storandt, M. (1990). Bender-Gestalt test performance in senile dementia of the Alzheimer type. *Psychology and Aging, 5*, 604–606.

Stoudemire, A., & Hales, R. E. (1991). Psychological and behavioral factors affecting medical conditions and DMS-IV. *Psychosomatics, 32*, 5–13.

Strachan, A. M. (1986). Family intervention for the rehabilitation of schizophrenia: Toward protection and coping. *Schizophrenia Bulletin, 12*, 678–698.

Strawbridge, W. J., & Wallhagen, M. I. (1991). Impact of family conflict on adult child caregivers. *The Gerontologist, 31*, 770–777.

Streissguth, A. P., Aase, J. M., Clarren, S. K., Randels, S. P., LaDue, R. A., & Smith, D. F. (1991). Fetal alcohol syndrome in adolescents and adults. *Journal of the American Medical Association, 265*, 1961–1967.

Striegel-Moore, R. H., Silberstein, L. R., & Rodin, J. (1986). Toward an understanding of risk factors in bulimia. *American Psychologist, 41*, 246–263.

Strober, M. (1991). Family-genetic studies of eating disorders. *Journal of Clinical Psychiatry, 52*(Suppl. 10), 9–12.

Strober, M., & Humphrey, L. L. (1987). Familial contributions to the etiology and course of anorexia nervosa and bulimia. *Journal of Consulting and Clinical Psychology, 55*, 654–659.

Sturgis, E. T., & Gramling, S. (1988). Psychophysiological assessment. In A. S. Bellack & M. Hersen (Eds.), *Behavioral assessment: A practical handbook* (3rd ed., pp. 213–251). New York: Pergamon.

Sullivan, H. S. (1953a). *Conceptions of modern psychiatry*. New York: Norton.

Sullivan, H. S. (1953b). *The interpersonal theory of psychiatry*. New York: Norton.

Suls, J., & Sanders, G. S. (1988). Type A behavior as a general risk factor for physical disorder. *Journal of Behavioral Medicine, 11*, 201–226.

Suppes, T., Baldessarini, R. J., Faedda, G. L., & Tohen, M. (1991). Risk of recurrence following discontinuation of lithium treatment in bipolar disorder. *Archives of General Psychiatry, 48*, 1082–1088.

Suzdak, P. D., Glowa, J. R., Crawley, J. N., Schwartz, R. D., Skolnik, P., & Paul, S. M. (1986). A selective imidazobenzodiazepine antagonist of ethanol in the rat. *Science, 234,* 1243–1247.

Suzdak, P. D., Schwartz, R. D., Skolnick, P., & Paul, S. M. (1988). Alcohols stimulate gamma-aminobutyric acid receptor-mediated chloride uptake in brain vesicles: Correlation with intoxication potency. *Brain Research, 444,* 340–345.

Swartz, M., Landerman, R., George, L. K., Blazer, D. G., & Escobar, J. (1991). Somatization disorder. In L. N. Robins & D. A. Regier (Eds.), *Psychiatric disorders in America: The epidemiologic catchment area study* (pp. 220–257). New York: Free Press.

Swedo, S. E., Leonard, H. L., Rapoport, J. L., Lenane, M. C., Goldberger, E. L., & Cheslow, D. L. (1989). A double-blind comparison of clomipramine and desipramine in the treatment of trichotillomania (hair pulling). *New England Journal of Medicine, 321,* 497–501.

Szasz, G., Stevenson, R. W. D., Lee, L., & Sanders, H. D. (1987). Induction of penile erection by intracavernosal injection: A double-blind comparison of phenoxybenzamine versus papaverine-phentolamine versus saline. *Archives of Sexual Behavior, 16,* 371–378.

Szasz, T. (1961). *The myth of mental illness.* New York: Harper & Row.

Tabakoff, B., & Hoffman, P. L. (1988). A neurobiological theory of alcoholism. In C. D. Chaudron & D. A. Wilkinson (Eds.), *Theories of alcoholism* (pp. 29–71). Toronto: Addiction Research Foundation.

Taber, J. I., Russo, A. M., Adkins, B. J., & McCormick, R. A. (1986). Ego strength and achievement motivation in pathological gamblers. *Journal of Gambling Behavior, 2,* 69–80.

Talbott, J. A. (1974). Stopping the revolving door: A study of readmissions to a state hospital. *Psychiatric Quarterly, 48,* 159–168.

Talbott, J. A., & Glick, I. D. (1986). The inpatient care of the chronically mentally ill. *Schizophrenia Bulletin, 12,* 129–140.

Tarasoff v. Regents of the University of California, et al., Cal. Rep., 14, 551 Pp., 2d, 334, 1976.

Tarnowski, K. J., Rosen, L. A., McGrath, M. L., & Drabman, R. S. (1987). A modified habit reversal procedure in a recalcitrant case of trichotillomania. *Journal of Behavior Therapy and Experimental Psychiatry, 18,* 157–163.

Teicher, M. H., Glod, C., & Cole, J. O. (1990). Emergence of intense suicide preoccupation during fluoxetine treatment. *American Journal of Psychiatry, 147,* 207–210.

Telch, M. J., Lucas, J. A., & Nelson, P. (1989). Nonclinical panic in college students: An investigation of prevalence and symptomatology. *Journal of Abnormal Psychology, 98,* 300–306.

Teri, L., & Gallagher-Thompson, D. (1991). Cognitive-behavioral interventions of treatment of depression in Alzheimer's patients. *The Gerontologist, 31,* 413–416.

Teri, L., Hughes, J. P., & Larson, E. B. (1990). Cognitive deterioration in Alzheimer's disease: Behavioral and health factors. *Journal of Gerontology: Psychological Sciences, 45,* P58–P63.

Teri, L., & Lewinsohn, P. M. (1986). *Geropsychological assessment and treatment.* New York: Springer.

Teri, L., Reifler, B. V., Veith, R. C., Barnes, R., White, E., McLean, P., & Raskind, M. (1991). Imipramine in the treatment of depressed Alzheimer's patients: Impact on cognition. *Journal of Gerontology: Psychological Sciences, 46,* P372–P377.

Terman, M., Terman, J. S., Quitkin, F. M., McGrath, P. J., Stewart, J. W., & Rafferty, B. (1989). Light therapy for seasonal affective disorder: A review of efficacy. *Neuropsychopharmacology, 2,* 1–22.

Terr, L. C. (1991). Childhood traumas: An outline and overview. *American Journal of Psychiatry, 148,* 10–20.

Thase, M. E., Frank, E., & Kupfer, D. J. (1985). Biological processes in major depression. In E. E. Beckham & W. R. Leber (Eds.), *Handbook of depression: Treatment, assessment, and research* (pp. 816–913). Homewood, IL: Dorsey Press.

Thigpen, C. H., & Cleckley, H. M. (1957). *The three faces of Eve.* New York: McGraw-Hill.

Thompson, J. K. (1990). *Body image disturbance: Assessment and treatment.* Elmsford, New York: Pergamon.

Thompson, L. W., Gallagher-Thompson, D., Futterman, A., Gilewski, M. J., & Peterson, J. (1991). The effects of late-life spousal bereavement over a 30-month interval. *Psychology and Aging, 6,* 434–441.

Thomson, A. D., Jeyasingham, M. D., & Pratt, O. E. (1987). Possible role of toxins in nutritional deficiency. *American Journal of Clinical Nutrition, 45,* 1351–1360.

Tienari, P., Sorri, A., Lahti, I., Naarala, M., Wahlberg, K. E., Moring, J., Pohjola, J., & Wynne, L. C. (1987). Genetic and psychosocial factors in schizophrenia: The Finnish adoptive family study. *Schizophrenia Bulletin, 13,* 477–484.

Tippin, J., & Henn, F. A. (1982). Modified leukotomy in the treatment of intractable obsessional neurosis. *American Journal of Psychiatry, 139,* 1601–1603.

Tobin, D. L., Johnson, C., Steinberg, S., Staats, M., & Dennis A. B. (1991). Multifactorial assessment of bulimia nervosa. *Journal of Abnormal Psychology, 100,* 14–21.

Torgersen, S. (1985). Relationship of schizotypal personality disorder to schizophrenia: Genetics. *Schizophrenia Bulletin, 11,* 554–563.

Torgersen, S. (1986). Genetic factors in moderately severe and mild affective disorders. *Archives of General Psychiatry, 43,* 222–226.

Torrey, E. F. (1988). *Surviving schizophrenia: A family manual* (rev. ed.). New York: Harper & Row.

Townsend, A., Noelker, L., Deimling, G., & Bass, D. (1989). Longitudinal impact of interhousehold caregiving on adult children's mental health. *The Gerontologist, 4,* 393–401.

Treaster, J. (1992, January 14). Colombia's drug lords add new line: Heroin for the U.S. *New York Times,* pp. A1, B2.

Treffert, D. (1989). *Extraordinary people: Understanding "idiot savants".* New York: Harper & Row.

Treffert, D. A. (1988). The idiot savant: A review of the syndrome. *American Journal of Psychiatry, 145,* 563–572.

Truax, C. B., & Carkhuff, R. (1967). *Toward effective counseling and psychotherapy: Training and practice.* Chicago: Aldine.

Tsai, L. Y., & Stewart, M. A. (1983). Etiological implication of maternal age and birth order in infantile autism. *Journal of Autism and Developmental Disorders, 13,* 57–65.

Tucker, G., Popkin, M., Caine, E., Folstein, M., & Grant, I. (1990). Reorganizing the "organic" disorders. *Hospital and Community Psychiatry, 41,* 722–724.

Tuma, A. H., & Maser, J. (Eds.). (1985). *Anxiety and the anxiety disorders.* Hillsdale, NJ: Erlbaum.

Turkel, H., & Nusbaum, I. (1986). Down syndrome and Alzheimer's disease contrasted. *Journal of Orthomolecular Medicine, 1,* 219–229.

Turner, E., Ewing, J., Shilling, P., Smith, T. L., Irwin, M., Schuckit, M., & Kelsoe, J. R. (1992). Lack of association between an RFLP near the D_2 dopamine receptor gene and severe alcoholism. *Biological Psychiatry, 31,* 285–290.

Turner, R. E. (1989). Pedophilia. In T. S. Karasu (Ed.), *Treatment of psychiatric disorders* (Vol. 1, pp. 617–633). Washington, DC: American Psychiatric Association.

Ueha, T., & Kuriyama, K. (1991). Ethanol-induced alterations in the function of cerebral GABA-$_A$ receptor complex: Effect on GABA–dependent $+^{36}+Cl^-$ influx into cerebral membrane vesicles. *Alcohol & Alcoholism, 26,* 17–24.

Uhde, T. W., Tancer, M. E., Black, B., & Brown, T. M. (1991). Phenomenology and neurobiology of social phobia: Comparison with panic disorder. *Journal of Clinical Psychiatry, 52*(11, Suppl.), 31–40.

Ullman, L. P., & Krasner, L. (1975). *A psychological approach to abnormal behavior* (2nd ed.). Englewood Cliffs, NJ: Prentice Hall.

U.S. Bureau of the Census. (1975). *Historical statistics of the United States: Colonial Times to 1970. (Part 1, Bicentennial ed.).* Washington, DC: U.S. Government Printing Office.

U.S. Department of Commerce. (1989). *Statistical abstracts of the United States* (109th ed.). U.S. Dept. of Commerce: Robert A. Mosbacher, Washington, D.C.: U.S. Government Printing Office.

U.S. Department of Education. (1985). *The school-age handicapped: A statistical profile of special education students in elementary and secondary schools in the United States.* Child Trends, Inc.: Washington, DC, Nicholas Zill. National Center for Education Statistics. NCES 85–400.

U.S. Department of Health and Human Services. (1988). *Vital statistics of the U.S., 1985: Volume 2. Mortality (Part A).* Hyattsville, MD: Author.

U.S. Department of Health and Human Services. (1990). *Seventh special report to the U.S. Congress on alcohol and health.* Rockville, MD: Author.

U.S. Department of Health and Human Services. (1991). Births, marriages, and deaths for 1990. *Monthly Vital Statistics Report,* 39, (12).

U.S. Department of Health and Human Services. (1992). *Advance report of final mortality statistics, 1989* (Vol. 40, No. 8, Suppl. 2). Hyattsville, MD: Public Health Service.

U.S. Department of Justice. (1989). *Children in Custody, 1975–1985.* Washington, DC: Author.

Ussher, J. M. (1991). *Women's madness: Misogyny or mental illness?* Amherst, MA: University of Massachusetts Press.

Vaillant, G. E., & Milofsky, E. (1980). Natural history of male psychological health: IX. Empirical evidence for Erikson's model of the life cycle. *American Journal of Psychiatry, 137,* 1348–1359.

Vaughn, C. E., & Leff, J. P. (1976). The influence of family and social factors on the course of psychiatric illness: A comparison of schizophrenic with depressed neurotic patients. *British Journal of Psychiatry, 129,* 125–137.

Vaughn, C. E., Snyder K. S., Jones, S., Freeman, W. B., & Falloon, I. R. (1984). Family factors in schizophrenic relapse. *Archives of General Psychiatry, 41,* 1169–1177.

Vela-Bueno, A., Soldatos, C. R., & Julius, D. A. (1987). Parasomnias: Sleepwalking, night terrors, and nightmares [Special Issue: Sleep disorders]. *Psychiatric Annals, 17,* 465–469.

ver Ellen, P., & van Kammen, D. P. (1990). The biological findings in post-traumatic stress disorder: A review. *Journal of Applied Social Psychology, 20,* 1789–1821.

Verwoerdt, (1976). *Clinical geropsychiatry.* Baltimore, MD: Williams & Wilkins.

Vestal, R. E., McGuire, E. A., Tobin, J. D., Andres, R., Norris, A. H., & Mezey, E. (1977). Aging and alcohol metabolism. *Clinical Pharmacology and Therapeutics, 21,* 343–354.

Vincent, K. R. (1990). The fragile nature of MMPI code types. *Journal of Clinical Psychology, 46,* 800–802.

Virkkunen, M. (1986). Insulin secretion during the glucose tolerance test among habitually violent and impulsive offenders. *Aggressive Behavior, 12,* 303–310.

Virkkunen, M., De Jong, J., Bartko, J., Linnoila, M. (1989). Psychobiological concomitants of history of suicide attempts among violent offenders and impulsive fire setters. *Archives of General Psychiatry, 46,* 604–606.

Virkkunen, M., Nuutila, A., Goodwin, F. K., & Linnoila, M. (1987). Cerebrospinal fluid monoamine metabolites in male arsonists. *Archives of General Psychiatry, 44,* 241–247.

Vitaliano, P. P., Russo, J., Young, H. M., Teri, L., & Maiuro, R. D. (1991). Predictors of burden in spouse caregivers of individuals with Alzheimer's disease. *Psychology and Aging, 6,* 392–402.

Volavka, J. (1987). Electroencephalogram among criminals. In S. A. Mednick, T. E. Moffitt, & S. A. Stack (Eds.), *The causes of crime: New biological approaches* (pp. 137–145). Cambridge: Cambridge University Press.

Volberg, R., & Steadman, H. (1988). Refining prevalence estimates of pathological gambling. *American Journal of Psychiatry, 145,* 502–505.

Vollhardt, L. T. (1991). Psychoneuroimmunology: A literature review. *American Journal of Orthopsychiatry, 61,* 35–47.

von Knorring, A. L., Bohman, M., von Knorring, L., & Oreland, L. (1985). Platelet MAO activity as a biological marker in subgroups of alcoholism. *Acta Psychiatrica Scandinavica, 72,* 51–58.

Wagner, E. E., Alexander, R. A., Roos, G., & Adair, H. (1986). Optimum split-half reliabilities for the Rorschach: Projective techniques are more reliable than we think. *Journal of Personality Assessment, 50,* 107–112.

Wakefield, J. C. (1987). Sex bias in the diagnosis of primary orgasmic dysfunction. *American Psychologist, 42,* 464–471.

Walaskay, M., Whitbourne, S. K., & Nehrke, M. F. (1983–1984). Construction and validation of an ego-integrity status interview. *International Journal of Aging and Human Development, 18,* 61–72.

Waldinger, R. (1986). Intensive psychodynamic psychotherapy with borderline patients: An overview. *American Journal of Psychiatry, 144,* 267–274.

Wallace, I., Wallechinsky, D., Wallace, A., & Wallace, S. (1980). *The people's almanac presents the book of lists #2.* New York: William Morrow.

Wallander, J. L. (1988). The relationship between attention problems in childhood and antisocial behavior eight years later. *Journal of Child Psychology and Psychiatry and Allied Disciplines, 29,* 53–61.

Wallander, J. L., & Hubert, N. C. (1987). Peer social dysfunction in children with developmental disabilities: Empirical basis and a conceptual model. *Clinical Psychology Review, 7,* 205–221.

Walsh, B. T., Stewart, J. W., Roose, S. P., Gladis, M., & Glassman, A. H. (1984). Treatment of bulimia with phenelzine: A double-blind, placebo-controlled study. *Archives of General Psychiatry, 41,* 1105–1109.

Walsh, B. T. (1991). Psychopharmacologic treatment of bulimia nervosa. *Journal of Clinical Psychiatry, 52* (Suppl. 10), 34–38.

Ward, C. D. (1986). Commentary on "Alzheimer's disease may begin in the nose and may be caused by aluminosilicates" [Special Issue: Controversial topics on Alzheimer's disease: Intersecting crossroads]. *Neurobiology of Aging, 7,* 574–575.

Washton, A. M., & Gold, M. S. (1987). Recent trends in cocaine abuse: A view from the National Hotline, "800-COCAINE". *Advances in Alcohol and Substance Abuse, 6,* 31–47.

Washton, A. M., Stone, N. S., & Hendrickson, E. C. (1988). Cocaine abuse. In D. M. Donovan & G. A. Marlatt (Eds.), *Assessment of addictive behaviors* (pp. 364–389). New York: Guilford Press.

Wasow, M. (1986). The need for asylum for the chronically mentally ill. *Schizophrenia Bulletin, 12,* 162–167.

Wasylenki, D. A. (1992). Psychotherapy of schizophrenia revisited. *Hospital and Community Psychiatry, 43,* 123–127.

Waterman, A. S. (1982). Identity development from adolescence to adulthood: An extension of theory and a review of research. *Developmental Psychology, 18,* 341–358.

Waters, E., Wippman, J., & Sroufe, L. A. (1979). Attachment, positive affect, and competence in the peer group: Two studies in construct validation. *Child Development, 50,* 821–829.

Watkins, J. G. (1984). The Bianchi (L.A. Hillside Strangler) case: Sociopath or multiple personality? *International Journal of Clinical Experimental Hypnosis, 32,* 67–101.

Watt, N. F., Anthony, E. J., Wynne, L. C., & Rolf, J. E. (Eds.). (1984). *Children at risk for schizophrenia: A longitudinal perspective.* Cambridge: Cambridge University Press.

Watzlawick, P., Weakland, J. H., & Fisch, R. (1974). *Change: Principles of problem formation and problem resolution*. New York: Norton.

Watzlawick, P., Jackson, D., & Beavin, J. (1967). *The pragmatics of human communication*. New York: Norton.

Wecker, L. (1990). Dietary choline: A limiting factor for the synthesis of acetylcholine by the brain. In R. J. Wurtman, Corkin, S., Growdon, J. H., & Ritter-Walker (Eds.), *Advances in neurology: Vol. 51. Alzheimer's disease* (pp. 139–145). New York: Raven.

Weddington, W. W., Brown, B. S., Haertzen, C. A., Cone, E. J., Dax, E. M., Herning, R. I., & Michaelson, B. S. (1990). Changes in mood, craving, and sleep during short-term abstinence reported by male cocaine addicts: A controlled, residential study. *Archives of General Psychiatry, 47*, 861–868.

Weinberg, T. S., & Kamel, G. W. L. (Eds.). (1983). *S and M: Studies in sadomasochism*. Buffalo, NY: Prometheus Books.

Weinberg, T. S., Williams, C. J., & Moser, C. (1984). The social constituents of sadomasochism. *Social Problems, 31*, 379–389.

Weiner, R. D., & Coffey, C. E. (1988). Indications for use of electroconvulsive therapy. In A. J. Frances & R. E. Hales (Eds.), *Review of psychiatry* (Vol. 7). Washington, DC: American Psychiatric Press.

Weingartner, H., Grafman, J., & Newhouse, P. (1987). Toward a psychobiological taxonomy of cognitive impairments. In G. G. Glenner & R. J. Wurtman (Eds.), *Advancing frontiers in Alzheimer's disease research* (pp. 249–262). Austin: University of Texas Press.

Weinstein, H. C., Teunisse, S., & van Gool, W. A. (1991). Tetrahydroaminoacridine (THA) and lecithin in the treatment of Alzheimer's disease: Effects on cognition, functioning in daily life, behavioural disturbances, and burden experienced by the caregiver. *Journal of Neurology, 238*, 34–38.

Weintraub, S. (1987). Risk factors in schizophrenia: The Stony Brook high-risk project. *Schizophrenia Bulletin, 13*, 439–450.

Weiss, G. (1990). Hyperactivity in childhood. *New England Journal of Medicine, 323*, 1413–1415.

Weiss, G., & Hechtman, L. T. (1986). *Hyperactive children grown up: Empirical findings and theoretical considerations*. New York: Guilford Press.

Weiss, J., Samson, H., & The Mt. Zion Psychotherapy Research Group. (1986). *The psychoanalytic process: Theory, clinical observation, and empirical research*. New York: Guilford Press.

Weiss, J. M. A., Davis, D., Hedlund, J. L., & Cho, D. W. (1983). The dysphoric psychopath: A comparison of 524 cases of antisocial personality disorder with matched controls. *Comprehensive Psychiatry, 24*, 355–369.

Weissberg, J. H., & Levay, A. N. (1986). Compulsive sexual behavior. *Medical Aspects of Human Sexuality, 20*, 129–130.

Weissman, A. (1987). The dysfunctional attitudes scale. In K. Corcoran & J. Fischer (Eds.), *Measures for clinical practice: A source book*. New York: Free Press.

Weissman, M. M. (1988). The epidemiology of anxiety disorders: Rates, risks and familial patterns. *Journal of Psychiatric Research, 22*, 99–114.

Weissman, M. M. (1990a). The hidden patient: Unrecognized panic disorder. *Journal of Clinical Psychiatry, 51* (11, Suppl.), 5–8.

Weissman, M. M. (1990b). Panic and generalized anxiety: Are they separate disorders? *Journal of Psychiatric Research, 24* (Suppl. 2), 157–162.

Weissman, M. M. (1991). Panic disorder: Impact on quality of life. *Journal of Clinical Psychology, 52*(2, Suppl.), 6–8.

Weissman, M. M., & Klerman, G. L. (1985). Gender and depression. *Trends in Neurosciences, 8*, 416–420.

Weissman, M. M., Klerman, G. L., Markowitz, J. S., Ouellette, R., & Phil, M. (1989). Suicidal ideation and suicide attempts in panic disorder and attacks. *New England Journal of Medicine, 321*, 1209–1214.

Weissman, M. M., Leckman, J. F., Merikangas, K. R., Gammon, G. D., & Prusoff, B. A. (1984). Depression and anxiety disorders in parents and children. *Archives of General Psychiatry, 41*, 845–852.

Weissman, M. M., Merikangas, K. R., & Boyd, J. H. (1986). Epidemiology of affective disorders. In J. E. Helzer & S. B. Guze (Eds.), *Psychiatry, affective disorders, and dementia* (pp. 105–118). New York: Basic Books.

Weisz, J. R., Weiss, B., Alicke, M. D., & Koltz, M. L. (1987). Effectiveness of psychotherapy with children and adolescents: A meta-analysis for clinicians. *Journal of Consulting and Clinical Psychology, 55*, 542–549.

Weller, R. A., & Halikas, J. A. (1985). Marijuana use and psychiatric illness: A follow-up study. *American Journal of Psychiatry, 142*, 848–850.

Wells, C. E. (1979). Pseudodementia. *American Journal of Psychiatry, 136*, 895–900.

Wender, P. H., Kety, S. S., Rosenthal, D., Shulsinger, F., Ortmann, J., & Lunde, I. (1986). Psychiatric disorders in the biological and adoptive families of adopted individuals with affective disorders. *Archives of General Psychiatry, 43*, 923–929.

Wender, P. H., Rosenthal, D., Kety, S. S., Schulsinger, F., & Welner, J. (1974). Cross-fostering: A research strategy for clarifying the role of genetic and experimental factors in the etiology of schizophrenia. *Archives of General Psychiatry, 30*, 121–128.

Werry, J. S., Reeves, J. C., & Elkind, G. S. (1987). Attention deficit, conduct, oppositional, and anxiety disorders in children: I. A review of research on differentiating characteristics. *Journal of the American Academy of Child and Adolescent Psychiatry, 26*, 133–143.

West, M., & Sheldon, A. E. R. (1988). Classification of pathological attachment patterns in adults. *Journal of Personality Disorders, 2*, 153–159.

Westen, D. (1991). Cognitive-behavioral interventions in the psychoanalytic psychotherapy of borderline personality disorders. *Clinical Psychology Review, 11*, 211–230.

Westen, D., Ludolph, P., Misle, B., Ruffins, S., & Block, J. (1990). Physical and sexual abuse in adolescent girls with borderline personality disorder. *American Journal of Orthopsychiatry, 60*, 55–66.

Whalen, C. K., & Henker, B. (1985). The social worlds of hyperactive (ADDH) children [Special Issue: Attention deficit disorder: Issues in assessment and intervention]. *Clinical Psychology Review, 5*, 447–478.

Whalen, C. K., Henker, B., & Hinshaw, S. P. (1985). Cognitive behavioral therapies for hyperactive children: Premises, problems and prospects [Special Issue: Cognitive behavior modification with children: A critical review of the state of the art]. *Journal of Abnormal Child Psychology, 13*, 391–410.

Whitbourne, S. K., & Tesch, S. A. (1985). A comparison of identity and intimacy statuses in college students and alumni. *Developmental Psychology, 21*, 1039–1044.

Whitbourne, S. K., Zuschlag, M. K., Elliot, L. B., & Waterman, A. S. (1992). Psychosocial development in adulthood: A 22-year sequential study. *Journal of Personality and Social Psychology, 63*, 260–271.

Whitfield, C. L. (1989). Co-dependence: Our most common addiction—some physical, mental, emotional and spiritual perspectives. *Alcoholism Treatment Quarterly, 6*, 19–35.

Wickramasekera, I. (1976). Aversive behavior rehearsal for sexual exhibitionism. *Behavior Therapy, 7*, 167–176.

Widerlov, E. (1988). A critical appraisal of CSF monoamine metabolite studies in schizophrenia. *Annals of the New York Academy of Sciences, 537*, 309–323.

Widiger, T. A. (1991). DSM-IV reviews of the personality disorders: Introduction to special series. *Journal of Personality Disorders, 5*, 122–134.

Widiger, T. A., Frances, A. J., Pincus, H. A., Davis, W. W., & First, M. B. (1991). Toward an empirical classification for the DSM-IV. *Journal of Abnormal Psychology, 100*, 280–288.

Widiger, T. A., Frances, A. J., & Trull, T. J. (1987). A psychometric analysis of the social-interpersonal and cognitive perceptual items for the schizotypal personality disorder. *Archives of General Psychiatry, 44*, 741–745.

Widiger, T. A. & Shea, T. (1991). Differentiation of Axis I and Axis II disorders. *Journal of Abnormal Psychology, 100*, 399–406.

Widom, C. A. (1978). A methodology for studying noninstitutionalized psycopaths. In R. D. Hare & D. A. Schalling (Eds.), *Psychopathic behavior: Approaches to research.* (pp. 71–84), Chichester, England: John Wiley.

Wiedl, K. H., Schöttner, B. (1991). Coping with symptoms related to schizophrenia. *Schizophrenia Bulletin, 17*, 525–538.

Wilbur, C. B., & Kluft, R. P. (1989). Multiple personality disorder. In T.B. Karasu (Ed.), *Treatment of psychiatric disorders* (pp. 2197–2216). Washington, DC: American Psychiatric Association.

Williams, G. D., Grant, B. F., Harford, T. C., & Noble, B. A. (1989). Population projections using DSM-III criteria: Alcohol abuse and dependence 1990–2000. *Alcohol Health and Research World, 13*, 366–370.

Windle, M. (1990). A longitudinal study of antisocial behaviors in early adolescence as predictors of late adolescent substance use: Gender and ethnic group differences. *Journal of Abnormal Psychology, 99*, 86–91.

Winnicott, D. W. (1971). *Playing and reality.* Middlesex, England: Penguin.

Winokur, G., Black, D. W., & Nasrallah, A. (1988). Depressions secondary to other psychiatric disorders and medical illnesses. *American Journal of Psychiatry, 145*, 233–237.

Wirak, D., Bayney, R., Ramabhadran, T. V., Fracasso, R. P., Hart, J. T., Hauer, P. E., Hsiau, P., Pekar, S. K., Scangos, G. A., Trapp, B. D., & Unterbeck, A. J. (1992). [Letter] *Science, 255*, 1445.

Wirak, D. O., Bayney, R., Ramabhadran, T. V., Fracasso, R. P., Hart, J. T., Hauer, P. E., Hsiau, P., Pekar, S. K., Scangos, G. A., Trapp, B. D., & Unterbeck, A. J. (1991). Deposits of amyloid B protein in the central nervous system of transgenic mice. *Science, 253*, 323–325.

Wise, T. N. (1985). Fethisism–Etiology and its treatment: A review from multiple perspectives. *Comprehensive Psychiatry, 26*, 249–257.

Wise, T. N. (1989). Fetishism and transvestism. In T. S. Karasu (Ed.), *Treatment of psychiatric disorders* (Vol. 1, pp. 633–646). Washington, DC: American Psychiatric Association.

Witkin, H. A., Mednick, S. A., Schulsinger, F., Bakkestrom, E., Christiansen, K. O., Goodenough, D. R., Hirschhorn, K., Lundsteen, C., Owen, D. R., Philip, J., Rubin, D. B., & Stocking, M. (1977). Criminality, aggression and intelligence among XYY and XXY men. In S. A. Mednick & K.O. Christiansen (Eds.), *Biosocial bases of criminal behavior* (pp. 165–188). New York: Gardner Press.

Witzig, J. S. (1968). The group treatment of male exhibitionists. *American Journal of Psychiatry, 125*, 179–185.

Woititz, J. G. (1983). *Adult children of alcoholics.* Deerfield Beach, FL: Health Communications.

Wolfe, L. (1978). The question of surrogates in sex therapy. In J. LoPiccolo and L. LoPiccolo (Eds.), *Handbook of sex therapy.* New York: Plenum Press.

Wolpe, J. (1958). *Psychotherapy by reciprocal inhibition.* Stanford: Stanford University Press.

Wolpe, J. (1973). *The practice of behavior therapy* (2nd ed.). Elmsford, NY: Pergamon.

Wolpe, J., & Lang, P. J. (1964). A fear survey schedule for use in behavior therapy. *Behaviour Research and Therapy, 2*, 27–30.

Wooden, W. S. (1985). Arson is epidemic—and spreading like wildfire. *Psychology Today, 19*(1), 23–28.

Wright, L. K. (1991). The impact of Alzheimer's disease on the marital relationship. *The Gerontologist, 31*, 224–237.

Wu, T. C., Tashkin, D. P., Djahed, B., & Rose, J. E. (1988). Pulmonary hazards of smoking marijuana as compared with tobacco. *New England Journal of Medicine, 318*, 347–351.

Wyatt v. Stickney, 325 F. Supp. 781 (M.D. Ala. 1971); 344 F. Supp. 343 (M.D. Ala. 1972).

Yates, W. R. (1991). Transient hypochondriasis: A new somatoform diagnosis? *Archives of General Psychiatry, 48*, 955.

Yesavage, J. A., Leirer, V. O., Denari, M., & Hollister, L. E. (1985). Carryover effects of marijuana intoxication on airline pilot performance: A preliminary report. *American Journal of Psychiatry, 142*, 1325–1329.

Yirmiya, N., & Sigman, M. (1991). High functioning individuals with autism: Diagnosis, empirical findings, and theoretical issues. *Clinical Psychology Review, 11*, 669–683.

Zametkin, A. J., Nordahl, T. E., Gross, M., King, A. C., Semple, W. E., Rumsey, J., Hamburger, S., & Cohen, R. M. (1990). Cerebral glucose metabolism in adults with hyperactivity of childhood onset. *New England Journal of Medicine, 323*, 1361–1366.

Zametkin, A. J., & Rapoport, J. L. (1987). Neurobiology of attention deficit disorder with hyperactivity: Where have we come in 50 years? *Journal of the American Academy of Child and Adolescent Psychiatry, 26*, 676–686.

Zarit, S. H. (1980). *Aging and mental disorders: Psychological approaches to assessment and treatment.* New York: Free Press.

Zarit, S. H., Eiler, J., & Hassinger, M. (1985). Clinical assessment. In J. E. Birren & K. W. Schaie (Eds.), *Handbook of the psychology of aging* (2nd ed., pp. 725–754). New York: Van Nostrand Reinhold.

Zarit, S. H., Todd, P. A., & Zarit, J. M. (1986). Subjective burden of husbands and wives as caregivers: A longitudinal study. *The Gerontologist, 26*, 260–266.

Zettle, R. D., & Hayes, S. C. (1987). Component and process analysis of cognitive therapy. *Psycholgoical Reports, 61*, 939–953.

Zilboorg, G., & Henry, G. W. (1941). *A history of medical psychology.* New York: Norton.

Zipurski, R. B., Lim, K. O., Sullivan, E. V., Brown, B. W., & Pfefferbaum, A. (1992). Widespread cerebral gray matter volume deficits in schizophrenia. *Archives of General Psychiatry, 49*, 195–205.

Zisook, S., & Shuchter, S. R. (1991). Depression through the first year after the death of a spouse. *American Journal of Psychiatry, 148*, 1346–1352.

Zorc, J. J., Larson, D. B., Lyons, J. S., & Beardsley, R. S. (1991). Expenditures for psychotropic medications in the United States in 1985. *American Journal of Psychiatry, 148*, 644–647.

Zubin, J., & Spring, B. (1977). Vulnerability—A new view of schizophrenia. *Journal of Abnormal Psychology, 86*, 103–126.

Zucker, R. A., & Gomberg, E. S. L. (1986). Etiology of alcoholism reconsidered: The case for biopsychosocial process. *American Psychologist, 41*, 783–793.

Zuckoff, M. (1986, December 1). Court test gets underway today for aversive therapy. The Boston Globe, p. 53.

The authors are indebted to the following for permission to reprint from copyrighted material:

•**Page 9** James McConnell and Dr. Ronald P. Philipchalk, figure from *Understanding Human Behavior*, seventh edition, copyright © 1992 by Holt, Rinehart and Winston, Inc., reprinted by permission of the publisher. •**Pages 36 & 37** American Psychiatric Association, "Severity of Psychosocial Stressors Scales: Adults, and Children and Adolescents," and "Axis V: Global Assessment of Functioning Scale." Reprinted from *Diagnostic and Statistical Manual of Mental Disorders*, third edition, revised, Washington, D. C. American Psychiatric Association. Copyright © 1987 and reprinted with permission. •**Page 59** J. Indicott and R. L. Spitzer, figures reprinted from "The Schedule for Effective Disorders and Schizophrenia," reprinted from *The Journal of General Psychiatry*, Vol. 35, 1978. •**Page 67** Charles G. Morris, figure from *Psychology: An Introduction*, seventh edition, Copyright © 1990, p. 301. Reprinted by permission of Prentice Hall, Englewood Cliffs, New Jersey. •**Page 70** Minnesota Multiphasic Personality Inventory. Copyright © by the Regents of the University of Minnesota 1942, 1943 (renewed 1970). All rights reserved. "MMPI" is a trademark of the University of Minnesota. •**Page 95** Erik Erikson, figure adapted from *Childhood and Society*, second edition, by Erik H. Erikson, by permission of W. W. Norton and Company, Inc. Copyright © 1950, © 1963 by W. W. Norton and Company, Inc. Copyright renewed 1978, 1991 by Erik H. Erikson. •**Page 105** Abraham H. Maslow, figure from "Hierarchy of Needs" from *Motivation and Personality* by Abraham H. Maslow. Copyright © 1954 by Harper and Row, Publishers, Inc. Copyright © 1970 by Abraham H. Maslow. Reprinted by permission of HarperCollins Publishers. •**Page 107** A. Jones and R. Crandall, Items from the "Self-Acualization Scale," from *Personality and Social Psychology Bulletin 12*, copyright © 1986. Reprinted by permission of Sage Publications. •**Page 123** Aaron T. Beck, table from "Steps Leading from Dysfunctional Attitudes to Negative Emotions," by Aaron T. Beck. Copyright © 1979 and reprinted by permission of the author. •**Page 123** Arlene Weissman, Items from the "Dysfunctional Attitude Scale," from *Measures for Clinical Practice: A Source Book*, by K. Coccoran and J. Fischer. Copyright © 1978 and reprinted by permission of Arlene Weiss-

man. •**Page 177** David H. Barlow, figures from *The Journal of Clinical Psychiatry*, Vol. 51 (12, suppl. A): pp. 17–23, 1990. Copyright © 1990, Physicians Postgraduate Press. Reprinted with permission of Physicians Postgraduate Press and the author. •**Page 178** A. Tuma and J. Maser, from *Anxiety and the Anxiety Disorders*. Copyright © 1985 and reprinted by permission of the publisher, Lawrence Erlbaum Associates, Inc. •**Page 182** W. C. Sanderson and D. H. Barlow, figure from *Journal of Nervous and Mental Disease*, Vol. 178, No. 9, pp. 588–591, "A Description of Patients Diagnosed with DSM-III-R Generalized Anxiety Disorder." Copyright © 1990 by Williams and Wilkins. •**Page 205** C. Ross, Items from the "Dissociative Disorders Interview Schedule," from *Multiple Personality Disorders*, copyright © 1989 by John Wiley and Sons. Reprinted by permission of John Wiley and Sons, Inc. •**Page 268** I. Elkin et al., Figures from *Archives of General Psychiatry*, Vol. 46, pp. 971–982, Copyright © 1989. Based on a National Institute of Mental Health study. •**Page 298** Irving I. Gottesman, from *Schizophrenia Genesis*, by Irving I. Gottesman. Copyright © 1991 by Irving I. Gottesman. Reprinted by permission of W. H. Freeman and Company. •**Page 356** Barry Reisberg, "Phases of Dementia." Reprinted by permission of The Free Press, a Division of Macmillan, Inc. from *Alzheimer's Disease: The Standard Reference* by Barry Reisberg, M.D. Copyright © 1983 by Barry Reisberg, M.D. •**Page 360** M. F. Folstein and P. R. McHugh, table from "Mini-Mental State," reprinted with permission from *Journal of Psychiatric Research 12*, copyright © 1975, Pergamon Press, Ltd. •**Page 381** Helen Annis, from "Expectancy Based Assessment Measures," published in *Inventory of Drinking Situations: Short Form*. Copyright © and reprinted by permission of Helen Annis, Addiction Research Foundation, Toronto, Canada. •**Page 381** G. A. Marlatt and J. R. Gordon, figure from *Relapse Prevention: The Treatment of Addictive Behaviors*. Copyright © 1985 and reprinted by permission of the publisher, Guilford Publications, Inc. •**Page 383** Helen Annis and C. S. Davis, figure from *Assessment of Addictive Behaviors*, p. 103. Copyright © 1988 and reprinted by permission of the publisher, Guilford Publications, Inc. •**Page 417** W. S. Agras, figure from *The Journal of Clinical Psychiatry*, Vol. 52 (10, suppl): pp. 29–33, 1991. Copyright © 1991, Physicians Postgraduate Press. •**Page 420** W. S. Agras, E. M. Rossiter, B. Arnow et al. Figure from *American Journal of Psychiatry*,

Vol. 149, pp. 82–87, 1992. Copyright © 1992, The American Psychiatric Association. Reprinted by permission of the publisher and author. •**Page 445** M. E. Giesecke, from "The Symptom of Insomnia in University Students." Reprinted from the *Journal of American College Health*, Vol. 35, pp. 215–221. Copyright © 1987.

PHOTO CREDITS